WESTERN INDIANS

WESTERN INDIANS

Comparative Environments, Languages, and Cultures of 172 Western American Indian Tribes

JOSEPH G. JORGENSEN
University of California, Irvine

Research Collaborators
Harold E. Driver
Donald G. Callaway
James L. Coffin
John Fox
Jon Hofmeister

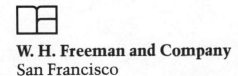

W. H. Freeman and Company
San Francisco

Sponsoring Editor: Richard J. Lamb
Project Editor: Patricia Brewer
Manuscript Editor: Kirk Sargent
Designer: Brenn Lea Pearson
Production Coordinator: William Murdock
Compositor: Graphic Typesetting Service
Printer and Binder: Arcata Book Group

Library of Congress Cataloging in Publication Data

Jorgensen, Joseph G   1934–
   Western Indians: comparative environments,
languages, and cultures of 172 western American
Indian tribes.

   Bibliography: p.
   Includes index.
   I. Indians of North America—The West. I. Title.
E78.W5J67   978'.00497   80–12564
ISBN 0–7167–1104–4

Printed in the United States of America

9 8 7 6 5 4 3 2 1

TO MY TEACHER,
HAROLD E. DRIVER,
AND
TO THE MEMORY OF HIS TEACHER,
ALFRED L. KROEBER

Contents

Preface

Western Indians analyzes, through comparisons, the relations among environments, languages, and cultures of the Indian societies of western North America. A full discussion of the focus of the book and the reasons for which it was researched and written are found in Chapter 1. In brief, *Western Indians* pulls together data on the Indian societies that inhabited the region from Yakutat Bay in Alaska to the northern Baja Peninsula of California, and from the Rocky Mountains to the islands along the Pacific Coast. Although there is a very extensive literature pertaining to the Indians of western North America, including the results of the cultural survey conducted under the direction of Alfred L. Kroeber at the University of California in the 1930s, until now that literature has not been used to full benefit. In this volume, and volumes to follow, the richly reported region encompassing six culture areas—Northwest Coast, California, Southern California, Plateau, Great Basin, and Southwest—receives extensive analysis.

We break from the traditional practices in anthropology, history, and cultural geography, and apply formal techniques to large sets of data to determine environmental areas, relations among sister languages of language families, and culture areas. Scholars and teachers in anthropology, American Indian history, comparative linguistics, cultural geography, and Native American studies, as well as interested nonprofessionals, should find these analyses of interest. This volume, however, is not organized around culture area or environmental area themes. In this volume we address the entire region of western North America, analyzing such topics as the nature and variation of Indian economic organizations at the time of first contact with Europeans and the relations between such topics as environment and economic organization.

We provide, then, empirically and formally obtained environment, language family, and culture taxonomies, but the text defines and describes phenomena such as technology, social organization, political organization, and ceremonialism; accounts for variation —similarities and differences—within those topics; and provides maps of the distributions of the majority of the variables that are analyzed in this volume. Hypotheses about American Indian ecology, kinship organizations, sodalities and cults, potlatches, and the like, which have interested scholars and nonprofessionals for the past fifty years, are evaluated, and many new explanations of the relations among environment, language, and culture are advanced.

Western Indians should find uses in university-level courses on American Indians taught in anthropology, cultural geography, history, and Native American studies departments, and should find further uses among professionals who wish to provide alternative explanations to the analyses provided here. Part of the large data base appears in the maps in Appendix D, but the entire coded and rated data set is available from the author so that retests and new tests of relations are possible.

Nonprofessionals with interests in the Indians of North America at the time of first contact with Europeans may find some of the technical discussions, such as those on kinship terminological systems or the relations among sodalities (cults) in California, heavy going, but for the most part technical, especially methodological, discussions are kept to a minimum for the sake of the narrative. Discussion of the formal methodology, for instance, appears in an appendix. Even the maps—so crucial to the study—are placed in an appendix, thus organizing them in one place and preventing disruption of the narrative.

About nine years have elapsed between the time the research on which this book is based was envisaged, and the publishing of the book. The plunge into the labyrinth of western North American Indian cultures, languages, and environments has been fascinating and extremely enlightening. Where I was raised, in the wilds of Utah, I was told that total immersion brought remission from sins. What I have learned from total immersion in western North American ethnography, the literature on the environments of the West, and the basic research on the languages spoken by Indians of the West is that it is well nigh impossible to avoid sins of omission in a study such as this, because the terrain is so vast and so complex, and because no mere mortal can comprehend all the relations that obtain among so many parts. Sins of commission, too, have no doubt flowed from my pen. Both types of transgressions, I suspect, will be pointed out by critics. It is unsettling to think that all of the work one undertakes in order to clear away errors can in the end leave a person so vulnerable, but vulnerability is the factor that makes social inquiry interesting, so, contradictorily, I welcome investigation of this work.

When I embarked on this research, my former teacher, Harold E. Driver, the person to whom this volume is dedicated, and whose monumental research on North American Indian societies has no challengers, was my research partner. We jointly created the sample of societies and mapped the strategy by which data would be collected. Shortly after the National Science Foundation awarded Jorgensen and the University of Michigan Grant number 2950, and Driver and Indiana University Grant number 2951, Driver became ill. We transferred part of his grant to the University of Michigan, and he later freed himself of the chore of analyzing and writing portions of the project, but he created the codes (definitions) for most of the environmental and technology variables and, in conjunction with his former student at Indiana University, James Coffin, rated those variables (see Appendices A and B). Harold Driver was the principal collaborator in the early research stages of the project. Moreover, he is the senior author of Appendix B, which compares the breadth and scope of the variables of Jorgensen and Driver's sample of western North American Indians with the ranges of topics in George Peter Murdock's worldwide sample (1967) and Harold Driver and William Massey's sample of North American Indian societies (1957). It is unfortunate that the health of my teacher and collaborator did not allow him to help me organize, analyze, and interpret all the data, but I am deeply grateful for his many contributions in the early going. Indeed, if Harold Driver had not suggested that we take on a study of all Indian societies north of Panama in 1964, during a little victory celebration in Bloomington following the defense of my dissertation, we would never have begun this project.

COLLABORATORS

Besides Harold Driver, several other scholars collaborated in the collection of data for this study. My former students at the University of Michigan, Donald G. Callaway and Jon Hofmeister, each worked for about two years reading ethnographies and rating vari-

ables, and Driver's former student, James Coffin, also rated variables. A description of their contributions appears in Appendix A.

John Fox, a former colleague of mine at the University of Michigan, was instrumental in the computer data management portion of the study. A sociologist, Fox tackled the gargantuan data set with relish and efficiency. He redimensioned my own nonmetric trees program so it would handle 172 tribes (73,000 pieces of information) rather than the 32 tribes which it originally handled. He created a program to allow us to test the reliability among the variable ratings of the researchers (Callaway, Coffin, Driver, Hofmeister, and Jorgensen), and redimensioned my own correlational and unordered matrix program so that it would catch thousands of coefficients (about 15,000 per run) in asymmetrical matrices, thus allowing us to pour the coefficients into my nonmetric trees program and the Guttman-Lingoes Non-Metric Multivariate Program Series. After consulting with Waldo Tobler, another Michigan colleague, and using programs of his recommendation, Fox and I also programmed the computer graphics that we used to map the distributions of most of the variables in the study. Working with John Fox was a pleasure, and his productive contributions paved the way for my analyses over the next several years. Even after John Fox moved on to professorships in Canada, he contributed to the solution of problems.

ACKNOWLEDGMENTS

Besides the NSF grants, I received a Horace H. Rackham Senior Fellowship from the University of Michigan to help complete the research. Several people helped in other important ways to complete this project. My former colleague at the University of Michigan, James Lingoes, aided me in understanding and using much more powerful nonmetric multivariate techniques than I had created during previous research ventures. Waldo Tobler provided expertise in spatial analysis and was extremely helpful in our efforts to generate computer-drawn maps of the variable distributions.

Bonnie Kendall, a former student of Harold Driver, collected published lexicostatistical materials and boiled down notes about them to a manageable size. Richard Newton converted my drafts of tree diagrams and two-dimensional representations to finished forms, and Maureen Killackey did the same thing for the base map and the conventional area maps. David Bowen drafted the kinship organization figures from my originals.

Rachell Keefe, with good humor and perseverance, typed the manuscript and all its revisions from what I had scrawled on long, lined, yellow pads. She deserves a medal.

The late Robert Heizer read the first draft of the manuscript very carefully and made many helpful criticisms. I am extremely grateful. David Aberle and Isidore Dyen made helpful comments on the comparative analysis of languages.

Several scholars read chapters of a second manuscript that I have written on the six culture areas of western North America. Although intended for the second volume, many of the comments and criticisms I received from those scholars have been helpful to me while I finished this volume. In particular, I am grateful to William W. Elmendorf for his help in the analysis of western American Indian languages and for his comments on Plateau and Northwest Coast cultures. I am also appreciative of the enlightening comments of Angelo Anastasio, Jerrold Levy, Don Fowler, Michael Moratto, Philip Drucker, Alfonso Ortiz, and Richard Clemmer.

My colleagues in the Program in Comparative Culture at the University of California, Irvine, among them Pete Clecak, Dickran Tashjian, and Jim Flink, provided the intellectual support and friendship that are necessary catalysts in any research project: on many occasions while flyfishing the great western rivers, Jim Flink has listened patiently to my tirades about how the rivers were expropriated from the subjects of this book.

Finally, Kathy, Brig, and Sarah held up well through the writing of this volume. Kathy gave me time to write, and I am in her loving debt.

January 1980   *Joseph G. Jorgensen*

WESTERN INDIANS

Chapter 1

Introduction

This volume is the first product of a comparative analysis of 172 Indian tribes of western North America. The present study seeks to analyze aboriginal environments and cultures from Yakutat Bay in Alaska to the northern part of Baja California, and from the Rockies to the Pacific Coast, as they were before contact with, and penetration by, Europeans.

The following pages will introduce readers to the comparative analysis of tribal environments, of languages, and of cultures. This application of comparative analysis is quite broad. The intention is to develop a picture of environmental, linguistic, and cultural similarities and differences in aboriginal western North America, and to offer explanations for many of these phenomena. Whereas "explanations" usually seek to remove a puzzle, to make matters plain and intelligible, many of the explanations offered herein are "concluding hypotheses," i.e., testable statements about relations among phenomena that will require testing with further data, especially data from several periods of time. Tests for many of these concluding hypotheses will be presented in subsequent volumes.

When the project was commenced in 1970 it was recognized as being too ambitious for presentation in a single volume. Its sheer size alone requires extensive exposition and analysis. For instance, comparable information on a comprehensive set of topics, referred to as "variables"* in the study, was identified, defined, and collected for analysis: 132 features of topography, climate, fauna, and flora were selected for measures of the environments, and 292 features of technology, subsistence economy, economic organi-

*See Appendix E.

zation, social organization (including demography and settlement patterns), political organization, sodalities, warfare, ceremonialism, shamanism, and related topics were selected for measures of the cultures. Lexical, phonological, and grammatical data pertaining to the languages of western North America were also collected.

The variables that were defined and classified for analysis for each of the 172 tribes represent nearly 73,000 pieces of information that have been correlated and analyzed in several fashions. In order to minimize technical and methodological discussions in the body of the text in this volume, most of the formal information pertaining to the conduct of the inquiry has been placed in the appendices. The variable code, for example, is reproduced in Appendix E: each variable is broken into subparts so that readers can see the range of measurement afforded by each variable. The way in which the variables were selected, and the research backgrounds of the scholars who made the ratings from the ethnographic and environmental sources, a test of the reliability of the ratings, and a discussion of the comprehensiveness of the variables are all found in Appendix A and Appendix B. The formal methods employed to analyze these data are discussed in Appendix C. The list of sample tribes is found in Appendix F. Maps showing how the information summarized in the variable code is distributed geographically by tribal area can be found in Appendix D.

Subsequent, more technical volumes will present explicit tests of concluding hypotheses offered here and other hypotheses drawn from evolutionary, functional, inferential historical, and neofunctional ecological modes of explanation. At several points

1

throughout this volume, however, many explanations that stem from these modes are evaluated.

TRIBES IN THE SAMPLE

A few words are in order about which Indian groups have been included in this study, which have been excluded, and how the tribes in the sample were defined.

From the approximately 250 ethnic units (usually referred to as "tribes" in the ethnographic literature) in western North America for which there is some ethnographic information, 172 were selected for this study. Unfortunately for students of western North America, even though anthropologists from the University of California conducted a Culture Element Survey in the 1930s in an attempt to fill in all large gaps, ethnographic data in sufficient quantity and quality were not then available for many tribes. That survey is of fundamental importance to the present work, nonetheless, and will be explained shortly. For the comparative study reported here, when ethnographic data pertaining to a tribe were too sparse, that tribe was excluded from the sample. Because Spanish policies and European-carried diseases ravaged tribes along the California Coast, some tribes, such as the Gabrieliño and Salinan of coastal California are poorly reported; nevertheless these two are included in the sample. The Chumash from the coastal region near Santa Barbara, and the Costanoans from the coastal region between San Francisco Bay and Monterey Bay were, however less well reported than either the Salinan or the Gabrieliño and have been excluded. European-introduced epidemics also wiped out most of the Kalapuya and neighboring Penutian-speaking tribes of western Oregon, and the Columbia Salish of the Plateau region. The information on these several groups was too meager to justify their inclusion: all of these societies hold considerable interest for a comparative study such as this, yet the reporting on these groups is so incomplete as to be useful only for illustrative materials and for conjecture. The lack of information about one of these societies—the Chumash—is particularly unfortunate. The Chumash are especially interesting because of their maritime, ocean-fishing economy, their proclivities for warfare (some scholars argue that they were especially militaristic, others that they were inordinately peaceful) and, perhaps, because of their development of the most complex political organization in California. John Harrington knew something about these people from working among them, and he filled out an element list for A. L. Kroeber's

Culture Element Survey (though he attempted to dissuade Kroeber from including Chumash data in the survey) and it is the least useful list in the entire survey.

Sparse ethnographic reporting was not the only reason for which tribes were excluded from the sample. Some closely related tribes, though well reported, were eliminated from the sample because it was deemed redundant to include them. Jorgensen's (1969) comparative analysis of thirty-five Salish tribes was used to select those twenty-four Salish tribes for the sample that were the most diverse and for which the most complete records were available. The comparative analysis by Driver et al. (1972) of North American tribes demonstrated that most of the thirty-two Western Shoshone, Northern Paiute, and Southern Paiute groups of the central and southern Great Basin for which information was available were so similar that it would serve no useful purpose to include every society in our sample. So the fourteen most heterogeneous and best-reported groups in the central and southern Great Basin were selected for the sample. The same procedure was followed in selecting Pomo (three), Miwok (three), and Wintu (three) groups, and some other groups in California, from the matrices of tribal similarities that accompanied the Culture Element Distributions.

At this point it should be made clear that the terms "tribe" and "tribal" are used here in the most convenient sense. Service (1962) popularized a definition of the tribe that was basically political. In his scheme, tribes were organizations of several different local residence-groups that were directed by councils of chiefs and whose kinship organizations were crosscut by sodality memberships. Tribal members recognized joint ownership of property and shared obligations to defend tribal property. In Service's definition, the tribe was an essential political organization that was more complex than a band, which was based principally on kinship criteria, and less complex than a chiefdom, which integrated political and economic criteria in its organization. Bands, tribes, and chiefdoms were viewed as levels of increasing evolutionary complexity in the organization of economic and political relations. Service's several definitions have little relevance for the cultural units in western North America, as we shall make clear as we proceed.

In this book, when "tribe" is used, it may be used to compare the Southern (Fort Rupert) Kwakiutl with the Haisla Kwakiutl, or the Walapai with the Northeast Yavapai, or the Yuma with the Southeast Pomo, yet not one of these groups would qualify as a tribe by Service's definition. On the other hand, each of the groups just mentioned is known as a "tribe" in the literature compiled by anthropologists, linguists, missionaries, travelers, government officials, and the like, and each has been so recognized for at least one of the following reasons: (1) the group occupied a common territory, and members spoke a mutually intelligible language or dialect of a language; or (2) the group occupied a common territory, and members possessed a similar culture; or (3) the group occupied a common territory, and members spoke a mutually intelligible language, and they shared a similar culture.

Political organization is not critical in such definitions. The Southern Kwakiutl, for instance, resided in scores of villages spread across northern Vancouver Island, adjacent islands, and the coast of British Columbia, but the village residents paid allegiance to no organization larger than the kinship groups to which they belonged, and there was generally more than one kinship group in a village. Yet the Southern Kwakiutl spoke a language that was not intelligible to the neighboring Salish and Nootka, nor even to the Bella Bella and Haihais Kwakiutl Indians. Moreover, the cultural differences between the Southern Kwakiutl and neighboring tribes were obvious. For the Southern Kwakiutl, language and culture coincided, but the many Southern Kwakiutl villages and demes within villages did not constitute a single political-territorial unit.

The Western Shoshone groups of Nevada have been recognized as tribes primarily on the basis of the territory that they frequented. For instance, the Reese River Shoshone and the Spring Valley Shoshone spoke dialects of the same language and possessed very similar cultures, but they occupied different territories and have been distinguished as separate cultural units, or tribes, on this basis.

As we assess economic, kinship, political, and ceremonial organizations, care will be exercised so as to distinguish the forms that the various territorial units took, but "tribe," or "group," or "culture," or "society," will be used from time to time to refer to—for instance—all the Southern Kwakiutl or Northern (Chilkat) Tlingit or Reese River Shoshone Indians.

Chapter 9, on political organization, analyzes governmental authority over territory in western North America, and a typology of political organizations is derived. Over 50 percent of all "tribes" in the sample recognized no authority greater than the *residential kinship group*. Polities restricted to residential kinship groups dominated areas with rich resources and dense populations, such as the Northwest Coast (with a few exceptions, such as the Tsimshian-speaking villages, some Nootkan winter villages, and some villages inhabited by the northwestern California Athapaskan speakers), yet they were also the dominant organizations in areas with meager resources and tiny populations, such as the southern and central Great Basin.

Local societies composed of several residential kin groups formally united into *villages* (known as *tribelets* in California) or *bands* were the next most common forms of political organizations. Bands were more mobile than villages. In the Rockies, bands usually convened during summer months and in the Plateau, bands usually convened during winter months. Villages (and tribelets), on the other hand, stayed together all year round, or during fall, winter, and spring.

Band organizations were relatively egalitarian, open, and simple, whether in the Plateau, the Rockies east of the Great Basin, or the Southwest (the Eastern Apaches, for example, in this last region). Yet village organizations varied from the simplicity of egalitarian Piman and Plateau settlements to the highly centralized Pueblo villages of the Tanoan speakers (San Juan, Taos, Isleta, Santa Clara, and others) and the Eastern Keres (Cochiti, Sia, Santa Ana, Santa Domingo).

The largest territorial groups were *tribes*, which were composed of several bands, the Flathead of the upper Columbia Plateau being an example, albeit an example perhaps dating from after rather than before contact with Europeans, and *districts*, which were composed of several villages, the Valley Nisenan of the Sacramento Valley being an example. Leaders of tribes and districts did not wield nearly so much authority as leaders of the Eastern Pueblo villages, so the territorial size of an organization was not closely related to centralization of political authority in western North America.

Although the societies of western North America were organized in a wide variety of political communities at the time of European contact, chiefs and other leaders seldom possessed the power to allocate strategic resources within their political communities unless those political communities were independent, residential kinship groups.

The important threads to follow as we set out to explicate and account for such complex and interdependent phenomena as economic, social, political, and ceremonial organization are the abundance, predictability, and storability of extractive resources (wild plants and animals) in western North America; the property ownership customs connected with strategic subsistence resources; and the considerable differentiation among languages in western North America.

A final detail about the groups discussed in this volume should be explained: it has to do with the names that are used to denote various groups.

Throughout this book "Nootkan," "Apachean," "Shoshonean," "Salishan" and other words with "-an" endings will be used from time to time rather than "Nootka," "Apache," "Shoshone," "Salish," and the like. Table 3-1 shows languages that compose the "-an" groups in western North America. By and large, "-an" suffixes refer to groups of societies that spoke the same language (e.g., Apachean, including Navajo and all Apache communities), or belonged to the same branch of a language family (e.g., Shoshonean, including Shoshone, Ute, Southern Paiute, Hopi, Tubatulabul, Cahuilla, and so forth), or belonged to the same language family (e.g., Salishan, including all coastal and interior Salish societies). In brief, "-an" endings can be considred pluralistic and are used to designate societies related through the inheritance and sharing of a mutually intelligible language, or

societies related through the inheritance of languages not mutually intelligible at the time of first contact with Europeans—languages that nonetheless emerged from a common mother language. The term "Tsimshian" is confusing because it refers to a set of communities speaking the same language—Tsimshian—as well as communities, such as Gitksan, which speak languages related to Tsimshian but not mutually intelligible with Tsimshian. When it is necessary to distinguish Tsimshian from Gitksan, or some specific Shoshone society from Shoshonean, distinctions will be made. Chapter 3 classifies western North American Indian societies on the basis of their genetic and typologic language relations.

A conventional representation of the tribal boundaries of western North America is shown in Figure 1-1. The units in our sample are all identified there,

Figure 1-1 *A conventional mapping of 172 tribal territories in western North America. Solid lines indicate language boundaries; dashed lines, dialect boundaries; dotted lines, territorial groups not sampled and territorial groups sampled but of the same dialect as other groups within the language or dialect.*

1 Northern Tlingit	46 Chimariko	91 Kaliwa	132 Shivwits Southern Paiute
2 Southern Tlingit	47 Trinity River Wintu	92 Akwa'ala	133 Kaibab Southern Paiute
3 Northern Massett Haida	48 McCloud River Wintu	93 Alkatcho Carrier	134 San Juan Southern Paiute
4 Southern Skidegate Haida	49 Sacramento River Wintu	94 Lower Carrier	135 Chemehuevi Southern Paiute
5 Tsimshian	50 Nomlaki	95 Chilcotin	
6 Gitksan	51 East Achomawi	96 Shuswap	136 Havasupai
7 Haisla Kwakiutl	52 West Achomawi	97 Upper Lillooet	137 Walapai
8 Haihais Kwakiutl	53 Atsugewi	98 Upper Thompson	138 Northeast Yavapai
9 Bella Bella Kwakiutl	54 Valley Maidu	99 Southern Okanagon	139 Southeast Yavapai
10 Fort Rupert Kwakiutl	55 Foothill Maidu	100 Sanpoil	140 Mohave
11 Bella Coola	56 Mountain Maidu	101 Columbia	141 Yuma
12 Clayoquot	57 Foothill Nisenan	102 Wenatchi	142 Kamia
13 Makah	58 Mountain Nisenan	103 Coeur d'Alene	143 Cocopa
14 Klahuse	59 Southern Nisenan	104 Kalispel	144 Maricopa
15 Pentlatch	60 Coast Yuki	105 Flathead	145 Pima
16 Squamish Salish	61 Yuki	106 Kutenai	146 Papago
17 Cowichan Salish	62 Yana	107 Nez Percé	147 North Tonto Western Apache
18 West Sanetch	63 Northern Pomo	108 Umatilla	148 South Tonto Western Apache
19 Upper Stalo	64 Eastern Pomo	109 Klikitat	149 San Carlos Western Apache
20 Lower Fraser	65 Southern Pomo	110 Wilshram	150 Cibecue Western Apache
21 Lummi	66 Wappo	111 Tenino	151 White Mountain Western Apache
22 Klallam	67 Patwin	112 Klamath	152 Warm Springs Chiricahua Apache
23 Twana	68 Northern Miwok	113 Modoc	153 Huachuca Chiricahua Apache
24 Quinault	69 Central Miwok	114 Wada-Dokado Northern Paiute	154 Mescalero Apache
25 Puyallup	70 Southern Miwok	115 Kidu-Dokado Northern Paiute	155 Lipan Apache
26 Quileute	71 San Joaquin Mono	116 Kuyui-Dokado Northern Paiute	156 Jicarilla Apache
27 Lower Chinook	72 Kings River Mono	117 Owens Valley Northern Paiute	157 Western Navajo
28 Tillamook	73 Chuckchansi Yokuts	118 Panamint Shoshone	158 Eastern Navajo
29 Alsea	74 Kings River Yokuts	119 Washo	159 Hopi
30 Siuslaw	75 Kaweah Yokuts	120 Reese River Shoshone	160 Zuni
31 Coos	76 Lake Yokuts	121 Spring Valley Shoshone	161 Acoma
32 Tututni	77 Yauelmani Yokuts	122 Ruby Valley Shoshone	162 Sia Keres
33 Chetco	78 Tubatulabal	123 Battle Mountain Shoshone	163 Santa Ana Keres
34 Galice Creek	79 Kawaiisu	124 Gosiute Shoshone	164 Santo Domingo Keres
35 Tolowa	80 Salinan	125 Bohogue Shoshone	165 Cochiti
36 Yurok	81 Gabrieliño	126 Agaiduku Shoshone	166 San Juan Tewa
37 Karok	82 Luiseño	127 Hukundika Shoshone	167 San Ildefonso Tewa
38 Hupa	83 Cupeño	128 Wind River Shoshone	168 Santa Clara Tewa
39 Wiyot	84 Serrano	129 Uintah Ute	169 Nambe Tewa
40 Sinkyone	85 Desert Cahuilla	130 Uncompaghre Ute	170 Taos
41 Mattole	86 Pass Cahuilla	131 Wimonuch Ute	171 Isleta
42 Nongatl	87 Mountain Cahuilla		172 Jemez
43 Kato	88 Mountain Diegueño		
44 East Shasta	89 Western Diegueño		
45 West Shasta	90 Desert Diegueño		

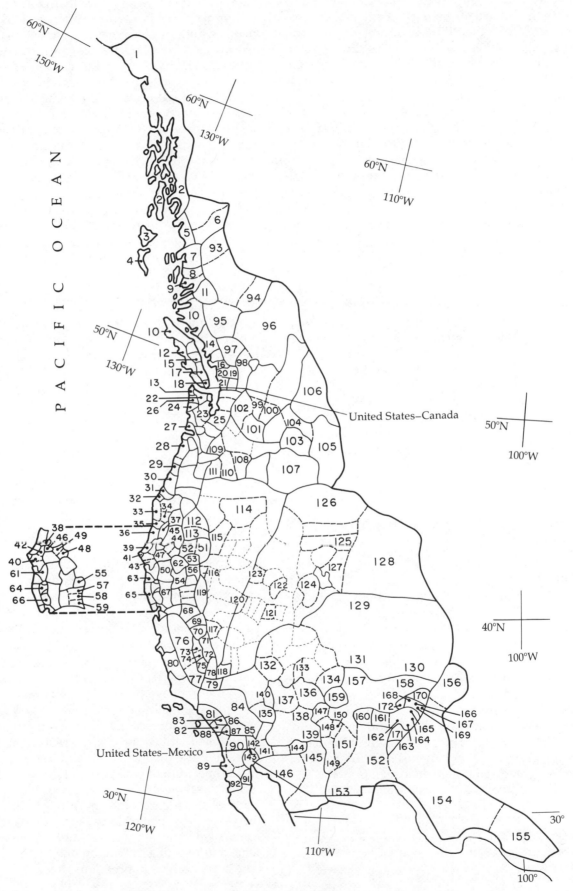

PACIFIC OCEAN

60°N
150°W

60°N
130°W

60°N
110°W

United States–Canada

50°N
130°W

50°N
100°W

40°N
100°W

United States–Mexico

30°N
120°W

110°W

30°
100°

from the Northern Tlingit (Chilkat) near Yakutat Bay, Alaska, to the Kaliwa of the northern Baja California peninsula. Except that the easternmost Utes and Apaches spilled out east of the Rockies, from west to east all of the tribes inhabited an area extending from the islands close to the Pacific shore to the Rocky Mountains.

Figure 1-2 represents the approximate centers of the tribal territories for the tribes in our sample. Figure 1-2 looks different from Figure 1-1 because it was drawn by computer (as is explained in Appendix C), and because the flat and square projection of the latitudinal and longitudinal quadrants magnifies distances the more northerly the tribes. Figure 1-2 is especially important because a large portion of the data that are analyzed in the following chapters are presented in distribution maps similar to Figure 1-2. About 240 of the 443 variables listed in Appendix E have been mapped and are included in Appendix D, and reference to these maps is made throughout the text. Figure 1-2 will serve as a guide to identifying tribes in the variable maps, since in those maps cultural and environmental attributes are designated with various symbols that always have the same location for each tribe, from map to map.

The conventional mapping in Figure 1-1 is also used as a basic illustration within several chapters of the text, to show cultural and environmental areas that have been determined through comparisons made within categories of variables.

WHY WESTERN NORTH AMERICA, AND WHY COMPARISONS?

Western North America was selected as the region to be analyzed because of the wealth of ethnographic and comparative lexical data that are available, and because of the robust theorizing that has been generated to account for cultural phenomena in the region.* Students of anthropological theory will recognize the theories in the following roster, which were advanced in large part to account for phenomena in western North America and that found applicability elsewhere in the world. The scholars who formulated these theories often found themselves the focus of worldwide debate about the adequacy of the theories they had advanced. This was true of Alfred L.

Kroeber's theories of inferential culture history for California and all of North America (1939); Ruth Benedict's notions of the basic personality structures of Northwest Coast and Pueblo cultures (1934); Elman Service's claims about the evolution of Great Basin bands and Northwest Coast chiefdoms (1962); Fred Eggan's cultural ecological generalizations about the relations among environment, kinship, and ceremonial organization throughout the Pueblos (1950); Julian Steward's theories of the relations between ecology and the sociocultural evolution of Pueblo villages and Great Basin bands (1937, 1938); and Harold Driver's generalizations about the interplay of evolution, history, and function in explaining girls' puberty rights, kinship organization, and other phenomena (1941, 1956, 1966). This is but a partial list of theories that have found wide applicability and have also provoked debates about their utility.

More recently, a number of young scholars have breathed new life into the study of aboriginal western North America. A form of neofunctional cultural ecology that ultimately leans heavily on the General System Theory of von Bertalanffy in defining culture as one part of a larger biological and abiological system has been employed by various anthropologists to account for the potlatch phenomenon on the Northwest Coast (Vayda 1961, Piddocke 1965, Suttles 1960 a, b); feasts, trade, wealth, and exchanges in California (Gould 1976, King 1976, Vayda 1966, Bean 1972); ritual in the Pueblos (Ford 1972); and demography and settlement patterns in the Great Basin (Thomas 1972). Students who owe some intellectual debts to ideas culled from French structuralism (as in the work of Claude Levi-Strauss), and semiotics (particularly the work of Victor Turner), have shed new light on the kinship and ceremonial organizations of the Southwest (Ortiz 1969, Hieb 1972, Lamphere 1969), and the mythologies of many tribes in western North America (e.g., see Levi-Strauss 1967, and a critique by Thomas, Kronenfeld, and Kronenfeld 1976).

The many theories that have been offered to account for various facets of Indian culture in western North America (with the exception of those of Driver and Kroeber) have practically always been advanced to explain something about one or two tribes, and have begged for explicit tests. Formal comparisons among many tribes and many variables, to determine whether these theories could withstand scrutiny over a wide spectrum of data pertaining to a large group of societies, seemed necessary. It may be the case that many of the theories that have been advanced over the years seem plausible because their authors have marshalled only a small amount of data, selecting some and rejecting others, on one tribe so as to illustrate preconceived impressions. In order to test these

---

*"Theory" is used in a nonspecialized sense of postulating relations among several phenomena. The "theory" accounts for the relations.

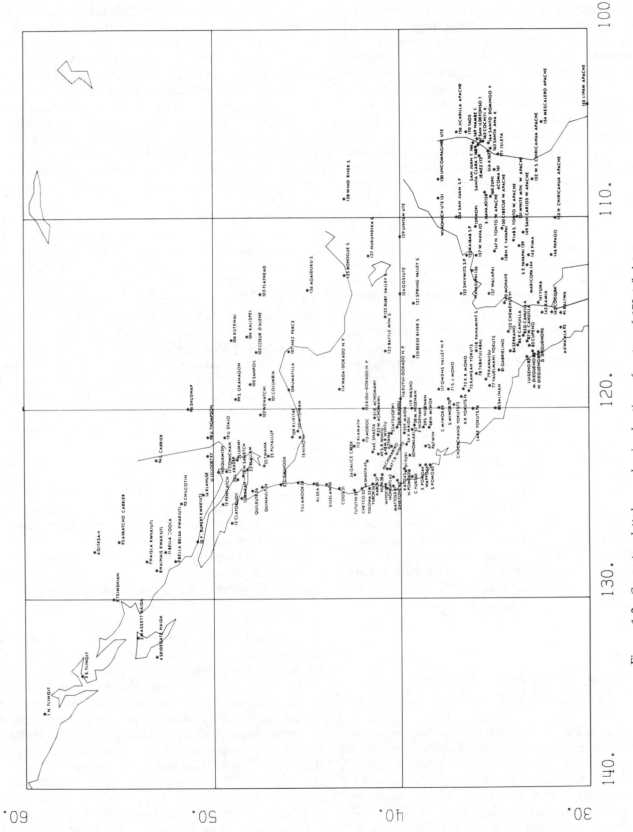

Figure 1-2 *Computer-plotted map showing locations of centers of 172 tribal ter-*
ritories in western North America. The mappings of variables in Appendix D follow
the format of this map. Tribe names are listed by number at Figure 1-1.

and other theories, it was necessary to define variables on a wide variety of topics and to collect information on those variables for a large sample of tribes distributed over a continuous geographic region.

Comparative analysis applied to many societies within a continuous geographic area has the strength of allowing the researcher to command ethnographic information on a large number of societies with greater depth and breadth than is possible for a worldwide sample of the same number of societies, while it forces ethnologists to recognize similarities and differences among tribes that are often overlooked by scholars who analyze one society in depth. By the method of making explicit comparisons of languages and cultures, the researcher becomes aware of the interactions among many cultures through such acts as trade, warfare, intermarriage, ceremonial attendance, or the intercommunity requests for shamans. This procedure alone helps the researcher to define a "regional ethnographic context" (Driver 1966; Jorgensen 1974; White 1975).

A comparative study of a continuous geographic region does not insure that, even if a person controls a vast amount of information, acceptable generalizations will be offered. Indeed, one of the most enduring charms of ethnology is that all of its theories are vulnerable, but one of its drawbacks is that the way in which competing theories are evaluated is usually through polemics. Perhaps this facet of the discipline adds to its spirited nature. A brief review of continuous-area comparisons of western North America seems to substantiate the foregoing: the debates among inferential historians, evolutionists, functionalists, structuralists, neofunctional ecologists, Marxists, and comparativists (whether employing continuous-area or world-wide samples and whether leaning toward inferential-historical, ecological, or evolutionary perspectives) began in anthropology 90 years ago and show no signs of abating.

COMPARATIVE STUDIES OF WESTERN NORTH AMERICA

As early as 1894, Franz Boas analyzed a corpus of folktale elements from several adjacent Northwest Coast and Plateau tribes, a tribe in eastern Canada, and a tribe on the Plains. He calculated the similarity for each pair of tribes and ordered the results in matrices—the more similar the tribes, the closer together they were placed in the matrix. Boas demonstrated that Northwest Coast tribes shared much in common, as did Plateau tribes, and that tribes from

those two areas were more similar to each other than to the Plains and eastern Canadian tribes. Boas hoped to learn why, even when adjacent tribes resembled each other, resemblances were only resemblances and not identicalities. That the tribes were connected historically through the acts of borrowing of tales and the inheritance of tales from a mother culture, whence daughter cultures separated and migrated, could not be denied, but there were not sufficient data on enough topics to begin to answer Boas's questions, nor were there firm, documented sources from which history could be reconstructed, and he never again carried out a formal comparison of cultural materials.

Alfred L. Kroeber, one of Boas's first students at Columbia University, moved to the University of California, Berkeley, upon achievement of his Ph.D. degree and set out to study the cultures and languages of California (see Driver 1962 for a detailed history of Kroeber's activities). Very early in his career he began using matrix analysis to organize interlanguage and intertribe relations, and relations among and within archeological sites. By the late 1920s, Kroeber had stimulated several students to follow him in using proximity measures (percentages of agreement and the like) organized in matrices to determine the clustering of ethnic units from the same period of time in continuous geographical areas. The goals in all of these studies were to classify the relationships among ethnic units or among aspects of the cultures of these units, such as the Sun Dance, and to reconstruct the history of the cultures or of certain aspects of the cultures, such as the Sun Dance. The "history" was, of course, wholly inferential, being surmised from the proximity coefficients.

In 1935, the first number in a series entitled *Culture Element Distributions* (CED) was published in the *University of California Publications in American Archeology and Ethnology*. That first number, "The Structure of California Indian Culture" by Stanislaw Klimek, is seldom cited, but it is a magnificent early example of comparative ethnological analysis applied to a single, continuous geographic region, and of the kinds of debates that generalizations about culture can engender, especially generalizations about the origins of culture. Kroeber, by now the preeminent student of California Indian cultures and languages, had invited Klimek, a European, to visit California and to use data that Kroeber had collected among the Indian communities of California over a 35-year period. Many of these data had been published in Kroeber's *Handbook of the Indians of California* (1925).

Klimek attempted to use Kroeber's data on about 800 cultural traits distributed among 60 tribes, intercorrelating tribes and traits. As he proceeded, Klimek learned that information on all 800 traits was not available for every tribe, so he reduced the number of traits to 411, heavily stressing items of material culture for which there was information for most of the 60 tribes. Klimek's comparisons of cultural inventories (the cultural traits shared by each pair of cultures) allowed him to determine culture areas (the groups of tribes that were most similar—that is, Q-mode analysis), as well as groups of traits (the traits that were most highly intercorrelated—R-mode analysis). Examples of Q-mode and R-mode analysis are the following:

Q-Mode: Tribe with Tribe

	Pomo	Wappo	Patwin
Pomo	X	.75	.50
Wappo		X	.70
Patwin			X

R-Mode: Trait with Trait

	Flat hat	Alnus decor	Overlay twining
Flat hat	X	.70	.60
Alnus decor		X	.65
Overlay twining			X

Klimek also made some gross correlations between culture areas and language dialect groups, and between groups of cultural traits and language dialect groups. Going a step further, he made some even cruder analyses of racial types, which he then compared with the language and culture distributions so as to reconstruct California Indian "history."

Inasmuch as practically none of the data used in the comparisons were obtained from various points of time in documented history, which would be necessary in order to compare tribes, languages, and physical types at say, three or more different times, the "reconstruction" was not based on a diachronic or temporal analysis at all. Rather, the data were drawn from the "ethnographic present," as was true for Kroeber's own studies as well. The ethnographic present refers, roughly, to a seemingly timeless period just before European contact. That period would be the early eighteenth century along most of the Pacific Coast, and somewhere between the mid-

sixteenth century and mid-eighteenth century for the rest of western America. The validity of the ethnographic present, then, depended upon the assumption that all data representative of that period, whether they were linguistic or cultural, were synchronic; that is, they were data from some single time immediately preceding European contact and subsequent influence, or from a period in which time is held constant, as opposed to diachronic.

After comparing aspects of culture, language, and human physical types, as these were evident in synchronic data, Klimek (1935) interpreted California Indian history from the correlations that were obtained. The assumptions on which the interpretation was based were that (1) people speaking dialects of the same language, and languages of the same language family shared a common history, having diverged from the same protolanguage (mother language); (2) tribes sharing the same cultural traits either borrowed them from their neighbors, or inherited them from the protoculture from which they diverged; (3) similarity of physical type meant genetic similarity—inheritance of the same physical features; and (4) arranging groups of cultural traits and clusters of tribes into scalograms—thus organizing sets of tribes on the basis of the similarity of their cultural inventories, and separating each set from all other sets—determined "cultural strata," which, when correlated with sets of tribes, determined "historical facts." Following is an example of a scalogram with two "strata" in Klimek's terminology:

		Tribes				
	Karok	Yurok	Wiyot	Mohave	Yuma	Chemehuevi
Flat hat	+	+	+			
Alnus decor	+	+	+			
Overlay twining	+	+	+			
Pottery: Paddle				+	+	+
U-Ladder cradle				+	+	+
Twined bags				+	+	+

(Culture trait)

When cultural strata were correlated, in the main, with tribes from the same language family, the traits in question were alleged to have had but a single origin, whence they received wider distributions through segmentation and migration of tribes from mother cultures. In Klimek's view, the "historical facts" drawn from synchronic data were not inferences, or even concluding hypotheses: they were *facts*. Klimek left no room in his theory for the independent invention of phenomena, and he showed no interest in assessing the possibility that people in similar environments might borrow traits because of environmental advantages in doing so.

Kroeber, interested in the relations between culture and environment but disposed to show that environmental effects were usually overridden by cultural forces and the histories of particular cultures, wrote a separate introduction to Klimek's work, in part because he strenuously objected to Klimek's reconstruction of the historical sequences of California Indians. But Kroeber was motivated by other reasons as well. For instance, Kroeber agreed that Klimek's formal methodology was sound, and that the clusterings of tribes (Q-mode), of cultural traits (R-mode), and of tribes with traits (cultural strata in scalograms) represented real progress over the methods used by Kroeber and his students, which were primarily in the Q-mode. But Kroeber was surprised that the data he and other scholars had collected on California tribes were so spotty. He pointed out that Klimek's analysis revealed the "extent of the deficiencies in existing knowledge" about California cultures, languages, and archeology. Yet Kroeber knew that the ethnography of California's tribes was much more systematically and completely reported than was the ethnography of the tribes of all other areas of western North America. Kroeber, with his unceasing interest in inferential history and the internal logical rules that he presumed were inherent in cultures, reasoned that if the historical sequences of California Indian cultures were to be reconstructed, some measure of relative sequence would have to be employed to do so. It was Kroeber's opinion that relative sequences could be posited by direct archeological evidence, or through comparison of cultural data on tribes throughout the rest of western North America, or through better classifications of the physical types or language types of each local society. Klimek's bold interpretations caused Kroeber to see clearly some of the shortcoming of his own work and to be uncomfortable about Klimek's conclusions.

Because the data available on California societies and societies in the adjacent regions were not sufficient to make the comparisons vital to reconstructions of historical sequences, Kroeber promptly initiated the Culture Element Survey from his base at the University of California, Berkeley, with the intention of collecting comparable data not only throughout California, but throughout the Northwest Coast, Plateau, Great Basin, and Southwest. Kroeber reasoned

that if explanations he, Klimek, or other comparativists advanced were to be warranted, to be supported, empirical data must be collected that, when compared, would support or reject the explanations.

Kroeber's colleagues, such as Edward Gifford, and his students, such as Harold Driver, Philip Drucker, Julian Steward, and Homer Barnett, were sent out to collect comparable information on topics ranging from technological items to magical practices. Although the Culture Element Survey was not begun until the mid-1930s, the investigators were told to seek the oldest and best-informed people in each society, and to record information these elders could give about the cultures of their grandparents. In other words, the ethnographers were asked to collect "recall ethnographies" about what native cultures were like prior to European contact.

Because the ethnographers checked off the responses of their informants on long lists of traits, recording pluses for elements that were present, and minuses for elements that were absent, the Culture Element Distributions that were published for each tribe became known as "checklists," though a more popular and pejorative referent used by anthropologists over the years has been "laundry lists." The lists were collected during the depths of the Great Depression, and many of the fledgling anthropologists found the job distasteful and mindless, a rote procedure leading nowhere, an exercise that robbed culture of everything—its life, its spirit, its intricate connections, and its sentiments. Many accepted their assignments for the modest stipend that was offered. Although many were in disagreement with the speed with which this vast ethnographic salvage project was conducted, some went on to write excellent areal monographs from their field data (see Barnett 1955, and Drucker 1951).

Kroeber, apparently, was undaunted. At the time his survey was undertaken, detailed monographs had been written on particular cultures by scholars of great skill and reputation, such as himself, Edward Sapir, Matilda Cox Stevenson, Franz Boas, Leslie Spier, Robert Lowie, Edward Gifford, Ronald Olson, Ruth Benedict, Elsie Clews Parsons, Frank Cushing, Edward Loeb, and Roland Dixon. Kroeber thought that even in the most intensive of these, some cultural items were invariably overlooked. The Culture Element Survey was intended to fill in the picture, to determine which cultural acts, objects, ideas, and sentiments were present, and which were absent, and to record the presence and absence for every society in western North America. Then, and only then, could comparative inquiry proceed and could warranted explanations be advanced.

Each researcher was given one or more assignments—these were to collect information from informants in several tribes from one geographic region, such as the Fraser and Columbia Plateau, or northwestern California, or the Oregon coast. As each researcher completed an assignment, either Kroeber or the researcher tallied the lists, obtained proximity coefficients for every pair of tribes, and organized the tribes into a matrix on the basis of their similarities. The most similar tribes were placed most closely together in the standard Q-mode format. For example, here are the Culture Element Distributions found by Barnett (1939) for Gulf of Georgia Salish tribes (boxes group the tribes that were found to have the greatest similarity):

	Pentlatch	Comox	Homalco	Klahuse	Slaiamun
Pentlatch	X	.91	.13	.22	.36
Comox		X	.36	.39	.76
Homalco			X	.86	.76
Klahuse				X	.74
Slaiamun					X

Kroeber or the researcher then made a few brief comparisons and published the lists and the ordered matrices. If the researcher wrote generalizations about the meaning of the matrices with which Kroeber disagreed, Kroeber supplied a note of his own.

Kroeber did not attempt to make formal comparisons of all of western North America, even though this was the specific reason he cited for embarking on the Culture Element Survey. It was Kroeber's view that one could not infer the history of California, as Klimek had done and, by implication, as Kroeber himself had done, without establishing control groups consisting of tribes and languages outside of California.

Kroeber's major comparative work on North America, *Cultural and Natural Areas of Native North America* (1939), was completed in final form in 1931. It is wholly impressionistic in methodology, and it was not rewritten to accommodate the new data that was made available by the Culture Element Survey.

In point of fact, the distributions from the Culture Element Survey are of value only if a scholar has read all of the traditional essay monographs and articles on the society in question. In that fashion the element lists can be understood because the elements can be checked against statements in the essays, and the new material that does not occur in the essays can be fitted into the picture that the essay creates. If there are no traditional monographs on a society, the element lists can be best understood if the researcher has comparative knowledge of related and neighboring tribes.

Harold Driver (1941, 1956, 1966, and with James Coffin 1975) employed the data made available by the Culture Element Survey, in addition to traditional ethnographic accounts, to push the continuous area methodology further than anyone else. His study of "Girls' Puberty Rites in Western North America" (Driver 1941) incorporated correlational analysis of tribes with tribes (Q-mode), traits with traits (R-mode), and traits with tribes (scalogram), much as Klimek had done, but his interpretations were a major break from those of Kroeber and Klimek. Driver integrated ecological, psychological, inferential history (as inferred from correlations of cultures with languages), documented history, native explanations, and physiological explanations into his overall explanation of girls' puberty rites.

His subsequent analyses were confined neither to girls' puberty rites nor to western North America (Driver 1956, 1966; Driver and Coffin 1975). They were addressed to the entirety of the North American continent, and in these studies Driver integrated functional, evolutionary, and historical theories to account for many aspects of North American Indian culture, but particularly kinship organization.

The intention in this volume and others that will follow it is to make a systematic comparison of the data that have been collected in such great quantity about western North American Indians in traditional ethnographies and in the Culture Element Survey, so as to provide empirically warranted generalizations about a broad group of topics that have animated students of culture for years.

THREE GENERATIONS OF ETHNOGRAPHY

Luckily, scholars of western North American Indians are blessed with a rich body of ethnographic literature purporting to represent Indian culture prior to extensive European contact. Perhaps no other region of the world is so well reported. Moreover, the traditional essay ethnographies as well as the Culture Element Distributions were researched and written by eminent scholars who were or are deeply involved in basic data collection as well as the theoretical issues of their periods. Without question, the region has provided the data base and the nexus for many of the most interesting and enduring debates in anthropology and comparative linguistics.

The first generation of scholars to undertake ethnologic and linguistic analyses of the tribes in western North America, working approximately between 1890 and 1930, reads like a Who's Who of American Anthropology. Franz Boas began his ethnologic career in the Arctic, but by the late 1880s had begun research on the Northwest Coast of North America. He studied many Northwest Coast tribes, but from 1885 to 1930 his central concern was with the Kwakiutl of British Columbia. Boas challenged the explanations of culture offered by the cultural evolutionists of his day (see White 1963), and subsequently exercised a profound influence on the nature of theorizing in American anthropology. Alfred Kroeber's important contributions to kinship analysis and inferential culture history, which drew him into debates with British functionalists, were at the center of anthropological debating for two decades. As was pointed out earlier, Edward Sapir, Elsie Clews Parsons, Edward Loeb, Ruth Benedict, Edward Gifford, Ronald Olson, Matilda Cox Stevenson, Robert Lowie, Frank Cushing, and Roland Dixon were among the other competent anthropologists who conducted basic ethnographic work in western North America in the first three decades of this century. The traditional essay monographs that they published on the tribes they studied range widely in quality and completeness, but all have been consulted in conducting the research for this volume. Some of the monographs are thin because researchers spent little time collecting information among some tribes. Many do not touch on topics that were not theoretically interesting during the period in which the research was conducted. Kroeber attempted to fill in such gaps with the Culture Element Survey, and during the same period—the 1930s—many young anthropologists with new theoretical ideas embarked on field research among the tribes of the West.

This second generation of scholars, most of whom conducted their field work in the 1930s, contributed enormously to the ethnographic picture of western North America, as well as to the theoretical debates of the time. Harold Driver, Homer Barnett, Julian Steward, Robert Heizer, William Duncan Strong, Cora DuBois, Ralph Beals, and Omer Stewart are some of the scholars who received their training at the University of California under Kroeber and Kroeber's colleagues Lowie, Olson, and Gifford. Most of these anthropologists, as well as some not mentioned here, participated in the Culture Element Survey, and then went on to contribute their own views to the an-

thropological debates that continued from the 1930s to the present.

A few of the prime ethnographers of this second generation and some of the theoretical areas in which they worked warrant mention. Homer Barnett's investigations of the Coast Salish, including his remarkable dissertation on the nature of the potlatch, have not been superseded for clarity or rigor. The potlatch phenomenon on the Northwest Coast has stimulated spirited theoretical debates for four decades. The potlatch has been explained from many anthropological perspectives, including the economic, evolutionary, French structuralist, and functional ecological modes. Later in this volume the potlatch is analyzed; the reader will find considerable support for Barnett's views. Harold Driver's contributions to comparative methodology and to a formal synthesis of evolutionary, historical, and functional explanations in kinship analysis stemmed from his field research in California. Julian Steward's ecological and evolutionary explanations grew from his extensive field work in the Great Basin and Southwest. As was stated earlier, these three anthropologists were products of training at the University of California by Kroeber or his colleagues.

Second-generation scholars trained at other major universities have also made significant contributions to the analysis of western North American culture. Leslie A. White, Fred Eggan, and Morris Opler, who received their training at the University of Chicago, and Mischa Titiev, who received his training at Harvard University, made critical contributions to the ethnography of the Puebloan and Apachean Indians; moreover, Eggan's theoretical contributions to the relations among environment, kinship organization, and ceremonial organization throughout the Pueblos has also influenced ethnology elsewhere in the world. Grenville Goodwin, Verne Ray, Erna Gunther, Burt Aginsky, Viola Garfield, Ruth Underhill, and Esther Goldfrank are other significant ethnographers of this second generation; their ethnographic work as well as their ethnological explanations have shaped this study. Most important, if these people had not collected the data about American Indian culture which were still available in the 1930s, a comparative study such as the one reported in this volume could not have been carried out.

A third generation of scholars interested in the Indians of western North America dates from about 1950. These scholars have conducted their research after the time when basic ethnographic data for the pre-European period could be reliably recalled by native informants. Following those scholars who shared concerns about what cultures were like at the time of European contact, and how they came to be that way, the research of this third generation has been directed toward analysis of the ethnographic materials collected by those scholars who preceded and often taught them—in essence, pouring old wine into new bottles. With the exception of ethnohistorical research, the period from 1950 on has been a time for digestion of what is available, rather than for the collection of new materials.

Evolutionary, functional ecological, French structuralist, and other modes of explanation have been advanced to account for kinship and ceremonialism in aboriginal California; for rank, slavery, and the potlatch on the aboriginal Northwest Coast; for economy and society in the aboriginal Great Basin; and for other phenomena. Many other questions have been pursued. For instance, increasing numbers of ethnologists of western tribes have been concerned mainly with modern affairs—modern religion, economics, kinship, politics, psychology, and the like. The work of these scholars does not concern us here, but it will in a future volume.

A few of the third-generation scholars who have addressed themselves to accounting for how, and why, western North American Indian societies were as they were at contact are David Aberle, Helen Codere, Elman Service, Marshall Sahlins, Wayne Suttles, Alfonso Ortiz, Keith Basso, Andrew Vayda, Edward Dozier, and Robert Murphy. Anthropological linguists, led by such scholars as Maurice Swadesh, Isidore Dyen, Kenneth Hale, Wick Miller, William Elmendorf, Mary Haas, and Patrick Wenger have, through innovative comparative methodologies, provided invaluable analyses of language relations in the West. These now make possible many inferences about historical relations among tribes and, in conjunction with comparisons of cultural and environmental data, make it possible to present the new interpretations of western North American culture that are contained in this volume.

In the process of collecting information, it was necessary to read every available ethnography—both essay-style and checklist—on each tribe. For each variable we recorded the sources and pages for all data and wrote notes about each variable. The information that resulted is voluminous: the variable worksheets on which sources and notes were recorded total about 2,500 pages, far too many to reproduce here. The compromise solution has been to publish the Bibliographic References Arranged by Tribe at the back of this volume to show the sources used for each tribe, and variable distribution maps to demonstrate the ratings of the tribes on about 240 of the 443 variables in the sample. Scholars who desire a complete listing of all the ratings for each society in the sample, or copies of pages that list the specific sources for each rating may request them from the author. In the text itself, references to authors have been kept to a bare minimum.

PART I

ABORIGINAL ENVIRONMENTS

Chapter 2

Environment

That western North America holds prospects of great riches for the intrepid venturer has fascinated Europeans and their American progeny ever since the first Spanish incursions into the Southwest in the sixteenth century. Then, even as they are today, the environments of the West were viewed with awe not only because of the challenge faced in conquering them but also because of their alluring beauty. The mountains harbored great mineral wealth; the ocean, straits, bays, and coastal rivers were abundant with sea mammals and large anadromous fish that spawned in fresh water; the coast ranges were heavily forested with enormous infestation-resistant trees; and the river systems, mountains, and lakes supported fur-bearing animals sought for their pelts and large game animals hunted for their skins. Not only were these riches available, but the land itself was eminently habitable. The American West, save the Northwest Coast region from Cape Mendocino in California northward through Alaska, was bathed in sun and provided vast open spaces defined by spectacular mountains.

The first Europeans to visit the West were Spaniards led by Coronado who, in 1540, sought the fabled Seven Golden Cities of Cibola in northern New Mexico. Coronado marched north into one of the most arid environments in western North America, and though he did not find mineral wealth, his party came upon the densely populated farming villages of the Pueblo Indians in the Rio Grande Valley. The Pueblos had coped brilliantly with thier environments, but these had not offered them the material riches Coronado sought. Before Coronoda left the area he rounded up and killed 200 Pueblo men because of the natives' reluctance to supply food, clothing, and women during the Spanish occupation. This led to more bloodshed as Pueblos fought back, only to be decisively defeated. Three subsequent Spanish expeditions plundered their way up and down the Rio Grande before 1598, when Juan Oñate went back to the Rio Grande Valley with the intention of colonizing it. If gold and silver were to be found, time would be needed for exploration, and the local populations would have to be controlled through colonization, which held the prospects of making some riches through farming and ranching. By Oñate's plan for colonization, *encomiendas* were created for each soldier in his charge. An *encomienda* was a land grant carrying with it the right of *repartimiento*. In brief, *repartimiento* granted the right of the landowner, the *encomendero*, to use the labor of local Indians. The profits from Indian labor were shared between the king and the *encomendero*. (See Spicer 1962 for a brief review of this history.)

Thus, from the first, the history of European enterprise in the West centered on the pursuit of extractable riches, and this soon became linked to colonization and farming. Always there were lands to be conquered, peoples to be harnessed or displaced, and prospects of wealth. The notion of abundances of resources in the West fueled men's ambitions in the eighteenth century and especially in the nineteenth century.

As late as 1893, some 28 years after the conclusion of the Civil War and 300 years after the first Spanish settled in the Southwest, Frederick Jackson Turner characterized the American West of the nineteenth century as an area of free land, a frontier that, through efforts to conquer it, provided an impetus for American development. In Turner's view, by 1893 the

17

West had been won, for the frontier had been closed. Although Turner and most other American historians until the past decade did not linger long on the matter of assessing the lives of Indians who occupied the land when it was said to have been "won," that is, when the environment rather than the Indians had been conquered, historians were surely correct in their assessments of western North America. The large scale and great diversity with which western resources were utilized had begun to leave noticeable imprints in nearly every region of the West by the end of the nineteenth century.

By 1893, salmon, cod, halibut, and whale were all being hauled from western waters by commercial fisheries, and the sea-otter had been harvested almost to extinction. The vast redwood and giant-sequoia forests of California and southern Oregon were being denuded, and lumbering teams were setting to work in the red- and yellow-cedar and Douglas-fir forests of Oregon, Washington, British Columbia, and southern Alaska. In rivers at the milling sites, where logs were stored or transported by floating, mill effluents, wood litter, and leached chemicals changed fish habitats and depleted the populations of salmon, steelhead, sturgeon, and lamprey. In nearly all the mountains of the West, miners were digging in search of copper, gold, silver, coal, asphalt, lead, iron, and other mineral treasures; the silts and minerals that leached from the mine tailings altered the biota of mountainsides and rivers.

As settlements grew, it became necessary to cut timber in nearby browse areas and forests for firewood, fences, barns, and houses, as well as for the railroad ties and telegraph poles that connected settlements. Deer, elk, and antelope populations in arid areas dwindled once such forests were reduced, and through competition with livestock raised by farmers.

In California, by clearing the oak forests and woodlands so that farms could be laid out, farmers also wiped out the several kinds of grizzly bears that were the major animal influents in the ecology of the sclerophyll forests.

The fragile soils of the intermontane regions of the West were not suited for the extensive agriculture and enormous irrigation systems implemented in them; they were soon overgrazed, and relations among native flora and fauna were changed forever. Alkaline flats were a common result of irrigation; flash floods eroded soils once overgrazing and overbrowsing had eliminated the naturally sparse cover of vegetation. Sagebrush and saltbush distributions increased in the impoverished soils, and large plant-eating animals began to diminish.

In the process of winning the West, the non-Indian populations had come to control the vast majority of the western environments as well; Indian populations, which had shrunk in size by about 90 percent, watched these environments often undergo marked transformations as most of the natural resources that had once supported Indians now became the spoils of others or were simply ruined.

In planning to analyze the environments of western North America for this book, it was desirable to establish a baseline that, so near as possible, would be representative of the period prior to massive occupations by non-Indians. The task was not simple because, as a result of that occupation, huge changes took place throughout the West, in forest and desert alike. It was deemed crucial to gather information on edible food sources in the native environments, the local topographies, the local precipitation, and the local climates.

SELECTION OF ENVIRONMENTAL AREAS

As a first step in analyzing the environments of western North America, a sample of 132 environmental variables was created, which included 7 variables to measure temperature, precipitation, and topography; 70 variables to measure animals (including land animals, acquatic animals, and birds); and 55 variables to measure wild plants. This may be the largest sample of environmental variables ever assembled and correlated. The geographical boundaries of the 172 culture units in the sample (Figures 1-1 and 1-2) were used to delineate the areas to be measured. The correlations among the assemblages of variables representing each tribal territory makes it possible to establish environmental areas for western North America at the time of European contact. Each area encompassed a set of tribal territories that were, on the whole, more similar to one another than they were to territories classified in other areas.

Geographically, the environmental areas analyzed ranged westward to the Pacific, from 60° N. Latitude 140° W. Longitude in the northwesternmost part to 30° N. Latitude 100° W. Longitude in the southeasternmost part, an area mainly to the west of the Continental Divide except in the south (the southeasternmost tribal environments were those just east of the Pecos River in Texas). Figure 2-1 shows the principal land forms, rivers, and lakes of the part of the West dealt with in this book.

During the planning, it was recognized that exhaustive environmental inventories for the geography depicted in Figure 2-1 could not be constructed

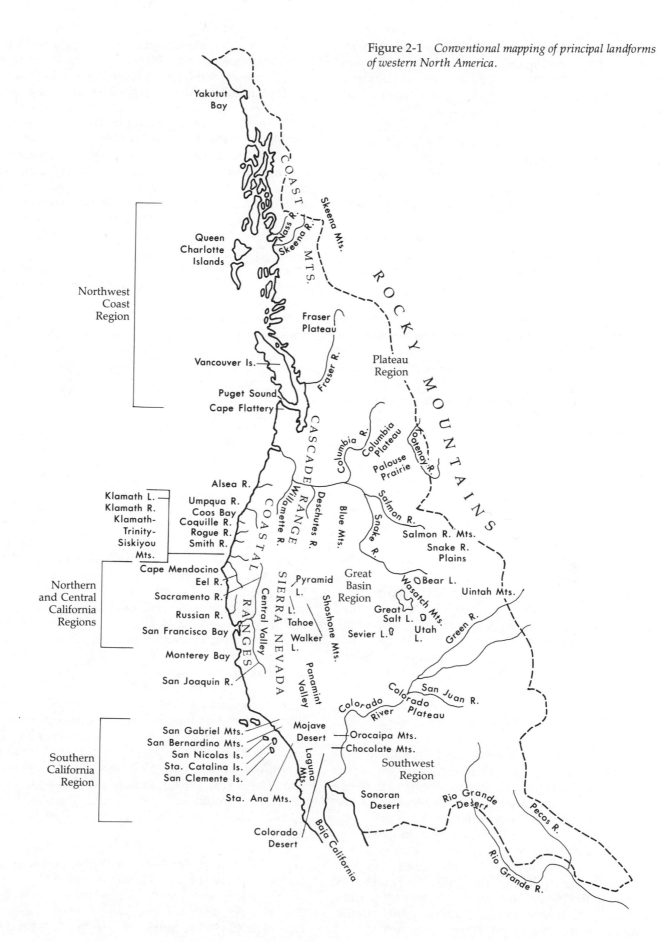

Figure 2-1 *Conventional mapping of principal landforms of western North America.*

because the biological and abiological environments of any geographical space comprise indefinitely many plants and animals, types of soils and water, elevations of terrain, and so forth. In order to have a general inventory for all of the area, from Yakutat Bay in Alaska on the north to the Mexico–United States border on the south, and from the Rocky Mountains on the east to the Pacific Ocean on the west, it was reasoned that any sample used should include large numbers of plants and animals that were important foods in native diets. Because of the relations among the variety and abundance of plants, the size, variety, and abundance of plant-eating animal species, and the size, variety, and abundance of predatory animal species, we sampled a wide variety of trees, grasses, forbs, succulents, cacti, and lilies among the plants, and we also took note of dominant plants in each area, regardless of whether or not the dominant was a direct food source for natives of the area. A dominant is a species that exercises considerable control over the organisms in a region. For instance, the coniferous forests of the north Pacific Coast were dominated by western red-cedar, western hemlock, Douglas-fir, and Sitka spruce. These enormous trees reduced the intensity of light on the forest floor and thereby influenced the ground cover and the animals in the area. Large mammals and large birds coped more effectively in the coniferous forests than did small mammals; therefore, bears, deer, and mountain goats were the major animal influents in these forests, and the red fox and porcupine were the minor influents.

As plants, plant dominants, and many land mammals were sampled, indicators of the relationships among plants and animals in an environment were generated. Dominant plant species were weighted two or three times as much as other plants, depending on their distribution in a tribal region. The entire list of the plants and animals analyzed in the sample is included along with other variables in Appendix E.

As for marine life, saltwater fish, anadromous fish, and freshwater fish were all sampled, and the total amount of fish available per year in each square mile of tribal territory was estimated by following Rostlund (1952). This provided us with sample measures of the variety of species available, as well as with the total amount of fish available to each Indian group. The distributions of sea mammals—all the way from whales to the sea-otter—were rated along the coast, but it was not possible to gain good measures of the abundance of these animals other than in the fact that more species of large whales plied the coast in the north than in the south. We also learned that most nineteenth- and twentieth-century whaling centered in northern waters, suggesting that populations of sea mammals were densest and perhaps also greatest in the northern waters. The greatest variety of sea mammal species, on the other hand, occurred in rookeries and migration routes along the coast of California, but species populations were neither as large nor as concentrated as they were farther north.

Shellfish and most birds proved too difficult to sample. Because hundreds of species of birds migrated up and down the Pacific Flyway each year, and because most of the major waterfowl, especially ducks, geese, and swans, flew across all the tribal regions in our sample, we could not easily distinguish among regions on this basis, and only four birds were sampled. Shellfish were even more difficult. They occurred everywhere along the coast, and the shellfish beds were used heavily by Indians and sea-otters alike. Because data on shellfish species and their distributions were uneven and incomplete, they have not been included in the sample.

ENVIRONMENTAL AREAS

General Trends Throughout Western Environments

The environmental inventories of all 172 tribal territories in the sample were intercorrelated, ranked, and mapped into a two-dimensional representation through the use of a nonmetric algorithm that determines the smallest distances among a number of points (correlation ranks) in a Euclidean space. Nine regions defined with relative clarity met our expectations about what the western North American landscape, including plants and animals, should look like, and these are shown in Figure 2-2. There, the environments of the coastal tribes form a tier from top to bottom on the right-hand side. Moreover, from Masset Haida (upper right) to Western Diegueño (bottom center) the environments fall into a rather neat set of distributions with ocean and island regions closer to the right-hand periphery, and territories on sheltered straits, bays, and sounds behind them on the left. The tribes that are farthest to the upper left within the Northwest Coast group (Northern Tlingit to Pentlatch and Klallam to Lower Fraser) are those of Puget Sound in Washington, of Georgia Strait in British Columbia, and of the Skagway–White Pass region in Alaska.

The division of the Pacific Coast into three areas shows a marked break between the northern and southern parts of the California coastline. The break would be less severe if the cultural information about the societies that occupied the central California coastal region between the areas of the Pomo and the

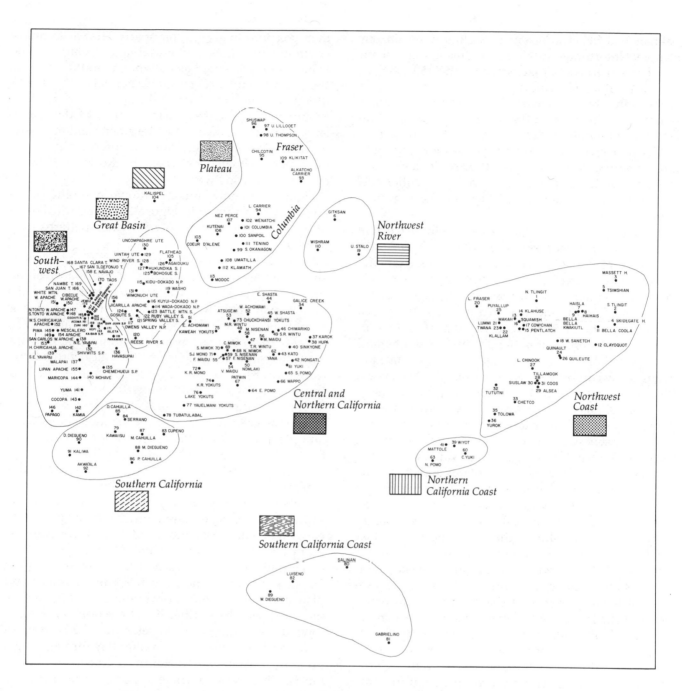

Figure 2-2 *Two-dimensional mapping of environments of the 172 tribal areas in western North America derived from the MINISSA nonmetric, smallest-space algorithm of Lingoes and Roskam (1971), applied to Driver's G coefficients based on 132 environmental variables (334 attributes of climate, topography, fauna, and flora).*

Salinan had been sufficient to include them in our sample. Unfortunately, the Coast Miwok, Costanoan, and Esselen tribelets that occupied the 150 miles of coastal territory from north of San Francisco Bay to Big Sur, and the Chumash, who occupied the 80 miles of coastal territory from the Salinan boundary to the Gabrieliño boundary, did not endure the imposition of Hispanic civilization and missionization, and only fragmentary information about them remains. Because the cultural data were so meager, neither cultural nor environmental variables for these groups were included.

In the upper center of Figure 2–2 are three clusters of environments representing, from north to south, the areas of the Skeena Mountains (for example, Gitskan and Alkatcho Carrier tribes), the Cascade Mountains (Tenino tribe), the coastal ranges (Galice Creek and Karok), and the area between the Sierra Nevada and the California coastal range (East Pomo). The three clusters in this tier are juxtaposed behind clusters representing the coastal areas in a fashion that is easily comprehended. For example, Northwest River environments of the interior mountain passes are more similar to Northwest Coast environments than to Southern California coast environments, as the relative closeness of clusters shows, and the closer a tribal territory is to the right-hand side of a cluster, the closer it is to the coastal mountains and the Pacific Ocean. Yet the geometric distances from the central clusters of interior environments in Figure 2–2 to the environments clustered at the left side of the figure (farther inland) are shorter than from the central clusters to the coastal environments. The major factor contributing to the wide separation of coastal environments from the environments that abut them on the east is the presence of sea mammals and ocean fishes. If shellfishes had been included in the sample, the tribal data points signifying coastal environments would have been plotted farther toward the right-hand side of the figure. It is apparent that, though the coastal environments and interior environments closest to the coast are arranged in the figure in a top-to-bottom and right-to-left order that matches well with their north-to-south and west-to-east relationships in geographic space, the same cannot be said of the Euclidian geometric distance representing difference between coastal and interior environments; the latter distance is markedly different from geographic distance and represents important ecological differences between the areas.

The third group of environmental clusters, farthest to the left in the figure, represents, from top to bottom, the north-to-south distributions of the major interior basins of western North America. As among the other two groups, the closer the territories are to the right-hand sides of the clusters, the more western

their positions in geographic space. The westernmost environments, those of Fraser and Columbia Plateaus, are represented as data points in the center of the figure, and are situated between the Rocky Mountains and the Coast Mountains and Cascade Mountains. The Great Basin, farther to the left, is situated between the Rocky Mountains and the Sierra Nevada. The Southwest cluster represents tribal environments situated between the Rocky Mountains and the Colorado River.

Figure 2–3 shows a conventional mapping of the environments shown in Figure 2–2. The tribal areas in Figure 2–3 are coded with the same patterns used in Figure 2–2.

Figure 2-4 is another representation of the relationships among the environments of the 172 tribal territories in the study. The treelike features of the dendrogram link tribal territories to their closest neighbors. Although the treelike diagrams oversimplify the relations among environments, showing them in only one dimension, they also provide information that is not provided in the smallest space-mappings, to wit: the vertical margins of the figure show the levels of similarity shared by pairs or by groups of territories. Except for the slightly aberrant placement of the Plateau territories and some of the territories in Southern California, the unaided eye can easily transform the one-dimensional dendrogram representation to fit the two-dimensional representation, and in so doing we can gain information about the percentage of similarities within and among environmental areas. From left to right, Figure 2-4 groups (a) the coastal environments at 60 percent average similarity, (b) the second-tier interior valleys at 72 percent, and (c) the third-tier interior basins and plateaus at 76 percent. Furthermore, within each of the three sets the northernmost environments occur toward the bottom of each set. Thus the Northwest Coast environments from Yakutat Bay through Puget Sound (or, from the Northern Tlingit to the Lower Fraser tribal areas), average 87 percent similarity, and so forth.

The separation of the coastal environments from those of the northern rivers and the California interior, and from all of the basins, plateaus, and canyonland environments is pronounced, and the differences are highly significant ($P < .001$). All of the interior environments, from the farthest west to the farthest east, and from north to south, averaged 67 percent similarity.

Later on in this chapter a brief sketch of the environmental regions corresponding to the main culture areas will be provided. For now, let us compare the distributions of several plants, animals, and climatological features for all the tribal territories of the West.

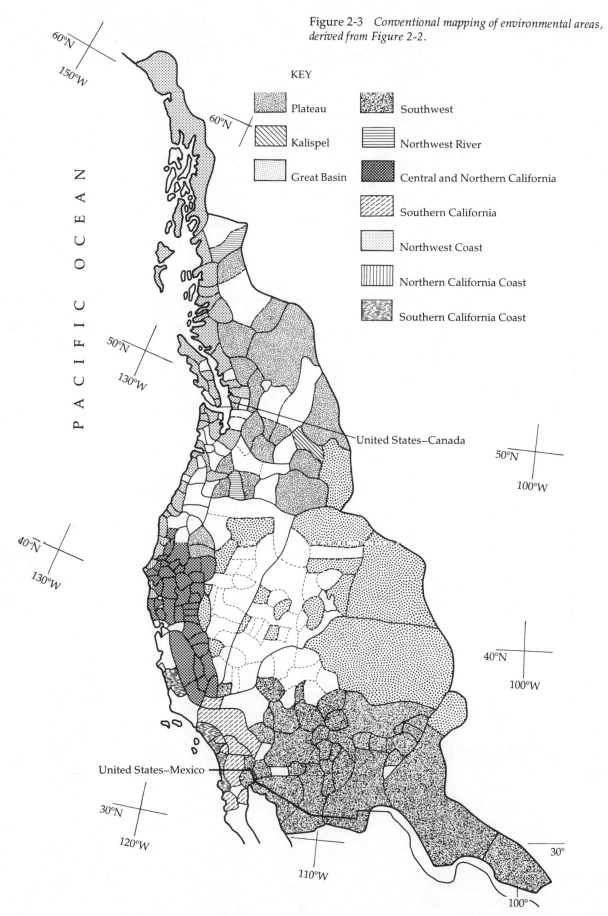

Figure 2-3 *Conventional mapping of environmental areas, derived from Figure 2-2.*

KEY

- Plateau
- Kalispel
- Great Basin
- Southwest
- Northwest River
- Central and Northern California
- Southern California
- Northwest Coast
- Northern California Coast
- Southern California Coast

PACIFIC OCEAN

United States–Canada

United States–Mexico

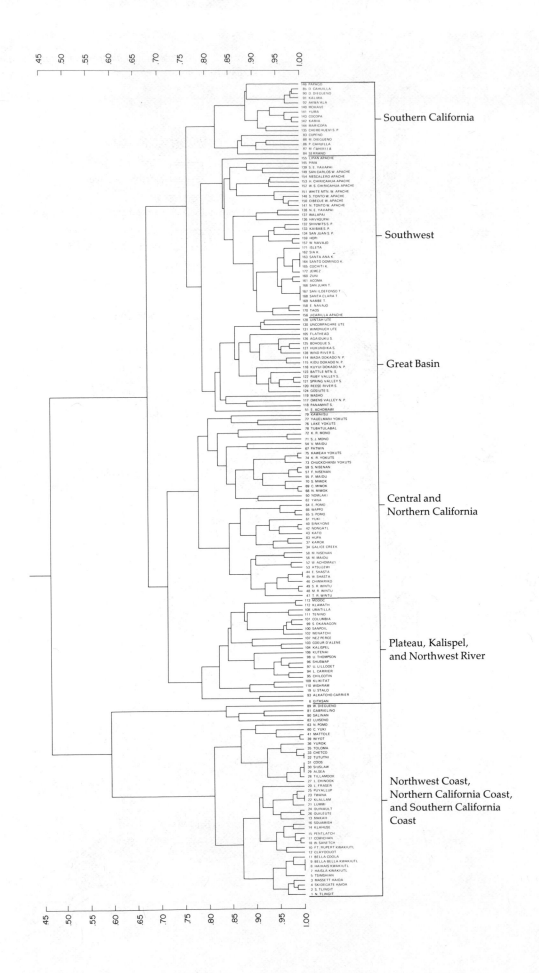

Figure 2-4 *Environmental tree: 1. Groupings of tribal territories derived from G coefficients based on 132 variables (334 attributes) which include measures of climate, topography, flora, and fauna.*

SOUTHERN CALIFORNIA

146 Papago
85 Desert Cahuilla
90 Western Diegueño
91 Kaliwa
92 Akwa'ala
140 Mohave
141 Yuma
143 Cocopa
142 Kamia
144 Maricopa
135 Chemehuevi Southern
    Paiute
83 Cupeño
88 Mountain Diegueño
86 Pass Cahuilla
87 Mountain Cahuilla
84 Serrano

SOUTHWEST

155 Lipan Apache
145 Pima
139 Southeast Yavapai
149 San Carlos Western Apache
154 Mescalero Apache
153 Huachuca Chiricahua
    Apache
152 Warm Springs Chiricahua
    Apache
151 White Mountain Western
    Apache
148 South Tonto Western
    Apache
150 Cibecue Western Apache
147 North Tonto Western
    Apache
138 Northeast Yavapai
137 Walapai
136 Havasupai
132 Shivwits Southern Paiute
133 Kaibab Southern Paiute
134 San Juan Southern Paiute
159 Hopi
157 Western Navajo
171 Isleta
162 Sia Keres
163 Santa Ana Keres
164 Santo Domingo Keres
165 Cochiti

172 Jemez
160 Zuni
161 Acoma
166 San Juan Tewa
167 San Ildefonso Tewa
168 Santa Clara Tewa
169 Nambe Tewa
158 Eastern Navajo
170 Taos
156 Jicarilla Apache

GREAT BASIN

129 Uintah Ute
130 Uncompaghre Ute
131 Wimonuch Ute
105 Flathead
126 Agaiduku Shoshone
125 Bohogue Shoshone
127 Hukundika Shoshone
128 Wind River Shoshone
114 Wada-Dokado Northern
    Paiute
115 Kidu-Dokado Northern
    Paiute
116 Kuyui-Dokado Northern
    Paiute
123 Battle Mountain Shoshone
122 Ruby Valley Shoshone
121 Spring Valley Shoshone
120 Reese River Shoshone
124 Gosiute Shoshone
119 Washo
117 Owens Valley Northern
    Paiute
118 Panamint Shoshone
51 East Achomawi

CENTRAL AND NORTHERN
CALIFORNIA

79 Kawaiisu
77 Yauelmani Yokuts
76 Lake Yokuts
78 Tubatulabal
72 Kings River Mono
71 San Joaquin Mono
54 Valley Maidu
67 Patwin
75 Kaweah Yokuts
74 Kings River Yokuts

73 Chuckchansi Yokuts
59 Southern Nisenan
57 Foothill Nisenan
55 Foothill Maidu
70 Southern Miwok
69 Central Miwok
68 Northern Miwok
50 Nomlaki
62 Yana
64 Eastern Pomo
66 Wappo
65 Southern Pomo
61 Yuki
40 Sinkyone
42 Nongatl
43 Kato
38 Hupa
37 Karok
34 Galice Creek
58 Mountain Nisenan
56 Mountain Maidu
52 West Achomawi
53 Atsugewi
44 East Shasta
45 West Shasta
46 Chimariko
49 Sacramento River
    Wintu
48 McCloud River Wintu
47 Trinity River Wintu

PLATEAU

113 Modoc
112 Klamath
108 Umatilla
111 Tenino
101 Columbia
99 Southern Okanagon
100 Sanpoil
102 Wenatchi
107 Nez Percé
103 Coeur d'Alene
104 Kalispel
106 Kutenai
98 Upper Thompson
96 Shuswap
97 Upper Lillooet
94 Lower Carrier
95 Chilcotin

109 Klikitat
110 Wishram
19 Upper Stalo
93 Alkatcho Carrier
6 Gitksan

COAST

89 Western Diegueño
81 Gabrielino
80 Salinan
82 Luiseño
63 Northern Pomo
60 Coast Yuki
41 Mattole
39 Wiyot
36 Yurok
35 Tolowa
33 Chetco
32 Tututni
31 Coos
30 Siuslaw
29 Alsea
28 Tillamook
27 Lower Chinook
20 Lower Fraser
25 Puyallup
23 Twana
22 Klallam
21 Lummi
24 Quinault
26 Quileute
13 Makah
16 Squamish
14 Klahuse
15 Pentlatch
17 Cowichan
18 West Sanetch
10 Fort Rupert
   Kwakuitl
12 Clayoquot
11 Bella Coola
9 Bella Bella Kwaikiutl
8 Haihais Kwakiutl
7 Haisla Kwakiutl
5 Tsimshian
3 Massett Haida
4 Skidegate
2 Southern Tlingit
1 Northern Tlingit

Climatic and Topographic Influences

The distribution of plant life in western North America does not produce sets of tribal environments that are identical to those produced by incorporating all of the other environmental variables in the sample. For example, in Figure 2-5, which compares the similarities of tribal environments in terms of flora, climate, and topography, the key factor that separates the environments is aridity. At the bottom of the figure, the Southern California, Colorado River Desert, and Southwest environments form a southern set, sharing about 64 percent similarity, and it is joined with the Great Basin and Plateau environments. These hot deserts, cold deserts, and semideserts not only received less precipitation than the Northwest Coast and Central California (the two next higher sets), but the precipitation patterns for the latter two regions were reversed: environments along the northern coast and in Central California gained their precipitation in the winters, and the

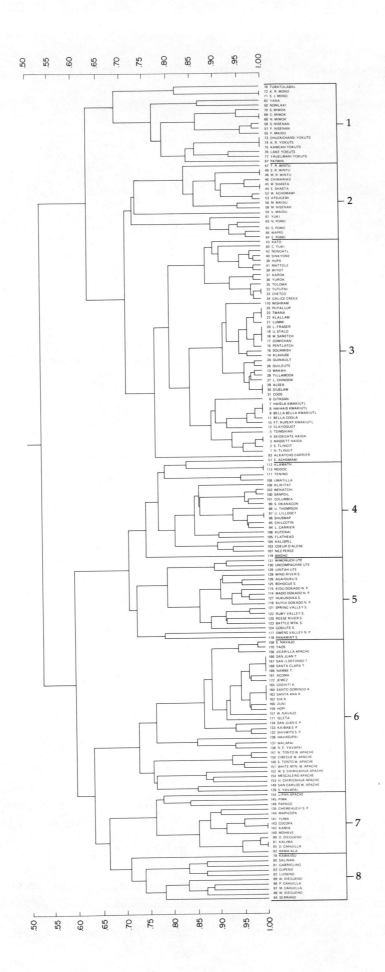

Figure 2-5 *Environmental tree: 2. Groupings of tribal territories of western North America derived from G coefficients based on 62 variables (185 attributes) which include measures of climate, topography, and flora.*

GROUP 1

78 Tubatulabal
72 Kings River Mono
71 San Joaquin Mono
62 Yana
50 Nomlaki
70 Southern Miwok
69 Central Miwok
68 Northern Miwok
59 Southern Nisenan
57 Foothill Nisenan
55 Foothill Maidu
73 Chuckchansi Yokuts
74 Kings River Mono
75 Kaweah Yokuts
76 Lake Yokuts
77 Yauelmani Yokuts
67 Patwin

GROUP 2

47 Trinity River Wintu
49 Sacramento River Wintu
48 McCloud River Wintu
46 Chimariko
45 West Shasta
44 East Shasta
52 West Achomawi
53 Atsugewi
56 Mountain Maidu
58 Mountain Nisenan
54 Valley Maidu
61 Yuki
63 Northern Pomo
65 Southern Pomo
66 Wappo
64 Eastern Pomo

GROUP 3

43 Kato
60 Coast Yuki
42 Nongatl
40 Sinkyone
38 Hupa
41 Mattole
39 Wiyot
37 Karok
36 Yurok
35 Tolowa
32 Tututni

33 Chetco
34 Galice Creek
110 Wishram
25 Puyallup
23 Twana
22 Klallam
21 Lummi
20 Lower Fraser
19 Upper Stalo
18 West Sanetch
17 Cowichan
15 Pentlatch
16 Squamish
14 Klahuse
24 Quinault
26 Quileute
13 Makah
28 Tillamook
27 Lower Chinook
29 Alsea
30 Siuslaw
31 Coos
6 Gitksan
7 Haisla Kwakiutl
8 Haihais Kwakiutl
9 Bella Bella Kwakiutl
11 Bella Coola
10 Fort Rupert Kwakiutl
12 Clayoquot
5 Tsimshian
4 Skidegate Haida
3 Massett Haida
2 Southern Tlingit
1 Northern Tlingit
93 Alkatcho Carrier

GROUP 4

51 East Achomawi
112 Klamath
113 Modoc
111 Tenino
108 Umatilla
109 Klikitat
102 Wenatchi
100 Sanpoil
101 Columbia
99 Southern Okanagon
98 Upper Thompson
97 Upper Lillooet

96 Shuswap
95 Chilcotin
94 Lower Carrier
106 Kutenai
105 Flathead
104 Kalispel
103 Coeur d'Alene
107 Nez Percé
119 Washo

GROUP 5

131 Wimonuch Ute
130 Uncompaghre Ute
129 Uintah Ute
128 Wind River Shoshone
126 Agaiduku Shoshone
125 Bohogue Shoshone
115 Kidu-Dokado Northern Paiute
114 Wada-Dokado Northern Paiute
127 Hukundika Shoshone
116 Kuyui-Dokado Northern Paiute
121 Spring Valley Shoshone
122 Ruby Valley Shoshone
120 Reese River Shoshone
123 Battle Mountain Shoshone
124 Gosiute Shoshone
117 Owens Valley Northern Paiute
118 Panamint Shoshone

GROUP 6

158 Eastern Navajo
170 Taos
156 Jicarilla Apache
166 San Juan Tewa
167 San Ildefonso Tewa
168 Santa Clara Tewa
169 Nambe Tewa
161 Acoma
172 Jemez
165 Cochiti
164 Santo Domingo Keres
163 Santa Ana Keres
162 Sia Keres
160 Zuni
159 Hopi

157 Western Navajo
171 Isleta
134 San Juan Southern Paiute
133 Kaibab Southern Paiute
132 Shivwits Southern Paiute
136 Havasupai
137 Walapai
138 Northeast Yavapai
147 North Tonto Western Apache
150 Cibecue Western Apache
148 South Tonto Western Apache
151 White Mountain Western Apache
152 Warm Springs Chiricahua Apache
154 Mescalero Apache
153 Huachuca Chiricahua Apache
149 San Carlos Western Apache
139 Southeast Yavapai

GROUP 7

155 Lipan Apache
145 Pima
146 Papago
135 Chemehuevi Southern Paiute
144 Maricopa
141 Yuma
143 Cocopa
142 Kamia
140 Mohave
90 Desert Diegueño
91 Kaliwa
85 Desert Cahuilla
92 Akwa'ala

GROUP 8

79 Kawaiisu
80 Salinan
81 Gabrieliño
83 Cupeño
82 Luiseño
89 Western Diegueño
86 Pass Cahuilla
87 Mountain Cahuilla
88 Mountain Diegueño
84 Serraño

interior regions gained the bulk of their precipitation during the summer months. The exceptions were the coniferous montane regions that interrupted the deserts and semideserts. The farther east the mountainous areas were from the coastal ranges, the Cascades, and the Sierra Nevada, the more precipitation received year round. Since some of the sets in Figure 2-5 do not coincide with the environmental regions that are referred to elsewhere, the sets are merely numbered from 1 to 8 instead of being identified with regional designations. Figure 2-6 is a conventional representation of the areas obtained in Figure 2-5.

The twenty-year average of annual precipitation for all of the tribal territories in western North America demonstrates that precipitation decreases markedly east of the Sierra, the Cascade Mountains, and the coastal ranges and increases in the mountainous pockets to the east. This can be seen in Map E-4 in Appendix D, which is a distribution of V-4, Appendix E.*

---

*The complete definition for each variable that has been mapped can be found in Appendix E.

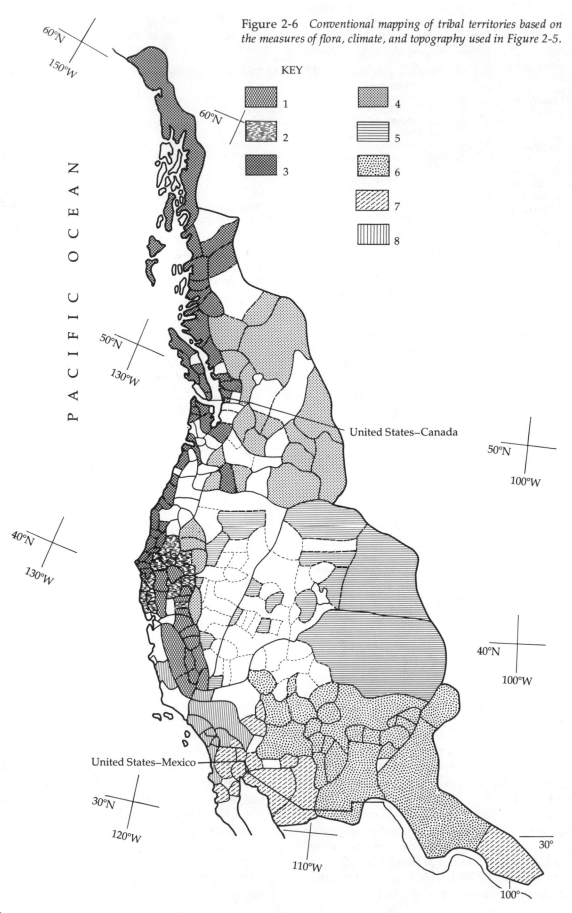

Figure 2-6 *Conventional mapping of tribal territories based on the measures of flora, climate, and topography used in Figure 2-5.*

KEY

1
2
3
4
5
6
7
8

PACIFIC OCEAN

60°N
150°W

60°N

50°N
130°W

40°N
130°W

United States–Canada

50°N
100°W

40°N
100°W

United States–Mexico

30°N
120°W

110°W

30°

100°

The distribution of many of the 132 variables comprising the biological and abiological phenomena analyzed in this chapter have been summarized in 15 maps located in Appendix D. The environmental features of western North America form distinct areal clusters, and these spatial clusters can be comprehended visually. The reader is encouraged to consult the maps in Appendix D in the course of reading this chapter.

The soils of the northern coastal region of western North America were acidic and rich, as they were constantly mulched by needles and other organic material that fell to the forest floor and fed the soil through the action of rain and favorable bacteria. Natural vegetation areas for each tribal territory can be seen in Map E-5, V-5. The Northwest Coast is dominated by conifers; that region is distinct from the (1) western pine regions of Northern California and the mountains to the east, (2) the pinyon–juniper areas of Central California, (3) the fragile alkaline soils and sandy soils that characterized the shadscale areas of the cold deserts of the northern Great Basin and Plateau, and (4) the creosote–mesquite (chaparral) areas of the hot deserts of the Southwest.

The temperatures for the tribal territories, drawn from the averages of their high and low readings for the months of January and July, provide information about the mildness of coastal climates—even in their most northern reaches—the extreme heat of the hot deserts of the Colorado River region, and the winter cold of the Fraser Plateau in the Canadian interior, to mention a few key features of western temperatures (Map E-6, V-6; Map E-7, V-7). The sparse vegetation and high altitudes in the areas east of the Sierra and the Cascades gave the soil little insulation against extreme temperatures; because there was little cloud cover, nighttime temperatures cooled rapidly throughout the year, and in the winter, daytime sunshine regularly sent temperatures well above freezing on the majority of days. The extreme range of temperatures on any day, summer or winter, could be 40 degrees. Although the hot desert areas did not normally experience such fluctuations, temperatures could dip below freezing on winter nights in the easternmost areas.

Flora Sampled

There were more than 600 species of wild plants in western North America at the time of the first Euro-

pean contact with Indians. How many of these species were used by various tribes for construction of houses and tools, for firewood, food, drinks, narcotics, and medicines is not known, but the number was surely very high. In a detailed analysis of the ethnobiology of the Eastern Apaches of the Southwest, Castetter and Opler (1936) noted the uses of more than 100 species, and they did not suggest that they had made an exhaustive list of all of the plants used by those tribes. Barrows (1900) noted 60 food plants used by the Cahuilla of Southern California and another 28 species used as narcotics and for medicinal purposes. The lists of plant uses are very long for every tribe, and especially so for tribes in the arid regions; as one can imagine, some were much more important than others. Lists of the most important food plants for each region are provided later in this chapter, in "Descriptions of Major Environments."

It was considered neither possible nor necessary to collect data on all of the wild plants in western North America. For instance, the Liliaceae (lily) family alone embraced 90 genera and species ranging from camas (genus *Quamasia* or *Camassia*), the most important root crop in the West with more than five known species, to the Joshua-tree (*Yucca brevifolia*) of the Mojave Desert. Instead, it was decided to select a small sample of the wild plants; toward this end, 55 species in several genera were selected. Often species from more than one genus occurred in an area and were used for the same purpose or in the same fashion. If the species were widely and abundantly distributed, they were treated separately. Otherwise, they were treated jointly as if they were one species. Table 2-1 lists all of the wild-plant genera in our sample in which more than one species were considered to be important food items in one or another tribal territory in western North America. Where a set of species has been bracketed, that set of species was weighted as if it were equivalent to a single species.

Because the total number of animals and plants studied here is so large (altogether 125 species or genera) it was decided to map plants into groups of those that were exploited in somewhat similar fashions, rather than to group them strictly by families or genera. For each tribal territory, the number of types of plants within each group was rank-ordered on the basis of how many species or genera in each plant-group occurred in the tribal area. Let us examine some of these groups briefly, since the rank orders provide good indicators of abundances of plants.

Of twelve species of oak and tan-oak (genera *Quercus* and *Lithocarpus*), all producers of edible acorns, ten were distributed most heavily in California, where they dominated the foothills and valleys of the

Table 2-1
Wild plant genera sampled, for which more than one species was deemed an important food item

Common name	Taxonomic name	Common name	Taxonomic name
Camas	* ⌈ *Quamasia quamash* *esculenta* three other spp. ⌋	Mescal	*A. deserti* *A. neomexicana* *A. palmeri* *A. parryi*
Common purslane	⌈ *Portulaca oleracea* *retusa* ⌋	Oak, blue	*Quercus douglasii*
Hackberry	⌈ *Celtis douglasii* *reticulata* ⌋	Oak, California black	*Q. kelloggii*
		Oak, California live	*Q. agrifolia*
Honey mesquite and other mesquites	⌈ *Prosopis glandulosa* *juliflora* *velutina* ⌋	Oak, California white or valley	*Q. lobata*
		Oak, Emory or scrub	*Q. emoryi*
Lambsquarter	⌈ *Chenopodium album* *capitatum* *fremontii* *leptophyllum* *murale* *rubrum* ⌋	Oak, evergreen or scrub live	*Q. undulata*
		Oak, Gambel or scrub	*Q. gambelii*
		Oak, interior live	*Q. wislizenii*
Lupine	⌈ *Lupinus littoralis* *polyphyllus* ⌋	Oak, maul or canyon live	*Q. chrysolepis*
Mescal	*Agave americana* *A. conesii*	Oak, Oregon white	*Q. garryana*

*Species that are bracketed were given a weighting equivalent to a single species.

interior (Map E-8, V-431). East of the Sierra grew two additional species of scrub oak. Both of these species grew in the Southwest and one grew in some territories in the Great Basin. In some foothill zones from southern New Mexico and Arizona through eastern Utah and western Colorado, scrub oak dominated.

Pines (*Pinus* spp.) that bore large, edible seeds were prominent in Indian diets wherever they occurred. The seeds from most pines were edible, but those that were preferred grew on the sugar pine (*P. lambertiana*), a 200-foot giant of the California Coast Range, the Sierra, and the Cascades; the digger pine (*P. sabiniana*) of the California foothills; the ponderosa pine (*P. ponderosa*) of all the western pine forests; the shore pine (*P. contorta*) of the Northwest Coast; and the lodgepole pine (*P.c. latifolia, P.c. murrayana*) of the interior mountains. Of all pines, two pinyons, *P. edulis* and *P. monophylla*, produced seeds so large that

they were referred to as nuts. These trees were distributed in large pinyon–juniper groves that dominated the vegetation in some of the foothill regions and on some of the mesas or plateaus throughout the Southwest and the Great Basin (Map E-9, V-432). Seed-bearing pines were abundant in the California foothills and mountains, including some that were not included in the sample made for this study. But on the coast, where the massive hemlock, redwoods, cedar, Douglas-fir, and Sitka spruce dominated, edible-seed pines did not fare well, except for the shore pine, which grew close to wind-swept coastal waters. Interior mountains from the Fraser Plateau to the Rio Grande desert were often dominated by western pine, lodgepole pine, and ponderosa pine. In the southern interior, where the vegetation was generally sparse (below the 40° N. Latitude), considerable food was provided by the co-occurrence of two or three pine species, including the pinyons, and two

Common name	Taxonomic name	Common name	Taxonomic name
Pine, digger	*Pinus sabiniana*	Indian millet a.k.a.	*Eriocoma cuspidata*
Pine, sugar	*P. lambertiana*	Serviceberry	*Amelanchior alnifolia*
Pine, shore	*P. contorta*		*florida*
			pallida
Pine, lodgepole	*P. c. latifolia*		*prunifolia*
	P. c. murrayana	Sunflower	*Helianthus annuus*
Pine, yellow or ponderosa	*P. ponderosa*	Sunflower	*H. aridus*
			bolanderi
Pinyon, double-leaf	*P. edulis*	Tan-oak	*Lithocarpus densiflora*
Pinyon, single-leaf	*P. monophylla*	Thistle	*Cirsium acaule*
			eatoni
Prickly-pear and cholla cactis	*Opuntia arborescens*		*virginianum*
	clavata	Wild potato	*Solanum fendleri*
	engelmanni		*jamesii*
	polycantha		*triflorum*
Saltbush	*Atriplex argentea*	Wild rye	*Elymus condensatus*
	cornuta		*sibiricus*
	nuttallii		*virginianum*
	philonitra		
Sand-bunchgrass, rice-grass, and Indian millet	*Oryzopsis hymenoides miliacae*	Yuccas (datil, Joshua-tree, soapweed, and Spanish saber)	*Yucca baccata*
			brevifolia
			glauca
			whipplei

scrub oak species; these grew in the mountainous and high plateau territories.

The majority of the edible-seed pine species occurred in the western pine forests and adjacent to the sclerophyll (predominantly oak) forests of California, and not across the breadth of other vegetation areas. The Indians of California, from north to south, had access to the greatest variety and number of edible seeds and nuts from trees.

Mesquite, yucca, cactus, and mescal were plants of the desert. Mesquites *(Prosopis juliflora* or honey mesquite, *P. glandulosa,* and *P. velutina),* were shrubby trees growing to 20 feet or more, and favored river banks, oases, and dry stream beds. Mesquite provided vast quantities of highly storable pods for eating. The leaves were cut and boiled and used for treating eyes irritated by desert heat and sand. Mesquite sap was also used for this purpose. On the Colorado River Desert from the present-day cities of

Needles on the north to Yuma on the south, the honey mesquite grew at two levels along the banks of the Colorado River and formed a continuous distribution at the highest level. Along this stretch, which winds for about 200 miles, the mesquite attained trunks eight inches in diameter. In the early twentieth century mesquite trees were greatly depleted for use as fuel for steamers on the Colorado River. Mesquite belongs to the pea family (Leguminosae), as does another important desert plant—the screwbean— *(Prosopis pubescens,* or *Strombocarpa* spp.) species of which are close relatives of the mesquite.

In Map E-10, V-433, these desert legumes have been grouped with the genus *Yucca* (Liliaceae family), in which are found soapweed *(Y. glauca),* Joshua-tree *(Y. brevifolia),* and other species, all of whose roots and flower fruits were eaten; prickly-pear and cholla cacti *(Opuntia* spp.) and giant sahuaro cactus *(Carnegiea gigantea),* all of the Cactaceae family, whose flowers, fruits, flesh and seeds were eaten and also made into an alcoholic beverage; and numerous species of mescal (*Agave neomexicana, A. parryi, A. desertii, A. utahensis, A. palmeri,* and *A. conesii*) of the Amaryllidaceae family. Hearts of the mescal flowers were roasted and eaten, and the leaves were used for their fibers.

Of the nineteen species of cactus, mescal, mesquite, screwbean, and yucca in our sample, all occurred south of the 40° N. Latitude. They were most abundant in the southern parts of the Southwest, from the Rio Grande Desert in the east through the Sonoran Desert in the center, to the Colorado River Desert in the west. Many of these plants occurred also in a lobe of the Mojave Desert west of the Colorado River, in the desert valleys to the west, and in what today are the Los Angeles and San Diego basins of Southern California, the mesquite and screwbean being especially abundant in the mountain valleys of southeastern California.

An extensive variety of seed-producing plants were widely distributed in the arid portions of the West. Among them were many genera and species of the Poaceae or Gramineae families. These grasses normally occurred in bunchgrass patches in the northern Great Basin, in the Sacramento Valley of California, and in parts of the Plateau, and as short grass in the grassland parts of the southeastern Great Basin and the southeastern Southwest. Grasses of many kinds were also sparsely distributed in the best-watered portions of the central Great Basin, but they were not dominant plants. The Asteraceae family was also well represented; indeed, the dominant vegetation in much of the arid west included genera of the Asteraceae. Many species of some of these plants could be found, such as sagebrush (*Artemesia* spp.), and along with creosote bush (*Larrea tridentata*) and saltbush (*Atriplex* spp.), these dominated much of the Great Basin.

Of these seed-producing plants, twelve species have been grouped together as "grasses" (Map E-11, V-434). "Grasses" is used as a convenient title rather than "edible seeds" or some other designation, because flowers and leaves were eaten nearly as often as the seeds. It is clear from the distribution that the greatest number of these grasses, shrubs, and forbs occurred in the Great Basin; the Southwest and the Plateau supported the next greatest distribution; and those areas were followed by Northern California and then by Southern California. The Northwest Coast, with its dominant forests, possessed the fewest number of these types of plants.

Because sagebrush (*Artemesia* spp.) was so widely distributed it was not measured in our sample, nor was chia or coastal sage (*Salvia* spp.), which provided excellent seeds for food. The major species and genera that were assessed were pigweed (*Amaranthus retroflexus*), whose stocks and seeds were eaten and which was cultivated in many forms; sotol (*Dasylerion wheeleri*), a shrub whose seeds and fruits were eaten; lambsquarter (*Chenopodium* spp.), broomrape (*Orobanche* spp.), sand-bunchgrass and rice-grass (*Oryzopsis* spp.), wild rye (*Elymus* spp.), and Indian millet (*Eriocoma* spp.), whose seeds were boiled and eaten; saltbush (*Atriplex* spp.), a shrub whose seeds were especially favored because of their salty taste; sunflowers (*Helianthus annuus,* and all other species), whose seeds were eaten (some species were cultivated); thistle (*Cirsium* spp.), whose seeds and hearts were eaten; and guaco (*Cleome serrulata*) and common purslane (*Portulaca oleracea*), flowering forbs whose seeds and flowers were eaten.

Roots, stalks, and seeds from the Liliaceae family, nuts other than acorns and pinenuts from shrubby trees, and berries from the families Rosaceae, Ericaceae, and Grossulariaceae, were all well represented in the wet foothills and along the river banks of the Northwest Coast, the Plateau, and Northern California. In Southern California, the Southwest, and the Great Basin, especially where there was little precipitation or stream and river water, very few of these plants occurred. The valleys of the Plateau, which received abundant water from the Columbia and Fraser River systems, but not from precipitation, had many well-watered root fields, as did the valleys of the Rocky Mountains and the Sierra. Berry bushes flourished along the river banks and shores. The combination of seeds, berries, roots, and nuts (of all kinds, including acorns and pines) in Northern California provided the inhabitants of that region with perhaps a greater variety and more abundant supply of plant foods than could be found in any other region in western North America.

Eleven species of roots, nuts, lilies, and berries have been included in the sample (Map E-12, V-435). The roots included yamp (*Carum gairdneri*), tobacco-root or bitter-root (*Valeriana edulis*), camas (*Quamasia* or *Camassia* spp.), wild potato (*Solanum triflorum* and other species), and sand-root (*Ammobroma sonorae*). The flowers were eaten, as were the roots, which were storable for years if dried. Berries included serviceberry (*Amelanchier alnifolia*), western hackberry (*Celtis douglasii*), and salal (*Gaultheria shallon*). Tiger-lilies (*Lilium* spp.) and the wokas or water-lily (*Nymphaea polysepala*) were extremely good sources of seeds and bulbs, and braken fern (*Pteridium aquilinum*) had edible roots, shoots, and buds. The western hazelnut or filbert (*Corylus californica*) and the California buckeye (*Aesculus californica*) were widely distributed in California—hazelnut in coastal Oregon as well—yet neither the buckeye nor filbert was used as heavily as acorns and pine seeds. The buckeye, which provided 23 percent protein by dry weight, was barely used at all.*

Fauna Sampled

Land mammals, sea mammals, shellfish, and fish were all important in the diets of many Indians in western North America; reptiles and invertebrates were less important. In general, the areas of sparsest vegetation, especially the cold desert and semidesert areas of the Great Basin, Plateau, and Southwest, were inhabited by fewer large mammals than were any other areas in western North America. Yet the mountains and plateaus in those three main regions, especially the Rocky Mountains, supported the greatest numbers and variety of large mammals. The mountainous areas east of the Coast Range, the Cascades, and the Sierra provided grasses, shrubs, and trees for graze and browse, which supported large plant-eating mammals; the foothills and bunchgrass prairie provided sufficiently open range to support medium-sized browsers. The creosote and sagebrush zones primarily supported small mammals and reptiles.

Because all of these zones were mixed in the Plateau, Great Basin, and Southwest, there the variety of all available animals was extensive, but the greatest abundances were in the eastern and northern regions along the Rocky Mountains of Utah, Colorado, Wyoming, Idaho, Montana, and British Columbia.

Medium-sized land mammals, especially deer, became the dominant mammals throughout the Northwest Coast and California, perhaps because natural selection favored them in those environments. Large omnivores such as brown bears, black bears, and grizzly bears, also occurred in large numbers in these areas. Deer found considerable browse; bears ate berries, roots, fish, and some mammals, including deer. Bears could sustain speeds of 35 miles per hour for great distances, and as a consequence they were highly effective hunters. What California—and even more so the Northwest Coast—lacked in variety of both small and large mammals was more than made up for with fish and large populations of deer. The

---

*Before the buckeye could be eaten, hydrocyanic acid had to be leached from it; however, tannic acid had to be leached from acorns, so this inconvenience probably did not cause buckeyes to be used lightly and acorns to be used heavily, though leaching aesculin from buckeyes requires more time than leaching the tannic acid from acorns.

coastal tribes supplemented these animals with sea mammals, shellfishes, and waterfowl.

Figure 2-7 is a one-dimensional representation of relations among the tribal territories based on 70 mammal, fish, and bird species. The differences between the coastal regions and all interior areas are overwhelming. The distribution of faunal territories is not identical to either the floral territories (Figures 2-5 and 2-6), or the areas derived from the total list of environmental variables (Figures 2-2, 2-3, and 2-4). The conventional mapping in Figure 2-8 makes this clear. For the most part the coast represented a continuous unit distinguished by the presence of sea mammals and fish, and by a heavy forest canopy that reduced the light reaching the ground below, hence reducing the variety of plants and plant-eating animals. The Southern California coastal territories were the least similar to the others, in part because of long summer droughts and the absence of tall forests. Many of the streams in Southern California dried up during the summer droughts, so only a very few rivers provided spawning areas for steelhead trout, and other species of anadromous fish are not known to have spawned in the Southern California region. The coastal valleys and foothills in this region did not have a heavy forest canopy (hence, greater light reached the ground, plants were scrublike and brushy, and large plant-eating animals were sparsely distributed). The southern California coast supported some deer, but small mammals dominated.

Land Mammals

Food chains linked plants, plant-eating animals, and flesh-eating animals in any territory. Wherever there were large numbers of plant-eating animals there were larger numbers of plants to support them. And wherever there were carnivores, there were larger numbers of plant-eating animals than carnivores, in order to support the carnivore populations. Most plants and animals were closely dependent on climate. For example, lush grasses and lush browse required considerable precipitation. Elk and bison, having body weights that averaged from 750 pounds (elk) to 1,500 pounds (bison), required large amounts of grasses and browse. As a consequence, elk and bison were not found in great numbers in the arid west, nor on the grassless Northwest Coast, but were found in the intermontane forests and grasslands along with the largest predators—wolves, grizzly bears, and mountain lions. Moose, caribou, and mountain sheep, whose body weights averaged from 300 pounds (sheep, caribou) to 1,000 pounds (moose) required young willows, balsam fir, birch, aspen, pop-

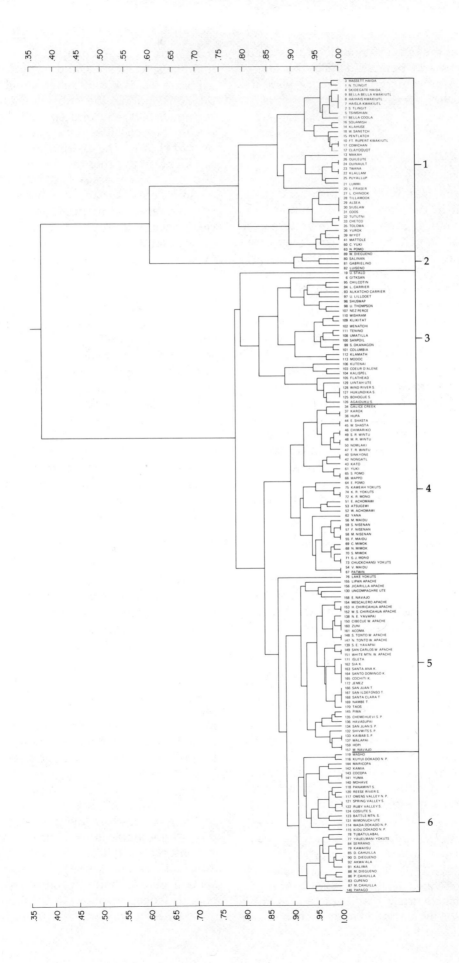

Figure 2-7 *Environmental tree: 3. Groupings of tribal territories derived from G coefficients based on 70 variables (149 attributes) which include land mammals, sea mammals, fish, and birds.*

GROUP 1

3 Massett Haida
1 Northern Tlingit
4 Skidegate Haida
9 Bella Bella Kwakiutl
8 Haihais Kwakiutl
7 Haisla Kwakiutl
2 Southern Tlingit
5 Tsimshian
11 Bella Coola
16 Squamish
14 Klahuse
18 West Sanetch
15 Pentlatch
10 Fort Rupert Kwakiutl
17 Cowichan
12 Clayoquot
13 Makah
26 Quileute
24 Quinault
23 Twana
22 Klallam
25 Puyallup
21 Lummi
20 Lower Fraser
27 Lower Chinook
28 Tillamook
29 Alsea
30 Siuslaw
31 Coos
32 Tututni
33 Chetco
35 Tolowa
36 Yurok
39 Wiyot
41 Mattole
60 Coast Yuki
63 Northern Pomo

GROUP 2

89 Western Diegueño
80 Salinan
81 Gabrieliño
82 Luiseño

GROUP 3

19 Upper Stalo
6 Gitksan

95 Chilcotin
94 Lower Carrier
93 Alkatcho Carrier
97 Upper Lillooet
96 Shuswap
98 Upper Thompson
107 Nez Percé
110 Wishram
109 Klikitat
102 Wenatchi
111 Tenino
108 Umatilla
100 Sanpoil
99 Southern Okanagon
101 Columbia
112 Klamath
113 Modoc
106 Kutenai
103 Coeur d'Alene
104 Kalispel
105 Flathead
129 Uintah Ute
128 Wind River Shoshone
127 Hukundika Shoshone
125 Bohogue Shoshone
126 Agaiduku Shoshone

GROUP 4

34 Galice Creek
37 Karok
38 Hupa
44 East Shasta
45 West Shasta
46 Chimariko
49 Sacramento River Wintu
48 McCloud River Wintu
50 Nomlaki
47 Trinity River Wintu
40 Sinkyone
42 Nongatl
43 Kato
61 Yuki
65 Southern Pomo
66 Wappo
64 Eastern Pomo
75 Kaweah Yokuts
74 Kings River Yokuts
72 Kings River Western Mono
51 East Achomawi

53 Atsugewi
52 West Achomawi
62 Yana
56 Mountain Maidu
59 Southern Nisenan
57 Foothill Nisenan
58 Mountain Nisenan
55 Foothill Maidu
69 Central Miwok
68 Northern Miwok
70 Southern Miwok
71 San Joaquin Western Mono
73 Chukchansi Yokuts
54 Valley Maidu
67 Patwin
76 Lake Yokuts

GROUP 5

155 Lipan Apache
156 Jicarilla Apache
130 Uncompaghre Ute
158 Eastern Navajo
154 Mescalero Apache
153 Huachuca Chiricahua Apache
152 Warm Springs Chiricahua Apache
138 Northeast Yavapai
150 Cibecue Western Apache
160 Zuni
161 Acoma
148 South Tonto Western Apache
147 North Tonto Western Apache
139 Southeast Yavapai
149 San Carlos Western Apache
151 White Mountain Western Apache
171 Isleta
162 Sia Keres
163 Santa Ana Keres
164 Santo Domingo Keres
165 Cochiti
172 Jemez
166 San Juan Tewa
167 San Ildefonso Tewa
168 Santa Clara Tewa
169 Nambe Tewa

170 Taos
145 Pima
135 Chemehuevi Southern Paiute
136 Havasupai
134 San Juan Southern Paiute
132 Shivwits Southern Paiute
133 Kaibab Southern Paiute
137 Walapai
159 Hopi
157 Western Navajo

Group 6

119 Washo
116 Kuyui-Dokado Northern Paiute
144 Maricopa
142 Kamia
143 Cocopa
141 Yuma
140 Mohave
118 Panamint Shoshone
120 Reese River Shoshone
117 Owens Valley Northern Paiute
121 Spring Valley Shoshone
122 Ruby Valley Shoshone
124 Gosiute Shoshone
123 Battle Mountain Shoshone
131 Wimonuch Ute
114 Wada-Dokado Northern Paiute
115 Kidu-Dokado Northern Paiute
78 Tubatulabal
77 Yauelmani Yokuts
84 Serraño
79 Kawaiisu
85 Desert Cahuilla
90 Desert Diegueño
92 Akwa'ala
91 Kaliwa
88 Mountain Diegueño
86 Pass Cahuilla
83 Cupeño
87 Mountain Cahuilla
146 Papago

lar, and bushier browse in profusion, to support their body weight, so they ranged in the northern intermontane forests, but not in the Sierra or coastal forests. The caribou occurred from Montana northwest into British Columbia, and the moose occurred as far south as the Uintah Mountains in Utah. Some kinds of mountain sheep adapted to the more arid canyons of the western deserts.

In general, there were greater numbers of mammals both small and large in the Rocky Mountain region than anywhere else in western North America. There were large deer populations and relatively large elk populations in California, along with a large grizzly bear population. Large deer populations for-

aged in the more penetrable areas of the Northwest Coast, and large populations of small mammals occurred in the Southwest, Great Basin, and semideserts of the Plateau (Map E-14, V-112).

The distribution of types of game in Map E-14 samples twenty animals from various food chains. Table 2-2 organizes them by relative size, weight, and distribution.

Distributions of game must be understood in relativistic terms. If all factors were held constant and all located mammals were in their optimal environments, the diffusely distributed jackrabbits could number as many as 200 animals per square mile (1,000 pounds). Elk, which moved in large herds

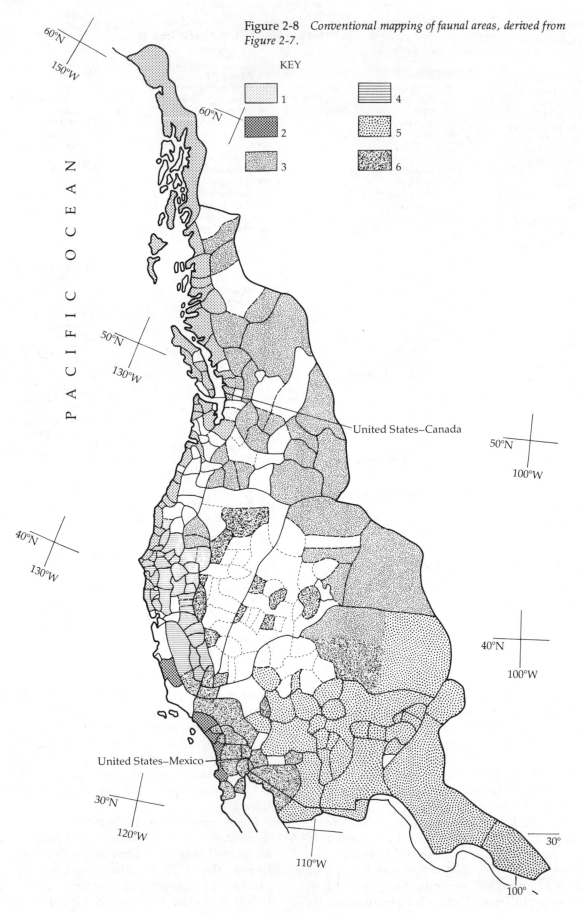

Figure 2-8 *Conventional mapping of faunal areas, derived from Figure 2-7.*

KEY

1
2
3
4
5
6

PACIFIC OCEAN

60°N
150°W

60°N

50°N
130°W

40°N
130°W

United States–Mexico

30°N
120°W

110°W

100°

United States–Canada

50°N
100°W

40°N
100°W

30°

Table 2-2
Mammals sampled: their relative weights, diets, and distributions

Common name	Taxonomic name	Average weight (pounds)	Diet	Distribution
SMALL MAMMALS				
Cottontail rabbit	*Sylvilagus* spp.	3	Plants	Diffuse
Jackrabbit	*Lepus* spp.	5	Plants	Diffuse
Porcupine	*Erethizon dorsatum*	25	Plants	Diffuse
Bobcat	*Lynx rufus*	30	Animals	Diffuse
Lynx	*L. canadensis*	35	Animals	Diffuse
Coyote	*Canis latrans*	45	Animals	Solitary
Beaver	*Castor canadensis*	50	Plants	Diffuse
MEDIUM-SIZED MAMMALS				
Gray wolf	*Canis lupis*	95	Animals	Packs
Antelope or pronghorn	*Antilocapra americana*	110	Plants	Small herds*
Mountain goat	*Oreamnos americanus*	110	Plants	Small herds
Cougar, mountain lion, puma	*Felis concolor*	180	Animals	Diffuse
White-tailed deer	*Odocoileus virginiana*	200	Plants	Small herds
Mule deer or black-tailed deer	*Odocoileus hemionus*	200	Plants	Small herds
LARGE MAMMALS				
Caribou	*Rangifer* spp.	300	Plants	Large herds
Mountain sheep	*Ovis canadensis*	300	Plants	Small herds[†]
Black bear	*Ursus americanus*	350	Plants and animals	Solitary
Elk	*Cervus* spp.	750	Plants	Large herds
Grizzly bear	*Ursus horribilis*	800	Plants and animals	Solitary
Moose	*Alces alces*	1,000	Plants	Small herds
Bison	*Bison bison*	1,500	Plants	Large herds

*Antelope herds of up to 300 animals occurred in the bunchgrass prairies above northeastern California and in the San Joaquin Valley. Herds of 500 or so occurred in the grasslands of Wyoming, eastern Utah, Colorado, and New Mexico. Smaller herds occurred elsewhere.

[†]In some regions of Idaho, Montana, Wyoming, and Utah there were more mountain sheep than there were deer.

through mountain meadows in the summer and through forest edges and lower valleys in the winter, required large territories so that only about five animals could be supported per square mile. Yet in comparing the mass of these two species per square mile, it can be seen that the optimal environments for each would support 3,750 pounds of elk to 1,000 pounds of rabbit. The payoff for hunters pursuing an elk herd or a bison herd would be much greater than for pursuing a few hundred lightning-swift rabbits. Although deer tended to herd in very small groups, their distributions throughout many areas were wide and diffuse, hence they were available to hunters.

Fish

Paramount among the fish of western environments were the five species of Pacific salmon that spawned in fresh water as far east as central Idaho, yet lived most of their lives in the ocean. Likewise, steelhead, white sturgeon, and the western sea-lamprey were ocean fish that plied the interior waters and contributed to the diets of Indians located near the spawning-rivers. Although they were less important than the foregoing, some populations of Dolly Varden char and cutthroat trout that spawned in rivers that emptied into the Pacific Ocean also went to sea. At coastal locations, there were both saltwater fish and anadromous fish. The montane lakes and fast-flowing rivers of the eastern slopes of the coastal ranges were filled with char and trout. Whitefish also inhabited the waters in the northern regions of the eastern slopes. The rivers of the Rocky Mountains south through Utah and Colorado produced many trout, and the lakes of the Great Basin and the rivers of the Southwest produced large suckers, minnows, and bottomfeeders, as well as some giant cutthroat trout (Map E-15, V-132).

Fish were in greatest abundance along the coast from San Francisco Bay northward, and along the river systems that emptied into the ocean in that same region. The drainages of the Sacramento River, Klamath River, Smith River, Columbia River, Fraser River, Skeena River, and all the minor coastal drainage systems in between annually produced upwards of 1,000 pounds of fish per square mile of tribal territory. In the Columbia, Fraser, and Skeena systems, vast quantities of fish occurred deep into upper reaches several hundred miles from the river mouths. The semidesert Fraser and Columbia Plateaus were crossed by networks of these remarkably fish-rich rivers, and many of the river valleys in these plateaus also supported dense fields of roots. Roots and fish provided food for Indians, and vegetation along the river banks stabilized the banks and provided habitation for freshwater shrimp and sculpins, which fed the fish. From the Klamath River southward, average quantities of fish dropped off to 600 and 700 pounds per square mile for the tribal territories located on the smallest and most distant tributaries. Even at that, the California Indians living on the Klamath River system had large amounts of fish, including salmon, sturgeon, lamprey, steelhead, cutthroat, and suckers.

Southern California, the Great Basin, and the Southwest were fish-poor, with a few interesting exceptions. Basin groups that were located near what remained of the massive Pleistocene lakes—lakes that once filled much of the Great Basin—had access to several species of large suckers, and huge cutthroat trout. The latter, known as Lahontan *(Salmo clarkii henshawii)*, often weighed more than 50 pounds. The Lower Colorado River territories provided large suckers, minnows, and other kinds of fish. The Rio Grande supported suckers and trout, and so did the mountain rivers of the Rockies and the most distant tributaries of the Columbia River system—the Snake, Salmon, and other rivers. Because the territories of the easternmost Shoshones and Utes were so large and the fish so localized, Map E-15 somewhat obscures the amount of fish that were available in concentrated areas of the montane region, though the average for the tribal territories is correct. Sturgeon, suckers, and trout were found along the Snake River, trout in the mountain rivers, and suckers in the lakes of these territories. In these localized areas of the Southwest and Great Basin there were sufficient fish in the slow-moving waters that poisoning was a practical means of extracting a catch. The density of fish must be relatively great for poisoning to yield a harvest without decimating the stock of fish, and the waters cannot be so fast as to render the poisons ineffective through rapid diffusion.

Anadromous species entered streams to spawn in such great numbers that the distribution of anadromous fish in western North America is an excellent guide to the quantity of fish used by Indians (Map E-16, V-125). Salmon and steelhead are included in Map E-16, but lamprey, sturgeon, Dolly Varden char, and cutthroat trout are not. The anadromous species that entered western rivers increased from south to north, as Map E-16 indicates. It can be seen that territories deep in the Middle Columbia and Upper Fraser systems were inhabited by as many as four species of these fish.

Table 2-3 lists anadromous species that were sampled, and their most southern distribution. The time of commencement of spawning runs each year is also indicated there. In general, spawning runs occurred over several months and fish were caught during the duration of the runs.

Several kinds of saltwater fish that fed in kelp beds along the coast, or made annual runs into the rivers, or spawned near the banks, were very important to California coastal dwellers and to the inhabitants of the Northwest Coast. Halibut and cod were large fish regularly sought by all island dwellers, and eulachon, smelt, and herring were small fish that ran in great numbers close to shore and up the rivers. These fish were all important sources of food. They were also important because of their relationships to the predatory sea mammals who followed right behind them: these were also hunted by natives. Sturgeon and sea-lampreys entered the rivers as well (Map E-17, V-442).

Table 2-4 lists the eight principal kinds of saltwater fish that were sampled.

Several species within four genera of freshwater fish complete the sample of fish (Map E-18, V-443). Many species of suckers (Castomidae) inhabited the lakes and rivers of the Great Basin and Southwest. Several species of lake whitefish *(Coregonus* spp.) and Rocky Mountain whitefish *(Prosopium* spp.) were distributed in the interior lakes and rivers, from Montana northward. Many subspecies of cutthroat trout *(Salmo clarkii)* occurred throughout the West, from the Cascade and Sierra ranges through the mountain rivers of the Rockies and as far south as the Rio Grande. Dolly Varden char *(Salvelinus malma)* inhabited river systems from the Klamath northward on the Coast, and interior rivers and lakes from Idaho and Montana northward. The many subspecies of rainbow trout *(Salmo gairdneri)*, including the ocean-going steelhead, had a wide distribution along the Pacific Coast, from Mexico to the Bering Sea region. Many had become landlocked in the area from California to British Columbia during the late Pleistocene. Several trout species of the Great Basin and Southwest had very restricted distributions, such as the red-band trout (not officially classified) of Oregon and Idaho, the Apache trout *(Salmo apache)* of Arizona, the gila

Table 2-3
Anadromous fishes sampled: their river ranges and the approximate time of year they served as a food source

Common name	Taxonomic name	Most southern range	Approximate month when spawning runs commence
Char, Dolly Varden	*Salvelinus malma*	Columbia River	June and December
Salmon, Chinook or king	*Onchorhynchus tshawytscha*	San Joaquin River	May
Salmon, chum or dog	*O. keta*	Rogue River	October
Salmon, coho or silver	*O. kisutch*	Sacramento River	September
Salmon, pink or humpback	*O. gorbuscha*	Gray's Harbor (Chehalis River)	August
Salmon, sockeye or red	*O. nerka*	Columbia River	July
Sea-lamprey, western	*Entosphenus tridentatus*	Sacramento River	—
Trout, cutthroat	*Salmo clarkii* and ssp.	Eel River	June and December
Trout, steelhead	*S. gairdneri*	Los Angeles River	November

Table 2-4
Saltwater fishes sampled

Common name	Taxonomic name	Deep- or shallow-water spawners*
Eulachon or candlefish	*Thaleicthys pacificus*	Shallow
Pacific cod	*Gadus macrocephalus*	Deep
Pacific halibut	*Hippoglossus stenolepsis*	Deep
Pacific herring	*Clupea harengus pallasii*	Shallow
Sardine or California pilchard	*Sardinops caerulia*	Deep
Surf smelt	*Hypomesus pretiosus*	Shallow
Western sea-lamprey	*Entosphenus tridentatus*	Shallow
White sturgeon	*Acipenser transmontanus*	Shallow

*Shallow water refers to rivers and coastal shores. Deep water refers to depths of two fathoms or more in the straits, bays, coves, or sea. Deep-water spawners were taken with hooks rather than nets, traps, weirs, impounds, and the like.

Table 2-5
Freshwater fish sampled

Common name	Taxonomic name	Freshwater habitat	Common name	Taxonomic name	Freshwater habitat
Char, Dolly Varden	*Salvelinus malma*		Trout, cutthroat	*S. c. tahoensis*	Lake Tahoe
				S. c. utahensis	Utah Lake
				S. c. virginalis	Rio Grande
Sucker	Fam. Catostomidae, genera *Catostomus, Chamistes, Deltistes, Pantosteus;* and *Xyrauchen texanus*		Trout, gila	*S. gilae*	New Mexico and Arizona
			Trout, golden	*S. whitei*	Western Sierra
Trout, Apache	*Salmo apache*	Arizona	Trout, rainbow	*S. gairdneri*	
				S. g. gilberti	Kern River
Trout, cutthroat	*S. clarkii*			*S. g. irideus*	
	S. c. alpestris	Flathead Lake		*S. g. kamloopsis*	Shuswap Lake
	S. c. bouveri	Idaho		*S. g. shasta*	McCloud River
	S. c. eremogenes	Washington		*S. g. whitehousei*	Babine Lake
	S. c. gibbsi	Deschutes River			
	S. c. henshawii	Lake Lahontan	Trout, red-band	No Linnaean designation	Oregon and Idaho
	S. c. lewisi	Snake River			
	S. c. macdonaldi	Rocky Mountains			
	S. c. pleuriticus	Colorado River	Whitefish, lake	*Coregonus* spp.	
	S. c. seleneris	Southeastern California	Whitefish, Rocky Mountain	*Prosopium* spp.	
	S. c. stomias	South Platte River			

trout (*S. gilae*) of New Mexico and Arizona, and the Paiute trout (*S. clarkii seleniris*) of southeastern California. To the west, over the crest of the Sierra, was another unique trout species, the California golden trout (*S. whitei*). Table 2-5 shows the freshwater fish that were sampled.

Sea Mammals

Predatory sea mammals could be found wherever there were large schools of ocean fish and extensive shellfish beds. Because rich kelp beds along much of coastal western North America supported many fish, rookeries of many predatory sea mammal species abounded which were sustained by the fish near the kelp beds. Moreover, large whales, which ate micro-organisms, invertebrates, and plant life, migrated along the coasts each year.

Twenty-nine species of sea mammals were sampled, ranging from the blue whale, which, as the largest animal that ever lived, attained lengths of over 100 feet and weights of up to 150 tons (and which was used for its bone and oil and as food if beached but was never hunted by Indians of the Pacific Coast), to the Pacific harbor porpoise, which seldom grew to six feet. The sea-otter (*Enhydra lutris*) also inhabited the coast (Map E-19, V-92). Although the Southern California coastal region was familiar to more species of sea mammals than were the areas along the Northwest Coast and the narrow inlets, straits, and short passages between the northwestern islands, the spawning fish drew many sea mammals to the shore, giving Northwest Coast people access to sea mammals that was better than most Southern California tribes had, especially access to the large whales.

Table 2-6 shows which sea mammals were sampled.

Following are brief sketches of the major environmental areas of western North America.

DESCRIPTIONS OF MAJOR ENVIRONMENTS

Northwest Coast

The Northwest Coast environment stretched for 1,800 miles, from Yakutat Bay in Alaska to Cape Mendocino in California, and varied in width from a few miles to 200 miles near the Fraser River at the border between the United States and Canada. In the

Table 2-6
Sea mammals sampled

Common name	Taxonomic name	Common name	Taxonomic name
Blackfish or pilot-whale, Pacific	*Globicephala scammonii*	Right-whale, Pacific	*Eubalaena sieboldii*
Dolphin, Gill's bottle-nose	*Tursiops gillii*	Seal, harbor	*Phoca vitulina*
Dolphin, Gray's-porpoise or spotted	*Stenella styx*	Sea-lion, California	*Zalophus californianus*
		Sea-lion, northern	*Eumetopias jubata*
Dolphin, northern right-whale	*Lissodelphus borealis*	Sea-otter	*Enhydra lutris*
Dolphin, Pacific	*Delphinus bairdii*	Sperm whale	*Physeter catodon*
Dolphin, Pacific bottle-nose	*Tursiops nuuanu*	Sperm whale, pygmy	*Kogia breviceps*
Dolphin, Pacific white-sided	*Lagenorhynchus obliquidens*	Whale, Baird's beaked	*Berardius bairdii*
Elephant-seal, northern	*Miroungo angustirostris*	Whale, blue or sulphur-bottom	*Sibbaldus musculus*
Fur-seal, Guadalupe	*Arctocephalus townsendii*	Whale, California gray	*Eschrichtius gibbosus*
Fur-seal, northern or Alaska	*Callorhinus ursinus*	Whale, fin-back	*Balaenoptera physalus*
Killer-whale, false	*Pseudorea crassidens*	Whale, goose-beak	*Ziphius cavirostris*
Killer-whale, Pacific	*Grampus rectipinna*	Whale, hump-back	*Megaptera novaengliae*
Porpoise, Dall's	*Phocenoides dallii*	Whale, Pacific beaked	*Mesoplodon stejnegeri*
Porpoise, Pacific harbor	*Phocoena vomerina*	Whale, sei	*Balaenoptera borealis*

north, high mountains rose steeply from the sea, and deep fjords cut through them. Precipitation was very great, averaging from 50 to 100 inches per year, with greater precipitation in the mountains and at some spots along the Coast, and less precipitation in rain shadows of peninsular and island mountains.

Enormous trees in dense rainforests covered the landscape. In the north, above 51° N. Latitude, western hemlock *(Tsuga heterophylla)* and Sitka spruce *(Picea sitchensis)* dominated other plants. Along the narrow coastal shores in the north, these trees attained heights of 200 feet. In the central area between 51° N. Latitude (northern tip of Vancouver Island) and 42° N. Latitude (southern Oregon) the coastal shore widened and from southern British Columbia the coastal environment extended over the Coast Range to the Cascades. In this region, western hemlock, western red-cedar *(Thuja plicata)*, and several firs, but especially Douglas-fir *(Pseudotsuga menziesii)*,

which grew taller than 250 feet, dominated other plants. In the southwesternmost part of Oregon and in northwestern California, redwood *(Sequoia sempervirens)*, which at maturity stood taller than 300 feet, dominated the forests.

Throughout the region, atmospheric humidity was high, fogs were frequent, soil was acidic and well-mulched, and temperatures were mild, averaging about 52° F annually. Only about 50 percent of possible hours of sunshine occurred along the coast; given the small amount of sunlight and the dense forest canopy, only shade-loving plants could grow below the tall trees. Ferns were especially successful, as was salal *(Gaultheria shallon)*, in the extremely dense undergrowth. The riverbanks were thick with willows *(Salix* spp.) and tall bushy plants such as salmonberry *(Rubus spectabilis)*, huckleberry *(Gaylussacia* spp.), and blackberry *(Rubus parviflorus* and *R. vitifolius)*.

Of mammals in this region, deer and elk dominated the coastal areas south of the 51° N. Latitude; deer alone dominated the north. Elk were not found above the 51° N. Latitude, but farther south they were able to graze on some grasses and pursued many kinds of browse. In the north, where the forests were dense and the coast was narrow, there was little grazing fodder. Deer principally ate salal, young Douglas-firs, ferns, willows, alder, and lichen (*Usnea* spp.). Mountain lions were the main predators of deer, and omnivorous bears ate berries, inner bark from trees, and large quantities of fish.

Fish were so abundant along the coast and in the rivers during the spawning runs that the waters are said to have boiled with them. Sea mammals were abundant, too, but especially so during smelt, herring, and eulachon runs.

Key edible plants for humans in the Northwest region include the following.

Common name	Taxonomic name
Blackberry species	*Rubus parviflorus* *R. vitifolius*
Braken fern	*Pteridium aquilinum*
Epos	*Carum oreganum*
Evergreen huckleberry	*Gaylussacia* spp.
Lupine	*Lupinus littoralis*
Salal	*Gaultheria shallon*
Salmonberry	*Rubus spectabilis*
Shore pine	*Pinus contorta*
Tiger-lily	*Lilium* spp.
Wapato or arrowhead	*Sagittaria latifolia*
Western hazlenut or filbert	*Corylus californica*
Wokas or water-lily	*Nymphea polysepala*

The Northwest River environments were somewhat colder and received more precipitation than the coastal regions. Moreover, they did not provide access to sea mammals or many shellfishes.

The Northern California coast between Cape Mendocino and San Francisco Bay was backed by redwood forests; at the coast itself, windswept cliffs plunged to the ocean. The rivers entering the ocean were smaller and carried fewer fish than the Sacramento and San Joaquin Rivers to the south or the large rivers farther to the north.

Northern and Central California

The environments of California showed considerable variation, yet the foothills that surrounded all of the coastal valleys as well as the Central Valley (the Sacramento Valley in the north and the San Joaquin Val-

ley in the south) were dominated by sclerophyll vegetation. Sclerophyll denotes the thick, tough, shiny, highly cutinized leaves of a wide variety of plants from over ten families, and these plants were distributed in three distinct kinds of plant habitats: forest, woodland, and chaparral. Forests were extensive groves of oaks with grass ground-cover. In woodlands, oaks were more scattered and were accompanied by madrone (*Arbutus menziesii*) and manzanita (*Arctostaphylos* spp.). Chaparral was predominatly brush or shrub sclerophyll. In general, the farther north and the higher the elevation in California, the greater the forest and woodland vegetation. The farther south and the lower the elevation, the greater the chaparral vegetation. The floor of the Central Valley was predominantly bunchgrass with stands of oaks close to the river courses and, in one southern San Joaquin Valley area, coastal sage. From the foothills around the Central Valley rose mountains (Sierra Nevada in the east, the Coast Range in the west, and the Trinity-Klamath-Siskiyou mountain ranges in the north) dominated by western pine.

Most precipitation occurred during the winter months. Summers were rainless. Usually less than one inch precipitation was registered from June through September. Precipitation was greater in the north than the south, and greater at the higher elevations than the lower. Per year, the mountain regions received from 22 to 50 inches and the valleys received from 16 to 38 inches precipitation. The climate was extremely mild during the winter months, seldom falling below freezing except at high elevations. Daytime summer temperatures were often extremely hot in the Central Valley, frequently soaring above 100° F. The foothills and the valleys of the coastal range were cooler. There, in general, the sun shone most days and winters were very mild.

The dominant animals of the sclerophyll regions were the grizzly bears (*Ursus horribilis californicus, U.h. tularensis, U.h. colossus*) that attained weights of over 1,000 pounds and ate nuts, roots, berries, deer, fish, elk, antelope, and rodents. Indeed, these mighty omnivores competed with Indians for identical food resources and occasionally dispatched and devoured Indians.

Deer were the dominant herbivores throughout the foothill regions of forest, woodland, and chaparral. They also ranged in the coastal sagebrush areas. In some places in the north there were perhaps as many as five per square mile. Antelope ranged in herds of up to 300 in the San Joaquin Valley. Golden eagles (*Aquila chrysaetos*) were the principal bird predator, and the California condor (*Gymnogyps californianus*) and coyote (*Canis latrans*) were the principal carrion eaters. As predators, coyotes mostly ate rabbits and rodents.

The major rivers of the San Joaquin and Sacramento drainages were laden with anadromous fish during the summer spawning seasons and sustained trout and other freshwater fish year round.

The nut-bearing trees that were most heavily used by Indians in Northern and Central California are listed below. Most grew in sclerophyll woodland, forest, and chaparral habitats. The pines were located somewhat higher on the mountains.

Common name	Taxonomic name
Oak, blue	Quercus douglasii
Oak, California black	Q. kelloggii
Oak, California live	Q. agrifolia
Oak, California white or valley	Q. lobata
Oak, interior live	Q. wislizenii
Oak, maul or canyon live	Q. chrysolepis
Oak, Oregon white	Q. garryana
Pine, digger	Pinus sabiniana
Pine, sugar	P. lambertiana
Pinyon, single-leaf	P. monophylla
Tan-oak	Lithocarpus densiflora

Southern California

Southern California had two rather distinct environmental areas: one, the littoral and the islands on the west, had greater precipitation and cooler summers than the other, the territories of the mountains, passes, and deserts to the east. The littoral territories also supported sea mammals, saltwater fishes, and large quantities of shellfishes, which provided a marked contrast with the interior.

The littoral was defined by the San Gabriel, Santa Ana, and Laguna Mountains on the east, and included Catalina, San Nicolas, and San Clemente Islands on the west. The interior territories stretched from the eastern sides of the San Gabriel, Santa Ana, and Laguna Mountains to the San Bernardino, Orocaipa, and Chocolate Mountains still farther east.

In the coastal region, sagebrush and bunchgrasses dominated the coastal plains, chaparral dominated the foothills, and sclerophyll forests occurred higher in the mountains. Groves of oaks were found in washes and along the sides of the undulating hills of the coastal region, and several kinds of coastal sage, yucca, cactus and some mescal also were mixed in the chaparral.

As in Central and Northern California, summer droughts of about four months were followed by several months of precipitation each year in the littoral and mountain areas of Southern California. Here, bunchgrasses grew abundantly on the plains and throughout the foothills and mountains during the wet season. Deer and grizzly bears ranged throughout the chaparral. Smaller mammals, including rabbits, were dominant in the sage and grass areas and were hunted by coyotes, eagles, bobcats, and hawks.

The deserts and foothills of the Southern California interior possessed many features of the littoral and many features of the hot deserts to the east. The foothills and passes were covered with coastal sage. Above this zone occurred sclerophyll chaparral, in which oak, yucca, and mescal were constituents. The low courses of mountain canyons and desert oases were lined with palms (Washingtonia filifera), mesquite, and screwbean. Above the chaparral, vegetation in the mountains facing these deserts was similar to that of the littoral, and included stands of sugar pine, single-leaf pinyon (P. monophylla) and two other Pinyon species—the Mexican pinyon (P. cembroides, a double-leaf pinyon), and the Parry Pinyon (P. parryana, a four-leaf pinyon). Cacti were more abundant throughout the interior territories and on eastward-facing slopes than in the littoral. Deer and grizzly bears ranged in the sclerophyll regions, but toward the valley floors rats and reptiles were the dominant animals.

The following list represents the most important native plant foods in Southern California.

Common name	Taxonomic name
Cherry, hollyleaf	Prunus ilicifolia
Cherry, wild, or wild plum	P. andersonii
Chia or coastal sage	Salvia spp.
Honey mesquite	Prosopis juliflora
Lambsquarter	Chenopodium spp.
Mescal	Agave desertii
Niggerhead or barrel cactus	Echinocactus cylindricus
Oak, California black	Quercus kelloggii
Oak, California live	Q. agrifolia
Oak, California white or valley	Q. lobata
Oak, evergreen or scrub live	Q. undulata
Oak, maul or canyon live	Q. chrysolepis
Oak, scrub	Q. dumosa
Pinyon, double-leaf	Pinus edulis
Pinyon, single-leaf	P. monophylla
Prickly-pear or cholla cactus	Opuntia spp.
Screwbean	Prosopis pubescens

Common name	Taxonomic name
Soft-leaf or Whipple yucca	*Yucca whipplei*
Saber, Schidiger, or Mohave yucca	*Y. mohavensis*
Sugar pine	*Pinus lambertiana*

Plateau

The Plateau was another unique environmental region in western North America. It was a vast, high, cold, semidesert seared by hot temperatures in the summer months and chilled by cold temperatures in the winter months. The western border of the Plateau was defined by the high Canadian Coast Mountains and the Cascade Range; the Plateau extended east to the Rocky Mountains. The Columbia and Fraser Plateaus lay in the dry rain shadow of the mountains to the west; potential storms made their way across the Plateau, to be caught in the east by the Rockies.

Although there were four relatively distinct sets of microenvironments within the Plateau, all four microenvironments shared the following qualities: precipitation was meager, ranging from 6 to 20 inches per year; valley elevations were quite high, from 3,000 to 4,500 feet above sea level; huge rivers carrying great quantities of water and fish cut through the valleys; large fields of roots abounded in the river valleys; and the adjacent mountains were forested with dominant western pines. The precipitation came in summer storms and winter snows, yet except for the mountainous Upper Columbia region of Idaho and Montana, these were not plentiful.

In the Upper Columbia microenvironment were river valleys, forests, and mountains on the edge of the Rocky Mountains. Bunchgrass prairies, mountain forests of hemlock, red-cedar, and white pine, forests of lodgepole pine and Douglas-fir, and of ponderosa pine, and valleys rich with roots, all were interspersed in a patchwork fashion on rugged terrain, which received from 17 to 20 inches of precipitation per year. The Upper Columbia carried fewer fish than the other drainages in the Plateau. Deer, elk, moose, and mountain sheep were abundant in this region. Caribou herds also ranged into the northernmost reaches of the Upper Columbia drainage. Grizzly bears and the black bear were omnivorous predators; wolf packs pursued the caribou and larger herbivores.

In another microenvironment, the Middle Columbia River drainage cut through basalt plains that were lower than any of the other valley floors in the Plateau. Here, lava flows from ancient volcanic activity covered an area about 10,000 miles square and apparently separated the relict hemlock and red-cedar forests of the Upper Columbia region from the coastal forests. The river cut through these desolate regions, called "scablands," and also through rich areas of loess deposits, called "Palouse Prairie." The loess was probably blown in over the basalt, and enormous floods then scraped clean about 2,800 square miles of the basalt, leaving "scablands."

The most northern parts of the Middle Columbia received 11 to 15 inches of precipitation, but in the southern portions only 6 to 9 inches accumulated. Antelope herds moved across the grasses of the Palouse Prairie, and deer, elk, mountain sheep, and mountain goats moved through the mountains on the peripheries. The Middle Columbia carried huge quantities of fish, and the root grounds apparently always produced large quantities of roots.

The Fraser River Plateau—the third microenvironment—was cold and had sparse sagebrush vegetation. Average annual precipitation here was 10 to 16 inches. Yet the mountains were heavily forested and the Fraser River carried from 800 to 1,000 pounds of fish per square mile of tribal territory throughout most of the region. Lakes were numerous and the rivers that fed and drained them were lined with berry bushes and willows. Although the variety of land mammals was few in comparison to the Columbia Plateau areas, moose herds feasted on the willows and shrubs around the lakes and rivers, and caribou herds moved along the edges of the region. Deer also browsed here.

The Klamath–Modoc Lakes region on the basaltic flows east of the Cascades forms the fourth microenvironment. It was also an area of meager precipitation that nonetheless possessed considerable water from rivers and lakes. The lakes attracted ducks, geese, and swans, and also supported dense growths of water-lilies. The Klamath River carried lamprey, suckers, sturgeon, salmon, steelhead, and trout, and the chaparral supported large deer herds and some elk. Root-grounds were abundant, as elsewhere in the Plateau.

The following list represents the wild plants most heavily used as food by Plateau Indians.

Common name	Taxonomic name
Bitter-root (Tobacco-root)	*Valeriana edulis*
Braken fern	*Pteridium aquilinum*
Camas	*Quamasia* spp.
Cat-tail	*Typha latifolia*
Huckleberry	*Gaylussacia* spp.
Serviceberry	*Amelanchior alnifolia*
Tiger-lily	*Lilium* spp.
Wild-onion	*Peucedanum canbyi*

Common name	Taxonomic name
Wild parsnip	*Heracleum lanatum*
Wild plum or wild cherry	*Prunus* spp.
Wild potato	*Solanum* spp.
Wokas or water-lily	*Nymphaea polysepala*
Yamp	*Carum gairdneri*

The Great Basin

The waters that entered the Great Basin, from the east slope of the Sierra Nevada to the west slope of the Wasatch Range, an arm of the Rocky Mountains, emptied into inland lakes or seeped into the aquifer on the valley floors. Many parallel chains of mountains stretched from north to south across the Basin. Associated with the mountains and the valley floor were several vegetation areas and their corresponding animals.

As recently as 10,000 years ago, the area of the Great Basin was largely inundated by vast Pleistocene lakes. What had then been lake bottoms subsequently became salty valley-floor soils, from which alkalies leached when water accumulated on them for any considerable period. Annual precipitation in this region was low everywhere, ranging from five inches in the Panamint Valley on the southwest to eighteen inches in the valleys along the western Wasatch mountain front. In general, the Great Basin was in the rain shadow of the Sierra, the mountain chains within the Basin being not so high as to catch many of the storms that pressed eastward. It was the eastern edge of the Great Basin—the Utah and Colorado Rockies, beginning with the Wasatch Range on the west (which annually received 150 inches or more of snow)—that drew the greatest precipitation. Considered generally, the region received winter snows as well as spring and late-summer precipitation. Average January temperatures were slightly above freezing, but because the sun usually shone, winter daytime temperatures were normally well above freezing. Summer temperatures climbed higher than 80 and 90° F in the north and beyond 100° F in the far south, but because the soil was little insulated by the sparse vegetation, and because the valley floors were from 2,500 feet (southwest) to 6,000 feet (north) above sea level, nighttime temperatures dropped to 60° or even 50° F. Low precipitation, cold winters, and sparse valley vegetation characterized this region: it was a cold desert cut up by semidesert mountains and plateaus.

The valley floors, especially the old lake beds, were dominated by saltbush (*Atriplex confertifolia*), also known as shadscale. West of Great Salt Lake an extensive salt desert occupied part of the floor of the ancient Pleistocene Lake Bonneville, and salt deserts from the ancient Lake Lahontan ranged across areas of western Nevada. Associated with the shadscale were sand bunchgrass (*Oryzopsis hymenoides*) and several tiny annual grasses (genera *Poa*, *Stipa*, and *Agropyron*) that appeared briefly each spring.

The dominant animals in the shadscale were the tiny kangaroo rats (*Dipodomys* spp.). Jackrabbits, several species of mice, and several species of lizards, all burrowing creatures, and several small, burrowing predators—coyote, badger, and red fox—made their homes throughout the shadscale. The burrowing owl (*Speotyto cunicularia*) hunted the kangaroo rats and insects. The sparse vegetation and the modest amount of protective cover surely favored these small burrowing animals over their competitors within the same environment.

The alluvial fans that bordered the ancient lakes were foothills washed from the many mountain chains. These areas were dominated by sagebrush (*Artemisia tridentata*) and sand bunchgrass, and they also supported winter-fat (*Eurotia lanata*), rabbitbrush (*Chrysothamnus* spp.), greasewood (*Sarcobatus* spp.), and several annual small grasses and low bushy plants.

In the sagebrush and bunchgrass areas, jackrabbits were abundant, and at one time antelope herds ranging in size from 20 animals (in the Southwest) to 500 (in eastern Utah) and up to 1,000 (in western Wyoming) grazed on the bunchgrasses and browsed through the tall sage, which often grew to six feet. It is probable that there were more than half a million antelope in the Great Basin and at its periphery beyond the Wasatch mountains in Utah, western Colorado, and western Wyoming, prior to European contact with native Americans. Coyotes and wolves were the dominant mammalian predators, and golden eagles, several hawks (*Buteo jamaicensis*, *B. swainsoni*, *B. regalis*, *Falco mexicanus*), and the great horned owl (*Bubo virginianus*) also preyed on the rodent, rabbit, and reptile populations.

All of the mammals of the cold desert were elusive: they were speedy and the small ones were burrowers as well. For the antelope, speed and mobility were important: these qualities allowed them to reach water holes and to move to grassy areas as the grasses matured. Because of their speed and because of limited human endurance, hunters were not especially successful in bagging them, and carefully organized drives were mounted when these animals were to be pursued. By the same token, jackrabbits, cottontail rabbits, and kangaroo rats were swift, darting animals that could jump well. Lizards moved quickly for short distances, and even locusts moved swiftly. The cold deserts selected for speed and mobility. The burrowing habits of these animals also helped to protect them in their otherwise exposed habitats.

The lake regions were ringed with tule or bulrush (*Scirpus acutus*) and cat-tail (*Typha latifolia*), and the lakes and rivers carried several species of large suckers and trout. Relict populations of giant Lahontan cutthroat (and other subspecies of cutthroat), rainbow, and red-banded trout were isolated in various watersheds of the Great Basin in post-Pleistocene times. The bald eagle (*Haliaectus leucocephalus*) was the dominant predator near the lakes. During the fall and spring, ducks, swans, and geese used the lakes, and pelicans and seagulls occupied them for much of the year.

Sagebrush, mountain mahogany (*Cercocarpus* spp.) and grasses dominated the mountains of the central Great Basin to an elevation of about 8,000 feet. Pinyon pine, and juniper (*Juniperus scopulorum* and *J. utahensis*) dominated from 8,000 to 9,500 feet, and above that level to 11,500, limber pine (*P. flexilis*) and bristlecone pine (*P. aristata*) dominated, gradually giving away to alpine meadows. Small deer herds browsed in the pinyon-juniper forests and down into the sagebrush during the winter months, and cottontail rabbits were found in the higher sagebrush and grass areas.

The contorted topography of the Great Basin, where ancient lake beds were interlocked with mountains, and where precipitation was much greater on the western and eastern peripheries than in the vast center, divided the region into several microenvironments. The first of these, the Washo area, the eastern slope of the Sierra, from Lake Tahoe east to the eastern Sierra foothills, provided well-watered valleys and a wide variety of mountain and foothill vegetation, and the most bountiful resources in the far western part of the Basin. The central Basin shadscale and sagebrush zones were the driest and provided the least plant food. The southern plateaus and canyons of the Colorado River area and the hot deserts on this southeastern periphery constituted a special area; so did the well-watered montane area, the Snake River Valley, and the Colorado Plateau, occupied by Utes and Northern Shoshones on the northern and eastern periphery of the Great Basin.

A list of the most important plant foods in the Great Basin follows. It does not list all plants used for food and does not reflect the enormous variety of grasses that were eaten.

Common name	Taxonomic name
Broomrape	*Orobanche* spp.
Camas	*Quamasia* spp.
Pinyon, double-leaf	*Pinus edulis*
Pinyon, single-leaf	*P. monophylla*
Saltbush	*Atriplex argentea* *A. confertifolia*
Sand-bunchgrass	*Oryzopsis hymenoides*
Screwbean	*Prosopis pubescens*
Sunflower	*Helianthus* spp.
Tobacco-root or bitter-root	*Valeriana edulis*
Thistle	*Cirsium* spp.
Wild rye	*Elymus* spp.
Yamp	*Carum gairdneri*

Southwest

Hot deserts, pinyon–juniper plateaus, shadscale river bottoms, creosote bush (*Larrea* spp.) deserts, alpine plant communities, and shortgrass plains were all interspersed throughout the Southwest. These diverse vegetation areas frequently occurred together within a small geographic area made up of river bottom, plateau, foothills, and mountains. As diverse as they were, the many vegetation areas shared one important feature—scanty precipitation—which served as an ecological leveller that made plant cover sparse, thus favoring plant-eating animals that were small. Except for the highest mountain communities, annual precipitation ranged from 3 to 20 inches, with wide fluctuations in every region. Precipitation accumulated during winters, late spring and summer, and long growing seasons and sun-filled days made agriculture possible practically everywhere, despite the meager precipitation. The Colorado River drainage and the Rio Grande drainage supplied predictable water and made agriculture successful in these arid regions.

On the high plateaus in northern Arizona and northern New Mexico, winter temperatures sometimes dipped to 0° F, though the sun usually shone and daytime temperatures normally were above freezing. These were regions of pinyon–juniper, sagebrush, bunchgrass plateaus, and shortgrass plains. On the hot Arizona–Sonora and Colorado River Deserts of southern Arizona, and the Rio Grande Desert of Southern New Mexico, winters were warmer, and for the Colorado River Desert, freezes were rare and the growing season exceeded 300 days annually.

The southern deserts supported varied and rich plant life, even though the characteristic plant dominants for each desert were spaced from ten to thirty feet apart. Creosote bush was present in all of the deserts, as were kangaroo rats, several species of mice, and several species of lizards. Hawks, owls, bobcats, and coyotes were the principal predators of the small mammals and reptiles. In the east, tarbush (*Fluorensia cernua*), mesquite, sotol, and ocotillo (genus *Fouquieria*) were dominant, and saltbush, several species of *Opuntia* and *Echinocactus* cacti, and mescal all had wide distributions. The Arizona–Sonora Desert was dominated by creosote bush, giant sahuaro cactus, and ocotillo. Here, mesquite, saltbush, smaller cacti, and mescal were also widely distributed. The Colorado River Desert possessed most of the plants of the other areas, but also hosted several plants that were sensitive to frost, such as desert ironwood (*Olnea lesota*) and smoke-tree (*Dalea spinosa*). Willows, cottonwood poplars, and mesquite occurred in very dense growths along the flood plains, and creosote dominated on the mesas above the Colorado River.

Large game, such as deer, were scattered in foothill grasslands and especially through the oak–juniper woodlands of the mountains in eastern Arizona and western New Mexico that bordered the hot deserts.

The following list of important wild food plants provides an indication of the extreme vegetational variation throughout the hot deserts, cold deserts, and semideserts of the Southwest.

Common name	Taxonomic name
Common purslane	*Portulaca oleracea*
Datil	*Yucca baccata* and other spp.
Giant sahuaro cactus	*Carnegiea gigantea*
Guaco	*Cleome serrulata*
Honey mesquite and other mesquites	*Prosopis juliflora* and other spp.
Indian millet	*Eriocoma cuspidata*
Lambsquarter	*Chenopodium* spp.
Mescal	*Agave* spp.
Oak, Emory	*Quercus emoryi*
Oak, evergreen or scrub live	*Q. undulata*
Oak, Gambel	*Q. gambelii*
Pigweed	*Amaranthus* spp.
Pinyon, double-leaf	*Pinus edulis*
Ponderosa pine	*P. ponderosa*
Prickly-pear and cholla cactus	*Opuntia* spp.
Saltbush	*Atriplex* spp.
Sand-root	*Ammobroma sonorae*
Serviceberry	*Amelanchier* spp.
Sotol	*Dasylerion wheeleri*
Western hackberry	*Celtis douglasii* and other spp.
Wild potato	*Solanum* spp.

PART II

ABORIGINAL LANGUAGE RELATIONS

Chapter 3

Language

There was extraordinary diversity among the Indian languages of western North America. In our sample, from the Tlingit in the far northwest corner to the Lipan Apache in the far southeast corner, at least 116 mutually unintelligible languages were spoken. The figure is probably conservative. Quite reasonably the total might be increased by ten percent, because many aboriginal Californians were either wiped out by diseases or removed to missions, or both of these disruptions occurred before their languages were recorded, and several groups in the Southwest, the Northwest Coast, and the Plateau had also been disrupted before investigations of their languages or cultures began.

Most of the 116 mutually unintelligible languages have been classified into larger genetic aggregations of one kind or another, though no single classificatory scheme or method for arriving at such a scheme has proved acceptable to all scholars interested in the inferential histories of American Indian languages. In the taxonomy used in this book, 104 of the languages are classified in 22 language families, and the remaining 12 languages are classified as 12 "isolates."* Ten of the isolates can be combined with some of the language families into phyla, and the remaining two iso-

lates are not known to have any close relatives. Figure 3-1 shows the distribution of language phyla and families throughout western North America. Table 3-1 shows the taxonomic classification of languages within these families and phyla.

An introductory discussion to the languages of western North America can be conducted first in the paradigm of genetic language relationships. Then we can shift to the paradigm of language diffusion across genetic boundaries. In the section entitled "Genetic Language Relationships," the "family" and "phyla" taxa we shall employ are presumed to embrace languages that are sisters of one another and daughters of a mother language (i.e., they are "genetically related"). Because there are no records of western North American Indian languages to reveal how, when, and in what ways daughter languages separated from a mother language, one task of comparative linguistics has been to reconstruct protolanguages, or mother languages, through systematic comparisons of the phonologies and morphologies of a set of languages that are presumed to have been sisters.

A comparative method that was developed in the study of Indo-European languages in the nineteenth century analyzed the predictable sound shifts that occurred within a language in certain phonetic environments. For instance, from the comparison of French and Latin it was possible to map the changes that occurred in the phonologies of the words in French that had been inherited from Latin, the preceding stage of the French language. "Laws" of regular phonetic changes were discovered from this procedure that allowed Indo-European researchers to demonstrate how and in what ways languages di-

---

*The Na-Dene phylum is said to be composed of two mutually unintelligible languages, Haida and Tlingit. In some taxonomies (e.g., Voegelin and Voegelin 1966), Na-Dene includes Haida, Tlingit, Eyak, and Athapaskan. As is pointed out below, the evidence supports an Eyak-Athapaskan family, but not as a member of the Na-Dene phylum. There is no evidence to support genetic connections between Haida and Tlingit either.

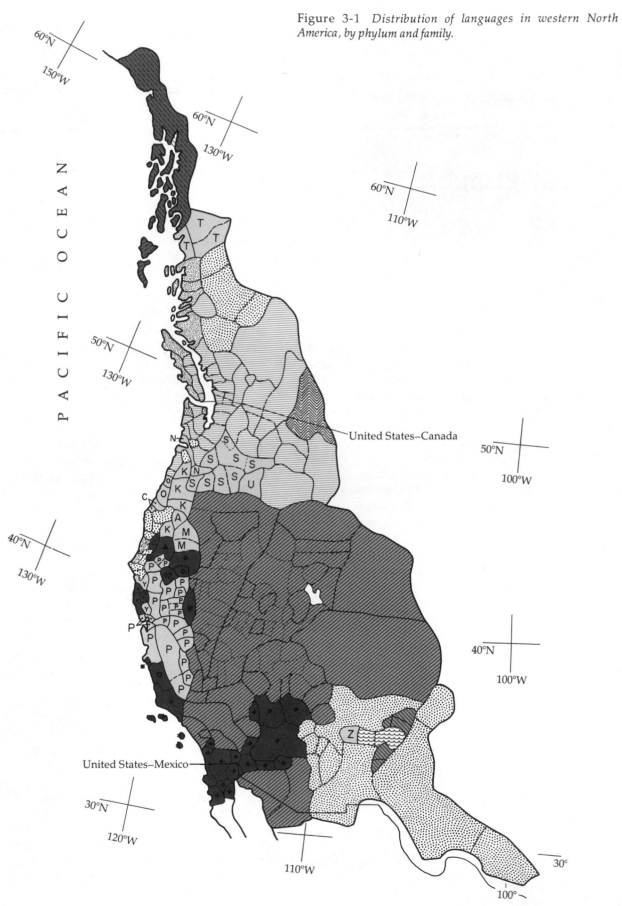

Figure 3-1 *Distribution of languages in western North America, by phylum and family.*

PACIFIC OCEAN

United States–Canada

United States–Mexico

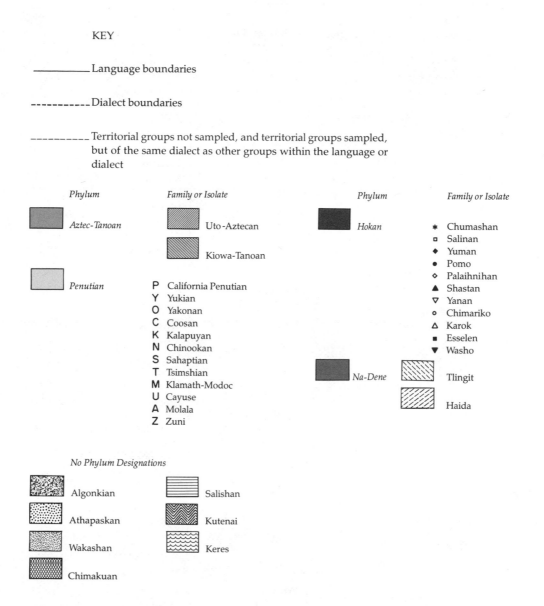

KEY

_____ Language boundaries

----------- Dialect boundaries

_____ Territorial groups not sampled, and territorial groups sampled, but of the same dialect as other groups within the language or dialect

| *Phylum* | *Family or Isolate* | | *Phylum* | *Family or Isolate* |

Phylum — Aztec-Tanoan

Family or Isolate
- Uto-Aztecan
- Kiowa-Tanoan

Phylum — Penutian

P   California Penutian
Y   Yukian
O   Yakonan
C   Coosan
K   Kalapuyan
N   Chinookan
S   Sahaptian
T   Tsimshian
M   Klamath-Modoc
U   Cayuse
A   Molala
Z   Zuni

Phylum — Hokan

Family or Isolate
- ✳ Chumashan
- ▫ Salinan
- ◆ Yuman
- ● Pomo
- ◇ Palaihnihan
- ▲ Shastan
- ▽ Yanan
- ○ Chimariko
- △ Karok
- ■ Esselen
- ▼ Washo

Phylum — Na-Dene

- Tlingit
- Haida

No Phylum Designations
- Algonkian
- Athapaskan
- Wakashan
- Chimakuan
- Salishan
- Kutenai
- Keres

verged from one another through systematic shifts of the sounds employed in those languages. These researchers were also fortunate enough to have written records that allowed them to match the sound shifts, or regular phonetic changes, that occurred between two languages with the time period in which those changes took place.* Thus, comparative linguistics was first and foremost an analysis of the histories of languages, and the nineteenth century method allowed explanations of how, when, and where

changes took place. Dyen (1973) has called this early form of historical linguistic inquiry into the changes that occurred in the history of a single language, such as French and its preceding form, Latin, "historical genetic linguistics."

Historical genetic linguistic methods have been adapted by students of North American Indian languages. Thus, two or more languages presumed to be genetically related because of recognizable similarities in grammatical forms (aspects of grammar or syntax), lexicons (words), or phonologies (sounds) between or among the languages, can be compared so as to discover whether regular phonetic changes have occurred in predictable environments, and studies of this kind have been made. Comparisons of

*Historical records in the form of dated written works are not available to account for every point in time when language branching occurred in the Indo-European family, but records are available for many languages in the family.

Table 3-1
Languages, language isolates, language families, and language phyla of western North America

Phyla	Family	Branch	Language
Aztec-Tanoan	Uto-Aztecan		Gabrieliño
			Luiseño
			Cupeño
			Cahuilla
			Serraño
			Tubatulabal
		Shoshonean	Kawaiisu
			Ute
			Mono
			Paviotso
			Shoshone
			Panamint
			Hopi
		Sonoran	Pima
	Kiowa-Tanoan		
		Tanoan	Tewa
			Tiwa
			Towa
			Piro
Penutian	California Penutian		Costanoan
			Lake Miwok
			Coast Miwok
			Bay Miwok (Saclan)
		Miwok-Costanoan	Plains Miwok
			Northern Sierra Miwok
			Central Sierra Miwok
			Southern Sierra Miwok
			Mountain Maidu
			Valley Maidu
		Maiduan	Northwestern Maidu
			Southern Maidu (Nisenan)
			Wintu
		Wintun	Patwin
			Nomlaki
			Northern Foothill Yokuts
		Yokuts	Southern Foothill Yokuts
			Valley Yokuts
	Yukian*		Yuki
			Wappo
	Yakonan		Siuslaw
			Alsea
	Coosan		Hanis
			Miluk
			Takelma
	Kalapuyan		Northern Kalapuya
			Central Kalapuya
			Southern Kalapuya
	Chinookan		Lower (Shoalwater)
			Upper (Kiksht)

*Not all agree on classification of Yukian as a Penutian language. Indeed, a principal scholar of the language, William Elmendorf (pers. comm.), does not accept this classification.

Table 3-1 *(continued)*
Languages, language isolates, language families, and language phyla of western North America

Phyla	Family	Branch	Language
	Sahaptian		Sahaptin Nez Percé
	Tsimshian		Coastal [†] River
	Isolate		Klamath-Modoc
	Isolate		Cayuse
	Isolate		Molala
	Isolate		Zuni
Hokan	Chumashan		Chumash
	Salinan		Salinan
	Yuman		River Delta Upland (Pai) Southern (California)
	Pomon		Southern Pomo Southwestern Pomo Northern Pomo Central Pomo Eastern Pomo Southeastern Pomo Northeastern Pomo
	Palaihnihan		Achomawi Atsugewi
	Shastan		Shastan
	Yanan		Yanan
	Isolate		Chimariko
	Isolate		Karok
	Isolate		Esselen
	Isolate		Washo
	Algonkian	Ritwan	Wiyot Yurok
	Eyak-Athapaskan		Canadian Pacific Apachean
	Wakashan	Kwakiutlan	Haisla Bella Bella Kwakiutl
		Nootkan	Nootka Nitinat Makah
	Chimakuan		Chimakum Quileute

continued on page 56

[†] Elmendorf (pers. comm.) reports that there may have been two Tsimshian languages spoken on the coast.

Table 3-1 (*continued*)
Languages, language isolates, language families, and language phyla of western North America

Phyla	Family	Branch	Language
	Salishan	Bella Coola	Bella Coola
		Tillamook	Tillamook
		Coast	Quinault
			Lower Chehalis
			Chehalis
			Cowlitz
			Twana
			Puget Sound
			Klallam
			Straits
			Halkomelem
			Nootsack
			Squamish
			Pentlatch
			Seshelt
			Comox
		Interior	Thompson
			Columbia
			Okanagon
			Kalispel
			Coeur d'Alene
			Lillooet
Na-Dene‡	Isolate		Tlingit
	Isolate		Haida
	Isolate		Kutenai
	Isolate		Keresan

‡It is highly doubtful that Tlingit and Haida were genetically related. At this time it is best to consider each of them to be isolates with no known relatives.

two or more languages spoken during the same period, roughly the late nineteenth century and early twentieth century for most of the American Indian languages that have been recorded, have yielded reconstructions of the presumed phonological and lexical forms from which the daughter languages diverged. The reconstructed form is called a protolanguage, but because protolanguages are reconstructed from synchronic comparisons,* the mother language

*Synchronic in this sense means that time is held constant and that, all things being equal, the sister languages were coequal and coterminous, even if in comparing four languages the data for one were collected in 1890 and the data for the other three were collected in 1930.

is inferential, so the taxonomy and the history, too, are inferential. Unlike the Indo-Europeanists, the students of North American Indian languages have not been able to specify where or when languages diverged. Nevertheless, language families have been reconstructed through the systematic comparisons of regular phonetic changes.

Many of the language families represented in Figure 3-1 have been reconstructed through these systematic comparisons. Uto-Aztecan, Sahaptian, Athapaskan, Kalapuyan, California Penutian, Pomo, and Kiowa-Tanoan are cases in point. Other language families for which there are considerable data suggesting genetic relatedness, but which have not been reconstructed into protolanguages through the methods of historical genetic linguistics, such as Salishan and Wakashan from the central Northwest Coast region, are presumed to constitute families. For the language families that have been reconstructed, as well as for language families that have been presumed to be related, the branching relations within each family (subgroupings within families) can be inferred through a set of methods broadly defined as "comparative genetic linguistics" by Dyen (1973).

The methodology most often employed in comparative genetic linguistics is lexicostatistics. In this methodology, a standard list of basic vocabulary is used to compare several languages—namely, all the languages in a language family for which identical basic vocabulary lists can be compiled. In principle, the basic vocabulary of a language is the set of words that have meanings for which common words can be expected to be found in any language. The words for meanings such as "eye" and "sky" are also presumed to be relatively unaffected by borrowing resulting from cultural contact. Words for technological implements, on the other hand, such as "hoe" and "winnowing tray," may well be affected by contact. It has become standard practice to use as a basic vocabulary list either a set of about 165–200 items (Swadesh 1950), or a more refined set of 100 items (Swadesh 1955). It is supposed that the words for the list of glosses (meanings) that comprise the basic vocabulary are likely to change over time as a result of the chronic tendency of language to change, rather than by virtue of any specific and unpredictable accidents of culture contacts.

The basic vocabularies of each pair of languages or dialects in the family are compared to determine which items are cognates and which are not. Cognate words in two languages or dialects for the same meaning, such as "sky," other things being equal, suggest retention from a prior language. The percentage of basic vocabulary cognates shared between each pair of languages or dialects allows for subgrouping of the languages within the language family. The classification is normally accomplished by some statistical technique such as cluster analysis.

The percentages of cognates shared among Salishan languages, for instance, have been classified by Swadesh (1950), who used impressionistic clustering techniques, by Dyen (1962), who used a formally explicit metric grouping procedure, and by Jorgensen (1969), who used a formally explicit nonmetric technique for finding the shortest distances in a Euclidian space. The three clustering techniques provide highly similar branchings.

One of the reasons that linguists have pursued their inquiries into the genetic relations among languages is to unravel the histories of American Indian languages. Historical genetic reconstructions and comparative genetic analyses allow us to make reasonable inferences about whether languages are closely related, or related only distantly, and by matching language similarities with spatial proximities among languages, we can make inferences about when groups diverged. The time factor "when" is vexing. One notable attempt to supply dates to divergences, called glottochronology, has foundered for several reasons,* but a concept that was a critical underpinning to glottochronology is still valid: namely, the less similar two related languages are on the basis of percentage of basic vocabulary cognates shared, the longer the period since they diverged. Relative time separations can be inferred, then, from the similarities and differences among languages.

The problem in understanding "what possibly happened" in western North American prehistory can be aided by a comparative linguistic analysis that sorts out the relationships among languages within a family. We address ourselves to the task in this and subsequent chapters.

Of the genetic descriptions in Table 3-1, we have discussed the meaning of language "family" but not of language "branch." In the course of time, languages change and, furthermore, they change in different ways in different areas. When changes accumulate and the dialect of one area ceases to have mutual intelligibility with the dialect of another area, the dialects are then said to belong to different languages. This process can, of course, be repeated and can be called branching after the way it might be represented in a family tree. The languages that result from branching are called daughter languages in relation to the language that has branched, which is called their "protolanguage." A language that has resulted from branching and then branches itself is, of course, a protolanguage to its daughter languages and a daughter language to its own protolanguage. Such a language is often called a mesolanguage to specify both relations at once.

In Table 3-1 "branch" is used synonymously with "mesolanguage." For instance, Uto-Aztecan had at least three mesolanguages, Shoshonean, Sonoran,

---

*For instance, glottochronological divergence rates were determined statistically by Lees (1953) on the basis of a 13-language sample that included 11 Indo-European languages, Coptic, and Chinese. The sample might be representative of Indo-European, but cannot be assumed to be representative of all of the world's languages.

and Aztec (Voegelin, Voegelin, and Hale 1962); they are diagrammed in this way:

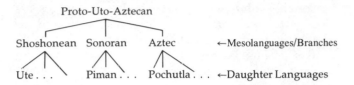

A "phylum" is a set of languages that are presumed to be related but for which there is no solid evidence to base claims that their relatedness is genetic. Some languages have been linked into a phylum on the basis of resemblances among verb stems. Other languages have been linked into phyla because of the manner in which verbs are affixed, and so forth. There is some evidence to support the claims for genetic relatedness among the languages in each of all four of the phyla in western North America—Aztec-Tanoan, Penutian, Hokan, and Na-Dene—but by far the strongest cases have been marshalled for the Aztec-Tanoan and Penutian phyla. We shall return later to the question of phylum relationships.

Before we proceed with a discussion of genetic relationships among languages and the manner in which languages diverged, it is critical to introduce an equally important dimension of inferential language history, the diffusion of features of language between genetically unrelated languages. Trade, marriage, slave-raiding, attendance at ceremonials, performances by shamans, and myth-telling sessions generated myriads of language contacts between people whose languages were unrelated genetically. Moreover, contacts were also made between people whose languages may have been genetically related but whose separation was so deep in the past that only a few of their genetic features remained, or between people whose languages were genetically related and mutually unintelligible even if many genetic features remained.

Evidences for diffusion of language features occur in phonology, lexicon, and grammar. In general, a feature of language is recognized as having diffused if it has a very wide distribution in one language family but a very narrow distribution in an adjacent language family. In some instances, these features appear to fit integrally into the systems of the former but perhaps less integrally into the systems of the latter. The picture can become more complex if, for instance, features diffuse from one unrelated language to another and then one of the language communities moves, carrying the borrowed feature with it, or a new language community migrates into the area and drives a wedge between the two language communities that once shared a common border.

Borrowing between unrelated languages and subsequent diffusions of those borrowings have created linguistic areas in which many shared resemblances spill across several language families. We shall address the evidence for diffusion of language features after we deal with the question of genetic relatedness.

Let us return now to the empirical problems of the relations among languages. We shall ask how it was that there was so much diversity among the languages of western North America, and why the cleavages were so deep and the variation so much greater along the whole of the Pacific Coast and the Southwest than in the vast expanses of the Plateau and the Great Basin.

GENETIC LANGUAGE RELATIONSHIPS

At the time of European contact there were 94 distinct and mutually unintelligible languages spoken along the Pacific Coast and in the Southwest, yet in the Great Basin and Plateau, the aggregate land mass of which was approximately equal to the combined mass of the Northwest Coast, Northern California, Southern California, and Southwest regions, only 18 mutually unintelligible languages were spoken. Some rules will be useful in interpreting the variation and inferring something from the interpretation.

In order to make sense of the linguistic variation and the geographic distribution of languages and dialects, it is necessary to assess the relations within each language family and, when possible, between language families. The rule that will be followed in assessing the historical depth of language variation can be stated: the greater the diversity of cognates shared among sister languages in the same territory, the more probable it is that the languages diverged in that area than somewhere else. To argue otherwise, one would have to assume that several distinct and already linguistically differentiated groups from the same language family, once located in many separate areas, subsequently migrated from their several different places into a common territory that they occupied at the time of contact with Europeans (Jorgensen 1969: 23–26). There is no plausible rationale to explain why several distinct members of the same language family occupying territories removed from each other would migrate, as a group or even in separate movements, to a common region. Perhaps the movements of one branch of languages within a family could be explained by chance, but it stretches credulity to account for several branches within one family, or for the distributions within several families, in such a fashion. So we assume that the greater the diversity within a language family in a common region, as measured by percentages of cognates shared, the more probable that the diversity developed *in situ* and that the region in question was the homeland of the family or the branch of the family.

Although language is subject to external influences, and modes of diffusion* operate on many languages to change them, it is still reasonable to assume that at some time a single protolanguage was spoken by a group of people. This entails the assumption that the group shared a common protoculture as well. To be sure, there could have been variation in both the language and the culture. For instance, it is most plausible to assume variation in individual speakers (idiolects), and it is plausible to assume that there could have been dialectical differences if there were several communities. If there were different communities, it is likely that different adaptations to an environment, different marriage practices, and other cultural practices would represent cultural variation within the protolanguage community.

It is even conceivable in the history of a language family that people speaking in a language—say, in the Eyak-Athapaskan family—dropped their native language and adopted the language of a neighbor from an entirely different family. In this regard, Drucker (1965) suggests that an Athapaskan-speaking group near Yakutat Bay dropped its language in prehistoric times and adopted the Tlingit language and culture as a result of trade contacts. The Tagish, a Canadian Athapaskan group of the interior lakes region east of the Northwest Coast adopted the Tlingit language through trade contacts with the Chilkat Tlingit during the nineteenth century, but they did not adopt Tlingit culture *in toto* (McClellan n.d.). According to Gordon Marsh,[†]a very few old Tagish still spoke Tagish as a second language in the 1950s. Drucker (1965) also claims that in late prehistoric times a Tlingit group was given land on the Nass River by the Niska and adopted Niska (Tsimshian) speech. On the basis of human morphological features, Elsasser and Heizer (1966) suggests that the Athapaskan-speaking Kato of the Northern California coast were once Yukian speakers.

---

*Diffusion includes analogic change where a concept, such as tense distinction between the remote and the recent past, is borrowed and worked into the phonology and grammar of the recipient language.

†Marsh provided a considerable amount of detail about Tagish moieties (in personal communications to David F. Aberle).

The case for the Tagish adopting Tlingit and a Tlingit group adopting Tsimshian are well grounded, and in neither instance would such adoptions of an alien language upset interpretations of homeland and language diversity. In both instances the borrowing speech communities were located adjacent to those speech communities from which the languages were learned and with which they had regular intercourse. A problem might arise, at least in the comparisons of languages and culture, if in the distant past a similar change of language took place and the borrowing group migrated and eventually gave rise to several daughter languages. If the original borrowers had not also fully adopted the culture of the speech community from which they had borrowed speech, interpretations of the relations between language divergences and cultural divergences could be in error. There is no way to test for a hypothetical situation such as the one above, and at this point cultural divergences from a protoculture are not our principal concern. As a working premise let it be assumed that at some time each protolanguage was spoken by a group of people who were not significantly differentiated dialectally or culturally.

The evidence for language diffusion among adjacent and genetically unrelated languages is compelling. The maximal diffusion is for a speech community to drop its language and borrow one from some other group. But the evidence for differentiation among genetically related languages that are separated from one another over large distances for long periods of time is even more compelling. It was determined through work on the Salishan language family that the greater the number of Salish language units occupying the geographic space between any pair of Salish languages, the lower the cognate similarity between the pair (Jorgensen 1969). The relations between pairs of Salish languages were reduced even further if genetically unrelated language units or mountain barriers separated the members of the pairs. The statistical inference to be drawn is that languages in contact influence each other, and the greater the distances across which contact is made between pairs of genetically related languages, the fewer the contacts and the less the influence between members of the pair.

When we direct our attention to Map 3-1 and Table 3-1 and recognize that the diversity in the languages along the coast and in the Southwest occurred within language families as well as between language families, we must assume not only that many language groups migrated to those areas but that, once there, they stayed and differentiated further.

This process not only took a long time—probably 6,000 years or so is required to account for all of the diversification if phyla members prove to be genetically related—but was also pinned to two phenomena, one environmental and the other cultural. As we have learned in our introduction to western North American environments, the natural extractive resources along the coast from Yakutat Bay to the United States–Mexico border were abundant and quite localized or nucleated. There was variation in abundance and localization, of course. On both sides of the Georgia Strait, for instance, natural extractive resources were abundant and diffusely distributed, but in the far north the best fishing sites occurred in a few areas, and in Southern California considerable distances often separated sources of good water. These many localized areas, with their varied and bountiful resources (as was true of California) or their less varied but extremely abundant resources (as was true along the Northwest Coast), lent themselves to language differentiation through cultural factors, such as the methods by which resource areas were exploited and the customs through which those areas were owned. It seems most plausible that the cultural concepts of private ownership of key resource sites and the jealous protection of them sped the process of language differentiation along its way by reducing contacts among local communities that had become rather fixed in place.

The language diversity among closely spaced, property-owning extractors from the same geographic locality and the same language family, such as the Wakashan, Salishan, or Pomo speakers, invites assertions about the interrelations among language, culture, and environment: in general, with regard to the West Coast of North America, one gains the impression that language differentiation was not a simple function of the time at which separation of sister dialects occurred,* nor can the variation among languages in a single area be solely accounted for through the immigration of many distinct languages to the same place. To be sure, migrations to the West Coast did occur over a period of several thousand years, with the most recent migrations occurring no more than perhaps 800 years ago (Pacific Athapaskans), and variations in the languages of these immigrants will be accounted for; but for practically every immigration there was also subsequent language diversification. Moreover, in the past 3,000 years, once people moved to the coastal area, including the

breadth of California, there is considerable evidence that the populations made successful technological adaptations to the many microenvironments and neither the adaptations nor the territories were easily forsaken. Once ensconced, people were not easily dislodged nor did they move readily. Yet once ensconced, populations along the Northwest Coast of North America (e.g., Salishan and Sahaptian speakers) and throughout Northern California and Southern California (e.g., Uto-Aztecan speakers) probably grew and fissioned. While mother cultures stayed put, fissioning and subsequent eastward migrations of daughter cultures most plausibly accounts for the Salishans in the Plateau, the Uto-Aztecans in the Great Basin, and, perhaps, the Sahaptians in the Plateau.

It may be inferred, in part on the basis of archeological summaries* and in part from the correlations of cultural phenomena with languages, that some groups with long histories of residence on the west coast (e.g., Hokan speakers, Salishan speakers) originally entered the region when population densities were very low. The immigrants located in nucleated resource zones that had high natural productivity given the extractive technologies possessed at the time in which the groups entered.

It is surely possible that there were some dislocations of sparse populations and that, say, Hokan speakers were not the first people in California or Salishan speakers were not the first people to penetrate the central Northwest Coast and adapt successfully to the wet forests. Archeological investigations along the Northwest Coast do not yet allow for a comprehensive, temporal picture of what happened there, but the earliest littoral subsistence economies were probably oriented toward shellfish collecting, with fishing and maritime adaptations coming later. Whether populations were displaced, who they were, and where they might have gone is not known.

The archeological evidence suggests that generalized gathering and hunting technologies that were widely distributed in the western North American archaic period—at least as early as 9000 B.C. in the interior regions and 5000 B.C. on the California coast—preceded specialized gathering technologies (acorn, mesquite, and shellfish microenvironmental adaptations, say, in early California) and more specialized fishing technologies (in the Plateau and parts of California), and that technological adapta-

---

*Bergsland and Vogt (1962: 115–158) demonstrated that the Old Norse spoken in Iceland in 1960 had not changed from the prior form of Old Norse spoken in Norway in 1000 A.D.

*For archeological summaries see Heizer (1971) for California; Sanger (1967) and Leonhardy and Rice (1970) for the Plateau; Jennings (1974) for the Great Basin; and Mitchell (1971) for the central Northwest Coast.

tions to rain forests, including development of woodworking tools and the competence to use them to build even-keeled boats (on the Northwest Coast) preceded technological adaptations to maritime subsistence economies. The maritime adaptations of the Gabrieliño and Chumash of Southern California were unique and probably followed specialized littoral adaptations.

Let us hypothesize that, in California and the west coast of North America, the mild winter climates and the stability, abundance, and localization of extractable natural resources in those areas (given the extant technologies of the groups that migrated there) allowed the earliest residents to establish themselves in areas of high natural plant and animal productivity. Moreover, the groups became sedentary for the greater part of each year, engaging in only modest movements, usually during summer months.

As community populations grew, most probably they fissioned, and the migrating groups—daughter groups as it were—sought new locales similar to the locales from which they migrated and in which adjustments would be relatively simple. The phenomenon of growth, fission, and migration, with "mother" cultures staying put, probably occurred time and time again, and dialectal and language differentiation proceeded as communication was cut off.

Other factors, cultural in nature, probably intervened to stimulate language differentiation. People ensconced in areas for generations probably began to lay claim to the resource areas that they exploited, that is, they appropriated areas for their private property. With increased population density, local fissioning, and immigration from other areas (say, the Penutian penetration into the interior of California), it is probable that protection of resource areas from trespass and poaching reduced communication among peoples from different communities and speeded language differentiation.

Contrariwise, in areas where resources were fluctuating or meager, or both, where intergroup mobility was high, and where private claims to extractable resources were few, dialect division was minimal, even when some areas had been occupied for long periods of time—say, 2,000 years. In part, the scanty language differentiation in the Plateau and Great Basin resulted from the recentness of the occupation of those areas by the people who resided there at the time of contact with Europeans. But relative language homogeneity also arose from the diffuse and not especially abundant distribution of strategic resources in those regions and the manner in which people adapted to those resources. From the Plateau through the Great Basin, people were extractors of wild plants and animals. Their private property concepts were weakly developed; resource areas were

often shared by several groups; and considerable contacts through intermarriage and ceremonial attendances were maintained among people who were separated by great distances for much of the year.

In this setting, by modifying Miller's (1970) hypothesis for a more restricted problem, we may say that dialect differentiation was probably minimized by considerable mobility of groups in areas of low population densities where there were few bounded speech communities, considerable migration between communities, no social stratification, and perhaps casual attitudes about language style. For the Great Basin and the Plateau, there was also considerable bilingualism, and as Miller (1970) points out for the Shoshone language of the Great Basin, all dialects were readily accepted as equal. Bilingualism was especially widespread in the central Great Basin. Whenever Great Basin peoples speaking mutually unintelligible languages came into contact, it was common for speakers of each language to learn the language spoken by their neighbors; therefore, ready acceptance of different languages was customary in the Great Basin, as was the ready acceptance of dialectal differences.

The Southwest poses an interesting problem. Some of the languages that were spoken at the time of contact with Europeans were apparently the progeny of language groups that migrated to the area more than three thousand years earlier and participated in the development of sedentary, horticultural life. They became localized in the arid Southwest around farming sites where water could be gained from rivers, springs, or wash-offs—places where water from storms could be contained in a drainage. Private claims were made to the farm sites, and a process of differentiation occurred that was somewhat similar to that which existed on the coast. Because of the aridity of the Southwest, there seems to have been a marked reduction in the number of farming villages and a retrenchment of the area of the farming cultures shortly before Athapaskans moved into the region. Thus, the Southwest was inhabited by small pockets of long-term residents, among whom there was considerable language diversity, and by wide stretches of short-term residents among whom there was only modest dialectal diversity.

What will be proposed here, then, is that language change proceeded more rapidly among Northwest Coast, California, and Pueblo tribes than among other tribes in western North America and, given extant technologies, environmental and cultural phenomena account for the differences. The factors beyond time alone that drove related languages apart by cutting off communication were migration, of course, but also the availability of concentrated, highly productive resource areas, private claims to them, and the ability of the claimants to maintain themselves over relatively long periods of time (several generations) from the same resource base in the same locale.

The separation of a speech community into dialects, and dialects into two or more mutually unintelligible languages went on for thousands of years. Some languages that appear to be genetically related, such as many of the members of the Hokan phylum and many, but by no means all, of the members of the Penutian phylum, diverged so long ago that genetic relations are not obvious. This seems the most plausible explanation.

To propose a general rule, if all things are equal and if there was a considerable lapse of time between contacts among two groups of people who shared the same language, two dialects developed. Dialect changes sometimes led to language changes. Yet dialect differentiation, and in turn, language differentiation, was hastened by privatization of resources in abundantly endowed, localized resource areas, and retarded by communitarian uses and sharing of resources in modestly endowed, diffuse resource areas.*

Many languages in western North America have been compared for the basic vocabulary that they share. We shall provide these data in our analysis of genetic relations. There are many other languages for which we do not have shared cognate percentages. For these languages interpretations will perforce be based on historical genetic reconstructions and some lexicostatistical measures other than percentages of cognates shared.[†] We shall call attention to the comparative data that are available as we proceed.

---

*As was pointed out earlier, glottochronological divergence rates were determined from a sample of thirteen languages from around the world—eleven Indo-European, one Chinese, and one Coptic. This sample *may* be appropriate for Indo-European languages, but one cannot generalize to the world from it, and one Indo-European language, Old Norse, studied by Bergsland and Vogt (1962), had not changed at all over a period of almost 1,000 years. While comparing the Indian languages discussed in this chapter, glottochronological rates were not used, though it is reasonable that, *all things equal*, languages would change at about the same rate.

[†] In a comparative study of Salish, Jorgensen (1969) measured the functional loads carried by the phonemes in the basic vocabulary lists to determine how similar or different languages were on phonological material. A student of Jorgensen (Wenger 1968) did a similar functional load study for the canonical shapes and phonemes of several languages in the Penutian phylum and later (Wenger 1973) for languages in several phyla.

The discussions of phyla and families that follow are brief and speculative. So as not to burden the reader with qualifications, let us proceed as if the footing were more firm than in fact it is.

Language Phyla and Families

Penutian Phylum

The evidence to support the genetic status of the Penutian phylum is strong, and new evidence is regularly being presented that firms up our knowledge of the connections among the languages. At the time of contact with Europeans, Penutian was composed of eight language families and four language isolates in western North America, another three language families in Mexico, and one language family in Bolivia. In western North America the majority of the languages were spoken from the Middle Columbia Plateau through the Oregon coast, and throughout the Central Valley and central coast of California. Two outliers, the Tsimshian family of the northern Northwest Coast and the Zuni isolate of the Southwest, completed the phylum in western North America. The Mayan, Mixe-Zoque, and Totonacan languages of Mexico, and the Chipaya-Uru of Bolivia will not be considered here. But the diversity of the western North American Penutians suggests that the homeland of proto-Penutian was in the north rather than in Mexico if, indeed, the Penutian phylum is a genetic unit.

The very deep separations among the languages along the Oregon coast from the Cascades on the east to the ocean suggest that this area was the homeland of the Penutians. Designating a time of origin is vexing, but it is plausible that 6,500 years ago the proto-Penutians were adapting to a riverine-based subsistence economy that included generalized hunting and some gathering. Quite possibly this occurred on the west side of the Rockies in the Fraser Plateau. At a very early time, fissioning of the parent group must have taken place. Among the Penutian speakers in western North America it is likely that the earliest separation occurred when the group that came to speak **Tsimshian*** was separated from a group that

---

*In the descriptions that follow, names of language families will be designated in boldface type where each is first discussed. Names of branches and languages within families will be designated in italic type. Dialects will not be given special typographic treatment.

moved slowly southward. Tsimshian, which was composed of two (perhaps three) languages spoken on the *Coast* and along the *Nass* and *Skeena* Rivers (Rigsby 1969) may have separated from its congener as early as 6,000 years ago. The Tsimshian languages were developed among the group that moved north and west.

It may have been that the southern Penutians followed the upper reaches of the Middle Columbia River through the Cascades, beginning 6,000 years ago. Some went as far as the river's mouth and others moved down the Lower Columbia (Willamette River drainage). As groups located, claimed fishing and gathering stations, and grew, new units broke off and pursued rivers such as the Alsea, Siuslaw, Coos, Umpqua, and Rogue, that cut through the Coast Range to the ocean.

On the Oregon coast from north to south, the **Chinookan** family was composed of two languages, *Shoalwater* (two dialects) and *Kitsht*. Chinookan seems to have been related only remotely to its nearest Penutian neighbors in the Plateau and south along the coast.

South of the areas where Chinookan was spoken and throughout the Willamette Valley was the **Kalapuyan** language family, composed of these four languages: *Northern Kalapuya* (with two known dialects), *Central Kalapuya* (with six known dialects), *Southern Kalapuya* (one known dialect), and *Takelma* (two dialects) (Swadesh 1965; Shipley 1970). Takelma, spoken on the upper and middle reaches of the Rogue River, was very distantly related to Kalapuya, but Shipley (1970) reconstructed a proto-Kalapuya-Takelma phonology, and Swadesh (1965) demonstrated with his 100-item basic vocabulary that 70 percent cognates were shared between Central and Southern Kalapuya.* Central and Southern Kalapuya

languages were surely different, and all the evidence suggests that Northern Kalapuya, spoken in the northwest corner of the Willamette Valley, was equally divergent from the other two. Takelma shared 48 percent cognates with Central Kalapuya, suggesting that Takelma was the first group to break away (Swadesh 1965).

The **Yakonan** family was composed of *Siuslaw* (two dialects) and *Alsea* (two dialects). The relationship between the two was distant and no cognate percentages have been worked out, though Pierce (1966) has demonstrated that cardinal numbers and actor morphemes in the personal pronouns of the Alsea and Siuslaw languages were similar in several features. These two languages were spoken on the Yaquina and Alsea Rivers (Alsea), and the Siuslaw and Lower Umpqua Rivers (Siuslaw). The Kiutsh dialect was spoken on the Lower Umpqua. The Yakonan languages seem to have been most closely related to the Coosan languages, which were located south of the Kiutsh dialect (Lower Umpqua River) of Siuslaw (Wenger 1973).

Coosan, like Yakonan, was composed of two languages, *Hanis* and *Miluk*. Hanis was spoken on the Coos River and northern Coos Bay, while Miluk was spoken on the Lower Coquille River and the southern slough of Coos Bay. Although they were located side by side, the two languages were very different in their cardinal number systems and similar in the phonological (but not possessive affixing) aspects of their pronominals (Pierce 1966).

Molala, a language isolate spoken in the southern Willamette Valley along the west side of the Cascades, may be distantly related to *Cayuse*, a language isolate on the Deschutes River, a tributary of the Middle Columbia on the east side of the Cascades, and Sahaptian, a language family on the Middle Columbia (Rigsby 1966).

Sahaptian was composed of *Sahaptin* (two dialects), spoken along the Middle Columbia, and *Nez Percé*, spoken on the Upper Columbia (Aoki 1966). The modest differentiation within Sahaptian, which was spoken from near the present-day city of The Dalles to northeastern Idaho, suggests a recent movement into the Columbia Plateau, perhaps no more than 800 to 1,000 years ago. Although there is not specific evidence to indicate as much, the migration might have begun from the Willamette Valley region on the west side or from the Deschutes River on the east side of the Cascades. If Sahaptian, Cayuse, and Molala prove to be distantly related members of one family, the linguistic evidence would support ancient differentiation among these groups, perhaps as old as 5,000 years, and perhaps centered on the east slope of the Cascades near the Deschutes River. One group

---

*Seventy-seven percent cognate retention on Swadesh's 100-item list and 70 percent on his 200-item list are the arbitrary points at which the distinction between language and dialect is drawn. If two speech communities shared 78 percent on the 100-item list, they are said to have been dialects of the same language. If they shared 76 percent they are said to have been separate languages. The dividing line is arbitrary because it is possible for two languages to have shared 80 percent or more cognates and still have been mutually unintelligible. It is highly doubtful, however, that languages sharing less than 77 percent on the 100-item list were mutually intelligible. The reason Swadesh's 200-item list requires only 70 percent cognates to distinguish languages is that as sample size increases, sample error decreases. Hence, only 70 percent is required on the 200-item list.

may have stayed on the Deschutes when another group of Penutians broke from it and moved through the Cascades.

What has not been worked out are the relations among Sahaptian, Molala, and Cayuse, or between any of them and Klamath-Modoc. *Klamath-Modoc* (two dialects) was a language isolate spoken in the Upper Klamath River and lakes region at the south end of the Cascades in Oregon and Northern California. The parent Klamath group probably located there early, perhaps 4,500 years ago. Whether they entered from the east, following the Deschutes River, or from the west, is not clear. The language differences between the Klamath and their nearest neighbors to the west, the Takelma, were considerable (Wenger 1973), but they may have been equally different from Sahaptian, Cayuse, and Molala.

The deep division within and among the five Penutian-phylum language families and three language isolates near the Oregon coast make this area the probable homeland of the Penutians, save for the early separation of Tsimshian.

The major, but not necessarily the earliest, movement into California was probably from the northeast, following the tributaries of the Sacramento River. Subsequently, groups fanned out around the foothills. Hokan speakers probably already inhabited the upper courses of the Sacramento drainage as well as the Trinity drainage of the Klamath River system. There is general agreement that **California Penutian** is one language family composed of four branches, *Maiduan* (four languages), *Miwok-Costanoan* (eight, but perhaps more languages),* *Wintun* (three languages), and *Yokuts* (three languages) (Pitkin 1962; Shipley 1966; Callaghan 1967). Phonological correspondences have been worked out and a proto-Penutian phonology has been reconstructed that embraces these languages (Shipley 1966; Callaghan 1967). On phonological criteria, the closest relation of California Penutian was Klamath (Shipley 1966). Wenger's (1973) grammatical data also suggest a connection between California Penutian and Klamath.

Except for the San Francisco Bay region, where Miwok established themselves to the north and Costanoan became ensconced to the south, the coastal

and mountain river valleys around the perimeter of California seem to have been previously claimed by Hokan. The Penutians may have dislocated some Hokan groups. Because of the known variation within Miwok-Costanoan on the coast and in the Bay region, it is probable that this was the first branch of the California Penutian family to enter what is now California. The Miwok-Costanoans probably pushed their way down the Sacramento River into the Bay region and eventually expanded southwest along the San Joaquin River.

For many years the *Yukian* language, composed of *Wappo* and *Yuki* (three dialects), has been considered to be a language family with no known relatives. The leading scholar of the Yukian languages (Elmendorf, pers. comm.) considers Yukian to be genetically independent of all other language families in North America. Both Kroeber (1925) and Driver considered Yukian to be representative of one of the earliest, if not the earliest, migration into California of a people whose progeny were still in California at the time of European contact. Wenger's (1973) comparative analysis of 52 grammatical features among twenty-one languages representing fourteen language families and isolates in California and Oregon classifies Yukian as a member of the Penutian phylum. Whether this affinity was caused by diffusion of grammatical and phonological features (areal effect) or because of inheritance from a protolanguage is not known. No comparative reconstruction has linked Yukian to other Penutian languages. Yukian's closest relationships were to Yokuts and Miwok. One possible explanation is that Yukian was the first Penutian-phylum group to enter California, doing so before the California Penutians entered and began diverging. Let us say that Yukian belongs to the Penutian phylum.

At contact, the Yukians were located on the coast and in the interior between Wintun, Pomo, and Athapaskan speakers. Although the Huchnom, Yuki, and Coast Yuki shared between 83 and 90 percent cognates, these dialects were so different that Elmendorf (1968) called them "dialectlike languages (see Table 3-2). Wappo, the other Yukian language, was spoken in the Napa River valley. It shared only 36 percent cognates with Yuki. The cleavage in the Yukian language family is deep and probably represents a separation that occurred within 1,000 years after the proto-Yukians entered northwestern California. Yukians must have entered California by 5,000 years ago.

A final language isolate, *Zuni* of the Southwest, has been classified as Penutian by Newman (1964) and Wenger (1968). Wenger's comparative analysis of Penutian canonical shapes placed Zuni as a distant member of the phylum, no closer to the California

---

*Broadbent and Callaghan (1960), and Callaghan (1967) think that there were six Miwok languages and at least one Costanoan language with seven or eight dialects. Costanoan was spoken over a 100-mile stretch from San Francisco Bay to Monterey Bay and quite likely was composed of several distinct languages, but most of the Costanoans either died or dropped their native language during the mission period.

Table 3-2
Yukian lexicostatistical relations: basic vocabulary

Language	Yuki	Huchnom	Coast Yuki
Wappo	36	35	35
Yuki		90	83
Huchnom			90

Source: Elmendorf (1968).
Note: Data based on Swadesh's 100-item list.

Penutian than, say, Takelma. It is plausible that Zuni split and began moving southeast from the southern Cascades or Sierra area as early as 4,000–4,500 years ago, perhaps at about the time that the California Penutians were penetrating California.

In Table 3-3 some of Wenger's (1973) comparative grammatical data have been reworked to demonstrate the relations among nine Penutian-phylum languages representing six language families and isolates. It is generally agreed that grammatical features change more slowly than phonological features and lexical features of a language. Wenger's painstaking analysis of 52 grammatical features provides us with an idea about how different and similar these several languages were.

Takelma, representing the Kalapuyan family, was most different from all other Penutian languages in this sample, and Coos and Siuslaw (Yakonan) were close pairs. Siuslaw was linked to Miwok, but Miwok fitted more securely into the California Penutian cluster. The representatives of the four California Penutian languages were demonstrably more closely re-

---

*It is a common practice to refer to Hanis and Miluk as Coos. When the author has not been able to ascertain which language has been referred to by Jacobs or other Coosan scholars, Coos is used.

Table 3-3
Penutian phylum grammatical relations

Family or Isolate	Language	Hanis	Siuslaw	Klamath	Maidu	Wintu	Yokuts	Southern Sierra Miwok	Yuki
Kalapuyan	Takelma	37	47	40	45	37	29	44	26
Coosan	Hanis		64	35	52	42	53	44	36
Yakonan	Siuslaw			35	51	52	53	65	46
Klamath-Modoc	Klamath				59	40	55	50	51
California Penutian	Maidu					66	63	48	31
California Penutian	Wintu						75	63	41
California Penutian	Yokuts							71	59
California Penutian	Southern Sierra Miwok								61
Yukian	Yuki								X

Source: Adapted from Wenger (1973).
Note: These figures represent the percentages of 52 grammatical features shared by each pair of languages. The percentage is an index of the number of shared items divided by the number of the 52 items that could possibly be shared given the aggregate grammatical features possessed by the two languages of each pair. Grammatical items among the 52 that neither language possessed were not used in the division, $\frac{a}{(a + b + c)}$, where a = common presences for 1 and 2, b = present in 1 but not in 2, c = present in 2 but not in 1.

lated than any other set and must represent more recent divergences than for most of the other languages. Klamath grammatical features suggest old ties to the California Penutians, as do the Yukian features.

Hokan Phylum

Although their distribution was broken by Athapaskan and Penutian languages, Hokan languages were distributed in an ovallike pattern around the periphery of California. In California, the Hokan phylum comprises seven families and four isolates. Two other families and two isolates were located in west Mexico, northeastern Mexico, southern Mexico, and elsewhere in central America. By far the greatest number of Hokan languages occurred in California, however; it is the probable homeland of Hokan. The Hokan phylum, if it is indeed a genetic unit, evidently is very old, because (1) so many language isolates were located nearly side by side in California, and (2) so many Hokan-speaking people occupied prime coastal and northern forest areas surrounding the Penutians located throughout the hot yet rich Central Valley and the adjacent foothills.

Table 3–4 adapts Wenger's (1973) figures for grammatical similarity among six Hokan languages representing two language families and four isolates in Northern California.

The greatest variation among the Hokan languages in California occurred in the north and it is likely, because of this variation, that early Hokan speakers moved into California down the Klamath-Trinity drainage or the Sacramento drainage and adapted to the forests and coastal valleys.

Although no one has reconstructed a proto-Hokan phonology or morphology, the grammatical similarities suggest that the Karok isolate and Achomawi language possessed deep resemblances, and that the Pomon family, the Yanan family, the Chimariko isolate, and the Washo isolate possessed deep resemblances. If Pomo, Yana, Chimariko, and Washo were congeners, the fissions and migrations must have occurred at a very early point in the history of the phylum, perhaps prior to the period in which the California Penutians spread throughout the Central Valley and eastern foothills of California. The extinction of some Hokan-speaking groups related to any or all of these languages may have been caused by Penutians, beginning as early as 4,500 years ago.

The **Pomon** language family inhabited a small and nearly continuous area in northern California bordered on the north by the Yuki, on the east by the Wintu, on the southwest by the Wappo, and on the

Table 3-4
Hokan phylum grammatical relations

Family or Isolate	Language	Chimariko	Yana	Pomo	Karok	Achomawi
Isolate	Washo	77	52	54	46	37
Isolate	Chimariko		60	49	41	41
Yanan	Yana			54	50	46
Pomon	Pomo				33	25
Isolate	Karok					60
Palaihnihan	Achomawi					X

Source: Adapted from Wenger (1973).
Note: The values were computed in the same manner as those in Table 3–3.

south by the Miwok. Surrounded as they were by several groups speaking remotely related Penutian-phylym languages, the Pomons themselves had separated into seven separate languages and several dialects. Without any question, this diversity developed over a long period of time, just as the probable divergence from some branch of Hokan took a long time.

Proto-Pomo phonology has been reconstructed (Webb, 1972), and Oswalt (1964) and Webb (1972) have calculated Pomo vocabulary relations among the seven Pomo languages, arriving at similar results with different word lists.

Table 3-5 suggests that *Northeastern Pomo* speakers split off first, perhaps being severed from contacts with their *Eastern Pomo* kinsmen by the Yuki. The Eastern Pomo and *Southeastern Pomo* fissioned next, followed by the *Northern Pomo*, who spread across a relatively wide expanse of territory all the way to the ocean. The *Southern, Central,* and *Southwestern Pomo* apparently grew from the Northern Pomo. Although they spoke mutually unintelligible languages, the Northern, Central, Southern, and Southwestern Pomo were significantly more similar than were the three eastern groups. It is evident that the Clear Lake area and the Russian River were the Pomo homelands.

The **Palaihnihan** language family, composed of two languages and several dialects spread over a continuous area in northeastern California, was very diverse. *Achomawi* and *Atsugewi* shared only about 44 percent basic vocabulary cognates on Swadesh's 200-item list,

Table 3-5
Pomo lexicostatistical relations: basic vocabulary

Language	Southern	Central	Northern	Eastern	Southeastern	Northeastern
Southwestern	76	76	64	53	52	50
Southern		76	66	56	57	53
Central			68	59	56	53
Northern				51	48	56
Eastern					57	49
Southeastern						46
Northeastern						X

Source: Oswalt (1964).
Note: Data are based on Swadesh's 100-item list.

Table 3-6
Yuman lexicostatistical relations: random vocabulary

Language	Dialect	Havasupai	Yavapai	Mohave	Maricopa	Cocopa	Diegueno
Pai	Walapai	95	91	63	57	54	50
	Havasupai		92	63	58	56	51
	Yavapai			62	57	54	51
River	Mohave				85	65	52
	Maricopa					76	52
Delta	Cocopa						61
California	Diegueno						X

Source: Winter (1957).
Note: Data are based on a *random* vocabulary list of 100 items. Kaliwa is missing. Campo has been deleted from Winters (1957) list because it is not clear whether Campo was spoken by the Kamia, the Tipai, or some other group.

according to Baumhoff and Olmsted (1964). The differences between Achomawi and Atsugewi were considerable, and the grammatical connection to Karok was very remote.

West of Palaihnihan, the **Shastan** family was composed of one language and many dialects, as was **Yanan,** to the south of Palaihnihan. There may have been several Yanan languages, but the Yana speakers had been hunted to extinction by whites by the time that the last living Yana Indian was discovered.

Chimariko and *Karok* in northwestern California, *Esselen* on the central California Coast south of the Costanoans, and *Washo* in eastern California were other Hokan language isolates. South of Monterey Bay, the little-known **Salinan** and **Chumashan** languages were spoken. Each of these language families had several dialects, and the Chumashans were organized into the largest villages and perhaps the most complex social and political units in California. Yet we know very little about them. It is plausible that there were several Salinan and Chumashan languages.

From the Chumash southward, Uto-Aztecan speakers filled the Los Angeles basin to what is today central San Diego County, and from the coast, Uto-Aztecan speakers spread inland throughout the Great Basin. South of the Uto-Aztecans, from the ocean to the Colorado River and on into Arizona, speakers of the **Yuman** language family resided.

Precursors of Yumans, or some other Hokan-speaking group, probably occupied the Los Angeles

basin and littoral before the Uto-Aztecans spread into these areas. The homeland for the Yumans was Southern California, where their primary adaptations were probably to the chaparral and woodlands of the low-lying coastal range and the higher mountains to the east.

The mesquite and screwbean groves and the extensive stands of mescal and cactus in southeastern California and also along the Colorado River may have drawn one group of Yumans to the Colorado River from southwestern California, while another group remained in Southern California. By the time of European contact there were five languages and many dialects of Yuman. *River Yuman* was spoken along the part of the Colorado River between the present-day cities of Needles and Yuma by the Mohave, Yuma, and Maricopa (who were later pushed on to the Gila River). *Upland Yuman,* or *Pai,* was spoken on the plateaus and the canyons of western Arizona by the Walapai, Havasupai, and Yavapai, and in Baja California by Akwa'ala (or Pai Pai). The Akwa'ala probably crossed the Colorado River and passed across the territories of several non-Pai speakers to locate in the northern Baja. *California Yuman* was spoken by the Diegueño in Southern California. *Delta Yuman* was spoken by the Cocomaricopa and the Cocopa on the Colorado River delta. *Kaliwa,* whose speakers located near the Akwa'ala, was a distinct language, and Kaliwa speakers probably were the first group to split from proto-Yuman.

The percentage relationships in Table 3-6 are not

computed strictly from either Swadesh's 100- or 200-word list. The cognates include items from those lists, but they were drawn at random from the larger vocabularies. Nevertheless, we gain an impression of the relations among some of the dialects and languages. The Pai dialects, River dialects, Delta language, and California language are represented. Kaliwa cognation was not available.

Aztec-Tanoan Phylum

The Aztec-Tanoan phylum, which is problematic, but less so than the Hokan and Penutian phyla, is thought to have embraced the languages of the **Uto-Aztecan** family and of the **Kiowa-Tanoan** family. At the time of contact with Europeans, Uto-Aztecan speakers controlled western Mexico north to the Gila and Salt Rivers of southern Arizona, the Valley of Mexico, and a vast swath of territory from the Southern California coast throughout the Great Basin and east through the Rocky Mountains. The *Hopi*, a Uto-Aztecan outlier, resided on the southern edge of Black Mesa in northeastern Arizona.

The Kiowa-Tanoan family was located along the Rio Grande in northern New Mexico, and in a few spots east of the river. One outlier, *Kiowa*, resided further east still on the southern Plains.

Uto-Aztecan, as reconstructed by Voegelin, Voegelin, and Hale (1962), was composed of three branches: *Aztec, Sonoran*, and *Shoshonean*. The Sonoran languages, spread over 700 miles from the Pima settlements on the Salt and Gila Rivers near the Colorado River in the north to Cora settlements in the Mexican state of Nayarit on the West Coast, was the most deeply differentiated of all Uto-Aztecan branches. The distribution of these languages spread from a center in what is now the state of Sonora in northwestern Mexico. It is probable that this area was the homeland of the Uto-Aztecans. Furthermore, if the phylum is a genetic unit, northwestern Mexico might also be the place where proto-Kiowa-Tanoan split from proto-Uto-Aztecan, perhaps 5,000 years ago. The division between Uto-Aztecan and Kiowa-Tanoan does not seem to be nearly so deep as many of the cleavages in Oregon-California Penutian or of only the intra-California cleavages in Hokan. Davis (1959) made "cursory comparisons," using Swadesh's 100-item basic vocabulary, between *Tarahumara* (a Sonoran branch language) and *Southern Paiute* (a dialect of Ute, a Shoshonean branch language) and five known Kiowa-Tanoan languages. The average cognate similarity between Southern Paiute and the five Kiowa-Tanoan languages, and between Tarahumara and the five Kiowa-Tanoan languages, was about 20

percent. Kiowa had the least relation to the Uto-Aztecan languages. One would expect the range of percentages of cognates shared between Kiowa-Tanoan languages and other languages from the Sonoran and Shoshonean branches to be about the same as the range with Tarahumara and Southern Paiute, though areal affects might well inflate Hopi-Tanoan percentages. If the phylum is genetic and it originally divided into a Kiowa-Tanoan branch and a Uto-Aztecan branch, then all three branches of Uto-Aztecan (given expected sampling error) should share the same range of similarity percentages with Kiowa-Tanoan. Davis's preliminary results suggest that such may have been the case for Aztec-Tanoan.

At an early date, perhaps as much as 4,000 years ago, the proto-Shoshoneans separated from the parent Uto-Aztecan group and moved northwest. Eventually, surely by 3,500 and 3,000 years ago, they crossed the Colorado River while moving toward the Laguna Mountains of Southern California. It is possible that Hokan speakers were already ensconced there and that the proto-Shoshoneans moved farther north and east to the Santa Rosa and San Bernardino Mountains. In all likelihood it was here, near the San Bernardino, San Jacinto, and Santa Rosa Mountains in southeastern California that the Shoshonean branch began to expand and fission perhaps 3,000 years ago.

Table 3-7 provides a selection of Shoshonean, Sonoran, and Aztec branch languages. Evidently the *Hopi* broke from their Shoshonean congeners and began moving eastward sometime between 2,500 and 3,000 years ago at about the same time that the precursors of the *Pima* and Papago were separating from their closest Sonoran kin and moving northward into southern Arizona. The Shoshoneans of Southern California (the *Serraño, Luiseño, Cupeño, Cahuilla*, and *Gabrieliño*) spread throughout the mountains and eventually across the littoral by perhaps 1,500 years ago. The *Tubatulabal* had moved north into the Kern River Valley even earlier. Some Plateau Shoshoneans, from a position most probably on the east slopes of the southern Sierra Nevada, moved across the Sierra to the west (the *Mono*, and *Kawaiisu*). Eventually, and very recently, perhaps only 1,500 to 2,000 years ago, the Plateau Shoshoneans who had remained east of the Sierra divided into *Shoshone, Paviotso* or *Northern Paiute*, and *Ute* languages as they spread across the Great Basin, into the Snake River Valley and the Rocky Mountains. The Great Basin was the area most recently occupied by Uto-Aztecans. The modest language and dialect differentiation within the Plateau Shoshonean group, the immense territory over which they were distributed, and the considerable amount of resemblances to

Table 3-7
Uto-Aztecan lexicostatistical relations: basic vocabulary

Language	Dialect	Southern Paiute	Ute	Shoshone	Comanche	Tubatulabal	Cahuilla	Hopi	Papago	Pima	Tepecano	Mayo	Tarahumara	Cora	Pochutla	Mecayapan	Zacopoxtla
Paviotso or Northern Paiute	Paviotso or Northern Paiute	59	67	65	73	40	38	41	38	32	33	37	29	33	30	25	23
	Southern Paiute		83	70	72	45	43	44	37	32	35	37	29	37	30	24	29
Ute	Ute			65	75	45	36	42	36	35	25	40	30	40	30	28	28
Shoshone	Shoshone				88	51	40	44	29	29	29	34	24	35	25	21	22
	Comanche					50	45	47	37	35	35	35	28	36	29	24	24
Tubatulabal	Tubatulabal						51	42	35	33	32	38	35	40	32	32	28
Cahuilla	Cahuilla							42	39	37	35	33	35	33	30	26	34
Hopi	Hopi								32	33	28	36	30	32	32	29	31
Pima	Papago									94	88	40	37	36	31	32	31
	Pima										81	42	38	34	26	33	29
	Tepecano											42	42	36	36	35	35
Mayo	Mayo												40	42	42	31	34
Tarahumara	Tarahumara													32	32	25	26
Cora	Cora														31	31	27
Pochutla	Pochutla															69	68
Mecayapan	Mecayapan																71
Zacopoxtla	Zacopoxtla																X

Source: Hale (1958). Recomputed to give percentage.
Note: Data are based on Swadesh's 100-item list.

California cultures attests to the relative recentness of the slow eastward movement of these people.

The Kiowa-Tanoan language family could have emerged from the archaic traditions of eastern Sonora or western Chihuahua in Mexico, and begun moving northeastward as early as 4,500 years ago. It is possible that the proto-Kiowa-Tanoans were part of the archaic tradition of rather sedentary pithouse-dwellers who spread northward along the Sierra Madre Occidental, and it can be speculated that they eventually helped develop the Mogollon Pueblo traditions. The precursors of modern Tanoans may well have moved north along the Rio Grande, though that is also speculation. How far north the precursors of the Tanoans migrated is anyone's guess. *Kiowa*, which least resembled the other Tanoan languages, may have become separated from proto-Tanoan as its speakers moved to the Plains, where they probably became pedestrian bison hunters, yet even some of the Tanoan pueblos of eastern New Mexico, such as Pecos Pueblo, were also on the edge of the Plains, so the Kiowa may well have split off at an early date from Tanoan, and may have adapted to a horticultural life at some time before venturing onto the Plains.

The other Tanoan languages—the *Tewa, Tiwa, Towa,* and *Piro*—were spoken in the Rio Grande Valley Pueblos. Tewa was spoken in several villages north of Santa Fe, New Mexico (and at one Hopi village in the historic period). Tiwa was spoken at what are now the towns of Taos and Picuris, close to the New Mexico–Colorado border, and at several villages (Sandia, Isleta, Tutahaco) near what is now Albuquerque. Towa was spoken at Jemez Pueblo, to the west of the Rio Grande Valley in New Mexico, and at Pecos Pueblo on the Pecos River in eastern New Mexico overlooking the Plains to the east. The Jemez people apparently migrated westward from a point on the Plains and became thoroughly influenced by Keresan speakers. Several Piro-speaking villages occupied a 100-mile strip along the Rio Grande south of Albuquerque. Linguistically, Piro was more similar to Tiwa than to other Tanoan languages, but apparently it was a distinct language about which we know very little (Davis 1959).

Table 3-8 shows lexicostatistical relations between Kiowa-Tanoan languages.

The considerable divergences among the Tanoan languages along a 200-mile strip of the Rio Grande Valley makes it plausible that their differentiation took place principally in the areas occupied by Tanoans at the time of contact with Europeans and in areas to the north and east of these. The archeology along the Rio Grande is inadequate to shed light on this because so little has been done there, but it may have been that the first Tanoans, at the edges of this

Table 3-8
Kiowa-Tanoan lexicostatistical relations: basic vocabulary

Language	Dialect	Taos	Tewa	Jemez	Kiowa
Tiwa	Isleta	83	57	48	23
	Taos		57	46	27
Tewa	Tewa			47	29
Towa	Jemez				26
Kiowa	Kiowa				X

Source: Davis (1959).
Note: Data are based on Swadesh's 100-item list.

region, were compressed southward and westward. Groups that spoke Tiwa and Piro formed a broken semicircle from north to south on the east. The Tewa may have been long-term residents in the center; the Towa may have contracted from the east; and the Jemez people may have moved across the territories of several established villages and located west of the Rio Grande. The Towa villages shared only 47 percent cognates with the other Tanoans, suggesting that they separated and settled into privately owned farming areas, perhaps on the east slope of the Rockies, overlooking the Plains, several centuries before speakers of Tiwa, Tewa and Piro separated. The most recent language division seems to have been the separation of Taos from Isleta. More than likely, Taos speakers moved north beyond the Towa- and Tewa-speaking villages within the past several hundred years.

Diversity similar to that registered among the Tanoan languages was commonplace wherever resource bases and subsistence technologies allowed people to settle for long periods, regardless of the proximity of neighbors. In fact, the proximity of neighbors can be said to have promoted long-term settlement and linguistic diversity, for private property concepts entailed the notion of protection of property: neither private property nor its protection was, initially, a stimulus to unrestricted movement and intercourse. Farmers were much of the time tied to their lands, and in the arid Southwest, travel was not easily undertaken. Even much of the trading was done through a few intermediaries in many of the farming villages. Whereas there is considerable evidence for trade objects moving between Mexico and the Pueblos, and the California coast and the Pueblos, trade contacts were probably conducted by a few traders, on foot, between villages. Evidence that Pueblo farmers mounted offensive raids, first-strike in nature, is not known.

Na-Dene Phylum

Two Northwest Coast languages, *Haida* and *Tlingit*, have often been classified as being co-members of a remotely related genetic group, Na-Dene. The Athapaskan language family and Eyak have often also been included in this group. There is no lexical evidence to link Haida to Tlingit on genetic grounds, and no lexical data to link either Haida or Tlingit to Athapaskan or Eyak on genetic grounds (Krauss 1972). The morphological structures of Haida and Tlingit showed some similarities, as did their classifier affixes (Krauss 1972); this similarity probably came about after long periods of isolation, through protracted contacts by which both the Tlingit and the Haida accommodated each other in order to expand their seafaring lives along the north Pacific coast. Levine (1976) has recently suggested that the evidence for a Haida-Tlingit connection rested on erroneous morphological classifications made by Swanton at the turn of the century. It is likely that the genetic relationship of the Haida and Tlingit languages was extremely remote, if the two did in fact stem from a common source, and that certain grammatical similarities found in the two languages during the nineteenth and twentieth centuries were products of subsequent diffusion. Speakers of Haida and Tlingit inhabited parts of the northern Northwest Coast before the Tsimshian expanded and began dislocating both Haida and Tlingit.

Eyak-Athapaskan Language Family

The **Eyak-Athapaskan** language family. (Krauss 1972) was the youngest and most widely distributed genetic group in all of western North America. South of Alaska, the distribution of Athapaskan dialects and languages suggests extensive migrations as well as shorter "leapfrogging" moves around and between groups that were already established. The family's full range was from northwestern Alaska to southern Canada, along the northern California and southern Oregon coasts, in two patches near the mouth of the Columbia River, and from the Four Corners area of Utah, Colorado, New Mexico, and Arizona, south almost to the Texas gulf coast.

Across this vast but noncontinuous expanse of western North America there were but eight Athapaskan languages, and five of these were spoken in Alaska. The homeland for the Eyak-Athapaskan family was in western Alaska. *Eyak*, spoken on the Alaskan coast northwest of where the Tlingit people were located, shared 32 percent cognates with its nearest Athapaskan neighbor in the interior, *Atna*, and 32 percent with the Navajo in the Southwest. Eyak undoubtedly split from proto-Athapaskan at least 2,500 years ago. Its sister language probably stayed intact for at least another 500 years. The Athapaskan family, exclusive of Eyak, which has only recently been proved to be a distant member, was reconstructed through the historical genetic method by Hoijer (1963).

The three Athapaskan languages represented in our study are *Canadian*, *Pacific*, and *Apachean*.* It is likely that the parents of these three languages moved southeast from Alaska, filling the subarctic region in western Canada about 1,500 to 1,000 years ago. The Canadian speakers established themselves in the northern fringe of the Fraser Plateau (Carrier and Chilcotin) probably by 500 years ago.

The earliest Pacific Athapaskans, including the parent group or groups of all the Athapaskan dialects of California and Oregon, such as Hupa, Mattole, Kato, Nongatl, Galice Creek, and Tolowa, had moved into the California–Oregon region, probably by following the interior valleys and their major rivers, by 600 to 800 years ago. They were surely the last language groups to penetrate the Northwest Coast and were sandwiched in among speakers of Penutian, Hokan, and Algonkian who were already there. Speakers of other Pacific Athapaskan dialects (presumably) were located in the Willapa Hills of southwestern Washington near Puget Sound, and near the mouth of the Columbia River of northwestern Oregon (Clatskanie). Not enough is known about these groups to speculate on their language histories, but like other Pacific Athapaskans, with the exceptions of Hupa, Tolowa, and Tututni, their cultures suggested recent and incomplete integration into the coastal life in which their non-Athapaskan neighbors were engaged (Elmendorf 1976).

The Apachean Athapaskans must have arrived in the Southwest no more than 500–700 years ago. They moved into the area at a time when Pueblo farming communities had been severely constricted and re-

---

*Dyen and Aberle (1974) separated Mattole from Hupic because it did not share 77 percent cognates with any other member of the dialect chain. Yet Mattole shared 76 percent with Hupa and Kato and was reconstructed (Hoijer 1963) into the Hupa, Mattole, Kato et al. chain, so Pacific is here classified as one language that includes Mattole, Kato, Hupa and others.

trenched. The constriction process among Pueblos had been proceeding for 300 years and was probably not completed when the Apacheans arrived. The Apacheans, including the Eastern Apaches, Western Apaches, and Navajos, located in areas entirely surrounding the Pueblos, and retained intelligibility among the dialects. The Kiowa Apache of the Plains were most different from the others in the language set, and Hoijer (1971) suggests that they separated from the other Apacheans in Canada, probably followed them down the eastern flanks of the Rockies, though not in contact with them, and then moved onto the Plains. The Apacheans, occupying an area about fifteen times the size of the Tanoan area, spoke but one language, whereas there were four languages and some deep dialect divisions among Tanoan.

Lexicostatistical relations among the Athapaskan languages are shown in Table 3-9.

The immense spread of Athapaskans in Canada, in the Southwest, and in two patches on the Pacific Coast—one distinct language (with several dialects) was spoken in each of these three areas—makes it clear that the movements into the three regions in western North America were recent. The relative recentness of penetrations is also inferred from the distributions of the dialects within areas. The dialects were spoken by people whose communities were surrounded by many other languages along the Pacific Coast and were spoken by people whose communities surrounded many sedentary farm villages representing several different languages in the Southwest. That Apachean averaged about 70 percent cognate similarity with Canadian and 68 percent similarity with Pacific, and that Pacific averaged about 65 percent similarity with Canadian, certainly suggest the separation of these three languages happened no more than 1,000 years ago. Apparently subarctic Canada was uninhabited before speakers of Athapaskan moved southeast from Alaska to fill it; they brought fully developed boreal-forest and lacustrine adaptations; some jockeying and dislodging may have taken place along the eastern slopes of the Coast Range in the northern Fraser Plateau, where Salishans were already established. Within the Canadian language, the people who spoke Carrier dialects held villages for much of the year, whereas the Chilcotin wandered much more than the Carrier. Not surprisingly, the Carrier dialects showed greater variation than the Chilcotin. The earliest Apachean and Pacific groups, however, probably migrated south across 1,000 miles of territory in which there were many occupants.

The Pacific group may have separated and moved south earlier than the Apachean group; however, the environments chosen by the Pacific Athapaskans were densely populated and rich in resources; in these, large groups could persist in small, impacted territories, and many different languages were spoken. Private claims to resources, and isolation followed by language diffusion among near neighbors, may have stimulated dialect differentiation among Pacific Athapaskans; by contrast, Apaches maintained more widespread Apachean-language contacts and communitarian uses of hunting and gathering areas in the arid Southwest. In support of the hypothesis stated earlier in the chapter, that ownership of concentrated resources leads to dialectal differentiation and language change, the more mobile Eastern Apaches, whose resources were not especially concentrated, showed less dialect variation than the semisedentary, partly horticultural Western Apaches and Navajo.

In his comparative study of 52 grammatical features, Wenger (1973) demonstrates that the Pacific dialects Hupa, Mattole, and Kato were much more similar internally than any one of them was similar to Navajo (see Table 3-10). Although the grammatical divergences took the same direction as the lexical divergences, they did not proceed at the same rate. This is probably a result of the influence of a heavy representation of grammatical features present in California and Oregon Algonkian, Hokan, and Penutian languages in Wenger's sample, and the diffusion of some of those grammatical items into the language of the Pacific Athapaskans from their non-Athapaskan-speaking neighbors. Nevertheless, all the Athapaskan languages shared high percentages of grammatical features when compared with Hokan and Penutian languages (see Tables 3-3 and 3-4), suggesting recent intrusion of Athapaskan peoples, yet marked divergences occurred among the Pacific dialects. The Kato dialect, which was spoken farthest south and adjacent to the Coast Yuki dialect, had diverged the most among the Pacific Athapaskan languages.

Salishan Language Family

The **Salishan** language family occupied a nearly continuous region from about the center of the east side of Vancouver Island to the area south of Puget Sound and eastward from the coast to the Rocky Mountains. In the north were the Bella Coola, separated from the Salish, who occupied an area north of the Columbia River, by Kwakiutl speakers, who probably severed an earlier connection of the Bella Coola and their Salishan congeners. The Tillamook, on the northern Oregon coast, were separated from other Salish by the Chinook. The Chinook may have moved into the region somewhat later than the Tillamook.

Table 3-9
Athapaskan lexicostatistical relations: basic vocabulary

Language	Dialect	Koyukon	Tanana	Atna	Ingalik	Kutchin	Han	Nabesna	Hare	Dogrib	Slave	Chipewyan	Beaver	Carrier	Sarsi	Hupa	Mattole	Kato	Galice	Navajo
Tanaina	Tanaina	56	58	63	59	57	60	61	55	52	56	59	46	61	56	48	45	47	54	55
Tanana	Koyukon	X	79	69	75	76	75	69	63	65	65	72	71	70	66	59	63	61	62	64
	Tanana		X	72	70	74	73	68	64	66	66	71	68	71	64	57	60	57	59	59
Atna	Atna			X	71	70	72	69	65	66	67	69	68	68	62	57	58	57	62	67
Ingalik	Ingalik				X	69	73	68	64	67	68	71	67	69	64	58	57	55	61	64
	Kutchin					X	84	81	74	74	73	79	75	77	69	64	69	68	69	71
	Han						X	82	74	74	74	79	76	77	61	61	64	64	67	70
	Nabesna							X	74	71	70	73	71	73	66	59	63	63	66	67
	Hare								X	86	85	83	78	76	72	65	63	68	73	71
Canadian	Dogrib									X	88	85	77	75	72	59	59	62	68	68
	Slave										X	81	83	77	70	61	58	63	68	69
	Chipewyan											X	78	83	79	64	65	68	73	76
	Beaver												X	78	75	64	61	66	70	70
	Carrier													X	73	63	62	66	71	73
	Sarsi														X	60	61	63	66	68
Pacific	Hupa															X	76	75	75	65
	Mattole																X	76	71	65
	Kato																	X	78	69
	Galice																		X	73
Apachean	Navajo																			X

Apachean Language

Dialect	San Carlos	Chiricahua	Mescalero	Jicarilla	Lipan	Kiowa Apache
Navajo	94	95	95	94	92	77
San Carlos	X	96	94	93	90	78
Chiricahua		X	97	95	93	78
Mescalero			X	96	95	78
Jicarilla				X	94	78
Lipan					X	78
Kiowa Apache						X

Pacific Language

Dialect	Hupa	Kato	Mattole	Coquille	Tolowa	Galice
Hupa	X	75	76	76	78	75
Kato		X	76	75	80	78
Mattole			X	72	74	71
Coquille				X	97	92
Tolowa					X	90
Galice						X

Source: Hoijer, in Deyen and Aberle (1974).
Note: Data based on Swadesh's 100-item list.

Table 3-10
Athapaskan grammatical relations

Language	Dialect	Mattole	Kato	Navajo
Pacific	Hupa	94	78	57
	Mattole		90	61
	Kato			62
Apachean	Navajo			X

Source: Adapted from Wenger (1973).
Note: Data are percentages of shared items from the aggregate inventory for each pair of languages, from a 52-item list.

In this nearly continuous geographic expanse encompassing Northwest Coast environments, the Cascade Mountains and the coastal ranges, the Middle Columbia Plateau, the Upper Columbia region of the Rocky Mountains, and the Fraser Plateau, the Salish had differentiated into at least 22 distinct languages and an unknown number of dialect groups within many of the languages (Jorgensen 1969).

The Salishan language has not been reconstructed by the historical genetic method, but Table 3-11 presents the comparative lexicostatistics for the family. The extremely low percentages of cognates shared within the Salish language has long been a puzzle (Elmendorf 1951; Kroeber 1955). But there can be little doubt that Salishan speakers occupied the Northwest Coast and the Plateau for a long time, and that the Fraser River drainage was their homeland. Three Salishan branches on the coast, composed of *Bella Coola* (one language), *Tillamook* (one language), and *Coast* (fourteen languages), demonstrate the great variability within Salish languages on the coast. Five of these languages and several distantly related dialects—*Straits* (two) and *Halkomelem* (two)—were spoken close to the Fraser drainage from the coastal ranges to the coast. East of the coastal and Cascade ranges, the *Interior* branch comprised six languages.

It is plausible that the proto-Salishans moved west down the Fraser River from the Fraser Plateau into the wet forests of the coastal range, adapting to a riverine-dominated subsistence economy. The original entry through the Fraser Pass may have taken place 4,500 years ago. As the Salishans became more proficient in their riverine pursuits—and it could have taken centuries to develop proficiency in the wet forests—Salishan peoples began expanding north and south. They may have filled unoccupied areas as they moved along and began making still further adaptations to maritime-riverine subsistence economies. Small family groups probably stopped at favorable locales, and stayed to claim those territories. The local populations grew and fissioned. Archeologists have yet to determine whether the spread of Salishan groups was made at the expense of other inhabitants.

Perhaps 2,500 years ago, a Salish group that had fully adapted to a riverine economy moved east from the wet coastal forests and into the east slope of the Coast Range; then began the phenomenon of slow growth and migration that eventually filled most of the Fraser Plateau, the Columbia Plateau, and the rugged mountainous area in between. The language diversity within the Interior branch was considerably less than the diversity within the Coast branch, yet the plateau people occupied more than twice as much territory as the coastal people. The reasons for the difference in language variations must be that the plateau people were relatively recent occupants of the interior, that subsistence resources were more diffusely and meagerly distributed, and that wide contacts were maintained and communitarian uses of resources were made by plateau people scattered over large areas: this cannot be said of the Coast Salish. Evidence to support these speculations will be amassed steadily throughout this book.

Wakashan Language Family

North of the Salishans, and south of Tsimshian on the coast and islands of British Columbia, and from Cape Flattery on the northern tip of the Olympic Peninsula northward through the eastern and northern parts of Vancouver Island, the Wakashan speakers controlled the ocean-side (as opposed to the Georgia Straits) territories of the central Northwest Coast.

Wakashan, like Salishan, has not been reconstructed by the historical genetic method. Swadesh (1953) recognized two branches of Wakashan, Kwakiutlan, and Nootkan. In comparing a representative of each branch on his 200-item basic vocabulary, Swadesh determined 30 percent similarity. The differences between the branches represented a deep cleavage that probably took place close to the Rivers Inlet region of the coast south of the Bella Coola River. Nootkan speakers may have moved to Vancouver Island and south to the Olympic Peninsula 2,500–3,500 years ago. The Kwakiutl may have expanded from the mainland to northern Vancouver Island during the maritime period of the past 2,500 years.

Nootkan comprised three languages: *Makah*, on the north tip of the Olympic Peninsula; *Nitinat*, along the southwestern part of Vancouver Island; and *Nootka*, along the central western portion of Vancouver Island (Haas 1969; Jacobsen 1969; Thompson 1970).

Table 3-11
Salishan lexicostatistical relations: basic vocabulary

Language	Dialect	Lower Chehalis	Satsop	Chehalis	Cowlitz	Twana	Nisqually	Snohomish	Skagit	Klallam	Lummi	Songish	Nootsack	Fraser	Nanaimo	Squamish	Pentlatch	Seshelt	Comox	Tillamook	Lillooet	Thompson	Shuswap	Columbia	Okanagon	Kalispel	Pend d'Oreille	Spokane	Coeur d'Alene	Bella Coola
	Quinault	57	43	41	36	22	23	23	24	22	22	21	22	20	20	14	15	16	18	16	17	18	17	16	17	15	14	13	17	12
	Lower Chehalis		51	50	43	27	21	20	20	18	20	19	19	19	17	16	14	17	17	15	18	17	17	17	17	14	14	15	17	13
Chehalis	Satsop			83	59	36	31	28	28	19	20	18	24	23	19	17	20	23	23	14	21	18	18	19	17	15	17	17	19	14
	Chehalis				66	39	32	31	32	22	21	19	25	23	21	17	20	20	25	17	19	19	18	18	17	16	17	15	16	12
	Cowlitz					38	30	28	27	20	21	18	19	21	19	15	18	19	25	16	19	21	19	20	18	17	18	18	18	15
	Twana						41	33	32	24	27	24	30	31	25	25	19	17	22	21	23	21	20	19	22	20	20	19	17	15
Puget Sound	Nisqually							75	71	31	39	34	43	36	33	32	26	25	24	19	24	24	21	20	21	21	21	23	19	15
	Snohomish								88	34	37	35	43	34	30	29	23	29	22	20	21	23	19	19	21	20	21	21	17	16
	Skagit									35	41	36	44	33	31	30	21	25	22	18	21	21	19	16	19	20	20	19	15	12
	Klallam										65	63	40	36	40	31	27	28	27	17	20	17	16	16	19	16	15	16	15	19
Straits	Lummi											73	47	45	47	35	30	34	28	16	21	20	19	18	16	16	15	16	17	17
	Songish												46	53	54	38	34	33	30	16	20	20	19	16	20	17	18	17	16	23
	Nootsack													58	56	48	35	31	31	20	26	20	19	18	20	17	18	18	18	16
Halkomelen	Fraser														73	50	42	34	35	23	28	23	19	17	20	18	16	16	19	23
	Nanaimo															59	38	34	27	20	25	22	17	16	18	15	14	14	17	22
	Squamish																33	31	27	20	22	18	15	14	13	13	12	12	14	18
	Pentlatch																	51	45	15	20	19	16	10	15	10	11	11	10	23
	Seshelt																		55	16	22	24	20	15	20	17	17	17	17	20
	Comox																			15	20	19	17	13	18	15	15	15	15	20
	Tillamook																				19	22	18	18	22	17	18	18	16	14
	Lillooet																					57	48	25	33	27	25	27	23	19
Thompson	Thompson																						75	34	47	37	38	36	34	17
	Shuswap																							34	50	40	39	39	32	14
	Columbia																								54	52	52	51	50	12
	Okanagon																									65	66	64	44	16
Kalispel	Kalispel																										93	85	55	11
	Pend d'Oreille																											86	55	11
	Spokane																												54	11
	Coeur d'Alene																													12
	Bella Coola																													X

Source: Swadesh (1950), reordered by Jorgensen (1969).
Note: Data based on Swadesh's 200-item list: 70 percent is arbitrary division between dialect and language.

Kwakiutlan also comprised three languages: *Kwakiutl,* on the northern portion of Vancouver Island and the adjacent mainland; *Bella Bella–Haihais,* near the mouth of the Bella Coola River in the Center of Kwakiutlan territory; and *Haisla,* near the Gardner Canal in northern Kwakiutlan territory.

On the basis of language features alone it is plausible that the Wakashan may have entered the Northwest Coast to the north of and somewhat later than the Salish migration down the Fraser. It may be that the proto-Wakashan moved south before splintering. They engulfed the Bella Coola Salish except on the east side, and it is likely that either they dislocated some Salish or inhibited the Salish from moving north beyond Bute Inlet.

Chimakuan Language Family

Adding to the complexity of languages spoken on the Northwest Coast was **Chimakuan,** whose two languages were *Chimakum,* spoken on the Puget Sound (eastern) side of the Olympic Peninsula, and *Quileute,* spoken on the ocean (western) side of the Olympic Peninsula. This isolated family was hemmed in by Makah and several Salish languages. Whenever it was that the proto-Chimakuan moved on to the Olympic Peninsula, it must have been more than 2,000 years ago. Swadesh (1955) used the historical genetic method to make a preliminary reconstruction, and he also compared the Chimakuan languages on his 100-item basic vocabulary. Quileute and Chimakum were 40 percent similar (Swadesh 1955), though separated by only about 50 miles of Klallam Salish territory. As elsewhere on the Northwest Coast, it is likely that contacts were minimal after separation into different private resource territories, and the contacts were further restricted by the Salish, who may have moved in between them.

Whether Chimakuan speakers entered the Olympic Peninsula shortly before Salishans moved in from the east and south and before the Makah entered from the north is not known, but it seems plausible that Chimakuans penetrated the region early and were engulfed. Perhaps some of their congeners were displaced.

Kutenai Language Isolate

Kutenai, composed of Upper Kutenai and Lower Kutenai dialects, has not been linked to any language family or phylum, though Sapir once suggested that it was a member of a macrophylum that included Wakashan, Algonkian, and Salishan. If Kutenai was related to any of these families, the relationship was so remote as to be undetected by others who have examined the language. Kutenai was spoken in the Kootenai (or Kootenay) River drainage and Kootenay Lake area of northern Idaho, northwestern Montana, and southeastern British Columbia.

Linguistically the Kutenai are an enigma. The dialectal differentiation appears to be recent in origin and the outcome of a migration from the Upper Kootenay River region (British Columbia) into the Lower Kootenai area of Montana and Idaho (Turney-High 1941). Archeologists have yet to provide clues on when the Kutenai arrived in the Upper Kootenay region.

Keres Language Family

Seven dialects of the *Keresan* language were spoken at seven Pueblos near the Rio Grande in central New Mexico. Near the San Jose River tributary of the Rio Grande, were the two mesa villages of Acoma and Laguna. These two dialects were closely related and more different from the other five dialects than any of the latter dialects were from one another (see Table 3-12). Acoma and Laguna have been classified as Western Pueblo cultures, while the other five dialects have been regarded as a bridge between Western and Eastern Pueblo cultures, more or less as a class of their own.

It is clear that Sia, Santa Ana, San Felipe, Santo Domingo, and Cochiti formed a relatively tight cluster of dialects. All seven dialects formed a chain that corresponded rather well to their geographic positions from south to north, with Acoma at one end and Cochiti at the other. The largest geographic break and the largest percentage of difference between adjacent dialects occurred between Laguna and Santa Ana (seven percent). The greatest differences between any pair of dialects was between Acoma on the south and Cochiti on the north, but Miller (1963), who reconstructed Keresan through the historical genetic method, reports that Acoma and Cochiti were mutually intelligible to speakers willing to accustom themselves to the other dialect. Thus, Acoma and Cochiti might be called "language-like" dialects, following Elmendorf's distinction between Yuki and Coast Yuki or Jorgensen's distinction between Ute and Southern Paiute.

It is likely that the proto-Keresans were longtime residents of the Pueblo Southwest and that their diversification throughout several villages was rela-

Table 3-12
Keresan lexicostatistical relations: basic vocabulary

Dialect	Laguna	Santa Ana	Sia	San Felipe	Santo Domingo	Cochiti
Acoma	98	89	89	86	86	84
Laguna		91	91	88	88	86
Santa Ana			99	96	96	92
Sia				97	96	93
San Felipe					98	95
Santo Domingo						94
Cochiti						X

Source: Davis (1959).
Note: Data are based on Swadesh's 100-item list.

tively recent, in perhaps the past 800 years. The homeland for proto-Keresans was probably on the western tributaries of the Rio Grande, where the Keresans were located when first contacted by Europeans. If precursors of the proto-Keresans were located in some other places in the Southwest, the inferences must be based on grounds other than dialect distribution. Archeological searches for a homeland prior to the Keresan villages of the time of contact have been contradictory.*

Algonkian Language Family

In the northwest region of California the *Wiyot* and *Yurok* languages of the **Algonkian** language family were spoken. The two languages were very different, so much so that the relations between them seem to have been remote, although they were spoken side by side on the California coast. Teeter (1964) and Hamp (1970) have demonstrated through phonologi-

cal correspondences* that Wiyot and Yurok stemmed from a common protolanguage, and that it was surely Algonkian. Ritwan has been proposed as the mesolanguage for Yurok-Wiyot, but that hypothetical language is disputed. Wenger's (1973) analysis of Wiyot and Yurok grammar demonstrates that of the aggregate of the 52 items present in Wiyot and Yurok, 87 percent were shared. Although Yurok and Wiyot phonologies and lexicon were considerably different, their grammars were still very similar.

Yurok and Wiyot have been puzzling because of the geographical distance between the groups who spoke these languages and their nearest Algonkian neighbors. At the time of European contact the Algonkian neighbors closest to the coastal groups were the Gros Ventre and Blackfeet of the high Plains, 800 to 1,000 miles to the northeast, beyond several major mountain chains.

Given the considerable divergence between Yurok and Wiyot it is reasonable to infer 1,500 years of separation into their coastal and riverine niches. Elsasser and Heizer (1966) have suggested resemblances between technological items from Fremont-Promontory culture deposits in northern Utah and Yurok-Wiyot villages in northwestern California. Fremont culture spanned a 900-year period from about 400 AD to 1,300 AD near Great Salt Lake. If the Yurok-Wiyot speakers moved west from the Great Salt Lake region, they must have done so before Fremont-Promontory settlements were established, perhaps splitting from a precursor of Fremont. Otherwise it is difficult to account for the considerable diversity between Yurok and Wiyot. A date of perhaps 1 AD may be presumed in order to account for something even more interesting, namely: the grammatical relations among Yurok, Hanis, and Takelma. Wenger (1973) has demonstrated that Yurok-Wiyot shared grammatical features with Hanis (Coosan family: Penutian phylum), spoken on the Oregon coast, and Takelma (Kalapuyan: Penutian), spoken on the Upper Rogue River. It is likely that the grammatical features diffused during a long period of protracted contact when Penutians, perhaps Coosans and Kalapuyans, and Algonkians all resided next to one another. The Athapaskans, much more recent migrants (600 to 800 years ago) to northwestern California and southwestern Oregon, formed a semicircle around the Algonkian speakers and separated them from Penutians. Of interest in this regard is the diffusion of phonological features between Oregon Penutians and Athapaskans

---

*See Ford, Schroeder, and Peckham (1972) for a set of opinions from archeologists that bring the Keresans from Chaco Canyon, New Mexico; Mesa Verde, Colorado; and the Puerco River, New Mexico.

---

*The historical genetic method was used in these analyses.

(Wenger, 1973), and among Algonkian speakers, Karok (Isolate: Hokan phylum) speakers, and Hupa (Athapaskan) speakers. Phonological features seem to have spread more rapidly than grammatical features, and the differences between the sharing of grammatical and phonological features appear to provide good clues to linguistic prehistory.

Language Differentiation and Property Concepts

The most profuse differentiation and the deepest cleavages among languages, whether of the same family or the same phyla, and the greatest number of different languages in the same geographic area were found along the coastal strip of western North America, in California, and in the Southwest. Each of these areas seems to have been occupied for long periods by successive generations of internally related groups of people, specifically, Penutians, Hokans, Wakashans, Salishans, and so forth. Yet the language diversity within families and phyla was not a simple phenomenon of time. Archeological evidence suggests that people occupied and moved through the interior plateaus and basins over a ten-thousand-year period, but there is no evidence to show if the earliest people to pass through these regions put down their roots or if their descendents were the generations found there by the first Europeans (Davis 1966; Fowler 1972). On the other hand, it seems quite evident that when groups moved to the coastal or southwestern regions during the past 5,000 years they put down their roots and stayed, and the populations found by the first Europeans were the progeny of many settlers who moved in from 5,000 to 2,000 years ago. A comparable situation was probably nonexistent in the interior basins and plateaus until 2,000 to 1,500 years ago; then people seem to have edged back toward the Rocky Mountains from positions near the Sierra, the Cascade Range, and the coastal ranges. Evidence will be adduced in the subsequent chapters to support these and other points, but some generalizations should be provided here to help us understand language and culture relations.

Along coastal western North America and in California, early inhabitants were able to develop subsistence economies that supported large groups for long periods in restricted locales. Everywhere in these areas we find the development of family, lineage (demonstrated unilineal descent group), sib (stipulated unilineal descent group), deme (demonstrated bilateral descent group), or village property ownership; protection of resource areas; and considerable language variation. Even when groups appear to have inhabited the coastal or California regions a relatively short time, such as the Algonkians, or an even shorter time, such as the Pacific Athapaskans, dialect differentiation appears to have proceeded rapidly. Indeed, where strategic resources were concentrated in a small area and were also abundant, private ownership and language differentiation went hand in hand.

In the Southwest, where early occupants became involved in the development of farming traditions, language differentiation within families over the past 3,000 years has been correlated with kinship and village ownership of strategic farming land. If language variation is viewed as distributions of different language communities over the landscape one can see that an even more complex patchwork pattern evolved during the past 1,000 years, as farming cultures contracted and retrenched.

In the Plateau and Great Basin, during the past 1,000 or 2,000 years, language diversification did not proceed at so rapid a pace as it did in the Southwest, and this was true for the Apachean and Pai speakers in the Southwest as well. Where strategic resource areas were diffuse and not especially abundant, their joint use was allowed, or access was provided to hunting and gathering territories by the recognized owners. This commingling must have inhibited dialectal variation and reinforced dialect chains for longer periods in these regions than was so along the coast, in California, or in the Southwest. Even among the Apacheans of the Southwest it was the Eastern Apaches, spread across wide territories, whose dialects diverged less than those of the more sedentary, partly horticultural Navajos and Western Apaches. And for the Canadian Athapaskans of the Fraser Plateau, the Carrier dialects, spoken by relatively sedentary people, diverged more than the Chilcotin dialects, whose speakers were mobile.

Archeologists may some day sort out the different rates of divergence by comparing probable occupation time-spans for the earliest Southern California Uto-Aztecans with Basin-and-Plateau Uto-Aztecans; Apachean Athapaskans with Pacific Athapaskans; and Coast Salish with Plateau Salish.

As a concluding hypothesis, let us say that differentiation proceeded much more rapidly, perhaps by 20 or 25 percent, among the coastal and California dwellers and among then sedentary village farmers of the Southwest than among the Basin dwellers, Plateau dwellers, or the Apacheans and Pais of the Southwest.

Only one-half of the picture is language differentiation, as has been suggested in a few places in the preceding discussion, but especially in the discussion of Algonkian–Penutian–Pacific Athapaskan relations. Of considerable importance to linguistic prehistory is the analysis of diffusion of language features. Therefore, let us turn our attention to the borrowing of language features.

DIFFUSIONAL LANGUAGE RELATIONS

The study of language diffusion in western North America has concentrated on relatively recent prehistory, perhaps the past 2,000 years for much of the West. Diffusion among Northwest Coast languages and among languages in Northern California must have begun even earlier. It has focused on the borrowing, as a result of contact, of words, phonological features, and grammatical features. The differentiations that proceeded along the coast and in California, we aver, were correlated with the immigration and spread of populations of extractors adapting to localized and bountiful environments; these adaptations led to isolation. But from at least 2,000 years ago, surely earlier in California, on the northern Pacific Coast, and in the sedentary Southwest, development of trade and numerous other mechanisms may well have brought near neighbors into frequent contacts. Intermarriages occurred; ritual organizations were created that integrated members from different language communities; shamans (medicine men and women) performed their skills in adjacent language communities, and so forth. Bilingualism and multilingualism became a characteristic feature of different language groups that had regular contacts, whether these languages were from the same family or different families. The communication ultimately led to diffusion of linguistic features between languages, and in some areas, such as northwestern, central, and southern California, the central and northern Northwest Coast, and the Plateau, linguistic features spilled across dozens of languages, creating the linguistic counterparts to culture areas.

Diffusion was not restricted to genetically unrelated language pairs spoken in areas having extensive common borders, but it is easier to detect diffusion between such pairs than it is between genetically related languages. In general, some linguistic features had a wide distribution in one language family but a narrow distribution in another family, only a few member-languages of the second family possessing the feature; if speakers of the languages in the second family that possessed the feature were known to have been in close contact with speakers of the language

family that exhibited a wide distribution of the traits, the latter are said to be the donors of the feature and the former are said to be the recipients. It is possible, too, for features to pass from a donor family to a recipient in still another family, and for the recipient to pass it on to other language communities within the same family, and for subsequent daughter languages to inherit the features. To further complicate the picture, features from one language family, say Salishan, can diffuse to Sahaptian, be modified within Sahaptian, and diffuse back to Salish. Logically, inferences of borrowing should be made only when features presumed to be borrowed have been proved not to be reconstructable in the protolanguage of the recipient language. Such reconstructions have not been worked out for more than a handful of the unique linguistic items that seem to have diffused in western North America. It is the very uniqueness of many of the items found in adjacent languages from different families and phyla, however, that suggests diffusion as the source of their transmission, rather than inheritance.

In an analysis of Salish, Jorgensen (1969) demonstrated that the fewer the number of mutually unintelligible language communities separating any two Salishan languages, the greater the percentage of basic vocabulary retained by that pair. It is highly plausible that diffusion through human contacts in trade, ceremonials, and intermarriage inflated the relations among near neighbors from the same language family, but it is difficult to ferret out the influences. On the other hand, when mountain barriers or a non-Salishan language separated two Salishan languages, the similarities between that pair of languages dropped significantly. The inference to be drawn is that intra-Salishan diffusion must have influenced intra-Salishan similarities. This point is raised here primarily by way of caution. It is very plausible that language features created in one family and diffused within the same family may inflate the genetic relationships of some members of these families.

In comparing languages from different language families and phyla, as among Algonkian, Penutian, Hokan, and Athapaskan, there is some evidence that lexical and phonological items diffused more readily than grammatical items. Furthermore, grammatical items in particular were subject to analogical change wherein a concept, such as that of possessive third person pronominals, was borrowed by one language, but the third person pronominal was reworked so as to fit the phonological rules of the recipient language.

By introducing topological and multivariate comparisons among many languages, Patrick Wenger (1973) has raised the level of language diffusion studies a notch. Wenger's path-blazing study analyzes phonological and grammatical features among twenty-one languages representing several language families and phyla in California, the Northwest Coast, and the Plateau culture areas. In his analysis Wenger sorted out genetic, diffusional, and analogical relationships among the languages. In one section of his study Wenger focused on the distribution of 52 grammatical traits among genetically unrelated language pairs that shared common geographic borders, and among those that did not. Wenger demonstrated that when common borders were extensive, including, perhaps, a major river drainage, the probability that grammatical features had diffused between the pairs was very high. On the other hand, genetically unrelated language units that shared common borders only slightly or had no common borders also shared fewer grammatical features.

In California, where language differentiation among members of the same family was often extensive, there was also considerable evidence for diffusion of phonological items, lexicon (words), and grammatical features among unrelated languages located close to one another, and there was evidence for loan translations in which grammatical and semantic traits were shared across many language families, but took distinct phonological forms in each language. These loan translations were cases of analogical development where the idea, but not the specific form, was borrowed and reworked.

An example of possible diffusion relations in northwest California and southwest Oregon, reinterpreted from Wenger (1973)*, will make the point. Four very distantly related Penutian phylum languages—Southern Sierra Miwok (California Penutian family), Takelma (Kalapuyan), Siuslaw (Yakonan), and Yuki (Yukian)[†]—all exhibited possessive pronominal suffixes and verbs that took personal pronoun suffixes. In addition, all but Yuki allowed verbs to take subject and object suffixes with the object preceding the subject. Two of these grammatical traits were observed by the Wiyot and Yurok (Algonkian), and two were observed by the Chimariko (Isolate: Hokan), but were not widely observed among other Hokan languages or any other California languages except Penutians. It is plausible that these traits were archaic Penutian grammatical features that were diffused to the Wiyot, Yurok, and Chimariko before the Athapaskans moved in and engulfed the Algonkians, cutting them off from the Penutians, and cutting off the Chimariko from the Algonkians and all Penutians except the Wintu (California Penutian), who shared one of the traits with Chimariko.

Years ago Melville Jacobs (1937, 1954) suggested that some representatives of the Coosan family (Penutian phylum) and California Algonkians may have shared a border prior to the arrival of the Athapaskans. Wenger (1973) demonstrates that Hanis (Coosan family) and Takelma (Kalapuyan) shared several grammatical features with Yurok and Wiyot. Given Wenger's analysis of archaic Penutian traits, the possibility of extended contacts between Algonkian and Penutian groups up and down the Rogue River and points south to the Klamath River for twelve hundred years or more are very good, as well they might have been between Algonkians and Coast Yuki to the south. Chimariko, too, was probably influenced by either the Algonkians, the Penutians, or both.

As for the entry of the Pacific Athapaskans into northwestern California and southwestern Oregon, Wenger (1973: 80–82) demonstrates that Hanis (Coosan) and Takelma, but especially Hanis, shared many phonological features with Pacific Athapaskans, their neighbors to the south. Although Hanis had several similarities with Algonkian on grammatical and phonological features, only phonological relationships stood out in Coosan-Athapaskan relationships. Wenger (1973: 81–82) reasoned that Coosan-Algonkian relationships were older* and Coosan-Athapaskan relationships were younger. The phonological terms in Wenger's analysis were involved in less complex relations with the entire language system than were the grammatical items, so his reasoning that the phonological items would change more readily than the grammatical is supportable.

Although linguists have been interested in "areal effects," or diffusion, among North American Indian languages at least since the Sapir-Boas controversy of the 1920s, about the difficulty and necessity of distin-

---

*Wenger (1973: 266) stressed the genetic relationship only among the Penutians, but the diffusional relationships between Penutians and Algonkian, and between either Penutians or Algonkians and Chimariko are evident.

[†]Classification of Yuki as a Penutian language is tentative. Yuki, too, may have been a recipient of the suffixes in question.

---

*Wenger could have added that Takelma-Algonkian relationships were older and Takelma-Athapaskan relationships were younger.

guishing genetic features from diffusional features of language,* much more attention has been paid to genetic relations. Indeed, the forms of generative and transformational inquiry that dominated American linguistics in the 1950s and 1960s sought rules to account for the internal logic of languages, and in so doing all but precluded the analysis of the influences of cross-language borrowings.† The findings reported in the present study do not yet make it possible to select a sample of phonological traits, vocabulary items, and grammatical features that were most probably diffused among languages and correlate them among the 172 units in the sample used in this book, so as to determine a "language area," within which area languages were more similar on the same set of diffusional features than were the languages outside the area. Driver (1969:47–50) suggests that languages change more slowly than culture. As evidence he demonstrates that there was extensive genetic language variation within a single culture area in North America. In working with the Salishan language family, Jorgensen (1969) was able to specify culture and language similarities and suggest more complex relations among environment, culture, and language than had previously been suggested. But neither Driver nor Jorgensen explored language diffusion in depth, to correlate diffusion of language with cultural and environmental accommodations. As stated earlier, the data are still too sparse to allow for correlational analyses such as these, but one can gain an impression of how vulnerable all aspects of language are to external influences from a brief review of areal features of language.

Northern Northwest Coast

The Haida, Tlingit, Tsimshian, Haisla Kwakiutl, Bella Bella Kwakiutl, and Canadian Athapaskans were both borrowers and lenders of words for edible animals, subsistence technology, slaves, and peacemaking ceremonies (Rigsby 1969). In general, words that were loaned were created in the area of their principal use. For instance, the Canadian Athapaskan term for "moose" was borrowed by coastal people. Moose occurred in the territories of Canadian Athapaskan speakers, but not normally in coastal regions. The

term for "herring rake," a technological item, was created by the Bella Bella Kwakiutl, who were principal users of the item, but the word was borrowed by others.

Among the Haida, Tlingit, and to a lesser degree the Canadian Athapaskans, there were general phonological similarities and classifier affixes, which most probably were diffused (Krauss 1972).

Central Northwest Coast

The central area of the Northwest Coast, especially the Wakashan, Chimakuan, and Salishan languages, used reduplication of nominal and verbal stems to indicate plenitude, distribution, and the diminutive (Sherzer 1973), and most of the languages in these families, plus Tsimshian (Penutian) also shared a complex of uncommon phonological traits, including lateral consonants, glottalized stops, glottalized continuants, labiovelar consonants, and back-velar consonants.

Southern Northwest Coast and Northwestern California

The Penutian languages of southwest Oregon, and the Penutian, Hokan, Athapaskan, and Algonkian languages of northwest California shared many features that not only allow us to infer something about contacts and migrations prior to the period of contact with Europeans, but also provide evidence to show how northwestern California language relations spilled over into northeastern and central parts of California, sometimes through migrations.

Use of consonantal symbolism to indicate the diminutive was a trait of the Hupa and Kato (Athapaskan); the Wiyot and Yurok (Algonkian); the Karok and Yana (Hokan); and the Hanis, Yuki, and Southern Sierra Miwok (Penutian) (Wenger 1973). Diminutive suffixes were common to the Hupa and Kato (Athapaskan); the Wiyot and Yurok (Algonkian); the Achomawi, Karok, and Yana (Hokan); and the Siuslaw, Klamath, Yuki, and Southern Sierra Miwok (Penutian) (Wenger 1973).* It is plausible that the consonantal symbolism and the suffixes that indicated the diminutive were old Penutian traits carried south

---

*See Swadesh (1951) for a review of the controversy about distinguishing genetic features from diffusional features in language.

†See especially Noam Chomsky (1965), *Aspects of the Theory of Syntax*, MIT Press, Cambridge, Mass.

---

*These and subsequent interpretations are drawn from Wenger (1973) when it appears that the data he has marshalled warrants diffusional interpretations. He has not argued for all of the following borrowings.

by the Sierra Miwok and diffused among the neighbors of Penutians in northern California.

Augmentative suffixes had a more narrow distribution among the following Penutian phylum languages: the Siuslaw (Yakonan), Klamath (Isolate), and Southern Sierra Miwok (California Penutian); the Kato and Hupa (Athapaskan); and in an analogous way, by the Wiyot (Algonkian), who expressed augmentation through consonantal symbolism. The idea or concept for expressing diminution and augmentation in these fashions may have stemmed from Penutian-Salishan contacts, but that is pure speculation. "Small," or "few," or "less" (diminutive), and "large," or "many," or "more" (augmentative) were central concepts in Northwest Coast culture, especially in relation to abundance, ownership, the life cycle, and prerogatives. That such concepts took special grammatical forms throughout the Northwest Coast and into parts of California is not surprising, and it is reasonable to believe the concepts probably penetrated into California by way of the Penutians.

There were many other features that linked the language families. The Algonkian uses of illative and ablative prefixes seem to have been analogically borrowed by Hanis (Coosan family: Penutian phylum). Penutian possessive-case ending may have been a loan translation analogically borrowed by the Achomawi and Atsugewi (Palaihnihan: Hokan) and Shasta (Shastan: Hokan). And productive nominalizing suffixes, probably a Penutian feature, were used by Penutians, Hokans, and Algonkians in southern Oregon and in the northern and central parts of California (Wenger 1973).

Central California

Callaghan (1964) has pointed out that Wappo (Yukian: Penutian), Eastern Pomo (Pomo: Hokan), Lake Miwok (California Penutian: Penutian), and Patwin (California Penutian: Penutian) shared consonantal stop series, retroflex dentals, a voiceless lateral, and glottalized semivowels. These four very distinct languages spoken around Clear Lake, California, therefore suggest extensive diffusion. The Northern Pomo (Pomo: Hokan), Yuki (Yukian: Penutian) and Maidu (California Penutian: Penutian) shared illative and ablative suffixes, perhaps borrowed by the Pomo.

Southern California

The Yuman (Hokan) language of Southern California spoken by the Diegueño, and River Yuman spoken by Yumans and Mohaves along the Colorado River, vari-

ously shared a complex of eight consonants and semivowels including several laterals with Serrano, Luiseño, Cupeño, and Cahuilla (all of the Uto-Aztecan family) spoken in Southern California (Sherzer 1973).

Plateau

The language communities in the Plateau were especially interactive. Aoki (1975) demonstrates that the Sahaptian (Penutian) and Interior Salishan languages shared labiovelar consonants, glottalized stops, and other unusual phones, many of which were diffused from the Northwest Coast complex. Sahaptians and Salishan also shared a feature of vowel alteration; Aoki (1975) reconstructed vowel alteration as a feature of Interior Salish that stemmed from a change in an earlier form of Coast Salish. Thus, Sahaptian borrowed the feature from Interior Salish.

Upper Chinook (Chinookan: Penutian) borrowed postfixes (Sapir 1907) and also developed a grammatical category to distinguish the recent and remote past through contacts with Sahaptin (Sahaptian: Penutian) (Silverstein 1974). Moreover, Chinookans analogically borrowed gender distinctions from Coast Salish before the Upper Chinook moved east to The Dalles, the major natural steps on the Columbia River, where it passes through the Cascades (Silverstein 1974).

Sahaptian and Nez Percé (Sahaptian: Penutian), Cayuse (Isolate: Penutian), Molala (Isolate: Penutian), and Klamath (Isolate: Penutian) all possessed similarities in their numeral stems and the manner in which numbers were formed: these were borrowed rather than inherited (Rigsby 1965).

Given the present state of inquiry, the evidence for grammatical and phonological diffusion in the Columbia Plateau is swamped by evidence for lexical borrowings. Not only did Salishans borrow from Sahaptians, and Sahaptians from Salishans, but in some instances Salishans borrowed back from Sahaptians words that had originally been borrowed by Sahaptians from Salishans (Aoki 1975).

Great Basin

Language differentiation in the Basin was modest, and bilingualism was extensive. That the regular interdialectal and interlanguage contacts leveled language distinctions through regular diffusion is most plausible. Some of the Uto-Aztecan speakers of the Basin (Plateau Shoshoneans) used prefixes to indicate the general character of the motion involved in an activity, and to indicate the specific body-part involved in an action (Kroeber and Grace 1960). These verb prefixes are rare in Uto-Aztecan, yet Wenger (1973) has demonstrated that these traits were also part of the speech of the Washo (Hokan) and Maidu (Penutian), who were neighbors of several Northern Paiute groups, and of the Pomo (Hokan); and existed also in the Penutian languages of Takelma and Klamath. Whether the instrumental prefixes on verbs were originally Hokan or Penutian is not known, but they were probably borrowed by Uto-Aztecans.

Washo (Isolate: Hokan) borrowed words from Miwok (California Penutian: Penutian) to the southwest, Maidu (California Penutian: Penutian) to the northwest, and Northern Paiute or Paviotso (Uto-Aztecan) to the east (Jacobsen 1966). Systematic inquiry into Uto-Aztecan lexical borrowings have not been undertaken, but the grammatical evidence suggests a long period of adjustment between Uto-Aztecans and non-Uto-Aztecans on the fringe of the Sierra, perhaps beginning well before the movements eastward through the Great Basin were begun.

PART III

ABORIGINAL CULTURE

Chapter 4

Introduction

Ever since Otis Mason (1896) postulated eighteen aboriginal cultural and environmental areas for the entirety of the Americas, the concept of culture areas has been used to classify cultures on the basis of their similarities and differences. Culture area schemes are useful pedagogical devices, because they allow scholars to reduce great amounts of complex data to a few generalizations. In brief, sets of tribes showing the most similar inventories of cultural acts, objects, and beliefs can be clustered together and separated at greater and greater distances from those sets of tribes that are most different from them culturally; treating cultural inventories in this way is analogous to the way environmental areas were treated in Figures 2-1 and 2-2.

Except for two culture area classifications of North America by Driver and his colleagues (Driver, Kenny, et al. 1972; Driver and Coffin 1974), all continent-wide culture-area taxonomies have been impressionistic. Driver was the first person to derive culture area schemes for an entire continent by intercorrelating tribal inventories.

Using culture area schemes to classify the tribes of the Northwest Coast (for example) as more similar to each other than they were to tribes of the Plateau or California made it possible to isolate many of the features that distinguished the Northwest Coast from neighboring regions to the south and east. Moreover, culture area taxonomies begged for explanations. Why, for instance, were Northwest Coast cultures different from California cultures? And why were Plateau cultures different from Great Basin cultures?

Although the units of comparison were rather gross—Northwest Coast versus California—the culture areas, once obtained, were not ends in themselves. They were used as the basis for further speculation, that is to say, they prompted scholars to ask further questions about how cultures in the same areas came to be as they were at the time of contact with Europeans, and why they were different from cultures in other areas.

Environment has often been regarded as important in explaining variations among cultures and in explaining similarities among cultures in an area. Kroeber (1939), Driver and Massey (1957), and many others have suggested that environmental factors placed some limits on the forms of cultural developments. Throughout his career, Kroeber also argued that culture areas were historical areas, that is, tribes that were embraced by the same culture area were similar not only because they occupied similar environments, but more importantly because they borrowed features of culture from one another, and because they inherited from their predecessors cultural features that were passed through the generations. As tribes from different historical traditions met, they borrowed features from each other, and these features diffused considerable distances from the creators or donors through "relay diffusion" or borrowing through intermediaries. Thus, borrowing and inheritance, the phenomena of historical contacts, were uppermost in Kroeber's explanations of cultural similarities and cultural developments.

The age area schemes of Clark Wissler (1926) were an attempt to explain how it was that culture areas formed in the Americas, and why tribes were similar. He hypothesized that most cultural features were created by one or a few tribes in the geographical center of an area (theoretically, the center of the area and diffusion from it would be thought of as a perpendicular circular cone), and that features—such as woodworking complexes or fishing devices and techniques—diffused outward at regular rates from the center to the peripheries of the area. By this hypothesis, it follows that the wider the distribution of the feature, the older the feature. Thus Wissler explained that the oldest cultural features in North America, such as the bow and arrow, had universal distributions, but recent traits were confined to small sets of tribes, but not all of the tribes, in the same areas.

The quest to uncover origins and histories through the synchronic distributions of cultural traits was basic to the work of Kroeber, Wissler, and Klimek. The various approaches and historical explanations offered by these scholars were never completely discredited, because a common origin is the most plausible explanation for similar traits that were shared by adjacent tribes speaking different languages, or shared by tribes from the same language family separated by considerable distances from each other, when the tribes that intervened between them did not possess the features in question.

Harold Driver (1941, 1956, 1966) pointed out that the problem with such schemes is that not only were they based on impressions rather than empirical tests, but that they did not distinguish similarities among those things that were alike but of different origins from similarities among those things that were alike and of the same origins. Driver (1956) pointed out that matricentered and patricentered societies in North America probably had several origins, but probably no more than one or two origins within each culture area that included, say, matrilineal tribes. For instance, along the northern Northwest Coast, the Haisla Kwakiutl, Gitksan, Tsimshian, Haida, and Tlingit groups practiced avunculocality, observed matrilineality, employed special avoidance behaviors between in-laws, and shared many of the same names for moieties and phratries. It is doubtful that there were four independent inventions of matricentered social organization in the region. On the other hand, Northwest Coast avunculocal-matrilineal systems were very different from Western Pueblo matrilineal systems in many details and the two most surely had different origins.*

The origin of matrilineality among the Apacheans, who also resided in the Southwest, could have been independent of both Pueblo and northern Northwest Coast matrilineality (Dyen and Aberle 1974).

Culture area delineations are not ends in themselves. But as classifications of tribes they provide many uses. Besides their pedagogical value, they provoke questions about history, evolution, function, and relations between culture and environment and culture and language. Moreover, culture areas can be used to draw stratified probability samples.† As a way to begin our comparative analysis of the cultures of western North America, we shall present a culture area scheme derived from a sample of 292 variables for the 172 tribes in the study.

The culture relations among the 172 units in our western North American sample do not fit perfectly with either genetic language relations or environmental areas. Perusal of Figures 4-1 and 4-2 shows this. But even a casual comparison of language, environment, and culture distributions suggests that within each culture area, language similarities correlated more closely with cultural similarities than did environmental similarities.

CULTURAL VARIABLES

The culture areas of western North America were derived from a comparison of all 172 tribes on 292 variables covering eight major topics of culture: (1) technology and material culture, (2) subsistence economy, (3) economic organization, (4) settlement pattern, demography, and community organization, (5) social and kinship organization, (6) political organization, sodalities, and warfare, (7) ceremoni-

---

*Following convention, the Hopi (including Tewa-speaking Hopi) and Zuni tribes comprise the Western Pueblos, as well as the two Western Keres villages of Acoma and Laguna. These societies observed matrilineal descent and, for the most part, relied on seeps, springs, and rainfall in raising their crops. The Eastern Pueblos embrace the Tewa-,

Towa-, and Tiwa-speaking villages of Taos, Isleta, Picuris, Pecos, Nambe, San Juan, Santa Clara, San Ildefonso, and Jemez, all located along the Rio Grande and Pecos River drainages. Their kinship organization was bilateral and they used canal irrigation in raising their crops. The Eastern Keres villages along the tributaries of the Rio Grande, such as Santa Ana, Santo Domingo, Sia, and Cochiti, are usually considered with the Eastern Pueblos unless specific distinction is necessary. The Eastern Keres villages have been called a "bridge" between Western and Eastern Pueblos (Eggan 1950), and are different in many cultural features from the Western Keres villages of Acoma and Laguna.

† The author has drawn such a sample for testing several hypotheses in the R-mode and in scalograms. The results of these tests will appear in future volumes.

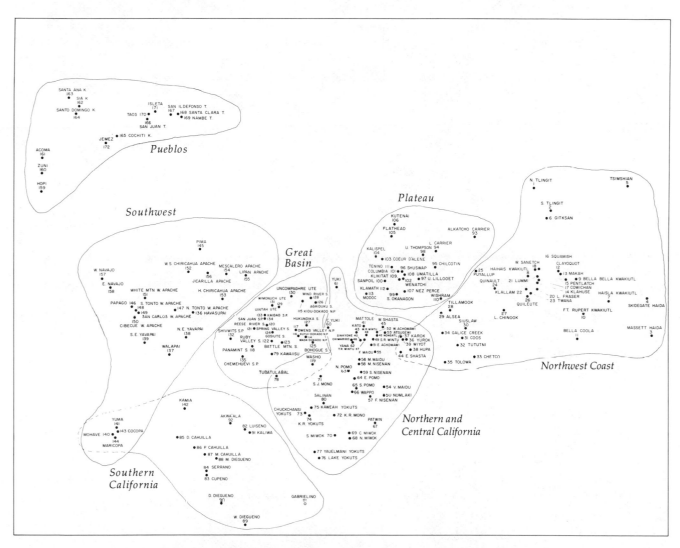

Figure 4-1 *Two-dimensional mapping of 172 western North American Indian tribes derived from the MINISSA nonmetric, smallest-space algorithm of Lingoes and Roskam (1971) applied to Driver's G coefficients based on 292 cultural variables (1,577 attributes).*

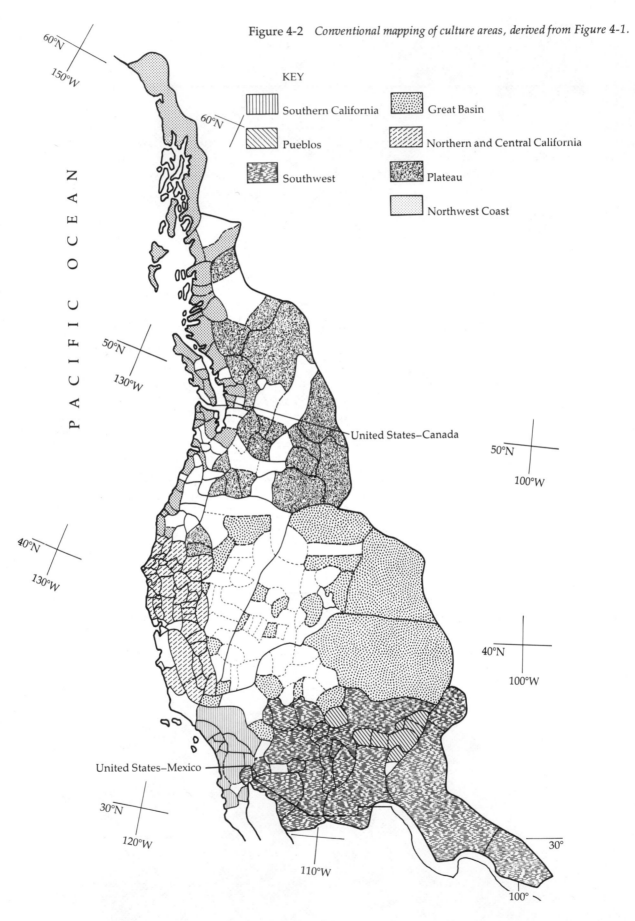

Figure 4-2 *Conventional mapping of culture areas, derived from Figure 4-1.*

KEY

⦀	Southern California	⦂	Great Basin
⧄	Pueblos	⧄	Northern and Central California
⦂	Southwest	⦂	Plateau
⦂	Northwest Coast		

PACIFIC OCEAN

60°N
150°W

60°N

50°N
130°W

United States–Canada

50°N
100°W

40°N
130°W

40°N
100°W

United States–Mexico

30°N
120°W

110°W

30°

100°

alism, including the life cycle, and (8) spirit quests, shamanism, causes of illness, and magic.*

A sampling of all eight topics was necessary in order to provide a representative description of what each culture was like, and in order to make systematic comparisons among all cultures and all cultural topics. As is pointed out in Appendix B, the Jorgensen–Driver sample employed here is the largest and most balanced list of cultural variables thus far used in comparative cultural inquiry. A brief overview of the variables within each topic follows: it should help the reader understand the range and variety of data on which the culture area analysis is based, and the rationale behind selecting these topics for inclusion.

1. *Technology* articulates people with their environments. We sampled 46 variables pertaining to material items and techniques for hunting, fishing, gathering wild plants, horticulture, food preparation and preservation, water transport, housing, clothing, and weaving.

2. *Subsistence economy* shows relative differences in the outcomes of the ways in which people articulated with their environments. Thirty variables were sampled. These covered information about the relative importance of agriculture, fishing, hunting, and gathering in the diet; whether the resources were produced or procured locally or whether they were obtained extralocally, and the amounts for each source; the nature or types of resources procured or produced, the manner in which they were transported and stored, and the duration of the storage.

3. *Economic organization* measures how production and extraction were organized: who owned, who inherited, who produced, who distributed, what was distributed, how distribution was conducted, and who had access to strategic resources. The 67 variables in the sample covered questions about the organization of labor by sex, age, specialization, and

task groups for subsistence pursuits, housing, the production of tools, and so forth. They also covered the organization of reciprocity and distribution of goods, including sharing of access to resources, gift exchange, barter and trade. Two further sets of variables dealt with the ownership and inheritance of property, including strategic resources for production.

4. *Settlement pattern, demography, and community organization* answers questions about the compactness, fixity, size, and density of community organizations, and whether there were important public structures, local subdivisions, and intracommunity residence patterns of significance. Nine variables assessed these topics.

5. *Social and kinship organization* pursues the relations among marriage, residence, descent, and kinship phenomena in organizing social, economic, and ceremonial life. We sampled 42 variables to measure who married, where couples resided, the relations between the families of the couple, the nature of family and household organization, the nature of descent reckoning, the economic and ceremonial organization of descent groups, and the kinship terminologies employed.

6. *Political organization, sodalities, and warfare* allows a determination of whether political organization existed beyond the kinship group, and if so, how that polity influenced defense, economic, and civic decisions. Using measurements of sodality organizations allows a probing of the nature of nonkin organizations within and between societies and their roles in ceremonial and political affairs, while questions about feuding, raiding, and warfare allow an assessment of intra- and intercommunity hostile relations and the ceremonial and military organization that attended them. Political organization, sodality, and warfare phenomena are often related, but they vary independently. The sample was composed of 34 variables measuring the complexity of polities within and among communities; modes of succession to leadership; spheres of political influence or power over organizing common defense; distribution of food in times of scarcity; provision of access to strategic resources; allocation of civic duties; and settlement of disputes. Sodalities were analyzed for their sex and age composition; roles in politics, raiding, warfare, and ceremonials; and their restricted or tribalwide nature. The set of raiding variables determines how often feuding, raiding, or warfare was engaged in, who engaged in it, what motivated it; whether there was special fighting regalia, special military organization, and special ceremonials for raiding and warfare.

7. *Ceremonialism, including the life cycle* measures whether societies performed ceremonies, and if so,

---

*The culture areas were determined by correlating each tribe with all other 171 tribes on 292 variables, using Driver's G coefficient. The 14,706 G coefficients were then rank-ordered and mapped in two dimensions with a multivariate algorithm (MINISSA) that locates the smallest distances in the Euclidean space for a number of points (rank coefficients) (see Lingoes and Roskam 1971). These methods are explained in Appendix C. The entire variable definition code for the 292 cultural variables, comprising 1,577 attributes, is found in Appendix E. Unfortunately the ratings for the 172 sample tribes on the 292 culture variables are too unwieldy to publish here, and readers interested in obtaining a complete copy of the ratings should contact the author.

how often, and for what purposes; who sponsored and who attended; whether gifts were given and who received them. The life cycle events of birth, maturation, marriage, and death are assessed so as to learn whether there was no observance at all, whether private or public ceremonies accompanied them, and of what features the ceremonies were composed. Thirty-nine variables were defined and rated on these topics.

8. *Spirit quest, shamanism, causes of illness, and magic* measures whether and how people gained supernatural power and the nature of that power; whether shamans and laymen gained the same kinds and amounts of power; and whether shamans developed skills and reputations that transcended their own communities. Theories of disease, especially theories about soul loss, spirit intrusion, and violation of interdictions are linked to shamans' performances and magic. Twenty-six variables were defined and rated on these topics.

In many of the eight topical areas, measures of intercultural contacts were sought, such as whether resource areas were shared, whether intertribal marriages were contracted, whether intertribal raiding was commonplace, whether attendance at ceremonies was intertribal, and whether shamans' performances were intertribal. These variables, and others similar to them, help to interpret intertribal relations throughout western North America.

CULTURE AREAS

The 172 culture units ("tribes") in Figures 4-1 and 4-2 fitted rather well into seven culture areas. By way of simplest interpretation, what this means is that the culture units within a broad geographical region shared more cultural features with their co-members than they did with culture units in other regions. The bulk of the units were easily classified within these culture areas for most of the culture topics. But for practically every topic one or more units took intermediary positions between two areas. Only in the Pueblo Southwest, where Pueblos were sufficiently distinct to be separated from all other Southwest cultures, were there no borderline placements of cultural units. Nevertheless, for simplicity, in our discussions we shall treat the culture areas as if they were synonymous with the main geographic regions of the West. A future volume on the Northwest Coast, California, Southern California, Plateau, Great Basin, and Southwest culture areas will offer more detailed analyses of each area than are possible here,

and the tribes that took intermediary positions between culture areas will also be discussed in particular.

In defining culture areas for the present volume, the Northwest Coast and California regions posed the largest taxonomic problems: several cultures ambiguously took places between the Northwest Coast and northern California areas.* Moreover, the connections of northern California tribes to the Great Basin and to Southern California were interesting, as were the connections of Southern California tribes to the River Yumans of the Southwest.

By focusing on the causes of the equivocal placements of many tribes, we learn a great deal about language, culture, and environment relations. For instance, when California tribes are analyzed—to the exclusion of other tribes in western North America— it is clear that the tribes of the northwestern part of California could as well be classified in the Northwest Coast area as in California.[†] These Californian groups had made unique adaptations to coastal and riverine life in the wet forests and to the oak woodlands. After Kroeber's (1925) analysis of the societies of the northwestern part of California, in which he described them as having made an unusual and independent adjustment to the wet-forest, riverine culture of the Northwest Coast, Kroeber and several other scholars chose to classify these societies as one of several variants of the Northwest Coast culture area. In this book we therefore follow the tradition established by Kroeber (1939) and affirmed by Driver and Massey (1957) and Drucker (1965): the northwestern California groups were considered to compose a southernmost province of the Northwest Coast and were analyzed as such, while emphasizing the avowedly California nature of this subarea.

---

*Throughout the book, "California" will be used to refer to both northern and central parts of present-day California, and "Southern California" will refer to the part south of the Tehachapi Mountains. It is sometimes convenient to refer to California without always specifying both northern *and* central parts, yet from time to time, as when describing different customs practiced north and south of San Francisco Bay, we shall distinguish between "northern" and "central." More often, tribal units along the northern California coast shared similarities with units within the Northwest Coast region, so it is practical to consider the northwestern part of California as a southernmost subregion of the Northwest Coast, as is explained above, in the text. Southern California is a distinct culture area.

[†]Hupa, Karok, Yurok, Wiyot, Nongatl, Mattole, and Kato.

Likewise, the analyses of California and the Great Basin demonstrated that the Tubatulabal and Kawaiisu fitted better in California than the Great Basin, while the Washo fitted better in the Great Basin than in California, so these three groups have been classified accordingly. Nevertheless, all three were intermediary and the important relations between these tribes and their Great Basin and California neighbors are recognized at appropriate places in the analysis.

The River Yumans of the Colorado River stood between the Southwest and the Southern California culture areas. The great difference between the River Yumans and the Southern Californians was that the former farmed and the latter did not. The separate analyses of the Southwest area and Southern California area placed the River Yumans more firmly in the Southwest. With the inclusion of the River Yumans and the Pueblos in the Southwest, all of the farming cultures in the contiguous geographic areas that comprise the Southwest could be analyzed together. The distinctiveness from one another of the River Yumans, Pueblos, and Pimans, all of whom were longtime resident farmers of the Southwest, and the distinctiveness of these three from the much less differentiated gatherers, hunters, and parttime farmers of the area, provide us with intriguing questions that beg for answers.

The complexity of the two-dimensional analysis (Figure 4-1) is simplified in the one-dimensional analysis of Figure 4-3. The tree diagram in Figure 4-3, with its clean, neat, and absolute branching, of course suggests the relations among the tribes were much more clean than they were in fact, but that is the nature of a one-dimensional analysis: closest pairs are placed side by side, while tied relations and next-closest pairs are placed elsewhere along a single dimension. Only the bridges that join the groups at the centroids give us a hint as to the complexity of the relations. The bridges are the main cross-bars joining all the pairs of tribes within main groups and represent the least distance or difference among all tribes linked within a group; in Euclidean space a centroid is a central point representing the least distance among all data points (here, "tribes") in that space. The Pueblo and non-Pueblo societies are bracketed together in Figure 4-3, though it is clear that the average similarity of the two sets of societies was low.

One advantage of tree diagrams is that they show the coefficient level at which pairs and groups of tribes are joined. Following are brief descriptions of the tribal memberships and geographical ranges in each of the culture areas of Figures 4-1 and 4-2. The coefficients referred to are those shown in Figure 4-3.

Northwest Coast

The tribes from Northern or Chilkat Tlingit, east of Yakutat Bay, Alaska, to Kato, near Cape Mendocino, California make up the Northwest Coast culture area. The group averages of the Kato and other groups in the northwestern part of California are found in the middle of the California group in Figure 4-3. Cultural diversity was considerable, but the area was not nearly so complex as the California and Southwest areas. The Northwest Coast tribes averaged about 55 percent cultural similarity, with a northern subarea in which tribes shared 75 percent similarity, a central subarea where tribes shared 68 percent similarity, a southern subarea with 74 percent similarity and a northwestern California subarea of 72 percent. Throughout this book we shall refer frequently to these subareas.

California

The tribes from Shasta in the north to Kawaiisu, near Tehachapi Pass in the south, and from the crest of the Sierra westward to the coast, formed the California culture area. In the one-dimensional analysis in Figure 4-3, the tribes of the San Joaquin drainage or the central California region were separated from northern California by the Great Basin and linked with Southern California tribes. The two-dimensional solution in Figure 4-1, on the other hand, placed the San Joaquin tribes in the California area rather than in Southern California. The differences among the tribes from the San Joaquin drainage subarea (64 percent average similarity), the subarea of the river valleys of the northern Coast Range (62 percent average similarity), the northern mountains and foothill subarea (67 percent average similarity), and the Sacramento Valley subarea (68 percent) were greater than the internal variation among the Northwest Coast tribes.

Southern California

The tribes of the Southern California area were very homogeneous, averaging 82 percent similarity without the two Baja Peninsula tribes (Akwa'ala and Kaliwa), and 70 percent with them. The Southern California culture units were located from the Los Angeles Basin on the south side of Tehachapi Pass to about the 30° N. Latitude in the Baja Peninsula, and from the Chocolate Mountains in the east to the San

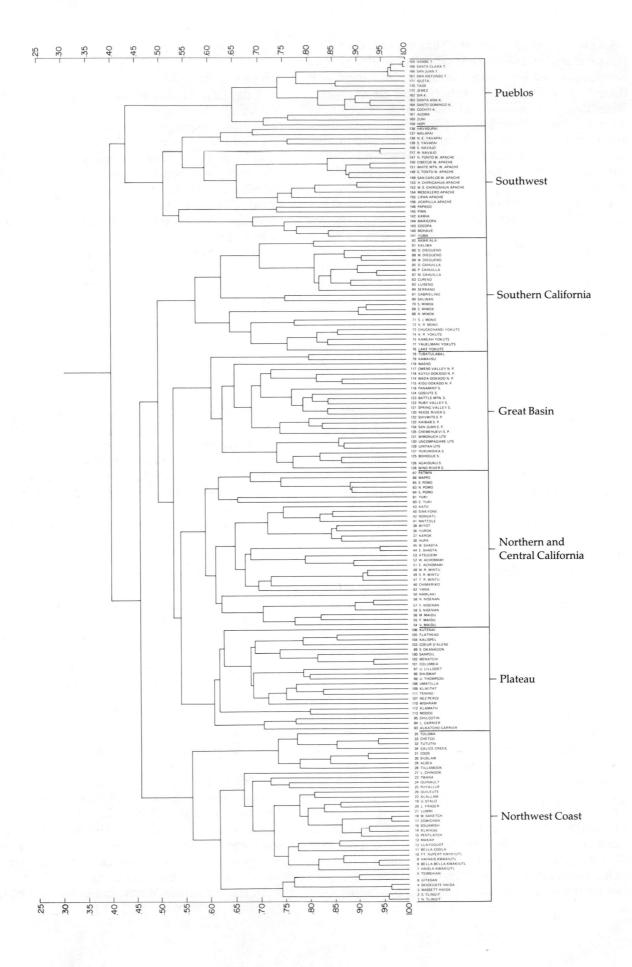

Figure 4-3 *Culture tree: 1. Groupings of 172 western North American Indian tribes derived from G coefficients based on 292 variables (1,577 attributes).*

PUEBLOS

169 Nambe Tewa
168 Santa Clara Tewa
166 San Juan Tewa
167 San Ildefonso Tewa
171 Isleta
170 Taos
172 Jemez
162 Sia Keres
163 Santa Ana Keres
164 Santo Domingo Keres
165 Cochiti Keres
161 Acoma
160 Zuni
159 Hopi

NON-PUEBLO SOUTHWEST

136 Havasupai
137 Walapai
138 Northeast Yavapai
139 Southeast Yavapai
158 Eastern Navajo
157 Western Navajo
147 North Tonto Western
    Apache
150 Cibecue Western Apache
151 White Mountain Western
    Apache
148 South Tonto Western
    Apache
149 San Carlos Western
    Apache
153 Huachuca Chiricahua
    Apache
152 Warm Springs Chiricahua
    Apache
154 Mescalero Apache
155 Lipan Apache
156 Jicarilla Apache
146 Papago
145 Pima
142 Kamia
144 Maricopa
143 Cocopa
140 Mohave
141 Yuma

SOUTHERN CALIFORNIA

 92 Akwa'ala

 91 Kaliwa
 90 Desert Diegueño
 88 Mountain Diegueño
 89 Western Diegueño
 85 Desert Cahuilla
 86 Pass Cahuilla
 87 Mountain Cahuilla
 83 Cupeño
 82 Luiseño
 84 Serrano
 81 Gabrieliño
 80 Salinan
 70 Southern Miwok
 69 Central Miwok
 68 Northern Miwok
 71 San Joaquin Mono
 72 Kings River Mono
 73 Chuckchansi Yokuts
 74 Kings River Yokuts
 75 Kaweah Yokuts
 77 Yauelmani Yokuts
 76 Lake Yokuts

GREAT BASIN

 78 Tubatulabal
 79 Kawaiisu
119 Washo
117 Owens Valley Northern
    Paiute
116 Kuyui-Dokado Northern
    Paiute
114 Wada-Dokado Northern
    Paiute
115 Kidu-Dokado Northern
    Paiute
118 Panamint Shoshone
124 Gosiute Shoshone
123 Battle Mountain Shoshone
122 Ruby Valley Shoshone
121 Spring Valley Shoshone
120 Reese River Shoshone
132 Shivwits Southern Paiute
133 Kaibab Southern Paiute
134 San Juan Southern Paiute
135 Chemehuevi Southern Paiute
131 Wimonuch Ute
130 Uncompaghre Ute
129 Uintah Ute
127 Hukundika Shoshone
125 Bohogue Shoshone

126 Agaiduku Shoshone
128 Wind River Shoshone

NORTHERN AND CENTRAL
CALIFORNIA

 67 Patwin
 66 Wappo
 65 Southern Pomo
 63 Northern Pomo
 64 Eastern Pomo
 61 Yuki
 60 Coast Yuki
 43 Kato
 40 Sinkyone
 42 Nongatl
 41 Mattole
 39 Wiyot
 36 Yurok
 37 Karok
 38 Hupa
 45 West Shasta
 44 East Shasta
 53 Atsugewi
 52 West Achomawi
 51 East Achomawi
 48 McCloud River Wintu
 49 Sacramento River Wintu
 47 Trinity River Wintu
 46 Chimariko
 62 Yana
 50 Nomlaki
 58 Mountain Nisenan
 57 Foothill Nisenan
 59 Southern Nisenan
 56 Mountain Maidu
 55 Foothill Maidu
 54 Valley Maidu

PLATEAU

106 Kutenai
105 Flathead
104 Kalispel
103 Coeur d'Alene
 99 Southern Okanagon
100 Sanpoil
102 Wenatchi
101 Columbia
 97 Upper Lillooet
 96 Shuswap
 98 Upper Thompson

108 Umatilla
109 Klikitat
111 Tenino
107 Nez Percé
110 Wishram
112 Klamath
113 Modoc
 95 Chilcotin
 94 Lower Carrier
 93 Alkatcho Carrier

NORTHWEST COAST

 35 Tolowa
 33 Chetco
 32 Tututni
 34 Galice Creek
 31 Coos
 30 Siuslaw
 29 Alsea
 28 Tillamook
 27 Lower Chinook
 23 Twana
 24 Quinault
 25 Puyallup
 26 Quileute
 22 Klallam
 19 Upper Stalo
 20 Lower Fraser
 21 Lummi
 18 West Sanetch
 17 Cowichan
 16 Squamish
 14 Klahuse
 15 Pentlatch
 13 Makah
 12 Clayoquot
 11 Bella Coola
 10 Fort Rupert Kwakiutl
  8 Haihais Kwakiutl
  9 Bella Bella Kwakiutl
  7 Haisla Kwakiutl
    Tsimshian
  6 Gitksan
  4 Skidegate Haida
  3 Massett Haida
  2 Southern Tlingit
  1 Northern Tlingit

Clemente, San Nicolas, and Santa Catalina islands 50 miles from the Pacific shore in the west.

Plateau

From the Alkatcho Carrier tribe at the northern tip of the Fraser Plateau to the Klamath and Modoc tribes along the Klamath River drainage near the southwesternmost tip of the Columbia Plateau, the Plateau tribes averaged about 62 percent similarity. Some general distinctions among the Fraser, Columbia, and

Klamath and Modoc tribes were evident, but language similarity was the best guide to cultural similarity within this area.

Great Basin

The Great Basin tribes were located from the Salmon River area in Idaho (Agaiduku Shoshone) to the Mojave Desert in California (Chemehuevi Southern Paiute) and from the Colorado Rockies (Uncompaghre Utes) to the Truckee River in the Sierra

(Washo). Overall the Basin tribes averaged 68 percent similarity. A neat distinction separated the tribes into two areas. The northeastern subarea in the Snake River and Colorado River drainage systems was occupied by Utes and Shoshones, who averaged about 74 percent similarity. The Great Basin proper and the canyons and plateaus of the Colorado River on its southern flank were occupied by Western Shoshones, Northern Paiutes, and Southern Paiutes, who averaged about 71 percent similarity. Washo joined both groups at 66 percent similarity.*

Southwest

The Southwest was the area of maximal cultural variation in western North America. The many tribes there averaged only about 43 percent similarity. The Pueblos shared 65 percent, the River Yumans 69 percent, the Pimas and Papagos 74 percent, and the Pais and Apacheans 55 percent. The Pais were, however, equidistant between Apacheans and River Yumans.

VARIATION AMONG CULTURAL CLASSIFICATIONS BASED ON DIFFERENT SETS OF VARIABLES

The foregoing culture areas were derived from 292 variables covering, as mentioned earlier, eight broad cultural topics. Appendix D contains distribution maps of about 240 of these variables, each map

---

*The Shoshone societies located south of the Snake River and west of the Great Salt Lake in the central Great Basin conventionally are referred to as Western Shoshones (Steward 1938), whereas the Shoshone societies along the Snake River, north of the Snake River, and east of the Great Salt Lake conventionally are referred to either as Northern Shoshones or less frequently as Eastern Shoshones (Lowie 1924; Steward 1938). We shall use "Northern" rather than "Eastern" to refer to the Bohogue (Fort Hall), Agaiduku (Lemhi, or Salmon-eater), and Wind River Shoshones, for examples. The distinctions between Western and Northern Shoshones were many, but the main differences were in their subsistence economies. The former depended more on seed and nut gathering and rabbit drives, the latter on big-game hunting and fishing.

---

number being identified with a "Cu-" prefix.* No two variables had identical distributions, so it was reasonable to ask whether greater variation among tribes occurred for some topics, such as economic organization, than for other topics, such as ceremonial organization and life cycle. In order to answer that question, the relations among the tribes on each of seven topics were analyzed, from technology through spirit quests (the variables of settlement patterns and social organization, because they were related conceptually and because there were few of the former, were joined to reduce the categories of variables from eight to seven). It was then found that no two topics created identical culture area taxonomies, and that the correlations among topics varied widely.[†] Some pairs of categories, such as technology and economic organization, produced groupings of tribes that conformed rather well to each other as well as to the culture areas determined by using all variables on all topics, while other topics, such as settlement pattern and social organization, produced groupings of tribes that did not match the overall culture area taxonomy. For instance, the settlement pattern, demography, and kinship and social organization variables formed clusters among the 172 tribes that distinguished them first by bilateral kinship versus deme and unilineal kinship criteria, and second by territorial proximity and language filiation distinctions. Normally territorial proximity alone is the best predictor of culture area membership, no matter what set of variables are used to classify tribes. The exceptions, we shall learn, are very interesting. The seven one-dimensional tree diagrams, which have been produced from the correlation matrices of 172 tribes on each topic, will accompany the discussions of the topics they represent, in subsequent chapters of this book, but we will use the results obtained in Figure 4-1 when referring to major culture areas.

Table 4-1 demonstrates the correlations among the seven cultural topics derived from correlating each 172-tribe matrix with every other matrix. We can see that economic organization, technology, and subsistence economy were much more closely related than

---

*The distributions of about 50 variables showed so little variation that there was no reason to publish them.

[†]The tribes were ordered on only one dimension. Two- or three-dimensional analyses would retain more detail and produce less simplified orderings, but the coefficient-of-association levels are lost when such analyses are done with the MINISSA technique, so it was decided to use one-dimensional orderings.

Table 4-1

Relations among correlation matrices of seven general categories of cultural variables for 172 western North American Indian societies

	Subsistence Economy	Economic Organization	Technology	Ceremony–Life Cycle	Settlement–Kinship	Politics–Warfare
Spirits–Witchcraft	.345	.358	.453	.397	.268	.243
Subsistence Economy		.707	.690	.418	.425	.335
Economic Organization			.704	.489	.504	.418
Technology				.570	.437	.367
Ceremony–Life Cycle					.380	.409
Settlement–Kinship						.353
Politics–Warfare						X

Note: Matrix of Pearson's r coefficients generated from Driver's G coefficients among all 172 tribes in each subsample. Each r coefficient is based on $(172) (171) / 2 = 14,706$ G coefficients.

were the other topics. It is not tautological to say that these three cultural spheres and their objects, activities, and beliefs were conditioned more by environment, the customs of neighbors, and the economic entailments among technology, subsistence, and the organizations for extraction and production, than where the other topics. The surprising thing is that the intertopic correlations for these three spheres are so high. The set of variables on polities, sodality, and warfare, and the set on spirit quests, shamanism, causes of illness, and magic correlate least well with the others. In western North America, and perhaps throughout the world, these cultural spheres are more subject to local variation and are more independent of one another than the technology, subsistence economy, and economic organization variables. But all correlations among the topics are positive, meaning that tribal scores tended to be similar, rather than different, on all topics. Moreover, all of the matrix correlations are highly significant (i.e., are not products of chance).

VIEWING THE RELATIONS AMONG TECHNOLOGY, SUBSISTENCE ECONOMY, AND ECONOMIC ORGANIZATION FROM A COMPARATIVE PERSPECTIVE

Let us briefly mention the relations among the three most highly correlated sets of variable topics in the cultural sample—technology, subsistence economy, and economic organization. The relations among these phenomena are especially interesting because of the prominent places they occupy in several current theories that purport to account for cultural adaptations and evolution, especially cultural materialism (see Harris 1978) and system ecology (see Bean and Blackburn 1976). Neither of those theories have been tested by empirical means on a comparative sample of societies or on a comparative and wide-ranging sample of variables. Since the analysis that begins in Chapter 5 is comparative, it is worthwhile before turning to that analysis to discuss why doubt must be cast on the validity of explanations offered by system ecologists and like-minded scholars of cultural adaptation who attempt to prove their theories on the basis of analysis of a single society.

The overriding feature of the material underpinnings of all of the western North American Indian cultures was the mixed usage of wild plants, land mammals, and fish in their diets. Birds, reptiles, and invertebrates were consumed as well, with large edible birds (ducks, geese, and swans) being more important along the riverine and lacustrine regions of the Pacific Flyway, reptiles being more important in the hot deserts of the Southwest, and invertebrates being more important in the Great Basin. None of these animals were principal items in the diet of any group.

Indeed, even the Northwest Coast tribes, highly dependent on fish, shellfish, and, in some places, sea mammals, gathered wild plants, as did the successful Pueblo farmers of the Southwest. In fact, the tribes in all areas of western North America were gatherers *and* hunters *and* fishermen, exploiting much of the total biomass in their regions. (In only a very small number of territories were fish so meager as not to be used in native diets.)

In assessing the environments of the western North American Indian societies in Chapter 2 we learned that hunting, gathering, and fishing were possible in all major environmental areas, but we also learned that environmental differences were considerable. For instance, great abundances of fish and shellfish were available on the Northwest Coast, occurring in an often inhospitable environment. Moreover, large game did not occur in parts of the Plateau, Southern California, Great Basin, and Southwest, and the medium-sized game in these regions, such as antelope, were extremely fast runners with remarkable endurance. Although environmental differences in combinations of plant cover, land mammals, water and water life influenced the adaptations made anywhere, they did not determine those adaptations.

It is possible to cite numerous examples in support of this. Pueblos gained most of their diets from farm products. Although the territories of the Pueblos were not nearly so conducive to agriculture as the areas of the Pimans and River Yumans in the Southwest, the latter tribes relied much less on agriculture than did the Pueblos. Southern California and California tribes did not farm, but many of them acquired firsthand knowledge about farming from the River Yumans who traded throughout their territories. The California tribes and Southern California tribes could have farmed, though they chose not to do so. Great Basin gatherers engaged in practically no farming at all, yet their precursors and cohabitants in much of the Great Basin had farmed for nearly 1,000 years. In point of fact, the Southern Paiutes did engage in a little farming, but their efforts were meager when compared with those of their accomplished dry-farming neighbors, the Hopis, and with those of their river-bottom-farming neighbors, the Havasupais and Mohaves. The Southern Paiutes had extensive contacts with people from all of these groups. Colorado River Yumans and Eastern Pueblos on the Rio Grande had relatively complex fishing technologies, yet the Eastern Pueblos did not extract fish in great abundances and the River Yumans, who hauled in much larger quantities of fish than the Eastern Pueblos, used fish to supplement their wild and cultivated plant diets.

In the Plateau, the bunchgrass prairies provided a wide number of edible grass seeds, yet only the Klamath, Modoc, Wenatchi, and Sanpoil tribes seem to have collected them; similarly, on the Northwest Coast, abundances of berries and nuts were not fully extracted, and mule deer and Sitka deer were not regularly pursued even though they occurred throughout the dense undergrowth.

The gross correlations among technology, subsistence economy, and economic organization alone suggest that there were close, but by no means uniform, relations among the way in which people articulated with their environments, gained their livelihoods from their environments, and organized themselves to own, inherit, extract, produce, distribute, and consume the goods from their environments. Because relations among the spheres of technology,

subsistence economy, and economic organization were close, special attention must be paid to all three. What will become evident is that language affinities are often better predictors of adaptations than are similarities of environments. Yuman speakers, for example, regardless of whether they occupied fertile river bottom land or desert oases, preferred to collect and store mesquite pods, screwbeans, and mescal hearts, even when they knew how to farm. The many representatives of the Penutian phylum provide another example of this phenomenon. At the time of first European contact those speech communities we have classified as Penutian were located in many environmental regions, including wet forests, the Great Central Valley of California, and the Columbia Plateau, and they probably settled in those regions after they had already developed a basic inventory of tools and techniques, including weirs, traps, single-point harpoons, and the like, which made successful riverine fishing possible. It is interesting in this light that the coastal Penutians, from the Tsmishians of British Columbia to the Costanoans near Monterey Bay, were aware of sea-mammal hunting, but they never acquired the technology, such as toggle-head harpoons with floats and detachable lines, or the techniques, such as task-group use of large canoes to pursue sea mammals, which were used by the most expert sea-mammal hunters in western North America, including the Kwakiutl, Nootka, Haida, and Quinault tribes. The Penutians were primarily fishermen, hunters of land mammals, and gatherers, even when many species of sea mammals traversed their shores. Other examples could be cited, but a generalization suffices: everywhere in western North America cultural features such as the aforementioned were more apt to override environmental similarities, given extant technologies, than were environmental similarities apt to override culture.

On The Evaluation of Cultural Adaptation from Comparative and Noncomparative Perspectives

Although A. L. Kroeber did not test for relations between environment and culture, in his grandest impressionistic work, *Cultural and Natural Areas of Native North America* (1939), he showed again and again, as Driver has pointed out, the "powerful dominance of history and culture over geography" (Driver 1962: 8). Kroeber (1939: 1) argues that while "cultures are rooted in nature . . . they are no more produced by nature than a plant is produced or caused by the soil in which it is rooted."

As for specific relations between environment and

cultural organization, it can only be implied that at best, environments impose broad limits in which many organizations (or adaptations) work, but even this statement must not be relied on too seriously, because the developments of complex technologies allow water to be moved thousands of miles through pumps and with gravity flow, that "the deserts shall rejoice, and blossom as the rose"; and complex technologies allow Eskimos on the polar ice cap to eat hot dogs with relish and to pursue their quarry on snowmobiles, and allow equatorial dwellers to eat ice cream cones. If we fix time, place, and circumstance solidly in the context of the seventeenth century western North America, however, we correctly conclude that canal irrigation (for example) would have been an unlikely adaptation where there was no predictable source of running water; that hunting would not be dominant where mammals and birds were sparse; and so forth. In the aboriginal context we focus on here, environments did provide some broad ranges within which a variety of adaptations were available. Indeed, it is very probable that prehistoric farmers who once occupied sites across the breadth and length of the Southwest—the Anasazi, Mogollon, and Hohokam cultures—contracted their distributions to a few favorable localities within this region following sustained drought or some other deleterious and protracted environmental forces that threatened subsistence and survival alike, whereas the island-dwelling tribes of the Wakashan language family developed sea-mammal hunting for less urgent reasons, to supplement their fishing subsistence economies in regions rich in sea mammals but less rich in game and edible plants. Some groups survived and others probably did not, but even the canal-irrigation people of the Southwest (the Pimans, Papagos, and Eastern Pueblos) and the fishing–sea-mammal hunting peoples of the Northwest Coast and Southern California "adapted" in different fashions.

"Ecological adaptation" has come to convey the meaning to some anthropologists that human, other animal, and plant populations interact in physical space in such ways that the human population—usually unwittingly, but not necessarily so—has optimized its viability: those who apply the term in this sense would, in brief, have humans enhancing their survival probabilities by "adapting" to other forms of life within some nonrational, self-regulating system. We term the system "nonrational" because human intentions, or reasons, or dispositions for causing humans to act as they do are not required. Anthropologists who advance such analysis cannot have studied more than a single society before doing so, and therefore exercise neither controls nor comparisons to support their generalizations and to demonstrate that the relations they perceive are real and determinate. By "real relation" is meant that variation in one part of the relation is accompanied by variation in the other; and by "determinate relation" is meant that controls have been exercised to show that no other sources of influence have intervened to affect the relation.

In this book we shall not claim this kind of optimized, nonrational ecological adaptation: *all* western North American tribes were practicing customs of one sort or another and occupying definable spaces at the time of first contact with Europeans; thus it is a trivial truth to say that all were ecologically adapted, for ultimately an adaptation is anything that works. It would, however, be quite another thing to allege that "whatever is" (e.g., the nature of the tribe's economic organization) "had to be" (e.g., the tribe's economy is organized as it is because it had to be so organized): such a lawlike explanation is a nonsequitur.

Let us briefly address the logical and theoretical underpinnings of system ecology, even though this current view of ecological adaptation is not supported by the analysis in this book.

One point of logic that is most relevant but that has been obscured by some recent advocates of system ecology in accounting for ecological adaptations is that at *any* point in time any culture unit is "adapted" to its environment. Unless relations among phenomena are specified and measured through systematic comparisons and controls for a sample of cultural units, there is no way to evaluate a generalization about the fit between natural environment and cultural environment, or between natural environment and social structure, or between cultural systems and biological systems, or whatever else one purports to explain.

In talking about adaptation, many anthropologists have acted as if all ecological systems are composed of sets of populations which operate in definable natural environments, which are alleged to have from minimal to maximal potential for carrying the several populations in their embrace. The natural environments, and all the relations among biological populations, are said to have specifiable relations with the human populations: thus, farmers are dependent not only on their seeds, the techniques they use to manage their crops, their storage techniques, their knowledge of precipitation patterns and soils, and the like, but also upon things that farmers need not or do not understand, such as the role played by ritual in adapting the human population to the environment. For instance, system ecologists claim that in order for the human population to *survive* (a key term), it must *adapt* (a key term because it describes a relation) to the other biological populations, and that all of these populations must adapt in their many interrelations in the environment.

This poses an interesting paradox: on the one hand, human populations (culture units) must maximize their survival potential by creating and optimizing customs to adjust to threats of all types. Thus, humans are conceptualized as rational, economic beings (that is, as the "economic man" defined in classical economic theory). On the other hand, this model of man as an economic maximizer is eschewed, since the system is also explicated as being a nonrational, self-regulating mechanism imposing lawful adaptations. If the populations become unbalanced—for instance, if the population of farmers outstrips its food supply because of a drought, and the drought likewise affects the wild plant and animal populations—human survival is threatened. The human population, so it is held, adapts to the environment without even knowing an adaptation is being made.

Adaptation, then, can be interpreted the way adaptation in evolutionary biology is: it is a nonrational or nonintentional process of adjustment. That is to say, the human population is part of a larger system of multivariate relations wherein an impulse generated or felt in one part influences the other parts, and the various populations must adapt to these impulses or die, that is, lose in the selection process. Human populations, it is contended, adapt themselves to changes in other populations and the natural environment through customs that control and regulate human population. Thus, human populations create and borrow techniques for subsistence and often, in unwitting response to impulses from elsewhere in the system they are part of, create customs that serve as controls and regulatory mechanisms so that the human population can survive. The notion of controls and regulatory mechanisms allows the analyst to understand systems as organizations of phenomena separate from the intentions, reasons, motives, and dispositions of the human agents in the system. Indeed, the system is alleged to be self-regulating (a nonrational model), and its behavior obeys lawful processes.

In a fashion reminiscent of the British functionalists of the 1930s and 1940s, Richard Ford (1972: 1–17) has claimed that certain ritual customs of Eastern Pueblos are not at all what Eastern Pueblos think they are. He says that the customs are regulatory feedback mechanisms for assisting the survival of the population by storing and redistributing food to people in need. The customs, then, are unwittingly integrated into a system that "assists" survival of the population when the needs of some people outstrip their ability to satisfy those needs. Moreover, the nature of the system is such that the needs of some people will become dire at regular intervals, and the regulatory mechanisms will "assist" survival at these periods. It

is not clear that anything of theoretical or empirical import turns on either Ford's or the general system ecology view of environment (biological as well as nonbiological) and culture relations, because the key relational terms, i.e., the key explanatory terms that clinch the argument, such as "assist" and "survival," are not defined and measured; the ranges for the variables in the system are not specified and measured; the meaning of the key term "effective variable" is not clear because it is not demonstrated why some variables are "effective" and others are not; and the like. Furthermore, no models have been deployed in which differential equations simulate a dynamic system, to show how survival is achieved through adaptations. In Ford's paper, for instance, he does not show that any segment of the Tewa Eastern Pueblo population was in dire need of food, or that ritual distribution of food satisfied the dire need.

It is indeed alluring to conceptualize culture in any fashion that appeals to lawful relations unencumbered by human decisions and the weight of human history—including its tenacious rational and nonrational characteristics. But the nonrational models of cultural evolutionary theory, system ecology, and functionalism, in uncovering some very interesting relations and providing some interesting and nontrivial generalizations, also obscure much of the substance of culture, language, and environmental relations.

Because technology, subsistence economy, and economic organization were closely related in western North America, and because all subsistence economies were mixed, only a more comprehensive comparative examination is of value in analyzing the relations among those phenomena. Let us begin by assessing these phenomena and seeing in what ways technologies were similar and different. We shall treat each sphere somewhat independently, though that these overlap will be obvious. Briefly, (1) technology and material culture measures tools and their uses, techniques of food extraction and production, and other products and techniques by which people articulated with their environments, and these topics are treated in Chapter 5; (2) subsistence economy measures the contributions of various types of foods to the local diet, the manner and places in which the foods were procured, the ways in which economic goods were transported, and the manner and duration of food storage, and these topics are discussed in Chapter 6; and (3) economic organization measures the organization of extraction and production, including the division of labor by sex, age, task groups, and specialization; the reciprocity, distribution, gifting, and sharing of access to resources; and the ownership and the inheritance of property. The topics in this group are dealt with in Chapter 7.

Chapter 5

Technology

The material items and techniques that articulated people with their environments matched reasonably well with the distributions of environments. But the physiographic, climatic, and biotic environments of the tribes did not stand in one-to-one relationships with their technologies. Figure 5-1, and Figure 5-2, which has been derived from it, demonstrate the closest pairs of associations of tribal technologies, and the geographical distributions of the branches.*

The specialized agricultural technology of the Pueblos, the aquatic animal and wood working technology of the inhabitants of the central and northern Northwest Coast, and the fishing and root-gathering technology of the Plateau tribes were more distinct than any of the more generalized gathering, hunting, and fishing technologies of California, Southern California, and the Great Basin, or mixed farming, gathering, and hunting technologies of the Southwest. The northwestern California cluster, for instance, was separated from the Northwest Coast tribes in Figure 5-1 because the northwestern Californians shared the balanophagy[†] technology and other technological items and techniques distributed widely among other tribes in California and Southern California. The River Yumans and Pimans, who practiced horticulture but who also fished and collected desert plants, were distinguished from the Pueblos and joined more closely to the Southern California gatherers.

---

*The branches for technology have been selected, arbitrarily, at the G coefficient of 50 or greater for cartographic representation in Figure 5-2.

[†] Acorn preparation and eating.

HUNTING TECHNOLOGY

Sea-Mammal Hunting

Sea-mammal hunting was highly specialized and developed most fully only in the central and northern Northwest Coast area. Successful sea-mammal hunting required harpoons, usually a large wooden boat to pursue the quarry unless rookeries were in coastal grottos, and great technical skill. Sea mammals were hunted by most tribes along the Northwest Coast, the Northern–Central California coast, and the Southern California coast. The most elaborate development of sea-mammal hunting occurred along the central and northern portions of the Northwest Coast. The most avid and successful sea-mammal hunters south of the Makah on the Olympic Peninsula were the Gabrieliño and Chumash of Southern California. The seafaring technology of the Southern Californians was different from the Northwest Coast forms in practically all respects, and undoubtedly developed independently of it, though the source of the detachable harpoon (toggle-headed) used by the Chumash and Gabrieliño is an enigma. The Northwest Coast versions of this kind of harpoon may have derived ultimately from the toggle-headed harpoons used in the Arctic more than 4,000 years ago. The complicated device probably diffused down the West Coast to northwestern California societies. Yet the device used by Chumash and Gabrieliño sea-mammal hunters may well have been invented independently in Southern California and may have been derived from a feature used on some arrows. These harpoons had single-barbed toggles with foreshafts inserted into heavier shafts. The Gabrieliño and Chumash seem to have hunted mostly small sea mammals, such as the

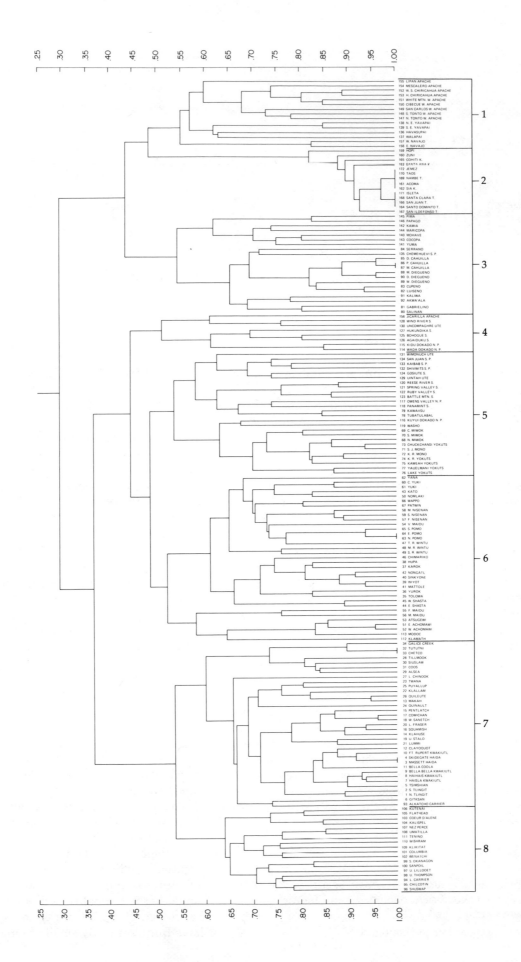

Figure 5-1 *Culture tree: 2. Groupings of tribal territories derived from G coefficients based on 46 variables (204 attributes) of technology and material culture.*

GROUP 1

155 Lipan Apache
154 Mescalero Apache
152 Warm Springs Chiricahua Apache
153 Huachuca Chiricahua Apache
151 White Mountain Western Apache
150 Cibecue Western Apache
149 San Carlos Western Apache
148 South Tonto Western Apache
147 North Tonto Western Apache
138 Northeast Yavapai
139 Southeast Yavapai
136 Havasupai
137 Walapai
157 Western Navajo
158 Eastern Navajo

GROUP 2

159 Hopi
160 Zuni
165 Cochiti Keres
163 Santa Ana Keres
172 Jemez
170 Taos
169 Nambe Tewa
161 Acoma
162 Sia Keres
171 Isleta
168 Santa Clara Tewa
166 San Juan Tewa
164 Santo Domingo Keres
167 San Ildefonso Tewa

GROUP 3

145 Pima
146 Papago
142 Kamia
144 Maricopa
140 Mohave
143 Cocopa
141 Yuma
 84 Serraño
135 Chemehuevi Southern Paiute

85 Desert Cahuilla
86 Pass Cahuilla
87 Mountain Cahuilla
88 Mountain Diegueño
90 Desert Diegueño
89 Western Diegueño
83 Cupeño
82 Luiseño
91 Kaliwa
92 Akwa'ala
81 Gabrieliño
80 Salinan

GROUP 4

156 Jicarilla Apache
128 Wind River Shoshone
130 Uncompaghre Ute
127 Hukundika Shoshone
125 Bohogue Shoshone
126 Agaiduku Shoshone
115 Kidu-Dokado Northern Paiute
114 Wada-Dokado Northern Paiute

GROUP 5

131 Wimonuch Ute
134 San Juan Southern Paiute
133 Kaibab Southern Paiute
132 Shivwits Southern Paiute
124 Gosiute Shoshone
129 Uintah Ute
120 Reese River Shoshone
121 Spring Valley Shoshone
122 Ruby Valley Shoshone
123 Battle Mountain Shoshone
117 Owens Valley Northern Paiute
118 Panamint Shoshone
 79 Kawaiisu
 78 Tubatulabal
116 Kuyui-Dokado Northern Paiute
119 Washo
 69 Central Miwok
 70 Southern Miwok
 68 Northern Miwok
 73 Chuckchansi Yokuts
 71 San Joaquin Mono
 72 Kings River Mono

74 Kings River Yokuts
75 Kaweah Yokuts
77 Yauelmani Yokuts
76 Lake Yokuts

GROUP 6

62 Yana
60 Coast Yuki
61 Yuki
43 Kato
50 Nomlaki
66 Wappo
67 Patwin
58 Mountain Nisenan
59 Southern Nisenan
57 Foothill Nisenan
54 Valley Maidu
65 Southern Pomo
64 Eastern Pomo
63 Northern Pomo
47 Trinity River Wintu
48 McCloud River Wintu
49 Sacramento River Wintu
46 Chimariko
38 Hupa
37 Karok
42 Nongatl
40 Sinkyone
39 Wiyot
41 Mattole
36 Yurok
35 Tolowa
45 West Shasta
44 East Shasta
55 Foothill Maidu
56 Mountain Maidu
53 Atsugewi
51 East Achomawi
52 West Achomawi
113 Modoc
112 Klamath

GROUP 7

34 Galice Creek
32 Tututni
33 Chetco
28 Tillamook
30 Siuslaw
31 Coos
29 Alsea

27 Lower Chinook
23 Twana
25 Puyallup
22 Klallam
26 Quileute
13 Makah
24 Quinault
15 Pentlatch
17 Cowichan
18 West Sanetch
20 Lower Fraser
16 Squamish
14 Klahuse
19 Upper Stalo
21 Lummi
12 Clayoquot
10 Fort Rupert Kwakiutl
 4 Skidegate Haida
 3 Massett Haida
11 Bella Coola
 9 Bella Bella Kwakiutl
 8 Haihais Kwakiutl
 7 Haisla Kwakiutl
 5 Tsimshian
 2 Southern Tlingit
 1 Northern Tlingit
 6 Gitksan
93 Alkatcho Carrier

GROUP 8

106 Kutenai
105 Flathead
103 Coeur d'Alene
104 Kalispel
107 Nez Percé
108 Umatilla
111 Tenino
110 Wishram
109 Klikitat
101 Columbia
102 Wenatchi
 99 Southern Okanagon
100 Sanpoil
 97 Upper Lillooet
 98 Upper Thompson
 94 Lower Carrier
 95 Chilcotin
 96 Shuswap

fur-seal, and usually dispatched them on land with clubs; the toggle-headed harpoon seems to have been used primarily to catch sea-otters and large tuna (Landberg, 1965).

From the Haida to the Quinault, the Northwest Coast tribes that occupied the offshore islands and the blustery West Coast employed a sea-mammal harpoon (Map Cu-3, V-138), similar to those used by Arctic sea-mammal hunters, which had a detachable toggle head and to which were secured inflated floats to slow and track the quarry. Lines were also attached so that the catch could be hauled in. Eastern neighbors who lived on sheltered bays and inlets did

not generally use floats, and did not pursue the largest sea mammals either.

Floats were not attached to harpoons by other coastal tribes, from the Chinook on the Columbia River to the Western Diegueño near what is today the Mexico–United States border. Floats made it possible to hunt whales because the securing lines could swing free of the hunters when the diving whale tried to escape. Sea-mammal hunters south of the Olympic Peninsula simply held onto securing lines, hence they pursued only the smaller seals, sea-lions, dolphins, and porpoises. The Chinook, who were consummate traders, had firsthand knowledge of sea-mammal

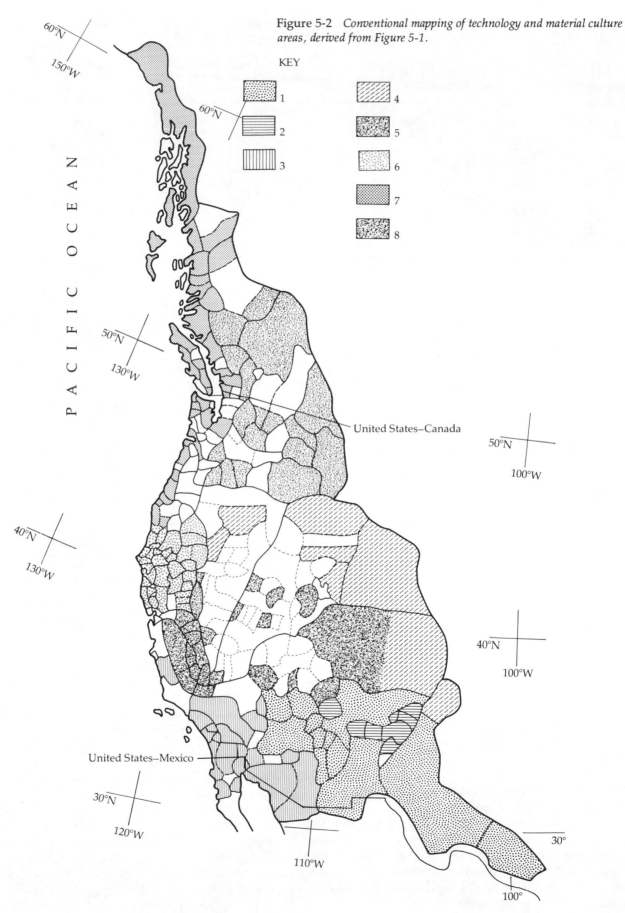

Figure 5-2 *Conventional mapping of technology and material culture areas, derived from Figure 5-1.*

KEY

1		4	
2		5	
3		6	
		7	
		8	

PACIFIC OCEAN

United States–Canada

United States–Mexico

hunting from their Salishan and Nootkan neighbors to the north, but they did not bother with game larger than seals and sea-lions unless these were washed ashore. It is likely that, south of the Columbia River, a good part of the sea-mammal hunting was conducted with clubs and spears during mating season. Animals could then be caught on the rocks and beaches of their rookeries.

Boats were required for successful sea-mammal hunting on the sea, and large boats that could hold lines, floats, harpoons, harpooners, and paddlers were required to hunt whales. Although a variety of dugout canoes were used throughout the Northwest Coast for (depending on the type of hull) fishing, sea-mammal hunting, transportation, and the like, south of the Olympic Peninsula dugout canoes were too small for successful whale hunting and were used instead to pursue smaller game. The Pomo used log rafts to pursue sea mammals on offshore rocks, but along the rest of the Northern and Central California coast the Penutian and Hokan speakers used balsa rafts fashioned from bundles of reeds and rushes.* They were used in all sheltered bays and wherever else water was navigable. Balsas were even used to paddle to kelp beds, if the beds were close to shore, either to hunt small sea mammals that foraged for fish there, or to catch the fish that ate the kelp or hid in the kelp beds (Map Cu-4, V-160).

Stands of redwood or mixed redwood and cedar forests grew in California as far south as Monterey Bay, but tribes south of northwestern California used neither redwood nor cedar for boats. Cedar, in particular, can be worked into boats, boxes, and planks with a few tools and the controlled use of burning. The California groups did not possess the tools or the techniques for employing them that were necessary for a more thorough exploitation of the ocean resources in their territories. As was indicated earlier, the environment provided resources for oceangoing boats, but Californians along the central coast did not, in general, avail themselves of those resources and did not follow the practices of their northwestern California neighbors. Abundances of acorns and shellfish in California obviated seafaring lives.

Unlike their neighbors on the central California coast, the Chumash and Gabrieliño of the Southern California coast and islands made plank boats up to 30 feet long and 4½ feet wide. They were radically different from Northwest Coast dugout canoes. Pine, juniper, or even redwood and cedar (from driftwood logs) were used to make these planks, which were then overlapped and joined with cordage covered with asphaltum. The boats were large enough to accommodate whaling crews, but the Chumash and Gabrieliño did not hunt whales. They sought seals, sea-lions, dolphins, and porpoises, and they used their boats, lines, hooks, and baskets to fish for sardines, swordfish (*Xiphias gladius*), halibut, rockfishes (*Sebastodes* spp.), and kelp bass (*Paralabrax clathratus*), several species of pelagic schooling fish, including yellowtail, bonito, skipjack, and tuna (*Seriola dorsalis, Sarda lineolata, Katsuwonus pelamus,* and *Thunnus alalunga*), and other ocean fishes unavailable to Californians and Southern Californians who did not have wooden canoes.

Land-Mammal Hunting

Stalking with bow and arrows and lances was the dominant mode of hunting medium-sized and large game practically everywhere in western North America. Because all tribes used bows made from one piece of wood, with and without sinew backing, called self bows, maps are not necessary to show their distributions. There was some regional variation in bow manufacture: Western Apaches glued twisted fiber onto their bows, for instance, and Utes, Northern Shoshones, and some Plateau dwellers such as the Flathead made bow staves from sections of mountain-sheep horn. The Utes and Northern Shoshones, and the Flathead, who were the most successful big game hunters in western North America, traded their bows and bow materials with Plains tribes. Snares, nooses, and other small traps, which were used primarily to catch small game, but also to catch deer, were used by all tribes; so these devices, as was also true for bow and arrow, have not been given map representation.

Devices along which, or into which, land mammals were driven were used by tribes in all areas but the Northwest Coast and the Southwest. Impounds, fences, and the like were the only means of successful hunting of antelopes, rabbits, and even invertebrates, such as crickets, that moved in herds or swarms, or that were spread out widely through the sagebrush and shadscale in the arid regions. Stationary fences made of stones, brush, sticks, logs, and whatever else was available were used in antelope and rabbit drives to channel the movements of the animals toward hunters who could dispatch them with clubs or spears, or into enclosures where hunters could use bows and arrows, clubs, or other objects to kill them. Sometimes antelopes and larger game, such as bison,

---

*Balsa means, of course, "raft," not the lightweight wood of *Ochroma lagopus*, which is not native to North America.

were driven over cliffs or into water. When driven into water, animals were pursued by hunters. Among the Klamath, for instance, women used canoes to pursue deer that had been driven into the lakes of the hunting territory.

Portable nets were used, especially in the Great Basin, in central California, and in parts of the Plateau, primarily to ensnare rabbits driven toward them in communal hunts (Map Cu-5, V-139). Crickets, locusts, and grasshoppers were driven into trenches and natural gulleys; once caught, they were roasted.

The widely varying techniques employed to drive animals in communal hunts throughout western North America were not used equally throughout all culture areas. Southwestern farmers and desert dwellers had access to a modest amount of game and, perhaps as a corollary, used few devices in their drives. In the Southwest it was a common practice for entire communities, under the direction of a leader and assistant, to encircle the animals, which were then driven toward the center of the encirclement. These communal rabbit drives and deer hunts were staged semiannually, if not more frequently, and held considerable ceremonial significance for many of the Pueblo and Piman groups. Devices would have made these drives more efficient. The southwesterners knew of rock impounds and nets for drives but seldom used them. Although deer dances, rabbit chants, and other communal rituals were staged with care, Southwesterners made meat a very small part of their diets, relying more on agricultural products and wild plants.

The Northwest Coast people, though they knew of many techniques and devices employed in game drives, used few of them. Fishing produced great abundances; small mammals were scarce, so not worth driving; and the medium-sized and large game animals throughout the area browsed in small groups in the dense forest undergrowth, making drives difficult. Above the 51° N. Latitude there were few species of medium-sized and large game animals.

Use of devices for drives, pitfalls, and deadfalls was more extensive in the northeastern sections of the Plateau, northern California, and the eastern Great Basin. All of these mountainous areas were bordered by grasslands. In the western pine forests and adjacent grasslands the varieties and amounts of game were large and the techniques used by individual hunters and communal hunting groups were more elaborate. Conditions favored hunting more in these areas than anywhere else in western North America (Map Cu-6, V-144; Map Cu-7, V-145).

Pitfalls, which were concealed traps of any sort into which animals fell, were sparsely used on the northern or central Northwest Coast; the most northern groups did not use them at all, even though pitfalls would have been efficient on deer runs. Nor were they used in Southern California or most of the Southwest, where ground and tree cover was sparse and game was scarce. Furthermore, sandstone beneath the thin soil cover of the Southwest and the hard clay soils of Southern California precluded pitfalls.

Deadfalls, or traps made of weights which fell on animals and either pinned or killed them when they tripped a mechanism, were used almost everywhere. Deadfalls were easier to build than pitfalls—which had to be excavated—and logs, stones, or both could be used for weights in deadfalls. Thus use of deadfalls evened out environmental differences between forested and treeless areas. In the Great Basin, Southern California, and the Southwest, timber was sparse and most deadfalls were made from rocks. In the Northwest and the Plateau, timber was abundant and logs were used.

Hunting with deadfalls and pitfalls, like stalking, was an individual or perhaps small group undertaking. The tribes most dependent on game tended to use tools and techniques that could be employed by individual hunters, such as stalking, pitfalls, deadfalls, snares, nooses, decoys, bows, clubs, and spears; but they acquired more animal protein from the coordinated hunting efforts of larger groups of hunters than from individual pursuits. In areas such as the Great Basin proper, the Southwest, the Northwest Coast, and most of California, where land-mammal hunting did not provide dominant contributions to diets, individual techniques were the principal hunting methods. Land-mammal hunting was not the dominant means of procuring food in either the most arid regions or in the rain forests.

Birds, especially waterfowl, were hunted throughout the coastal regions, and along the watercourses of the inland flyways. Among coastal tribes, bird hunters went out on quiet bays at night and threw nets over unsuspecting water fowl. Another technique was to erect nets and, by frightening the birds, to cause them to fly into the nets. In the interior, especially in the central part of California and the Great Basin, decoys were made from tule rushes and bird skins, to lure birds which were then caught with nets or bows.

FISHING TECHNOLOGY

The vast tonnages of fish that lived among the kelp beds off the Pacific shore, and the even greater tonnages of salmon, steelhead, sturgeon, eulachon, smelt, and herring that entered the tidewaters along the coast, were extracted by a wide variety of techniques, from poisoning to trapping. Native suckers, whitefish, and trout abounded in the ancient lakes of the Great Basin, and along the Rio Grande and Colorado River in the Southwest, and techniques were also developed to catch fish in these regions. Although there were exceptions, the greater the amount of fish available to a tribe, the greater the number of fish-extracting techniques the tribe possessed. Indian fishermen were wise, however, and usually relied on the techniques that brought in the most fish with the least effort. For example, on some tidewater flats, Salishan Indians of the central Northwest Coast merely constructed rock impounds and collected fish caught behind when the tide went out; and in parts of the Great Basin and Southwest, where waters were slow and fish concentrations high, poisoning techniques were frequently used.

The greatest number of fish were taken along the Northwest Coast, followed by California, and in these regions nets, traps, and weirs were the principal devices used to haul them in (Map Cu-8, V-142; Map Cu-9, V-143). On the other hand, tribes in the most arid regions, unless they lived near waters abundant with fish, as did the River Yumans and some Eastern Pueblos of the Southwest and a few Great Basin lake dwellers, did not possess any of these devices. Hook and line were the least efficient techniques for extracting fish from the ocean but, with the exception of the fish harpoons used by Gabrieliño and Chumash, were about the only tools available for the job. Along parts of the coast, especially where sea-mammal hunting dominated, trolling with hook and line for large fish such as halibut or tuna also was a well developed technique. These aspects of a maritime adaptation most probably occurred independently in the central and northern parts of the Northwest Coast and in Southern California.

Small hand nets made from plant fibers were known and used by all but a few fishermen. Gill nets and seines were restricted more to use in the dense fish populations of California, the Plateau, and the Northwest Coast. Seines, which were long nets with sinkers attached to one edge so that they could be held vertically, were often long enough to be stretched across an entire spawning stream. The nets could then be drawn tight, encircling the fish moving up the stream. Hand nets or dip nets, the latter hung from a sturdy wooden arm, were frequently used in conjunction with weirs. They were a major fishing device for Plateau fishermen, who used them at the natural falls that occurred along the interior rivers. The fishermen would position themselves on rocks or platforms and net salmon and steelhead as they at-

tempted to jump over the falls to reach their spawning grounds.

Weirs, which were part of the fishing technology of the fish-rich areas, were barriers made of rocks, latticework, brush, or anything else capable of stopping fish from moving, but not so tightly made as to stop the passage of water. Rock impounds constructed in straight lines or semicircles on tidal flats only required people to go out and pick fish up after the tide went out. Along rivers and streams, dip nets, hand nets, scoop nets, or spears were often used to catch fish at weirs. Walkways were often constructed atop the weirs across Northwest Coast streams, and fish were hauled in with dip nets, spears, or leisters by people on the walkways.

Traps attached to weirs, which caught fish migrating up rivers on their spawning runs, such as salmon and steelhead on the coast and suckers and trout in the Great Basin, were especially effective devices. Indeed, traps woven from sticks and reeds were so efficient and energy-saving that their use throughout the Northwest Coast and in California accounted for the extraction of most fish along the rivers in these regions.

Fish spears were used in conjunction with weirs. There were two types in wide usage. The leister had a three-pronged head; to each prong was attached a barbed point. The impaled fish was usually caught by at least two barbs, and this made it much easier to land a fighting fish, especially salmon and steelhead, which weighed from 10 to 70 pounds. South of the Columbia River, only simple one-pointed spears were used (Map Cu-10, V-144), though a three-pronged spear has been reported as used by the Gabrieliños.

It is plausible that the early adaptation to riverine life made by Penutians, even those along the southern Oregon coast, preceded the development of the leister. Use of the leister did not diffuse south of the Columbia River, and among all fishing tribes beyond the central and northern Northwest Coast only the Plateau Penutians and Plateau Salishans acquired leisters. These devices probably entered the Plateau through central Northwest Coast contacts. On the other hand, the fish harpoon with two detachable points, gill nets, seines capable of being stretched across rivers, and basketry traps were all spread throughout the fish-rich areas of California wherever Penutians located. Most of these items were also used by the non-Penutian groups in the northern areas of California, who added the less complex single-pointed fish harpoon to their inventory (Map Cu-11, V-145). The Penutians did not use the single-pointed device, preferring the more effective double point, which their ancestors may have introduced to the region.

Just as the California Penutians knew about single-pointed fish harpoons but did not use them, it is probably significant that most of the Plateau tribes did not use the double-pointed harpoon, even though they knew about them. Throughout the central and northern Northwest Coast and along the Middle Columbia and northward in the Plateau, the leister was used more widely and effectively than the fish harpoon, double or single pointed. The leister was probably adopted on the Northwest Coast after Penutians had moved into the Lower Columbia drainage and into California. Adoption of leisters by Penutians on the Middle Columbia may have been important to the spread of Plateau Penutians upriver along the Middle Columbia, where impaling fish that attempted to jump the falls was a major extractive technique. Single-pointed harpoons made from reeds were employed on the Southern California coast, but here, trolling and use of hook and line were of equal importance for ocean fishing (kelp bass and bottom fish), while leisters were of considerable importance for procuring spawning steelhead along the rivers.

Herring rakes were used along the Northwest Coast to spear and rake herring and sardine out of the dense schools in which they traveled. This ingenious device was not used outside the area, though gaffs—shafts with a hooked end—were used in a raking fashion by some tribes along the Northern California coast with the intention of "gaffing" fish.

Hook and line were used not only for trolling off the coastal shores, but also in lakes and rivers. Except among the specialized sea-mammal hunters of the Northwest Coast and the maritime people of Southern California, trolling and shore casting did not produce big yields of fish, yet the technology for this kind of fishing had wide distribution. For example, composite fishhooks, made of several pieces joined together, were used not only throughout the Northwest Coast but also throughout the Plateau, and simpler barbed and curved fishhooks were used throughout the Great Basin, central California, and Southern California. On the Columbia River system, inland tribes as far west as the Bohogue Shoshones on the Snake River used hook and line to catch the enormous white sturgeon, which weighs several hundred pounds. In such instances, hook and line were certainly worth the patience expended to catch fish.

There is no doubt but that the wide variety of devices and techniques used to catch fish, which included even attracting them with fire or poisoning still bodies of water, underscores the importance of these animals to natives in most tribal territories where they were available, but all groups did not extract equal proportions of fish resources relative to the local abundance of fish.

Shellfishes

Shellfish collection required very little technology—only a stick to pry some species loose from rocks or to dig them out of the soft mud flats and sands, and baskets to carry them. Knowledge of the dangers of "red tide,"* which was fatal to many fish, and which contaminated shellfish, was fundamental. Natives dived for certain beautiful shells that were valued as prestige economy items and used for units of measure. *Dentalium* spp. (tusk shells), *Haliotis* spp. (abalone), and *Olivella* spp. (olive shells) in particular were collected through diving because shells retrieved with living organisms in them had more luster than those that did not. Clams, mussels, and crabs of a wide variety were collected along the entire coast and in all the tidewater regions of western North America.

GATHERING TECHNOLOGY

Simple extraction of wild plants either codominated with some other food source, or was the single most important source of food among most of the tribes of California, Southern California, the Great Basin, and the Southwest. There can be little doubt but that the adaptations in all of these areas were built upon ancient and generalized subsistence economies, which anthropologists usually refer to as "archaic." That is not to say that the tribes in all of these areas were the progeny of the archaic extractors of the same areas. Parts of the Great Basin, for instance, were occupied by gatherers for more than 10,000 years, and Uto-Aztecans probably moved into the Great Basin from southeastern California beginning no more than 2,000 years ago, eventually replacing many farmers in the eastern parts of the Basin.

---

*"Red tide" occurs when dinoflagellates, tiny plants in plankton (usually *Gymnodinium*), proliferate and disrupt the balance of sea life. When populations are especially dense, they give the ocean water a red color; animals in the marine food chains are killed and humans eating contaminated sea animals are made ill by red tides.

Penutians probably entered California with a rather specific pine or hemlock forest riverine economy; in all likelihood, after contacting other archaic cultures already in this region, they became more generalized in their new localities in the Central Valley and the tidewater areas of California, where acorns and shellfish abounded. In general, the extractive economies of the arid West, though based on rather modest arrays of tools, were highly developed and effective at the period of European contact. They seem to have been that way for precursor groups for several thousand years.

For the most part, wild-plant extraction required few skills, few tools, and practically no controls of the environment. Occasionally, the gathering of wild plants did require some environmental management: in California, fire was used intermittently to inhibit undergrowth and to encourage grasses and oak forests and woodlands; in parts of the Great Basin wild seeds were irrigated; and on the Colorado River wild seeds were sown and then irrigated.

In the Northwest Coast and the Plateau, natives predominantly collected roots, nuts, and berries; south of the Plateau, the foregoing items as well as tons of seeds were collected each year; and gatherers who ranged south of the 41° N. Latitude were likely to collect cactus and mescal hearts. In the transitional zones, between the Great Basin and the hot deserts, cacti were added to the plant fare. The dichotomy between those who collected seeds and those who did not is of interest and probably can be accounted for in a simple way: seed gathering was tedious work and seeds were not collected when other plants were abundant. Northwest Coast residents had access to grass and water-lily seeds but did not collect them; likewise, Plateau residents had access to many varieties of bunchgrass seeds on the loess soil of the Palouse Prairies and in mountain meadows but did not collect them. Of all tribes of the Northwest Coast and the Plateau, only the Wenatchi and Sanpoil, in the Middle Columbia semidesert, and the Klamath and Modoc, adjacent to California and the Great Basin, collected seeds from grasses and water-lilies.

The division in the utilization of plants between the Plateau and Northwest Coast tribes and the tribes of the four southern regions is in part a reflection of riverine and maritime adaptations, and abundant root grounds in the river valleys of the north. Roots and fishes were sufficiently abundant to obviate extensive and tedious seed gathering. On the other hand, the plant-collecting technology, including the seed-gathering techniques of the southern regions, stemmed from a 10,000-year-old tradition in the arid Great Basin. Between 8500 BC and the time of European contact knowledge of a huge number of edible plants of many species accrued through successive generations and diffused with successive occupations, throughout the entire fish- and game-sparse regions east of the Sierra and west of the Rockies. Plant collection of many types, including seeds, became integrated with the hunting of deer, shellfish, and fish in Southern California and California, and with the hunting of large game in the Rockies. The protracted development of wild-plant extraction techniques for seeds, leaves, nuts, roots, and berries must have been correlated with movements of gatherers, many millennia ago, from the Great Basin into California and from the Great Basin into the Southwest. More recently, movements of Uto-Aztecans from northern Mexico into Southern California and from Southern California throughout the Great Basin again spread seed-gathering subsistence economies through the region. The Plateau and Northwest Coast did not share equally in this long process, and inhabitants of these northern regions had less use for seed gathering than the southern groups, even through Northerners did use wild plants.

In California, Southern California, the Great Basin, and the Southwest at the time of contact with Europeans, seed beaters, grinders, basketry winnowing trays, parching baskets, and other implements used in seed-gathering technology had become fundamental in subsistence economies. These implements had their origins in prehistoric periods beginning more than 10,000 years ago. They probably reached nearly complete development by 5,000 years ago, or about the time that the progenitors of Northwest Coast tribes were beginning their wet forest and riverine adaptations.

None of the preceding is meant to suggest that wild plants were not important to the northern peoples. Roots, berries, and nuts contributed from one-third to nearly one-half of the diets of the majority of Plateau tribes, but systematic extraction of grass seeds could have pushed the percentage of wild plants in diets as well as the total plant food consumption much higher. However, the seed-gathering traditions were not picked up in the North even though seed gatherers such as the Klamath and the Northern Paiutes made frequent contacts with the Middle Columbia River tribes, and contacts between seed gathering Northern Shoshones and Upper Columbia River tribes were also frequent.

So far, we have focused only on the importance of seed gathering among southern tribes and the absence of seed gathering among northern tribes: that this is but a single example of many dichotomous relations between tribal areas and available food, others of which could also be focused on, almost goes without saying, yet the wide variety of food plants in the total biomass of each of the six culture areas of western North America is often overlooked. Many kinds of plants, perhaps more than 250, were collected and used by the inhabitants of western North America for food, drink, medicine, or narcotics. Barrows (1900) noted 60 food plants and 28 medicinal, narcotic, and stimulant plants used by a single tribe—the Cahuilla of Southern California. Castetter and Opler (1936) noted more than 100 plants used by the Mescalero and Chiricahua Apaches of the Southwest, and their listing was not complete. Bye (1972) studied 49 plants used by Southern Paiutes, and Smith (1972) analyzed 29 plants used for medicinal purposes alone among the Western Shoshones. In this book there has been no attempt to list all the plants which were known to be used because the number was so large, but the principal plants in the diets mentioned by leading scholars for the tribes in each area have been included in our sample.

Seed Collecting and Preparation

Seeds were knocked from plants with the use of woven basketry seed-beaters by all seed collectors except the Apacheans, Northern Shoshones, and Utes, who beat seed-bearing plants with bundles of sticks. Some Southwesterners used both sticks and basketry devices. Seeds were almost universally beaten into large, conical burden baskets. The sedentary River Yuman farmers, who also harvested seeds along the river bottoms near their residences, used large pottery containers for storage in addition to basketry containers, while the mobile, mountain-dwelling Utes, Northern Shoshones, and Apacheans used hide containers or both basketry and hide containers. It is significant that Utes, Northern Shoshones, and Apacheans not only relied less on grasses than their western neighbors, and used sticks rather than basketry devices to beat seeds, but they also had access to many hides, either through hunting or through regular contacts with Plains people who predominantly used hides for containers. This was especially true for Utes, Northern Shoshones, Jicarilla Apaches, and Mescalero Apaches (Map Cu-12, V-146).

Before seeds were stored or eaten they were parched, usually by placing seeds in a container of glowing coals and shaking it. In Northern California and the Great Basin, seed parching was done mainly in basketry containers, whereas in the Southwest and Southern California, pottery containers predominated. In the Southwest the use of pottery for parching was correlated with agriculture* and was introduced to the region about two thousand years ago, after baskets had been used to parch wild seeds for several millennia. Pottery containers were the only kind used for parching seeds by the Pueblos, the River Yumans, and Southern California Yumans; both pottery and basketry containers were used by Pimans and the Southern California Uto-Aztecans (Map Cu-13, V-158).

After parching, the seeds were milled between stones. One stone (the mano) was held in the hand and ground against the other, a basinal or flat slab (the metate) on which the seeds were placed. The round or oval-shaped milling stone used throughout the Great Basin and California is the earliest type found in the prehistoric West and was probably reintroduced from California by the Great Basin Shoshoneans when they entered the latter region (Map Cu-14, V-156). Rectangloid milling stones date from the beginning of agriculture in the Southwest and were of a more recent type. In the Pueblos, a third type was used, the stones being set in bins or troughs, but in other communities they were portable. Among the Yumans in Southern California and the Southwest, and among Pimans in the Southwest, two or even all three types of milling stones were used. The use of the round or oval form among the Yumans is interesting, because it most probably antedated agriculture, but the rectangular stones clearly date from the beginnings of agriculture. Whether Uto-Aztecans brought a tradition of using rectangular stones with them when they entered Southern California or learned to make them from the Yumans

---

*In this book we have defined agriculture as a complex of techniques used in the production of plants for food or for other purposes. That complex included preparing the soil, planting the seeds, weeding and tilling the soil, harvesting the crop, and storing a seed crop and a crop for consumption (eating, drinking, smoking, weaving). Water management through irrigation or diversion techniques was part of the agricultural complex as we have defined it here. Agriculture has been distinguished from incipient horticulture. Several societies watered and collected wild seeds, and some also were known to have planted wild seeds, but they did not practice other techniques in the agricultural complex. Whether for the production of food crops or nonfood crops, this practice has been called incipient horticulture. The agricultural complex in western North America is correlated with other features, such as true loom weaving, rectangloid milling stones, pottery, and the contruction of rectangular stone-walled houses, all of which originated in Mexico.

is still undecided, though it seems increasingly probable that they adopted both the rectangular milling stone for seed grinding and the manufacture of pottery for parching, boiling, and storage from Yumans.

Seeds and other plant foods were boiled over direct fires wherever people had pottery. The principal pottery area in western North America was the Southwest. Nevertheless, some crude pottery was also produced by tribes in Southern California, and in parts of Northern California and the Great Basin (Map Cu-15, V-152). On the other hand, stone boiling, the dropping of hot stones into baskets of water, was practiced by everyone but the Yuman speakers, the Pueblos, and the Pima and Papago, and underscores the long agricultural tradition and relative sedentariness of each of these groups. The Uto-Aztecans beyond the Southwest and the Apacheans within the Southwest all made pottery but were never as competent potters as the Pueblos, Pimans, and Yumans, and usually were more mobile as well. As a rule of thumb, the greater the mobility of a people, the less practical it was to use ceramic pots as containers: quite simply, pots broke. Nevertheless, pottery was used for boiling by the Southwest Apacheans, the Uto-Aztecans outside of the Southwest, and by the Yokuts, who were California Penutian neighbors of the Uto-Aztecans, but it was never used exclusively for this purpose. On the Northwest Coast, at least for large feasts, dugout canoes were filled with water and hot stones were dropped into them for cooking.

Some of the technological items required for collecting and processing seeds were also used in other forms of collecting, most notably as burden baskets and as utensils for boiling. Only a few additional implements were required for collecting nuts, berries, fruits, and roots. Except roots, most of these foods were collected by hands; a pole was all that was required for bending branches or for knocking nuts from the higher branches in trees. Even then, men often climbed the trees and shook the limbs, thus dispensing with the need for poles. Roots were dug with a long pointed stick (Map Cu-16, V-147).

Root Collecting

The Plateau tribes were the ultimate root collectors, and they used crutch-handled sticks, as did many of their neighbors on the Northwest Coast. Many of the well-watered valleys of the Plateau and Northwest Coast were rich with edible roots, and the crutch-handled stick, which formed a Y-shape under the

arm, was a better tool for digging large quantities of roots than the straight-handled stick, since it provided support while allowing the digger to apply force from the shoulder and back. Some Plateau root grounds were so rich that a woman could dig a year's supply for her family in less than one week. The straight-handled stick was also used on the Northwest Coast, sometimes for digging roots but more often for prying shellfishes from rocks.

Extraction and Preparation of Nuts, Pods, Berries, and Fruit

Poles used to knock acorns from trees were employed wherever pine nuts, pine seeds, juniper berries, acorns, or mesquite and screwbean pods were important in local diets. Thus, poles were used throughout California, Southern California, the Great Basin, and the Southwest (Map Cu-17, V-148).

Mescal blades were used to cut the leaves from agave (mescal) and yucca by most Southwesterners and some Great Basin people residing in mescal and yucca regions, but not by Puebloans. Cactus tongs, two sticks or splints of wood bound together to serve as tongs to secure and remove cactus fruit, were used by most tribes in the Southwest and Southern California.

As is apparent from our survey, wild-plant gathering and processing technology relied on tools that were little more than sticks, and on receptacles and milling stones, all of the utmost simplicity. Even ingenious tools such as cactus tongs were no more than simple grasping devices. Such basic items were used for many millennia in western North America. Subsequently, many of them became modified during a period of perhaps three thousand years as the grand invention of agriculture spread from a wild plant-gathering base in Mexico, gradually to replace subsistence economies based on the extraction of wild plants in the Southwest.

The task of acorn preparation led to several refinements in gathering technology. Although acorns were used by most tribes who had access to them, in California a balanophagy technology developed that allowed for rapid processing of the acorns. Acorns required leaching of tannic acid from the nut. Grinding the acorns speeded the leaching process; the pulverizing was done with stone pestles in large wooden mortars carved into the sides of logs. Once the nuts had been reduced to meal, the acorn meal was placed in a sand basin and water was poured over the meal to leach it. An earlier leaching technique was to submerge acorns in mud for about one year. Leaching by submersion in mud was used only in the regions of the Northwest Coast and Plateau that possessed oak trees with edible nuts. There were few oaks in Klamath territory, but the Klamath gathered and pulverized hazel nuts. It is likely that the Klamath taught the pulverizing technique to the Klikitat, who inhabited an area near The Dalles (Map Cu-18, V-153).

Other methods of preparation were also used. The simplest method was merely to roast the acorns. In some places, acorns were eaten raw, regardless of the tannic acid. Both methods were used on Vancouver Island, in the Great Basin beyond the eastern slopes of the Sierra, and in the Southwest. It is fair to say that acorns were not consumed in great quantity by any group that relied solely on roasting or that ate them raw. Still another method was used by the Chiricahua Apaches, who boiled acorns in lye, a technique used also in the Great Lakes and eastern Plains regions. Whether the Apaches independently discovered the process is not known. The most effective technology for processing acorns was pulverization, mentioned earlier. It developed in the area in which oaks dominated the sclerophyll forests, woodlands, and chaparral. The pulverizing–soaking–draining invention, which greatly speeded the leaching process, probably increased the importance of acorns in the diets of Californians and Southern Californians, and may well have originated at the time the Miwoks and Yokuts moved into the foothills, mountains, and valleys of the San Joaquin drainage area. The inhabitants of central California's San Joaquin drainage used the technique exclusively, as did the Southern Californians. Indeed, alternatively, the technique could have been developed in Southern California, from a similar technique used for grinding corn by River Yumans. Wherever it developed, acorn pulverization must have spread rapidly and increased the importance of acorns in diets.

Various forms of wooden food mortars were used. In California, these were hollowed into the sides of logs. The wooden food mortars used in the western Great Basin along the eastern border of California, in Southern California, and in the River Yuman area were hollowed into the ends of logs. The two mortar types probably had different origins. Southern Californians and the Yumans and Pimans of the Southwest used their mortars to grind mesquite and screwbean. Plateau people, whose end- and side-hollowed wooden mortars were equipped with handles, used mortars primarily for crushing berries, and seem to have developed this variant themselves (Map Cu-19, V-155).

Some of the techniques used to prepare plant foods were also used for meats, and it is plausible that the techniques were extended to meat preparation from their uses for plants. For instance, stone food mortars made from portable slabs or blocks were used throughout northern California and the Plateau to pulverize fish and to pound roots. Upper Columbia people, the Utes, and the Northern Shoshones all used them to pound slices of venison, and among Utes and Northern Shoshones bison, into pemmican. Portable hollowed stone mortars were used for plant foods, including acorns, in Central and Southern California, parts of the Great Basin, and by some Apacheans in the Southwest (Map Cu-20, V-154).

Meat Preparation

Fish or mammal meat was prepared for storage by slicing and drying, or by pulverizing and drying. Even when dried, putrefaction could occur unless the meats were frozen or constantly aired in the sun. In Southern California, the Southwest, and part of the central Great Basin—all places where game was sparse and relatively unimportant as a food source—meat was sun- and air-dried only. Inasmuch as a hot sun usually shone, and since except at rabbit and antelope drives the quarry was usually consumed before putrefaction set in, a temporary technique such as this worked. In California, the Northwest Coast, and the Plateau, fish were hauled in by the ton during four or five months of the year, precipitation was heavy, and overcast days were frequent, so a more permanent means of curing was needed, and fish were smoke-dried, or smoke-dried and pulverized. Smoking and pulverizing were also used on mammal meats, extensively so among Northern Shoshones, Utes, and Upper Columbia Plateau people (Map Cu-21, V-157).

FARMING TECHNOLOGY

At the time of contact with Europeans maize (corn) was cultivated by all Southwestern tribes, albeit minimally by some Pai speakers and Apachean speakers (Map Cu-22, V-149). The oldest farming traditions in the Southwest unquestionably developed from techniques for cultivating maize (*Zea mays*), beans (*Phaseolus* spp.), squashes (*Cucurbita* spp.), cotton (*Gossypium hirsutum*), and many other domesticated plants all of which were dispersed from places of origin in Mexico. Rectangloid bin-shaped milling stones, pottery, and stone architecture were all related features in a cultural "package" that diffused north to the Southwest. Nevertheless, four separate prehistoric farming traditions can be identified, known as Fremont, Anasazi, Mogollon, and Hohokam, and these overlapped in the region where they developed, from northern Sonora in Mexico to northern Utah, and from eastern New Mexico to eastern Nevada. The Hohokam tradition, in northern Sonora and southern Arizona, appears to have been brought into that area intact, but the other farming traditions appear to have developed *in situ*, at bases previously used predominantly for gathering, following the utilization of domestic crops, pottery techniques, and the like.

By the middle of the sixteenth century the agricultural communities of western North America had contracted to several Western Pueblos (Hopi, Zuni, Acoma, Laguna) predominantly dependent on seeps, springs, and wash-offs for water; a few Eastern Pueblos (Nambe, Santa Clara, San Juan, San Ildefonso, Isleta, Picuris, Taos, Pecos) dependent on the Rio Grande and the Pecos River; Jemez Pueblo and a few Eastern Keres Pueblos (Sia, Santa Ana, Santo Domingo, Cochiti) dependent on irregularly running western tributaries of the Rio Grande, seeps, springs, and wash-offs. There were several Pima and Papago farming communities on the Salt and Gila Rivers and on some less predictable streams farther south, in southern Arizona and northern Sonora. There were also several groups of Yuman farmers on the Colorado River—the Mohave on the north, to the Cocopa on the Colorado River delta in the south. The Walapai, Havasupai, Yavapai, and Apacheans were less ambitious farmers than the Pueblos, Pimans, and River Yumans. The Apacheans were, of course, recent interlopers.

Critical to all farming enterprises in the hot, arid Southwest was water, and all tribes except some of the Apacheans perfected some form of irrigation for their local areas to control its use (Map Cu-23, V-150). The Eastern Pueblos practiced farming with an irrigation system of canals, dams, ditches, and gravity flow; the Eastern Keres groups used dams, ditches, and terraces; and Western Pueblos used dams and terraces. The Pimans, including the Papago wherever conditions permitted, used irrigation systems consisting of main canals, which were much larger than the canals of the Eastern Pueblos, side ditches, and auxilliary wing-fences (portable fences erected so as to be wide at the mouth where run-offs could be collected and narrow at the exit so the water could be directed), dams, and dykes to control water after each of two floods every year. The Pimans planted two crops per year, to coincide with the flooding. The River Yumans, who also received two floods each year, employed no techniques other than flood irrigation and capillary water action and planted but one crop per year, even though they knew of the Piman practice of digging a major canal from a river and then digging several side ditches to control the flow of water to a field. The River Yumans gathered fish and the highly storable mesquite and screwbean pods more extensively than the Pimans, and relied less on cultivatable crops.

The Pais used ditches or natural flood-irrigation techniques, and the Apacheans, if they employed any water control techniques at all, controlled natural flood waters with wing-fences, dykes, and dams (Navajo), or used ditches and obstructions to divert water (some Western Apaches). The Apacheans evidently learned most of their impoundment and diversion techniques from the Western Pueblos, but never farmed so vigorously as those sedentary people.

Very few hand tools were required for the intensive horitcultural methods of the Southwestern farmers (Map Cu-24, V-151). Principal among them was an all-purpose tool for digging, planting, and weeding. Most Apacheans employed a simple pointed stick, identical to a wild-plant-gatherer's digging stick, for all purposes. The Western Navajos followed the Pueblo practice of leaving a branch stub near the base of the stock so that the stick could be pushed down deeply into the soil with the foot. End-bladed tools for excavating ditches and building dams, and swordlike tools for weeding were additional tools used by Pimans, some Yumans, and Pueblos. Hopis is also used an antler rake.

River Yumans, Pimans, some Pais, and some Navajos all planted in the rich alluvium deposited by semiannual or annual floods on the plains adjacent to rivers and streams. Most other farmers in the Southwest dug deeply into the dry soil and planted independent clusters of maize, beans, and squashes every few feet.

As mentioned above, farm products were milled on rectangular stones and boiled in pottery containers. Inasmuch as the oval or round stones had been used to grind the hard seeds of desert and semidesert plants for thousands of years, the transition to grinding maize on rectangloid slabs or bins was simple. Maize was processed either into a gruel by boiling, or it was rolled into thin slabs of bread called *piki* which were fried on hot stones. Whereas wild seeds had been eaten in the gruel form, fried bread is associated with the advent of horticulture.

Structures for Food Storage

Farm produce was highly storable, in general, as were the acorns collected by Californians and all of the seeds, nuts, and pods collected in the desert.

Mesquite, screwbean, grass seeds and the like could be stored in the dry environments of desert regions for years. The quantities of storable food collected in the Great Basin generally did not make storage necessary beyond a few months or a year, but seed crops to be used in future planting in the Southwest were always stored for at least one year, if not for many more, and food crops, too, were stored for more than one year.

Because of the importance of the storability of food in the subsistence economy, that topic will be addressed in the following chapter. Here we shall examine how and where food was stored. Customs varied: the River Yumans of the Southwest and Southern California tribes, for example, used more types of storage places than other groups in western North America, and the tribes with the most durable foods tended in general to build special structures or special rooms as dominant places for storage (Map Cu-25, V-212).

Among the Pueblos, food was sun-dried and stored in a separate room in each family's house, or, in earlier times, before Apacheans and Utes penetrated the region, in separate granaries (small stone-walled rooms formed by enclosing an area beneath a rock overhang). The dry climate allowed food and seed crops to be stored a long time in these dark rooms, where rats rather than rot posed the greatest threat.

The River Yumans and Pimans, and tribes of Southern California, who stored food in large pots, beneath overhangs, in shade houses (four corner posts supporting a roof), inside houses, and in pits, predominantly erected wooden platforms in these storage places and placed extremely large coiled baskets on them. The baskets were filled with mesquite, screwbean, acorns, pine seeds and, among the River Yumans and Pimans, maize, beans, amaranth, and other farm products. The coiled baskets were often five or six feet high, so large that women stood inside them to weave the coils.

The more mobile Eastern Apaches, Pai, and peoples of the Great Basin used rock shelters, caves, and pits for storage, and the Western Apaches used these places and shade houses. The Plateau people, who were also rather mobile during part of the year, used rock shelters and caves, but also used either platforms in their houses or special scaffolds on which they placed smoked mammal and fish meat so as to keep the meat dry, well-aired, out of the reach of carnivores and omnivores, and frozen during the winter.

The more sedentary people of California stored their considerable acorn crops in tall, cylindrical, twined baskets that were propped up with poles outside their houses. They also stored many foods in baskets inside their houses.

Along the Northwest Coast from Cape Mendocino to Yakutat Bay, most food was stored on platforms or hung from rafters inside the house. In some areas of extremely high rainfall, such as Cape Flattery, at the northwest tip of the Olympic Peninsula, the smoked meat was hung from rafters in the house and roof slats were removed so that the meat would be aired whenever skies cleared. Rot, which set in quickly in this region, made it impractical to store food in caves, shelters, or pits, but watertight boxes within the house were used for storing oils, water fowl, sea-mammal blubber, and certain other foods.

HOUSING

During at least one season of the year most Indians in western North America moved from permanent to temporary residences. Very frequently this entailed building one or more temporary houses. The more often people moved, the less probable it was that these temporary houses would be very substantial, and the more probable that they would be either portable structures, such as the hide tipis used by the easternmost Utes, Shoshones, and Apaches, or temporarily occupied lean-tos, caves, rock shelters, or brush structures. The variety of houses throughout the West in general is awesome, and the variety in California alone is especially remarkable. Although similarities are discernible among California houses, for instance (all variations seem to have been produced by making small changes in a basic form), the variations are distinct enough to form types, based on clear historical and often environmentally influenced differences. Essentially, most structures in western North America had simple circular bases and either domed or conical roofs. The more permanent structures had excavated semisubterranean floors, or tunnel entrances, or both. The correlation of these features suggests they are variations on very ancient patterns, and divergences away from these features are worth special attention.

Housing in one or another area of western North America appears to have been influenced by such different forces as (a) diffusion of a "package" of agricultural and agriculture-related traits from Mexico; (b) a wet-forest environment and the technological skills to cope with it; and (c) degree of sedentariness (the more sedentary a group, the more probable that its houses would be substantial and relatively permanent). Here our attention will be focused on the dominant types of winter houses, which were usually occupied for the greatest portion of each year by a tribe (in conjunction with this discussion, see the following: Map Cu-26, V-161; Map Cu-27, V-162; Map Cu-28, V-163; Map Cu-29, V-164; Map Cu-30, V-165; Map Cu-31, V-166). The Northwest Coast was dominated by multiple-family houses made of planks, rectangular and up to 60 feet long and 20 feet wide. Usually the roofs were gabled (two equal pitches), but some had only one pitch (though generally smaller than gabled houses, one one-pitched roof house was over 500 feet long). The houses were constructed of cedar planks or, for less well-to-do families, of bark pieces, either material being lashed to beams, corner posts, and side posts that were set into semisubterranean floors. In coastal Oregon, only the gabled roof protruded above the ground, as the floor was completely excavated, and in northwestern California, three sides and a level floor were often excavated in a hillside so that three walls were partially underground. Yet from north to south the houses were basically similar and shared the widespread California and Plateau features of having semisubterranean floors. Moreover, many houses in the most southern part of the Northwest Coast had the equivalent of sod or dirt walls. It is probable that excavated floors and sod walls stem from an Upper Paleolithic development in the far north, perhaps even in Asia, that became widespread as early as 5,000 years ago in the Plateau and other westernmost regions of North America. Part of the Northwest Coast adaptation to a wet-forest environment entailed development of a woodworking technology, which may have led gradually to the use of plank roofs and eventually to rectangular floor plans and semisubterranean floors, above which long cedar-plank walls could be placed. Further archeological research is needed to determine if this is indeed how such houses evolved.

The Fraser and Columbia Plateau tribes predominantly built circular semisubterranean earth lodges, with conical roofs that were constructed with a lattice work of roof poles in the north and a radiating arrangement of roof poles in the south. The Athapaskans in the Fraser region of the Plateau used a double lean-to (gabled roof) which was similr to the roofs on central Northwest Coast plank houses. The Athapaskan houses did not have perpendicular walls or semisubterranean floors.

Throughout California and Southern California, houses with domed (but neither flat nor conical) roofs predominated. The walls were covered with thatch, mats, or even sod (though sod covering was not used in Southern California). The floors were excavated and had tunnel entrances. Around the northern and eastern perimeters of California, in the mountainous regions, roofs tended to be conical.

To the east, across the Great Basin, rather crude conical tipis, called wickiups, were built. They were covered with thatch, bark, or brush; some had tunnel entrances. Wickiups were unexcavated, generally being built on erect four-pole frames. In the easternmost part of the Great Basin hides were sewn together and used to cover the wickiups.

In the Southwest, the Pueblos, Pimans, and River Yumans each had distinct house forms and each form had a long history in its territory. The Pueblos resided in rectangular, flat-roofed houses constructed either of stones cemented together with adobe (mud and fiber) or of adobe plastered over wall-frames made of poles. In many villages the houses were stacked up in multistory fashion. The Pimans excavated a rectangular floor about 25 feet by 18 feet, rounded the shorter ends slightly, and raised wall poles to which thatch was attached. The thatch was often plastered with adobe, and sod was thrown against the lower walls. The thatch roofs were given two very gentle pitches, so as to look almost flat. The River Yumans built rectangular houses about the same size as Piman houses, though these were not excavated. The roof of the Yuman house was nearly flat, but it sloped in four directions from the center toward each wall. Sand covered the roof and sand was also heaped against the thatch wall covering.

Most of the Apacheans built small domed houses with thatch or bark coverings and a covered or tunnellike entrance (not excavated). Circular structures such as these, with minor variations (for example, a conical roof, or no tunnellike entrance) occurred in so many places in North America that the basic Apachean type may have been one brought into the area by the earliest Apacheans when they entered from the north, which is most plausible, or the type may have been adapted from the conical form used by the Upland Yumans (Yavapai, Havasupai, Walapai), and the residents of the Great Basin.

The Southwestern Pueblos, Pimans, and River Yumans must have acquired rectangular floor plans in conjunction with pottery, domesticated crops, and rectangular milling stones from Mexico, whereas the circular, semisubterranean, earth-covered, tunnel-entrance tradition most probably stems from Siberia, as Driver has suggested.*

---

*Driver's analysis of these relationships is as reasonable today as it was two decades ago (Driver and Massey 1957: 302–310).

CLOTHING

The clothing of western North American Indians was influenced by dominant forms of subsistence, environmental resources, and style. For instance, tribes in the mountainous regions of the Rockies and adjacent chains tended to make land mammals a large part of their diets and to wear skin and fur clothing during the colder months. Northwest Coast natives, during the long wet season generally wore capes, hats, and skirts woven from plant fibers. These items could withstand rot while shedding water. In the hot, dry areas of California and Southern California, the Great Basin, and the Southwest, very little clothing was worn during summer months; however, capes, robes, or blankets were woven from rabbit skins or bird feathers, and, if larger mammals were available, occasionally made from a single hide. In the mountains and foothills of California there was more medium-sized and large-sized game than in Southern California, most of the Southwest, and most of the Great Basin, and regional variations in clothing, especially in the use of coverings made from single hides, were somewhat influenced by this environmental factor. Yet clothing was also correlated with the subsistence economy: the animals regularly hunted and the plants regularly extracted were also influencing factors.

The woven clothing of many Northwest Coast, Plateau, and northern California tribes shared some basic features, though a distinctively different style made the clothing of each region unique (Map Cu-32, V-167; Map Cu-33, V-171; Map Cu-34, V-172).

The Northwest Coast people wore wide-brimmed, woven rainhats, usually conical in shape. Women wore plant-fiber skirts that hung to their knees, a woven plant-fiber cape, and often a woven plant-fiber apron in the front. Men might wear a tunic woven from plant fibers during the summer months and wear waterproof ponchos in the fall. But in the winter, Northwest Coast men normally wore either a robe made of skin, with the fur or hair intact, or a rectangular robe woven from mountain-goat wool or dog hair. Skin robes with fur left on them resisted rot longer than the dehaired robes of the drier climates to the east. Fur caps, either brimless or with small visors, completed the basic winter wear on the Northwest Coast (Map Cu-35, V-168).

In California, Southern California, and the Great Basin there was considerable overlap in clothing features. Brimless basketry hats, skirts and breechclouts of either unwoven plant fibers or hide, aprons of hide or plant materials worn in the front and back, and robes made by weaving many rabbit skins together were commonly worn throughout all three areas,

showing a basic unity in these features, which were probably brought to the Basin from California by the Great Basin Shoshoneans (distributions of these features are shown in Map Cu-36, V-170; Map Cu-37, V-174; Map Cu-38, V-175; Map Cu-39, V-176; Map Cu-40, V-177; and Map Cu-41, V-178).

Use of plant materials in clothing tended to dominate more in the Great Basin than in California or Southern California. California tribes, in particular, produced elegant capes woven with bird feathers and robes made of either one large hide or several smaller ones sewn together, which distinguished this clothing from that of the other areas.

By the time observers contacted the Plateau tribes at the beginning of the nineteenth century, the Plateau groups had been heavily influenced by the clothing style of the Plains, yet they also wore clothing features common to the Northwest Coast and to Penutian speakers in California as well. Plateau clothing, more than the clothing of any other area, showed a strong mixture of influences. For instance, brimless basketry rainhats were worn by women (a trait associated with Penutian-speaking groups throughout the Oregon coastal and California areas and shared by Uto-Aztecans in Southern California and the Great Basin). For winter wear, brimless fur caps were worn (this practice was common on the Northwest Coast and in the Great Basin), as were fur robes made from one large hide (a widely distributed trait among Penutian speakers) and semitailored fur robes made from many small pieces sewn together (a trait of the Northwest Coast) (Map Cu-42, V-169).

The dominant articles of clothing worn in the early nineteenth century by Plateau men and women, and in the eighteenth century by Ute and Northern Shoshone men and women, were semitailored buckskin shirts and dresses, which had flaps for sleeves that extended down to the elbows (Map Cu-43, V-173). Breechclouts were made from hides. Moccasins were soft-soled and fashioned from a continuous piece of buckskin, just as they were on the Northwest Coast and through the Subarctic. These moccasins were one of the types worn by Utes and many Apacheans at the time of contact with Europeans. The soft-soled moccasin was worn almost everywhere people used snowshoes (Driver and Massey 1957: 328). The Apacheans probably introduced this type of moccasin into the Southwest. Otherwise those natives of the Southwest, Great Basin, and California who wore moccasins made a two-piece variety with hard soles (Map Cu-44, V-179). Other cold-weather wear for Plateau people were mittens made from buckskin or from fur. Mittens, of course, helped the wearer in carrying items and withstanding cold while hunting or traveling during the winter months. It is interesting that California Penutians and some of their neighbors in northern California used mittens and fur muffs (one roll of fur with two ends into which hands were inserted), but the more southern Penutians in California used only fur muffs (Map Cu-45, V-181). These items may well indicate retention of a paleo-Plateau trait among the Penutians.

Plateau clothing, adapted both for rain and snow, was most likely influenced by clothing worn on the Plains, on the Northwest Coast, and in the Subarctic. Nevertheless, several features of clothing may well have been developed in the Plateau region several thousand years ago and subsequently been carried south into California by Penutian speakers. It is plausible that basketry rain caps without brims, brimless fur caps, semitailored fur robes (perhaps subarctic in origin) and fur muffs were carried into California and influenced the clothing styles among some societies adjacent to Penutian speakers.

Pueblo Indians in the Southwest wore clothing made of cotton cloth. Women wore a dress fashioned from a rectangular piece of cotton cloth that was tied over one shoulder and secured by a belt. Hard-soled moccasins and wrapped buckskin leggings were worn on the feet and legs. Men wore a cotton breechclout around which was wrapped a cotton cloth kilt, secured by a woven belt. Cotton shirts were worn by men. These were rectangular pieces of cotton cloth with a hole in the middle for the head, and ties along the sides. Pueblo Indians also wore hard-soled moccasins. In cold weather, blankets woven of strips of rabbit fur were worn, as was the practice elsewhere in the Southwest, Great Basin, northern California, and Southern California. Sandals woven from plant materials were worn among the Western Pueblos and had wide distributions among Yuman and Uto-Aztecan speakers in the Southwest and in its bordering areas. Plaited sandals made of plant fibers were worn in the Southwest by successive generations for over 1,000 years; woven sandals preceded these by several thousand years in pre-agricultural times in the Great Basin and Southwest (Map Cu-46, V-180).

Cloth made of domesticated cotton had its origin in Mexico, but Pueblo use of cotton was distinctive. Pueblo men wove beautiful belts and kilts for ceremonial clothing to be worn on ritual occasions. These cotton items were thoroughly integrated in the distinctive ritual and agricultural lives of these people. Shells, acquired through trade from California over a 2,000 year period, and semiprecious stones such as turquoise were used in jewelry worn primarily by men.

WEAVING

Mats, bags, and baskets were essential to the adaptations made by the Indians of western North America. Some of the woven articles used included clothing, siding and roofing for houses, fish traps, and receptacles for cooking, carrying, and storage. Not only were many articles woven for many separate purposes, but western Indians in general were exquisitely competent at the twining, coiling, and plaiting techniques used to produce these various articles.

Twining was the technique that predominated on the Northwest Coast and in the Plateau. It had the advantage of forming a tight weave while retaining considerable flexibility. Basketry rainhats, for instance, were twined. In twining, the warp (or foundation) strands (in a basket these became vertical at the sides of the basket) were woven with pairs of weft (or filling) strands that were twisted once before being passed around each pair of warp strands. This technique was used everywhere in western North America.

Coiling produced less flexible baskets than did twining. In coiled baskets, the warp formed a foundation of horizontal strands, and the weft was used to sew the warp together by going over and under each warp strand. Massive coiled baskets were used for granaries in Southern California and among the River Yumans and Pimans. They were able to stand independently and could support the weight of hundreds of pounds of mesquite, screwbeans, or acorns. The cylindrical baskets in which central California natives stored acorns, on the other hand, were twined, and they had to be propped up with poles in order to support the weight of the acorns.

Plaiting was a simple technique in which no distinction was made between warp and weft. Warp and weft strands were the same size and were woven over and under each other to produce (usually) flat rectangular objects to be used for house covers, house flooring, raincoats, sandals, and the like (Map Cu-47, V-182).

Blankets, robes, shirts, dresses, and pants were often woven with the aid of weaving frames, or even looms in the Southwest. Most groups in the Plateau, southern Northwest Coast, and northern California used no devices at all. The same was true for the Apacheans, with the exceptions of the Navajos.

The northern Northwest Coast tribes used either a horizontal bar or a taut cord from which hundreds of linear warp threads made of mountain-goat wool were hung. The weft was twined through the warp to make handsome Chilkat blankets. The name is derived from the Chilkat Northern Tlingit who produced beautiful versions of the blanket.

Two-bar devices were used in California, Southern California, the Great Basin, and by some Salishan and Nootkan speakers on the Northwest Coast and in the adjacent Fraser Plateau. In California, Southern California, and the Great Basin, two bars were staked horizontally into the ground (that is, the device was used flat), though some of the two-bar devices used in California were made of vertical posts between which the warp was strung horizontally. Rabbit-skin blankets (for robes) were woven on these devices. A central Northwest Coast form seeems to have developed from the simple one-bar or cord form used in the northern subregion. The central Northwesterners used two horizontal bars, one above the other, so that the warp was vertical. Dog-hair and goat-hair blankets and cedar-bark mats were woven on these devices (Map Cu-48, V-183).

The Pimans and Pueblos of the Southwest possessed true looms, which were two-bar devices equipped with heddles to separate the alternating warp strands. A weaver could throw the weft yarn all the way through the warps once a heddle had opened a path, and while the warps were open a batten would be inserted to push the weft down against the preceding courses. When the heddle was closed a comb was used to pack the weft tightly into place.

Pueblo and Piman women were excellent weavers, and among the Piman and Hopi, where weaving and woven articles of cotton cloth were important in ritual affairs, men did most of the weaving of those articles. Among the Hopi, weaving was done in the kivas, underground ceremonial chambers. Keresan and Tanoan weaving was done by both men and women. There is little doubt but that weaving devices (heddles, spindlewhorls to spin yarn, battens, and combs), cotton, and weaving techniques were diffused from Mexico as part of the agricultural complex that slowly transformed Indian culture in the Southwest.

Chapter 6

Subsistence Economy

The majority of tribal subsistence economies in western North America were dependent on a wide variety of wild plant, fish, and mammal resources, including, among most coastal tribes, sea mammals and shellfish. In conjunction with fish, marine resources were important to the coastal tribes not only for subsistence, but also for the cultural relations that were developed among these tribes. In the Southwest, domesticated crops were added to the wild plant fare; indeed, they were the most important staple in many communities. Even among Southwestern tribes in which domesticates were not the principal staple, they exercised a profound influence on those tribes and their relations with their neighbors. In some areas, then, the importance of a small number of food items—sometimes only one or two—overshadowed all others. In other areas, a host of food items was collectively important, but no single item was critical in and of itself. The contributions made by various types of food to the local diet, the places where the food was procured, the manner in which it was procured, and the ways in which goods were transported and stored aligned tribes into groupings considerably different from the groupings based on environmental factors and somewhat different from those based on technological factors.*

Figure 6-1 reveals that a deep division exists between the subsistence economies of the tribes located in inland Southern California and the Southwest (and some peripheral tribes) on the one hand, and all remaining tribes on the other. The Piman–River Yuman cluster, comprising Pima, Papago, Yuma, Mohave, and Cocopa, is exceptional, however: it cannot be placed with the tribes whose subsistence economies were consistent with the arid, hot desert.

Quite simply put, all of the tribes that are grouped in the major branching at the upper end of Figure 6-1, from Desert Diegueño to San Juan Tewa, occupied arid inland regions south of the 37° N. Latitude; they did not procure many fish through extraction or trade; either they raised and stored domesticated crops (one crop per year) or collected and stored wild plants, or both; and they transported goods primarily by human carriers. This cluster of plant-dependent groups, paradoxically, occupied water-scarce regions. The tribes were localized around water sources and exercised considerable controls over water use as well as controls over the plants they grew or extracted food from. Storage was a critical concern, and plants were stored for long periods—two years or more—by most of the tribes in the cluster.

At the lower end of Figure 6-1, from the Alkatcho Carrier to the Pima all tribes had multiple sources of food, but the two features that seem to draw them all together at a very basic level of similarity and differentiate them from the desert branch was access to, and use of, fish; moderate storability of food; waterways that were used for access to other tribes for trade, or bodies of water that were jointly used by two or more tribes; and watercraft to move small or medium-sized loads.

The Piman–River Yuman branch is the anomaly that links the two major branches. Whereas the Pimans and Yumans fished and used watercraft, they also farmed and collected wild plants which they could store for very long periods. The Pimas de-

---

*See Figures 2-2 and 2-4, also Figure 5-1.

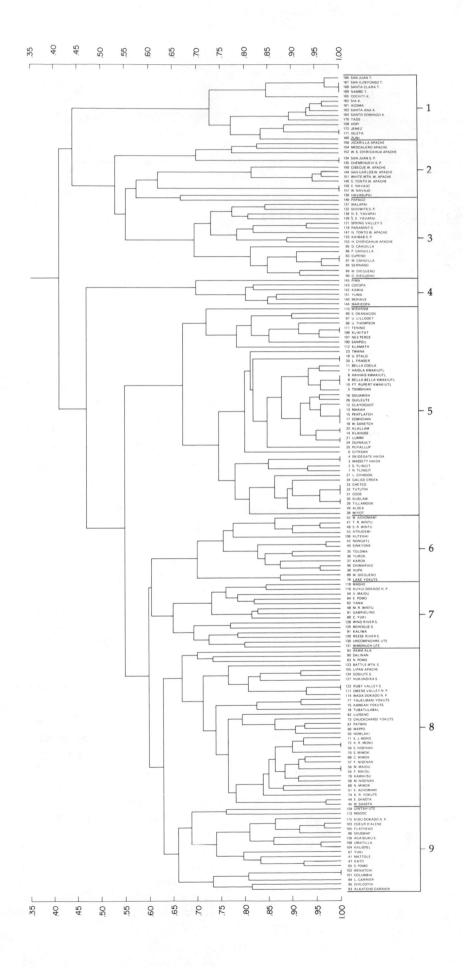

Figure 6-1 *Culture tree: 3. Groupings of tribal territories derived from G coefficients based on 30 variables (182 attributes) of subsistence economy.*

GROUP 1

166 San Juan Tewa
167 San Ildefonso Tewa
168 Santa Clara Tewa
169 Nambe Tewa
165 Cochiti Keres
162 Sia Keres
161 Acoma
163 Santa Ana Keres
164 Santo Domingo Keres
170 Taos
159 Hopi
172 Jemez
171 Isleta
160 Zuni

GROUP 2

156 Jicarilla Apache
154 Mescalero Apache
152 Warm Springs Chiricahua
     Apache
134 San Juan Southern Paiute
135 Chemehuevi Southern
     Paiute
150 Cibecue Western Apache
149 San Carlos Western
     Apache
151 White Mountain Western
     Apache
148 South Tonto Western
     Apache
158 Eastern Navajo
157 Western Navajo
136 Havasupai
146 Papago

GROUP 3

137 Walapai
132 Shivwits Southern Paiute
138 Northeast Yavapai
139 Southeast Yavapai
121 Spring Valley Shoshone
118 Panamint Shoshone
147 North Tonto Western
     Apache
133 Kaibab Southern Paiute
153 Huachuca Chiricahua
     Apache
85 Desert Cahuilla
86 Pass Cahuilla

83 Cupeño
87 Mountain Cahuilla
84 Serrano
88 Mountain Diegueño
90 Desert Diegueño

GROUP 4

145 Pima
143 Cocopa
142 Kamia
141 Yuma
140 Mohave
144 Maricopa

GROUP 5

110 Wishram
99 Southern Okanagon
97 Upper Lillooet
98 Upper Thompson
111 Tenino
109 Klikitat
107 Nez Percé
100 Sanpoil
112 Klamath
23 Twana
19 Upper Stalo
20 Lower Fraser
11 Bella Coola
7 Haisla Kwakiutl
8 Haihais Kwakiutl
9 Bella Bella Kwakiutl
10 Fort Rupert Kwakiutl
5 Tsimshian
16 Squamish
26 Quileute
12 Clayoquot
13 Makah
15 Pentlatch
17 Cowichan
18 West Sanetch
22 Klallam
14 Klahuse
21 Lummi
24 Quinault
25 Puyallup
6 Gitksan
4 Skidegate Haida
3 Massett Haida
2 Southern Tlingit
1 Northern Tlingit

27 Lower Chinook
34 Galice Creek
33 Chetco
32 Tututni
31 Coos
30 Siuslaw
28 Tillamook
29 Alsea
39 Wiyot

GROUP 6

52 West Achomawi
47 Trinity River Wintu
49 Sacramento River Wintu
53 Atsugewi
106 Kutenai
42 Nongatl
40 Sinkyone
35 Tolowa
36 Yurok
37 Karok
46 Chimariko
38 Hupa
89 Western Diegueño
76 Lake Yokuts

GROUP 7

119 Washo
116 Kuyui-Dokado Northern
     Paiute
54 Valley Maidu
64 Eastern Pomo
62 Yana
48 McCloud River Wintu
81 Gabrielino
60 Coast Yuki
128 Wind River Shoshone
125 Bohogue Shoshone
91 Kaliwa
120 Reese River Shoshone
130 Uncompaghre Ute
131 Wimonuch Ute

GROUP 8

92 Akwa'ala
80 Salinan
63 Northern Pomo
123 Battle Mountain Shoshone
155 Lipan Apache
124 Gosiute Shoshone

127 Hukundika Shoshone
122 Ruby Valley Shoshone
117 Owens Valley Northern
     Paiute
114 Wada-Dokado Northern
     Paiute
77 Yauelmani Yokuts
75 Kaweah Yokuts
78 Tubatulabal
82 Luiseño
73 Chuckchansi Yokuts
67 Patwin
66 Wappo
50 Nomlaki
71 San Joaquin Mono
72 Kings River Mono
59 Southern Nisenan
70 Southern Miwok
69 Central Miwok
57 Foothill Nisenan
56 Mountain Maidu
55 Foothill Maidu
79 Kawaiisu
58 Mountain Nisenan
68 Northern Miwok
51 East Achomawi
74 Kings River Yokuts
44 East Shasta
45 West Shasta

GROUP 9

129 Uintah Ute
113 Modoc
115 Kidu-Dokado Northern
     Paiute
103 Coeur d'Alene
105 Flathead
96 Shuswap
126 Agaiduku Shoshone
108 Umatilla
104 Kalispel
61 Yuki
41 Mattole
43 Kato
65 Southern Pomo
102 Wenatchi
101 Columbia
94 Lower Carrier
95 Chilcotin
93 Alkatcho Carrier

pended less on wild plants than the Papago or River Yumans, in that Pimas raised two main crops per year, which reduced the necessity of long-term storage, while River Yuman abundances of mesquite and screwbean mitigated the need for long-term storage of any particular food.

The conventional mapping of the subsistence economy areas in Figure 6-2 has been accomplished by selecting bridges at .65 G or higher.* The similarity

among the tribes on the basis of the subsistence economy variables was about 10 percent greater in each region than it was for technology. For instance, in Figures 6-1 and 6-2, the tribes of the Northwest Coast, the Middle Columbia Plateau, and the western fringe of the Fraser Plateau, from Chetco on the south to Northern (or Chilkat) Tlingit on the north and to Sanpoil on the east, averaged about 67 percent similarity. The predominance of fish in the diets of these people was so great as to overshadow all other measures of their subsistence economies. On the other hand, the technological similarities among these many tribes averaged only about 53 percent.

Let us turn our attention to the way in which sub-

---

*It will be recalled that Driver's G = percent for these data. The Apachean and peripheral Pai–Southern Paiute cluster averaged only about 55 percent similarity.

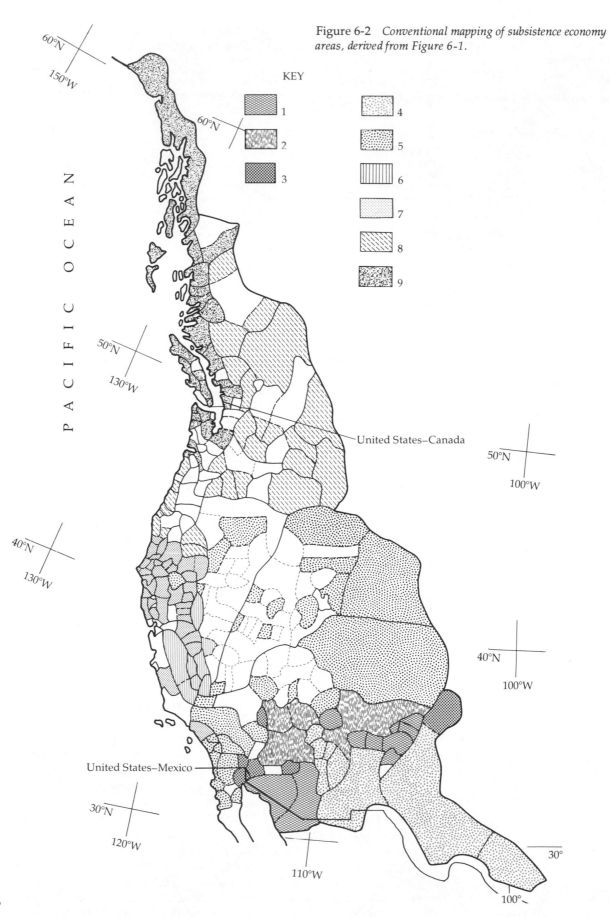

Figure 6-2 *Conventional mapping of subsistence economy areas, derived from Figure 6-1.*

KEY

1
2
3
4
5
6
7
8
9

PACIFIC OCEAN

60°N
150°W

60°N

50°N
130°W

40°N
130°W

30°N
120°W

United States–Mexico

110°W

United States–Canada

50°N
100°W

40°N
100°W

30°

100°

sistence economic patterns were distributed in western North America so that we can understand what features influenced the branching among tribes in Figure 6-1.

AGRICULTURE

The development of agricultural subsistence economies in western North America was stimulated by the diffusion of crops and techniques to the Southwest from Mexico. The transition from archaic extraction to the limited growing of maize may have begun as early as 4,000 years ago, preceding the diffusion of some aspects of maritime technologies from the Arctic to Northwest Coast tribes and the subsequent development of maritime subsistence economies in the Northwest. Both agriculture and seafaring subsistences were based on specialized technologies that were highly productive. Agriculture in the arid west required control of water, and maritime adaptations required the control of people and boats while on water—including technologies for procuring animals from the water. In Figure 6-1, most of the tribes at the upper end from Maricopa to San Juan Tewa engaged in some farming. The exceptions were the Uto-Aztecans (Cahuilla, Gabrieliño, Cupeño, Serraño, Luiseño), and Yumans (Diegueño, Kaliwa, Akwa'ala) of Southern California who did not farm but who had access to very storable wild plants, whilch they stored for lengthy periods.* The Southern California tribes employed many features of gathering and storing technology that were similar to those of their neighbors in the Southwest. The emphasis placed on agriculture in the native subsistence economy was greatest among the Pueblo and Pima tribes and the Mohave tribe, all of whom gained the majority of their food from this pursuit, and least among the few Shoshone tribes in the Great Basin who irrigated some wild seeds and, for the Spring Valley Shoshone tribe, maize (Map Cu-50, V-184).[†]

A small amount of produce gained through agriculture and incipient horticulture was not used for food.

---

*Bean and Lawton (1976: 25–29) suggest that agriculture, at least incipient horticulture, where wild seeds were irrigated, was present in Southern California prior to European contact. The data are inconclusive.

[†]It is believed that maize was cultivated by the Spring Valley Shoshone prior to European contact: they could have acquired maize from Europeans, but could also have acquired it from the Southern Paiutes to the south of them, before European contact.

Incipient horticulture means that crops were not planted but that either food plants or nonfood plants were watered and harvested; agriculture of nonfood crops means that planting, tending, and harvesting were all done, but the produce was not used for food. Several Great Basin tribes watered and tended wild grasses which they ate (hence, this would count as incipient horticulture of food crops), but the dominant crop of people who employed only the simplest techniques to nourish wild plants was tobacco, which was used as a narcotizing agent rather than for food. *Nicotiana attenuata*, which was a wild species in the Great Basin and Plateau, was *collected* by Basin dwellers, yet it was *planted* and tended by some Plateau tribes (hence, for them this is counted as agriculture of a nonfood crop). *Nicotiana bigelovii*, a wild species in California, was collected by the Yokuts groups and the Tubatulabal, yet it was planted and tended by other California groups. *Nicotiana bigelovii* (and the closely related *N. quadrivalvus* and *N. multivalvus*) became diffused to the Oregon coast and into the Plains where tobacco was cultivated. On the Northern Northwest Coast *Nicotiana* spp. grew wild, yet were also cultivated.

Although tobacco had a wide natural distribution and was used for its narcotizing agent by scores of tribes, most of these same tribes did not transfer their knowledge of cultivating tobacco, or tending tobacco, to food plants (Map Cu-51, V-185). The heartland of agriculture in western North America was the Southwest, where tribes raised maize, beans, squashes, sunflowers, cotton, tobacco, and tended several other species of semidomesticated plants such as agave (mescal), panicgrass, and barnyard grass (Map Cu-52, V-186).

The Pima and Papago tribes and the River Yuman tribes cultivated the greatest number of types of crops, but they were actually less dependent on those crops than were the Puebloans, who had less abundance of wild plants in their territories. Furthermore, the Pima, Papago, and River Yuman tribes treated many wild crops as if they were cultigens (V-187). Screwbean, mesquite, and sahuaro cactus were fermented into alcoholic beverages by these people, probably following the Piman practice of fermenting maize gruel. These alcoholic beverages assumed importance in Piman and River Yuman ceremonial life.

In the Southwest, the people who produced the most crops and were most dependent on them did not trade *for* agricultural produce (Map Cu-53, V-188). Yet considerable trading and ceremonial feasting were conducted by Pueblos, Pimans, and River Yumans with other tribes located in the Southwest and on its peripheries by which maize, beans, and squash were moved to people who did not produce crops at all, or who produced very few crops. Furthermore, some tribes, especially the Apacheans, who engaged in some farming, but also the Utes, who did not, raided Pueblo villages for food and booty, and Apacheans also raided Pima villages along the Salt and Gila Rivers for food.

In order for us to understand how people subsisted, let us distinguish locally produced food in the diet from food that was acquired extralocally from other tribes through trading, raiding, or ceremonial feasting, or through some combination of those means (Map Cu-54, V-190; Map Cu-55, V-191). It is evident that the major producers did not acquire crop foods from their neighbors, but the Southern Paiutes, Utes, Apacheans, and Pais, and the Papago, Desert Diegueño, and Desert Cahuilla tribes gained as much as ten percent of their diets from farm products raised by Pima, River Yuman, and Pueblo farmers. Of these, the Apacheans and Utes most often raided for food, and the other groups gained farm products primarily through trade and feasts to which they were invited. Two River Yuman societies, the Mohave and Yuma, were never raided against successfully, but the Pimas and Pueblos were vulnerable and the Pueblos, in particular, often traded with Apacheans and Utes, and served as their hosts at ceremonial feasts, at least during the equestrian period, beginning in the eighteenth century, and probably prior to the sixteenth century. It is surely plausible that the sedentary Pimas and Pueblos served as hosts to the mobile Utes and Apacheans so as to reduce the frequency of raids and to gain access to products and byproducts of hunting and wild-plant gathering.

Although Apacheans and Pais did some farming, agricultural products beyond what they produced locally were desired for the variety they provided in the diet and for the high storability of the extralocal crops. Moreover, cultivated crops were nutritious, especially so when eaten with meats, which provided iron, nitrogen, and salts which more completely metabolized the proteins in beans and more effectively utilized the nutrients in maize and squash.

Salt (sodium chloride) was an extremely important item in the diets of all people in western North America who subsisted primarily on plant foods, whether cultivated or not. As the salt in the body is depleted, it tends to be replaced in the blood stream by potassium, which is highly concentrated in plant foods and which may cause the body to require salt. Whether salt was craved for biochemical reasons, to maintain salt in the blood, or whether plant-eaters merely enjoyed the taste of salt is not known. Whatever the case may have been, salt was traded widely from its sources and was an important trade stimulus

in the Southwest and California (Map Cu-56, V-159). In addition to salt acquired through trade, salty plants, such as saltbush (*Atriplex* spp.), were introduced in gruel for flavor or to replenish body salt levels.

Dogs and turkeys were the only domesticated animals raised in western North America. Although dogs were kept by practically all tribes, they were raised for eating only by the Yokuts in northern California, yet most central Northwest Coast tribes and several tribes in the northern and central parts of California ate dogs ceremonially (Map Cu-57, V-193). Other tribes used them variously for hunting, to stand watch, for transportation (some Plateau tribes, Utes, and Northern Shoshones) or as sources of wool (primarily along the Northwest Coast). Apparently there were few attempts to domesticate other animals, though turkeys were bred and raised by the Hopi and Zuni tribes and among some Tanoan-speaking Pueblos, for feathers. Many Apacheans captured live turkeys and kept them for pets. Turkeys were not an important food source, nor were dogs. It is interesting, nevertheless, that the sedentary Pueblos, who seem to have needed meat in their diets because of the meager amount they procured in hunting and because of the restriction of their hunting territories after the Apacheans moved into the region, did not eat turkeys or dogs. On the other hand, trade with Apacheans and Utes supplied some meat to the Pueblos. Ceremonialism was so fundamental in Pueblo life and the need for feathers consequently was so great that these cultural features apparently outshadowed any inclinations to eat turkeys.

It is clear that most tribes practiced agriculture—the raising of some domesticated product—either raising dogs, tobacco, or both, but that agriculture for food crops was the focus of the subsistence economy only in the arid Southwest, and that the people who farmed the least in that area gained access to crops by means other than farming.

AQUATIC ANIMALS—FISH, SHELLFISH, SEA MAMMALS

Fish, shellfish, and sea mammals in enormous amounts were exploited by the people of the Northwest Coast, somewhat less so by the coastal people of Southern California (Gabrieliño and Chumash in particular), and less still by the inhabitants on the northern and central coast of California. Although shellfish and sea mammals were important along the coast, with shellfish being prominent both on the Southern

California coast and farther north and sea mammals being more prominent along the northern coastline, fish were everywhere the dominant, or codominant aquatic animal procured (Map Cu-58, V-194; Map Cu-59, V-195).

The importance of aquatic animals in native diets can be seen in Map Cu-58, but reference to Figure 6-1 will be instructive. The Northwest Coast group from Wiyot in northwestern California to Northern Tlingit in southern Alaska gained the major amounts of their food from aquatic animals (Map Cu-58). The Haida and Tlingit groups—geographically far northern tribes—are placed closest to the southernmost Northwest Coast groups in Figure 6-1 because all the tribes in this cluster gained about 60 to 75 percent of their sustenance from aquatic animals. The branch above them in Figure 6-1 from Gitksan to Twana, essentially the tribes of the central Northwest Coast subarea, gained from about 75 to 90 percent sustenance from aquatic animals. The Plateau branch, above the central Northwest Coast branch (but including also the Klamath–Wishram group), gained about 50 percent sustenance from fish. At the bottom of Figure 6-1 is clustered a mixed group of tribes from the Plateau, Great Basin (Northern Shoshones, Utes), and the northern part of California, all of whom gained from 30 to 50 percent of their sustenance from fish. This major branch of the tree, which groups together tribes from several areas that depended heavily on aquatic animals, also tends to place geographic neighbors most closely together within the branch.

The importance of the extraction of wild plants and the hunting of mammals and other animals varies among the areas that were predominantly dependent on fish, or where fish contributed the modal amount to subsistence. In California the importance of fish, plants, and mammals varied considerably, as can be seen in Figure 6-1 by comparing groups 8, 7, and 6, from West Shasta to West Achomawi. The tribes from Lake Yokuts to West Achomawi, which are clustered in group 6, were the most dependent on fish of all societies in the central and northern parts of California, but these same tribes were also heavily dependent on plants. We shall return to these topics.

A testimony to the importance of fish is that they formed at least a tertiary food source almost everywhere that fish were available. There were some exceptions along the middle reaches of the Colorado River and some of its tributaries: the Southern Paiutes of this region lived on the plateaus above these large but sluggish bodies of water, and they did not extract the fish that were available. This was true of the San Juan Southern Paiutes, for example. Map Cu-58 demonstrates that the tribes in the interior of

the northern part of California and the Plateau were great consumers of fish, and that residents of the Great Basin and Southwest, with the exception of most of the Southern Paiutes, also extracted fish heavily in certain favorable locales, such as along spawning-streams of lakes and along the lower course of the Colorado River. In Map Cu-60, V-196 we see the probable amount of locally procured fish in tribal diets.

Unlike the most agriculture-dependent cultures in the Southwest, who did not trade for farm crops or secure them from neighbors by other means, the people who were most dependent on aquatic animals also traded for them, as was the case in the northern part of California and the Plateau, or acquired them through joint use of fishing stations, as was done in the Plateau, or acquired them through gifting and feasting, as the tribes on the Northwest Coast did. Where fish were least abundant, throughout the interior of Southern California, the Southwest, and the Great Basin, they were not traded for, nor were they given as gifts or provided at feasts, yet many Northern Paiutes and Western Shoshones jointly used a few key fish-resource areas, such as Walker Lake and Pyramid Lake in Nevada, and some other localities (Map Cu-61, V-197; Map Cu-62, V-198). The Battle Mountain Shoshone of the Great Basin, who had no fish resources of their own but shared Northern Paiute areas to the west, gained more than ten percent of their sustenance from fish.

Whereas many Plateau groups traded for fish with coastal tribes or with Plateau neighbors located closer to river mouths than themselves—where fatter and tastier fish could be obtained*—only the Chilcotin acquired more than ten percent of their total diet from fish gained from their neighbors.

The specific manner in which fish, farm products, and other foods were bartered or moved among communities will be introduced here but will be discussed more fully in Chapter 7, "Economic Organization." Joint use by several tribes of key fishing resource areas recognized as belonging to a single tribe was common in the Plateau, where households were also recognized as owners of fishing stations, and in the Great Basin, but not in California. In the Southwest, where agricultural crops were traded (to the interior tribes), gifted, or shared in feasts, use of all the principal tribal food resources was strictly limited to tribal owners.

---

*Anadromous fishes do not feed when they begin their spawning journeys.

HUNTING—LAND MAMMALS, BIRDS, REPTILES, INVERTEBRATES

Whereas agriculture provided the dominant source of food for many tribes in the Southwest, and extraction of aquatic animals provided the dominant source of food for all Northwest Coast tribes and many tribes in the northern part of California, along the Southern California coast, and in the Plateau, hunting of land animals and birds provided the dominant sources of food only for the easternmost Utes and Shoshones, in the Wyoming and Colorado Rockies (Map Cu-63, V-199). In part, this is a reflection of the aridity of most western terrain and the modest amount of large and medium-sized game to be found throughout the various regions. Yet it is most evident that hunting could have been the dominant source of subsistence among many tribes in the northern foothills of California and the mountainous regions of the Plateau, where hunting was instead a secondary subsistence pursuit. North of San Francisco Bay in California fish and acorns were plentiful, and roots and fish were plentiful in the mountain and lakes region of the Upper Columbia Plateau. Even the Uintah Utes, occupying the easternmost portion of the Great Basin, could have been more dependent on large game such as elk, mountain-sheep, and bison, and medium-sized game such as deer and antelope, but fish and edible wild plants were available as well. Apparently the Nez Percé, Kalispel, Flathead, and Coeur d'Alene of the Upper Columbia Plateau chose to maintain larger winter settlements than could have been supported with hunting alone, whereas tribelets in the northern part of California, whose bountiful wild-plant and fish resources could support rather dense populations, were not easily able to expand their hunting ranges against their well ensconced neighbors. In order to have been more dependent on hunting, then, those societies located in regions where large numbers of mammals roamed in herds would have had to forsake what were relatively large and sedentary populations, and would have had to abandon large winter villages for large summer encampments. Winter villages subsisted in large part from stored food, whereas summer villages subsisted from communal hunting activities, and in the northern parts of California such a dependence on hunting would have necessitated encroaching on the territory of numerous hostile neighbors.

Indeed, it is plausible that in the northern and central parts of California, acorn and fish resources were instrumental in supporting large populations while allowing people to localize in small territories to which they laid claim and whose boundaries they protected. Hunting, too, was conducted in these rather small regions. For game to be caught in enough quantity for it to be the dominant food source, it must be pursued across large territories, so availability of game does not mean that concentrated and sedentary tribal populations based their subsistence on game. Where game did provide a subsistence, mobility for much of the year was required: this was so for the Utes and Wind River Shoshones, and for some of the tribes in the mountainous zones of the Plateau. Yet even in the Plateau—where game could be pursued and was—tribes such as the Nez Percé, Kalispel, Shuswap, and Kutenai gained considerably more of their diets (60 to 85 percent of the diet) from fish and wild plants than from game.

The conclusion to draw from this is that fish, with the appropriate technology, such as weirs with traps, harpoons, and nets, were easy to secure, were nutritious, and stored well. Moreover, people traded for fish without difficulty. Wild plants such as the acorns used by California tribes and the roots used by the Plateau tribes were extracted even more easily than were fish with weirs and traps, and either independently or in conjunction with dried fish allowed relatively large populations to convene and subsist on the stores for a long time. Hunting, even when large herds of game were present, was seldom preferred to more sedentary and more predictable extractive pursuits. Except for the easternmost Utes and Shoshones, and perhaps the Flathead, big-game hunting did not become the dominant subsistence pursuit for any of the tribes in western North America, even after the introduction of the horse, though products of the chase did become more prominent seasonally among groups from the Great Basin and Plateau who ventured onto the Plains.

Maps Cu-64 and Cu-65 (V-200) demonstrate that tribes who extracted game most heavily pursued large game, especially in herds. Where game was a secondary source, deer, supplemented with elk, mountain sheep, or antelopes were hunted. In Southern California (Map Cu-64), the Great Basin, and the Southwest (Map Cu-65), where most animals were small, animals of practically every size—reptiles, mammals, birds, insects—were pursued. On the Northwest Coast, waterfowl were more important than they were in most other places in the West.

Most hunting was conducted within the territory of each tribe (Map Cu-66, V-201), but deer, in particular, were also acquired through trade, which is how some game was obtained by the Lower Chinook and Wishram tribes and several tribes north of San Francisco Bay in California and in the Southwest (Map Cu-67,

V-202). A few Great Basin groups allowed their neighbors access to game, sometimes to stalk deer and sometimes for deer drives. In the Great Basin, communal antelope hunts, where several local groups joined together, were the principal reasons tribes convened. Small game, such as rabbits, rats, and less common animals, such as lizards and grasshoppers, were seldom acquired extralocally by any tribe in western North America. What was oftenest sought extralocally were deer and elk and byproducts from them such as hides, and the people who sought them usually exchanged fish, acorns, or farm products for these goods.

The amount of land mammals procured through trade or joint use of territories was modest, and few tribes engaged in these methods of procuring game. In fact, many fewer tribes acquired land-mammal byproducts extralocally than gained fish from outside their own territories. No tribes gained more than ten percent of the food in their diets by these methods except the Lower Chinook, who were active fishermen and renowned traders. The Pueblos and Pimas had little local animal fare in their diets and undoubtedly benefited from their acquisition of meat through trade with the Apacheans, Utes, and Papagos (Map Cu-68, V-203). As a rule, however, it should not be assumed that the potential usefulness of items abundant in one region but relatively unavailable in another is always a good guide to exchanges of resources between regions. Many tribes in the Southwest, Southern California, and the Great Basin who did not have abundant medium-sized mammals in their territories could have benefited from extralocal access to meat but did not acquire it. Some of the factors that conditioned extralocal access were proximity to game in another territory and means of transportation. For example, fish and animal byproducts (hides, mainly) could be transported between tribes along the rivers of the Plateau, Northwest Coast, and in northern parts of California by canoes. Among the sedentary Pueblos, game brought to them was most often carried on the backs of the Apacheans and Utes who dwelled in the mountains and canyons nearby. Pimas acquired some game from the Papagos, who also transported goods on their backs. Other Southwest inhabitants and Southern Californians did not have ease of access to game outside their own regions, though they possessed wild plants to trade for such goods when they were available. Most Great Basin dwellers had neither access to abundant resources in other areas nor an abundance of goods to use in trade. Joint use was the technique they often employed to acquire game (antelope) and fish.

GATHERING OF WILD PLANTS

Wild-plant gathering was the predominant means of food acquisition in most of the Great Basin, the area north and south of San Francisco Bay in California, and Southern California, and it was the dominant or codominant source of food in the Southwest for all people except the Pueblos and Pimas. In the northern areas of California and across the Plateau wild-plant gathering was also a secondary food source. Only on the Northwest Coast and among the Pueblos, where wild plants provided from 5 to 25 percent of the food in the diets, were they a tertiary food source (Map Cu-69, V-204; Map Cu-70, V-208).

Figure 6-1 distinguishes among the several combinations of extraction: gathering, hunting, and fishing where gathering was dominant. Near the bottom of the figure, in group 8, the acorn-gathering tribes from West Shasta to Yauelmani Yokuts were dependent on plants (which provided 45 to 55 percent of the diet), hunting (25 to 35 percent of the diet), and fishing (15 to 30 percent), in that order. Just above that branch, the Wada Dokado Northern Paiute–Battle Mountain Shoshone branch shared the same order of importance among extractive food sources, but different proportions (plants made up 50 to 60 percent of the diet; land animals 25 to 30 percent; and fish 15 to 25 percent). The Yana–Washo branch, at the top of group 7, reversed the dominance of land animals and fish, and the tribes in the Wimonuch Ute–Wind River Shoshone branch (bottom of group 7), located geographically at the northern and eastern peripheries of the Great Basin, gained as much, or nearly equal, sustenance from hunting as from gathering. The top of the figure shows that extractors in the interior of Southern California and throughout the Southwest desert rarely ate fish but depended heavily on wild plants for most of their food.

Regional differences in the *predominant* crops gathered are striking. Northwest Coast and Plateau people gathered roots and berries. California tribes, central and northern, gathered acorns, pine seeds, and pine nuts. Southern California tribes collected acorns, pine nuts, and chia, and as was also the practice of the Colorado River Desert people, collected mesquite pods, mescal hearts, and cactus fruits. The Western Apaches, ranging from the mountains through the deserts, had access to a wider variety of plants than all other tribes, but the plants were not so abundant as in California. Great Basin dwellers were collectors of many plants. Although seed plants predominated, grasses by themselves probably did not contribute more than a small part of the diets (Map Cu-71, V-205).

Wild plants were sought from neighboring and more-distant tribes about as often and about as extensively as fish were sought. Dried berries and roots were traded in the Plateau, but more often neighboring tribes were allowed to share root and berry grounds, as was also the practice in the Great Basin. In California, acorns and fish were traded in much the same way; some species of acorns, such as those from the tan-oak, were preferred over other species and all were given an order of preference. Fish, venison, or even less-preferred acorns might be exchanged for more-preferred acorns (Map Cu-72, V-206). The amounts of plant food gained extralocally was usually less than ten percent of the total diet (Map Cu-73, V-207).

ON ACQUISITION OF FOOD FROM NEIGHBORS

The manner in which access to the food resources of neighbors was achieved varied, but most of the Indians of western North America either traded for food, raided for food, were guests at feasts, were given access to neighboring resource areas, or gained some of their neighbor's resources through some combination of these methods. Joint access predominated in the Great Basin, trade was dominant in California, ceremonial feasting and gifting were the means of access on the Northwest Coast, the combination of raiding and trading were the means in the Southwest, and so forth. In general, movements of food between areas were greatest where human carriers did not have to do most of the work (Map Cu-74, V-209). Important exceptions were the River Yumans, who regularly walked as far as the California coast, and the northern Northwest Coast tribes, who walked through the unnavigable mountain passages to exchange with interior people. Boats, especially the large dugout canoes and plank canoes, expedited movements among near neighbors, and the presence of such boats correlated highly with movements of food and chattels (Map Cu-75, V-210).

FOOD STORAGE

Among the people most dependent on highly storable wild plants or agricultural produce in the San Joaquin Valley of California, in Southern California, and in the Southwest, food was stored two years and more. Yet among most other tribes food was seldom stored longer than one year. Even the Pimas and some River Yumans seldom stored food for more than one year, though it might be expected that these tribes would have developed surpluses, since the Pimas produced two food crops and River Yumans produced one crop each year and also collected and stored large quantities of mesquite pods and mescal hearts. The northern tribes of California could have stored acorns and other nuts for much longer than one year, but they seldom did so, depleting their annual stores by hosting many feasts and extracting deer, fish, or whatever else was available throughout each year (Map Cu-76, V-213). On the Northwest Coast, dried fish rotted after a half year or so, and tribes in this region expected to draw from natural abundances as needed, as did the Great Basin dwellers, who moved frequently and stored whatever abundances accumulated between movements. The hard seeds and nuts of the Great Basin stored well but were seldom plentiful enough to last longer than one winter season.

Chapter 7

Economic Organization

The preceding assessment of subsistence economy drew us into several brief discussions of economic organization. We learned, for instance, that practically all tribes acquired some foods from their neighbors or from their neighbors' resource areas. In assessing the extralocal sources of food, we touched on the manner in which food was acquired. In the preceding chapter it was sufficient to distinguish trade, ceremonial feasts, raids, and joint access to resource areas as major mechanisms for moving food among communities; in this chapter we shall explore the more complex fashion in which ownership, distribution, extraction, and production were organized.

One of the most persistent assertions about American Indians is that they recognized communal use of subsistence resources and did not recognize private property. There is a kernel of truth to this generalization about property concepts, though it would be misleading to consider the assertion other than superficial, for the nature of individual and group ownership of subsistence resource areas, houses, movable property, and even the privileges to perform certain dances or wear certain insignia varied greatly among the culture areas in western North America.

In Chapter 3 it was proposed that the principal factor that contributed most greatly to the profusion of languages in western North America was the abundance of localized resources throughout the Northwest Coast and California, which allowed small groups to become self-sufficient for long periods of time in small regions. What must have stimulated language differentiation within the language families and phyla was the concept of private ownership and the willingness of groups to defend property to which they claimed the exclusive right to extract resources or produce crops.

Concepts of communitarian and private property should be defined so that we may account for the private interests held by economically autonomous groups and recognize the communitarian access to the property accorded members of each of those units. In the Great Basin, for instance, private property concepts were minimally developed; year-around residence-groups were small and followed a complex extracting schedule that varied with plant and animal abundances as they occurred each year. Nevertheless, some Great Basin and Southwest peoples laid claims to eagle nests so that only the owners of those nests could catch the eagles that nested in them. But since eagles were used for shamanistic and religious purposes rather than for subsistence purposes, it can be argued that nests were claimed for the common good. There is also indication that some families among the westernmost Great Basin dwellers claimed temporary ownership of pinyon trees, and the Western Shoshone and Southern Paiute farmers appropriated their farm plots as private property. Beyond these items, and a few pieces of movable property, hunting, fishing, and gathering resource areas were available to everyone in each camp of families. Moreover, rich resource areas around lakes, or in pinyon–juniper forests, or on antelope prairies were shared with people from several camps who might speak several languages and who often joined communally for such undertakings as antelope drives. Trading was done to an infinitesimal degree in the central area of the Great Basin. Only on the western edges, where contacts were maintained with California societies, and eastern edges, where contacts were maintained variously with Plains, Plateau, and Southwest societies, was trading engaged in to any notable extent.

In the Plateau, fish and root resources were concentrated at several key fishing stations and river valleys throughout the Columbia and Fraser River drainages, but most other extractive resources were diffusely distributed across the scablands and cold semideserts of the Plateau. Key resource areas, such as fishing stations, were most often appropriated by kinship groups within bands or villages, rather than by the larger units, and that was also true for many root-producing areas. An improved hunting site such as a deadfall might even be claimed as private property by the man who erected it. As a matter of fact, Plateau ownership concepts of key resource areas were strikingly similar to Northwest Coast private property concepts, yet in practice they were not applied to so many forms of property in the Plateau as on the Northwest Coast, and the private properties, at least the resource areas, were not regarded as inviolable.

Although Plateau people tended to recognize kinship-group rights to the ownership of fishing stations, these same kinship groups, following a simple request, made their resource areas available to people from other kinship groups and even from other language groups. Access by owners and their guests to resources, whether communally owned or privately owned, communal feasting, and extensive trading were hallmarks of Plateau society. So even when private property ownership was recognized, nonowners were generally accorded access to those resources. Thus, Great Basin and Plateau societies were very similar in awarding open access and encouraging communitarian use of resources, even though Plateau concepts of private ownership were more highly developed than those of their Great Basin counterparts.

Owners of private property along the Northwest Coast, in California, Southern California, and the Southwest, on the other hand, tended not to provide access to their key resource areas to people other than the owners. What will be important to our analysis here and in subsequent chapters are the ways in which indirect access to products by nonowners was accomplished throughout western North America, and the differences between property that was owned by the entire community and property that was owned by smaller units within those communities.

Figures 7-1 and 7-2, in which tribes are compared on the basis of 67 variables measuring economic organization, correlated more closely with the culture area taxonomy derived from all 292 variables than did any other subclassification of the cultural variables. The high correlations among economic organization, subsistence economy, and technology demonstrate the importance of these in establishing overall cul-

tural similarity. It is not easy to avoid sounding mechanical, even trite, while emphasizing the critical nature of the economic base to the shaping of the rest of the culture. We are not making an argument for economic determinism when we point out that the relations between economic and noneconomic features of culture were positive and rather high, though considerable variation obtained. Rather, we recognize that economic mechanisms were extremely influential in cultural organization, and they were often well integrated with, and deeply embedded in, kinship, religious, and ceremonial aspects of culture. It is very clear, in fact, that economic organization was much more important than environment, given a similar technology, in shaping cultural responses to an environment.

It is also clear that economic organization was very much influenced by nonpredictable features of tribal and language-family histories. For instance, Pueblo and Piman canal-irrigation farmers in the Southwest possessed economic organizations that were different from one another in many important respects not attributable to technology or environment. River Yumans, who resided in an environmental context very similar to that of the Pimas and who possessed many features of technology and subsistence economy similar to those of the Pimas, had a much different economic organization from the Pimas. Plateau fishermen and root extractors could have been organized much as were California extractors, or Northwest Coast extractors, but the economic organizations of all three varied significantly from one another, as we will see below. Much of this variation was due to rather arbitrary developments that were conditioned by different natural environments, different technology, and contacts among people from different tribes, and we may just as well wonder why the economic organizations in these three regions were not more similar than they were. In the discussions of languages, it was seen that there were similarities among tribes occupying the same environmental regions, and that there were also many similarities between sister languages spoken by tribes occupying different environmental regions, and even language similarities between neighboring tribes occupying adjacent areas in a similar natural environment, who were not linguistic congeners. Such variability prepares us for what will be found when examining economic organization.

Economic organization was deeply embedded in kinship, religion, and ceremony, and we may expect to find that in the facets of culture for which these were important economy was likewise important, yet because subsistence economies were also adapted to natural environments through technology and economic organizations in ways that are simply fortuitous and arbitrary, we should expect to find non-predictable phenomena important in influencing the nature of cultural phenomena.

The major division in Figure 7-1 separates the Southwest, at the top of the figure, from all the other economic organization areas, yet within the Southwest four distinct branches emerge at 62 percent or greater average similarity. The uppermost group is the disparate Pueblo–Piman group (1), representing the persistence of sedentary, private-property-owning cultures who had farmed in the Southwest for at least 2,300 years. The Pai–Navajo branch (2), at 63 percent similarity, is a cluster of semisedentary farmers and gatherers; at the time of contact with Europeans, the Pais perhaps farmed less than they did a century before this contact, and the Navajos increased their farming following contact with Pueblos. The River Yuman branch (3) represents a set of farming, gathering, fishing cultures extending back to at least 500–800 AD, people who were expert traders and raiders. The Apachean branch (4) was composed of seminomadic communities that possessed mixed gathering, hunting, farming, and raiding economies and that exercised considerable influence on the economic organizations of the sedentary tribes and the Pais.

At the bottom of the figure is the northern and central Northwest Coast branch (9), which, at 67 percent average similarity, was characterized by kinship-group ownership of private property and ceremonial gifting and feasting. The Plateau and southern Northwest Coast branch (8), at 64 percent similarity, was characterized primarily by trade, barter, and feasting, but the Plateau also was characterized by joint use of tribal resource areas. The northwestern California societies of the Northwest Coast culture area and northern California societies of the California area formed a branch (7), at 63 percent similarity, that embraced two types of property ownership. In the northwestern part of California (the Tolowa–Kato cluster in branch 7), individual men owned the key resource sites. Elsewhere in northern California tribelets* owned the resource areas, though some family-owned property was recognized within tribelet boundaries. The northern California

and northwestern California societies in branch 7 were characterized by extensive bartering and feasting, and zealous protection of tribelet resources. The central California branch (6), at 70 percent similarity, was characterized by feasting, trading, protection of resource areas, and tribelet ownership of all but gathering sites. The Great Basin and Southern California branch (5), at 74 percent similarity, cluster the patrilineal sib†communities of Southern California who traded, guarded their resources, and dealt reciprocally, through moiety organizations‡, with other communities, and, interestingly, the bilateral family camps of the Great Basin who did not possess moieties, had little to trade, and provided free access to most of the resource sites that they claimed. These two regions exhibited more similarity in the ways labor was organized in each than in features of ownership and distribution.

OWNERSHIP AND INHERITANCE

A good way to begin assessing economic organization in western North America is to compare different concepts of ownership and inheritance. We shall comment first on some general trends in what constituted ownership and who owned property, before comparing ownership customs within regions; finally, inheritance will be dealt with.

father's house or to establish a new house nearby (patrilocal postnuptial residence). In northern California tribelets were predominantly composed of many patribilateral lineal households in one or more settlements—usually a central village and one or more outlying hamlets—observing bilateral descent. In central California each tribelet comprised a single localized patrilineage among the Miwok and Costanoan, multiple patrilineages among Salinan, some Yokuts, and some Mono, and many patribilateral lineal households among Kawaiisu, Tubatulabal, and other Yokuts and Mono.

† Patrilineal sib, or patrisib, is a unilineal descent group in which the members are linked through stipulated or presumed descent to a male ancestor. A sib is composed of two or more lineages. Lineages are demonstrated unilineal descent units in which membership is traced to an ancestor through explicit genealogical reckoning.

‡ Moiety, or dual division, is the organization of a community or network of communities into two parts. The criteria for membership vary. Lineages, sibs, sodalities, residence, and other criteria can be employed to determine membership. The two divisions maintain reciprocal obligations of some sort.

*A tribelet is a politically autonomous and discrete territorial unit. Leadership in such a unit was nominal, but a tribelet recognized and defended a territory and jointly sponsored ceremonies. Among many tribelets, "patribilateral lineal households" were integral to the organization of the society. Such households comprised co-residing kinspeople of from three to five families tracing their descent bilaterally, yet to a common ancestor, usually the head of the household. Men brought their wives to reside in their

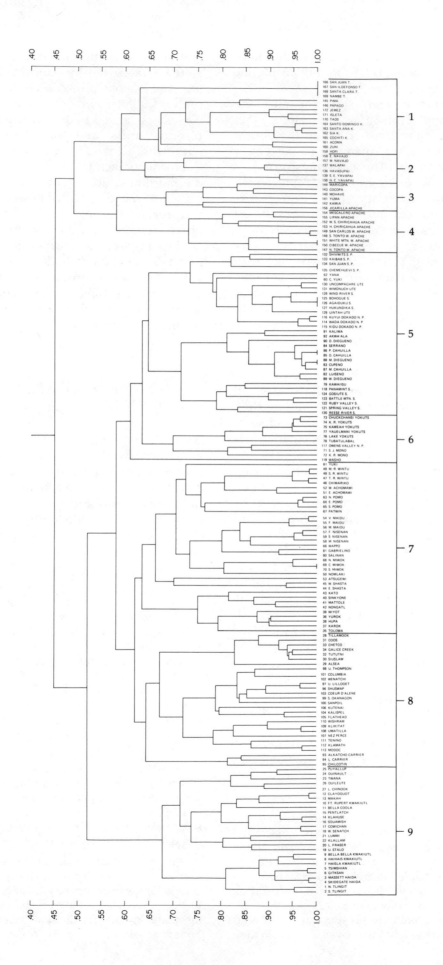

Figure 7-1 *Culture tree: 4. Groupings of tribal territories of western North America derived from G coefficients based on 67 variables (409 attributes) of economic organization.*

GROUP 1

166 San Juan Tewa
167 San Ildefonso Tewa
168 Santa Clara Tewa
169 Nambe Tewa
145 Pima
146 Papago
172 Jemez
171 Isleta
170 Taos
164 Santo Domingo Keres
163 Santa Ana Keres
162 Sia Keres
165 Cochiti Keres
161 Acoma
160 Zuni
159 Hopi

GROUP 2

158 Eastern Navajo
157 Western Navajo
137 Walapai
136 Havasupai
139 Southeast Yavapai
138 Northeast Yavapai

GROUP 3

144 Maricopa
143 Cocopa
140 Mohave
141 Yuma
142 Kamia
156 Jicarilla Apache

GROUP 4

154 Mescalero Apache
155 Lipan Apache
152 Warm Springs Chiricahua Apache
153 Huachuca Chiricahua Apache
149 San Carlos Western Apache
148 South Tonto Western Apache
151 White Mountain Western Apache
150 Cibecue Western Apache
147 North Tonto Western Apache

GROUP 5

132 Shivwits Southern Paiute
133 Kaibab Southern Paiute
134 San Juan Southern Paiute
135 Chemehuevi Southern Paiute
62 Yana
60 Coast Yuki
130 Uncompaghre Ute
131 Wimonuch Ute
128 Wind River Shoshone
125 Bohogue Shoshone
126 Agaiduku Shoshone
127 Hukundika Shoshone
129 Uintah Ute
116 Kuyui-Dokado Northern Paiute
114 Wada-Dokado Northern Paiute
115 Kidu-Dokado Northern Paiute
91 Kaliwa
92 Akwa'ala
90 Desert Diegueño
84 Serrano
86 Pass Cahuilla
85 Desert Cahuilla
88 Mountain Diegueño
83 Cupeño
87 Mountain Cahuilla
82 Luiseño
89 Western Diegueño
79 Kawaiisu
118 Panamint Shoshone
124 Gosiute Shoshone
123 Battle Mountain Shoshone
122 Ruby Valley Shoshone
121 Spring Valley Shoshone
120 Reese River Shoshone

GROUP 6

73 Chuckchansi Yokuts
74 Kings River Yokuts
75 Kaweah Yokuts
77 Yauelmani Yokuts
76 Lake Yokuts
78 Tubatulabal
117 Owens Valley Northern Paiute
71 San Joaquin Mono
72 Kings River Mono
119 Washo

GROUP 7

61 Yuki
48 McCloud River Wintu
49 Sacramento River Wintu
47 Trinity River Wintu
46 Chimariko
52 West Achomawi
51 East Achomawi
63 Northern Pomo
64 Eastern Pomo
65 Southern Pomo
67 Patwin
54 Valley Maidu
55 Foothill Maidu
56 Mountain Maidu
57 Foothill Nisenan
59 Southern Nisenan
58 Mountain Nisenan
66 Wappo
81 Gabrieliño
80 Salinan
68 Northern Miwok
69 Central Miwok
70 Southern Miwok
50 Nomlaki
53 Atsugewi
45 West Shasta
44 East Shasta
43 Kato
40 Sinkyone
41 Mattole
42 Nongatl
39 Wiyot
36 Yurok
38 Hupa
37 Karok
35 Tolowa

GROUP 8

28 Tillamook
31 Coos
33 Chetco
34 Galice Creek
32 Tututni
30 Siuslaw
29 Alsea
98 Upper Thompson
101 Columbia
102 Wenatchi
97 Upper Lillooet
96 Shuswap

103 Coeur d'Alene
99 Southern Okanagon
100 Sanpoil
106 Kutenai
104 Kalispel
105 Flathead
110 Wishram
109 Klikitat
108 Umatilla
107 Nez Percé
111 Tenino
112 Klamath
113 Modoc
93 Alkatcho Carrier
94 Lower Carrier
95 Chicotin

GROUP 9

25 Puyallup
24 Quinault
23 Twana
26 Quileute
27 Lower Chinook
12 Clayoquot
13 Makah
10 Fort Rupert Kwakiutl
11 Bella Coola
15 Pentlatch
14 Klahuse
16 Squamish
17 Cowichan
18 West Sanetch
21 Lummi
22 Klallam
20 Lower Fraser
19 Upper Stalo
9 Bella Bella Kwakiutl
8 Haihais Kwakiutl
7 Haisla Kwakiutl
5 Tsimshian
6 Gitksan
3 Massett Haida
4 Skidegate Haida
1 Northern Tlingit
2 Southern Tlingit

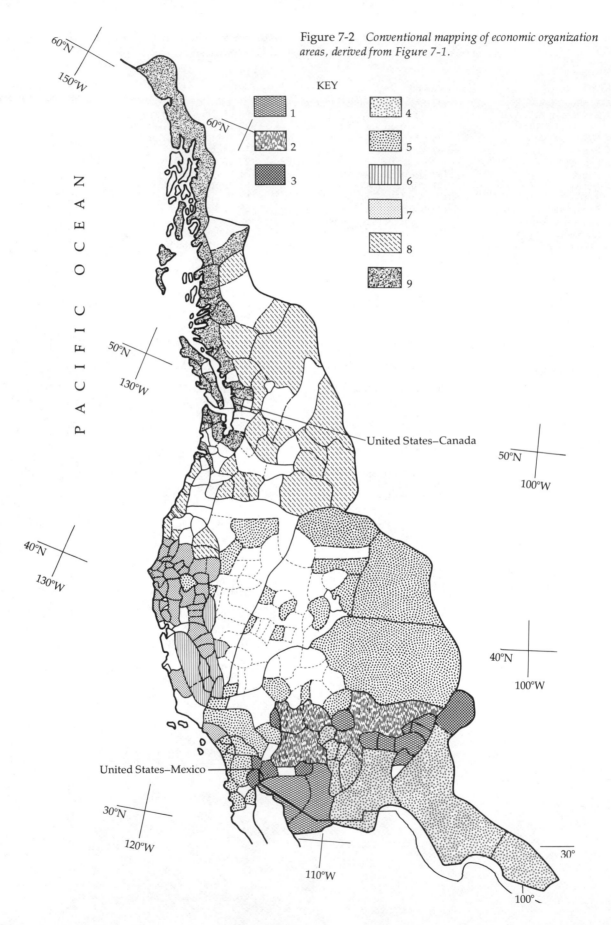

Figure 7-2 *Conventional mapping of economic organization areas, derived from Figure 7-1.*

KEY

1
2
3
4
5
6
7
8
9

PACIFIC OCEAN

United States–Canada

United States–Mexico

Concepts of private property were most highly developed on the Northwest Coast and were extended to resource extraction areas of all kinds (fishing, hunting, and gathering sites), houses, all manner of movable or corporeal property (chattels, including slaves, as explained in V-271, V-272, and V-273), and a wide range of incorporeal property, including special dances, heirlooms, crests, songs, spirit possessions, and the like.* Private property in many corporeal and incorporeal forms was recognized in California, Southern California, and among the sedentary tribes in the Southwest, but not to the extent that it was recognized throughout Northwest Coast culture.

In certain regions, ownership was closely correlated with the concentration of resources, the abundance of resources, and the uses to which resources were put. For example, in the Great Basin and most of the Southwest the majority of the extractable subsistence resources were diffusely distributed over extensive terrain, so except for people who farmed, it was impossible to settle around a single resource area which could be appropriated for exclusive use. The River Yumans and some Apacheans were exceptions: the River Yumans claimed as property extensive groves of mesquite and mescal and stands of giant cactus; the mobile Western and Chiricahua Apaches, though they moved seasonally between mountains and deserts, nevertheless recognized gathering and farming areas as the private resource areas of sibs and bands.

Similarly, on the Northwest Coast, wild-plant gathering sites, key hunting sites, key fishing sites, houses, and house sites were all claimed by localized kinship groups even though extraction of wild plants from root and berry grounds was not important to subsistence. All of these extractable-resource sites were located in restricted pockets along coastlines, riverbanks, and in a few well watered valleys (Map Cu-78, V-266).

Within the Yurok, Wiyot, Karok, Hupa, Tututni and Tolowa villages of the northwestern area of California, men appropriated gathering sites (mainly oak trees), fishing stations, and improved hunting sites within range of their houses for their immediate families. The same man owned the house in which his family resided and the site on which it was built.

Farther south, from the western edge of the Sacramento Valley to the coast in northern California, tribelets owned and controlled the key fishing, hunting, and gathering sites, though individual persons within tribelets might appropriate oak trees, or even branches of oak trees, from year to year. Just to the east, in the central and eastern Sacramento Valley, patrihouseholds owned the key gathering sites within tribelet territories. Hunting sites and fishing sites, on the other hand, were less often appropriated by patrihouseholds,* though in a few communities individual persons or patrihouseholds did own fishing sites or hunting sites, or both. In still other communities, individual persons owned some property, but all the rest was vested in the entire tribelet (Maps Cu-79, V-267; Cu-80, V-268).

House ownership correlates closely with private ownership of key resource areas and with the number of families occupying the house. The greater the claim to private ownership of resource areas by individuals, families, or localized kinship groups larger than a family, the more probable that ownership of their house was also claimed by the same group that claimed the resources (Map Cu-82, V-270).

By far, most ownership among Northwest Coast tribes was vested in localized, residential kinship

---

* "Corporeal property" is tangible and consists in a physically material body of some sort, such as a boat, a fishing station, a farm plot, or an ear of corn. It can be movable, i.e., chattels, such as slaves, or not, such as a stretch of river. "Incorporeal property" is intangible and constitutes a right that has no physical existence. Although a Northwest Coast family crest was a tangible object, and a spirit dance was a tangible act, the spirit that each represented had no physical existence, yet the right to claim ownership of the family crest's spiritual being or of a spirit that was embodied in a dance step was recognized, and such property is incorporeal.

* "Patrihouseholds" comprise "patribilateral lineal households" (p. 131 fn) and "patrilineal lineal households." The difference between the two forms is solely in descent reckoning. We use the general term *patrihousehold* when finer distinctions are not required. Both types observed patrilocal postnuptial residence in which the groom takes his bride to reside in or near his father's house and to form an economic unit with his father, hence *patri-* in the first part of the term. There was little generation depth in either the patrilineal or patribilateral forms of the household, with descent traced to the head of the household in each. Among Oregon Athapaskans and some other societies, households observed patrilineal descent, whereas among other patrihousehold societies bilateral descent was observed.

Although it may seem contradictory, "lineal" in patribilateral or patrilineal "lineal" households does not refer to descent but to co-residing families spread across two and perhaps three generations, e.g., a man (household head) and his wife, their sons, their son's wives, and the unmarried children of those couples, and perhaps a son's son, his wife, and his unmarried children. See V-302 for definitions of family household types.

groups, not in the individual person. These groups were matrilineages* in the northern and patridemes† in the central subareas; patrihousehold and individual ownership was more frequent in the southern and in the northwestern California subareas. In times before contact with Europeans, matrilineages, patridemes, and patrihouseholds were the ultimate autonomous political and economic units throughout the majority of Northwest Coast communities; indeed, all of the exceptions to this pattern seem to have developed late in pre-Contact times, among (a) the Athapaskan-speaking tribelets of northwestern California, who were certainly not fully adapted to coastal life; (b) the Tsimshian speakers, who possessed village organizations as well as matrilineages; and perhaps (c) some Central and Northern Nootkan winter villages. Inasmuch as most Northwest Coast villages were composed of more than one localized kinship group, most had more than one politically and economically autonomous organization.

The concept of privatization extended to fewer corporeal and incorporeal objects throughout California (northern and central) and Southern California than it did on the Northwest Coast, but the major resource areas in California were always owned by entire tribelets, whereas some specific resource sites within the tribelet-owned resource areas might be recognized as belonging to patrihouseholds, lineages, or even individual persons. It is plausible to assume that

the fractionation of private property throughout California and the emergence of tribelets resulted as a response to crowding, competition for resources, and because of the highly concentrated nature of several bountiful types of resources in small areas; what resulted was a complex tapestry of property ownership by individual persons, families, kinship groups, and tribelets.

Throughout Miwok territory in central California, key hunting, fishing, and gathering sites were owned by patrilineages. Miwok patrilineages constituted monolineage communities, so we can refer to patrilineages here as autonomous political and economic units for the Miwoks. Yet the Yokuts who lived south of the Miwoks in multilineage tribelets and who, like the Miwoks, spoke California Penutian languages emphasized tribelet ownership for everything but key gathering sites. Within a Yokuts tribelet, a group of related men, or a group of women who worked together as gatherers, often appropriated gathering areas for their own use.

The ownership of gathering areas in California by units smaller than tribelets, such as lineages, patrihouseholds, and groups of kinspeople who extracted together is noteworthy. It is plausible that California Penutians originally moved into California as patrilineal groups. Initially they may well have appropriated riverine resource sites, but in the sclerophyll regions they may have become less dependent on river resources and more dependent on plant resources. As these groups grew and fissioned in northern California, conflicts may have arisen between one and another of these groups and between them and tribes who had located in the area before them. It is conceivable, for example, that population growth, skirmishes, and appropriation of some resources and expropriation of others led to the formation of tribelets, perhaps at first through combinations of several lineages scattered throughout a contiguous region, who joined together to protect the larger territory, or through the growth of a single lineage and the subsequent fractioning of property interests until communal rights were established. It is also plausible that the patrilineages themselves may often have given way to bilateral descent and to smaller households in the north, and to the multilineage tribelets that typified the Yokuts and Patwin groups in central Califonia.* Nonetheless, among some California Penutians, patrilineages remained intact, even though among others, the patrilineages became

---

*Localized "matrilineages" were organizations of kinspeople who demonstrated their descent by tracing it to a common female ancestor. Usually a matrilineage included the families of sisters spread over three or more generations. On the Northwest Coast the localized matrilineages observed avunculocal residence so that when a son married, he moved from his father's maternal home and took his bride to his mother's brother's house.

†"Patridemes" were organizations of kinspeople who, although their descent organization was bilateral so that both the mother's and father's sides were emphasized in kinship reckoning, demonstrated their descent to a common deme ancestor by tracing it through *either* the father's side *or* the mother's side. It was possible, then, to align with mother's or father's kinspeople. After marriage, however, a man practically always took his bride to live with the families of his brother(s), father, paternal uncle(s), and paternal grandfather; yet if prospects were better for the couple in the wife's deme than the husband's deme, that couple might choose to reside with the wife's father's family. Hence, a patrideme comprised a core of male kinsmen. The "matrideme" would be the matrilocal (bride takes husband to reside in her mother's camp) counterpart of the patrideme.

---

*Evidence from Penutian kinship organization adduced in the following chapter supports this hypothesis.

grouped into multilineage tribelets. Wherever they were grouped into larger tribelets, the tribelets owned some of the same types of resources that were owned by individual lineages in the monolineage communities. It is plausible that tribelets not only replaced the autonomy of lineages but also replaced lineages as property-controlling units. The Miwoks and Costanoans of central California were organized into communities of independent lineages and were not grouped into larger tribelets before Contact, and their monolineage communities may best represent the early Penutian economic, social, and political organization.

Northwest Coast tribes could have followed a course of events similar to that proposed for Northern California patrilineages, forming autonomous political and economic units larger than localized kinship groups prior to contact with non-Indians, but only the Coast Tsimshian villages did so,* and other Northwest Coast tribes responded to crowding and competition by following the contradictory procedures of raiding, on the one hand, and developing a complex intervillage ceremonial gifting and feasting tradition, on the other.

In Southern California, water sites, gathering sites, houses, and house sites were owned by patrisibs, which were the ultimate units of political and economic autonomy in that region. Hunting territories, which supported little game, were not protected so vigorously as gathering sites, which produced remarkable stores, and water sites (springs and seeps located at oases), which were vital to existence.

In the Southwest and among some peripheral farming cultures in the Great Basin, farming resource areas were always treated as private property, whether owned by whole villages, lineages, or even small units. These farming areas were the most productive resource areas, and the land parcels as well as the crops were treated as inviolate; all farmers owned their farming sites. Other kinds of resource areas were not protected as private property, except for key gathering sites among Yuman speakers and some Eastern Pueblos, and key gathering and hunting sites among most Apacheans. In each Eastern Pueblo village, ownership of both corporeal and incorporeal property was vested in the sodality leadership, and nuclear families were given usufruct rights to village-owned property. On the other hand, Western Pueblo localized matrisibs owned the most important in-

corporeal properties in their villages. Among the Western Pueblos, Jemez Eastern Pueblos, and the Navajos, matrisibs owned farm sites. Among the Yuman speakers, individual men claimed ownership of farming and gathering sites for their immediate families. Among the Western Apacheans, gathering sites, hunting sites, and some farming sites were owned by matrilineages, though other farming sites were private property of individual persons. The Eastern Apacheans also owned farming sites either as individual persons or through matridemes. The Chiricahua Apaches also recognized hunting and gathering sites as matrideme property. Chiricahuan matridemes, in all but descent reckoning, were comparable to the Western Apachean matrilineages in economic ownership (Map Cu-81, V-272).

Ownership among Plateau tribes was sometimes vested in patrihouseholds, sometimes in individual persons, and sometimes in villages or bands. Plateau concepts of ownership are of special interest because of the manner in which access to privately owned resources was granted by owners to nonowners, and because of how communitarian uses and intercommunity relations were emphasized in Plateau communities over kinship-group or family uses. Although the Plateau tribes recognized private property in several forms, access to those properties was much more similar to the communitarian practices of Great Basin tribes and the more nomadic tribes in the Southwest than it was to Southern California, California, or Northwest Coast uses.

Inheritance (V-274 to V-287) of control over key resources usually was bestowed on the eldest and most competent son of the person who served as the steward for the property in the patrilineal and bilateral societies. In the matrilineal societies on the Northwest Coast, the eldest sister's son succeeded to the position of steward of the kinship group's property. In the Southwest, matrilineal inheritance was vested in women for farm property, though their brothers were vested with control over the lineage's rituals.

In the Plateau, in the southern areas of the Northwest Coast, and among the less sedentary groups in the Southwest, competence was a more important criterion for succession to stewardship of resources than was inheritance. In California, competence demonstrated by the accumulation of wealth was the principal criterion for succession to tribelet and patrihousehold stewardship.

An important point to bear in mind about ownership and inheritance is that ownership of key resources was practically always vested in a group of people rather than an individual. The northwestern California and southern subareas of the Northwest Coast represent the only real exceptions to this

---

*The centralized polities of the Athapaskan-speaking Nongatl, Sinkyone, Mattole, and Kato tribes will be discussed in Chapter 9.

generalization. In the central and northern subareas, when one man was selected as the steward of a group's property, all members of that group were co-owners of that property and he was their representative: the highest-ranking member of each kinship group was extolled by his kinspeople whom he represented at great ceremonies, but he did not have the right to dispose of his kinship group's strategic resources or incorporeal property.

ECONOMIC DISTRIBUTION

Food and other movable properties were distributed within and among communities in a wide variety of ways in western North America. Trade was only one of many mechanisms employed, and it may have been the least important of all of them in pre-Contact times, even though it was an extremely widespread means of effecting exchanges of things among tribes. Reciprocity, gifting, feasts, redistributive gifting, raids, and allowance of joint access to resource areas were all important means of distributing property. Distribution mechanisms were least pretentious in the Great Basin and most elaborate throughout the Northwest Coast, where they became the centerpiece of Northwest Coast culture during the early period of contact with Europeans.

In western North America, the organization of distribution should be thought of as separate from ownership only for analytic purposes, and both ownership and the organization of distribution are more realistically viewed if not separated from kinship organization except for analytic purposes. All of these organizational phenomena were intricately bound together in native understanding and practice and they formed clearly defined patterns within complex areas, being influenced by such factors as the resources or limitations of the environment, the technology used to manipulate the environment, the organization of extraction or production, and the competition among neighbors for resources.

For instance, across a distance extending roughly from San Francisco Bay in northern California to the Siskyou-Sierra region in the northeast, hunting territories more or less defined tribelet territories and were the common property of tribelets which the tribelets defended from trespass. Within tribelet areas, however, improved hunting sites such as deadfalls were often claimed as the private property of specific patribilateral households, or even of the men who developed them. There was other fractionation of ownership, as we have seen. In the wider area trade was highly developed, so that food and chattels

moved great distances from their sources. Baskets, preferred types of acorns, pulverized fish, dried shellfish, venison, woodpecker scalps, feathers of many kinds, ornamental shells (such as those of *Olivella*, *Haliotis*, and *Dentalium* genera) and a much longer list of items were moved in many directions from their sources, and shells from the California coast were traded as far away as the Pueblos in the Southwest. Northern Californians had boats to ply the rivers and trails for moving between and across territories.

Yet native Californians seldom had contact with anyone beyond the distance of one or two tribelets. They knew their closest neighbors well and protected their territories from them, but entered into feasts and trading with them. Within their home communities native northern Californians had an equally well developed sense of trade. They often sold objects to their own kinspeople by using standard values that had been established throughout the region, such as trading one hand's-width of *Dentalia* shells for some quantity of pulverized fish, or they higgle-haggled over the worth of some object until an acceptable bargain was struck. The recognition of private property within the tribelet, bargaining among kinspeople and nonkinspeople within the tribelet, and protection of resources against trespass was a combination of practices unique among the concepts of ownership and distribution in western North America.

For instance, in the Plateau, some private property was also recognized as belonging to kinship groups and individuals within the community, bargaining was also common among kinspeople and nonkinspeople from the same community. Yet in the Plateau, joint access was provided to private resource areas, gifts to kinspeople and nonkinspeople were given often without the expectation of return, and goods were also reciprocated without bartering. The differences in the resource areas in the northern part of California and the Plateau might be thought to account for the different treatment of community resources and private resources in these regions. Except for fishing stations and root grounds, Plateau resources were diffuse and relatively scarce across the scablands and cold semideserts of the Middle Columbia and the Fraser Rivers. Dugout or bark canoes were used to ply the rivers, and tribes from considerable distances commingled, traded, and jointly used Plateau resources. Northern California resources were more localized, more bountiful, and more easily procured. This led to larger populations, more crowding since there was less space in which to expand, and a greater emphasis on keeping that which belonged to families or individuals.

The problem with this argument is that it suggests, by an analogous line of thinking, that Plateau people, having less abundant resources than northern Californians, would have worried all the more shrewdly about their own survival, so would have had a greater reason than Californians to higgle-haggle in the hope of driving a hard bargain, to withhold gifts, and to deny access to their resources.

Similarly, arguments that depend on contrasts between locally abundant and widely dispersed resources cannot be sustained when a brief comparison is made with the Northwest Coast. In that area, the climate was mild, resources were abundant and concentrated in certain areas, population was dense, property was owned by kinship groups and was protected against trespass, and there was the constant threat of raid. Yet there was practically no bargaining or higgle-haggle *within* communities. Reciprocity mechanisms and excessive gifting were the foundations of economic relations among kinspeople and nonkinspeople within a community, and though bargaining and the uses of standard values occurred between people from distant communities—communities often several hundred miles apart—regular formal procedures were established through intermarriage and joint attendance at ceremonies, by which trade relations were transformed to gifting relations, and by which access to resources rather than denial of such access was provided among widely scattered people. The world in which Northwest Coast and Plateau tribes lived seemed large and expansive, whereas to the northern Californian the world seemed much more restricted. The distribution organizations for California and the Northwest Coast are easily rationalized: both fitted beautifully into their cultural and natural environments. Either set of mechanisms could have worked in the other region instead, and the mechanisms used on the Plateau could have worked in California or the Northwest Coast, but that is not how things were.

Let us turn to an assessment of the various organizations of distribution in western North America, accounting for similarities and differences wherever plausible. Economic organizations make more sense when analyzed in terms of several related variables rather than when a single variable is analyzed at a time, so let us first present the data variable by variable, then generalize about the relationships among the economic variables within and among culture areas.

The variable maps in Appendix D that are pertinent to this discussion are separated into sets, one of which deals with local or intracommunity economic relations, and one of which deals with extralocal or intercommunity economic relations. Each set deals with major topics such as reciprocity, redistribution, gifting, barter or trade, access to strategic resources,

and the ceremonialism or etiquette involved in these transactions.

Local Economic Distribution

The types of reciprocity that occurred in the many communities throughout the West are shown in Map Cu-83, V-249. In reciprocity transactions a donor gives something to a recipient, such as food, a basket, or a pot. It is expected that the recipient will give something in return in the future.

Balanced reciprocity, which was by far the dominant mode in western North America, was an exchange of equal amounts between donors and receivers. The receiver did not need to repay immediately but was expected to repay at some time. Generalized reciprocity, which occurred in conjunction with balanced reciprocity in northwestern California and in the central and northern subareas of the Northwest Coast, was the practice of a kinship group leader or (in northwestern California) a nominal chief giving much more than they received in return. It was generalized because the kinship group chiefs and village chiefs gave to everyone in their groups. Negative reciprocity occurred along the central and southern parts of the Northwest Coast. In these transactions the donors received much more in return than they gave originally.

Forms of local redistribution were most complex along the West Coast, as is demonstrated in Map Cu-84, V-256. Local redistribution* refers to the practice by which some individual or group collects chattels and food from several people and then redistributes these, in the form of feasts, gifts, or both, to people not related to the giver. On some occasions, however, gifts were also redistributed to people who were related to the giver. Individuals, heads of kinship groups (lineages, demes, sibs, households), and chiefs of residential groups (such as villages or localized bands) usually directed the redistributions.

Barter is treated synonymously with trade in this study and distinguished from reciprocity and gifting (Map Cu-85, V-261). Barter in the local community means that two people either bargained over the val-

---

*Throughout this study "redistribution" is defined as the centralized collection of food and/or chattels by kinship groups, sodalities, villages, or some authority followed by the distribution of these chattels and/or food to people other than those who produced and collected it, but perhaps including those who produced and collected it.

ues of the two items they were exchanging, or they used standard values to establish the worth of an item being traded. The most commonly used standard values in western North America were strands of prized shells of such species as *Dentalium*, *Haliotis*, and *Olivella*. Standard equations were used to fix the price, say, of a basket of pulverized acorns. Some sort of trade went on in the majority of local communities, except in the central and northern parts of the Northwest Coast and in Southern California, where reciprocity, redistribution, and gifting dominated economic transaction, and among the camps in the central Great Basin and Apachean groups in the Southwest, where reciprocity and gifting dominated. Exceptions occurred, then, among groups that possessed the most resources and chattels, and groups that possessed the least.

Gifting differs from reciprocity in that gifts were given ostensibly with no strings attached. The giver simply gave to the receiver. In practice, however, it was bad form if the recipient did not give a gift in return at some time. On the Northwest Coast, for instance, the giving of gifts within the community at the naming ceremony for one's daughter (or son) was critical. Without a gift-giving ceremony the community would not recognize the girl's incorporeal property right to the name that was bestowed upon her. Although recipients of the gifts at these and related ceremonies were not bound to repay, recognition of the girl's right to use the name bestowed upon her was fully established only at a subsequent ceremony sponsored by another family in the local community. The girl's father was invited to attend the ceremony and would be given gifts appropriate to the name he had originally claimed for his daughter at the ceremony he had sponsored for her. The family sponsoring the second distributive ceremony recognized the parents' claim, while making a claim of some sort for their own family. The more the second host gave, the stronger the claim of the parents to the rights, prerogatives, or statuses they sought for their daughter at the distribution they sponsored on her behalf.*

Gifting within the local communities was most de-

veloped in the Northwest Coast and Plateau areas, as is shown in Map Cu-86, V-262; in both of these regions, consideration of rank, kinship relations, and affinal relations were important in gifting. Elsewhere in western North America, with the exception of a few California communities, a person's relative rank had little to do with gift exchange. And among northern California tribelets, some Middle Columbia Plateau villages, and the easternmost Shoshones and Utes, gifts were exchanged between any people, not only between kin and affines.

In most communities, all residents either had free access to local food-resource areas such as fishing and hunting sites or could gain access to the resources by requesting the favor from the owners (Map Cu-87, V-251; Map Cu-88, V-254). In some situations owners might invite affine or friends to share their resource areas, often in conjunction with a local ceremonial occasion. In a very few Northwest Coast and Southwest farming communities, access to private property was denied to local residents.

Etiquette, or some formality such as requesting food in a particular way, or reciprocating a chattel in a culturally approved fashion, attended practically all of the reciprocity transactions along the Northwest Coast, and attended many similar transactions in northern California, the Plateau, and the Southwest. In the Great Basin, central California, and Southern California, special etiquette was not required for reciprocating. It was enough to take something without asking, or to receive something without asking, and to reciprocate. It is evident that the correlation between etiquette and ceremonialism in reciprocity within the local community was only loosely correlated with private property ownership (Map Cu-89, V-252) but was highly correlated with local barter. This implies that even balanced reciprocity was attended by some formality in the areas where barter was practiced within the local community, and that barter and reciprocity were clearly distinguished.

Local redistributions in all but two tribes (the Tubatulabal and Southern Pomo of California) were attended by some ceremonialism which marked these gift-giving transactions. In the majority of local redistributions attending such events as child namings, girl's puberty ceremonies, or first-fruits ceremonies, all recipients were treated equally in the amount and quality of the gifts they received. But throughout the central, northern, and northwestern California subareas of the Northwest Coast, ceremonies always attended redistributions and the recipients received goods unequally. In general, the highest-ranking people received the best and the most goods, and they also received them earlier in the ceremony than lower-ranking people. The forms

---

*Distribution follows the usage of Homer Barnett (1955) who distinguished between intracommunity distributions sponsored by a family on behalf of a child, and intercommunity distributions sponsored by a kinship group on behalf of one of its members. On the Northwest Coast the intervillage distributions, known by the Chinook jargon term, potlatch, most probably grew by extension from intravillage distributions. Distributions and potlatches are discussed on page 145.

and styles of redistributions in the northern and central subareas on the one hand, and the northwestern California subarea on the other, were very different and most probably had different origins.

Extralocal Economic Distribution

Economic transactions between people from two communities, especially reciprocal transactions, were commonplace. By and large, reciprocity between people from different communities was balanced (Map Cu-91A, V-255). The exceptions to giving about as much as one received were few. For instance, there is little evidence that the Apacheans reciprocated or gifted with people from neighboring communities. Most of their economic transactions with people from other communities were through trading, raiding, attending ceremonies (with feasts), and sharing access to resources. The Uto-Aztecans of central California (Mono, Kawaiisu, Tubatulabal) and some of the Yokuts tribelets in that region did not reciprocate outside their own tribelets. Their economic transactions with people from other communities practically always took the form of gifting. In the central and northern Northwest Coast, some communities were dominated by people who either gave more than they received or who were involved in balanced transactions (Haida, Tsimshian, some Kwakuitlan and some Salishan societies); some received much more than they gave (the Tlingits were negative donors); and some were characterized both by balanced transactions and by receiving more goods than they gave (e.g., many Gulf of Georgia Salishan chiefs). These Northwest Coast groups integrated reciprocity into a part of a complex intercommunity and intracommunity exchange system that made special recognition of individual and kinship-group rank, and in some instances (the Tsimshian groups, for example), even village rankings. These rankings were of maximal importance in extralocal redistributions (V-256; see Map Cu-84, because the distributions are identical for local and extralocal redistribution). Individuals, not entire communities, were invited to attend intercommunity ceremonials and were given gifts on the basis of their ranks and the ranks of their kinship groups. In California, the Plateau, and the Southwest, the recipients of goods at extralocal redistributions were not ranked and their gifts were equal. Throughout these societies both extralocal reciprocity and redistribution were attended by formalities that called attention to the importance of the transactions (Map Cu-91B, V-258).

Most of the same societies who so carefully redistributed and reciprocated goods among their neighbors—especially the farming villages in the Southwest, the successful gatherers in Southern California, the semisedentary tribelets of California, and the kinship groups of the central and northern Northwest Coast—generally denied access to subsistence resource areas to all nonowners. Among a few groups in the southern subarea of the Northwest Coast, however, individual persons granted access to their privately owned resources. This was done only after the proper formalities, and usually in conjunction with bargaining as well (Map Cu-92, V-257; Map Cu-93, V-260). On the other hand, the Apacheans and Pais of the Southwest, the people of the Great Basin, and most Plateau groups provided access only to some of their principal resource areas (but not to farmland). The diffuseness of the resources in the arid regions occupied by these extractors may have stimulated this practice. Resources were seldom so concentrated in small regions as to be the principal sources of food for a group, so claiming control over resource areas seldom meant that the owners were the only users, and other people were allowed to use some key properties. Sharing in this fashion may have been an advantage in that it promoted reciprocal uses of territories among Great Basin and Southwestern extractors. In the Plateau, however, where key fish and root resources were located in concentrated places and were frequently very abundant, joint use of resources seems to have stimulated trade, gifting, and reciprocity, so should not be equated with Great Basin and Apachean–Pai practices.

Barter and trade between individuals from different communities were common everywhere but in the Great Basin and Southern California, where reciprocity and gifting dominated. Barter was most developed in California, the Northwest Coast, and the Plateau, where everyone was free to bargain. Standard values were used somewhat less widely in these regions, though they were the only form used in transactions among most northwestern California people. It is not a coincidence that, in all of western North America, rights to individual ownership of property were most highly developed in northwestern California. Wealth and the individual responsibility for wealth were very important considerations among these people. In the Southwest, most of the predominant farming societies relied on a form of trade in which standard values were not used and in which bartering was conducted only between strangers: friends were given gifts, instead. Only the Western Pueblos differed from this pattern and bargained with everyone (Map Cu-94, V-263; Map Cu-95, V-264).

Some form of gifting went on between people from different communities within practically every tribe in western North America except among the Apacheans (Navajos excluded) and Western Pueblos in the Southwest, and some Hokan speakers in northern California. In California, where tribelets or patrisibs were represented by leaders, leaders were the people who most often exchanged gifts. Along the Northwest Coast, gifting most often was conditioned by rank and by the kinds of relations engaged in by in-laws and kin of donors and receivers alike from different communities (Map Cu-96, V-265).

Again and again we have seen how private property concepts were most highly developed along coastal western North America and in the sedentary Southwest. In these areas, since barter, reciprocity, gifting, redistribution, and sharing of access to privately owned resources were complex and often intertwined with the functions of kinship and ceremonial organizations, distributive mechanisms were also the most elaborate. A review of the distribution organizations in the culture areas of the West will allow us to piece together how distribution varied among areas, and to account for the variation.

ECONOMIC DISTRIBUTION: AREAL PATTERNS

Great Basin Reciprocity

In the Great Basin, balanced reciprocity and gifting between people in the same communities as well as between people from different communities were by far the dominant modes of distribution of goods throughout the area. Usually no formality was involved in the transactions. As a matter of fact, reciprocity in the Great Basin was so informal and generous that it could be called simply "giving" rather than balanced reciprocity were it not the case that donors and receivers reversed roles, often following long gaps between transactions.

The very egalitarian and generous ways of Great Basin dwellers carried over to their resource areas, to which all members of the local communities had equal access, people from other communities generally being granted access with little or no formality. Gifting rather than barter or redistribution characterized most transactions between members of different communities; for example, friends and affines (relatives-in-law) from different communities were reciprocated or gifted.

There was some bartering with strangers, though people in the Great Basin proper had little to barter.

The Utes, who traded animal byproducts among the Pueblos for farm products, were the principal intercommunity traders in the Great Basin. Their trading was conducted by special groups of men who journeyed to the villages carrying animal products. The Utes were also the principal raiders in the Great Basin, often raiding the Pueblo villages, but raiding was more a post-Contact phenomenon made possible by the use of horses than a pre-Contact phenomenon.

The paucity of trade items among most Great Basin groups, the weakly developed notion of private property, and the emphasis on reciprocity and gifting as the mode of exchange were the underpinnings of the flexible and open economic organizations of the local groups in the area. Great Basin economies contrasted markedly with the economic organizations of the neighboring tribes in California, Southern California (whence the Great Basin dwellers originally migrated), and the Southwest. It is most plausible that the paucity of game and the erratic quantity and diffuse distribution of other food sources influenced the maintenance of the reciprocal-based economies in the Great Basin. Reciprocity moved goods without strict accounting, from the people who possessed them to people who did not. Repayment could come at any time.

This is not to argue that by dint of ecological necessity the Great Basin people had to develop reciprocating and resource-sharing economies, but in so doing, they obviated most competition for local abundances, and perhaps they obviated offensive raiding as well, at least in the central portions of the Great Basin. Ownership of key resources could have been claimed by many Basin groups, but it was not. If Southern Paiute and Western Shoshone farmers had been more vigorous in their horticultural pursuits, they could have become as sedentary as the Western Pueblos, but in fact, farming was not much developed by Great Basin groups, nor were the best fisheries appropriated by camps that frequented them. Instead, resources were open and available to all, and the extracted goods were stored only for brief periods; the natural environment itself was the Great Basin's best storehouse, its generosity characterizing also those who drew from it.

Plateau Egalitarian Exchanges

Some private ownerships (of improved hunting sites), some patribilateral household and deme ownership (of fishing stations and houses), and some communal—that is, band or village—ownership (of gathering and hunting territories) were recognized among most Plateau groups. Although some resources such as root grounds were localized and important for subsistence, root grounds were usually communally owned and access to them was often allowed neighboring groups. The importance of this practice is that root grounds and some other key properties were not owned and controlled in the same fashion they were among Northwest Coast kinship groups. Access was regularly provided to people from different bands who spoke different languages from the owners. Moreover, these key properties were not jealously guarded against poachers and trespassers, as they were in California. As was pointed out earlier, the similarities and differences among organizations of distribution in Northern California, the Northwest Coast, and the Plateau demonstrate that many different forms of economic exchange worked (or were "adaptive") in somewhat similar contexts.

Plateau people fished at their own stations, inviting other people from their own community and from different communities to join them in the task with each person being the sole owner of his personal catch. Fishermen caught fish, and their wives filleted and pulverized them. Fish byproducts were traded, either by standard values or hard bargaining. Fish byproducts were also gifted, reciprocated, and used in feasts sponsored by owners for nonowners. These various kinds of economic transactions were how most types of movable property available to Plateau tribes, such as baskets, hides, furs, and canoes and paddles were exchanged, while access to strategic food resources, such as root grounds, was made available as well.

The great fisheries and root grounds became centers of economic, social, and ritual relations among people speaking several languages and representing many bands, who walked or moved down the rivers to key spots in dugout and bark canoes during the salmon and gathering seasons and, upon arrival, engaged in all sorts of economic transactions as well as contracting marriages, gambling, attending storytelling sessions, and participating in feasts. The social and ritual relations that linked these activities, drawing together people from considerable distances and many tribes, created a more expansive social world and a wider set of amicable contacts than the natives of Northern California had; and relations among Plateau people were more egalitarian and access to resource areas more freely granted than on the Northwest Coast. The raiding skirmishes that followed poaching between northern California tribelets, and the raids for booty, slaves, and even territory that occurred on the Northwest Coast were largely nonexistent in the pacifistic Plateau. The egalitarian

social and ritual network into which economic transactions were woven must have obviated most internal raiding in the Plateau.

No simple rationalization adequately explains why Plateau economic practices were so different from northern California and Northwest Coast practices. A reasonable explanation must account for such fortuities as providing neighbors access to strategic resources and basing an entire economic organization on open exchanges. The cultural style of the Plateau differed sharply from the Northwest Coast, but the roots of Plateau culture were surely planted in the Northwest Coast, and Plateau and Northwest Coast tribes influenced each other for centuries. Although family or kinship group-ownership of fishing stations was a practice of Penutians and Salishans throughout both the Coast and Plateau, the coastal people controlled their fishing sites much differently than did the Plateau people. And in the Fraser Plateau, modest intertribal redistribution ceremonies similar to potlatches on the Northwest Coast varied from the coastal pattern in that guests were gifted and feasted in an egalitarian fashion rather than a ranked fashion.

Plateau people emphasized generosity, gifting, reciprocity, and feasting, and they eschewed raids and battles just as Great Basin people did, but Plateau dwellers had more to exchange and more to lose than Great Basin people had. Plateau people also emphasized barter, much as in northern California, yet they used every nonhostile mechanism known in western North America to exchange and grant access to property beyond trade. Winter Spirit Sings,* interhousehold visiting, first-fruits ceremonies (ritual observances in conjunction with the first harvest of some resource each year, such as salmon or camas roots), salmon harvests, naming ceremonies, and marriage ceremonies were interhousehold and intervillage mechanisms for distribution of goods in ways other than engaging in explicit trade through standardized values or bargaining.

California Barter

The recognition of individual rights of ownership and control of strategic food resources was more highly developed throughout northern and northwestern

---

*Winter Spirit Sings were ceremonies held recurrently during each winter season in practically all Plateau villages. Hosts fed guests at these affairs, but guests often brought gifts of food with them and offered them to hosts. Winter Spirit Sings are analyzed in Chapter 10, "Ceremonialism."

California and along the Oregon Coast than anywhere else in western North America. Concomitantly, the greatest development of intracommunity barter (bargaining and standardized values), even between kinspeople, also occurred among the tribes in that region. In the central area of California, intracommunity bartering was restricted to people who were not kinsmen. All other mechanisms, such as gifting, reciprocity, and redistribution, operated within and between communities, but the manner and contexts in which such exchanges occurred distinguished California from other areas.

Wealthy men often gave more than they received to their kinspeople and to others in their tribelets because it was expected of them if they wished to be influential in tribelet affairs, especially if they wished to become chiefs and to direct the intertribelet feasts that were often associated with important ceremonies. Guests from adjacent tribelets were invited to attend feasts that stretched over periods of several days. The tribelet members contributed food for the feast, if they wished to, and often they provided food as gifts to be taken home by their guests.

Guests were often suspicious that they might be poisoned (by witchcraft) or harmed at these occasions. Yet these occasions were also times to negotiate marriages, to trade property, and to watch shamans' performances. In this setting, the host tribelet attempted to demonstrate its good intentions toward its guests, yet it also sought to demonstrate the resolve of the tribelet to protect itself and the power of the tribelet to be successful in that resolution. Although people were invited from several communities scattered in all directions from the host community, people from tribelets separated by more than one tribelet's territory from the host were seldom invited and were often regarded as enemies.

Although northern California Indians traveled easily in the abundant waterways of the northernmost area and central Californians traveled easily by foot, the world of California Indians was quite small and except for shamans, personal travel was very limited. On the other hand, goods traveled many miles from their point of origin, usually being relayed from community to community through traders in each community. Guest traders would bargain or use standard values to exchange goods with resident traders who, in turn, would trade with people in adjacent tribelets. In California it was acceptable to barter food, baskets, knives, or anything else of value. When bargaining went on between kinsmen in the same community, it was usually over some item produced by a specialist, and not food. Among the Yurok, Wiyot, Karok, Hupa, Tolowa, and Tututni of northwestern California, a subarea of the Northwest

Coast, economic distribution was unique, paralleling neither California nor Northwest Coast practices. Food was not traded within communities at all. It was plentiful and given away at feasts and as gifts.

Many of the tribelets in northern California, as was pointed out earlier, stood out from the tribes in all other areas because they recognized private property rights for some people within the tribelet. Northern California was unique, too, in that bargaining occurred between kinspeople and nonkinspeople within the tribelets, and in that entire tribelets protected resource areas against trespass. Although each of these customs was known or practiced in other areas, only in northern California did they all come together and did they include recognition of private property among people whose movements and contacts were restricted to such small areas.

Northwest Coast Hierarchical Distributions

Along the Northwest Coast, from the southern through the northern subareas, key strategic resources were owned by kinship units rather than villages, tribes, or chiefdoms. Supervision of these resources was also vested in the kinship groups, who exercised paramount authority. The Tsimshian speakers in the north, in northwestern California the Mattole, Sinkyone, and Nongatl (all Athapaskan speakers), and the Yurok, Wiyot, et al., were exceptions to this generalization. There is no doubt that the Tsimshians developed village-political and, during the historic period, chiefdom-political hegemony over some aspects of resource supervision as they expanded north along the coast, displacing both Haida and Tlingit peoples. It may also have been that the Mattole, Sinkyone, and Nongatl were organized into villages with jurisdictional authority over kinship groups because they, too, entered the coastal region of northwestern California after the groups in the northern California interior through whom they passed had already formed into tribelets. If there were no unconfederated family groups to displace, only tribelets, the Athapaskan response to encountering Northern California tribelets may have been to consolidate and migrate in a single group. If, on the other hand, Athapaskans squeezed some people from coastal territories, it may have been because these were organized into anarchistic communities much like the Yurok and Karok: such people would most easily be forced from their territories by organizations larger than themselves. Whatever the case, the Mattole, Sinkyone, and Nongatl were bordered on the south and east by tribelets who defended their own territories.

Among all other Northwest Coast groups, kinship units owned property and the members of each kinship group sponsored economic distributions of a ceremonial nature that linked together people from different kinship groups in the same communities and affines from different communities. What evolved in response to the need for development of a grand distribution system in an area where resources were rich and raiding was a constant threat was one stabilizing mechanism that may well have made unnecessary the Tsimshianlike development of political hegemony of the few over the many. It is as if competition was waged on a single level, where ceremonial and economic mechanisms channeled this competition. The Tsimshians, as it were, perhaps operated on another level, since they came into direct conflicts with Haida and Tlingit lineages. Yet even among the Tsimshians, lineages owned property, though the ranking lineage chief also controlled village property.

The salient feature of the organization of distribution among Northwest Coast kinship groups were the *distributions* themselves. These were intravillage and interhousehold affairs attending birth, naming, puberty, marriage, death, and several other events in a person's lifetime which were causes for parents to sponsor a feast and distribute gifts to everyone in their local community in the name of the family's child: it was for the child that each distribution was sponsored. These distributions were among the principal mechanisms for local exchanges of goods, and they were held with such regularity that goods were constantly moving among households.

Distributions which, more than likely, were expanded to an intervillage scale during the period of contact with Europeans became known by the Chinook jargon word "potlatch," which may have derived from the Nootkan word for "gift," *potshatl*. In these affairs a kinship-group chief collected food and chattels from all members of his kinship group, an enormous set of feasts was prepared, and influential and highly ranked guests were invited from many highly ranked kinship groups near and far. In addition to being treated to the feast, each guest was provided gifts on the basis of that person's rank among all other guests. These affairs were not wholly one-sided. In their canoes guests also brought gifts of fish and other food to the feast. (See Barnett 1938 for an unsurpassed analysis of the potlatch, and Barnett 1955, Drucker 1951, and Drucker and Heizer 1967 for other excellent analyses.)

Among residents within the local communities on the northern and central Northwest Coast there was no barter, either through the higgle-haggle of bargaining or through standard values. Yet access to resource areas was denied to nonowners. Gifting, in the context of distributions, moved goods among and between kinship groups, and reciprocity, too, was basic to intracommunity exchanges. Reciprocity between people in different kinship groups did not occur often: most reciprocity was within the kinship group, the chief being expected to give much more than he received and to be generous in hosting meals. Within each kinship group, people reciprocated goods on a balanced basis, the most opportune period for reciprocation being just prior to a distribution planned by a kinsman, since at that time goods were borrowed from their kinspeople by the parents sponsoring the distribution and added to whatever the parents had produced or accumulated through attending distributions since last sponsoring a distribution themselves. After they gave the goods away at the distribution for their child they were called upon to repay their kinspeople only when the kinspeople planned to sponsor distributions of their own.

The chief usually lent more toward each distribution than anyone else, and it was expected that he would receive much more in return than he gave. This form of negative reciprocity had the support of the members of the kinship group because, by paying back all they had received, plus much more that they had accumulated and produced since originally borrowing from the chief, they could help to maintain the position and good name of their kinship group. The distributions and potlatches sponsored by chiefs always included the entire kinship group, even when the events honored a chief's son or daughter.

Intercommunity exchanges beyond potlatches included barter by reliance on standard values and by bargaining. But they were also consummated through extensive gifting between affines. Most high-ranking families sought to arrange marriages in distant villages, in order to draw themselves into a wider ceremonial network and establish additional gifting and reciprocating contacts as well as trade contacts (after the arrival of Europeans). Access to certain resource areas, such as shellfish beds, were often provided to affines as a form of etiquette and hospitality, which strengthened the bonds between the kinship groups.

It is very likely that the development of the potlatch from distributions was a rather recent phenomenon stimulated by the desire of Europeans for furs and hides and the desire of Northwest Coast natives for trade goods, such as pieces of copper, which they could give away in order to enhance their local and regional ranking (see Barnett 1955, Drucker 1951, and Drucker and Heizer 1967). During the Contact period Northwest Coast populations were decimated by epidemics, but at the same time trade goods were sought increasingly by coastal Indians just as pelts and hides were sought increasingly by Europeans. Paradoxically, though raids across greater and greater distances may have been initiated to secure pelts, furs, and other items of European interest, potlatching probably developed as a means of reducing hostile contacts. Although the potlatch did not do away with raiding, people who established amicable contacts in distant villages through intermarriages and ceremonial participation did not normally raid those villages, nor were they raided by them. The worlds of Northwest Coast natives, especially of the highest-ranking members of the highest-ranking kinship groups, in some senses became more amicable and much larger than they had been prior to contact, yet paradoxically raids, too, were conducted farther and farther from home villages.

Raids were always a threat to coastal dwellers, and resource areas were always guarded from trespass. Only invitations, normally extended to affines, gave access to resource sites to nonowners; and there is no evidence that the people who extended such invitations did this often or that they invited others to use key areas such as fishing stations.

The hierarchical nature of gifting and the absence of local barter and local nonowner-access to kinship-group resource areas distinguished organization of the economic distributions among the highly independent Northwest Coast kinship groups from the tribelets in Northern California and the bands and villages in the Plateau.

Among the Indians of two subareas of the Northwest Coast—along the southern Northwest Coast and in northwestern California—individuals, patribilateral families, some patrilineal families, and for the Mattole, Sinkyone, and Nongatl, even villages owned property. The Indians of these subareas never developed potlatches, suggesting either that potlatches were relatively recent phenomena, or that the societies on the Oregon coast and in northwestern California were beyond the mainstream of central and northern Northwest Coast culture. The histories of the two areas seem to be quite different, so that many of the similarities between the regions, such as kinship-group ownership of property, may be old and independently arrived-at traits. Even interpersonal economic relations diverged from the practices to the north. For instance, in these more southern areas intracommunity barter even between kinspeople was common, though kinspeople were more apt to reciprocate or offer gifts to one another than to bargain. Generalized reciprocity in which a wealthy person gave more than he received was common in northwestern California. But in coastal Oregon, balanced and negative reciprocity were the only forms of reciprocity practiced, and negative reciprocity predominated.

Along the Oregon coast, a unique set of practices developed. Hard bargaining was conducted during trade. Even a so-called reciprocity transaction took the form of an unequal exchange between someone who desired goods and someone who possessed goods that were desirable. The person whose goods were sought received more for his property than did the person with whom he exchanged. In general, the people who possessed the most desirable items were the wealthiest men in the communities. The gains that accrued in reciprocity and trade transactions were not then redistributed for the good of the kinship group, as was the case farther north. Except for perishables that were eaten, goods were accumulated by the owners, and prestige items such as obsidian blades and woodpecker scalps were especially prized.

The Tillamook on the northern Oregon coast sponsored modest distributions at naming ceremonies in which kinspeople and nonkinspeople were guests at a feast. Gifting, on the other hand, was restricted to kinspeople. The economic transactions of Oregon coastal people operated more in the trade and negative-reciprocity modes than in the gifting and redistribution modes. These people provide a most interesting contrast to central and northern Northwest Coast tribes in the way in which wealth was used to establish social position. In Oregon and northwestern California, the wealthiest men sponsored displays of wealth during the winter. Although they were helped to host feasts for local residents and neighboring villages by other members of the host community, who also contributed food to the feast, the wealthy men did not part with the property that they displayed at these feasts: these prestige items were displayed so as to enhance the positions of their owners and their immediate families, but not to enhance the position of a larger kinship group.

Inasmuch as the southern and northwestern California Northwest Coast people had appropriated localized resource areas in which abundances were predictable, the bartering in which they engaged allowed them to accumulate more goods for prestige, since they did not require more for survival. Although private property concepts existed in this area, and bargaining and negative reciprocity between kinspeople or nonkinspeople occurred within communities, the tribelets common in the California culture area did not form among people in northwestern California or along the Oregon coast: extended family households were the ultimate sovereign units, instead. The tribelets in the interior of northern

California observed the same property concepts and engaged in the same modes of economic transactions within their communities as their neighbors along the coast in northwestern California and Oregon, yet in coastal Oregon there were neither tribelets to protect and integrate small families nor potlatches to connect larger kinship groups in an areal economic system. Therefore it is likely that neither the potlatch nor tribelet, nor Oregon coastal organizations were necessary mechanisms for articulating social and economic relations in these areas of dense population, abundant and concentrated resources, and extractive subsistence adaptations, yet all three worked and probably any one of them could have worked in any one of these areas.

The anarchistic Yurok, Karok, Hupa, and Wiyot tribes of northwestern California differed from the other Northwest Coast groups in that many villages sponsored an elaborate cycle of what anthropologists call first-fruit rites, or world renewal ceremonies. Several villages sponsored dances and feasts spaced over the year and these festivities were integrated in a cycle. Guests were drawn from many villages to each host village in the cycle for a feast and celebration. Guests were also invited from communities that did not sponsor festivities in the cycle, such as Tolowa, Tututni, and Chilula. Although northwestern California individuals and families were ranked, a giveaway system such as the potlatch did not occur. These people, too, sponsored winter wealth displays.*

Southern California Sib and Moiety Reciprocity

Throughout Southern California among the Uto-Aztecan- and Yuman-speaking groups, patrisibs owned water sites as well as all gathering and hunting sites within definite territories. Patrisibs were the maximally autonomous political and economic groups in Southern California, and there was but one sib in each territory. The patrisibs were composed of two or more patrilineages who stipulated their descent from a common ancestor. Women married into a sib, leaving their natal community, and became members of their husband's sib.

Sib property was available for use by all members of the sib, but nonmembers were not granted access. As in areas to the north within California, should poachers trespass on sib property and be detected, a

battle would ensue. Within the sib each family owned the food it collected, but there was considerable reciprocation in distribution of food between sibmates. These exchanges were balanced so that in the long run people received about as much as they gave.

Barter within the sib was unheard of, yet redistribution of food by family heads to others in the sib at events such as birth and naming ceremonies were prominent features of Southern California life. The balanced egalitarian nature of reciprocity and redistribution in Southern California contrasted with Northwest Coast practices, and the absence of local bartering, bargaining, or the use of standard values in inter-community bargaining contrasted with northern California practices.

Intercommunity exchanges were developed around a moiety system that organized most patrisibs into either "wildcat" or "coyote" divisions. Ceremonies were sponsored for moiety reciprocals; that is, "coyotes" hosted "wildcats" and vice versa. Feasts accompanied the ceremonies, and gifts were often exchanged between lineage and sib leaders from the opposite moieties. The moiety-alignment of property-owning kinship groups meant that all economic transactions were conducted with extralocal groups.

In many ways the patrisibs were similar to the demes and lineages along the Northwest Coast, where there was no political organization larger than the kinship unit (except among the Tsimshians, some Athapaskans, and some Central and Northern Nootkan winter villages), and where lineages and sibs were aligned into exogamous moieties and phratries,* just as Southern California sibs were organized into moieties. In both regions kinship, political, and economic autonomy was retained by the property-owning units. The ritual relations among sibs and between moieties may have obviated larger and more centralized political organization. Moiety organization proscribed marriages within the moiety and prescribed reciprocal ceremonial sponsorship in which moiety mates from many sibs joined together to play host to their opposites.

People from different sibs often bartered goods they produced, but neither bargaining nor standard

---

*See Chapter 10, "Ceremonialism."

---

*Exogamy means to marry outside of some group, in these instances outside of one's lineage, sib, moiety, or phratry. A phratry was any organization in which the number of lineages or sibs was greater than two. Sibs of Tsimshian speakers and of the Haisla Kwakiutl were organized into four phratries, yet these paired with moieties of the Haidas and Tlingits for intermarriage.

values were used in those transactions. Hard-bargaining would have been bad form. Even when Mohave or Yuma (a.k.a. Quechan) traders visited Southern California groups, Southern California traders either accepted the first offer made by these River Yuman traders, or did not exchange at all.

In Southern California, the egalitarian and equal nature of reciprocity, redistribution, and moiety exchanges were complemented by the nonbargaining fashion in which intercommunity barter was conducted. Yet springs and resource areas were stoutly defended against trespass, and people from other sib communities, whether belonging to the same or different moieties, were not allowed to use local resources. In comparing Southern California with other regions, the importance of water in Southern California cannot be overlooked, nor can the general abundance of resources when making comparisons with the Northwest Coast. In Southern California there were concentrated areas of abundant, predictable, and storable foods, but these areas were frequently separated by considerable distance. Oases were not abundant. Along the Northwest Coast, on the other hand, ocean or riverine sources of fish were available for everyone and populations were closely spaced throughout all but the northernmost region. In that region fjords were deeper, mountains rose more steeply from the sea, and there were fewer wide riverbanks and coastal plains. It was precisely in the northernmost region that exogamous moieties developed, perhaps in response to political economic concerns. The exchange of women and the creation of affinal ties among otherwise competitive groups may well have been one solution to the maintenance of kinship groups as property-owning units, but by no means did these social relations do away with all raiding. As with relations established through potlatching—which were integrated with moiety membership on the northern Northwest Coast—moiety mates and moiety reciprocals who intermarried and participated in one another's ceremonies were not apt to mount raids against each other.

In the northern Northwest Coast, access to resources, especially exotic and locally variable resources, was sometimes granted to affines (moiety opposites in those communities), yet resources in general were abundant on the Northwest Coast, so kinship groups could probably allow some access to their resource areas by nonowners without jeopardizing the local group's food supply. Southern Californians, on the other hand, protected their property and mounted raids against trespassers, though they did not mount offensive raids, which the Northwest Coastal groups did. The stress on balanced reciprocity and equality in economic transactions in this hot, arid region ran counter to the Northwest Coast emphases on rank, accumulation of wealth, and conspicuous and competitive distributions.

Southwest: Traders, Raiders, and People in Between

Economic distribution in the Southwest had a much greater range of variation within and between tribes than in any other culture area. Differences in sedentariness, forms of resource-area ownership, amounts and types of raiding, and importance of farming to subsistence strongly influenced differences in economic distribution in the Southwest. The Pueblos, Pimans, and River Yumans were more sedentary than the Apacheans or the Pais, and they were also more dependent on farming than Apacheans or Pais were. The Yuma and Mohave groups among the River Yumans were also energetic traders, traveling from the California coast to the Pueblos, and were devastating raiders, frequently wreaking havoc on other River Yumans, including the Maricopa on the Gila River, and the Cocopa on the Delta. Mohave and Yuma raiding, trading, and wild-plant gathering proclivities were engaged in at the expense of greater dependence on farming. The choice to pursue raiding and trade had a marked effect on economic distribution in the Southwest. Apacheans, too, were raiders and traders and even less dependent on farming than the River Yumans. Apacheans frequently raided both Pueblo and Pima farming villages for farm products, however, whereas the Mohave and Yuma groups raided for booty, and for the prestige that accrued through war honors.

The raiding and trading behavior of the Apacheans and of the Mohave and Yuma River Yumans undoubtedly exerted considerable influence in shaping the nature of Southwestern economic and social organizations in the sixteenth and seventeenth centuries. Northeastern and Western Yavapais were fearful that if they farmed they would be attacked by Apache raiders. The Pima and Papago settlements were regularly attacked in the winters, their crops stolen and their villages burned, and many Pima groups were ultimately dislocated by Apachean raiders. Apacheans raided Pueblo villages from time to time, but also conducted trading ventures with these villages, so the specter of attack lurked behind the act of trading. The Pueblos were cut off from traditional sources of game by the expanding Apachean populations. For their part, Pueblos fiercely defended their farm sites from pilfering and prevented access to them by people who were not privileged to raise crops there. Yet Pueblos traded farm products with Apacheans and Utes for meat and animal byproducts, and they traded with Pais, who were intermediaries for River Yumans, for goods from places as far away as coastal California.

Equal reciprocity characterized interpersonal transactions throughout the Southwest, so in that sense the area differed from northern California and the Northwest Coast and was similar to the other regions of western North America. Residents within the groups that were the most dependent on crops and the most sedentary engaged in some bartering with people in their own communities to whom they were not related, but relatives did not barter with one another. They either reciprocated on an equal basis or they extended gifts. Some redistribution by family heads to everyone else in the community on certain occasions in the lives of their children also distinguished the groups of the Southwest from those of all other areas. A few gifts were collected and redistributed by parents to members of their communities in various ceremonies that attended the life cycles of their children. The distributions were modest in quantity of gifts and few in number in comparison with Northwest Coast distributions. Beyond the nuclear families, sodalities* in the Pueblos also collected food and provided feasts for the larger communities on ritual occasions.

Explicit redistributions between or among communities, between kinship groups in separate communities, or between sodalities in more than one community were not practiced among the Pueblos, though kinspeople, guests from other Pueblos, and guests from among the Apacheans were feasted at many Pueblo ceremonies. Among the River Yumans and the Pimans, local communities reciprocated by hosting feasts and drinking ceremonies (at these, an alcoholic beverage made from Sahuaro cactus was consumed). In each community the food and beverage was collected by the sponsors of the occasions and redistributed to the community members and their guests.

Among the Pueblos, River Yumans, and Pimans, intervillage bartering was similar to intravillage bartering. Friends, rather than kinspeople, were given gifts; bargaining characterized transactions between strangers. In these communities, even in the River Yuman communities, attempts were made to estab-lish friendships with strangers and to exchange gifts rather than to barter. The contrast between the practices of Pimans and River Yumans and those of the Apacheans and Utes to the north was marked. The Utes and Apacheans sought to bargain or to use standard values in all of their economic transactions with people from different communities. The differences in modes of transactions between the less sedentary hunting and gathering groups and the more sedentary farmers were not complete. The Apacheans in the Southwest and the Utes from the Rocky Mountains exchanged meat and animal byproducts for food and articles of Pueblo manufacture but were not easily drawn into economic relations based on friendly gift exchanges. The rather innocuous and mobile Papago tribe and Pai tribes,* on the other hand, exchanged animal byproducts with the Pima villages and River Yumans for agricultural products through reciprocating and gifting, and through joint attendance at ceremonials. Bartering was conducted only between strangers.

Thus, differences in intracommunity exchange mechanisms were not solely attributable to farming lifestyles versus mixed hunting-gathering-farming lifestyles but were also attributable to the effectiveness of Apachean and Ute raiding behavior. Apache and Ute groups posed a threat to Pueblos and were treated with care in bargaining. Yet Pueblos attempted to befriend Apaches in barter transactions. Pai groups and the Papago groups posed no threat to the River Yuman tribes and the Pima villages and exchanged goods with them through reciprocity, gifting, and ceremonial transactions.

Among the Pai groups, the Yavapais often squabbled with the Walapais, raiding them from time to time, but all the Pais remained friendly with the River Yumans and appear to have served as a buffer between them and the Apaches.

Whereas the Apacheans were aggressive raiders and traders, they were also more communitarian than the Pueblos, Pimans, and River Yumans. Apacheans recognized key farming, gathering, and hunting territories as the exclusive properties of sibs and bands,[†] yet access to these resources was granted to neighbors who desired to use the gathering and hunt-

---

*Sodalities were selective organizations into which people were initiated. They drew their membership from several kinship groups in each society. Sodalities are described in Chapter 9.

*The Southeastern Yavapai joined Western Apaches in aggressive raiding ventures. They posed a threat to Pueblos, Pimas, and Maricopa.

[†]Several matrisibs were organized into each band among the Western Apaches, and several matridemes were organized into each band among the Eastern Apaches. This is explained more fully in Chapters 8 and 9.

ing territories. Even farmland, which was owned by sibs among the Western Apaches, could be used by people from other sibs if they joined with the owners and co-resided in their territory. These practices were identical to those of the Havasupai and Walapai.

Pueblos, Pimans, and Yumans were much more dependent on crops and farmland than were the Apacheans. Owners and users allowed no access to their farmlands, and within the villages members of different sibs or unrelated families bartered their goods, whereas relatives formally gifted one another. Between communities there was an attempt to create friendships between trade partners so that transactions would be recognized as gift exchanges. This procedure may have represented a ritualistic extension of the property-ownership rights of the sedentary people, which they hoped nonowners would recognize. The more communitarian Apacheans reciprocated, provided access to their private resources, though on a very restricted basis if the resource was farmland, and did not barter with people from their own communities. Bartering with and raiding among the dominant farming communities served as constant reminders of the political, economic, and ceremonial differences between Apacheans and their neighbors.

ORGANIZATION OF EXTRACTION AND PRODUCTION

Organization for the extraction of plants, fishes, and other animals, and organization for the production of crops, houses, baskets, and other movable properties exhibited remarkably little variation across culture areas in western North America, but where variation occurred, it was often meaningful and it correlated with other important differences between areas. In the following assessments, care has been taken to distinguish work by sex, by task-group, and by specialization. It is not enough to know whether one sex contributed most of the labor for a particular task. It is also important to know whether individual persons, *ad hoc* groups of two or three people, or task-groups* did the work required in each project, and

---

*Throughout, "task groups" are defined as units of co-workers who regularly—daily, seasonally, or annually—coalesced to accomplish some task. Each member need not have provided the same resources, skills, or labor to accomplish the task. Membership was rather stable over a period of a few years.

whether or not work was accomplished by specialists or by laymen. Specialists were recognized as possessing unique gifts for, or expertise at, some pursuit. Often specialists were considered to possess supernatural power which allowed them to be particularly effective at their work.

Craft Organization

The crafts, such as potting, weaving, hide-working, and wood-working, were almost universally tasks engaged in by an individual person, or tasks carried out by one person and a few helpers. By far the greatest development of craft specializations occurred in the Northwest Coast where people not only trained to become proficient at their work but, to aid them in their specialties, they also acquired spirit helpers either through vision quests or through apprenticeship and purchase from older craft specialists.

The weaving of nets, baskets, and mats was done by all groups in the West and was almost universally done by women. Weaving is a very old craft in western North America, at least as old as 10,000 years, and it is highly plausible that it was always a female task, the exceptions to this being the Mohave and Yuma (River Yumans), the Pimans, and the Pueblos where cotton cloth was woven either by men or by both men and women (Map Cu-97, V-214, V-217 to V-219). Male weaving of cotton cloth correlated rather closely with male dominance in agricultural labor. For example, among the Pueblos (with the exception of the Tewa villages) and the Pimans, men grew the cotton and also wove the cloth. Among the Tewa villages, though men grew the cotton, men and women wove the cloth. Among the River Yumans both men and women raised cotton and both also wove the cloth it was used for. The introduction of cotton seems to have followed the advent of agriculture in the Southwest. Inasmuch as cotton was the only material that men wove, it is likely that they began weaving only after cotton was introduced into agriculture and at a time when agriculture became preeminent in ceremonial and religious affairs. Many of the objects that were woven from cotton were used exclusively in ceremonials by Pueblos and Pimans, but that was not the case for the River Yumans, who had a meager ceremonial life. Thus, it may be that the relation between men and cotton-weaving was conditioned by the importance of ceremonialism in village affairs as well as the role of males in farming.

Among societies with sophisticated fishing technologies, men wove the basketry traps that were attached to weirs. These were men's tools because men dominated fishing pursuits everywhere in western North America. Men were not specialists at the weaving task; rather, all men in the fishing societies learned the skills. On the other hand, though all women learned how to do some form of weaving—twining, coiling, plaiting, or all three—only specialists made baskets in a few Salishan groups and among the Makah groups of the central Northwest Coast, throughout northwestern California, northern California, and Southern California, and among a few Ute, Southern Paiute, and Western Apache groups. On the Northwest Coast some women gained supernatural powers through vision guests, which enabled them to produce fine baskets and blankets from mountain-goat wool or dog hair. These items were valued as potlatch and distribution goods (V-217 to V-219). The belief that special skills emanated from supernatural helpers and that those skills could be sold by a specialist to an apprentice was consonant with the emphasis given property rights on the Northwest Coast, where people had exclusive rights to some incorporeal and corporeal properties.

In California and among the mobile people on the peripheries of the settlements of sedentary Southwest farmers, the baskets of certain makers were sought in trade, so it is convenient to call those producers whose goods were desired specialists. California basketry, which was especially fine, was traded widely; Apache basketry was desired by Pueblo villagers; and Southern Paiute basketry was desired by the Navajo groups (Map Cu-98, V-215).

As for hide- or leather-working, which involved scraping and at times dehairing flesh and drying, smoking, or otherwise treating the skins of animals, this was performed by men throughout most of the tribes in the Southwest, the Great Basin, and California, and predominantly by men but also by women along the Northwest Coast. The distribution of male dominance in hide-working throughout these areas suggests that male dominance was old, and it probably was associated with the modest importance that hide-working assumed in these societies. When large hides were plentiful and used for clothing, on the other hand, the hide-working tasks were normally accomplished by women. For example, on the Northwest Coast, though fur robes and hats for winter were highly prized, clothes woven by women from plant fibers dominated year-round dress, and in California, an area of mild climates, worked hides were not especially important in clothing, nor were they in the Southwest, with the exception of the Apacheans, from whom buckskin was important in men's and women's dress. In the eastern peripheries of the Great Basin, buckskin apparel was worn

among the Utes and Northern Shoshones of the Rocky Mountains, and it was the most important item in year-round clothing throughout the entire Plateau. Among these last groups—Apacheans, Utes, Northern Shoshones, and Plateau tribes—women rather than men contributed most of the labor in hide-working (Map Cu-99, V-220, V-221 to V-222), just as they did in weaving the plant fiber clothing worn in the Great Basin and Northwest Coast.

We have seen that among the societies in which hunting of medium- and large-sized land mammals contributed heavily to subsistence, these animals were more abundant than elsewhere, and it is evident that women worked the hides once the animals had been caught. The custom of female dominance in leather-working among Utes and Shoshones, as well as the techniques of hide preparation and clothing manufacture, were probably relatively recent borrowings of practices from the Plains. The Plateau customs, on the other hand, may have originated in either the Subarctic area or the Plains. The adoption of hide clothing was especially recent for many Middle Columbia Plateau tribes and for those tribes of the Northwest Coast which located near the mouths of the Columbia and Fraser Rivers. The Haidas and Tlingits in the far North, however, may have employed the custom for many centuries, taking the practice with them to the coast and the islands. The people along the most western stretches of the Columbia and Fraser Rivers did not depend much on large game. They traded for hides with tribes in the interior, and the women adopted the practice of working them.

Pottery-making was almost entirely the task of women. It is likely that both the original technique for making pottery and the role of women in its manufacture diffused northward from Mexico along with male dominance in farming, male weaving of cotton, and the rest of the agriculture-related complex. Among the Gabrieliño, who used steatite bowls more than pottery, and also among a few Western Shoshone groups, men made pots. These innovations did not catch on elsewhere (Map Cu-100, V-223). Pottery among Western Shoshones was rare, however, and not suitable for carrying long distances.

Specialists manufactured pottery in less than half of the tribes in which pottery was manufactured, but specialization was present both in societies where pots were the dominant receptacles (e.g., the Pueblos) and where they were the least important receptacles (e.g., the Apaches and the Luiseño). In some societies, even though all women made pots, the pottery of some women was preferred and traded. In other societies only a few women made pots (true in central California as well as of the Apaches), and they traded their wares. There was no positive correlation between use of pots and specialization (Map Cu-101, V-224; V-225).

The construction of balsas, bark canoes, plank canoes, and dugout canoes of all sizes and shapes was a male task and the use of these canoes in fishing and transport was also a male undertaking. Specialization in the task was restricted to the coastal and Plateau tribes that made canoes from wood. Among the groups that produced watercraft from reeds, tule, and other marsh plants, all men learned how to make them. It is plausible that the Penutians entered California before dugout canoes had been developed in western North America, and that the Penutians and their Hokan neighbors made do with balsas. Yet on the Southern California coast, either the Gabrieliño (a Uto-Aztecan-speaking group) or the Chumash (Hokan speakers) developed plank canoes. Both of these Southern California groups were using them at the time of first contact with Europeans. The Northwest Coast specialists often retained assistants to help them burn, chisel, stretch, and shape huge cedar logs into canoes. The task of preparing keels for different seagoing purposes was difficult, and good canoe-builders were able to accumulate payments in food and movable properties that they could then dispense at distributions and potlatches (Map Cu-102, V-226; Cu-103, V-227; V-228).

The houses that predominated among most tribes in western North America for the longest portions of each year were substantial structures built to last for several years. In California, the Northwest Coast, the Plateau, and among the most sedentary tribes in the Southwest, men often in patrilineally related task-groups built and occupied the houses. Matrilineally related males built Western Pueblo houses, while patrikinspeople built Tlingit houses, with help from some affines. Among the tribelets in the San Joaquin drainage in central California men and women joined together in task-groups, and in the Southwest women often plastered the walls. But the larger and more substantial houses throughout western North America were built predominantly by male kinsmen, even if they did not occupy them, as was the case among the Western Pueblos (Map Cu-104, V-229; Map Cu-105, V-230; Map Cu-106, V-231).

House-building tasks were assigned to women or to combinations of women and men among the Apaches of the Southwest and among Great Basin tribes where brush or hide-covered wickiups predominated. These houses were either portable, or they were built quickly and abandoned after short periods of use. As a rule of thumb, the less sedentary the group the more probable that houses were used for only brief occupations and that women, or men and women together, built them. Specialists directed construction at Zuni and Taos Pueblos. Beyond those communities, practically all specialists were located on the Northwest Coast, where they were called in to set the corner posts and mount the center and side beams; the same people who carved elegant masks and built the canoes, watertight boxes, and coffins also did the infrastructural work on these houses.

Organization of Extraction

Gathering of wild plants, whether the pursuit dominated the subsistence economy or was inconsequential to it, was women's work (V-232 to V-234). Plant gathering, which seems to have either dominated or co-dominated the earliest subsistence economies in western North America (from as early as 10,000 years ago) was probably always the work of women, but at the time of Contact in California, the Great Basin, and the Southwest or wherever seeds, nuts, or pods from trees or the giant cactus were collected, men joined women in harvesting and hauling the food. So did children and the aged. It is instructive that in societies where wild plants dominated subsistence, and where among such plants tree crops were the backbone of subsistence (pinyon, oaks, mesquite), men joined women in the tasks of collecting them. Indeed, whenever any particular wild plant crop, such as mescal, contributed a large percentage of a group's annual food, it was likely that men and women joined together to collect or haul it. Among the more generalized gatherers, i.e., people who gathered small amounts from many different plants, such as the Great Basin tribes, the Pais, and the Apaches, men, children, and the aged helped not only with extraction of the most important plants but with some other gathering tasks as well.

Gathering, except for knocking cones, nuts, and pods from trees, or trimming the leaves and cutting the hearts from mescal, usually required little team effort and no specialization. Men would often climb the trees and shake them or hold branches while women picked, or wield the poles that were used to knock cones down. Nevertheless, throughout the Northwest Coast and California, women, or women and men accomplished most of the gathering in small task-groups. In part, this was done to have company while doing the work, but often the harvests of tree crops or mescal hearts were so rich that task-groups were required to move the food quickly. (This was true also in gathering roots from the rich beds of the Plateau.) Moreover, in the entire coastal region as far east as the Sierra, and also in the Upper Columbia

River drainage, the nuts, roots, and berries gathered for tribal use were also foraged for by bears, including grizzly bears, who were constant threats to human gatherers. The massive grizzly bears were the major mammals and most dangerous predators in the California hills and mountains and women went out together in part to keep watch on their flanks, to protect against grizzly-bear attacks (Map Cu-107, V-235).

If gathering was overwhelmingly a female task, hunting was overwhelmingly a male task, so much so that distribution maps are not needed (V-236 to V-237). In the areas where cricket, rabbit, antelope, or deer drives were held, especially in the Great Basin and areas peripheral to it, women joined men in frightening or directing the animals. The drive was the exclusive communal hunting technique in many of the Eastern Pueblos. Among the Klamath, where deer were driven into the water, women usually killed the animals from their positions in canoes. Where gathering pursuits dominated subsistence but the products from communal hunts were also important, which was true in arid areas in general, men and women joined forces in many of the gathering and hunting pursuits.

Elsewhere hunting was primarily conducted by stalking: a lone hunter or a few men would join together to track and secure game (Map Cu-108, V-239). It has often been said that affines hunted well together for large herd animals such as bison, caribou, and antelope, that required concerted and organized effort for large, successful kills. Hunting groups composed of affines did not dominate among most societies in western North America. Especially in the ambilocal communities of the Great Basin and Plateau, affines and kinsmen often hunted together in communal undertakings as well as in small-scale stalking ventures. In the Rockies and the adjacent territories to the east and west where hunting made a greater contribution to the food supply than in most of the Great Basin and Plateau, some hunting groups were predominantly composed of affines (Utes, Wind River Shoshone, Eastern Apaches, and Kutenai); some were predominantly patrikinsmen (Agaiduku Shoshone, Nez Percé, Coeur d'Alene); and some were mixed groups of kinsmen and affines (Flathead and Kalispel). There seems to have been a tendency toward composing hunting groups principally of affines among the people most dependent on large game of all types (large herd and small herd animals). The Agaiduku Shoshone, Nez Percé, and Coeur d'Alene hunting groups had the fewest affinal relations in them, but these tribes also resided around fish resources for part of the year, and that actively influenced the composition of their fishing groups, which were predominantly corps of patrikinsmen.

The same combinations conducted hunting operations.

Fishing and sea-mammal hunting was as much a male-dominated pursuit as was land-mammal hunting, but women collected most of the shellfish, and along the Northwest Coast and throughout the Plateau where spawning fish could be caught in vast numbers, women hauled and filleted the fish that the men caught. So just as men joined women in major tasks of gathering nuts, seeds, and pods from trees in areas where those foods were extremely abundant, so did women join men in catching and processing fish where fish were abundant and had to be collected and processed quickly (Map Cu-109, V-240, V-241).

In most areas when there were abundances of fish, task-groups of men related through their patrikinsmen (either bilaterally or patrilineally) joined together to accomplish some fishing labor, such as building weirs and traps, or even herding fish through the rivers toward seines and other devices. The custom of using task-group labor in extracting fish very likely went hand in hand with the appropriation of fish resource-areas by kinship groups throughout much of the West. Indeed, in many communities families owned fishing stations even though the communities were bilaterally organized tribelets.*

The societies that were most dependent on fish and that had the greatest abundances of fish available to them almost always had fishing specialists who either directed the task-groups or who performed rituals considered vital to the conduct of successful fishing. Northern California tribelets often had several specialists but along the Northwest Coast there was very often but one in each kinship group, and that person was usually someone other than the specialist in hunting sea-mammals (Map Cu-111, V-243).

Extraction of plants, land animals, and aquatic animals was organized very similarly throughout western North America on the basis of sex, but the amount of cooperation between the sexes while working at the same tasks varied: in any two regions men helped at some gathering pursuits in—let us say—California, but not the Northwest Coast, and—to use the converse example—women helped out during the major fish runs on the Northwest Coast, but not in California. In large part such differences stemmed from the greater abundances of acorns in California and fish on the Northwest Coast and the importance of each of these resources in the respective subsistence economies. Yet in the Great Basin, men and

---

*In Chapters 8 and 9 a reconstruction of bilateral tribelets from patrilineages is offered.

women joined forces in many gathering and hunting tasks, but great abundances of neither plant nor animal foods were available to them. In the Great Basin it was a matter of mustering all available hands in order to collect a small surplus. In California and the Northwest Coast, it was a matter of collecting vast surpluses that could be feasted and gifted away. But whether in areas of sparse and unpredictable resources, or abundant and predictable resources, extractors had to move fast when nature provided the surplus.

In the Great Basin, gathering was more often an individual and hunting more often a communal venture than elsewhere. Very few task-groups were formed, and they were usually formed *ad hoc* when camps convened. Plants were diffuse and sparse, so task-groups would not have helped procure more of them, and small, burrowing animals and fast desert browsers could only be hunted successfully in drives by people who did not expect to gain more food than was needed to support a group that stayed together for only brief periods in each year.

On the Northwest Coast, in the Plateau, and California, task-groups stood out in fishing, sea-mammal hunting (mainly along the Northwest Coast), housebuilding, root gathering (a few tribes), and acorn gathering (California). Most often the task-groups were composed of patrikinsmen and emphasized the property-owning nature of the groups that worked together. Ownership and labor were evidently related very closely to abundant and concentrated resources (such as fish and acorns) and to the houses in which owners resided. It is plausible that task-group labor in fishing and ownership of fishing sites preceded task-group labor and ownership of gathering sites. Except for tree crops, gathering seldom required teamwork. The Northwest Coast gatherers formed teams in part to keep company, in part to maintain watchful eyes on their perimeter, and in part to haul and dry roots and berries from the fields to camp. Yet ownership of gathering sites probably resulted from the general Northwest Coast practice of kinship-group appropriations and the competition among kinship groups to maintain their ranking or their wealth. It is doubtful that the economic relations of task-group labor or the importance of wild plant foods in Northwest Coast diets caused Northwest Coast residents to appropriate gathering areas.

Organization of Production

The advent of agriculture in the Southwest must have brought about a basic transformation in the sexual division of labor. Whereas women were the gatherers of wild plants at the time of European contact, and probably did most of the gathering prior to the introduction of agriculture, the principal work in preparing the soil, sowing the seeds, digging and maintaining irrigation systems, and harvesting agricultural crops was men's work. The most crop-dependent peoples of the Southwest relied on men for farming, while women and children helped with the weeding and some harvesting activities. The women also prepared the crops for storage (Map Cu-112, V-248; V-245).

Among the Apaches, who probably learned how to farm in the Southwest, but who could have brought the techniques with them from the Plains, men and women contributed about equal amounts of labor. The Apaches were not very dependent on crops, at least not upon those that they raised themselves; Apache men moved on raiding and trading ventures frequently; and they used only the most rudimentary water-diversion techniques. The more sedentary River Yuman men and women also shared the farm labor, even though Yuman predecessors had probably been farming since 500 AD, if not 200 years earlier. Yet these people did not develop irrigation techniques beyond diversions, and the men were actively engaged in trading and raiding, and also joined women at mesquite, screwbean, mescal, and Sahuaro cactus harvests.

It is evident that the more dependent people were on crops, the more sedentary were their communities, and the more likely that men were the principal farmers. The Pueblos and the Navajos, whose agriculture followed the Hopi model, recognized agricultural specialists who possessed either supernatural powers or who directed rituals critical to successful farming, and who also directed the farming operations (Map Cu-113, V-246). The more modest farmers of the Southwest and along the southern fringe of the Great Basin did not have specialists among them, nor did the Pimans, though the Pimans recognized leaders who organized collective pursuits such as canal digging and clearing.

Among the Western Pueblos and Navajos, male affines formed task-groups to provide for the sib into which they married, and as members of their own sibs they performed rituals that were critical to successful farming and maintenance of their sisters' land. Among the Eastern Pueblos and the Pimans, task-groups of male patrikin joined to work their land. For some undertakings they even formed into village-wide groups to share their labor (Map Cu-114, V-247).

The task groups of the Eastern Pueblos and the Pimas provided one of the most interesting contrasts in the organization of production in all of western North America. All lived in villages composed of bilateral kinsmen, and all employed irrigation techniques with main canals, tributary ditches, and diversionary devices to control water. In the Eastern Pueblos and among most Eastern Keres, theocratic village leaders exacted labor from villagers to maintain the ditches and to raise some crops for the village storeroom, controlled by these leaders. The village leaders possessed the power to banish people who did not obey, to reallocate land to people as they saw fit, to cause people to participate in communal rituals, and to assign them houses in which they could reside. Among these pueblos, family "ownership" of farms and houses, as we have defined them earlier, are better understood as rights to use ownership (usufruct), with ownership being ultimately vested in the village leaders.

Among the Pimas and Papagos the villages were predominantly formed around male bilateral kinsmen who brought their wives to live with them. Each one was a patrilocal deme. Garden plots passed from father to sons, yet the land was considered to be owned by all Pimas or Papagos, past and present, so the land farmed by each family was owned in usufruct. The deme headman could direct the men of his deme only through suasion and esteem, not through the real power of coercion. He could not banish people or reassign land. There were no community fields, and when ditches were to be cleaned, or new canals to be dug, or dams to be built, several villages cooperated to do the work. The villages worked communally and reciprocally to open the major canal, and then the demes worked communally and reciprocally to open their tributaries. When the work was completed, the families chose their parcels of land. From that time on, the main canal was cleared by the men of each village along their portions of its course. The men were often organized by their headman to do so, but they had no obligation to follow his instruction. In contrast to the Eastern Pueblos and many Eastern Keres villages, Pimas and Papagos developed extensive canals among several villages with no more than kinship-group labor, nominally directed by kinship-group headmen. It is clear that centralization of control over the means of production

was not necessary to truly massive aboriginal waterworks. The Piman hydraulic enterprise, much more energetic in scope than its counterparts among the Eastern Pueblos and Eastern Keres, was much less organized. On the other hand, other aspects of Piman craft organizations and their organizations of extraction and house production were very similar to those of the Eastern Pueblos and Eastern Keres.

The contrast between Piman and Eastern Pueblo organizations of production is interesting to us because several scholars have alleged that Eastern Pueblo and Western Pueblo social organizations differed because canal irrigation was present in the east but not in the west (Wittfogel and Goldfrank 1943, Eggan 1950, Dozier 1970). Sib organizations have been hypothesized as the proto organizations among all Pueblos before the Eastern Pueblos developed canal irrigation. Canal irrigation, it is postulated, required more centralization than was afforded by sibs in order to control the intricate demands of societies whose subsistence economies were based upon it. Hence, the Eastern Pueblos developed village-wide sodalities with leaders to direct irrigation, and eventually to direct all other communal aspects of the society.

The example of the Piman speakers refutes the claim that centralization was required to control "the intricate demands of an irrigation society" (Dozier 1970: 132). With little more organization than reciprocity and good will, Pimans developed and maintained waterworks much larger and more complex than those of the Eastern Pueblos. Moreover, the Pimans received less annual precipitation than the Eastern Pueblo villages, and were as beseiged by Apachean raiders after the early sixteenth century as were the Eastern Pueblos. In fact, because River Yumans, Apaches, and Southeast Yavapais attacked them, the Pima villages were more beleaguered than the Eastern Pueblos. It is a distinct possibility that Eastern Pueblo village organizations became more centralized, either after initial responses to Coronado's vicious stay among them, or after forced changes to their society during the long period of local Spanish domination beginning in 1598.

Chapter 8

Social Organization

INTRODUCTION

Settlement pattern, demography, and community organization were all intricately related to many aspects of kinship and social organization. For the sake of simplicity, 51 variables covering these several topics have been correlated and ordered here.* Figure 8-1 demonstrates that the similarities among tribes based on complexes of social organization, demography, and community organization variables differ considerably from the alignments based on technology, subsistence economy, and economic organization. Whereas those three aspects of culture were correlated with each other at about 70 percent average similarity, the relations among the tribes based on social organization variables averaged only about 45 percent similarity with the technology and economy sets (see Table 4-1, in Chapter 4).

These results demonstrate that rather similar technologies, subsistence economies, and economic organizations can operate in rather different social organization contexts, and vice versa. Comparison of Figures 8-1 and 8-2 with Figures 7-1 and 7-2 will make the point clear.

In Figure 8-1 nine principal statistical groups emerge. By and large the groupings cluster tribes that shared contiguous territories. Yet the Eastern Pueblos (at the bottom of the figure), who observed bilateral descent, have been separated from the matrilineal descent Western Pueblos and Keresans (at the top of the figure), who observed matrilineal descent; and the

matrilineal-descent tribes of the northern Northwest Coast form a cluster at the top of the figure and are separated from the other Northwest Coast clusters, most of which observed bilateral descent (group 6 in the figure). It is evident that tribes whose environments and economies were very similar often possessed social organizations that were fundamentally different.

In Figure 8-1, the tribes in which people traced their descent unilineally, either through the maternal or paternal side, are placed toward the top in groups 1 to 5 (from the Haida groups at the very top through the Nomlaki), and the societies observing bilateral descent are placed at the bottom (from the Nambe Tewa, in group 9, through the Tolowa, in group 6). Inspection of the bridges between each set of most-closely related tribes shows that the similarities among the clusters of tribes observing unilineal descent were not strong. The northern Northwest Coast cluster (group 1) stands out as the most unique set in western North America, while the Western Pueblo–Keresan Pueblo set (group 2) is next most unique.

There were considerable differences among bilateral-descent societies as well. The Tewa (Eastern Pueblo groups, in group 9) were most aberrant, but on the whole the largest kinship units among the groups from Nambe Tewa to Upper Stalo (groups 9 and 8 in Figure 8-1) were "lineal" families composed of one nuclear family in the senior generation and two or more families in the junior generation, and they predominantly observed patrilocal residence; that is, the groom took his wife to reside in or near his father's house. The groups in Figure 8-1 from Lipan Apache through Tolowa (groups 7 and 6), though observing bilateral descent, tended to be organized into

---

*See Appendix E, Variables 281–331.

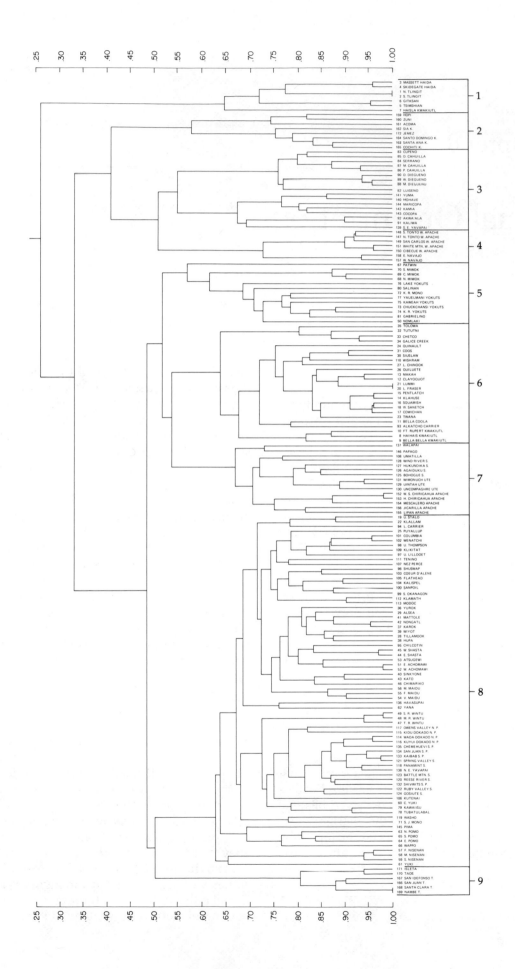

Figure 8-1 *Culture tree: 5. Groupings of tribal territories of western North America derived from G coefficients based on 51 variables (286 attributes) of settlement pattern, demography, community organization, and social and kinship organization.*

GROUP 1

3 Massett Haida
4 Skidegate Haida
1 Northern Tlingit
2 Southern Tlingit
6 Gitksan
5 Tsimshian
7 Haisla Kwakiutl

GROUP 2

159 Hopi
160 Zuni
161 Acoma
162 Sia Keres
172 Jemez
164 Santo Domingo Keres
163 Santa Ana Keres
165 Cochiti Keres

GROUP 3

83 Cupeño
85 Desert Cahuilla
84 Serrano
87 Mountain Cahuilla
86 Pass Cahuilla
90 Desert Diegueño
89 Western Diegueño
88 Mountain Diegueño
82 Luiseño
141 Yuma
140 Mohave
144 Maricopa
142 Kamia
143 Cocopa
92 Akwa'ala
91 Kaliwa
139 Southeast Yavapai

GROUP 4

148 South Tonto Western
    Apache
147 North Tonto Western
    Apache
149 San Carlos Western
    Apache
151 White Mountain Western
    Apache
150 Cibecue Western Apache
158 Eastern Navajo
157 Western Navajo

GROUP 5

67 Patwin
70 Southern Miwok
69 Central Miwok
68 Northern Miwok
76 Lake Yokuts
80 Salinan
72 Kings River Mono
77 Yauelmani Yokuts
75 Kaweah Yokuts
73 Chuckchansi Yokuts
74 Kings River Yokuts
81 Gabrielino
50 Nomlaki

GROUP 6

35 Tolowa
32 Tututni
33 Chetco
34 Galice Creek
24 Quinault
31 Coos
30 Siuslaw
110 Wishram
27 Lower Chinook
26 Quileute
13 Makah
12 Clayoquot
21 Lummi
20 Lower Fraser
15 Pentlatch
14 Klahuse
16 Squamish
18 West Sanetch
17 Cowichan
23 Twana
11 Bella Coola
93 Alkatcho Carrier
10 Fort Rupert Kwakiutl
8 Haihais Kwakiutl
9 Bella Bella Kwakiutl

GROUP 7

137 Walapai
146 Papago
108 Umatilla
128 Wind River Shoshone
127 Hukundika Shoshone
126 Agaiduku Shoshone
125 Bohogue Shoshone

131 Wimonuch Ute
129 Uintah Ute
130 Uncompaghre Ute
152 Warm Spring Chiricahua
    Apache
153 Huachuca Chiricahua
    Apache
154 Mescalero Apache
156 Jicarilla Apache
155 Lipan Apache

GROUP 8

19 Upper Stalo
22 Klallam
94 Lower Carrier
25 Puyallup
101 Columbia
102 Wenatchi
98 Upper Thompson
109 Klikitat
97 Upper Lillooet
111 Tenino
107 Nez Percé
96 Shuswap
103 Coeur d'Alene
105 Flathead
104 Kalispel
100 Sanpoil
99 Southern Okanagon
112 Klamath
113 Modoc
36 Yurok
29 Alsea
41 Mattole
42 Nongatl
37 Karok
39 Wiyot
28 Tillamook
38 Hupa
95 Chilcotin
45 West Shasta
44 East Shasta
53 Atsugewi
51 East Achomawi
52 West Achomawi
40 Sinkyone
43 Kato
46 Chimariko
56 Mountain Maidu
55 Foothill Maidu

54 Valley Maidu
136 Havasupai
62 Yana
49 Sacramento River Wintu
48 McCloud River Wintu
47 Trinity River Wintu
117 Owens Valley Northern
    Paiute
115 Kidu-Dokado Northern
    Paiute
114 Wada-Dokado Northern
    Paiute
116 Kuyui-Dokado Northern
    Paiute
135 Chemehuevi Southern
    Paiute
134 San Juan Southern
    Paiute
133 Kaibab Southern Paiute
121 Spring Valley Shoshone
118 Panamint Shoshone
138 Northeast Yavapai
123 Battle Mountain Shoshone
120 Reese River Shoshone
132 Shivwits Southern Paiute
122 Ruby Valley Shoshone
124 Gosiute Shoshone
106 Kutenai
60 Coast Yuki
79 Kawaiisu
78 Tubatulabal
119 Washo
71 San Joaquin Mono
145 Pima
63 Northern Pomo
65 Southern Pomo
64 Eastern Pomo
66 Wappo
57 Foothill Nisenan
58 Mountain Nisenan
59 Southern Nisenan
61 Yuki

GROUP 9

171 Isleta
170 Taos
167 San Ildefonso Tewa
166 San Juan Tewa
168 Santa Clara Tewa
169 Nambe Tewa

demes. Demes were unilineal-like kinship groups composed of several families representing three or more generations who co-resided year around, either in bands or villages, and though bilateral, they traced descent to a common ancestor. The branching that places the bilateral-descent societies into one group where "lineal" families were the largest kinship units and another group where demes were the largest kinship units, comprises many societies that, though similar in kinship organization, were very different in

political organization, as we shall see in the following chapter. The tribelets tracing bilateral descent in the northern part of California, for instance, were more complexly organized than the Great Basin family camps, yet the two sets of societies in which bilateral descent was observed averaged about 65 percent similarity in features of social organization.

It is evident that similar features of social organization can be shared by groups at several levels of political complexity, and that political inferences should

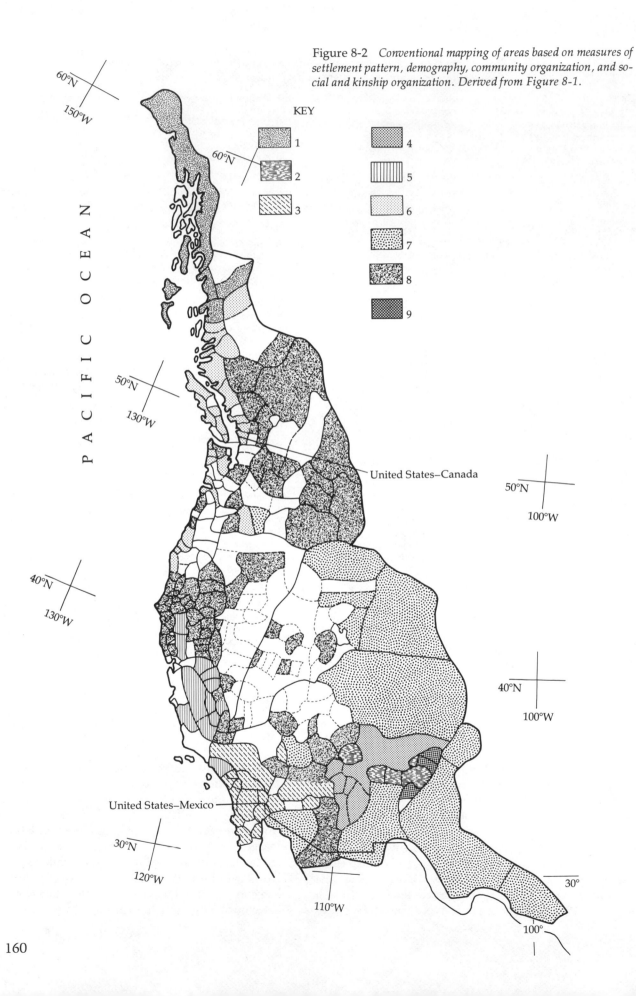

Figure 8-2 *Conventional mapping of areas based on measures of settlement pattern, demography, community organization, and social and kinship organization. Derived from Figure 8-1.*

KEY

1
2
3
4
5
6
7
8
9

PACIFIC OCEAN

60°N
150°W

60°N

50°N
130°W

40°N
130°W

30°N
120°W

United States–Mexico

110°W

50°N
100°W

40°N
100°W

United States–Canada

30°

100°

not be hastily drawn from features of social organization. The Tanoan Eastern Pueblo villages and the camps in the central Great Basin traced descent bilaterally and recognized the nuclear household, composed of a couple and their children, as being independent. Yet the Eastern Pueblos had the largest and most compact populations and the most complex and centralized political organizations in western North America. Kinship groups among Eastern Pueblos were not sovereign and autonomous political and economic units, and relations among kinspeople were much less important than political and religious organizations. The Great Basin dwellers, except along the eastern slopes of the Sierra and among the Northern Shoshones and Utes, were the smallest and most diffuse populations in western North America. They did not develop political organizations at all. Great Basin nuclear families joined into family camps of from 12 to 25 people for perhaps eleven months of each year, but they were free to leave those camps if they so desired.

The following data suggest that economic considerations played major roles in shaping social organization. Very often features of kinship and social organization, especially marriage and postnuptial residence customs, the relations between the families of the husband and wife, the nature of family and household organization, and even descent reckoning and kinship terminologies were shaped by economic considerations. And in many instances, as has been suggested above, kinship considerations were secondary in importance to political considerations.

Among the societies predominantly based on agriculture in the Southwest, the aquatic-animal-dependent societies of the Northwest Coast, the mixed gatherers, hunters, and fishermen of California, and the gatherers of Southern California, kinship-group residence and community residence were relatively fixed for each person and each family. The inflexibility of local residence-group membership in these areas stood in marked contrast to the flexibility of local residence-group membership throughout the Plateau, Great Basin, and among the more mobile Pais and Apacheans in the Southwest.

In the former areas, territory ownership was more important and language differentiation was greater than in the latter areas. Yet in Southern California, California, and the Northwest Coast, diffusion of language features across several language families and phyla was marked, and groups that were located side by side shared similar kinds of sodalities and ceremonies. The variations in the ceremonial and sodality organizations, however, were bewildering and served to emphasize the discreteness of each autonomous political group, be it a tribelet of a few hamlets, a compact village, or a localized kinship group within a larger village or in a separate and distinct village. The similarities suggest that there were extensive social contacts even though the diversity among ceremonial and sodality organizations suggested local reworking of themes that were distributed throughout wide areas.

Among many of the unilineal societies in which the local kinship groups were economically and politically autonomous, moieties, or the organization of each descent group into one of two divisions, regulated many relations among kinship groups in the absence of greater centralized political organization. Distributions, potlatches, wealth displays, and feasts were used throughout the Northwest Coast to establish relations between autonomous and predominantly bilateral kinship groups and to maintain the ranked position of those kinship groups. Other mechanisms were used to draw people together from basically competitive, property-owning kinship groups of inflexible membership. In the northern and central parts of California and among the Eastern Pueblos and Eastern Keres, for example, political units emerged.

The differences between the groups that recognized relatively fixed membership and strict private-property concepts and those that recognized flexible membership and communitarian use concepts of property provide strong contrasts. We shall offer postulates to account for the various organizations as we proceed.

SETTLEMENT PATTERN AND DEMOGRAPHY

The permanency, compactness, and population size of communities varied widely in western North America from the seminomadic family camps of as few as twelve people among some of the Western Shoshones to compact villages of up to 1,000 people among some of the Eastern Pueblos. Although the data on the Chumash of the Southern California coast are meager, Spanish observers reported villages of as many as 1,400 people among them.

The permanency, size, and compactness of settlements, assessed together, provide a rough index to the general complexity of the local cultures in terms of crafts, trade, sodality organizations, ceremonials, and the like, but the index does not accurately reflect the "carrying capacity" of the local environments given the technologies that were employed. Carrying capacity refers to the size of the population that can be sustained in any area given the nature of the population's technology and subsistence economy. There is good reason to believe that Northwest Coast populations based solely on extraction could have been larger than those found at first white Contact. The pre-Contact groups of California, especially those that occupied the region north of San Francisco Bay, also could have been organized into more compact and politically centralized villages and could have maintained larger populations. Resources were abundant throughout these areas and watercraft and waterways were available to transport goods and people. People from many communities convened to eat vast quantities of food, and on the Northwest Coast enormous amounts of movable property were circulated. Yet political and economic organizations capable of maintaining large populations never developed. Alas, political organizations did not emerge to quell enmities among competing groups. Ceremonial, sodality, and kinship mechanisms were the principal means by which localized kinship groups and tribelets interacted. Nevertheless, in all of western North America, California tribelets and Northwest Coast villages (composed of one or more autonomous kinship groups) were second and third, respectively, after the Pueblo, in permanence, compactness, and size of their local communities and the population densities of their territories.

The most sedentary and permanent settlements were occupied by the Pueblos, Pimas, and Maricopa in the Southwest, the cluster of northwestern California tribes that forms a subcategory of the Northwest Coast tribes, and some of the Pomo of northern California. All occupied their settlements throughout the year, and each settlement was maintained for long periods of time—very long periods for the Pueblos. The Hopi village of Oraibi, for instance, was occupied continuously from about 1000 AD to Contact, and it is still occupied. The Mohave and Yuma villages were only slightly less permanent, being occupied throughout the year but periodically moved following unusually extensive flooding of the river plains (Map Cu-116, V-281). The Pueblo, Pima, and northern California villages were compact settlements of houses, villages of the Pueblos and Pimas usually having either a central courtyard, ceremonial chambers, or both (V-286), and those in California having a main dance house that was larger than the dwelling structures (Map Cu-117, V-282).

Along the Northwest Coast, winter villages were occupied for seven or eight months each year, and then the villagers moved to a principal summer site for four or five months; from there small groups often ventured for short periods. Both principal locations were used indefinitely, and some people stayed in the winter villages the year around. In each of the Northwest Coast villages the leading kinship groups usually had one large house suitable for spirit dancing, wealth displays, or other ceremonials. In northwestern California and among the River Yumans, settlements were less compact, straggling along rivers.

The Plateau tribes that were located at key fishing sites, such as at The Dalles and Celilo Falls on the Columbia River and at key points on the Fraser, Bulkley, and Skeena Rivers, lived in semisedentary settlements similar to those of the Northwest Coast. Other Plateau dwellers, inhabitants of the Great Basin, and the Pais and Apacheans of the Southwest occupied winter villages for a few months each year, but they were settlements of dispersed homesteads rather than compact villages, and there were no central plazas or ceremonial houses in those communities. During the spring, summer, and fall months the communities created several temporary camps as they moved from one locality to another in quest of resources.

The Utes, Wind River Shoshones, Pais, and Apaches concentrated into their largest populations during the summer period: the Apaches and Pais to farm, and the Utes and Wind River Shoshones to hunt large game. Raiding and trading groups from among the Utes ventured away from the main bands during the summer. During the winter periods these groups disbanded and organized into smaller residential units. Among the Apaches and Pais, winter periods were times for foraging, and for the Apaches, times for visiting, trading with, and raiding Pima, Papago, and Pueblo villages.

A few Apaches, Utes, and Salishan speakers of the Upper Columbia drainage were nearly fully nomadic. It is not clear whether this occurred after first contact with Europeans, in conjunction with the advent of the horse, or before Contact, in conjunction with adaptations to big-game hunting and gathering, which would have taken the Utes and Salishans through several mountain, foothill, and grassland zones and the Chiricahua Apaches through mountains, canyons, and deserts; this way of life, which combined transitory settlements of dispersed homesteads and subsistence economies based on extraction of considerable resources from several biotic zones, could have been sustained by pedestrian as well as equestrian people.

It is noteworthy that the most nomadic people did not necessarily have the fewest resources: though the population in each local settlement was small, during the summer months these small populations convened to form a population greater than the largest local population of most of the more sedentary people. The most nomadic communities had more access to bison and other large game than all other people in western North America, and their forays after large game could support the large group that convened for a few months (Map Cu-118, V-283; Map Cu-119, V-284). The seminomadic peoples of the Great Basin did not convene into large summer or winter groups.

Community population size is a deceptive indicator of the availability of resources, the duration for which food was stored, and the complexity of many features of local culture such as ceremonial or craft organization. Perusal of Map Cu-118 demonstrates that local populations for most of the Northwest Coast villages south of Cape Flattery, for example, consisted of fewer than 50 people. Several Pima and Southern California communities had similar populations. Map Cu-119, however, shows that the population densities of the tribal territories in which these villages or communities were located were from 1 to 25 people per square mile, whereas all other local communities having fewer than 50 people were found in tribal territories where densities were from below 1 person per five square miles to 1 person per square mile. Territorial densities on the Northwest Coast, in California, Southern California, and the agricultural Southwest were relatively high, though the sizes of local communities were not always a good indicator of the density of territories. Only among the Pueblo villages were both community size and tribal population density great, and only among some Great Basin and Southwest foragers were both community size and tribal population density small.

The explanation for this phenomenon is straightforward. Throughout the territories comprising the southern Northwest Coast (which includes northwestern California), one or a few local kinship-groups made up small, nonpolitically aligned villages, yet there were many villages within short distances of one another. In each village the kinship groups owned private property; since individual property rights were most highly developed here and settlements were straggled along the rivers in northwestern California, and further, each settlement was divided by individual property rights, this fractionation of property without political consolidation made village boundaries hard to define among the anarchistic families of this densely populated area. Even in the area north of Cape Flattery, villages tended to be composed of few more than 100 people, but the villages were very closely spaced throughout the Salishan area, as were rich extraction sites, so tribal densities were great.

A similar phenomenon occurred throughout California and Southern California. In areas of California where population densities were as great as 25 people per square mile, three or four small communities were scattered about a central hamlet. The set of small communities was organized into a tribelet, with other tribelets surrounding on all sides. The densely populated Miwok and Costanoan regions in California contained scattered communities in which independent lineages lived, each one localized in its own territory, but often in close proximity to other lineages. In Southern California each related set of lineages was grouped into a sib. Whereas lineages might scatter for part of the year, they convened as localized sibs in compact communities around springs during the winter months. The territories in which each sib located were from 5 to 50 times as densely populated as some territories in the Great Basin: yet some of the Southern California local communities, at least during the part of the year in which lineages scattered, were often not much larger than some Great Basin communities.

The impressive force of private property—whether invested in individual persons, families, or larger kinship groups—in shaping the size of local communities in otherwise heavily populated areas cannot be denied. In the absence of more complex political centralization, property-owning communities were small and independent. Among the Pueblos and the central and northern Northwest Coast people, ceremonial relations (ceremonial relations and political controls among the Eastern Pueblos and the Tsimshians), coordinated the largest villages. Coordination of the same kind could have been exercised among the Pimas, who lived in small deme-villages of perhaps 50 people, and the River Yumans, whose small villages were straggled along the river banks, but such coordination was not effected.

Whereas the most compact, permanent, and largest villages formed where populations were most dense and extractive and farming resources were rich, many small communities also formed in these environments. What militated against larger local communities and political organization was the concept of private property invested in individual persons (and their immediate families), or in localized kinship groups, or in small tribelets.

Among the local communities in the Plateau, Great Basin, and parts of the Southwest, population density was small and the flexibility of local group-membership was great. Individual persons (and more typically families) could move from one local community to another. Throughout these communities access was provided to communal and kinship group-owned resources. In areas where population density was great—among the extractors in the Great Basin, Plateau, and Southwest—the community organizations were flexible, allowed communal access, and were small; they stood in marked contrast with the community organizations of the Pima farmers and the extractors of Southern California, California, and, in general, most of the Northwest Coast, which were inflexible, allowed private ownership, and were also small.

Abundances of resources, either those that occurred in nature or those that were produced from farming, correlated positively with population density but not with political and economic organization. That is to say, predictable, storable, and abundant food supplies generated the highest population densities in western North America, but these factors were not sufficient to generate complex and centralized political and economic organizations. The variety of ceremonial, sodality, and kinship mechanisms that were invoked to coordinate closely spaced, independent, and competitive communities will engage us in many places throughout the rest of this book.

KINSHIP AND SOCIAL ORGANIZATION

There was a marked difference between the flexible social organizations of the Great Basin and Plateau, and the inflexibility of most organizations along the Northwest Coast, in the central and northern parts of California, in Southern California, and in the Southwest. In some part the differences in the openness of the social organizations between these two blocs of culture stemmed from the manner in which tribes gained their livelihoods, and the localization and abundances of resources in their areas, but the manner in which ownership and use-rights to strategic resources were recognized proved to be much more important in determining whether or not group membership was flexible.

Marriage

An assessment of kinship and social organization with marriage is valuable in that it allows us to set the stage not only for learning who married whom, but whether the families of the bride and groom entered into long-term and formalized relations, and whether these relations had economic or political importance. An assessment of these leads quite logically into an examination of postnuptial residence and its implications for political and economic relations. Did the couple reside in the husband's or wife's community, and with the husband's or wife's parents, or in some

other arrangement? We shall determine these things and account for the relations that obtained.

Cousin Marriage

Among societies in which unilineal descent is observed,* throughout the world the frequency of marriages between cousins has always been high. Cousin marriages among the tribes of western North America were often consummated between the children of brothers and sisters ("cross-cousin" marriages in which one parent of the bride and one parent of the groom were siblings of the opposite, or cross, sex) but not between children of brothers or between children of sisters; in some instances between the children of sisters or the children of brothers ("parallel-cousin" marriages in which one parent of the bride and one parent of the groom were siblings of the same, or parallel, sex) but not between cross-cousins; and in a few instances, marriages were approved between both parallel-cousins and cross-cousins (see Figure 8-3).

In western North America, even though 34 percent (sixty) of all societies observed unilineal descent (20 percent patrilineal and 14 percent matrilineal), only 11 percent (nineteen) of all societies approved marriages between first cousins (i.e., cousins whose parents included siblings among them), and five of those societies observed bilateral descent (Map Cu-120, V-294). Marriages between second cousins (whose grandparents included siblings among them) were approved by 16 percent (27) of all societies, and nine of those societies observed bilateral descent (Map Cu-121, V-295).

At the time of European contact it was abundantly clear that cousin marriages were approved in very few tribes; that second-cousin marriages were more acceptable than first-cousin marriages; and that only the matrilineal societies of the northern Northwest Coast, the patrilineal Athapaskan societies of the southern Northwest Coast, and the patrilineal Patwin and Miwok societies of the central part of California, among all unilineal societies, approved of marriages between first and second cross-cousins. The vast majority (84 percent) of western North American societies disapproved of cousin marriages altogether,

---

*Descent is an ideological phenomenon. In unilineal descent individual persons recognize and assign kinship relations through the mother's female relatives (these are matrilineal) or the father's male relatives (these are patrilineal). Bilateral descent recognizes and assigns kinship relations through both sides.

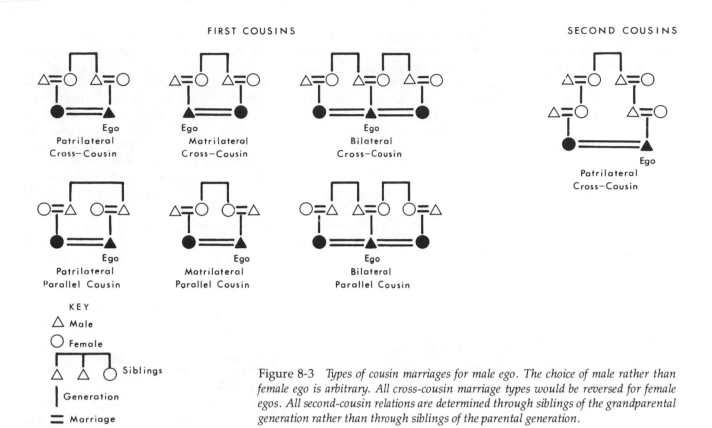

Figure 8-3 *Types of cousin marriages for male ego. The choice of male rather than female ego is arbitrary. All cross-cousin marriage types would be reversed for female egos. All second-cousin relations are determined through siblings of the grandparental generation rather than through siblings of the parental generation.*

or they did not condone marriages between cousins closer than the third degree of removal (great grandchildren of siblings in the great grandparental generation) (Map Cu-122, V-296).

Among most societies, whether unilineal or bilateral in custom of descent, cousin marriages were not desired, even though each cross-cousin marriage could have served to align two unilineal descent groups. As a matter of fact, only the patrilineal Athapaskans of southern Oregon and the patrilineal Patwin of the central part of California systematically aligned patrilineages through intermarriage. These people often selected matrilateral cross-cousins as mates, thereby exchanging women and men between lineages.

The other unilineal societies in which cross-cousin marriages were sometimes contracted were those of the northern Northwest Coast. These matrilineal societies approved marriages with matrilateral as well as patrilateral cross-cousins, and the Haisla Kwakiutl also approved marriages between patrilateral parallel-cousins. Although cross-cousin marriages and even patrilateral parallel-cousin marriages were approved among these societies, cousins per se were not sought in marriage. Rather, marriages were sought between people in opposite moieties, whether or not they were cousins.

Throughout the northern Northwest Coast, matrilineages comprised each group of people who traced their descent to a known, common matrilineal ancestor. These descent groups were further organized into several named matrisibs in which the members stipulated that they descended from a common maternal ancestor, even if they could not demonstrate the genealogical relations among the matrilineages that composed each matrisib. The Haida and Tlingit further organized the matrisibs into two divisions, or moieties, while the Tsimshians and Haisla organized their matrisibs into four divisions, or phratries. The moieties and phratries were marriage-regulating units, and people had to seek mates outside their own division. It was crucial to marry outside one's lineage, sib, and division, whereas it was not crucial to seek a cross-cousin. For marriages between people in moiety and phratry societies, the phratries were lumped into two divisions and paired with the moieties.

Cousin marriage was an insignificant factor in mate selection among the Miwok of the central part of California, who were patrilineal, as well. These societies, too, were composed of lineages organized into moieties, and the important thing was to marry a person from the opposite moiety rather than to align with any particular patrilineage. South of the Miwok, the patrilineal Yokuts, patrilineal Kings River Mono, and bilateral San Joaquin Mono of the central part of California were also organized into moieties which regulated marriage. The emphasis was not only to marry outside one's lineage and moiety in this part of California, and outside one's lineage, patrisib, and moiety in Southern California, but to marry someone from another community as well.

Exogamy, Endogamy, Agamy

The practice of marrying someone from outside one's lineage, sib, moiety, or phratry is "exogamous," as is marrying outside of one's community. It is plausible that cross-cousin marriage once had a wider distribution along the Coast, in California, and in Southern California than it had at the time of European contact. In each of those areas there may have been periods when unilineal-descent groups, especially among the Penutian speakers and perhaps also among the Uto-Aztecan and Hokan speakers, formed task-groups and appropriated resource areas. As they settled around their resources in independent communities, the monolineage communities (single-lineage communities) may have engaged in marriages between cross-cousins.

At the time of European contact the form of exogamy emphasized among all the extractive-based unilineal societies* was to find a partner not only beyond the moiety or phratry but also beyond the community. Marriage partners were also sought outside the community in bilateral societies (Map Cu-123, V-298). In fact, 70 percent of the societies from the Akwa'ala on the south to the Chilkat Tlingit on the north predominantly practiced community (settlement) exogamy, i.e., a person sought a mate from outside his or her own settlement.[†] In the remaining 30 percent of societies there was no clear preference (that is, agamy was observed) for marriage outside

---

*All unilineal societies in the Northwest Coast, California, and Southern California culture areas were based on extraction rather than production.

[†] Exogamy can take many forms. Among them are kinship group exogamy, community (settlement) exogamy, speech community exogamy, and political organization exogamy. If a kinship group is exogamous its members seek mates outside their own group. If a moiety is exogamous its members seek mates outside their own moiety. There are, then, many forms of exogamy. For instance, a member of a Kaweah Yokuts tribelet would seek a mate outside his or her kinship group, moiety, settlement community, and perhaps, tribelet (politically organized community), but perhaps not outside his or her speech community (people speaking a mutually intelligible Yokuts language).

(exogamy) or inside (endogamy) the community. Within some of the largest villages throughout western North America, endogamy was practiced; in these villages it was possible for people to find mates from other lineages (Patwin and Salinan tribes), from an opposite moiety (some Yokuts and Tlingit), or from other phratries (Tsimshian); likewise, within the largest villages in the bilateral tribelets of northern California endogamous marriages were arranged. Yet even in the ostensibly agamous Northwest Coast villages, children from the highest-ranking kinship groups obtained marriage partners from other villages, and in northern California tribelets where mates could be found inside or outside the village or the tribelet (thus agamous), children from the wealthiest families obtained partners from other communities: even in agamous communities,* therefore, exogamy was often preferred and leading kinship groups and leading families married outside their communities. In this manner alliances were created between distant kinship groups on the Northwest Coast, and between leading families among adjacent tribelets in northern California.

Marriage outside the community was emphasized by the most prestigious kinship groups and by the leading families in agamous societies, and by everyone in the other societies located in the abundantly endowed coastal strip in far western North America. This practice suggests that marriage was an important mechanism in creating formal relations among competitive groups who, for the greatest part, had but a minimum of political organization. Among the societies in the northern part of California, where intense bartering was conducted, and among many Northwest Coast societies from the northwestern area of California through the Salishans of the central area, families even sought brother–sister-exchange marriages (brothers from one family each married sisters from another family, or a brother and sister from one family married their opposites from another family) (Map Cu-124, V-297).

The pressure to marry outside one's community, whether defined formally between moieties or among ranked kinship groups, or informally between communities within and among tribelets, created myriads of affinal relations among localized kinship groups and among tribelets. The predominantly exogamous communities of the Northwest Coast, the central and northern parts of California, and Southern California were matched by the patrideme communities of the Pimas in the Southwest. Members of Pima demes

---

*Agamy characterizes a community in which some marriages are outside the community and some inside. There is no predominance of either form and no rule for agamy.

sought marriage partners from other communities: the woman moved to her husband's village. Yet among the Pueblos, endogamy, which was the opposite of exogamy, dominated in the villages. An endogamous village was one in which marriage partners were from the same community. In each of the Pueblo villages, whether Western or Eastern, or inhabited by Eastern Keresans, in one sense all village members were either co-owners of farmland or had access to it, even in the Western Pueblos where matrilineal sibs owned the land. Although the Western Pueblo sibs owned land, the sibs were hierarchically organized in terms of rituals relating to the use of the land, which it was the prerogative of each sib to perform, and each sib gained land on the basis of the rituals in its custody. Alliances were constantly struck among people from different sibs in the same village so that access to prominent rituals, and its corollary, access to land, would be enhanced. Within the Western Pueblo villages a person could not marry someone from his own sib, his father's sib, or his mother's father's sib. Marriage rules, then, proscribed long-term alignments between sibs in favor of a wide net of affinal relations for most sibs. Control of agricultural land and the most important rituals, whether by design or by fortuity, did not become centralized in the hands of three or four sibs. Whereas one sib (the "bear" sib) in each Hopi village was recognized as the rightful owner of all Hopi land, ritual support from other sibs was critical to the maintenance of land. The various sibs in each village joined forces to control land ceremonially, and to maintain the land within the village through endogamy. The Eastern Pueblos eschewed cousin marriages, and expected marriage partners to be from the same villages, though some exogamous marriages occurred in all the villages.

Throughout the Great Basin, Plateau, and among the most mobile groups in the Southwest, agamy predominated. The preferences in the Ute communities for exogamy were the exceptions. Because cousin marriages were not allowed or were allowed only between distant cousins, people in these societies sought mates when two or more local residence-groups convened for a ceremony, or at root-gathering grounds, or some other occasion, but there were no formal or ceremonial relations among such organizations as ranked kinship groups, moieties, phratries, or sibs to weld them together.

Plural Marriages—Polygyny, Polyandry

In order to understand differences in marriage practices we must expand our discussion to include plural marriages, gifting at marriage, and postnuptial residence practices. Plural marriages (Map Cu-125, V-292) are referred to as "polygamy." Polygamy took several forms in western North America, such as "sororal polygyny" wherein co-wives of the same man were sisters, "nonsororal polygyny" wherein co-wives of the same man were not sisters, "general polygyny" wherein some co-wives were sisters and some were not, and "fraternal polyandry" wherein co-husbands of the same woman were brothers.

Polygamous marriages occurred in the vast majority (79 percent) of western North American societies, and the forms polygamy took were almost always sororal polygyny, or sororal polygyny coupled with nonsororal or general polygyny. The incidence of polygyny exceeded 10 percent only in a handful of groups, and they were predominantly in the Northwest Coast and Plateau (Map Cu-126, V-291). In these societies alliances between families were sought in all directions, and surpluses of fish or of fish and roots made it possible for up to one-fourth of the men to support more than one wife. The ability to provide for wives in western North America seems to have been a very important factor in whether or not there was a high proportion of polygamous marriages in a society. High proportions of such marriages occurred only in societies in which men made the greatest contribution to subsistence. But factors other than surpluses operated to prompt the creation of polygamous marriages. For instance, men did most of the farming among the Pueblos, but in the Western Pueblos they farmed on their wives' lands, so they did not control the subsistence resource base, and in the Eastern Pueblos they farmed on village land, so did not control that base either. Thus, in western North America, the contributions of men to subsistence seem to have been important in providing a context for polygyny; but high incidences of polygyny occurred primarily in extractive societies in which large surpluses could be stored and in which men controlled the subsistence resource areas. Even among the matrilineal Tsimshians and Tlingits where there were high incidences of polygyny, men and their sister's sons controlled the resource areas of the matrilineage.

It is possible to account for a good portion of the polygyny in our sample through the custom of the sororate, wherein a man took his deceased wife's sister (or perhaps her terminological sister) for his wife. In all but 16 tribes in western North America the sororate was practiced. In all but 21 societies the levirate was also practiced, wherein a woman took her deceased husband's brother (or perhaps terminological brother) for her husband (V-293). In practice, sororal polygyny was most often a form of "anticipated sororate" in which a man married his wife's younger sister, though his wife was still living.

Polygyny was rare in some California tribelets and Southern California sibs. In these mixed extractive economies wild plant gathering was important, as was the woman's role in procuring wild plants. Polygyny was conspicuously absent among the Pueblos, where strict monogamy was the rule. For the Pueblos, not only did marriage rules act against the formation of strong and lasting alliances between families, but neither did they allow women or men to accumulate multiple mates. Furthermore, gift exchanges between families of the bride and groom before, during, or after marriages were not common. It is as if bonds were expected to be transitory, and were solely expected to serve the couple. Gift-exchange customs did not bind the families of the husband and wife into reciprocal arrangements of long duration. In California, where surpluses could perhaps have supported more polygamous unions than existed in fact, the tendency was toward very limited, even rare, polygyny.

The contrast in amounts of polygyny between Northwest Coast–Plateau societies and California societies may well not have been influenced by the presence of the sororate, or abundant resources, or male control of resource areas, as these features were common to all three areas. Yet male contributions to subsistence were greater in the Northwest Coast and Plateau, and families among tribes in both areas sought wider and more extensive trade contacts and ceremonial relations, which were cementable through marriages. Successful men were encouraged to gain more than one wife from more than one community. Indeed, co-wives in the Plateau and Northwest Coast were not predominantly sisters, and general and nonsororal polygyny prevailed. Northwest Coast and Plateau people travelled considerable distances by canoe for ceremonial occasions, and Plateau people traded with coastal people. Gifting attended trading, marriages occurred between coastal and interior people, and in the Bulkley and Skeena drainages, Plateau people assumed the opposite moiety names of their coastal trading partners and gifted them. Plateau and Northwest Coast marriage practices were influenced by many of the same things and even by each other.

Gift Exchange—Before, During, and After Marriage

Whereas the practice of gifting was a widespread feature attending life-cycle events on the Northwest Coast, especially in the form of distributions among the Salishans and their neighbors, the same practice could have been carried into the Plateau by the Salishans, or borrowed from coastal people through trade, ceremonial, and marriage relations at a later date. Intermarriages between Salishan speakers and Sahaptian speakers in the Plateau were accompanied by gifting. Kinship terms and other features of language diffused among these groups, and it is very likely that many of the borrowings were stimulated by intermarriages (see Aoki 1962, 1966, 1975). It is plausible that the practice of elaborate and equal gift exchanges between Plateau families diffused from Salishans to Sahaptians in the context of wider relations that included extensive reciprocating, trade, joint use of some resource areas, and ceremonial participation.

The practice of exchanging gifts between families of the bride and groom before, during, and after marriages and the nexus of relationships in which the gifting patterns were embedded in the Northwest Coast and the Plateau were consonant with the extensive travel undertaken by these people and their concerted efforts to formalize relations between widely separated people. In northern California, on the other hand, people traveled only short distances: even people living on the navigable rivers did not travel far. People who were caught considerable distances from their home communities might be treated as poachers and repulsed. Even trade and ceremonial relations were maintained within and between neighboring communities in northern California. Marriage alliances, too, were between people from communities in the same tribelet or neighboring tribelets. Yet in the Plateau visitors were welcome, and on the Northwest Coast visitors, especially prospective suitors and their families, always entered a village bearing gifts.

There were differences in Northwest Coast and Plateau practices, to be sure. In about one-half of the societies on the Northwest Coast gifts between families before marriage were most often unequal, the groom's family giving more than the bride's family gave in return. Unequal exchanges of this sort approached a "bride price," that is prestation* for women was made at a greater rate than the prestation for men. Among the Haida and Haisla Kwakiutl, who were matrilineal, the prestation pattern was reversed (that is, it was "dowrylike"), the bride's family giving more than the groom's. The inequality of Northwest Coast exchanges was consonant with their ranking systems and with the general practice of the couple residing in the home of the groom's father or male paternal relatives (residence was therefore patrilocal or virilocal), or the groom's maternal uncle (residence

---

*"Prestation" refers to obligatory presents ostensibly given as gifts.

was avunculocal): unequal exchanges marked the removal of the women from her paternal home (Map Cu-127, V-299). In the Plateau, where gift exchanges tended to be equal, there was no ranking system.

Gift exchange between families of the bride and groom also occurred in some northern California societies and among the Apacheans in the Southwest. Such exchanges were almost always unequal in favor of the bride's family. In northern California and along the southern Northwest Coast unequal gift exchange was frequently coupled with "bride service" in which the groom worked for a year or longer for the bride's parents at everyday tasks such as hunting, fishing, house-building, and so forth. In these areas, where the concept of personal private property was highly developed and where kinsmen often bartered for special goods, postnuptial residence was strictly patrilocal. Bride service had a rare distribution outside of the coastal areas of northwestern California and Oregon, and the interior of northern California, just as gifting after marriage was almost completely restricted to the Northwest Coast and the Plateau (Map Cu-128, V-300; Map Cu-129, V-301).

The forms of gifting, before and after marriage which favored the bride's family among some Western Apaches, and the bride service, which favored the bride's family among the Chiricahua Apaches, are interesting because these groups practiced matrilocal postnuptial residence (the couple resided with the bride's matrisib among the Western Apaches and Navajo and the bride's matrideme among the Chiricahua). We might expect to find a dowrylike arrangement inasmuch as strict compensation was usually required for the spouse who left the natal home and moved into the home of his or her spouse. Such was not the case among the Apacheans or the Great Basin tribes who practiced bride service. In these societies women performed the bulk of the gathering of wild plants and, where farming was practical, women were codominant with men in farming labor. Rather than serving as compensation for losing an important laborer, bride service can instead be rationalized as representing the husband's need to prove that he was worthy to share in the fruits of his wife's labor: it was proper etiquette to establish that proof. On the other hand, the Apacheans observed matrilocality, whereas only some Great Basin dwellers did (the Utes and Wind River Shoshones). Ambilocality (residing with the family of the bride or the groom, depending on which prospects looked better at the time) was the dominant postnuptial residence practice in the Great Basin. It is unlikely that the bride service custom among Great Basin dwellers was prompted by compensation for the loss of the female from one family, or by proving the male's worth to the bride's family. On the other hand, throughout the

Plateau, Great Basin, and among the most mobile people in the Southwest, there was great flexibility in postnuptial marital arrangements: families were relatively free to leave one camp or band and move to another. Even the matrilocal matrisibs of the Western Apaches were flexible in membership. The customs in these many societies—the way they owned, used, or owned *and* used strategic resources—were markedly different from the customs that prevailed among the inflexible kinship groups, villages, and tribelets that controlled resources in California, Southern California, the Pueblos, and the Northwest Coast.

Postnuptial residence looms as an important factor in economic organization and in social organization, and certainly in marriage practices. We shall pay special attention to the relations among these phenomena.

RESIDENCE AND FAMILY HOUSEHOLD

Residence of the Couple After Marriage

Fixed postnuptial residence, overwhelmingly "patrilocal" (where the husband and wife resided with the husband's father), predominated throughout the Northwest Coast, California, and Southern California culture areas. "Avunculocality" (where the husband and wife resided with the husband's mother's brother) was a variation on the patrilocal theme in the northern Northwest Coast, whereas "virilocality" (where the husband and wife resided with or near the husband's male kinsmen) was practiced among a few California tribelets. Whether patrilocal, virilocal, or avunculocal, these forms of residence after marriage meant that couples resided with male kinspeople of the husband, and the communities into which people moved, whether bilateral tribelets or localized kinship groups, owned the key strategic extractive resource sites. Movements of families out of these communities was extremely rare.

In Southern California, the bride not only moved to her husband's patrisib community, but she also became a member of his sib, thus entitling her to use the sib's key gathering resources and water sites. She also became a member of her husband's moiety, joining with that moiety to host certain ceremonies for the moiety to which she belonged prior to marriage. The Southern California tribes, by absorbing women into the patrisib communities into which they had married and placing the bride in a new context in which she ceremonially reciprocated with the moiety to which she once belonged, made the woman a total member of her husband's sib. Postmarital gift exchanges between families of the bride and groom were made unnecessary by the moiety relations that, in a general fashion, kept them in contact as ceremonial opposites who were obligated to host each other on certain occasions.

Among the Pima and River Yuman farmers, residence was predominantly patrilocal and there was little shifting of families after they once became established, unless an entire Pima patrideme or Yuman patrilineage relocated so as to open new farmland. Mohave couples broke this pattern and often resided wherever their economic prospects were best (they were ambilocal).

Among Pueblos, residence was matrilocal among the Sia (Eastern Keresan), and either "neolocal" (where the couple established a new home without regard to the residence of the parents of either) or ambilocal among the other Eastern Keresans and the Tanoans; in the predominantly endogamous Pueblos, residence was fixed within all villages, and families did not move among villages after they had once been formed; and for the Western Pueblos, residence was matrilocal. Thus, not only were Western Pueblo families bound into villages, but residency within these villages was inflexibly arranged with the bride's mother's family (Map Cu-130, V-305).

From Yakutat Bay to the Gulf of California, and throughout the most sedentary Southwestern villages, there were few couples who did not observe the dominant forms of postnuptial residence. The youngest sons of the lowest-ranking patridemes and patribilateral families in the central and southern Northwest Coast often went to live with the family of the bride (residence was matrilocal yet with the bride's paternal relatives). Choice in the location of residence (ambilocality) was available to those lowest-ranking couples from the lowest-ranking kinship groups. In northern California there was a modest amount of "uxorilocality" (where the couple resided near the wife's patrikinsmen). This postnuptial residence practice was sometimes desired by a man's father-in-law, if the father-in-law had no sons, or by the newly married couple, if the economic prospects were better among the bride's kinsmen. In the northern part of California, the practice of bride service often caused the couple to reside initially and temporarily with the bride's family, but also patrilocal tribelets in the central area of California that did not practice bride service also expected the couple to reside for some period in the bride's household (Map Cu-131, V-306; Map Cu-132, V-307).

Only the concentration of ambilocal societies northwest of San Francisco Bay—several Pomo, Wappo, Coast Yuki, and Kato tribelets—did not observe patrilocality, and only the Coast Yuki and Kato expected the couple to begin their residence with the bride's family.

The point of the limited variation in forms of postnuptial residency among the societies along the coastal strip of western North America and throughout California, Southern California, and the sedentary communities in the Southwest as well, was that the couples became fixed in some community—some kinship group or village, and so forth—through which they gained access to privately owned resources. The Californians, with their narrow world of immediate contacts, sent their sons to live temporarily with their brides' families; and the bilateral people of the Northwest Coast, who had extensive contacts with groups near and far, allowed the lowest-ranking couples to locate wherever they could get the best deal and exchanged gifts with all families into which their children had married.

The Great Basin, Plateau, and more mobile Pais and Apacheans of the Southwest did not so rigidly fix the membership of their local residence-groups. Even though some of these groups owned concentrated resource areas, the areas were not controlled nearly so stringently as they were along the entire Coast of western North America, in the interiors of California and Southern California, and in the sedentary-farming regions. In the Great Basin, most residence was ambilocal and families could splinter from camps at any time and relocate with another camp.

In the Plateau, most tribes observed patrilocal residence, but a few observed ambilocal and even matrilocal residence. For each of these societies, those that practiced matrilocal residence observed an initial period of patrilocality, and those that practiced patrilocality observed an initial period of matrilocality. These practices had the effect of causing the couple to reside in the bride's community and the groom's community for some length of time. Subsequently, it was always possible for a couple to relocate with the family of either partner, or even to establish themselves in a new band or village. Most Plateau resources were either treated as communal and available to all in the residence group or as privately owned, access being granted within the residence group.

The Western Apaches in the Southwest represented a half-way point between localized, resource-owning matrilineages (local segments of nonlocalized matrisibs), and flexible bands. Postnuptial residence was matrilocal, so that a man moved into his wife's matrilineage and the couple farmed on her land. Yet unrelated people could join the sib segment, on request, and work the farmland if some were available. The localized segments of matrisibs were also free to join with adjacent localized groups to form bands, which they did in order to hunt, raid, and trade. Yet the localized sib-segments were also free to splinter from one band and to join another. Thus, Western Apache sibs had the flexibility of hunting and raiding bands as well as the localized food-resources of farmers. Even the localized sib-segments were flexible in allowing new families to join them, yet the recruits had to submit to the authority of the local headman.

The Eastern Apaches, Utes, and Wind River Shoshones observed matrilocal residence, and the families were organized into matridemes which, in turn, joined with several other matridemes to form hunting and gathering bands. Families were free to leave their demes and attach with any band for hunting and raiding. The fluidity of movements of the bands as they sought gathering and hunting resources made them much less sedentary than the Western Apaches or the fishermen of the Plateau, and also prompted some flexibility of band membership.

The Pais were similar to most Plateau tribes in observing initial temporary matrilocal residence followed by more permanent patrilocal arrangements or by ambilocality. The Southeast Yavapai, who came under the influence of the Western Apaches, were exclusively matrilocal and were organized into matrisibs and bands on the Apachean model.

Among all of the people in the interior of western North America who were not predominantly farmers, who were not dependent on localized resources, or who were dependent on localized *and* nonlocalized resources (Plateau), fluidity of movement and flexibility of families characterized their basic social organizations. Marriages could not be contracted between first or second cousins. It was hoped that marriage would not be contracted between genealogical kin at all. Postnuptial residence customs either allowed for a choice or expected couples to reside first with the family of one partner in the union, then with the other. Subsequent movements of families were welcomed, also, and access was provided to resources by the group with whom residence was established. The contrast between extractors and modest farmers of the interior, and the coast-based extractors and dominant farmers of the Southwest, is most intelligible when the whole bundle of factors including marriage rules, community exogamy practices, gifts accompanying marriage, polygamy customs, postnuptial residence, and the abundance and localization of resources are considered together. In this light the rather inflexible membership of the localized resource-owning groups in the regions rich in aquatic animals and wild plants, on the one hand, and among the people most dependent on agriculture, on the other, can be understood. The people in these areas worked out a set of mechanisms to relate to neighbors while maintaining

control of their own resources. Moieties, phratries, gift exchange, bride service, and the like are but a few of the mechanisms, along with barter, ceremonial gifting, and sodality performances, that were variously employed in the articulation of neighbors. Of course feuding, raiding, and a few instances of warfare also plagued many of the localized kinship groups, tribelets, and villages.

Family Household Forms

The family households that were formed or expanded with each new marriage were influenced by the postnuptial residence custom that was observed. Thus, from the central Northwest Coast through the Plateau, and throughout the central and northern parts of California, Southern California, and the Colorado River region, patrikinsmen formed the nucleus of the various family households and the communities. The size and composition of family households, on the other hand, varied considerably (Map Cu-133, V-304; also V-302 and V-303).

A "family household" comprised the co-residential kinship units living under one or a few adjacent roofs, which shared some domestic functions, such as the distribution of food, or child rearing or training, or preparation of some meals, or the like (see Figure 8-4). The simplest family household was the "independent nuclear household" composed of a husband, wife, and their unmarried offspring. These forms dominated in the Great Basin, the San Joaquin Valley of Central California and the Eastern Pueblos, and for quite different reasons in each area. In the Eastern Pueblos, kinship was of minor importance when compared with village and village sodality organization. Large groups of people living in small and independent nuclear families were packed into apartment-house-like structures in compact villages. Residence was either neolocal and assigned by the village leaders or, if the couple moved near one of their parents because a room was available, ambilocal.

The Yokuts of the San Joaquin Valley and foothills of the southern Sierra lived in patrilocal independent nuclear families. Several families related through the patriline formed independent households in near proximity, and several such lineages comprised most villages.

Among the Uto-Aztecan neighbors of the Yokuts, independent but related households, either virilocal or patrilocal, tended to cluster together. Throughout the Great Basin proper, on the other hand, ambilocal independent households were grouped into small family camps that foraged over the countryside, los-

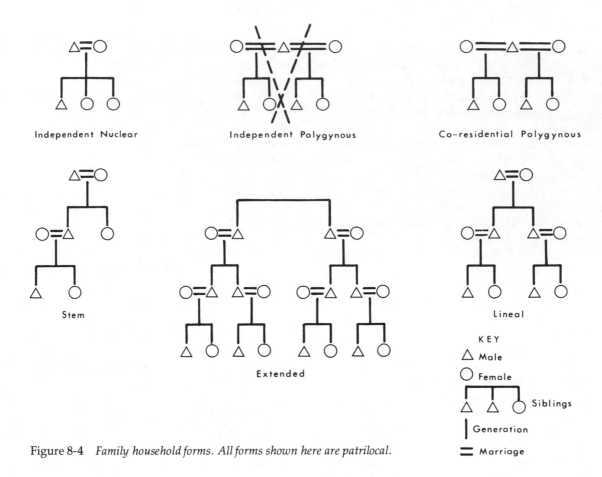

Figure 8-4 *Family household forms. All forms shown here are patrilocal.*

ing and gaining nuclear family households from time to time. The family household was the basic unit of organization in the Great Basin, whereas independent nuclear families were embedded in complex economic, political–religious structures in the Eastern Pueblos, and in patrilineages in the San Joaquin Valley.

"Polygynous family households" occurred in most societies in western North America, but except for a few societies, the incidence of such households was meager. Where polygynous households approached codominance with a household of another type, polygynous households have been shown on the distribution map (Map Cu-133). When a husband, his wives, and their unmarried offspring shared the same house the polygynous household was termed "co-residential"; when each wife and her offspring had separate abodes, the households were termed "independent." Co-residential polygynous family households occurred among the Athapaskans on the southern Oregon coast and form a patch on that part of Map Cu-133, but this particular household form was actually codominant with "lineal" family households (which will be described below), and occurred in villages that were composed of patrilineal kinsmen.

"Stem family households" normally were composed of a husband and wife, their unmarried children, and perhaps one married child and that person's family. Stem families, which were larger than nuclear yet smaller than lineal families, linked two families from two generations. Stem families were the dominant types among the Miwok groups in central California. The Miwok resided in monolineage communities, i.e., localized patrilineages in which the single lineage was the sole owner of all strategic resources in its designated territory. South of the Miwok, the Yokuts, who may well have evolved multilineage tribelets out of monolineage communities, also were organized into patrilocal and independent nuclear family households that were smaller than Miwok stem families. Yokuts patrilineages retained control over key gathering sites, but other extractive resource areas were owned by the multilineage tribelet. It is plausible that ownership roles of Yokuts patrilineages were reduced during the same period in which those roles were being assumed by the multilineage tribelets. A process such as this would account for family households being smaller and less complex among the Yokuts than among the Miwok.

"Lineal family households" dominated throughout northern California, Southern California, the Pla-

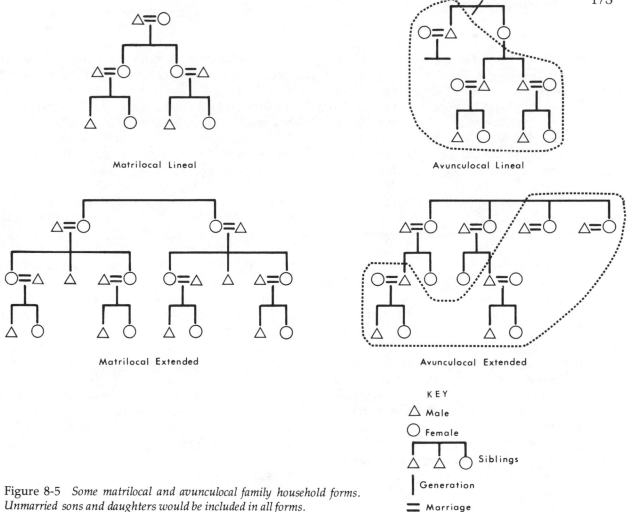

Matrilocal Lineal

Avunculocal Lineal

Matrilocal Extended

Avunculocal Extended

KEY

△ Male

○ Female

△ △ ○ Siblings

| Generation

= Marriage

Figure 8-5 *Some matrilocal and avunculocal family household forms. Unmarried sons and daughters would be included in all forms.*

teau, the Apachean groups in the Southwest, and much of the Northwest Coast. Lineal family households included one family of procreation in the senior generation, and at least two procreating families in a junior generation. Throughout most of the northern subarea of California, the Northwest Coast, and the Plateau, family households observed patrilocal or virilocal residence and bilateral descent. Thus we may call these "patribilateral lineal households." Among the central Northwest Coast groups several patribilateral lineal households were organized into economically and politically autonomous patridemes which, except for unilineal descent rules, were equivalent to large localized lineages. A village comprised one or more demes. In the southern and northwestern California subareas of the Northwest Coast patribilateral lineal households and patrilineal lineal households (the latter among Oregon Athapaskans) tended to be the ultimate autonomous political and economic units.* Several such units composed a vil-

lage. In northern California, patribilateral lineal households were subsumed under tribelet organizations, but in the Plateau they were organized into dispersed villages, yet these households retained greater flexibility of movement than was the case for the same type of households in the coastal and California regions.

In Southern California lineal families observed patrilocal residence and were clustered into patrilineages and patrisib communities recognizing a priest-chief. In many ways these family households were similar to the households just to the north in the California culture area and in the central and northern parts of the Northwest Coast culture area. They had less autonomy than units in the Plateau, which could move if they desired, and in the southern (including northwestern California) subareas of the Northwest Coast, where the family households were economically autonomous.

Among the Apacheans, lineal families observed matrilocal residence; among the Tlingit they observed avunculocal residence. Matrilocal and avunculocal family households are represented graphically in Figure 8-5.

*See definitions of patribilateral lineal household, patrilineal lineal household, and patrihousehold (page 135).

"Extended family households," which included two related families of procreation in at least two generations, were restricted to some central and northern Northwest Coast tribes and to the Western Pueblos. Among the Western Pueblos, families observed matrilocal residence and resided in adjacent apartments which belonged to the matrilineage. Each extended family was a segment of the lineage. Among the Salishans on the Northwest Coast one or more patribilateral extended family households owned and occupied large plank-houses and constituted demes that were politically and economically autonomous. Farther north the Haidas, Tsimshians, and Haisla Kwakiutl practiced avunculocal residence and matrilineal descent. The extended families were either segments of lineages or entire lineages that occupied large plank-houses and owned property.

It should be clear to the reader that similar family household types in different areas, such as the patribilateral lineal households of the Plateau and the patribilateral lineal households of northern California, often had vastly different amounts of autonomy and ownership rights, and different kinship relations and relations to other family households in their communities. There was a tendency for the people who had access to, and control over, the greatest resources to co-reside in family households larger than independent nuclear arrangements, but the Eastern Pueblos, whose kinship relations were less dominant than their village sodality organizations, and the Yurok and some other northwestern and northern California groups were exceptions to the trend. House size was not a foolproof predictor of family household type either, because some people with small and portable houses (for example, Apaches) also formed lineal households. Yet the trend was for larger houses to be occupied by the more complex family household types.

DESCENT AND DESCENT GROUPS

Introduction

Descent is an ideological variable that distinguishes how individuals recognize and assign kin relations. Descent reckoning is distinguishable and varies independently from household residence forms, descent groups, inheritance, and succession. These phenomena are often conflated in the social organization literature, and the mistake is understandable because people who were recognized as kinship relatives often co-resided in descent groups through which property was inherited and through which succession to authority occurred. If all of these practices did not co-occur in a society, some combination of them often did, and they were important in the organization of the society. There can be no question that these several features vary independently from one another. Good demonstrations of the relations among some of these phenomena were provided by Driver (1956, 1966) when, working with a comparative sample of about 280 Indian tribes north of Panama, he showed that (all things being equal and given an indefinite amount of time*) aspects of economic and kinship organizations tended to integrate, or adjust to one another, within societies. These adjustments, Driver averred, followed a regular and predictable sequence in which changes in the division of labor by sex triggered changes in postnuptial residence practices which in turn triggered changes in land tenure practices and, subsequently, changes in descent reckoning, kinship terminologies, and in-law avoidance customs. It was Driver's postulate that whichever sex contributed most to the daily sustenance of the kinship unit would be the sex that would determine where the couple lived after marriage. The same sex would own and inherit land, own the house, bring their spouses to reside in their own houses, and so forth. Driver also postulated that once a rule of descent, such as matrilineality, became established, it reinforced the postnuptial residence and land tenure rules that preceded it. Thus, Driver (1956) envisaged feedback from descent to other features of kinship and economic organization. He suggested that kinship organization, in general, was resistant to change and that the reinforcing nature of feedback mechanisms helped account for kinship organizations that were not "fully integrated." Societies that were not fully integrated were those in which—say, as among the Hopi—the division of labor was dominated by men but residence was matrilocal, tenure was matrilineal, descent was matrilineal, and kinship terminologies were of the Crow type. Even if a society became fully integrated, given Driver's definition, at some point in time—change being postulated as an ever-occurring phenomenon—adjustments toward integration would be challenged by such factors as the migration of a community into a new environment in which their subsistence economy and labor

---

*The interpretation of temporal sequences from a set of "steady-state" variables is a "stochastic process," or, a partial-ordering law. Driver correlated data from a single, pre-Contact time period and inferred a stochastic process.

needs might change, or intermarriage with people from other communities whose kinship organization were different from their own, or the borrowing of horticultural practices by people who previously had not been horticultural, and the like.

This cyclical hypothesis of kinship development did not propose that some forms of kinship organization represented more complex evolutionary stages than other forms, only that it was possible for kinship organizations encompassing a host of variables to change and become integrated in another fashion as the organization of extraction or the organization of production (specifically, the sexual division of labor), which dictated the form of integration changed. Key parts of this hypothesis were formulated by E.B. Tylor (1889) nearly a century ago in an evolutionary framework that argued for the transformation from matrilineal to patrilineal societies through a "remove" stage; they were reformulated and demonstrated by Murdock (1949); and they were reformulated and demonstrated by Jorgensen (1966) on the basis of worldwide samples.

The importance of the "cyclical," "lag," or "main sequence" kinship organization hypothesis (all being synonyms by which the postulate is known) is that it posits regular relationships among economic and kinship phenomena that recur again and again around the world. There are, however, many shortcomings in the hypothesis, as well. For instance, as in any synchronic hypothesis, there are no tests for actual historical sequences; and as in all synchronic cross-cultural studies, there are no foolproof methods to distinguish between tribes that possess similar kinship organization features (variables) because they inherited or borrowed them from a common source and tribes that independently invented those same features. This puzzle is known as "Galton's Problem" because the statistician Sir Francis Galton, after hearing E. B. Tylor read his famous paper in 1888, asked him how many culture units in his worldwide sample were historically related and how many were independent: the rate of dependency and interdependency would influence Tylor's statistical results. Tylor could not answer the question because he did not know in what way the cultures in his sample were related.

In this study we have assumed that tribes related by language have inherited some common cultural features and that features have also diffused among tribes that share common territories. We have also assumed that some inventions occurred independently. But whenever and wherever inventions occurred, such as the creation of moieties, or phratries, or sodalities, these phenomena almost invariably diffused from their creators to other societies, either through inheritance or borrowing. Because our sample is geographically continuous, includes practically all of the tribes in western North America for which there are extensive ethnographic records, and has been analyzed for variables that were present in each culture as well as variables that were absent, we are in a position to suggest plausible explanations for the creation and diffusion of kinship organization features. In the following analysis we bring much more data to bear than were considered by Tylor (1889), Murdock (1949), Driver (1956, 1966), or Jorgensen (1966), but some of the hypotheses advanced in the earlier studies will be germane to us here.*

Descent Reckoning

Descent reckoning was the way by which kinspeople distinguished relatives. It was not a level or a stage in an evolutionary scheme of social organization. In western North America "bilateral descent" dominated in all areas but the Southwest, central California, Southern California, Athapaskan-speaking tribes located close together on the Oregon Coast, and the northern Northwest Coast (Map Cu-134, V-308).

In bilaterality, or nonunilineal descent, individual persons were considered equally related to kin traced through males or through females. Distance, or the number of genealogical links, rather than the sex of the connecting link, was used to differentiate kinspeople. Bilaterality is a kinship-ordering criterion of great variability, and of especially great interest to us in our analysis of western North America. For instance, the seminomadic Western Shoshone of the Great Basin lived in tiny family camps the membership of which was flexible, and they observed bilateral descent. The semisedentary Salishans of the central Northwest Coast formed large, localized kinship groups, membership in which was relatively inflexible, and most observed bilateral descent. And the large Eastern Pueblo villages were sedentary, membership was inflexible, and bilateral descent was observed. Thus, bilateral descent was observed by societies in which there was great variety in flexibility of group membership, sedentariness, local group size, and overall cultural complexity. We shall return to this later in our analysis of descent groups.

Patrilineal descent, wherein individuals em-

---

*Extensive synchronic and diachronic multidimensional tests of these and other hypotheses in the R-mode (variables with variables) will be made in future volumes.

phasized membership within a line of descent traced through males, was restricted to the Oregon Athapaskans, many of the California Penutians from the Nomlaki on the northwest through the Yokuts on the south, one Mono tribelet adjacent to the Miwoks of the southern Sierra, the Southern California Uto-Aztecans, and the Yumans. The continuous distribution of patrilineality from the west side of the Sacramento Valley to northern Baja California appears to represent at least two parallel developments of patrilineal organizations. The California Penutians may have brought patrilineal concepts with them into California from the river drainages to the north, and some of the northern California Penutians (Maidu, Nisenan, and some Wintun speakers) changed to bilaterality and organized into tribelets in that region while retaining several patrilineal features.*

The Yumans and Southern California Uto-Aztecans, on the other hand, appear to have developed patrilineal descent independently in Southern California, or perhaps the Yumans practiced patrilineal descent and passed it on to the Uto-Aztecans with whom they formalized marriage and ceremonial behavior through a pan-Southern California moiety organization. The Southern California patrilineal system appears to have been younger than the Penutian system because it had neither Omaha-type kinship terminologies nor in-law avoidances, and both of these features of kinship organization appear to develop late in the life histories of patricentered kinship organizations (Driver 1966; Jorgensen 1966).†

The evidence suggests that the patrilineal-descent systems of the central and northern parts of California and of Southern California, including the River Yumans, developed independently from one another, but the evidence also suggests that a considerable number of features of social, sodality, and ceremonial organization that may have been developed in Southern California, such as moiety organizations, mourning-anniversary ceremonies, and Jimson-weed

(Datura) drinking sodalities, diffused in various forms and combinations as far north as the Pomo, Yukians, and Maidu, and played significant roles in intra-tribelet, intertribelet, and interkinship group affairs. We shall, of course, return to these matters.

Societies observing matrilineal descent occurred in the northern Northwest Coast among the Haida, Tlingit, Tsimshians, and the Haisla Kwakiutl; and among the Carrier Athapaskans on the Bulkley and Skeena drainage. Matrilineal descent also was observed in the Southwest among the Navajo and Western Apaches, Southeast Yavapai, Hopi, Zuni, and both Eastern and Western Keresan Pueblos. One of the notable things about matrilineality was that it spread across five distinct and probably unrelated, yet adjacent language groups in the Northwest Coast and Plateau, and spread among four distinct and unrelated language groups in the Southwest. The evidence that will be provided below suggests that the Haisla Kwakiutl, Tsimshians, and probably the Carrier all borrowed the concept of matrilineal descent-reckoning, moiety-phratry concepts, and in-law avoidances from the Haidas and Tlingits. In the Southwest, the Keresan, Hopi, and Zuni Pueblos probably continued the practice of matrilineal descent-reckoning from a prehistoric Anasazi period, whereas the Apacheans may have brought matrilineality with them to the Southwest, as Dyen and Aberle (1974: 373–383, 422–423) contend, or may have borrowed the concept from matrilineally organized farming societies on the Plains, where they also may have borrowed in-law avoidance customs. Avoidances were not practiced by Pueblo people, and the Western Pueblos and Eastern Keresans also used different types of kinship terminologies—by and large the Western Pueblos employed the type known as Crow, whereas the matrilineal Apacheans generally employed an Iroquois-type system. The differences and the similarities between Pueblo and Apachean kinship organizations will be mentioned below, but it is evident that the Hopi sib system had a significant impact on the Navajo sib system, so that no matter where or when some of the Apacheans acquired matrilineality, the Hopi organization influenced the Navajo organization after the two groups came into contact. The Southeast Yavapai borrowed matrilineality from the Western Apacheans, with whom they intermarried and joined forces on raiding ventures.

Descent, an ideological variable, tells us how people viewed their kinship relations, whereas descent groups organized people in various discrete combinations of kinspeople. It is possible, for instance, to describe kinship units with reference to marriage customs, descent, and residence, as well as

---

*Such as Omaha-type kinship terminological systems and in-law avoidances, to be discussed later.

†Patricentered refers to a cluster of kinship organization variables that have a patri, that is, father-son, bias: patrilocal residence, patri-inheritance, patri-succession, patri-ownership (tenure), patrilineal descent, patrilineal descent groups, Iroquois-type or Omaha-type cousin terminologies, bifurcate collateral-type or bifurcate merging-type avuncular and aunt terminologies, and father-in-law daughter-in-law avoidance customs. A majority of such traits constitutes "patricentered." Conversely, matricentered refers to matri-biased variables.

by reference to location, internal relationships, joint activities, the ownership of corporeal and incorporeal property, and relationships between and among units. Because each of these features can vary independently from all other features, the differences between two matrilineal kinship units, say, could be marked. The presence of matrilineal descent in two societies is only one indication of similarity.

Demonstrated Descent Groups: Demes and Lineages

A simple way to distinguish kinship units is to determine whether or not a group of people *demonstrated* descent from a common ancestor by tracing descent to that ancestor (Map Cu-135, V-309). Where descent is demonstrated, or reckoned, claim to membership in the unit is validated by an acceptable demonstration of genealogical connection with another member of the line. The "demonstration" need not coincide with the actual genealogical tree. In western North America demonstrated descent groups occurred among bilateral societies as well as unilineal societies, so lineality, alone, was not necessary to define descent-group organization by the criteria employed here.

Throughout the Plateau, Great Basin, the northern part of California, the tribes of northwestern California considered part of the Northwest Coast culture area, and in the Eastern Pueblo villages of the Tanoans there were no kinship units at all. Each person recognized a "kindred" of bilateral relations traced both through the father's side and the mother's side. Full siblings shared identical kindreds, but beyond siblings, each kindred was unique. Therefore kindreds were not localized groups that owned property, performed activities, and so forth. Indeed, because kindred memberships varied with each ego, every person usually belonged to several kindreds or networks of people related to some specific person. Figure 8-6 shows three partial bilateral kindreds and shows that whereas siblings share identical kindreds, children of siblings belong to kindreds that vary from the kindreds of their parents and from the kindreds of their cousins, e.g., father's sister's children and mother's brother's children. In the Tanoan Pueblos and the tribelets of the California culture area, kinship relations were not so important as membership in villages and tribelets, yet kindreds in these societies provided each person with a set of kinspeople from among whom a mate could not be chosen and between whom reciprocity and gifting was commonplace. Yet among the people residing in

the northern part of California and northwestern California (Northwest Coast culture area), even some bartering went on among kinspeople.

Great Basin and Plateau residents probably relied much more upon their kinspeople and less upon village and tribelet membership than did individuals in either California or the Eastern Pueblos. Kinspeople from different Great Basin communities or Plateau communities not only reciprocated, gifted, and attended each other's ceremonies, but the postnuptial residence patterns of the tribes in these areas—being either ambilocal or initially matrilocal followed by permanent patrilocality—the flexibility of economic organizations, and the fluctuating nature of the resources on which Great Basin and Plateau extractors subsisted also lent themselves to movements of individuals, usually families, from one residence group to another, thus joining kindred mates of either the husband or the wife. Kindreds, then, appear to have had greater significance for Great Basin and Plateau residence-group organizations than for the less flexible residence-groups in the Pueblos and throughout the northern part of California.

Kindreds, of course, were not restricted to bilateral societies. Individuals in each society in which unilineal descent was observed also had kindreds, but in societies observing patrilineal descent, paternal kinspeople usually formed task-groups, owned property together, aided each other, and the like, whereas in matrilineal societies maternal kinspeople provided the kinship nexus.

One of the interesting facets of bilateral descent is that it occurred both among the Great Basin societies, which were among the simplest in western North America, and among the Tanoan Eastern Pueblos, which were among the most complex. In the Great Basin, bilateral kinship lent itself to great flexibility and fluidity of movement, yet in the Eastern Pueblos bilaterality correlated with the diminution of the importance of kinship bonds and the considerable importance of a moiety organization that was essentially two sodalities joined into a tribal religious-political system. The two divisions in each village alternated in exercising authority for their village. Whereas bilaterality provided the kinship flexibility so useful to people dependent on a fluctuating resource base, it also occurred among societies in which kinship was of little importance beyond regulating marriage and celebrating the life cycles of family members.

Yet in marked contrast to Great Basin societies on the one hand and Eastern Pueblos on the other, organizations which observed bilateral descent, which practiced patrilocal residence, and which were localized around strategic resources that they owned occurred throughout much of the Northwest Coast.

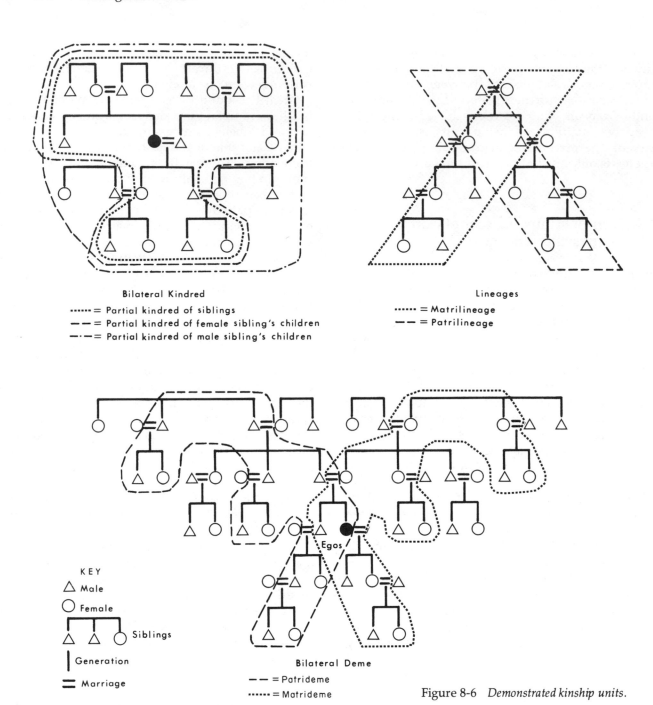

Figure 8-6 *Demonstrated kinship units.*

These units owned incorporeal property, including myths, songs, ceremonial prerogatives, kinship-group histories, kinship-group crests, and heirlooms. They were hierarchically ranked internally by birth order and genealogical proximity to the kinship group's chief so that the earlier the birth and the closer the child was to the chief, the higher the rank (son or daughter of the chief was closer than the son or daughter of the chief's younger brothers, and the older children were more highly ranked than the younger). Among the Wakashan, Chimakuan, Chinookan, and Salishan speakers of the central Northwest Coast, these kinship units formed "patridemes" which, except for the practice of bilateral descent, were very similar to unilineal descent groups.

Demes

"Demes" are groups of people demonstrating descent from a common ancestor regardless of the sex of the connecting ascendants, which are united by some additional criterion, such as unilocal postnuptial residence or collective ownership. *De facto,* some of the recognized descendants of a given ancestor are potential members and others are actual members of the unit. For instance, in Figure 8-6, the patrideme is drawn so as to exclude all of the married women (sisters and daughters of the deme's members) because they leave their father's and brother's houses and move into the houses of their husbands' and their husbands' patrikinsmen. Yet the woman retains membership in her natal deme, and the right to return, and her children can claim residence in her deme. Furthermore, a daughter can bring her husband to reside in her patrideme. Such was sometimes done among the lower-ranking families within central Northwest Coast demes (Map Cu-136, V-312).

Among the Kwakiutl, at least in historic times, a man often chose to reside in his mother's patrideme (*numaym*), or to assume names and prerogatives in all demes to which he was a potential member so as to enhance his own position and that of his children. This probably was a phenomenon of the historic period when populations dwindled and wealth multiplied. There were many names of deceased ancestors to claim, and many goods to be distributed or destroyed at potlatches so as to lay claim to the names. Although patrilocality was the dominant mode of residence, we have signified the considerable practice of ambilocality among the more highly ranked Kwakiutl persons in Map Cu-136.

Demes, because they were bilateral, provided flexibility for members, which was not so common for unilineal kinship societies. Yet along the central Northwest Coast the demes not only practiced patrilocal residence, but the members of each deme were also part owners of their kinship group's crest and mythologized history, and they owned other corporeal and incorporeal property in common. Each deme was also ranked and the members of each deme sought to contract prestigious marriages with highly ranked people from highly ranked demes so as to maintain their own rankings. Furthermore, each deme sponsored potlatches, feasts, and dances, and deme members aided one another when one of their kinspeople sponsored a distribution. The deme's ranking, as well as each person's ranking within the deme, was maintained through cooperative giving. So central Northwest Coast patridemes, each of which was composed of one or more patrilocal extended families, were very similar to corporate unilineal descent groups except that the demes were somewhat more flexible in that potential members could become actual members by not observing patrilocal residence (Map Cu-137, V-313).

The patrilocal bilateral kinship groups of the southern Northwest Coast were smaller than demes, usually being composed of patribilateral lineal families with modest generational depth. Each unit owned property and was ranked in terms of its wealth, but the families did not have the size or historical continuity of demes. The patridemes of the Pimans recognized farm lands that ultimately belonged to the entire deme, past and present, but in point of fact each family head guided his own household and laid claim to specific parcels of land; demes were not ranked nor did they own deme houses; and the deme leader or village headman possessed only nominal authority. (Map Cu-138, V-315).

The matridemes of the Utes, Wind River Shoshones, and Eastern Apaches were mobile, year-round residence groups composed of women predominantly related through the maternal line, their spouses, and their unmarried sons. As among patridemes, potential members often became actual members when a son brought his wife to reside in his mother's deme. A difference from patrideme structure, however, was that a man who had married into the deme, rather than a male (or female) member of the deme, served as its leader. Usually, but not always, leadership entailed directing hunts when the demes were separated from larger groups. Matrilocal residence and localization of winter hunting territories were the phenomena that distinguished these matridemes. But the matridemes of the Rocky Mountains were much more flexible and mobile than the patridemes of the Northwest Coast. Whereas the patridemes were localized around abundant resources, the matridemes extracted diffuse, rather abundant, yet fluctuating resources from a large area. The resources extracted by Utes, Eastern Shoshones, and Eastern Apaches were less localized than those on the Plateau, and more abundant than those in the Great Basin. In these hunting and gathering societies a man moved from his natal deme to his wife's deme, reversing the Northwest Coast practice.

These matridemes were different from the Northwest Coast patridemes in ways other than leadership. Northwest Coast people were, in general, internally ranked within their demes on the basis of birth order and genealogical proximity to the chief, and the demes were ranked relative to other demes throughout the region on the basis of ritual prerogatives that they possessed, the sumptuousness of the potlatches they hosted, and perhaps the power that they exercised over the most abundant resource areas. The matridemes of the extractors of the Rocky Mountains and the southern Rio Grande region, on the other hand, were egalitarian, so that each person was treated equally and statuses within the demes were differentiated only on the basis of cumulative knowledge, generation, sex, and age. Moreover, the matridemes were not differentiated with respect to prestige, privilege, or power. The matridemes within the tribes that inhabited the easternmost parts of western North America were residence groups that moved together and extracted together year around. They also jointly sponsored certain ceremonies. But basically the matridemes were egalitarian, nonhierarchical kinship groups, and the cermonies or rituals they performed were modest and few in comparison with those sponsored by Northwest Coast demes (Map Cu-139, V-317; Map Cu-140, V-320).

Matridemes did not own corporeal property, such as hunting territories to which they laid exclusive claim, or even movable property such as a headman's house. They often claimed incorporeal property in the form of the rituals they sponsored, but such incorporeal property was often identical, or at least highly similar, to the property of neighboring demes. The matridemes were fluid in membership; several demes coalesced as bands during the hunting seasons of spring, summer, and fall and exploited resource areas in a communitarian fashion. The demes based on gathering and hunting were as open to new members, flexible, and mobile as resources were diffuse, whereas movement of personnel among the patridemes dependent on localized aquatic animal resources primarily befell the lowest-ranked men. High-ranking men tended to bring their wives to their father's house, but a low-ranking man might move to the house of his wife's father. It is evident that where demes were localized around strategic resources they were politically and economically autonomous, competitive, and ownership of strategic resources was matched by ownership of incorporeal property that distinguished each deme and legitimized the history of each autonomous group. The two types of property—economic and ethereal—marked each deme's position in the competitive ranking system (Map Cu-141, V-322; Map Cu-142, V-324).

Before moving on to a discussion of groups that demonstrated unilineal descent, some comparisons between the demes of the Utes, Shoshones, and Eastern Apaches should be made with the bilateral organizations in the Plateau. The Lillooet, Carrier, Wishram, and Umatilla were located near abundant fisheries and all were organized into egalitarian and nonhierarchial demes which owned fish and root resource sites. Other Plateau groups did not have kinship organizations larger than patribilateral lineal families. The resource base alone does not account for the differences in kinship organizations in the Plateau. The abundant root and fish resource sites of the Nez Percé, Columbia, and other Plateau tribes could have supported deme organizations, but demes were not present in these groups. Throughout the Plateau, in both the deme societies and those that had no kinship groups larger than patribilateral lineal families, the largest kinship units often laid claim to strategic resources, but they also made those resource areas available to relatives, friends, and neighbors who asked to use them. There is some evidence, however, that the patrideme societies were more prone to internal feuding (i.e., feuds between two demes in the same community), than were the Plateau societies that were not organized into demes.

The bilateral societies of the Plateau, deme and nondeme, possessed much of the flexibility and mobility of the deme societies among the Northern Shoshones and Eastern Apaches, but the Plateau groups moved less often and families probably splintered off less often. The relative stability of Plateau communities may have been made possible by the resource base of anadromous fishes and roots, both being much more localized and predictable resources than were the large herd-animals that foraged in the mountains and the wild plants that were distributed throughout the mountains and deserts. It is plausible that Plateau kinship organizations represent a transition from the localized, corporate kinship groups predominant on the coast to the band or village organizations predominant in the interior. Some private property concepts, such as ownership of fishing stations, may have been retained among demes and patribilateral lineal families in the more diffuse resource areas of the Plateau. Yet these kinship units were egalitarian and nonhierarchical. Indeed, through a bevy of mechanisms such as gifting, joint use of resources, ceremonial participation, and hospitable feasting, Plateau tribes resembled the communitarian and mobile bands composed of matridemes. Yet the matridemes coalesced into bands only so long as they were successful at procuring food. The predictability of Plateau resources allowed for more dense populations than were possible in the regions inhabited by the Utes, Shoshones, and Eastern Apaches.

Lineages

The forms of unilineal descent demonstrated by groups were either matrilineages or patrilineages. Matrilineage members traced their descent through the female line, whereas members of patrilineages traced their descent through the male line. In western North America not one of the matrilineages formed a separate and distinct community unit by itself: they were always aggregated with other matrilineages. Yet some matridemes formed independent winter communities among Utes and Wind River Shoshones, some patridemes formed year-round independent villages on the Northwest Coast, and among the Miwoks and Costanoans of central California, patrilineages, prior to Contact, formed monolineage communities. It is interesting that matrilineages did not form monolineage communities either among the mobile Apacheans, the sedentary Western Pueblos, or the northern Northwest Coast tribes. In each society several lineages constituted a year-round community. Furthermore matrilineages were everywhere only segments of larger and more distantly related kinship groups called sibs. We shall return to the question of matrilineages and matrisibs.

Societies that were composed of patrilineages but not of stipulated descent groups such as patrisibs occurred among the Athapaskans of coastal Oregon, among many California Penutians from the Nomlaki Wintun in the northern part of California to the Yokuts in the San Joaquin Valley of the central part, also among the Hokan speaking Salinan of the Salinas Valley and the central California coast, and among some of the Mono, who were Uto-Aztecan speakers in the southern Sierra of the central part of California.

All of these patrilineal societies except the Miwok and Costanoan—California Penutians who occupied a continuous belt from the Marin County coast north of San Francisco to Monterey Bay in the south, thence east to the Sierra—were organized into multi-patrilineage communities. Among the patrilineal societies each lineage was localized in only one community* and practiced patrilocal residence. Furthermore, each lineage owned some incorporeal property, such as rituals and totems, but in the multilineage villages of California, lineages seldom owned important corporeal property, such as strategic resource areas. If patrilineages in California's multilineage villages owned resource areas, they were usually gathering sites.

The small patrilineages in the multilineage Athapaskan villages along the Oregon Coast owned all strategic resource sites. This practice was consonant with that of other localized kinship groups on the Northwest Coast regardless of the number of such units in a village. The monolineage communities of the Miwok also owned all strategic resources in the territories that they claimed.

It is plausible that when the California Penutians and Yukians penetrated California, they did so as mono-patrilineage units and followed the major rivers. The lineages may well have planted their roots at spots where they extracted fish, but like other California extractors, they also collected acorns and hunted the relatively abundant deer in their areas. It is plausible that as lineage populations grew under these conditions, they splintered and migrated to new localities. The monolineage villages of the Miwok and Costanoan may well represent the original form of the localized kinship groups in California, at least the Penutian form of such groups.

All other California Penutians were either organized into multilineage villages, or villages of many patribilateral lineal families that observed bilateral descent. In all such instances the kinship groups were joined into two or more communities, and these communities formed tribelets. It was the tribelet that owned and protected property and that defended its territory. Tribelets were the political, economic, and in some senses, the ceremonial counterparts of the monolineage communities.

Consolidation of several populations in one locality was not common in California. Even in the multilineage and the bilateral tribelets, lineages and families tended to be settled where they regularly exploited some food resources. The amalgamation of several lineages into single tribelets may have come about as Penutian and Hokan speakers began crowding the available space, causing the small lineages to seek greater safety in larger numbers. If the genesis of multilineage tribelets occurred in this fashion, upon merging, lineages would have been required to foresake most of their private property, or at least to share that property with other lineages in the tribelet. Such appears to have been the practice among Yokuts, Patwin, and Salinan. It is likely that even lineages disappeared among the Maidu, Nisenan, and Wintu. Kinship-terminology evidence suggests that these Penutian societies may well have changed from patrilineal to bilateral descent-reckoning, and it is my impression that this change came about through the development of tribelet organizations. The evidence that Wintu, Maidu, and Nisenan were once patrilineal comes from their kinship terminologies, which cover a range, from the patrilineal Omaha-type for the Wintu, employed also by most other California Penutians, through the unilineal Iroquois-type cousin terms used by the Maidu (Maiduan), to the bilateral Hawaiian-type cousin terms

---

*Lake Yokuts and Salinan were exceptions. Lineages often had segments in more than one community.

used by the Nisenan (also Maiduan). The Maiduans, and especially the Nisenan seem to have gone further toward full integration of cousin terms with bilateral descent organization than the Wintu (Wintun), but the many tribelets among the Wintu, Maidu, or Nisenan also employed terms for uncles and aunts that correlated positively with unilineal descent, and they also observed in-law avoidance customs.

The importance of kinship terminology types and in-law avoidance customs in inferring changes in kinship systems was postulated by Driver (1956, 1966). In his "cyclical lag" hypothesis he contended that kinship terms for first-ascending-generation relatives (parents, uncles, aunts), changed more slowly than terms for relatives of ego's generation (sibling and cousins), and that changes in in-law avoidance customs occurred following changes to use of first-ascending-generation kinship terms. The Wintu, Maidu, and Nisenan were bilateral; among these societies only the Nisenan employed sibling and cousin terms which seldom correlated with unilineal descent systems; and all employed first-ascending-generation terms and in-law avoidances that correlated with unilineal descent systems. It is highly plausible that all California Penutians were patrilineal before any of them became bilateral, and it is plausible that the earliest California Penutians were organized into monolineages before the Patwin (Wintun branch) and Yokuts (Yokuts branch), undoubtedly independently from one another, formed multilineage villages and tribelets. The most plausible explanation for the changes toward bilaterality is that these accompanied the diminution of kinship-group importance in owning corporeal property, forming common defenses, and performing rituals. Among the multilineage tribelets, the lineages retained control of some totems and rituals, and in scattered instances, some gathering sites. It is likely that the earliest Penutians to enter the northern part of the California culture area became competitive with Hokan speaking tribelets with whom they came to occupy closely spaced territories along the river courses of the northern part of California. At the time of European contact the greatest incidence of bilaterality occurred in this region. Settlements were somewhat more distantly spaced and the territories claimed by groups were larger in central California, where the greatest incidence of monolineage and multilineage tribelets occurred.

Among all of the patrilineage societies in the central and northern parts of California, relations among kinspeople were egalitarian, except for the Nomlaki and the Salinan, who ranked people on the basis of wealth and power. Relations among patrilineages were egalitarian in all of the multilineage villages. If amalgamation of lineages occurred, an apparent condition of the tribelet was the relinquishing of proprietary claims to resources by lineages, and with that went the basis for ranking lineages. Among the Miwok, on the other hand, lineages were ranked into a very minimal hierarchy on the basis of prestige. That is, some lineage communities were considered to be more prestigious than others, perhaps because of the abundance of their resources and the sumptuousness of the ceremonies they sponsored.

Whereas none of the patrilineages were organized into patrisibs, and all but the Lake Yokuts and Salinan lineages were localized, moiety organizations were spread throughout all of the patrilineal tribelets except the Nomlaki (Wintun branch speakers of California Penutian in the Sacramento Valley), lumping each lineage into one of two divisions. In the multilineage villages both moieties were represented, and in the monolineage communities each community belonged to one or the other division (Map Cu-143, V-311).

Many California tribelets, whether they reckoned descent patrilineally or bilaterally, were divided into two moieties, or divisions, each performing rituals or games for their opposites. Indeed, the sponsoring of games and rituals was the common denominator of moiety organization among all the California tribelets that possessed them. Among the Yokuts and the Miwok, moieties also regulated marriage so that people whose lineages belonged to the same moiety could not marry. Moieties played exceedingly important roles in providing a framework for relations between lineages and between communities, so much so that the moiety concept may well have diffused from the patrilineal Southern California Yumans and Uto-Aztecans, who likely created the concept independently of other moiety organizations in western North America, northward through the patrilineal Yokuts, Miwok, Mono, and Patwin, to several bilateral societies including the Wappo, Pomo, Kato, and Yuki,* and also the Washo (Map Cu-144, V-319).

Stipulated Descent Groups: Sibs

We shall return to the meaning of moieties and phratries later. Let us first analyze the many patrilineal societies in Southern California that were organized

---

*The Western Kuksu societies, discussed below (pp. 191–192, 232–236), comprise the various Pomo, Wappo, Kato, and Yuki tribelets. These bilateral descent societies possessed nonexogamous moieties.

into *stipulated* descent groups, because it appears that the moiety organizations throughout California were borrowed, in concept, from a Southern California version associated with the Southern California sib organizations.

In a group in which descent is stipulated, membership in the line is asserted and presumed rather than demonstrated. Stipulation of membership establishes a putative kinship bond between any two members. "Sibs" are groups in which unilineal descent is stipulated. When sibs are localized, they are usually composed of two or more lineages located in the same place. When they are nonlocalized, the lineages, or sib segments, that compose the sibs are located in separate communities (Map Cu-145, V-310).

Patrisibs

In Southern California, patrisibs comprising several patrilineages were localized around water sites, which they owned. They also owned and defended the wild plants within their territories. Each localized patrisib was directed by a hereditary leader who served as priest-chief. He was the steward of the patrisib's fetish, a sacred bundle of ritual paraphernalia which served to link the sib to its leader and to the sib's property for time immemorial. The priest-chief lived in, and the principal fetish was stored in, a ceremonial house that belonged to the sib (Map Cu-146, V-314).

The patrisibs of Southern California observed the interesting custom of granting membership in her husband's sib to a wife. Thus, Southern California patrisibs were compromise kin groups that incorporated in-marrying women while losing their outmarrying women. Murdock (1949) and Driver and Massey (1957) have referred to these compromise stipulated-descent groups as "clans," in order to distinguish them from sibs that do not incorporate spouses of members. That distinction is not followed here.

Within the patrisibs all members were regarded as equals. There was no ranking based on birth order, wealth, or other such criteria (Map Cu-147, V-316). Some patrisibs, however, were recognized as more prestigious than others, and the basis for such estimation appears to have been the water sites and gathering resources that the sibs controlled (Map Cu-148, V-321). Not only did the Southern California patrisibs own water sites, gathering sites, and a sacred fetish bundle, but the priest-chief was authorized to settle disputes with other sibs over territorial infractions and to direct key rituals of the sib (Map Cu-149, V-323; Cu-150, V-325; Cu-151, V-318).

Patrisibs in Southern California were competitive, and prior to Spanish contact, with but one exception, there is no evidence that several patrisibs formed multisib tribelets so as to form united fronts or to reduce competition by joining together. After Spanish contact, several Desert Cahuilla sibs formed a winter community, as did several Desert Diegueño sibs. But prior to contact only the Cupeño, a Uto-Aztecan group, organized into multisib communities. The significance of the multisib communities of the Cupeño was considerable for all of Southern California, and undoubtedly for much of the California culture area, because it appears that some Western Diegueño sibs joined the Cupeño multisib community, and this accommodation may have led to the creation of moieties in Southern California: it appears that the Cupeño not only organized into multisib tribelets, but that sibs of the Cupeño and the most northern Western Diegueño (the latter Yuman speakers) organized themselves into a joint tribelet in which the Diegueño sibs were classified as "wildcat" and the Cupeño sibs were classified as "coyote." Each moiety performed rituals for its opposite, and the moieties also regulated marriages so that a person always sought a mate from the opposite division. Thus the customs of marrying outside of one's moiety into the opposite moiety and of assuming the obligation to perform ceremonials and engage in games with the opposite moiety, which were practiced throughout all of Southern California, probably began with the Cupeño and Western Diegueño. Their concepts most probably spread to the adjacent tribelets and, subsequently, northward into the central areas of California. The evidence for this assertion is tantalizing even though an iron-clad argument cannot at present be advanced. For instance, at the time of contact all Southern California Yuman sibs, except those among the Kaliwa and Akwa'ala, were classified as "wildcat" or "coyote." It is possible that the wildcat and coyote distinctions spread among the many localized sibs through regular contacts, especially through marriage and subsequent ceremonial participation, so that some Yuman groups were coyotes and others were wildcat. The same was true for the Uto-Aztecan speakers. At the time of contact, the transactions between two or more localized patrisib communities were conducted in the nexus of ceremonial relations—whether they were marriages, attendance at major ceremonials, or counsels of leaders representing their independent sibs.

The wildcat was an important mythological creature among all Yuman speakers, in and beyond Southern California, whereas the coyote was an important mythological character among all Shoshonean Uto-Aztecan speakers, in and beyond Southern California. As Strong (1929) pointed out, each language group contributed a mythological character to the ceremonial relationship between moieties. It is further evident that marriage relations in one generation, through offspring of the unions, created kinship bonds in subsequent generations. These ceremonial and marital bonds were formed between sibs of opposite moieties speaking the same language (e.g., Gabrieliño), speaking different languages from the same language family (e.g., Gabrieliño and Luiseño), and speaking languages from different language families (e.g., Cahuilla and Diegueño). The patrisibs, whether of the same moiety or opposite moieties, and whether jointly sponsoring rituals or as guests at rituals, were always competitive. Moiety organizations, with their ameliorative structure, most surely have helped to obviate raiding and other hostile competition by providing a charter and a ground plan for relations between independent sibs.

It is most plausible that the moiety concept diffused from Southern California northward into the central part of California. Some of the same symbolism that was used to distinguish Southern California moieties was used to distinguish the Yokuts and Miwok moieties, and some of the same ceremonials that were fundamental to Southern California moieties were also important moiety ceremonials for these California groups (especially the Mourning-Anniversary ceremony and the Eagle ceremony). "Down" and "up" directional symbolism and "red" and "black" color symbolism were used in both areas, though rather than "coyote" and "wildcat," the Miwoks used "land" and "water" or "wet" and "dry" names for moieties, whereas some of the Yokuts used "up" and "down" and others used "coyote" and "wildcat." Yokuts "up" paired with Miwok "water" moieties for ceremonial purposes, whereas Yokuts "down" paired with Miwok "land" moieties.

Among the multilineage Yokuts, though both moieties were represented in most tribelets, opposites from *different* tribelets entertained and married one another. The integration of territorially distinct, economically and politically autonomous tribelets, whether single lineage (e.g., Miwok and Costanoan), single sib (e.g., Cahuilla), multiple lineage (e.g., Salinan, Yokuts, Patwin), or multiple sib (Cupeño) was the hallmark of moiety organization in the Southern California culture area and northward, in the California culture area too: where moieties diffused to bilateral tribelets among the Pomo, Wappo, Kato, and Coast Yuki, intertribelet games were engaged in between, and performances were conducted for, reciprocals. Among some of the most southern Yokuts and Mono who were bilateral rather than patrilineal, there were no moieties, but among these people tribelets reciprocated one another much in the same fashion that opposite moieties from opposite tribelets reciprocated among the patrilineal Yokuts and Mono. The diffusion of moiety customs to bilateral tribelets, even when moieties themselves were not adopted, seems incontrovertible.

Whereas it seems evident that moieties lent themselves to the maintenance of unilineal descent groups in Southern California and in central California inasmuch as they were used to regulate marriage and to sponsor all of the key ceremonials, they did not regulate marriage among the bilateral tribelets in the northern part of California. Moreover, they appear to have been more recent accretions to the bilateral cultures than to the patrilineal cultures in central California and Southern California.*

In contrast to the localized patrisib societies of Southern California were the nonlocalized patrisib societies among the River Yumans of the lower Colorado River area. The River Yumans differed from the Southern California Yumans in so many ways that River Yumans were classified about halfway between the Southwest and Southern California in the two-dimensional analysis of Figure 4-1. It is plausible, nevertheless, that as early as 1,800 years ago the proto-Yumans were organized into patrisib communities, perhaps residing in the deserts and mountains of the southeastern part of California, and along the mesquite-rich banks of the Colorado River. This period most likely antedated the developments of moieties by Southern California Yumans and the adoption of farming by River Yumans.

Yumans in Southern California and the Southwest resided near mesquite and screwbean groves, and water sites. At a very early point in their prehistory the proto-Yumans probably focusing their gathering activities on mesquite and settled at productive water sites, from which they ventured to gather other plants in the surrounding region. At the time of contact with Europeans the areas that were most rich with oases, mesquite, screwbeans, mescal, cactus, and pineseeds were owned and occupied by localized patrisibs. It is plausible that the patrisibs grew from localized patrilineages. As the lineage population grew in the new location and eventually formed a sib, it was probably only a matter of time before lineages segmented from the sib and relocated at a water site and gathering area of its own which it claimed as private property.

It is plausible that the River Yumans (specifically, the Maricopa, Cocopa, Halchidoma, Kaveltcadom, Yuma, and Mohave) spread along the Colorado River

---

*See the comparative discussion of moieties in "Moiety Organizations," later in this chapter.

from the Gulf of California to the Grand Canyon. The river banks were covered with dense stands of honey mesquite, and the year-round availability of flowing water made it possible for groups to expand rapidly while not being restricted to oasis water sites, such as spring and seeps. Fish provided proteins and minerals that were otherwise difficult to obtain in the Colorado River desert. Farming, which appears to have been introduced perhaps by 300 AD but at least by 600 AD, came to provide from one-third to one-half of River Yuman diets.

It is likely that the presence of mesquite and abundant water allowed River Yumans to grow, fission, and expand up and down the river and into the Imperial Valley west of the Colorado River. The advent of farming, the presence of rich alluvial flood plains, one or two floods a year (depositing fresh alluvium), and a capillary water supply from the river probably accounts for the differences between the localized patrisibs of Southern California and the nonlocalized patrisibs of the River Yumans. Among the River Yumans it was possible for a man, his wife or wives, his unmarried children, and perhaps a married son and his family to branch off from a patrilineage and to move to an unoccupied farming site which they marked off and defended against trespass, even from members of their own lineage and sib. Thus, as patrisibs grew, small segments split off and sought new farm land. When the river changed course in certain areas and inundated farm lands, that too precipitated movements. As a consequence, some segments of a lineage stayed in one place, while their kinspeople—lineage and sibmates—moved on; yet each new localized group did not become an independent patrisib. The splintering groups were too small for that and they retained the identity of their patrisib. Thus patrisibs became nonlocalized, each one forming patchwork distributions within the various River Yuman tribes.

The counterpart of the independent patrisib tribelets among the Southern California Yumans and Uto-Aztecans became the tribes, or "nationalities" (as Kroeber often referred to them), of the River Yumans. The Mohave recognized internal affinities among all nonlocalized patrisibs as did the Yuma. These "national" sentiments could be drawn upon in times of warfare to muster pan-Yuma or pan-Mohave forces. And frequently Yuma and Mohave would join forces to battle an enemy, such as the Maricopa and Cocopa, as well.

The River Yumans engaged in little ceremonialism, were consummate traders, and were the masters of raiding for prestige and military honors. The Southern California patrisib tribelets, on the other hand, developed elaborate ceremonialism which they channeled through a moiety organization network that aligned them as "sames" and "opposites." Moreover, they were neither aggressive traders nor offensive raiders, yet the trading and exchanging that was accomplished was conducted in the nexus of moiety relations. Even in the presence of moiety organization, Southern California patrisibs guarded their territories and water sites jealously, and some feuds and raiding between sibs surely occurred. But competitive patrisibs, when organized into moieties, took on a set of ritual obligations that mitigated competition over resources, while recognizing the inviolability of those resources. The different outcomes in social organization in Southern California and along the Colorado River were no doubt influenced by the advent of farming on the river, and the difference in water resources in the two regions. The invention of moiety relations was a nonpredictable event that need not have occurred, but which, having occurred, served to align competitive tribelets in an ameliorative fashion. The contrast between River Yuman warfare and meager ceremonialism, on the one hand, and the complex ceremonial yet modest feuding and raiding activities in Southern California, on the other, was marked. That the groups in both regions came from a common source is incontrovertible, as were the relationships they maintained through River Yuman trading ventures. River Yumans could have developed moiety relations through their dealings with Southern California patrisibs, or, of course, they could have developed them independently of the Southern California societies but they did not. There is no evidence that the River Yumans were ever organized into moieties.

Various synonymous forms of the mourning-anniversary ceremony, the widespread practice of burning images in memory of the deceased, were performed in Southern California, where the ceremony was the ultimate moiety affair highlighting the performance of a host of rituals, including feasting, first-fruit ceremonies, the honoring of the sib, its deceased members, its newly born, its pubescent women, and the sib's land. Among the River Yumans, though the entire tribe was invited to ceremonies, just as moiety "sames" and "opposites" were invited to patrisib ceremonials in Southern California, these affairs were much attenuated and focused on honoring deceased individuals and their war exploits. It is plausible that among the River Yumans, whose patrisibs became nonlocalized and where warfare became a favorite pasttime, the annual mourning ceremony was changed from an early version in which patrisibs, their deceased members, and their territories were honored to one that focused on individuals and their exploits. The lessened importance of patrisibs with the advent of farming, increased importance of individual exploits in warfare, and the strength of tribal sentiments (embracing all Yuma, or all Mohave, for example) could account for a change in focus. In Southern California, where patrisibs became even more firmly rooted with the invention of moieties, annual mourning ceremonies not only celebrated patrisibs, but also the relations of sibs to resources, the living, the dead, the future (girls' puberty and naming ceremonies), and to their moiety opposites.

Matrisibs

Matrilineages, regardless of the tribes in which they occurred in western North America, were always organized into matrisibs. Furthermore, except for the Acoma Pueblo, all matrisibs were further organized into moieties or phratries. Unlike some patrilineal societies, there were no monomatrisib communities. So the contrast with groups that observed patrilineal descent, in which there were both monolineages and monosib communities, with or without moieties (there were no phraties), is interesting. No simple explanations can be given for this phenomenon. There were matrilineal farming societies, such as the Western Pueblos, Eastern Keres, and Navajos, and patrilineal farming societies, such as the River Yumans. There were patrilineal societies dependent upon aquatic animals, such as the Oregon Athapaskans, and matrilineal societies dependent upon aquatic animals, such as the northern Northwest Coast tribes. There was a host of patrilineal societies with mixed extractive economies in California and Southern California, but only the Western Apaches, who farmed, gathered, and hunted, approximated that description among matrilineal societies, and Western Apache matrilineality was closely linked to farming and farming-site ownership rather than to the extractive aspects of the Western Apache economy.

Two things that practically all patrilineal and matrilineal societies shared were rather permanent settlements where the lineages and sibs were located for much of the year, and predictable and abundant resources, either extractive or productive. There was no necessary relationship between lineality and the sex that provided most labor toward sustenance. Among the Pueblo (matrilineal) and Piman (bilateral) farmers men did most of the farming, yet among the Apachean (matrilineal) and River Yuman (patrilineal) farmers, women did at least half of the work. As we have seen, the groups most dependent on farming gained most of their farm labor from men. The West-

ern Apaches and River Yumans relied less on farm products than either Pueblos or Pimas. Although Western Apache and Yuman men farmed less, they raided, traded, and for the Yumans, fished more than women. Western Apache and Yuman women did the bulk of the gathering in those societies.

Among all of the aquatic animal-dependent societies, matrilineal and patrilineal, men were dominant in procuring the aquatic animal fare. So division of labor is not a useful key in determining lineality among sedentary aquatic animal extractors.

Our assessment has made it clear that sedentary, localized people who controlled abundant resources, whether extractive or productive, were aligned on patrilineal, bilateral, or matrilineal criteria. If anything, matrilineality was dominant among farming societies; patrilineality was dominant among mixed extractive economics which emphasized wild plant gathering; and bilaterality occurred in all types of subsistence economies. Although matrilineality in western North America was restricted to farming and aquatic animal-extracting societies, both of which subsistence pursuits were male dominated, ownership, inheritance, and succession criteria among the matrilineal societies of the Southwest had little in common with those of the northern Northwest Coast.

Along the northern Northwest Coast, since avunculocal residence was customary after marriage, a groom would leave his father's house and matrilineage and take his bride to reside in his mother's brother's house and lineage (the groom's matrilineage). Ownership of the lineage's houses, strategic resource sites, crests, heirlooms, names, dances, and other incorporeal property was retained by the men of the lineage. Similar to the patrisib organization of Southern California, northern Northwest Coast lineages were organized into matrisibs, yet unlike the patrisibs of Southern California, Northwest Coast sibs did not own strategic resource sites (they were owned by lineages, instead) and a woman did not become a member of her husband's sib at marriage. She retained rights and obligations in her own sib, and as we have pointed out, her sons took up residence in her brother's house (the sib house) at marriage. The northern Northwest Coast matrisibs were named, they shared common mythological histories, and the members of each sib shared a corporate liability for the actions of their sib mates in their own community.

Although northern Northwest Coast matrisibs did not own houses or extractive resource sites, nor were they led by chiefs, they owned incorporeal property, such as myths and crests, and the lineages within each sib were ranked so that a sib chief was vested with control of the sib incorporeal property. Yet sibs were too large to be effective economic units, so they were essentially marriage-regulating units: members of the same sib could not marry. Most sibs were composed of lineage segments distributed in several communities (nonlocalized sibs) so that a person who traveled some distance from his home community could establish formal relations in the communities to which he traveled merely by finding his sibmates. Even if sibmates had never laid eyes on one another and could not trace their relationship through a strict genealogy, they stipulated a relationship and the stranger, while residing in the community, became a kinsman who was not only liable for his own actions, but also was liable for the actions of his sibmates.

Beyond the matrisibs, northern Northwest Coast societies were further organized into moieties (Haidas and Tlingits) and phratries (Tsimshians and Haisla Kwakiutl). As in Southern California, the moieties were named, exogamous groups. Yet unlike the Southern California moieties, which performed a wide variety of rituals for their opposites and were essential to intersib affairs, Haida and Tlingit moieties performed no similar ritual tasks. Beyond marriage regulation within each moiety, moiety mates recognized affinity by sharing a common crest and totem ("raven" and "wolf" for Tlingits, "raven" and "eagle" for the Haidas). Among the several Tsimshian and Haisla Kwakiutl groups, sibs were organized into phratries rather than moieties. The phratries of these people used all the moiety names of the Haidas and Tlingits ("raven," "eagle," and "wolf") plus a fourth (either "fireweed" or "killer whale," depending on the society in question). For marriages between phratry and moiety societies, the Tsimshian or Haisla Kwakiutl phratries were lumped ("raven" and "fireweed" or "killer whale"; "eagle" and "wolf") and paired with the corresponding moieties of the Haida and Tlingit; members of opposite moieties, paired and lumped in this way, were marriageable. Thus a "wolf" could not marry an "eagle," but could marry a "raven."

The mythological histories of the moieties and phratries were important incorporeal property of each unit, but the sibs that composed each moiety seemed to share those histories in rather arbitrary ways. The relationships among the sibs in each moiety or phratry were complex and surely not the product of common genealogical heritage. It is possible that the Haidas and Tlingits consciously created moieties to effect marriages between groups, and that the named moiety concept spread to the Tsimshians and Haisla Kwakiutl, who subsumed groups of sibs under each of the three moiety names while adding a mythological favorite of their own for the fourth phratry (either "fireweed" or "killer whale"). The evidence that the moiety concept diffused through intermarriage is strong. Intermarriages among the four language groups were numerous, and all but the Haisla Kwakiutl also observed avoidance relations between mother-in-law and son-in-law (and between other relatives-in-law for the Haidas and Tlingits). In-law avoidance customs proscribed parents-in-law and children-in-law from talking directly, eating together, and looking eye to eye. Intertribal marriages were not only contracted between moiety or phratry opposites, but the parents-in-law and children-in-law observed special behavioral relations. In-law avoidances were not observed among the bilateral and patrilineal people on the Northwest Coast. In western North America these customs were restricted to the northern Northwest Coast matrilineal societies, the patrilineal California Penutians and some of their neighbors, and the Apacheans. In these three clusters, in-law avoidance customs were surely distinct developments, and among the northern Northwest Coast people who observed the custom, the Tlingits or Haidas were most probably the donors of the custom to the Tsimshians. This inference is based on the more mature development of the matrilineal kinship systems of the Haidas and Tlingits (see "Relations among Terminological Classifications," later in this chapter).

The importance of moiety–phratry organizations throughout the northern Northwest Coast was manifold. The seafaring people could find marriage partners in distant communities in a socially sanctioned way. Lineage leaders were constantly seeking men and women of high rank to become brides or grooms of members of their lineages and to create visiting, gifting, and potlatching relationships between the lineages. The moiety–phratry organizations helped make this possible. These were ways to establish formal affinal relations and to increase the contacts of each lineage segment. Furthermore, the extension of phratry and moiety membership to interior tribes with whom northern Northwest Coast people traded for furs made trade partnerships profitable and predictable.

Although trading, gifting, and potlatching relations were established, the autonomy of each lineage was maintained, and the lineages joined through marriage were always competitive in the areal ranking system. The basic competition was contradicted by a father's concern for his son's welfare, however; after marriage a father encouraged his son to use the father's matrilineage's resources in any way the son saw fit, except for potlatching. If the married son, who lived avunculocally in his own lineage house, used the father's kinship-group's resources for gifts when he sponsored a potlatch, the son would be promoting his own matrilineage (and that of his mother's) at the expense of his father's, yet doing so with resources from his father's lineage. Such an act was not permissible. If a wife wished to help her own lineage prepare for a potlatch, she would return to her lineage's resource areas to do so. If she borrowed berries, fish, or nuts from the resources of her husband's matrilineage, she had to gain permission to do so and also had to pay back the loan sometime in the future.

Thus, whereas moiety–phratry organization formed relations among moiety members throughout a large area of the Northwest Coast through crests, myths, and a vague sense of kinship, and though they formalized relations between moieties through marriage, moiety "sames" and "opposites" were always competitive, and their basic competitiveness was evident in distributions, feasts, potlatches, dancing-society performances, and raiding.

The basic competition among northern Northwest Coast matrilineages, each of which owned fishing, gathering, and hunting sites, houses and house sites, sacred myths, crests, and other incorporeal property, was about identical to the competition among Kwakiutl, Nootka, Salish, and Quileute demes. Individuals in each lineage were ranked, the highest-ranking being the firstborn son and the firstborn daughter of each lineage chief. The lineage chief, who was the steward of all lineage property, was frequently the oldest man in the lineage. Succession to the chief's position was by the oldest son of his oldest sister. Although each lineage member was ranked, and though each lineage was ranked within its sib as well as ranked within the wider geographic area, relations within lineages and sibs were egalitarian. In short, members of lower rank within lineages contributed to the potlatches* hosted by their lineages and directed by their chiefs, but relations among lineage mates were equal, except that chiefs and rich men often gave more to their kinspeople than they received in return.

The Western Pueblos (Hopi, Zuni, Acoma, Laguna), Eastern Keres (Sia, Santa Ana, Santo Domingo, Cochiti), and Jemez Towa possessed localized matrilineages and nonlocalized matrisibs. All practiced sib exogamy and matrilocal residence after marriage, so that matrilineages were composed of cores of women related through the matriline, their spouses, and their unmarried children. In the Western Pueblo villages, each matrisib owned a house which was occupied by a lineage segment of the sib. The head of that household was the sib mother, whereas her oldest brother, who resided in his wife's home, was the sib father. The lineages in each Western Pueblo sib were ranked into minimal hierarchies on the basis of prestige. The Hopi lineages went still further and ranked lineage segments within each sib on the basis of their genealogical proximity to the sib mother. Genealogical proximity was measured lineally and collaterally. For instance, the oldest daughter of the sib mother was her closest lineal female relative and most likely would succeed her in the sib house. Her next oldest daughter's family would be second in line, and so forth. Thus, the lines of sisters became collateral, and the closer the female collateral relative, the more likely that her segment might occupy the sib house at some time.

The internal ranking of sibs in a minimal fashion based on birth order among the Western Pueblos was not matched among the Eastern Keres, but there was a minimal hierarchical ranking among Eastern Keres sibs based on prestige. The prestige had nothing to do with land, house, or incorporeal property ownership, because the Eastern Keres sibs did not own property. Rather, ceremonial and political leaders were selected from certain sibs, and the sibs regulated marriage and generated camaraderie among members. Among the Eastern Keres Pueblos, villagewide political-ceremonial organizations owned land and guided the destiny of the villages, while families had usufruct rights to the land.

Among the Eastern Keres at the time of European contact, or shortly thereafter, matrilineal relatives did not loom as large in lineage, sib, or community affairs as they did in the Western Pueblo villages. It is unclear why the Eastern Keres, who possessed matrilineages, matrisibs, and who designated certain sibs as more important than other sibs in contributing ceremonial leaders, did not also invest corporeal and incorporeal property ownership in sibs. It is reasonable to assume that at one time, perhaps only a couple of centuries or so before European contact, Keres matrisibs owned property and rituals, and had only nominal village organizations, much as the Western Pueblos. It may well be that the Eastern Keres organized into centrally controlled villages with village ownership of land as a response to contacts with Tewa Pueblos in the past seven hundred years, but the influence of Spanish Catholics, with their emphasis on the nuclear family, their requirements of Indian labor to work the farms of priests, soldiers, and some *encomenderos*, and their opposition to native

---

*See the discussion of Northwest Coast hierarchical distributions in Chapter 7.

religion—much of it administered through sibs in the Western Pueblos—may have led to the diminution of sibs as property-owning and ritual-directing units among the Eastern Keres: control of native rituals passed into the hands of medicine societies (sodalities) rather than kinship groups sometime after contact with the Spanish.

Dozier (1970) attributes the dissipation of sib control over land and ceremonials among Eastern Keres to the emergence of incipient irrigation agriculture among them and to their contacts with the bilateral Eastern Pueblos. According to Dozier, centralized control was required for successful irrigation. Medicine societies usurped sib functions, and matricentered emphases in kinship, economic, and ceremonial behavior gave way to nonkinship controls under the stimulus of irrigation techniques learned from the Tanoans.

As we have seen in the Piman case, kinship groups can maintain large irrigation works without centralized authority, and kinsmen can even contribute food to their nominal leader simply in appreciation for his leadership and because it was good form to do so. Centralized control beyond the kinship group was not necessary in the Piman case and probably was not necessary in the Eastern Keres case either.

It may well be that both the Eastern Pueblos and the Eastern Keres were pushed toward village control and bilaterality by Catholic priests who required Indian land and Indian labor to work that land for their own sustenance, and the Spanish Catholic insistence on monogamous marriages and Christian practices among the Pueblos. The questions about when canal irrigation was introduced to the Eastern Pueblo and Eastern Keres villages, when village leaders began calling on all the able-bodied men to perform communal duties and to work the farms of village leaders, and when kinship groups lost their property ownership rights and the control of ceremonials may be of a piece, and the answers to these questions may be found in either pre-Contact or post-Contact relationships. Some solid archeological investigations of when the Eastern Pueblo and Eastern Keres villages were first settled and when canal irrigation was first practiced would be helpful in solving the problem of the growth of village organization at the expense of kinship organization.

The Jemez Towa, a matrilineal Tanoan group on the Jemez River, probably changed from bilateral organization to matrilineal descent through intermarriage with Keres people. All other Tanoans were bilateral, and even Jemez matrilineal organization seems to have been superimposed over a basic bilateral organization (Ellis 1964). The Jemez and Eastern Keres examples suggest not only that matrisibs can persist in village organization, they can even be adopted

after village organizations have been created (Jemez), or they can be adopted through migration and resettlement (Hopi Tewa). For the Eastern Keres and the Jemez, the lineages and sibs did not hold ownership to key resource or incorporeal property, but they were viable kinship-regulating units from whose midst certain sodality officials had to be selected.

The Western Pueblos did not develop village organizations, though among the Zuni, councils of priests, and among the Western Keres, councils of sodality leaders directed ceremonial activities in conjunction with sib leaders. Among the Hopi, only the council of sib leaders directed the ceremonial affairs of the village. The lineages and sibs among the Western Pueblos were politically and economically autonomous, retaining ownership of land, yet the sibs were also ranked hierarchically in relation to the ceremonies that they controlled. The relations among sibs through their controls over discrete but mutually important ceremonies that articulated them to the land, to water, to the gods, and to one another was accomplished through kiva societies that were associated with the sibs.

Kiva societies were ceremonial organizations attached to each sib and were composed of the men of the sib plus others who had been initiated from the community. The leaders of these societies were the brothers of the "mothers" of each sib. The highest-ranking sibs controlled the most important rituals in Western Pueblo mythology. There was no village organization to assume control over all rituals or over the land.

Except among the Tsimshians, western North American matrilineal sibs that owned key resource areas were autonomous, yet they always convened in multisib communities that bound the sibs together through some ritual or marriage-regulating organization. The avunculocal Tsimshian sibs were actually cores of males related through the maternal line, but they were also organized into villages and chiefdoms. Everywhere else the matrisibs were cores of female kinspeople who were organized only nominally through moiety intermarriages, or through a ceremonial calendar and mythology. Corporate matrilocal matrisibs seemed to need other matrisibs in their midst in order to persist as land-owning units. The same was not true of patrilineages or patrisibs. Furthermore, matrisibs that were organized into villages did not control key resource areas, whereas patrilineages among some Yokuts and Patwin multilineage tribelets were able to retain a few key extractive resource sites. It seems that though village organizations tended to select against corporate unilineal descent groups in western North America, patrilineal and avunculocal–matrilineal groups retained more control over private resources in village or tribal organization than did groups that observed matrilocal residence and matrilineal descent.

Among the Pueblos there was a further close association between land, myth, and ritual. For the matrilineal Pueblos it was an all or none proposition: if they owned land they controlled rituals and if they did not own land they did not control rituals. If village organizations usurped either ritual control or land, they usurped both. It is plausible that the Eastern Keres sibs relinquished rituals and productive land when they created village organizations. There is no simple explanation for the inability of matrisibs to retain land or ritual when they were not autonomous.

The Hopi and Zuni sibs were organized into unnamed exogamous phratries. If a local sib became very small, or had no female members, a woman from another sib in the same phratry might become the sib mother of that sib. As among Northwest Coast phratries, there was only a vague notion of kinship among the sibs in each phratry, but unlike Northwest Coast phratries or moieties, there were no myths or crests to tie phratry mates together.

The Western Pueblos, then, emphasized kinship relations and kinship control over land and ritual. Their phratry organizations were part of the kinship nexus of the societies. As vaguely related sets of matrisibs they married outside their own boundaries, and rituals, or perhaps even a female member, could be transferred from one sib to another within the phratry if there were an extraordinary reason for this. The Eastern Pueblos were organized on village principles with dual sodalities alternating each half year in guiding the village. These dual sodalities, or nonkinship moieties, did not regulate marriage and were not critical in maintaining relations among kinship groups. Thus, Eastern Pueblo moieties were extremely crucial in the management of Eastern Pueblo ritual, political, and subsistence affairs. It can be said that Eastern Pueblo moieties transcended kinship organization.

MOIETY ORGANIZATIONS: SOME FURTHER COMPARISONS

Moieties in Unilineal Descent Societies

As we have seen, moiety organization in western North America varied significantly in the manner in which membership was attained, and in the activities in which moiety mates and opposites engaged. But with only a few exceptions, all of the societies observing unilineal descent that were organized into moieties used those moieties to regulate marriage. On the other hand, no society observing bilateral descent used moieties to regulate marriage, though a few bilateral descent societies in the northern and central parts of California and in the Southwest had moiety organizations. The importance of moieties and phratries in organizing marital alignments among kinship groups in and between many matrilineal and patrilineal tribes in western North America is inescapable. For instance, in the northern Northwest Coast members of the same Haida and Tlingit moieties shared a vague sense of kinship, common ownership of myths and symbols, and did not intermarry. Rituals were not sponsored by moieties for their opposites.

In the northern and central areas of California and in Southern California most of the patrilineal Miwok, Yokuts, Salinan, Uto-Aztecan, and Diegueño groups possessed moieties that regulated marriages, shared common myths and symbols, entertained and bartered with their moiety opposites, and performed rituals for their moiety opposites. As in the northern area of the Northwest Coast, it appears that moieties were superimposed over unilineal descent groups. Moreover, it is plausible that moiety organizations, in their marriage-regulating roles, facilitated external relationships among sovereign kinship groups, i.e., groups that not only laid claim to strategic resources, but also recognized no jurisdictional authority higher than themselves. Moieties might also have been instrumental in allowing unilineal kinship groups to maintain their lineal integrity by establishing formal expectations between groups, and, perhaps, restricting competition among kinship groups.

For Southern California societies and the moiety societies of the central California area, elaborate moiety rituals were at the center of intertribelet affairs, and at the center of these rituals was the mourning-anniversary ceremony. The mourning ceremony appears to have been developed in Southern California and may well have diffused northward along with the moiety concept. Earlier it was pointed out that there were many similarities among the symbolisms found in Southern California moieties and those of moieties elsewhere in California; this was true for the rituals as well.

In the northern Northwest Coast region, moieties (and phratries among the Tsimshians and Haisla Kwakiutl) did not perform rituals. Potlatches were sponsored by independent kinship groups (Tsimshians also had village potlatches), and spirit-dancing and spirit-singing sessions were cosponsored by leading people from the ranking kinship groups in a village. There is little doubt that moieties among the matrilineal people of the Northwest Coast had a separate origin from the moieties among the patrilineal people of the California culture area and the Southern California culture area.

Moieties in Societies Reckoning Descent Bilaterally

The several Pomo, Wappo, Yuki, and Kato tribelets of the region north of San Francisco Bay observed bilateral descent. Their hamlets and tribelets were confederations of many bilateral families. Nevertheless, for some ceremonial occasions these bilateral people were organized into nonexogamous moieties. Apparently a wife joined her husband's moiety, while adult sons joined their father's moiety. Moieties competed in games, organized for ritual sweating, and hosted their local opposites to feasts. When attending a ceremony in an adjacent community or adjacent tribelet, visitors sought their moiety mates, with whom they sat during the ceremony. The societies with nonexogamous moieties also shared many similarities in their sodality organizations, so many in fact that the same societies have been classified as composing the "Western Kuksu" area (see "Sacred Public Performances: Integration and Separation" in the following chapter). Not only did nonexogamous moiety membership extend across tribelets, but "the pole ceremony," in which men attempted to scale a greased pole, was sponsored by these nonexogamous moieties. The pole ceremony, and probably the moiety concept, seems to have been borrowed from the patrilineal Patwin, Miwok, or Costanoan societies to the south, and reworked so as to accommodate bilateral descent customs and intertribelet visiting. The ultimate source of the pole ceremony, at least on the West Coast, seems to have been the Gabrieliño, who performed it in conjunction with a more extensive first-fruits celebration which itself was only one part of a larger set of ceremonies related to tribal initiations. These initiations also included the creation of sand paintings. A pole ceremony was also known and practiced among the Pueblos in the Southwest, as were sand paintings. The Southwestern, Southern California, and California versions of the Pole Ceremony may have had a common origin.

The bilateral groups among the Pomo, Wappo, Kato, and Yuki possessed moieties that feasted and entertained within their own villages but they also joined with their equivalents from other villages to entertain their opposites, both those from their home communities and from other communities and tribelets. This aspect of reciprocal moiety behavior, regardless of kinship connections among moiety mates, allowed for formalized arrangements wherein people from the same moiety in the same tribelet could participate as cohosts and, in so doing, banter with, entertain, and provide feasts for their opposites. Their opposites reciprocated. The ability to mix people from several villages and tribelets as hosts and recipients among these competitive and defensive tribelets was not a dominating feature of intercommunity life, but moiety organization lent itself to intertribelet affairs. In ritual affairs and even in intercommunity affairs, moieties among Wappo, Pomo, Yuki, and Kato tribelets were overshadowed by sodality organizations referred to as Kuksu cults and ghost societies (discussed in the following chapter). Moieties among the bilateral California people were probably recent, and they were not nearly so important as they were among the patrilineal people.

In the Southwest, both the bilaterally descended Pima and Papago possessed nonexogamous moiety organizations. Villages were divided into "coyotes" and "vultures" among the Papago, and into "red ants" and "white ants" among the Pima. The two halves bantered, and though they were not active in all Piman ceremonies, in some ceremonies half of the dancers were from one division and half from the other, and they complemented each other in jests, games, and dance performances. There is no evidence that moieties ever regulated marriage among these bilaterally descended people, or even that they performed rituals for their opposites. It is possible that ritual obligations of the two halves were more numerous, were complementary, and were more important in village affairs before European contact, during the Hohokam period, when large villages were spaced along the Salt River, Gila River, and adjacent drainages, than they were at the time of contact, though there is no evidence to support such an inference. It is clear that moiety activities were not central in Pima and Papago affairs after their contact with the Spanish and after a century of protracted struggles with Apacheans to maintain themselves in their riverside locations.

Pima and Papago moiety organization bore scant resemblance to the moieties of Southern California and most probably developed independently. The Eastern Keres and the Eastern Pueblos, who reckoned descent bilaterally, the moieties were ceremonial and political sodalities. Among most Eastern Keres, who reckoned descent matrilineally, moieties were ceremonial rather than kinship groupings. Only at the Eastern Keres Pueblo of Santa Ana were the nine matrisibs organized into moieties, six in one and three in the other. For most Eastern Keres Pueblos, moiety membership was determined by whether people lived on the north side or south side of a village.

The dual organizations of the Eastern Pueblos were more complex than simple directional divisions, though they, too, were organized into north and south sections. The Eastern Keres probably adopted moieties from the Tanoans. The Tewa, for instance, were organized into Summer people and Winter people. Each half possessed its own set of leaders and was charged with directing the village and its ceremonial life for half of the year. These two moiety divisions alternated the running of village affairs.

Thus, though Eastern Pueblo moieties were not kinship organizations, they exercised far more power than the moiety organizations among all other bilaterally or unilineally descended societies that possessed moieties in western North America. Eastern Pueblo (Tanoan) moieties could allocate resources, coordinate community activities, coerce labor, and the like.

It is conceivable that the many densely populated, competitive, resource-owning, largely sedentary, bilateral tribelets north of San Francisco Bay*, who recognized neither the leadership of strong kinship groups nor powerful political hierarchies but who did form moieties for entertainment and for some ceremonial performances, could have possessed organizations with centralized political and ceremonial authority, much as had the Tanoans. Yet the California groups did not possess such organizations. A favorite explanation for the centralization of authority in political–religious leaders in the Eastern Pueblos had been the need for those Pueblos to manage water for agriculture. This argument is not sufficient because the Pima had more extensive water works than the Eastern Pueblos, and they created and maintained them without centralized authority.

The creation of moieties among the Pima, Papago, and Tanoan Eastern Pueblos, all bilateral people, is a puzzle. The moiety organizations did not regulate marriage, align competitive kinship groups, or conduct key mourning ceremonies for their opposites. Furthermore, Piman moieties were totally inconsequential when compared to Tanoan moieties. Whether moieties for both stemmed from a common source is not clear, but it is possible. The bilateral groups in the California culture area who possessed moieties most surely borrowed the concept from their patrilineal neighbors in that same area, and used them so as to maintain some formal relations among people in distant communities. Both joining the moiety of one's father and maintenance of formal relations among distinct political communities were moiety practices among patrilineal people in central California and throughout Southern California.

The incidence of moiety or dual organization in bilateral-descent societies in western North America was exceedingly rare. Whereas the moiety principle undoubtedly diffused to some bilateral groups in the northern part of California, many bilateral groups in that area did not adopt the principle. Yet in the Southwest, the moiety principle seems to have diffused from the bilateral Tanoans to the matrilineal Eastern Keres, who at about the same time were probably forsaking the principles of corporate matrisibs in their social, economic, and political organization. Moiety organizations could be made compatible with bilaterality, as the Tanoans demonstrated, and as on a less crucial scale, the Pimans and several societies north of San Francisco Bay demonstrated, but by and large, moieties seem to have served as marriage-regulating devices that aligned competitive unilineal kinship groups. The origin of Tanoan moieties remains an enigma. The Piman moieties may have had roots in a unilineal-descent society. The Wappo, Pomo, Yuki, and Kato moiety concept must surely have been borrowed.

KINSHIP TERMINOLOGIES

Kinship terminology systems were the sets of terms used by individuals in each tribe to distinguish among types of relatives, such as among father, father's brother, and mother's brother, and among all the relatives by blood (consanguineal) or marriage (affinal relatives or in-laws). In this book we have classified the terminologies used in each tribe into sets of terminology types (see V-326 to V-331) so that similarities and differences among systems can be assessed.

Murdock's (1949) monumental analysis of 250 societies from around the world and Driver's (1956, 1966) brilliant analysis of 280 North American Indian societies have demonstrated many regular relations among kinship-terminological types used to classify cousins and relatives of the first ascending generation (parents and their siblings), and between these kinship terms and other aspects of social and economic organization, such as division of labor, postnuptial residence, land tenure, descent, and kinship avoidance customs. Earlier these studies were referred to as "main sequence," or "kinship lag," or "kinship cycle" or "cyclical lag" hypotheses of kinship development. Aberle (1961) and Jorgensen

*Pomo, Wappo, Yuki, and Kato.

(1966) have confirmed many relations in the "main sequence" hypothesis, but no one using large samples of societies from around the world or throughout North America has dealt systematically with kinship-terminological types other than for cousin and first-ascending-generation relatives.

In the following pages we go beyond previous studies and assess the terminological types for siblings (brothers and sisters), second-ascending-generation relatives (grandparents), and second-descending-generation relatives (grandchildren), as well as for cousins and first-ascending-generation relatives. As the kinship terminology maps reveal, types of kinship terms were not distributed at random across western North America. Furthermore, the statistics* that have been employed here to measure the relations between and among the terminologies show that five loose but discernible systems link types for cousins and first-ascending-generation relations but that sibling, grandchildren, and grandparent terminologies in these systems were highly variable. The five "systems" are loose because the statistical measures also demonstrate considerable variation within each of the five systems; that is, the systems were only partially ordered.

The intricacies of the variation and the interpretation of the variation will be treated in a subsequent volume devoted to particular questions about kinship and extrakinship organization. At this juncture it is important to point out that kinship terminologies correlated highly with language-family membership so that tribes that spoke related languages very often employed kinship-terminological systems that were similar. The evidence that the kinship terminologies employed by tribes speaking sister languages were sometimes different is not surprising, for groups fissioned, migrated, and made new adaptations to environments and neighbors. Often new subsistence adaptations occasioned changes in economic, marriage, descent, or political organization, or in some combination of those phenomena. Very often it seems that change in descent organization was attended by change in kinship terminologies. Indeed, though we have only synchronic data with which to work, the principal tenets of the lag hypothesis are supported here. These tenets hold that kinship-terminological systems are slow to change, but they do so in response to changes in descent, residence, and other features of social and economic organization.

At the end of this chapter we shall discuss the five loose systems and cite the variation within them. Before doing so it is important to outline the major features of western North American kinship terminologies. Two features that loomed large as organizing principles in the kinship terminologies of western North America's Indians were "bifurcation" and "collateralization."

"Bifurcation" means that terms distinguished relatives by sex (males from females) or by the sex of the relative through which ego traced his or her relationship to another relative. These terms could be used for relatives of any and all generations.

"Collateralization" means that ego's lineal relatives (parents, grandparents, children, and grandchildren) were distinguished from the siblings of ego's lineal relatives and the descendants of any of those relatives.

"Merging" and "lineal" features were less prominent in the kinship terminologies of western North America, but these features were present in many systems. There is considerable synchronic information which supports the inference that lineal features often developed from bifurcate collateral features, and that merging features also developed from bifurcate collateral features. Furthermore, there is more evidence that bifurcate collateral features also could develop from merging features. These are not minor points in a theologic treatise, as will be explained below.

A "merging" feature in a kinship system is a term that is used for both lineal and collateral relatives, that is, a term that merges relations of both types under one classification. For instance, when one term is used for father, father's brother, and mother's brother, all of the lineal and collateral first-ascending-generation males are merged. Merging was not uncommon for second-ascending-generation relatives (grandparents) and second-descending-generation relatives (grandchildren). For first-ascending-generation relatives, however, simple merging terms (referred to as "generational") were not used in western North America except in two Pueblos. Rather, "bifurcate merging" terminologies, which merged some lineal and collateral relatives— say, mother and mother's sister—under one term but distinguished father's sister by another term, were important. Bifurcate merging terminologies were frequent among societies observing unilineal descent and much less frequent among bilateral societies.

"Lineal" terms distinguished lineal relatives (mother, father, grandmother, grandfather, children, grandchildren) from collateral relatives (mother's sister, mother's brother, and so forth). Lineal terms were especially characteristic of some bilateral-

---

*See Appendix C for a discussion of Pearson's ϕ and Goodman and Kruskal's τ.

descent societies where organized bilateral kinship groups were the ultimate political and economic unit.

The dominance of bifurcation and collateralization in western North America was evident in the kinship terminologies used for relatives of all generations. Very often bifurcation and collateralization were joined in the same terms to create "bifurcate collateral" types. In each instance, relatives were distinguished by their collaterality (i.e., collaterals were differentiated from lineals), by their sex, and by the sex of the connecting relative.

Not only were bifurcate collateral features distributed widely, but they correlated with many bilaterally descended societies in the Great Basin, Southwest, California, and Plateau. Furthermore, features of bifurcate collateral terminology also correlated wth unilineal societies in the Southwest, Southern California, and California culture areas, though the associations were not quite so strong as with bilateral societies. The compatibility of bifurcate collateralization with unilineally, especially patrilineally descended societies, and also with societies observing bilateral descent, is a key to inferring change in kinship and extrakinship organization from synchronic data. The evidence suggests that bifurcate collateral terminologies were not only compatible with some bilateral and some unilineal descent systems, but that bifurcate collateral terminologies could have been transformed rather easily into bifurcate merging terminologies on the one hand or lineal terminologies on the other. The transformation either way required the shift of only one term and meaning (see Figure 8-7). By the same logic, transformations from lineal to bifurcate collateral, or from bifurcate merging to bifurcate collateral also required only one terminological change.

Driver, in his 280-society sample of North American Indian tribes north of Panama, discovered that when bifurcate collateral mother–aunt terms were employed in societies observing unilineal descent, they often coexisted with bifurcate merging terms for mother–aunt relationships (Driver and Massey 1957). From the widespread practice of using two types of first-ascending-generation terms, with bifurcate collateral dominating, Driver inferred that bifurcate collateral terms often preceded bifurcate merging terms, and that bifurcate merging terms developed from them following the related developments of unilocal residence and unilineal descent. But just as bifurcate merging terms could develop from bifurcate collateral terms in the presence of unilineal descent organization, so could bifurcate collateral terms develop from bifurcate merging terms in the presence of bilateral descent. Driver further surmised that during the period of first European contact and thereafter, many

societies changed from unilineal to bilateral forms of descent reckoning. This "cyclical," "lag," or "main sequence" kinship hypothesis posited interdependences among terminological types and other aspects of kinship organization, yet it also posited that every part of a kinship system did not change at the same time, so that perfect correlations among the many features of kinship organization need not have occurred for any large sample of tribes. On the other hand, the hypothesis accounted for variations from perfect correlations.

Among the Penutian speakers, especially the California Penutians, the evidence suggests that their early form of kinship organization centered on patrilineal descent, that siblings and parallel cousins were merged and distinguished from cross-cousins, that mother and mother's sister were merged and distinguished from father's sister, and that father and father's brother were merged and distinguished from mother's brother. Whereas the California Penutian system was somewhat more complex than this (generational skewing created a mature Omaha-type system*), features of bifurcate merging dominated the terminologies. Among the Miwok, Patwin, and many Yokuts, these descent and kin-term features were extant at the time of contact with the first Europeans. Among the Wintu and Nomlaki the kin-term features were present, but descent was bilateral. And among the Maidu and Nisenan groups, descent was bilateral, kin terms were bifurcate collateralizing for the first-ascending generation, and either Hawaiian (merging siblings and cousins) or Iroquoian (merging siblings and parallel cousins, but distinguishing cross-cousins). The several unilineal types of kinship terminologies associated with bilateral descent among the Wintu, Maidu, and Nisenan groups—all of whom were located in the northern part of the California culture area—the importance of bilateral tribelets in owning, sharing, and protecting property, and the scant evidence for bilateral kinship groups larger than patribilateral lineal families suggest that the more northern California Penutians underwent rather systematic transformations from organizations in which independent patrilineage, bifurcate merging, and Omaha-type kinship were features to bilateral tribelets in which kinship terminologies varied, some retaining the old kinship system and some acquiring terminologies that were collateralizing.

Evidence for pre-Contact transformations from bifurcate collateral to lineal systems comes from the

---

*Omaha, Hawaiian, Iroquoian, and other cousin-terminological systems are defined later in the chapter.

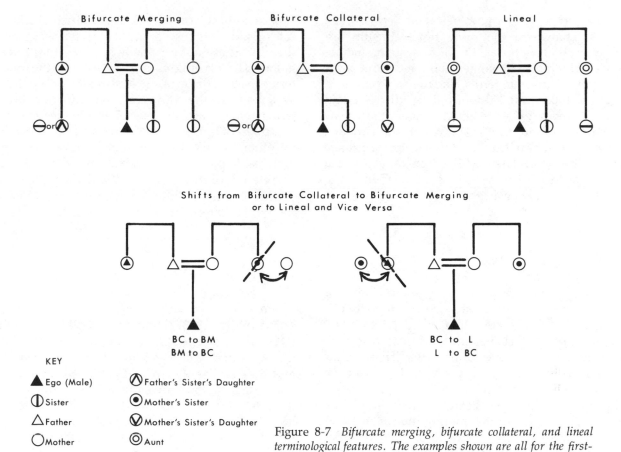

Figure 8-7 *Bifurcate merging, bifurcate collateral, and lineal terminological features. The examples shown are all for the first-ascending generation and the ego generation.*

Salishan speakers of the Plateau and the Northwest Coast. It is not clear whether a bifurcate collateral system preceded a lineal system or vice versa, but Driver (in Driver and Massey 1957) suggests, by inference, that bifurcate collateral was the prior form for most North American Indian societies, whereas Elmendorf (1961), in his reconstruction of Salishan kinship terms, posits that a collateralizing system was the prior form. In the main, collateralizing systems were employed by Salishans in the Columbia Plateau, and lineal systems were used in the Fraser Plateau and on the Northwest Coast. Transformation either way would have been possible with only very simple changes of terms. Either collaterals were merged (from collateral to lineal), or they were bifurcated (from lineal to collateral).

Because the migration into the Fraser and Columbia Plateaus seems to have been from the area near the Fraser River and the Canadian coastal range, because the movement seems to have been more recent than the movement north and south along the coast, and because the coastal kinship-terminological features and some Fraser Plateau features were predom-

inantly lineal, for the Plateau a transformation of terms from lineal to collateral will be posited in this book. This does not preclude that an even earlier transformation from collateral to lineal may have accompanied successful penetration of the wet forests. On the coast the Salishan patribilateral demes were the ultimate economic and political units, whereas in the interior demes were restricted to the Lillooet. The kinship units in most Plateau groups were not larger than patribilateral lineal families. Furthermore, flexible local communities composed of several bilateral families shared common territories. The kinship-terminology differences correlated with other kinship- and extrakinship-organization differences.

The correlations among kinship and extrakinship variables obtained in the studies by Murdock (1949), Driver (1957, 1966), Aberle (1961), and Jorgensen (1966) were not fortuities. Collateralization, given the appropriate conditions, transforms into lineal or merging features. And all things being equal, kinship terminologies do not seem to change rapidly. They appear to lag behind the changes made in other features of kinship organization. And finally, all terminologies in a kin-terminological system do not appear to change at the same time. Kinship terminologies, then, appear to form systems whose parts are vulnerable to changes in related parts of the culture. Yet because kin terms, like the basic words in Swadesh's 100- and 200-word lists, discussed in Chapter 3, seem to be retained longer than some other features of culture (or language), the variation in kinship terms within and between language families, when correlated with other variables, can embolden us to infer directions of change, even though the data are synchronic.

Grandparent Terminologies

The geographical distribution of the several ways for classifying grandparents is depicted in Map Cu-152, V-326. Figure 8-8 diagrams the features of each terminological type. Bisexual and bifurcate bisexual terms dominated in every culture area. These terms distinguished grandparents by sex, or by sex of the connecting relative (father or mother). Whereas all grandparents could have been merged under one term by dropping the term denoting the sex of either the grandparent or the connecting relative from either the bisexual or bifurcate bisexual types, merging terminologies had a narrow distribution, being restricted to the Coast Salishan and Wakashan speakers. For western North America, at least, merging terminologies for grandparents were restricted almost solely to bilateral patrideme societies, and therefore seem to be a special feature of the cultures of the central Northwest Coast who developed a unique kinship system.

Variations of bifurcate bisexual types and matriskewed types were common among unilineally descended societies in Southern California (the patrilineal Uto-Aztecans), the Southwest (the matrilineal Western Apaches, whose skewing was the reverse of the patrilineal Uto-Aztecans), and in the central part of the California culture area (some Miwok and Yokuts). The less frequently used kin terms were not distributed at random. For instance, Southern California Uto-Aztecans merged paternal grandparents under one term while distinguishing maternal grandfather from maternal grandmother. No other Uto-Aztec groups so classified grandparents. All others used bifurcate bisexual terms, except Hopis (who used only bisexual terms). The Western Apaches merged maternal grandparents under one term while distinguishing paternal grandmother from paternal grandfather.

Because of the predominance of bisexual and bifurcate bisexual types, grandparent terms in and of themselves are not especially important for interpretation. The exceptions are, of course, the merging terms used in the central Northwest Coast patrideme systems and the variations on bifurcate bisexual terms in many unilineal societies. On the other hand, grandparent terms were closely associated with terms for other classes of relatives in some sets of kinship systems. In particular, grandparent–grandchild terms correlated highly and positively, as did grandparent–first-ascending-generation terms. We shall discuss the interrelation among these kin terms next.

Grandchildren Terminologies

There were more types of terminologies used for grandchildren (V-327) than for any other class of relatives in western North America except siblings (brothers and sisters). Some types occurred rarely, and they are combined and exhibited on a separate map. Map Cu-153 shows the distribution of the dominant terminology types and some of the rare types. Map Cu-154 shows the geographical distributions of the rare types. The rare types were concentrated in the northern areas of California, but as was the case for grandparent terms, the distributions of grandchildren terms, too, were not random. Each rare type was usually restricted either to sets of neighbors from the same language family, or to neighbors regardless of their language affinities. Figure 8-9 diagrams the terminological types for grandchildren.

Simple bisexual terminologies were rarely used for grandchildren but frequently used for grandparents. When they were used for grandchildren they were usually reciprocals of grandparent terms (the terms used by grandparents for grandchildren, often with a diminutive affix, were also used by grandchildren for grandparents). Bifurcate terms were primarily restricted to Yuman speakers; merging terms were represented especially heavily among the unilineage and patrideme societies of the Northwest Coast and California culture areas; south of there, Southern California Uto-Aztecans used terms intermediate between bifurcate and "bifurcate speaker's sex," wherein male speakers used a different term for a daughter's children than did female speakers, yet both used the same term for a son's children. A glance at the grandchildren–grandparents maps (Cu-152; Cu-153) will help the reader understand the following correlations between the terminological types for the two: bisexual grandparent term–

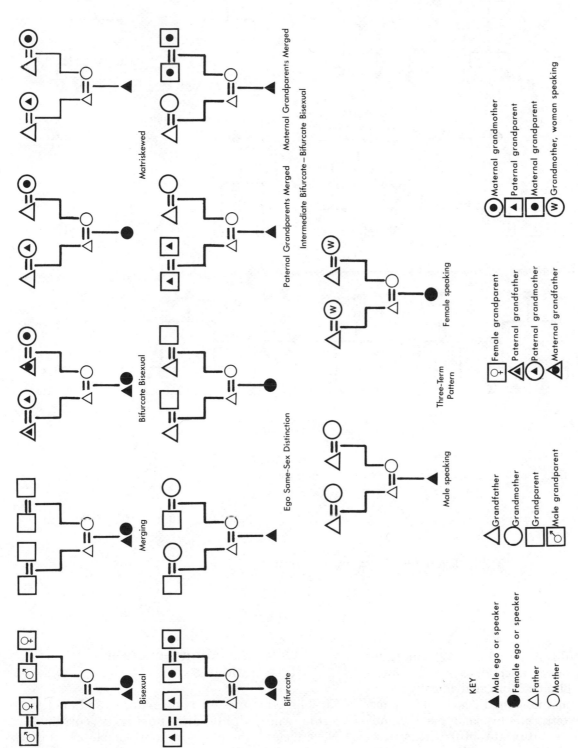

Figure 8-8 *Grandparent classifications.*

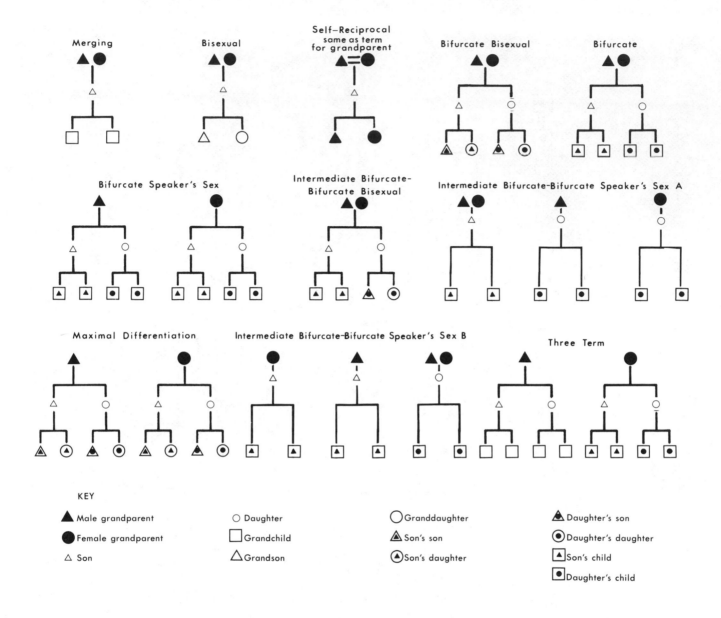

Figure 8-9 *Grandchildren classifications.*

merging grandchild term ($\phi = .49$), merging grandparent–merging grandchild ($\phi = .47$), intermediate bifurcate–bifurcate bisexual female grandparent/self-reciprocal grandchild ($\phi = .47$), intermediate bifurcate–bifurcate bisexual male grandparent/intermediate bifurcate–bifurcate speaker's sex A grandchild ($\phi = .43$), intermediate bifurcate–bifurcate bisexual grandchild ($\phi = .21$), and bifurcate bisexual grandparent–bifurcate grandchild ($\phi = .22$). The correlations of the rare types were almost entirely restricted to tribes belonging to the same language families, as the maps demonstrate.

First-Ascending-Generation Terminologies

Kinship-term types for fathers–uncles and mothers–aunts were highly and positively correlated. Nevertheless, there was a considerable amount of variation in usage wherein, say, bifurcate collateral terms which distinguished mother's brother's from father's brother's (i.e., distinguishing the sex of the connecting relative) and also distinguished them by their ages relative to the ages of mother and father (i.e., distinguishing father's elder brother, etc.), were

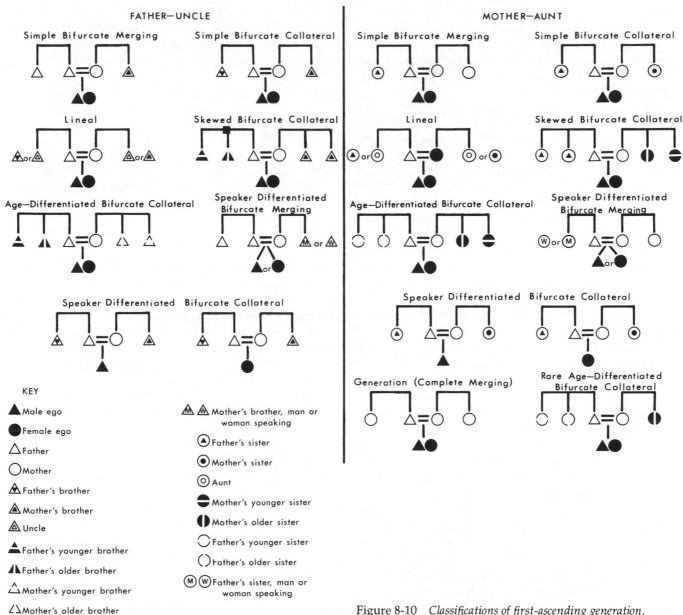

Figure 8-10   *Classifications of first-ascending generation.*

not used for aunts. The corresponding terms for aunts might be skewed or simple bifurcate collateral. Indeed, when variation occurred it was very frequently a discrepancy between two ways to bifurcate and distinguish collaterals, and the variation, again, was usually restricted to linguistically related groups, near neighbors, or both.

Map Cu-155 (V-328) shows the distribution of terms for fathers–uncles, and Map Cu-156 (V-329) shows the geographical distributions of terms for mothers–aunts. A quick glance at the two maps reveals that the following terminological types are highly correlated for the two sets of relatives: lineal ($\phi = .94$), simple

bifurcate collateral ($\phi = .79$), bifurcate merging ($\phi = .72$), and skewed bifurcate collateral ($\phi = .70$). Figure 8-10 diagrams the kinship terminological types for first-ascending-generation relatives.

Lineal first-ascending-generation terminologies were restricted almost completely to the patribilateral deme societies of the central Northwest Coast (Salishans and Wakashans). Simple bifurcate merging terms were distributed among unilineal descent societies and some bilateral descent societies, such as the Wintu of the northern part of California, which appear to have been patrilineal at an earlier period. Whereas bifurcate collateral terms were distributed among societies observing bilateral and unilineal descent, skewed bifurcate collateral terms for both aunts and uncles were closely correlated with unilineally descended societies of the Uto-Aztecan speakers and Yuman speakers in Southern California and the Southwest.

First-ascending-generation terms correlated highly and positively with both grandparents and grandchild terminologies. It appears that specific forms of second-ascending- and second-descending-generation terms more often correlated within several tribes from the same language family where cousin terminologies among the same groups varied. First-ascending-generation terminologies correlated rather highly with cousin terms, but cousin terms did not correlate very highly with grandparent and grandchild terms. A plausible explanation is that first-ascending-generation terms served in an intermediary position between cousin terminologies and terms for other classes of relations. By far the greatest variation occurred between simple bifurcate collateral first-ascending-generation terms and four types of grandchildren terms (self-reciprocal, bifurcate speaker's sex, intermediate bifurcate–bifurcate bisexual, and intermediate bifurcate–bifurcate speaker's sex B). All four grandchild types correlated significantly, but barely so, with bifurcate collateral terms (ϕ range .18 to .24, $\phi \leqslant .05$). These results may well show the sensitive function served by bifurcate merging terminologies in kinship change. Other first-ascending-generation terms (averaging the relations between father–father's-brother terms, and mother–mother's-sister terms) had more clearcut relations with grandchild and grandparent terms: for example, bifurcate merging correlated with merging grandchild ($\phi = .22$), and bisexual grandparent ($\phi = .27$); lineal correlated with merging grandparent ($\phi = .50$) and merging grandchild ($\phi = .54$); age-differentiated bifurcate collateral correlated with self-reciprocal grandchild ($\phi = .44$); skewed bifurcate collateral correlated with bifurcate grandchild ($\phi = .56$), intermediate bifurcate–bifurcate speaker's sex A grandchild ($\phi = .27$), bifurcate bisexual grandparent ($\phi = .32$), and intermediate bifurcate–bifurcate bisexual male grandparent ($\phi = .24$). The skewed bifurcate collateral correlations are interesting because they divide into two sets, one Yuman (bifurcate bisexual grandparent, bifurcate grandchild) and the other Southern California Uto-Aztecan (the two intermediate bifurcate–bifurcate bisexual forms). The convergence of first-ascending-generation terms (and cousin terms) between Yumans and Southern California Uto-Aztecans (who intermarried in Southern California) and the changes in Southern California Uto-Aztecan grandparent and grandchild terminologies suggest an accommodation toward Yuman kinship-term types. They were unique to Southern California Uto-Aztecans and did not appear among their congeners in the Great Basin, in the central part of California, or in the Southwest.

Sibling Terminologies

Fully eighteen types of terminologies were used to distinguish among siblings (V-330). In line with the bifurcate collateralizing nature of most kin terms in western North America, sex distinctions and relative age distinctions were regular features of the terminologies. Map Cu-157 (V-330) and Cu-158 (V-330) show the geographical distributions of the sibling terminology types, and Figure 8-11 diagrams them.

Dravidian terminologies, which distinguished sex as well as relative age, were employed in more than half of all societies, and these terms were equally compatible with unilineal and bilateral descent systems. East Polynesian terminologies, which distinguished relative sex and also relative age for siblings of the speaker's sex, were restricted solely to the Tlingits and Haidas of the northern Northwest Coast. Yoruban terminologies, which merged siblings of the opposite sex but distinguished them by relative age, were employed by most patrideme societies as part of their unique kinship system. The bilateral Tewa used Yoruban-type terms, but so did the matrilineal Western Apaches. Algonkian terminologies, which distinguished older siblings by sex but younger siblings only by relative age, were employed in a few bilateral and patrilineal societies. As was true for the terminologies used for other classes of kinsmen, sibling terms in and of themselves do not tell us much about general regularities in kinship organization. On the other hand, East Polynesian-type terms had a unique distribution, as did Yoruban (central Northwest Coast patridemes, Western Apaches, and Tewa Pueblos) and Yukian (Yuki and River Yuman) and these distributions represent clearcut historical-geographical relations within a language group (River Yumans) or in a larger area (central Northwest Coast).

Cousin Terminologies

Types of terms for cousins and first-ascending-generation relatives have long been used as keys to understanding kinship systems. Very frequently in societies where there were bifurcate merging first-ascending-generation terms, it was also the case that

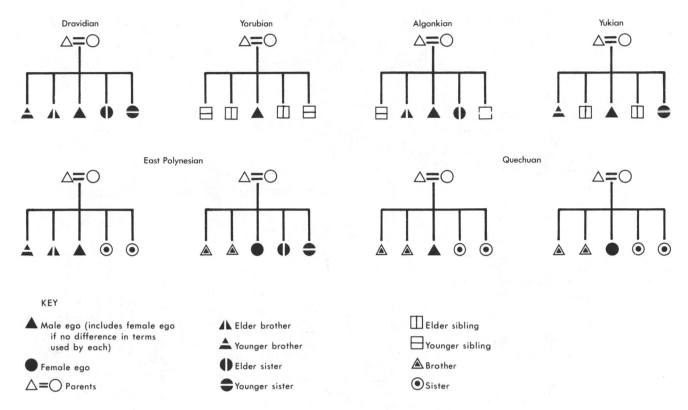

Figure 8-11 *Predominant sibling classifications.*

parallel cousins were merged with siblings under one term and distinguished from cross-cousins. As we pointed out above, parallel cousins were children of siblings of the same sex, and cross-cousins were children of siblings of the opposite sex. Around the world it was common among societies that made distinctions among cross- and parallel cousins that cross-cousins were marriage-eligible whereas parallel cousins were not. Cross-cousin marriage, however, was rare in western North America, even among societies that made cross- and parallel-cousin distinctions, so the practice of cousin marriage did not cause cross- and parallel-cousin distinctions to persist. Nevertheless, bilateral cross-cousin marriages were preferred on the northern Northwest Coast, and matrilateral cross-cousin marriages were preferred among the Miwok. These societies also had moieties, yet most moiety societies prohibited cross-cousin marriage. It may be that if cousin-marriage attended the development of cross- and parallel-cousin distinctions, the practice disappeared from most of the unilineal societies in western North America, perhaps especially with the stimulus of moiety and phratry developments. Map Cu-159 (V-331) shows the geographical distribution of the five types of cousin terminologies employed in western North America. Three of them, Iroquois, Omaha, and

Crow, made cross- and parallel-cousin distinctions. Hawaiian merged all relatives of both sexes in the same generation. Eskimo merged parallel and cross-cousins but distinguished them from siblings (see Figure 8-12).

Although bifurcate collateralizing kin terminologies were prominent for other classes of relatives, not one of the tribes in our western North America sample used the maximal bifurcate collateral terms for cousins (known as Sudanese). In such a classification siblings are distinguished from parallel and cross-cousins and further distinctions are made between parallel cousins and cross-cousins on the basis of the sex of the relative connecting ego and cousin.

Iroquois-type terminologies make the cross- and parallel-cousin distinctions, but Crow and Omaha go one step farther. The latter two skew generations so that terms used for some relative in descending generations are also used for some relative in ego's generation, and even for some relatives in ascending generations. In the Crow-type system, the term for father's sister is applied to father's sister's daughter, father's sister's daughter's daughter, and so forth. The term for father is applied to the sons of all those whom ego calls father's sister. As has been pointed out for several decades, a key feature of the Crow system is that persons of the same sex in certain maternal lineages

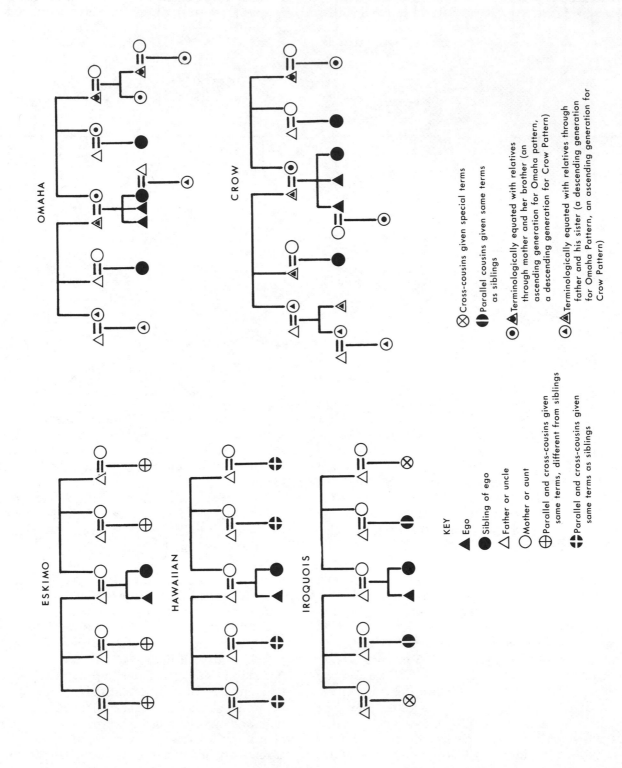

Figure 8-12 *Cousin classifications.*

are called by the same term (e.g., "father's sister" is the term for the women in ego's father's lineage, and "father" is the term for the men in ego's father's lineage). There are a few exceptions to these features inasmuch as, in some instances, a kin term used to classify lineage members of the same sex is also used for someone who does not belong to the lineage (often "grandfather" and in some societies "grandmother" are used for people who do not belong in the same lineage).

The correlation between Crow-type cousin terms and matrilineal descent is high in the world, and was high in western North America ($\phi = .48$). The Western Pueblos, and the Santa Ana and Sia Keresans among the Eastern Keres, and the Haidas and Tlingits of the northern Northwest Coast all observed matrilineal descent and employed Crow-type cousin terminologies. It is probable that all Keresans observed matrilineal descent and employed Crow-type cousin terms at one time, but some of these systems have undergone change away from Crow terms toward Eskimo terminology in the past century (White 1942; 1962; Eggan 1950), either under Tanoan influence, Spanish influence, or influences from both sources.

Omaha-type cousin terminologies are a mirror image of Crow-type terms, and throughout the world and in western North America they correlated highly with patrilineal descent ($\phi = .33$). In western North America, Omaha-type terminologies were restricted to Penutian speakers in California and some of their Pomo neighbors. Most of the Penutian speakers who used Omaha-type terms also observed patrilineal descent at the time Europeans first contacted them, but some of the most northern Wintu were bilateral, as were the Pomo. Above it was inferred that many of the California Penutians in the northern part of the California culture area, specifically the Wintu, Maidu, and Nisenan tribelets and perhaps the Penutians of Oregon had shifted toward bilaterality from an Omaha-type patrilineal base.

Iroquois-type terminologies made cross- and parallel-cousin distinctions that, with relative ease, could have been transformed either to the Hawaiian type, which merged all cousin and siblings, or to Crow or Omaha types, which maintained cross- and parallel-cousin distinctions while skewing generations. Iroquois terms correlated rather highly with patrilineally descended systems ($\phi = .30$) as well with matrilineal descent ($\phi = .23$). Among the patrilineal tribes the Southern California Uto-Aztecans, the Yumans, and the Oregon Athapaskans employed Iroquois terms. Among the matrilineal tribes the Navajos, Western Apaches, Haisla Kwakiutl, and Tsimshians employed Iroquois-type cross- and parallel-cousin distinctions. In conditions of unilineality it is reasonable to conclude that Iroquois-type terms could be generated from either Eskimo (by extension of sibling terms to parallel cousins) or Hawaiian-type terms (by creating new terms for cross-cousins) with but one terminological change. It is plausible that Southern California Uto-Aztecans began using Hawaiian terms and abandoned Iroquois terms because Hawaiian terms were used by practically all other Uto-Aztecan speakers in western North America. On the other hand, Dyen and Aberle (1974) infer that the Hupa Athapaskans of the Northwest Coast subregion that extends south into northwestern California adjusted their terminology from Iroquois to Hawaiian in the context of bilaterality. It is possible, of course, that the Iroquois terms were an earlier form for Uto-Aztecans and that the Papago and most Shoshoneans transformed their terms to Hawaiian types as their subsistence economies and descent organizations changed. As for the Maiduans (California Penutians) in the northern part of California, who employed Iroquois-type cousin terms, it is inferred that they changed from Omaha to Iroquois in the context of bilaterality, whereas the several Nisenan (Southern Maidu) groups, all of whom were bilateral, transformed to Hawaiian, perhaps after abandoning Omaha-type terms for Iroquois terms first. The Nisenan, then, may have proceeded one step farther in the change cycle than did their northern congeners, the Maidu. The greater complexity of the Omaha and Crow systems did not readily allow for direct and simple changes to Hawaiian-type terminologies.

Hawaiian-type terms occurred in every culture area of western North America except Southern California. Inasmuch as Southern California was totally dominated by patrilocal, patrilineal sibs and moiety organizations, it is not surprising that terms which correlated highly with bilateral descent systems were not present in Southern California.

Eskimo-type terms were restricted to the Tanoan villages, to some of the Eastern Keres villages adjacent to the Tanoan villages, to the Reese River Shoshones (who possessed an aberrant system in general), and to the Mattole Athapaskans on the northern coast in California. The development of Eskimo-type terms among the Eastern Pueblos, where they were the only terms used in Tanoan society but often overrode Crow-type systems among the Keresans, was consonant with the importance of village moiety organizations rather than kinship organization, and bilateral descent rather than unilineal kinship, especially matrisib organizations.

Cousin terminologies correlated more highly with first-ascending-generation terms than with any other kinship classification. The following correlations between cousin and first-ascending-generation terms average mother, mother's sister (mother–aunt) and father, father's brother (father–uncle) into a single coefficient representing first-ascending-generation terms unless otherwise specified: Hawaiian/lineal (ϕ = .36); Eskimo/age-differentiated bifurcate collateral (ϕ = .35); Iroquois/skewed bifurcate collateral mother–aunt (ϕ = .28), and several low positive scores between Iroquois and bifurcate merging father–uncle (ϕ = .10), bifurcate merging mother–aunt (ϕ = .04), and skewed bifurcate collateral father–uncle (ϕ = .04); Crow/bifurcate merging mother–aunt (ϕ = .40), and bifurcate merging father–uncle (ϕ = .11); and Omaha/bifurcate merging father–uncle (ϕ = .28) and bifurcate merging mother–aunt (ϕ = .13), and age-differentiated bifurcate collateral mother–aunt (ϕ = .17). Crow and Omaha types reversed strengths on bifurcate merging terms for father–uncle and mother–aunt, reflecting the patrilineal and matrilineal skewing of these two systems.

Relations Among Terminological Classifications

Taken singly and in pairs, first-ascending-generation and cousin terms tell no more about kinship organization than do the terminologies for other classes of kinspeople. At the beginning of this section it was mentioned that many of the kinship terminologies fitted into five loose systems. The five systems provide partial order at best to the various types of terminologies assessed here, and each system seems to reflect two or more shaping processes.

The first process might well operate in all societies given appropriate conditions. The second process seems to stress the uniqueness and peculiarities of historical context, including the uniqueness of sets of societies belonging to a common linguistic tradition.

The first process is inferred from a set of rather close correlations among forms of descent reckoning and certain cousin and first-ascending-generation terminologies. These correlations suggest regular relations among features of kinship organization that recur under certain conditions, namely, unilineal descent generates Iroquois cousin terms and either bifurcate merging or some form of bifurcate collateral first-ascending-generation terms. Patrilineality and patrilineal descent groups generate Omaha-type

cousin terms with generational skewing features which create unique types of bifurcate merging first-ascending-generation terms. Matrilineality and matrilineal descent groups generate the mirror image of the Omaha-type system. In western North America, Crow and Omaha types appear to be "mature" matrilineal and patrilineal systems which may have developed from Iroquois-type cross- and parallel-cousin distinctions among rather sedentary societies. By "mature" is meant that the terminological features distinguished several lineages, rather than simply cross- and parallel-cousin distinctions. It is reasonable to infer that in order for a system to develop that made those distinctions, not only did a relatively long period of time pass, but few changes in other aspects of the kinship organization disrupted the development of the terms during that period; and once established, the terms influenced the descent and tenure systems that preceded them. When changes occurred such as, perhaps, the posited change toward the development of tribelets and bilateral descent among the various Penutians in the northern part of California, the original systems may well have undergone changes toward terminologies that did not specify lineages or even cross- and parallel-cousin distinctions.

In a similar vein, the regular development of patrideme organizations on the central Northwest Coast may well have been accompanied by the development of Hawaiian cousin terms, lineal first-ascending and first-descending-generation terms, and merging second-ascending and second-descending-generation terms. This constellation of kinship terminologies marked the unique patriskewed (in terms of residence, corporeal and incorporeal property ownership, and succession) yet bilaterally descended societies of the Northwest Coast. Why Omaha-type systems did not develop in the same context is not clear. In preceding sections relations between descent forms, marriage practices, and diffuse and abundant resources have been posited. Whatever the reason may have been, the lineal system on the central Northwest Coast embraced Wakashan and Salishan speakers in a regular development to a mature bilateral system. There are other examples such as the occurrence of Eskimo terms and self-reciprocal bisexual terms for grandparents and grandchildren among the Tewa, where kinship was probably less important in organizing economic, social, political, or religious affairs than anywhere else in western North America.

The second process that can be inferred from the variation in kinship terminologies is the role of common history shared by groups. For instance, it seems likely that the Yumans developed patrilineality,

Iroquois-type cousin terms, and skewed bifurcate collateral first-ascending-generation terms in a context of patrilocal residence and kinship-group claims to resources. The Southern California Uto-Aztecans, in environments adjacent and similar to those of the Yumans of Southern California, veered from the practices of their Uto-Aztecan congeners in western North America and were organized very similarly to Southern California Yumans, with whom they intermarried, were coordinated in an area-wide moiety system, and shared similar cousin and first-ascending-generation terms. Other aspects of their terminological systems were different but suggest definite accommodations toward Yuman practices (see Table 8-1). The similarities seem to reflect the merging of their histories in the past 1,500 years or so.

The distribution of kin terminologies exhibits non-random patterns, but the distributions, as for the Yuman and Southern California Uto-Aztecans, must be understood in their historical contexts. Variation from what would be expected according to the main-sequence kinship-hypothesis very frequently reflected the uniqueness of sets of cultures which shared some aspects of common language histories.

Inspection of Table 8-1 suggests that much of the variation in the five systems correlates with historical differences that may be inferred from language relations and geographic proximity among groups.

"Type I, Generalized Unilineal," includes the patrilineal Southern California Uto-Aztecans and the Yumans. It also includes the matrilineal Western Apaches and Tsimshians–Haisla Kwakiutl, who were similar in two terminological features, yet different as to the first-ascending-generation terms they used. The Maiduans, who were bilateral, possessed features common to the other unilineal Iroquois-type systems. In the generalized unilineal type there was a pronounced usage of second-ascending and second-descending-generation terminologies that were intermediate between bifurcate and bifurcate bisexual, and intermediate between bifurcate and bifurcation on the basis of the speaker's sex.

"Type II, Bilateral," includes variants of "mature lineal" and "generalizing collateral" systems. The mature lineal system includes the Salishans and many Wakashan speakers of the central Northwest Coast. With little variation these patrideme societies used Hawaiian cousin terms, lineal first-ascending and first-descending-generation terms, and merging second-ascending and second-descending-generation terms. This unique constellation of traits distinguished the central Northwest Coast people from the unilineal tribes to the north and the bilateral but demeless tribes to the east. This system, which distinguished lineals from collaterals, emphasized lineal relations in a bilateral society. The importance of lineal inheritance and succession within bilateral demes has been amply discussed above. It is likely that the kinship-term system reflects those kinship-related phenomena of the deme system.

The generalizing collateral forms were used by most Salishan and Sahaptian residents of the Plateau, Uto-Aztecans of the Great Basin, and Eastern Apaches of the Southwest. This system, which distinguished lineals from collaterals, and distinguished collaterals on the basis of their sex and the sex of the connecting relative and also made relative age distinctions, dominated among the tribes that tended to be the most mobile through the year and to have the most diffusely distributed resources. Kinship organization was much more flexible in these societies, at least in the ability for family households to move and to exercise authority, than in the patrideme societies on the Northwest Coast. Whereas fission and fusion of collaterals and affines in camps, villages, or bands was common in the Plateau, Great Basin, and Eastern Apache areas, such changes were much less frequent in the less flexible organizations of the central Northwest Coast, where property ownership was invested in the localized kinship groups.

"Type III, Bilateral," is distinguished from the lineal and collateral type. In the lineal and collateral forms, kinship organizations such as demes, bilateral lineal families, and even camps of related nuclear families exercised considerable autonomy. The demes and family households made decisions which could not be countermanded. In the nondeme societies of the Plateau, Great Basin, and Eastern Apache areas, authority beyond the family households was only nominal. Yet in Type III, the families were independent and nuclear (hence "nuclearizing"). Throughout most Tanoan villages considerable authority was invested in village organizations. The Eskimo terms, which distinguished lineals from collaterals in ego's generation, were probably borrowed by some of the Eastern Keres villages as they moved away from matrilineal organization where kinship groups were economically and politically autonomous, toward moiety and village organizations.

"Type IV, Patrilineal," represents the "mature" patrilineality of some Penutian kinship systems, and the Pomo variations of that system.

"Type V, Matrilineal," represents the "mature" matrilineal kinship systems of the Western Pueblos and Eastern Keres, with variation by language groups for second-ascending and second-descending-generation terms. The Haidu and Tlingit system, with variation, was different in some important details

Table 8-1
Five loose types of kin terminological systems in western North America

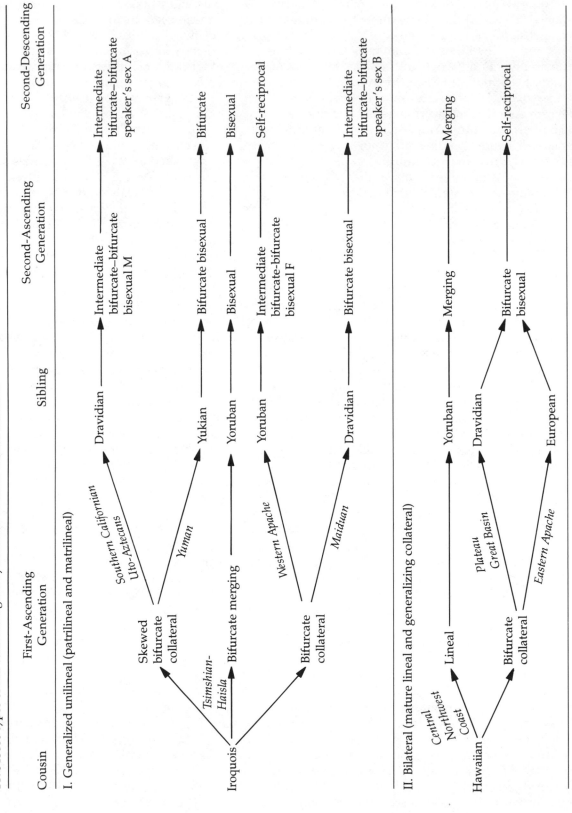

| Cousin | First-Ascending Generation | Sibling | Second-Ascending Generation | Second-Descending Generation |

I. Generalized unilineal (patrilineal and matrilineal)

Skewed bifurcate collateral → Dravidian → Intermediate bifurcate–bifurcate bisexual M → Intermediate bifurcate–bifurcate speaker's sex A

Southern Californian Uto-Aztecans

Yuman

Bifurcate merging → Yukian → Bifurcate bisexual → Bifurcate

Tsimshian-Haisla

→ Yoruban → Bisexual → Bisexual

Iroquois →

→ Yoruban → Intermediate bifurcate-bifurcate bisexual F → Self-reciprocal

Western Apache

Bifurcate collateral → Dravidian → Bifurcate bisexual → Intermediate bifurcate–bifurcate speaker's sex B

Maiduan

II. Bilateral (mature lineal and generalizing collateral)

Central Northwest Coast

Lineal → Yoruban → Merging → Merging

Hawaiian →

Bifurcate collateral → Dravidian → Bifurcate bisexual

Plateau Great Basin

→ European → Self-reciprocal

Eastern Apache

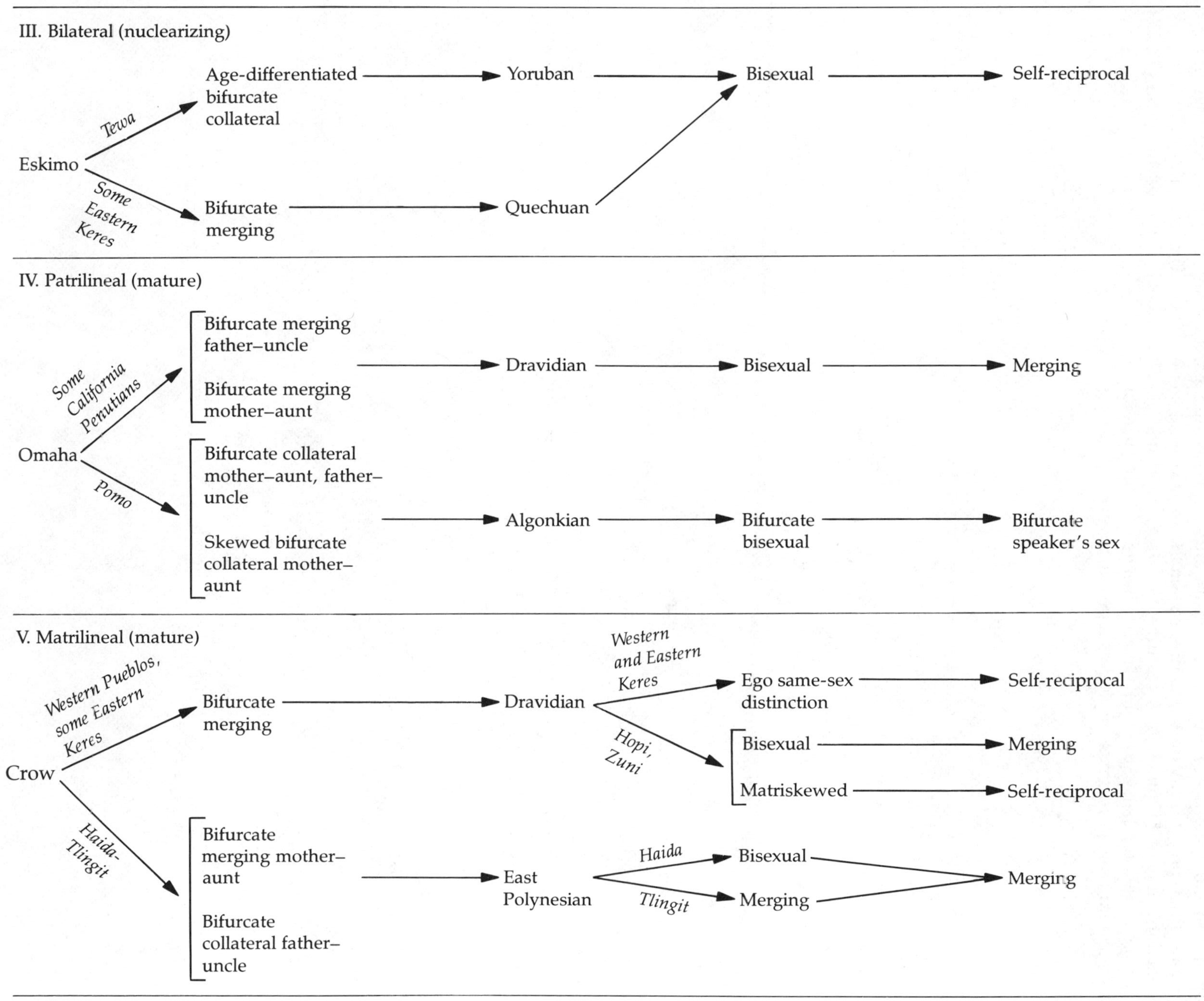

III. Bilateral (nuclearizing)

Eskimo → Age-differentiated bifurcate collateral → *Tewa* → Yoruban → Bisexual → Self-reciprocal

Eskimo → Bifurcate merging → *Some Eastern Keres* → Quechuan → Bisexual

IV. Patrilineal (mature)

⎰ Bifurcate merging father–uncle
⎱ Bifurcate merging mother–aunt → *Some California peninsums* → Dravidian → Bisexual → Merging

⎰ Bifurcate collateral mother–aunt, father–uncle
⎱ Skewed bifurcate collateral mother–aunt → Omaha, *Pomo* → Algonkian → Bifurcate bisexual → Bifurcate speaker's sex

V. Matrilineal (mature)

Crow → Bifurcate merging → *Western Pueblos, some Eastern Keres* → Dravidian →
  → *Western and Eastern Keres* → Ego same-sex distinction → Self-reciprocal
  → *Hopi, Zuni* → Bisexual → Merging → Matriskewed → Self-reciprocal

Crow → ⎰ Bifurcate merging mother–aunt
      ⎱ Bifurcate collateral father–uncle → *Haida-Tlingit* → East Polynesian →
  → *Haida* → Bisexual → Merging
  → *Tlingit* → Merging → Merging

[207]

from the Pueblo systems. "Mature" matrilineality and patrilineality represents my impression, based on the correlations among terminological features and descent organization, that Crow and Omaha lineage-skewing terminological types were developed from cross- and parallel-cousin distinctions that did not cross-cut generations. The maturation to Crow or Omaha, as stated above, followed unilineal descent organization.

Chapter 9

Political Organization, Sodalities, and Warfare

INTRODUCTION

Western North American Indian groups developed a variety of political organizations, but on the whole they were simple and the authority invested in leaders was nominal. Indeed, it was not so much clearly acknowledged authority as it was suasion, which leaders exercised because of the prestige and respect accorded to them, that characterized the leadership of most groups in western North America.

Sodalities, which were organizations whose members were not primarily determined by kinship or co-residence, took several forms and were directed toward several ends in western North America. Some sodalities were "tribal"-wide for all people of both sexes. Other tribalwide sodalities were for men only; some were for women only. And many sodalities were restricted to a select group of men or women within a tribe. Whereas sodalities in western North America were practically always sacred organizations, or organizations whose bases of legitimization were through connections to other-worldly phenomena, such as spirits, creatures from a mythical period, and the like, these sodalities were rarely political. Because sodalities were legitimized through supernatural sources, their authorities and prerogatives were not challenged. On the other hand, because sodality memberships crosscut kinship and co-residential alignments within societies, and because sodalities frequently sponsored ceremonies, or cured the sick, or educated and initiated the young into tribal life, or defended villages against attack (in a few

societies), or engaged in some combination of these activities, sodalities often occupied important niches in the social and political structure of their communities. In some societies sodality leaders were also the tribal leaders (as among the Valley Maidu, Foothill Maidu, and most Pueblos); in others, sodality leaders were principal assistants to the chiefs (true for much of the northern part of the California culture area), or leaders of several sodalities formed alliances, often shortlived, which, as powerful cliques, governed through religious and kinship suasion (Western Pueblos).

Although most sodalities in western North America were sacred organizations, they were not restricted to religious affairs. To the contrary, they provided some communitywide political cement both within societies that recognized only kinship-based authority in which jurisdictional hierarchy did not transcend the localized kinship group (most of the Northwest Coast), and within societies in which sodalities controlled political affairs (the Tewa villages). Yet all societies did not have sodalities. As a point of fact, sodalities occurred mainly among Pueblo, Southern California, California, and central and northern Northwest Coast societies. In brief, they occurred among many of those aboriginal societies in the West in which settlements were relatively sedentary, subsistence resources were considerable, and in which food resources were stored for long periods of time, or in which access to considerable subsistence resources was possible throughout the year, regardless of the duration of storage (e.g., people in the northern and central parts of California had access to foods throughout the year, as nature provided its own storage, and Southern California, Pueblo and Northwest Coast tribes had highly storable resources).

Because sodalities were formally and informally important in political affairs we discuss them in this section of the book. It will be clear, however, that sodalities, as privileged organizations whose major affairs were justified by a supernatural world, were focused as much on the supernatural world as they were on everyday events, including the events of the political worlds of western Indians.

Warfare, raiding, and feuding are topics that have also been included in this chapter. Warfare, by our definition, was a political act. It was a conflict between two groups each of which possessed definite leadership, military tactics, and the expectation that a series of battles could be endured. The motives for warfare varied from territorial expansion to glory and prestige, but warfare was always engaged in by political units or by definite factions within political units (e.g., warriors). By this definition there was little warfare in western North America, but there was considerable raiding. A raid was a single, small, military engagement of short duration motivated for any of several reasons. Feuds were conflicts between families, sibs, or some other form of kinship group, for which no formal mechanisms for resolutions existed.

Warfare, raids, and feuds, the differences among them, and the manner in which these various types of conflicts were resolved, were related to political organization, or the lack thereof, and to sodalities. For this reason it was decided to deal with these loosely related topics in one chapter.

The conflation and classification of political organization, sodality, and warfare variables in a single statistical analysis has yielded a culture tree that represents neither clearcut regional–cultural area groupings, as were evident in the classifications of the total cultural inventory and the domains of technology–material culture, subsistence economy, and economic organization (to compare these classifications, look again at Figures 4-1, 4-3, 5-1, 6-1, and 7-1) nor a clearcut culture-type grouping of the sort evident in the classification of settlement pattern and social organization variables (Figure 8-1). At the upper end of Figure 9-1 (see also Figure 9-2) we see that the Pueblos were organized into two distinct geographic sets—Hopi and Zuni in one (group 2), and all Keresans and Tanoans in the other (group 1); some of the Upper Columbia groups formed a distinct geographic set (Flathead, Coeur d'Alene, Kutenai, making up group 3) as did some of the tribelets of the Sacramento Valley and its western borders (Mattole to Southern Pomo, in group 4), and most of the Northwest Coast groups from Tsimshian and Gitksan south to the Lower Chinook (group 5). At the bottom of Figure 9-1, the River Yumans formed a distinct geographic cluster (group 20). Each of these sets stand out because of certain special developments of political organization, or sodality organization, or warfare, or some combination of developments of these phenomena. For example, whereas Western Pueblos, Eastern Keres Pueblos, and Tanoan Pueblos all possessed sodalities, the dual sodalities (nonexogamous moieties)* of most Tanoan Pueblos possessed the authority to control governmental functions. Government was centralized in the Eastern Keres Pueblos, and had some centralized aspects in the Western Keres Pueblos, but not through sodalities. Centralization of authority did not occur at the Hopi and Zuni Pueblos, though a priesthood at the Zuni villages controlled ceremonial affairs. And as further examples, though Clayoquot Nootka, Tsimshian, and Gitksan societies had the most complex political organizations on the Northwest Coast, their raiding patterns and dancing-society organizations linked them to their southern neighbors. The unique political organizations and raiding complex of the River Yumans distinguished them from their neighbors, from the Western and Eastern Apache raiders, and from the raiders of the Northwest Coast. Most of the specialized developments occurred among groups located in contiguous territories. Even where raiding was highly developed, such as among the River Yuman, Apachean, and Northwest Coast groups, either the differences in the local raiding complexes, the presence or absence of sodality organizations, or the nature of the political organizations served to distinguish among these three raiding complexes. The effects of historical relations in similar environments (neighbors tended to have similar types of sodalities and to engage in similar raiding patterns) are evident.

Although some tight clusterings appear in a few regions, the remarkable thing about Figure 9-1 is the general similarity among tribes from Salinan, at the bottom (in group 19), to Reese River Shoshone, at the top (in group 8). This distribution, joined at an average similarity of 64 percent, encompasses 61 percent

---

*In Chapter 8 we refer to the dual sodalities among the Eastern Pueblos (Tanoan speakers) and Eastern Keres Pueblos (Keresan speakers) as "nonexogamous moieties." We refer to these nonexogamous moieties here as either dual sodalities or nonexogamous moieties. These organizations were tribalwide, and membership was not based on kinship or marriage criteria.

of all tribes in western North America. Nominal government, a paucity of sodalities, and defensive raiding patterns characterized many of these groups, but the variation was wide. In order to ferret out unique constellations within this large set, branches were selected at several levels, from 87 percent to 65 percent average similarity. These sets are mapped in Figure 9-2.

It is evident from the clustering that many of the tribes at the lower end of Figure 9-1 are classified in sets which include members from two or more culture areas (compare with Figures 4-1 and 4-3). For instance, group 19, the set above that of the River Yumans, includes members from Achomawi in the northern part of the California culture area on the north to Gabrieliño in Southern California on the south. The set above that, group 18, includes such geographically disparate groups as Sinkyone, near the northwestern California coast, to Wind River Shoshone, in the Wyoming Rockies. Whereas a few of the sets of tribes in the lower part of the figure were distinguished by a few features, e.g. the Southeast Yavapai to Western Navajo set (group 15) comprised Eastern Basin and Southwest offensive raiders; the Thompson to Haida and Klamath set (group 14) comprised offensive raiders of the Fraser Plateau, Klamath Lakes region of the Plateau, and northern Northwest Coast; the San Juan Southern Paiute to Reese River Shoshone set (group 8) comprised the least warlike and least governed people in western North America. Figure 9-1 does not order the tribes of this section into easily interpreted regional patterns. It is probable that clearer divisions would have been obtained if the number of variables used in the analysis had been doubled, or if we had separated political, sodality, and warfare variables.

POLITICAL ORGANIZATION

In the introduction to this volume it was pointed out that most Indian groups in western North America recognized only nominal authority and had minimal political organizations. There was, however, considerable variation among these minimally organized groups as to how they defended property, allocated scarce resources, settled internal disputes, waged raids and counterattacks, and conducted other affairs which entailed political decisions.

In order to measure differences in political organization, variables were created to assess leadership, succession, territoriality, and authority over such key decisions as how resources were allocated in times of shortages, how access was gained to strategic re-

sources, whether civic labor and duties were assigned, whether alliances were formed, and whether crimes were punished. Whereas the information about authority seems best able to answer the questions about the nature of power in political organizations, the simplest introduction to the political organizations of the Indians of western North America might be gained by looking first at the political-territorial units (V-334), then turning to discussions of leadership, succession, and spheres of authority.

Government and Territorial Organization

In this study we determined three types of political-territorial units: (1) residential kinship-groups; (2) villages or bands; and (3) districts or tribes (Map Cu-161, V-334). The simplest and numerically most dominant political organization was the *residential kinship-group* that had no formal ties with any other group, even if several such kinship units lived side by side in the same community. Undoubtedly this is a very modest form of political organization and, many western North American localities, especially in the Great Basin, might best be described as having no political organization at all. Yet the range of cultural complexity among groups that recognized no authority beyond the residential kinship-group was wide, stretching from the nuclear family organizations within the small, ambilocal, bilateral family camps of the Great Basin proper to the matrilineages and patridemes of many Northwest Coast groups, some of the patrilineage communities of central California, and the patrisibs of Southern California.

Residential Kinship-Groups

The simplicity of many Great Basin cultures was marked by the free fashion in which families could leave one camp and attach to another, sharing in the resources available in the new area. Among some groups in the Plateau and among most Pai-speaking groups in the Southwest, the same kind of movement was possible and no firm and well-specified authority was invested in the leaders. Leadership was by precept and advice in these small, nonstratified, unranked, noncompetitive groups.

In the Northwest Coast the vast majority of patridemes, patrilineages, matrilineages, and patribilateral lineal families were politically autonomous as well as economically autonomous. The territory controlled by each residential kinship-unit was its strategic resource sites. If there were several kinship

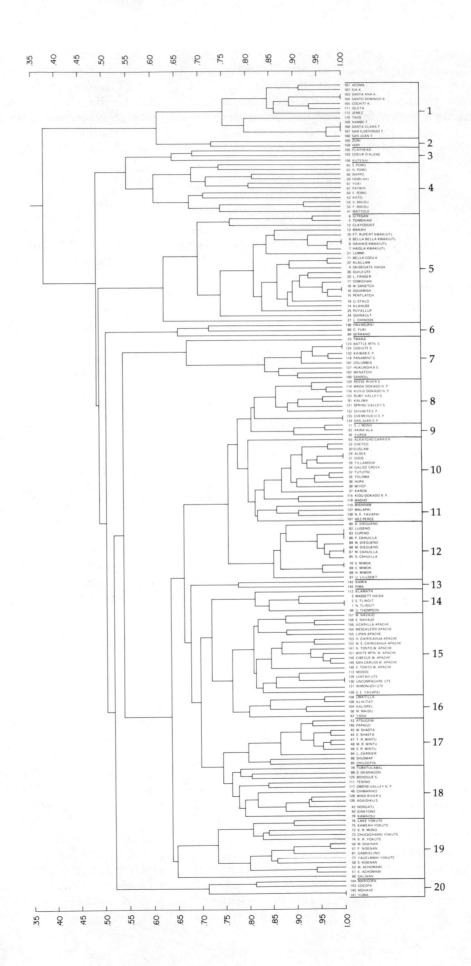

Figure 9-1 *Culture tree: 6. Groupings of tribal territories derived from G coefficients based on 34 variables (158 attributes) of political organization, sodalities, and warfare.*

GROUP 1
161 Acoma
162 Sia Keres
163 Santa Ana Keres
164 Santo Domingo Keres
165 Cochiti Keres
171 Isleta
172 Jemez
170 Taos
169 Nambe Tewa
168 Santa Clara Tewa
167 San Ildefonso Tewa
166 San Juan Tewa

GROUP 2
160 Zuni
159 Hopi

GROUP 3
105 Flathead
103 Coeur d'Alene
106 Kutenai

GROUP 4
65 Southern Pomo
63 Northern Pomo
66 Wappo
50 Nomlaki
61 Yuki
67 Patwin
64 Eastern Pomo
43 Kato
54 Valley Maidu
55 Foothill Maidu
41 Mattole

GROUP 5
6 Gitksan
5 Tsimshian
12 Clayoquot
13 Makah
10 Fort Rupert Kwakiutl
9 Bella Bella Kwakiutl
8 Haihais Kwakiutl
7 Haisla Kwakiutl
21 Lummi
11 Bella Coola
22 Klallam
4 Skidegate Haida
26 Quileute
20 Lower Fraser
17 Cowichan
18 West Sanetch
16 Squamish
15 Pentlatch

19 Upper Stalo
14 Klahuse
25 Puyallup
24 Quinault
27 Lower Chinook

GROUP 6
136 Havasupai
60 Coast Yuki
84 Serrano

GROUP 7
23 Twana
123 Battle Mountain Shoshone
124 Gosiute Shoshone
133 Kaibab Southern Paiute
118 Panamint Shoshone
101 Columbia
127 Hukundika Shoshone
102 Wenatchi
100 Sanpoil

GROUP 8
120 Reese River Shoshone
114 Wada-Dokado Northern Paiute
116 Kuyui-Dokado Northern Paiute
122 Ruby Valley Shoshone
91 Kaliwa
121 Spring Valley Shoshone
132 Shivwits Southern Paiute
135 Chemehuevi Southern Paiute
134 San Juan Southern Paiute

GROUP 9
71 San Joaquin Mono
92 Akwa'ala
36 Yurok

GROUP 10
93 Alkatcho Carrier
33 Chetco
30 Siuslaw
29 Alsea
31 Coos
28 Tillamook
34 Galice Creek
32 Tututni
35 Tolowa
38 Hupa
39 Wiyot
37 Karok
115 Kidu-Dokado Northern Paiute

119 Washo

GROUP 11
110 Wishram
137 Walapai
138 Northeast Yavapai
107 Nez Percé

GROUP 12
90 Desert Diegueño
82 Luiseño
83 Cupeño
86 Pass Cahuilla
89 Western Diegueño
88 Mountain Diegueño
87 Mountain Cahuilla
85 Desert Cahuilla
70 Southern Miwok
69 Central Miwok
68 Northern Miwok
97 Upper Lillooet

GROUP 13
142 Kamia
145 Pima

GROUP 14
112 Klamath
3 Massett Haida
2 Southern Tlingit
1 Northern Tlingit
98 Upper Thompson

GROUP 15
157 Western Navajo
158 Eastern Navajo
156 Jicarilla Apache
154 Mescalero Apache
155 Lipan Apache
153 Huachuca Chiricahua Apache
152 Warm Springs Chiricahua Apache
147 North Tonto Western Apache
151 White Mountain Western Apache
150 Cibecue Western Apache
149 San Carlos Western Apache
148 South Tonto Western Apache
113 Modoc
129 Uintah Ute
130 Uncompaghre Ute

131 Wimonuch Ute
139 Southeast Yavapai

GROUP 16
108 Umatilla
109 Klikitat
104 Kalispel
56 Mountain Maidu
62 Yana

GROUP 17
53 Atsugewi
146 Papago
45 West Shasta
44 East Shasta
47 Trinity River Wintu
48 McCloud River Wintu
49 Sacramento River Wintu
94 Lower Carrier
96 Shuswap
95 Chilcotin

GROUP 18
78 Tubatulabal
99 Southern Okanagon
125 Bohogue Shoshone
111 Tenino
117 Owens Valley Northern Paiute
46 Chimariko
128 Wind River Shoshone
126 Agaiduku Shoshone
42 Nongatl
40 Sinkyone
79 Kawaiisu

GROUP 19
76 Lake Yokuts
75 Kaweah Yokuts
72 Kings River Mono
73 Chuckchansi Yokuts
74 Kings River Yokuts
58 Mountain Nisenan
57 Foothill Nisenan
81 Gabrieliño
77 Yauelmani Yokuts
59 Southern Nisenan
52 West Achomawi
51 East Achomawi
80 Salinan

GROUP 20
144 Maricopa
143 Cocopa
140 Mohave
141 Yuma

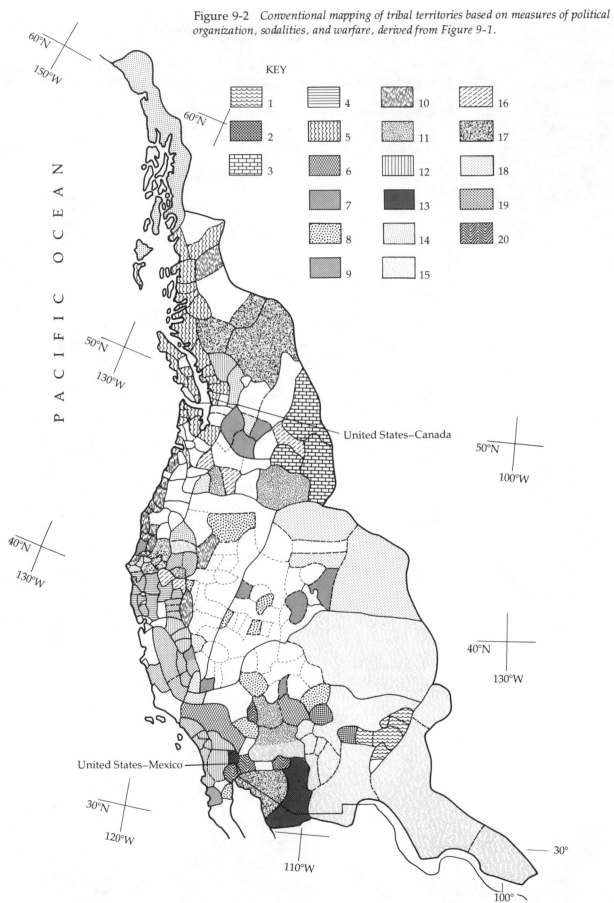

Figure 9-2 *Conventional mapping of tribal territories based on measures of political organization, sodalities, and warfare, derived from Figure 9-1.*

KEY

1		4		10		16	
2		5		11		17	
3		6		12		18	
		7		13		19	
		8		14		20	
		9		15			

PACIFIC OCEAN

United States–Canada

United States–Mexico

groups in a village—with the exception of the Tsimshian villages, some Central and Northern Nootkan* summer villages, and the Mattole, Sinkyone, and Nongatl villages—there were as many political units as there were kinship units. Each residential kinship-unit possessed its own chief, protected its own resources, allocated its own resources, and settled its own disputes. Yet in these ranked societies, the chiefs of each residential kinship-group in a village often convened in order to discuss the scheduling of village affairs, and might even form *ad hoc* alliances to protect against raids, or to mount counterattacks. Among the Haidas, Tlingits, and the Haisla Kwakiutl, moiety and phratry relations formally crosscut kinship groups and villages, but did not provide political organization beyond the residential kinship-group.

The patrilineages organized into single-village communities (monolineages) among the Miwok and Costanoan groups in the central part of California, and the patrisibs among the Uto-Aztecans and Yumans of Southern California were, like the demes and lineages of the Northwest Coast, economically and politically sovereign. Kinship groups, either lineages or sibs, owned and administered territories which included water sites and all key food-gathering sites. Relations with most neighbors were formalized through moiety organizations.

---

*Only two Nootkan societies have been included in our sample—the Clayoquot representing the Central Nootkan tribes and the Makah representing the Southern Nootkan tribes (Drucker 1951). There were five Northern Nootkan tribes (Chickliset, Kyuquot, Ehetisat, Nuchatlet, and Moachat), perhaps nine Central Nootkan tribes (Hesquiat, Ahousat, Clayoquot, Ucluelet, Toquat, Uchucklesit, Ohiat, Tsishaat, and Hopachisat), and two Southern Nootkan tribes (Nitinat and Makah). In retrospect the author feels that he should have included at least one Northern Nootkan society in the sample, perhaps the Moachat, for whom some eighteenth-century accounts are available. The principal scholar of the Central and Northern Nootkan societies, Philip Drucker, did not cover any Northern Nootkan societies in his *Culture Element Distributions: XXVI Northwest Coast* (1950), and his monumental *The Northern and Central Nootkan Tribes* (1951), though a sensitive comparative analysis, does not facilitate ferreting out cultural information on 292 topics for any particular Northern Nootkan tribe, so a Northern Nootkan tribe was not analyzed statistically. On the other hand, Drucker (1951) assesses Northern and Central Nootkan political organizations before and after the time of first European contact in some detail, so we use this information and refer to it at several points in this chapter.

The differences in size, cultural complexity, complexity of intergroup relations, and locally available subsistence resources among Great Basin nuclear families, Northwest Coast demes and lineages, Miwok and Costanoan patrilineage villages, and Southern California patrisib organizations were remarkable, yet not one of these groups, except for the Northwest Coast societies mentioned above, were organized into political units larger than residential kinship groups. It is accurate to say that the political units of the type that we have called "residential kinship-group" ranged from the absence of political organization (central Great Basin) to political organizations fully embedded in kinship organization (Miwok and Costanoan villages, and sibs of Southern California), and to those fully embedded in ranked kinship organizations (Northwest Coast).

Villages and Bands

Sometimes local societies were composed of several residential kinship-groups which, when united, recognized a common leadership and a common territory, and recognized no jurisdiction beyond the local organization; we have classified such political units as bands or villages.

Bands, as among the Apacheans, Eastern Shoshones, Utes, some Yavapai groups, and some Plateau groups, such as the Shuswap and Upper Thompson, and perhaps also the Coeur d'Alene and Flathead, formed into residential units for only part of the year. Eastern Shoshones and Utes dispersed into local deme communities of 60 or more people under a headman during the winter months, but in the summer periods several such communities convened into large residential units that recognized common territories. Each aggregation was directed by a band chief and his assistants. Special groups would split off from bands during the summer periods for raiding, trading, and hunting ventures. The Western Apaches and Southeast Yavapai reversed this pattern. During the summer periods they resided in sib communities that were located near their water and farm sites. During the winter periods several sibs formed into flexible bands, and it was during these periods that such bands usually conducted raids on sedentary villages.

The Western Apache sibs protected their private farm sites, watering sites, and some gathering sites, but entire bands recognized hunting territories. Thus, the Western Apaches combined the advantages of localized kinship-groups, private-property rights, and predictable food products, with the flexibility of mobile hunting, raiding, and trading bands.

The Eastern Apache local deme communities were about the same size as the Ute and Eastern Shoshone demes, yet they seem to have coalesced into bands rarely. They hunted and collected plants in their own territories for much of the year, but might join with members of other local deme communities to embark on a bison hunt or a raiding venture. Although characterized by mobility, the Eastern Apaches seem not to have organized into large summer or winter bands so regularly as the Utes, Eastern Shoshones, Western Apaches, and Southeast Yavapai. When they did, the most influential headman most probably directed the group, but he was advised by the other headmen.

The Upper Thompson and Shuswap of the Fraser Plateau, and the Coeur d'Alene and Flathead of the Upper Columbia region, each organized several winter villages of perhaps 100 people per community into large summer bands. Every band was directed by a chief with assistance of leaders from each winter village. The territories for such bands were the aggregate hunting territories of all the winter villages in the band. During the summer bison hunts in the historic or post-Contact period, both Coeur d'Alene and Flathead equestrian bands coalesced into tribes, but it is not clear whether these tribal organizations were created in the pedestrian, pre-Contact period. It is likely that they were not, and that bands did not merge until horses were acquired and the Upper Columbia people could hunt over a much expanded terrain, including the western flanks of the Great Plains.

Band-type organizations were restricted exclusively to the hunters and gatherers in mountainous regions who had access to several biotic zones and relatively abundant resources, including some large game and herd animals. These resources were, however, diffuse and, when the animals are considered, mobile. Likewise, the bands were mobile. The Western Apaches, though not occupying regions abundant in large game, had the advantages of storable agricultural products to help sustain them during part of each year. The Western Apaches could hunt, gather wild plants, and farm during summer periods as localized sibs, and trade, raid for farm products from more southern neighbors, and hunt as bands during the winter periods. The contrast of the seasonal patterns of the Western Apache bands with the fission and fusion of the Ute, Eastern Shoshone, Flathead, and Shuswap bands in the more northern areas, and with the Eastern Apaches, who formed bands irregularly and then only during summer bison hunts, was marked and most surely related to the environmental and economic differences among the bands in western North America.

Villages, in our taxonomy, were the equivalents of bands in many respects, though they demonstrated a much wider range of organizational complexity than that which characterized bands. Village political organizations embraced and coordinated several kinship groups, and villages had more permanency throughout each year and over many years than did bands.

An interesting point about village organizations is that they ranged from the simplicity of Plateau winter villages, composed of perhaps five or six multiple family lodges (bilateral lineal families) directed by a headman whose ultimate authority was suasion, to the Tewa villages of the Eastern Pueblos, in which sodality leaders, appointed to their positions, possessed sufficient authority to exact labor, allocate resources, and even banish people from the community.

For the pre-Contact period there is little evidence that any political organizations were more complex than the Pueblo villages of the Tanoans and Eastern Keres. There were, on the other hand, some political organizations that, for certain purposes such as warfare (River Yumans), or for protection and ceremonial purposes (the Nisenans and the Salinans of California), embraced many villages or hamlets spread over wide regions. We shall discuss these territorial organizations in the following section. Although River Yuman tribes, for instance, integrated people distributed over territories larger than those of the Eastern Pueblo villages for some purposes, those purposes were few and authority was never so final as it was among the Tanoans and the Eastern Keres Pueblos.

There is some evidence that the Chumash of California (see Landberg 1965: 34–35) were welded into loose federations in which several villages, some as large as 1,400 people, and satellite hamlets were directed by a principal chief from the principal village of each federation. The authority invested in such chiefs, who for intervillage affairs dominated the chiefs of each village, is only scantily understood. Prior to European contact, then, the Chumash may well have been organized into "districts" of ranked villages and concomitant ranked chieftancies capable of controlling subsistence activities, protecting district boundaries, and punishing people who did not attend intervillage affairs. If the Chumash were organized in such a fashion they would constitute the most complex territorial organizations in western North America prior to Contact. On the basis of our current knowledge, however, the Eastern Pueblos, though organized only into single, autonomous villages, were the most complex, even though their hegemony did not extend beyond the village.

The simplest village organizations were those of the Pima and Papago groups and the majority of Plateau groups. In the Plateau, villages of 100 people or more convened during the winter in permanent communities of several lodges. Each village selected a chief from among the household heads. Among the Pimas, villages were composed of two or more pat-ridemes organized under a leader whose authority was based principally on prestige and good will. He coordinated central irrigation projects (excavation and cleaning), and formed alliances with neighbors on *ad hoc* houses both for irrigation projects and for common defenses when attacked by Apacheans or River Yumans.

At a more complex level than the Plateau and Pima villages were the "tribelets" of California. "Tribelet" was Kroeber's (1966) term for a village community that often encompassed three or four settlements—one was a principal winter village with a large dance house, and the others were small satellite hamlets at short but varying distances from the principal village. In the northern part of the California culture area, from the Sierra to the coast, it was common for tribelets to be composed of many kinship groups, usually patribilateral families of modest size (stem or lineal families). Whereas the tribelet was not the sole land-owning group—in various ways families or lineages, depending on the kinship organization of the tribelet in question, often owned and controlled strategic resources of one type or another within the tribelet—tribelet members shared a common territory whose boundaries they and their neighbors recognized, in which the tribelet members hunted. The tribelet protected the entire area against trespass, even though private claims of families or lineages to some of the strategic resources within many areas were recognized.

As was asserted in previous chapters, it is possible that the tribelets of the northern part of the California culture area arose from the aggregation of several discrete, autonomous, property-owning kinship groups, perhaps the majority of which were unilineal descent groups much like the monolineage Miwok communities at one time. The tribelets of the northern part of California were not the exact equivalents of the independent kinship-groups of the Northwest Coast, Southern California, or the monolineages of the central part of the California culture area, because some forms of property were usually owned by families within each tribelet rather than by the tribelet as community property. It was specifically the owner-ship of key strategic resources by kinship groups that seems to have been the major factor inhibiting the development of political organization in the richly endowed extractive regions of the far West.

Territories for the tribelets of the northern part of California, then, are best understood as the property boundaries defended by the group. The factor of de-fense against poaching, in conjunction with the prac-tice of joint sponsorship of feasts and rituals, marked these interesting political communities. The political communities that were formed in the densely popu-lated and culturally and linguistically diverse areas of Northern California, on the other hand, did not award great authority to chiefs, especially in regard to the control of many of the key resources within each tribelet's boundaries.

The tribelets in Northern California tended to be composed of many patribilateral families (several lineages among the Patwin), whereas in the San Joa-quin Valley of Central California most were com-posed of several patrilineages each (Yokuts and Mono groups) and the remainder were composed of pat-ribilateral families (some Yokuts, the Mono, the Kawaiisu, and the Tubatulabal). North of the San Joa-quin tribelets the Miwoks and Costanoans resided in sovereign patrilineage communities, and south of Tehachapi Pass, the Uto-Aztecans and Yumans of Southern California were organized into sovereign patrisibs.

Although the San Joaquin tribelets in general pos-sessed larger territories than the Miwok lineages and integrated more kinship groups than either the Miwoks or the Southern California sibs, from the Miwoks on the north to the Western Diegueño on the south, each tribelet and residential kinship-group community possessed moieties or their equivalents (reciprocating lineages in different villages in some instances, and reciprocating villages in others) which helped to regulate relations among neighbors. If the neighboring sibs or lineage communities were of the same moiety they joined forces in order to sponsor some feasts and certain ceremonials. If they were moiety opposites, they sponsored key events for each other and, more than likely, exchanged women in marriage.

Among the San Joaquin tribelets, though both moieties were usually represented in each tribelet, each moiety in each tribelet would host its opposite from a different tribelet. The presence of moieties in intertribelet affairs in the central part of the California culture area and in Southern California may well have been instrumental in obviating either the pro-tracted raiding northward in California or the devel-opment of bilateral kinship-organizations (and the concomitant loss of some kinship control over private strategic resources), or both. In the San Joaquin drainage, from the northernmost Miwok village southward, the shadings from independent lineage communities (Miwok), into multiple lineage tribelets (Yokuts, Mono), and bilateral tribelets (Yokuts, Mono) suggests a developmental political sequence in which kinship and ceremonial organization were the princi-pal organizing factors.

The most complex and centralized political organi-zations in western North America were the villages among the Tanoan and Keresan Pueblos in the Southwest where, for the most part, sodalities or dual sodalities (nonexogamous moieties) with supreme ritual authorority transcended kinship groups and controlled political and many principal economic affairs.

The Tsimshian villages of the northern Northwest Coast were somewhat less organized than the Tanoan and Keresan villages, whereas the pre-Contact Central and Northern Nootkan summer villages of the central Northwest Coast and the Mattole, Sinkyone, and Nongatl villages of northwestern California were somewhat less organized than those of the Tsimshians.

Among the year-round Tanoan, Eastern Keres, and Tsimshian villages, resource areas were set aside and owned by village chiefs. Members of any and all sibs (in Tsimshian and Keresan villages) and families (among the Tanoans) could be required to work to procure food from those areas and give them to the chiefs. Moreover, all sibs in each Tsimshian village contributed goods and food upon demand of its chief when potlatches were sponsored in the name of the village. In the Tewa villages, family members contributed labor to maintain the storehouses of the sodality chiefs and assistants, and to sponsor ceremonials. In the event of food scarcities, chiefs of Tanoan, Eastern Keres, and Tsimshian villages had the authority to allocate subsistence resources in the village, no matter who procured them. Many Tanoan and Eastern Keres village authorities even exercised the power to punish crimes and to evict families from farmland and from the village. In other Tanoan and Eastern Keres villages, and in Tsimshian villages, arbitrators were called in to settle disputes.

The Clayoquot Nootka society, a Central Nootkan society, was similar to Northern Nootkan societies in that summer villages were composed of residents of several winter villages, and each winter village was composed of one deme or more. So summer villages brought together many demes, each with its own leader and with its independent ranking relative to the other demes. The summer village was allied under the direction of a principal chief and several lesser chiefs representing the high-ranking demes. During the summer they organized for common defense and sponsored ceremonials. In the post-Contact period, the summer village chief allocated civic duties and organized raiding parties, but even then the Nootkan political organizations were never so centralized as those of the Tsimshians, who, during the post-Contact trade period, created chiefdoms incorporating two or more villages.

The Mattole, Nongatl, and Sinkyone Athapaskans of northwestern California were organized into villages, each directed by a chief whose closest assistant was a shaman. These villages provided a considerable contrast to the neighboring Hupa, Karok, Yurok, and Wiyot, who had no political organization beyond the family. It is plausible that these Athapaskans were the most recent people to settle in northwestern California, and that in order to secure a territory, they had to force their ways in among the residential kinship-groups to the north, and the tribelets (or their precursors) to the south and east who already occupied territories in the region.

Districts and Tribes

The largest political territorial units in pre-Contact western North America did not allocate as much control of community and personal affairs to their leaders as did the Tanoan and Keresan villages. *Districts* are defined as political units comprising two or more villages. *Tribes* were the more mobile counterparts of districts, being composed of several bands. Structurally, districts and tribes differed only in that districts were organizations that encompassed relatively sedentary villages, whereas bands, as we pointed out, were flexible and relatively mobile organizations.

It is possible that the Flathead and Coeur d'Alene possessed tribal organizations prior to Contact, but it is also likely that tribes emerged only after the Upper Columbia people acquired the horse; the latter view will be maintained here. During the equestrian period, several bands convened during the summers when communal bison hunts were possible. Large hunts were most successfully undertaken on horseback because horses provided the mobility necessary to pursue bison herds for extended periods. During the summer periods, at least in the nineteenth century, tribal organizations were invoked that provided defense, formed alliances, allocated civic duties to members, punished crimes, and distributed scarce food resources. The authority was lost, of course, when the tribes disbanded each fall. Large quantities of fish and roots allowed the winter villages of the Coeur d'Alene and Flathead to be rather more sedentary than the Shoshone and Ute bands to the southeast.

District organizations, on the other hand, very probably were of pre-Contact origin among the Salinans and the Nisenan peoples of California, the River Yumans of the Southwest, and among the poorly reported Chumash of California. Each of these groups had access to large quantities of storable resources, were sedentary for much of the year, and possessed political organizations that, for some issues, made decisions that affected residents of several villages.

The villages that composed the Nisenan districts of the northern part of the California culture area performed collective ceremonials and formed alliances for defense. The River Yuman tribes—Mohave, Yuma, Maricopa, Cocopa—stretched over vast regions along the Colorado River; hamlets were dispersed along the river banks adjacent to good farmland and stands of mesquite. The various River Yuman districts, or "nationalities" as Kroeber (1925) called them,* farmed and protected their common boundaries. But centralized control was almost completely limited to the conduct of intertribal warfare. Among the Salinans, organization does not seem to have operated except to marshal defensive alliances among villages (tribelets).

Let us turn our attention to leadership and the realms of authority, so as to gain better understanding of the aboriginal polities of western North America.

Leadership and Realms of Authority

Nominal authority, whose principal form was suasion, invested either in a kinship group leader or, when several kinship groups coalesced, some respected person in the group, was standard in much of the West (Map Cu-162, V-332). Centralized leadership beyond the residential kinship-group was absent among many Kwakiutl, Salish, and Great Basin communities, the communities of Southern California, and among the Yurok, Karok, Hupa, Wiyot, and Akwa'ala. When there were several demes in the same Kwakiutl or Salish village, each one remained essentially autonomous, though the chiefs of the demes, who were no more than leaders of their respective kinship groups, frequently gathered to discuss the scheduling of ceremonies and some other village affairs.

In only slightly lesser degree this was true for the pre-Contact Haidas, Tlingits, and all other coastal groups with the exception of the Central and Northern Nootkans, the Tsimshian groups, and the Mattole, Nongatl, and Sinkyone groups. Each Haida and Tlingit matrilineage was directed by a chief, yet Haida and Tlingit villages, at least in post-Contact times, also had village chiefs who were empowered to guide ceremonial affairs. Such chiefs did not possess authority over the village for common defense (Map Cu-163, V-335), the allocation of food during times of scarcity (Map Cu-164, V-336), or power to allocate access to subsistence resources (Map Cu-165, V-337).

The importance of kinship groups in controlling access to their private resources all of the time, and to their food in times of scarcity, was evident in Southern California and on the Northwest Coast, even among the Nootkans, who had more complex village organizations than either the Haidas or the Tlingits. It appears that investiture of private resource ownership in kinship groups was the principal deterrent to the formation of complex political organizations throughout most of the Northwest Coast, including organizations for common defense. The same factor must have been operating in Southern California where sibs were localized and separated from other sibs; but the effect of private property ownership seems to have been even more powerful among Northwest Coast societies in which several different kinship groups often resided in the same village and occupied ranked positions that were determined, ultimately, by the goods they gave away, hence, the resources they controlled. That is, the goods people gave away were a function of the resource base of the kinship group and the kinship labor that was invested in extraction and production from that base.

Haida and Tlingit chiefs, similar to kinship-group leaders in most other societies which recognized no authority beyond the residential kinship-group, did not have the authority to demand that people in these communities who did not belong to the leader's kinship group join together in common defense. In the post-Contact era there were households of propertyless people who worked in the households of the ranking lineages, and not even these people could be forced into battle or into labor in the name of the village. Haida and Tlingit chiefs could, however, draw together the kinship-group chiefs in order to form alliances on temporary bases as exigencies of the moments required (Map Cu-166, V-339), but then again, any and all chiefs in any multiple kinship-group village on the Northwest Coast could do this.

The principal fashion in which Tlingits and Haidas differed from the societies that did not recognize authority beyond each residential kinship-group was that Haida and Tlingit village chiefs could organize several kinship groups within the village for ceremonial purposes, but they could not conscript members to conduct civic duties for ceremonials or other purposes (Map Cu-167, V-338). This was modest political organization indeed.

The Karok, Yurok, Hupa, and Wiyot lived in hamlets that were straggled along rivers. They had no centralized authority. They had only powerful men

---

*See Chapter 8 for a discussion of the possible development of River Yuman "nationalities" from the development of multilocal sibs.

who gained and maintained their reputations through the accumulation of wealth and its manipulation. They were central to community affairs, such as sponsorship of world-renewal ceremonies, but they possessed no authority.

Throughout the central and western portions of the Great Basin, and in most Pai territory in the Southwest, the political issues were not how to retain and protect strategic resources, but how to find them. The scarce and diffuse resources of those regions supported so few people that private ownership of strategic resources was not a critical issue, though common defense, at least through alliances, held some importance to the Pais who, from the 1500s, were flanked on the east by Navajos and Apaches and on the west by the River Yumans. Families could move from camp to camp—permanently or as temporary residents. There can be little doubt that flexible organizations of this type, where fissions and fusions were not unusual, were correlated with at least three factors: the fluctuating resources of the intermontane areas, the whims of particular families, and the competencies of the various headmen who emerged as leaders.

A Great Basin headman developed a reputation for being knowledgeable and successful, and this was attested to as families joined his camp. They were under no obligation to stay, and might well move on, attaching to a new camp following a collective fishing venture or a successful antelope drive, or a pleasant round-dance. The leaders of the camps had no authority over resources or people, but they were respected and, through suasion, scheduled the subsistence movements of the group, gave advice about ceremonies, and the like.

The emphasis on competence in leadership without control characterized the headmen of Great Basin groups, Pais, the Akwa'ala, and some Plateau groups. In general, competence was more critical than inheritance in determining leadership. The same thing was true in band societies, yet in band societies the chiefs exercised authority over some decisions, and did not guide merely through suasion. Families were usually free to leave bands, but while attached to bands they were directed by a chief and his council. Chiefly councils were usually composed of several local residence-group headmen, and the most prestigious of them, usually because of his knowledge and his success in directing hunts, protecting the group, directing raids, and so forth, was the chief.

The authority of band chiefs and their counsels were restricted to the periods during which the bands were convened, and usually extended to mounting raids and directing the group's defense against raids, and in a few instances forming alliances (examples being the Wind River Shoshone, Agaiduku Shoshone, Chiricahua Apache, Flathead, and Coeur d'Alene). During the post-Contact period, Flathead and Coeur d'Alene chiefs were empowered to allocate scarce food and punish crimes, whereas the Coeur d'Alene chiefs also allocated civic duties to people in the tribe and allocated access to tribal subsistence resources to people from other tribes (Map Cu-168, V-340). Except for the punishment of crimes, which was within the authority invested in the majority of village chiefs in the Columbia Plateau, the other authority invested in Coeur d'Alene and Flathead leadership was unusual for band organizations, and may be the result of increased contacts with Plains people during the historic period, when summer congregations of bands became very large, being replete with large horse herds, and authority over camp affairs became a critical factor in the organization of bison-hunting societies on the northern Plains.

In general, band chiefs gained their positions through competence, though it was not uncommon for leaders to be sons of leaders. Chiefly counsel was followed in subsistence pursuits, in deciding when to move camp, and on deciding whether to aid a neighboring band in distress. Authority to punish people who did not obey these decisions was lacking.

Village organizations varied widely in the authority invested in village leaders. In the Plateau, chiefs were successful heads of bilateral lineal families who were counseled by other prominent household heads. In about half of the Plateau villages the chiefs and their assistants directed the defense operations. In general, the Plateau villages were very pacifistic. They did not regularly raid other Plateau villages, and only the groups on the periphery of the area developed defensive raiding to any degree. Yet the emphasis on pacifism and, as we have already seen, trade and the sharing of resource areas was not without structure. Leaders were selected for their competence, and leaders or their designates practically everywhere had the authority to punish crimes within the village, such as murder, adultery, or some other acts that were considered to be criminal. The relative harmony and generosity of these villages were not solely supported by good will. Authority was delegated within the village so that disruptive acts could be controlled.

Pima villages were directed by a chief, himself the leader of one of the patridemes in the village. Other deme leaders counseled the chief. The Pima village leaders organized the men in the village for common defense, and in the historic period, when they were besieged by protracted raids from the Apaches and warfare with the Yuma, they made alliances with other Pima villages on *ad hoc* bases. Pima chiefs did not have sole authority over the allocation of farm resources, but with the consent of the several families in each deme they allocated farmlands along the canals and ditches, and directed the digging and cleaning of the main irrigation canals. Their authority in allocating civic duties, such as the canal projects, as well as land allocation, was nominal. The chief's will could be resisted, but villages respected their leaders and, out of respect and good will, generally followed the advice of the chief and his counsel. The authority of Pima chiefs and their counsels stands in striking contrast to the authority invested in the leaders of the Pueblo canal-irrigation societies, thereby providing a severe challenge to the "hydraulic hypothesis" advanced by Wittfogel and Goldfrank (1943) and supported by many subsequent scholars (see Eggan 1950, Dozier 1970). The "hydraulic hypothesis" postulates a sufficient relationship between the need to control water in a society whose subsistence economy was based on canal irrigation, and the centralization of political authority in offices that would control the water system as well as make other key decisions in the society. Pima waterworks were huge and complex for the aboriginal Southwest, yet the authority system was based principally on suasion, respect, and good will.*

The tribelets in the northern part of California selected leaders in several ways. Among Valley Maidu and Foothill Maidu groups the leaders of the principal sodalities also directed the tribelets. Elsewhere in the California culture area, prestigious leaders frequently inherited their positions through the patriline, but leaders of the Wappo and some neighboring Pomo groups succeeded to leadership through the matriline. Among the Yokuts groups there were at least two principal chiefs in each tribelet, one representing each moiety. The bilateral Yokuts groups often had more than two chiefs, and they normally acted as counsels.

The chiefs of all California tribelets practically always received advice from the heads of the leading families, or from sodality leaders, or from powerful shamans. As a matter of fact, a single shaman, either as a leader in a sodality organization, or simply as an independent operator, very frequently exercised authority nearly equal to that of the chief, and many of their decisions were announced jointly.

Chiefs of California tribelets directed the defense of the village against raids and poachers, made alliances with neighboring tribelets, sponsored the principal intervillage feasts, and allocated some civic duties in conducting the feasts, public rituals, and building the large dance house in each principal village.

In a few tribelets (Yokuts, Patwin, Nomlaki, Yuki, for examples) the leaders could call on the villagers to pool and redistribute their food resources during periods of scarcity, or for moiety rituals (Yokuts, Mono), but they did not control the access of tribelet members to subsistence resources, and they seldom exercised the power to punish crimes (Maidu chiefs, who were also the leaders of the sacred sodalities, had limited authority to settle disputes, as did Yokuts leaders). Arbitrators attempted to settle most internal disputes stemming from crimes.

In California, the political organizations of the tribelets were oriented much more toward external affairs and external threats than toward internal controls. It may have been the case that shamans and sodality leaders, with their privileged knowledge and the specter of supernatural power at their service, exercised subtle social controls through intimidation (e.g., see Gayton 1930).

Western Pueblo settlements were multiple sib villages, and in some ways these villages were more centrally organized than, say, most of the multideme and multilineage villages of the Northwest Coast, but they delegated much less authority to village leaders than the Eastern Pueblos. At the several Hopi villages, including Hano (Hopi Tewa), and at the Western Keres village of Laguna, the separate lineages (local segments of the sibs) controlled kiva (sodality) ceremonies, and the male leader of each lineage was the "father" of that lineage. In this position he oversaw the ceremonial functions of his lineage's sodality, and he joined with other kiva-sodality leaders in forming factions that deliberated about village affairs. Although the leader of the "bear" sib was usually regarded as the "village father" and controller of the most important ceremonies in the annual calendar, the village father was unable to conscript labor for the common good, demand food storages from village residents and redistribute them in times of scarcity, assign or reassign farm sites that did not belong to his lineage, or commit his village to alliances with other villages. Beyond the religious authority and suasion invested in the leaders of each kiva society, or the temporary factions that they formed, there was little authority in the villages.

At Zuni Pueblo a somewhat higher level of village integration was achieved through a bow priesthood that coordinated the annual rituals and the performances of the villagers in those rituals. It is likely that the priesthood emerged through the coordination of rituals that were once invested in the sibs, and this may well have occurred in the post-Contact period. Political authority to allocate civic duties, to form alliances,

---

*See Joseph G. Jorgensen, n.d., "Comparative Traditional Economics and Ecological Adaptations."

to allocate farmland, or to pool and redistribute food in times of scarcity, was not invested in the Zuni priesthood.

The numbers and constancy of lineages or sibs at any point in time in Western Pueblo village history varied. Eggan (1950) has pointed out that many sibs died out through the lack of child-bearing women. Undoubtedly, the rituals that were critical to the annual ceremonial calendar were transferred from one to another sib and kiva society when the kinship groups that controlled rituals could no longer continue to control them (Eggan 1950). It is plausible that at Zuni Pueblo in historic times, as the population dwindled, the sodalities and the priesthood gained some independence from the lineages or sibs and provided stability to the ceremonial affairs of the village.

At Acoma, the other Western Keres village (along with Laguna), the "antelope" sib chief was the chief of the village. He and his sib could organize the village for common defense, redistribute the food that belonged to sibs in times of scarcity, allocate farm land, allocate civic duties in preparing for ceremonials, and control the kiva societies. Yet kinship groups retained ownership of their farm land and houses, and kinship group leaders counseled with and influenced the antelope sib chief.

Whereas Zuni may well represent that a centralized ceremonial organization could be created somewhat independently of kinship groups from several ceremonial organizations that were at one time controlled by kinship groups, Acoma may well represent that political authority could be invested in a sib chief whose duties at one time were restricted to that of ceremonial leader of the village. Whereas each Hopi village did not empower its village fathers, residents of Acoma did, and whereas the Zuni created a priesthood that crosscut kinship groups, and vested it with some power, the Acoma and Hopi did not follow suit.

The distinctive powers retained by matrilineal kinship-groups separated the Western Pueblos from Eastern Keres and Tanoan Pueblos. As we have already pointed out, the Eastern Keres and Tanoan Pueblos did not invest power in kinship groups, and their villages were more integrated and more centrally controlled in economic, social, ceremonial, and warfare matters than all other political communities in western North America.

Sodalities were important to all Western Pueblos in the sense that even when kinship groups owned and controlled certain kiva societies and their ceremonials, the kiva societies recruited members from many lineages beyond the lineage of the controlling kinship group. A person might belong to several kiva societies, and the ceremonial bonds that held people together who were not kinsmen were the essence of community integration. There was much less integration and much less delegation of absolute authority in Western Pueblo villages than in the villages along the Rio Grande and its tributaries, as we have pointed out above.

The Mattole, Sinkyone, and Nongatl villages of northwestern California possessed chiefs who, along with shamans, scheduled the moves of villages during their subsistence pursuits, scheduled the times when ceremonies would be held, assumed nominal sponsorship of ceremonies, and requested that villages contribute foods for ceremonials, which the chiefs would redistribute. But chiefs could not require villages to support the chiefs' subsistence needs with food and shelter. Rather, chiefs gave more than they received. Chiefs were vested with the authority to punish disruptive crimes within the village—thus demonstrating an important difference between these Athapaskans of northwestern California and other societies on the Northwest Coast, and an important similarity with their neighbors to the south (Yuki, Northern Pomo)—to form alliances with other villages, and to organize and direct common defense. The authority to organize and direct the defense operations of the village was invested in most political authorities in the tribelets of the northern subarea of the California culture area but not among the groups of the northwestern California or the southern subareas of the Northwest Coast. It was speculated earlier that the centralization of authority over warfare and the control of crime within the village among the Mattole, Nongatl, and Sinkyone chiefs could well have stemmed from the competition to secure resource areas in a region already inhabited by people who had laid claim to resources that they protected with vigor and resolve.

The authority invested in Nootkan summer chiefs, Tsimshian village chiefs, Keresan sodality chiefs, and Tanoan dual-sodality chiefs has been discussed earlier in the section on "Government and Territorial Organization."

Among the territorial groups organized at the district level, the Nisenans and the River Yumans provide an interesting contrast. The chief and his counsel in each Nisenan district exercised considerable power over the major ceremonials, formally inviting hundreds of villagers from beyond each district to attend. Chiefs hired shamans to perform witchcraft, in part as a means of maintaining social control. District chiefs had little influence beyond ceremonial affairs, however. Village chiefs, rather than district chiefs, directed common defense, redistributed community food in times of scarcity, and called villagers to defend the village and to build the large dance houses. In conjunction with shamans, they also punished crimes within the villages. If covillages in a district were attacked, the village leaders could form alliances, and in such situations the district chief might be instrumental in influencing several villages to join together in defense of one village's territory.

In light of the authority invested in village chiefs and their counsels, and the loose districts which convened to sponsor ceremonies and operate under the control of a district chief when they did so (Voegelin 1942), it is interesting that the Nisenans were earlier considered to be "simple" in political and ceremonial organization by many people who attempted to piece together their ethnography (see Kroeber 1925, Beals 1933). Although the village leadership did not control access to all of the key subsistence-resource areas within their territories, the Nisenans, at the village level, allocated as much power to chiefs as the most centralized tribelets, and went them one better in their loose district organization.

The River Yuman "tribes," as was postulated in the preceding chapter, grew from prior localized sib-organizations. In the context of a river locale, where fish were plentiful, yet the nature of specific sites along the flood plains for farming was somewhat unpredictable following floods, and where the wide distributions of mesquite and screwbeans provided large amounts of food, the Yuman patrisibs became multilocal in distribution and lost their corporate functions. The tribes, or districts in our typology, emerged. This larger body was a "nationality" (Kroeber 1925) in sentiment, and it drew together primarily to wage war under the direction of war leaders, yet war leaders did not possess authority beyond drawing men from the dispersed hamlets together to wage wars of offense and defense. For the Mohave, for instance, who thought of themselves as a "national entity" (Kroeber 1925), war chiefs were the most respected of all leaders, though shamans, directors of tribal entertainments, and hereditary chiefs of the many sibs also participated in kinship and extrakinship government. War leaders, as the most revered leaders, rallied Mohaves to wage raids, and also committed Mohaves to alliances with the Yumas, their neighbors to the south. Entertainment directors drew people from near and far for festivals; and great shamans brought the nation together for cremations of deceased war leaders. War leaders governed battles with a hierarchy of officers below them. The emphases on war leaders, feats of bravery in battle, and the pursuit of, and fulfilling of, dream experiences that tested each man's mettle—causing them to do battle against great odds if necessary—were more obvious among the River Yumans and more integral to the fiber of their culture than anywhere else in western North America. Among Northwest Coast raiders, men often sought to fulfill

dream instructions by leading successful raids, but warriors *per se* did not enjoy the prominence that they enjoyed among the River Yumans. On the other hand, no River Yuman leader of any sort could allocate civic duties, or confiscate or assign farmland or gathering sites. Hereditary chiefs of the local segments of sibs could sometimes redistribute scarce food among sibmates and others who had joined the hamlet, but mostly such chiefs directed by suasion. Their defense and offense roles had long ago been usurped by war leaders.

Mode of Succession of Political Leaders

The manner by which political leaders succeeded to their positions varied, but in general, succession was based on achievement, though other factors, especially inheritance of position coupled with achievement, were involved (Map Cu-169, V-333). The role of succession through kinship varied. In general, the more variable the resource base and unpredictable the food supply, the less important the role of inheritance in succession to authority. Inheritance of positions of leadership was most prominent among the California Penutians and the Southern California Uto-Aztecans. Most of these groups were patrilineal or they possessed strong patricentered biases. In these societies positions of leadership passed from father to son, or from a man to his nearest patrikinsmen. Such a mode of succession was certainly compatible with the nature of the property-owning groups and the local moiety organizations among the Miwok, Yokuts, and Patwin societies in California, and Uto-Aztecans in Southern California. In these societies, patrilineages or patrisibs were either the sole land-owning and residential groups or, as among the Yokuts and Patwin, several such units comprised the tribelet. Among the Patwin one person served as the principal leader and other kinship group leaders formed a council, but among the Yokuts, either two moiety chiefs and their councils of kinship leaders, or several chiefs possessed equal authority (true of the Kaweah and Lake Yokuts). The Kaweah and Lake Yokuts stood out from most other California Penutians in that among them personal leadership qualities, influence, and prestige were necessary in addition to inheritance in order to attain positions of leadership. If the oldest son of a chief did not possess the requisite skills for leadership, a younger son or perhaps a brother's child would succeed to the position.

A combination of inheritance in the maternal line—from a chief to his sister's son—and possession of high rank and prestige through wealth, especially through potlatching and participation in winter ceremonials, marked the succession of chiefs in the northern subarea of the Northwest Coast. Whereas inheritance was emphasized in succession, it was critical that the aspirant to the position had been successful in accumulating and distributing wealth. Among tribes in other subareas of the Northwest Coast, from the Kwakiutl groups through the Mattole, no matter whether they were bilateral or patrilineal in descent organization, the accumulation of wealth, positions of relative rank, and demonstrated qualities of leadership outweighed factors of inheritance in determining succession to leadership. The emphasis in these societies, clearly, was on individual achievement and the demonstration of successes. Nevertheless, the son of a chief was more apt to succeed the chief than was someone else in the society.

Throughout the Plateau and among most of the Great Basin groups that recognized leaders, chiefs or headmen were usually succeeded by one of their sons, but invariably it was one who was recognized as possessing the qualities of leadership, a person of prestige and influence who could speak for a community.

Succession practices in the Southwest were differentiated on the basis of whether groups were Apachean (demonstrated ability to lead was more important, in general, than inheritance), Yuman (first dreaming of the acquisition of power,* then demonstrating that power had been acquired by proving to be a successful war leader), Western

Pueblo (kinship succession was the most prominent feature, and the oldest brother and sister in the matrilineage that possessed the highest-ranking kiva society were keys to succession inasmuch as the ceremonial chieftancy and nominal political chieftancy passed in the matriline from the chief to his sister's son), Eastern Pueblo (kinship succession was the least important feature, leaders being appointed by the medicine and war sodalities among the Keresans, and by alternating moieties—i.e., dual sodalities— among the Tanoans), or Pais and Pimans (leadership qualities were more prominent than kinship in succession).

In all of western North America the Tanoans and the Eastern Keres had the most centralized governments, and these groups alone invested the authority to name successors in such nonkinship bodies as dual sodalities, war sodalities, and medicine sodalities.* The memberships of these nominating and legitimizing groups crosscut the many kinship organizations in these societies—from nuclear families to matrisibs.

On the Modest Size of Political Units and the Modest Authority Invested in Leadership

The preceding discussions of territoriality, leadership, realms of authority, and succession have demonstrated that political development in western North America was modest. It was rare that what political power was invested in chiefs or in chiefs and their councils integrated more than one village or even transcended the powers of kinship groups to manage their own affairs. As we have learned, nearly half of the Indian societies in the West recognized residential kinship-groups as the ultimate level of jurisdiction.

The distribution of such modest political organization in such widely different culture areas as the Northwest Coast, Southern California, the Great Basin, California (Miwok and Costanoan groups), the Plateau, and the Southwest suggest that complex political organization was not necessarily correlated with the abundance of resources, the localization of

---

*To the River Yumans, "dreaming" was the basis of everything in life (Kroeber 1925: 754). Shamanistic power, myths and songs, bravery and fortune in war, a man's success with women, and special abilities were all acquired through dreaming. River Yumans were raised in a context in which dreams were emphasized and in which dreams, in conjunction with song cycles whose bases were in dreams, were related like stories were. Thus, without benefit of Jimson weed (Datura spp.) or other narcotizing agents, River Yumans dreamed, and often a dream would contain information about bravery, supernatural events, or song cycles that the recipient had already learned from his elders. The dreamer, however, organized the stories of supernatural events and song cycles according to the unique messages he received in his dreams, so that perhaps no two people possessed complete or identical knowledge of a myth that integrated, say, Mohave song cycles and tales of supernatural events. In this way each dreamer could possess a variant of the truth, and the most successful warriors demonstrated the power of their own dreams through their actions. Jimson weed was used to facilitate dreaming to acquire luck in gambling, but gambling luck, or gambling magic as we refer to the phenomenon in Chapter 11, is a special form of power distinct from the supernatural power crucial to other aspects of River Yuman life.

---

*Whereas the war sodalities among Eastern Keres villages were known to have given approval to the appointment of village chiefs, the chief of each village was the chief of the medicine sodality and his assistants also belonged to that sodality. See "Sodalities as the Organizations of Political, Economic, and Social Control" in this chapter (pages 239–240).

resources, the competition for resources, or with subsistence economies dominated by food production as opposed to food extraction. Indeed, whereas competition for resources may well have led to kinship-group property-ownership concepts and the maintenance of kinship-group sovereignty throughout the Northwest Coast, Southern California, and for the Miwok and Costanoan groups of California, in the Great Basin the competition for diffuse and unpredictable resources may well have led to the communitarian nature of resource sharing and the absence of political development. Whereas the routes to minimal political organization and no political organization appear to be rational in areas of localized abundance as well as diffuse scarcities, neither was a *necessary* outcome of competition. Some pairs of groups in similar and competitive contexts, such as the Tsimshian and the Haida groups, the Mattole and Wiyot groups, some Northern and Central Nootkans and the Southern Kwakiutl, the Northern (Plains) Miwok and the Patwin, and the Western Keres and the Eastern Keres, all developed quite different political organizations, yet coexisted in neighboring territories whose environments were very similar.

In our discussion of economic distribution in Chapter 7, we pointed out that California and Northwest Coast solutions to property ownership, barter, and gifting varied significantly, yet that the practices in the two areas could have been similar. There were no compelling reasons beyond fortuities to account for the differences in the economic organizations in those areas. In political organization as well, there was variation among groups that could have been organized in the same fashion. Whereas each political organization was rational in the sense that the accommodations struck among and between kinship groups over territory, defense, and the like seemed logical and reasonable, any one of several forms of political organization could have served most of the groups along the coast.

Nevertheless, the major portion of the Northwest Coast was inhabited by kinship groups whose members recognized no authority greater than themselves. The Tsimshians, who recognized villagewide authority invested in the chief of the most prominent sib, and the Central and Northern Nootkans, who recognized a chief and assistants (other deme chiefs) vested with limited authority over their summer villages, were the exceptions in the central and northern Northwest Coast. The Mattole, Nongatl, and Sinkyone villages in the northwestern California subregion of the Northwest Coast were the exceptions in that these villages were composed of several kinship groups under the direction of a chief, assisted by a shaman. These village organizations differed from tribelets in the California culture area in that greater

authority was invested in those Athapaskan village chiefs.

Tsimshian expansion at the expense of their Haida and Tlingit neighbors was undoubtedly aided by the development of centralized village organization among the Tsimshians, and the Mattole, Nongatl, and Sinkyone societies may well have been able to establish themselves in the Cape Mendocino region precisely because they organized into villages for mutual protection. For the greatest part, however, property-owning kinship groups were the ultimate sovereigns throughout the entire Northwest Coast. The claims of kinship groups to private property were probably an early development in the prehistory of the Northwest Coast, and kinship-group ownership rights, which were woven into an areawide ranking system, must have been persistent as well.

In California, the emergence of small tribelets as property-owning and property-defending groups seems to represent the consolidation of several kinship groups in each tribelet. In the process of consolidation into tribelets—either through the growth of one kinship group or the aggregation of several kinship groups—the liquidation of property ownership rights invested in individual kinship groups most probably occurred. Political organization was modest in these tribelets. It is likely, indeed, that many kinship groups in California retained their independence and sovereignty until late in the Contact period (as among the Miwoks), and in Southern California, several related lineages retained their sovereignty as sibs. Then, in the nineteenth century, several lineages were pushed together in single communities among the Miwoks, and several sibs were pushed together among some Diegueño and Cahuilla groups. Thus, the tribelets in the northern part of the California area may have emerged in the context of crowding and competition; yet in similar but less crowded contexts, the Miwoks, Costanoans, and groups making up the northwestern California cluster did not develop tribelets.

Among the Pimans, the Western Pueblos, and the Western Apaches, either demes or sibs (or their localized segments, lineages) owned property. Any political organization with jurisdiction over kinship groups in these societies was organized for the purposes of defense, or ceremonies, or raiding, so power invested in leaders was nominal. Yet among the Eastern Keres and the Tanoans, highly integrated political units existed that controlled corporeal and incorporeal property. Enormous powers were invested in these ruling bodies. There are no obvious reasons why organizations similar to the Eastern Pueblos did not occur among the Pimans and Western Pueblos, but they did not. Community control over key strategic resources was the exception rather than the rule among the societies in western North America that had localized and abundant resources.

Bands emerged in the mountainous regions where medium- and large-sized migratory game were abundant, yet where resources in general were diffusely distributed over the terrain. Even the game required some pursuit, and the bands that hunted game most often did so by following leaders who were competent hunt leaders. The Western Apaches were exceptional in that localized kinship groups in mountainous areas farmed and gathered, whereas the bands that integrated many localized kinship groups shared hunting territories and plundered the resources of farmers to the south, at least in early historic times. The localized resources of Western Apache sibs were distinguished from the resources of Western Apache bands. Among the Coeur d'Alene and Flathead bands, both localized fisheries and localized root grounds allowed for storage of food and the maintenance of rather stable winter villages, yet bands shared in these productive territories. Key hunting territories that had been improved with pitfalls, deadfalls, and the like, on the other hand, were owned by families close to the winter village, but the hunting territory in general was available to all members of the band and their guests. Flathead, Coeur d'Alene, and Shuswap bands most surely grew from the simpler winter village organizations throughout the Plateau, but did so in the specific context of the availability of game occurring in large herds in the mountainous regions where successful pursuit of game often required both teamwork and free access to wide territories. Protection too was necessary while pursuing migrating herds.

The genesis of Eastern Shoshone and Ute bands from the nonpolitical family camps of the Great Basin, and of Western Apache raiding and hunting bands from sibs and, eventually, multilocal sibs, appears obvious. The former were not composed of kinship units that made claims to private resources, but the latter were.

Bands, then, were highly correlated with organizational requirements for successful hunting in mountainous regions, and perhaps with raiding and protection from raids. Nonpolitical family camps, on the other hand, correlated highly with diffuse and scarce resources. The wide variety of nominal political organizations for the rest of western North America are best understood as accommodations among localized and property-owning kinship groups to get along with one another. The Eastern Keres seem to have stripped their matrilineal kinship groups of all key authorities, but only among the Tanoans were family organizations fully dominated by political–religious authority. As has been suggested above, Tanoan bilaterality, dual sodalities (nonexogamous moieties), and centralized political-religious authority were, conceivably, phenomena of post-Spanish contact.

SODALITIES

Sodalities, as we have defined them, were organizations whose members were not primarily determined by kinship or co-residence. Members of sodalities, then, were usually drawn from several kinship organizations within a society so that people from two or more kinship groups (families, demes, lineages) with separate economic interests belonged to the same extrakinship organization. Invariably, these organizations gained their legitimacy and their special charters through connections to spirits or gods in a supernatural world. The charters usually set forth the sacred history of the sodality, which explained how and in what ways various spirits created, or were forever connected to, the living culture. Some spirits brought medicine and healing which were then invested in the sodalities, some brought rain, some protection, and so forth. Not only did the sodalities have sacred dimensions which accounted for the present world by connecting it to the supernatural, thus rendering their basic premises immune to challenges from the profane and everyday world, but the sacred information was passed on through the generations so that each group of initiates maintained the information in secrecy.

The sacred information gained from supernatural beings was preserved by the sodality and passed to each initiate, either individually or in a group, through a formal ritual. The initiation rituals were important events in the affairs of each sodality, yet they were but a small part of their overall operations which, for the societies of the Northwest Coast, California, and Southern California, included some private performances (for sodality members only) and some public performances (for the entire community as well as guests from other communities) each winter. For Pueblo sodalities, private and public performances were sponsored throughout the year following an elaborate calendrical cycle which focused on the vernal and autumnal equinoxes, the winter and summer solstices, and the growing seasons for the domesticated crops (seasons of fertility, maturation, and harvest).

Sodalities were not present within all aboriginal groups in western North America. In point of fact, they were present among only a minority of cultures at the time of contact with Europeans, including most central and some northern Northwest Coast societies, most California and Southern California societies, and the Pueblo societies of the Southwest (Map Cu-170, V-341; Map Cu-171, V-342).

Tribal sodalities occurred in many California, all Southern California, and most Pueblo societies. They were the most encompassing forms of sodalities. Some tribal sodalities were composed of all adult males and females in the society; in some northwestern California societies and some California societies there was one separate tribal sodality for men and one separate sodality for women; and in some other California societies, all Southern California, and some Pueblo societies, tribalwide sodalities existed for men only.*

Other sodalities were *restricted* organizations. Membership in these groups was restricted to a select group of men, or a select group of women, or a select group that included both men and women in each society. Among central and northern Northwest Coast societies, the masked-dancing sodalities, which were restricted to a select group of high-ranking males and females (high-ranking males only among the Klahuse Salish), were the only sodalities in those communities. Restricted sodalities, in addition to tribal sodalities, were well developed among most societies in the northern part of the California culture area and the Pueblos.†

The Kutenai and Flathead, two groups located on the edge of the Plains, possessed restricted military sodalities that were more similar to the sodalities among Plains societies during the equestrian period than to the pre-Contact sodality organizations in other parts of western North America. It is plausible that Kutenai and Flathead military societies were created during the equestrian period. On the other hand, the Kutenai had a formal society of shamans, each member having received power from the Bluejay Spirit, that performed private cures and pub-

lic rituals; Flathead shamans also received power from the Bluejay Spirit and staged joint performances at a spirit dance but did not form a restricted sodality. The Bluejay complex, in which people received power through spiritual contacts with the Bluejay Spirit, was common throughout the Columbia Plateau. The complex was associated with spirit dancing—another widely distributed ceremonial phenomenon on the Plateau—but only among the Kutenai was there a sodality of Bluejay shamans with their own public ceremony. Among the Flathead several Bluejay-empowered shamans performed at the same ceremonies but not in coordinated fashion, either through explicit dance steps, songs, myths, or organization. The military and medicine sodalities of the Kutenai appear to have been stimulated by Plains models, and the Bluejay society among the Kutenai may have been a fusion of Plateau beliefs with the Plains concept of sodalities.

Sodalities as Intracommunity and Intercommunity Organizations

Tribal and restricted sodalities, with the exception of military sodalities among the Kutenai and Flathead societies, occurred along the Northwest Coast, in California, in Southern California, and among the Pueblos in the Southwest. The tribes in these areas that possessed sodalities shared all of the following features: (1) inflexibility in their postnuptial residence patterns, that is, there was little free movement of families from one community to another after settling in a community, though once settled they would move *with* that community; (2) relative sedentariness, so that permanent villages were occupied for more than half of each year (usually eight months to twelve months) and returned to regularly; and (3) some private property ownership of key strategic resources was invested in kinship groups. Several tribes in western North America that did not have sodalities also had these same three features of relative sedentariness, kinship-group ownership of property, and postnuptial-residence stability. Examples are the Pima, some of the northernmost groups in California (Wintus, Shastas, and their neighbors), and most groups in the southern subarea and northwestern California subarea of the Northwest Coast. A few groups, such as the Tanoan and Eastern Keres Pueblos, possessed sodalities but did not recognize private ownership of key strategic resources by kinship groups. These Eastern Pueblo societies differed from all other societies with sodalities, to wit: among the Eastern Keres Pueblos and the Tanoans, sodality or-

---

*In California, tribal sodalities in which all adult males and females were members could be found among the Eastern Pomo, some Miwok groups, the Kings River Mono, and the Kaweah Yokuts; and such sodalities existed also among the Pueblos, the Hopi, the Keresans, and the Jemez Towa (all the matrilineal Pueblos with the exception of the Zuni). California societies in which there were separate tribal sodalities, one for men and one for women, were those of the Mattole, Sinkyone, Kings River Yokuts, and Yauelmani Yokuts. Tribalwide sodalities for men only existed among the Kato, Yuki, Coast Yuki, Southern Pomo, Patwin, Lake Yokuts, and Salinan groups; these were also a feature of the Zuni and the Tewa Pueblos.

†The Wappo, Nomlaki, Maidus, and the Serraño groups possessed restricted sodalities only.

ganizations controlled the political, economic, and religious activities of their communities, and the leaders of these sodalities were the political leaders of the communities. It was surely not fortuitous that dual sodalities (nonexogamous moieties) among the Tanoan villages and medicine sodalities among the Keresan villages ultimately controlled the economic, political, religious, and curing functions within the society. They centralized political and economic control at the expense of kinship groups (bilateral families among the Tanoans, matrisibs among the Keresans) (Map Cu-172, V-344).

Most sodalities did not possess the powers of the Eastern Keres and Tanoan sodalities (Table 9-1). The sole feature that all sodalities shared, whether tribal or restricted, was a belief that each was derived from a supernatural source.

Each sodality in western North America was obligated to sponsor ritual performances on some regular basis—e.g., during the winter period for Northwest Coast dancing societies and California Kuksu cults (which will be discussed later in the chapter), and year-round for the Pueblo sodalities. Tribal sodalities, of course, performed rituals for all of the adult members of the tribe, and often for the uninitiated children as well, whereas restricted sodalities everywhere* also performed public rituals (Map Cu-173, V-345). The specific rituals performed by sodalities for the public varied, but they were drawn from a broad range of topics. Sodality rituals were addressed to the greatest number of topics among the Pueblos where weather control, crop fertility, curative functions, war preparation, and cleansing after battle were focuses for performances. The fewest purposes for sodality ceremonies were served by the masked performances given by privileged members of Northwest Coast sodalities. In these rituals, members reenacted the behavior of the spirits from whom the rights to stage privileged performances were gained. The masked dances of these societies were staged by people who owned the incorporeal property and rights which they displayed, and who always put on some performances before public audiences.

So whether sodalities had few or many functions, the one that practically all shared in common, aside from explicit initiation ceremonies, was the sponsoring of ritual and ceremonial trappings, such as feasts, perhaps gifting, games, gambling, and social dancing, which might accompany the public performances.

---

*The single known exception to this practice occurred in the Nomlaki society, whose sodalities did not perform publicly.

Table 9-1
Functions of sodalities

Culture area	Religious performances	Health and curing	Political services	Economic services	Political-economic control
Northwest Coast	+				
Northern California	+	+			
Central California	+	+			
Southern California	+	+			
Northern California Maidu	+	+	+		
Western Pueblos	+	+	+		
Tanoan–Eastern Keres Pueblos	+	+	+	+	+

Initiations varied in their complexity. In California and Southern California novices were separated from the rest of society and underwent extensive training in "schools." Sodality leaders taught the novices the sacred meanings of their cult and tribal histories, and for the first time the novices would come to understand the sacred meaning of some of the ritual acts and objects they had previously seen in public performances. The same was true in the Pueblos, where novices were separated from their families for a period and underwent extensive training, alternately being challenged, perhaps whipped or made to endure ordeals, and finally becoming a member of the sodality. As a new member, each person was obligated to the sodality and responsible for its well being. Each group of novices that underwent initiation together developed special bonds and a camaraderie that went beyond kinship lines and kinship obligations.

Let us reiterate that sodalities occurred only among those societies that could store considerable amounts of food each year, or could extract considerable amounts of food throughout the year. They also occurred where postnuptial residences were rather fixed, settlements rather permanent, and property concepts were rather well developed. It is interesting, therefore, that where private property concepts were most highly developed, along the Northwest Coast, many societies had no sodalities at all, and those that possessed them restricted membership to the highest-ranking members of the most important kinship groups. The sodalities reflected the ranking system, and sodality initiations, much like the potlatches that followed them, were restricted to the highest-ranking people.

By contrast, Plateau dwellers were more mobile and had more diffuse as well as fewer resources than their Northwest Coast congeners, yet adhered to a religious system that stressed individual acquisition of spirits and subsequent spirit dancing and spirit singing which reenacted spirit encounters. The Plateau people possessed no sodalities, but the winter ceremonials that they sponsored, which were open to all, without initiation, and in which spirit encounters were dramatized, were related very clearly to Northwest Coast dancing societies. In all likelihood, the two areas shared several aspects of a common cultural substratum in which spirits, spirit quests, and individual encounters were basic ingredients.* But the central and northern Northwest Coast developments of privileged dancing societies, replete with initiations, were never evident in the Plateau, where communitarian interests outweighed kinship group and private individual interests.

The differences between the Plateau and the Northwest Coast are important because they shed light on a possible transition within some Northwest Coast societies from assumptions and practices about that which was supernatural and sacred—assumptions shared in common with some Plateau societies. On the Northwest Coast, in the presence of kinship-group ownership of property, permanence of settlements, fixity of residence, and abundant localized resources on the one hand, yet the general absence of centralized polities on the other, sodalities based on incorporeal property (spirit privileges) occupied positions of considerable social and ceremonial importance. These sodalities served to distinguish the high-ranking from the low-ranking people, but they also served to integrate people who were not kinsmen in either the same community or different communities by providing common club membership and ritual gatherings. With the possible exception of the Bluejay shamans' society among the Kutenai, comparable groups did not exist in the Plateau, where a communitarian approach to religious rituals and shared access to resource areas predominated.

Sodalities can be ranked on the basis of the things that they did in each society. Among the Northwest Coast communities, sodalities engaged in the fewest activities of all sodalities in western North America, but among the Tanoan and Eastern Keres Pueblos, sodalities controlled the political, religious, and (in part) economic life of the community. It is reasonable to understand sodalities in western North America as having evolved in conjunction with political organization from simple to complex. The simplest sodalities were those that operated in lieu of strong centralized polities (Northwest Coast). Somewhat more complex were those that provided bonds among people not necessarily related by kinship in definite but weakly centralized polities (northern California). Still more complex were those sodalities in which sodality leaders were also the political leaders (Maidu and Southern Nisenan groups). The most complex sodality organizations provided the basic form to economic, social, and ceremonial relations (Western Pueblos), and even provided the government in which sodality leaders directed governmental and major economic affairs (Tanoan and Eastern Keres Pueblos). As corollaries of these politically related activities of sodalities, the greater the relationship between politics and sodalities, the greater the number of activities engaged in by sodalities. For example, curing, warfare, weather control, and economic activities increased roughly as sodalities exercised greater control over governmental issues.

In the following discussions we shall treat sodalities in the order of the number of activities in which they engaged, from the Northwest Coast through the Pueblos. This will provide us with a reasonable assessment of the differences in sodality organizations.

It is not clear how many independent origins there were of sodalities, but the sodalities of the Northwest Coast, of the northern subarea of California, of the central subarea of California, of Southern California, and of the Pueblos probably represent four independent developments. The analysis that follows will support a postulate that the specific differences among the sodalities in the four regions stem from separate origins, yet the similarities in contexts among the regions—relative sedentariness, goodly amounts of localized storable or extractable resources, fixity of postnuptial residence, and private-property ownership—provided the basis for competition among groups and possibly led to the development of sodalities in lieu of centralized polities. Among the Tanoan and Eastern Keres Pueblos, the sodalities became the centralized polities.

Sacred Public Performances: Integration and Separation

The public performances of sodalities everywhere drew people together from many kinship groups and, more often than not, drew guests from other communities as well. Outside of the Eastern Pueblos, the meager political organizations among the tribes

---

*See Chapters 10 and 11 for analyses of Plateau–Northwest spirit concepts and ceremonialism.

that were the most sedentary, least flexible, least mobile, and in which kinship groups owned private property were, perhaps, mitigated by the presence of sodalities. These sodalities regularly drew the communities together and, for most of the tribelets in the California culture area, the sib communities in Southern California, and the Pueblo villages of the Southwest, organized major portions of the entire adult community into a club with secret knowledge and sacred duties to perform. As members of these sodalities, initiates learned either tribal secrets or restricted sodality secrets, or both. These secrets were shared and protected by all members, thus creating and maintaining special bonds among them.

It is certainly of interest that, with the exceptions of the Tsimshian villages and the summer villages of the Central and Northern Nootka, the societies of the Northwest Coast, which had the most meager political development of the societies along the western edge of the continent, extended the principle of kinship-group ownership of property to more resources and to more incorporeal phenomena than any other group of societies in western North America. In the societies of the northwestern California subarea and the societies in the southern subarea of the Northwest Coast culture area, not only was political development meager, but there were no sodalities at all. In the central and northern clusters (excluding the Tlingits and some Haidas) sodality membership was restricted to high-ranking persons who gained membership either through spirit encounters, or by inheritance, purchase, or as gifts (in the more northern areas). Potlatches were sponsored so as to validate a person's initiation to a dancing society, i.e., to validate the initiate's right to assume a dance, a mask, a song, and the myth that tied them together. The sodalities themselves were restricted in membership to people who possessed the privilege to perform dances and wear masks. In such sodality membership the principles of private property ownership, inheritance, succession, and individual kinship-group rights and prerogatives—invested in some members of each kinship group—were stressed. The highest-ranking representatives of the kinship groups—demes or lineages—were initiated into the societies. Each dance was the incorporeal property of some kinship group, and the dance performance was the enactment of the encounter between a famous ancestor of the family and a spirit-being. The spirit-being also taught the person a dance and bestowed on that person the right to perform it. Thus, future generations performed both the dance that was learned from the spirit-being and enacted the encounter with the spirit.

Dances were ranked and ordered, just as kinship groups and people within them were ranked and ordered. The initiation rituals usually excluded the public, and at these times the initiates simulated possession by the spirits they would later impersonate. At the end of the initiation sessions the novices were ritually "captured" by the members of the societies who exorcized the spirits, placed some taboos on the novices, and eventually provided the initiates with full membership in the dance society. The higher the rank of the dancer, usually, (a) the more dances in which he or she performed; (b) the higher the order of the dances; and (c) the more important that member's role in the dances (i.e., the more important the ceremonial perogatives). Men had more privileges than women, and high-ranking men had more privileges than people of lesser rank. People of low rank, needless to say, were not initiated at all.

So the dance societies of the Northwest Coast, initiations to which required sponsorship of potlatches, replicated the focus of the social and economic structure on ranking and on private property. Thus, people were separated on the basis of rank, and on the basis of membership and nonmembership. Yet the societies integrated high-ranking people from different kinship groups in the same community, as well as people from distant communities, for these performances. And though the highest-ranked dances were usually restricted to society members, the dances of the lower order were open to the public, so low-ranking people from many kinship groups convened to watch performances and to lend confirmation of the prerogatives of those who ranked above them, regardless of family.

In perpetrating the ranking system, the relations among kinship groups and the leaders of those groups were emphasized, as were the respective domains of power and control of each kinship group and its dancers. Drucker (1940) notes that dance performances in one series, "Shamans' series," among the Kwakiutls and Tsimshian groups, according to informants, were regularly followed by the murder of a low-ranking individual. The Shamans' series dancing performances, which were the most important ceremonies in the winter ceremonial period, were for initiated, high-ranking people only. Perhaps to underline the supernatural importance of membership, and the more basic distinction between high-ranking and low-ranking people, nonmembers were put to death if they saw any part of these particular performances. Drucker's (1940) informants also suggested, however, that whether or not a low-ranking person saw part of a performance, someone of low rank would be put to death following a set of Shaman's dances: thus, the implication was that the structural relation between members and nonmembers was to be reinforced by the sacrifice of a low-ranking nonmember regardless of the behavior of the person who was put to death.

Dancing societies among Northwest Coast tribes, in the absence of political organization,* integrated high-ranking families by drawing them together yet distinguishing them on the basis of rank. The exclusion of low-ranking people who were not members of dancing sodalities from observing some dances, even to the point of murdering those who observed part of such a dance, accentuated the basic hierarchical structure of Northwest Coast society. General public attendance at low-order dances allowed nonmembers to watch dance society members exhibit some of their special privileges. As often as not, the low-ranking nonmembers were watching the high-ranking members of their own kinship groups perform, and their performances were inspirational to such nonmembers who even contributed food and gifts to initiates from their kinship group who, in turn, sponsored potlatches after the dances. The potlatches that followed high-order dances were closed to nonmembers. Nevertheless, whether member or nonmember of a dancing society, and whether high-ranking or low-ranking, winter ceremonials were times to fraternize and feast with people in one's own community, and with people from other communities. Such events led to marriage contracts, invitations to potlatches, and the like.

Although the dance societies on the Northwest Coast trumpeted the importance of kinship groups and the high-ranking people within them, they also provided an arena in which family secrets became the special knowledge of nonfamily members throughout the sodality, and in which people from many independent kinship groups regularly convened to ballyhoo their respective worths. The Northwest Coast societies had the least political integration, the fewest governmental functions, and placed the greatest emphasis on private property of all of the relatively fixed residential and rather sedentary groups in western North America. The dance societies that emerged among many of these Northwest Coast groups did so, it appears, following the development of the distribution system and ranking system. For many, such as the Central and Northern Nootkans, sodalities were adopted very recently, perhaps in the potlatch

period (Drucker, 1940). The sodalities performed fewer services for the communities in which members lived than the other sodalities in western North America. Indeed, they emphasized privilege rather than responsibility, and that privilege included a social statement to the effect that dance-sodality members were supernaturally sanctioned for roles that were superior to those of the lower ranks, yet all were integrated into the same social order. Those who were not members were instructed not to violate any of the interdictions attending sodality operations.

The Northwest Coast sodalities, as Drucker (1940) pointed out many years ago, most probably originated among the more northern Kwakiutl groups, such as the Bella Bella, Haihais, and Haisla Kwakiutls, and spread to their Southern Kwakiutl, Northern Nootkan, Salishan, Tsimshian, and Haidan neighbors. The genesis of the dance societies themselves, however, probably stems from an earlier religious syndrome widely distributed throughout the Plateau and the central Northwest Coast in which youths sought spirit-helpers in individual vision-quests and enacted their encounters in ceremonials sponsored during the winter and referred to by ethnologists as "winter spirit sings and spirit dances." Whereas vision-quests were practiced on the Plateau and along the Northwest Coast at the time of contact with Europeans, on the Plateau, quests were engaged in by all males and females, but Northwest Coast quests were engaged in by a minority of each sex. Individual vision-quests in both areas were distinct from dancing sodalities, but not from spirit dancing and spirit singing. For instance, the dancing sodalities of the northern Salishan groups of the Georgia Straits (e.g. Comox, Klahuse), the Kwakiutls, and Tsimshian and Haida groups were marked by special initiations which were separate from vision-quests, but which simulated spirit encounters. These encounters were dramatized in privileged performances. The more southern Coast Salishans of the Georgia Straits, such as the Cowichan and Nanaimo, had dance sodalities, but performances of dances were not ordered and any high-ranking person with an encounter to express could join. The practice of the Coast Salishans at the southern end of the Georgia Straits was reminiscent of both the dancing societies to the north and the Plateau Salish practice to the east (Jorgensen 1969). The Plateau Salish did not have sodalities, but during the winter season they performed spirit sings and spirit dances. Anyone who encountered a spirit on a vision-quest could be a dancer and singer. The Plateau Salish pattern was present among the Sahaptin neighbors of the Salish to the south (Ray 1939, Jorgensen 1969).

---

*Tsimshian groups and Central and Northern Nootkans were exceptions. All had weakly developed dancing sodalities and probably borrowed the dancing society concept from the Kwakiutls after they had developed centralized polities. See Drucker (1940) for inferences about the recency of dancing sodalities among the Nootkans.

The importance of the spirit-quest to the origin of dancing societies is apparent. It is plausible that from a widespread practice of individualized questing for a guardian spirit, and the enactment of the spirit encounter in song and dance as a public affair (rather than as the privilege of a sodality), the Kwakiutls created sodalities to sponsor privileged performances. The sodality members were people who inherited, received as a gift, or were able to purchase their membership into a sodality and pass through its initiation ceremony, which itself was a simulation of a spirit encounter. The individual vision-quest was not a critical element of initiation at all, yet the simulated spirit encounter was. Among coastal peoples, vision-questing was probably engaged in by a minority of each sex in each generation, and it resulted in spirit encounters that brought special skills to the recipients. In the southern part of the Georgia Strait, on the Olympic Peninsula, and in Puget Sound, dancing sodalities were composed of these people. In the north a successful vision-quest was not an entrée to such a society.

In the Plateau the successful recipients of visions did not form sodalities. Their winter spirit sings and spirit dances were communitarian and open to all who wished to dramatize their encounters. The performances sought the good health and well-being of all in attendance, and the good health was to be a gift from the spirits. Thus, anyone who gained a spirit was eligible to sing and dance and to do so for the good of all. The Plateau practice, though borne of the individual spirit-quests engaged in by practically all male and females, focused on the community. The Northwest Coast sodalities, by formally organizing and focusing on select individuals and their families, did not stress the common good and, more than likely, came to be distinguished from the vision quest and the spirit singing and spirit dancing complex.

Public Performances and Curing Societies

The sodalities of the California and Southern California culture areas sponsored private and public ceremonials, and some also performed curing services for members of the community. The compositions of the sodalities were much different from those on the Northwest Coast. In practically all California tribelets and Southern California sibs, sodality membership was accorded (a) either to all men or (b) to all men and to all women, each in a separate sodality of the "tribal" type, or to all men and all women in a single sodality of the "tribal" type. Rank and private property were not considerations for membership or for positions in the sodalities.

Although the sodalities in the part of California north of San Francisco Bay engaged in spirit impersonations with the uses of masks and dances, the spirits that were impersonated were not similar to any of the plethora of individualized spirits impersonated by Northwest Coast dancers. And though sodalities in the northern subarea of California, the central part (San Francisco Bay to the Tehachapi Mountains) of the California culture area, and Southern California were of the tribal types and had curative powers, the sodalities among the societies of the northern subarea, generally referred to as "Kuksu" and "Ghost" cults, were markedly different from the sodalities of the central part of the California culture area and Southern California, which have been referred to as "Toloache" sodalities. The Toloache societies were based on the ingestion of *Datura stramonium* (Jimson weed), a psychoactive plant. The members of these sodalities did not impersonate spirits. A more complex form of the Toloache cult among the Gabrieliño of Southern California, called "Chungichnish," centered on a deity and required certain ritual dances, but it was distinct from the Kuksu organizations of the northern subarea of California.

As was true for the Northwest Coast, the Kuksu sodalities of Northern California and the Toloache sodalities of central California and Southern California invited members from parallel or similar sodalities in neighboring tribelets or sib communities to attend some of their rituals, private and public. It is surely significant that these people, who jealously guarded their kinship group and tribelet property from trespass and, in Southern California and north of that area in California at least, who were suspicious of the actions of their neighbors, formally invited their neighbors to attend sodality performances in their communities.

The principal community of each tribelet in the California culture area possessed a large dance house in which ritual performances were staged and in which guests were housed. One Southern Nisenan tribelet in the northern part of the culture area had five large houses and could host over 1,000 guests. Although the sodality performances were intended in part to generate good will, the guests invited to any performance were always suspicious of the powers of the ranking shaman and the evil ends to which those powers might be used on behalf of the tribelet chief. Visitors usually entrusted their care to the host chief, and by housing guests in large dance-houses built specially for such occasions chiefs could discharge their obligations to their guests. But as we mentioned above, several societies north of San Francisco Bay used nonexogamous moiety affiliations to help maintain visitors at sodality and tribelet ceremonies.

Although guests were invited from several adjacent tribelets, the Kuksu sodalities of the northern part of California, from the Sacramento drainage on the east to the coastal valleys in the west, were ritual performing cults that were distinct, often remarkably so, from tribelet to tribelet. Indeed, the involutions and embellishments that must have occurred in each tribelet's sodalities—once the concept of sodality-formation was adopted by a tribelet—in their specific myths, beliefs in specific spirits, the attributes of those spirits, and the ritual performances attendant to those spirits, were complex. So even though scores of tribelets formed a large sodality network in which ritual performances overlapped in content and style, and even though neighbors formed attendance networks at sodality performances from the northern coastal region of the California culture area to the Sierra, the differences among sodalities were as striking as the similarities. The diversity suggests that ideas initially very similar received very different embellishment among independent tribelets whose worlds were small and circumscribed and whose borders were always subject to violation.

In the Sacramento drainage and coastal valleys to the west, tribal sodalities and restricted sodalities were extremely influential in, and central to, tribelet affairs. The tribelets in the coastal valleys (Yukians, Pomos, the Kato, and Coast and Lake Miwoks)* formed what we shall refer to following tradition as the Western Kuksu area. For these tribelets, Kuksu was only one of several specific spirits, such as Hesi, Akit, and Shalnis, around which specific, restricted dance sodalities formed in each tribelet, but because Kuksu was generally the most important spirit impersonated in the tribelets of the coastal area, the many dance sodalities of the northern part of California—east and west alike—are all referred to as Kuksu cults. The Western Kuksu area usually had one restricted sodality per tribelet, yet each sodality might impersonate several spirits. And even though Shalnis, Kuksu, Hesi, and a few other spirits were all impersonated, the variation from tribelet to tribelet in initiation ceremonies, specific features of dance performances, specific ritual interpretations for each dance and each spirit, and combinations of spirits impersonated was considerable. For example, myths attributed to Kuksu in one tribelet's sodality might be attributed to Hesi in another. Once the idea for spirit-impersonating sodalities diffused, styles of performance, initiation, and interpretation were embellished

upon, transformed, and added to by every tribelet in the Western Kuksu area (Kroeber 1932, Loeb 1932b).

The Western Kuksu area was distinct from the Eastern Kuksu area* in that the Western groups, plus the Patwin, not only had Kuksu sodalities, but they also possessed tribal sodalities composed of all the men in one sodality (Yuki, Coast Yuki, Kato, and Southern Pomo) or all the men and women in one sodality (Eastern Pomo). Novices were initiated into these tribalwide sodalities, which were commonly known as Ghost societies, when between the ages of ten and thirteen. For up to three years they attended schools where the secrets of the tribe and the importance of spirits was taught to them, and where many spirits of the tribal dead were impersonated. Furthermore, all tribelets of the Western Kuksu area possessed nonexogamous moieties in which every member of a tribelet belonged either to the moiety of his or her father, or to the husband's moiety. When attending public sodality performances in a foreign tribelet, or when attending tribelet-sponsored ceremonials in another tribelet, a visitor joined his or her moiety equivalents in the host community and enjoyed the performances and the feasts with them. The visitors also joined their moiety equivalents in competitive games against the opposite moiety in that tribelet. Thus, the Western Kuksu area, comprising several tribelets and many differences in sodality performances, myths, and the like, was connected through nonexogamous moieties and through general similarities in Kuksu, Shalnis, Hesi, and other Kuksu-type beliefs and practices, and through their similar beliefs in and sponsorships of tribal wide Ghost sodalities.

Beginning in the late teenage years for people who already belonged to the Ghost society, and for some women among the Southern Pomo, Northern Pomo, Kato, and Yuki groups who were not members of the Ghost society, a second initiation into the Kuksu sodality took place.

The roles played by women in Western Kuksu sodalities were considerably greater than the roles played by women in Eastern Kuksu sodalities, and they were also greater than the roles played by women in the Ghost societies. Only among the Eastern Pomo were women incorporated in Ghost societies. As for Kuksu sodalities, both women and

---

*Neither Lake Miwok nor Coast Miwok have been included in the statistical analysis of the western American Indian sample.

*The Western Kuksu area embraced the Kato, Yuki, Coast Yuki, Coast Miwok, Lake Miwok, Wappo, and the Pomo groups; the Eastern Kuksu area embraced the Valley Maidu, Foothill Maidu, Valley Nisenan (not included in the statistically analyzed sample), Patwin, and Nomlaki groups.

men belonged to one sodality among the Southern Pomo, the Kato, and the Eastern Pomo tribelets, but men also had a separate sodality that was independent of women. Among the Northern Pomo tribelets men and women had separate sodalities. The Wappo and Coast Yuki sodalities were for men only.

The Ghost societies propitiated ghost spirits and through myth and ritual tied the present communities to the past. Except among the Eastern Pomo, women were excluded from these quasipolitical and economic affairs. Kuksu performances, on the other hand, focused on curing the sick and bringing good health to all participants, and curing functions were invested in entire societies which, in general, were open to women.

Sodality membership was not dependent on a vision-quest, and in fact individual persons among tribelets in the northern part of California, except for shamans, did not seek supernatural power. It may well be that women served relatively large functions in Western Kuksu sodalities because in the Western Kuksu tribelets, where large, rather closely spaced, agamous, and ambilocal settlements dominated, women had more permanence of place throughout life than in the Eastern Kuksu area. Women definitely had greater political influence and more numerous ritual roles in the western sodalities. Given the functions of women in sodalities, it is likely that male initiations preceded female initiations into cults, and that curative functions associated with Kuksu sodalities in the Western Kuksu area were deemed proper pursuits for women.*

The Eastern Kuksu area was similar to the Western Kuksu area in that visitors from other tribelets were invited to attend and participate in performances and the festivities that attended them, while the chiefs gathered contributions from the many independent families to feed the guests. Yet in the Eastern area, there were no tribalwide sodalities, except among the Patwin, who served as a "bridge" to the Western Kuksu area much as the Keresans served as a "bridge" between Tanoan and Western Pueblo kinship organizations. In the Eastern Kuksu area, all of the sodalities were restricted, and rather than having only one Kuksu sodality, or one chapter for men and one chapter for women, as was common in the western area, tribelets possessed as many as three sodalities. Here Hesi and Akit sodalities rather than the Kuksu sodality were for men only, again with the exception of the Patwin society, which had one chap-

ter for men and one chapter for both men and women.

Among the tribelets of the Eastern Kuksu area, especially among the Maidu and the Valley Nisenan groups, the dual chiefs of the tribelets were also the chiefs of the Akit and Hesi sodalities. They gained their secular authority directly from their sacred roles as leaders of these key sodalities. Other ranking sodality members served as counselors to the chiefs.

The distinction between Eastern Kuksu and Western Kuksu tribelets is interesting because women were denied membership in Kuksu sodalities, and neither tribal sodalities nor nonexogamous moieties existed in the Eastern Kuksu tribelets. Moreover, sodality leaders among some Eastern Kuksu tribelets were also political leaders. Women in the eastern area were not denied roles in curing and healing, but they had to perform such tasks as shamans—a role that was denied to women in the western area. On the other hand, women in the Western Kuksu cults provided curing services through sodality membership.

It is plausible that in the eastern area, which was dominated by California Penutian speakers, where community exogamy rather than agamy and patrilocality rather than ambilocality were practiced, and where communities, in general, were less closely spaced than those in the Western Kuksu area, women throughout their lifetimes were not drawn into sodalities because they were less fixed in place than were men, and were also less fixed in place than either women or men in the Western Kuksu area. There were no tribal sodalities for youths, and the Eastern Kuksu sodalities were restricted to men in their late teens and older. So in the Eastern Kuksu area, female contacts with initiations took place at about the time in which they moved to their husband's communities. Whereas a woman in the Eastern Kuksu area did not join a sodality, she could become a shaman, usually later in life when she was established in her husband's community.

There can be little doubt but that sodalities in the northern part of California were primarily male organizations. In those tribelets where political roles were explicitly delegated to sodality leaders, women were excluded from membership. On the other hand, the Western Kuksu area tribelets, plus the Patwin and the Nomlaki groups, who did not invest political power in sodality leaders, possessed tribalwide sodalities to connect the present generation with the past, which, in effect, contributed spiritual bonds to the tribal community. Both in the eastern and the western areas, however, tribelet interests usually superseded the interests of particular kinship groups, and sodality members formed bonds that transcended kinship ties and organized them for collective

---

*See the further analysis of this phenomena in the shamanism section of Chapter 11.

purposes. Both tribal and restricted sodalities were instrumental in providing religious cement for each tribelet inasmuch as such entities protected boundaries, dealt formally with neighbors, and recognized family ownership of some properties.

In the California culture area there were several ritual and ceremonial bridges between the societies of the northern subarea and the central subarea. Interestingly, though, sodalities formed only one small bridge in a much larger network of connections, and the sodality bridge appears to have been extended from the north to the central part rather than from the central to the north in the California area, yet many other ceremonial connections with the north undoubtedly originated in the San Joaquin area and the coastal regions farther south. The Salinan groups of the Salinas Valley and coastal regions sponsored Kuksu-type sodalities. The stimulus for such sodalities probably came from their Costanoan neighbors to the north. Yet the Kuksu-type sodalities among the Salinans were tribalwide for all males, rather than restricted in membership, as was the case for Costanoan and Coast Miwok communities.

The principal ritual and ceremonial bridges between central and northern California were the mourning-anniversary ceremony (sometimes called the annual mourning ceremony) in the foothills and valleys along the Sierra on the east, and the pole ceremony and nonexogamous moieties* in the foothills and coastal valleys of the Western Kuksu area. Ceremonialism receives greater attention in Chapter 10. Suffice it to say at this point that the mourning anniversary ceremony comprised a paramount series of rituals conducted by River Yumans, Southern California Yumans and Uto-Aztecans, and tribes in the eastern-central part of California. The pole ceremony, which was a competition among men to scale a pole and grab feathers attached to the top, was integrated in the mourning-anniversary ceremony often as part of the first-acorn ritual among most Southern California tribes and some in the California culture area. Among the tribes of the Western Kuksu area, where Ghost societies held sway, the pole ceremony was performed, whereas the mourning-anniversary ceremony was not.

As variation among the many tribelets that possessed Kuksu cults was extensive, the variation in the performances of the mourning-anniversary cere-

mony from tribe to tribe was also extensive. But in general the mourning ceremony was a constellation of ritual acts and beliefs that integrated propitiation of all deceased, and the subsequent burning of images and gifts; several dances performed by specially qualified dancers who might impersonate condors, eagles, or other animal spirits; and first-acorn rituals. In Southern California, naming-rites, girls' puberty rites, and several other rituals focusing on the sacred charter of the sib were included.

In the northern part of the California culture area, the Maidus and Nisenans of the Eastern Kuksu area performed mourning-anniversary ceremonies, but were not organized into moieties and did not sponsor versions of the tribalwide Ghost sodalities that were so common in the Western Kuksu area. Years ago, Kroeber (1925) suggested that the Maidus and Nisenans once possessed Ghost sodalities but dropped them after adopting the mourning ceremony because the two forms for propitiating the dead were incompatible. Both Ghost sodality performances and mourning ceremonies linked the living generations to their deceased ancestors, but did so with different ritual acts and different explanations. Furthermore, the mourning ceremonies performed in the central part of California and in Southern California were associated either with moiety obligations or some other form of reciprocating obligations among lineages, villages, or tribelets. But moieties or their equivalents were not created among the Maidus and Nisenans, whose sodality leaders were the tribelet chiefs. Yet the moiety concept, reworked in a nonexogamous form, was probably borrowed by the Western Kuksu people, who did not also borrow the mourning ceremony.

The Maidus and Nisenans had worked some concepts of the Ghost society into their Kuksu cults, just as the Wintus, Mountain Maidu, Northern Miwok, and Central Miwok tribelets performed some Kuksu-type spirit impersonations and dances without having benefit of Kuksu sodalities. There is no simple answer as to whether the Maidus and Nisenans dropped the Ghost society whereas the other groups dropped the Kuksu cults. It is possible, in fact, highly plausible, that all accreted aspects of these sodalities to their ritual lives without adopting the sodalities that bore them. What is certain is that the mourning ceremony was performed by tribes from south to north along the entire western slope of the Sierra, and it was one obvious ritual link between the Kuksu areas to the north and the Toloache sodality areas to the south. Moreover, one small part of the mourning ceremony of Southern California tribes—the pole ceremony—most probably made its way into the Western Kuksu area from the south, probably in con-

---

*See the discussion of moieties in Chapter 8. Nonexogamous moieties of the Western Kuksu area were probably reworked from the patrilineal exogamous moiety model in the central part of California.

junction with nonexogamous moieties. Thus the Western Kuksu area adopted moiety concepts, possibly in conjunction with the pole ceremony, but did not adopt the mourning ceremony. It is plausible that the presence of Ghost sodalities in the Western Kuksu region inhibited the acceptance of the mourning ceremony. The point is that from south to north, influences were felt in the eastern and western areas, but each area responded to different impulses. My hunch is that the Eastern Kuksu tribelets did not possess Ghost sodalities before coming in contact with people who practiced the mourning-anniversary ceremony, and this may have made them more receptive to adopting the mourning ceremony than they would have been had they possessed Ghost cults. They accepted the mourning ceremony in a rather complete form. Because Hesi and Akit sodality leaders were also principal chiefs of the tribelets, this too may have provided reasons for rejecting both Ghost sodalities and the moiety concepts.

The sodalities in central California communities, from the Northern Miwok to the Yauelmani Yokuts, are called "Toloache" sodalities. In point of fact, these tribalwide sodalities extended all the way south through the Western Diegueño in the Southern California area. In Southern California, the Toloache sodalities included only the males in each sib community, whereas in central California, only the Lake Yokuts group excluded females from membership. All other central California groups either integrated all men and women in the same group, or had separate chapters for each sex.

Toloache cults—those which, as mentioned earlier, were based on the ingestion of *Datura stramonium*, or, Jimson weed—may well have been created by the Gabrieliño from what were once societies of shamans. The narcotizing agents of *D. stramonium* were used by shamans throughout parts of the Southwest, and throughout the Toloache societies of central California and Southern California, to gain dreams and dream instructions, and to aid in curing functions. Toloache societies were everywhere involved with questions about sickness, death, and dying, too. Initiates into Toloache sodalities were taught the spiritual significance of sickness, death, and dying. Because parts of the ritual acts, objects, and philosophy of Gabrieliño Toloache societies occurred throughout much of Southern California and central California, it is likely that the Gabrieliños of Southern California integrated *D. stramonium* with a philosophy about life and death and created the Toloache sodalities. Membership in the Toloache sodality among Gabrieliño and all other societies that adopted versions of the Toloache was extended to many people who were not shamans.

Toloache sodalities were explicitly sacred in nature. They stressed the importance of moral lessons and mystical powers, and they prepared members for their own spiritual lives and to fulfill obligations within their sibs (Southern California), lineages, or communities (central California). *D. stramonium* could be taken only under strictest controls, so novices were given close instruction on how, how much, and when to take it. In the Southern California versions of the Toloache sodality, novices were often subjected to ordeals such as being buried in ant hills. They also watched, and later participated in, fire dances in which members danced over hot coals. Furthermore, Toloache cults in many Southern California sib communities also constituted a secret society of warriors who, from the ages of seven or eight, were prepared to fight if necessary. Ground-paintings made from sand and other natural substances were central features in the Toloache initiations, and depicted various aspects of mystical connections with the supernatural; the isolation of members for long periods in communal men's houses—schools for novitiates—was also common.

It is likely that a still later development among the Gabrieliño and Chumash societies was superposed on the Toloache sodalities. It came to be known as "Chungichnish" after the Chungichnish deity. Principal features of the Chungichnish sodalities were figures sculptured from steatite (a mineral abundant on Santa Catalina Island off the coast of Los Angeles), a basic myth about the world, a further development of sacred ground paintings, and the concept of Chungichnish as a deity who commanded performances.

The Toloache sodalities, concerned as they were with sickness and curing, living and dying, were linked to the development of the mourning ceremony. As with the use of *Datura stramonium*, the mourning ceremony had a wider distribution than the Toloache observances. It is plausible that the mourning ceremony preceded the development of the Toloache cults, but also developed in conjunction with them, for the Toloache sodalities, too, came to sponsor special mourning ceremonies for their deceased members. The interests in death and dying were central to the mourning ceremony and to Toloache ceremonies. Moreover, the joint interests in the individual and the kinship group are evident in both Toloache and mourning ceremonies.

As we pointed out in Chapter 8, moieties were the principal sponsors of mourning ceremonies throughout the predominantly patrilineal societies of Southern California and the central part of the California culture area, where the ceremonies were intertribal affairs. Toloache sodalities among these societies, on the other hand, were predominantly intratribal organizations with curing functions that were composed of members from one or more patrilineages. Among the Maidus and Nisenans of the Eastern Kuksu area there were no moieties and the mourning ceremonies were sponsored by each tribelet. The political organization of the valley- and foothill-dwelling Maidus and Nisenans invested principal authority for tribelet affairs in the sodality chiefs. It is plausible that the concept of moieties, which was more than likely joined with the mourning ceremony as the two diffused northward, was rejected by these bilaterally organized Eastern Kuksu area tribelets as extraneous to their kinship-group, intracommunity, and intercommunity affairs.

Membership in Toloache sodalities comprised people who crosscut the several kinship groups in the multilineage tribelets, but in the unilineage Miwok communities and the Southern California sib communities membership was, of course, drawn from a single kinship group. Among these tribes it was the moieties, rather than the sodalities, that served to integrate people from several communities. Within the communities in which both moiety divisions were present, such as among the Yokuts tribelets, the leaders of the exogamous moieties, rather than the sodalities, were often the dual tribelet chiefs. Sodalities could, however, draw together members from several chapters on an *ad hoc* basis. Toloache societies provided common spiritual knowledge, whereas exogamous moieties obligated their opposites through marriage and ritual.

Toward Political and Economic Powers Invested in Sodalities

As was mentioned above, sodalities among several Maidu and Nisenan tribelets not only performed public and private rituals, but nominal political authority for tribelet affairs was invested in the chiefs of the two principal sodalities. The chiefs were responsible for staging their tribelets' most important rituals, including calling on tribelet members to provide food and support and assuring the well-being of guests; distributing food in times of scarcity; and organizing the protection of their tribelet's territory, which might include the formation of temporary alliances. Although Maidu and Nisenan chiefs could not demand that their subjects obey, they held positions of esteem and exercised considerable suasion. The practical authority allocated to Maidu and Nisenan sodality chiefs, that is, the decisions they rendered that prompted compliance in daily, seasonal, and annual affairs, far outstripped the authority invested in sodality leaders

elsewhere in the California culture area, and among Southern California and Northwest Coast societies. Indeed, these were the only societies west of the Sierra, Cascades, or Canadian coastal ranges to delegate political control to sodality leaders. This simple form of tribal authority was not based in kinship. Rather, it was based on the sacred and nonchallengeable ideology that explained the Akit and Hesi cults. Thus, sanctified authority that was exercised over all members of each sodality most probably came to be extended over all people in the tribelet through the sacred positions of the chiefs of each sodality. These leaders were counseled by the ranking sodality leaders. Whereas many sodality functions were specifically intertribelet affairs among the Maidus and Nisenans, as was also the case among most other groups in the northern subarea of California, moieties were not borrowed by Nisenans from neighbors to the south in order to facilitate ceremonial or ritual relations with other communities. It is interesting that the nonexogamous moiety organizations among the tribelets of the Western Kuksu area were only weakly developed and these tribelets also sponsored pole ceremonies. Moreover, the Western Kuksu tribelets did not place tribalwide political authority in their Kuksu cult leaders.

It is conceivable, then, that the sacred authority invested in sodality leaders was extended from sodality to tribelet affairs among many Maidu and Nisenan tribelets. This could have selected against the adoption of nonexogamous moieties. In the Western Kuksu area, many tribelets presumably adopted moieties yet reshaped them so as to make them nonexogamous, as well as adopting the entertainment they afforded, and the pole ceremony in conjunction with first-acorn ceremonies. Reciprocals (opposites) in one's own community entertained each other on some occasions, and during "Big Times"* reciprocals from other communities also engaged in entertaining each other.

The roles played by sodalities and sodality leaders in Western Pueblo societies were referred to earlier in the section on political organization. The Western Pueblos were organized into corporate matrilineal kinship groups that owned land, controlled certain kiva ceremonials, and made the key decisions affecting the collective affairs of the matrilineage. On the other hand, all female and male youths between the ages of six and ten among the Hopi, the Hano (a Tewa-speaking Hopi village), and Western Keres villages were initiated into tribal-wide Kachina sodalities. Only males were initiated into the Kachina

---

*See Chapter 10 for a discussion of "Big Times."

society at Zuni Pueblo. The Kachina sodality for each tribe was associated with underground ceremonial chambers called "kivas," which also served as the places in which ceremonial objects were made and stored. Unmarried men slept in the kivas, and kivas were also places where restricted sodalities, here collectively called kiva cults, met and where secret rituals were performed.

The Kachina cult impersonated a vast array of spirit beings, believed to be the ancestral spirits of each tribe, through masked dancing performances. Various spirits were believed to watch over the land, bring rain, cure the sick, protect the village, create well-being in the community, and so forth. The Kachina cult, in drawing members from all kinship groups and imposing ritual obligations on all members, forced recognition of community concerns rather than individual or kinship-group concerns.

Political and some ceremonial but not economic authority in the Acoma Pueblo villages was centralized in the "antelope" sib, but no other Western Pueblo recognized so much centralized authority. The Zuni recognized the centralization of ceremonial control in the "bow" priesthood, but political and economic control was not allocated to that group. In the absence of centralized political organization, the important role played by ritual organization in coordinating community affairs cannot be overemphasized. Kachina cults brought all men and women together in sacred ceremonials that were absolutely vital to the well-being of their societies. They propitiated the ancestral spirits and petitioned them for help by showing respect and good intentions in their dance performances at prescribed rituals.

Kiva ceremonials other than the tribal initiations of the Kachina cults, it will be recalled, were sponsored by kiva societies. There were several such societies in each Western Pueblo tribe. The kiva societies were owned by sibs, but at Zuni the bow priesthood, and at Acoma the antelope sib, ultimately dominated the *kiva* societies.

Kiva societies performed different kinds of ceremonials, and if a person wanted to become active in the religious and political life of the community, he or she had to be initiated into a kiva society as well as the Kachina cult. Kiva societies focused on directing tribal initiations, retaliatory warfare, hunting, medicine and curing, rainmaking and the fertility of crops, and social control (the last through clown sodalities). As Eggan (1950) and Dozier (1970) separately have pointed out, at Hopi, the most arid of the Western Pueblo territories, rainmaking ceremonies were emphasized. The Hano (Hopi Tewa) and Zuni tribes gave equal emphasis to rainmaking and curing ceremonies. The Western Keres Pueblos emphasized curing ceremonies. It was not coincidental that water was more predictable in the eastern area than in the western area, and that rainmaking ceremonies received more attention in the west than in the east.

Whereas political and ceremonial control was centralized in the antelope sib at Acoma, nothing comparable occurred in the other Western Pueblos. It would have been logical for the "bear" sib to centralize political authority among Hopi sibs if specific kinship-group authority for each sib waned, but the bear sib was not granted such authority in any Hopi village. Among the Western Pueblo communities the kiva societies, with their sacred ritual duties to perform, provided the nexus for informed political control and some specific social and political services. For instance, male sibmates from the bear sib were initiated into the kiva society of their sib, but some people who did not belong to the bear sib were also induced to join that sib's kiva society. The same was true for other sodalities. In this fashion kiva sodalities drew together people from several sibs. Factions were developed and nourished through sib-leaders' memberships in overlapping kivas, but factions did not evolve into political communities. Even at Zuni Pueblo the bow priesthood, which may have evolved from the concentration of several rituals in the hands of a few kiva sodality leaders, controlled ceremonial, rather than political and economic affairs, but they did so with the cooperation of sib leaders.

The factions provided some political cohesiveness among the several kinship groups, though the cohesiveness was not long-termed. Other political ends, at least toward social control, were served by the clown societies, which employed humor verging on ridicule in ritual masks, dance, and pantomime to reverse accepted patterns of social, economic, and ritual behavior by celebrating disapproved behavior. Warrior sodalities, often two per tribe, at one time cooperated in waging defensive warfare to protect each Western Pueblo from external threats.

Women among the Western Pueblos* not only were initiated into the Kachina cult, but they also were initiated into exclusively female sodalities. There were one or more sodalities for women in each Western Pueblo with ceremonial functions related to human fertility, plant fertility, caring for enemy scalps, and tribal well-being (Map Cu-174, V-343; Map Cu-175; V-346).

Matrilineal kinship groups among the Western Pueblos never abrogated all of their ceremonial or ritual functions, not even at Acoma. Yet at Acoma

---

*Except at Zuni Pueblo.

Pueblo, one matrilineal group became dominant in decision-making over all others, and their medicine and curing ceremonies, invested in the antelope sib, were paramount cult ceremonies.

Sodalities as the Organizations of Political, Economic, and Ceremonial Control

The Eastern Keres villages possessed Kachina cults, medicine sodalities, dual (nonexogamous moiety) sodalities, warrior sodalities, and clown sodalities. If the Kachina cult, which sponsored rainmaking ceremonies, had ever been the dominant sodality in Keresan life, it was not dominant at the time of contact with Europeans. Indeed the medicine sodalities were the most important associations in every Eastern Keres village. The Kachina cult in each Eastern Keres village addressed itself to rainmaking, but it was neither a tribalwide sodality, as among the Western Pueblos, nor was rainmaking so important to the Eastern Keres villages as it was to Western Pueblos. The importance of sodalities in Eastern Keres social, political, and economic life was much greater than was the case for sodalities among the Western Keres. Conversely, the role played by matrilineal kinship groups in Western Keres societies was much more important than the roles played by their counterparts in Eastern Keres societies.

Eastern Keres tribal sodalities (dual organizations or nonexogamous moieties) were similar to those of the Tanoans. That is, in each Eastern Keres village there were two sodalities (moieties), whose memberships, except at Santa Ana Pueblo, were not based on kinship-reckoning criteria, and which were associated with the two kivas in each village.* The Eastern Keres dual sodalities were ceremonial in nature and membership could change throughout life, depending on where a person lived in the village (north side or south side). Tanoan dual sodalities, on the other hand, were more than ceremonial organizations. The leaders of Tanoan dual sodalities alternated in controlling village affairs.

Eastern Keres sodalities, such as warrior and clown, in addition to the Kachina society and the tribal nonexogamous moieties (dual sodalities), were ultimately directed by the medicine sodality in each village. It was the medicine sodalities that coordinated

all communal activities and, more specifically, the village chief and his assistants were medicine men. Not only did the village chief in each Eastern Keres village belong to a medicine sodality, but he also belonged to a clown sodality. Thus, communal well-being, personal health, and social control were functions overseen by the sodalities to which the chief and his assistants belonged, and they gained their moral and political authority from the sanctity of their positions within their sacred organizations.

It has been reported by Dozier (1970) that at one time the priests of the warrior sodalities also joined the medicine and clown sodality leaders in managing the communal affairs of Keresan villages, but during the period of earliest Contact (mid-sixteenth century), if not before, authority came to be centralized in a village chief who belonged to both the medicine and clown sodalities. This chief and his principal sodality brethren, that is, the leading priests of the medicine and clown sodalities, directed communal affairs. Control over Eastern Keres political, economic, and ritual life most probably was transferred from matrisibs to a village priesthood. Although Eastern Keres villages were basically egalitarian and democratic, the village chief and his council could confiscate houses, usurp farmland and chattels, and banish people from the village.

Tanoans probably achieved village integration based on nonexogamous moiety (dual sodality) rather than kinship principles earlier than their Eastern Keres neighbors. The dual sodalities of the Eastern Keres were organized along spatial dimensions which separated one half of the village from the other. Spatial division was also a prominent feature of Tanoan dual sodalities and probably was borrowed by the Keresans. Yet aside from the spatial features of the dual sodalities, among the bilateral Tanoans it was the dual organizations, rather than matrisibs or medicine sodalities, that occupied the positions of premier importance in controlling communal life. The social, ceremonial, economic, and political controls which were localized in the leaders of the dual sodalities were greater than the controls exercised by other leaders in western North America.

Tanoan nonexogamous moieties were associated with winter and summer seasons and winter and summer symbolism. There was one large ceremonial structure, or kiva, in each village that was used communally. The two moieties alternated at each equinox in directing the communal ceremonies in the kiva, and in directing the economic, political, and social affairs of the village. The villages had double chieftanships, one chief and his key assistants coming from each moiety. The villagers at Isleta, perhaps, went one step farther than those in other Tanoan vil-

---

*As mentioned in Chapter 8, Santa Ana Keresan dual sodalities were comprised of six and three matrisibs respectively. Recruitment to dual sodalities in the other villages did not follow kinship lines.

lages in centralizing political control in a town chief who was more important than either moiety chief, while at Taos, one moiety chief was considered dominant year around. The chiefs of the moieties, literally the ranking priest in each moiety and their principal assistants, did all of the following: they allocated housing sites to village members; controlled farm sites by allowing families to work plots; directed the repair and construction of the communal kiva for which labor was exacted by the chief's authority; directed the cleaning of the plaza for ceremonials, again by exacting labor; coordinated hunts, warfare, planting, and harvesting; exacted labor and directed the construction and cleaning of irrigation ditches; coordinated the purification rites; organized and directed the communal dances; and maintained the solar ceremonial calendar to which the village's agricultural life was calibrated. Beginning sometime during the Spanish colonial period, when a system of secular authority was imposed on the villages, the moiety chiefs nominated and installed the governors of the villages. The secular organizations were clearly post-Contact phenomena.

Membership in nonexogamous moieties was tribalwide for men and women, but the female role did not include participation in the dances except for one fertility rite associated with the Kachina cult. As among most other sodality organizations in western North America, women occupied less prominent positions.

In addition to dual sodalities, the Tanoan villages had kiva sodalities for hunting, warfare, clowns, and medicine. Among the Taos, Picuris, and Isleta villages it was the kiva sodalities that organized such specific activities as the communal hunts, retaliatory warfare, and curing rituals under the direction of the moiety chiefs. The Tewa villages also had kiva sodalities, but they were less dependent than their counterparts at Taos, Picuris, and Isleta.

Dozier (1970) suggests that the clown and medicine sodalities among the Tanoans were borrowed from the Keresans. There is no doubt that these sodalities were less important, less numerous, and less developed among the Tanoans than among the Keresans. Hunting and warfare sodalities, as well as the nonexogamous moiety organizations, were most probably created by the Tanoans. Later these sodalities were probably diffused to the Keresans during their period of contact with Tanoans on the Rio Grande. Warfare and hunting were especially important sodalities in the Tanoan villages. The Tanoan positions in the Rocky Mountains of northern New Mexico, the eastern foothills of that chain, and on the periphery of the western Plains, where game was abundant and threats of attacks were not un-usual, may well account for the central position occupied by war and hunt sodalities among the Tanoans.

Members were recruited to nonexogamous moieties and sodalities in a similar fashion. People usually joined their father's moiety, but they could change moiety membership if they shifted their residence in the village or for some other reason, such as marriage, in which the marital partners joined the same division. Parents could also encourage a child to join specific kiva sodalities, or a person could join a sodality if he or she was ill and pledged herself to the sodality, or if people dreamed a recurrent dream that they were to join a sodality. Initiation into the medicine, warfare, hunting, and clown sodalities bound a member to service for life.

The Kachina cult, too, occurred in Tanoan villages. The cult of the dancing masked gods most probably diffused to the Tewa from the Eastern Keres (Parsons 1929, 1939). The Kachina cult was never so important among the Tanoans as it was further west. The Kachina sodalities among the Tewa villages were dual, organized along moiety lines, yet were under the supervision of a separate Kachina leader, and were restricted to males. All males in each moiety were initiated at puberty. At each initiation a woman, a nonmember, participated in the ritual, but the same woman could participate only once. The Kachina cult focused on rainmaking and good health among the Tewa. At Isleta and Taos, Kachina cults were not borrowed, though beliefs and some other traditions about Kachinas penetrated these societies.

It is plausible that weak forms of dual sodalities (nonexogamous moieties), warfare-, and hunting-sodalities which were so central to Tanoan communal life diffused to the Keresans through precept, intermarriage, exchange, and joint ceremonial participation with Tanoans, just as Kachina cults, medicine, and clown sodalities, so central to the Keresans, might have been borrowed in subdued form and importance by the Tanoans. It is clear that in both Tanoan and Eastern Keres villages, kinship groups were not, in general, central to political, economic, social, or ceremonial affairs. Those affairs were controlled by the village chiefs, drawn either from the medicine sodalities (Eastern Keres) or dual sodalities (Tanoan).

WARFARE

In the introductory section of this chapter we pointed out that warfare, by our definition, was a political act engaged in by two groups, each possessing definite leadership, military tactics, and the expectation that a series of battles could be endured. There was little warfare in western North America by this definition. This is not to say that some groups in western North America were not warlike, or that feuding and raiding did not occur intermittently in many societies. Nevertheless, so far as we know, only the River Yumans in the Southwest and the Tsimshians of the Northwest Coast engaged their neighbors in protracted warfare for territorial gain. And the neighbors with whom Tsimshian and River Yuman tribes battled—the Haidas and Tlingits, in particular for the Tsimshians, and the Maricopa, Halchidoma, Kaveltchadom, and Cocopa groups for the Yuma and Mohave among the River Yumans—do not appear to have constituted political–military units so well organized as their opponents.

One of the most obvious and interesting aspects of the cultures of western North America's Indians at the time of contact with Europeans was that so few societies actually engaged in persistent offensive warfare, or even raiding,* yet the *prospects* of armed altercations deeply influenced the internal organizations and external relations of these aboriginal societies. Of the social organizations so far examined—moiety ceremonials in Southern California and in the central part of California; sodality ceremonies and tribelet ceremonies in the northern subarea of California; distributions, spirit-sings, dancing-sodalities, and moieties along the central and northern Northwest Coast; and feasting, gift exchange, and joint access to resources in the Plateau—all seem to have been related to creating and maintaining nonhostile ties with neighbors within one's own community and beyond.

In point of fact, there were few societies at contact that had the reputation of being persistent offensive raiders (Map Cu-176, V-358). By our measure, "frequent" offensive raiders were those who mounted more than four raids per year. Although few in number, the societies that engaged in frequent offensive raids caused considerable concern to their neighbors, near and distant. This was especially true during the early Contact period. Northern Northwest Coast groups, and the Kwakiutls and Nootkans of the central Northwest Coast, raided one another as well as communities as far south as Puget Sound and as far east as the passes into the Plateau and Subarctic regions. Tsimshian raiders were even successful in dislocating some Haida and Tlingit communities.

The Upper Thompson of the Fraser Plateau raided Halkomelem Salish villages on the coast as well as some of their Shuswap and Upper Lillooet neighbors

in the Plateau. In the Columbia Plateau, the Klamath and the Modoc made bellicose forays. Offensive raiding of Plateau communities by warriors from other Plateau villages was the exception rather than the rule, and the Modoc, Klamath, and Upper Thompson turned much of their fury onto tribes beyond the Plateau.

The Chumash of the central California coast are said to have been frequent fighters whose battles most often were waged between Chumash tribelets. The totality of California and Southern California was deeply influenced by poaching, raids, and the threat of raids, but offensive raiding was only modest throughout these areas and battles were of short duration and usually were terminated as soon as someone was hurt. The Nisenan tribelets and the Patwin tribelets of the Sacramento delta region was exceptional. They are said to have mounted more offensive raids than the average California tribelet. The California situation, in general, was paradoxical because whereas the threat of warfare was omnipresent, offensive raiding was only moderate. Nevertheless, practically all California and Southern California groups engaged in some raiding, defensive or offensive.

The Apacheans and the River Yumans of the Southwest were the dominant raiders in that region. It is likely that Apachean raids against their Southwestern neighbors began in the pre-Contact period, but was intensified after the Apacheans acquired horses. River Yuman militarism probably had an even older history in the Southwest that was quite independent of the Apacheans. The Apacheans plundered, whereas the Yumans gained spiritual and personal aggrandizement through raids. This is not to say that some Yuman warfare was not waged for territorial gain, but most warfare was not so waged.

The Utes on the eastern edge of the Great Basin raided the Southern Paiutes to the west and the Pueblos to the south in pre-Contact times, but like the Apaches, after the Utes acquired horses they raided tribes in all directions. The mobility provided by the horse stimulated Utes, Apaches, Navajos, and even some Shoshones, Northern Paiutes, and eastern Plateau dwellers such as the Nez Percé, Flathead, and Coeur d'Alene to engage in conflicts with people that they had not encountered prior to the advent of the horse. For the most part, however, let us attempt to restrict this analysis to the preequestrian period.

It is reasonable to ask whether offensive raiding and warfare could have had significant responsibility for shaping the contours of many western North American Indian societies—their internal features and external relations—when so few societies were known to have been aggressive offensive raiders. We

*See the definition of raiding given earlier in the introduction to this chapter.

can best begin to answer this question by looking at what groups defended against raids, and how often they did so. We shall also assess how groups prepared to do battle with their enemies, yet we will very soon have to turn to other issues such as the varieties of feuding, raiding, warfare, and also property and territory concepts, and the cultural variables that attended them, so as to gain a fuller understanding of the manner in which feuding, raiding, and warfare influenced the societies of western North America.

The incidence of defensive raiding (Map Cu-177, V-359) was not a perfect corollary of the incidence of offensive raiding. For instance, the societies of the northern Northwest Coast and some of the societies of the central Northwest Coast mounted frequent raids and also defended against attacks. In the same region, however, many Salishan societies defended against raids, particularly from the seafaring societies to the north, much more often than they mounted raids against other communities. Quite clearly, then, whether or not Northwest Coast communities were active offensive raiders, they frequently had to defend themselves against attacks.

The Northwest Coast pattern holds for most of western North America; that is, societies that mounted frequent offensive raids also had to defend themselves frequently against raids. This was true for the Upper Thompson, Klamath, and Modoc groups of the Plateau, the Patwin tribelet and the Nisenans of California, and the Utes of the eastern Great Basin. Furthermore, neighbors of these aggressive people who did not mount many offensive raids themselves, frequently defended themselves against raids from these aggressors, so they were intimately involved in raiding complexes.

The clearest exception to this pattern was in the Southwest. The River Yumans and most Apacheans were inveterate raiders, yet they were seldom, if ever, attacked on their home turfs. That is undoubtedly because both were such powerful fighting forces and because their victims were generally sedentary agriculturists. As was true for the other areas of western North America, however, many of the societies that sustained the brunt of Apachean and River Yuman attacks—such as the Cocopa, Pima, and Maricopa Yumans, Pueblos, and some Yavapai groups—defended against raids. In historic times many of these societies defended themselves against warfare from these same aggressive tribes. There can be little doubt that raiding, warfare, and the threats of both were influential forces in shaping aspects of the social, political, and ceremonial organizations of many groups in western North America. For instance, defense against raids became the responsibility of warrior sodalities throughout the Pueblos, and those sodalities occupied positions of considerable impor-

tance within each Pueblo. One of the responsibilities, but not the sole responsibility, of one of the divisions of the Chungichnish and Toloache sodalities in Southern California was to protect the sib communities from attack. The Shastas, who were not known to send raiders, unprovoked, into other communities, marshaled potent and well-disciplined warriors when attacked by the Modoc, and the Pimas massed large and moderately successful armies to withstand Apachean and some Yuman attacks in late historic times. It is not clear whether Yuman forces attacked Pimas in the precontact and early historic periods.

Although several societies had specific organizational structures to mount and to defend against raids, the development of permanent military organizations was rare, whether they were restricted sodalities with the sole purpose of militaristic encounters, or standing armies with definite leadership. The Clayoquot Nootka and the Makah on the Northwest Coast had military organizations with ranked leaders, but other Northwest Coast societies did not. Nootkan war chiefs wore special insignia and were probably able to conscript the services of all able-bodied men for large battles which usually pitted one Nootkan village or summer village against another (Map Cu-178, V-363).

The River Yumans, who were perhaps the most consummate warriors in the Southwest, possessed informal associations of warriors. These men had high prestige which they began to achieve when as young as four years of age by being subjected to various ordeals. Later, they were taught to use bows and arrows and war clubs, and they began to dream about warfare. If such dreams occurred at the time of puberty, they were construed as a sign of success, and led to participation in a war party and membership in the informal association of warriors. Most men were warriors, but only a few belonged to the informal association. The members of the association led the parties; the forces they led were divided into groups on the basis of the weapons they used (bows, spears, and clubs). As on the Northwest Coast, attacks were by surprise.

The Pueblo warrior sodalities, as we have mentioned, defended villages against attacks from Utes to the north, Apacheans, and even Plains tribes. Informal warrior groups among the Utes were neither sodalities nor standing armies, and the warriors in the Toloache and Chungichnish sodalities did not have warfare as their major calling.

It is clear that permanent military organizations were not widespread. What is of interest is that permanent military organizations were as often created for defensive purposes (the Pueblos) as offensive (Nootkans and River Yumans). Yet the groups whose purposes were primarily defensive were restricted to the sedentary societies of the Southwest.

It is obvious that there was not a positive relationship between permanent military organizations and the frequency of raids, offensive or defensive, but all societies that possessed permanent military organizations either raided frequently, were raided frequently, or both.

Fighting regalia such as special clubs and spears, shields, breast plates, bows, headdresses, insignias, and the like, and public ceremonies in preparation for battles and following the return of warriors are other measures of either militarism or the impact of raids and the threat of raids on societies (Map Cu-179, V-364; Map Cu-180, V-365). It is most evident from the distribution of fighting regalia and pre- and post-battle ceremonies that the vast majority of western North American societies either prepared for battles with special rituals (usually dances) or sponsored post-battle ceremonies to purify warriors and applaud their successes, or both.

Special fighting weapons were used in the majority of societies as well, and majority of these units also had armaments and special dress for their warriors.

We can see from the distribution maps in Appendix D that fighting regalia and public war ceremonies (Maps Cu-179 and Cu-180) correlated with the dominant raiding clusters (Map Cu-176) on the Northwest Coast and in the Southwest, so that societies that raided frequently were frequently raided, they possessed special fighting regalia, and they sponsored ceremonies before and after battles. But some of these features also occurred throughout most of the northern and central subareas of California, in Southern California, and the Plateau as well. Only a few societies in the Great Basin, Southern California, and the Plateau did not have special paraphernalia for battles and particular ceremonies to celebrate the occasions. Thus, it is plausible to conclude that most people prepared for battles, even if they engaged in them very seldom, but the people who engaged in the fewest altercations—inhabitants of the central Great Basin, the Middle Columbia portion of the Plateau, and many of the Southern California Uto-Aztecans—did not have the accoutrements and trappings of battle. That is, societies that rarely or never mounted raids, and were rarely raided, did not have fighting regalia and did not sponsor public ceremonies.

It is the "in-between" societies that are of considerable interest. By "in-between" societies is meant those societies that possessed the accoutrements of battle but seldom engaged in hostile conflicts, or did so, by and large, defensively. We note that the Salishans of the Northwest Coast and the Pimans and Pueblos of the Southwest were raided frequently.

They possessed fighting regalia, but except for the Tewa their public warfare ceremonies always followed conflicts rather than preceded them. The defensive nature of their operations were emphasized in this relationship. The "in-betweenness" (in terms of having fighting regalia and public ceremonies attending conflicts) of societies in Southern California, some Plateau societies, and some defensive Southwestern societies such as the Pais, who were not known even to have been attacked very often, will become clear in the following discussion.

It is apparent that property concepts, territoriality, and the abundances of localized resources were highly instrumental in shaping the relations among adjacent societies. The nature and incidence of duels, feuding, raiding, and warfare, associate albeit roughly with the abundance, localization, and storability of resources, and the ownership rights that people exercised over their resources and territories. Ceremonial relations that specifically recognized property rights and linked neighbors in ritual activities, as among California and Southern California moieties, mitigated conflicts by offering recognition to potential enemies, even though the host of a ceremony might use the occasion to parody or belittle the "enemy's" (the other moiety) fighting capabilities.

Let us assess duels, feuds, raids, and warfare, from the least complex to the most complex conflicts, in that order.

Duels

Duels were encounters between two individuals in the same community. Duels have not been reported by the ethnographers who investigated most of the tribes in our sample (V-349), so firm generalizations about the occurrence of duels cannot be offered, but a few words are needed about duels between members of the same River Yuman communities, which were noteworthy. When floodwaters destroyed farm boundaries, or someone transgressed on another person's farm, the disputants, if they could not settle their differences amicably by talking, engaged in a shoving battle. If that did not settle the issue, they had a stick fight. The winner set the new boundaries. No one in any of the River Yuman societies possessed the authority to settle the property dispute, and so no one intervened. Friends of the combatants might be enlisted to join the shoving fight, but not to adjudicate it. In general, among River Yumans, when individual persons, rather than kinship groups, owned private property, problems usually were resolved directly between individual property owners. Rather than having a state apparatus to oversee the litigation, as in the case for complex societies, individuals had to decide what was fair. The River Yumans used controlled stick fights. The Yurok, who also recognized personal property rights over key resource areas, killed poachers, but in many other issues where property was transgressed, the Yurok disputants settled their problems by bargaining. At the conclusion a payment was made in *Dentalium* shells by the party who lost the argument and had agreed to a sum in settlement.

What is of interest in western North America in regards to private property claims made by individual persons is that societies that recognized private ownership of key strategic resources had the most meager political organizations. The River Yuman districts were "nationalities" for waging raids and warfare and for joining in mourning ceremonies, but little else. Yurok, Karok, Hupa, and Wiyot villages were straggling hamlets of individual property owners. Each straggling hamlet cosponsored ceremonials, but little else was done communally. Contrarily, in those societies where the political organizations were most centralized and exercised the greatest control (the Eastern Keres and Tanoan pueblos), productive resource sites were ultimately controlled by the political-religious hierarchy. The "state" usurped, rather than protected, individual property holdings. Indeed, as can be faintly seen in the nature and number of duels, feuds, and offensive raids, there was generally a decrease of each activity with the loss of individual and kinship-group control over productive property.

Feuds

Feuds were conflicts between two families, lineages, sibs, demes, or other kinship groups. A glance at Map Cu-181 (V-350) will confirm that only the Pueblos, Pimans, and Mohaves and Yumas of the River Yumans, are reported as not countenancing feuding between kinship groups within the tribe. Religious–political hierarchies in the Pueblo villages controlled the internal social relations of each village, whereas Pima internal affairs were rather amicable and disputes were negotiated with a third party. Feuds are not reported for most Plateau and Great Basin societies at all, but when feuds were reported for people living in these areas, and in the Southwest, they were usually confined to kinship groups in the same community, or in adjacent communities of the same political unit, and the incidence of feuding was light. It is not a coincidence that, in general, the Pla-

teau dwellers, the Apacheans and Pais of the Southwest, and the residents of the Great Basin all provided free access to their hunting territories and made few claims to private property. With the exception of Apachean farming and gathering sites,* even when private resource areas were recognized, the owners regularly provided access to those areas to others.

Along the coastal strip of western North America and east to the Sierra and Colorado River Desert in California, however, it was a different story. In these areas feuds were engaged in between kinship groups from the same community, different communities from the same political unit (sib, village, tribelet, and so forth), and between kinship groups from different communities that were not aligned in language, culture, politics, or some combination of those features. From the Tlingits on the north to the Cocopa on the south, there was some feuding over fishing stations, oak trees, mesquite trees, water rights, house sites, and other issues.

The relation between the high incidence of feuding and the recognition of kinship-group ownership over some strategic resources is undeniable. Among the Northwest Coast and Southern California communities where kinship units, by and large, were the ultimate possessors of key resource areas, feuding was rampant and kinship groups sought retribution through reprisals. Among all of those societies arbitrators could be called upon to mediate feuds that got out of control. It is safe to say, however, that there were many more cultural mechanisms to control feuds among kinship groups in the central subarea of California and in Southern California than were available in the Northwest. The Northwest Coast societies could establish and maintain relations between kinship groups through distributions, feasts and, for some northern people, moiety alliances. In Southern California the lineages of each sib community were drawn together by common ownership of a sib bundle, recognition of a priest-chief, membership in a Toloache sodality, common moiety obligations, and the mourning-anniversary ceremony.

In the California culture area where tribelets were most frequently composed of several kinship groups—unilineal in the San Joaquin area and bilateral in the northern areas—tribelet territory was recognized and defended; but as is pointed out in Chapter 7, some key resources were practically always

---

*These resource areas were owned by sibs among Western Apache bands, and by demes among Eastern Apache bands.

recognized as the properties of specific kinship units. Poaching from these resources could, and often did, generate feuds. It may be speculated that political tribelets emerged when several related kinship groups coalesced and formed united fronts that recognized common territories. Kinship groups which did so very likely relinquished many property rights. It is noteworthy that among most Pomo, Yuki, Kato, Maidu, Nisenan, and Yokuts tribelets, feuds were settled by tribelet leaders who had the authority to intervene in protracted disputes (see Map Cu-168, V-340, discussed at "Leadership and Realms of Authority," earlier in this chapter). Furthermore, Ghost cults tied all tribesmen in the Western Kuksu area to a common ownership of the land and to one another for time immemorial, and Hesi and Akit societies did the same thing for the Eastern Kuksu tribes. Yokuts were bound by the Toloache sodality moieties, and the annual-mourning ceremony.

On the other hand, among the Miwoks, whose tribelets were single patrilineage communities, similar in many respects to Southern California sib communities, and among the multipatrilineally organized Patwin and Nomlaki communities, arbitrators mediated feuds between property-owning groups. Besides feuding over resources, higgle-haggle in economic transactions also correlated with feuding between kinship groups, so property concerns often precipitated feuds (see Map Cu-85 and Map Cu-94). It is highly plausible that when kinship groups relinquished private property rights as part of the expectation of tribelet membership, sodalities and tribelet officials gained authority to settle disputes between kinship groups within the tribelet. Conversely, the greater the ownership rights of kinship groups, the more likely that arbitrators would be called to mediate problems.

To reiterate, from the Tlingits on the north to the Cocopa on the south, there was feuding, and the incidence of feuding correlated with the ownership and control of strategic resources by kinship groups and the absence of political authority to settle those disputes. Among the bilateral tribelets and some multilineage tribelets of California, the political community, frequently through sodalities, was vested with power to settle feuds.

The Southwest represented an even more complex and unusual picture of feuding. Western Apache matrisibs were known to feud. Inasmuch as the matrisibs owned and protected garden and wild-plant tracts, it is not surprising that feuds emerged over these and other property issues. Eastern Apache matridemes also feuded, and they, too, recognized kinship group ownership of certain gathering tracts.

On the basis of practices among other societies in western North America in which kinship groups owned key resource areas, we would postdict that Western Pueblo matrisibs, too, would feud, but they did not, at least they did not engage in a series of protracted reprisals. Two Western Pueblo kinship groups who were at odds might try to enlist other kinship groups in the village to aid them in manipulating village affairs (to develop factions), but to feud would have been bad form, something unacceptable to the Puebloan way of life. Inasmuch as kiva sodalities controlled land, health, and protection, and Kachina societies controlled rain, all village members were obligated to participate in some collective actions for common ends, whereas kinship groups sought to avoid overt hostilities.

In the Eastern Keres and Tanoan villages, where the sodalities formed religious-political hierarchies, kinship groups owned little over which they could squabble, and the village officials exercised ultimate authority over the behavior of villagers. Feuding was not tolerated. It would have disrupted the Puebloan way.

It is interesting that the Pimas, Mohaves, and Yumas were not known for protracted feuding. Along with the Pueblos, these societies were the most sedentary and the most agriculture-dependent of all groups in western North America. As we have pointed out, River Yumans resolved farmland disputes at the level of the duel. Perhaps as part of a long adaptation to sedentary farming life, the dominant agricultural life in the arid Southwest selected against feuding so that people could control the preplanting, planting, weeding, and harvesting seasons without fear. The parttime farmers and raiders of the Southwest, such as the Navajos and Western Apaches, were relative newcomers to farming and to the region. It is plausible that they expanded their domains at the expense of some of the sedentary farmers, and that they even increased their raiding capabilities and proclivities with the advent of the horse. They did not expand at the expense of the River Yumans, who were exceptional warriors.

The River Yumans were a paradox in the Southwest. They farmed some, controlled productive mesquite groves, and seldom feuded, but often raided—even going to war in the historic period, when they dislocated the Kaveltchadom and Halchidoma, harassed the Maricopa, and attacked the Pimas. Yet the River Yumans did not raid for food, just as they did not feud for food. Food was exchanged and gifted at ceremonies as in other sedentary Southwestern societies, not fought over. It bears repeating: the old agricultural tradition in the Southwest selected against feuding and, as we shall see next, against raiding for food.

Raiding

If agriculture in the arid Southwest selected for (a) sedentariness around sources of water, (b) ritual feasting and trade between farmers and extractors, and (c) against raiding for food and the control of strategic resources, it also made societies vulnerable to attack and promoted defensive raiding skills (see Maps Cu-176 and Cu-177, discussed earlier). The principal raiding clusters were the (1) northern and central Northwest Coast, and (2) the Southwest. Klamath, Modoc, and Upper Thompson groups on the Plateau were also successful raiders. As we have pointed out, practically all societies from which frequent offensive raids were mounted also had to defend against raids (River Yumans were an important exception) but all people who defended against raids and formed counter-raids were not frequent offensive raiders. For instance, raiding had great impact on the organization of California, Southern California, Plateau, Pueblo, and Pima societies, most of whom raided their neighbors infrequently, if at all. Yet all were prepared for raids. Encounters between California Indians were brief, and the raiding party and the defensive party usually halted a fight and ran following the first injury. A small encounter was usually sufficient to reestablish boundaries, to quell immediate enmities, at the same time also sufficiently reinforcing suspicions. The Pimas marshaled large armies to protect themselves from Apachean attacks. The Maricopas called on large forces, which often included Pimas, to protect against Yuma–Mohave attacks, and so forth.

Let us assess the motives for raids with an eye toward understanding what they were about.

It is unmistakable that practically all societies shared one motive for mounting raids, namely, to avenge the death of a warrior (Map Cu-182, V-356). Thus, offensive raiders and those they attacked could become locked into escalating raids if one party was not willing either to quit the battle, or to fight only when attacked. Beyond societies that form offensive raiding clusters, most societies were willing to make a foray or two for retribution, but preferred to defend their home turf. Many Great Basin and Plateau groups did not raid at all.

The next most common motive among the greatest number of tribes to mount raids was to avenge poaching (Map Cu-183, V-357). It goes without saying that before poaching can be avenged, someone has poached fish, women, acorns, crops, water, or some other valuable resource. Thus, some group has conducted a small raid and another group has retaliated. The important point is that many more groups avenged poaching than were known to raid for economic booty (Map Cu-184, V-351). Another way to put it is that defenders were more generalized, whereas offenders were more specific. A few groups harassed many. Tlingits, for instance, at least in historic times, were known to raid as far south as Puget Sound, and River Yumans penetrated to the central California coast, preferably for trading, but also raiding if necessary.

It is significant that all of the groups in the principal offensive-raiding clusters mounted raids for economic booty. Economic booty is defined as all chattels that could be carried, especially food, for the Apacheans and Utes. The River Yumans did not raid for food, but raiding parties would take food on occasion. There can be little doubt that economic motives were important for the Apacheans and Utes, and perhaps even for the northern Northwest Coast groups and the Nootkans in pre-Contact and early Contact times (post-"ethnographic present"). But economic motives surely were not principal among the River Yumans, the Klamath and Modoc groups, and the Salishans of the Gulf of Georgia. Even the Kwakiutls and more northern tribes seem to have had important motives besides booty.

Among all of the principal raiding tribes, bravery and valor were rewarded, so men sought to become successful raiders. This was true among the River Yumans, Apacheans, Utes, Klamath, Modoc, Upper Thompson, and most northern and central Northwest Coast groups (Map Cu-185, V-354). Members of warrior sodalities in the Pueblos gained prestige from retaliatory raiding, but nowhere else was raiding a route to prestige. Prestige was not only gained as a secondary effect of raiding for booty, but it was, in conjunction with dream instructions, sufficient reason to initiate a raid. That is, instructions received in dreams and considered to have great supernatural importance provided a key reason for leading or joining raids among the River Yumans and a few Salishan groups (Map Cu-186, V-355), and prestige accrued to the successful raider. These reasons, regardless of booty or other incentives, were sufficient to cause people to embark on raids.

The distinctive nature of River Yuman raiding was marked by the near absence of economic motives and the modest amount of booty garnered by raiders during their raids. River Yuman men dreamed of power and sang to acquire supernatural power from a diffuse, impersonal force. The dream-recipient received prescriptions for battle—instruction that had to be followed—and the supernatural power in songs emboldened the warrior to accomplish great feats. Victory in battle was sufficient in and of itself. Economic gain was not important except as evidence of victory. The River Yumans, after all, controlled considerable storable resources, and no one challenged them in their home territories. Moreover, they could have produced much more food from farming had they chosen to. A few Salishans mounted raids when, as part of their vision-quests, they received instructions to do so in their dreams. The goal was to achieve prestige, but one means of so doing was in acquiring chattels on the raids which could then be redistributed at distributions and potlatches. Whereas all Northwest Coast people could use the booty they acquired in raids for gifts at distributions and potlatches, only some of the Salishans, including the Bella Coola, tied the raids in with vision-quests and dream instructions.

Among all societies in western North America that condoned offensive raiding, women were stolen on raids. Thus, the tribes in the principal raiding clusters sought women to take back to their home communities. Frequently women stolen on raids became wives of their captors (Map Cu-187, V-352). There were several societies in California and the Great Basin which did not grant prestige to warriors yet which conducted raids for women, specifically for wives. These raids were small in scale and, unlike Northwest Coast and River Yuman raids, did not seek to kill all men in the community under seige.

Raiding for slaves was a trademark of Northwest Coast raiding felt by victims in the Plateau and as far south as the California culture area (Map Cu-188, V-353). Slaves were traded, sold, and given at potlatches among the Northwest Coast tribes; they were even put to death at funerary potlatches for the ranking chiefs of the northern Northwest Coast tribes. Whereas slaves usually worked like everyone else, in some societies they were more ornamental than productive. The burdensome slave was a testimony to the owner's wealth and enhanced his prestige. Some of the tribes of the Middle and Upper Columbia regions became heavily involved in slave-trading in historic times.

On the Correlates of Offensive Raiding

The societies in the principal offensive raiding clusters sanctioned raids as means to gain prestige, women, and booty. The prescriptions to conduct raids from dreams were restricted to a few Salishans and the River Yumans and most probably represented independent origins inasmuch as the raiding patterns of Salishans and River Yumans were different in the key particulars of motive: prestige was of ultimate importance to the River Yumans, whereas booty and slaves enticed the Salishans. As for dream instructions, Salishans gained instructions on vision-quests, but River Yumans did not quest for visions and were not a part of the vision-quest–guardian-spirit complex at all. They received dreams through singing.

Raids to avenge deceased warriors were nearly ubiquitous; raids to avenge poaching occurred in most places where resources were localized, abundant, and stored. It is likely that at various times in the prehistories of the Northwest Coast, California, Southern California, and the horticultural Southwest, raids for food and food resource areas established defensive raiding postures among rather abundantly endowed people and, in these contexts, only where there was the least amount of political organization and where localized kinship-groups were corporate did offensive raiding become institutionalized. The most noticeable exceptions to this generalization were the River Yumans, whose raiding patterns were unique. River Yuman sibs were neither localized nor corporate. It is plausible that "nationalities" (e.g., all Yumas) replaced localized sibs and "nationalities" mobilized for warfare. Southern California Yumans were organized into corporate sibs, on the other hand, that were further organized into exogamous moieties, and moiety organizations sought to avoid warfare while regulating the affairs of moiety mates and opposites from different sib communities.

On the Correlates of Warfare

As we have defined warfare, it was a conflict between two groups which possessed definite leadership, military tactics, and the expectation that a series of battles could be endured (V-361 to V-365). We did not uncover much evidence of warfare in western North America by this definition. Nevertheless, at least two groups in historic times, the Tsimshians of the Northwest Coast and the River Yumans, are known to have attacked and displaced some of their neighbors and to have appropriated their territories. It is known that some Central and Northern Nootkan groups, such as the Clayoquot, in the historic period expanded against their neighbors, as did some Southern Kwakiutl groups but on the whole, most Northwest Coast societies prior to long European contact had scanty political organizations and raids and reprisals accounted for most of their conflicts.

The small sizes of most political units in western North America, the prevalence of feuding, and the widespread practice of retaliatory raiding lend themselves to a picture of the pre-Contact period that included the localization, expansion, and subsequent migration of small groups of people, most often kinship relations. As groups settled and began using resources in an area they marked off for themselves, they more often defended the area than tried to incorporate more area under their domain.

Chapter 10

Ceremonialism

INTRODUCTION

Ceremonies occupied prominent positions in the annual affairs of most Indian communities in western North America. Ceremonies were held on a wide variety of occasions and, ostensibly, for a wide variety of purposes. By explicit ritual incantation and beliefs, aspects of local subsistence economies were often linked with supernatural and extraordinary forces of the spirit world. "First-fruits ceremonies," for example, were held so as to propitiate cultivated crops, salmon, wild seeds, acorns, or some combination of these subsistence-economic resources by some groups. Communal hunts, too, were often attended by rituals which sought success in the hunt as well as the propitiation of the animals being hunted.

In many societies there were ceremonies that prepared warriors for battle or cleansed them after battle, or both, linking the prospects of warriors, as well as their successes in battle, with supernatural phenomena. And through ceremonies people in many societies acquired names and new statuses at various points in their lives—most often in conjunction with the life crises events of birth, puberty, marriage, and death.

Public ceremonies that sought both the well-being and good health of the community, as a collectivity, and the individual persons within the community, were not performed in some areas of western North America, such as the Great Basin and the southern, central, and northern areas of the Northwest Coast, whereas they were the principal ceremonies among most tribes in the Southwest, Southern California, and California. Private ceremonies that were addressed solely to curing specific persons rather than to the general well-being of all persons were widely distributed.

The foregoing does not exhaust all focuses of ceremonies in western North America, and some ceremonies, especially those among the Pueblos, the sib communities of Southern California, the tribelets of the San Joaquin drainage and coastal valley regions of California, and the relatively unorganized, independent, anarchistic, straggling settlements along the Klamath River in northwestern California, combined the propitiation of key subsistence resources with supplication for community and individual well-being.

Few societies performed ceremonies for all of these purposes or on all of the occasions associated with them, and some societies—particularly most of the Pais of the Southwest, and the Southern Paiutes, Western Shoshones, and Northern Paiutes of the Great Basin—sponsored very few ceremonies at all. Moreover, rituals performed by some groups for success in hunting, or to commemorate birth, or to effect cures for personal sickness were private, perhaps family affairs, whereas among other groups, rituals sponsored for similar purposes were elaborate public affairs.

There can be little doubt that the interplay among factors of environment, subsistence, economy, social organization, and polity, within and between communities, helps to account for the various emphases and focuses that ceremonialism received in western North America. It is not coincidental that most Western Shoshones, Northern Paiutes, Southern Paiutes, and Walapai, Yavapai, and Havasupai groups sponsored modest public ceremonies on *ad hoc* bases, and that the ceremonies were invariably associated with the food supply. Local communities among these groups were tiny, scattered over wide territories, and fluid in membership; local environments were not abundant in extractive resources; and some subsistence-resource areas, such as fish-spawning sites, pinyon groves, and grasslands, were available to any and all who wished to use them. Indeed, modest impromptu ceremonies of rejoicing for the abundances at one locality or another were the major reasons for public ceremonialism among these societies. Pais, in their buffered niches between Apachean raiders to the east and Yuman raiders to the west, sponsored rituals to help protect themselves in battle, but the regular performance of communal rituals to make the world whole or to recognize transitions from one status in life to another did not occur. The subsistence adaptations did not allow for several local communities to convene on regular bases, and the communities were so small and so devoid of centralized direction and explicit social and economic boundaries as to provide no impetus for the ritual celebration of the political and social community.

Among the Pueblo villages, on the other hand, key resource areas were localized and were owned either by villages or kinship groups within villages. Crops were abundant, were storable, and were stored. Where kinship organizations owned key resource areas, sodality organizations drew their memberships from several kinship groups, and these sodalities performed a repertoire of prescribed ceremonies for crop fertility, protection of the village, good health, the common good, and so forth. Where villages owned strategic resource sites, kinship organization was muted, and sodalities, usually dual in nature, coordinated and directed the prescribed ceremonial calendar.

Again, it is not a coincidence that people with abundant, predictable, and storable food supplies produced on localized sites which they owned, who organized into large, sedentary villages and were threatened by raids from less sedentary Apacheans and Utes, sponsored dozens of public ceremonies throughout the year, and that these ceremonies, among their principal purposes, promoted the common good, sought success in farming, asked for good health, and promised success in defense of the community. In order to sponsor public ceremonies that lasted for several days and were replete with feasts for large numbers of people, there must have been resources to do so; and in order to seek the common good, some community of adherents had to believe that there was a common good, a public weal, to promote. Such communities of adherents in western North America most often belonged to a political and economic unit, such as a village or tribelet. The Karoks, Yuroks, and Hupas were notable, but explainable, exceptions to the rule. We deal with this matter below.

In short, political and economic communities had to exist before they could be propitiated and before their members could seek a common good. A prerequisite to the formation of such communities was a resource base of relative abundance in which either several types of foods were extractable throughout the year, as in California, or large quantities of storable foods could be extracted or produced during one or two periods of the year, as in Southern California, the Northwest Coast, and the agricultural Southwest.

Although an abundant resource base was a prerequisite to the formation of villages, tribelets, districts, and the like, many societies with abundant resource bases did not form political communities larger than localized kinship groups. This was true, as we have pointed out in several places, for Northwest Coast societies, except the Tsimshians, perhaps the Central and Northern Nootkans, and the Sinkyone, Mattole, and Nongatl Athapaskans of northwestern California. The Tsimshians and Oregon Athapaskans sponsored prominent public ceremonies in behalf of entire political villages, but most Northwest Coast societies did not, even though the public ceremonial life along the Northwest Coast was resplendent with performances sponsored by kinship groups. Along most of the Northwest Coast, localized kinship groups, individual persons within those units, and the corporeal and incorporeal property owned by those groups were the recipients of ceremonial attention.

In preceding chapters we called attention to the relations among resource control and ownership, kinship organizations, political organizations, sodalities, moieties, and warfare. Ceremonial organization is of a piece with these complexly related phenomena. Ceremonialism cannot be explained through simple comparisons with environments alone, storable resources alone, political organization alone, or any other single factor. It is clear, however, that considerable resources were required in order to sponsor public ceremonials, and that the purposes of ceremonials varied systematically with resource bases, the ways in which resources were exploited, and the types of political and economic organizations of the groups that sponsored them. Villages, districts, tribelets, and bands sponsored public ceremonials that reaffirmed their political and economic communities. The Great Basin, Southwest, and Northwest Coast people who recognized no authority beyond the localized kinship group did not reaffirm, through ceremonies, political communities that did not exist, yet Northwest Coast ceremonials were integrally related to the kinship and economic order.

In western North America, moiety organizations or sodality organizations or both were associated with the elaboration of ceremonials and ceremonial organizations. As a rule of thumb, the more elaborate the ceremonial calendar, the more probable that sodalities or moieties were present, and wherever such organizations occurred, guests from adjacent tribes were formally invited to attend ceremonies—often as a reciprocal obligation. Kinship organizations, then, such as most moieties,* and nonkinship organizations, such as sodalities, not only organized people within local communities for kinship, economic, political, ceremonial, and, sometimes, warfare purposes, but also coordinated people between communities for ceremonial purposes. In this and other senses, then, ceremonialism was part of a complex mosaic that included kinship organization, political organization, environmental base, relations between communities, and the like.

Before proceeding with the analysis of ceremonialism in western North America, it is appropriate to provide some definitions of key terms, such as *ceremony, sacred, profane, ritual, cyclic rites,* and *crisis rites.*

A *ceremony* is a performance of any set of regularized practices (actions) and beliefs (thoughts), often with the use of special objects, that is set apart for certain occasions. In western North America, some ceremonies were performed for entire political communities, such as a tribelet. Sponsoring tribelets almost always invited guests to attend from other tribelets in which the language spoken was the same as that of the host group, and depending on the region in which the sponsoring tribelet was located, guests might be invited from political units in which the native language differed from that of the host community. At the other extreme, some ceremonies were private affairs, perhaps for a girl and her family. Ceremonies could be predominantly sacred, predominantly profane, or so mixed that both kinds of attitudes were displayed throughout the performance.

By *sacred* is meant that people held attitudes relative to some objects (such as carved masks), to some practices (such as whirling eagles attached to thongs through the air, and to some beliefs (such as the conviction that supernatural power was embodied in, and inherent in, songs), which not only set such

things apart and forbade their improper use, but which, adherents maintained, were also parts of an unchallengeable supernature. The sacred attitude, then, sanctified some object, acts, and ideas so that they were considered to be beyond mortal challenge. As Durkheim (1912) pointed out at the turn of the twentieth century and as White (1949) reaffirmed, there is nothing inherent in an act, object, or idea that is itself sacred: at any ceremony some songs may be sacred, others not; it is the projection of beliefs on to something that makes that thing sacred and that makes it become a symbol for something else.

By *profane* is meant that people held attitudes that were unsanctified about many ceremonial acts, objects, and ideas. Practices such as the distribution of gifts in some societies, objects such as woven blankets that were given as gifts, and beliefs such as the belief that it was good form to join a dance when invited to do so, might well be regular and expected aspects of ceremonies but were not considered beyond mortal challenges: they were, in short, not sacred. Yet these same acts, objects, and ideas, by dint of tradition, were considered to be very much of a piece with the ceremony.

Frequently, scholars distinguish between ceremony and *ritual.* That distinction will not be attempted here. Ritual is often regarded as a set of practices through which participants relate to the sacred, whereas ceremony has a wider use and includes profane acts and observances. In western North America, most sacred observances were embedded in a ceremonial context that included many acts that, though profane, were performed especially as parts of ceremonies. For instance, formal feasting, singing, dancing, gifting, shamans' performances, and drama could all be either sacred or profane in definition, and as either kind, all were often integral and expected parts of ceremonies, whereas other explicitly profane acts such as canoe races, foot races, and other forms of recreation—competitive and noncompetitive—also were parts of many large gatherings. Ceremonies, then, drew people together for performances of sets of regularized practices, in which acts, objects, and beliefs—sacred and profane—were set apart from everyday activities.

As a rule of thumb, the larger the ceremonial gathering, the more probable that fraternization would lead to reciprocal invitations from guests to their hosts, and to courtships, marriages, and the like. In the large, public context, ceremonial gatherings encouraged the participation in profane acts beyond sacred ritual practices simply because access to the profane was so available among people; it stretches the imagination to think that hosts and guests at public ceremonies attended for sacred

---

*Eastern Pueblo nonexogamous moieties were nonkinship or dual sodalities. The same was true for Pima-Papago and Wappo-Pomo-Kato-Yuki (Western Kuksu) moieties. See Chapter 9.

reasons alone. Rather, secular motives for courtship, feasting, recreation, gifting, and the like were of major importance in many public ceremonies, and probably of some importance in all ceremonies.

The balance between sacred and profane emphases in ceremonies was not always at equilibrium. For instance, among central and northern Northwest Coast societies, distributions, potlatches, and winter spirit-performances emphasized social positions and other profane ends while recognizing the sanctity of the incorporeal property owned by individual persons. Yet the profane character of northern and central Northwest Coast ceremonialism certainly outweighed its sacred character. Ceremonial gatherings in Southern California, on the other hand, emphasized sacred phenomena through prescriptive observances of death, naming, girls' puberty, the inherent powers invested in the sib's priest-chief and fetish bundle, the relations between reciprocating moieties, and so forth. Yet these ritual gatherings, too, were spiced with jests, symbolic threats, happy feasting, and so forth. No hard rule is required to distinguish ritual from ceremony in western North America. Both sacred and profane attitudes attended ceremonial practices. This is not to suggest that the differences between sacred and profane are not of interest. Indeed, we shall examine some reasons advanced to explain why ceremonials in some areas were demonstrably more sacred or more profane than ceremonials in other areas, but the distinction between ritual and ceremonial is not fruitful in studying western North America, so the terms will be used interchangeably.

Over the years the practice has become well established to distinguish *cyclic group-rites* from *crisis rites*.* Cyclic group-rites are recurrent and fixed ceremonies that have significance for most, if not all, of the members of the social group in which they are performed. Their performances are often correlated with rhythmic changes of nature, such as the sequences of the sun and moon, or the seasons of the year. Yet they are also correlated with periods of heightened economic activity.

Crisis rites mark special events in the life of each person: birth, puberty, marriage, and death. These are the so-called biological crises, and the ceremonials connected with these critical but normally

expectable events have been called "the rites of passage" by Van Gennep (1960). They are so named because the events involved transitions from one social status to another. Crisis rites, however, can refer to any ceremonial that is not performed on a fixed schedule. Indeed, pre- and postwarfare ceremonials can be called crisis rites, as can all manner of curing ceremonies.

Crisis rites have been said to be important to the individual for whom the rite is sponsored and to affect others only through their relations to that person. Such was surely so for Northwest Coast societies in which the transitional crises of life were celebrated with public distributions and potlatches. Yet such was surely not so for most of the tribelets of California, sib communities of Southern California, and Apachean bands of the Southwest. Among these groups, public ceremonies associated with death, girls' puberty, male initiations, and birth, either singly or in some combination of purposes, were the primary rituals. Not only were these ceremonials more important to the group than to any specific individual undergoing transformation, but individual ends were muted by, and subservient to, collective ends. Indeed, these ceremonies not only represented the political and economic group—the collectivity—but in California and Southern California they served to tie the living generations with all past generations.

Rather than *ad hoc* affairs that were performed for each woman when she experienced her first menses, or when each child was born, or when each person died, crisis rituals in the California and Southern California culture areas were cyclic, recurrent, fixed affairs. They were performed every year, every two years, or every three years depending on the size of the tribe in question, and whether or not that tribe was organized into moieties. On these ritual occasions, all puberties, or all births, or all deaths that had occurred since the performance of the last ceremony for a similar purpose were celebrated collectively. Societies with moiety organizations, or their equivalents, often reciprocated major rites on alternating years.

As for cyclic group-rites, whereas these had significance for most members of the social group in which they were performed, those groups were not always composed of everyone in the same community. For instance, among many coastal Salishan villages, no matter how many patridemes resided in those villages, each deme employed its own ritualist and sponsored its own ceremony when the first sockeye salmon made its way to the deme's fishing territory each year. The ritualist, after giving thanks for the first salmon that he caught, after treating the salmon with songs, and after shaking feathers onto it and

---

*The term "recurrent group-rite" is used synonymously with "cyclic group-rite." See Norbeck (1961) and Lessa and Vogt, eds. (1972) for examples; the term "rites of passage" (Van Gennep 1960) is used synonymously with "crisis rites."

performing other ritual acts, ate the fish. Following the ritualist, the next people to eat fish were the highest-ranking members of the deme. These modest affairs, while giving thanks for salmon and propitiating them so that they would return in great numbers in subsequent years, also distinguished the rights of each deme to its fishing sites and to the fish that passed through them. While setting each deme and its properties off from every other deme, including those in the same village, these first-salmon rites also distinguished among personal ranks within each deme.

Among competitive Northwest Coast groups, it was the style to use both cyclic rites, such as first-salmon ceremonies, and crisis rites, such as funerary distribution to maintain the competition by asserting and retaining position, to distinguish property rights, and to clarify social rankings of individuals and their kinship groups. Thus, cyclic rites on the Northwest Coast were shaped so as to resemble crisis rites, whereas most crisis rites among California tribelets, for instance, had only the tiniest consequences for individuals and were, in fact, shaped into primary cyclic rites that were addressed to maintaining harmonious and prescribed relations with the gods, with deceased ancestors, and with neighbors, and they affected all members of the sponsoring community.

It is probable that any prescribed ritual, whether related to a life crisis or not, can become cyclic and recurrent. Yet a distinction between crisis rites and cyclic rites in general is that gain or loss of societal members motivates birth and death ceremonies. Unless human sacrifice becomes involved, there is no gain or loss of societal members in cyclic rites.

Chapters 7, 8, and 9 demonstrated that relations between abundances of resources and amount of sedentariness did not always correlate with complexity of political and economic organization. Variations in regional relationships influenced political and economic organization, and the same held true for ceremonial organization. There was, nevertheless, a perceptible relationship among the amount and storability of resources that were exploited, sedentariness, political-economic organization, and ceremonial organization. From the scarce and diffuse resources of the Great Basin, with its anarchistic, egalitarian, flexible, tiny, and mobile communities, to the abundant, localized, predictable, and storable resources of the Eastern Pueblos, with their politically centralized, stable, large, and sedentary communities, ceremonialism varied from extremely simple to very complex. In the Great Basin proper, ceremonialism was characterized by very modest public performances sponsored on *ad hoc* bases, which few people outside the local residence group attended. The

ceremonials were performed in celebration of food supplies, and they entailed few ritually prescribed or proscribed acts and objects. There was only the simplest integration of beliefs with performance. Eastern Pueblo ceremonialism, on the other hand, was characterized by many elaborate, prescribed public and private performances sponsored throughout a ceremonial year. Many guests attended the public ceremonials, which were coordinated by leaders of one of the nonexogamous moieties (dual sodalities) and performed by various sodalities, depending on the ritual. Ceremonial purposes were complex and varied, ranging from propitiation of crops to seeking to make the world complete, and to promoting the health and common good of the village community. The more complex the ceremonies, the more numerous their focuses. The most complex ceremonies in western North America made individual persons, kinship groups, and their particular interests subservient to political-economic communities and their ends, and made the community of living and breathing souls less powerful than its deceased ancestors or its even more powerful array of spirits, who oversaw Pueblo affairs.

Ceremonies varying in complexity and purpose between those performed in the Great Basin and those performed among the Pueblos are of considerable interest because they show special emphases that developed within culture areas, as well as interareal correlations between similar types of ceremonial organizations and similar types of political organizations. Let us turn to culture area analysis before assessing interareal relations.

CEREMONIAL AREAS

Figures 10-1 and 10-2 demonstrate the areal patterning of ceremonial organizations in western North America. Differences were considerable among tribes, so much so that the average similarity overall was only 28 percent. Within each of the areas shown on the ceremony map (Figure 10-2) it is clear that variation was equally marked (as can be seen by comparing Figures 10-1 and 10-2). In fact, there was greater variability within and among culture areas for ceremonialism and life-cycle observances than for any of the other major categories of culture as we have defined them in this study. It appears that even when sets of societies from the same culture area shared many ceremonial features, most of those same societies embellished and innovated so as to make their repertoire of ceremonies, and the acts, objects, and beliefs they comprised readily distinguishable.

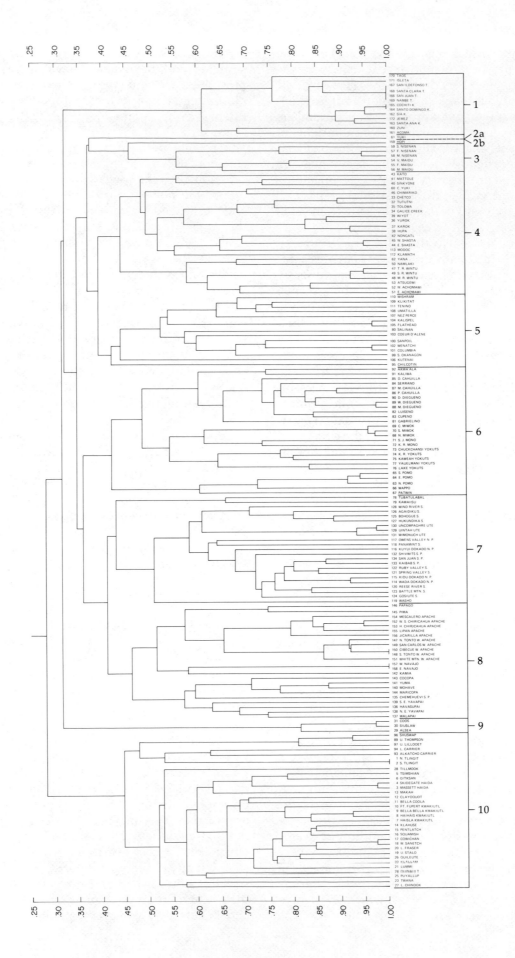

Figure 10-1 *Culture tree: 7. Groupings of tribal territories derived from G coefficients based on 39 variables (237 attributes) of ceremonialism, including life cycle.*

GROUP 1

170 Taos
171 Isleta
167 San Ildefonso Tewa
168 Santa Clara Tewa
166 San Juan Tewa
169 Nambe Tewa
165 Cochiti Keres
164 Santo Domingo Keres
162 Sia Keres
172 Jemez
163 Santa Ana Keres
160 Zuni
161 Acoma

GROUP 2A

61 Yuki

GROUP 2B

159 Hopi

GROUP 3

59 Southern Nisenan
57 Foothill Nisenan
58 Mountain Nisenan
54 Valley Maidu
55 Foothill Maidu
56 Mountain Maidu

GROUP 4

43 Kato
41 Mattole
40 Sinkyone
60 Coast Yuki
46 Chimariko
33 Chetco
32 Tututni
35 Tolowa
34 Galice Creek
39 Wiyot
36 Yurok
37 Karok
38 Hupa
42 Nongatl
45 West Shasta
44 East Shasta
113 Modoc
112 Klamath
62 Yana
50 Nomlaki
47 Trinity River Wintu

49 Sacramento River Wintu
48 McCloud River Wintu
53 Atsugewi
52 West Achomawi
51 East Achomawi

GROUP 5

110 Wishram
109 Klikitat
111 Tenino
108 Umatilla
107 Nez Percé
104 Kalispel
105 Flathead
80 Salinan
103 Coeur d'Alene
100 Sanpoil
102 Wenatchi
101 Columbia
99 Southern Okanagon
106 Kutenai
95 Chilcotin

GROUP 6

92 Akwa'ala
91 Kaliwa
85 Desert Cahuilla
84 Serraño
87 Mountain Cahuilla
86 Pass Cahuilla
90 Desert Diegueño
89 Western Diegueño
88 Mountain Diegueño
82 Luiseño
83 Cupeño
81 Gabrieliño
69 Central Miwok
70 Southern Miwok
68 Northern Miwok
71 San Joaquin Mono
72 Kings River Mono
73 Chuckchansi Yokuts
74 Kings River Yokuts
75 Kaweah Yokuts
77 Yauelmani Yokuts
76 Lake Yokuts
65 Southern Pomo
64 Eastern Pomo
63 Northern Pomo
66 Wappo
67 Patwin

GROUP 7

78 Tubatulabal
79 Kawaiisu
128 Wind River Shoshone
126 Agaiduku Shoshone
125 Bohogue Shoshone
127 Hukundika Shoshone
130 Uncompaghre Ute
129 Uintah Ute
131 Wimonuch Ute
117 Owens Valley Northern
     Paiute
118 Panamint Shoshone
116 Kuyui-Dokado Northern
     Paiute
132 Shivwits Southern Paiute
134 San Juan Southern Paiute
133 Kaibab Southern Paiute
122 Ruby Valley Shoshone
121 Spring Valley Shoshone
115 Kidu-Dokado Northern
     Paiute
114 Wada-Dokado Northern
     Paiute
120 Reese River Shoshone
123 Battle Mountain Shoshone
124 Gosiute Shoshone
119 Washo

GROUP 8

146 Papago
145 Pima
154 Mescalero Apache
152 Warm Springs Chiricahua
     Apache
153 Huachuca Chiricahua Apache
155 Lipan Apache
156 Jicarilla Apache
147 North Tonto Western
     Apache
149 San Carlos Western
     Apache
150 Cibecue Western Apache
148 South Tonto Western
     Apache
151 White Mountain Western
     Apache
157 Western Navajo
158 Eastern Navajo
142 Kamia
143 Cocopa

141 Yuma
140 Mohave
144 Maricopa
135 Chemehuevi
139 Southeast Yavapai
136 Havasupai
138 Northeast Yavapai
137 Walapai

GROUP 9

31 Coos
30 Siuslaw
29 Alsea

GROUP 10

96 Shuswap
98 Upper Thompson
97 Upper Lillooet
94 Lower Carrier
93 Alkatcho Carrier
1 Northern Tlingit
2 Southern Tlingit
28 Tillamook
5 Tsimshian
6 Gitksan
4 Skidegate Haida
3 Massett Haida
13 Makah
12 Clayoquot
11 Bella Coola
10 Fort Rupert Kwakiutl
9 Bella Bella Kwakiutl
8 Haihais Kwakiutl
7 Haisla Kwakiutl
14 Klahuse
15 Pentlatch
16 Squamish
17 Cowichan
18 West Sanetch
20 Lower Fraser
19 Upper Stalo
26 Quileute
22 Klallam
21 Lummi
24 Quinault
25 Puyallup
23 Twana
27 Lower Chinook

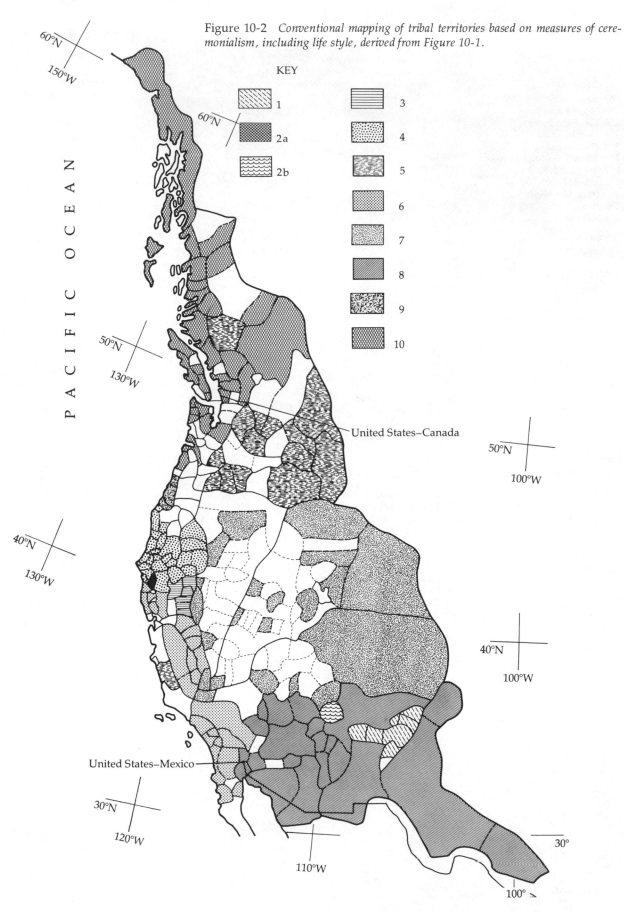

Figure 10-2 *Conventional mapping of tribal territories based on measures of ceremonialism, including life style, derived from Figure 10-1.*

KEY

1	2a	2b	3	4
5	6	7	8	9
10				

PACIFIC OCEAN

United States–Canada

United States–Mexico

Differences were measurable, even between neighboring societies whose members attended each other's ceremonies, intermarried, and effected other interactions. Witness, for examples, the variation within and between Eastern and Western Kuksu sodalities, and within and between Eastern and Western Pueblo sodalities. The average similarity for the areas stretched from a high of 62 percent among Pueblo groups (group 1, at the upper end of Figure 10-1), to a low of 42 percent among Central and Southern California groups (group 6, at the center in Figure 10-1).* The clustering of societies within continuous geographic areas fits the general pattern that we obtained when using the total cultural inventory (Figure 4-1) and most major categories of culture within the total (Figures 5-1, 6-1, 7-1, and 8-1).†

In previous chapters we have organized our analyses of societies to coincide with the culture area taxonomy obtained from correlating all cultural variables in the sample (Figure 4-1). The ceremonial area taxonomy is sufficiently interesting and varies enough from the culture area taxonomy to justify the use of the former to organize the analysis in this chapter. Several nontrivial inferences about cultural relations can be inferred from the groupings obtained here, as will be clear to the reader. For instance, we join the central and northern Northwest Coast and separate that set from the southern Northwest Coast. Moreover, northwestern and northern California are joined, thus separating the former from the Northwest Coast and the latter from the California culture areas.

The Pueblos, with their complex ceremonial calendar of agricultural and nonagricultural rituals, and the central and northern Northwest Coast tribes, with their highly developed distributions, potlatches, and winter dancing ceremonies, which were so closely integrated with the life cycle and the kinship ranking system, stand out on opposite ends of Figure 10-1 as having possessed the most distinctive ceremonial repertoires in western North America.

Pueblo ceremonials were addressed to the human community's obligations to the gods, community well-being, harmonious relations, good health, a renewed world, and success in agriculture. Either, as among the Eastern Pueblos, individuals and kinship organizations were of little significance or, as among

the Western Pueblos, matrisibs had considerable economic and ritual importance, but ceremonial activities and beliefs, even sodality membership, formally crosscut kinship interests and made kinship units subservient to the gods.

Northern and central Northwest Coast ceremonies, on the other hand, were focused on the life cycle, on personal and kinship group prerogatives and privileges, on property ownership, and on personal and kinship-group rankings in an areal ranking system. Northwest Coast ceremonies were elaborate, competitive, and predominantly profane. For the most part, distributions and potlatches sought to benefit only one person and that person's kinship group, whereas masked ceremonials, of winter performed by dance societies, demonstrated the rights and privileges of a select few.

The differences between cooperation, community emphasis, and questing for the general good, all in the prescribed ceremonial calendar of the Pueblo villagers, and the emphases on splendid, *ad hoc* ceremonials in behalf of people undergoing transformations in life, which typified ceremonies in the Northwest Coast culture area, represent points at opposite extremes, both of which were achieved by rather sedentary people who had abundant, storable resources: some of these people were food extractors, others food producers.

Pueblo Ceremonialism

The Pueblos, though surrounded by Apacheans and in contact with River Yumans, Pais, and Pimans, were sufficiently different from these neighbors in ceremonial practices to be set off from them at a considerable distance (groups 1 and 8 in Figure 10-1). Among the Pueblos, cyclic rituals, which were intended to generate community health and well-being, were the ultimate prescribed rituals in their annual ceremonial calendars. The rituals were performed for all of the people in the village, and wittingly, all villagers played a part in the successful performances, no matter what their kinship-group or sodality affiliations. Although sodalities controlled ritual performances, the rituals were more important than the sodalities themselves. In Western Pueblo societies, rituals could be transferred from sodality to sodality, if such was necessary, to keep the performances alive. The transfer of a ceremonial from one kiva sodality to another could occur, for instance, if the sib that owned the kiva ritual had no male members who could assume control of the ceremony. When sib membership dwindled to such a point, the

---

*See Figure 10-1 to determine the average similarity (in percentage) within each area, and the subsets within areas as well.

†Figure 9-1, on political organization, sodalities, and warfare was most clearly aberrant: there, societies were clustered in a crazy-quilt pattern.

ritual might be transferred to the son of the sib father (thus transferring the ritual to the sib of the father's wife). It might also be transferred to another sib in the same phratry if the sib that originally sponsored the ritual could no longer do so. The rituals were important because they gave legitimacy to society itself. Among the Pueblos, prescribed ceremonies were correlated with changes in the sequences of the sun at summer solstice (the longest day of the year, about June 21, when the sun is at its highest point in the south); winter solstice (the shortest day of the year, about December 21, when the sun is at the lowest point in the north); and at vernal equinox (about March 21) and autumnal equinox (about September 21), times when the sun is about midway between its most southern and northern positions, days and nights then being about equal in duration. Yet Pueblo ceremonies were also correlated with heightened economic activities, so much so that Ortiz (1969) has pointed out that the Tewa Pueblos recognized the four-part ritual year (two solstices and two equinoxes) with special ceremonies, yet Ortiz also notes that the basic ritual division was dual, distinguishing the summer, or agricultural cycle, from the winter, or nonagricultural cycle. A high dependency on agriculture was correlated with the greatest elaboration of an annual ceremonial calendar in western North America, and with an emphasis not only on the behaviors of the sun, moon, and the seasons, but on the economic activities of the seasons and the sacred aspects of all these phenomena.

In Pueblo ideology and practice, individual persons, kinship groups, and all things within the society were subordinate to, and integrated by, the supremely important ceremonial cycle and the gods that were represented in masked dances in various rituals of that cycle. The sanctified position of the gods could be reaffirmed, and the communal well-being obtained from their spiritual largesse, only if the proper rituals were performed in the specified way by specially qualified sodalities and their leaders: this condition not only defined the relations between Pueblo populations and their gods but also defined relations among members of a Pueblo and made clear their expectations. Groups of persons, not individual persons, were initiated into a ceremonial life—at the very minimum villagers were initiated into a tribalwide Kachina sodality (Western Pueblos), or into a dual sodality (Eastern Pueblos). The initiates were drawn into a complex ceremonial calendar that made the interests of each initiate subordinate to the common good.

So, whereas individualized crisis rites were either private and modest or not recognized ceremonially at all, public crisis rites to mark initiations of groups of individuals of about the same age into the principal sodalities were prominent in Pueblo culture, for their transition to ceremonial adulthood was recognized when these initiates assumed obligations in the ceremonial organization. Although great ritual fanfare was not attached to the funeral for each person, death occupied a very special place in Pueblo ideology. Death served to transform humans into ancestors, whereupon they became supernatural beings. The Eastern Pueblos, both Tanoans and Eastern Keres groups, made the mythological link between living and past generations explicit in acts and observances by sponsoring annual rituals to commemorate all dead ancestors.

Pueblo ceremonies required officiants who had committed entire complex rituals to memory. The gods that were honored in masked performances were envisaged as personalized spirit-beings. Among the Hopis, rainmaking ceremonies were the special province of the tribalwide Kachina sodality, and in Hopi mythology, the rainmaking ceremonies themselves were prescribed by the gods who gave Hopis land and crops. It was believed that deceased Hopis descended to the lower world of a two-part (upper and lower) cosmos. In the lower world of the dead they transformed to Kachinas and assumed the forms of clouds, where they manifested themselves as rainfall. The ceremonial ties between living and past generations, natural and supernatural phenomena, focused as they were on bringing rain to crops and making crops grow, were complete and circular. From life came death, yet from death came life.

Pueblo cosmologies had horizontal as well as vertical dimensions that were associated with color symbolism, and with the powers of various gods. The dimensions, symbols associated with them, and gods varied from Pueblo to Pueblo, but the cosmology for each Pueblo set boundaries around the world, defined its center, and defined the ritual obligations that obtained between the natural and the supernatural, and between the mortal and immortal.

Even shamans were suppressed as individual operators in the Pueblos and were organized into medicine societies. Rather than being independent practitioners, members of medicine sodalities performed ceremonies to effect cures as a group. The ceremonies were complex and were committed to memory. This is not to say that members of medicine societies were all equal. At public performances the members of the societies were capable of remarkable feats of legerdemain, but they were members of explicit sodalities to which all members devoted themselves for life—usually being initiated after a personal sickness and cure. As initiates, they were trained to cure, learned the same rituals, and later performed for private and public causes.

As we have seen, the medicine sodality in each

Eastern Keres Pueblo was especially important, being responsible for appointing the village chief from its membership and, through that chief, controlling political and ceremonial affairs of this village.

Pueblo agricultural rituals through which successful planting, maturation, and harvesting of crops were sought, especially production of rain to bring these about, were but part of the annual ceremonial calendar defined by the equinoxes and solstices. In its nonagricultural phase, communal dancing, game rituals, and war rituals were performed to protect the community, make the world whole, and to prepare the world for farming even though people did not farm at that time of the year. The rituals were undertaken in two steps. The first involved retreats into kivas by ritual leaders for prayer and preparation. Later, masked performances were staged in which supernaturals appeared.

There were differences between Western and Eastern Pueblos in their periods of greatest ceremonial activities. In the east, the greatest activity occurred between the autumnal and vernal equinoxes, that is, in the nonagricultural cycle. In the west it was the obverse. It is possible that two related phenomena account for the differences. Western Pueblo farmers were dependent on seep-water and rainfall; matrisibs owned land; matrisibs controlled kivas and their rituals; and centralized political authority was never developed. The greatest ritual activity of Western Pueblos was addressed to producing rainfall and making crops grow; this activity also expressed the interdependencies of sibs and their obligations to the gods. Eastern Pueblos depended more on main-canal irrigation and less on seeps and rainfall than the western groups; but much more important is that centralized authorities responsible for the agricultural land, the main ditches, and the houses also were responsible for directing the ceremonial life among Tanoans and the Eastern Keres groups. The ceremonies of the agricultural cycle were focused on producing rain and making crops grow, as in the west, but the Summer sodality (one nonexogamous moiety), controlled all the agricultural ceremonies. The Winter sodality (the other nonexogamous moiety) controlled all the ceremonies that expressed the unity of the religious-political-economic community. It is likely that Eastern Pueblo winter ceremonials expressed the unity of political communities that were never achieved among Western Pueblo matrisib villages.*

All of the following provided ceremonial integration where there was not complete centralization of a political and economic community: the integration of Western Pueblo ritual performances into a ceremonial calendar prescribed in Western Pueblo ideology by their gods; the performance of the rituals by kiva sodalities composed of members from many sibs, even though each kiva sodality and its ceremonies was controlled by a particular sib; and the tribal initiation into the Kachina cult, coupled with transformation into Kachinas at death.

Northern and Central Northwest Coast

In marked contrast to the Pueblos, northern and central Northwest Coast societies (represented at the bottom of Figure 10-1) paid scant attention to the cycles of the sun and the moon, and their ceremonials were not sponsored for the common good. Neither individual persons nor kinship groups were made subordinate to a centralized polity or to an integrated set of gods. Even the Tsimshian villages were not nearly so centralized as Eastern Pueblo villages. Life crisis events, and the masked performances of the winter ceremonials—which appear to have grown from vision-quests at puberty—became the main focuses of ceremonial life. Birth, puberty, marriage, and death, especially when these things happened among the wealthy, were marked by colorful distributions, replete with naming ceremonies, gifting, feasting, privileged displays of masked dancing, and singing.* The intent of distributions was to secure the social position of the individual person and his or her kinship group. The distributions stressed notions of property control through inheritance of resources, privileges associated with incorporeal property, succession to positions within the kinship group, and individual and kinship-group rights and prerogatives, which were ranked in comparison with all other kinship groups in the general region in which each person and his kinship group resided.

Whereas distributions and the potlatches that most probably grew from them did not stress community well-being, or village integrity beyond the kinship group (except for Tsimshian villages), or the common good, potlatches explicitly promoted interkinship-group, intervillage, and intertribal comparisons of resource control and wealth. The bases of these comparisons were in the nature of the resource areas that people controlled and from which they could ac-

---

*For an analysis of the differences between Tanoan and Eastern Keres political and ceremonial organization, see Chapter 9.

*See Chapters 7 and 8 for discussions of economic, kinship, and rank considerations of distributions and potlatches.

cumulate wealth. Moreover, potlatches were catalysts to intermarriages among people from distant villages and different language groups.

The winter ceremonials of northern and central Northwest Coast societies were similar in many beliefs, acts, and objects, even though dancing sodalities were most highly developed among the Kwakiutls. Throughout the entire region, individual persons, at around the time of puberty, went on lonely and physically demanding quests in order to gain spiritual help in specialized pursuits such as raiding, hunting, shamanism, woodworking, and weaving. If a spirit was encountered, the lone searcher received from that spirit instructions about a song, a prescribed way to paint his or her face, a cry, costume items that represented the spirit, and an exhibition that mimicked the spirit and recreated the encounter. The spirit encounter was subsequently validated by the community at winter performances.

Barnett (1955) has pointed out that winter ceremonials varied among Salishans, though all basically were performances in which each recipient of a spirit encounter recreated that encounter, including privileged song and costume performances. In the Puget Sound area, Salishan people such as the Puyallup, Nisqually, Skokomish, Snohomish, and others convened in large dance-houses to sing and dance, each individual recreating his or her encounter. The sessions were unorganized in the sense that anyone with a spirit helper could perform, and each performance was unique to the possessor of supernatural aid. Among the Salishans to the north, in the Gulf of Georgia region, spirit dancing and singing was unorganized. In these villages, too, each participant demonstrated his or her spirit-endowed privileges and unique spirit encounter. Like the Puget Sound Salishans, Gulf of Georgia Salishan spirit dancers at Cowichan, Sanetch, Nanaimo, and many other villages did not have dance sodalities which performed explicit series of dances, but they differed otherwise from Puget Sound Salish in that all new dancers had to be initiated by established dancers; this was not required in the area around Puget Sound.

Farther north still, the Comox and Pentlatch Salish at the northern end of the Georgia Strait had organized dancing sodalities into which people were initiated if they had acquired, through inheritance, gift, or purchase, the right to perform a simulated spirit encounter. That is to say, Comox Salish did not reenact their personal encounters with spirits. Rather, they simulated a spirit encounter said to have been experienced by a long-deceased ancestor in their deme. The simulated spirit encounter was a property of the deme that one member of the deme was privileged to display. Thus, winter ceremonials

among the most northern Salish of the Georgia Strait area—those closest to the Kwakiutls—enacted spirit encounters, but these enactments were not personal encounters of the privileged performers. They were prestigious displays, formalized in content and style, so that at any point in time—no matter whatever member of whatever generation of the deme received the right to simulate the deceased ancestor's encounter—the performance entailed the same song, costume, dance, and so forth. These performances, inherited through the deme and recognized by other demes and other communities through potlatches that claimed the right to display the spirit and claim the spirit name, were symbols of the performer's position within the deme and of the deme's position among other demes in the wider community.

Drucker's (1940) analysis of Kwakiutl, Nootkan, Tsimshian, Haidan, and Bella Coola (Salishan) winter ceremonials shows that there were several coordinated Northern Kwakiutl (Bella Bella, Haihais, Haisla, Wikeno) dancing societies—Shamans', Dluwulaxa, and Nutlam—and that these sodalities performed a systematic, ranked series of dances. Yet at base, each of the dances in the cycle reenacted an ancient spirit encounter, and each dancer inherited the right through his or her kinship group, legitimized through a potlatch, to join the appropriate sodality and perform the dance. This, of course, was similar to the practices of the Comox and Pentlatch Salish along the Georgia Strait. The various Southern Kwakiutl, Tsimshian, Haidan, Nootkan, and Salishan dance cycles were not arranged so systematically as those of the Northern Kwakiutls. It is most likely that from the Northwest Coast and Plateau base of the vision quest, and from the re-creation of each vision encounter in the winter spirit dances and sings, the Northern Kwakiutl groups developed dancing sodalities and the concept of inherited performances. The practice must have diffused north and south from the Haisla, Haihais, Bella Bella, and Wikeno Kwakiutl groups to other Kwakiutls and to adjacent tribes.

No matter whether the winter ceremonials were organized and coordinated by sodalities or were unorganized, and no matter whether a person reenacted his or her own encounter, or that of a deceased ancestor, the successes of individual persons and the stations occupied by their kinship groups were dramatized in winter performances.

The inheritance of privileged performances and the distribution of worldly goods through potlatches were so vital to membership in dancing sodalities that, among several Kwakiutl groups and some of their neighbors, uninitiates had to avoid dance houses during the entire rituals, but could attend one night of dancing (Drucker 1940). Furthermore, un-initiates were barred from the potlatches that followed winter ceremonial performances, even when the initiates were high-ranking members of their own demes or sibs (depending on the society). This was not true for other kinds of distributions and potlatches, where all people in the kinship group that sponsored the affair attended and contributed to it.

In accenting the gradations of rank, the winter ceremonials replicated secular rankings. The higher the rank, the greater the number of ceremonial prerogatives owned by the sodality member. Wherever winter ceremonial prerogatives were based on ancestral encounters with spirits, the ritual organizations served to divide, rather than integrate, people in the same villages and wider regions.

Central and northern Northwest Coast ceremonialism celebrated each person, each kinship group, and the private corporeal and incorporeal properties of those kinship groups (invested in individuals in the dancing sodalities). Although highly secularized and addressed to the ranking system of the kinship and economic order, Northwest Coast ceremonialism also recognized the sanctity and supernatural powers inherent in crests, songs, dances, masks, and names. It legitimized the individual person and his or her kinship group.

Southern Northwest Coast

The societies strung along most of the Oregon Coast were similar to their neighbors north of the Columbia River in availability of subsistence resources, concepts of kinship-group ownership of strategic resource sites, and the presence of residential kinship-groups as the ultimate sovereign units.* Yet throughout this southern subarea of the Northwest Coast, economic distributions were not welded into ceremonies, potlatches were not sponsored, and the ceremonial organization in the region suggested little or no sustained contacts with the societies to the north, where potlatching and winter ceremonials were dominant features of life. Southern Northwest Coast ceremonials were simple in concept and modest in performance, and had meager attendance. The marked differences from the central and northern sections of the Northwest Coast cannot be attributed to the variations between southern and central North-

---

*Oregon Athapaskans also shared features with northwestern California and the coastal Penutians.

west Coast environments (see Figure 2-2), or to basic differences in property ownership practices. In fact, it is very likely that the relations between wet-forest adaptations, localized fishing stations, and kinship-group ownership of strategic resources were developed independently more than once along the Northwest Coast. The differences in other aspects of economic organization, such as the failure of groups along the Oregon Coast to create redistribution mechanisms and the ceremonial elaborations of redistributions into potlatches, suggest different spheres of associations for the people who resided north and south of the Columbia River. Whereas Kwakiutl, even Tlingit, raiders were known to journey south into Puget Sound, contacts between central and southern Northwest Coast villagers were few.

Consonant with Oregon Coast notions of property ownership, as well as similar notions elsewhere along the Northwest Coast, rank, prestige, and wealth were important features of ceremonial organization. But the ceremonial manifestations of these ranking phenomena were so different from the more northern coastal cultures as to suggest either an independent development of this secular focus along the Oregon Coast, or a common and ancient substratum for all Northwest Coast cultures harkening to the earliest localization of kinship groups around productive resource areas. A relative ranking system based on the abundance and predictability of resource areas may have developed to distinguish among residential kinship-groups. The more productive properties may have generated more wealth for their owners, and a commensurate social ranking.

Only the Tillamook villages sponsored distributions of any type, and they were much smaller in scope than the distributions sponsored by their Salishan congeners around Puget Sound and along the Washington coast. Nevertheless, the ranking of extended families throughout the Salishan and Penutian communities along the Oregon Coast was an important feature of the social organization, and it was also important in the ceremonial life of the area. At dances held in large houses at irregular times during the winter seasons, heads of the most prominent households displayed their wealth.

People from many villages were invited to attend these two-night affairs in which individual performances, often quite competitive, highlighted the dancing. Wealthy men, frequently with the help of their families, displayed their otter skins, obsidian blades, woodpecker scalps, and other precious items. As with the dancing, wealth-demonstrations too were competitive, as men jockeyed to demonstrate their importance. They did not give the wealth away at the conclusion of the dance, though one rich man would usually host the affair in conjunction with his kinspeople.

Some leaders owned the songs that they sang, but lent them to all singers. Thus, ownership was recognized, but the use of the song was extended to people other than owners. There were no dancing orders, and no formalized sequences of dances. The main body of the dancing was imitative of hunting and may have re-created the vision experiences of each dancer. Added features that distinguished the Oregon Coast from the more northern regions were a male–female dance conducted with obsidian knife blades, which imitated a battle between the sexes, and a quick side-stepping dance for pairs of women, done inside the dance house.

The winter dances performed along the Oregon Coast were not focused on the life cycle, or on first-fruits ceremonies. On the other hand, the imitative animal and hunting sequences that sought abundances of game, and the communal weeping that followed the dancing, suggest that commemoration of the dead, as well as reenactment of spirit encounters from vision quests at puberty, were basic to these individualistic gatherings. The belief—widely spread throughout the Plateau, the Northwest Coast, and the Plains region beyond the Rockies—that a spirit helper could be obtained through an individual vision quest, may ultimately account for the imitative dances associated with southern Northwest Coast winter wealth-displays.

To be sure, winter dances provided opportunities for wealthy persons to assert their positions relative to one another. Yet these winter ceremonies did not celebrate the various transitional stages in the life cycle, which the distributions and potlatches of the tribes north of the Columbia River did, nor were they full-blown wintertime spirit-sings and dances associated with spirit quests and their reenactments, found farther north along the coast and in the Plateau to the east. Oregon coastal people did not dance with masks to represent family prerogatives. Moreover, the only stage of the life cycle that received much attention in the southern subarea was birth, for which private naming ceremonies were sponsored which were attended by feasts and the distribution of gifts to family members. These affairs were not held in conjunction with winter displays.

Public winter ceremonials in the southern subarea of the Northwest Coast, then, were not focused on the life cycle, or the food cycle, or community health, yet they ballyhooed the wealthy and their rights to control strategic subsistence-resource areas. The ceremonials clearly recognized the relations between small kinship groups and their leaders, emphasizing the productive resources and celebrating the economic success of those leaders.

Winter dancing and wealth displays, in which woodpecker scalps, otter skins, obsidian blades, and white deerskins were exhibited by their owners, were sponsored by Oregon Athapaskans near the California border, and the display of the same kinds of prestige items also occurred in northwestern California. It is obvious that all the Oregon coastal groups and those of northwestern California shared some similar features, probably through a loose network of connections maintained by intervillage attendance at winter dances, where they saw one another's practices. Yet the Oregon Athapaskans and northwestern California societies were sufficiently different from the Penutian and Salishan speakers of the Oregon Coast to be grouped with several societies from the northeastern California interior (group 4 in Figure 10-1). Public ceremonies for each woman at her first menses, and a complexly integrated cycle of ceremonies devoted to the propitiation of fish, acorns, and deer distinguished the northwestern–interior northern California cluster of societies.

Northwestern and Northern California

The ceremonies of northwestern California societies were sufficiently different from the other Northwest Coast societies to be distinguished from practically all of them. Group 4 in Figure 10-1 lumps these societies at a low level of similarity with their Athapaskan neighbors in northwestern California and southern Oregon (the Tolowa, Tututni, and Chetco) and with their interior neighbors of northern California (Yana, Wintu, Chimariko, and so forth). The subsistence economies of the northwestern California societies were much less dependent on fish, sea-mammals, and shellfish than were the subsistence economies of most northwest Coast groups. We have observed concomitant differences between northwestern California societies and other Northwest Coast groups in their economic, social, and political organizations. It is highly likely that the cultures of northwestern California represent adaptations to wet-forest environments that were, for the most part, independent of adaptations and influences from more northern tribes.

The primary rituals of the Karok, Yurok, Hupa, and probably the Wiyot, propitiated the key subsistence resources in their environments, celebrated the firmness and wholeness of the world, and sought good health for, and good will among, the world's inhabitants. For these tribes, the world was the Klamath River and adjacent regions (Kroeber 1925). Unlike most of the groups in the southern cluster of the Northwest Coast, the northwestern Californians celebrated each girl's transition to womanhood with a public ceremony. The sponsorship of these public ceremonies linked them with their interior neighbors, yet the interior people did not sponsor elaborate ceremonials in conjunction with subsistence resources.

The unique constellation of northwestern California ceremonials suggests that though females were publicly selected for special treatment at puberty, and wealthy individuals displayed their prestige with items of wealth, neither kinship groups nor individual persons received other recognition worthy of special mention. To the contrary, the many straggling and anarchistic Karok, Yurok, and Hupa hamlets shared common obligations to propitiate salmon, acorns, and deer, to enrich the world and make it whole, and to foster good health. In many obvious ways these ritual focuses were the antithesis of Northwest Coast culture. Furthermore, these focuses were contradictory to the unorganized structure of northwestern California social and economic organization.

It was in northwestern California that individual ownership of resources, as opposed to ownership by kinship groups, was most highly developed. No real authority was invested in any person beyond one's own patribilateral lineal household. Yet neither individuals nor their households were the sole sponsors of ceremonials; and neither individuals nor households were the center of attention in ceremonials. Ceremonials, which included several days of feasting and dancing in each village that helped sponsor the cycle, were no-host affairs nominally directed by the community's wealthiest man, alone or with the codirection of a shaman. All households in the community contributed, but not from duress or obligation to the wealthy leader. Instead, the households in each community acted on common obligations to remake the world each year.

There is no doubt that personal wealth was more important among the coastal groups than among the interior groups, even though wealthy men exercised considerable influence in most interior communities. The Oregon Athapaskans, as we have pointed out, sponsored wealth displays in conjunction with winter dancing, in which they represented animal spirits, whereas the wealthiest men among the Yuroks, Karoks, Hupas, and Wiyots usually represented their communities. The important points, it seems, are that the ceremonials of the northwestern California people not only emphasized renewal of the world, but that the world-renewal theme (the name by which anthropologists refer to this ceremonial cycle) was an obligation of people from many communities and many language groups, people who competed for ownership and control over resources.

There was no formal organization to integrate the ceremonials that these peoples sponsored, but people from the Karok, Yurok, and Hupa villages were invited to ceremonials sponsored by each community, and the performances of the various villages were scheduled so as not to overlap. Moreover, Wiyot, Tolowa, Tututni, and Chilula people from the coast, and Shastan people from the interior, attended these ceremonies.

The ceremonies did not distinguish tribelets *qua* tribelets: each sponsoring community was only one of several distinct sponsoring communities; but each sponsor was, in actuality, a coalescence of several families from the anarchistic and straggling settlements along the Klamath called villages. So without formal village organizations, or a formal ceremonial organization, the Karoks, Yuroks, and Hupas were integrated into a prescribed cycle, a concatenated series of rituals that propitiated the first salmon, the first acorns, and the plenitude of deer, and that reestablished the world, created new fire, prevented disease, and averted calamity for another year or, perhaps, two. The rituals, then, focused on the good of the community, the well-being of individuals, and the bountifulness of nature.

Throughout the many communities, at specific times, ritualists performed specific acts and staged dances in specific sacred structures (houses, or sweat-houses, or lean-tos, depending on ritual prescription). The most prominent of the dances were the Jumping Dance and the White Deerskin Dance. The former made use of woodpecker-scalp headbands, the latter albino deerskins and long obsidian blades. Either singly, or together, these two dances were performed in ceremonies sponsored at thirteen separate communities in the cycle. Moreover, at each of these thirteen communities these particular dances were repeated from one or two successive days up to sixteen days, again depending on prescription. Songs added complexity to the performances in each community, as did scores of variations on ritual themes. Nevertheless, the Karoks, Yuroks, Wiyots, Hupas, Tolowas, Chilulas, and Shastans, speaking several different languages, created a tight ceremonial world that underscored their common purposes rather than their differences.

The ceremonial accommodations made among the people of northwestern California stand in striking contrast to their individualistic social and economic orders. The world-renewal cycle varied more from the central and northern Northwest Coast ceremonial patterns than did the ceremonials of the Oregon Coast tribes. The evidence from the southern and northwestern California subareas of the Northwest Coast suggests that arguments for the necessity of distributions and potlatches to distribute locally variable resources have been significantly overdrawn (see Piddocke 1965; Suttles 1960).

The tribelets of the Northern California interior, the Coast Yuki, and the Athapaskan Nongatls, Katos, Sinkyones, and Mattoles formed several distinct subsets within the Northern California–Northwestern California ceremonial area. All of these tribelets were distinguished from the northwestern California communities through the performance of tribelet-sponsored ceremonies called "Big Times" or "Big Soups." Big Times were several days of feasting and dancing, usually performed in a large communal house, and usually under the supervision and directorship of a chief and a shaman. When tribal larders were full, one tribelet would sponsor a Big Time, with most households in the tribelet contributing food for the feasts. Sometimes food was also offered as "take-home" gifts to visitors. Guests were invited from adjacent tribelets in all directions by means of messengers carrying knotted strings which they gave to leading men in each tribelet, each knot representing a day prior to the Big Time.

Singing, dancing (often by Kuksu cults), feasting, and games occupied the time of guests and sponsors alike. The guests often brought food to the festivities, so the Big Times were not asymmetrical distributions of food from sponsors to guests.

Big Times varied in their structures from tribelet to tribelet. Dance costumes, dances, the number of days of the performances, and so forth, were a bit different for every tribelet. Yet Big Times were performed by all tribelets in California, from the Wintu and Shasta on the north to the Yokuts on the south.* Big Times, more than any other ceremonial, epitomized the organizations of tribelets and their relations with neighbors. They were communal festivities to which neighbors were invited, which were reciprocated by neighbors. Throughout the Western Kuksu area reciprocation was facilitated by nonexogamous moieties. Each tribelet protected its boundaries and was suspicious of its neighbors, yet neighbors were invited. Even at Big Times guests were wary of the power of shamans who were instrumental in the ceremony and it was incumbent on the tribelet chief who sponsored the ceremony to insure a safe visit for the guests.

Big Times, while providing points of contact with neighbors, also reinforced differences among neighbors. Big Times were not the same as the world-renewal ceremony. World renewal stressed common purposes among many property owners, from many localities, speaking several languages.

The tribelets of the northern interior of the California area performed public rites recognizing each girl's puberty transition that were similar in many details to those sponsored in northwestern California.* These tribelets also performed some Kuksu songs and dances at Big Times, though they were not organized into Kuksu cults. Thus, these interior tribelets of northernmost California shared similarities with all California tribelets in sponsoring Big Times, with the Eastern and Western Kuksu tribelets in performing some Kuksu-type songs and dances, and with northwestern California tribelets in sponsoring public ceremonies at the puberty transition of each female.

Northeastern California

The Maiduans comprised a distinct ceremonial area that we call Northeastern California (group 3, Figure 10-1). Except for the northernmost tribelets of interior California (Wintus, Shastans, Achomawis, *et al.*), all tribelets in the California culture area as defined in chapter 4 possessed special ceremonies and special ideologies about the relations between the living and deceased generations and the unity of both within the tribelet. As will be recalled, the Western Kuksu tribelets made the connection through their tribal-wide Ghost societies and the rituals that they sponsored. The Eastern Kuksu tribelets, particularly the Maidus and Nisenans, made the connection between the living, the deceased, and the continuity of the tribelet through mourning-anniversary ceremonies.[†] It is evident that Maiduan ceremonies were different and distinct even though they were similar to Western Kuksu ceremonies in some ways, similar to Big Times sponsored throughout the entirety of the California culture area in many ways, and similar to mourning-anniversary ceremonies sponsored by societies in the central California area in some ways.

Mourning ceremonies were important rituals in cultures ranging from the Maidus in the north to the

---

*The "Fiestas" of Southern California tribes, mentioned later in connection with ceremonies of Northern Paiutes, were similar to Big Times, but they seem to have been post-Contact phenomena that gained importance when the elegant Mourning-Anniversary Ceremony withered.

*Girls' puberty rites and other life crises are discussed below.

[†]Mourning-anniversary ceremonies also go by the names "Annual Mourning" and "Mourning." No matter what name is used, all shared many similar features, though performances were locally variable. Some tribelets sponsored them annually, some biannually, and so forth.

Kaliwas of Southern California and the River Yumans of the Southwest in the south. Among the tribelets south of San Francisco Bay, the mourning ceremony was the most important public ritual in each tribelet's repertoire. But among all groups ranging from the Eastern and Western Kuksu tribelets to the River Yumans, death rituals were of great importance, whether or not mourning ceremonies were sponsored. Rather than emphasizing differences among people, as was the practice on the Northwest Coast, mourning ceremonies and Ghost society rituals stressed continuity of relations among members of the same tribelet. They were rituals for tribelets or collectivities, rather than for individual persons and their kinship groups.*

Initiation ceremonies for boys and sometimes for girls at puberty, as was demonstrated in the sodality section of the preceding chapter, were also of great importance for groups ranging from the Kuksu areas through the Toloache and Chungichnish zones of Southern California. These ceremonies, too, created similarities among people within tribelets and made explicit their obligations to the sodalities, to the supernatural, and to their communities. Puberty ceremonies in California, then, did not create distinctions among people and celebrate individual persons, though they most frequently created distinctions between the sexes.

The public and communal features of male and sometimes female puberty initiations, and mourning and ghost ceremonials, defined and celebrated tribelets as boundary-protecting groups. California ceremonials did not sanctify the autonomy and importance of particular kinship groups (which Northwest Coast ceremonials did) or the ritual unity of independent households scattered over a wide region (which was focused on in northwestern California tribelets).

Along the eastern half of the Sacramento Valley, and eastward to the crest of the Sierra, the many Maidu and Nisenan tribelets were distinguished from their neighbors in the northern part of the California area, as well as from their neighbors to the south and as far west as the Pacific Coast (group 3, near the top, in Figure 10-1). As we have pointed out, they shared Kuksu cult features but not Ghost society features with the Western Kuksu area; and shared mourning ceremonies but not the Toloache sodality with units to the south of them. The Maidus and Nisenans sponsored Big Times, as did all tribes in the northern parts of California, and conducted public girl's-puberty ceremonies for each woman at her first menses, as did their neighbors in the northern part of the California area.

Earlier chapters mentioned the complex tapestry of rituals, sodality organizations, and moiety organizations that spread across the California culture area, the Southern California culture area, and extended as far south as the River Yuman area. The complexity can be understood from any of a number of vantage points. It is possible to speculate about the historical origin, subsequent borrowing, and subsequent elaboration of rituals, among other things. I have chosen to suggest that the development of tribelets as boundary-defending units was most simply demonstrated in ceremonials by Big Times. Sodalities, which crosscut kinship interests within tribelet communities, and moieties or their equivalents,* which established obligatory relations between communities, were more complex social developments that were inextricably bound with ceremonials and that further defined the internal structure of tribelets. Moieties were especially prominent features of ceremonial life where unilineal kinship-groups flourished. And when mourning ceremonies or Kuksu dances were hosted, Big Times were often staged at the conclusions.

Big Times and the battery of other sacred rituals performed on ceremonial occasions among California tribelets variously served to legitimize, and put beyond mortal challenge, each tribelet and its sodalities. The stamp of uniqueness for each tribelet came from the considerable variation among tribelets in the performance of, and beliefs about, such things as the nature of Kuksu, Hesi, or Akit spirits.[†] It was possible for Eastern Kuksu area tribelets to differ from one another and from Western Kuksu tribelets in sacred beliefs, acts, and objects associated with Kuksu performances, all of which undoubtedly had a common origin, and for Western Kuksu tribelets to possess Ghost societies and nonexogamous moieties whereas Eastern Kuksu societies did not; yet many Eastern Kuksu tribelets performed mourning-anniversary ceremonies, whereas Western Kuksu tribelets did not. And mourning ceremonies were more complex in the San Joaquin area than they were among the

---

*The exceptions were the Miwok monolineages and Southern California sibs. Mourning ceremonies among these people, however, specifically linked lineages or sibs with their moiety opposites. Furthermore, each Southern California sib was composed of several lineages and was equivalent in size to a multikinship-group tribelet.

---

*Opposite and reciprocating lineages, or reciprocating communities.

[†] See the section on sodalities in Chapter 9.

Maidus and Nisenans. On the other hand, Toloache sodalities were less important to internal affairs among San Joaquin groups than were Kuksu sodalities among the Maidu and Nisenan groups.

The performances of mourning ceremonies among groups ranging from the Maidus on the north to the River Yumans in the south were public affairs in which guests from adjacent regions and different sibs, tribelets, or districts were specifically and formally invited to attend the death and burial of a deceased member of the group, as well as to commemorate all deceased members of the group who had died prior to the current ceremony. Oratory, singing, feasting, wailing, moaning, the burning of gifts which were offered to the deceased, and the burning of images of the deceased were parts of all mourning ceremonies. Among the Maidus and Nisenans, mourning ceremonies defined the districts (tribes) and linked the living members with the past. Big Times of feasting, dancing, and gambling were sponsored by Maidu and Nisenan tribelets following their versions of the mourning ceremony. Farther south, among the Miwok, Yokuts, Mono, and Kawaiisu tribelets, and among the sibs of Southern California, the mourning ceremony was integrated into performances with several different combinations of rituals and, depending on the tribe, they were often sponsored, at least in part, by moiety reciprocals.

California and Southern California

The California and Southern California ceremonial area taxonomically is perhaps the most confusing of all ceremonial areas, at least it may seem so as the reader compares the combinations of societies that co-occur in this area with the classifications of those societies in previous chapters. As stated above in explaining the differentiating of the Northwest Coast culture area into three ceremonial areas, we have sought throughout to maintain consistency in referring to societies and the culture areas in which they are classified. To do so we have used the culture area taxonomy derived from the multidimensional analysis of 292 variables for 172 societies. Yet the cultural phenomena pertaining to ceremonials do not produce the same culture areas that we obtained with our total sample of cultural phenomena. As we have seen in our discussion of the northwestern California societies and some of their near neighbors in the interior, and our discussion of the Northeastern California ceremonial area, the California culture area and the California ceremonial areas are not isomorphic.

In the ceremonial area that we have labeled "California and Southern California," some, but not all, societies in the California culture area, as defined in Chapter 4, are classified along with all Southern California societies in a single area. All of the ceremonial areas are interesting, but this area is especially interesting because the combination and permutations of ceremonial observances and practices within the area, and the similarities of these observances and practices to ceremonial observances and practices in Northeastern California allow us to hypothesize about nontrivial relations that encompass all of the California and Southern California culture areas.

The California and Southern California ceremonial area (group 6 near the center in Figure 10-1) draws together in three separate subsets societies from the Southern California culture area (all), the central subarea of the California culture area (the Miwoks, Yokuts, and Monos), and the northern subarea of the California culture area (the Pomos, Wappos, and Patwins—i.e., most of the societies that constituted the Western Kuksu area). The Pomo-Wappo-Patwin group, hereafter referred to as the Western Kuksu group for simplicity, was most different from the other two inasmuch as these tribelets did not perform a mourning ceremony at all. The mourning ceremonies of central California groups incorporated Big Times, mourning, the burning of effigies, shamans' performances, first-acorn rituals, war dances, and other components over a period of several days. Nevertheless, propitiation of deceased ancestors and recognition of the sacred links uniting the living, the dead, and their common ownership of tribelet territories provided the underpinnings for mourning ceremonies, as well as for the Ghost societies. The former represented the Central California and Southern California groups; the latter represented the Western Kuksu groups. These many societies possessed moieties (exogamous for the patrilineal societies and nonexogamous for the bilateral descent societies of the Western Kuksu area) and sponsored first-acorn ceremonies, though in different contexts. And the Miwok of the San Joaquin area sponsored many Kuksu-type spirit impersonation dances, even though they did not have Kuksu sodalities. In this respect, the Miwok were similar to the Wintu and Shasta.

Big Times were held following either Kuksu performances or mourning ceremonies, or whenever large quantities of food had been accumulated. In the Central California and Western Kuksu areas, as in the Northern and Northwestern California ceremonial areas, the Big Times were directed by a chief, usually in conjunction with a shaman. On these occasions, guests were housed in large dance houses, feasted, and joined in dancing and singing. Moieties often entertained each other and competed in some games; Kuksu dancers and Ghost dancers performed for the groups in the Pomo area; and all spectators—guests and hosts—often watched shamans perform feats of legerdemain, such as ventriloquism, or rattlesnake handling, sometimes in competitive performances.

Guests were invited under friendly circumstances, though they attended with some trepidation. Shamans were the causes of much of the fear, at least in the Western Kuksu area and in the adjacent northern part of the California region, because they were believed to smite enemies as well as cure friends. Because guests were potential enemies and because shamans occupied positions as directors or codirectors of public ceremonies in which guests were invited from other tribelets and other language communities, the guests were often suspicious of their hosts' actions. These contradictions of pleasure and fear were inherent in a shaman's power, but they were also inherent in intertribelet relations in the northern part of California, where each tribelet defended its boundaries against trespass yet invited its neighbors to feast and dance with them in an atmosphere charged with the power of shamans.

Among the San Joaquin and Southern California groups, on the other hand, where patrilineal exogamous moieties or their equivalents played very prominent roles in the ceremonial affairs of their opposites, even shamans from opposite moieties were invited to attend and to join the local shamans in performances at mourning ceremonies. Lineages, multiple lineages, sibs, and reciprocating villages—all who participated in the moiety phenomenon—were able to define themselves and recognize others in amicable ceremonial relations. Yet these were the same people who jealously guarded their resources against poachers. The differences between moieties were underlined on ceremonial occasions through rough jesting in songs and games in which moiety opposites were ridiculed as enemies—though friendly ones.

Shamans' performances were delightful and awe-inspiring at the same time. The competition among shamans demanded that everyone in attendance recognize the power and potential harm that could be inflicted were ritual relations not so well established on both sides, but they also displayed the individual powers of the shamans, regardless of their moiety–tribelet affiliation.

As was pointed out in Chapter 8, nonexogamous moieties existed among the Western Kuksu area societies and exogamous moieties existed in Southern California, and throughout the Central California area. Only in the latter two areas did moieties draw opposites into explicit ritual obligations while defining marriage-eligible partners. Among the Western Kuksu people moiety organizations were less formal. What has not been made clear up to this point is the

manner in which the exogamous moiety system in Southern California, while coordinating egalitarian sibs into explicit ritual relationships, also laid the ceremonial base for defining each sib as distinct and economically autonomous. In the Southern California culture area moiety reciprocals were also obligated in the sponsoring or directing of ceremonies that recognized the transitions of statuses of birth, girls' puberty, and death for their opposites.

Common themes among the societies of the California and Southern California ceremonial area were the roles of moieties or their equivalents in performing games for their opposites and in sponsoring the pole-climbing ritual attached to the first-acorn ceremony. But even the moieties and the rituals they sponsored varied among groups. Moieties among the Western Kuksu groups were weakly developed and primarily they provided recreation and games, whereas among the groups of the central part of California and in Southern California, they regulated intersib and intertribelet relations and were deeply involved in the entirety of the mourning ceremony.

The life crisis events among communities in the central part of California and Southern California were channeled toward initiating members into lineages, sibs, moieties, sodalities, or some combination of those organizations, whereas among the Western Kuksu societies they were focused on sodalities, including tribeletwide sodality initiation alone. Yet in all of the societies of this ceremonial area, ritual connections between all the living and all the deceased were expressed. Contrary to the Northwest Coast practice, individual persons were not singled out and celebrated in ways that allowed each person to be recognized to the exclusion of all others, and subsequently to occupy unique niches in the society. Girls' puberty rites were less important in the central part of California and the Western Kuksu area than in Southern California or the northern part of the California area, except among the Miwoks to the east of San Francisco Bay. Rites for this transition either were not performed, or they were performed on a private and restricted basis. Among the Miwoks and the Southern California groups, public girls' puberty rites were performed for girls by their moiety opposites.

The Southern California societies, when contrasted with societies of the Northwest Coast, best exemplify how different ceremonial organizations could be even when the ultimate political and economic organizations of each area were, by and large, localized kinship groups, and when the subjects of the rituals themselves were the life crisis events.

Along the central and northern Northwest Coast, life crisis events—distributions and, at a later date, potlatches—substantiated claims to personal privileges and prerogatives embodied in names. Through the ceremonial acquisition of names and related privileges, each person could achieve a ranking relative to others within and outside the kinship group, and each kinship group could be ranked relative to all others. Only members of the kinship group could use kinship-group property, except by invitation. Naming conferred each kinship-group member with rights to their collective property, yet set each person apart in the ranking system. Shortly after puberty only a select number of persons from high-ranking kinship groups were initiated into dancing societies, and the sodalities were not envisaged as mechanisms for the common benefit of any political unit.

In Southern California, sibs owned and protected property. At birth, sib naming ceremonies established a person as a member of the fathers' sib and moiety, but they did not rank the persons who were named. Moreover, sibs were not hierarchically ranked. Membership in a sib defined obligations to sibmates, moiety mates, and moiety opposites, and sib rituals stressed the sib collectivity and ritual obligations to moiety opposites. Whereas births were attended by a formal public naming ceremony and two subsequent namings, girls' puberty by a formal public ritual, male puberty by sodality initiations into Toloache or Chungichnish societies, marriage by a moiety feast and gift exchange, and death by effigy burning, in every instance the sib took precedence over the individual. For instance, a group of boys of about the same age were inducted into the Toloache and Chungichnish sodalities at the same time. Several girls were collectively given a puberty ceremony. All children born since the last mourning ceremony were named in a single naming ceremony. And all people who had died since the last mourning ceremony were collectively recognized at one mourning ceremony. Moreover, most of these events were integrated into the mourning ceremony, so all events were ceremonialized when this was performed, once every few years, usually once each one- to three-year period, depending on whether there had been any deaths during the period. As a consequence, no individual person stood out: the sib, alone, stood out.

The mourning-anniversary ceremonies among Southern California groups were the ultimate ceremonies, and like the Toloache sodality, the ritual acts, objects, and beliefs were markedly sacred, much more so than was true for Northwest Coast distributions or winter ceremonials. Mourning ceremonies were spread out over many days and required active participation from moiety opposites. The ceremonies honored both the recent and ancient dead, through wailing, moaning, singing, dancing, gifting, and burning effigies, but the entire mourning-an-

niversary repertoire of ritual focuses included birth-naming ceremonies, which replaced deceased members with the most recent additions to the sib by birth, and linked the two eternally: from death comes life, and from life comes death. Southern California sibs also incorporated the Eagle Ceremony, a set of whirling dances, symbolically linked the living with the dead, into their mourning-anniversary ceremony, and the sacred fetish bundle of each sib, too, was renewed at the mourning-anniversary, thereby confirming the sib's power and his sacred position as priest-chief. Furthermore, as part of the mourning-anniversary the water from one of the sib's most strategic springs was asperged, linking the sib to its most precious resource. Finally, in the mourning-anniversaries of many sibs, girls' puberty rites, directed by moiety opposites (men initiated their daughter's daughters into the opposite moiety), prepared women for marriage and subsequent removal to the moiety of their maternal grandfather. The muting of individual ambition, the sacredness of the proceedings, the submerging of personal motives, and the interplay of moieties were not even vague reflections of Northwest Coast affairs. Not even marriage potlatches between Haida and Tlingit moieties and paired Tsimshian and Haisla phratries reflect on Southern California practices.

The mourning ceremonies of Southern California, in stressing sib membership, and the sanctity of kinship groups and their rights, also recognized the sanctity of moiety reciprocals. It was the collectivity rather than the individual member, reciprocity rather than unbalanced relations, equality rather than hierarchy, and sacred rather than secular ceremonialism that distinguished Southern California ceremonialism from Northwest Coast ceremonialism. It was not coincidental, surely, that whereas Southern California natives, like their counterparts in the California culture area, were suspicious of their neighbors, they engaged in less raiding, offensive and defensive, than the natives of the Northwest Coast. Finally, the mourning ceremonies sponsored by Mono, Yokuts, Miwok, Salinan, and Maiduan were not nearly so complex as those in Southern California and did not reaffirm sacred authority of priest-chiefs as was the case in Southern California.

Plateau

In much of the ceremonialism that was sponsored by societies in the Plateau, one can discern the egalitarian and communitarian counterpart of the ranked and privileged ceremonies of the northern and central Northwest Coast. The major ceremonial complex among Plateau tribes (group 5 in Figure 10-1) was the winter Guardian-Spirit Dance. Based on the vision quests for guardian spirits at puberty undertaken by practically all males and females among Plateau societies, winter spirit-dances were held during a two- or three-month period around the winter solstice. It was believed that guardian spirits made annual visits at that time.

In these ceremonies, spirit encounters were re-created in dance, song, and shamanistic performances. Participation in the dancing and singing was open to anyone who possessed a spirit; moreover, anyone and everyone could attend the performances as a spectator. There were no secret sodalities and no named and traditionally performed dances that were passed from generation to generation. Each dance re-created the personal spirit encounter of the dancer.

Dances were sponsored either by prominent shamans, whose powers were attributed to extraordinary spirit encounters, or by any other respected spirit dancer. They were staged so as not to overlap or conflict with ceremonials sponsored by adjacent communities. Dancers and spectators were invited to the sponsoring village from neighboring villages and from other villages as far distant as people wished to travel. All guests were feasted and given gifts of equal amount, but the people who had travelled the farthest were often the first to receive gifts.

Songs and dances were individually led by people who possessed spirits, and shamans, in particular, conducted special performances of sleight-of-hand, and escape tricks. During seances shamans performed acts of ventriloquism or gave speeches in strange voices. Among a few groups, power contests among shamans were also conducted during winter ceremonials. The dancing usually took place at night in a large house over periods of four or five days (depending on how many members of the tribe took part in the ceremony).

The Klamaths on the south, the Athapaskan Carriers on the northwest, and the Kutenais on the northeast were least like the other Plateau tribes. Winter spirit dances among the Klamaths featured shamanistic performances; Carrier and Chilcotin groups sponsored irregular, one-night sings; and the Kutenais did not have winter dances at all, though anyone among the Kutenais who possessed a guardian spirit could perform publicly to forecast events with the help or his or her spirit, and the Bluejay shamans' society was a special version of spirit dancing restricted to a select group.

The winter guardian-spirit dance-complex required initiation, but there was no sodality, as there was among the Comox Salish of the Georgia Strait, into which the initiate was inducted. The initiate in the

Plateau simply participated in an inaugural dance in order to demonstrate possession. Among the Fraser Plateau Salishans (Lillooet, Upper Thompson, Shuswap), the winter performances tested the spirit songs of initiates and sought an abundant food supply. But throughout most of the Plateau, the winter ceremonial season sought, through the annual visitation of guardian spirits, to bring good health and well-being to everyone.

The communitarian and egalitarian nature of the feasting and gifting that accompanied the Plateau ceremonies differed considerably from Northwest Coast practices. Winter dances on the coast, whether or not they were performed by dancing sodalities, were followed by potlatches or wealth displays. On the northern and central Northwest Coast, feasts and distributions of gifts correlated the social worth of the recipient with the liberality of the donor—the effect was to publicize ranked social statuses. In the Plateau neither kinship groups nor individual members were given gifts that denoted social status, nor were dances and songs ranked and performed as privileges of ownership. Spirit performances, as well as the gifting and feasting associated with them, were common to the Northwest Coast and the Plateau, and they probably had a common origin. The abundant and localized resources, of the Northwest Coast, that region's dense populations, its sedentary winter villages, concepts of property, kinship organization, and ranking system were all of a piece with the ceremonial organization of the Northwest Coast.

Each Plateau village and band did not distinguish itself from all similar communities, as was the practice of the tribelets of California. But similar to California tribelets and Northwest Coast kinship groups, Plateau dance sponsors invited people from far and wide to attend their ceremonials, yet only in the Plateau were guests treated as honored equals, and only here were distinctions of the local political community unimportant. Conviviality marked these ceremonies, just as conviviality marked other relations among Plateau communities.

First-fish ceremonies were performed at the major fishing spots on the Columbia and Fraser drainages, almost always as intertribal affairs. The same was true for first-fruits ceremonies associated with the collection of roots at major gathering grounds. On these occasions gambling was especially prominent, and teams from various communities engaged in hand-and-stick games, among other gambling diversions. The hand-and-stick game was played with marked and unmarked sticks. One team would sing and beat rhythmically on a log with sticks as it attempted to deceive the opposite team as to who possessed the marked and unmarked sticks. Members of the opposite team would attempt to guess the whereabouts of the sticks. If they guessed correctly, the sticks were given to them to hide. If they guessed incorrectly too often, they lost whatever they had waged. The best gamblers were considered to possess special supernatural powers for the task. Rather than hoard their winnings, however, successful gamblers shared them by hosting many of the intertribal feasts that attended first-fruit ceremonies or foregatherings for trade.

Thus, the major ceremonials of Plateau groups were based on individual vision-quests at puberty, but they were performed to bring good health and to promote the common good rather than to enhance individual statuses, whereas first-fruits ceremonies were occasions for public rejoicing and intertribal use of resources, rather than annual affirmations of kinship group or tribelet property rights.

Great Basin

Great Basin (group 8, Figure 10-1) ceremonialism was less complex, ceremonies were sponsored less frequently, and fewer people attended ceremonies than anywhere else in western North America, except among the Pai societies of the non-Pueblo Southwest. Among most of the tiny Western Shoshone, Southern Paiute, and Northern Paiute communities, ceremonies were *ad hoc* affairs, often no more than circle dances, feasts, and gambling, directed by a shaman or by a headman who also was a shaman. At fish-spawning locales, or prior to a communal antelope hunt, or at a rich pine-nut harvest when two or more camps convened, hunt leaders might simulate, say, antelope behavior, and attempt to make the antelopes vulnerable to their spears and arrows through magical acts such as scraping together a notched and unnotched stick, dancing, and singing. Circle dances in which women and men danced sideways around a circle were parts of most such affairs, but these foregatherings to antelope hunts were not regular in performance, and did not celebrate anything other than a bountiful harvest or the prospects of a successful hunt.

On the far western side of the Great Basin culture area, the Northern Paiutes of the Owens Valley and immediately adjacent areas attended Big Times and mourning ceremonials sponsored by the Western Monos and Miwoks on the western side of the Sierra. In turn, the Northern Paiutes hosted Big Times (called "Fandangos or Fiestas" in post-Contact times) and even mourning ceremonies, on irregular bases. Although modest mourning ceremonies were sponsored from time to time, Big Times, following successful seed harvests or rabbit hunts, were the major ceremonials of these people at the edge of the California culture areas. The Northern Paiutes of the Big Pine and Bishop areas undoubtedly borrowed the moiety reciprocating concept, *sans* moieties, from their California neighbors on the west side of the Sierra. On an alternating, biannual basis, these communities hosted Big Times for each other to which they also invited Western Monos and Miwoks from across the Sierra.

On the eastern side of the Great Basin culture area, the Ute and Shoshone bands of the Rocky Mountains and the Snake River drainage convened for intra- and interband ceremonials at several times during the year. The greater ceremonial activity of the Utes and Shoshones, contrasted with the ceremonialism of their congeners in the Great Basin proper, was unquestionably a product of a greater abundance of subsistence resources—particularly medium-sized herd mammals—larger community size, band organization, and warfare. All of the Utes and Shoshones performed the basic Great Basin repertoire of circle dances in conjunction with successful hunting and gathering activities, but their largest and most important ceremonies were usually sponsored in the spring.

Among Utes, the primary ritual was the Bear Dance. Each band sponsored one between February and March, each year. People from adjacent bands were invited, the dances being scheduled so as not to conflict, and the guests were fed by the hosts while in attendance. The dances were directed by a shaman (bear-dance chief) and several helpers. The ceremony lasted about ten days, with dancing activity increasing each day though ending each night. An orchestra played musical rasps (the notched and unnotched sticks also used for antelope-charming) on a drum resonator, or log, to simulate the awakening of bears from hibernation. Women chose partners and then the dancers formed two lines, women in one, men in the other. For several days, the lines of dancers would advance and retreat, simulating the increased activities of bears as they resumed their hunting and cohabitation practices. On the final day, the dance lines would break into couples and the couples would begin dancing to exhaustion, each woman and man trying to run the other into the ground and to gain dominance in so doing. Finally, a pubescent girl and her partner would fall in exhaustion: they were charmed by a shaman who rubbed a rasp over them. This was followed by a feast, gambling, and more singing.

By performing the bear dances, Utes sought to invoke Puwa, a diffuse force, for a change in the weather from that of winter to that of the onset of spring. But they sought much more, including good health for all, fertility for women, and hunting and gathering success. Bears were believed to enjoy robustness, good health, and prowess in both sexual and food-gathering pursuits. Utes desired the same things, but they also wanted to be protected from bears during the spring. Indeed, so concerned were they for this that a menstrual hut would be constructed adjacent to the brush enclosure in which the bear dances were held, and girls who were honoring or experiencing their first menses stayed inside the hut so as not to offend the bears.

Some Shoshones (Agaiduku) performed bear dances, and others (Bohogue, Hukundika, and Wind River) performed circle dances for general blessings, warm weather, and to make the grasses grow. During the equestrian period the Wind River Shoshones adopted the Sun Dance (the most majestic of Plains Indians ceremonies) as their primary ritual, and they also sponsored naming events for prestigious warriors and leaders. But prior to the early nineteenth century, circle dances were their main ritual fare, though Utes and Eastern Shoshones, perhaps prior to the equestrian period, performed war dances in preparation for battle, and scalp dances to purify warriors upon their returns from raids.

The public ceremonial activities of Utes and Shoshones were confined primarily to the spring, summer, and fall (the reverse of Plateau and Northwest Coast practices), when food was plentiful. At these times local residence-groups convened into bands, and interband contacts were made through hunting, gathering, and fishing expeditions. The band and interband meetings drew many more people together than was possible in the central and western portions of the Great Basin. Yet like their Great Basin congeners, Utes and Shoshones did not mark the life cycle with public ceremonies. Ute and Shoshone emphases on good health, community well-being, and heightened economic activity were but elaborations on Great Basin themes. But bear dances and their public equivalents among the Eastern Shoshones correlated with the reconvening of the bands each year, whereas the rituals associated with warfare correlated with the offensive raiding that was made possible by their mobile, hunting life-styles. It is not coincidental that the band and village societies of the Plateau, the band societies of the eastern Great Basin, and the Apachean bands of the Southwest, each in their own ways practiced communal rituals that called for good health and well-being for their own members and for all visitors, but that did not make clear distinctions between territorial boundaries of hosts and guests and did not threaten guests with the specter of shamans employing power for malevolent ends. Predominant band exogamy, the fluidity of band membership, and the open policies of hunting-territory use seem to account for the egalitarian and communitarian nature of band rituals in western North America.

Non-Pueblo Southwest

The Athapaskan-, Yuman-, and Piman-speaking tribes of the Southwest were distinguished as three separate clusters within the non-Pueblo Southwest (group 8 in Figure 10-1). The ceremonialism of the non-Pueblo groups was sufficiently different from the Pueblos to separate these two sets of tribes by a considerable distance in the tree diagram, whereas the differences among the non-Puebloan subareas suggests differences in the histories of the three language groups.

Yumans and Pimans, for instance, had long histories of residence in the Southwest. The Hohokams, the most likely precursors of the Pimans, were probably ensconced in southern Arizona by 400 BC, and Hakataya Patayan farmers on the Colorado River plains, the most likely precursors of the River Yumans, were raising crops by between 300 and 600 AD. It is plausible that the progenitors of the River Yumans acquired domesticated crops from the Hohokam, and there is little doubt but that subsequent trade and ceremonial contacts were established among River Yumans and Pimans, River Yumans and Pueblos, Pueblos and Pais, River Yumans and Pais, and Pais and Pueblos. In still more recent times, the Apacheans entered the Southwest. All of the Apacheans, but particularly the Navajos and Western Apaches, maintained contacts with Pueblos. Pueblo ceremonial practices exercised great influence on Apachean rituals, but the differences among Apachean and Pueblo ceremonials, between Navajo and Apache ceremonies, and the focus of Pueblo and Apachean ceremonials were very different.

The River Yumans, unlike their agricultural and sedentary neighbors, had very little ceremonialism in their lives. As we have learned, River Yumans were consummate traders and raiders. They farmed much less than was possible on the flood plains of the Colorado River, but they also gained large quantities of storable food from mesquite and screwbean trees. Fish, too, were available in considerable quantities. The principal ritual gatherings and foregatherings of the River Yumans did not center on changes in the weather or the quest for food. The life cycle did not receive special public attention either, even though the major River Yuman ritual was a mourning ceremony which, in some features, was similar to the ritual staged by Southern California Yumans and all other tribes as far north as the Maidus.

The Pais (Upland Yumans) are not known to have sponsored mourning ceremonies until 1889, when the ritual came to them as part of a religious movement coterminous with the Ghost Dance. Thus, the mourning ceremony was most elaborately developed among Southern California Yumans, was present but not nearly so elaborate among River Yumans, and was absent, as far as we know, among Pais prior to its introduction as part of a religious movement in 1889. Whether Pais sponsored mourning ceremonies before they spread into the relatively inhospitable areas that they occupied at the time of Contact with Europeans is not known.

As will be recalled, among the Southern California Yumans, mourning ceremonies were their most splendid and encompassing ritual affairs, integrating first-fruits observances with tribal mourning, the naming of children, and male and female initiation. As we learned, sib communities were aligned into reciprocating moieties, and the resources of each sib, particularly the springs and mesquite groves, their priest-chiefs, and their sib fetishes were reaffirmed in this elaborate ritual. Trespass was not allowed on Southern California sib property, yet intersib raiding was minimal, suggesting that raiding was, perhaps, influenced by the obligations of moiety membership. Some Southern California Yumans performed ceremonies following raids, but raiding was not a favorite avocation or a well-developed art in Southern California.

Among the River Yumans, however, warfare occupied the central place in the Mohave and Yuma mourning ceremonies. The Cocopas and Maricopas, on the other hand, were more similar to Southern California Yumans, inasmuch as they did not celebrate warfare. But they were distinct from Southern California Yumans, too, because they engaged in very little ritual dancing at their ceremonial affairs. They danced even less than the Mohaves and Yumas.

It is most probable that the warfare theme in Mohave and Yuma rituals was their own creation. None of the River Yumans were organized into localized corporate sib communities, and none possessed moiety organizations either. Their mourning ceremonies transcended smaller communities and were tribalwide, for all Mohaves or all Yumas. Thus, nonlocalized sibs may well have become organized, for ceremonial purposes at least, into what came to be known as the Mohaves, Yumas, and so forth, with the advent of farming along the Colorado River (see Chapters 8 and 9).

It matters not which River Yuman tribe we assess:

mourning ceremonies were sponsored only upon the death of prominent leaders—in warfare or otherwise. All members of the tribe (Yuma, Mohave, Cocopa, and so forth) were invited to attend the ceremony, hosted by the sib and friends of the deceased. The Mohaves and Yumas usually performed mourning ceremonies solely for great war leaders, with Mohaves inviting Yumas, and Yumas inviting Mohaves to attend, much as they did when joining forces in battle. Their allegiances to each other were deep. It is doubtful that all Mohaves and Yumas, scattered in hamlets distributed over approximately 250 miles along the Colorado River, attended each mourning ceremony, but representatives from most communities must have appeared.

Mohave and Yuma mourning ceremonies were directed toward warfare and the warfare accomplishments of the deceased. Songs were sung recalling the importance of the power that had been gained through dreaming for success in warfare. Speeches lauding the accomplishments of the deceased were offered, and a mock battle was staged. Effigies of the deceased were erected on stakes. In turn, the effigies were sprinkled with corn pollen—the use of which had wide currency in Pueblo and Piman rituals and was invariably connected with fertility. The corn pollen that was sprinkled on the images made a symbolic connection of the deceased with future generations. The images were then hoisted and carried in a line-dance. Gifts were made to them, and the lot—images and gifts—was burned.

The militaristic theme also occurred in the Mohave and Yuma ceremonies that preceded and followed warfare. Postvictory celebrations were grander affairs than prewar rituals and attracted participants from both tribes. Dance leaders, who were shamans, directed the construction of large dance houses. In conjunction with residents from their community, they provided feasts for all who attended. The postwarfare rituals were made up of dancing and of long song cycles reiterating travels of warriors from a spirit world and their encounters, mock battles, and resultant victories.

The modest trace of maize ceremonialism in the mourning ceremony, the meager interest in promoting community well-being and adjusting community affairs to the seasonal changes in environment, and the focus on warfare separated the River Yumans from both Southern California and Pueblo ceremonialism. For an area that could have supported greater farming, larger populations, and centralized polities, River Yuman ceremonial organization was as unique as the ceremonial organization of the Northwest Coast tribes. Rather than symbolizing the differences between moieties, hence distinguishing localized sibs, sib resources, and sib leadership, the Mohaves and Yumas celebrated their ceremonial brotherhood, particularly their desire to come to the aid of their brothers in times of warfare.

The Pimans (Pimas and Papagos), if they were the progeny of the Hohokams, most probably performed elaborate rituals in the pre-Contact period. The major archeological sites of the Hohokam have revealed ceremonial centers with ball courts. Even in the late Contact period, the Piman ceremonial year was fairly rich. Although it was much less elegant than the complex ceremonial calendar performed by Pueblo sodalities, Piman ceremonialism was more similar to the Pueblo focus on crops, rain, good health, and well-being than was the case for the militaristic River Yumans.

The primary Piman ceremonial was named Vikita. Vikita was held about the time of the winter solstice every year. Communities staggered the performances so that each community had to sponsor the event only once every four years. Vikita, as Pueblo winter solstice ceremonies were, was a prescription to hold the world together, to replenish it, and to vitalize all Pimans. Even prayer sticks, so common in Pueblo ceremonies, were made by Pimans from turkey down feathers and were used in ceremonies aimed at bringing rain and good health. About July, probably following the harvesting of the first crops each year among the Pimas, who raised two crops per year, both Pimas and Papagos gathered large quantities of sahuaro fruits and made alcoholic beverages from them. During a Sahuaro Ceremony each participant drank to satiation with the expectation that this would cause rain to saturate the crops and raise the rivers for the next growing season.

Planting of summer crops began only after the sahuaro ceremony. The planting rituals continued at each village to which participants at the ceremonies returned. Effigies of crops were created that simulated corn. Shamans sang songs to cause the corn to grow, and masked dancers carried effigies of rain clouds while singing for supernatural power to cause rain.

Although the masked dancing was not so complex as among the Pueblos, when crops matured, a Green-Corn Ceremony would be held during which masked dancers personified the sun and moon, and corn pollen would be sprinkled by other dancers as if to create fertility and to bring good health. It is possible that the rituals associated with the raising and maturing of corn were more complex before Contact and included ceremonial ball games.

Although ball games in court yards were not played in the late nineteenth century, a period for which we have direct evidence, other ceremonial games and tests of endurance were present in Piman rituals. After the crops had been harvested and stored in the autumn, villages that harvested especially large yields invited neighboring villages to rejoice with them and engage in competitions of various sorts. In subsequent years, neighbors reciprocated.

The postharvest ceremonies were times to rejoice, but also to prepare for the coming agricultural cycle. Pimans, unlike residents of the Pueblos, lived along rivers that normally flooded twice each year and allowed for two crops each year. It is plausible that the postharvest ceremonies were held following the first harvest, while Vikita ceremonies were sustained by surpluses from the second harvest. Pima ethnography is meager, so most of our information comes from the desert-dwelling Papagos, who farmed less than the Pimas, but whose ceremonials match many details that have been reported for the Pimas. Whatever the cause may have been, the postharvest ceremony in the autumn was not intended to bring rain, but it was intended to bring luck for rain. Intervillage games, intervillage song challenges, and a long kickball race were parts of the postharvest ceremony that were intended to bring hosts and guests the good luck of abundant rain and good health. The Papagos may have stressed luck for rain more than the Pimas.

Vikita ceremonies, like sahuaro ceremonies, sought to bring rain and success. The prayer sticks that were distributed at Vikita ceremonies were stuck upright in fields by some farmers to simulate corn; other people dropped them along the way—to bring good luck— as they made salt pilgrimages to the Gulf of California. Pilgrimages for supernatural power were common among the Pueblos and among Uto-Aztecans in the Sonoran region of Mexico, as well as among Pimans. The salt pilgrimage had special meaning for Pimans because salt was in the ocean and oceans were water: thus salt pilgrimages were thought to be related to bringing water, or rain.

Whereas Piman ceremonials helped individuals attain good luck through prayer sticks, salt pilgrimages, and "naming" events (where the names of people were honored), in the main, Piman ceremonials sought good health and agricultural success for all. Beyond the friendly competition between villages at the postharvest ceremony that promoted the success of reciprocating villages, a communal rabbit drive, which opened the summer prior to the sahuaro ceremony, and a communal deer hunt, which opened the winter prior to the Vikita ceremony, both brought community well-being. The Piman people, with little centralization of ceremonial, political, or economic control, maintained an informal set of reciprocating arrangements through which they shared the burden of a rather complex ceremonial calendar each year.

The Apacheans, including the Navajos, were unusual in the Southwest because their ceremonialism did not emphasize the central themes of agriculture or community well-being. Western Apache sib communities annually sponsored green-corn and harvest ceremonies, but they were not large public affairs. For the most part, Apacheans were as aberrant as the Yumans in this regard. Apachean ceremonialism was oriented toward the restoration of good health and the maintenance of a pleasant and long life for each person. The rationales for the performance of most ceremonial activities were ailments of individual persons, which were perceived to be caused by the intrusion of spirit objects, and which could be removed only by shamans who possessed special knowledge of particular curing ceremonies.

The influence of Pueblo ceremonialism on Apachean practices is undeniable. Apacheans performed masked dances, used corn pollen symbolism in some ceremonies, and made sand paintings in order to restore ailing patients to good health. Sand paintings were used among the Pueblos in initiating youths, as was also the practice in Southern California, and in curing rites. Cahitans (Uto-Aztecan speakers) on the Sonoran coast of Mexico (not covered in our sample of western North America) also made sand paintings of guardian animal spirits, later rubbing the sand on their bodies to make them well. It is most plausible that the Apacheans, particularly the Navajos, adopted and embellished upon the Pueblo and more general Southwestern and Sonoran practices of using sand paintings for curing rites, and coupled with this masked dancing, the use of corn pollen, and notions of a bounded and layered universe.

The "sings" of Apacheans were specific rituals performed by specially qualified shamans for specific *ad hoc* occasions. The Pueblo influence here also seems undeniable. The sings were hosted by the localized sib communities among Navajos and Western Apaches, and they included feasts to which all members of the community plus guests from other communities were invited. Of all Apachean curing ceremonies, the sings performed with the aim of achieving protection from lightning and rattlesnakes seem to have been the most important public affairs, yet public puberty rites for girls were also well-developed among all Apacheans. As was true for the curing sings, girls' puberty rites, too, were performed individually for each pubescent girl, rather than for a group of girls. As Driver (1941) pointed out years ago, Apachean public girls'-puberty rights were anomalous in the Southwest and, with their emphases on running, working, and dancing, were similar to the girls'-puberty rights in the northern part of the California culture area and the northern part of the Plateau culture area. It may well be that Apachean girls'-puberty rites, which were quite different from the group puberty rites for girls in Southern California where rest features rather than work features dominated the performances, were part of the cultural baggage that Apacheans brought with them into the Southwest.

The Apacheans seem to have adopted many of the ritual acts and objects of their sedentary agricultural neighbors in the Southwest, and some of their beliefs as well, such as a layered and bounded cosmos. Nevertheless, the focus of Apachean ritual was on individual curing, the transition of each girl to womanhood, and raiding. Both preraiding rituals and postraiding purification ceremonies were prominent. Everyone in the community shared in the ritual, but the rituals were those of noncentralized units who emphasized shamanistic curing, female transitions, and purification of warriors rather than community purposes. The niches occupied by Apacheans were different from all other Southwesterners, and no matter how many ritual acts, objects, and beliefs they borrowed from their sedentary neighbors, the distinctive focuses of Apachean ceremonialism did not bend the will of the individual so as to accommodate community concerns. Yet the general good health of all Apacheans who attended sings was analogous to open blessings provided to all members of the sponsoring band and its guests among Utes and Shoshones.

PUBLIC CEREMONIES

Comparisons of some of the salient features of ceremonial practice as they have been uncovered in the areal survey will enhance our understanding of some basic features of ceremonialism for all of western North America. In our analysis of sodalities and in the preceding sections of this chapter we learned that some ceremonies were private, for an individual person or some select group, and others were public, for the entire community and even for guests from other communities. Some ceremonies were major in importance, such as mortuary potlatches on the northern Northwest Coast, and some were minor, such as first-fruits ceremonies among people in the same area. We also learned that some ceremonies were distinctly profane and secular in belief and purpose, whereas others were predominantly sacred. Let us turn to brief comparisons of these and other factors.

Major public ceremonies were those which drew

most members of a sponsoring group, usually a political unit such as a kinship group, a band, a tribelet, a village, or a district together and which were considered major in importance by the participants—sanctified events. Inspection of Map Cu-190 (V-366) confirms that the northern, central, and northwestern California subareas of the Northwest Coast, California, Southern California, and the Pueblos were the culture areas in which the greatest ceremonial activity occurred. The Oregon coastal tribes, with their rich resources, were irregular hosts of winter ceremonials, whereas Southern California sibs, with more modest resources, engaged in a rigorous ceremonial year, reciprocating as hosts and guests through their moiety system.

In general, the tribes with either the largest and most storable food supplies or the most constantly predictable food supplies, culled from areas rather restricted in size (fishing stations, mesquite groves, farm plots), sponsored the greatest number of ceremonies on regular bases. The River Yumans and Oregon coastal people were interesting exceptions. We can generalize that food was necessary to large public rituals, but by no means sufficient to cause elaborations of ceremonialism.

It is also interesting that practically all tribes in western North America invited guests from adjacent communities to attend their most important public ceremonies (Map Cu-191, V-367). Indeed, on all of the following occasions guests were invited to ritual gatherings: Northwest Coast potlatches, winter ceremonials, and world-renewal ceremonies; California Big Times and mourning ceremonies; Southern California and River Yuman mourning ceremonies; Plateau winter spirit-performances; Apachean sings; Piman Vikita and sahuaro ceremonies; Ute bear dances; and the entire Pueblo ceremonial calendar. Even the residents of two or more family camps in the Great Basin were pleased to celebrate a good harvest together, and Oregon coastal winter wealth-displays, too, drew people from several kinship groups.

Ceremonials brought together friends and potential enemies, people who owned some specific resources, and people who, conceivably, might compete for these same resources. The inescapable generalization is that ceremonies were not for sponsors alone. Even if, year after year, performance after performance, ceremonies served to sanctify the kinship group, or the village, or to restore a person's health, they also provided arenas for amicable contacts among neighbors.

This is not to suggest that all ceremonies were similar in their intentions or in any other dimension. That is patently false. Some ceremonies were more sacred,

some more profane; some sought to heal, some to prepare for war, and some to bring rain (Maps Cu-192 and 193, V-368 and V-369). Some were sponsored by communities, some by kinship groups, some had no formal sponsors at all, and so forth (Map Cu-192, V-368; Map Cu-193, V-369; Map Cu-194, V-372).

The major public ceremonies of the Pueblos, Columbia Plateau villages (winter spirit-dances and sings), central and northeastern California tribelets (mourning), Southern California sibs (mourning), Western Kuksu area tribelets of the northern part of the California culture area (Ghost society), and households in the northwestern part of California (world renewal) were predominantly sacred affairs that were sponsored either by whole political communities, their sodalities, or their moieties, to promote the physical and spiritual well-being of the people in the community, including the healthiness of relations among members of the community. For all but the Plateau villages these ceremonies were invariably prescribed as obligations to deceased ancestor spirits and even higher orders of spirits who had formed some sorts of covenants with the living. These covenants were beyond mortal challenge, and they were maintained through ritual. Except for the northwestern California households (Wiyots, Yuroks, and Hupas), the sponsors of these ceremonies were organized into political units that recognized common territorial boundaries that they defended and that were prescribed as inviolable. Northwestern California households laid private claims to ownership of their inviolable property. Plateau villages provided access to their resource areas after proper requests or invitations, but the other communities in this set did not. It is significant that no society in the set mounted frequent raids against their neighbors or anyone else, and that except for the Keresans, none of the societies mounted many retaliatory raids. It is plausible that the political and raiding contexts of tribes nourished the sacred nature of their rituals. The tribes were seldom challenged mortally, and their rituals were beyond mortal challenge.

Two exceptions, but not in terms of offensive or defensive raiding, were the northwestern California households and the Middle Columbia Plateau village and bands. In northwestern California, ritual obligations were shared among many communities of small and independent property owners. There were no political communities, but independent households coalesced for ritual purposes. Moreover, the independent households did not allow access to their private resources; they collected wealth with great care; they did not trade food, but they gave food away at feasts and ceremonies. If there was a community, it was a loose, ceremonial collectivity composed of several anarchistic and straggling villages speaking several different languages, villages that recognized common ritual obligations to keep the world whole. In the Middle Columbia Plateau, ritual obligations were prescribed for persons who possessed guardian spirits. Although villages and bands did not sponsor prescribed rites, individual persons within villages did; yet everyone in the community contributed to the success of a winter spirit-dance and spirit-sing with food and lodging for guests and participants. Plateau bands and villages provided nonowners with easy access to their resources on request and invitation. The similarity between Plateau and northwestern California was that hamlet, band, and village communities were organized into large and loose ceremonial networks in which communities sponsored the same kinds of ceremonies, attested to the sacredness of each ceremony, attended the ceremonies sponsored by other communities in the network, and did so amicably. In California, Southern California, and among the Pueblos, moiety and sodality organizations created similar networks among neighbors.

Of the several societies whose major ceremonies were either predominantly profane in nature—social singing, dancing, games, feasting, fraternizing—or perhaps equally mixed between profane and sacred elements, all but those of the Great Basin, and the Pais, either mounted frequent offensive raids or defensive raids, or they were suspicious of trespass, raids, and sorcery. There can be little doubt but that neighbors of offensive raiders, such as Ute and Apachean bands, River Yuman districts, northern and central Northwest Coast villages and residential kinship-groups, Nisenan districts, and Modoc and Yana tribelets were influenced by their nemeses and often mounted defensive raids to combat them. What is interesting about the major ceremonials sponsored by the offensive raiders, and some of the ceremonials sponsored by the communities that retaliated, is that the ritual affairs were salted with social singing, dancing, feasting, and games. Either kinship groups sponsored the affairs, or there were no formal sponsors and the direction was under the nominal control of shamans. Moreover, regardless of the purposes for which the defensive raiding societies ostensibly sponsored rituals, the offensive raiders frequently sought to promote the well-being of one person, rather than the common good, in their public ceremonies. It was also true, of course, that people other than the person for whom the ceremony was sponsored benefited from it, but a single moral community was not the prescribed sponsor or beneficiary.

Notwithstanding the importance of spirit encounters, or the acquisition of prerogatives and privileges through inherited spirit encounters, northern and central Northwest Coast distributions, potlatches, and winter performances were characterized by secular focuses, as were Ute bear dances and Maidu Big Times. Neither single political communities nor networks of independent kinship groups or communities sponsored ceremonials in which beliefs placed the continuity of the tribe or network of tribes and its rituals beyond mortal challenge. The profane nature of singing, dancing, and games stimulated fraternization and perhaps, good will, but not obligatory social and ceremony relations.

In the northern interior of California one can see the mix of sacred and profane rituals very clearly. Maidu Kuksu cults (Hesi, Akit, and so forth) sponsored sacred spirit impersonations, and cult leaders directed the sacred mourning ceremonies, but Maduans, and all other tribelets of the northern part of the California culture area, sponsored Big Times to which neighbors were invited about whom the hosts were suspicious. Although there were ceremonial linkages, there were no supernatural sanctions and prescriptions that motivated ritual obligations among the groups. Moreover, most of these tribelets were raided, from time to time, by Modoc, Yana, Patwin, or Nisenan warriors and the victims, in turn, mounted retaliatory (defensive raids). Force and the threat of force were omnipresent in the northern part of the California area. The ceremonial network that linked tribes together did not link the various tribelets into a sacred and prescribed ceremonial order. Big Times generated both camaraderie and suspicion among the participants.

It may have been the case that the more people regulated their intertribal affairs through ceremonial participation, the more likely that those relations would be obligatory, sacred, and regular (annual at least), while the less probable that the parties of the relationship would challenge the resource ownership rights of others. The Northwest Coast kinship groups, with their glorious ceremonial year, were the most notable exceptions. But the puzzling development of Northwest Coast culture, with its emphasis on kinship-group property, kinship-group rankings, ceremonial rankings, raiding, and ad hoc ceremonial sponsorship in order to maintain rankings, elevated ceremonialism to a lofty but secular position in which regulation was a series of ad hoc affairs through which individuals and kinship groups endeavored to maintain themselves. It was the material demonstration of generosity, and the challenge to provide even more, that always left the claims of Northwest Coast kinship groups and Tsimshian villages unresolved and open to mortal doubt.

Gifting at public ceremonies primarily occurred

among central and northern Northwest Coast groups, Plateau, California, and Southern California groups, and the non-Yuman tribes of the Southwest (Map Cu-195, V-370; Map Cu-196, V-371). As we have seen in previous chapters, gifting at central and northern Northwest Coast ceremonials was an explicit measure of rank. The highest-ranking guests were the first to receive gifts and also received the greatest amount of gifts. Everywhere else that gifts were given, they were either equal in quality and amount for all, or perhaps somewhat better gifts were given to people who made the greatest contribution to the success of the ceremony.

The contrast between gifting practices of the Northwest Coast and those of California, Southern California, the Plateau, and the non-Yuman tribes of the Southwest were marked, but nowhere were the differences more extreme than among Plateau groups. The dominant practice in the Plateau was, at the conclusion of winter ceremonials, for everyone in attendance—guests and hosts—to contribute to a pool of gifts that were then distributed. People who had worked the hardest at the ceremony might receive more than others, but in general everyone received the same amount.

Among the gifting societies in California, the practice was to exchange gifts between hosts and guests, though Miwok and Yokuts moiety members for whom ceremonies were sponsored often gave more generously to their reciprocals who made especially notable efforts on their behalf. In Southern California, on the other hand, ritual hosts always gifted their guests rather than exchange with them. Although gifting between moiety reciprocals was highly developed, the amount and quality of gifts were equal for all.

Among the Pueblos, the villages or sodalities that sponsored ceremonies also provided gifts to guests. Again, people who contributed heavily to successful performances were singled out for special gifts, but most guests received equal gifts.

Reciprocity characterized Apachean ceremonial gift exchange.

It is evident that ceremonial gifting among practically all western North American groups that engaged in the practice was either equal in amount, or it was weighted slightly toward guests who made especially significant contributions to the ritual. The groups that engaged in ceremonial gifting of this type also sponsored ceremonials that were predominantly sacred in nature. These same groups were not warlike and seldom engaged in defensive raiding. I am emboldened to say that the ceremonial gifting which distinguished among recipients only on the bases of their contributions to rituals emphasized the sacred

nature of the events, the comradeship between and among participants, and the integrity of the ceremonial network. The exception was provided by the Apacheans, who either reciprocated equal gifts or received gifts as guests. It may well be the case that the Apachean practice was learned from the Pueblos or Pimans.

With the exceptions of the Apacheans, most of the same Indian communities in western North America that gifted at public ceremonials also were the loci of private ceremonies that were sponsored by restricted groups within the community (Map Cu-197; V-373). These groups were, of course, the spirit-impersonating sodalities of the Northwest Coast, California, and the Pueblos; the Toloache sodalities of central California, and the Toloache and Chungichnish sodalities of Southern California. Although prior to first Contact the Plateau groups did not have sodalities, except, perhaps for the Kutenai Bluejay shamans' society, initiation dances for novices who subsequently performed at winter spirit ceremonies were restricted to members and novices. Private ceremonies performed by and for restricted groups occurred where ceremonial organization was elaborate, but in turn, restricted groups often contributed to the organization and further elaboration of public ceremonials, as well as participating in both private and public ceremonials sponsored by other communities in the ceremonial network. Northwest Coast sodality members danced in communities other than their own, as did Plateau spirit dancers. California Kuksu and Toloache members attended ritual performances away from home, and so forth.

The very ritual acts, objects, and beliefs that made people, their restricted organizations, and their communities unique, also linked people into wider ceremonial networks, as Map Cu-197 demonstrates, and brought communities into gifting relations.

THE LIFE CYCLE: PRIVATE AND PUBLIC OBSERVANCES

Some ceremonial acts, objects, and beliefs attended birth, puberty, and death in most societies. We dealt with marriage—a social transition that takes place over a wide time range following puberty—in Chapter 8, on social organization. The transitions in the life cycle were not treated equally in all societies. Some singled out girls' puberty for the greatest ceremonial attention; many singled out death; the northern and central Northwest Coast societies emphasized each transition in the life cycle with public ceremonials;

denizens of the Great Basin did not sponsor public ceremonies for any of the transitions of life.

Even though some societies sponsored public ceremonies at the life crisis events and others did not, similar ceremonial acts and beliefs were shared by many tribes across wide geographic regions, regardless of whether they performed the acts publicly or privately, for an entire community group of pubescents, say, or for one pubescent at a time. As for Kuksu-type performances, among the Wintus, Shastas, and Miwoks dances and impersonations could be borrowed without borrowing the sodality organizations that performed them. Moreover, acts, objects, and beliefs associated with life's transitions that were spread across wide regions could precede the development of public rituals, and undoubtedly many did.

Birth

There is little doubt but that pregnant women were regarded as special people. Scores of ceremonial practices and beliefs guided their behavior prior to parturition, at parturition, and shortly thereafter. But a few of these phenomena were sampled for the analysis made here.

In all societies in western North America pregnant women were removed from the mainstream of everyday life and secluded somewhere (Map Cu-198, V-374). The Oregon Athapaskans, Western Apaches, Eastern Keres groups, and Yumans were unique in allowing husbands to remain in the house with their wives without any further seclusion of the woman. This practice was primarily restricted to the Southwest where stone and sand architecture dominated and where other building materials were scarce. Among other Southwestern societies women stayed in the house and the men left. The practice of using entire houses for seclusion, with men leaving during the period of removal, was common throughout the central part of California and in Southern California. The Oregon Athapaskan and Western Apache practice of allowing men to stay with their wives may represent the retention of a trait that was shared by the precursors of both groups before the Apacheans migrated into the Southwest. The evidence for this is meager, but Oregon Athapaskans were not bordered by anyone else who practiced this custom, whereas Western Apaches, who lived in brush wickiups in mountainous areas, easily could have constructed temporary quarters for the man.

Throughout the Great Basin, the northern part of California, the Plateau, and the Northwest Coast the practice was to isolate pregnant women in special huts or brush enclosures, though many coastal Salishans and Tsimshians sequestered women in curtained sections of the large plank houses. The north/south distinction between occupying specially built huts (in the north) and occupying houses, often evacuated by men (in the south), with a few exceptions is clear. An interesting aspect of the seclusion of women at parturition is that very similar structures and practices accompanied seclusion at puberty. In Southern California, for instance, Yuman women were placed outdoors in a pit; at puberty they were not only secluded in a pit but were often covered with sand, as well.

The removal of women from the normal routines of their societies served notice of the importance, and the potential danger, of parturition. During parturition most societies had one or two special positions that parturients were taught to use to ensure proper deliveries (Map Cu-199, V-375; Map Cu-200, V-376). Sitting was the dominant position in the non-Pueblo Southwest, in Southern California, and among the Wakashan speakers along the Northwest Coast. Kneeling dominated among the Great Basin societies and Keresan speakers, squatting was common in the central part of California, reclining among Salishans of the coast and Fraser Plateau, and so forth. The distributions were clearly linked to language families such as Wakashan and Salishan, or societies from the same language family occupying contiguous areas (Great Basin Uto-Aztecans), or to societies in contiguous regions speaking languages from several families. It is plausible that these distributions reflect two factors: inheritance (retention) of customs that were practiced by the precursors of these societies, and borrowing through intermarriage. There are no obvious physiological, environmental, economic, or other factors that would account for the distributions of these customs. Nor are there obvious explanations beyond fortuities, that is, the unpredictability of history, in which a belief and practice emerged and was subsequently maintained, to account for the definite and nonrandom areal distributions of attitudes toward the birth of twins (Map Cu-201, V-377) or the ritual numbers that were associated with the actions of women and their husbands before, during, and after parturition, or the ritual numbers associated with the care of the newborn (Map Cu-202, V-378). Indeed, in most societies the ritual number of times that ceremonial acts were performed, such as bathing the parturient, or the number of days that taboos were observed, such as the days when a husband did not speak, and the like, were most often duplicated in ceremonial practices attending other life crises, the story-lines of myths and tales, and other features of culture.

In the Southwest, where cultures differed considerably in ceremonial details, cosmologies tended to divide the world into four layers, four directions, and, perhaps, up and down dimensions, the ritual number four or a multiple of four (two times four or three times four, and so on) was the dominant ritual number. Intermarriage and joint participation at public ceremonies and myth-telling sessions must account for the diffusion of the ritual number four among so many diverse societies. Great Basin tribes, southern Northwest Coast tribes, and most Plateau dwellers preferred "five," or a simple multiple of five. "Three" and its multiples had currency among Palaihinan speakers (Hokan phylum) in the northern part of California, Salinan (also Hokan) in the central part of California, among some Yokuts groups adjacent to the Salinan speakers, and among the Kaliwa (Yuman family, Hokan phylum) in northern Baja. The use of the number three suggests early Hokan retentions and interlanguage contacts between Salinan and Yokuts groups, much as the use of four in the Southwest, or among the Salish and Wakashan on the Northwest Coast, and five in the Basin, Plateau, and Oregon Coast suggest both retentions and historical contacts.

Material items of similar structure associated with birth, such as the cradles in which babies were placed, were distributed over very wide regions, suggesting that material items, even if they varied in design from tribe to tribe, were often uniform. Material objects, such as cradles, might have diffused more readily than ritual acts and beliefs associated with the life crisis events (Map Cu-203, V-379; Map Cu-204, V-380), though Driver (1941) suggests that such was not the case for material items associated with girls' puberty observances.

Cradles, for instance, could be moved from the locale in which they were made to a far distant location, where they were eventually copied, through trade, gifting, migrations, or some combination of these and other mechanisms. Throughout the central part of California, Southern California, the Great Basin, and the non-Pueblo Southwest, the cradle pattern prevalent in the central part of California was used in which basketry, slats, or rods made up the basic structure, whereas in the northern and northwestern parts of California, unique sitting-type cradles fashioned from basketry were dominant. Plant materials that could be easily woven were available in these regions, but the dominant trees of the regions, such as oak, pinyon, and others, did not lend themselves to woodworking. The greatest variation in cradles occurred on the Northwest Coast, where woodworking with soft native cedar was a well-developed art. In that area hollowed boards, dugouts, and sewn boxes were used. In the Plateau, where native lumber was available but was harder than the cedar of the Northwest Coast, bark or straight boards formed the basic structures for cradles.

Naming the baby or the infant was, perhaps, the most important feature associated with birth among most societies in western North America. The ceremonial acquisition of names among Northwest Coast people was the efficient cause, or manifest reason, for most distributions and potlatches. On the Northwest Coast the names that were claimed at their ceremonial occasions were considered to embody spirits and to carry with them certain rights and privileges. The highest ranking people acquired the names that granted the most prestigious privileges, and they also acquired the greatest number of names. Among most Northwest Coast groups, names could be inherited from the mother's kinship group, or the father's kinship group, and could be achieved through spirit quests or potlatches, though among the matrilineal people of the northern Northwest Coast it was common for a person to acquire his or her most important name from a matrilineal relative (Map Cu-205, V-381; Map Cu-206, V-382; Map Cu-207, V-383; Map Cu-208, V-384; Map Cu-209, V-385).

On the Northwest Coast, then, ceremonial naming, a practice normally associated with birth and infancy to recognize each new member of a family and the community, most plausibly became extended to all other life crisis events, including marriage, and to many *ad hoc* occasions when a person acquired names merely through achievement (the sponsoring of potlatches). Individuals and their kinship groups sought again and again to secure their ceremonial and social positions, to make their names good. The names and the prerogatives that such incorporeal property entailed were used on ceremonial occasions, while nicknames or common names were used throughout the youthful lives of most Northwest Coast inhabitants.

At the other end of the ceremonial ladder, the Pais and Great Basin people used only common names, and normally did not assign them until late infancy or early childhood. The practice in these societies was to wait until the child had lived long enough to acquire some recognizable characteristic, or had lived long enough to associate something of interest with his or her being to confer a name. Neither public nor private ceremonies were associated with naming, and almost anyone could confer the name. Most likely it was someone who recognized something about the child's behavior and tagged the child with a monicker that conveyed whatever had been recognized.

In between the complex elaboration of Northwest Coast practices and the basic, simple practices of

Great Basin and Pai peoples were the practices of everybody else. Plateau societies showed resemblances to the Northwest Coast in using nicknames and also bestowing names at infancy, puberty, and adulthood. Names acquired through vision quests, of course, were incorporeal property. But Plateau names were bestowed by anyone, rather than predominantly maternal and paternal relatives. Moreover, the ceremonies that attended naming events in the Plateau were not nearly so glorious as those on the Northwest Coast. Only the westernmost Fraser Plateau Salishans sponsored anything akin to distributions, and they were modest in comparison with Coast Salishan potlatches and distributions. Nevertheless, the closer the Plateau tribe was located to coastal tribes, from the Fraser Plateau through the Columbia Plateau, the more probable that public ceremonies with gifting (equal for all in attendance) and fasting would be hosted by the parents of the recipient at that person's *most important* naming event. Public ceremonies for families that included a feast with, perhaps, the distribution of a few gifts by the parents of the infant were the extent of the ceremonies sponsored by the more eastern tribes. The diminution of Northwest Coast ceremonial influence from west to east in the Plateau seems an inescapable conclusion from the distribution of these data, though multiple names were important everywhere in the Plateau.

The combination of multiple names, each of which was recognized as incorporeal property, and the bestowal of these names at public ceremonies, was not unique to the Northwest Coast and Plateau region. Quite independently, it appears, Southern California Uto-Aztecans and Yumans employed nicknames as well as special sib names that were bestowed at birth and again near puberty. The names were always bestowed by patrilineal relatives and were awarded during the naming portion of the mourning ceremony. Although the sib names were kept secret, they were culled from deceased ancestors more than one generation removed from the recipient. The spiritual connection that was made between past and living patrikinspeople through naming was an important feature of the Southern California sib system.

Farther north in California, people tended to use nicknames as well as special ceremonial names—not incorporeal property—that were bestowed during infancy or early childhood. The correlation between who bestowed names and the local descent systems was perfect. Patrilineal relatives among the patrilineal groups from Nomlaki through the Yokuts bestowed names, whereas both maternal and paternal relatives bestowed names among the bilateral Maidu, the bilateral Wintu, and the Yokuts groups that were

bilateral. Public feasts accompanied naming events among some of the patrilineal California Penutians, but the bilateral Maiduan branch of that family sponsored only private affairs. The other bilateral groups of the northern part of California, mostly Hokan-phylum members, paralleled the naming practices of the bilateral Penutians in many details, though only the Pomos, Wappos, and Yukis hosted ceremonies, and they were private affairs.

It is plausible that where unilineal kinship organization or its equivalent (Northwest Coast demes) was operative and societies were relatively sedentary, naming was an important feature of social organizations, so much so that kinship group names were honored and treated as sacred. Those who bestowed them and those who received them were ritually linked to past generations and to the places in which deceased generations once resided. The names provided spiritual and kinship continuity and were publicly honored.

Among the bilateral tribelets of the northern part of the California culture area, naming was not nearly so prominent as among the unilineal groups, and in many of these same societies in the California culture area Ghost, Kuksu, Akit, and Hesi spirits loomed much larger than specific deceased ancestors with whom unilineal people identified.

The Pueblos bestowed ritual names on children either at birth (Western Pueblos) or during infancy (Eastern Pueblos). No particular person from the maternal or paternal side was expected to bestow the ritual name among the Eastern Pueblos, but names among the matrilineal Western Pueblos were bestowed by the child's paternal relatives, rather than maternal relatives, stressing the obligations of the father's sib and the relations between a child and his or her father's sib.

Individual life crisis events, in general, received small ceremonial play among the Pueblos. At naming the donor of the name also gave a gift to the recipient of the name, and the parents of the child gave a gift to the person who bestowed the name.

Hopi children also received adult ceremonial names in conjunction with their initiation into the tribal Kachina cult. This was a group affair, of course, that was accompanied by a feast. Although all initiates were treated collectively, individual ceremonial names were received from the sibswomen of the "ceremonial father." A "ceremonial father" was selected by the parents of the child, but did not belong to the sib of either parent. The emphasis was on making ritual connections outside one's own sib or father's sib.

So whereas naming had ceremonial significance among Pueblos, the collective tendencies of Pueblo life, even among the matrilineal descent Pueblos in which matrilineal descent was observed, softened the importance of family names.

Girls' Puberty

Girls' puberty will receive our attention here, much as boys' initiations commanded most of our attention in the section on sodalities in Chapter 9. Yet neither this discussion, nor the discussion of boys' initiations, fully exhausts the question of puberty rites, and we shall touch on the topic again in Chapter 11 when we address the question of spirit quests.

In a masterful study of girls' puberty rites in western North America conducted many years ago, Driver (1941) identified several areas, in each of which girls' puberty customs were distinctive—Northwest Coast; Plateau; Great Basin; Southern California; the three closely related northern, northwestern, and central areas of California; Pueblos; the Athapaskan Southwest; and the River Yumans–Pais. These areas match closely the tribal alignments that we have determined on the basis of ritual features that attended birth.

It is significant that public puberty rites for girls were sponsored on the Northwest Coast in the northwestern and northern parts of California, in Southern California, and among the Apacheans in the Southwest, but nowhere else in all of North America save for the human fertility motif in Ute bear dances and the establishment of puberty huts near bear dances for first menstruants. The idea to associate girls' puberty with public ceremonies may have been borrowed by the Utes from the Jicarilla Apaches during the post-Contact period. Inasmuch as eastern North America was dominated by matrilineal societies, yet these societies did not sponsor public ceremonies for girls at puberty, and the matrilineal Tlingits and Western Pueblos* did not sponsor public ceremonies for pubescent girls, it is doubtful that public ceremonies for pubescent girls was a feature of matrilineal societies. Rather than being linked to descent, girls' puberty observances, especially public observances, seem to have been related to fishing, hunting, and gathering subsistence-economies. The societies that enjoyed the greatest abundances from their extractive subsistence-economies were often the same societies that sponsored public girls' puberty ceremonies (Map Cu-210, V-394; Map Cu-211, V-395).

---

*Hopi girls who had experienced their first menses during the year were able to join one of three womens' societies at about the time of the tribal initiation each year.

Driver (1941) identified several ritual acts, objects, and beliefs in relation to a woman's first menses that were universal in western North America. It was generally believed, for instance, that the menstrual discharge was dangerous, indeed, that it polluted spiritual and material things such as the successful promotion of certain ceremonials, success in hunting ventures or fishing ventures, and the good health and well-being of people who came in contact with the menstruant, other than those with special qualifications for contact. It was universally believed that the menstruant herself was not in control of the dangerous discharge—thought to be a supernatural power in material form—and during this period she was susceptible to harm. To avert trouble she had to observe sundry explicit taboos during the period. Finally, in all western North American societies it was believed that a woman's actions during her first menses determined her behavior through her adult life.

As was characteristic of all life crisis observances, whether or not there was a public ceremony at the conclusion, menstruants were removed from the rest of society and secluded. During seclusion the menstruants underwent a transitional period of training with an attendant who instructed them on restrictions of food and drink; taught them not to scratch their bodies with their fingers but to use a special scratching stick; taught them the restrictions of, or expectations about, work during the menstrual period or thereafter; taught them the restrictions about bathing and changing clothes at the end of seclusion; and instructed them about avoidances of men in general, and hunters, fishermen, and gamblers in particular, during subsequent menses. At the conclusion of seclusion the woman was introduced to society with some public fanfare on the Northwest Coast (distributions or potlatches), throughout California, Southern California, and the Apachean Southwest (see Maps Cu-210 and Cu-211). Private ceremonies for the menstruant and her proctor, or for the menstruant's kinswomen and female friends from the local community, were sponsored by a few societies along the Northwest Coast, in California, or in areas adjacent to Athapaskan communities where public rites celebrated the transition (Map Cu-212, V-396).

The universal distribution of these phenomena among western North American tribes suggests that girls' puberty rites were practiced very early in the prehistory of the area. There is no evidence that the observances were recent phenomena. The universals also suggest that regional differences were generated from a common base of beliefs and practices that were part of the ideological baggage of hunting, fishing, and gathering adaptations.

It is especially interesting that the Pueblos, who paid the least attention to girls' puberty, were also the most dependent on agriculture of all people in western North America, and the bulk of their ceremonial calendar was devoted either to agriculture, the preparation for agriculture, or attempts to make the community well and whole. Hopi women could be initiated into women's sodalities, Eastern Pueblo women could be initiated into medicine sodalities, and so forth, but these were not puberty rite events. Even among the Hopi, who paid more attention to a girl's first menses than was so in other Pueblos, did not treat the individual menstruant with great fanfare.

As Eggan (1950) noted for the Hopi, the differences in observation of first menses among First Mesa, Second Mesa, and Third Mesa villages were marked. On First Mesa, where contacts and intermarriages with Navajos were most frequent, girls supervised by women who had gone through the same procedure would grind corn inside their father's sister's house during the initial menstrual period, and did not eat fresh food, hot food, or salt. At the conclusion of menstruation their hair would be arranged in two circles ("butterfly whorls"), one on either side of the head, and a feast would be held for villagers. On the Third Mesa, where Navajo contacts were minimal, the ceremony was performed in much the same way but was "not thought to be connected with puberty," although it was thought to be a prerequisite for marriage (Eggan 1950). It is plausible that Navajo practices influenced Hopi practices, but Hopi Pueblo villages were less centralized politically than all other Pueblo villages, and the modest puberty ceremonies for women at the Hopi Pueblo villages but not at the other Pueblos, may reflect the importance of kinship groups in Hopi economy and society.

This brief aside is more important than may be apparent. Driver's (1941) analysis of Apachean puberty rites demonstrated that they influenced other practices in the Southwest. Pimans, for instance, sponsored public dances and feasts at the conclusion of each girl's period of seclusion, in which the dance sequences and many other practices were nearly identical to the Apachean sequences, and the Apachean dance routines were very similar to those of northwestern California and southern Oregon—the heart of Pacific Athapaskan occupation. Driver inferred that the Athapaskans carried the concept of the public ceremonial for each girl from the northern Fraser Plateau region (the Carriers performed such rites) to the northern part of the California region and to the Southwest. The ceremony for each girl was characteristic of the north Pacific Coast, whereas the dance routines were probably added by the Athapas-

kans. Little features, such as drinking through a tube, were practiced by Carrier and Chilcotin Athapaskans in the far northern reaches of the Plateau, and by several Salishan groups, by Apacheans in the Southwest, and by practically no one else. The custom may have been used by Pacific Athapaskans at one time but was subsequently dropped.

The evidence supports Driver's surmise. Moreover, though many Apacheans gained some of their sustenance from farming, foremost they were hunters, gatherers, and mobile raiders who kept most menstrual taboos intact. If Driver is correct, public ceremonies at puberty were created on the Northwest Coast, borrowed by Athapaskans many centuries ago, and carried to the northern part of the California region and to the Southwest region, whence they diffused. The public ceremonies in Southern California developed independently. But ritual acts (such as drink taboos), objects (such as scratching sticks), and beliefs (such as in the danger of the menstrual flow) associated with the first menses preceded all public ceremonies.

The following distribution maps sample only 33 of the 425 traits identified by Driver (Map Cu-213, V-386; Map Cu-214, V-387; Map Cu-215, V-388; Map Cu-216, V-389; Map Cu-217, V-390; Map Cu-218, V-391; Map Cu-219, V-392; Map Cu-220, V-393). The 33 attributes are organized into eleven variables (see Maps Cu-210 to Cu-212 as well). No two variables had identical distributions, but distinguishing aspects of Southern California, the Apachean Southwest, the northern part of California, and the Northwest Coast are obvious.

Girls' puberty ceremonies in Southern California were sponsored during the mourning ceremonies, and rather than hosting a separate ceremony for each pubescent girl, all girls who had experienced their first menses since the last public ceremony were secluded in a ceremonial enclosure. They were painted with the color and patterns of their moiety, and the ceremony was directed by a leader from the reciprocal moiety (their mother's sib). The public ceremony was performed only once for each set of girls, thus distinguishing it from the ceremony in the northern part of the California culture area, and the postmenstruants did not dance, thus distinguishing the ceremony from both those of the Apacheans and the northern Californians.

As we have suggested earlier, group female initiations in California, Southern California, and the Pueblo Southwest probably were developed after group male initiations, though individual observances at puberty for males and females undoubtedly antedated male initiations.

Death

As was true for ceremonies that attended the life crises of birth, puberty, and marriage, death was a time of great ceremonial activity on the central and northern Northwest Coast, and as was true for the other crisis events the higher the rank of the deceased, the grander the distribution or potlatch sponsored in his or her honor. The most prominent men among the Northwest Coast communities, specifically the chiefs of the kinship groups, the village chiefs among the Tsimshians, and the highest-ranking chiefs among the Nootkans, not only were honored by great potlatches, but memorial potlatches held one year later were sponsored in their memories. The intention was not only to remember the deceased chief, but to make good the claim of the son, or sister's son who succeeded him, to the chief's position and to some of his rights and prerogatives. Other rights and prerogatives would be claimed at subsequent potlatches (Map Cu-221, V-404).

The glorification of the individual's incorporeal property rights and the interareal ranking of his kinship group was not the intention of the mourning ceremonies and ghost society funerals sponsored by California tribelets or Southern California moieties. Although these people too held funerals for each deceased, as well as memorial public ceremonies subsequent to the funeral, the public ceremonies—even when they were sponsored specifically for only one decedent—were affairs for the entire tribelet, the entire tribalwide sodality, or for the sib plus all moiety mates and reciprocals who wished to attend. The California and Southern California ceremonies specifically remembered all deceased ancestors. The living offered gifts to the deceased spirits which were burned.

In post-Contact times the Eastern Pueblos observed the Roman Catholic All Souls' Day once each year, in which the solidarity of each village was reaffirmed. Reports are contradictory about whether Eastern Pueblo villages sponsored annual mourning ceremonies prior to Spanish contact. The question cannot be resolved here, but one point is interesting: whatever the origin of annual mourning for all of the village's deceased may have been, Ortiz (1969) makes it clear that the Tewas connected naming ceremonies with mourning ceremonies—thus linking the newly arrived and the eternally departed—through symbolic inversions in ritual that were not at all Christian but that were clearly original with the Tewas. Either the Eastern Pueblos adapted their periodic mournings to a Catholic ritual, or they reworked All Souls' Day to be consonant with their own beliefs.

The manner in which deceased were prepared for disposal and removed from houses, the manner in which houses and personal property of the deceased were treated, and other phenomena distinct from public ceremonies, collectively formed rather distinct areal clusters which, except for the obvious similarities between Southern California and California societies, matched the major culture areas that we determined with our overall measures of cultural relations. Certain economic influences, such as the way in which the houses in which people died were treated, were unmistakable. For instance, large houses that took a long time and considerable effort to build were treated much differently from lean-tos and wickiups.

In general, the deceased were removed from the living, prepared for disposal, mourned over through wailing, and then disposed. The final separation was brief and simple in the Great Basin, but it was attended by the grandest possible tribal ritual in Southern California.

When death appeared imminent, if the dying person was in his or her house, most societies preferred to let the person die in this place (Map Cu-222, V-401). The Southern California, River Yuman, Pimans, and Eastern Pueblos, however, desired to move the person out of the house before expiring, or as soon after as possible. The hasty removal of the corpse among the tribes in the foregoing areas was influenced, no doubt, by the beliefs people held about the spirit of the deceased. Free, and on its own, the spirit could be dangerous, yet as a member of the eternal community it required proper treatment. The Southern California sibs and the Yuman groups of the Southwest burned houses that people expired in, but the Pueblos merely exorcised the room in which a person died. Exorcism made sense when compared with the alternative of burning down apartment houses constructed of stone, mud, and timber (Map Cu-223, V-402). For Western Pueblos, timber was scarce.

The small, conical, bark- or thatch-covered houses of the central California Indians were burned, as were the brush-covered wickiups of Great Basin and Apachean people. Such houses had short life expectancies anyway. But the substantial semisubterranean lodges of the Plateau, the smaller but still substantial earth and timber lodges of northern California, and the plank houses of the Northwest Coast were all exorcised and temporarily abandoned. Northeastern California tribelets observed the greatest number of alternatives. Some houses were torn down and rebuilt elsewhere, some were destroyed, and some were abandoned forever. In general, the more substantial the house, the less probable that it would be abandoned forever or destroyed.

The way in which the deceased was removed from the house is interesting. In a custom observed all the way down the Northwest Coast, including all Pacific Athapaskans, and extending into the northern interior of California, the deceased were removed through a hole in the wall, perhaps by removing a slat. This practice was followed by a few Plateau tribes, including the Carriers, as well as the Apacheans in the Southwest. Except for the Apacheans, whenever the dead were removed through a hole in the wall, the house was exorcised yet kept intact (Map Cu-224, V-400). It is very plausible that, along with certain birth and puberty customs shared by other Athapaskans* but unique to the Southwest, this custom was brought by Apacheans who migrated to the Southwest, who subsequently yielded to the prevailing practice among people who built small brush houses of burning the house. Some Great Basin people did not remove the dead at all. They merely burned the house down around its deceased occupant.

Corpses were usually extended and wrapped in a hide, mat, or blanket, but areal variations were striking. In California, Southern California, and among the Yumans in the Southwest, the body was placed in

a receptacle in a pit for cremation. On the Northwest Coast, bodies were placed in small shed houses, wooden boxes, or canoes above the ground: the more important the deceased, the more elegant the receptacle. Inhumation was the practice in the Plateau and the northern part of California, whereas a rock cairn sufficed for most Great Basin and Apachean societies (Map Cu-225, V-397; Map Cu-226, V-398; Map Cu-227, V-399).

Funeral ceremonies for each deceased person, rather than for all deceased persons as among the Southern California mourning ceremonies, were more elaborate on the Northwest Coast than anywhere else. Specialists often were paid to prepare the corpse. Mourners and wailers were hired to watch over the corpse and wail through the night. And specialists in pallbearing and undertaking often placed the corpse in its final resting place.

In the central and northern Northwest Coast, and in some places in the Plateau, the widespread practice of burying much of the deceased's property with the deceased was extended to slaves, who were sacrificed for the event, though in some societies, slaves were set free (Map Cu-228, V-403). Either custom showed the largesse of the former owner and the remaining kin. An analogue to this practice, but using dogs rather than slaves, occurred throughout the California culture area, parts of the Plateau, and among Utes and Eastern Shoshones. In historic times favorite horses of Utes and Shoshones were put to death at the death of the owner.

The Navajo practice of putting slaves to death (Reichard 1941) may have been a retention of a practice shared with the Plateau Athapaskans. Yet no other Southwestern Apacheans are known to have sacrificed dogs or slaves.

---

*Namely, the customs are the following: birth—Oregon Coastal Athapaskans and Apacheans allowed men to stay in the house with women during parturition seclusion; girls' puberty—Fraser Plateau Athapaskans and Apacheans required menstruants to drink all water through tubes; dancing—Pacific Athapaskans and Apacheans conducted similar dance sequences; death—Fraser Plateau Athapaskans and Navajos put a deceased owner's slaves to death.

Chapter 11

Spirits and Shamanism

The belief in personal control of supernatural power, usually through a spirit helper of some sort, and the belief in specialists who gained their powers directly from supernatural sources through visions, dreams, or trances, were bound together in the predominantly hunting-, gathering-, and fishing-based societies of western North America. The specialists were shamans (medicine men or women), types of healers who operated with a theory of disease that held that sickness was caused (a) by some foreign item, such as a stick possessed of or directed by supernatural power or a spirit, that entered the body either through witchcraft or chance; (b) by the loss of a person's soul or spirit helper, either through chance wandering, fright, or theft; and (c) by violation of taboos or proscriptions against certain behaviors. Any of these things could cause a healthy person to become an invalid.

Thus the belief in supernatural forces, the belief that some people gained power through direct contact with the supernatural, a theory of disease that attributed sickness to supernatural intrusions or losses (soul wanderings or thefts), and a belief that the shaman could cure illnesses, were collectively implied by the presence of shamanism in any society. For this reason all of these topics are dealt with in this final chapter.

Priests were ceremonial practitioners of a different sort than shamans. Priests acted as intermediaries between humans and the supernatural. Rather than acquiring their positions through dreams, visions, or trances, or through specific quests, they were usually appointed, or perhaps they inherited, their positions. As priests they learned codified and standardized prayers or formulae.

In the Southwest, the distinction between priest and shaman was not always crystal clear, especially among the Apacheans (Western Apaches and Navajos) who had been influenced by ideas practiced in Pueblos about cosmogony and ceremony, but whose theories of power and curing were different from those among the Pueblos.

Priests and priesthoods occurred among the tribes most dependent on agriculture, such as the Pueblos, where the most common ceremonials were public rites performed on a year-round basis. Shamanism correlated most highly with hunting, gathering, and fishing societies, yet also with the societies that mixed horticultural pursuits with extractive pursuits (Pimans and River Yumans). It was among the Apacheans, the most recent interlopers and farmers in the Southwest, that beliefs associated with priesthoods—codified and standardized rituals that derive their sanctity from a myth—were most mixed with shamanistic beliefs. Navajo curers were priests, whereas Apache curers were much more like shamans. Eastern Apaches sought visions, yet Western Apaches, even shamans, did not. And Navajo priests who conducted curing sings relied on shamans, such as hand-tremblers, to diagnose illness for them.

In Southern California, the Gabrieliño, Luiseño, and others possessed intricate cosmologies that bestowed power to priest-chiefs who, in turn, put the sib's myth to memory, kept the sib's sacred fetish, directed the sacred sib ritual during the Mourning Ceremony, and oversaw the Chungichnish cult with its strong ethical prescriptions and proscriptions. Among these nonfarming, yet sedentary people, in a manner somewhat akin to Pueblo and Navajo practice, some supernatural power was beckoned through rather standardized rituals based on a formalized cosmology, yet shamans were also important in these societies. In western North America, the more formalized and standardized the cosmology, the less probable that supernatural power was obtainable through questing, and the more probable that if anyone attained power through a quest, that person would be a shaman, not an ordinary person (layman).

The theories of disease in the societies that had priesthoods and integrated their mythologies with formalized and standardized ritual practices were not much different from the theories of disease that were common among the extractive societies. The difference was that among the Pueblos, cures belonged to medicine societies, and the power to cure was invested in the rituals of these societies, whereas cures were dependent upon the proper performance of the rituals. The members of medicine societies, once initiated, devoted their lives to the calling. This avocation usually included the sponsorship by the sodality of one public ritual each year for the benefit of the entire community. Although Navajo "singers" (priests with formal knowledge of sings, such as "Beauty Way," "Blessing Way," and the like) did not form sodalities, they were not shamans either. They gained and used power through knowledge of standardized rituals learned from another singer.

Culture Tree 8 (Figure 11-1) and Figure 11-2 demonstrate that beliefs about the causes of illness, the nature of the powers of shamans and laymen, the ways in which powers were acquired, and related phenomena were all much more uniform throughout western North America than were ceremonial and life crisis observances.*

The Plateau and Northwest Coast tribes in which individual vision quests for guardian spirits loomed large in importance for most males and many females are set off at the bottom of Figure 11-1 (group 13).

Near the top of the figure is (a) the Pueblo–Navajo–Western Apache set (group 5), in which curers did not pursue individual vision quests; and (b) the set (group 4) composed of the majority of Southern California Uto-Aztecans, Great Basin Uto-Aztecans and Yumans, among whom laymen did not seek individual visions and some yet not all shamans sought power through dreams. For most of these tribes, shamans received their power unsought. At the far top of Figure 11-1 (in group 1), the Eastern Apaches, who sought visions, are distinguished from

their western congeners of group 5, who did not; yet the theories of disease, and even the themes in the curing procedures of Eastern and Western Apacheans, were similar. The major difference was in the greater accommodations to Pueblo-type practices made by Western Apaches and Navajos. The Shasta were unique, as can be seen in Figure 11-1 (group 2), because the majority of their shamans were women rather than men.

To the left- and right-hand sides of the center of Figure 11-1 are several sets of California and Northwest Coast tribes, and one set that combines Eastern Shoshones, Utes, and Diegueños (group 7). In practically all of these tribes, if there were vision quests at all, they were restricted to a few men and a few women who sought to become shamans, but most of the shamans received their powers either through inheritance, or dreams, sought or unsought.

From bottom to top, Figure 11-1 roughly represents, first, the diminution of the individual vision quest for guardian spirits for laymen and shamans, and second, the diminution of the importance of the vision quest for shamans.

ACQUISITION OF SUPERNATURAL POWER

At least two general beliefs about supernatural power coexisted in most Indian societies in western North America. One belief was that a diffuse and impersonal supernatural force pervaded the universe. It was referred to as *puwa* by Utes, *box* by Eastern Shoshones, and by other names by other tribes. The belief is best known anthropologically by its Melanesian name *mana*. Associated with *mana*, or the diffuse and impersonal force, was the notion of taboo. The force had measurable power, much like electricity, that could injure the person who did not know how to use it. One had to recognize supernatural power, and to observe the proper prescriptions and proscriptions in its use, because being impersonal, its effects could help or harm depending on the user's qualifications.

The notion of a diffuse and impersonal force that pervaded the universe was not only basic to most Indian tribes in western North America, but another basic belief was that supernatural power could be localized in specific spirits and specific objects. Bears, badgers, eagles, ravens, wolves, killer-whales, mountain-lions, foxes, rattlesnakes, and Thunderbirds were among the more popular spirit beings; yet deceased ancestors, the sun, moon, winds, and rain, were also recognized as the loci of personal spirits.

---

*The statistical bridge at which all societies are joined in Figure 10-1 is 28 percent, whereas that bridge is 45 percent in Figure 11-1.

Localized spirits in material form, such as a rock carved to resemble, or having the natural shape of a frog, which was carried by Zunis to ward off harm, or to make a person well, or a bundle full of mysterious items, which symbolized the sacred knowledge and rights of a Southern California sib, were known as fetishes—items with power in and by themselves. The belief in both personal and impersonal forms of power in many tribes meant only that the diffuse and impersonal force frequently took personal forms.

The way in which supernatural power was acquired, which was a prerequisite to becoming a shaman, varied throughout western North America, not only for shamans, but for laymen or ordinary people as well. North American Indians were unique throughout the world in that laymen, especially among hunters and gatherers, sought and acquired supernatural power to help them in their subsistence pursuits. On the Northwest Coast, competence at other skills, such as woodworking, canoe making, basket and blanket weaving, were gained through successful quests for and support from spirit helpers.

Perhaps no religious phenomena in North America is better known than the individual vision quest for guardian spirits (Map Cu-230, V-405; Map Cu-231, V-406; Map Cu-232, V-407). Throughout the Plateau and most of the Northwest Coast, at a time usually either a little before or at puberty, parents and grandparents began preparing their children for the individual ordeal of seeking a vision, which would culminate, it was hoped, in an encounter with a spirit. The child was counseled about what to expect during a vision when a spirit, usually in animal form, would reveal itself to the supplicant. In a series of procedures prior to the quest, the youth went without food or water for periods of increasing length, boys went on overnight vigils, and both boys and girls swam in cold rivers or pools. Eventually, on some winter night, the boy would go off by himself, fast, sleep in the forest or some isolated spot, plunge into cold water again and again, and perhaps scratch his body with conifer boughs or thorns. The girl's quest was less rigorous, and she did not move far from the house. After a day or two for girls, and several days for boys, and while experiencing the exhilaration of religious supplication and physical exhaustion, the seeker might be successful and dream that his or her soul encountered a spirit, who provided food and counsel, bestowed a song, perhaps a dance step, and perhaps a gift—such as woodworking skills, or the ability to become industrious and attractive, or the prospects of becoming a shaman. If seekers did not receive visions, they might attempt to gain them on subsequent quests. After puberty, however, if women had not received a vision, they seldom pursued spirit helpers again because they were now ready for marriage. Men married a little later and might pursue visions until that time.

If a person's vision quest made him sick, the sickness represented a sign, interpreted by shamans who were called in for counsel, that the seeker's soul had been taken by a spirit. When a shaman retrieved the lost soul, the successful retrieval was a sign that the vision recipient was to become a shaman. To achieve so demanding a skill required more quests and greater rigor in the quests.

As we have learned above, successful encounters with spirits and the acquisition of help from spirits gave recipients the right to be initiated into winter dance ceremonies in the Plateau in which spirit encounters were reenacted. On the Northwest Coast practices varied. Among most Coast Salishans, for instance, vision recipients could join the winter dances and dance sodalities in which they reenacted their encounters or performed more stylized dances. These dances were attended by potlatches and feasts. From the Comox and Klahuse Salish northward to the Haida, however, the dancing societies were formalized, the dance choreographies were standardized, and membership was inherited or purchased, and validated with a potlatch. Some societies were specifically for shamans, others were for people of high rank who were not shamans. This is not to suggest that visions were not important to the more northern tribes. Not only did they reenact the spirit encounters of their deceased ancestors, but the high-born (high-ranking people) also experienced personal visions which they validated with public feasts.

The Eastern Apaches and Wind River Shoshones were more similar to the Indians of the Plateau and the Plains than to their western neighbors. Among these groups the majority of males and females sought spirit helpers through vision quests. In all likelihood, the Wind River Shoshones acquired the practice from the Kiowa or Comanche tribes on the Plains. Whether the Mescalero Apaches carried the practice with them to the Southwest, or borrowed the practice from their neighbors on the southern Plains is not clear, but is reasonable to surmise that the Eastern Apache practice was retained from an earlier period.

The circumstantial and distributional evidences for retention of the Eastern Apache practices from a period prior to the migration into the Southwest gains support from the Oregon Athapaskan and Plateau Athapaskan practices. For example, Navajos did not seek visions, and the Western Apaches believed in something akin to a dream-journey in which shamans (not all individual persons) gained power

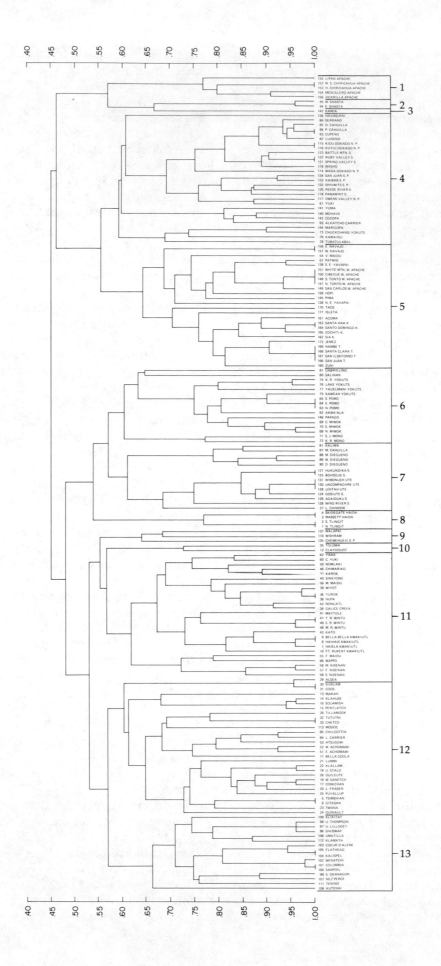

Figure 11-1 *Culture tree: 8. Groupings of tribal territories derived from G coefficients based on 26 variables (101 attributes) of spirit quests, shamanism, causes of illness, and magic.*

GROUP 1

155 Lipan Apache
152 Warm Springs Chiricahua Apache
153 Huachuca Chiricahua Apache
154 Mescalero Apache
156 Jicarilla Apache

GROUP 2

45 West Shasta
44 East Shasta

GROUP 3

142 Kamia

GROUP 4

136 Havasupai
84 Serraño
85 Desert Cahuilla
86 Pass Cahuilla
83 Cupeño
82 Luiseño
115 Kidu-Dokado Northern Paiute
116 Kuyui-Dokado Northern Paiute
123 Battle Mountain Shoshone
122 Ruby Valley Shoshone
121 Spring Valley Shoshone
119 Washo
114 Wada-Dokado Northern Paiute
134 San Juan Southern Paiute
133 Kaibab Southern Paiute
132 Shivwits Southern Paiute
120 Reese River Shoshone
118 Panamint Shoshone
117 Owens Valley Northern Paiute
61 Yuki
141 Yuma
140 Mohave
143 Cocopa
93 Alkatcho Carrier
144 Maricopa
73 Chuckchansi Yokuts
79 Kawaiisu
78 Tubatulabal

GROUP 5

158 Eastern Navajo

157 Western Navajo
54 Valley Maidu
67 Patwin
139 Southeast Yavapai
151 White Mountain Western Apache
150 Cibecue Western Apache
148 South Tonto Western Apache
147 North Tonto Western Apache
149 San Carlos Western Apache
159 Hopi
145 Pima
138 Northeast Yavapai
170 Taos
171 Isleta
161 Acoma
163 Santa Ana Keres
164 Santo Domingo Keres
165 Cochiti Keres
162 Sia Keres
172 Jemez
169 Nambe Tewa
168 Santa Clara Tewa
167 San Ildefonso Tewa
166 San Juan Tewa
160 Zuni

GROUP 6

81 Gabrieliño
80 Salinan
74 Kings River Yokuts
76 Lake Yokuts
77 Yauelmani Yokuts
75 Kaweah Yokuts
65 Southern Pomo
64 Eastern Pomo
63 Northern Pomo
92 Akwa'ala
146 Papago
69 Central Miwok
70 Southern Miwok
68 Northern Miwok
71 San Joaquin Mono
72 Kings River Mono

GROUP 7

91 Kaliwa
87 Mountain Cahuilla
88 Mountain Diegueño

89 Western Diegueño
90 Desert Diegueño
127 Hukundika Shoshone
125 Bohogue Shoshone
131 Wimonuch Ute
130 Uncompaghre Ute
129 Uintah Ute
124 Gosiute Shoshone
126 Agaiduku Shoshone
128 Wind River Shoshone
27 Lower Chinook

GROUP 8

4 Skidegate Haida
3 Massett Haida
2 Southern Tlingit
1 Northern Tlingit

GROUP 9

137 Walapai
110 Wishram
135 Chemehuevi Southern Paiute

GROUP 10

35 Tolowa
12 Clayoquot

GROUP 11

62 Yana
60 Coast Yuki
50 Nomlaki
46 Chimariko
37 Karok
40 Sinkyone
56 Mountain Maidu
39 Wiyot
36 Yurok
38 Hupa
42 Nongatl
34 Galice Creek
41 Mattole
47 Trinity River Wintu
49 Sacramento River Wintu
48 McCloud River Wintu
43 Kato
9 Bella Bella Kwakiutl
8 Haihais Kwakiutl
7 Haisla Kwakiutl
10 Fort Rupert Kwakiutl
55 Foothill Maidu
66 Wappo

58 Mountain Nisenan
57 Foothill Nisenan
59 Southern Nisenan

GROUP 12

29 Alsea
30 Siuslaw
31 Coos
13 Makah
14 Klahuse
16 Squamish
15 Pentlatch
28 Tillamook
32 Tututni
33 Chetco
113 Modoc
95 Chilcotin
94 Lower Carrier
53 Atsugewi
52 West Achomawi
51 East Achomawi
11 Bella Coola
21 Lummi
22 Klallam
19 Upper Stalo
26 Quileute
18 West Sanetch
17 Cowichan
20 Lower Fraser
25 Puyallup
5 Tsimshian
6 Gitksan
23 Twana
24 Quinault

GROUP 13

109 Klikitat
98 Upper Thompson
97 Upper Lillooet
96 Shuswap
108 Umatilla
112 Klamath
103 Coeur d'Alene
105 Flathead
104 Kalispel
102 Wenatchi
101 Columbia
100 Sanpoil
99 Southern Okanagon
107 Nez Percé
111 Tenino
106 Kutenai

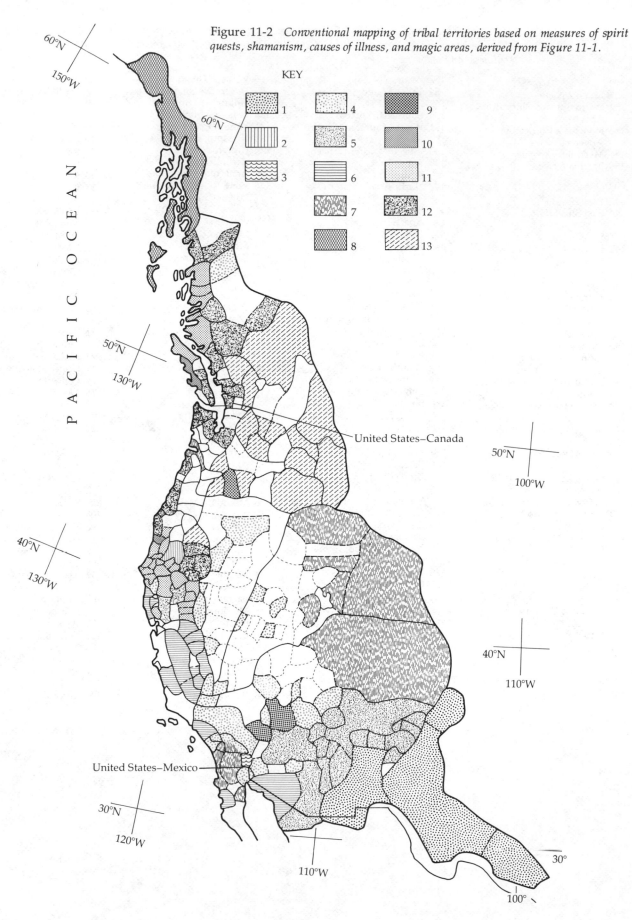

Figure 11-2 *Conventional mapping of tribal territories based on measures of spirit quests, shamanism, causes of illness, and magic areas, derived from Figure 11-1.*

KEY

1 2 3 4 5 6 7 8 9 10 11 12 13

PACIFIC OCEAN

60°N
150°W

60°N

50°N
130°W

40°N
130°W

United States–Canada

50°N
100°W

40°N
110°W

United States–Mexico

30°N
120°W

110°W

30°

100°

through various sources similar to spirit helpers, such as water, fire, eagles, or snakes. Most male and female Carrier and Chilcotin tribe members of the Fraser Plateau, and members of Athapaskan tribes on the Oregon coast sought visions. The latter is noteworthy because the Oregon Athapaskans were the only groups in the Oregon coastal region to do so. As a matter of fact, except for the Achomawi and Atsugewi, visions were not pursued at all, or they were restricted to a small minority of shamans throughout the northern part of California, northwestern California, and the Oregon coast. It is plausible, then, that Oregon Athapaskans and Eastern Apaches retained and continued to pursue individual vision quests even though their neighbors, including some Athapaskans, did not seek visions. That is, whereas a few California Athapaskan shamans sought visions, they fitted in with the prevailing practice in the area. Western Apache shamans recognized dream journeys in which the dreamer travelled to sources of animal and natural phenomena power which were embodied in animal spirits, much as did the Pimans and Yumans, and Navajos did not pursue visions. It is plausible that the Western Apaches, influenced by Yuman, Piman, and Pueblo practices, and the Navajos, influenced by Pueblo practices, innovated on the prevailing themes of their neighbors.

Throughout the California culture area, most individuals did not believe that they could gain control over supernatural power. Everywhere in western North America people were wary of supernatural power, but the differences between those who sought power (Northwest Coast and Plateau), and those who did not, or who did so in a most limited fashion, were marked.

In the California culture area it was possible for some persons to seek power, but few did so. Power was bestowed on most shamans in dreams, even though it was not sought. And many, if not most, who gained power were frightened by it. We shall return to this point in our discussion of the nature of shamanism in California below.

In the central part of California, in conjunction with Toloache initiations and subsequent membership, novices ingested *Datura stramonium*, or Jimson-weed, and experienced dreams in which they gained personal power to keep them healthy through life. The same was true for Toloache and Chungichnish members in Southern California. The critical difference was that the dreams brought good life and good health, but not the power required for special skills.

In fact, wherever *Datura* was used, from the Miwok tribelets on the north to the Pimans and Pais in the Southwest (Map Cu-233, V-408), dreams were sought which would bring a person confidence and good health. Such dreams, then, brought personal power for everyday life and everyday affairs. Among the Pimans, River Yumans, and Pais there were no Toloache sodalities, but *Datura* ingestion in conjunction with singing sessions to stimulate dreams were engaged in by shamans. Among River Yumans, young men might also seek protection in warfare. Pimans coupled their dreaming–singing sessions with long pilgrimages to the Gulf of California for salt, whereas River Yumans, who emphasized warfare, coupled their dreaming–singing sessions (long song-cycles) with individually conducted raids that tested the power of their dreams and songs to make them brave.

Throughout the Great Basin, vision quests for individuals were not practiced. In a few societies, primarily Ute and Eastern Shoshones, where there were contacts with either Plains or Plateau tribes, some shamans might go to a place in which power was believed to be localized, but there was no rigorous quest, not even anything matching the singing-dreaming sessions of the River Yuman, Pai, and Piman shamans. On the other hand, all Great Basin people believed that a bit of the impersonal power that pervaded the universe had to be localized in each person and in each living thing. This force was life itself, and it came to a person through the mere fact of birth, not through a spirit encounter.

If individual vision quests for spirit helpers occurred primarily as a response to the desire for skills to make people successful in hunting, fishing, gathering, and other subsistence economy and economic pursuits, one would be hard pressed to explain the absence of quests among the dwellers of the Great Basin and the Pais, for not only were these people extractors, but their resources were more diffuse and less abundant than anywhere else in western North America. On the other hand, as a requisite of life these people believed that each person had to possess some power. This belief may have obviated the individual spirit quest.

SHAMANS

Beliefs about shamans and their powers, the distinctions between shamans and laymen, and the roles that shamans played in their home communities, neighboring communities, and even far-distant communities, were related to four factors of economic, social, and political organization. It appears that (1) the more dependent people were on hunting, fishing, and gathering for subsistence, the more pronounced were individual vision quests for shamans and laymen alike.* But even among societies with extractive-based subsistence economics, (2) the most sedentary communities, in which (3) centralized political authority was exercised over many households, and in which (4) sodalities were present, individual vision quests by laymen did not occur, and vision quests by shamans were rare. Shamans, in fact, usually acquired their power by means other than vision quests. Although the ethnographic information on the topic is spotty, the number of shamans in hunting, gathering, and fishing societies that were also sedentary, that recognized political authority beyond the household, and that possessed sodalities were fewer than in the more anarchistic hunting, gathering, and fishing societies. Moreover, there was a distinct tendency for shamans in the more centralized, extractive-based societies either to be organized into loose societies of shamans whose only tasks were to initiate, thereby to control, the credentials of new shamans (as among the Wintu, Shastan, and Achomawi tribes and some other tribes in the northern part of California), and to sponsor shamans' power contests in which shamans competed in displaying their powers. Whether or not loosely organized shamans' societies such as these occurred within a society, shamans in California tribelets assisted in the control of the ceremonial affairs of the community, usually in league with the chief or chiefs. In the northern part of California, few people wanted to become shamans at all, in part because a person could not always control the power he or she thought was possessed, in part because possession of power carried great responsibilities, and in part because a prevailing practice was to kill shamans whose cures did not work. When a cure did not work, the shaman was suspected of evil intent.

Shamans, in all western North American societies in which they occurred, cured the sick. Many, too, forecast events, gave counsel, attempted to influence the weather, and did other miraculous things. But in the more politically centralized societies there were fewer shamans, their numbers were often controlled by loose organizations of shamans that initiated new shamans, and the individual virtuosity of shamans was under more control, sometimes under the threat of death for failure to cure, or for suspicion of witchcraft. Shamans assisted chiefs, and from positions of strength and favor, often coerced members of their own communities to participate in ceremonies. From

these positions they also posed threats to the well-being of members of other communities, particularly those who visited, say, a Big Time sponsored by a tribelet in California.

It may well have been the case that with (a) the acquisition of agriculture and the dependence for subsistence upon it; (b) an agricultural cosmogony that recognized seasons and cyclic events; and (c), the development of sodalities to conduct standardized ceremonials in centralized political communities, that though theories of disease were the same as for extractors, curing was transferred to codified rituals in the hands of initiates. Individual virtuosity gave way to the collectivity, yet the collectivity of medicine societies performed for the public at least once a year.

In the communities of the California and Southern California culture areas shamans demonstrated their individually possessed, awe-inspiring powers in public displays, even in power contests among shamans. That medicine societies were created through transition from a loosely organized society of individual shamans, or even from the concept of public power contests that did not require society membership, seems plausible. Indeed, only simple transitions would have been necessary to organize shamans into a group with the authority to initiate new shamans; and only some standardization of shamans' performances would have been required to create regularized public performances by a medicine society.

On the Northwest Coast, where extractors were sedentary, there was next to no political centralization, save for the Tsimshian tribes, some Nootka tribes, and the Athapaskan cluster in the northwestern part of California. It is interesting that, as Drucker (1940) suggests, of all the winter dance sodalities in the central and northern Northwest Coast, shamanistic beliefs and practices, in the Shaman's society as well as the other dance societies, "contributed more heavily to the form of the rites" than any other aspect of native culture. Shamanistic beliefs and practices provided the vision quest, healing, and plots for dramas requiring legerdemain, masks for the impersonation of spirits, mythology, lay figures, hereditary prerogatives of shamans, and so forth. The dances were codified and coordinated, but shamans were still independent operators, medical virtuosos, much as the kinship groups from which shamans came were independent. The Northwest Coast did not satisfy the requirement for political centralization. This may explain why shamans were numerous and of high rank. Their performances, even codified performances, and the performances of others at winter ceremonials up and down the coast, trumpeted their individuality and uniqueness, their privileges and prerogatives. In other societies with

---

*The Great Basin societies were obvious exceptions. Pai societies engaged in some farming.

extractive-based economies in which either sodalities or independent shamans'-initiating societies were present, shamans were important, but few in number, whereas priests (singers) and curing sodalities occurred in the farming societies (Map Cu-234, V-409).

In extractive-based economies, then, it appears that sedentariness, political centralization, and the development of sodalities and sodality initiations selected against free access of any and all to spirit powers, and selected against the proliferation of shamans, which by nature was individualistic and threatening. Shamanism was threatening because supernatural power, used for malevolent ends, could jeopardize the political fabric. Yet supernatural power in the hands of a few qualified people who were in league with chiefs or priest-chiefs could not only heal the sick, but threaten enemies and local recalcitrants, and keep these powers in full view at shamans' power contests and in ceremonial affairs.

The manner in which shamans acquired their power and the difference between the powers of shamans and laymen provide evidence for the preceding suggestions about the nature of shamanism in various kinds of extractive-based economies (Map Cu-235, V-410; Map Cu-236, V-411). In the Plateau shamans and laymen went on similar quests, but shamans gained greater power than laymen, often through the acquisition of spirit helpers, even specialized spirits for particular types of healing and skills. On the Northwest Coast, though vision quests usually began in the same way for most seekers, people who inherited the right to become shamans had special training, and all shamans acquired distinctive power for their specialties. What is crucial about Northwest Coast shamanism was the distinctiveness of the training and of the prerogatives that were associated with the vision. Northwest Coast shamans could join dance sodalities, cure the sick, and so forth, but unless they were chiefs, they did *not* exercise greater power than a chief in allocating kinship group resources or anything else. The nature of the ranking system made shamans unique but also restricted them to their specialties.

In the northern and central parts of California and in Southern California, either power came unsought in dreams—which were frequently denied by the recipients who did not want them—or at a late stage in life. Perhaps after a woman had raised her family, or after a man was involved in a special way in sodality affairs, these people would seek spirit helpers through rigorous training and dancing. Power from a guardian spirit—either an animal or the spirit of a deceased shaman—was implanted in the prospective shaman by means of a "pain," which took the form of a small, sharp object. Throughout northwestern California and elsewhere in the northern part of California, shamans alone possessed supernatural power. In the Toloache and Chungichnish areas, members gained personal power that was less in amount, if not less in specialized spirits, than shamans. The notion that power could vary in amount most often meant that some people controlled more of the diffuse, impersonal supernatural force than others. It did not need to stem from more spirits, or specialized spirits.

As we have described, in the Great Basin everyone possessed some power, whereas shamans gained greater amounts, usually unsought. Western Apache shamans gained power unsought as well, whereas Navajo singers and Pueblo medicine society members acquired the use of power by learning and performing rituals.

Sex of Shamans

In the majority of Indian societies in western North America, most shamans were men. Among the Uto-Aztecan-speaking communities of Southern California, and to the north among the Salinan and some Yokuts groups, shamans were exclusively men (Map Cu-237, V-412). All these societies were patricentered in residence and descent. In societies where shamans were predominantly but not totally male, men shamans treated the most serious illnesses, and they were also called upon to influence the weather and to forecast events. In these same societies, almost invariably, women shamans were assigned less important tasks—sometimes referred to as "household shaman" pursuits. Household-type tasks included administering to girls at puberty; administering to women with menstrual cramps; aiding women who were experiencing difficult parturitions; and caring for minor ailments of household members. In the predominantly patrilocal communities of the California culture area, women seldom became shamans until middle age. By this time their children were usually grown, and the woman herself was ensconced in her husband's community. Given the general suspicion with which people regarded shamans in California, it is not surprising that women, who tended to hail from communities other than the community in which they resided with their husband did not become shamans until they were well established in their husband's community.

Throughout the egalitarian family camp and band societies of the Great Basin and among the Eastern Apaches, male and female shamans were perhaps equal in numbers. Among the Eastern Apaches, men were the most powerful shamans. They possessed the most important curing rituals (curing techniques learned in spirit encounters), and it was the curing rituals that were sponsored for the restoration of good health that was the basic concern of all Apacheans, Eastern and Western, even through public girls' puberty rites were the most important collective ceremonials. Throughout the Great Basin, men and women shamans could be of equal prominence, yet even in those societies, more male shamans tended to be prominent than women.

There is no simple explanation for the differences in the importance of shamanistic functions for men and women. There must be something more basic than the distinctions between societies that observed patrilocal residence and those that did not. In the egalitarian, anarchistic, and ambilocal communities throughout the Great Basin, even when female shamans were prominent, they were outnumbered by prominent male shamans.

The answer may lie in the entire body of beliefs that attended women in hunting, gathering, and fishing societies. Women at first menses, subsequent menses, and during pregnancy were universally regarded as either possessing, or being possessed by, special powers that were dangerous to men (the unqualified), dangerous to the women themselves unless special taboos were observed and special precautions were taken, and dangerous to all other living things, especially the animals that inhabited land and water and that were vital to subsistence. Powers such as these were not to be trifled with, by men or women. When women became shamans, they usually administered to female problems. In many societies in the central and northern parts of California, such practices were restricted more to older women, perhaps even postmenopausal women.

There was a cluster of societies along the Oregon coast (all tribes but the Athapaskan), northwestern California (all tribes but the Athapaskan, with the exception of the Hupa), and the northern part of California (the Shastan), in which not only the majority of shamans were women, but they were also the most powerful shamans. Inasmuch as Algonkian speakers (Yurok–Wiyot tribes), Hokan speakers (Shastan–Karok tribes), Penutians speakers (Coos–Alsea–Siuslaw tribes), and Salishan speakers (Tillamook), formed this unique cluster, it is plausible that the custom was developed before the Athapaskans penetrated the region, but was diffused among many adjacent societies. The Hupa, Athapaskan speakers who became nearly indistinguishable from the Karok and Yurok tribes in basketry, ceremonial practices, and many other aspects of culture, probably adopted the practice of allowing women to com-

pose the majority of shamans, whereas the other Athapaskans did not. Yet even the Tolowa, Tututni, Sinkyone, and Nongatl tribes and others recognized as many male as female shamans, though males were considered more powerful. Among the Nootka tribes there were more women than men shamans, but these tribes also considered men more powerful.

As late as 1942, in a reassessment of Yurok shamanism, Kroeber was puzzled as to how and why women came to be the dominant shamans in the region. Through ceremonial wood gathering for the sweat house some men gained "luck" (power) to accumulate wealth, sometimes through gambling. Others became brave by diving into cold and turbulent water. But men did not gain power to cure the sick through dreams or through "doctor-making" dances—which were the two routes to becoming shamans. Indeed, dreaming and dancing were the ways in which daughters of shamans usually became shamans. In all of these societies, and among the adjacent Wintu and Athapaskan tribes as well, wealth in prestige items (woodpecker scalps and the like) could be accumulated through shamanistic practices.

Somehow women came to dominate the practice among these societies, such as Coos, Alsea, Tillamook, Yurok, Karok, Wiyot, and Hupa, which were amorphous yet relatively wealthy in subsistence resources, prestige items, and trade goods. The combination of small and independent households, considerable resources, and rather sedentary yet unorganized communities, except for ceremonial purposes among the Yurok, Karok, Hupa, and Wiyot was unique in western North America, as was the preponderance of female shamanism. Shamans were not put to death if their cures failed, though that was the fate of many shamans elsewhere in California: instead, if the cure failed, the shaman merely repaid the fee she received. So the specter of death for incompetent or malevolent shamans did not exist and could not have deterred them. If anything, men might have desired to become shamans because the practice, as for modern physicians, was lucrative. It is easy to see why Kroeber had no explanation, no hypothesis, no guess to account for the preponderance of female shamans in the area. It was unique, and no explanation can be advanced here either.

Shamans' Impersonations, Disguises, Possessions, and Trances

Shamans used masks or disguises representing their spirit powers while performing curing techniques throughout much of the Northwest Coast and parts of the Plateau. In these same areas, of course, winter ceremonial performances reenacted spirit encounters, and on the Northwest Coast, shamans often formed restricted sodalities to enact shamanistic dramas with the use of masks (Map Cu-238, V-413). Masks too were used throughout the Southwest by Pueblo medicine societies and Piman curers who undoubtedly had a long history of masked performances, but also by Navajos and Apacheans who mounted masked performances in conjunction with cures and sings.

Navajos and Pueblos represented gods with their masked performances. In the performances on the Northwest Coast and in the Plateau, however, shamans were often believed to become possessed by the spirit they represented, that is, by their own spirit helper. This belief had especially wide currency in Siberia and among Eskimos, but was not so widely believed in western North America, being restricted more to the northwestern regions adjacent to the Arctic, which was the possible source of the belief (Map Cu-239, V-415).

Throughout the California culture area, but not in the region dominated by women shamans, it was believed that men gained power from the grizzly bear, and those who did so had the power to turn themselves into grizzlies and destroy enemies. Grizzly-bear shamans wore bear disguises, and though all gained their power from bears, many were believed not only to be possessed by bear spirits but to transmute to bears as well.

The belief in possession by a supernatural spirit did not prevail in Southern California, the Southwest, and the Great Basin, but trances occurred in which shamans appeared to lose contact with the ordinary world and to hobnob with spirits from whom power and instructions were gained. In the *Datura*-using societies, shamans often entered trance states, perhaps aided and abetted by long, hypnotic song cycles among Pimans, River Yumans, and Pais. Some Western Apachean, Zuni, and Tewa shamans also went into trances brought on by bear spirits, in particular. This belief in bear-spirit trances, common to spirit possession and even transmutation among California Penutians, may have been carried to the Southwest by the Zuni (Penutians), or it may have stemmed from an even earlier belief that prevailed among prehistoric hunters and gatherers in western North America.

Serpents, in general, were thought to be sources of great power, but in the societies of the California, Southern California, and Great Basin culture areas, and among the Pais, some shamans gained their power from rattlesnakes. These shamans demonstrated their control over these dangerous reptiles in public displays. Among the Yokuts societies and throughout Southern California, rattlesnake shamans would convene to perform intricate juggling and manipulating acts with rattlesnakes publicly, and, of course, they possessed the power to cure snakebite. Among Great Basin Uto-Aztecans, Pais, and the more northern Californians, more modest public displays with rattlesnakes were known (Map Cu-240, V-414).

The Hopi Snake-kiva society performed a Snake ritual every other year, alternating with the Flute ritual, in which sodality members performed dances with rattlesnakes. At Acoma, too, rattlesnakes were used ceremonially. Whether public rattlesnake displays in the Pueblos share a common origin with shamanistic displays in Southern California is not known, but tribes in each area also used snake motifs in sand paintings associated with curing and initiation rites. Trade contacts between the regions were of extremely long duration, so it is plausible that they came to share some similarities in ceremonial motifs.

The Navajos and Apaches did not handle rattlesnakes or possess sodalities for which initiation using snake motifs was employed. But the rattlesnake motif was a prominent feature in Apachean sand paintings associated with curing ceremonies.

SHAMANS AND DISEASE

Among all societies in western North America in which there were shamans, only the Walapai tribe was reported not to have recognized some shamans as performing more miraculous feats than others. It is probable that the reporting for the Walapai is not accurate. Reputations were based on performances. The shoddy performer might be killed in the northern and central parts of California, and shamans who were suspected of using their power maliciously might be killed in many societies elsewhere (Map Cu-241, V-416).

Shamans' reputations earned in one community were often extended to another community to which shamans were invited (Map Cu-242, V-417). In point of fact, except for a cluster of aggressive Tlingit and Haida societies, a cluster of aggressive Nootka, Southern Kwakiutl, and northern Coast Salishan societies, a cluster of aggressive Eastern Apaches, a cluster of suspicious societies in the northern part of California, and a few Great Basin societies that had few contacts with people speaking languages different from their own, some notable shamans were known to be invited either to perform at shamans' contests, or to effect cures, in communities other than their home communities, including communities speaking different languages from their own. Shamans' reputations spread over considerable distances. Both fear and respect were accorded great shamans, and if problems within one community were severe, fears would often be overcome and shamans from distant communities and different tribes would be summoned.

It is plausible that shamans from different language communities were not summoned by the Northwest Coast, Eastern Apache, and Nisenan groups precisely because each of these clusters of societies comprised offensive raiders who were suspicious of their neighbors, as well as suspect to those neighbors, wherever power of any sort, whether physical force or supernatural force, was at issue.

It is understandable that shamans would be summoned from near and far to effect cures, because a basic theory of disease was shared by most tribes. Emphases differed, and central and northern Northwest Coast people, for example, believed that they suffered and died more often from soul loss or loss of their guardian spirit, whereas the people from the southern Northwest Coast through the northwestern part of California subscribed to the view that they more often suffered and died from the intrusion of objects into their bodies (Map Cu-243, V-418; Map Cu-244, V-419).

Intrusions of some sort were reported for every tribe in western North America except the Alkatcho Carrier. Some California culture area and Southwestern tribes attributed most foreign intrusions to objects—known as "pains" in California—whereas both spirits and objects were recognized as the efficient causes of sickness elsewhere. For object intrusions, the nearly universal treatment was a sucking cure in which a shaman put his mouth on the patient's chest or other afflicted part, depending on the diagnosis, and produced an object from inside his mouth. For spirit intrusions, the spirit was sometimes sucked out. Other techniques included fanning, pressing the shaman's head to the afflicted person's body, and luring the spirit out through songs.

Illnesses caused by the loss of a spiritual entity were not completely restricted to societies in which vision quests for guardian spirits were pursued, but the belief that the loss of *spirit helpers* brought about sickness was restricted to those Plateau and Northwest Coast societies in which spirit helpers were gained through vision quests. The loss of a soul, or a person's own spiritual entity, as opposed to loss of a spirit helper, occurred in all but a few societies in the California and Southwestern culture areas.

The cure for soul loss or spirit-helper loss was to retrieve it. Most frequently the shaman would go into a trance. At such times his power would allow his own soul to journey to the Land of the Dead, or some other supernatural place, and bring the spirit helper or soul back.

The reporting on the causes of foreign intrusion and spirit entity losses is, by and large, sketchy. Some ethnographers pursued such questions in great detail, but most did not. Consequently, though it is hoped the following maps are accurate, it is possible that they are inadvertently misleading: Map Cu-245, V-420; Map Cu-246, V-421; Map Cu-247, V-422.

It was almost universally reported that people attributed foreign instrusions to (a) sorcery performed by a shaman with evil intent; (b) magic performed by anyone who knew how to do it; or (c) supernatural forces, such as ghosts or spirits, that performed on their own, independent of human actions.

The loss of spirit entities, like the causes of foreign intrusions, were attributed to shamans with evil intentions, to people other than shamans performing magic, and to supernatural forces operating independently of human actors. Yet soul loss also came about through the violation of certain taboos and by rather whimsical causes, such as a soul wandering off on its own volition while a person slept, or its being frightened away during a particularly bad dream. However the soul- or spirit-loss came about, the patient felt discouraged and possessed little energy. If a spirit was intruded into a person's body, the patient experienced some of the same symptoms as in spirit loss, but often, as among the people of the Great Basin, suffered from "fevers" as well as ennui and disphoria.

Most shamans' cures included the use of songs (chants), and sucking, fanning, or blowing. Dancing, spirit impersonations, masks, various feats of legerdemain—including ventriloquism—sand paintings, fetish bags (medicine bags), and trances were also used.

MAGIC

Magic was based on the assumption of impersonal supernatural power, a concept that was basic to the beliefs of many people in western North America. Great Basin Uto-Aztecans, as we have learned, believed that all living things needed some power for life itself. But ceremonialism, vision quests, reenactments of spirit encounters, were more often supplicative than manipulative. Through ritual people often sought to conciliate the personal powers of gods or lesser spirits so as to request favors. This was especially true among the Pueblos.

Magic was not supplicative. It was a formula or a set of formulas in which impersonal powers were manipulated in order automatically to make use of them. But as different as manipulation and supplication were in concept, both were often used together. For example, Pimans created effigies of corn and stuck them in the ground so as to make corn grow, and they satiated themselves with sahuaro cactus so as to cause rain to fall. These were magical, manipulative acts whose formulas caused impersonal power to work. In the same ceremonies, Pimans also made offerings to the four cardinal directions, sang songs requesting favors from the cloud and sun spirits, and performed other supplicative acts. It is not always clear how and in what way magical and religious acts were intertwined in Piman rituals and in the rituals of many other tribes. Some standardized ritual acts were symbolic, and the beliefs on which they were pinned were supplicative, whereas other acts were based on the magical assumption that certain formulae caused impersonal powers to make things happen.

Sir James Frazer (1922) defined the "General Law of Sympathetic Magic," which held that things act on each other at a distance through a secret sympathy. The actions are wholly impersonal, impulses being transmitted from one to the other as if by telepathy—by what Frazer described as a "kind of invisible ether." The "ether," of course, was a belief in impersonal forces.

The "General Law of Sympathy" yields two kinds of magic: "imitative magic" (based on the principle that "like begets like"), and "contagious magic" (based on the principle of "contact," which holds that things once conjoined must remain in the same sympathetic relation forever after, even if subsequently separated). For examples, in the former, an imitation of growing corn will—say—cause corn to grow. In the latter, a fingernail clipping could be used to affect the person from whom it had been taken.

Some forms of magic were reported for all tribes in western North America, but the reporting is spotty. Magic, especially personal uses of magic, was not a topic that people readily talked about, in part, of course, because impersonal powers could be used for malicious as well as beneficial purposes, and not a small amount of sickness and death was attributed to malicious performances of magical acts. Magical acts with malicious intent, which were performed in secret to harm rather than help, are those often referred to by anthropologists as "black magic" and "witchcraft." "White magic," on the other hand, is that used for beneficial purposes. The definition becomes sticky, however, because what is beneficial for one tribe, say, the elimination of enemies, is not beneficial for the victims of that magic. Naroll (1961) demonstrated that ethnographers and other observers sel-

dom collected information on witchcraft, sorcery, or black magic unless they had been in the field for a year at the least, or longer: it was not something people talked about freely. Basso (1969) points out the difficulty that he encountered in getting people even to acknowledge that he had asked them questions about witchcraft.

It is plausible that the sketchy and incomplete reporting of magic (V-423 to V-430) stems from the short periods in which ethnographers were normally in the field and the reluctance of people to talk about witchcraft or black magic to strangers. That beliefs in magic are still very much alive among Indians in many communities is evident.* For imitative magic, in particular, reporting is inconclusive (Map Cu-248, V-425, and V-423 to V-425). Many ethnographers reported that imitative magic was absent, yet the belief was reported as present for a few societies in every culture area save the southern Northwest Coast. It may well have been practiced everywhere.

White imitative magic was performed in mourning ceremonies where images of the deceased were burned, thus liberating the spirits of the decedents. Among the Pima communities, dancers imitated maize as singers sang songs to "sing it up," i.e., to cause the maize to grow through magical song formulas. Black imitative magic was the only kind of imitative magic reported on the Northwest Coast. The Quinault tribe, for instance, imitated the wind by repeatedly dropping a log into the water, and they imitated hunters and animals by creating images of them and attaching them to the logs: storms were summoned in this way which, like the "storms" whipped up when the logs dropped into the water, prohibited hunters and fishermen from pursuing game and fish.

It should be noted that in many societies anyone could perform imitative magic, and the same was true for contagious magic (Map Cu-249, V-428). The power was impersonal, and all a person needed was the formula to make it work. Intent need not even have been a factor in making it work, and the same is true even today. For instance, a Navajo recently explained the withered and distorted arm—a birth defect—of his daughter as being caused by his unintentional actions. Prior to his wife's parturition he drove the opening of an empty beer can onto a fragile new branch of a sacred evergreen tree, twisting the can as he pushed it. The branch was mangled and distorted, as was the child's arm at birth.

---

*See Basso's (1969) analysis of Western Apache witchcraft and Colson's (1974) assessment of Pomo witchcraft, for examples.

One only needs knowledge of its magical formula to make the impersonal power work. For this reason probably more societies than have been recorded on the distribution maps believed that anyone, not only "specially qualified" people, could perform magic. In the literature what was usually meant by "special qualification" was that the practitioner of magic was a shaman or ritualist. Some select people, such as ritualists, were called on to perform magic, usually for a fee. This reporting may only scratch the surface and miss the point that anyone could perform magic so long as they know a formula. For instance, imitative charms such as frog- or owlshaped stones, and contagious charms such as an eagle claw or a strand of hair from a great shaman, might be placed in a bag, and though the bag might harbor several spirits, these spirits were all impersonal: they worked for anybody and for any purpose that the possessors of them sought. Such charms were known as *fetishes* which were useful to anyone who possessed them. The Kiowa *T'ame*, or Sun Dance doll, had power in and of itself. It came into the possession of Utes, who still often display it at modern sun dances: it is as good for the Ute as it was for the Kiowa.

Contagious magic is much better reported than imitative magic. Such practices as that of treating the navel cord and afterbirth in a special way were widely followed. Navel cords were buried in anthills so as to make the child industrious; or tacked on a cradle, for if they were lost the children would not prosper; or hung around the neck, ultimately to be placed in a medicine bundle at puberty. Afterbirths were often hung in the crotches of trees so as to grow and return to their owners, or were buried so as not to be eaten by carrion eaters, since its ingestion by carrion-eaters would affect a woman's ability to have additional children. The list of contagious magic beliefs and practices is long.

An example of contagious black magic from the Quinault tribe gives the idea of how it works and, perhaps, why people were wary to talk about it. A person who wished to stop someone or some deme from fishing might place some salmon hearts inside clam shells, place the clam shells in a piece of rotten wood, and bury the rotten wood in a secret place. Fish would not proceed beyond that point until the magic was removed because the fish would become "sleepy." A person who was discovered performing such magic was killed, so black magic was a very secret undertaking.

Gambling was an important activity in western North America, especially among Plateau, Great Basin, Southern California, and non-Pueblo cultures of the Southwest. In all of these culture areas, some people were recognized to be better gamblers than others, either because they carried charms that gave them success, or because they performed magic that caused others to play recklessly and foolishly and gave the performer of the magic an advantage (Map Cu-250, V-429).

Gambling magic was often suspect, even feared, and those who possessed such magic were seldom desired on opposite teams. Yet to have such a person on one's own team in a hand-and-stick game (in which marked and unmarked sticks were hidden from the opposition) was a desired advantage. In the Plateau, where gambling was an important intertribal event, successful gamblers might have assuaged fears about their powers by sponsoring huge intertribal feasts from their winnings.

Love charms and magic (Map Cu-251, V-430) that caused a woman to be irresistible to a man, or vice versa, was sketchily reported, but it was probably as widespread as gambling magic. It was even reported among some of the Pueblos.

APPENDICES AND BIBLIOGRAPHIES

Appendix A

Variable Ratings and the Reliability of Judgments

When we formulated our research design and created the variables to be analyzed, we were confronted with several problems, most of which stemmed from the enormous size of the sample cases (S) times sample variables (V): total size is 172 S × 443 V. Our first problem was to allocate case and variable rating duties among the five research associates. We reasoned that if we divided the 172 cases into five nearly equal groups (34 or 35 cases in each) and assigned each associate to rate all variables for each case in his group, we might well introduce huge amounts of bias beyond that which might appear in each ethnographic report for each case. Biases are defined as errors that result from factors which dispose the errors to occur in one direction rather than at random. Biases need not reflect either the conscious or unconscious subjectivity of the ethnographer or the informant during the primary research (in the field), or the analyst during secondary research, but these desires can create bias nevertheless.

Let us illustrate with a hypothetical example from primary research among the Northern Pomo Indians of California. Suppose that when an ethnographer among the Pomos observes Northern Pomo life and asks Pomos to recall Pomo cultural practices and observances prior to extensive Euro-American contact, two types of bias—one from the informant and one from ethnographer—can be introduced to the ethnographer's report. Furthermore, the context of the primary observation can or cannot dispose the ethnographer to bias the report. Among the Northern Pomos, let us say that the informant is asked a question about the ownership and inheritance of oak trees. It is possible that the ethnographer expects that groves of oaks were owned by patrilocal bilateral lineal families and nominal ownership was inherited by the most competent son of the dominant family of each lineal family upon the death of the previous owner. Unconsciously the ethnographer may phrase the question in such a way as to elicit the response he expects. Indeed, if the question is phrased in such a way that the

expected response is more or less valid in the mind of the Northern Pomo informant, that person may well respond positively, even if the Northern Pomo's conception of ownership and inheritance is somewhat vague, or at variance with that of the ethnographer.

The bias may also be exacerbated by the expectations of the informant and the context of the interview. For instance, it may well have been that the informant, interviewed on a reservation in the depths of the Great Depression, was in need of the informant's fee that would be paid to him, and he or she did not want to offend the ethnographer and jeopardize future fees. Or it may have been that the informant simply did not want to offend the ethnographer as a matter of pride, and systematically responded in a positive fashion. Or it may have been that the informant wished to deceive the probing, snooping ethnographer, and chose to respond with erroneous information. Or it may be that the informant did not know, but supplied an answer anyway. Whatever the case may be, bias can be created by the informant and the ethnographer. In addition, bias can be created by the secondary, comparative researcher.*

---

*An early discussion of bias in field research appears in Driver (1938) and a few other such discussions have appeared in the past 15 years, e.g., Naroll (1962: 77–106; 1970: 927–945) and Köbben (1967b: 3–34). Less rigorous but nonetheless interesting papers in Jongmans and Gutkind, eds. (1967) touch on problems of bias in field work—see there the contributions of den Hollander (pp. 1–34), Köbben (pp. 35–55), and De Josselin de Jong (pp. 89–101). Yet, in a 600 page book on the subject of ethnographic field research edited by Freilich (1970), bias receives only four pages of informal treatment; and in a much more rigorous book on anthropological research by Pelto (1970), bias receives no treatment at all.

We shall not attempt to list all potential forms of bias in secondary research, but one ubiquitous source comes from selective reading of ethnographic reports so that information favorable to the rater's predilections or hypotheses is found. Such bias can emerge through several practices, to wit: interpreting and rating variables as present on the basis of indirect evidence so as to confirm one's hypotheses, even when one cannot find information which confirms that judgment; or failing to interpret and rate a variable as absent when indirect evidence points toward absence of the variable. Another source of bias can come from the selective use of ethnographic reports. For instance, if three different ethnographers reported land tenure customs within a Pueblo society but only one ethnographer classified land tenure in the fashion that met with the rater's expectation, the rater might use the rating that was favorable to his own preconception as the "correct" empirical interpretation. Still other sources of bias might be a rater's systematic and arbitrary rejection of reports written by missionaries, or functionalists, and the like, regardless of the competence of the observers and the length of time the observers spent with the Indians about whom they reported.

In our study we tried to come to grips with secondary research bias by (1) formulating a multitude of hypotheses which specified so many variables that it would be difficult for the principal investigators or their research associates to rate each variable for each case so that all of the hypotheses might become validated; (2) defining and rating close to 100 variables for which there were no explicit evolutionary, ecological, functional, or structural hypotheses to integrate them; (3) staffing the project with researchers from, and using independent library resources at, two universities— Indiana University and the University of Michigan—rather than one, to reduce the probability of convergence of ratings through discussions among the researchers and through seeing marginal notes made in the ethnographies by the first researcher to use each source; (4) not making explicit to the three research associates all of the hypotheses formulated by Jorgensen and Driver, the principal investigators; and (5) dividing the rating duties by topical sets of variables, e.g., ceremonialism and life-cycle events, shamanism, spirit quests, causes of illness, and magic, all of which were rated by Jorgensen, rather than separating duties by sets of tribes.

We reasoned that allocation of duties by variable topics for all the tribes would make it difficult for any person to rate all of the variables pertinent to one or more hypotheses, because most of the hypotheses integrated variables among several topics. Furthermore, each rater would be able to formulate a picture of the entire range of variation for each variable assigned to him. Thus, as he read and learned more, previous ratings could be adjusted in light of new information. For instance, a rater might be puzzled about whether the large Salishan and Kwakiutl villages, which were typified by their potlatches, abundant resources, raiding proclivities, and deme headmen who served in various capacities as economic redistributors, and the like, should be rated as (1) residential kinship-group societies, (2) villages, or (3) districts, for V-334, or "Government and territory." Provisional rating into some category would be made in the rater's notes, and those ratings

would be changed, if necessary, or made more firm, once the rater had analyzed the material from, say, the Mattole, Nongatl, and Sinkyone tribes of northwestern California, or the Tewa Pueblos of New Mexico, and could compare the nature of chieftanship, territorial control, warfare behavior, and the like, of these several groups.

There is also the problem of introducing bias through loss of perspective of the whole: had each rater rated all of the variables for a few tribes selected at random, or for all of the tribes in a particular continuous area, the comparative information necessary in order to rate variables in a statistically reliable fashion might have been lost. Indeed, we felt that a partial picture constructed from viewing, say the Northwest Coast tribes only, might cause a bias in ratings that exaggerated either the differences or the similarities of those tribes with, say, California groups. So in attempting to control for bias, we also attempted to create depth of understanding among raters of several variables, realizing that this procedure, too, can introduce bias. What we hoped for was that if bias emerged, we could detect it from a few reliability tests among the raters, and our research design included overlap in the ratings of what we considered to be *some* key variables in order to test for the reliability of judgments among raters.

As it turned out, each researcher had so many variables to rate that all of us read practically every source on every tribe in detail (over about a 1½-year period from May 1971 through December 1972). It was necessary to read most sources *in toto*, or nearly so, because information on economic reciprocity, say, occurs among ceremonial topics, ceremonial topics occur among subsistence-economy sections, and the like. For an anthropologist, no experience can be more instructive about the intertwined nature of economy, kinship, polity, and religion among tribal peoples than reading several hundred ethnographies on 172 tribes. We were aware of this before we began the inquiry, of course, but it is nonetheless impressive to read hundreds of ethnographies in several formats and from several points of view and see, again, the intertwining. We created many variables to account for intertwined relations, such as among kinship, economy, and ceremony, for analytical purposes. Yet for these, as for more "isolated" or "independent" topics, some of the variables we typologized as ceremonial were to be found in subsistence economy, some that we typologized as economic organization were to be found in material culture, some that were classified as kinship were to be found in life-cycle or games sections, and so forth. By necessity, then, we all read practically all the ethnographies.

Any recruit to comparative method who has access to a set of the Human Relations Area Files (or microfiles)—and both Indiana University and the University of Michigan are HRAF member institutions—can begin to learn about the embedded and interwoven nature of various culture-information subjects simply by referring to one or two of the three-digit subject-index entries for the HRAF materials on some society: a three-digit topic, such as "Gambling 525," may lead the investigator to sections of ethnographies devoted to economics, ritual, entertainment, sickness and health, magic, and elsewhere as well. The HRAF sources have been processed by specialists who read and reread monograph upon monograph for all content classifiable by the *Outline of Cultural Material* subject-index scheme (described in Appendix B). The task for us five research associates was simpler because we read monographs for only about 60 cultural variables each (excluding the 150 environmental variables rated by Driver, or by Coffin, or created from these ratings through combining several of them, such as the species of oaks present in a society's territory, by Jorgensen on the computer), but the HRAF subject-indexing procedure was useful in suggesting how we should procede to analyze the variables assigned to each of us. One can learn from the HRAF that a thorough researcher must comb many sections of every ethnography for information on practically any variable.

On the whole, our research team was not composed of raw recruits to comparative method or to North American Indian studies. Indeed, we controlled a large amount of background information before we began.

THE RESEARCH ASSOCIATES

In the 1930s, Harold E. Driver conducted much of the primary field work among several California tribes incorporated in the sample. Not only did he conduct the basic field work, but he carried out the only formal reliability study on primary North American Indian data known to us (Driver 1938)* by comparing traditional ethnographic reports with Culture Element Distribution reports (University of California "checklists", as explained in Chapter 1), including his own. Specifically, he tested for the reliability of ethnographers with ethnographers, informants with informants, and even the reliability among some groups of variables from four tribes in California and Oregon. Somewhat to his own surprise he demonstrated that the reliability of culture element material is fairly high, with reliability coefficients ranging from 87 to 97 percent, and percentages of agreements ranging from 84 to 91. Reliability, in this context, is a measure of whether two or more ethnographers, or two or more informants, or the same informant at different points in time, or the same ethnographer at different points in time report the same answers to the same (or similar) questions. In short, various combinations of reports can be reliable, that is, consistent; but not correct, that is, not capable of yielding an accurate picture, or true description of the custom, belief, relationship or the like. From this early study of Driver's we have some basis from which to evaluate the information culled from Culture Element Distributions and traditional essays used in our study. The sources agree in the same directions overall. More will be said about this below.

Aside from contributing to the primary research on which this study is based, Driver also inquired into California Indian ethnohistory pursuant to Indian Claims Commission hearings; and he conducted several comparative studies pertaining to Indians of western North America (see Driver 1941), and North American Indians in general (see Driver and Massey 1957, and Driver and Coffin 1975). He thus brought considerable knowledge of Indian culture and comparative methodology to the project.

Joseph Jorgensen worked for and conducted primary research among Utes and Shoshones in four Rocky Mountain states (1964, 1972), and though he spent considerable time pursuing information about the nature of these cultures at Contact, he was probably 25 years too late to get copious information about that period. Nevertheless, the kinship, shamanistic, and ceremonial information he learned over the years is 92 percent in agreement with comparable information gathered in the 1930s by Anne M. Smith (1974) and Omer C. Stewart (1942). In 1963–1964 Jorgensen spent a year doing ethnohistorical research among documents pertinent to the eastern Shoshoneans in general. Jorgensen has also conducted comparative secondary research on the cultures and languages of the Salish Indians of western North America (1969) and the aboriginal ecology and economy of Indians of the Southwest (1973), so his expectations about the range and diversity of cultural features, as well as his ability to define and measure those features, were rather well formed when this study was undertaken. He was able to modify variables in the coding and rating process with relative ease.

Donald Callaway was a Ph.D. candidate at the University of Michigan when he joined the research team. He had written a master's thesis on River Yuman warfare and specialized in comparative inductive inquiry. He has completed a year of field research among the western Navajos. For his dissertation he inductively analyzed warfare and raiding in western North America using some of the data collected here.

Jon Hofmeister was also a Ph.D. candidate at the University of Michigan when he joined the research team. In 1969 Hofmeister published a formal comparative study of 16 California and Plateau tribes, so he brought expertise in western North American Indians and comparative method to the project. Furthermore, he had taught for two years at the University of Montana before he joined us. Hofmeister has conducted field work on economics and social organization in American Samoa.

James Coffin was a doctoral candidate at Indiana University when he joined the project. For his dissertation he inductively analyzed the Driver–Massey (1957) sample of variables among North American Indian tribes in both the Q-mode and the R-mode. Although Coffin had done only a little field work among the Navajos, he was grounded in comparative inquiry and North American Indian studies.

RATING ASSIGNMENTS

Jorgensen and Driver agreed to create variables covering nine broad topics. For the most part the definitions for sections I ("Natural environment") and II ("Technology and material culture") were created by Driver, and sections III–IX were created by Jorgensen. Yet, after Jorgensen and

---

*Subsequent reliability studies of ratings made by secondary researchers in cross-cultural investigations are those by Swanson (1960) and Rohner and Katz (1970).

Driver arrived at their initial definitions, they reviewed all the work and made sure that definitions could be changed to accommodate whatever empirical information might be encountered that would not otherwise fit some variable. Raters were also given discretion to change variable definitions after consultation with Jorgensen and Driver.

This is the breakdown of the ratings.

Variable set	Total variables	Rater
I. Natural environment		
Wild plants	55	Coffin
All other variables	80	Driver
II. Technology and material culture		
All variables	45	Driver
III. Subsistence economy		
All variables	29	Callaway
IV. Economic organization		
Division of labor	35	Callaway
All other variables	34	Coffin-Driver
V. Settlement pattern, demography, and community organization		
All variables	7	Callaway
VI. Social and kinship organization		
All variables	41	Hofmeister
VII. Political organization, sodalities, and warfare		
Warfare	16	Callaway
All other variables	27	Hofmeister
VIII. Ceremonialism, including life cycle		
All variables	38	Jorgensen
IX. Spirit quest, shamanism, causes of illness, and magic		
All variables	26	Jorgensen

RELIABILITY AND AGREEMENT BETWEEN JUDGMENTS

In cleaning up the data set before we began our analysis, Dr. John Fox ran "wild" code-checks to see whether ratings occurred outside the categories that had been established for each variable. For instance, if a variable had four attributes, and several tribes were rated at attribute number 5 for that variable, we then checked the notes, ratings, and punch cards in order to determine and correct the errors.

Next, we used an ingenious program written by Dr. Fox to make consistency checks, from which we obtained the information on which we based our reliability and agreement tests. In our consistency checks, we tested to determine whether the attributes of variable "a," if they should be consistent with the attributes of variable "b," were in fact consistent with the attributes at "b." That is to say, we tested to find out whether some set of attributes of variable "a" was equal to some specified set of attributes of variable "b." If inconsistencies occurred, the computer printed out the list of societies in which they occurred and we then checked for errors (or bias) in the ratings. To our delight, we obtained high agreements and reliability, exclusive of petty and correctable errors, for the variables we checked. The results may be products of unknown bias, but we doubt it.

We wished to know whether Driver, working at Indiana University and possessing extensive background knowledge, would rate differently than Callaway, working at Michigan, on the topic of subsistence resources. So, unknown to Callaway, we chose a ranked variable about the relative amount of fish used by each tribe to measure the agreement between the raters. Driver rated V-133 ("Relative amount of fish used as food by tribe"), and Callaway rated V-194 ("Focal fishing") and V-196 ("Probable percentage of diet contributed by fish, shellfish, and large aquatic mammals procured locally"). Although they are not identical variables, because of the overwhelming dominance of fish in the diets of all but one of the tribes in the sample which procured aquatic animals of all types, the three variables measured the same thing. V-133 and V-196 contain five ordinal steps, and V-194 contains four ordinal steps (ordinal steps are ranked nominal attributes in an ordinal scale). The agreements and disagreements between the raters on the 172 society sample follow:

Researcher and variable	Agree	Disagree	Percentage agreement
Callaway's V-196 and Driver's V-133	162	10	94
Callaway's V-194 and Driver's V-133	162	10	94

The disagreements between Driver and Callaway were not systematic, so they do not suggest different biases. Driver rated six societies as more dependent on fish than did Callaway, and Callaway rated four societies as more dependent on aquatic animals than did Driver. There was not a single instance in which their disagreements were more than one ordinal rank apart.

Hofmeister and Coffin were compared on economic organization and kinship organization variables and agreed on practically all ratings for which we tested. Coffin's V-269 ("Ownership of farming sites . . .") and V-270 ("Ownership of house") were tested against Hofmeister's V-322 ("Ownership of corporeal property by demonstrated kinship unit") and V-323 ("Ownership of corporeal property by stipulated kinship unit"). Here we would be able to determine two things, to wit: (1) whether Coffin and Hofmeister agreed that corporeal property was recognized, and (2), whether Coffin and Hofmeister agreed about the general composition of the groups that owned the properties. Whereas Coffin's variables discriminated among types of kinship groups, Hofmeister's lumped kin groups under demonstrated and stipulated. The differences are, we think, due to random errors because they are almost nil (3 in 344 ratings), and because Hofmeister and Coffin never laid eyes on one another or even exchanged notes. If bias was operating it was not easily identifiable by us:

Researcher and variable	Agree	Disagree	Percentage agreement
Coffin's V-275 and Hofmeister's V-329/V-330	169	3	98
Coffin's V-276 and Hofmeister's V-329/V-330	172	0	100

Jorgensen and Hofmeister were compared on sodality and ceremonial variables. Here we wanted to know whether Jorgensen and Hofmeister, both working at Michigan, agreed whether sodalities were present, if they were restricted in membership, and whether they performed private or public rituals or both. Hofmeister's V-344 ("Functions of restricted sodalities") and V-345 ("Restricted sodality: participants and spectators"), and Jorgensen's V-372 ("Sponsorship and performance of all public ceremonies") and V-373 ("Private ceremonies performed by restricted sodalities or the like") showed only two disagreements.

Researcher and variable	Agree	Disagree	Percentage agreement
Hofmeister's V-344 and Jorgensen's V-372	172	0	100
Hofmeister's V-345 and Jorgensen's V-373	170	2	99

It is probably the case that the percentage agreement between Jorgensen and Hofmeister is inflated because they worked at Michigan and were in constant contact. Nevertheless, they did not see each other's notes or ratings until the project was completed. Although undetected bias might have been operating, if so, it did not play a significant role. It seems safe to infer this on the basis of high agreements achieved by the other combinations of raters at different locations and on different topics.

Overall we feel that two things contributed to the high agreement among the raters: the good quality and large amount of information about the Indians of western North America in the standard ethnographic sources; and the schematic Culture Element Distribution reports of the University of California, which included a vast amount of information about *absences* of things, which is a kind of information rarely given in the standard essay-style field report. We further feel that though our agreement tests are few, the agreements obtained are probably representative. We conducted another 50 specific comparisons between raters, but were restricted to presence–absence information, so these will not be reported here. For instance, V-149 ("Maize cultivated at time of first contact with Europeans"), rated by Driver, was compared with Callaway's V-245–248 to be sure that when Driver rated a society as "1. cultivation absent," so did Callaway, and vice versa. Other comparisons among attributes for the same variables, however, were not relevant because they asked questions which were not comparable. Except for coding or key-punching errors, we did not find disagreements about presence or absence, and have not included the results from these gross comparisons.

The results of our correlational and multivariate analyses, we contend, have not falsely confirmed or falsely invalidated our propositions, and we feel that our empirical generalizations, therefore, are not based on unreliable ratings.

Appendix B

Sampling in the Q-Mode

Comparison of the Jorgensen–Driver Sample with the Samples of Murdock (1967) and Driver–Massey (1957)

By Harold E. Driver and Joseph G. Jorgensen

Although there have been a number of recent discussions of the ethnic unit and how to draw samples of ethnic units in the R-mode (Naroll 1964; Naroll and Cohen 1970; Helm 1968; Murdock and White 1969; and McNett 1968), there has been no comparable discussion of how to define and sample cultural and social inventory for comparisons of a Q-type (ethnic unit with ethnic unit, as in Jorgensen's (1969) analysis of Salish cultures and languages) or of a joint Q- and R-type (ethnic units with culture variables, as in Carneiro's (1970) scalogram analysis of cultural evolution). Jorgensen (1969) sought to provide equal numbers of variables for technology, social organization, and religion, and to include variables (such as descent and kinship terminologies) whose distributions conform to hypotheses about regular development, as well as variables (such as types of hats worn) whose distributions are not accounted for by such hypotheses. But this procedure was wholly judgmental. Carneiro (1970), on the other hand, sought only those variables which formed a simplex (unidimensional scalogram) of cultural development. His judgments, then, were conditioned by the assumptions of a simplex and the hypothesis of general cultural evolution. Neither of these procedures are acceptable in our view, though the first procedure is justified more easily than is the second. Since in the study reported in this book we have sought to test hypotheses as well as to derive configurations of cultural relatedness, as a consequence, we tried to provide balance in six categories of environmental variables and eight categories of cultural variables, and we sought to in-clude variables, especially those we did not expect would be subsumed under hypotheses of development or cycling, which would help us determine the nature of tribal interre-lationships.

Although we did not create our sample by consulting the *Outline of Cultural Materials* (hereafter referred to as OCM) of Murdock et al. (1961), the latter is the best-known and most readily available inventory of cultural variables that can be used to make comparisons among the sampling traits (that is, cultural variables) of several samples. The OCM is the subject index of the Human Relations Area Files (or HRAF), described in Appendix A. The HRAF is a large classified repository of information on about 300 of the world's societies. The OCM lists 631 specific variable topics (locatable by reference to three digits) under 88 classes of topics (indexed with two digits). Although the number of cultural variables for all of the world's ethnic units, past and present, would be infinite, and any list of topics (variable classes) is only partial, finite, and a product of whatever one or more scholars considered to be important when creating their lists, most lists, as acts of commission, exclude topics that were presumed to be irrelevant to the study at hand. Furthermore, most lists, by such acts of commission and omission, unintentionally exclude any topics that their compilers have not thought about; thus bias probably occurs in all lists, including the OCM, but the amount of bias and its effects on results in most studies is not known: we hoped to be able to assess the amount and effects of such bias in our study.

The OCM is a product of many scholars working over a period of 24 years (from 1937 to 1961, during which time four revisions were made in the subject code). Because of the large size of the inventory, the large number of scholars who worked on its preparation and revisions, the large number of specific studies whose topics were added to the index, and the larger number of ethnographic, historical, and other such materials read by these researchers on more than 300 cultures around the world, it is our impression that the OCM is the best empirical universe of cultural variable topics available. Although we did not know how representative it might be of the universe of cultural variables (all of those variables that have been defined or can ever be defined), we thought that a relatively good sample of the entire range of this inventory could be obtained by drawing an equal number of variables from each of the OCM's three-digit categories, yet the variables would also need to apply to the ethnic units selected for comparison.

Of the 631 three-digit topics in the OCM, however, only 412 are germane to the three samples we shall compare in this appendix. For instance, the OCM categories numbered from 101–147 and from 181–198 do not contain conventional cultural content and are best eliminated. A considerable number of the remaining categories, such as "Chemical industries, 381–389," do not apply to any tribal or peasant societies and will not appear in samples of their social and cultural inventory.

Moreover, 130 OCM three-digit categories should be eliminated because they are not germane to any North American Indian ethnic unit, including those in Meso-America. This seemed appropriate to us in that our present sample is composed of 172 Indian societies from western North America. Following are the categories thus deleted from the comparison; the three-digit categories are preceded by the verbal caption and number of the two-digit category under which they are subsumed:

Communication 20: 204–207; Records 21: 213–217; Food quest 22: 228; Food processing 25: 253–258; Food consumption 26: 265; Exploitative activities 31: 315; Processing of basic materials 32: 327; Building and construction 33: 334, 336, 337; Structures 34: 348; Settlements 36: 365, 367; Energy and power 37: 371, 375–379; Chemical industries 38: 381–389; Capital goods industries 39: 391–399; Machines 40: 401–407; Tools and appliances 41: 414; Marketing 44: 446, 447; Finance 45: 451–458; Labor 46: 467, 468; Land transport 49: 493–499; Water and air transport 50: 502–504, 506–509; Recreation 52: 528; Entertainment 54: 541–549; State 64: 642; Government activities 65: 654; Political behavior 66: 664–669; Justice 69: 697, 698; Armed forces 70: 706, 707; Military technology 71: 711–719; Health and welfare 74: 741–748; Ecclesiastical organization 79: 797; Exact knowledge 81: 811, 813, 815; Education 87: 873, 875, 876. Our 150 environmental variables do not occur in the OCM.

As a means of evaluating the size and scope of the topics in our western North American Indians sample, we made comparisons, using the OCM list of variables (or culture variable topics), among (1) our sample, (2) the Driver–Massey (1957) sample of North American Indians including those of Mexico, and (3) the Murdock (1967) sample of societies from around the world. We took the position that

Table B-1

Comparison of the Murdock and Driver–Massey samples for the OCM three-digit categories

		Murdock (1967)		
		Present	Absent	Total
Driver–Massey (1957)	Present	18	34	52
	Absent	38	322	360
	Total	56	356	412

any two samples could be compared to each other in terms of the number of OCM three-digit categories shared, the number present in the first but not in the second, the number present in the second but not in the first, and the number absent in both samples. Following for each of the three samples, the OCM three-digit categories represented in each are shown, and a comparison of each combination of two samples is made.

The OCM categories included in Driver and Massey (1957) follow. Food quest 22: 222, 224–227; Animal husbandry 23: 231, 235, 237; Agriculture 24: 241, 249; Food processing 25: 251, 252; Food consumption 26: 262, 263; Drink, drugs, indulgence 27: 273, 276; Leather, textiles, and fabrics 28: 285, 286; Clothing 29: 291, 292, 294; Adornment 30: 302, 304; Exploitative activities 31: 311; Processing of basic materials 32: 321, 323, 325; Structures 34: 342, 343; Equipment and maintenance of buildings 35: 352; Settlements 36: 361; Energy and power 37: 372, 373; Capital goods industries 39: 391, 394; Tools and appliances 41: 411, 412, 415; Labor 46: 462; Travel and transportation 48: 481, 482; Land transport 49: 492, 493; Water and air transport 50: 501; Living standards and routines 51: 515; Marriage 58: 582; Family 59: 591; Kinship 60: 601, 602; Kin groups 61: 611; Military technology 71: 714; Ecclesiastical organization 79: 796.

The three-digit OCM categories included in Murdock (1967) are: Food quest 22: 222, 224, 226; Animal husbandry 23: 231, 233; Agriculture 24: 241–246, 249; Leather, textiles, and fabrics 28: 282, 286; Exploitative activities 31: 311; Processing of basic materials 32: 323, 325; Building and construction 33: 333; Structures 34: 342; Settlements 36: 361; Property 42: 428; Exchange 43: 431; Labor 46: 462; Water and air transport 50: 501; Recreation 52: 524; Social stratification 56: 563–565, 567; Marriage 58: 583, 587; Family 59: 591, 594–596; Kinship 60: 601, 602, 605; Kin groups 61: 611–618; Community 62: 621, 622, 627; Justice 69: 692; Religious beliefs 77: 776; Sex 83: 834, 836; Reproduction 84: 846; Infancy and childhood 85: 857; Adolescence, adulthood, and old age 88: 882.

Out of a total of 412 three-digit categories only 18 were included in both Driver–Massey (1957) and Murdock (1967). The commonly excluded categories number 322. These and other figures are shown above in Table B-1.

Converting some of these figures to proportions, Murdock (1967) used only .136 of the total of 412 three-digit

Table B-2
Comparison of the Jorgensen-Driver and Driver-Massey samples for the OCM three-digit categories

		Jorgensen–Driver western Indians sample		
		Present	Absent	Total
Driver-Massey (1957)	Present	32	20	52
	Absent	105	255	360
	Total	137	275	412

Table B-3
Comparison of the Jorgensen–Driver and Murdock samples for the OCM three-digit categories

		Jorgensen–Driver western Indians sample		
		Present	Absent	Total
Murdock (1967)	Present	36	20	56
	Absent	101	255	356
	Total	137	275	412

categories; and Driver–Massey (1957) used only .126 of the same total. The proportion of overlap in the two samples is only .044.

For these comparisons we have eliminated the 150 variables from the Jorgensen–Driver sample which pertain to the environment. The following categories appear in the present sample of Jorgensen–Driver. Food quest 22: 222, 224–227; Animal husbandry 23: 231, 235, 237; Agriculture 24: 241–244, 248; Food processing 25: 251, 252; Food consumption 26: 262; Drink, drugs, and indulgence 27: 276, 277; Leather, textiles, and fabric 28: 281, 283–286, 288; Clothing 29: 291–294; Exploitative activities 31: 313, 314; Processing of basic materials 32: 323; Building and construction 33: 332, 333, 335; Structures 34: 342; Tools and appliances 41: 411–413, 415, 417; Property 42: 421–426, 428; Exchange 43: 431, 432, 436–439; Labor 46: 462, 463; Travel and transportation 48: 482, 489; Land transport 49: 492; Water and air transport 50: 501, 505; Individuation and mobility 55: 551, 553–556; Social stratification 56: 561, 562, 567: Interpersonal relations 57: 571, 574–576, 578, 579; Marriage 58: 581–588; Family 59: 591–595; Kinship 60: 601, 605; Kin groups 61: 611–619; Community 62: 621–624, 626–628; Territorial organization 63: 631, 632, 634; Law 67: 674: Armed forces 70: 701, 704; War 72: 726–728; Sickness 75: 751, 753–756; Death 76: 763–766; Religious beliefs 77: 776, 777; Religious practices 78: 781–789; Ecclesiastical organization 79: 796; Reproduction 84: 841, 844; Adolescence, adulthood, and old age 88: 881. A comparison of these categories with those of Driver–Massey is given in Table B-2.

Converting some of the frequencies of Table B-2 to proportions, it is apparent that the Jorgensen–Driver sample used .333 of the total of 412 categories, a proportion more than twice as great as the .126 used by Driver–Massey. The proportion of overlap in the two samples is .078.

A comparison of the Jorgensen–Driver sample with that of Murdock (1967) is shown in Table B-3.

When some of the frequencies in Table B-3 are converted to proportions, we find that Murdock used only .136 of the total number of categories, as compared with .333 for Jorgensen–Driver. The proportion of overlap is .087.

Although none of the three samples compared was chosen from the OCM at random or from any other comprehensive list of subject categories at random, the larger sample of Jorgensen–Driver gives a broader coverage than

the other two and includes more two-digit categories as well as three-digit subcategories. The tree diagrams and the many groupings of ethnic units in this volume would appear to be more meaningful than the classifications derived in the same way from the Murdock (1967), (Driver et al. 1972), or the Driver–Massey samples (Driver and Coffin 1975).

Further, it should be pointed out that the Jorgensen–Driver sample area includes less than half of the North American continent and does not include Meso-America. If the three-digit categories in the OCM were further pruned to eliminate all categories not present in the Jorgensen–Driver areal universe, the proportion of the relevant total in the Jorgensen–Driver sample would be higher than .333; an estimate would be that it might reach .400. It is, therefore, a much larger sample for its area than the other two samples.

In order to provide another dimension to our understanding about the types of variables in the three samples, we may use the eight basic variable categories created by Jorgensen–Driver (excluding the environmental variables) to group the two-digit OCM subjects that appear in the three samples. These comparisons will allow us to gain a gross impression of the range of topics covered by each study. Table B-4, it should be pointed out, masks a considerable amount of information, as can be intuited from the following: the Jorgensen–Driver sample includes 292 cultural variables encompassing 1577 attributes; the Murdock sample includes 44 variables and more than 424 attributes (exact number is not known); and the Driver–Massey sample includes 153 variables and 625 attributes.

It is apparent that the Driver–Massey sample represents more technology and subsistence economy topics relative to the other six categories than do the other two samples. Moreover, both the Driver–Massey and the Murdock samples are underrepresented for categories 7 and 8 (in proportion to all categories).

Let us collapse these eight categories into the three or so frequently used by ethnologists to divide culture into major analytical categories: I, technology and subsistence (Jorgensen–Driver categories 1–2); II, economic, social, and political organization (3–6); and III, ideology and ritual (7–8). And let us add the OCM inventory to the comparisons by classifying the 69 two-digit subjects that are appro-

Table B-4

Comparisons of Jorgensen–Driver (western Indians), Driver–Massey (1957), and Murdock (1967) samples for the OCM two-digit categories as classified by the Jorgensen–Driver eight-topic scheme

Jorgensen–Driver western Indian topics	Frequency of OCM two-digit categories		
	Driver–Massey	Murdock	Jorgensen–Driver
1. Technology	7	3	8
2. Subsistence economy and material culture	10	7	9
3. Economic organization	1	3	4
4. Settlement pattern, community organization	2	2	2
5. Social and kinship organization	4	5	5
6. Political organization, sodalities, and warfare	1	1	4
7. Ceremonialism, and life cycle	1	2	5
8. Spirit quest, shamanism, causes of illness, and magic	0	1	3

Table B-5

Comparisons of the *Outline of Cultural Materials*, Jorgensen–Driver (western Indians), Driver–Massey (1957), and Murdock (1967) samples for the OCM two-digit categories as classified into three supercategories

Supercategory	Frequency and proportions of OCM two-digit categories			
	Driver–Massey	Murdock	Jorgensen–Driver	Outline of cultural materials
I. Technology and subsistence	17 (.680)	10 (.400)	17 (.680)	25 (1.000)
II. Economic, social, and political organization	8 (.276)	11 (.379)	15 (.517)	29 (1.000)
III. Ideology and ritual	1 (.067)	3 (.200)	8 (.533)	15 (1.000)

priate for our samples in terms of our most general typology of classes of cultural variables. Table B-5 shows that if we establish the observed OCM frequent for each of the three types of variables as the expected (E) proportion ($E = 1.000$), the Jorgensen–Driver sample has the most balanced proportional representation of OCM two-digit subjects relative to the distribution of variables in the OCM inventory. Furthermore it is by far the largest sample of culture variables ever analyzed. Certain questions are raised, of course, about the distribution of topics in the OCM, particularly the ratio of type III variables to types I and II. One suspects that fewer type III categories appear in all samples and the OCM because of (1) the difficulty of acquiring comparable information on these topics, which is in part influenced by (2) the general historical trend in ethnology, which, until very recently when an upsurge of structuralist inquiry altered that trend, was toward the analysis of material culture and social organization. Whereas we made a concerted effort to include type III variables in the Jorgensen–Driver sample, we approximate the proportional representation of type III to all variables in the OCM, to wit: proportion of III in OCM = .278; proportion of III in Jorgensen–Driver = .250. Murdock's III = .136, and Driver–Massey = .040.

Appendix C

Formal Methods

In conducting the comparative analysis of *Western Indians* it was important to follow formal procedures so that we could demonstrate that relations were *real* and determinate. In nontechnical language, we sought to compare the relations among tribes (cultural inventories), among tribal environments, and among languages, or, in matrix analysis language, we sought to make a Q-mode comparison, so as to demonstrate the closest and most distant relations among all environments, tribes, and languages. "Real" in statistical language means that whenever tribes *A* and *B* practice the same customs 1, 2, and 3, they will be more similar than if they do not practice those customs. It is not enough to know whether a pair of tribes is very similar, or very different, we must also determine the similarity of a pair of tribes in relation to all other tribes. In order to assess the meaning of any relationship between a pair of tribes, we controlled that relationship by comparing each member of the pair with all other tribes in the sample. We sought to exercise controls by measuring the relations among tribes. In Figure 2-2, for instance, the 172 tribal environments form $\frac{172 \times 171}{2} = 14{,}706$ pairs of relations, and all of these pairs had to be analyzed in order to reduce the 14,706 relations to a two-dimensional mapping of the 172 tribal environments.

Thus, formal comparisons were controlled, whether in our analyses of tribes or of variables. The methodology for comparisons and controls requires brief explication, and can best be understood as part of the overall research design (see Appendices A and B for discussions of samples and sampling reliability).

THE MEASURES OF RELATIONSHIP

In order to determine the similarity or dissimilarity of a pair of tribes on several variables it is necessary to compare the tribes and measure the comparison. For measures in the Q-mode, Jorgensen chose to use Driver's G coefficient, a measure of association closely related to Pearson's coefficient r, which is exceptional in that it eliminates the *d* cell in a conventional four-cell table.

$$\text{Driver's G} = \frac{a}{\sqrt{a+b} \ \sqrt{a+c}}.$$

A four-cell table is, conventionally,

		Tribe 1	
		+	−
Tribe 2	+	*a*	*b*
	−	*c*	*d*

where *a* = attributes of variables that are the same for tribes 1 and 2, *b* = the attributes of variables that are present in tribe 2 but absent in tribe 1, *c* = the attributes of variables that are present in tribe 1 but absent in tribe 2, and *d* = the attributes of variables in the total sample of variables for all tribes that are absent in both tribes 1 and 2. By excluding the *d* cell, the relations between pairs of tribes are not inflated by common absences.

For example, we measured each pair of tribes for their relationship on the total inventory of cultural variables, of which there are 292 in our sample. The 292 variables embrace 1,577 attributes, an average of nearly 7 attributes for each variable. Each society was rated for every one of the 292 variables. Because every variable comprises a set of mutually exclusive attributes, each society was necessarily rated on one but only one attribute for each variable. The variable "Local agricultural products in the diet" is composed of ranked (ordinal) attributes, to wit: (1) 0 percent, (2) 1–10 percent, (3) 11–25 percent, (4) 26–50 percent, and (5) 51–100 percent. Each culture unit was rated for one of these ordinal attributes. By rating each culture unit for all 292 variables we obtained a measure of the relationship for each pair of tribes on the entire inventory of cultural information. The same procedure was followed in measuring environmental relations.

For example, the Haisla Kwakiutl shared the same attributes as the Klallam Salish on 176 cultural variables and were different from them on 102 variables. Thus, a four-cell table indicating this would be:

Klallam Salish

		+	−	
Haisla	+	$a = 176$	$b = 102$	278
Kwakiutl	−	$c = 102$	$d = 1{,}118$	1,220
		278	1,220	1,498

Driver's G is calculated as follows:

$$G = \frac{a}{\sqrt{a+b}\ \sqrt{a+c}}$$

$$G = \frac{176}{\sqrt{176+102}\ \sqrt{176+102}}$$

$$G = \frac{176}{278}$$

$$G = .63$$

The total number of variables ($a+b$ or $a+c = 278$) does not add up to 292 (all possible variables) and the total number of attributes (1,498) does not add up to 1,577 (all possible attributes) because there were a total of 79 attributes distributed among fourteen variables for which no ethnographic information was availabe for either the Klallam Salish or the Haisla Kwakiutl. The table shows that whenever the same attribute is shared, an entire variable is accounted for in the a cell. Because variables are mutually exclusive and inclusive, whenever the Haisla practiced a custom that the Klallam did not practice (cell b), the Klallam practiced a custom that the Haisla did not practice (cell c). As a consequence, $b = c$. The d cell represents all 1,118 attributes of the 278 variables that neither culture unit practiced. Because the number of attributes that neither member of a pair shared was potentially unlimited, and because $b = c$, Driver's G can be interpreted as the percentage of agreement between each pair of tribes. That is, Driver's G of .63 for the total cultural inventory means that a pair of tribes were similar on 176 variables and different on 102, or 63 percent in agreement. Driver's G varies between .00 and 1.00.

In a few sections, but most notably in the analysis of kinship organization variables in Chapter 8, on "Social Organization," Pearson's ϕ has been employed to measure correlation between two nominal variables; it is the form of Pearson's r appropriate for qualitative data such that

$$\phi = \frac{ad-bc}{\sqrt{(a+b)(a+c)(b+d)(c+d)}}.$$

The ϕ coefficient varies between +1.00 and −1.00, so in the following example of the correlation between matrilineal descent and Crow-type cousin terminologies, the relation is high and positive: whereas most of the societies in western North America that practiced Crow-type cousin terms (80 percent) also observed matrilineal descent, only one third of the societies that practiced matrilineal descent also used Crow-type terms. Thus the relation is positive and high, but not perfect (+1.00). The four-cell table indicating this would be

Crow-type cousin terms

		+	−	
Matrilineal	+	8	15	23
descent	−	2	131	133
		10	146	156

Pearson's ϕ is calculated as follows:

$$\phi = \frac{(8)(131) - (2)(15)}{\sqrt{(8+15)(8+2)(15+131)(2+131)}}$$

$$\phi = .48$$

Only 156 societies in the 172 society total sample had information on both descent reckoning and cousin terminological types, so the sixteen societies for which information on either descent or cousin terms were missing were dropped from the calculation.

THE UNIDIMENSIONAL AND MULTIDIMENSIONAL, NONMETRIC, MULTIVARIATE ANALYSES

In analyzing the relations among culture units (Q-mode), two multivariate techniques have been used. Both are nonmetric techniques for finding the shortest distances in Euclidian spaces, but based on different algorithms. The unidimensional method, referred to as Jorgensen's Nonmetric Trees (see Jorgensen 1969), preserves some metric information in that bridges between the closest pairs show the level of Driver's G at which the pair is joined (the highest G level is the shortest distance between the two points). For groups larger than two members, the bridges show the centroid (geometric center of gravity, or the shortest distance among all points in the group) for all Driver G's among all culture units in the group. Professor John Fox redimensioned Jorgensen's Nonmetric Trees program to order indefinitely many variables (of societies and environments) in a single matrix.

The second method, called MINISSA by its authors (Roskam and Lingoes 1970; Lingoes and Roskam 1971), as used here is a multidimensional scaling program which converts coefficients of similarity (Driver's G) for a square matrix (Q-mode) to distances from a specified Euclidian distance function, and maps the distances into a set of ranks using special tie-breaking procedures. The relations among environments or cultures, as measured by ranks, are solved in as many dimensions up to 10 as are necessary. For complete analyses see also Guttman (1968), Lingoes (1965, 1968, 1971, and Lingoes and Roskam 1971).

The Guttman–Lingoes Coefficient of Alienation, K, is used to measure the amount of variation explained for solutions in two dimensions or greater. As a rule of thumb, K = .15 is employed as a reasonable fit. That is, about 85 percent of the variance among all of the points in the matrix is explained when K = .15. In general, the higher the dimensionality, the lower the K. On the other hand, the lower the dimensionality, the simpler the interpretation of complex phenomena.

In the Q-mode, the mapping of ranked G scores required only two dimensions for extremely good fits. The dimensions can be interpreted by looking at the front to back, and side to side, relations among points.

MINISSA, as dimensioned by James Lingoes for the University of Michigan's IBM 360-67 computer, can determine the smallest space relations for only 100 variables at a time. A second procedure in Professor Lingoes' MINISSA software makes it possible to fit indefinitely many variables to the fixed points (the first 100 variables). Professor John Fox wrote a program for our large matrices of variables that allowed us to discover the most heterogeneous units in the total matrices. For instance, when our matrices contained all 172 societies, Dr. Fox's program allowed us to select all societies from the matrix that had no G score with any other society higher than .60, or .50, or .80 (whatever cut-off line we selected). By trial and error we learned that when between 50 and 60 societies were selected by our method to determine the most heterogeneous tribes, the solutions were quick and economical. We fixed the relations among those 50–60 points (societies) in two or more dimensions; then, using Professor Lingoes conditional-fit option, found the positions of the remaining societies by entering all remaining societies (ranked variables) one at a time. In other words, the positions of the remaining societies were determined by the positions of the fixed configuration to which they were added.

COMPUTER MAPS OF THE VARIABLES

In order to provide a graphic display, a picture as it were, of the distributions of the attributes within each variable, the approximate centers of the tribal territories for each sample unit was recorded in West Longitude and North Latitude coordinates. Professor Waldo Tobler provided us with coastline coordinates for western North America. Professor John Fox and the author supplied coordinates for some major rivers and lakes, and Professor Fox wrote a program for the CalComp Graphic Plotter that allowed us to select one variable at a time and plot the distributions of the attributes within each variable. Maps for about 260 of the 430 variables were thus drawn.

Appendix D

Variable Distribution Maps

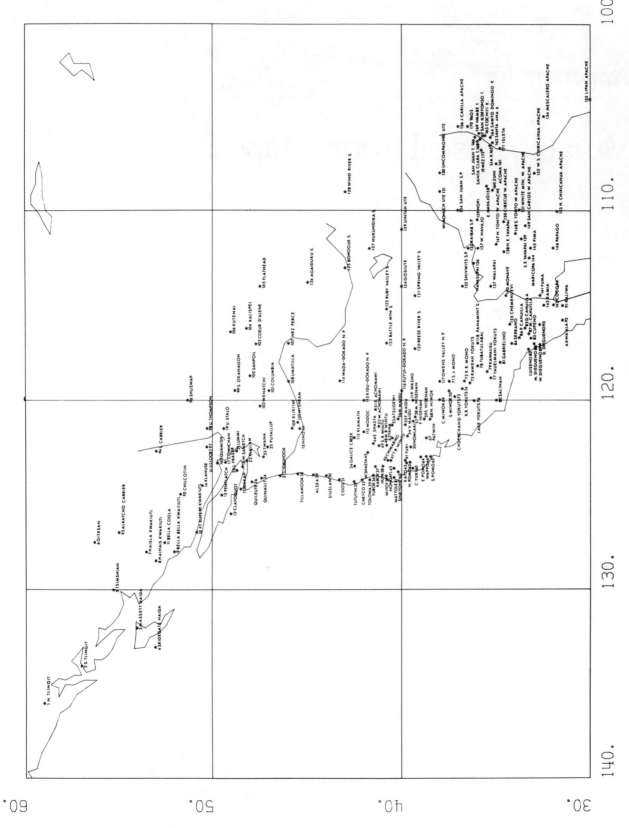

Computer-plotted map showing locations of centers of 172 tribal territories in western North America. The mappings of variables in Appendix D follow the format of this map. Tribe names are listed on the opposite page.

316

1 Northern Tlingit
2 Southern Tlingit
3 Northern Massett Haida
4 Southern Skidegate Haida
5 Tsimshian
6 Gitksan
7 Haisla Kwakiutl
8 Haihais Kwakiutl
9 Bella Bella Kwakiutl
10 Fort Rupert Kwakiutl
11 Bella Coola
12 Clayoquot
13 Makah
14 Klahuse
15 Pentlatch
16 Squamish Salish
17 Cowichan Salish
18 West Sanetch
19 Upper Stalo
20 Lower Fraser
21 Lummi
22 Klallam
23 Twana
24 Quinault
25 Puyallup
26 Quileute
27 Lower Chinook
28 Tillamook
29 Alsea
30 Siuslaw
31 Coos
32 Tututni
33 Chetco
34 Galice Creek
35 Tolowa
36 Yurok
37 Karok
38 Hupa
39 Wiyot
40 Sinkyone
41 Mattole
42 Nongatl
43 Kato
44 East Shasta
45 West Shasta

46 Chimariko
47 Trinity River Wintu
48 McCloud River Wintu
49 Sacramento River Wintu
50 Nomlaki
51 East Achomawi
52 West Achomawi
53 Atsugewi
54 Valley Maidu
55 Foothill Maidu
56 Mountain Maidu
57 Foothill Nisenan
58 Mountain Nisenan
59 Southern Nisenan
60 Coast Yuki
61 Yuki
62 Yana
63 Northern Pomo
64 Eastern Pomo
65 Southern Pomo
66 Wappo
67 Patwin
68 Northern Miwok
69 Central Miwok
70 Southern Miwok
71 San Joaquin Mono
72 Kings River Mono
73 Chuckchansi Yokuts
74 Kings River Yokuts
75 Kaweah Yokuts
76 Lake Yokuts
77 Yauelmani Yokuts
78 Tubatulabal
79 Kawaiisu
80 Salinan
81 Gabrieliño
82 Luiseño
83 Cupeño
84 Serraño
85 Desert Cahuilla
86 Pass Cahuilla
87 Mountain Cahuilla
88 Mountain Diegueño
89 Western Diegueño
90 Desert Diegueño

91 Kaliwa
92 Akwa'ala
93 Alkatcho Carrier
94 Lower Carrier
95 Chilcotin
96 Shuswap
97 Upper Lillooet
98 Upper Thompson
99 Southern Okanagon
100 Sanpoil
101 Columbia
102 Wenatchi
103 Coeur d'Alene
104 Kalispel
105 Flathead
106 Kutenai
107 Nez Percé
108 Umatilla
109 Klikitat
110 Wishram
111 Tenino
112 Klamath
113 Modoc
114 Wada-Dokado Northern Paiute
115 Kidu-Dokado Northern Paiute
116 Kuyui-Dokado Northern Paiute
117 Owens Valley Northern Paiute
118 Panamint Shoshone
119 Washo
120 Reese River Shoshone
121 Spring Valley Shoshone
122 Ruby Valley Shoshone
123 Battle Mountain Shoshone
124 Gosiute Shoshone
125 Bohogue Shoshone
126 Agaiduku Shoshone
127 Hukundika Shoshone
128 Wind River Shoshone
129 Uintah Ute
130 Uncompaghre Ute
131 Wimonuch Ute

132 Shivwits Southern Paiute
133 Kaibab Southern Paiute
134 San Juan Southern Paiute
135 Chemehuevi Southern Paiute
136 Havasupai
137 Walapai
138 Northeast Yavapai
139 Southeast Yavapai
140 Mohave
141 Yuma
142 Kamia
143 Cocopa
144 Maricopa
145 Pima
146 Papago
147 North Tonto Western Apache
148 South Tonto Western Apache
149 San Carlos Western Apache
150 Cibecue Western Apache
151 White Mountain Western Apache
152 Warm Springs Chiricahua Apache
153 Huachuca Chiricahua Apache
154 Mescalero Apache
155 Lipan Apache
156 Jicarilla Apache
157 Western Navajo
158 Eastern Navajo
159 Hopi
160 Zuni
161 Acoma
162 Sia Keres
163 Santa Ana Keres
164 Santo Domingo Keres
165 Cochiti
166 San Juan Tewa
167 San Ildefonso Tewa
168 Santa Clara Tewa
169 Nambe Tewa
170 Taos
171 Isleta
172 Jemez

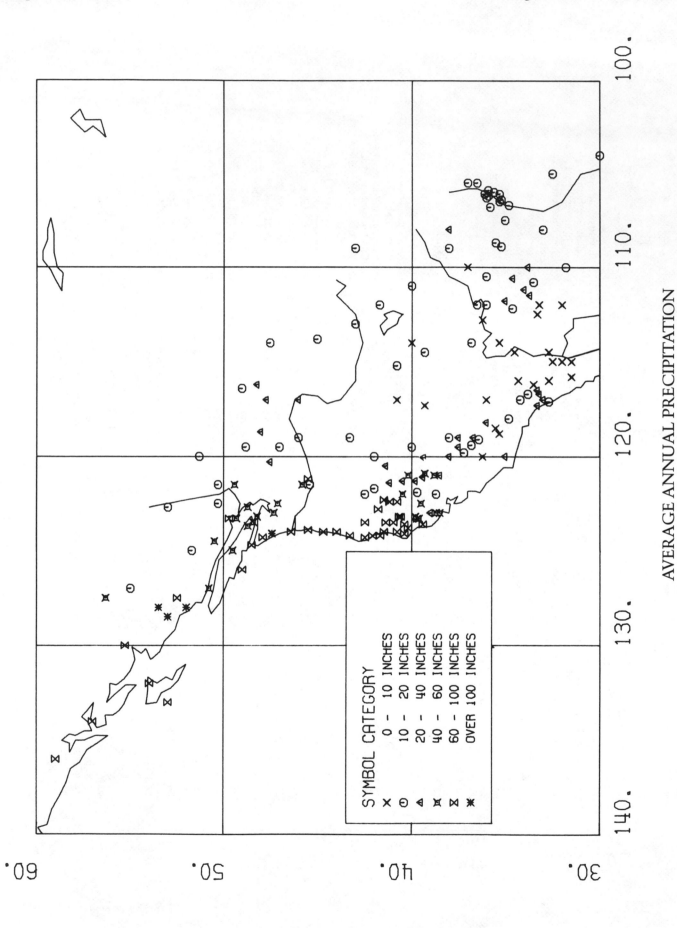

AVERAGE ANNUAL PRECIPITATION

SYMBOL CATEGORY

X	0 - 10 INCHES
⊖	10 - 20 INCHES
◀	20 - 40 INCHES
⋈	40 - 60 INCHES
⋈	60 - 100 INCHES
✳	OVER 100 INCHES

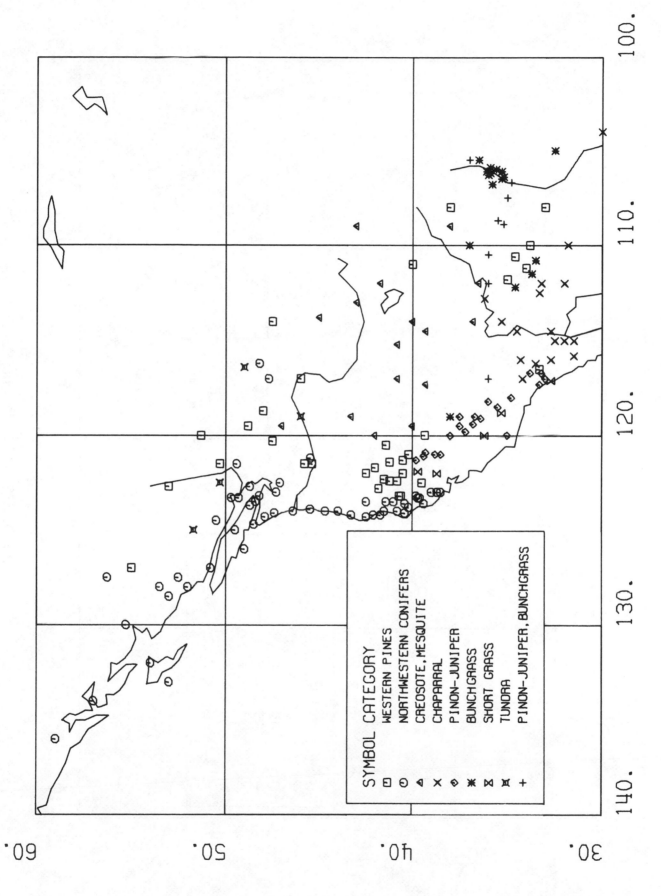

NATURAL VEGETATION AREAS

SYMBOL CATEGORY

⊟	WESTERN PINES
⊖	NORTHWESTERN CONIFERS
◁	CREOSOTE,MESQUITE
✕	CHAPARRAL
◇	PINON-JUNIPER
✳	BUNCHGRASS
⋈	SHORT GRASS
⋈	TUNDRA
+	PINON-JUNIPER,BUNCHGRASS

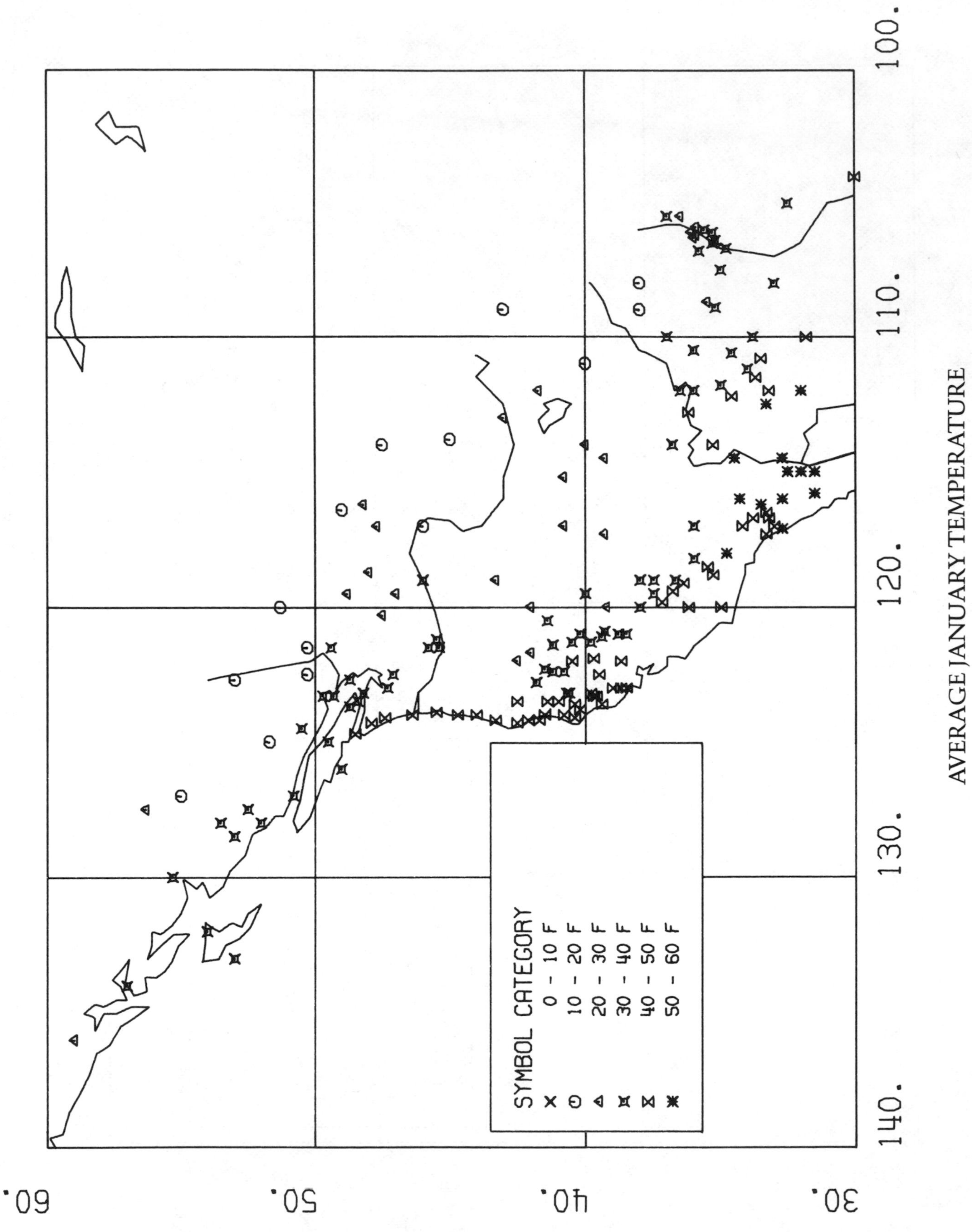

AVERAGE JANUARY TEMPERATURE

SYMBOL CATEGORY

X	0 - 10 F
⊖	10 - 20 F
◁	20 - 30 F
⋈	30 - 40 F
⋈	40 - 50 F
✳	50 - 60 F

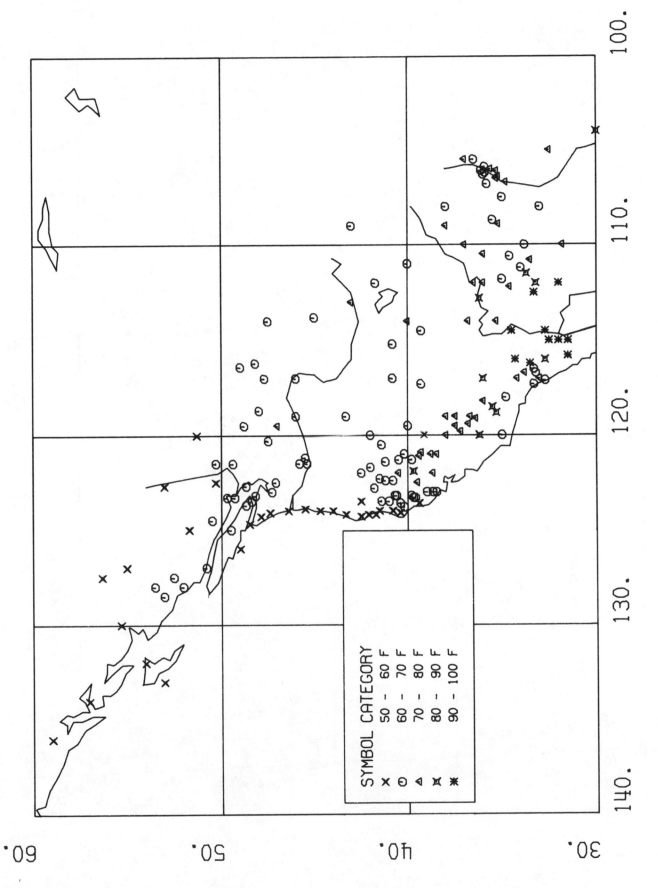

AVERAGE JULY TEMPERATURE

SYMBOL CATEGORY

X	50 - 60 F
Θ	60 - 70 F
◁	70 - 80 F
✕	80 - 90 F
✳	90 - 100 F

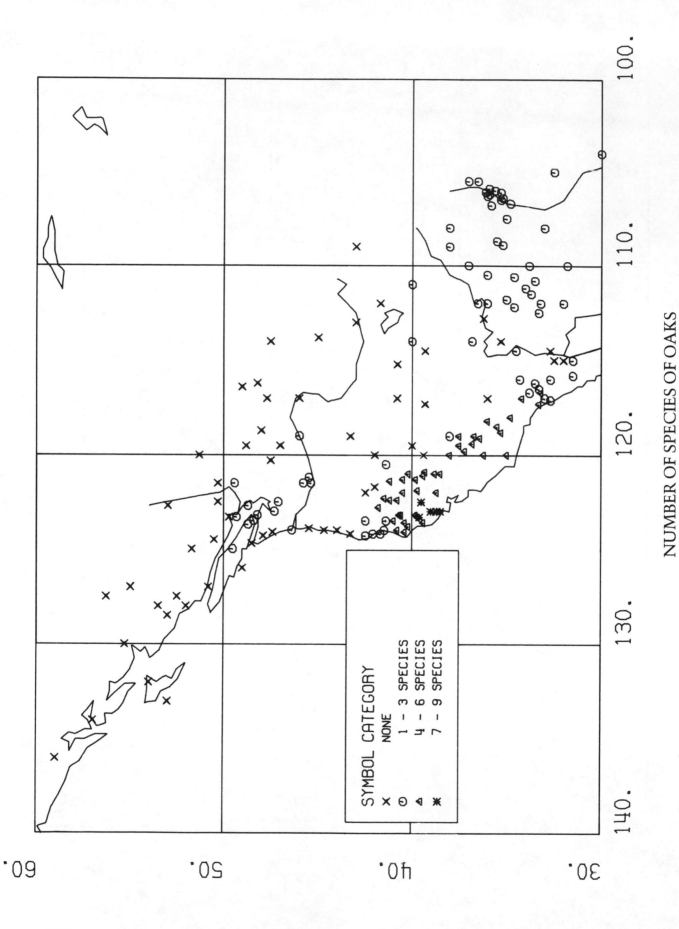

SYMBOL CATEGORY

X	NONE
⊖	1 - 3 SPECIES
◁	4 - 6 SPECIES
✳	7 - 9 SPECIES

NUMBER OF SPECIES OF OAKS

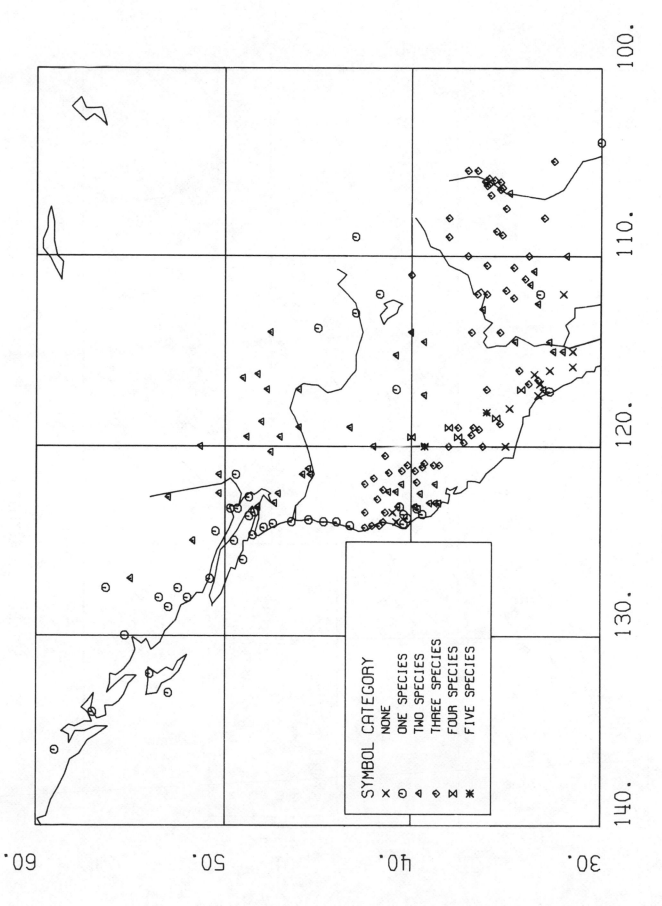

NUMBER OF SPECIES OF PINES

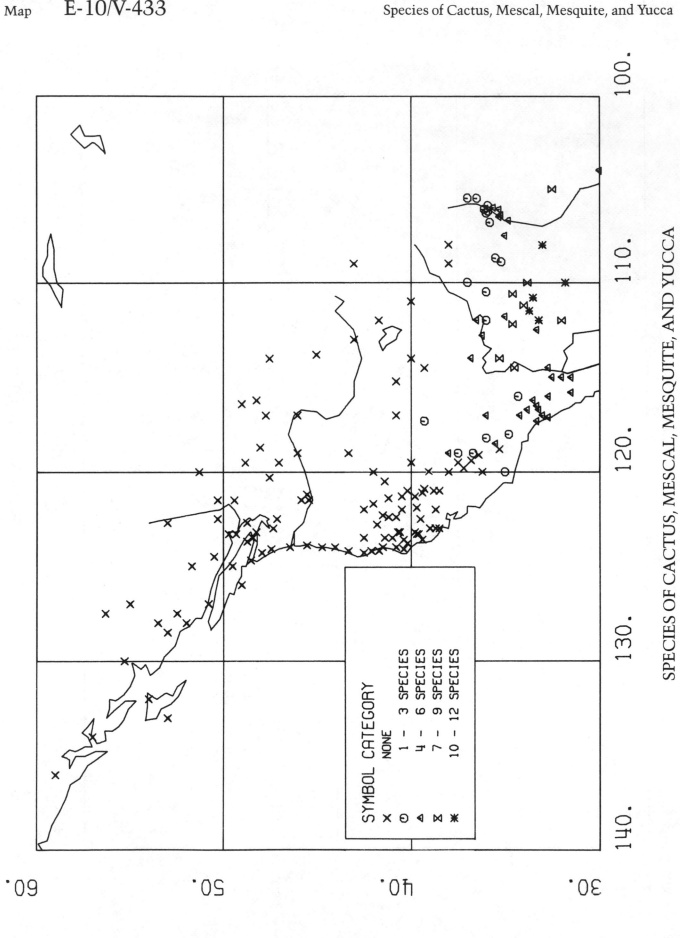

SPECIES OF CACTUS, MESCAL, MESQUITE, AND YUCCA

SYMBOL CATEGORY
NONE
X   1 — 3 SPECIES
⊖   4 — 6 SPECIES
◁   7 — 9 SPECIES
⋈   10 — 12 SPECIES
✳

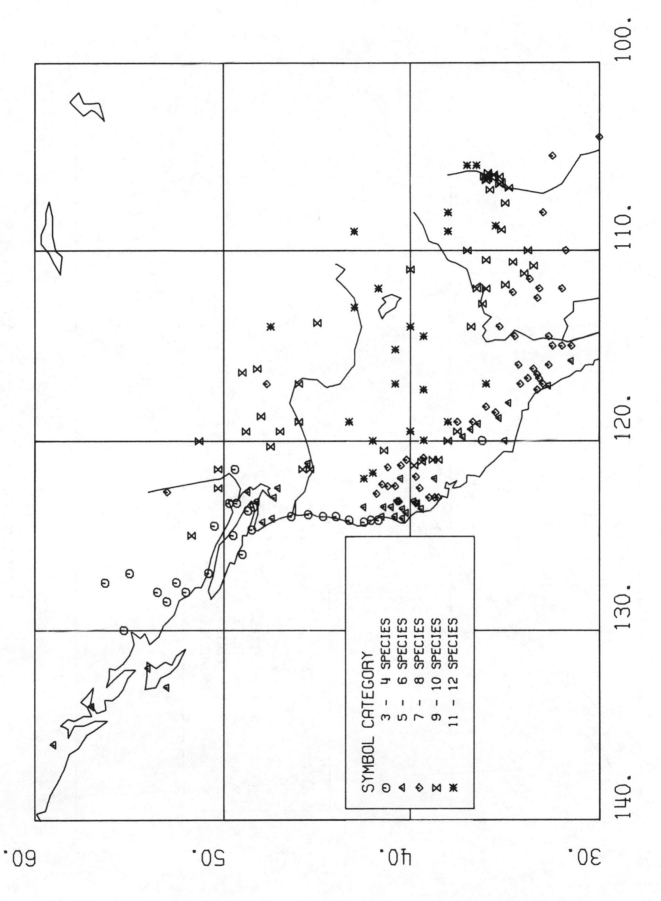

NUMBER OF SPECIES OF GRASSES

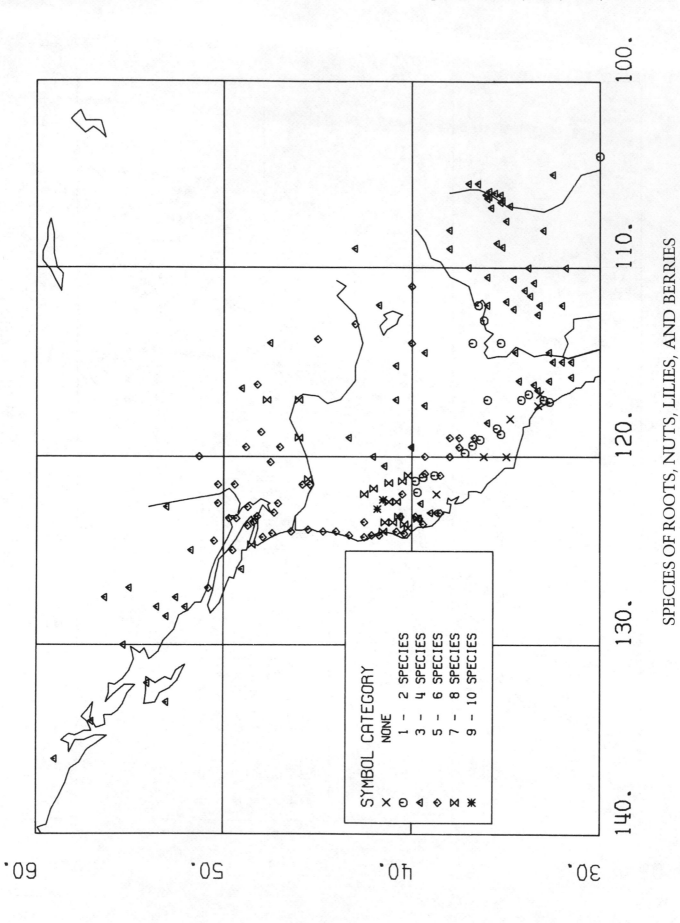

SPECIES OF ROOTS, NUTS, LILIES, AND BERRIES

SYMBOL CATEGORY

X   NONE
⊖   1 – 2 SPECIES
◁   3 – 4 SPECIES
◇   5 – 6 SPECIES
⋈   7 – 8 SPECIES
✳   9 – 10 SPECIES

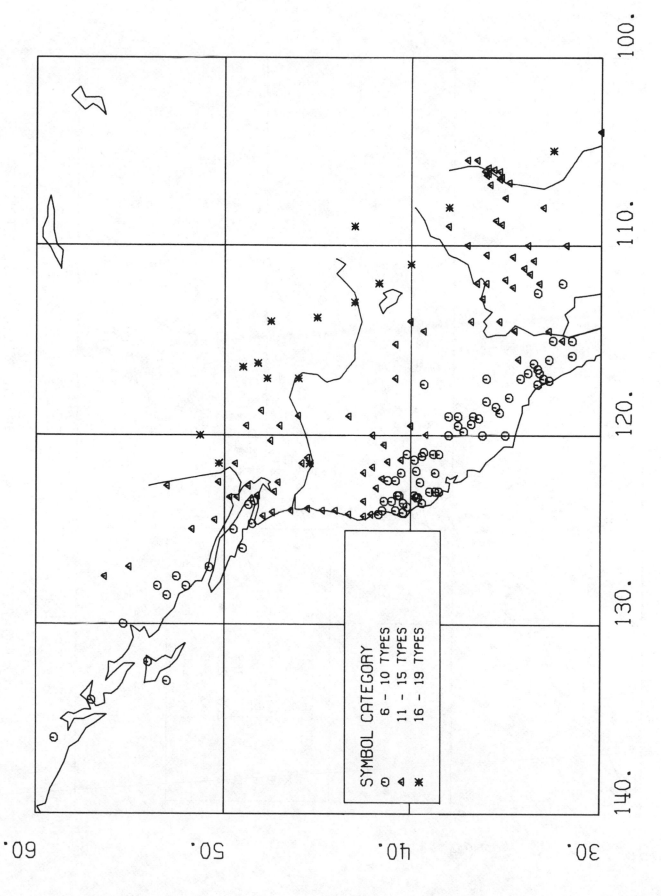

SPECIES OF LAND MAMMALS AVAILABLE

SYMBOL CATEGORY
⊖ 6 – 10 TYPES
◁ 11 – 15 TYPES
✳ 16 – 19 TYPES

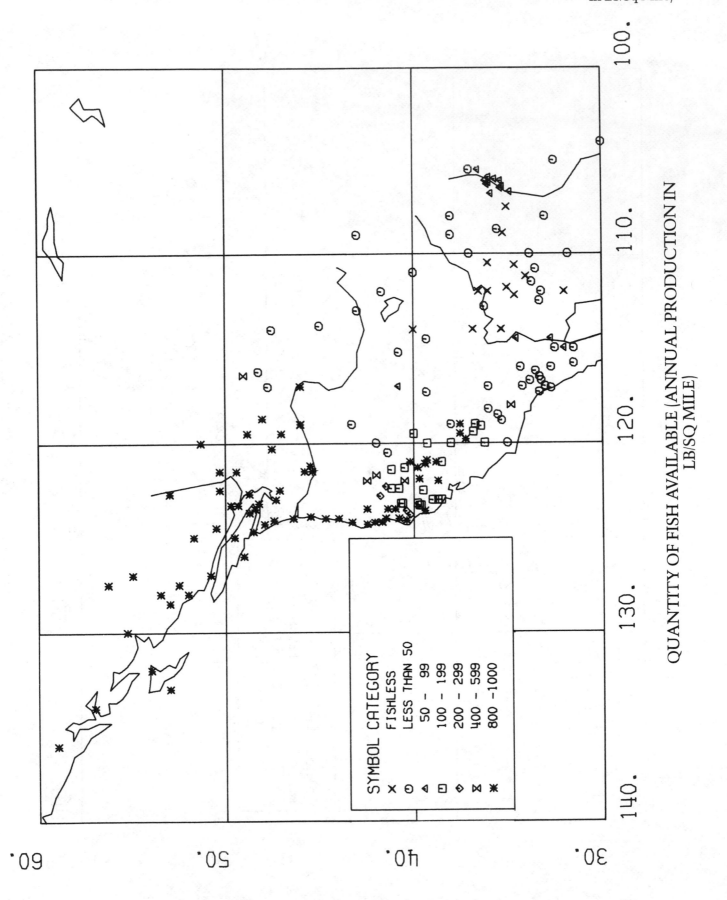

QUANTITY OF FISH AVAILABLE (ANNUAL PRODUCTION IN LB/SQ MILE)

SYMBOL CATEGORY

FISHLESS
LESS THAN 50
50 - 99
100 - 199
200 - 299
400 - 599
800 -1000

X Ø ◁ ⊟ ◇ ⋈ ✳

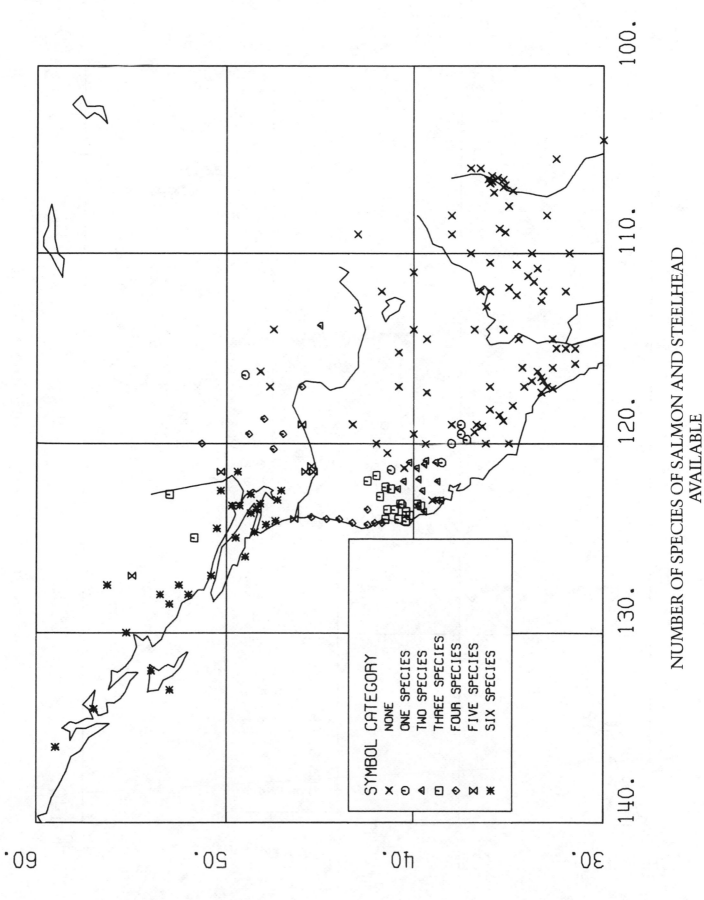

NUMBER OF SPECIES OF SALMON AND STEELHEAD
AVAILABLE

SYMBOL CATEGORY

Symbol	Category
X	NONE
⊖	ONE SPECIES
◁	TWO SPECIES
⊟	THREE SPECIES
◇	FOUR SPECIES
⋈	FIVE SPECIES
✳	SIX SPECIES

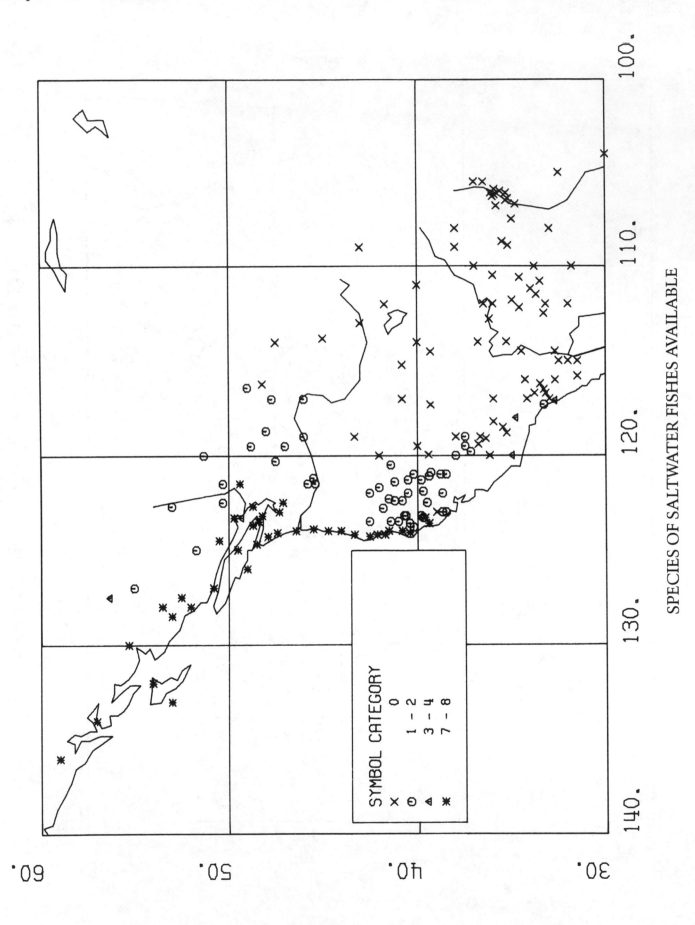

SYMBOL CATEGORY

X	0
Θ	1 – 2
◁	3 – 4
✳	7 – 8

SPECIES OF SALTWATER FISHES AVAILABLE

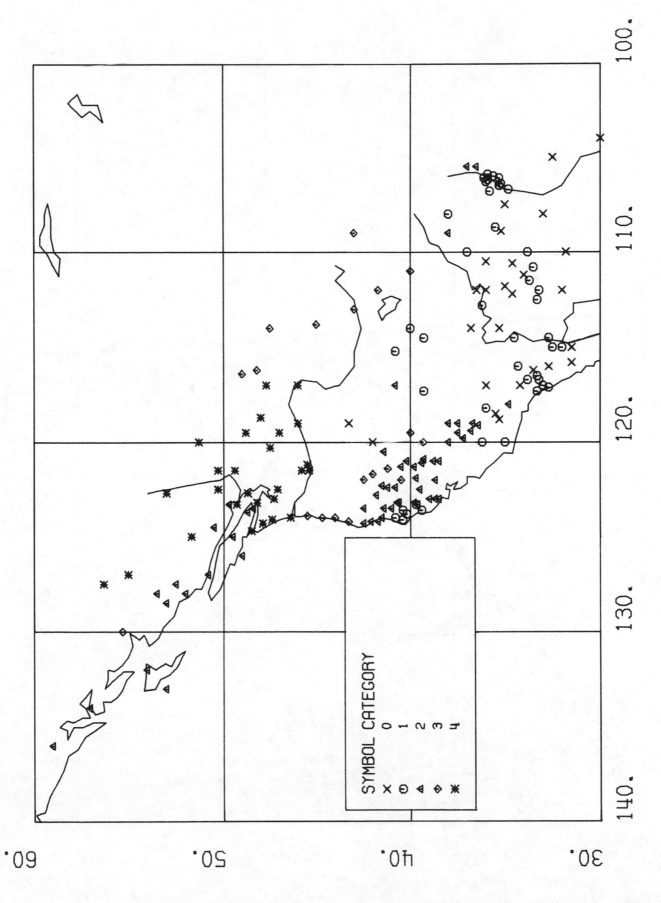

SPECIES OF FRESHWATER FISHES AVAILABLE

SYMBOL CATEGORY

0	✕
1	⊖
2	◁
3	◇
4	✳

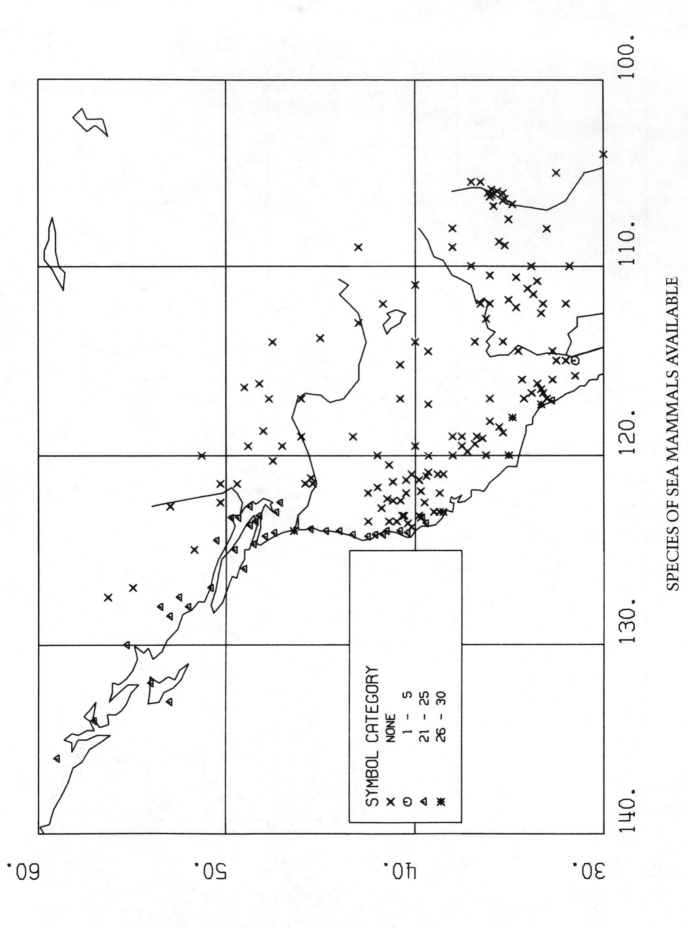

SYMBOL CATEGORY

X	NONE
⊖	1 - 5
◁	21 - 25
✳	26 - 30

SPECIES OF SEA MAMMALS AVAILABLE

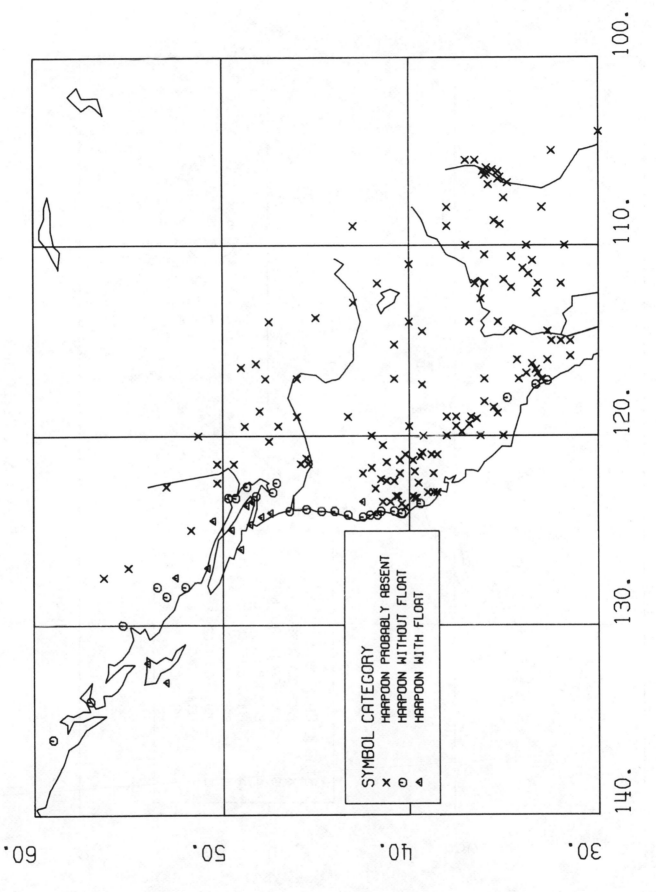

HARPOON USED TO CATCH SEA MAMMALS

SYMBOL CATEGORY
HARPOON PROBABLY ABSENT
HARPOON WITHOUT FLOAT
HARPOON WITH FLOAT
×   ⊖   ◁

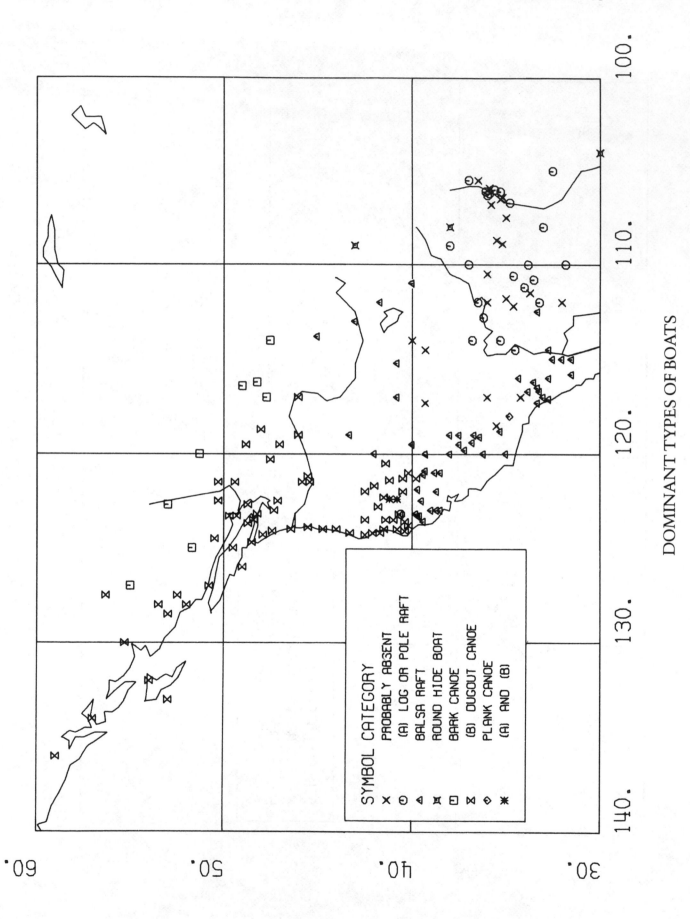

DOMINANT TYPES OF BOATS

SYMBOL CATEGORY

PROBABLY ABSENT
(A) LOG OR POLE RAFT
BALSA RAFT
ROUND HIDE BOAT
BARK CANOE
(B) DUGOUT CANOE
PLANK CANOE
(A) AND (B)

X ⊖ ◁ ⋈ ⊟ ⋈ ◇ ✳

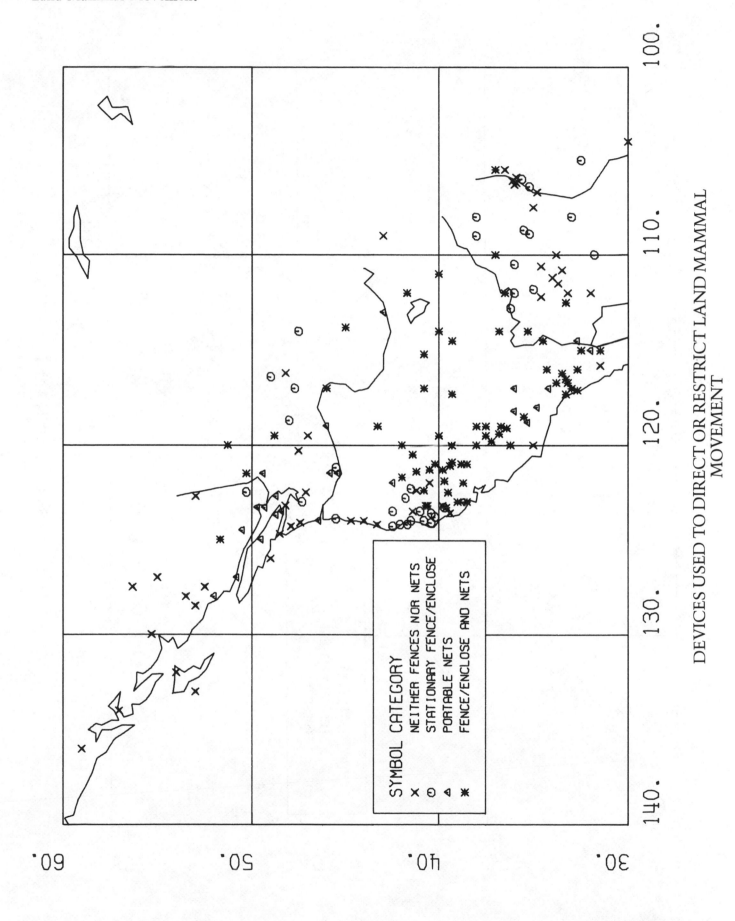

SYMBOL CATEGORY
NEITHER FENCES NOR NETS
STATIONARY FENCE/ENCLOSE
PORTABLE NETS
FENCE/ENCLOSE AND NETS

X   ⊖   ◁   ✳

DEVICES USED TO DIRECT OR RESTRICT LAND MAMMAL
MOVEMENT

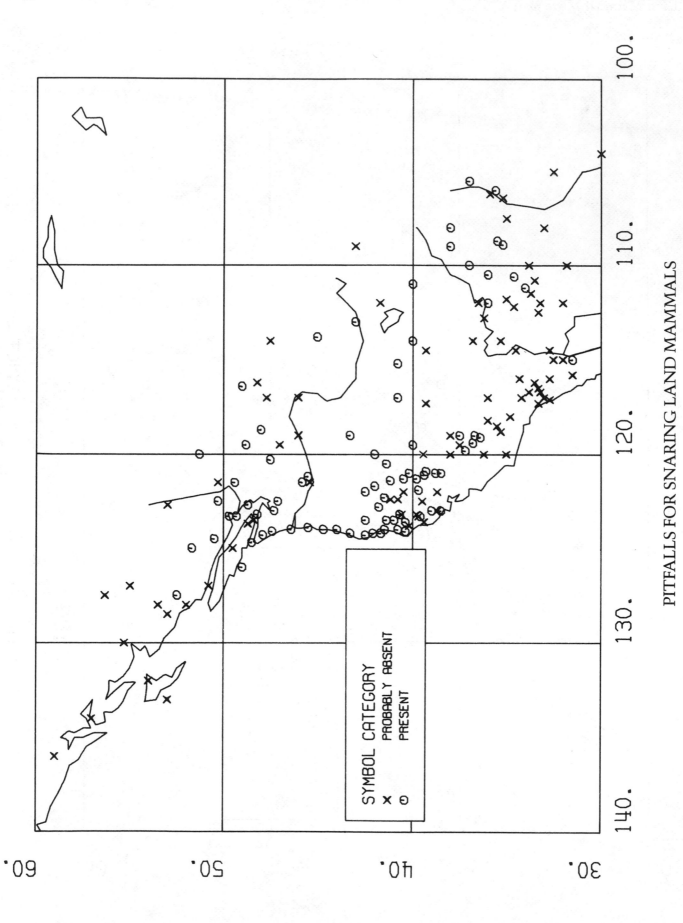

SYMBOL CATEGORY
X PROBABLY ABSENT
⊖ PRESENT

PITFALLS FOR SNARING LAND MAMMALS

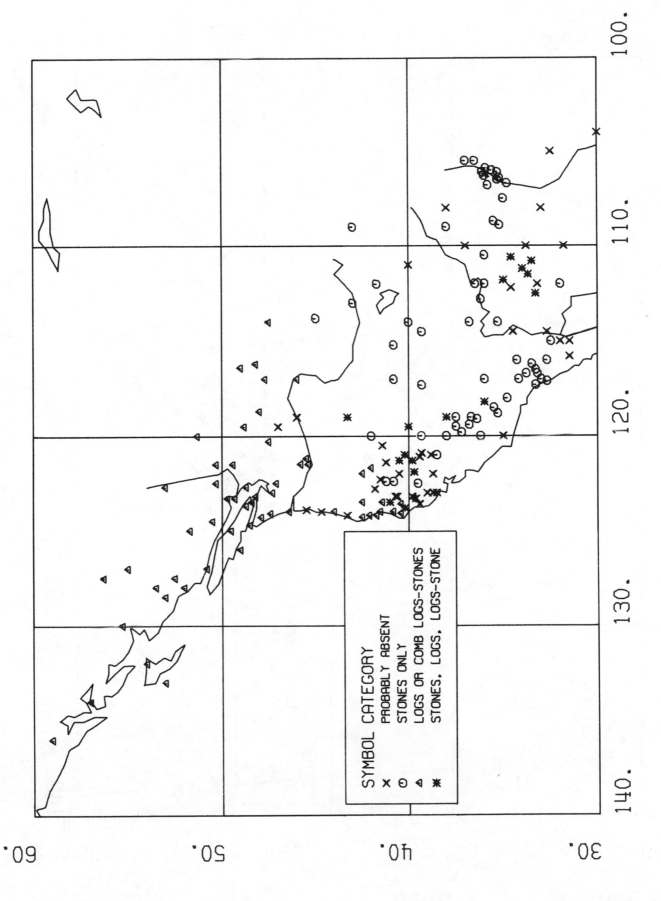

SYMBOL CATEGORY
X   PROBABLY ABSENT
⊖   STONES ONLY
◁   LOGS OR COMB LOGS-STONES
✳   STONES, LOGS, LOGS-STONE

DEADFALLS FOR SNARING LAND MAMMALS

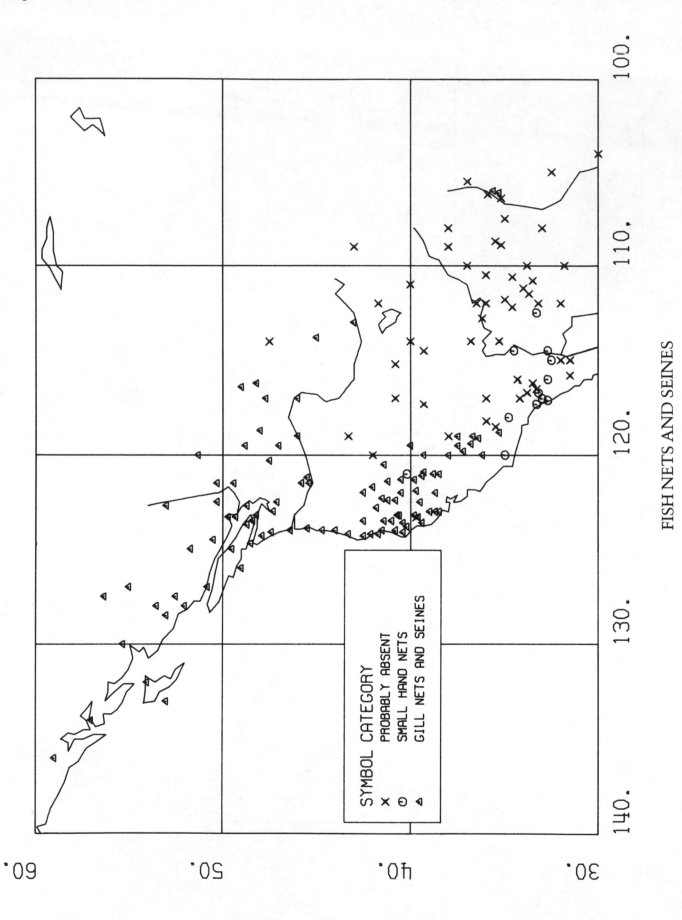

FISH NETS AND SEINES

SYMBOL CATEGORY
X   PROBABLY ABSENT
⊖   SMALL HAND NETS
◁   GILL NETS AND SEINES

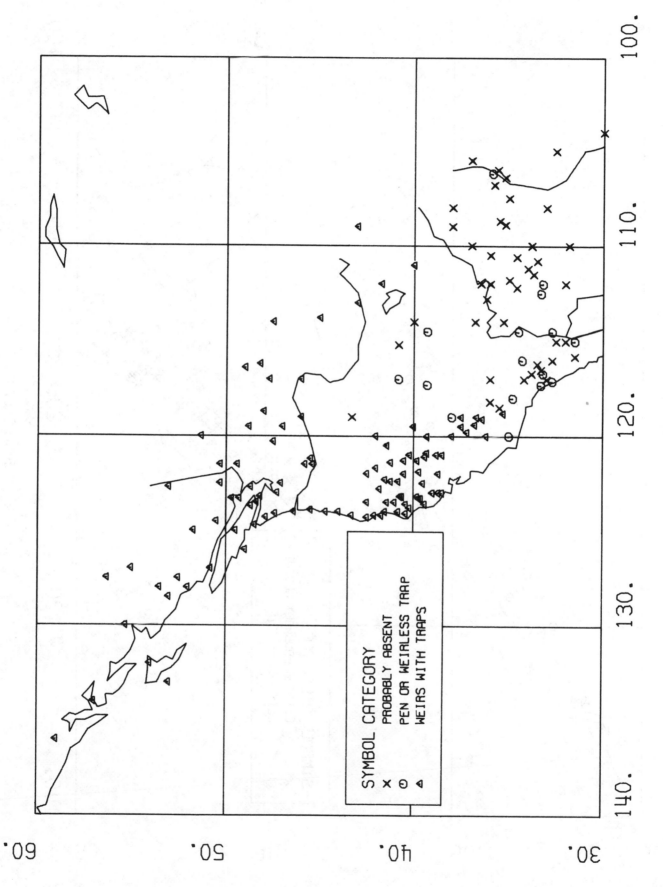

FISH WEIRS AND TRAPS

SYMBOL CATEGORY
X   PROBABLY ABSENT
⊖   PEN OR WEIRLESS TRAP
◁   WEIRS WITH TRAPS

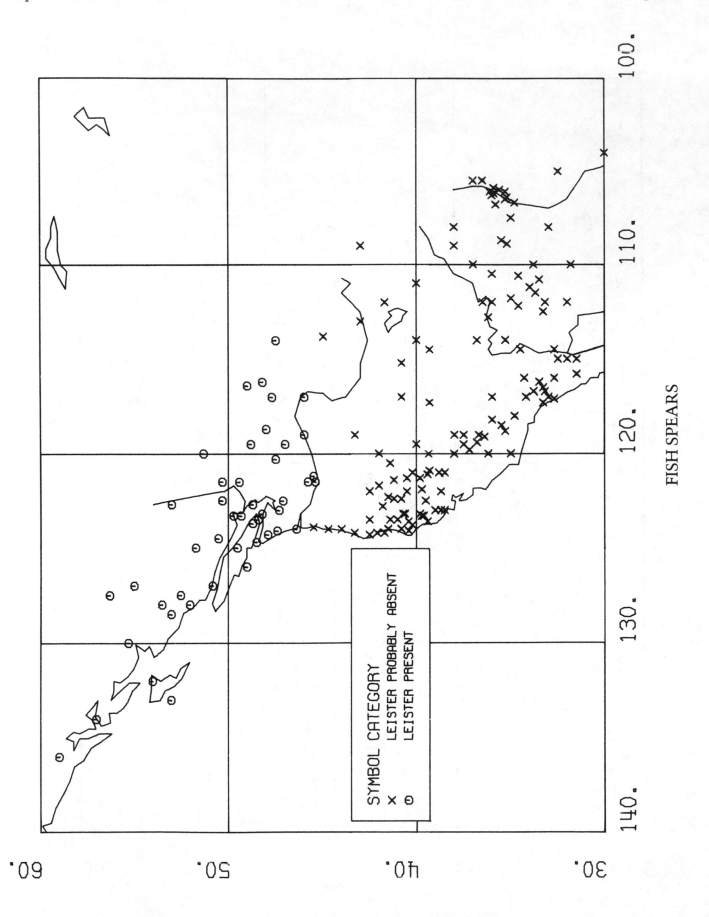

FISH SPEARS

SYMBOL CATEGORY
x   LEISTER PROBABLY ABSENT
⊖   LEISTER PRESENT

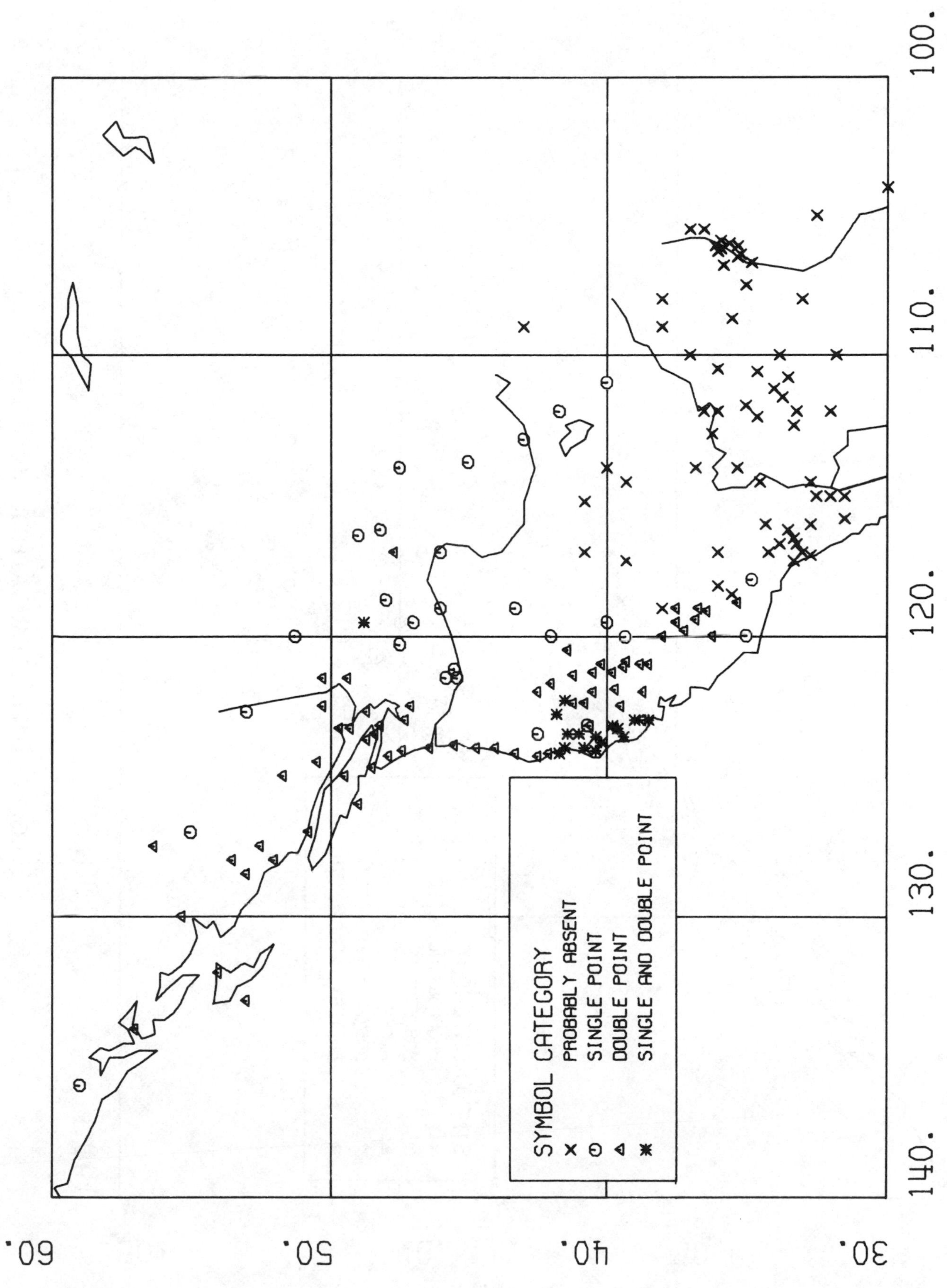

SYMBOL CATEGORY
× PROBABLY ABSENT
⊙ SINGLE POINT
◁ DOUBLE POINT
✱ SINGLE AND DOUBLE POINT
100.
110.
120.
130.
140.
30.
40.
50.
60.

FISH HARPOONS

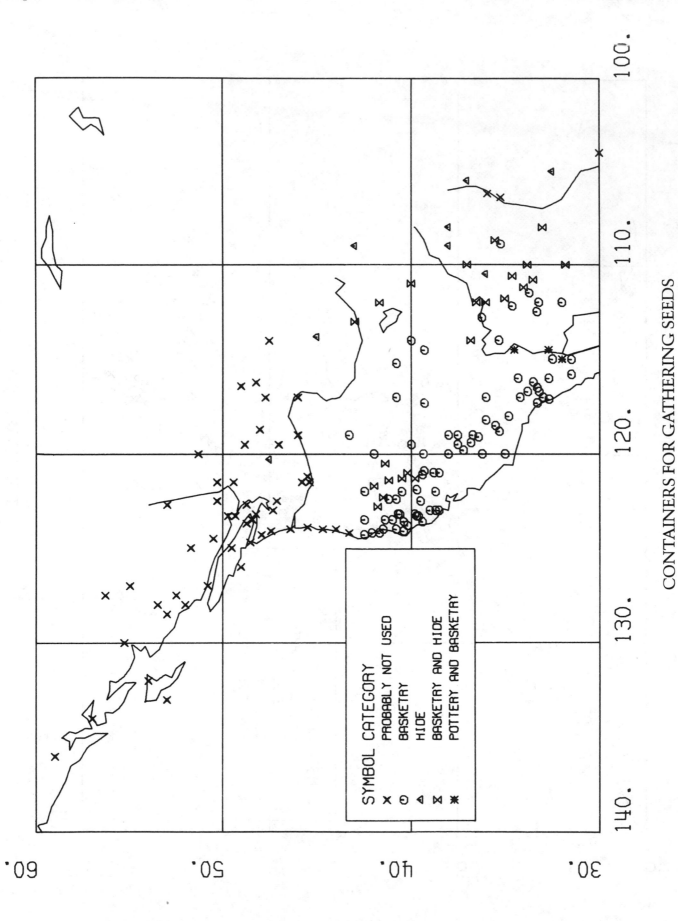

CONTAINERS FOR GATHERING SEEDS

SYMBOL CATEGORY

✗	PROBABLY NOT USED
⊖	BASKETRY
◁	HIDE
⋈	BASKETRY AND HIDE
✳	POTTERY AND BASKETRY

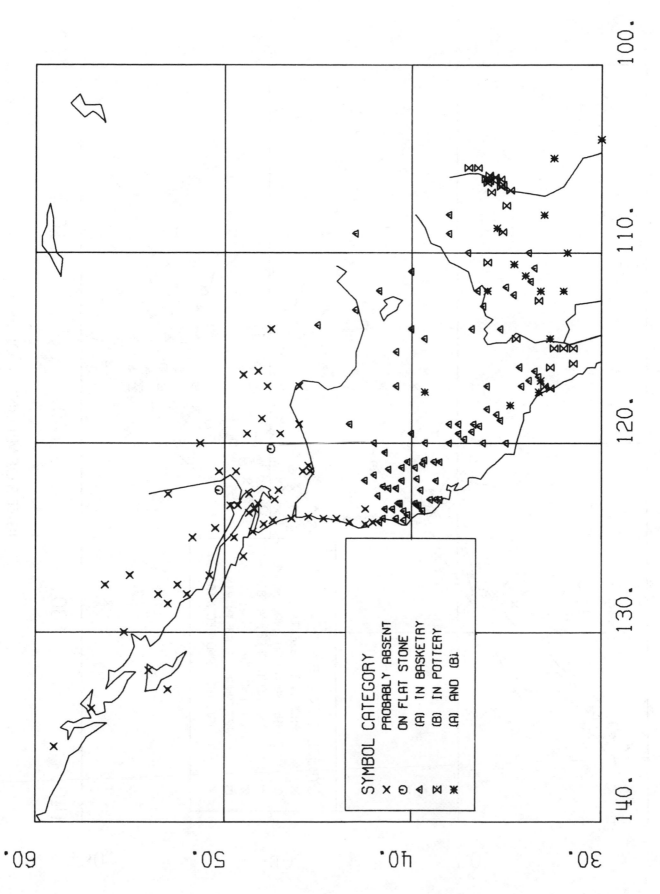

SEED-PARCHING IMPLEMENTS

SYMBOL CATEGORY

X	PROBABLY ABSENT
Θ	ON FLAT STONE
◁	(A) IN BASKETRY
⋈	(B) IN POTTERY
✳	(A) AND (B)

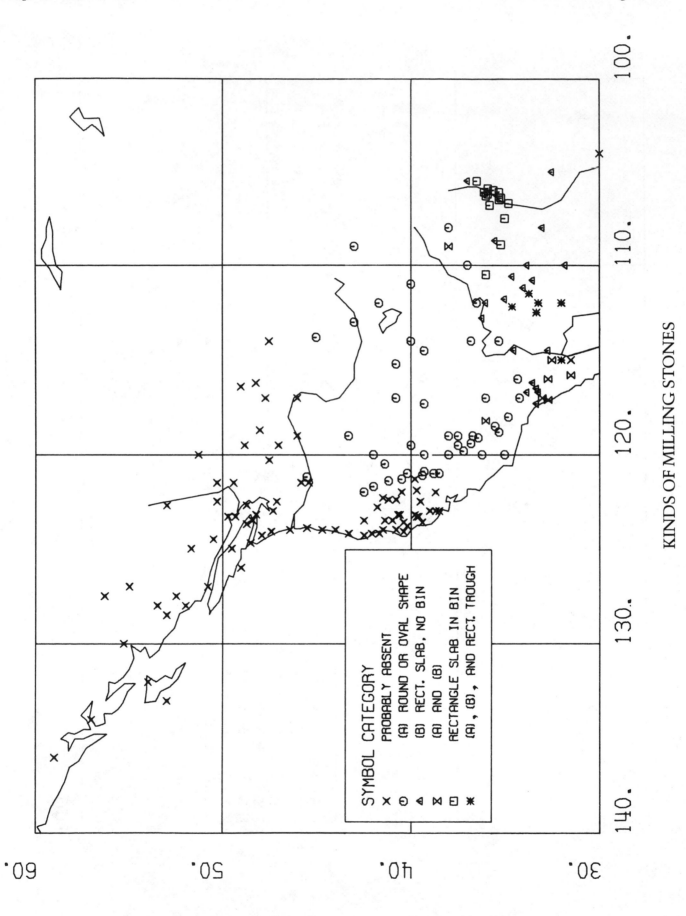

SYMBOL CATEGORY
X   PROBABLY ABSENT
⊖   (A) ROUND OR OVAL SHAPE
◁   (B) RECT. SLAB, NO BIN
⋈   (A) AND (B)
⊟   RECTANGLE SLAB IN BIN
✳   (A), (B), AND RECT. TROUGH

KINDS OF MILLING STONES

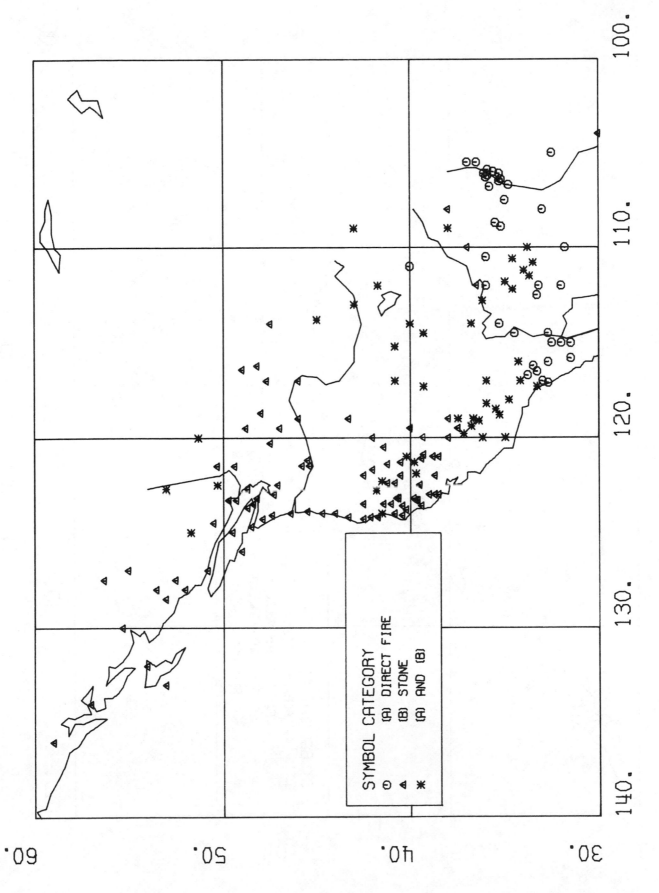

METHOD OF BOILING FOOD

SYMBOL CATEGORY
Ө (A) DIRECT FIRE
◁ (B) STONE
✳ (A) AND (B)

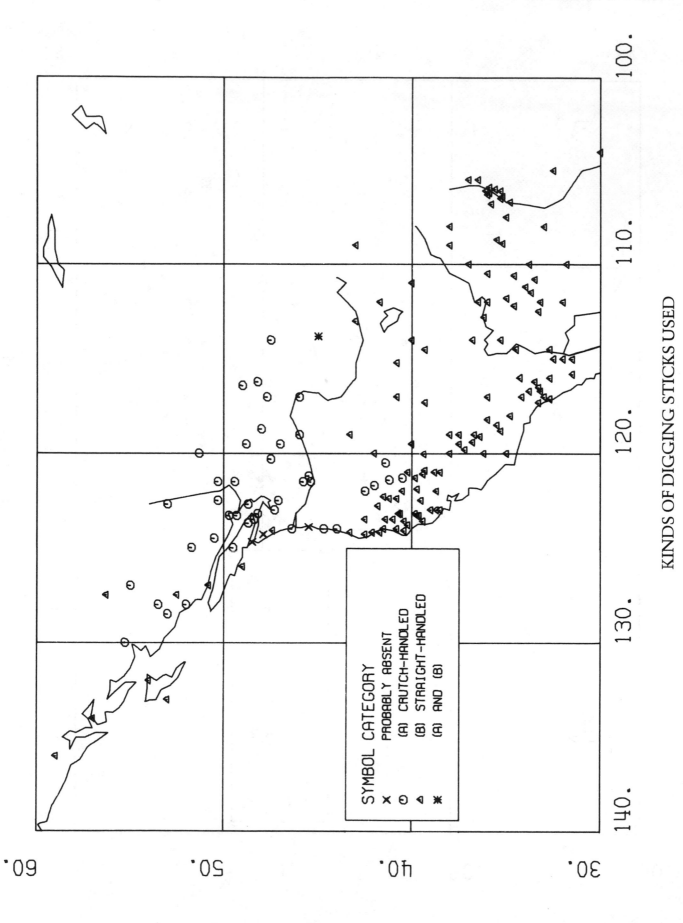

KINDS OF DIGGING STICKS USED

SYMBOL CATEGORY
PROBABLY ABSENT
× (A) CRUTCH-HANDLED
⊖ (B) STRAIGHT-HANDLED
◁ (A) AND (B)
✳

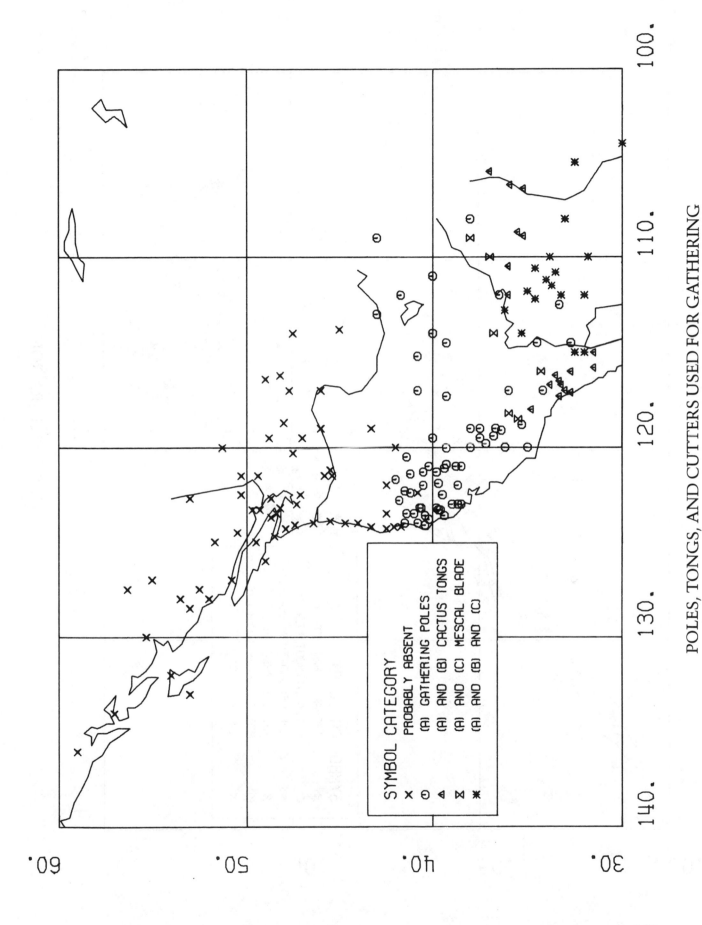

POLES, TONGS, AND CUTTERS USED FOR GATHERING

SYMBOL CATEGORY

✗	PROBABLY ABSENT
⊖	(A) GATHERING POLES
◁	(A) AND (B) CACTUS TONGS
⋈	(A) AND (C) MESCAL BLADE
✳	(A) AND (B) AND (C)

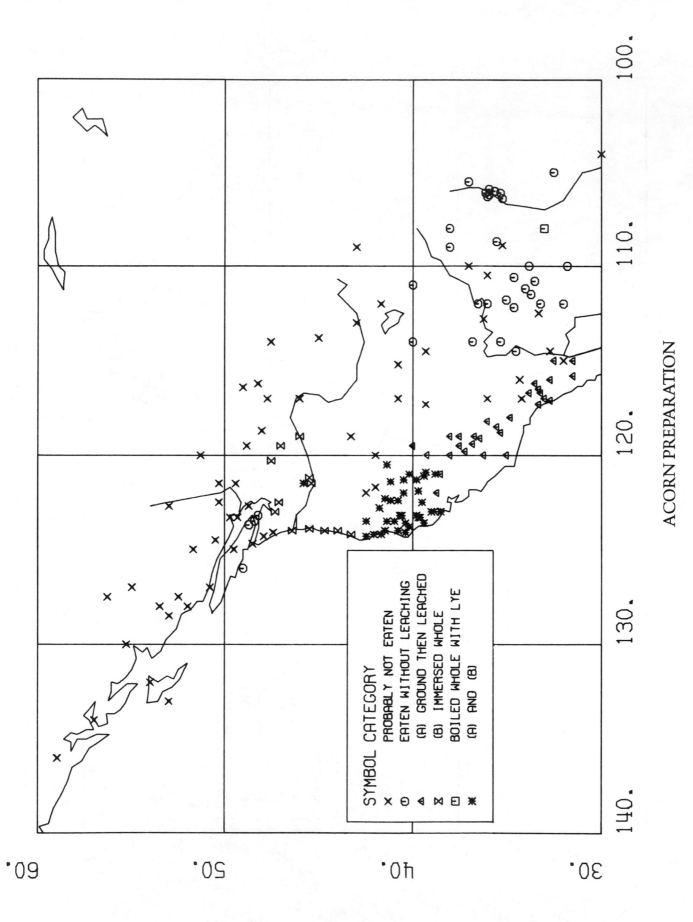

ACORN PREPARATION

SYMBOL CATEGORY
X   PROBABLY NOT EATEN
⊖   EATEN WITHOUT LEACHING
◁   (A) GROUND THEN LEACHED
⋈   (B) IMMERSED WHOLE
⊟   BOILED WHOLE WITH LYE
✳   (A) AND (B)

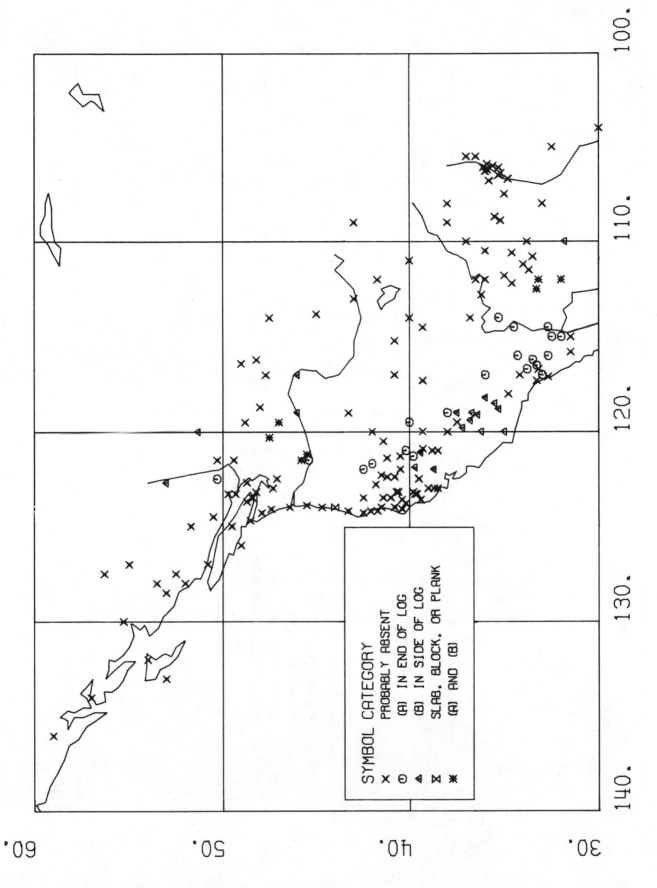

SYMBOL CATEGORY

✕	PROBABLY ABSENT
⊖	(A) IN END OF LOG
◁	(B) IN SIDE OF LOG
⋈	SLAB, BLOCK, OR PLANK
✴	(A) AND (B)

WOODEN FOOD MORTARS

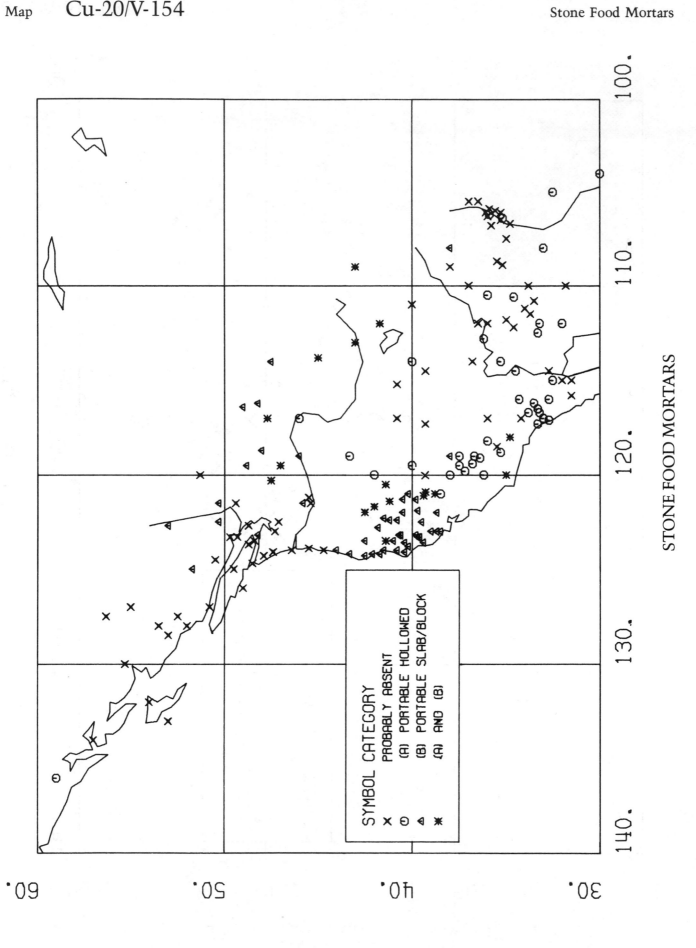

STONE FOOD MORTARS

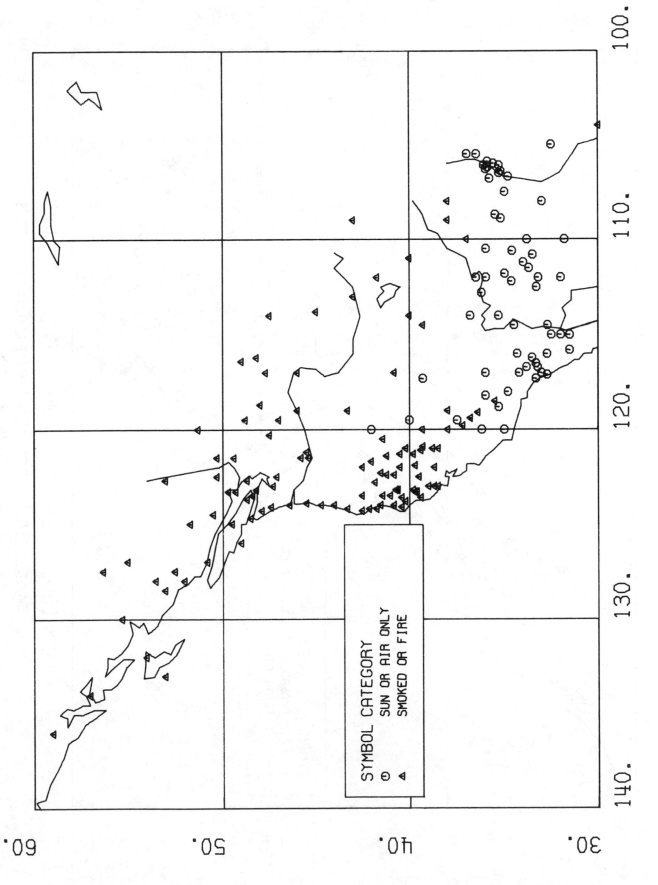

METHOD OF DRYING MEAT

SYMBOL CATEGORY
⊖ SUN OR AIR ONLY
▲ SMOKED OR FIRE

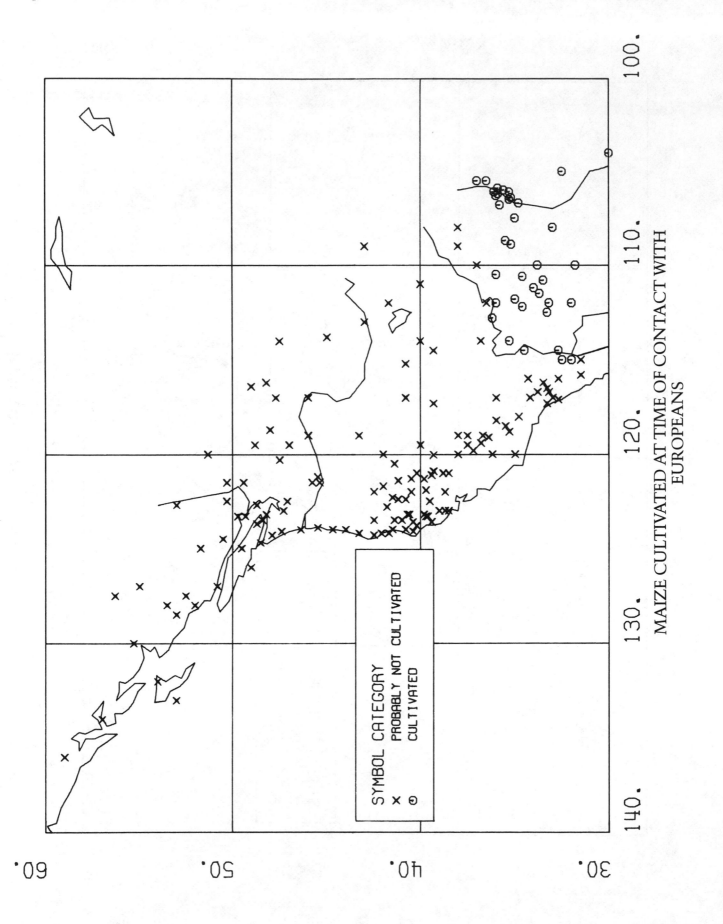

SYMBOL CATEGORY
PROBABLY NOT CULTIVATED
CULTIVATED

MAIZE CULTIVATED AT TIME OF CONTACT WITH
EUROPEANS

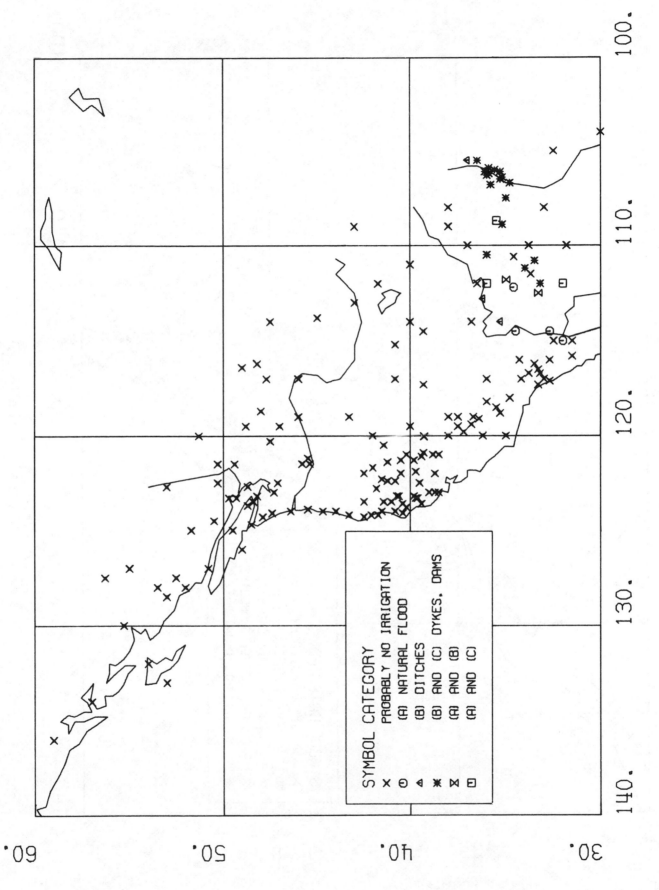

IRRIGATION OF CULTIVATED PLANTS

SYMBOL CATEGORY

	PROBABLY NO IRRIGATION
X	(A) NATURAL FLOOD
⊙	(B) DITCHES
◁	(B) AND (C) DYKES, DAMS
✳	(A) AND (B)
⋈	(A) AND (C)
⊟	

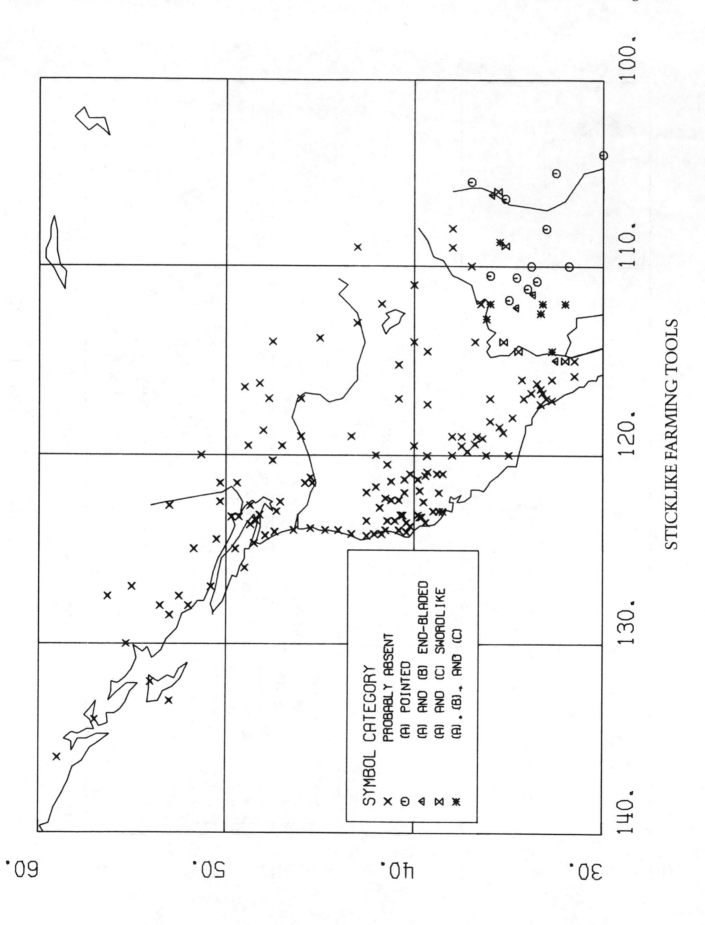

STICKLIKE FARMING TOOLS

SYMBOL CATEGORY

X	PROBABLY ABSENT
⊖	(A) POINTED
◁	(A) AND (B) END-BLADED
⋈	(A) AND (C) SWORDLIKE
✳	(A), (B), AND (C)

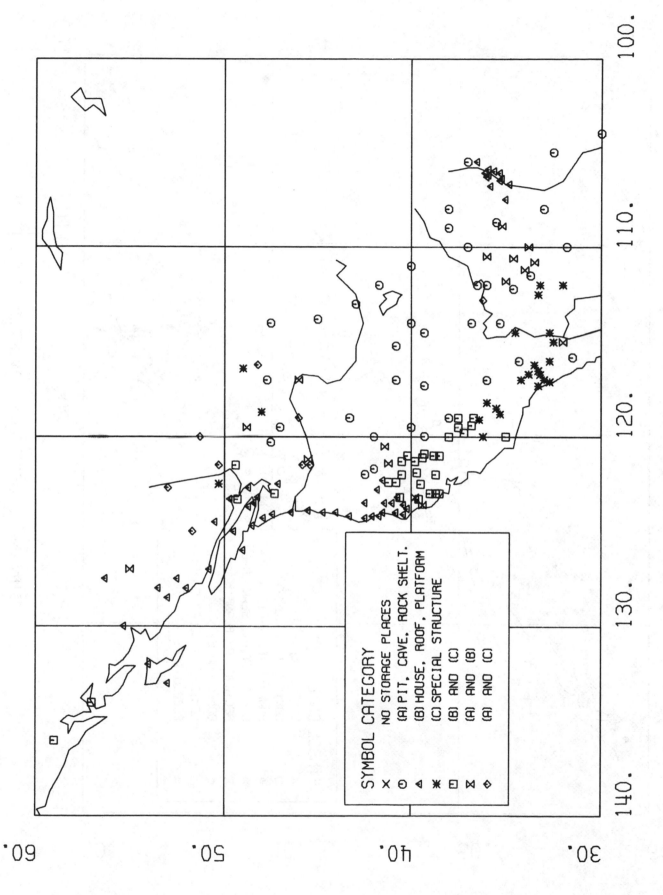

DOMINANT STORAGE PLACES FOR FOOD

SYMBOL CATEGORY
X   NO STORAGE PLACES
⊖   (A) PIT, CAVE, ROCK SHELT.
◁   (B) HOUSE, ROOF, PLATFORM
✳   (C) SPECIAL STRUCTURE
⊟   (B) AND (C)
⋈   (A) AND (B)
◇   (A) AND (C)

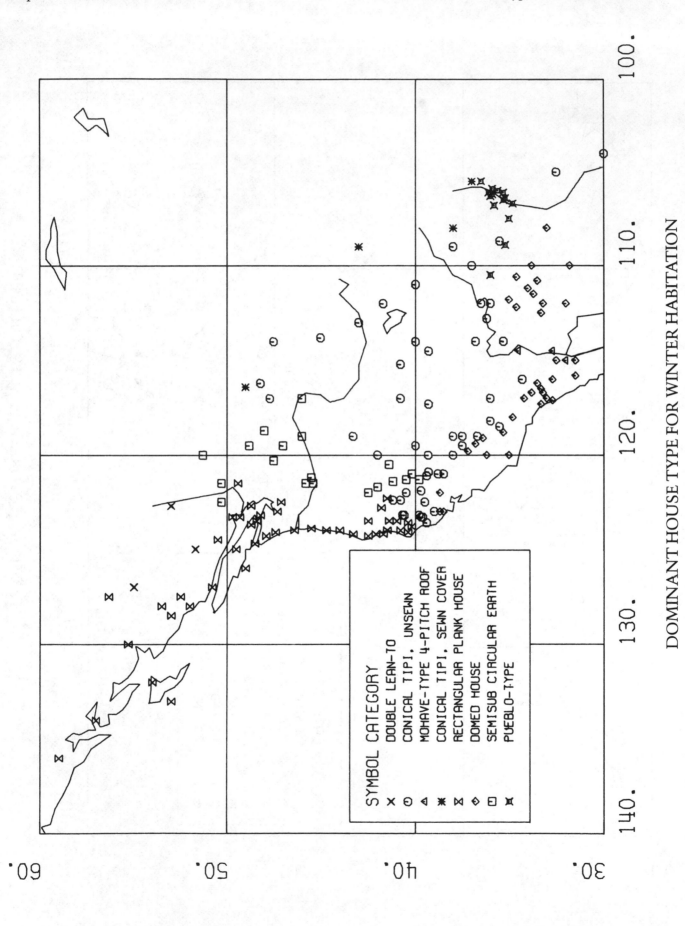

DOMINANT HOUSE TYPE FOR WINTER HABITATION

SYMBOL CATEGORY

✕	DOUBLE LEAN-TO
⊖	CONICAL TIPI, UNSEWN
◁	MOHAVE-TYPE 4-PITCH ROOF
✳	CONICAL TIPI, SEWN COVER
⋈	RECTANGULAR PLANK HOUSE
◇	DOMED HOUSE
⊟	SEMISUB CIRCULAR EARTH
⋈	PUEBLO-TYPE

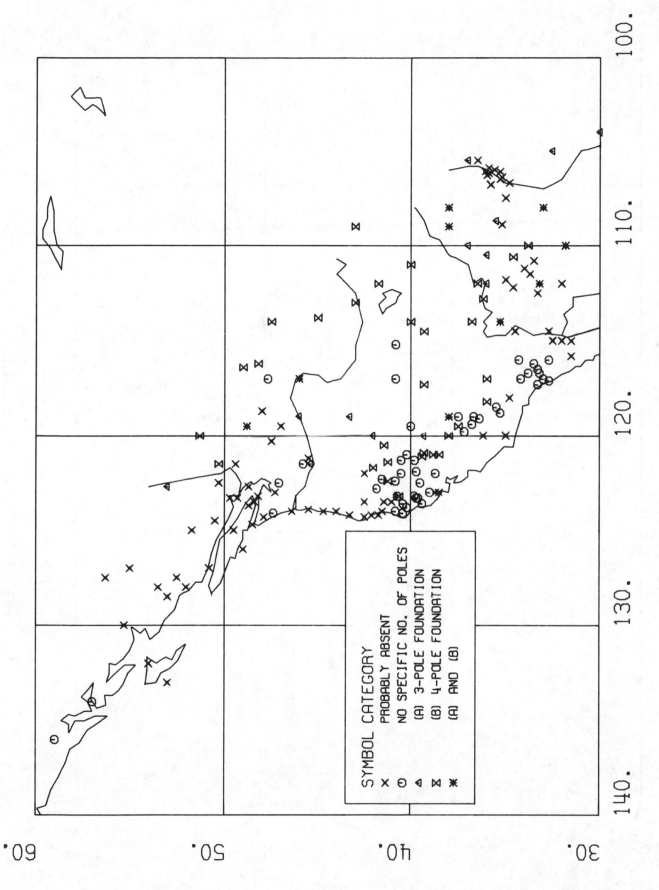

CONICAL AND SUBCONICAL DWELLINGS

SYMBOL CATEGORY

	PROBABLY ABSENT
	NO SPECIFIC NO. OF POLES
	(A) 3-POLE FOUNDATION
	(B) 4-POLE FOUNDATION
	(A) AND (B)

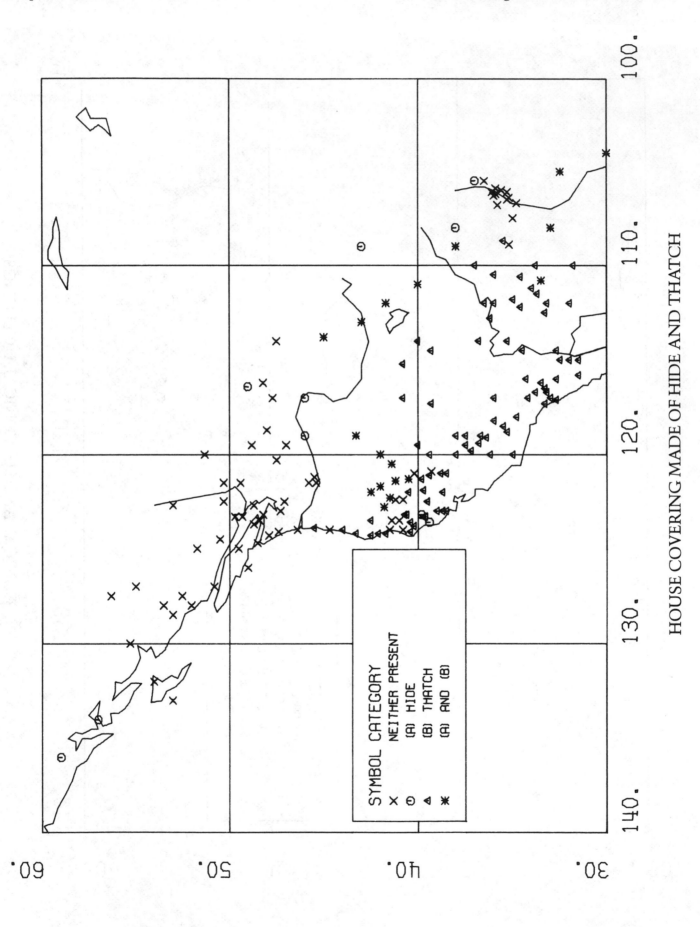

HOUSE COVERING MADE OF HIDE AND THATCH

SYMBOL CATEGORY
NEITHER PRESENT
(A) HIDE
(B) THATCH
(A) AND (B)

X   Θ   ◁   ✳

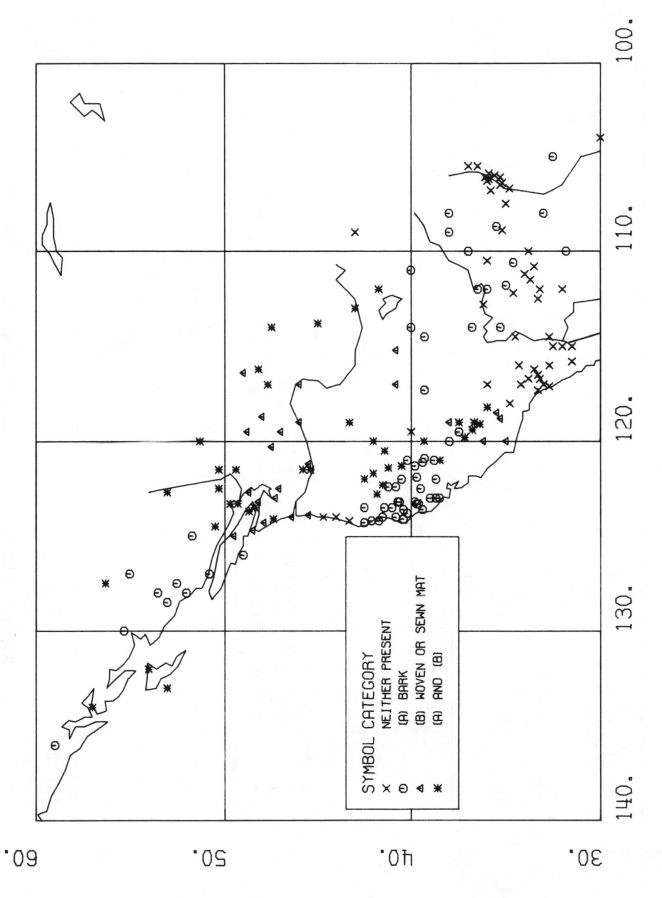

HOUSE COVERING MADE OF BARK OR MATS

SYMBOL CATEGORY
X   NEITHER PRESENT
⊖   (A) BARK
△   (B) WOVEN OR SEWN MAT
✳   (A) AND (B)

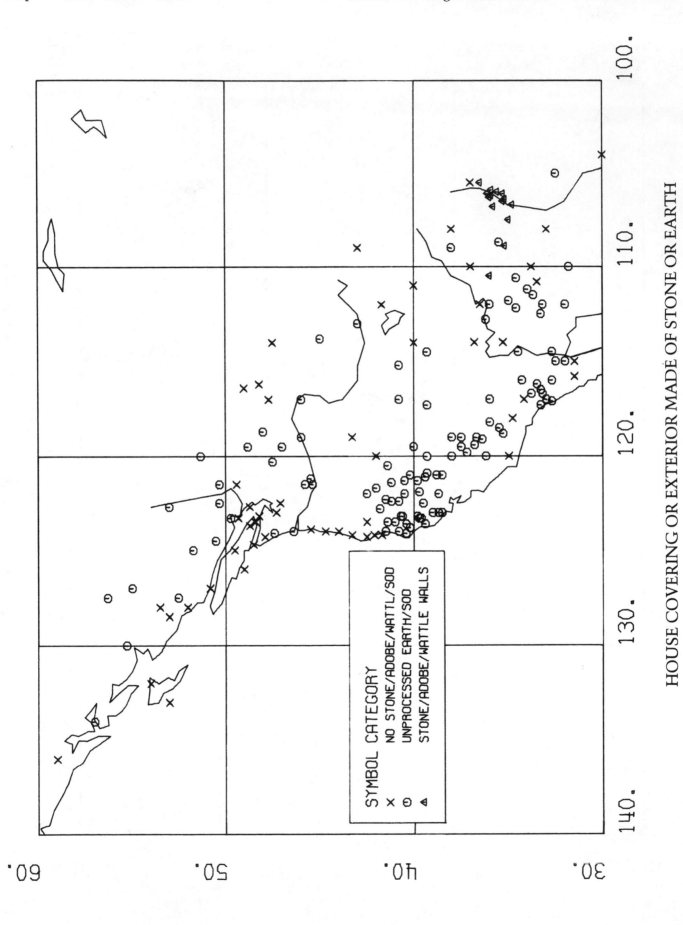

SYMBOL CATEGORY
X   NO STONE/ADOBE/WATTL/SOD
⊖   UNPROCESSED EARTH/SOD
◁   STONE/ADOBE/WATTLE WALLS

HOUSE COVERING OR EXTERIOR MADE OF STONE OR EARTH

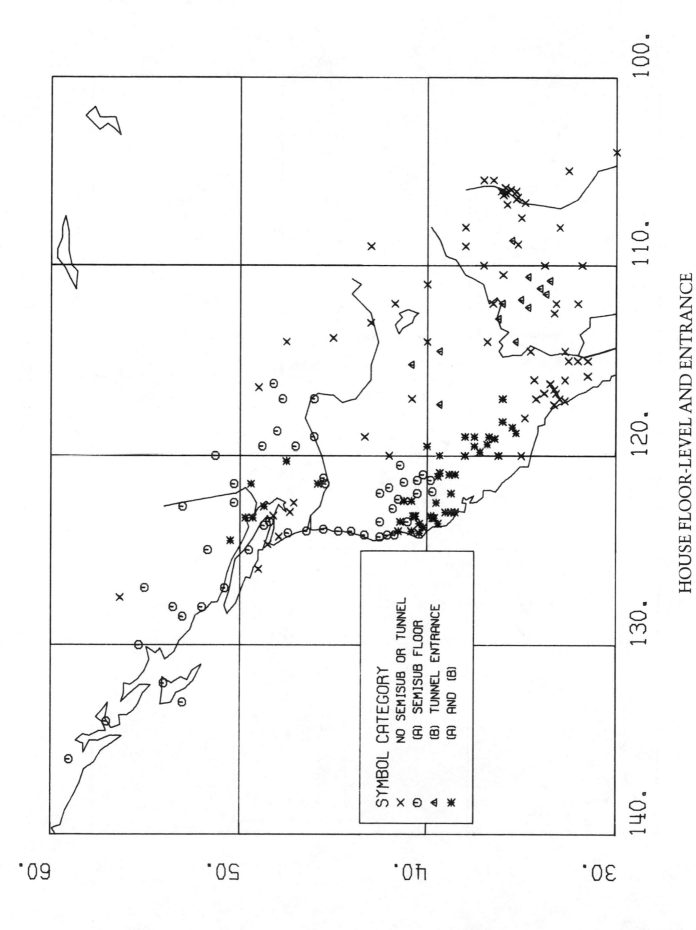

HOUSE FLOOR-LEVEL AND ENTRANCE

SYMBOL CATEGORY

X NO SEMISUB OR TUNNEL
⊖ (A) SEMISUB FLOOR
◁ (B) TUNNEL ENTRANCE
✳ (A) AND (B)

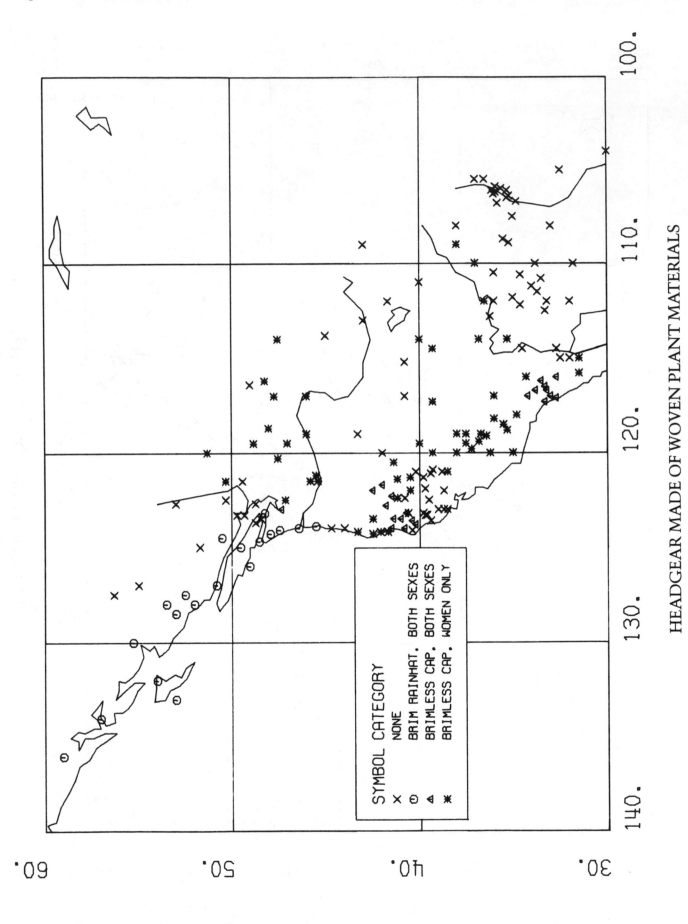

HEADGEAR MADE OF WOVEN PLANT MATERIALS

SYMBOL CATEGORY

X	NONE
⊖	BRIM RAINHAT. BOTH SEXES
◁	BRIMLESS CAP. BOTH SEXES
✳	BRIMLESS CAP. WOMEN ONLY

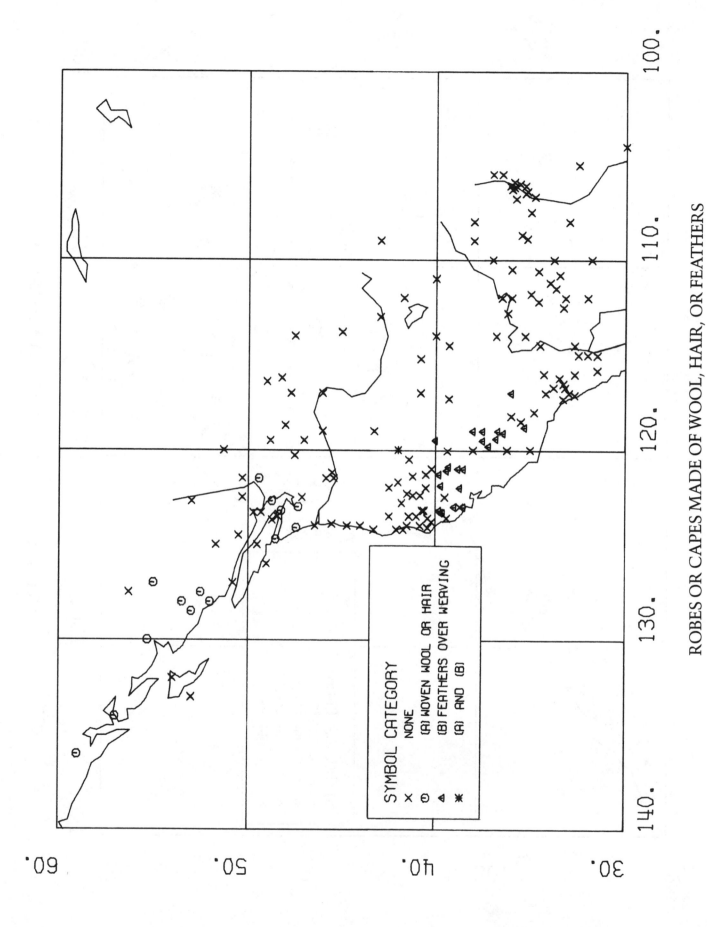

SYMBOL CATEGORY
NONE
(A) WOVEN WOOL OR HAIR
(B) FEATHERS OVER WEAVING
(A) AND (B)

× ⊖ ◁ ✳

ROBES OR CAPES MADE OF WOOL, HAIR, OR FEATHERS

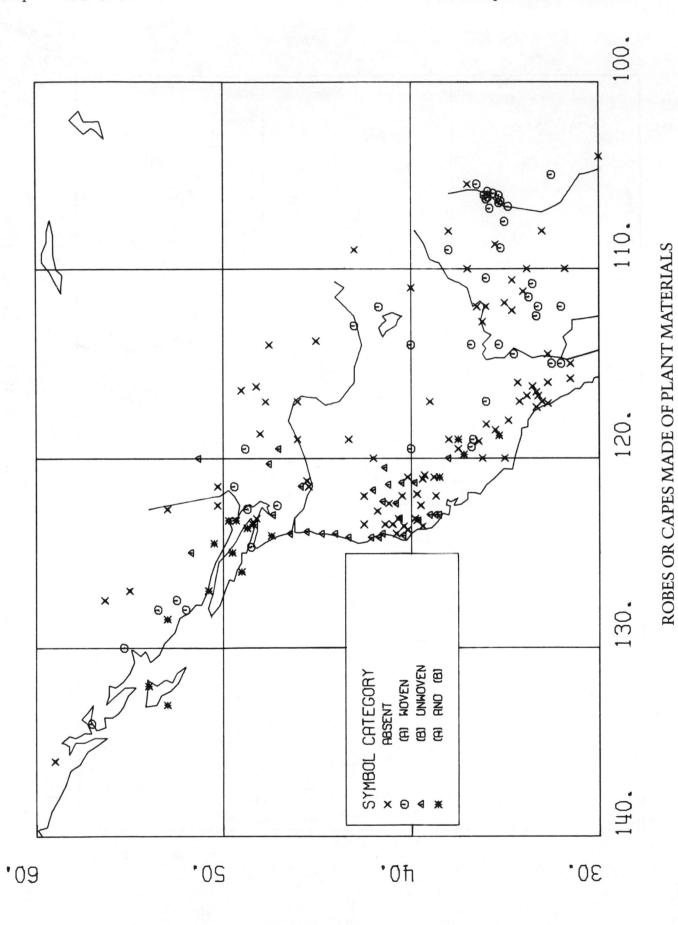

ROBES OR CAPES MADE OF PLANT MATERIALS

SYMBOL CATEGORY
ABSENT
(A) WOVEN
(B) UNWOVEN
(A) AND (B)

×   ⊖   ◁   ✳

100.

110.

120.

130.

140.

60.

50.

40.

30.

SYMBOL CATEGORY
        NONE
    X   (A) BRIMLESS FUR CAP
    ⊖   (B) FUR CAP WITH VISOR
    ◁   (C) BUCKSKIN CAP
    ◇   (A) AND (C)
    ⋈   (A) AND (B)
    ✳

HEADGEAR MADE OF HIDE OR FUR

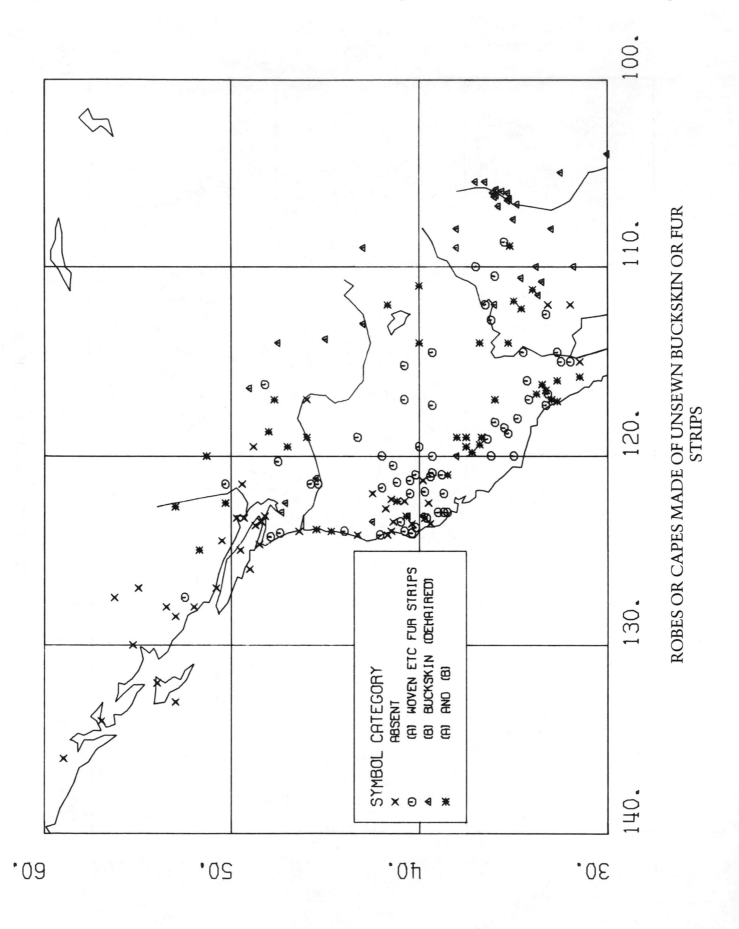

ROBES OR CAPES MADE OF UNSEWN BUCKSKIN OR FUR STRIPS

SYMBOL CATEGORY

X	ABSENT
⊖	(A) WOVEN ETC FUR STRIPS
◁	(B) BUCKSKIN (DEHAIRED)
✳	(A) AND (B)

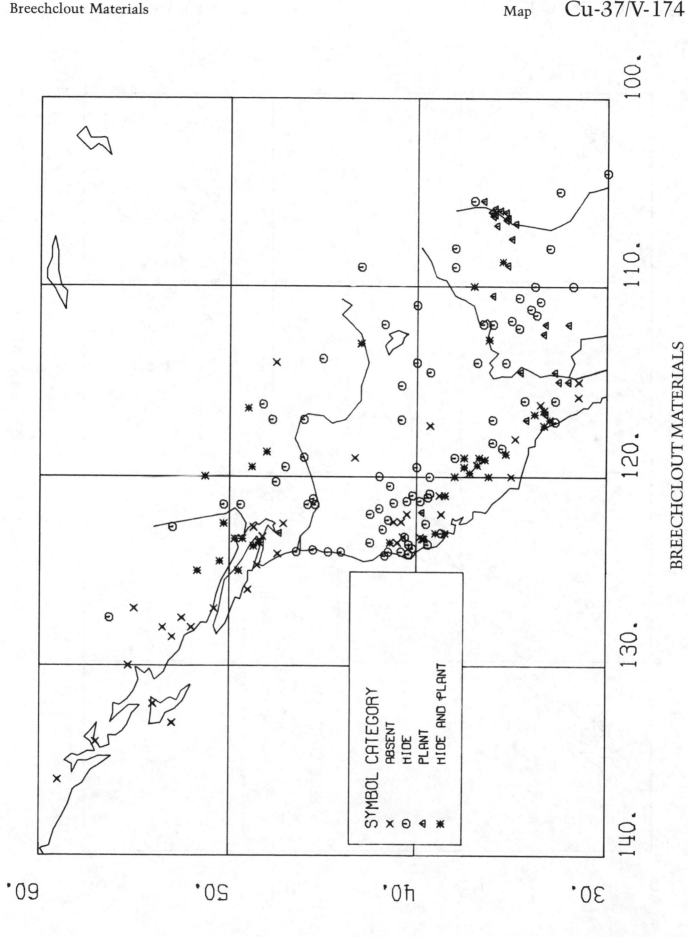

BREECHCLOUT MATERIALS

SYMBOL CATEGORY
ABSENT
HIDE
PLANT
HIDE AND PLANT

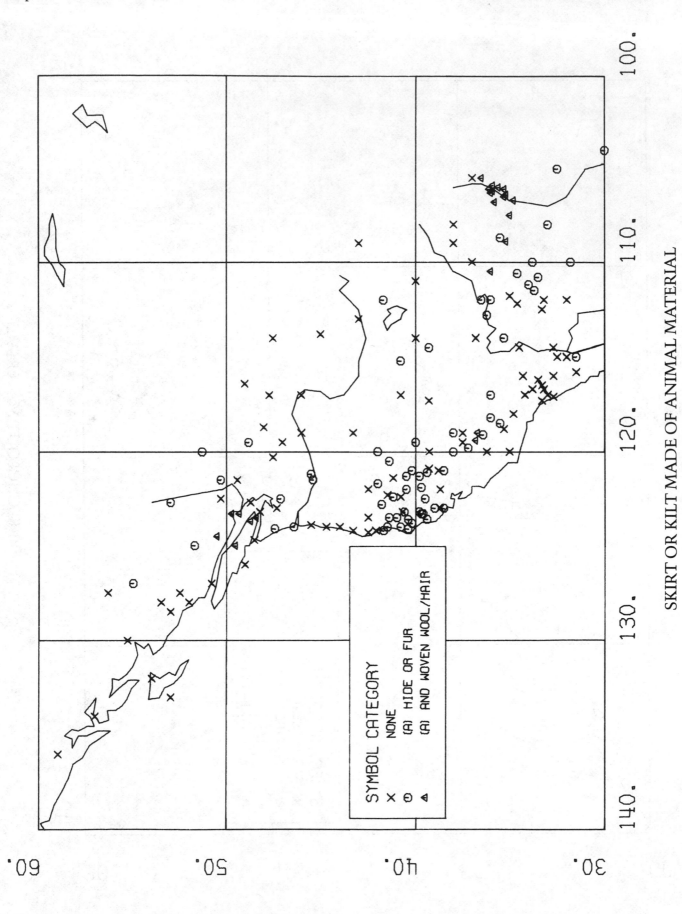

SKIRT OR KILT MADE OF ANIMAL MATERIAL

SYMBOL CATEGORY
NONE
(A) HIDE OR FUR
(A) AND WOVEN WOOL/HAIR

X
⊖
◁

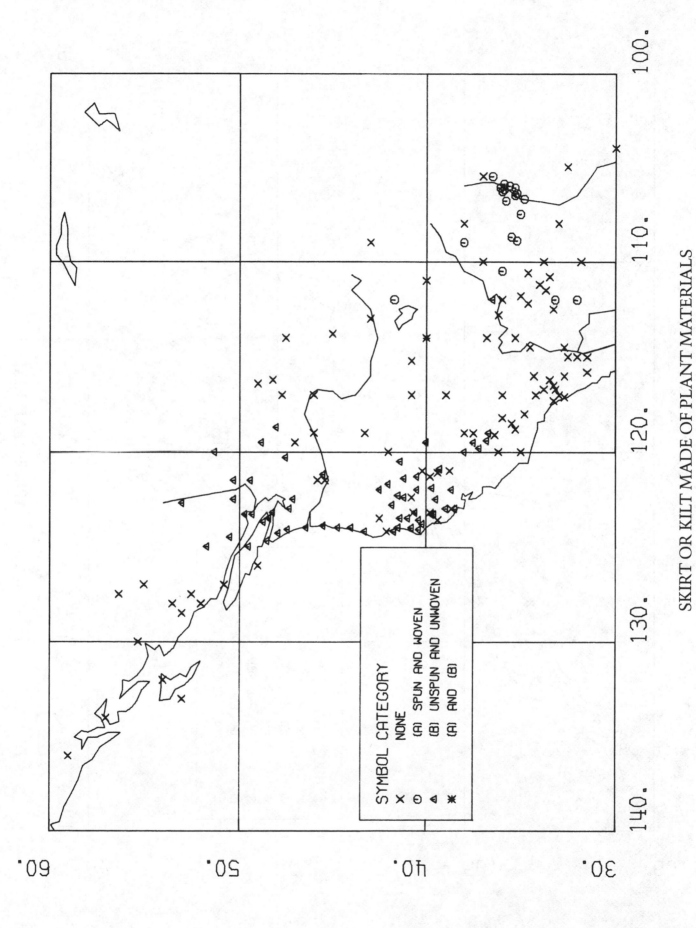

SKIRT OR KILT MADE OF PLANT MATERIALS

SYMBOL CATEGORY
X   NONE
⊖   (A) SPUN AND WOVEN
◁   (B) UNSPUN AND UNWOVEN
✳   (A) AND (B)

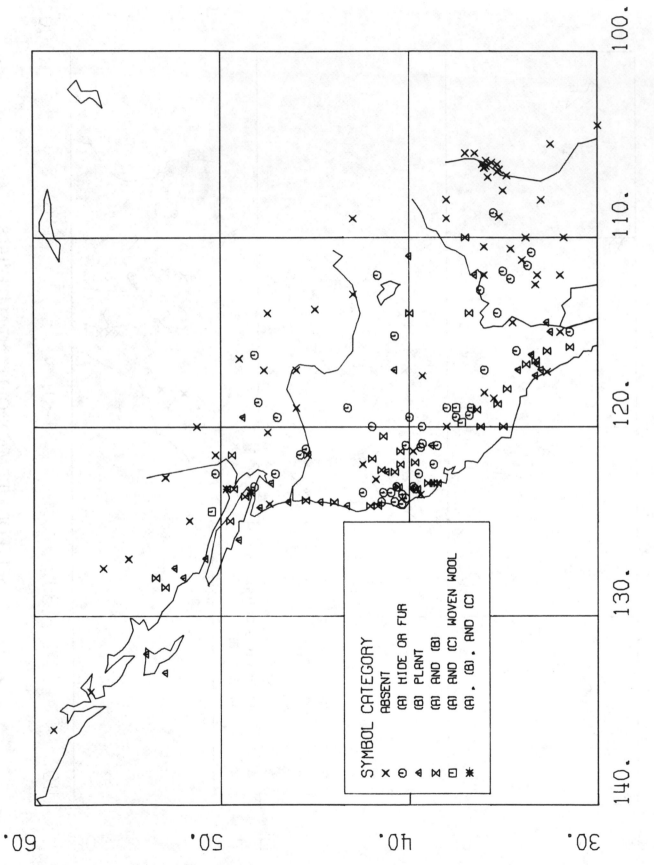

APRON MATERIALS

SYMBOL CATEGORY

✕	ABSENT
⊖	(A) HIDE OR FUR
◁	(B) PLANT
⋈	(A) AND (B)
⊟	(A) AND (C) WOVEN WOOL
✳	(A), (B), AND (C)

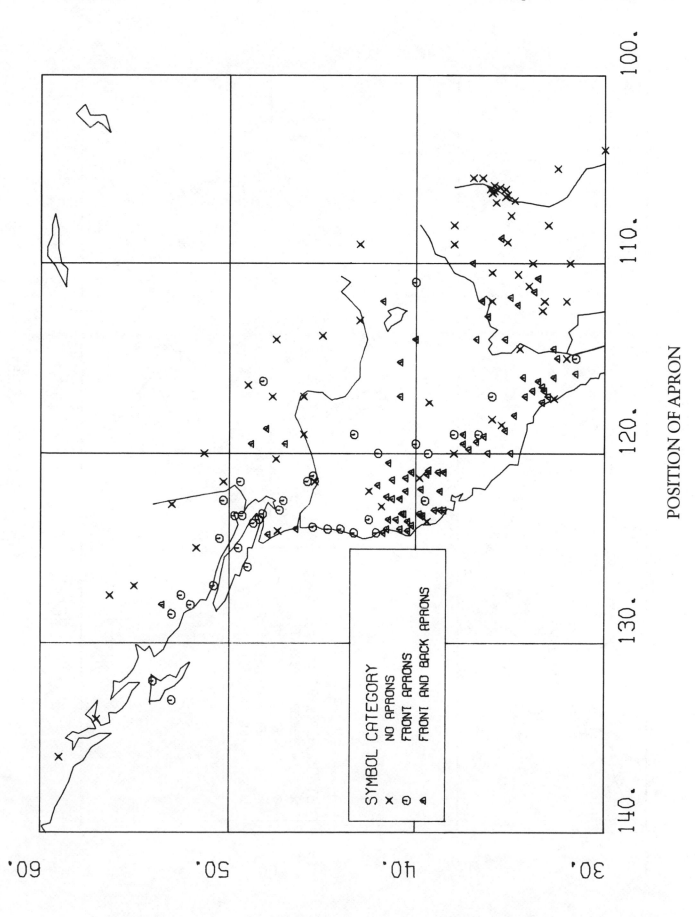

POSITION OF APRON

SYMBOL CATEGORY
× NO APRONS
⊖ FRONT APRONS
◁ FRONT AND BACK APRONS

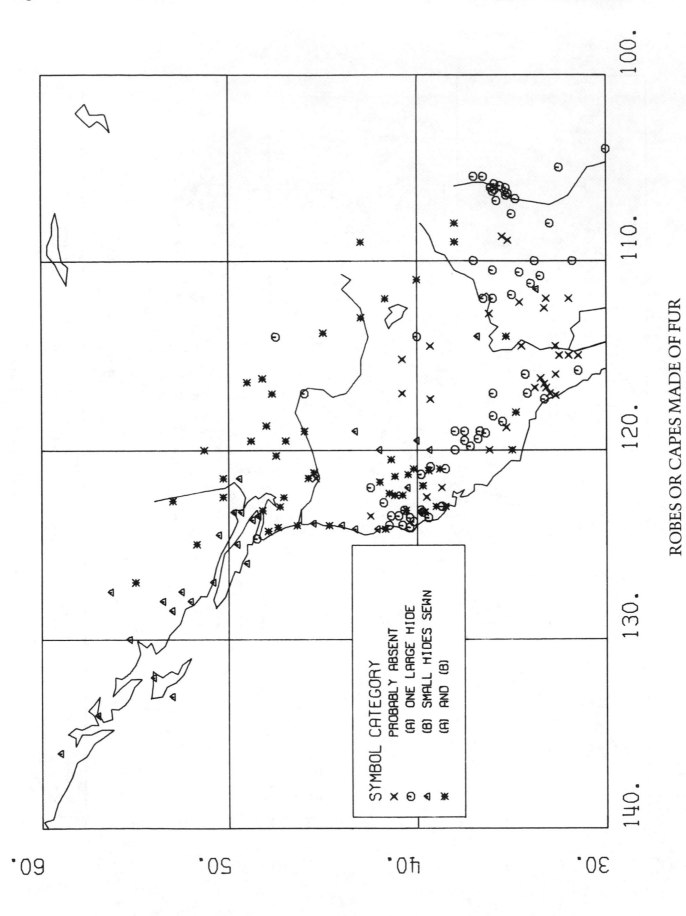

SYMBOL CATEGORY

PROBABLY ABSENT

(A) ONE LARGE HIDE

(B) SMALL HIDES SEWN

(A) AND (B)

× ⊖ ◁ ✳

ROBES OR CAPES MADE OF FUR

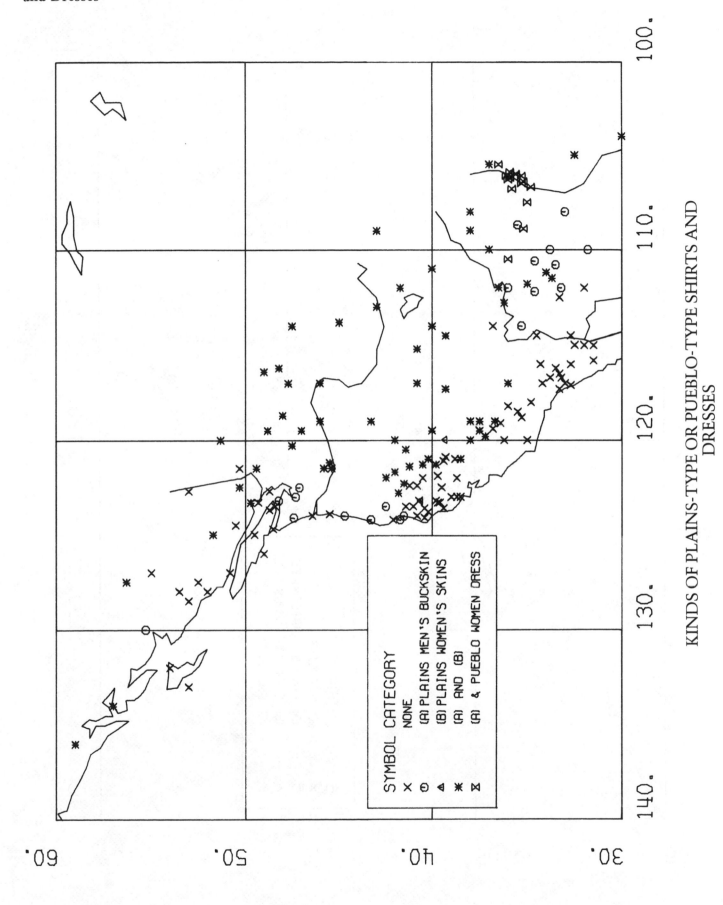

KINDS OF PLAINS-TYPE OR PUEBLO-TYPE SHIRTS AND DRESSES

SYMBOL CATEGORY

X	NONE
⊖	(A) PLAINS MEN'S BUCKSKIN
◁	(B) PLAINS WOMEN'S SKINS
✳	(A) AND (B)
⋈	(A) & PUEBLO WOMEN DRESS

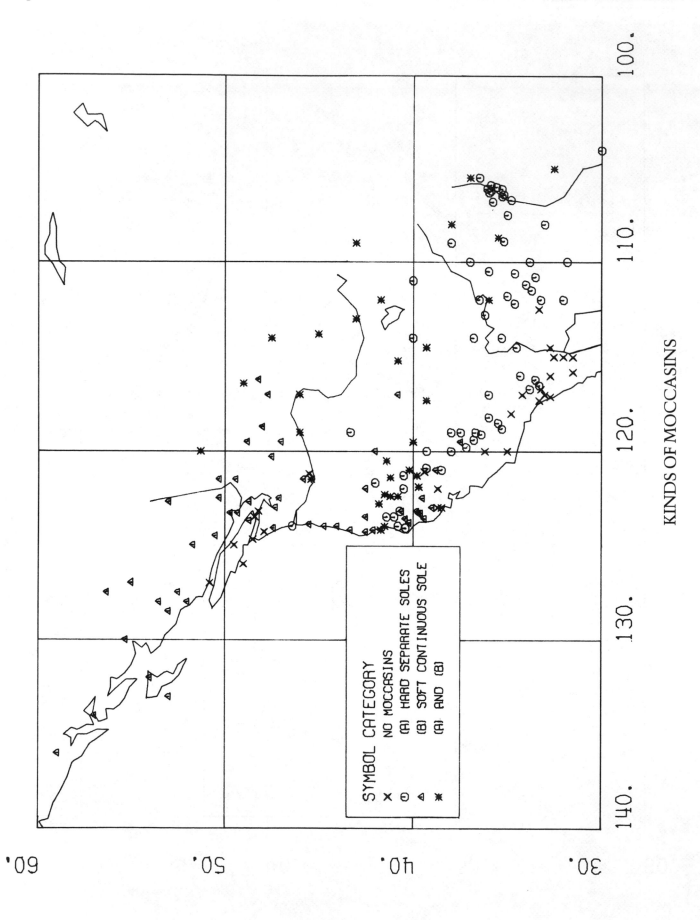

KINDS OF MOCCASINS

SYMBOL CATEGORY

	NO MOCCASINS
X	(A) HARD SEPARATE SOLES
⊖	(B) SOFT CONTINUOUS SOLE
◁	(A) AND (B)
✳	

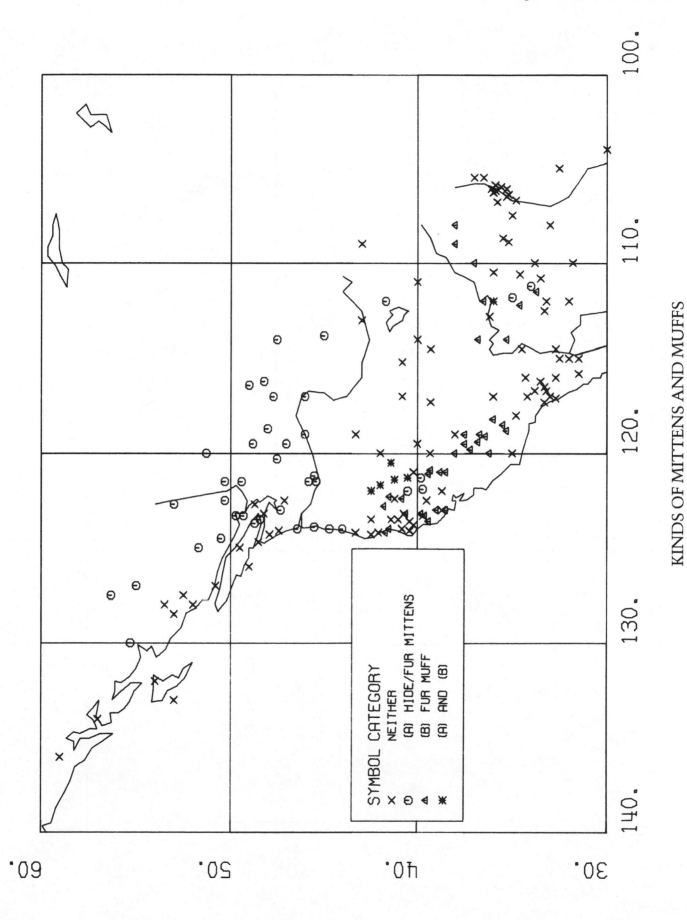

KINDS OF MITTENS AND MUFFS

SYMBOL CATEGORY
NEITHER
(A) HIDE/FUR MITTENS
(B) FUR MUFF
(A) AND (B)

X   ⊖   ◁   ✳

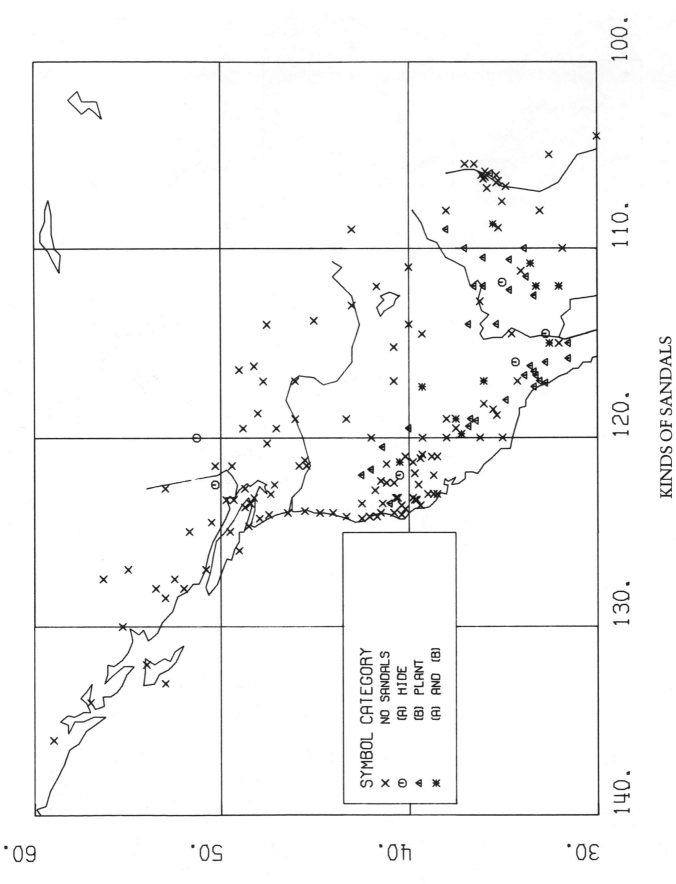

KINDS OF SANDALS

SYMBOL CATEGORY
X   NO SANDALS
⊖   (A) HIDE
◁   (B) PLANT
✳   (A) AND (B)

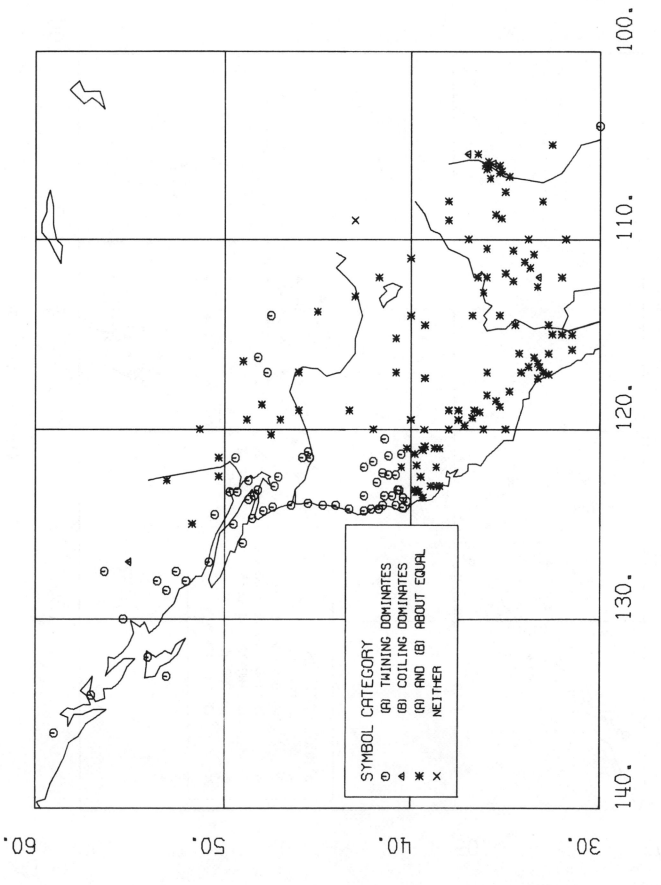

SYMBOL CATEGORY
⊖ (A) TWINING DOMINATES
△ (B) COILING DOMINATES
✳ (A) AND (B) ABOUT EQUAL
✕ NEITHER

TWINING AND COILING BASKETRY WEAVES

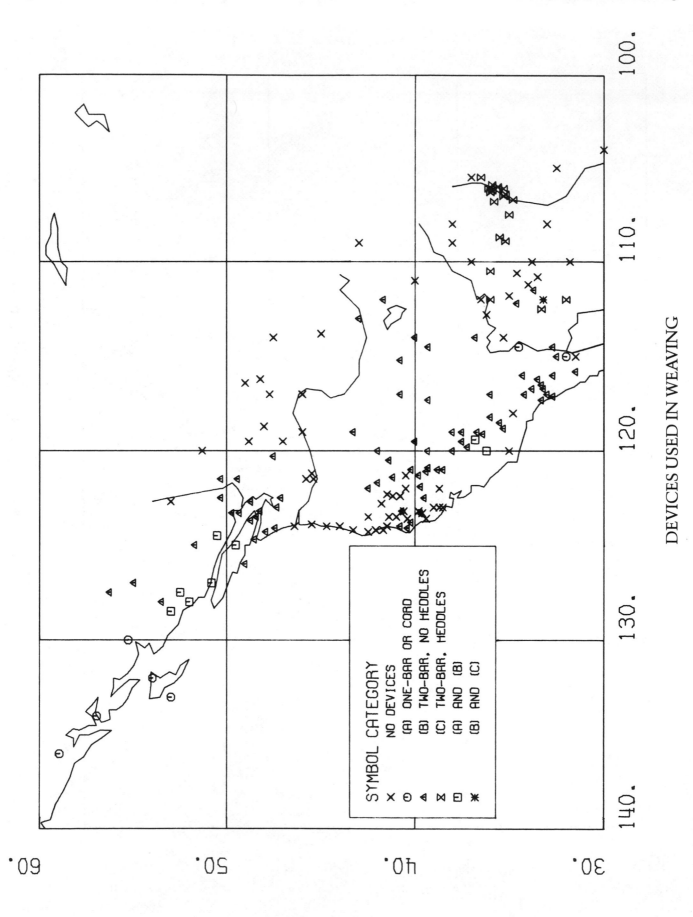

DEVICES USED IN WEAVING

SYMBOL CATEGORY

×	NO DEVICES
⊖	(A) ONE-BAR OR CORD
◁	(B) TWO-BAR, NO HEDDLES
⋈	(C) TWO-BAR, HEDDLES
⊟	(A) AND (B)
✳	(B) AND (C)

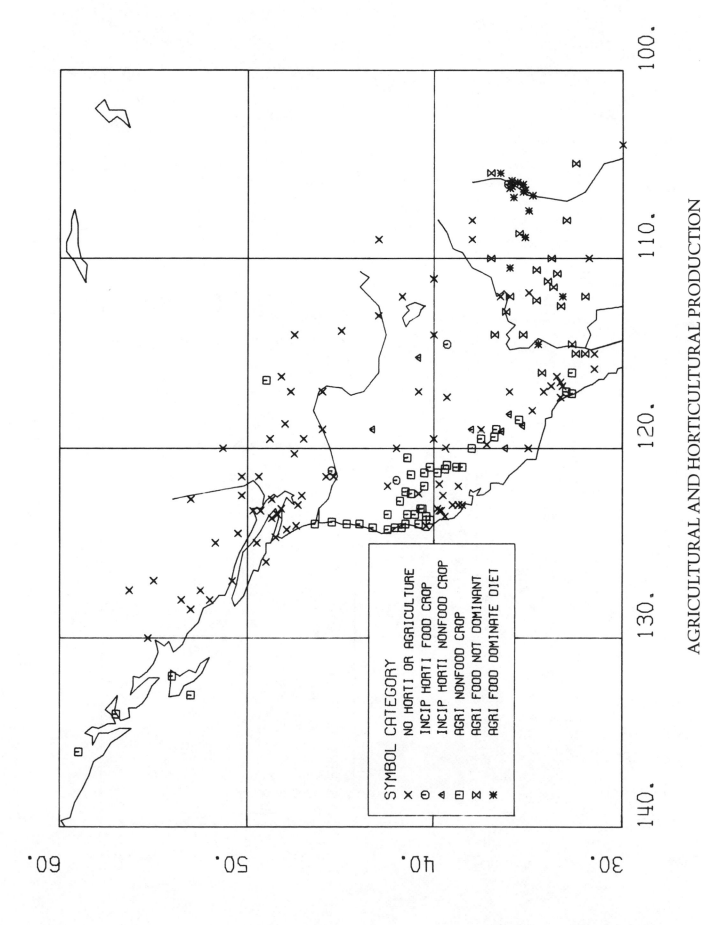

AGRICULTURAL AND HORTICULTURAL PRODUCTION

SYMBOL CATEGORY
X   NO HORTI OR AGRICULTURE
⊙   INCIP HORTI FOOD CROP
◁   INCIP HORTI NONFOOD CROP
⊟   AGRI NONFOOD CROP
⋈   AGRI FOOD NOT DOMINANT
✳   AGRI FOOD DOMINATE DIET

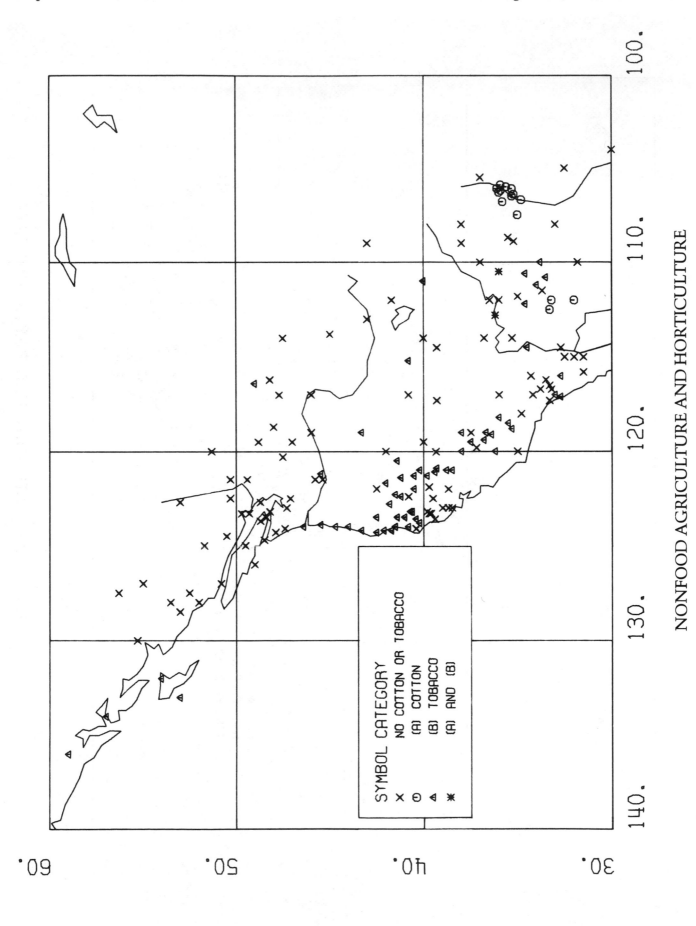

NONFOOD AGRICULTURE AND HORTICULTURE

SYMBOL CATEGORY
NO COTTON OR TOBACCO
(A) COTTON
(B) TOBACCO
(A) AND (B)

X   ⊖   ◁   ✳

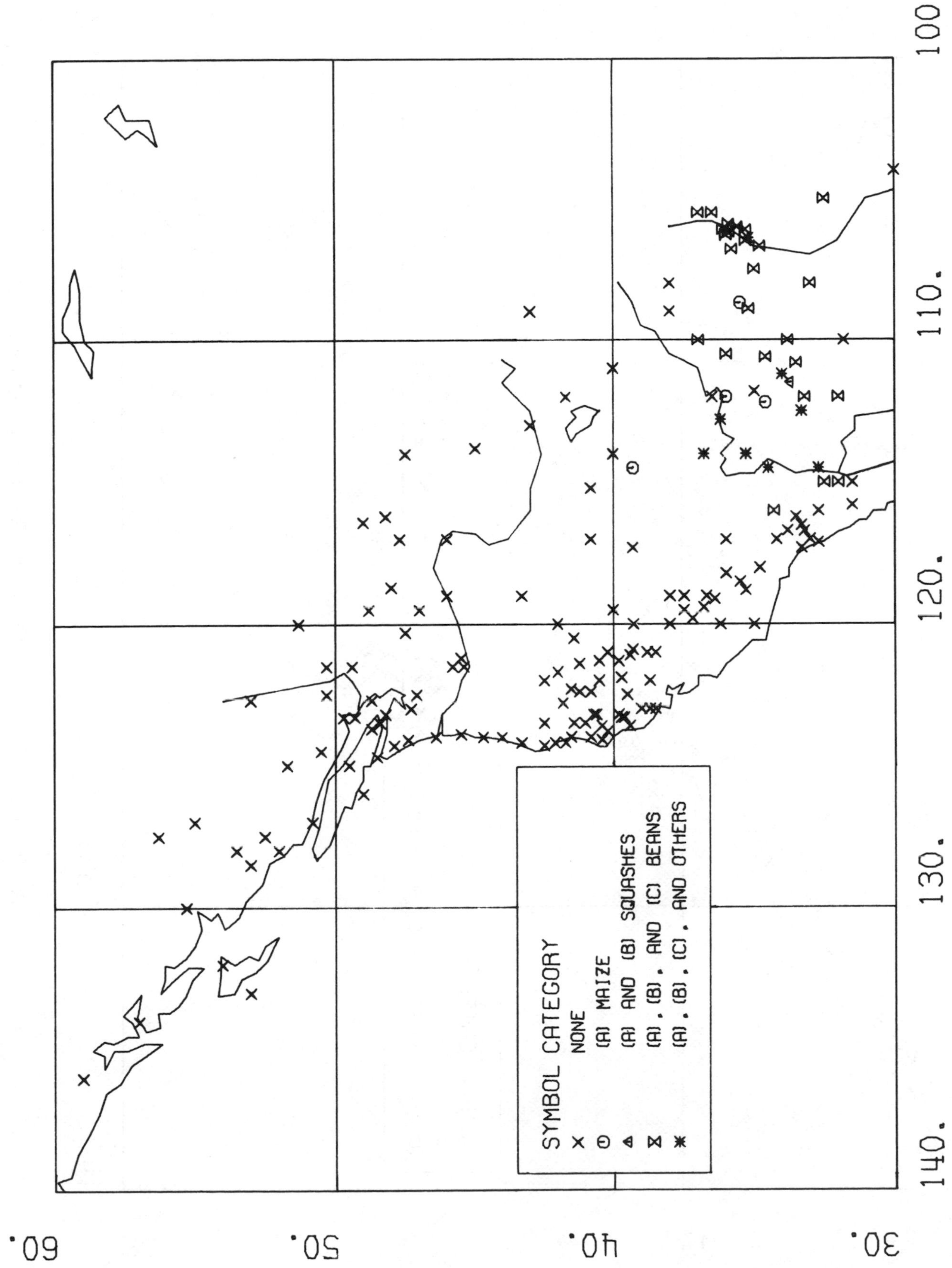

FOOD PRODUCTS GROWN

SYMBOL CATEGORY
×   NONE
⊖   (A) MAIZE
◁   (A) AND (B) SQUASHES
⋈   (A), (B), AND (C) BEANS
✳   (A), (B), (C), AND OTHERS

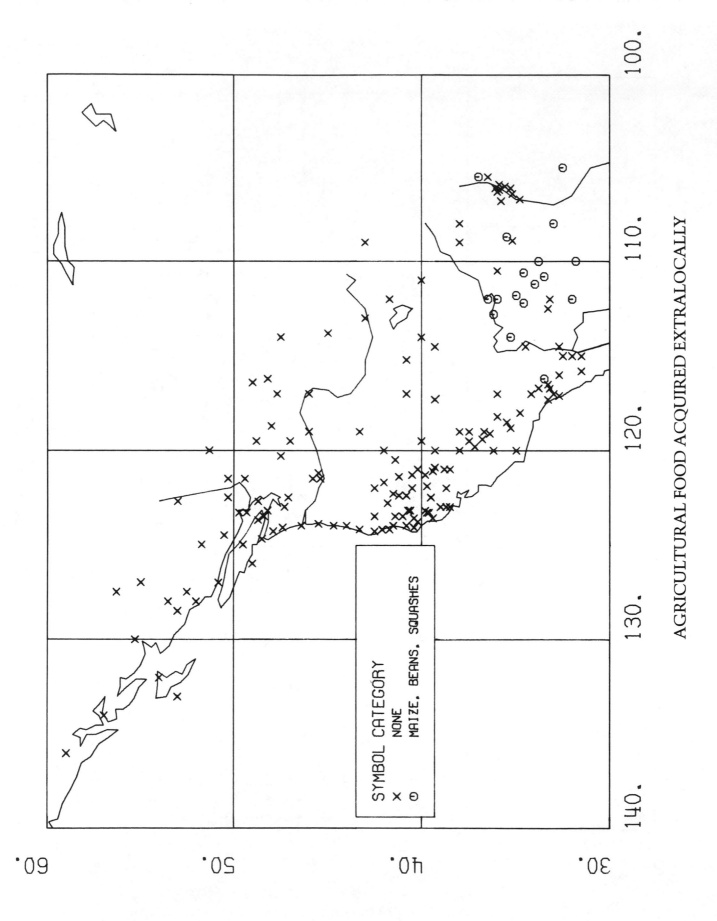

AGRICULTURAL FOOD ACQUIRED EXTRALOCALLY

SYMBOL CATEGORY
X   NONE
Ө   MAIZE, BEANS, SQUASHES

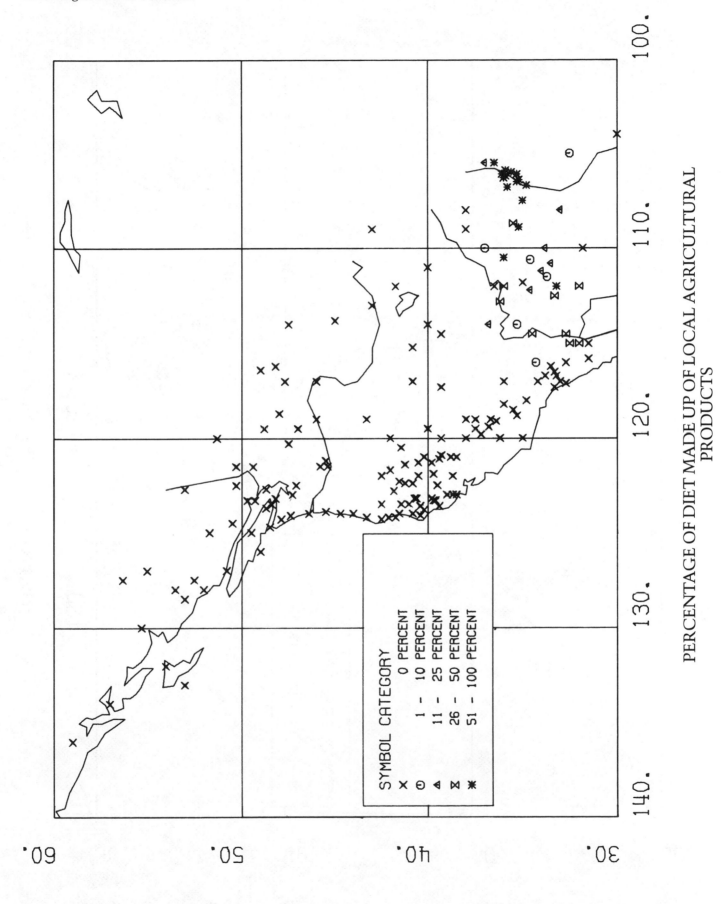

PERCENTAGE OF DIET MADE UP OF LOCAL AGRICULTURAL PRODUCTS

SYMBOL CATEGORY

X	0 PERCENT
Θ	1 – 10 PERCENT
◁	11 – 25 PERCENT
⋈	26 – 50 PERCENT
✳	51 – 100 PERCENT

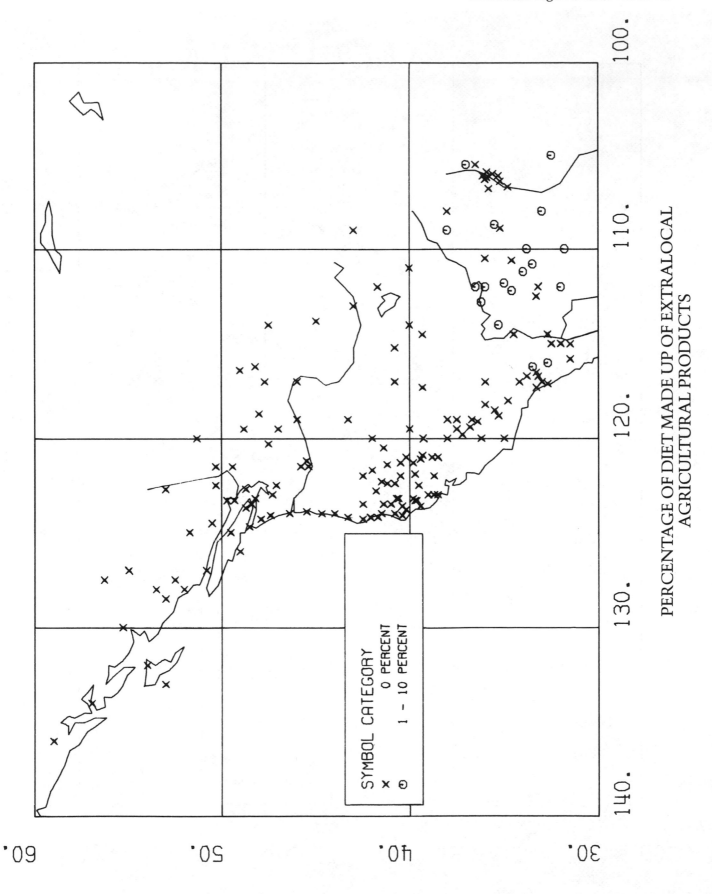

SYMBOL CATEGORY
×   0 PERCENT
⊖   1 - 10 PERCENT

PERCENTAGE OF DIET MADE UP OF EXTRALOCAL
AGRICULTURAL PRODUCTS

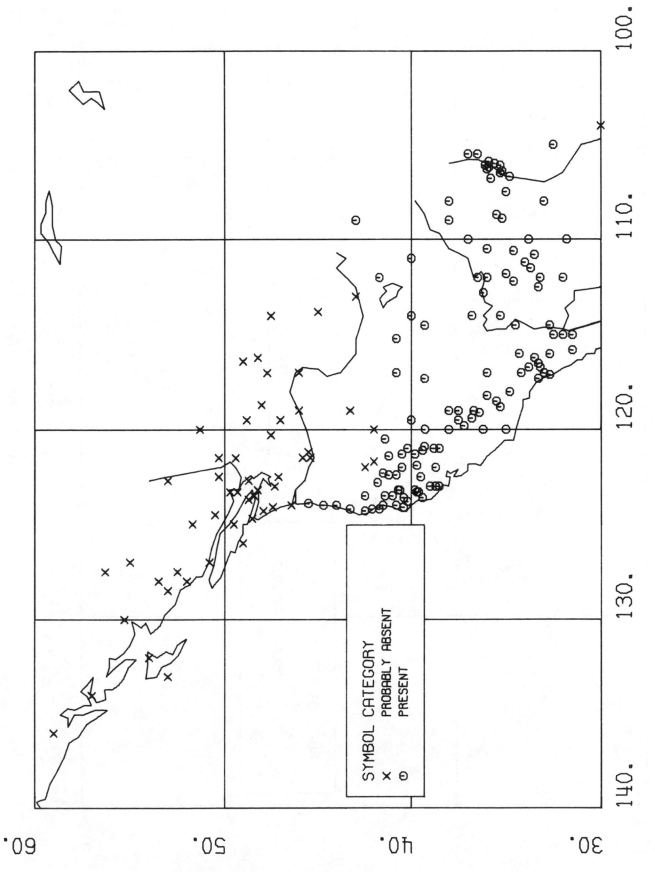

SALT ADDED TO FOOD

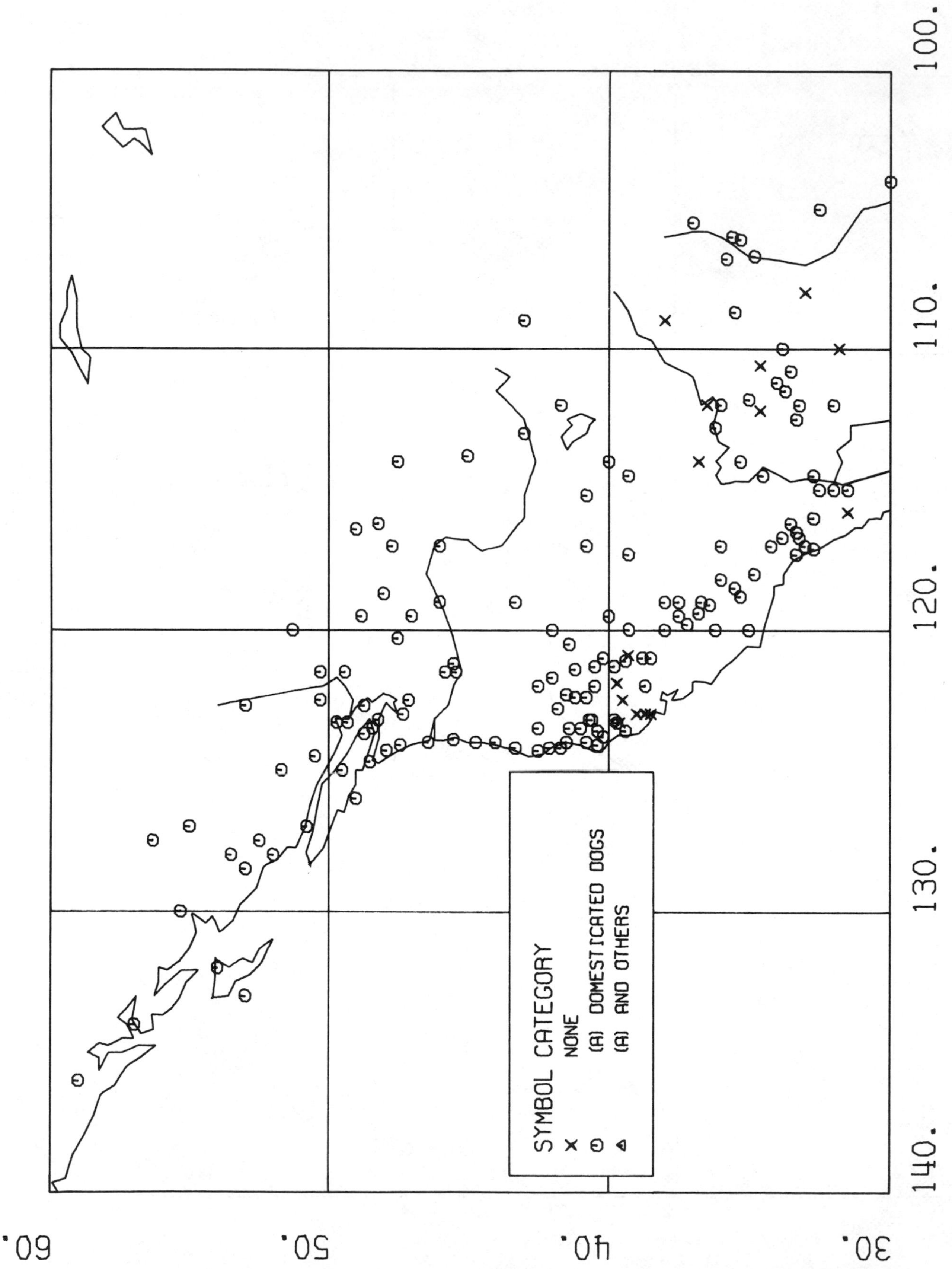

SYMBOL CATEGORY
× NONE
ʘ (A) DOMESTICATED DOGS
△ (A) AND OTHERS
100.
110.
120.
130.
140.
60.
50.
40.
30.

ANIMAL HUSBANDRY

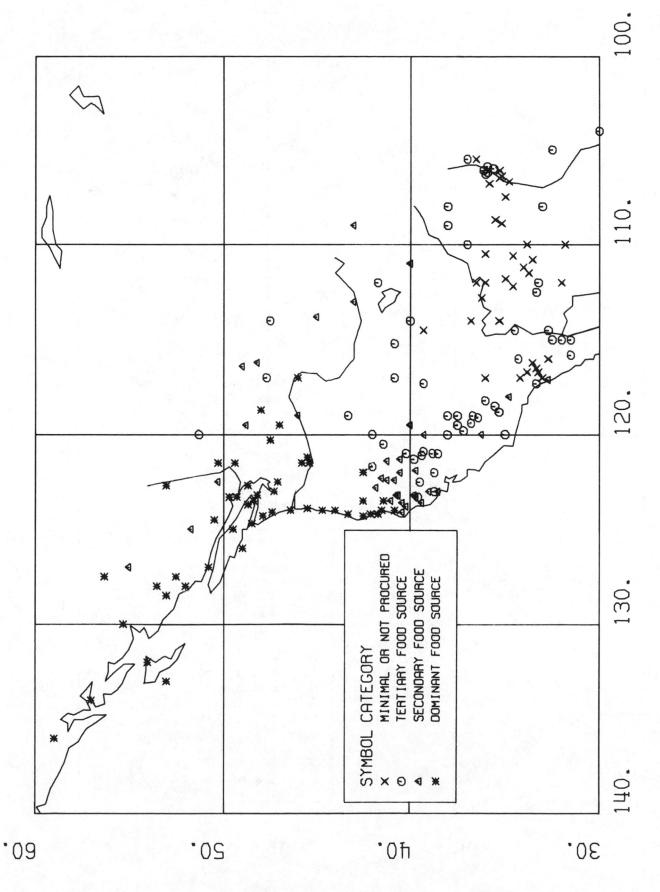

AQUATIC ANIMAL CONTRIBUTION TO DIET

SYMBOL CATEGORY
X   MINIMAL OR NOT PROCURED
⊖   TERTIARY FOOD SOURCE
◁   SECONDARY FOOD SOURCE
✳   DOMINANT FOOD SOURCE

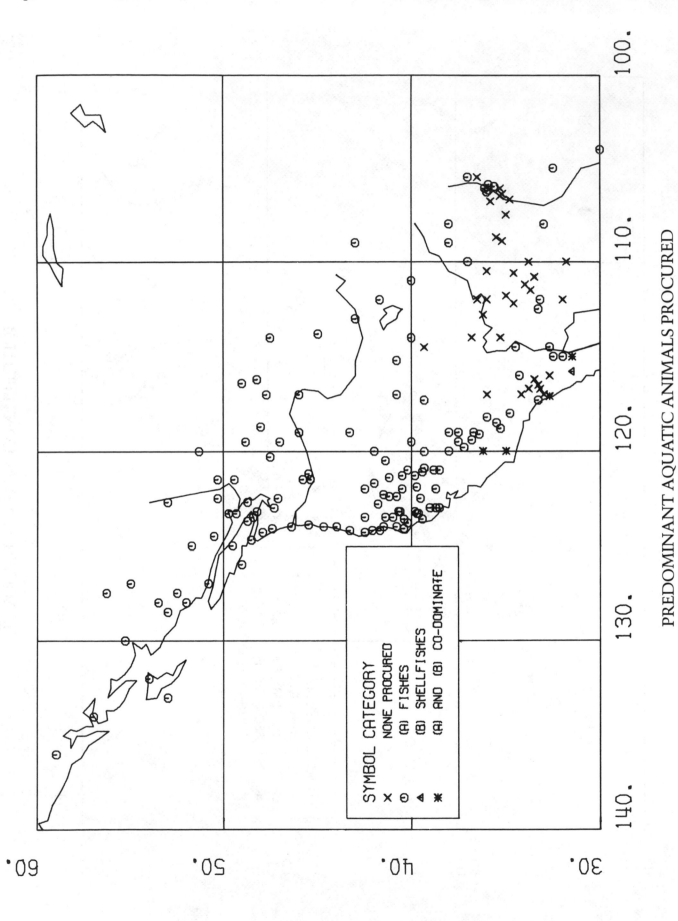

PREDOMINANT AQUATIC ANIMALS PROCURED

SYMBOL CATEGORY

X	NONE PROCURED
⊖	(A) FISHES
◄	(B) SHELLFISHES
✳	(A) AND (B) CO-DOMINATE

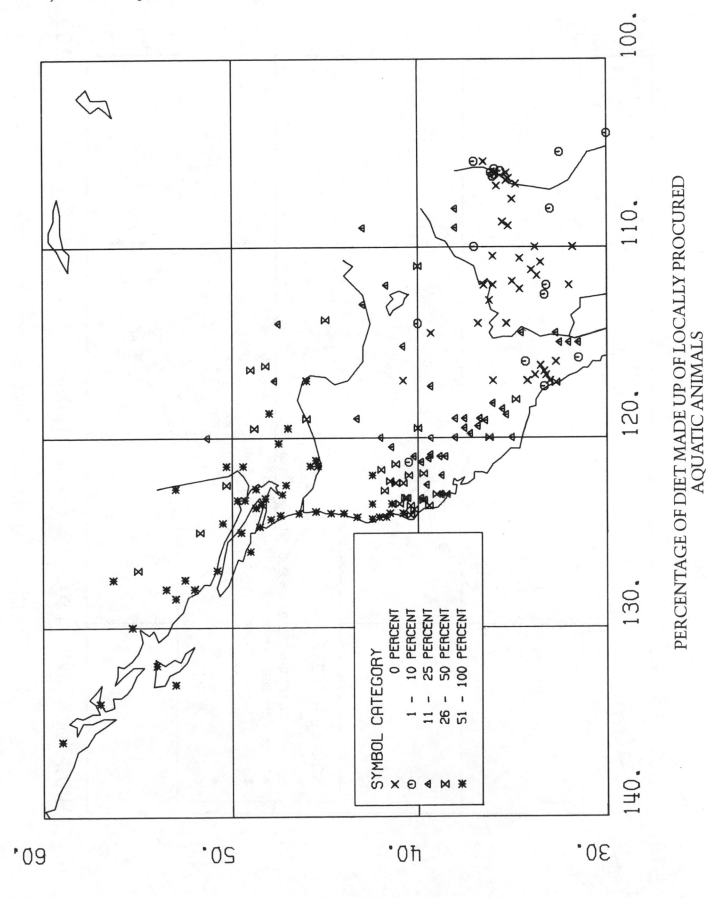

PERCENTAGE OF DIET MADE UP OF LOCALLY PROCURED
AQUATIC ANIMALS

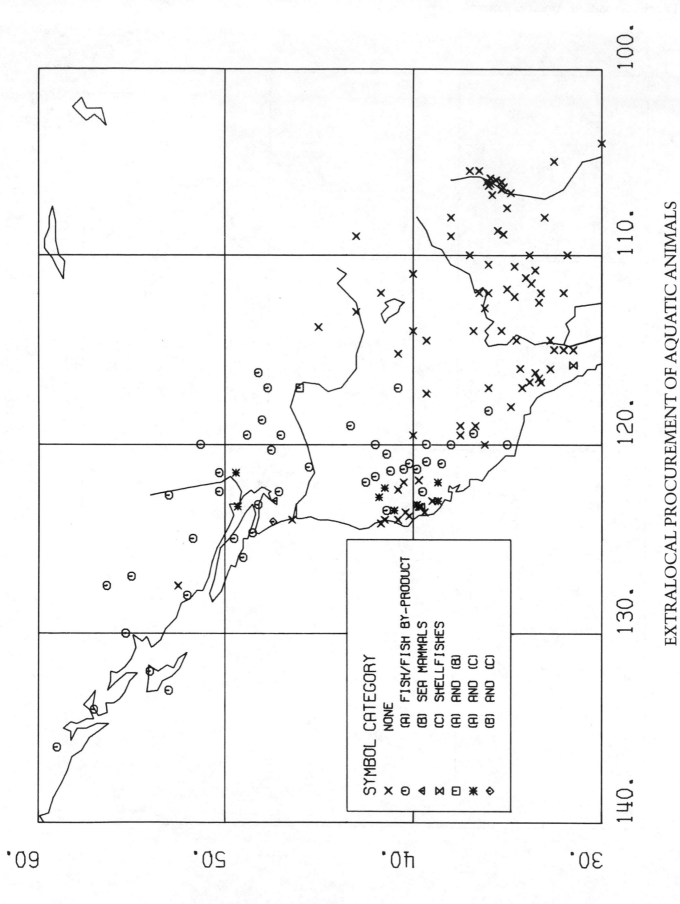

SYMBOL CATEGORY
NONE
X   (A) FISH/FISH BY-PRODUCT
⊖   (B) SEA MAMMALS
◁   (C) SHELLFISHES
⋈   (A) AND (B)
⊟   (A) AND (C)
✳   (B) AND (C)
◇

EXTRALOCAL PROCUREMENT OF AQUATIC ANIMALS

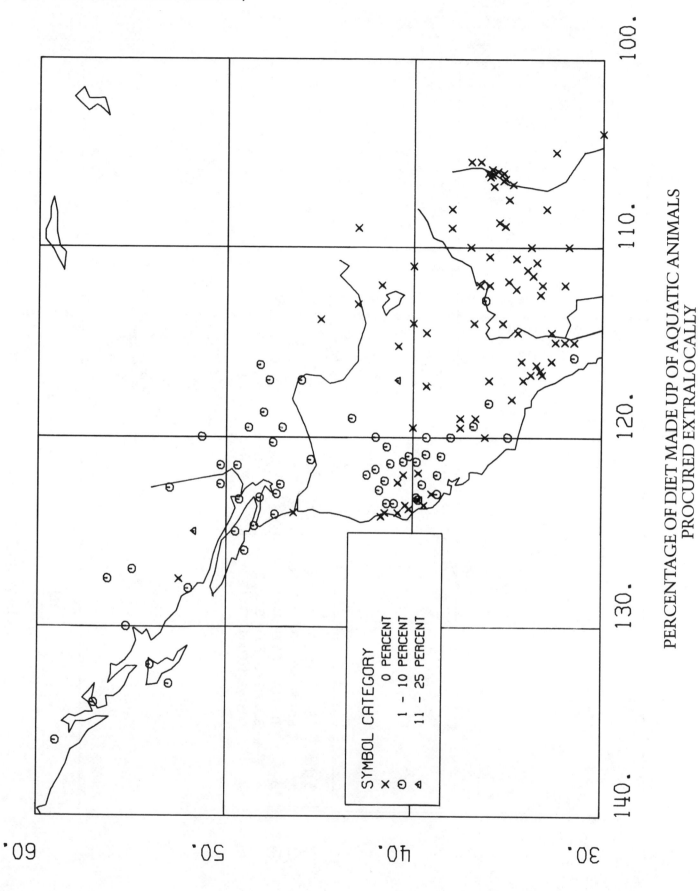

SYMBOL CATEGORY

X   0 PERCENT
⊖   1 - 10 PERCENT
◁   11 - 25 PERCENT

PERCENTAGE OF DIET MADE UP OF AQUATIC ANIMALS
PROCURED EXTRALOCALLY

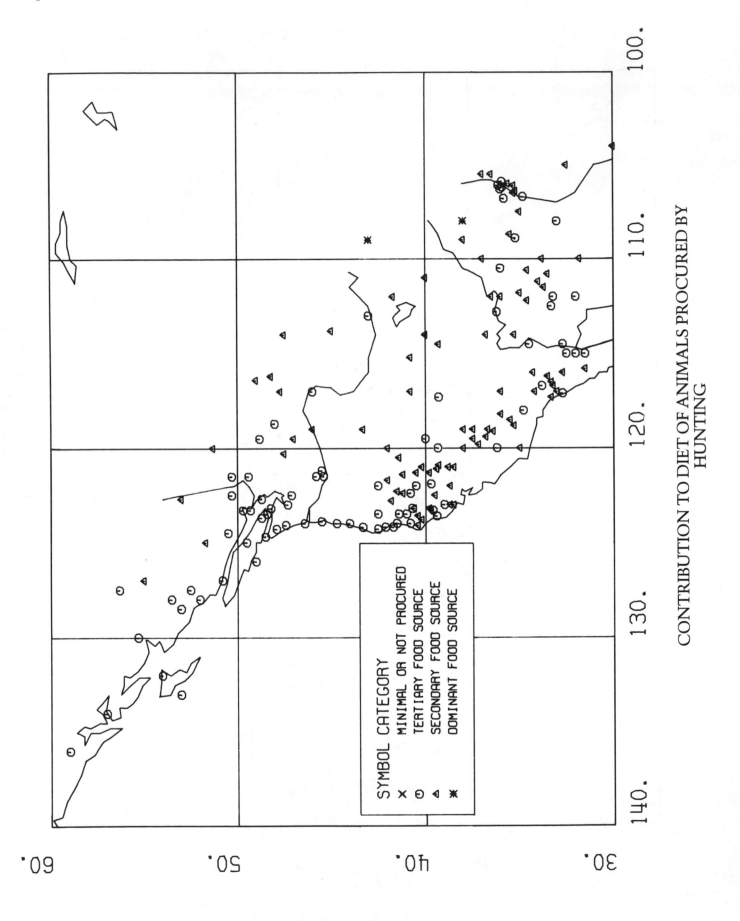

CONTRIBUTION TO DIET OF ANIMALS PROCURED BY HUNTING

SYMBOL CATEGORY

X   MINIMAL OR NOT PROCURED

⊖   TERTIARY FOOD SOURCE

◁   SECONDARY FOOD SOURCE

✳   DOMINANT FOOD SOURCE

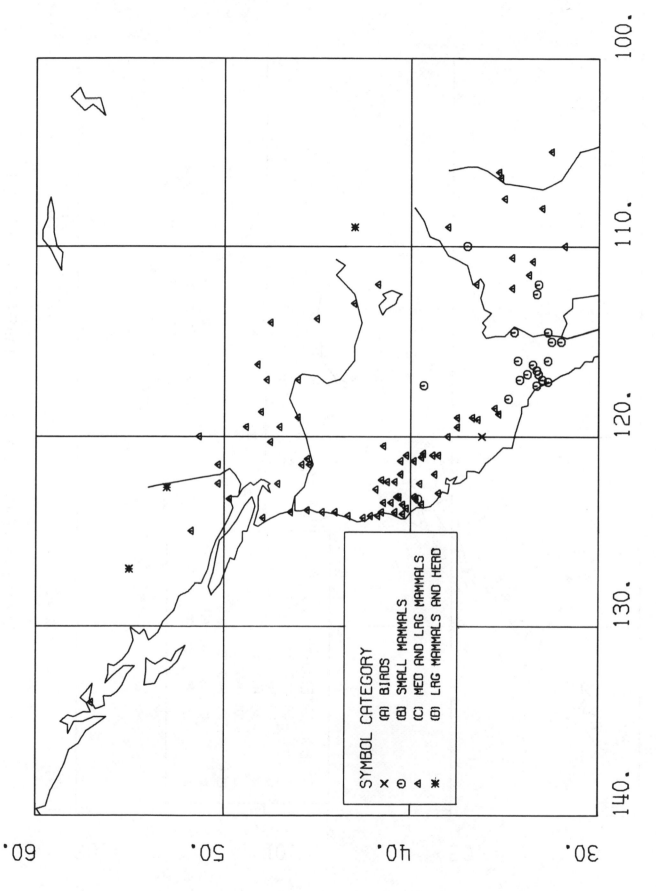

PREDOMINANT BIRDS AND LAND MAMMALS HUNTED, A

SYMBOL CATEGORY
X   (A) BIRDS
⊖   (B) SMALL MAMMALS
◁   (C) MED AND LRG MAMMALS
✳   (D) LRG MAMMALS AND HERD

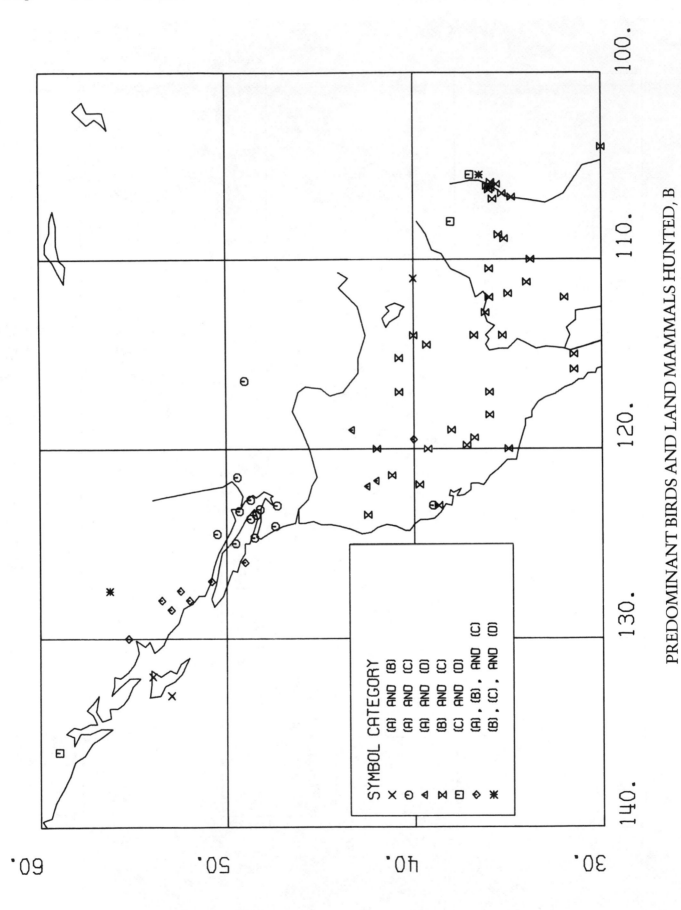

PREDOMINANT BIRDS AND LAND MAMMALS HUNTED, B

SYMBOL CATEGORY

Symbol	Category
X	(A) AND (B)
⊖	(A) AND (C)
◁	(A) AND (D)
⋈	(B) AND (C)
⊟	(C) AND (D)
◇	(A), (B), AND (C)
✳	(B), (C), AND (D)

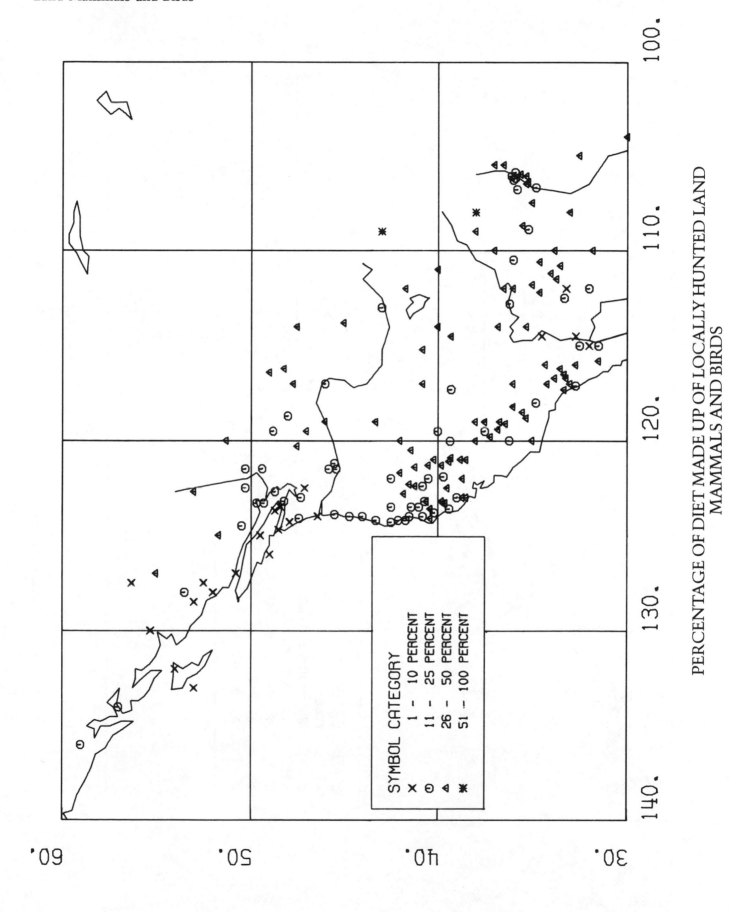

PERCENTAGE OF DIET MADE UP OF LOCALLY HUNTED LAND
MAMMALS AND BIRDS

SYMBOL CATEGORY

X	1 – 10 PERCENT
Θ	11 – 25 PERCENT
◁	26 – 50 PERCENT
✳	51 – 100 PERCENT

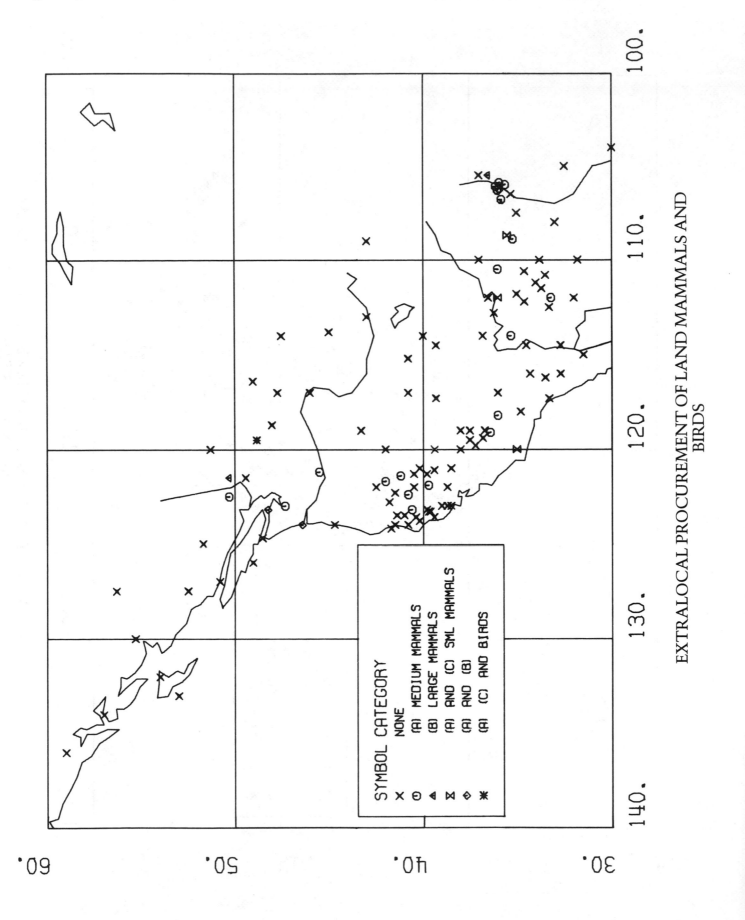

EXTRALOCAL PROCUREMENT OF LAND MAMMALS AND BIRDS

SYMBOL CATEGORY
NONE
(A) MEDIUM MAMMALS
(B) LARGE MAMMALS
(A) AND (C) SML MAMMALS
(A) AND (B)
(A) (C) AND BIRDS

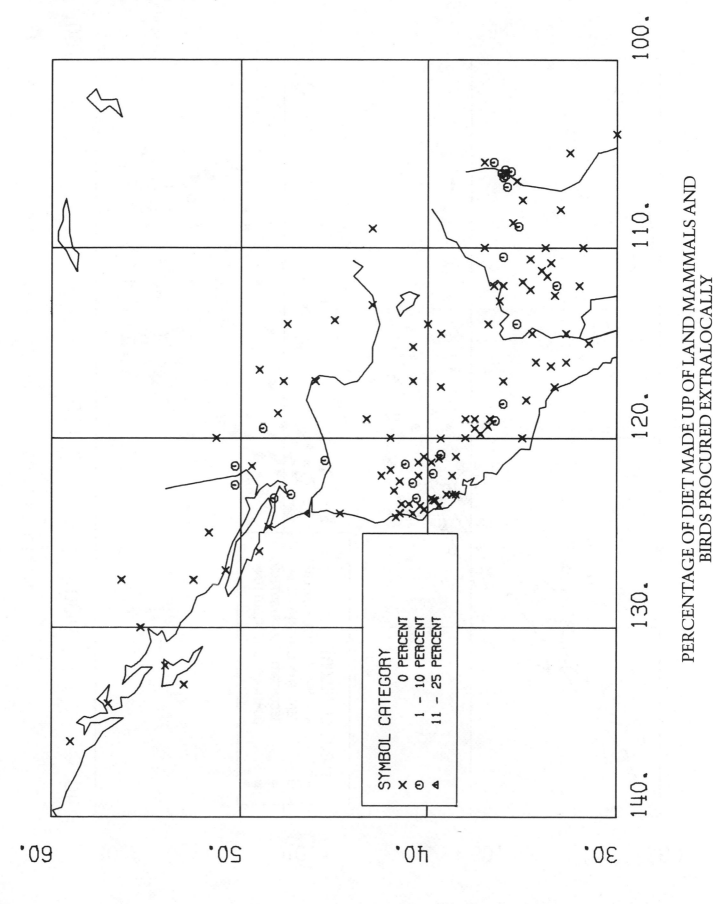

SYMBOL CATEGORY
X   0 PERCENT
⊖   1 - 10 PERCENT
▲   11 - 25 PERCENT

PERCENTAGE OF DIET MADE UP OF LAND MAMMALS AND
BIRDS PROCURED EXTRALOCALLY

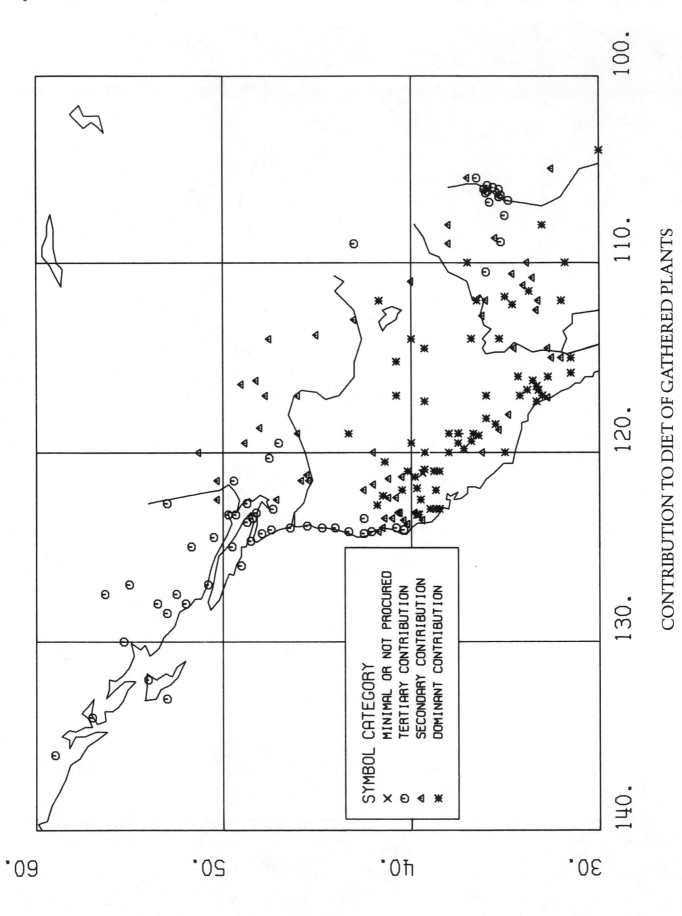

CONTRIBUTION TO DIET OF GATHERED PLANTS

SYMBOL CATEGORY
X   MINIMAL OR NOT PROCURED
⊖   TERTIARY CONTRIBUTION
◁   SECONDARY CONTRIBUTION
✳   DOMINANT CONTRIBUTION

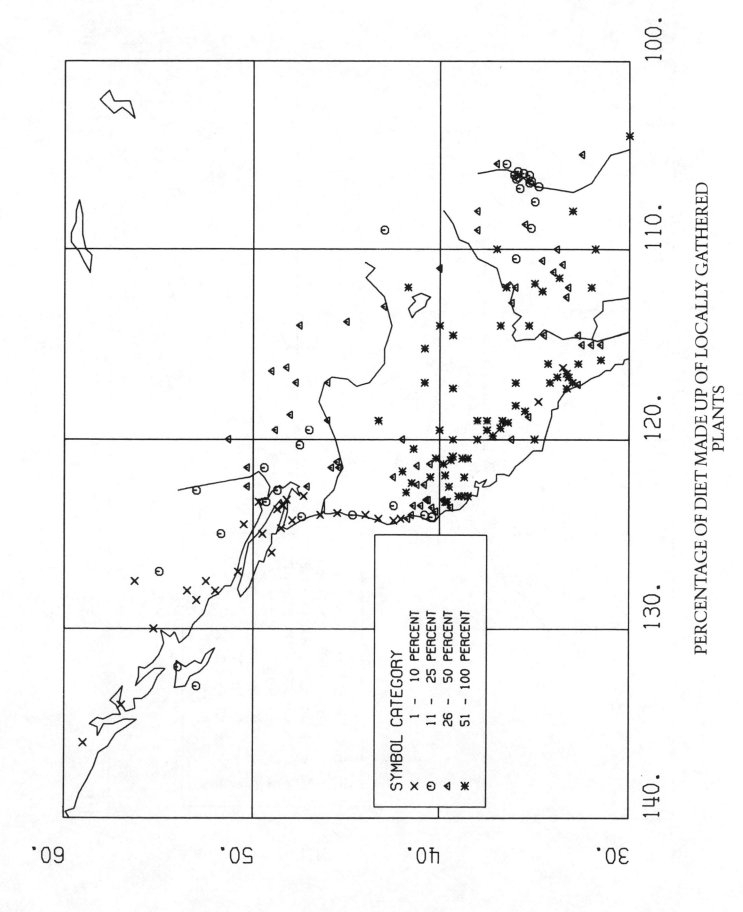

PERCENTAGE OF DIET MADE UP OF LOCALLY GATHERED PLANTS

SYMBOL CATEGORY

✕	1 – 10 PERCENT
⊖	11 – 25 PERCENT
◁	26 – 50 PERCENT
✳	51 – 100 PERCENT

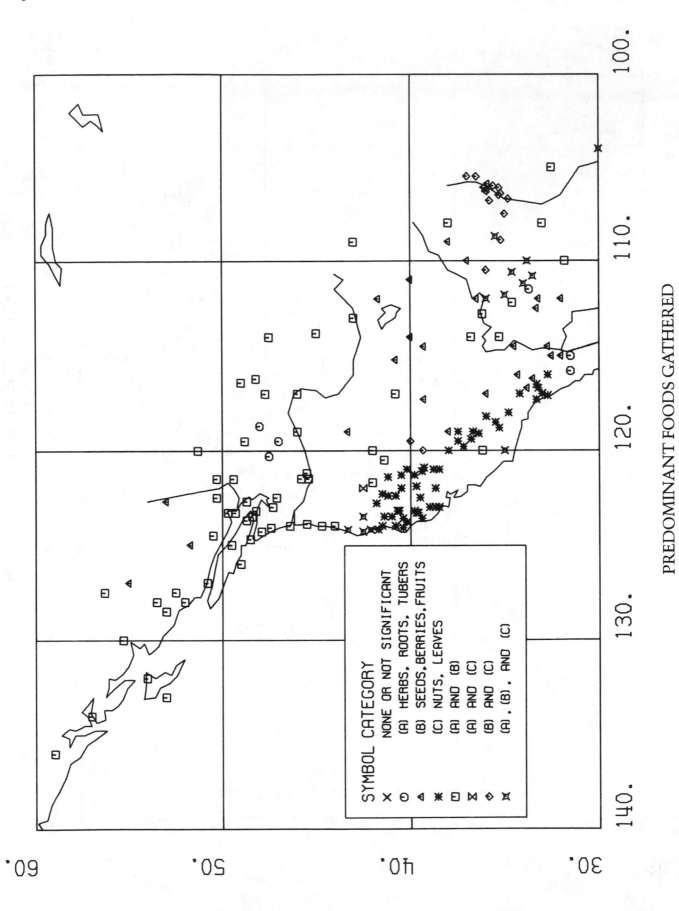

PREDOMINANT FOODS GATHERED

SYMBOL CATEGORY

NONE OR NOT SIGNIFICANT
(A) HERBS, ROOTS, TUBERS
(B) SEEDS, BERRIES, FRUITS
(C) NUTS, LEAVES
(A) AND (B)
(A) AND (C)
(B) AND (C)
(A), (B), AND (C)

X ⊖ ◁ ✳ ⊟ ⋈ ◇ ⋈

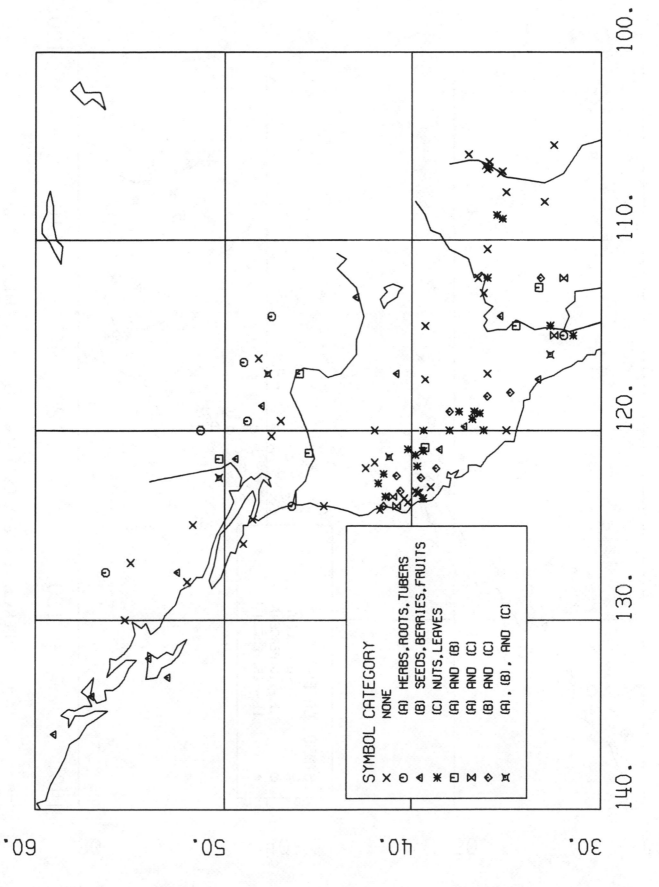

SYMBOL CATEGORY
NONE
×   (A) HERBS,ROOTS,TUBERS
⊙   (B) SEEDS,BERRIES,FRUITS
◁   (C) NUTS,LEAVES
✳   (A) AND (B)
⊟   (A) AND (C)
⋈   (B) AND (C)
◇   (A),(B), AND (C)
⋉

EXTRALOCAL PROCUREMENT OF GATHERED PLANTS

Percentage of Diet Made Up of Gathered Plants
Procured Extralocally

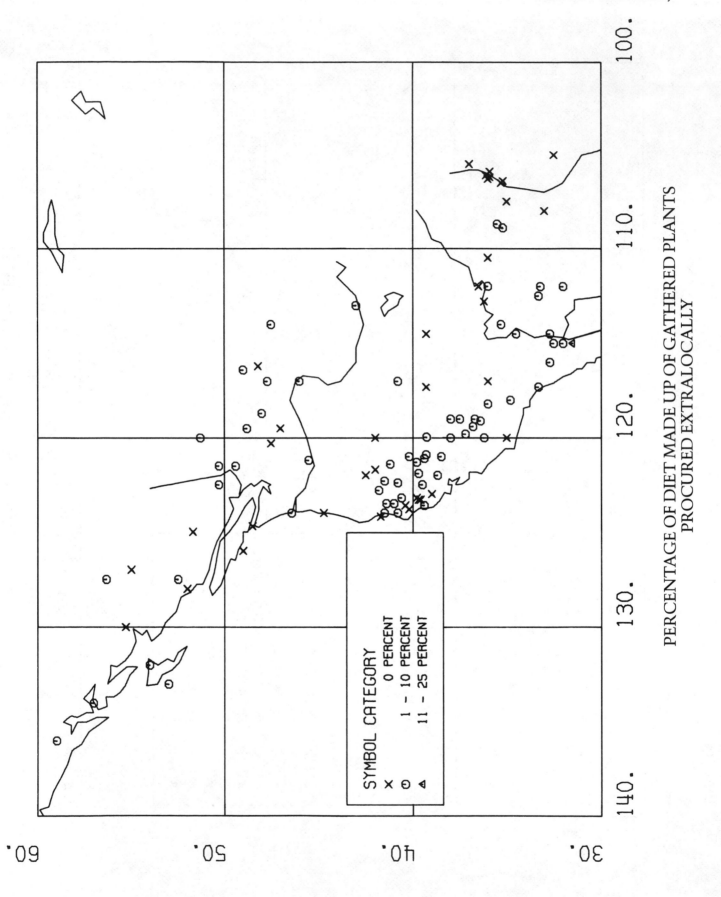

PERCENTAGE OF DIET MADE UP OF GATHERED PLANTS
PROCURED EXTRALOCALLY

SYMBOL CATEGORY

×	0 PERCENT
⊖	1 - 10 PERCENT
◢	11 - 25 PERCENT

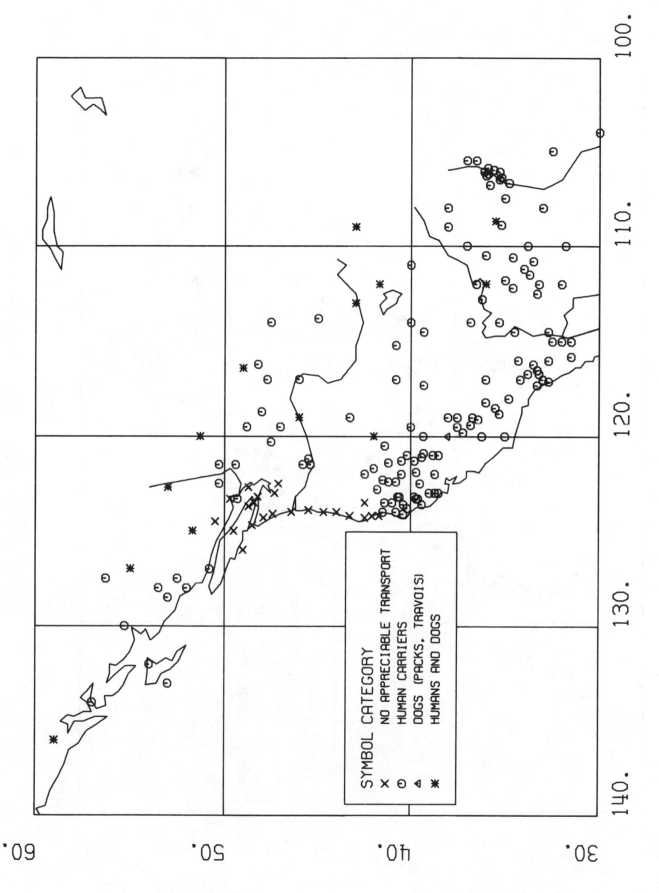

DOMINANT LAND TRANSPORT OF GOODS

SYMBOL CATEGORY
X   NO APPRECIABLE TRANSPORT
⊖   HUMAN CARRIERS
◁   DOGS (PACKS, TRAVOIS)
✳   HUMANS AND DOGS

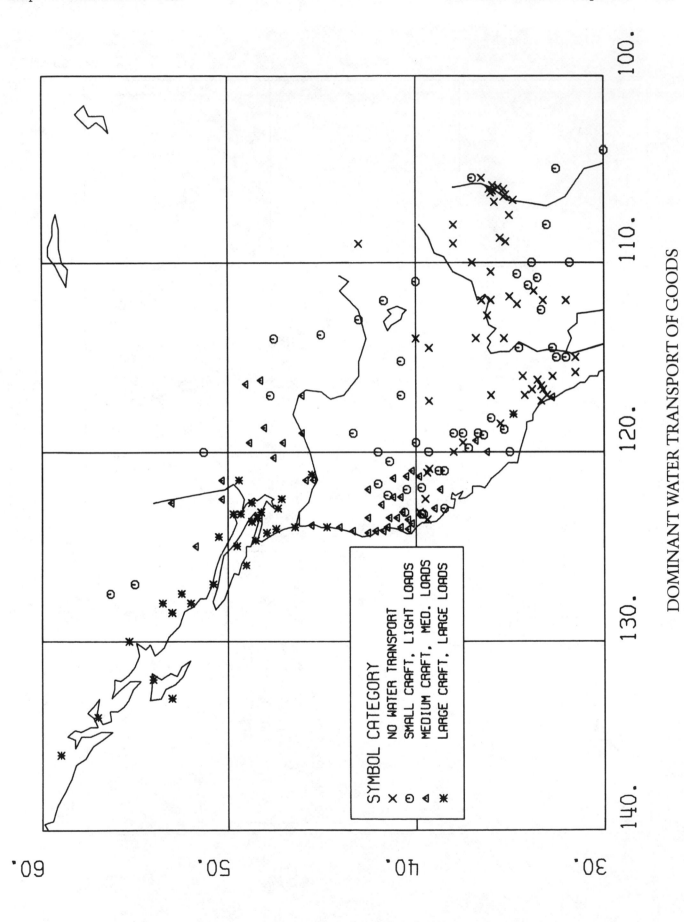

DOMINANT WATER TRANSPORT OF GOODS

SYMBOL CATEGORY
NO WATER TRANSPORT
SMALL CRAFT, LIGHT LOADS
MEDIUM CRAFT, MED. LOADS
LARGE CRAFT, LARGE LOADS

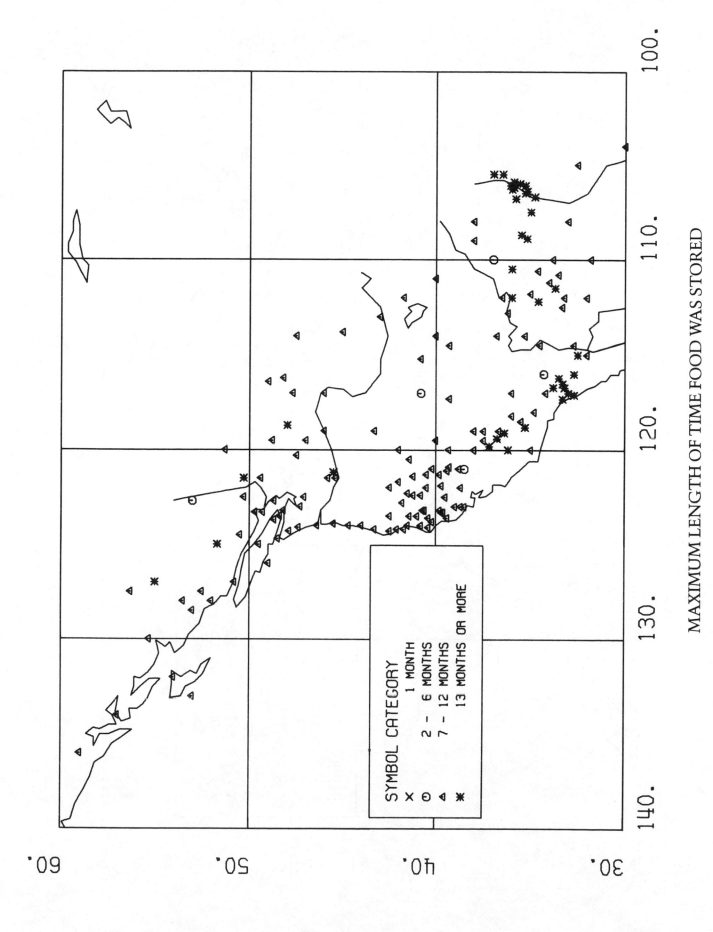

MAXIMUM LENGTH OF TIME FOOD WAS STORED

SYMBOL CATEGORY
X   1 MONTH
⊖   2 – 6 MONTHS
◁   7 – 12 MONTHS
✳   13 MONTHS OR MORE

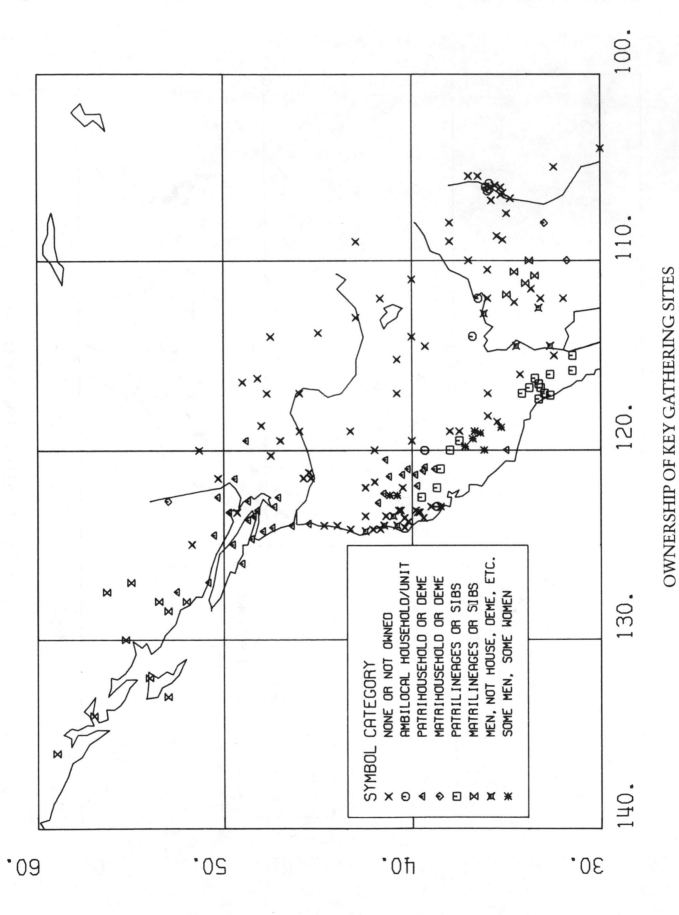

OWNERSHIP OF KEY GATHERING SITES

SYMBOL CATEGORY

✕   NONE OR NOT OWNED
⊖   AMBILOCAL HOUSEHOLD/UNIT
◁   PATRIHOUSEHOLD OR DEME
◇   MATRIHOUSEHOLD OR DEME
⊟   PATRILINEAGES OR SIBS
⋈   MATRILINEAGES OR SIBS
⋉   MEN, NOT HOUSE, DEME, ETC.
✳   SOME MEN, SOME WOMEN

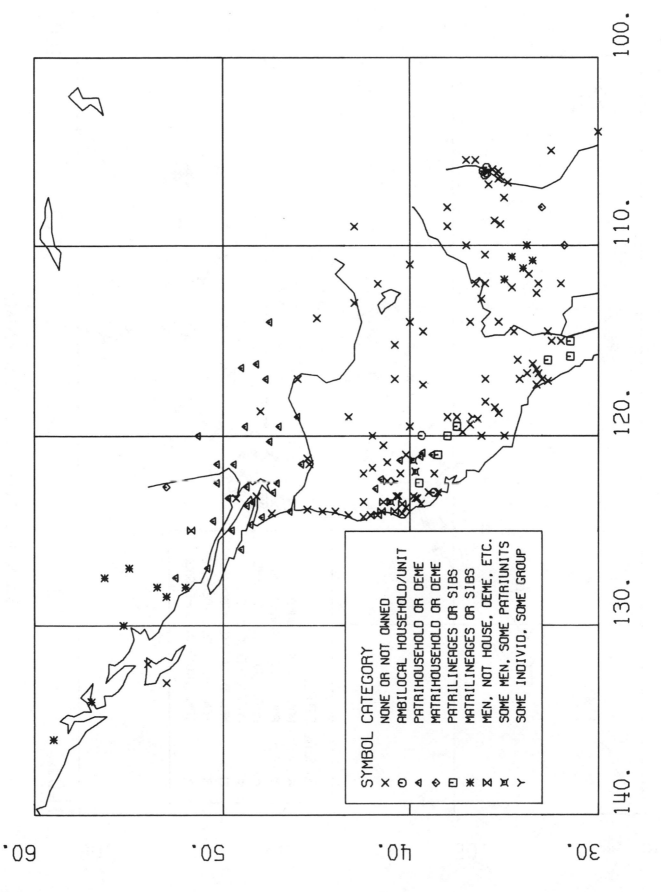

OWNERSHIP OF KEY HUNTING SITES

SYMBOL CATEGORY
X   NONE OR NOT OWNED
⊖   AMBILOCAL HOUSEHOLD/UNIT
◁   PATRIHOUSEHOLD OR DEME
◇   MATRIHOUSEHOLD OR DEME
⊟   PATRILINEAGES OR SIBS
✳   MATRILINEAGES OR SIBS
⋈   MEN, NOT HOUSE, DEME, ETC.
⋈   SOME MEN, SOME PATRIUNITS
Y   SOME INDIVID, SOME GROUP

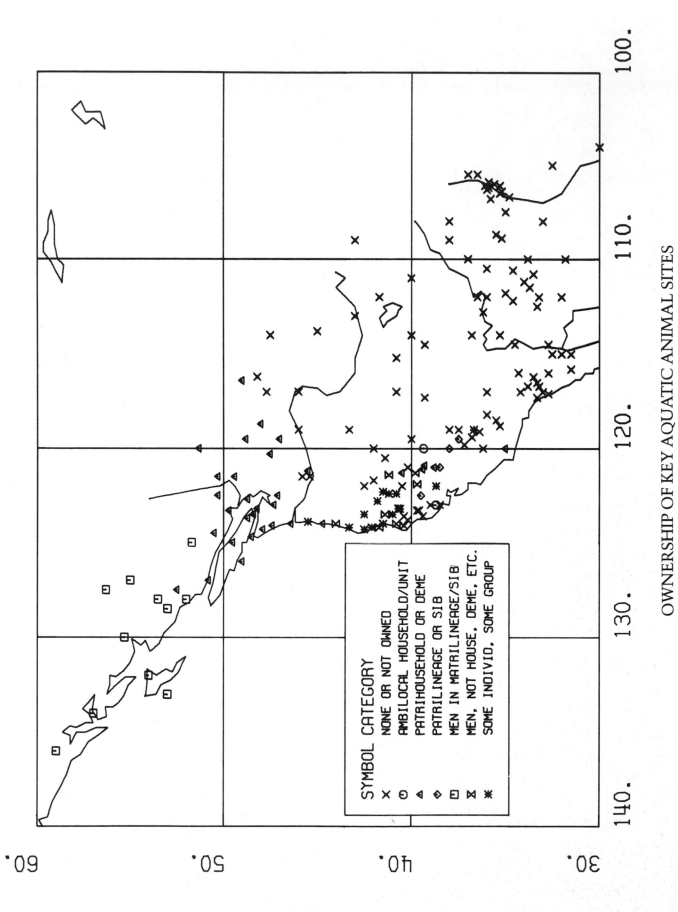

OWNERSHIP OF KEY AQUATIC ANIMAL SITES

SYMBOL CATEGORY
- ✕   NONE OR NOT OWNED
- ⊙   AMBILOCAL HOUSEHOLD/UNIT
- ◁   PATRIHOUSEHOLD OR DEME
- ◇   PATRILINEAGE OR SIB
- ⊟   MEN IN MATRILINEAGE/SIB
- ⋈   MEN, NOT HOUSE, DEME, ETC.
- ✳   SOME INDIVID, SOME GROUP

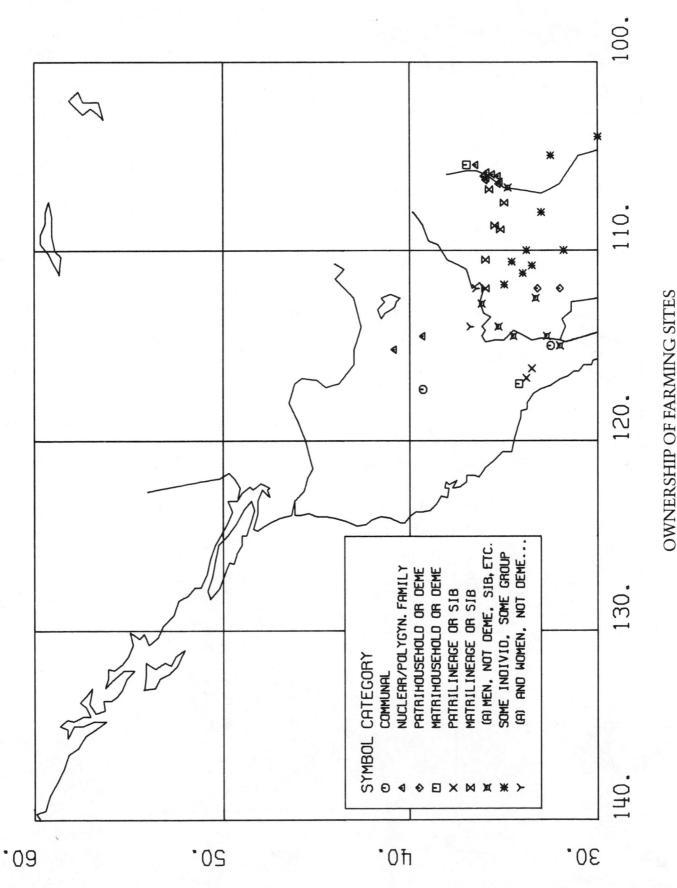

OWNERSHIP OF FARMING SITES

SYMBOL CATEGORY
COMMUNAL
NUCLEAR/POLYGYN. FAMILY
PATRIHOUSEHOLD OR DEME
MATRIHOUSEHOLD OR DEME
PATRILINEAGE OR SIB
MATRILINEAGE OR SIB
(A) MEN, NOT DEME, SIB, ETC.
SOME INDIVID, SOME GROUP
(A) AND WOMEN, NOT DEME...

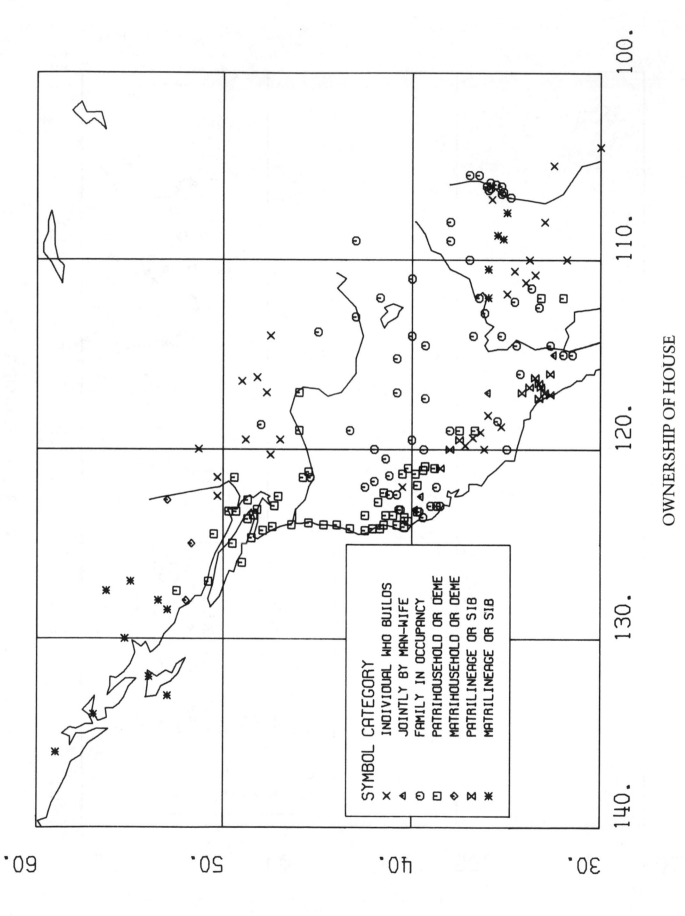

OWNERSHIP OF HOUSE

SYMBOL CATEGORY
INDIVIDUAL WHO BUILDS
JOINTLY BY MAN-WIFE
FAMILY IN OCCUPANCY
PATRIHOUSEHOLD OR DEME
MATRIHOUSEHOLD OR DEME
PATRILINEAGE OR SIB
MATRILINEAGE OR SIB

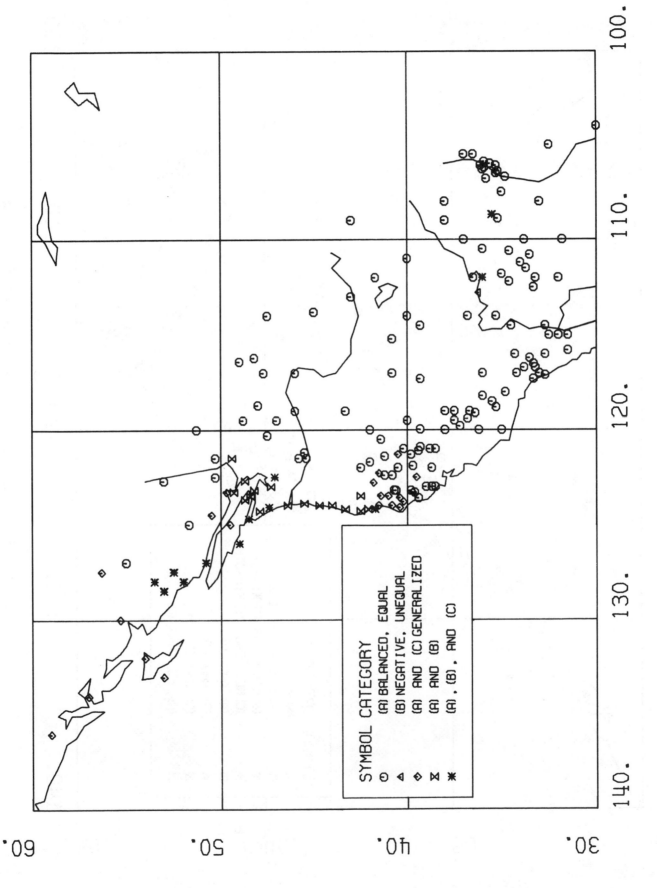

LOCAL RECIPROCITY OF FOOD AND CHATTELS

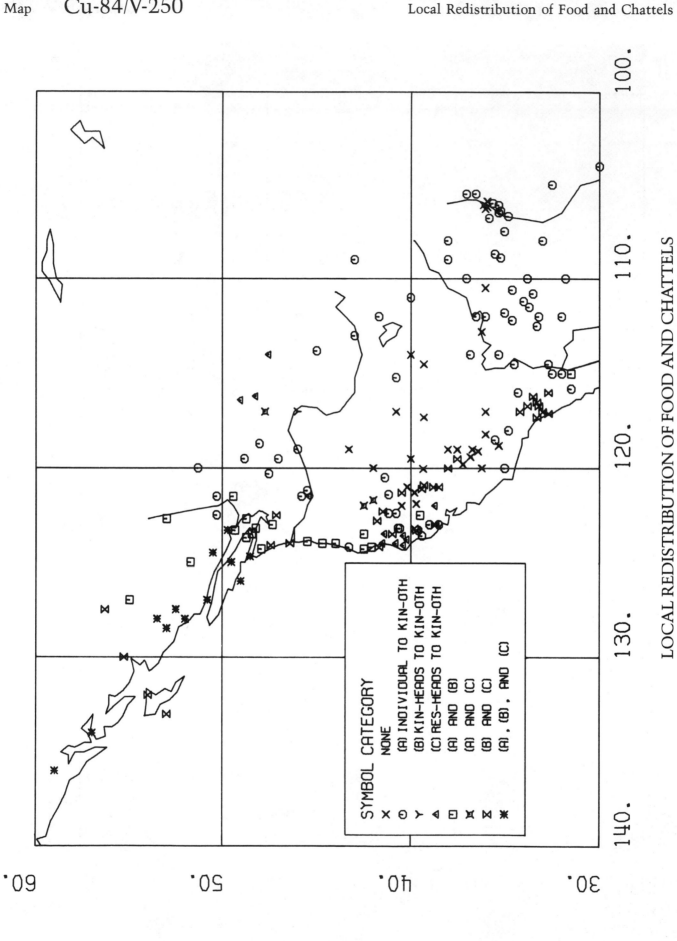

SYMBOL CATEGORY

	NONE
X	(A) INDIVIDUAL TO KIN-OTH
⊖	(B) KIN-HEADS TO KIN-OTH
Y	(C) RES-HEADS TO KIN-OTH
◁	(A) AND (B)
⊟	(A) AND (C)
⋈	(B) AND (C)
⋈	(A), (B), AND (C)
✳	

LOCAL REDISTRIBUTION OF FOOD AND CHATTELS

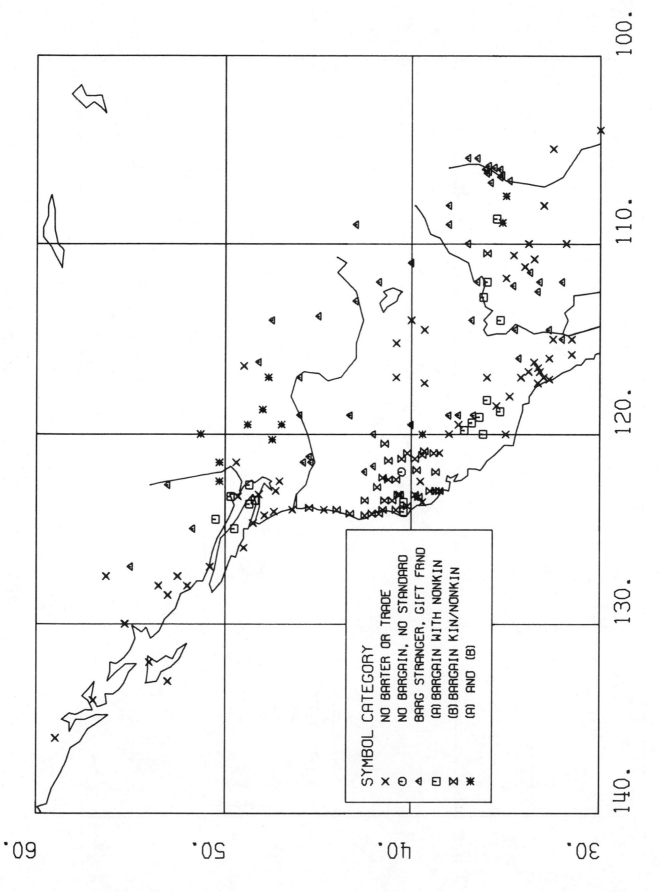

BARTER OR TRADE WITHIN LOCAL COMMUNITY

SYMBOL CATEGORY

X	NO BARTER OR TRADE
O	NO BARGAIN, NO STANDARD
◁	BARG STRANGER, GIFT FRND
⊟	(A) BARGAIN WITH NONKIN
⋈	(B) BARGAIN KIN/NONKIN
✳	(A) AND (B)

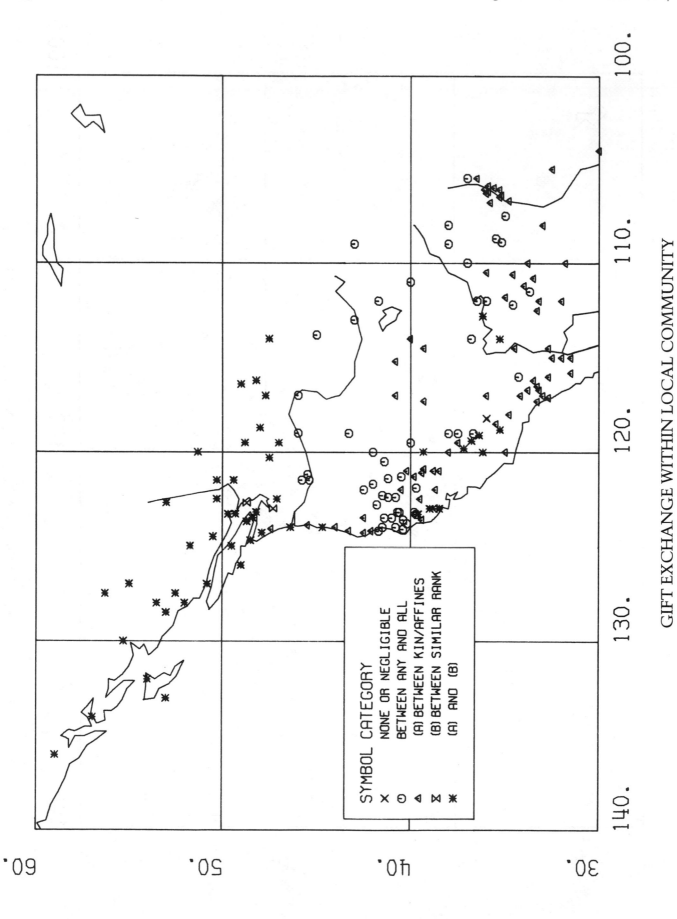

GIFT EXCHANGE WITHIN LOCAL COMMUNITY

SYMBOL CATEGORY

X   NONE OR NEGLIGIBLE
Ө   BETWEEN ANY AND ALL
◁   (A) BETWEEN KIN/AFFINES
⋈   (B) BETWEEN SIMILAR RANK
✳   (A) AND (B)

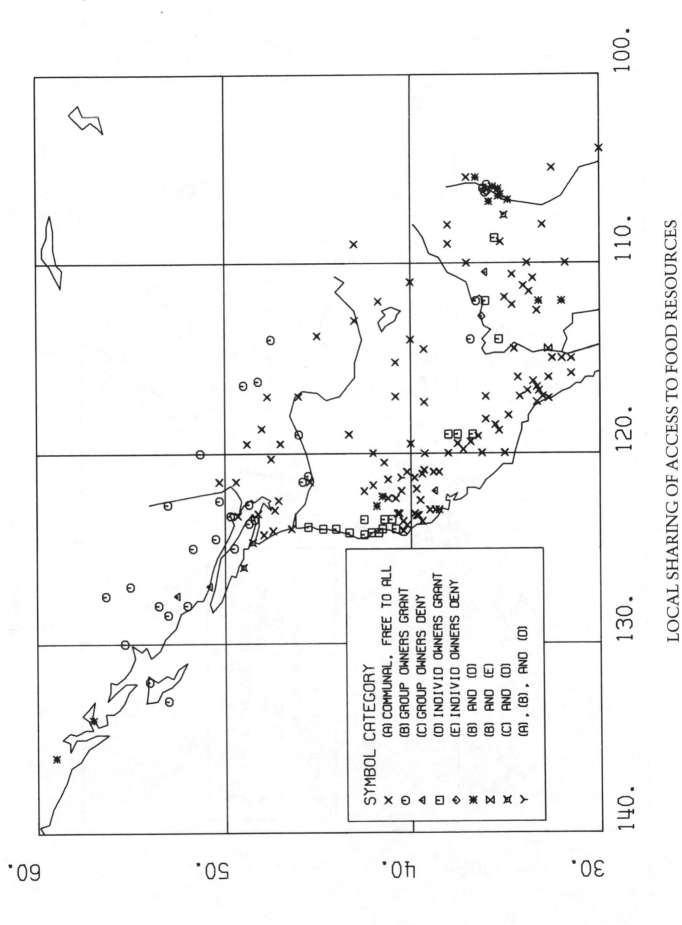

LOCAL SHARING OF ACCESS TO FOOD RESOURCES

SYMBOL CATEGORY

(A) COMMUNAL, FREE TO ALL
(B) GROUP OWNERS GRANT
(C) GROUP OWNERS DENY
(D) INDIVID OWNERS GRANT
(E) INDIVID OWNERS DENY
(B) AND (D)
(B) AND (E)
(C) AND (D)
(A), (B), AND (D)

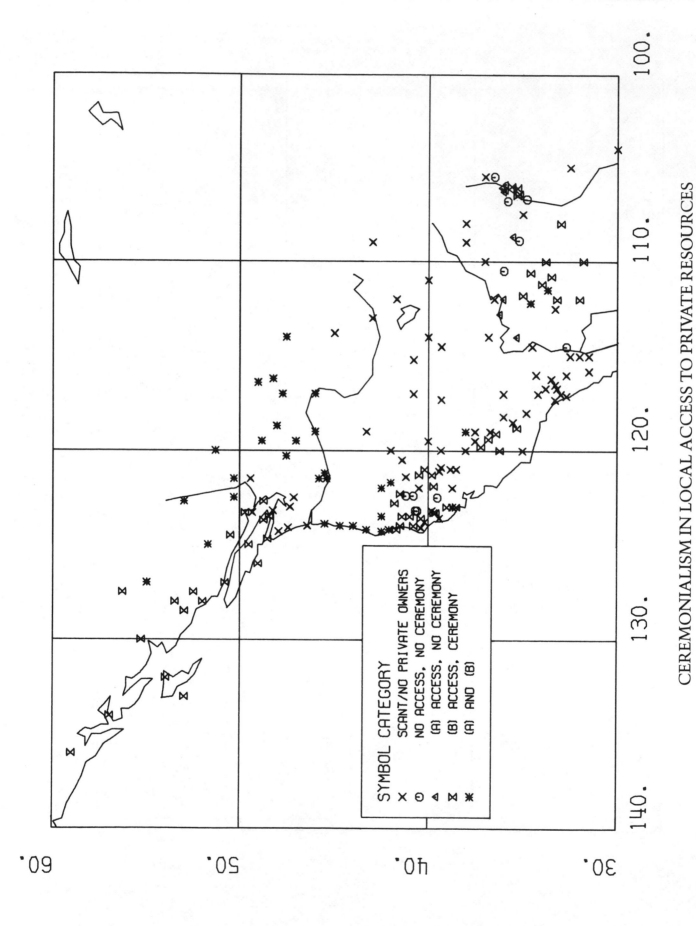

CEREMONIALISM IN LOCAL ACCESS TO PRIVATE RESOURCES

SYMBOL CATEGORY

X	SCANT/NO PRIVATE OWNERS
⊙	NO ACCESS, NO CEREMONY
◁	(A) ACCESS, NO CEREMONY
⋈	(B) ACCESS, CEREMONY
✳	(A) AND (B)

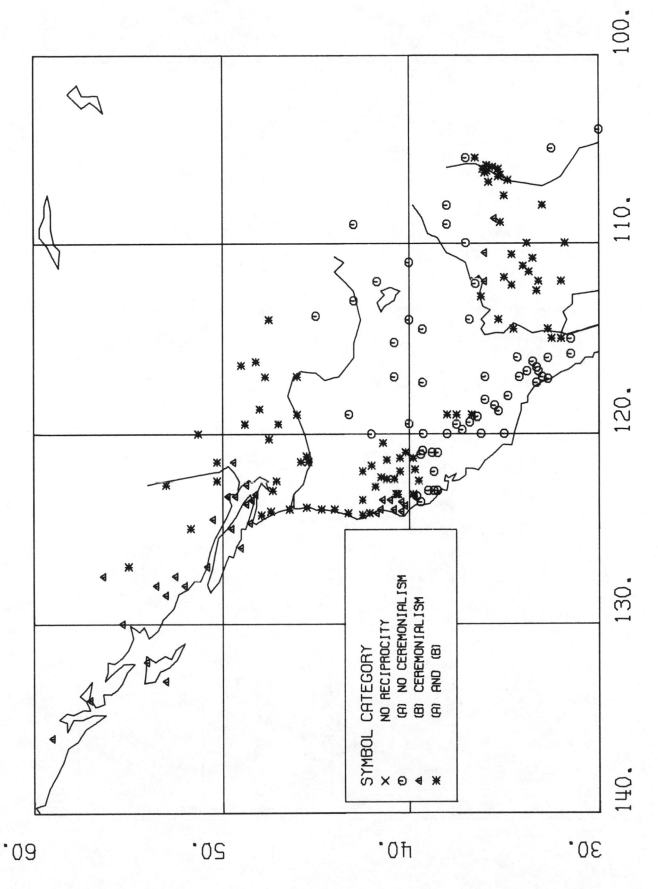

CEREMONIALISM IN LOCAL RECIPROCITY

SYMBOL CATEGORY

	NO RECIPROCITY
X	
⊖	(A) NO CEREMONIALISM
◁	(B) CEREMONIALISM
✳	(A) AND (B)

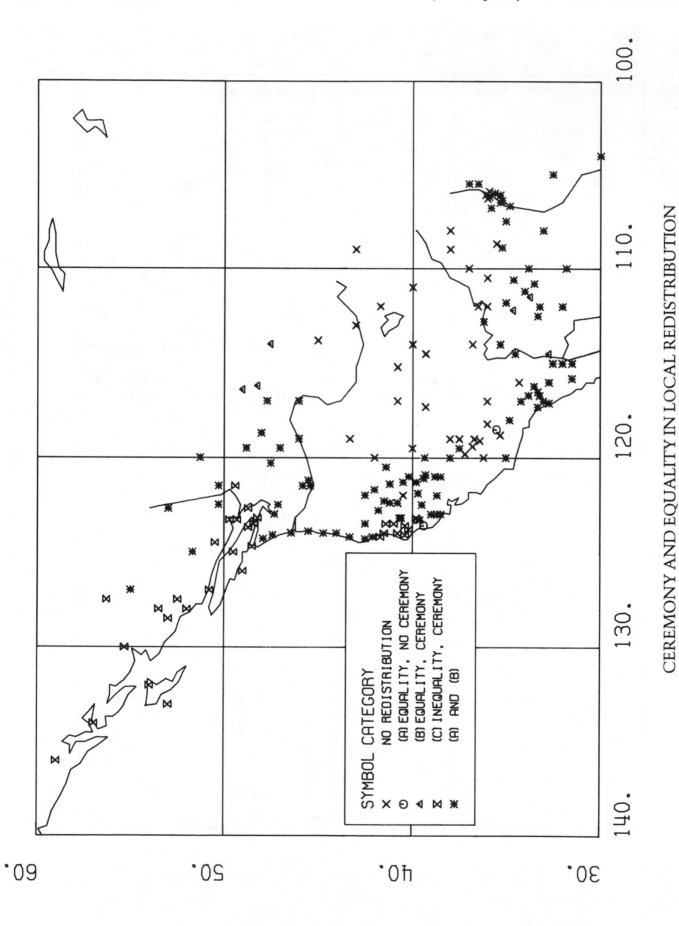

CEREMONY AND EQUALITY IN LOCAL REDISTRIBUTION

SYMBOL CATEGORY
    NO REDISTRIBUTION
(A) EQUALITY, NO CEREMONY
(B) EQUALITY, CEREMONY
(C) INEQUALITY, CEREMONY
(A) AND (B)

X
⊖
◁
⋈
✳

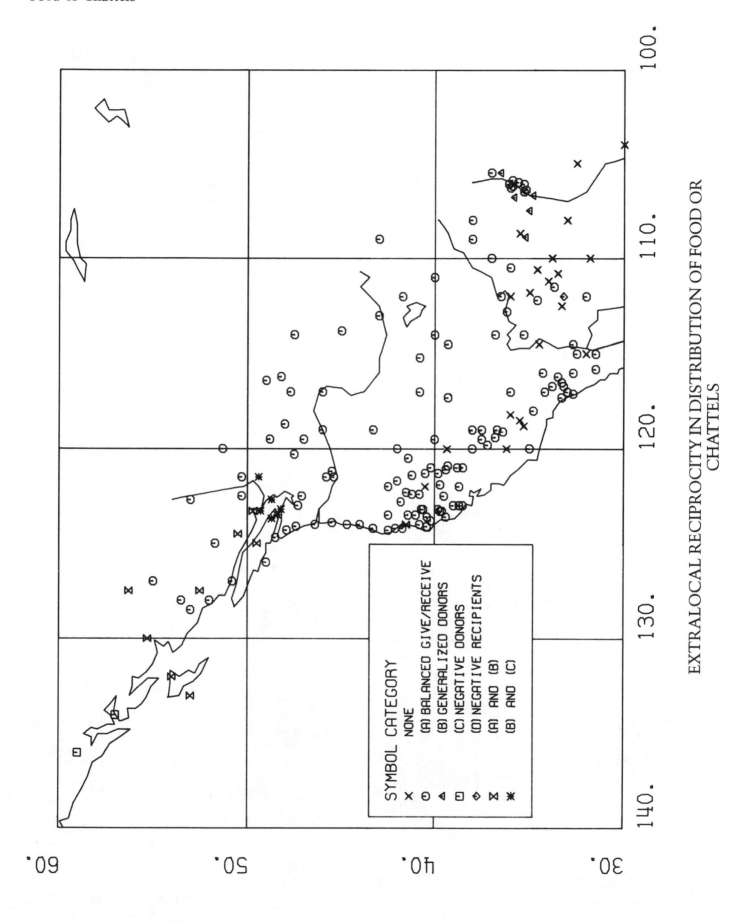

SYMBOL CATEGORY

	NONE
X	(A) BALANCED GIVE/RECEIVE
⊖	(B) GENERALIZED DONORS
◁	(C) NEGATIVE DONORS
⊡	(D) NEGATIVE RECIPIENTS
◇	(A) AND (B)
⋈	(B) AND (C)
✳	

EXTRALOCAL RECIPROCITY IN DISTRIBUTION OF FOOD OR CHATTELS

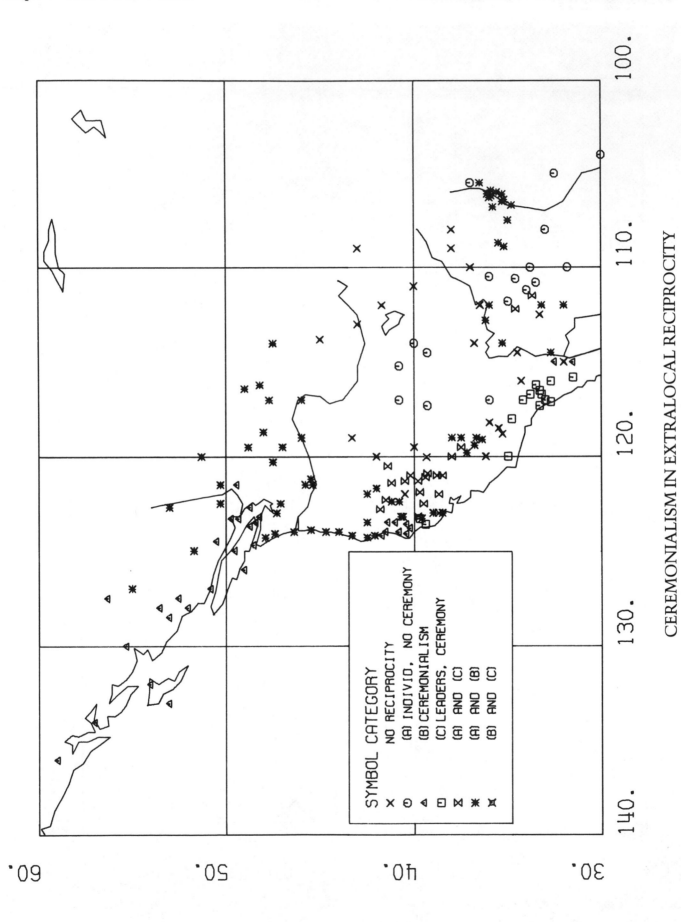

CEREMONIALISM IN EXTRALOCAL RECIPROCITY

SYMBOL CATEGORY
NO RECIPROCITY
X   (A) INDIVID. NO CEREMONY
⊖   (B) CEREMONIALISM
◁   (C) LEADERS, CEREMONY
⊟   (A) AND (C)
⋈   (A) AND (B)
✳   (B) AND (C)
⋈

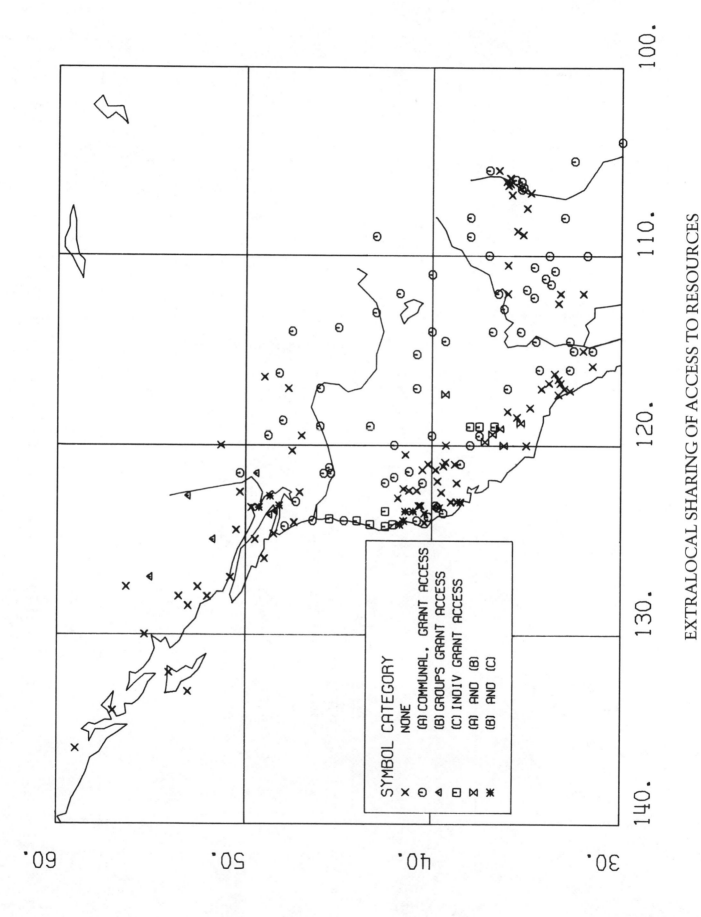

EXTRALOCAL SHARING OF ACCESS TO RESOURCES

SYMBOL CATEGORY
X	NONE
⊖	(A) COMMUNAL, GRANT ACCESS
◁	(B) GROUPS GRANT ACCESS
⊡	(C) INDIV GRANT ACCESS
⋈	(A) AND (B)
✳	(B) AND (C)

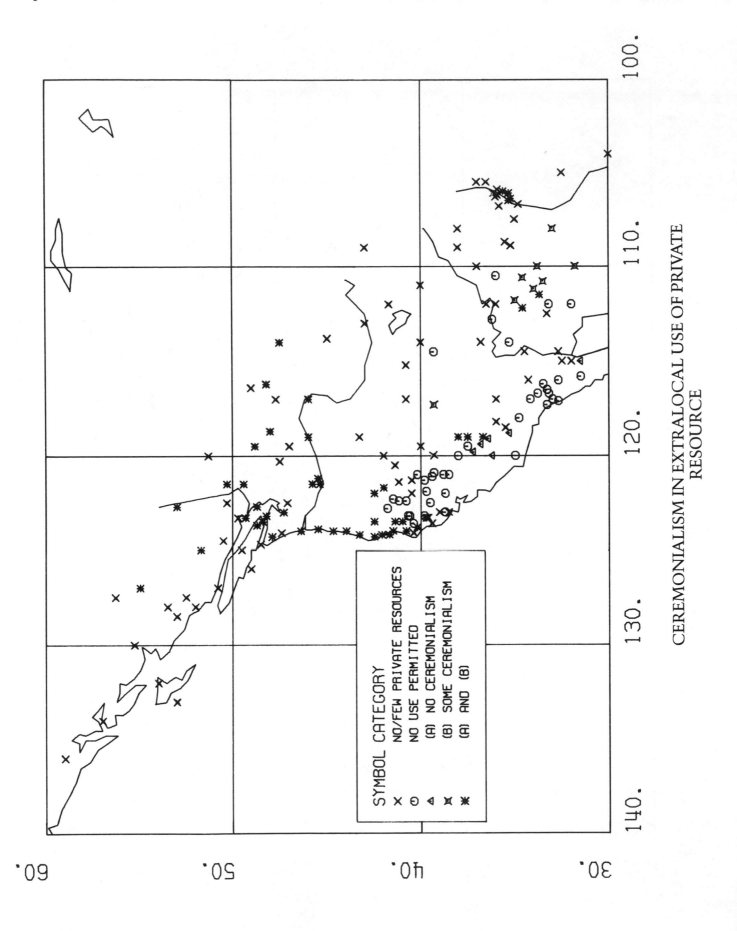

CEREMONIALISM IN EXTRALOCAL USE OF PRIVATE
RESOURCE

SYMBOL CATEGORY
NO/FEW PRIVATE RESOURCES   X
NO USE PERMITTED   ⊖
(A) NO CEREMONIALISM   ◁
(B) SOME CEREMONIALISM   ⋈
(A) AND (B)   ✳

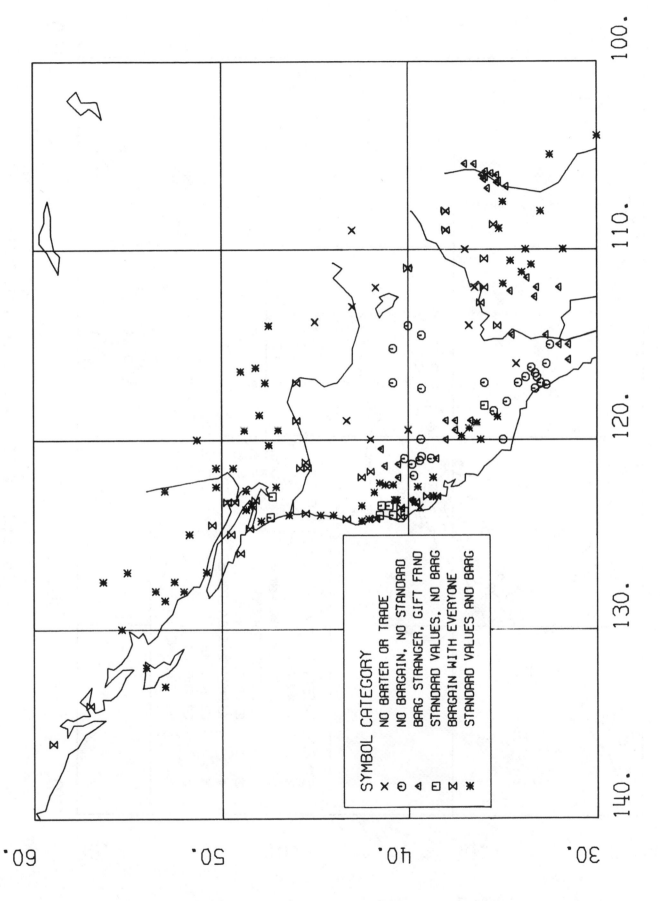

BARTER OR TRADE BETWEEN COMMUNITIES

SYMBOL CATEGORY
X NO BARTER OR TRADE
⊖ NO BARGAIN, NO STANDARD
◁ BARG STRANGER, GIFT FRND
⊟ STANDARD VALUES, NO BARG
⋈ BARGAIN WITH EVERYONE
✳ STANDARD VALUES AND BARG

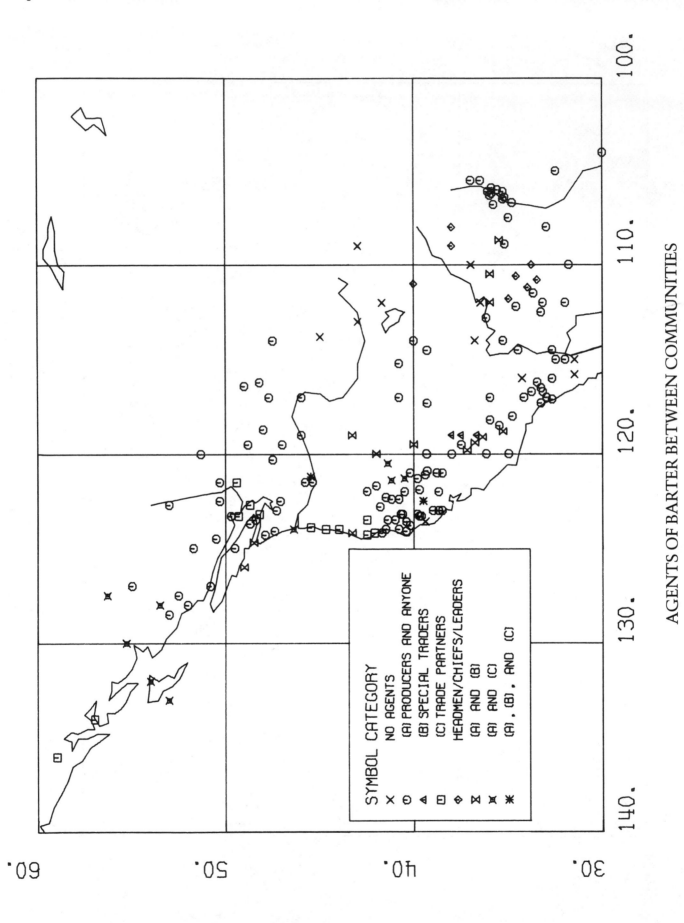

AGENTS OF BARTER BETWEEN COMMUNITIES

SYMBOL CATEGORY
NO AGENTS
(A) PRODUCERS AND ANYONE
(B) SPECIAL TRADERS
(C) TRADE PARTNERS
HEADMEN/CHIEFS/LEADERS
(A) AND (B)
(A) AND (C)
(A), (B), AND (C)

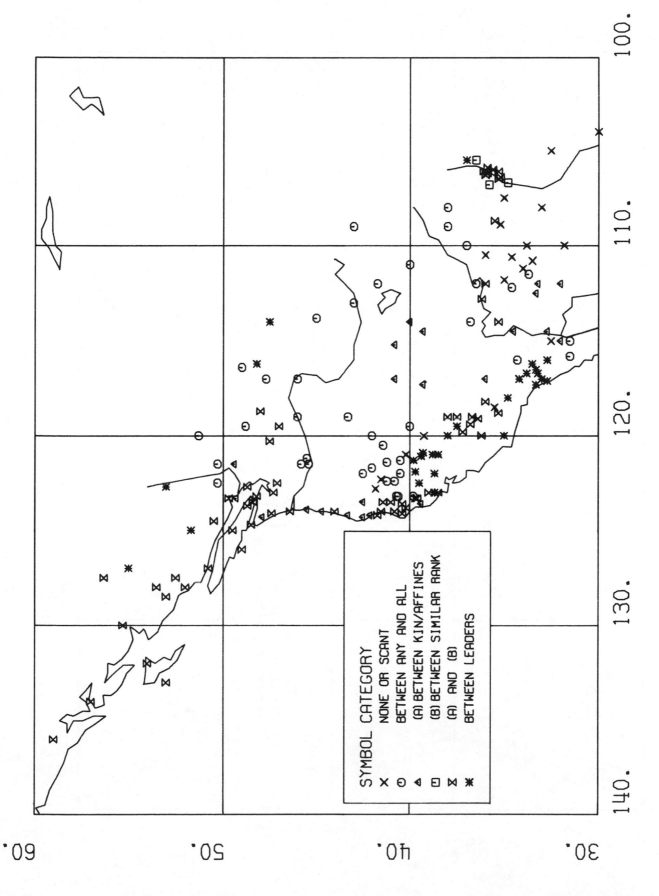

GIFT EXCHANGE BETWEEN COMMUNITIES

Sexual Division of the Labor of Weaving Nets,
Baskets, or Mats

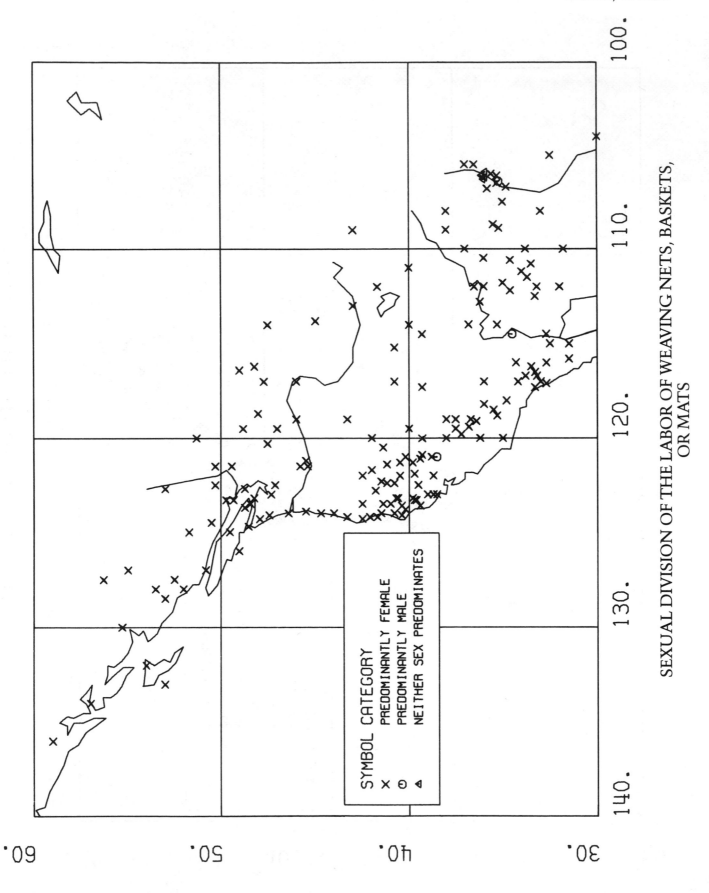

SYMBOL CATEGORY

×   PREDOMINANTLY FEMALE

⊖   PREDOMINANTLY MALE

◁   NEITHER SEX PREDOMINATES

SEXUAL DIVISION OF THE LABOR OF WEAVING NETS, BASKETS,
OR MATS

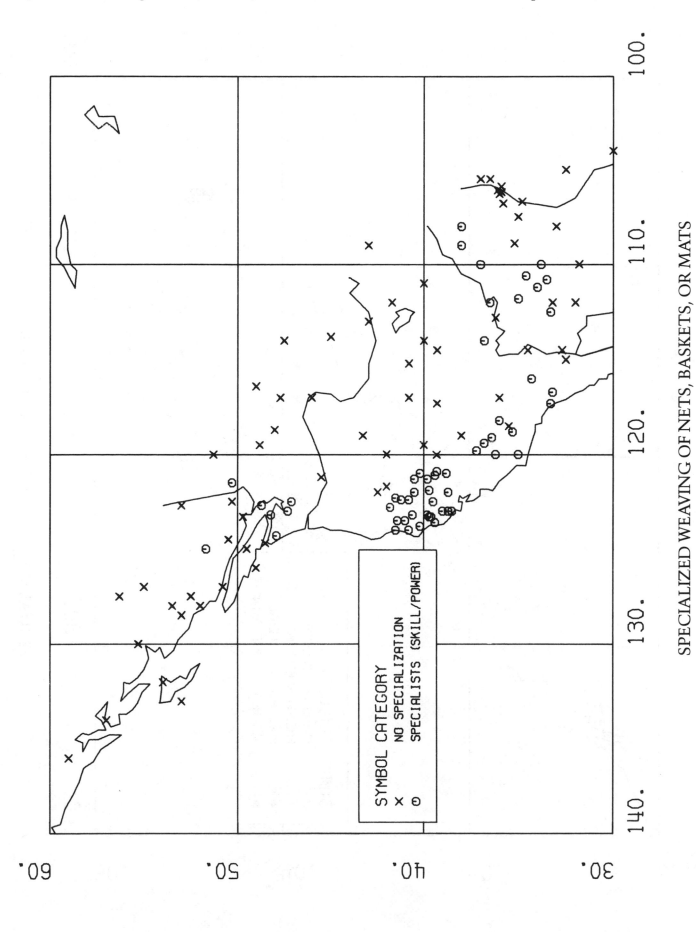

SPECIALIZED WEAVING OF NETS, BASKETS, OR MATS

SYMBOL CATEGORY
X   NO SPECIALIZATION
⊙   SPECIALISTS (SKILL/POWER)

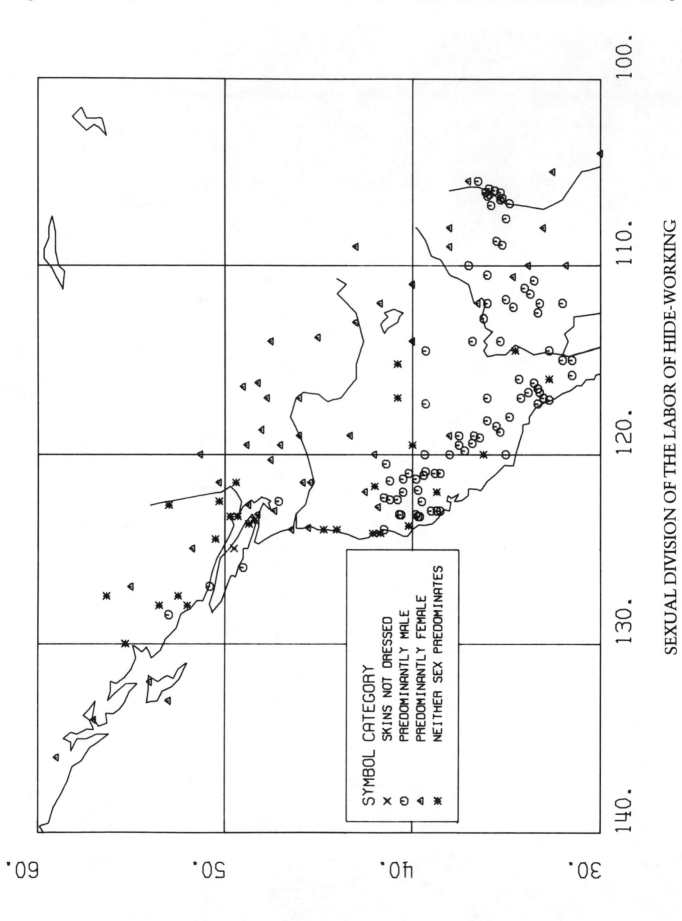

SEXUAL DIVISION OF THE LABOR OF HIDE-WORKING

SYMBOL CATEGORY

X	SKINS NOT DRESSED
⊖	PREDOMINANTLY MALE
◁	PREDOMINANTLY FEMALE
✳	NEITHER SEX PREDOMINATES

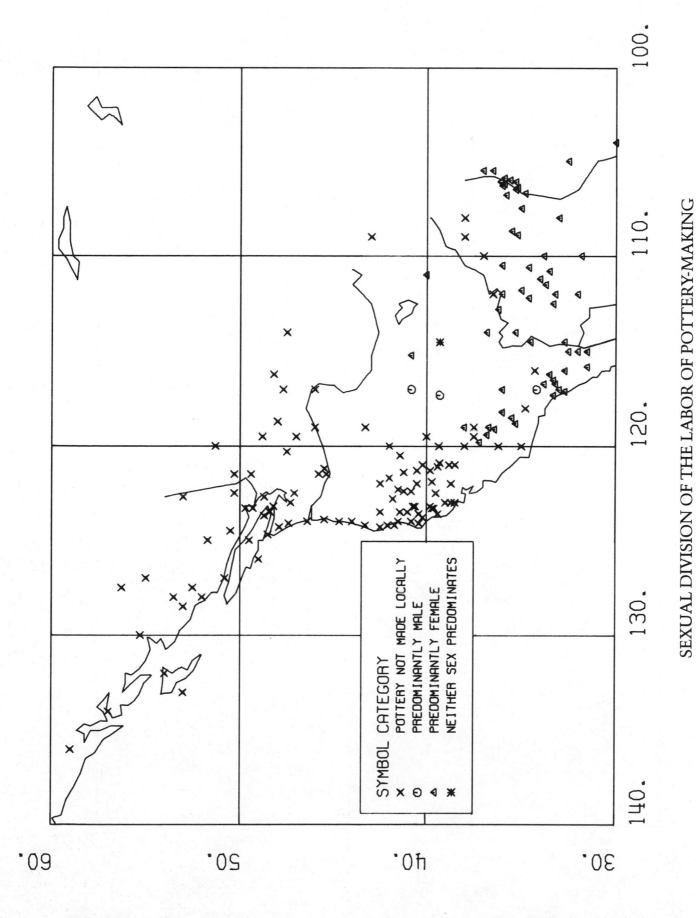

SEXUAL DIVISION OF THE LABOR OF POTTERY-MAKING

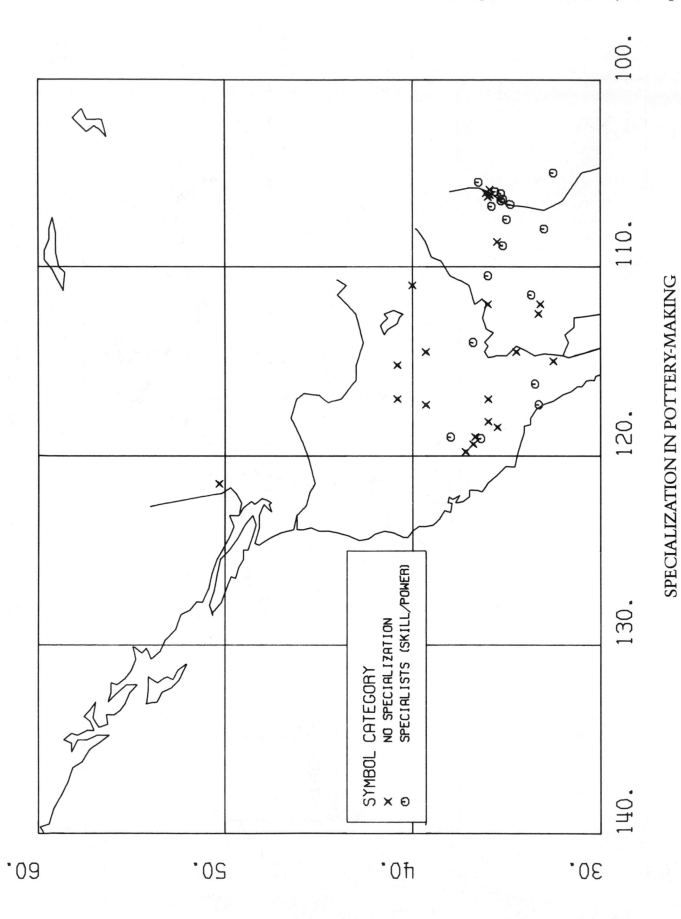

SPECIALIZATION IN POTTERY-MAKING

SYMBOL CATEGORY
X   NO SPECIALIZATION
⊖   SPECIALISTS (SKILL/POWER)

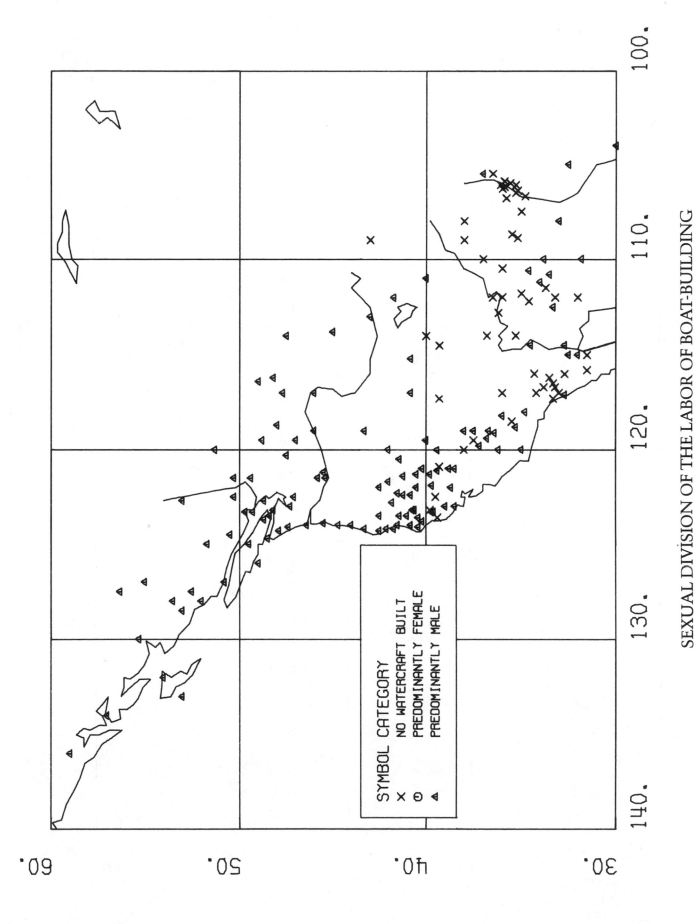

SYMBOL CATEGORY
X   NO WATERCRAFT BUILT
⊕   PREDOMINANTLY FEMALE
◁   PREDOMINANTLY MALE

SEXUAL DIVISION OF THE LABOR OF BOAT-BUILDING

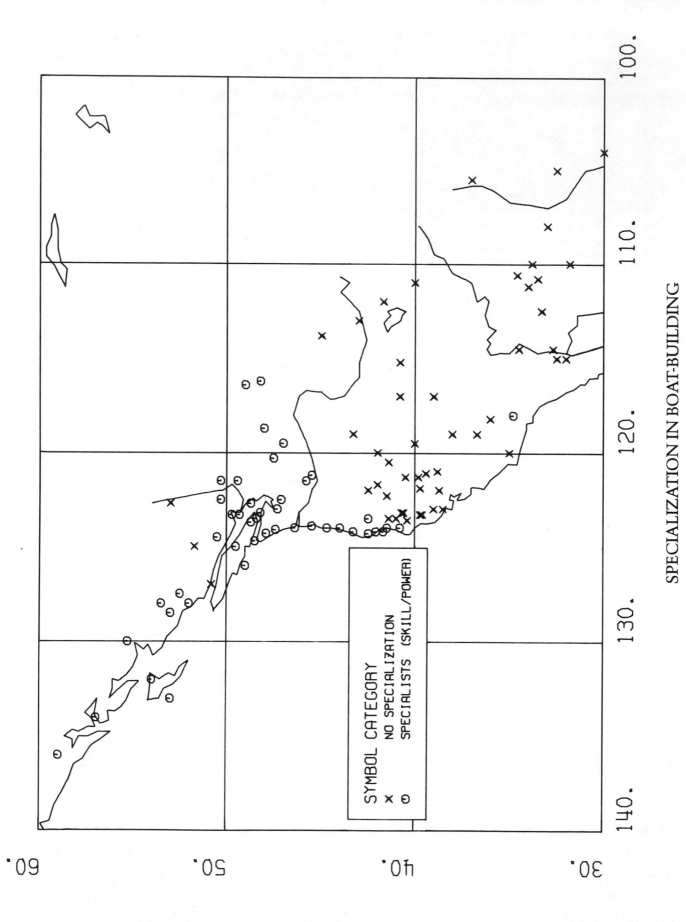

SPECIALIZATION IN BOAT-BUILDING

SYMBOL CATEGORY
× NO SPECIALIZATION
⊖ SPECIALISTS (SKILL/POWER)

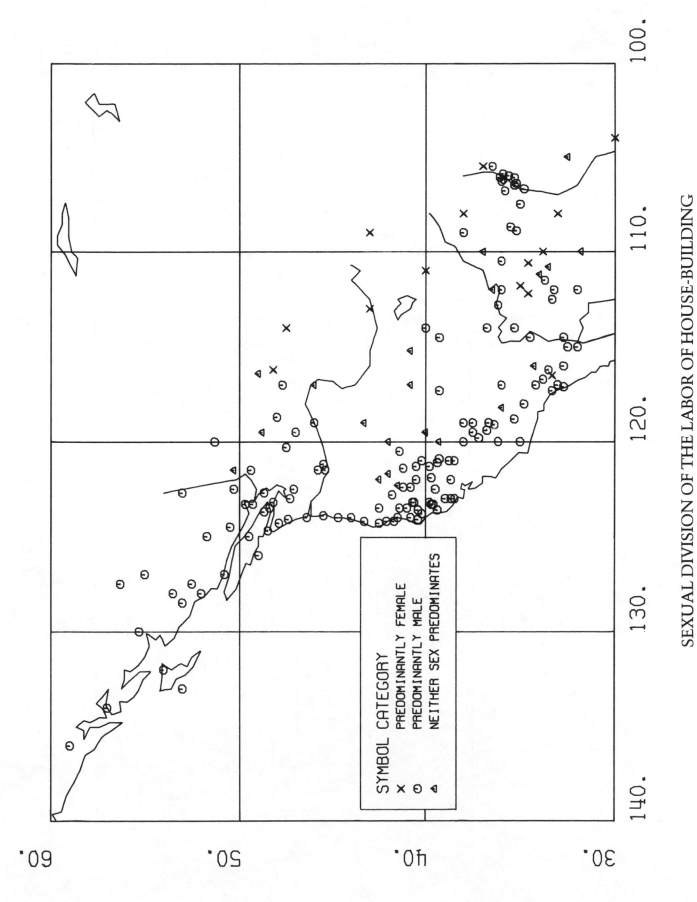

SYMBOL CATEGORY
× PREDOMINANTLY FEMALE
⊖ PREDOMINANTLY MALE
◁ NEITHER SEX PREDOMINATES

SEXUAL DIVISION OF THE LABOR OF HOUSE-BUILDING

SPECIALIZATION IN HOUSE-BUILDING

SYMBOL CATEGORY

X	NO SPECIALIZATION
Θ	SPECIALISTS (SKILL/POWER)

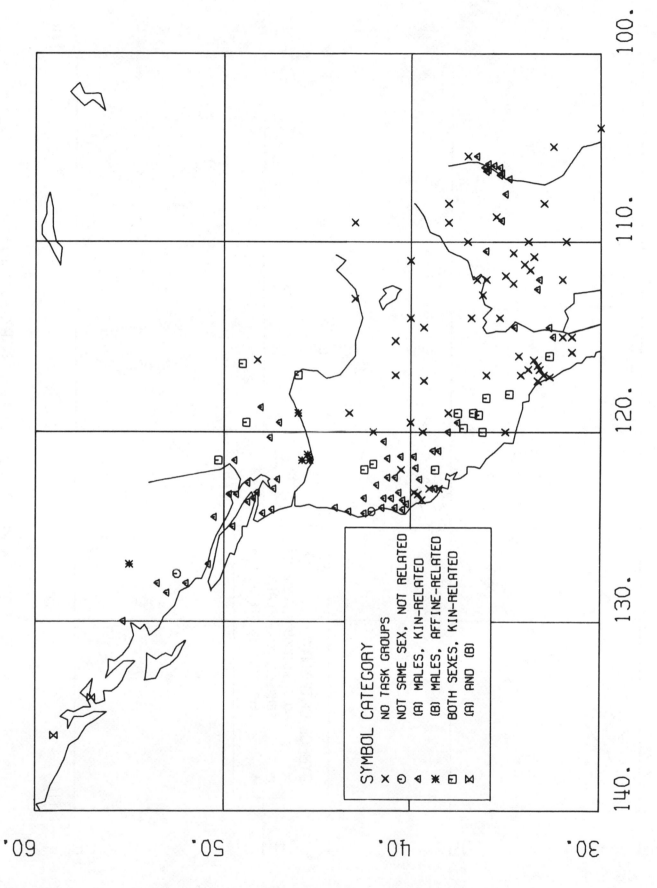

TASK-GROUP COMPOSITION IN HOUSE-BUILDING

SYMBOL CATEGORY

X NO TASK GROUPS
⊖ NOT SAME SEX, NOT RELATED
◁ (A) MALES, KIN-RELATED
✳ (B) MALES, AFFINE-RELATED
⊟ BOTH SEXES, KIN-RELATED
⋈ (A) AND (B)

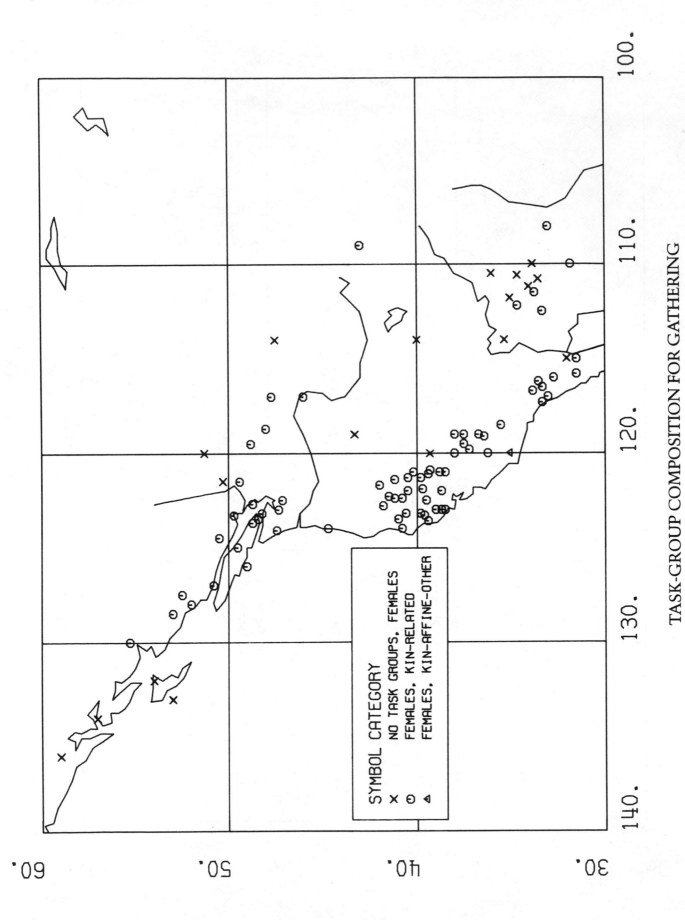

TASK-GROUP COMPOSITION FOR GATHERING

SYMBOL CATEGORY

X   NO TASK GROUPS, FEMALES
⊖   FEMALES, KIN-RELATED
◁   FEMALES, KIN-AFFINE-OTHER

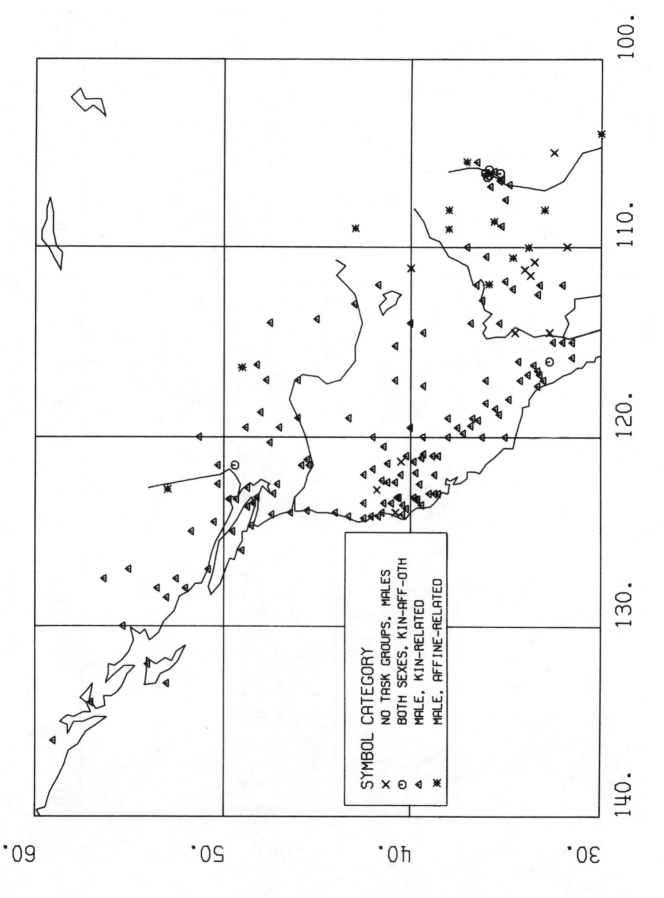

SYMBOL CATEGORY

X NO TASK GROUPS, MALES

⊖ BOTH SEXES, KIN-AFF-OTH

◁ MALE, KIN-RELATED

∗ MALE, AFFINE-RELATED

TASK-GROUP COMPOSITION FOR HUNTING

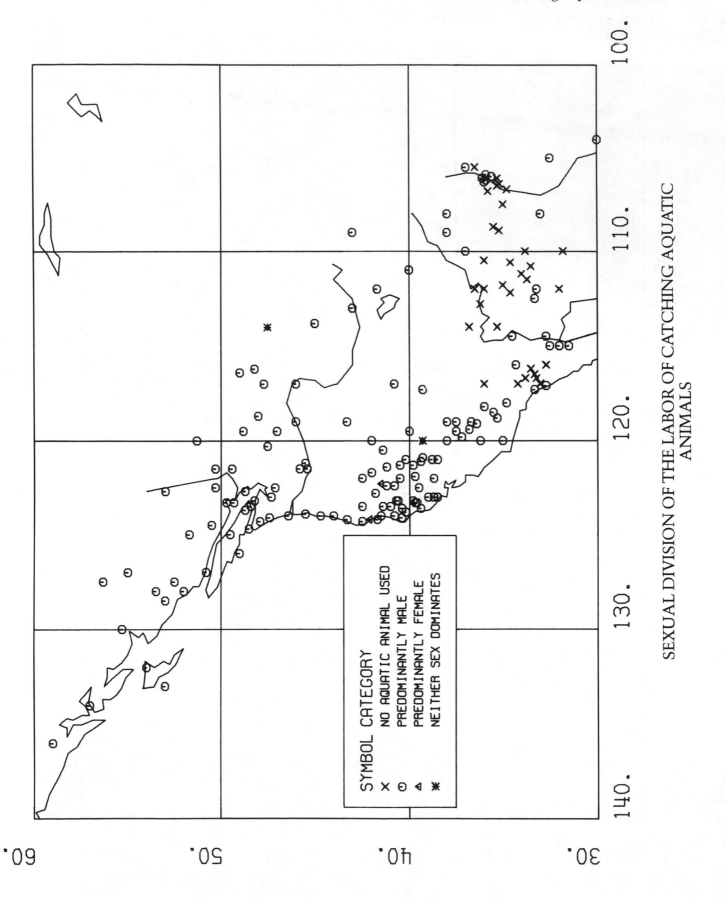

SEXUAL DIVISION OF THE LABOR OF CATCHING AQUATIC
ANIMALS

SYMBOL CATEGORY

×	NO AQUATIC ANIMAL USED
⊖	PREDOMINANTLY MALE
◁	PREDOMINANTLY FEMALE
✳	NEITHER SEX DOMINATES

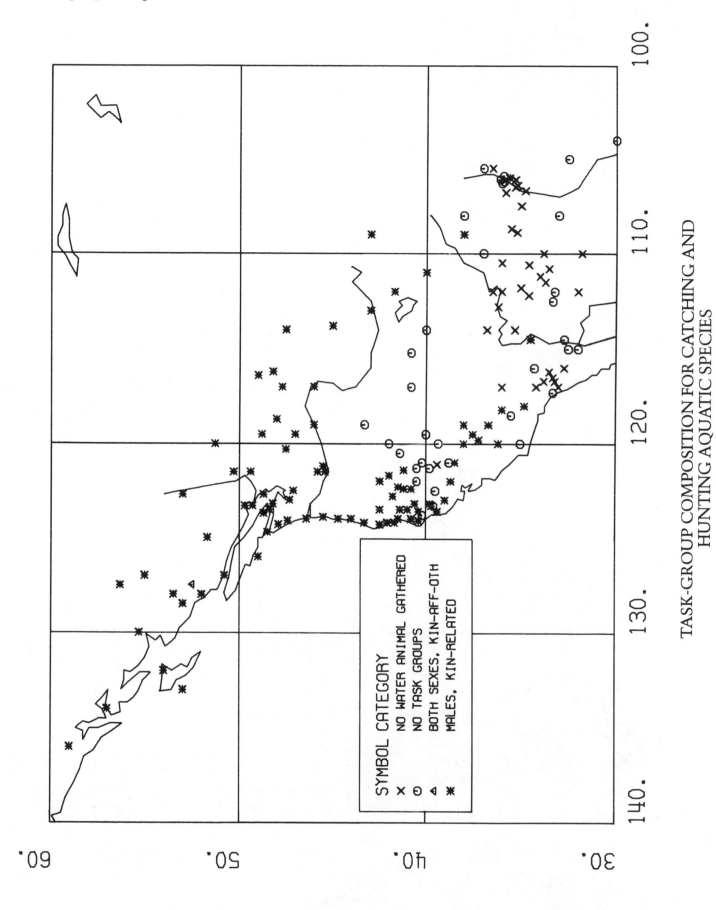

TASK-GROUP COMPOSITION FOR CATCHING AND
HUNTING AQUATIC SPECIES

SYMBOL CATEGORY
X   NO WATER ANIMAL GATHERED
⊖   NO TASK GROUPS
△   BOTH SEXES, KIN-AFF-OTH
✳   MALES, KIN-RELATED

Specialization in Fishing or Hunting for
Aquatic Animals

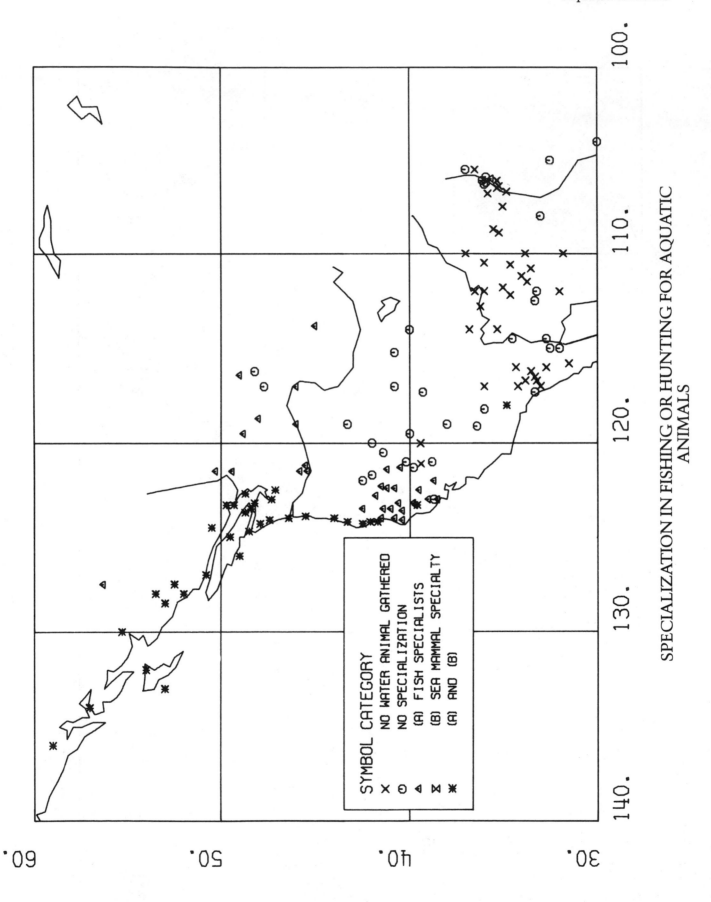

SPECIALIZATION IN FISHING OR HUNTING FOR AQUATIC
ANIMALS

SYMBOL CATEGORY
X   NO WATER ANIMAL GATHERED
⊖   NO SPECIALIZATION
◁   (A) FISH SPECIALISTS
⋈   (B) SEA MAMMAL SPECIALTY
✳   (A) AND (B)

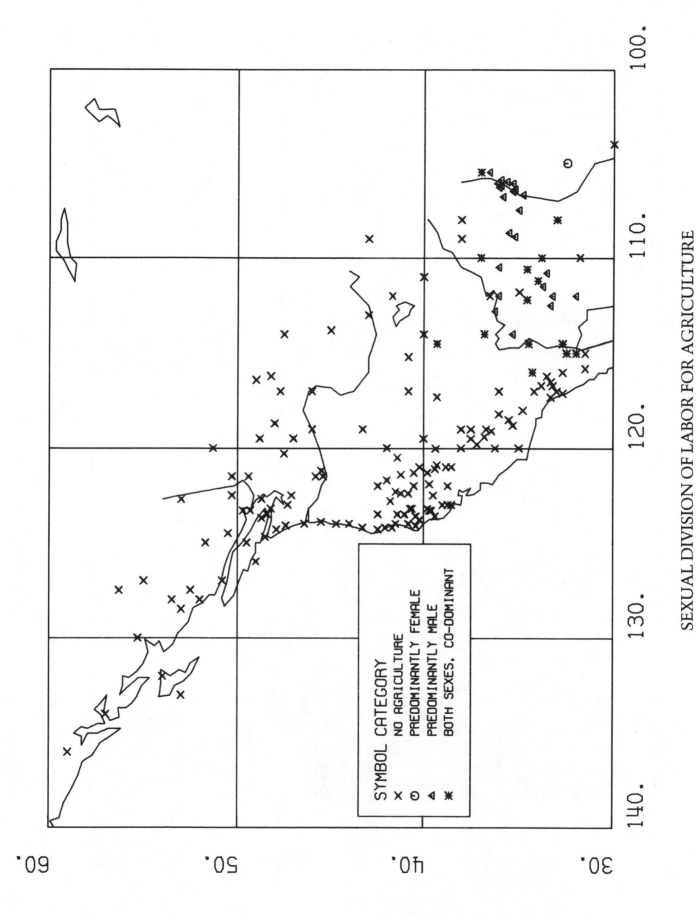

SEXUAL DIVISION OF LABOR FOR AGRICULTURE

SYMBOL CATEGORY
NO AGRICULTURE
PREDOMINANTLY FEMALE
PREDOMINANTLY MALE
BOTH SEXES, CO-DOMINANT

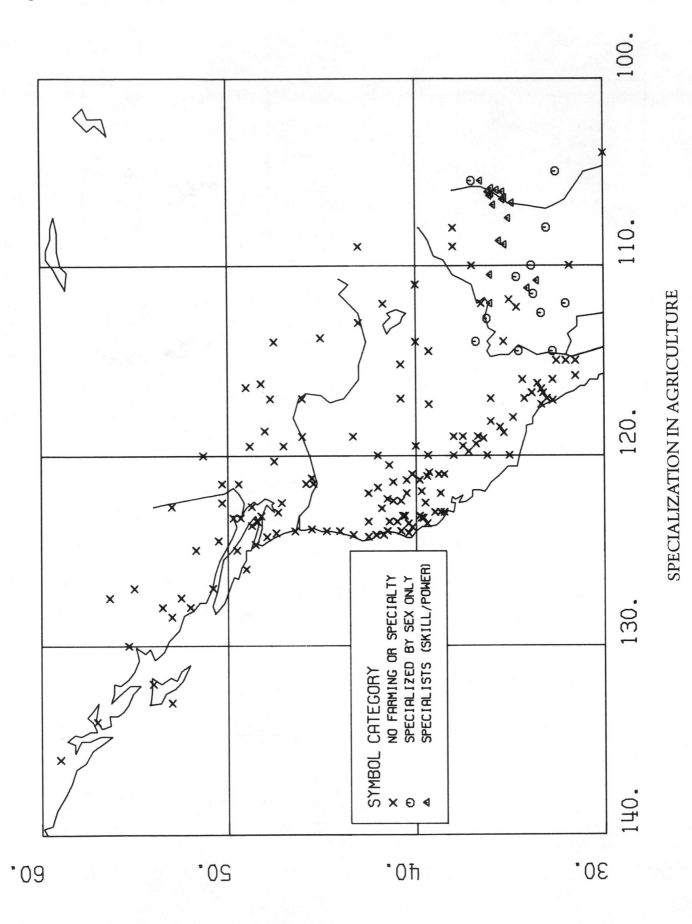

SPECIALIZATION IN AGRICULTURE

SYMBOL CATEGORY
× NO FARMING OR SPECIALTY
⊖ SPECIALIZED BY SEX ONLY
◢ SPECIALISTS (SKILL/POWER)

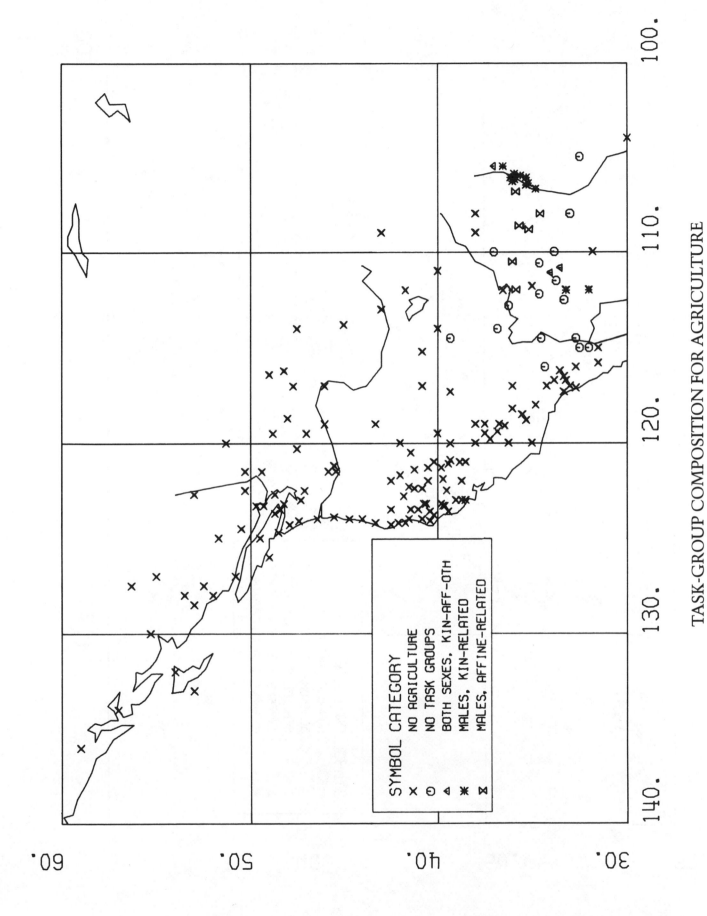

TASK-GROUP COMPOSITION FOR AGRICULTURE

SYMBOL CATEGORY
X   NO AGRICULTURE
⊖   NO TASK GROUPS
◁   BOTH SEXES, KIN-AFF-OTH
✳   MALES, KIN-RELATED
⋈   MALES, AFFINE-RELATED

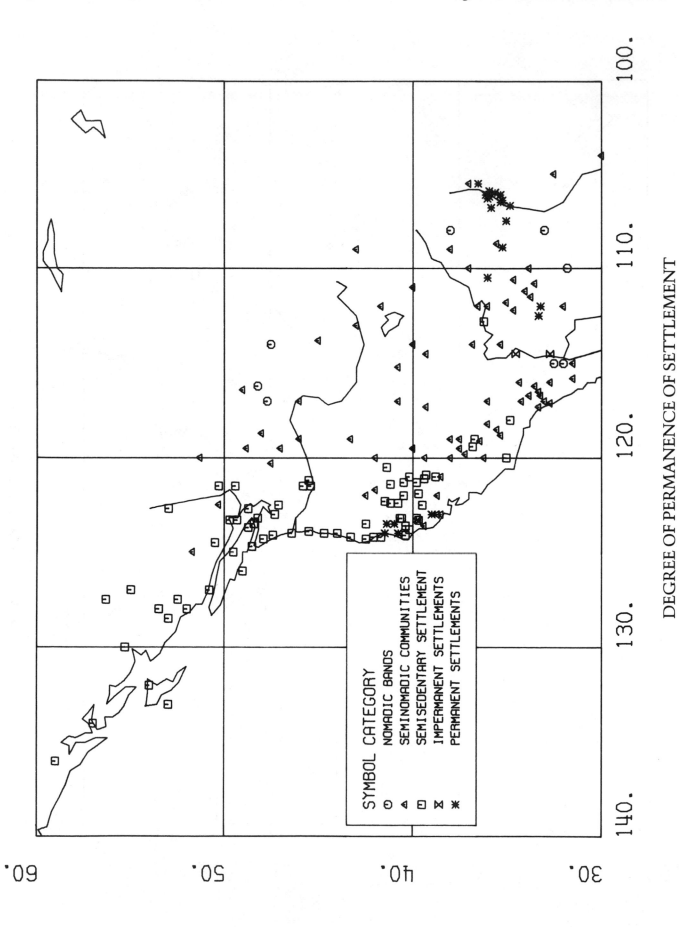

DEGREE OF PERMANENCE OF SETTLEMENT

SYMBOL CATEGORY

Θ	NOMADIC BANDS
◁	SEMINOMADIC COMMUNITIES
⊡	SEMISEDENTARY SETTLEMENT
⋈	IMPERMANENT SETTLEMENTS
✳	PERMANENT SETTLEMENTS

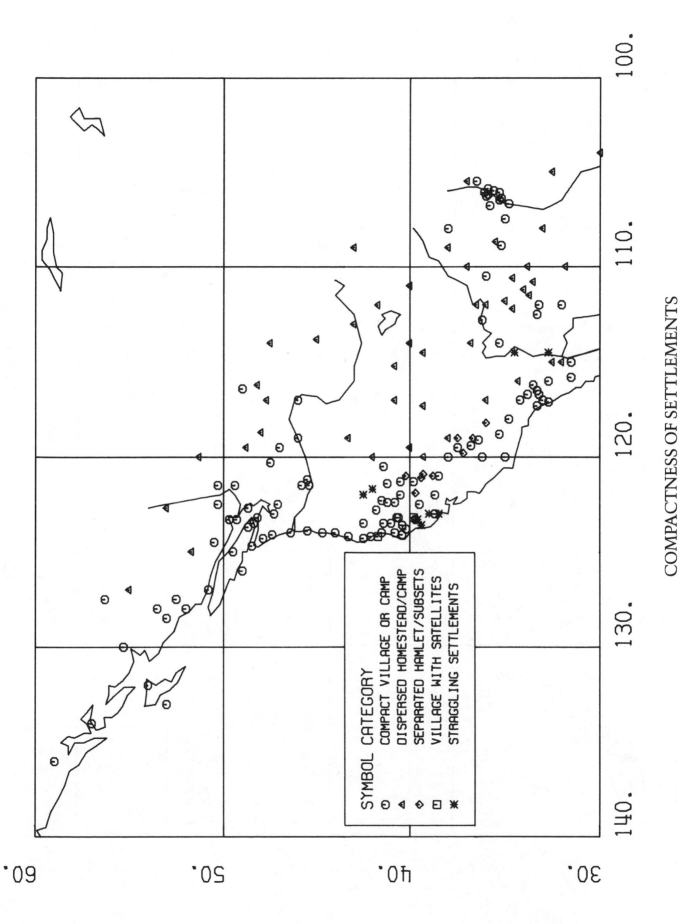

COMPACTNESS OF SETTLEMENTS

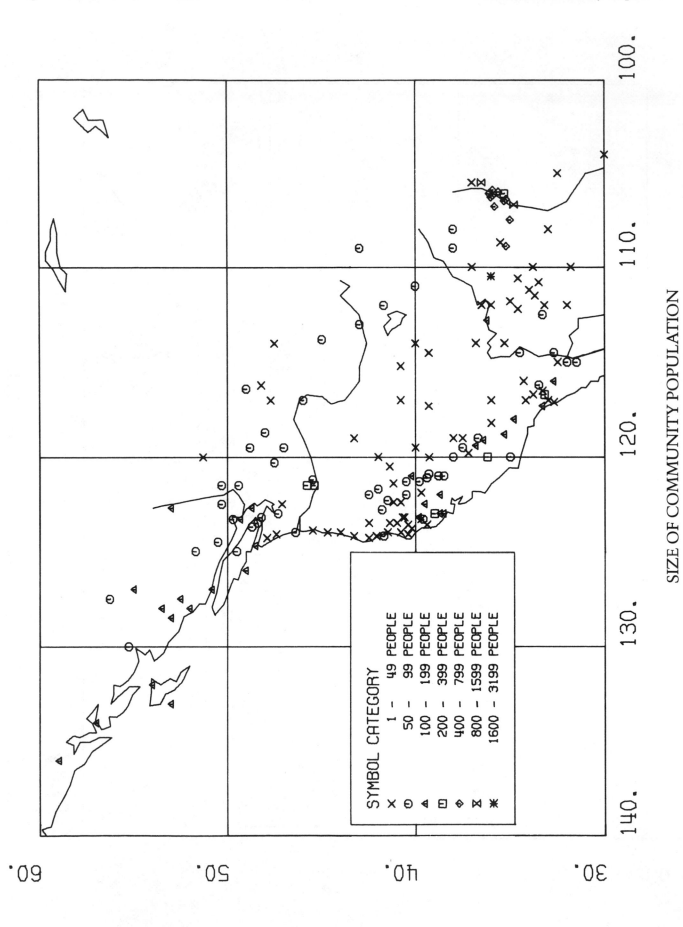

SIZE OF COMMUNITY POPULATION

SYMBOL CATEGORY

SYMBOL	CATEGORY
X	1 - 49 PEOPLE
⊖	50 - 99 PEOPLE
◁	100 - 199 PEOPLE
⊟	200 - 399 PEOPLE
◇	400 - 799 PEOPLE
⋈	800 - 1599 PEOPLE
✳	1600 - 3199 PEOPLE

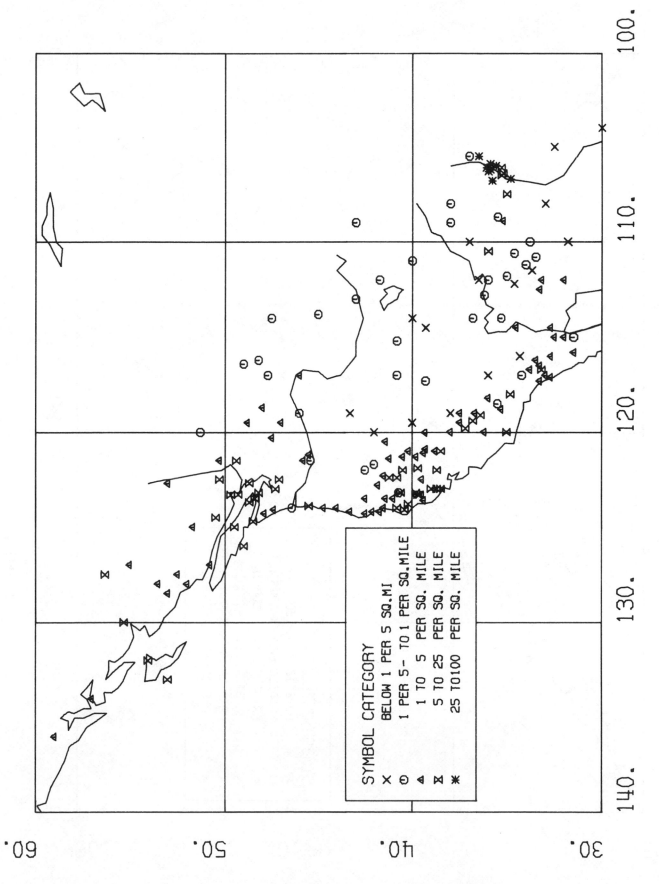

POPULATION DENSITY OF TRIBAL TERRITORY

SYMBOL CATEGORY
X   BELOW 1 PER 5 SQ.MI
Θ   1 PER 5 - TO 1 PER SQ.MILE
◁   1 TO 5 PER SQ. MILE
⋈   5 TO 25 PER SQ. MILE
*   25 TO100 PER SQ. MILE

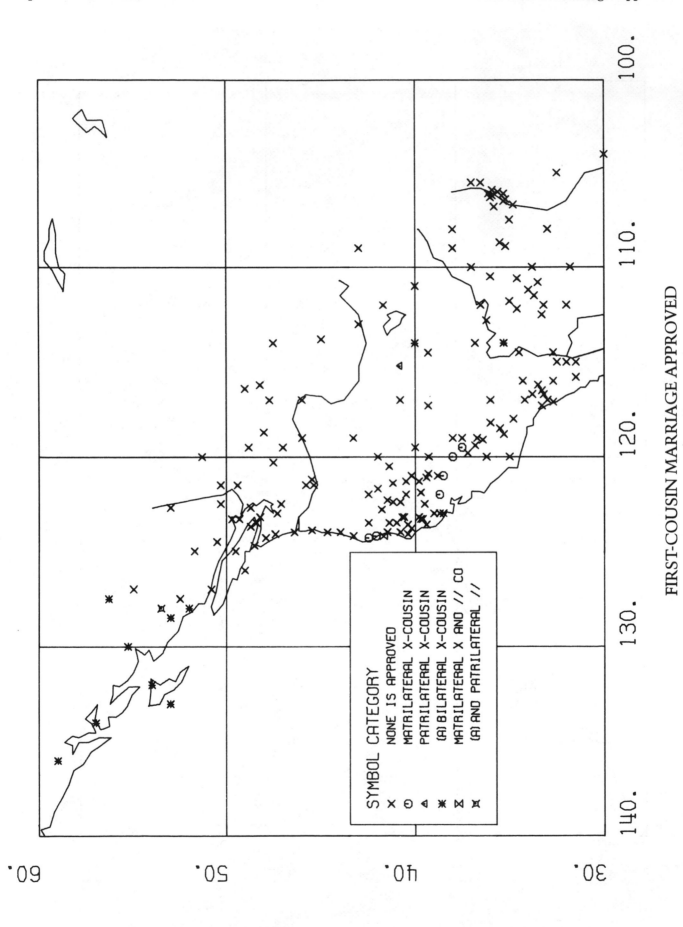

FIRST-COUSIN MARRIAGE APPROVED

SYMBOL CATEGORY

X	NONE IS APPROVED
⊖	MATRILATERAL X-COUSIN
◁	PATRILATERAL X-COUSIN
✳	(A) BILATERAL X-COUSIN
⊠	MATRILATERAL X AND // CO
⋈	(A) AND PATRILATERAL //

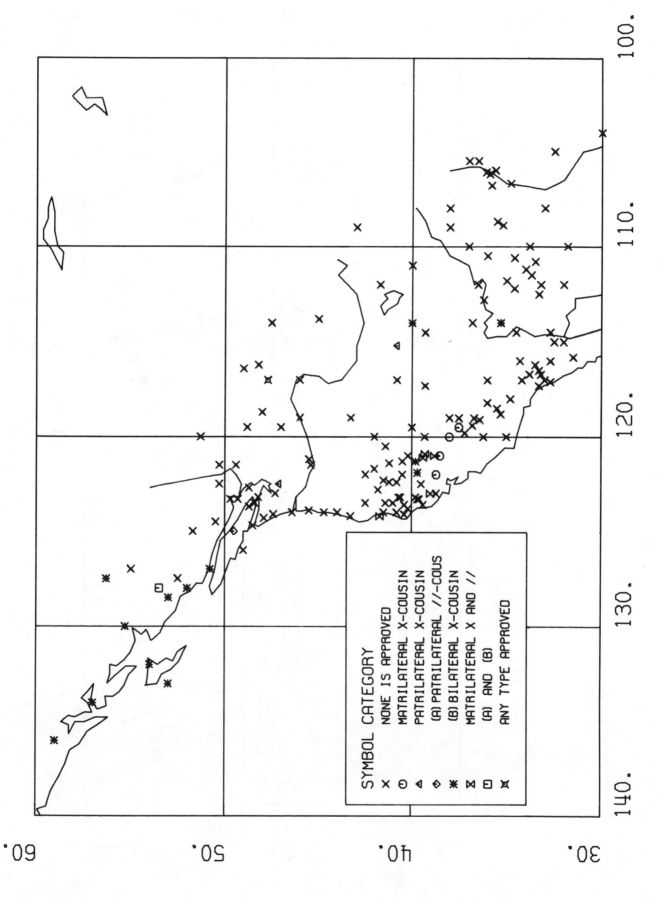

SECOND-COUSIN MARRIAGE APPROVED

SYMBOL CATEGORY

Symbol	Category
X	NONE IS APPROVED
⊙	MATRILATERAL X-COUSIN
◁	PATRILATERAL X-COUSIN
◇	(A) PATRILATERAL //-COUS
✳	(B) BILATERAL X-COUSIN
⋈	MATRILATERAL X AND //
⊟	(A) AND (B)
⋈	ANY TYPE APPROVED

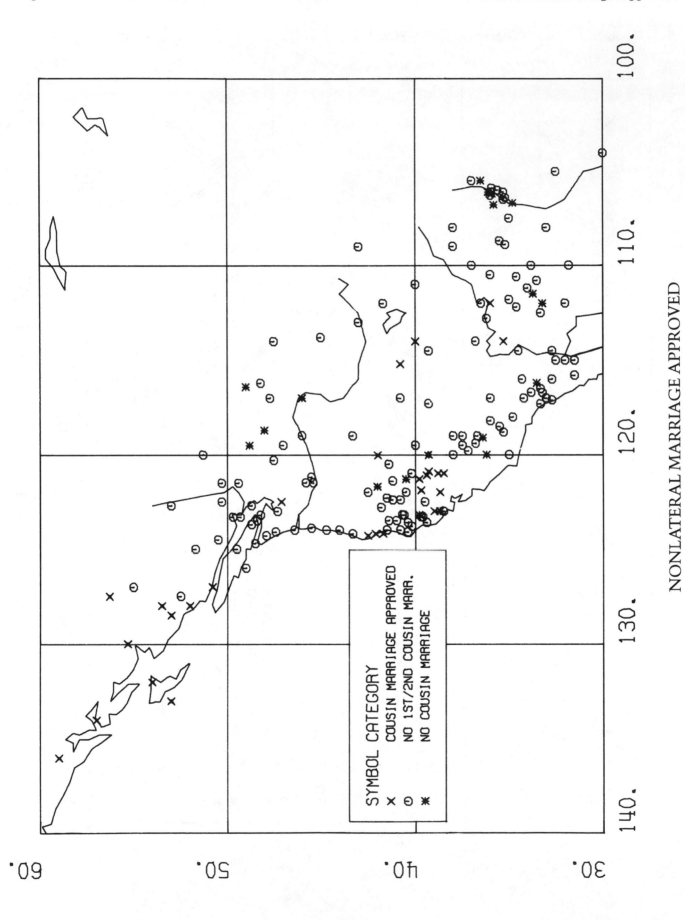

NONLATERAL MARRIAGE APPROVED

SYMBOL CATEGORY
× COUSIN MARRIAGE APPROVED
θ NO 1ST/2ND COUSIN MARR.
✳ NO COUSIN MARRIAGE

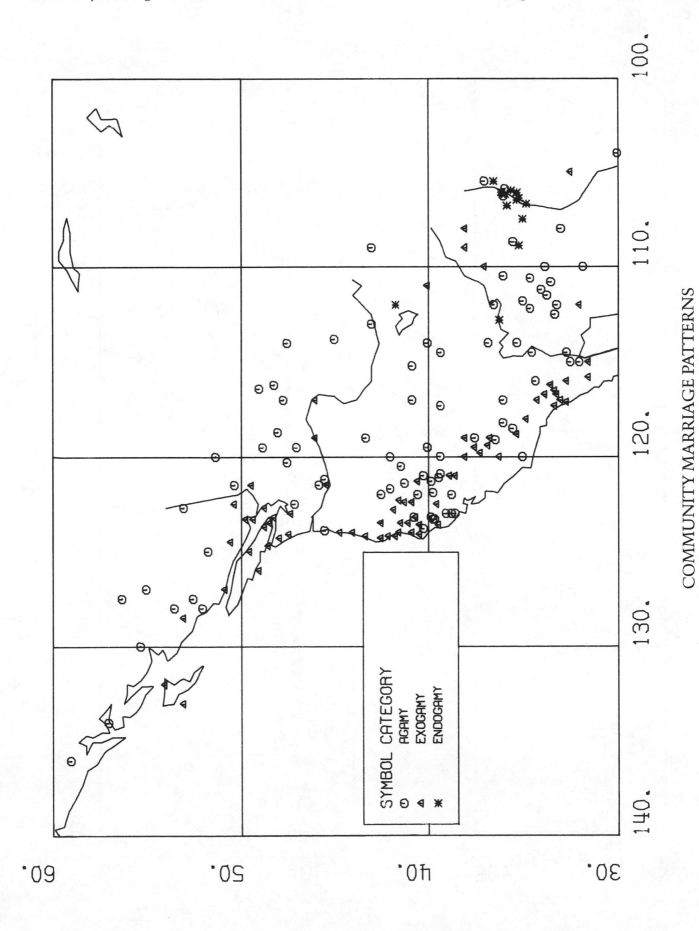

COMMUNITY MARRIAGE PATTERNS

SYMBOL CATEGORY

⊖ AGAMY

◁ EXOGAMY

✳ ENDOGAMY

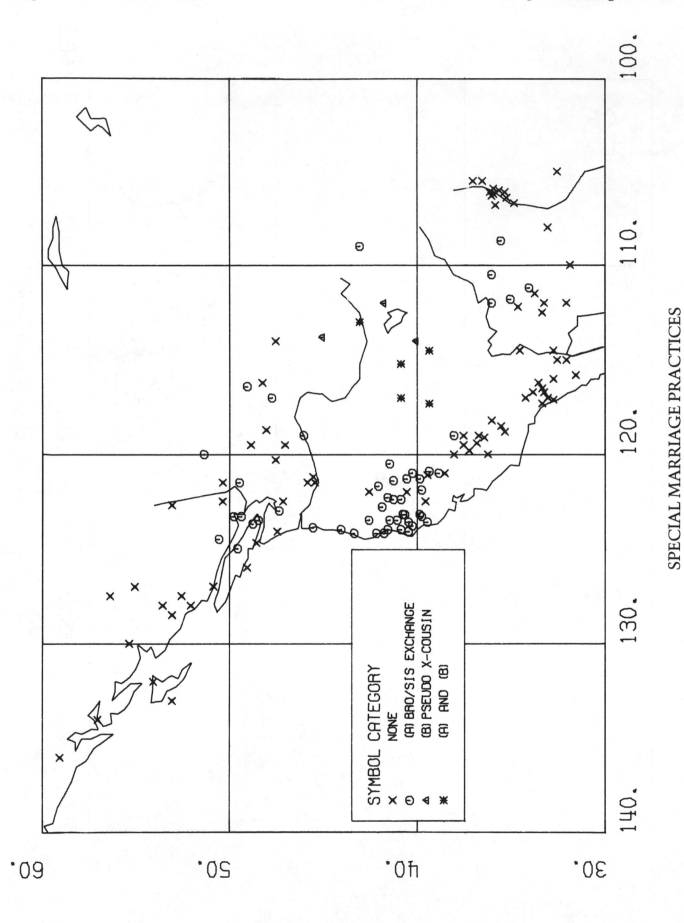

SPECIAL MARRIAGE PRACTICES

SYMBOL CATEGORY
            NONE
    X   (A) BRO/SIS EXCHANGE
    ⊖   (B) PSEUDO X-COUSIN
    ◁   (A) AND (B)
    ✳

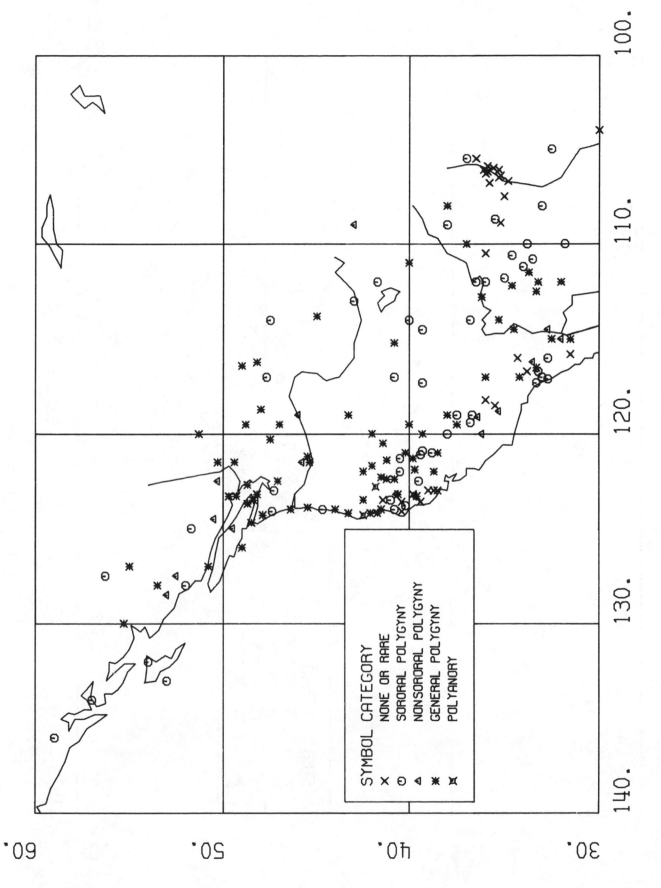

DOMINANT FORM OF POLYGAMY

SYMBOL CATEGORY

X	NONE OR RARE
⊖	SORORAL POLYGYNY
◁	NONSORORAL POLYGYNY
✳	GENERAL POLYGYNY
⋈	POLYANDRY

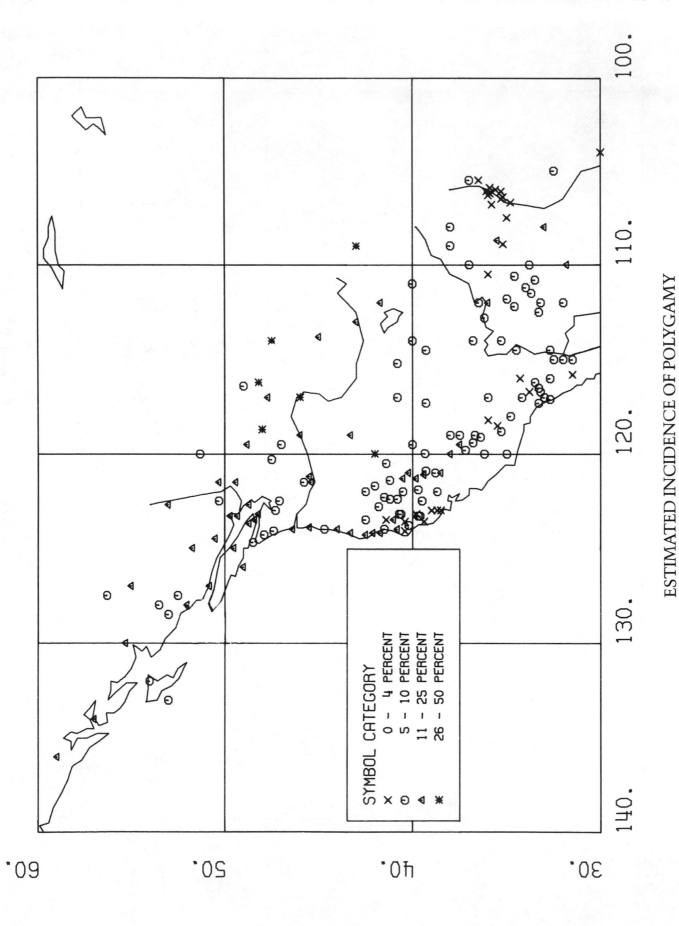

ESTIMATED INCIDENCE OF POLYGAMY

SYMBOL CATEGORY

	0 - 4 PERCENT
X	5 - 10 PERCENT
⊖	11 - 25 PERCENT
◁	26 - 50 PERCENT
✱	

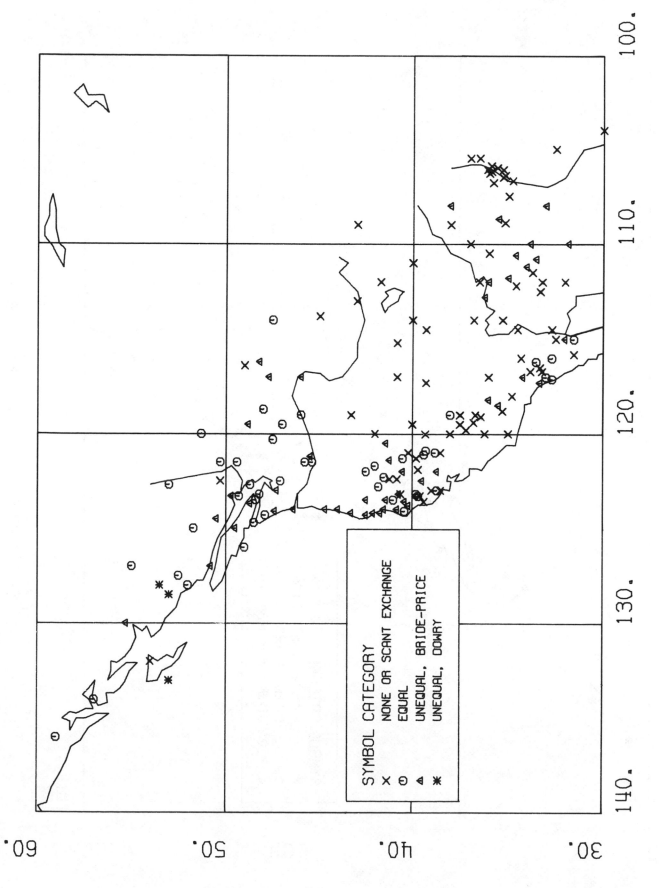

GIFTS BETWEEN FAMILIES BEFORE MARRIAGE

SYMBOL CATEGORY

X	NONE OR SCANT EXCHANGE
⊖	EQUAL
◁	UNEQUAL, BRIDE-PRICE
✳	UNEQUAL, DOWRY

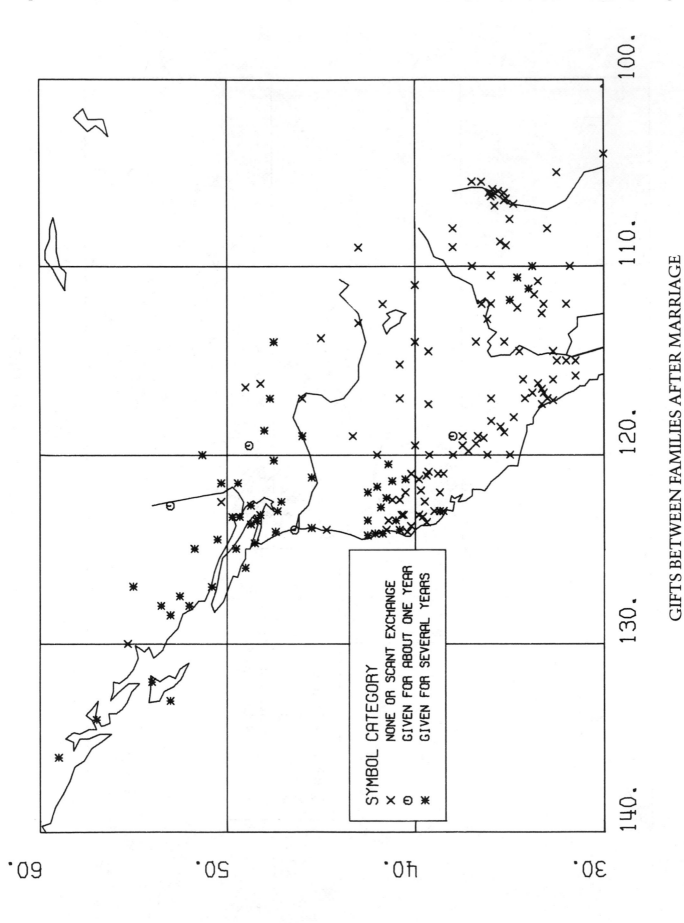

GIFTS BETWEEN FAMILIES AFTER MARRIAGE

SYMBOL CATEGORY
X   NONE OR SCANT EXCHANGE
⊖   GIVEN FOR ABOUT ONE YEAR
✳   GIVEN FOR SEVERAL YEARS

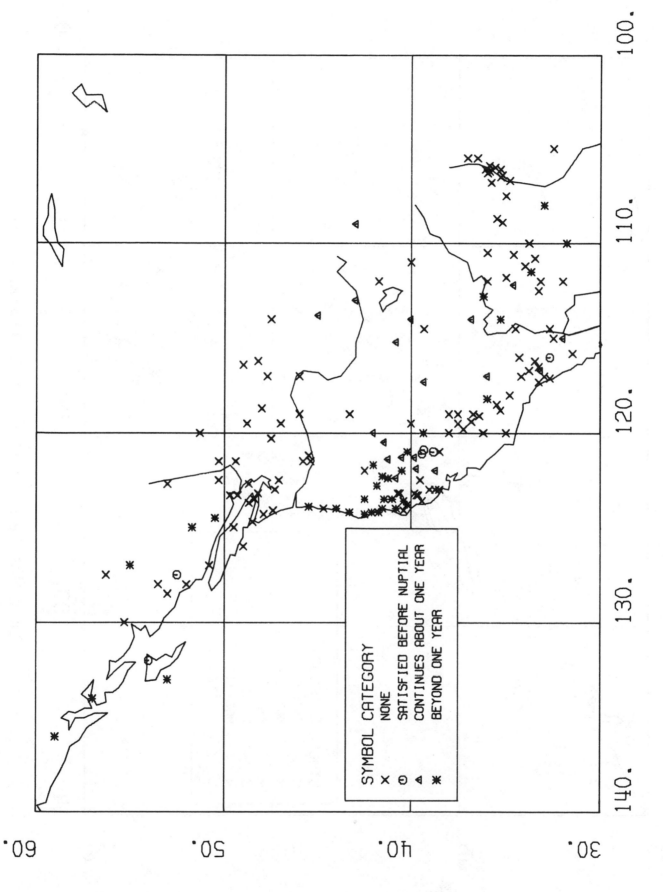

DURATION OF BRIDE SERVICE AFTER MARRIAGE

SYMBOL CATEGORY
X   NONE
⊖   SATISFIED BEFORE NUPTIAL
◁   CONTINUES ABOUT ONE YEAR
✳   BEYOND ONE YEAR

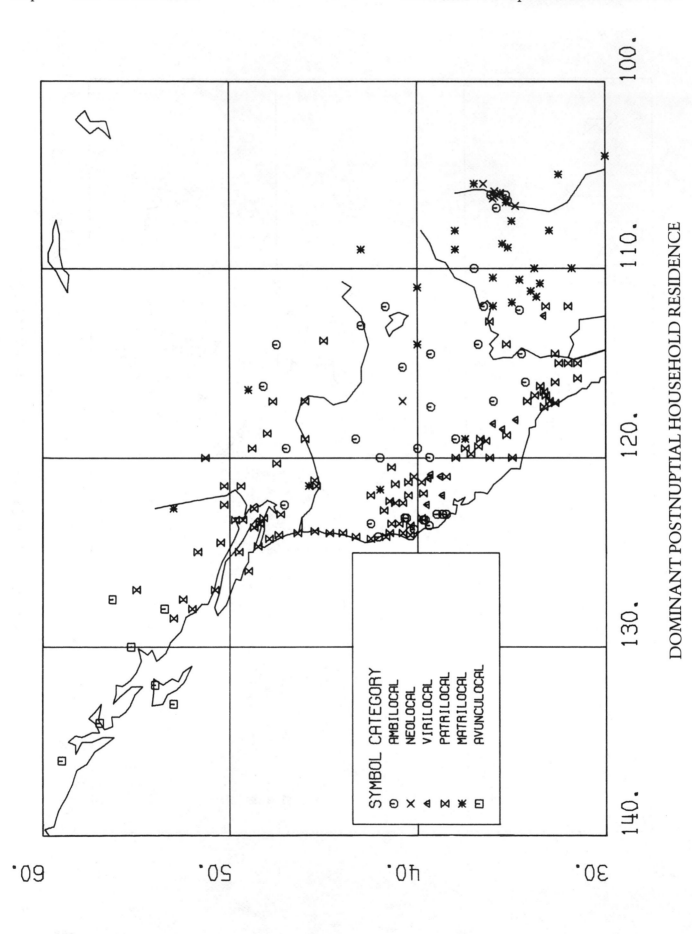

DOMINANT POSTNUPTIAL HOUSEHOLD RESIDENCE

SYMBOL CATEGORY
⊖ AMBILOCAL
× NEOLOCAL
◄ VIRILOCAL
⋈ PATRILOCAL
✱ MATRILOCAL
⊟ AVUNCULOCAL

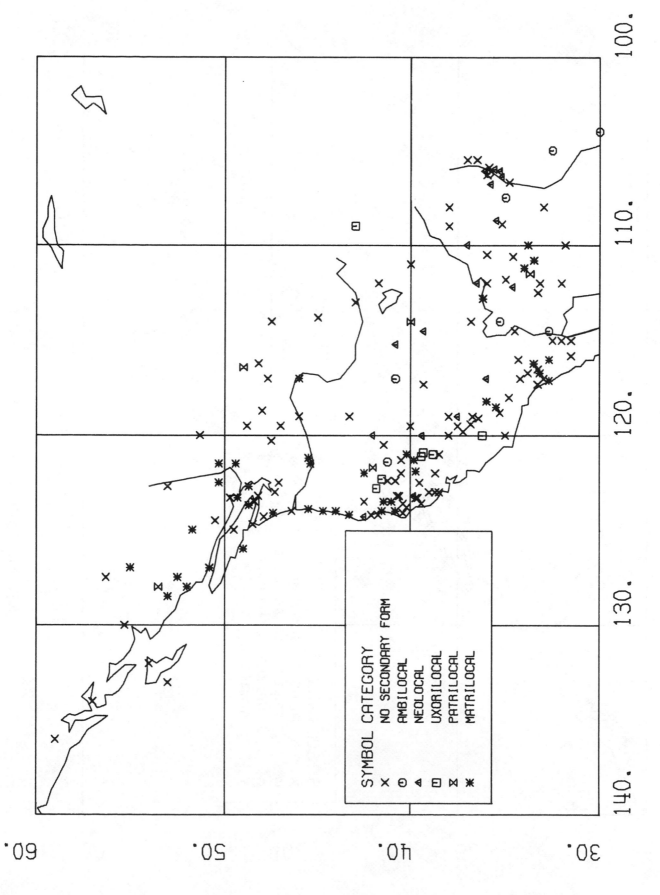

SECONDARY POSTNUPTIAL HOUSEHOLD RESIDENCE

SYMBOL CATEGORY
X   NO SECONDARY FORM
⊖   AMBILOCAL
◁   NEOLOCAL
⊟   UXORILOCAL
⋈   PATRILOCAL
✳   MATRILOCAL

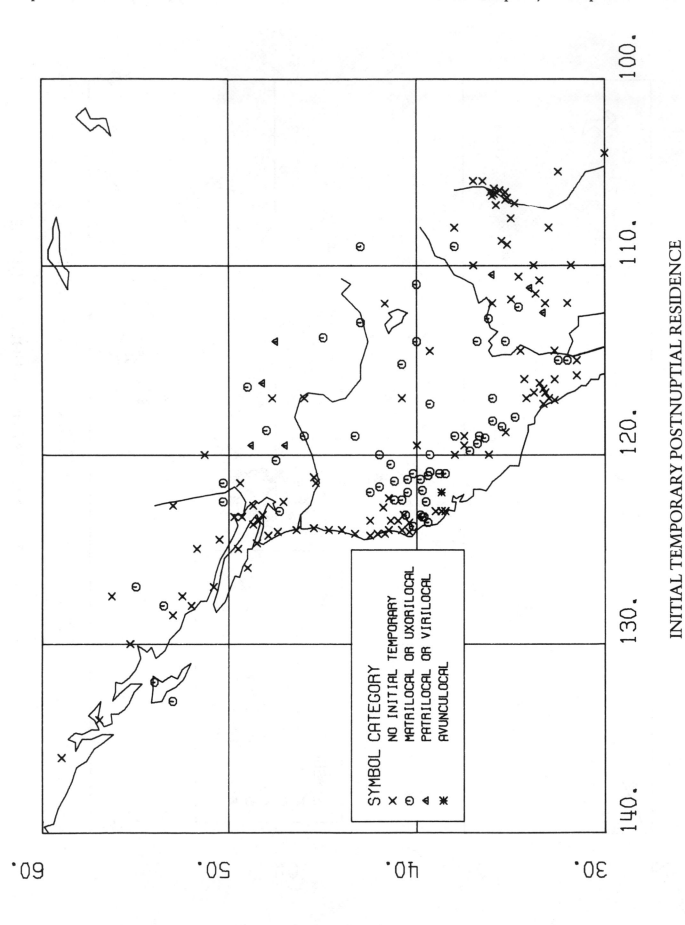

INITIAL TEMPORARY POSTNUPTIAL RESIDENCE

SYMBOL CATEGORY
X NO INITIAL TEMPORARY
⊖ MATRILOCAL OR UXORILOCAL
◁ PATRILOCAL OR VIRILOCAL
✳ AVUNCULOCAL

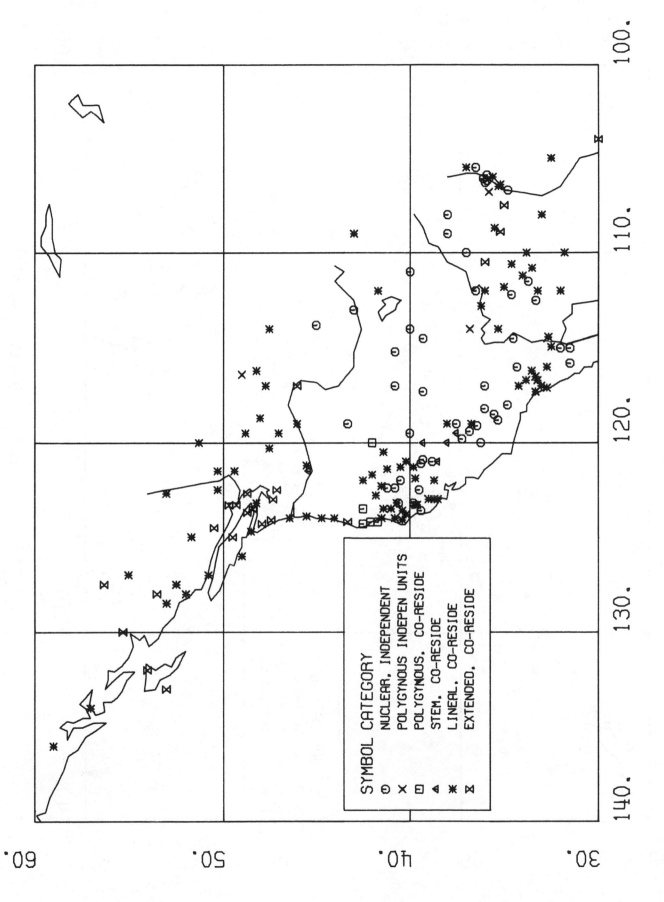

DOMINANT FAMILY HOUSEHOLD FORMS

SYMBOL CATEGORY
⊖ NUCLEAR. INDEPENDENT
✕ POLYGYNOUS INDEPEN UNITS
⊡ POLYGYNOUS. CO-RESIDE
◄ STEM. CO-RESIDE
✳ LINEAL. CO-RESIDE
⋈ EXTENDED. CO-RESIDE

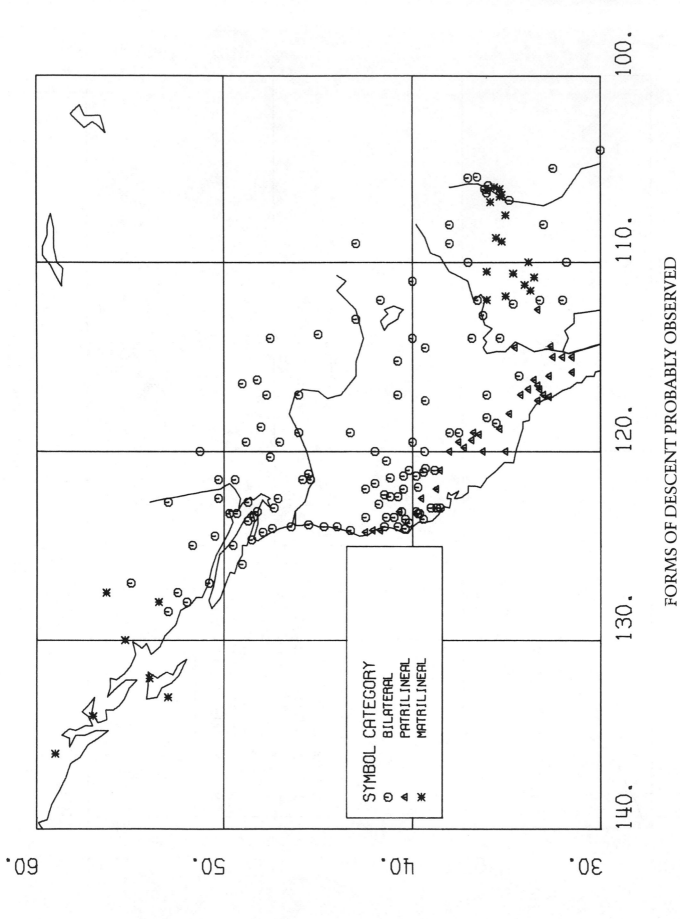

FORMS OF DESCENT PROBABLY OBSERVED

SYMBOL CATEGORY

Ɵ   BILATERAL

◄   PATRILINEAL

✳   MATRILINEAL

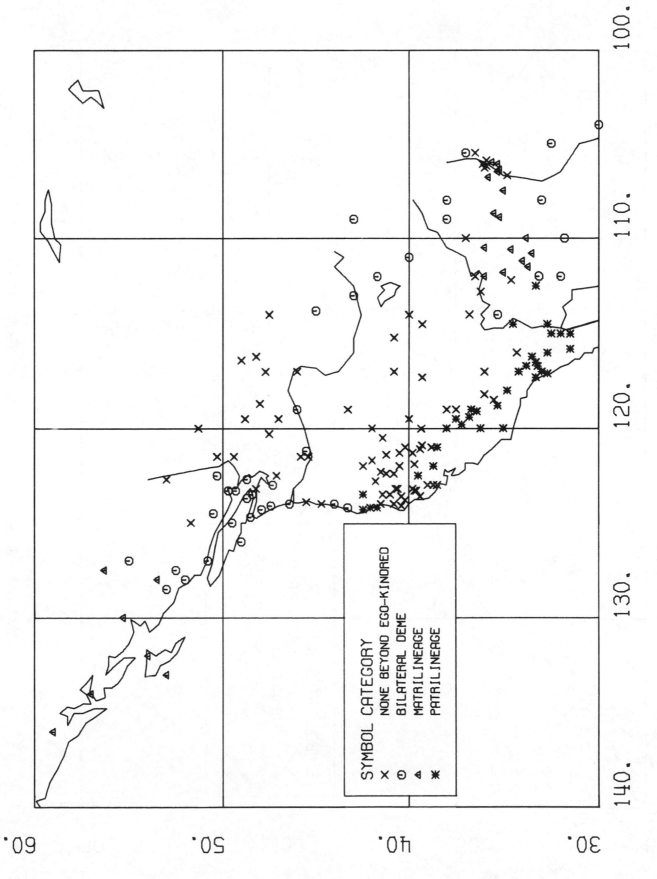

FORMS OF DEMONSTRATED KINSHIP UNITS

SYMBOL CATEGORY

×	NONE BEYOND EGO-KINDRED
⊖	BILATERAL DEME
◁	MATRILINEAGE
✳	PATRILINEAGE

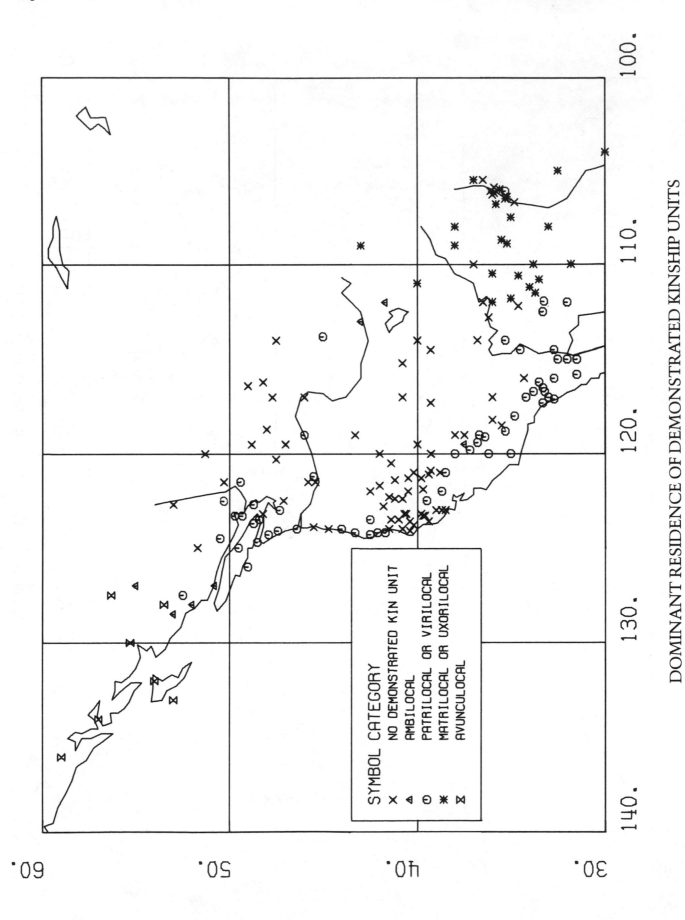

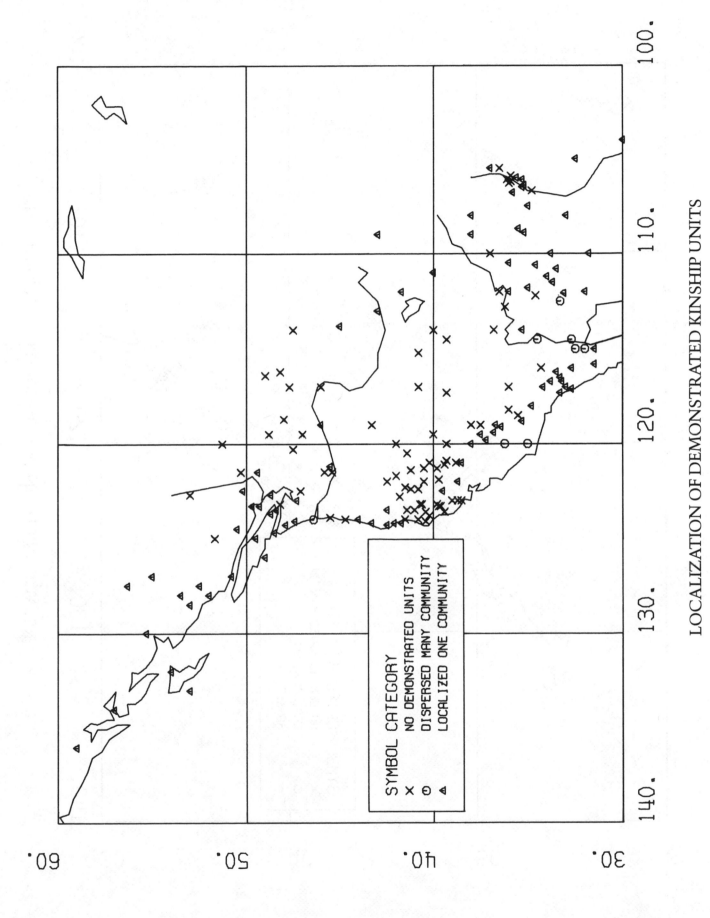

SYMBOL CATEGORY
X   NO DEMONSTRATED UNITS
Θ   DISPERSED MANY COMMUNITY
◁   LOCALIZED ONE COMMUNITY

LOCALIZATION OF DEMONSTRATED KINSHIP UNITS

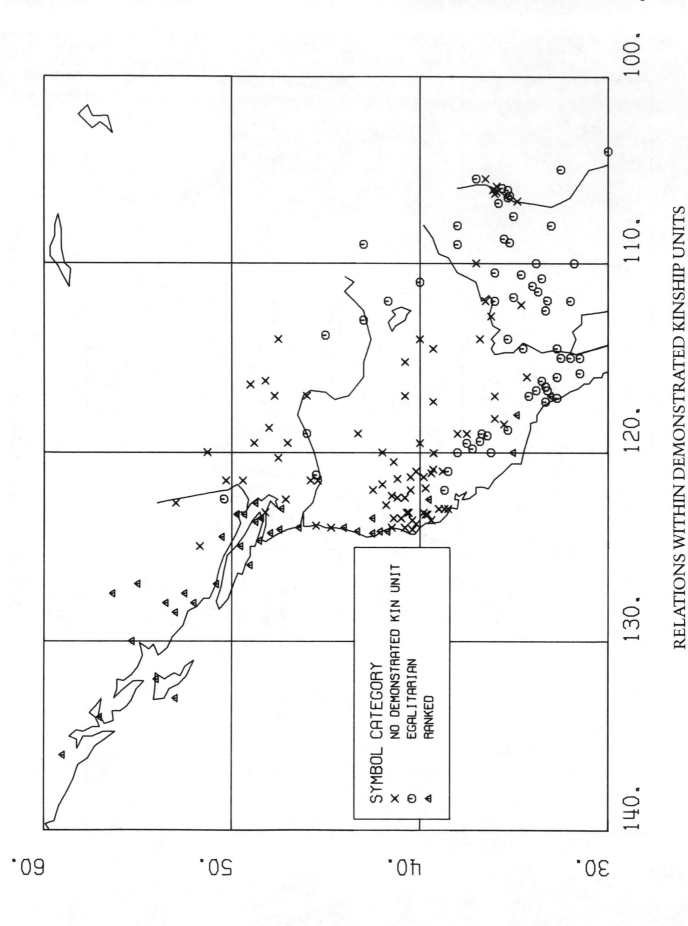

SYMBOL CATEGORY

	NO DEMONSTRATED KIN UNIT
X	
⊖	EGALITARIAN
◁	RANKED

RELATIONS WITHIN DEMONSTRATED KINSHIP UNITS

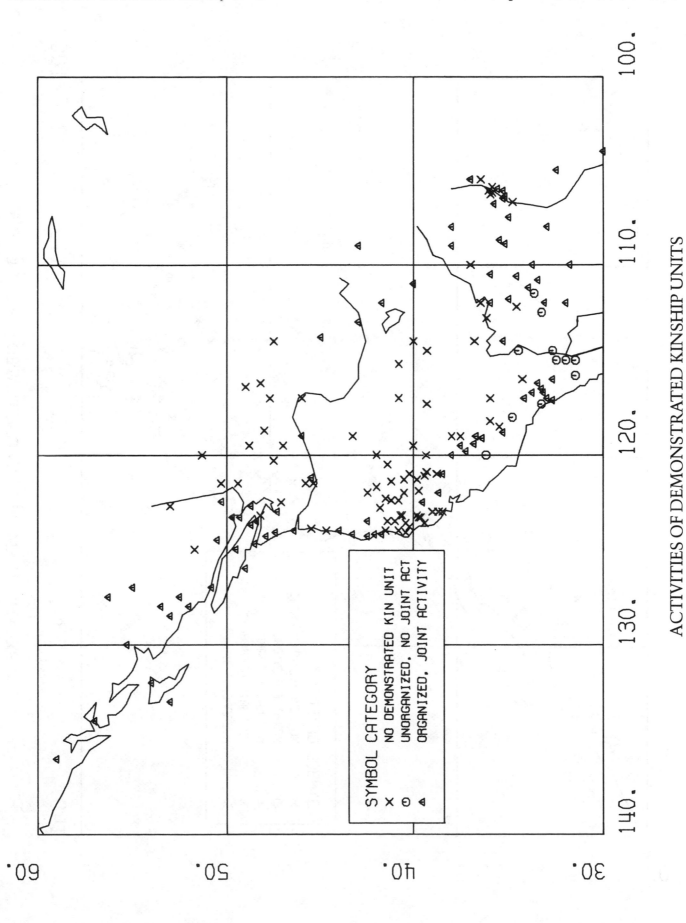

ACTIVITIES OF DEMONSTRATED KINSHIP UNITS

SYMBOL CATEGORY
×   NO DEMONSTRATED KIN UNIT
⊙   UNORGANIZED, NO JOINT ACT
◁   ORGANIZED, JOINT ACTIVITY

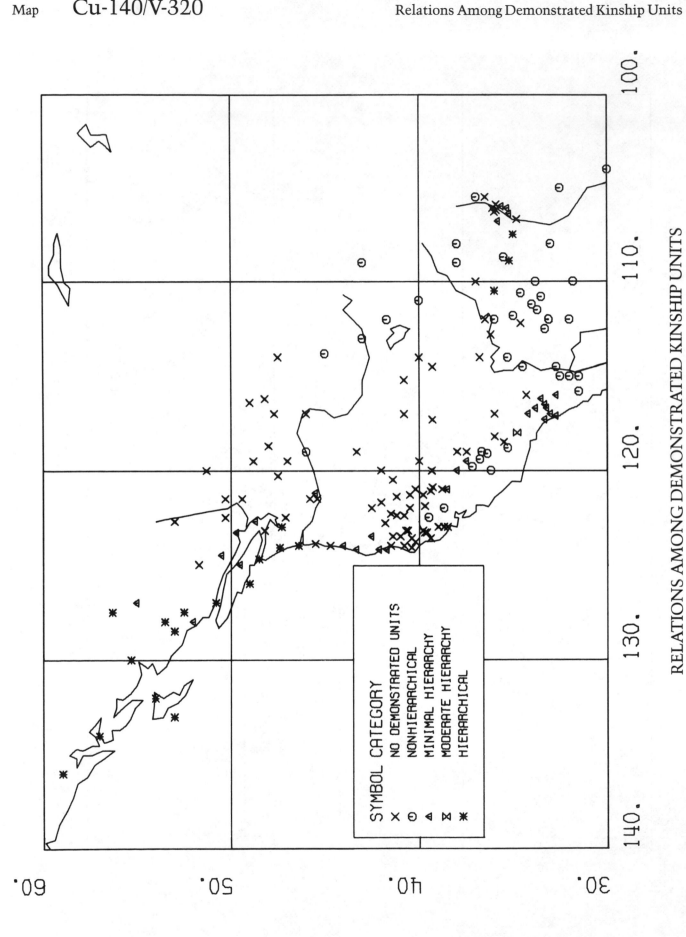

RELATIONS AMONG DEMONSTRATED KINSHIP UNITS

SYMBOL CATEGORY

X	NO DEMONSTRATED UNITS
⊖	NONHIERARCHICAL
◁	MINIMAL HIERARCHY
⋈	MODERATE HIERARCHY
✳	HIERARCHICAL

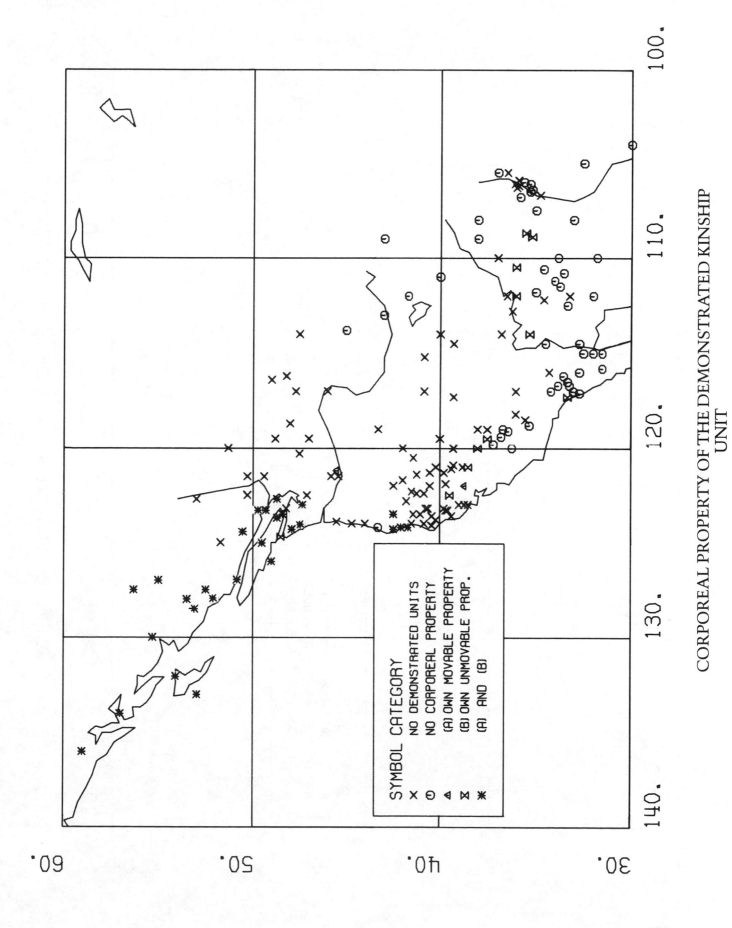

CORPOREAL PROPERTY OF THE DEMONSTRATED KINSHIP UNIT

SYMBOL CATEGORY

X	NO DEMONSTRATED UNITS
⊖	NO CORPOREAL PROPERTY
◄	(A) OWN MOVABLE PROPERTY
⋈	(B) OWN UNMOVABLE PROP.
✳	(A) AND (B)

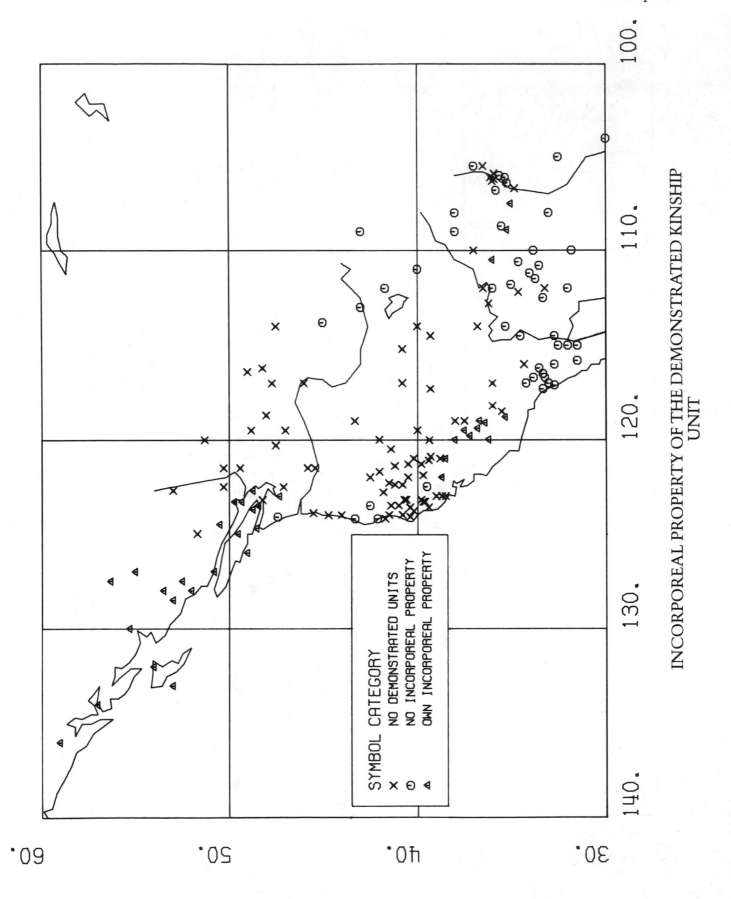

INCORPOREAL PROPERTY OF THE DEMONSTRATED KINSHIP
UNIT

SYMBOL CATEGORY

X	NO DEMONSTRATED UNITS
⊖	NO INCORPOREAL PROPERTY
◁	OWN INCORPOREAL PROPERTY

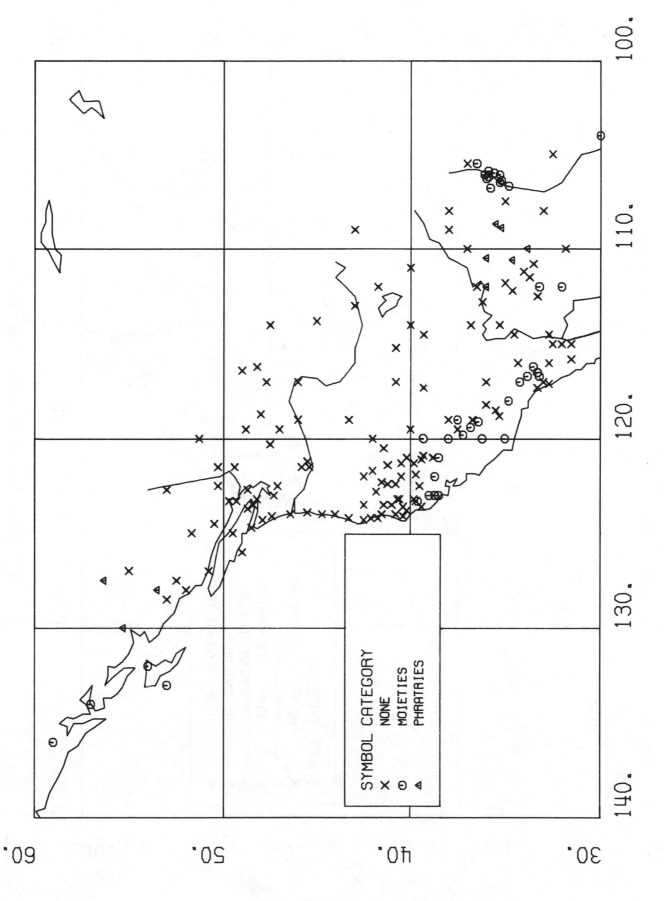

KINSHIP UNITS BEYOND SIBS AND SEPTS

SYMBOL CATEGORY
NONE
MOIETIES
PHRATRIES

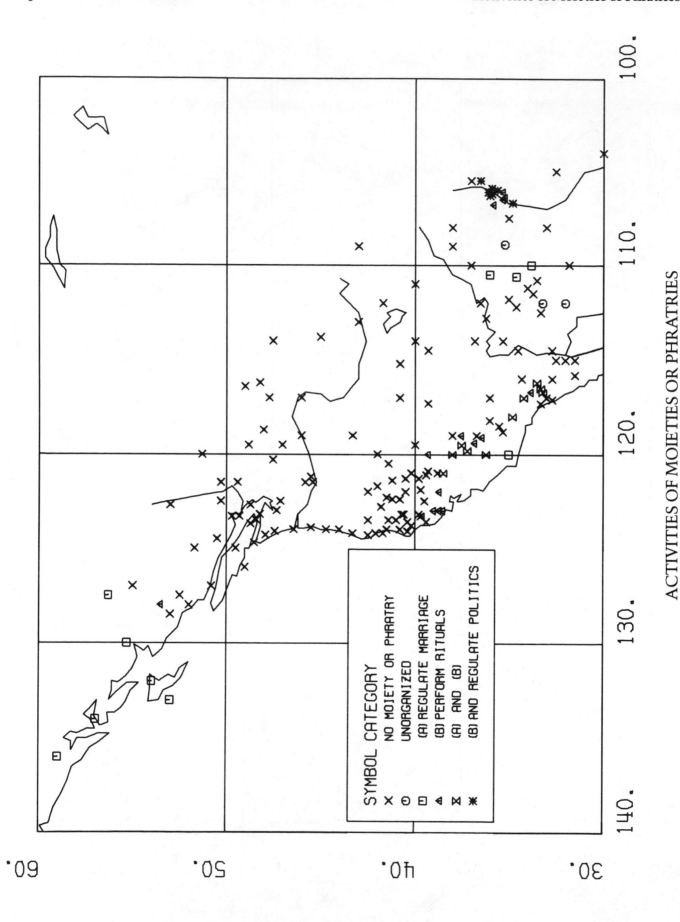

ACTIVITIES OF MOIETIES OR PHRATRIES

SYMBOL CATEGORY

X	NO MOIETY OR PHRATRY
⊖	UNORGANIZED
⊟	(A) REGULATE MARRIAGE
◄	(B) PERFORM RITUALS
⋈	(A) AND (B)
✳	(B) AND REGULATE POLITICS

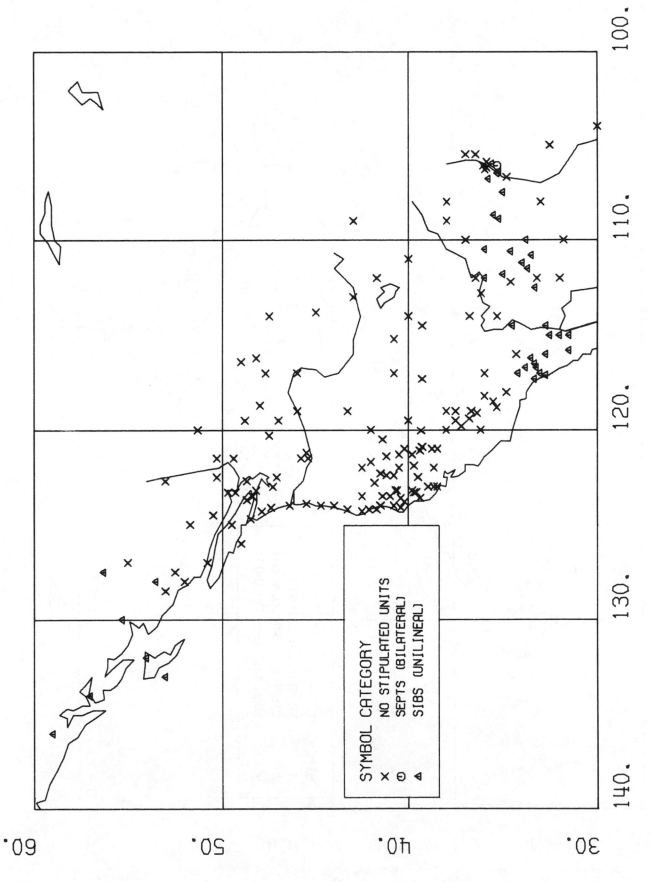

STIPULATED DESCENT UNITS

SYMBOL CATEGORY

×	NO STIPULATED UNITS
⊖	SEPTS (BILATERAL)
◁	SIBS (UNILINEAL)

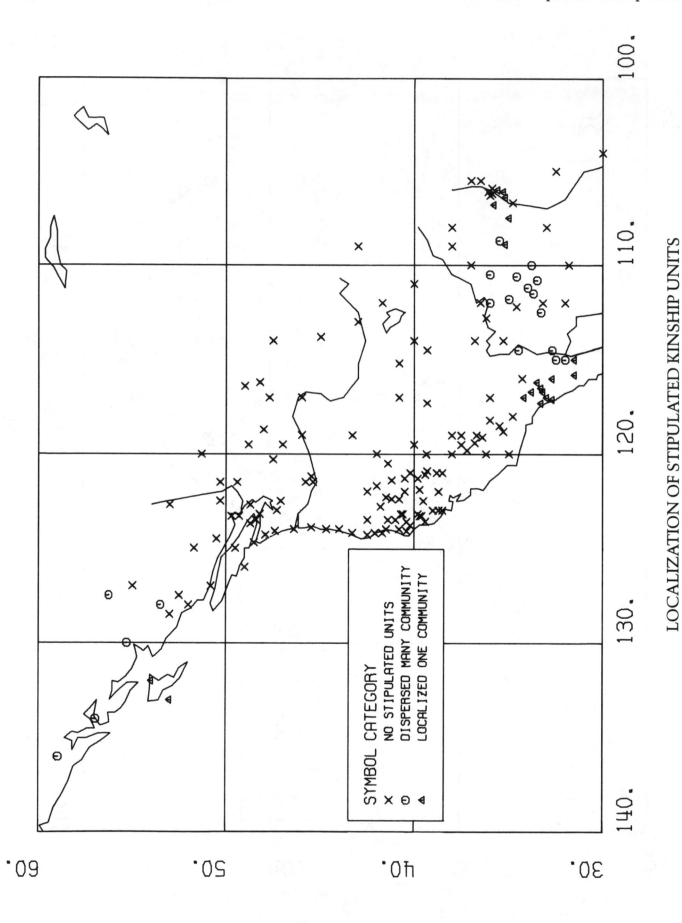

LOCALIZATION OF STIPULATED KINSHIP UNITS

SYMBOL CATEGORY
X NO STIPULATED UNITS
⊖ DISPERSED MANY COMMUNITY
◁ LOCALIZED ONE COMMUNITY

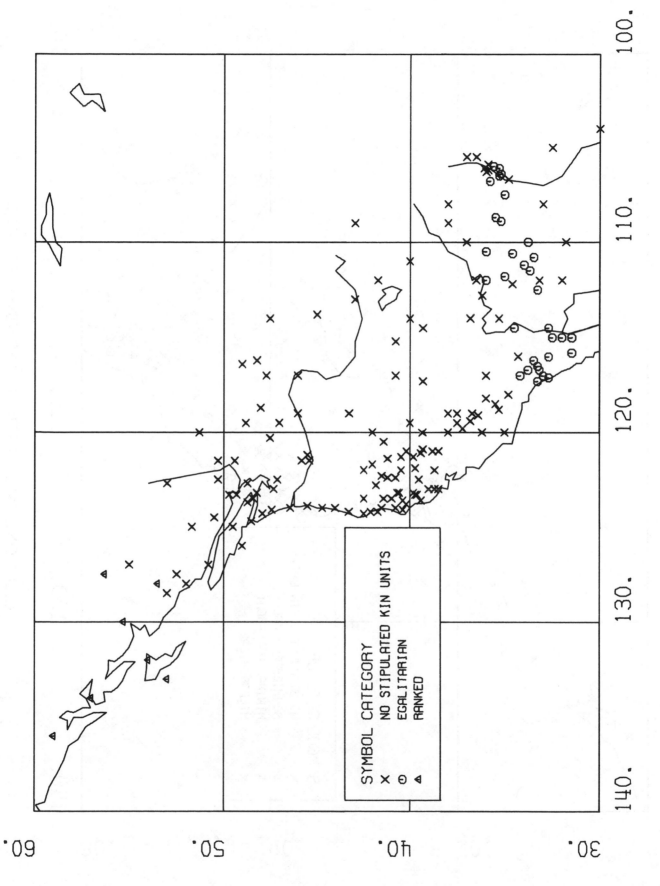

SYMBOL CATEGORY
X   NO STIPULATED KIN UNITS
Θ   EGALITARIAN
◁   RANKED

RELATIONS WITHIN STIPULATED KINSHIP UNITS

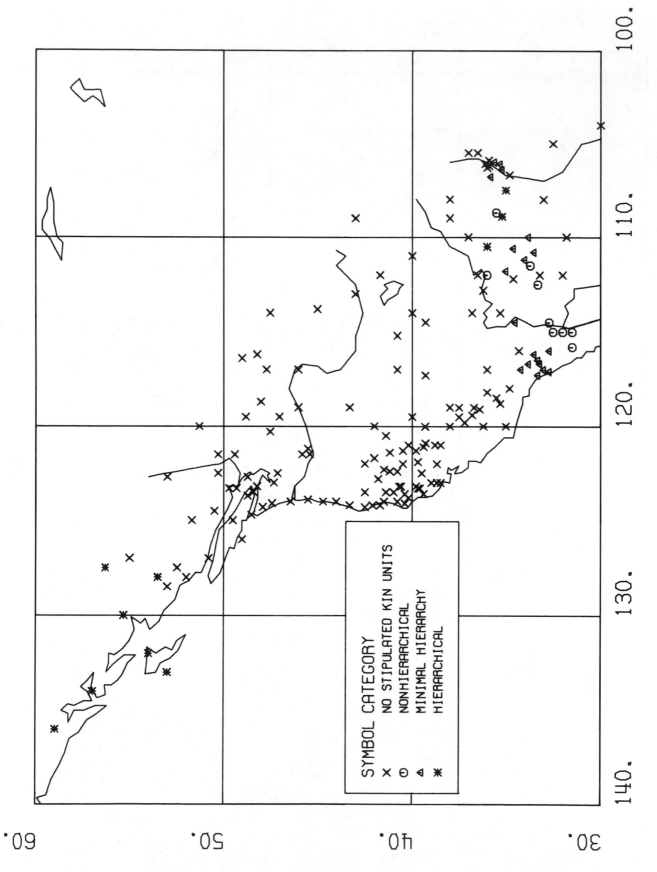

RELATIONS AMONG STIPULATED KINSHIP UNITS

SYMBOL CATEGORY
× NO STIPULATED KIN UNITS
⊖ NONHIERARCHICAL
◁ MINIMAL HIERARCHY
✳ HIERARCHICAL

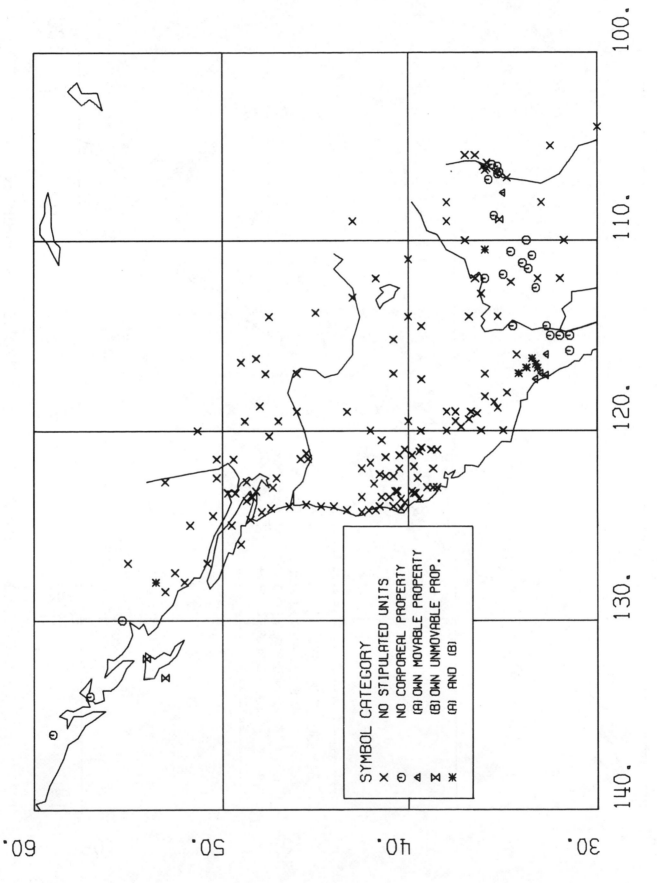

CORPOREAL PROPERTY OF THE STIPULATED KINSHIP UNIT

SYMBOL CATEGORY
X   NO STIPULATED UNITS
⊖   NO CORPOREAL PROPERTY
◁   (A) OWN MOVABLE PROPERTY
⋈   (B) OWN UNMOVABLE PROP.
✳   (A) AND (B)

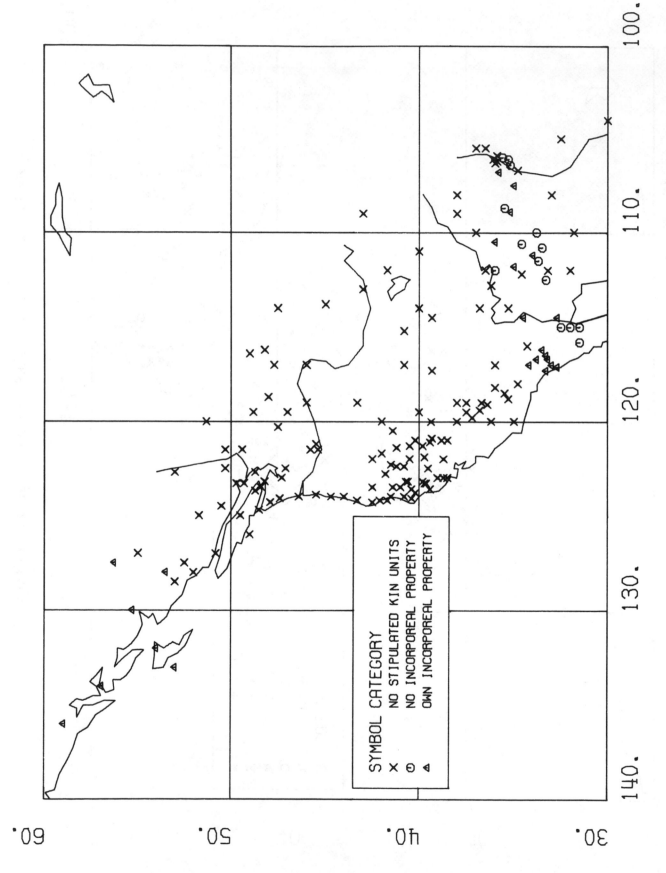

SYMBOL CATEGORY
X   NO STIPULATED KIN UNITS
⊖   NO INCORPOREAL PROPERTY
◁   OWN INCORPOREAL PROPERTY

INCORPOREAL PROPERTY OF THE STIPULATED KINSHIP UNIT

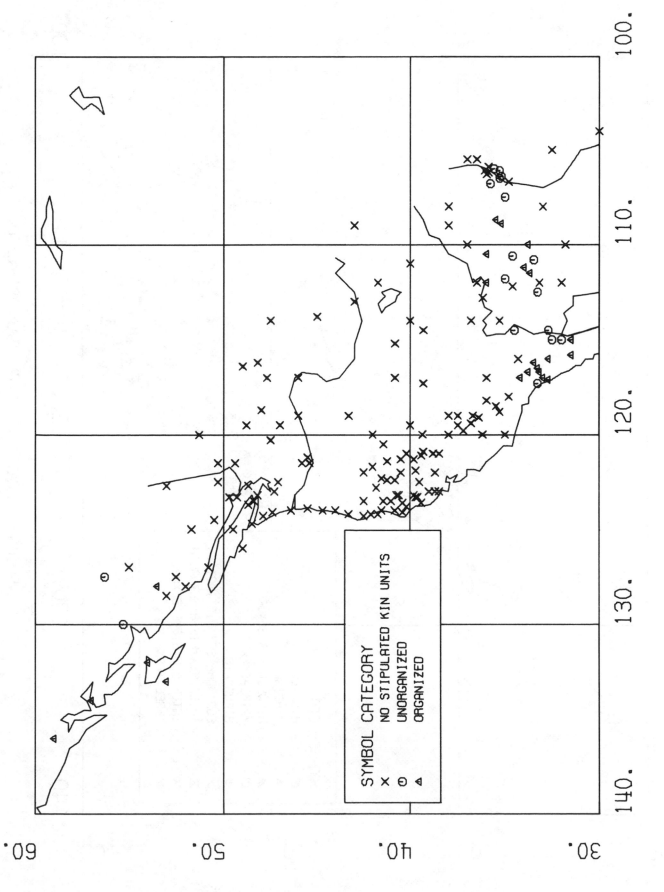

SYMBOL CATEGORY

	NO STIPULATED KIN UNITS
X	
☉	UNORGANIZED
◁	ORGANIZED

ACTIVITIES OF STIPULATED KINSHIP UNITS

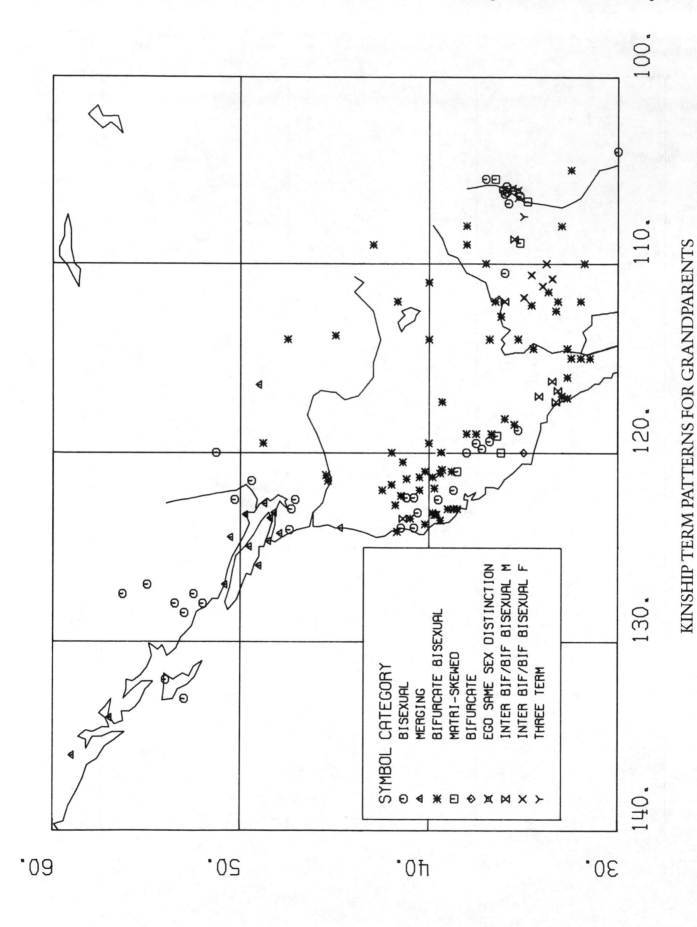

KINSHIP TERM PATTERNS FOR GRANDPARENTS

SYMBOL CATEGORY
⊖ BISEXUAL
◁ MERGING
✳ BIFURCATE BISEXUAL
⊟ MATRI-SKEWED
◇ BIFURCATE
⋈ EGO SAME SEX DISTINCTION
⋈ INTER BIF/BIF BISEXUAL M
✕ INTER BIF/BIF BISEXUAL F
Y THREE TERM

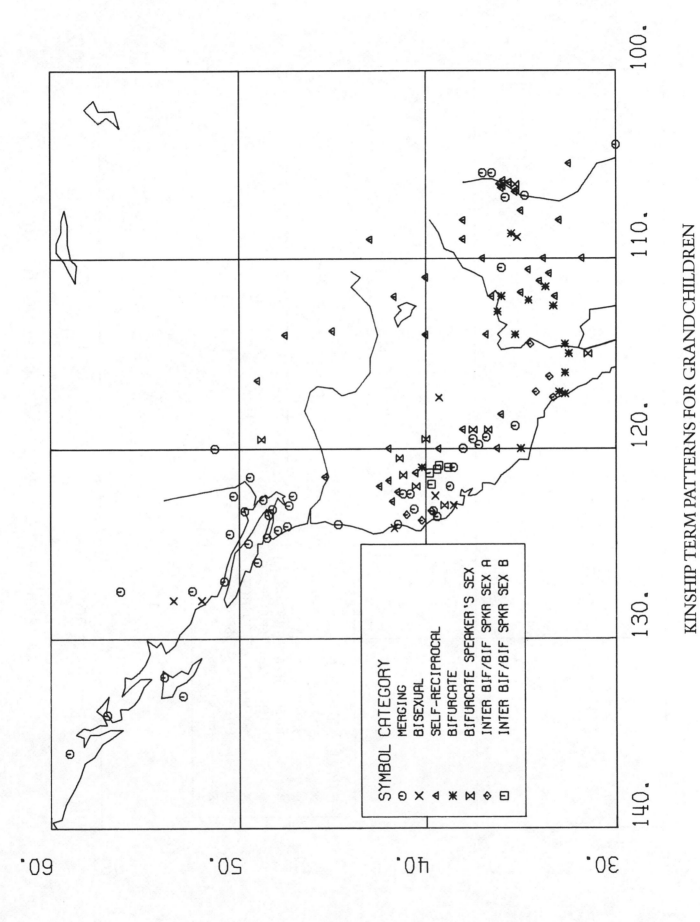

SYMBOL CATEGORY

MERGING
BISEXUAL
SELF-RECIPROCAL
BIFURCATE
BIFURCATE SPEAKER'S SEX
INTER BIF/BIF SPKR SEX A
INTER BIF/BIF SPKR SEX B

KINSHIP TERM PATTERNS FOR GRANDCHILDREN

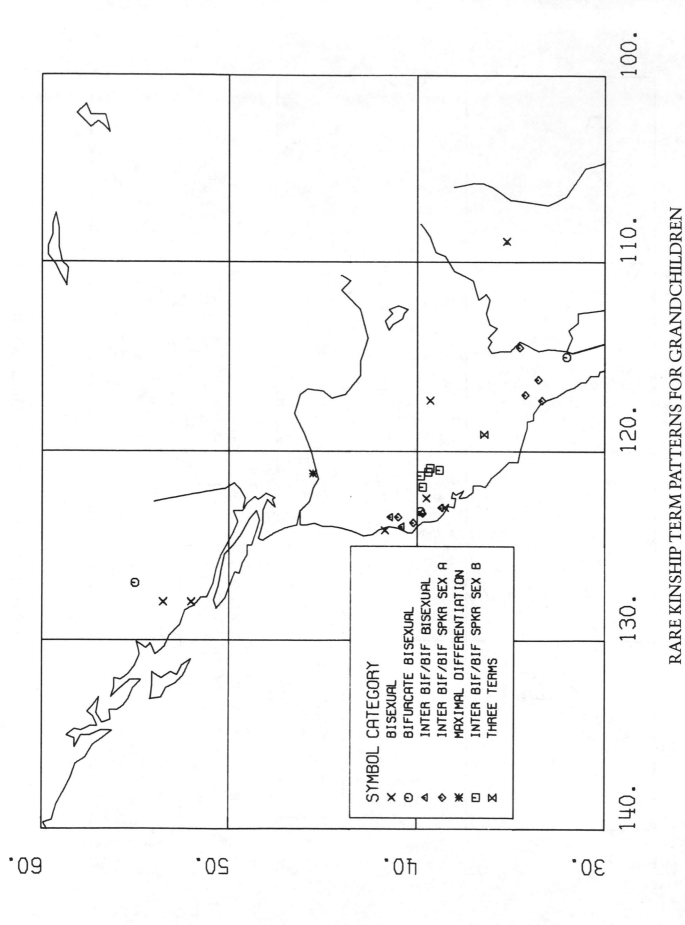

RARE KINSHIP TERM PATTERNS FOR GRANDCHILDREN

SYMBOL CATEGORY
X   BISEXUAL
⊖   BIFURCATE BISEXUAL
◁   INTER BIF/BIF BISEXUAL
◇   INTER BIF/BIF SPKR SEX A
✳   MAXIMAL DIFFERENTIATION
⊟   INTER BIF/BIF SPKR SEX B
⋈   THREE TERMS

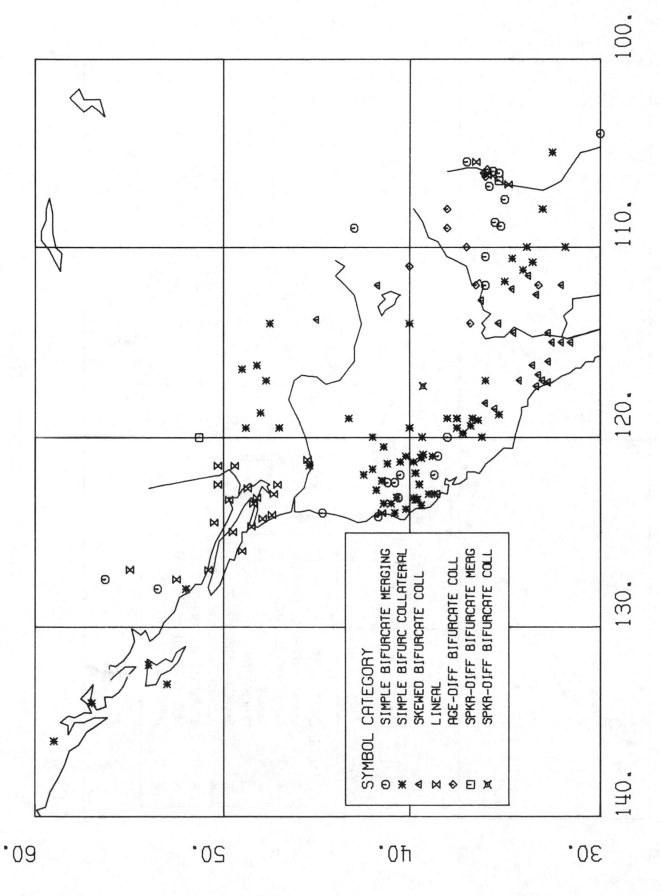

KINSHIP TERM PATTERNS FOR UNCLES

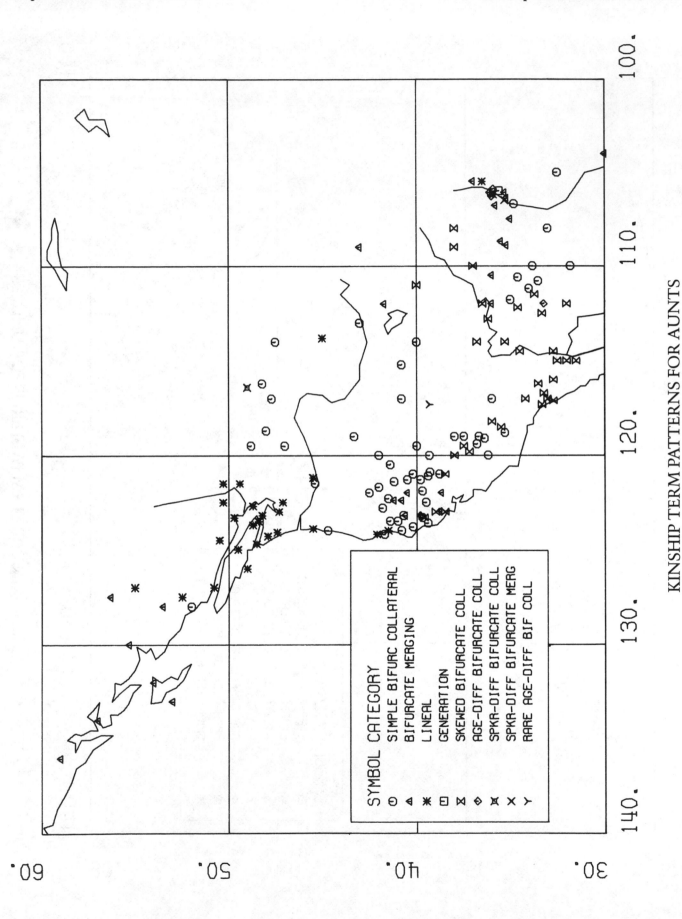

KINSHIP TERM PATTERNS FOR AUNTS

SYMBOL CATEGORY

⊖ SIMPLE BIFURC COLLATERAL
◁ BIFURCATE MERGING
✳ LINEAL
⊟ GENERATION
⋈ SKEWED BIFURCATE COLL
◇ AGE-DIFF BIFURCATE COLL
⋈ SPKR-DIFF BIFURCATE COLL
✕ SPKR-DIFF BIFURCATE MERG
Y RARE AGE-DIFF BIF COLL

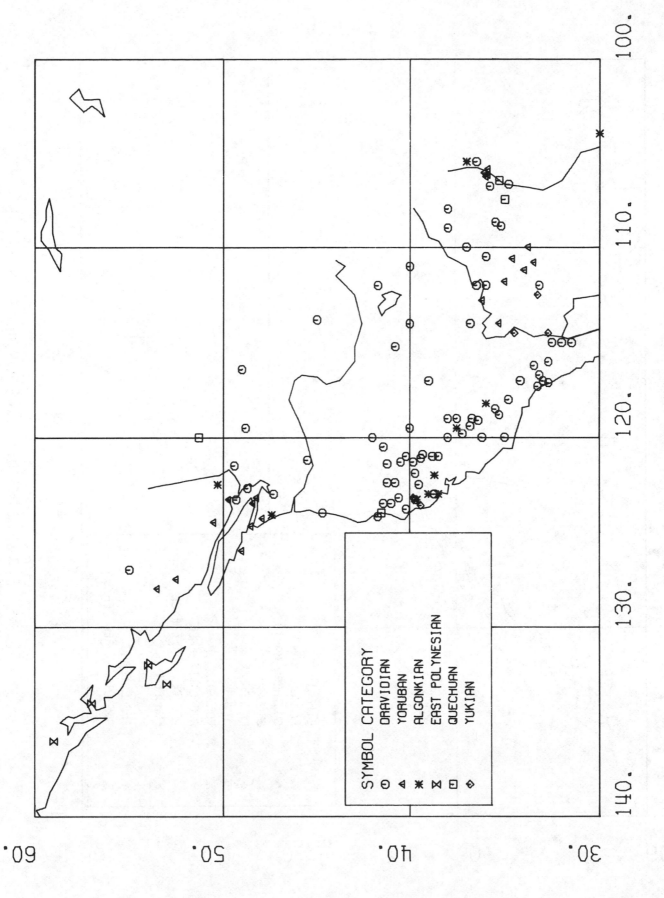

KINSHIP TERM PATTERNS FOR SIBLINGS

SYMBOL CATEGORY
Θ   DRAVIDIAN
◁   YORUBAN
✳   ALGONKIAN
⋈   EAST POLYNESIAN
⊟   QUECHUAN
◇   YUKIAN

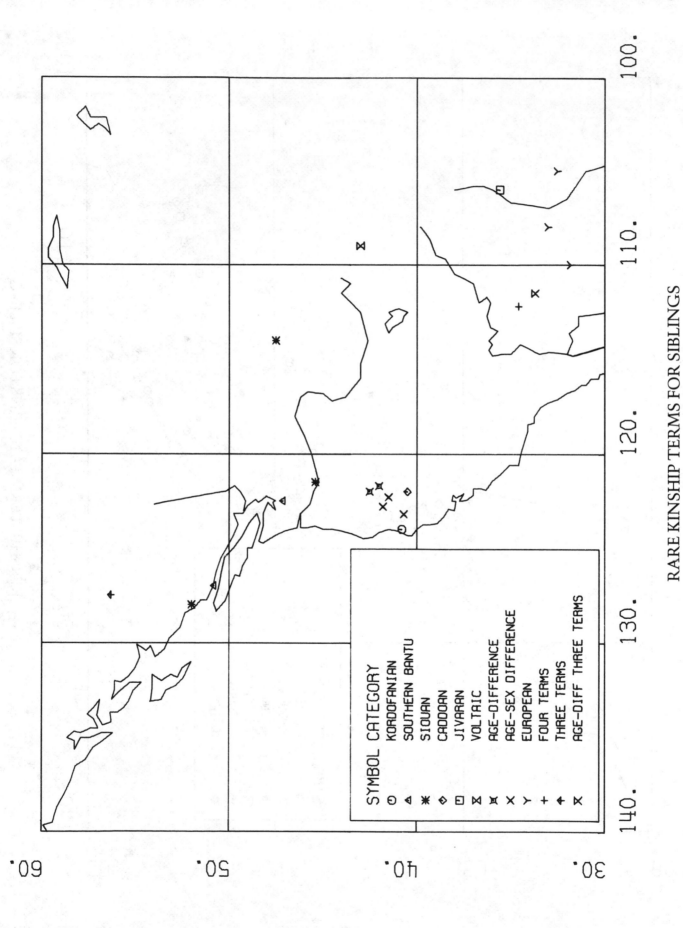

RARE KINSHIP TERMS FOR SIBLINGS

SYMBOL CATEGORY
KORDOFANIAN
SOUTHERN BANTU
SIOUAN
CADDOAN
JIVARAN
VOLTAIC
AGE-DIFFERENCE
AGE-SEX DIFFERENCE
EUROPEAN
FOUR TERMS
THREE TERMS
AGE-DIFF THREE TERMS

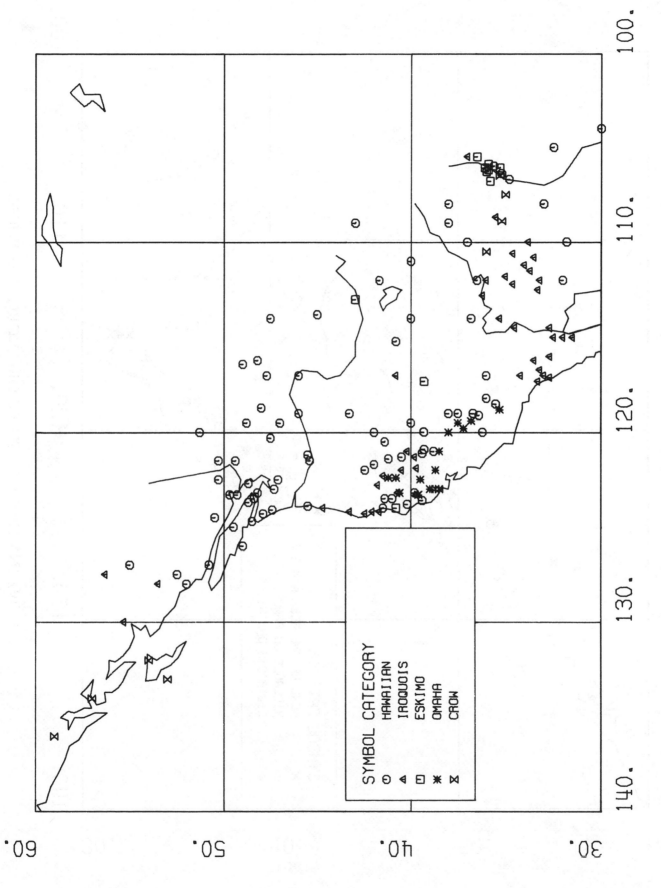

KINSHIP TERMS FOR CROSS AND PARALLEL COUSINS

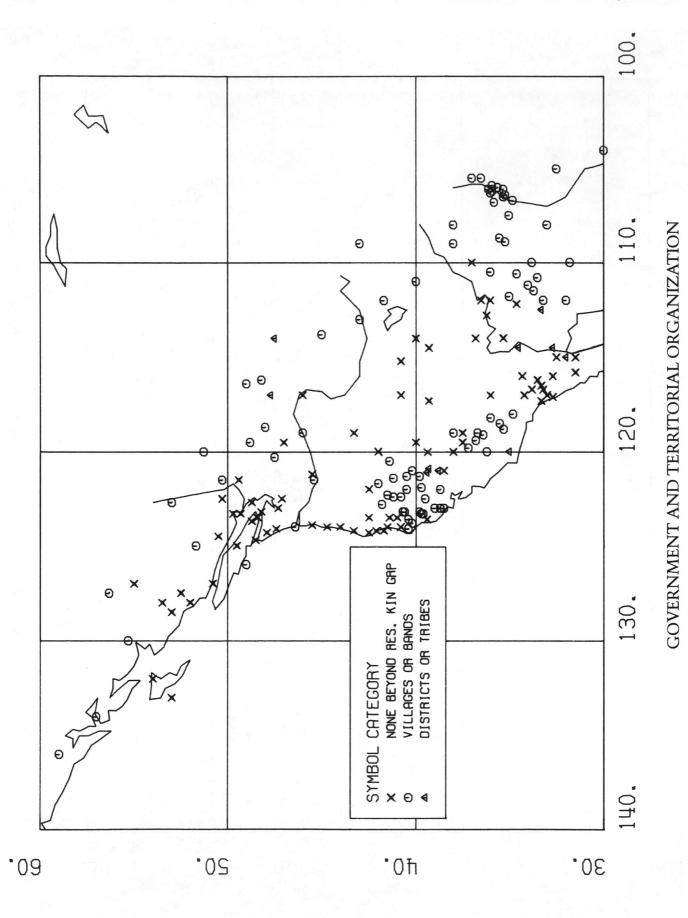

GOVERNMENT AND TERRITORIAL ORGANIZATION

SYMBOL CATEGORY
X   NONE BEYOND RES. KIN GRP
⊖   VILLAGES OR BANDS
◁   DISTRICTS OR TRIBES

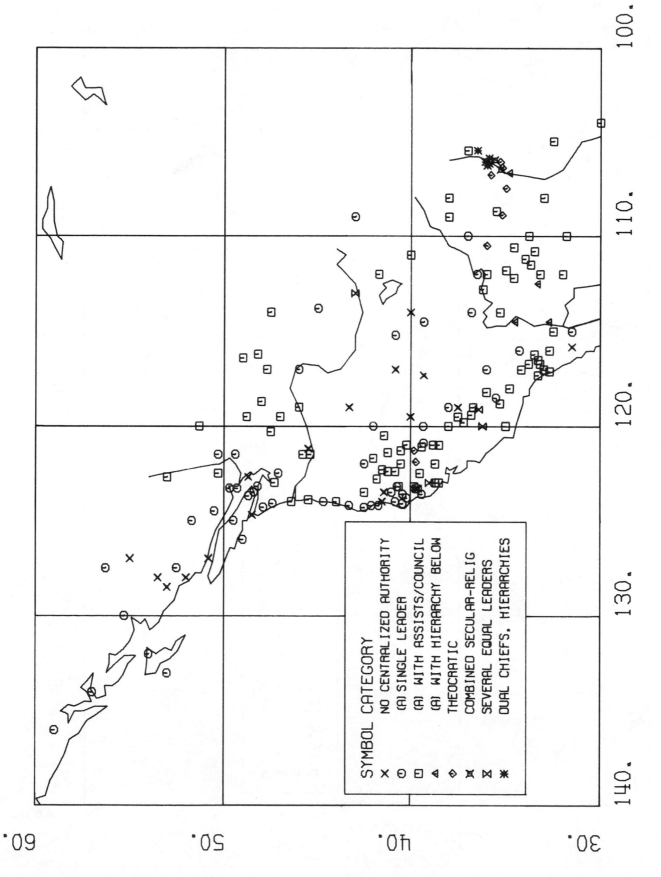

LOCAL COMMUNITY POLITICAL LEADERSHIP

SYMBOL CATEGORY
X   NO CENTRALIZED AUTHORITY
⊖   (A) SINGLE LEADER
⊟   (A) WITH ASSISTS/COUNCIL
◁   (A) WITH HIERARCHY BELOW
◇   THEOCRATIC
⋈   COMBINED SECULAR-RELIG
⋈   SEVERAL EQUAL LEADERS
✳   DUAL CHIEFS. HIERARCHIES

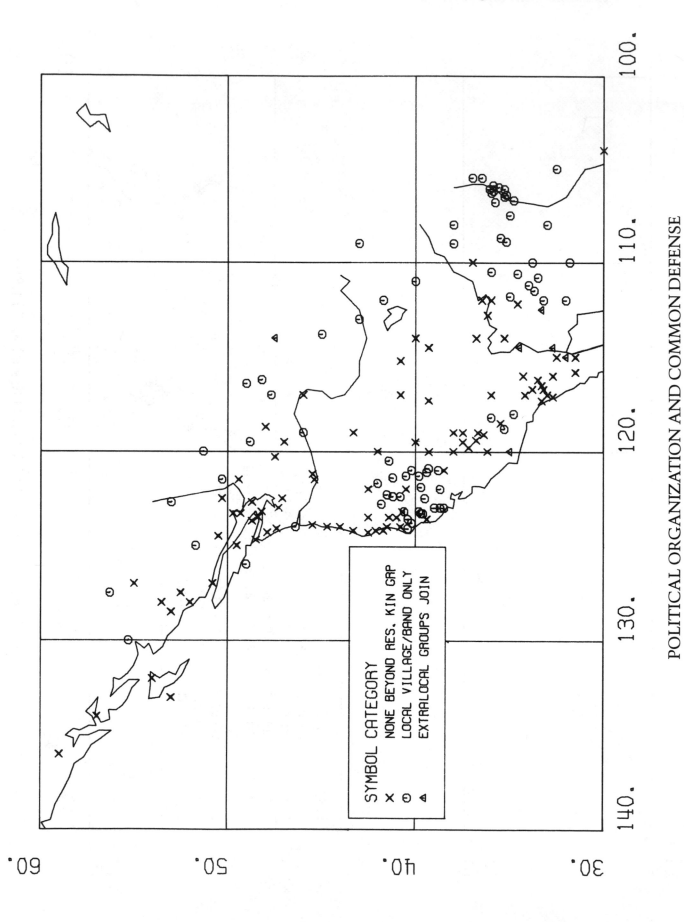

POLITICAL ORGANIZATION AND COMMON DEFENSE

SYMBOL CATEGORY

NONE BEYOND RES. KIN GRP   X

LOCAL VILLAGE/BAND ONLY   ⊖

EXTRALOCAL GROUPS JOIN   ◁

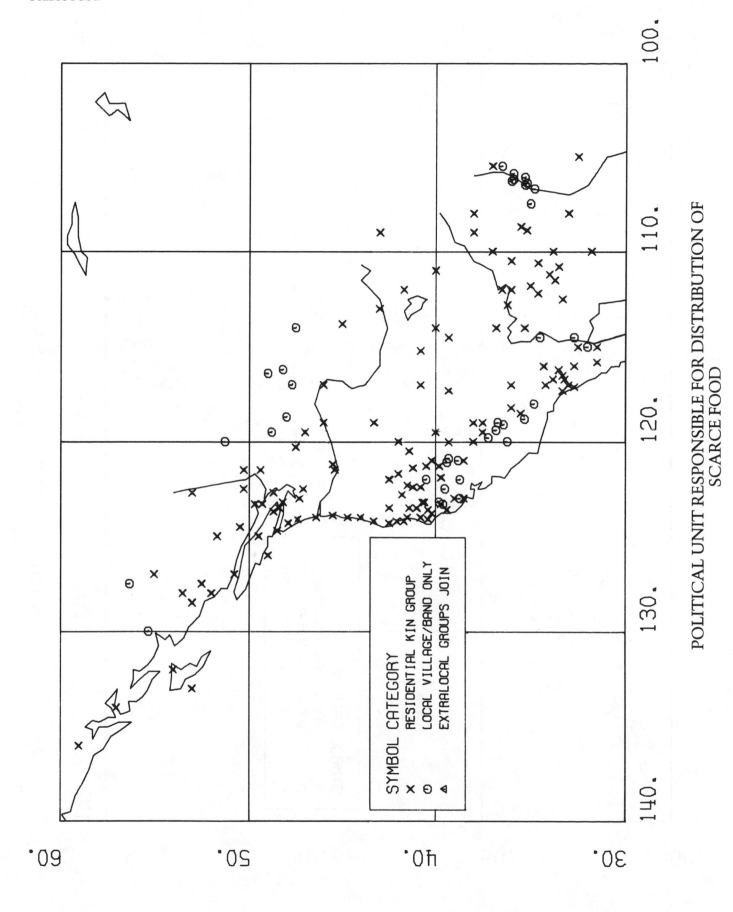

POLITICAL UNIT RESPONSIBLE FOR DISTRIBUTION OF
SCARCE FOOD

SYMBOL CATEGORY
X   RESIDENTIAL KIN GROUP
⊖   LOCAL VILLAGE/BAND ONLY
▲   EXTRALOCAL GROUPS JOIN

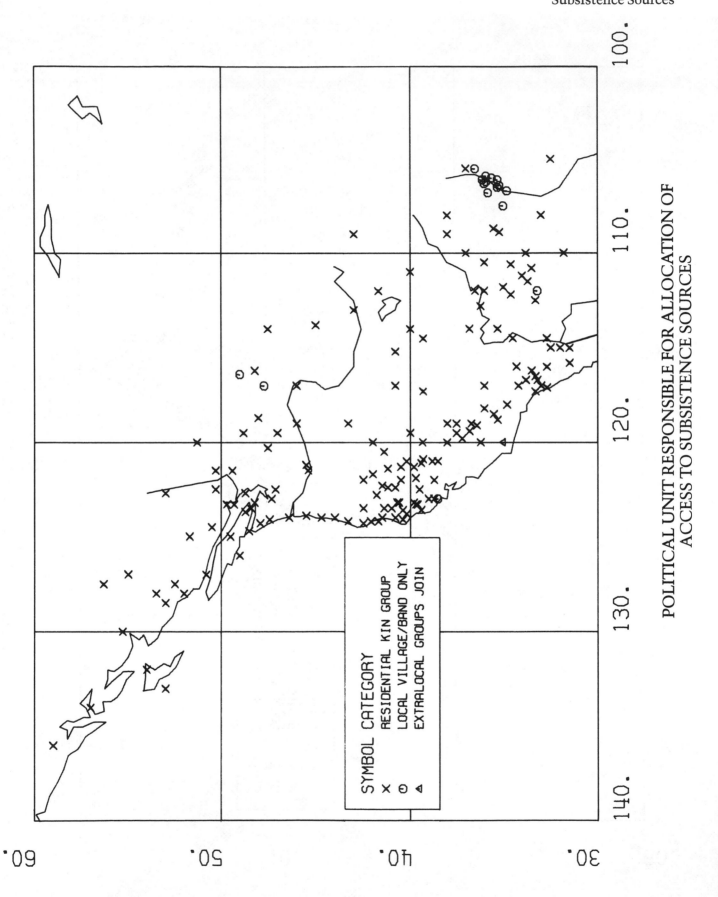

POLITICAL UNIT RESPONSIBLE FOR ALLOCATION OF
ACCESS TO SUBSISTENCE SOURCES

SYMBOL CATEGORY
X   RESIDENTIAL KIN GROUP
⊖   LOCAL VILLAGE/BAND ONLY
▲   EXTRALOCAL GROUPS JOIN

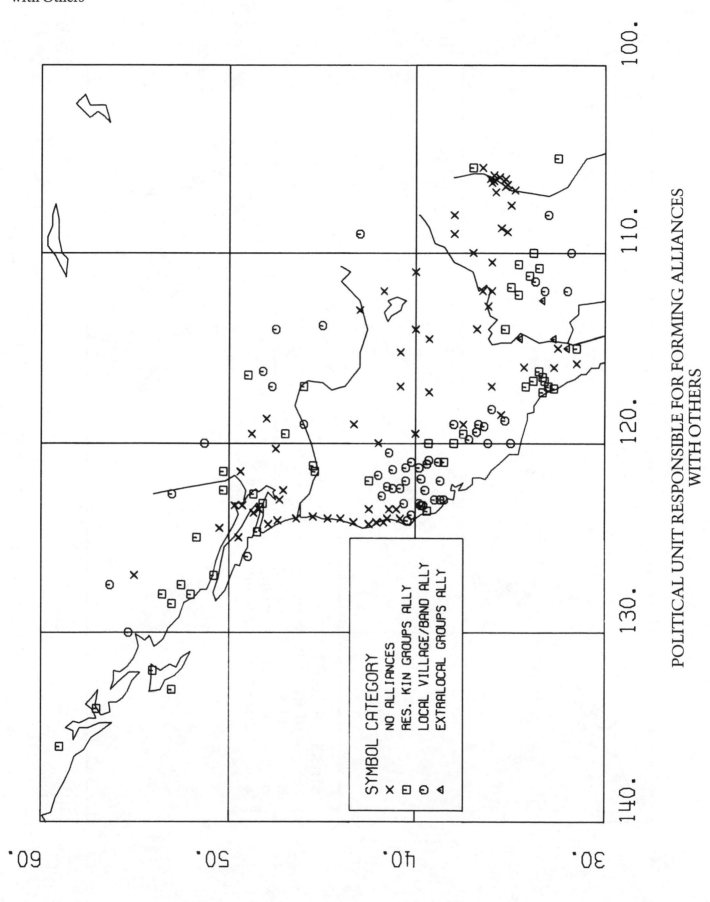

POLITICAL UNIT RESPONSIBLE FOR FORMING ALLIANCES
WITH OTHERS

SYMBOL CATEGORY
X   NO ALLIANCES
⊟   RES. KIN GROUPS ALLY
⊖   LOCAL VILLAGE/BAND ALLY
◁   EXTRALOCAL GROUPS ALLY

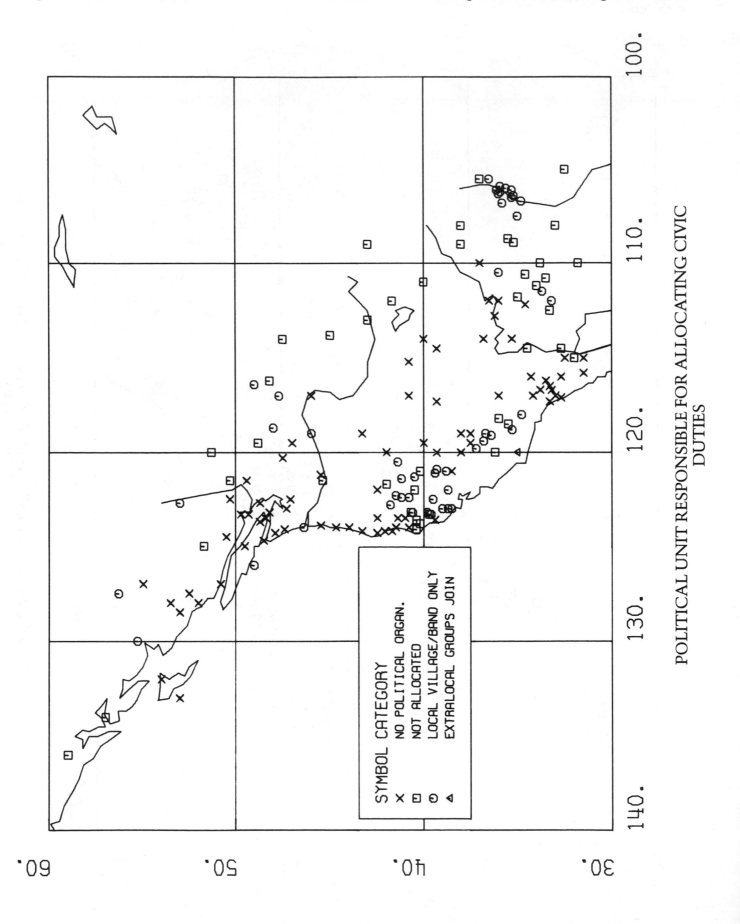

POLITICAL UNIT RESPONSIBLE FOR ALLOCATING CIVIC DUTIES

SYMBOL CATEGORY

X   NO POLITICAL ORGAN.
⊟   NOT ALLOCATED
⊙   LOCAL VILLAGE/BAND ONLY
◁   EXTRALOCAL GROUPS JOIN

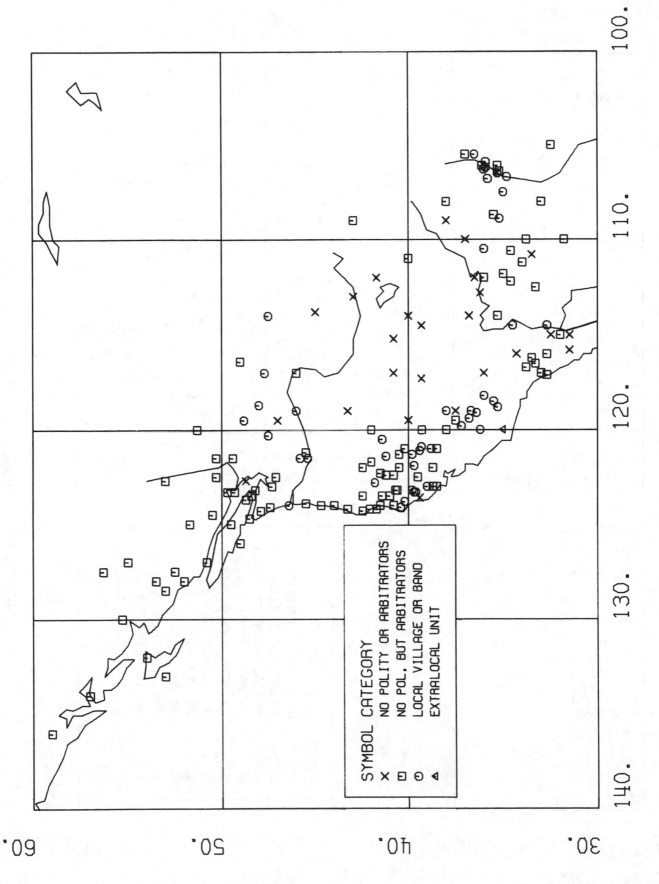

POLITICAL UNIT RESPONSIBLE FOR PUNISHING CRIMES

SYMBOL CATEGORY
× NO POLITY OR ARBITRATORS
⊟ NO POL. BUT ARBITRATORS
⊖ LOCAL VILLAGE OR BAND
◢ EXTRALOCAL UNIT

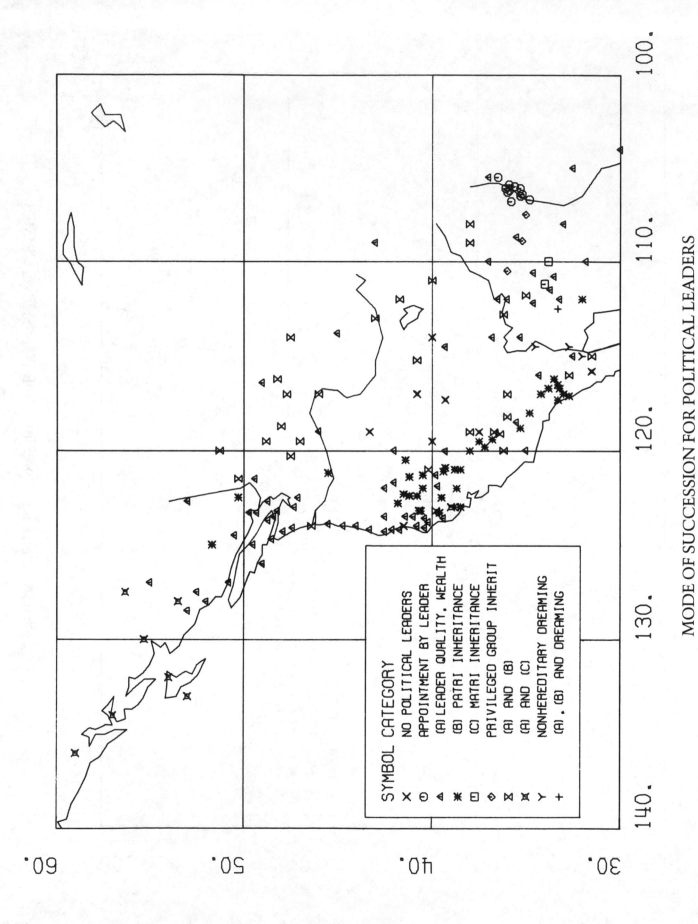

SYMBOL CATEGORY

X	NO POLITICAL LEADERS
⊖	APPOINTMENT BY LEADER
◁	(A) LEADER QUALITY, WEALTH
✳	(B) PATRI INHERITANCE
⊟	(C) MATRI INHERITANCE
◇	PRIVILEGED GROUP INHERIT
⋈	(A) AND (B)
⋈	(A) AND (C)
Y	NONHEREDITARY DREAMING
+	(A),(B) AND DREAMING

MODE OF SUCCESSION FOR POLITICAL LEADERS

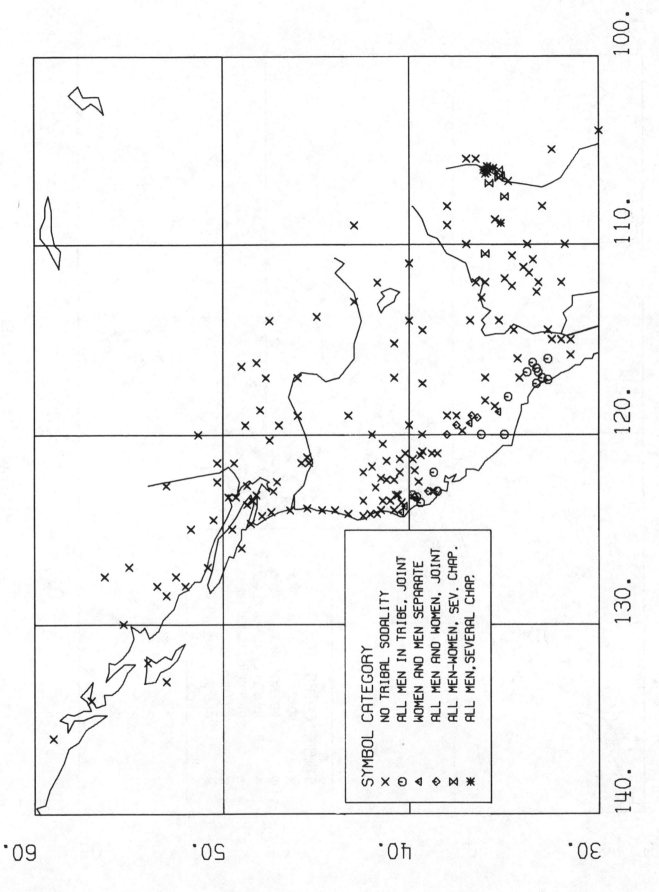

NATURE OF TRIBAL SODALITIES

SYMBOL CATEGORY
X   NO TRIBAL SODALITY
Θ   ALL MEN IN TRIBE, JOINT
◁   WOMEN AND MEN SEPARATE
◇   ALL MEN AND WOMEN, JOINT
⋈   ALL MEN-WOMEN, SEV. CHAP.
✳   ALL MEN, SEVERAL CHAP.

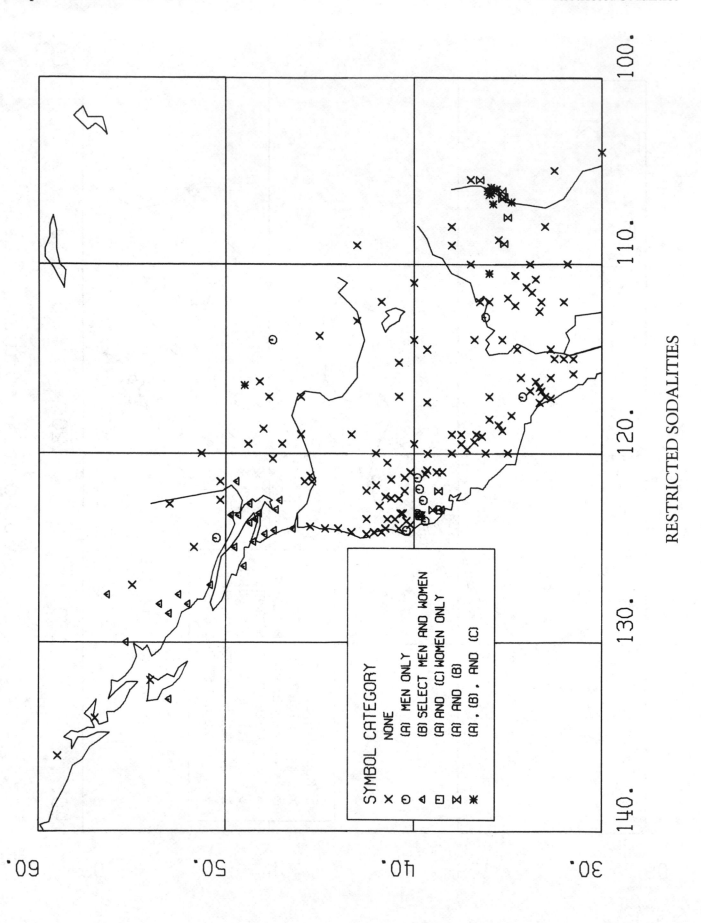

RESTRICTED SODALITIES

SYMBOL CATEGORY
NONE
X   (A) MEN ONLY
⊖   (B) SELECT MEN AND WOMEN
◁   (A) AND (C) WOMEN ONLY
⊟   (A) AND (B)
⋈   (A), (B), AND (C)
✳

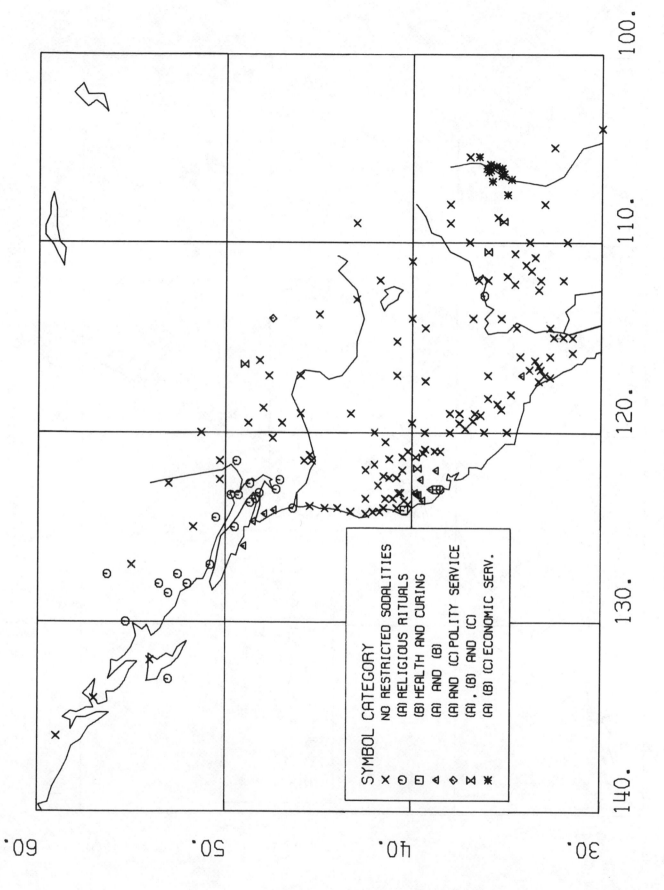

FUNCTIONS OF RESTRICTED SODALITIES

SYMBOL CATEGORY

Symbol	Category
X	NO RESTRICTED SODALITIES
⊖	(A) RELIGIOUS RITUALS
⊟	(B) HEALTH AND CURING
◁	(A) AND (B)
◇	(A) AND (C) POLITY SERVICE
⋈	(A) . (B) AND (C)
✳	(A) (B) (C) ECONOMIC SERV.

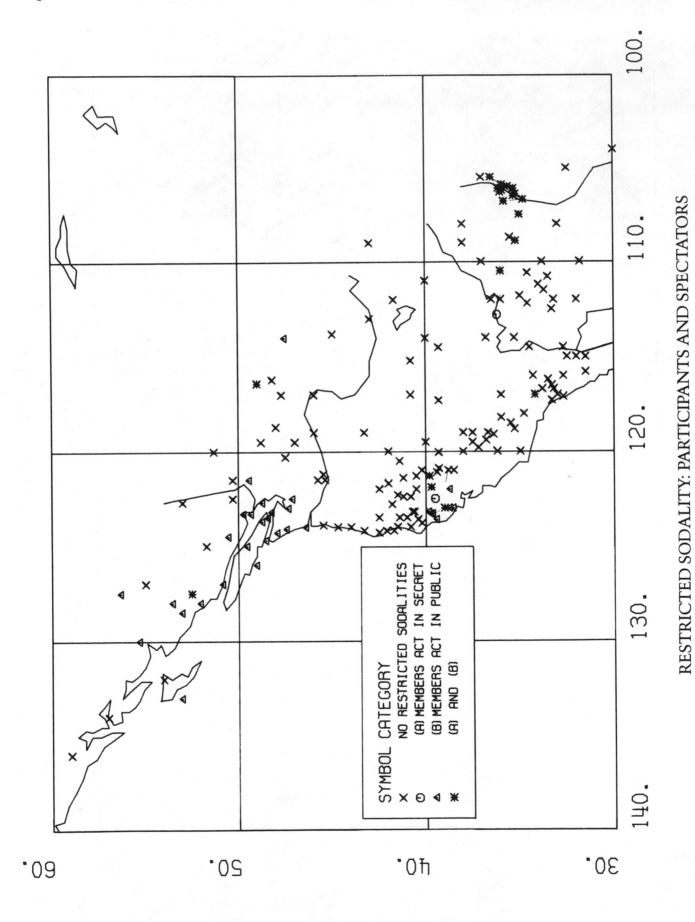

RESTRICTED SODALITY: PARTICIPANTS AND SPECTATORS

SYMBOL CATEGORY

	NO RESTRICTED SODALITIES
X	
⊖	(A) MEMBERS ACT IN SECRET
◁	(B) MEMBERS ACT IN PUBLIC
✳	(A) AND (B)

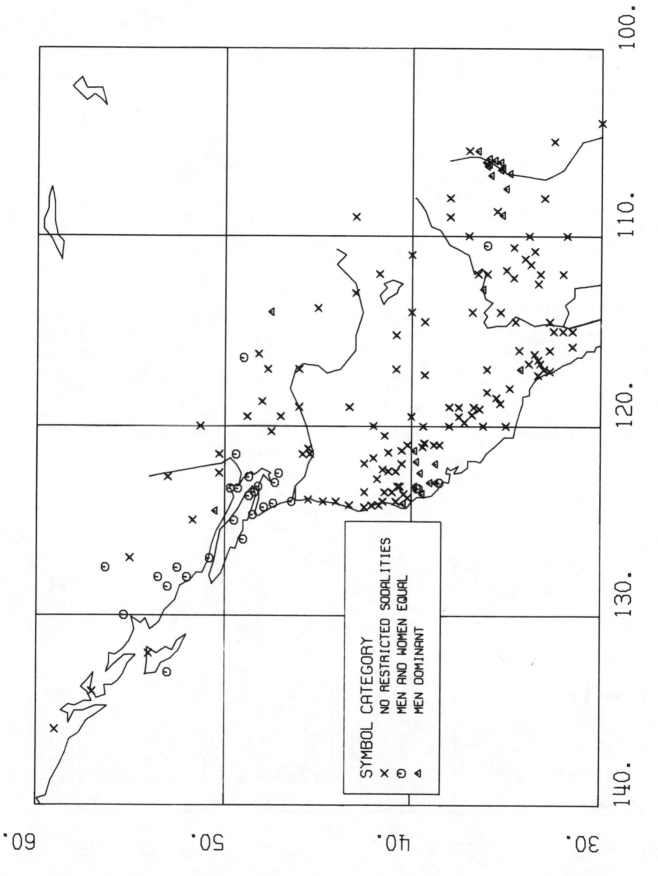

SEX DOMINANCE OF RESTRICTED SODALITIES

SYMBOL CATEGORY

X	NO RESTRICTED SODALITIES
⊖	MEN AND WOMEN EQUAL
◁	MEN DOMINANT

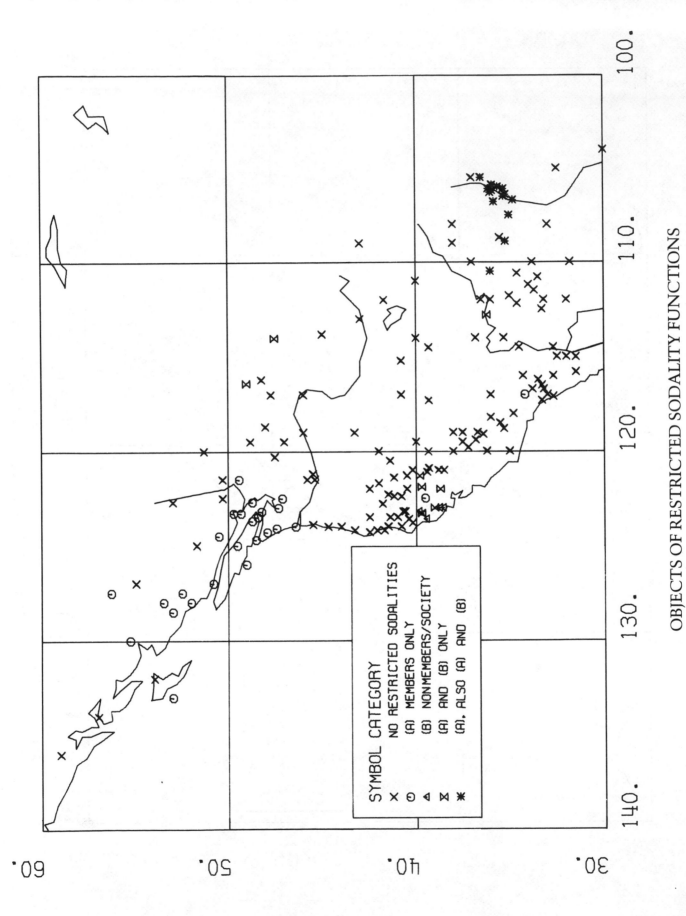

OBJECTS OF RESTRICTED SODALITY FUNCTIONS

SYMBOL CATEGORY
X   NO RESTRICTED SODALITIES
⊖   (A) MEMBERS ONLY
◁   (B) NONMEMBERS/SOCIETY
⋈   (A) AND (B) ONLY
✳   (A), ALSO (A) AND (B)

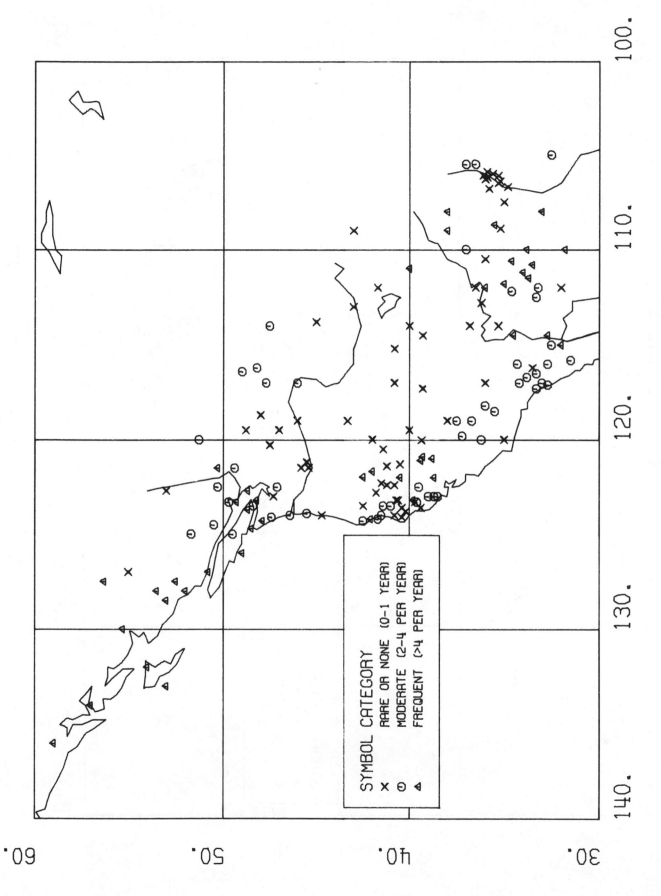

INCIDENCE OF OFFENSIVE RAIDING

SYMBOL CATEGORY
X   RARE OR NONE (0-1 YEAR)
⊖   MODERATE (2-4 PER YEAR)
◁   FREQUENT (>4 PER YEAR)

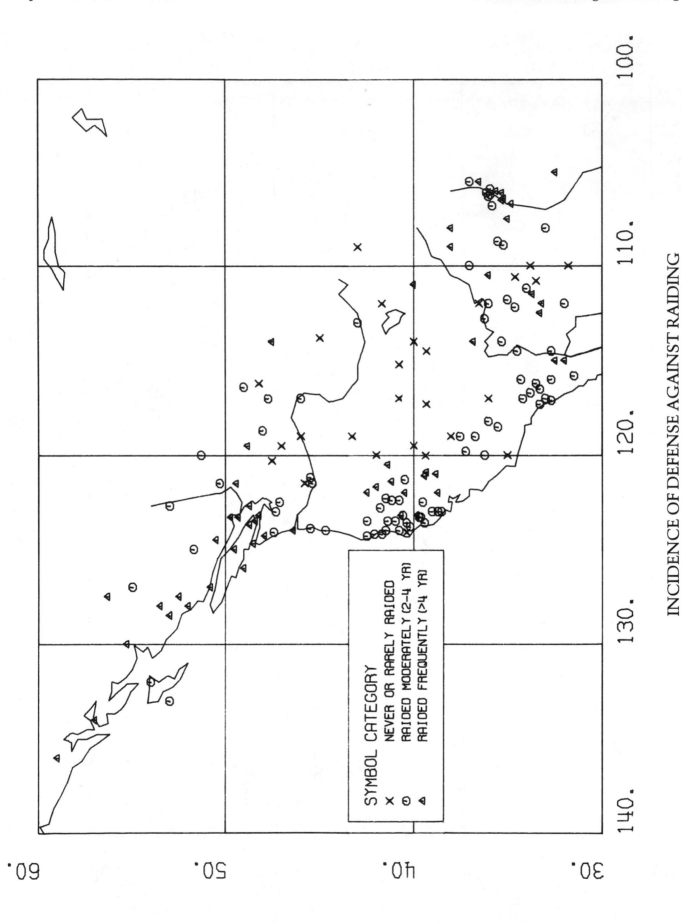

SYMBOL CATEGORY
X   NEVER OR RARELY RAIDED
⊖   RAIDED MODERATELY (2-4 YR)
◁   RAIDED FREQUENTLY (>4 YR)

INCIDENCE OF DEFENSE AGAINST RAIDING

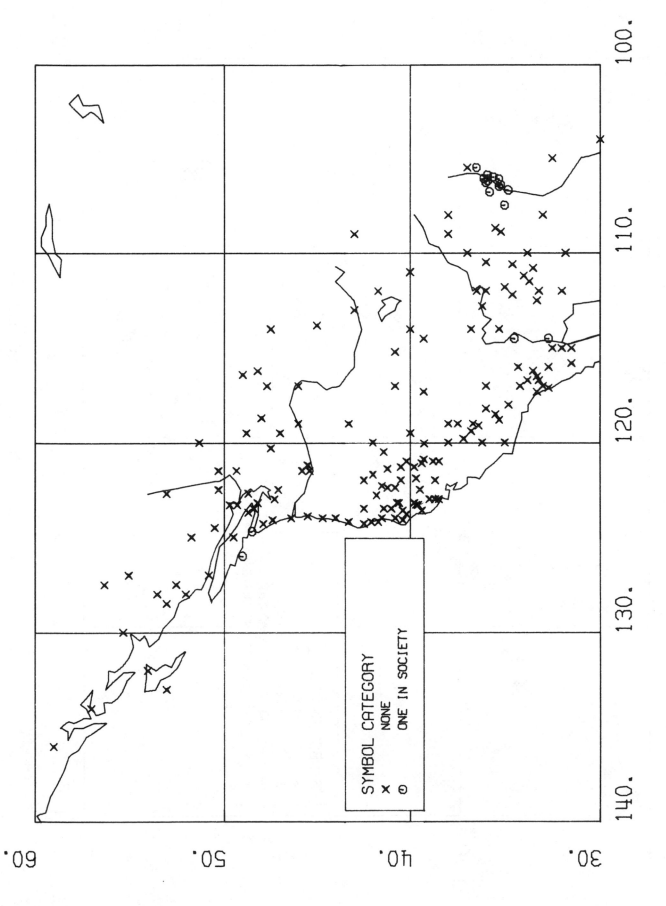

PERMANENT MILITARY ORGANIZATION

SYMBOL CATEGORY
X   NONE
⊖   ONE IN SOCIETY

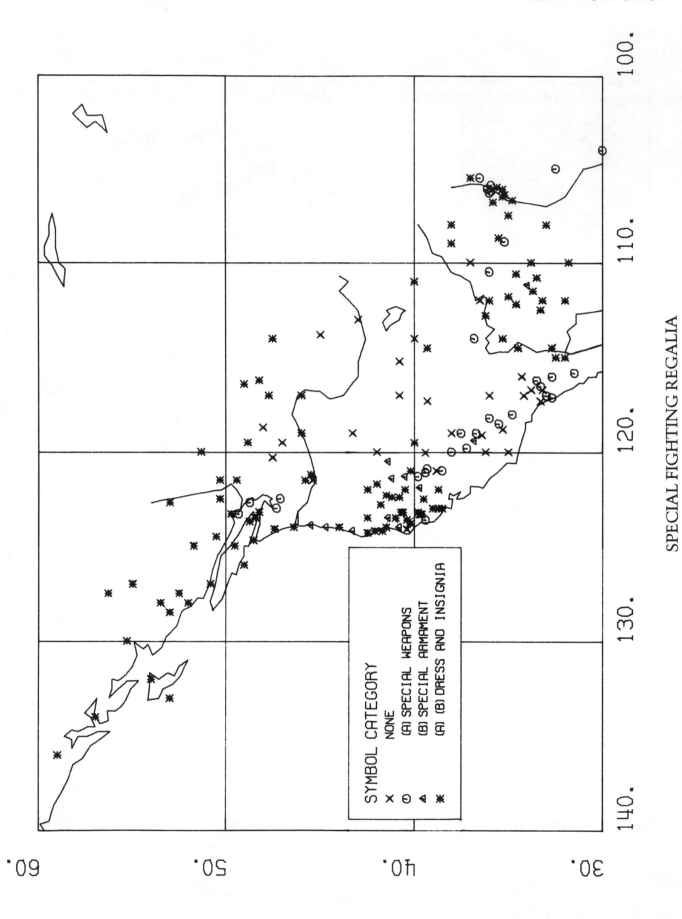

SPECIAL FIGHTING REGALIA

SYMBOL CATEGORY

X	NONE
⊖	(A) SPECIAL WEAPONS
◁	(B) SPECIAL ARMAMENT
✳	(A) (B) DRESS AND INSIGNIA

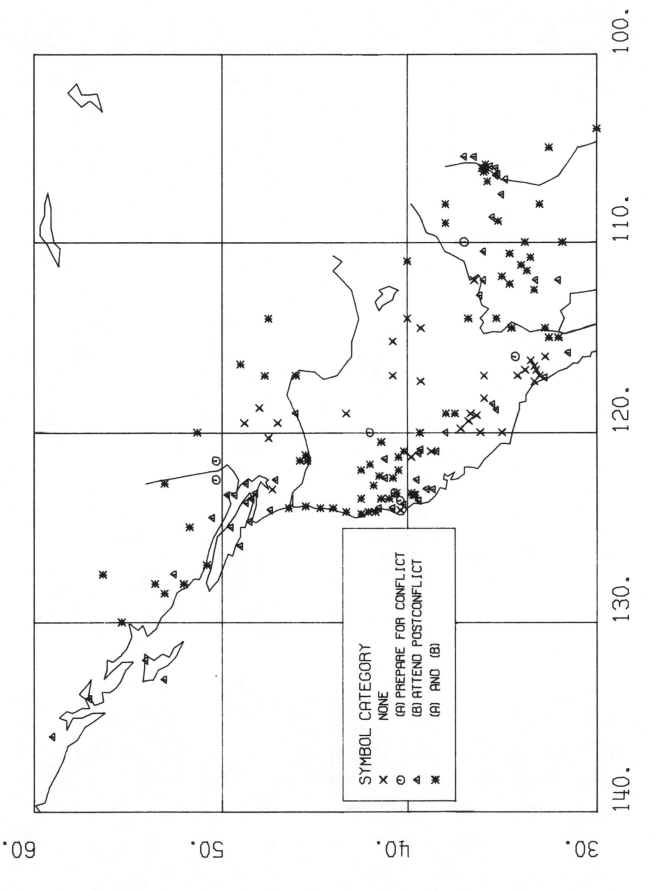

SYMBOL CATEGORY

X	NONE
⊖	(A) PREPARE FOR CONFLICT
◁	(B) ATTEND POSTCONFLICT
✳	(A) AND (B)

PUBLIC CEREMONIES ASSOCIATED WITH WARFARE OR RAIDS

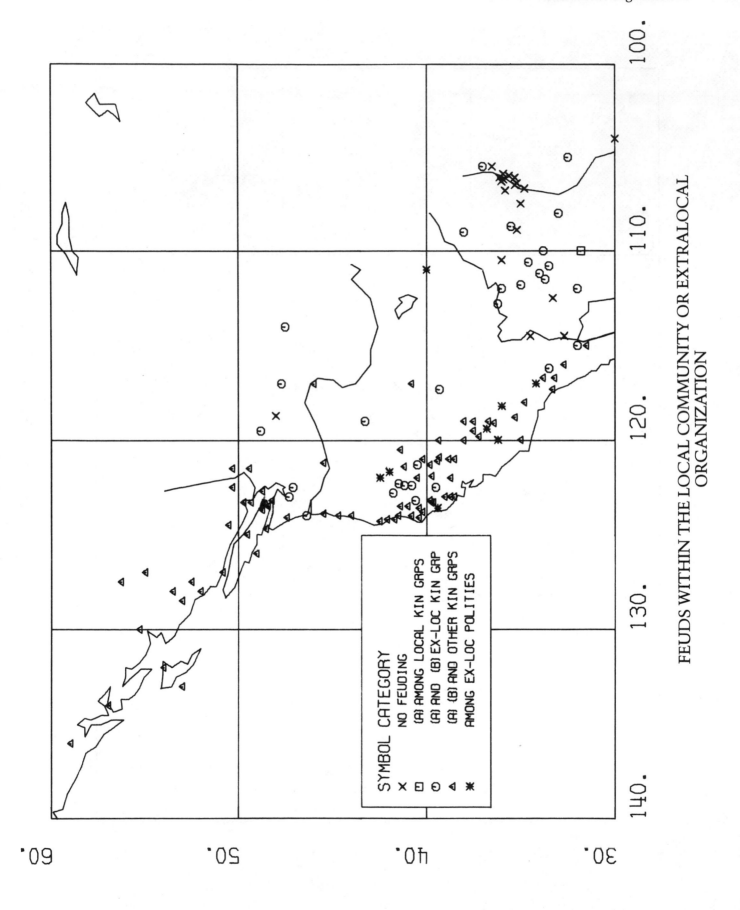

FEUDS WITHIN THE LOCAL COMMUNITY OR EXTRALOCAL
ORGANIZATION

SYMBOL CATEGORY
 X   NO FEUDING
 ⊟   (A) AMONG LOCAL KIN GRPS
 ⊖   (A) AND (B) EX-LOC KIN GRP
 ◁   (A) (B) AND OTHER KIN GRPS
 ✳   AMONG EX-LOC POLITIES

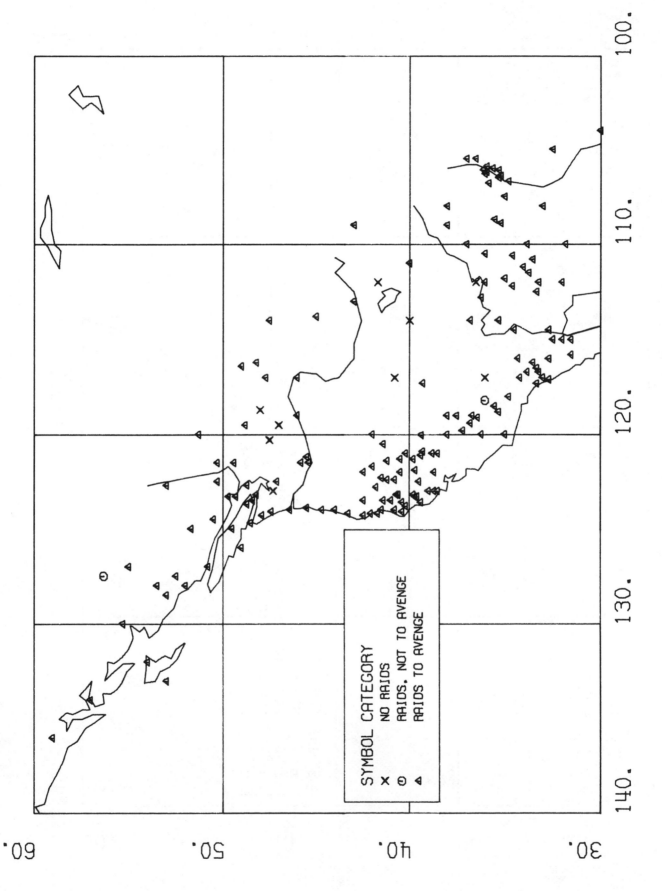

RAIDS TO AVENGE THE DEATH OF A WARRIOR

SYMBOL CATEGORY
X   NO RAIDS
⊖   RAIDS, NOT TO AVENGE
◁   RAIDS TO AVENGE

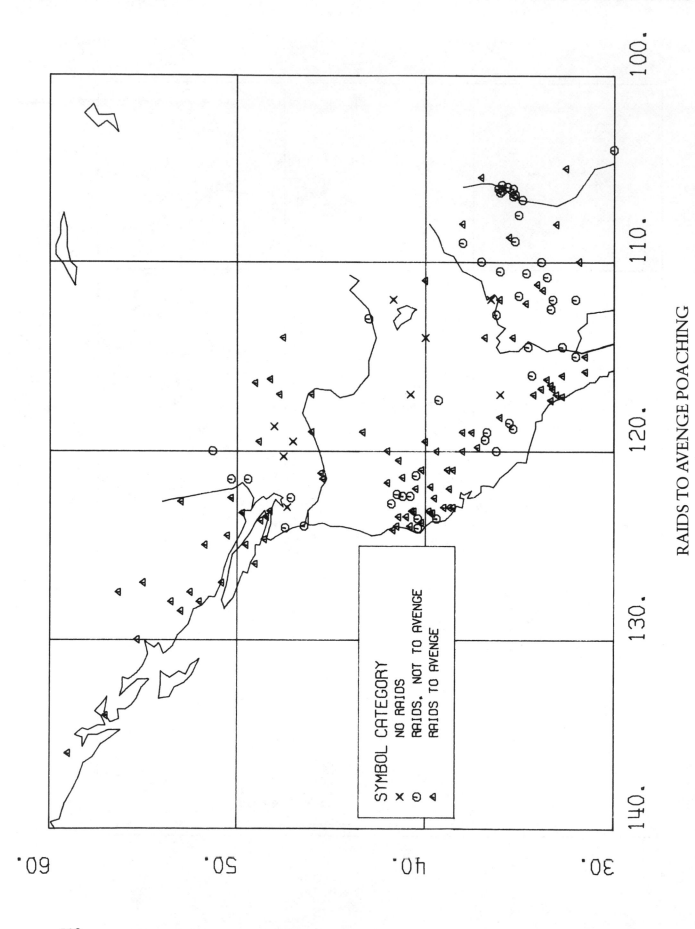

RAIDS TO AVENGE POACHING

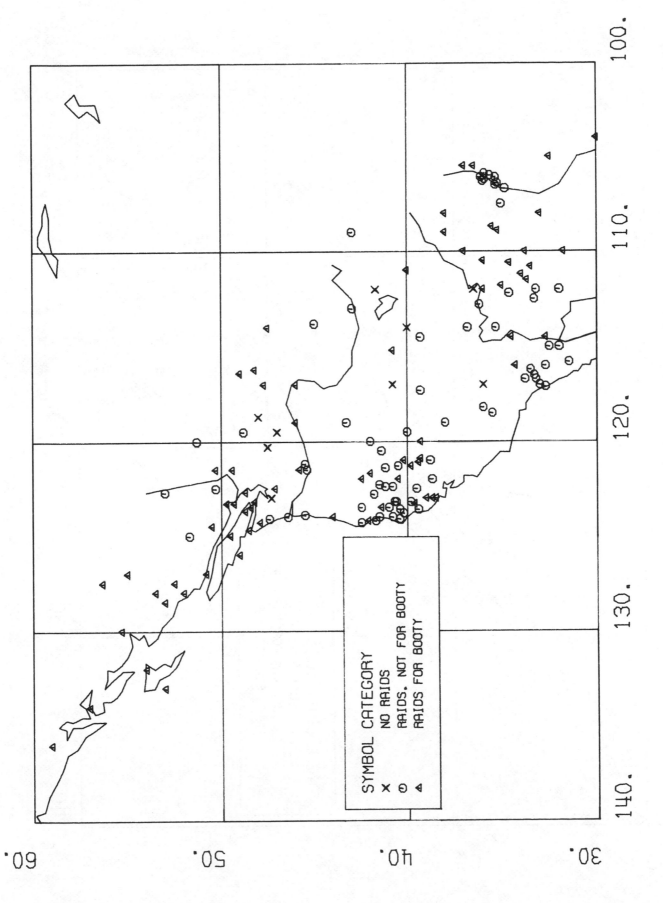

RAIDS FOR ECONOMIC BOOTY

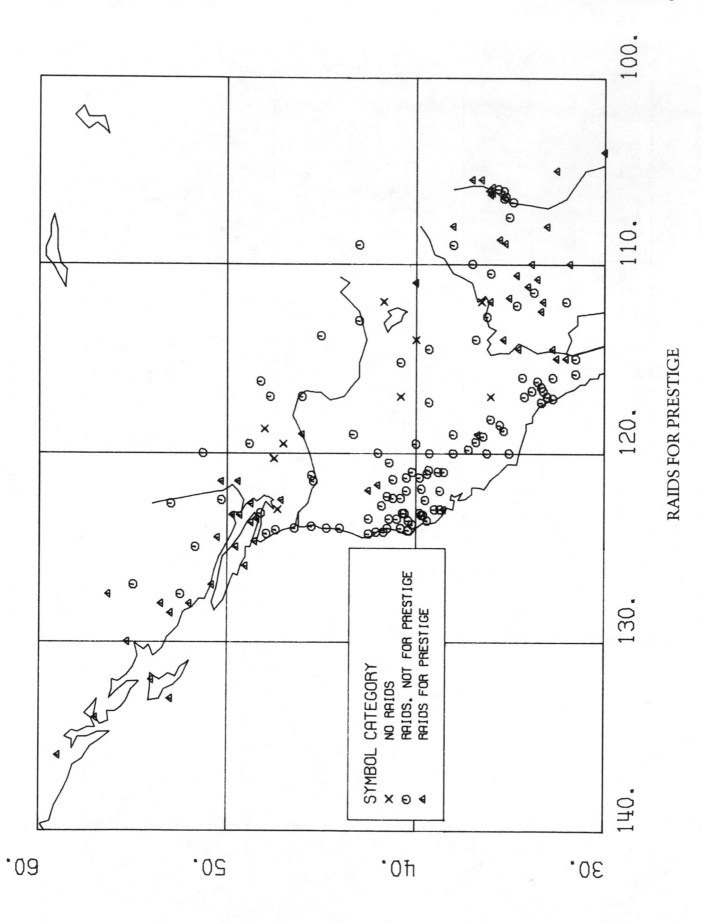

RAIDS FOR PRESTIGE

SYMBOL CATEGORY
X   NO RAIDS
Θ   RAIDS, NOT FOR PRESTIGE
◁   RAIDS FOR PRESTIGE

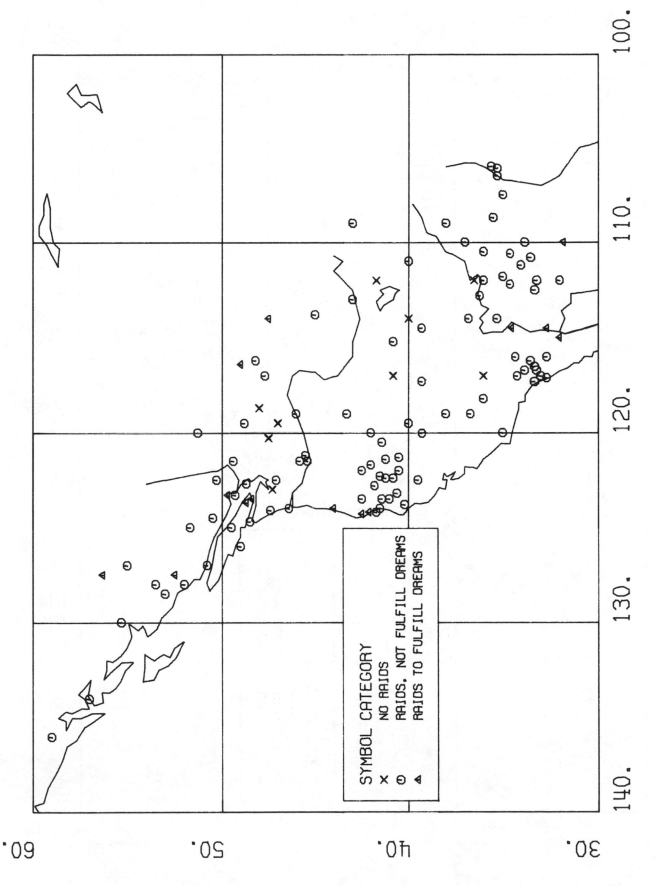

RAIDS TO FULFILL VISIONS OR DREAM INSTRUCTIONS

SYMBOL CATEGORY
X   NO RAIDS
⊖   RAIDS, NOT FULFILL DREAMS
◁   RAIDS TO FULFILL DREAMS

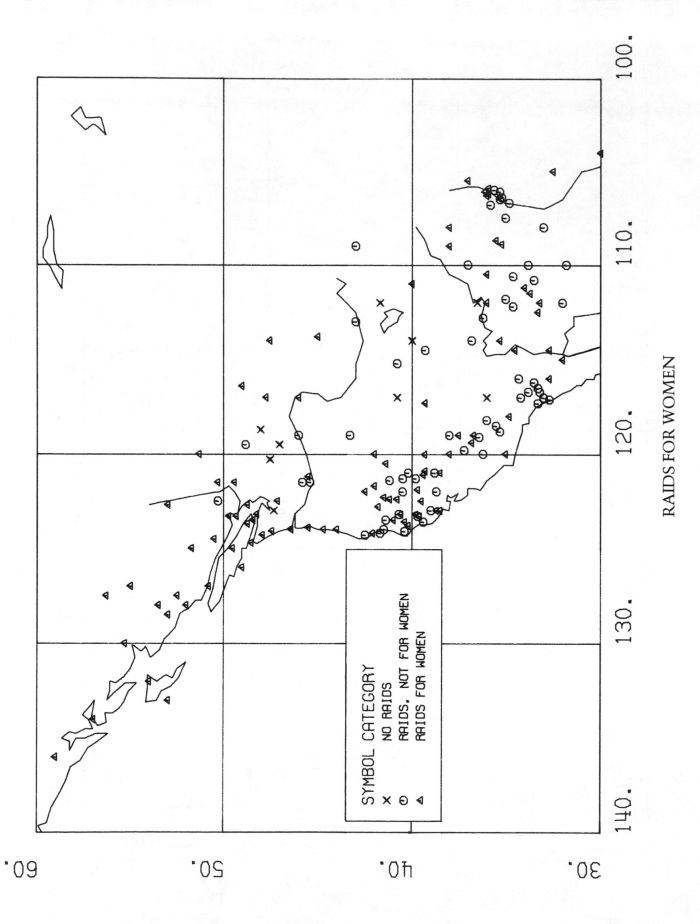

RAIDS FOR WOMEN

SYMBOL CATEGORY
X   NO RAIDS
⊖   RAIDS, NOT FOR WOMEN
◁   RAIDS FOR WOMEN

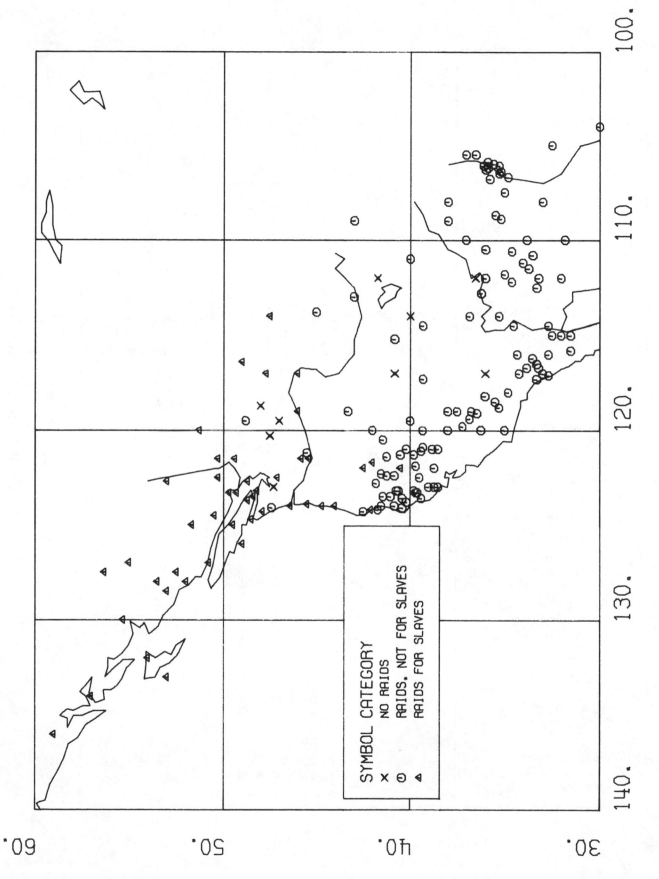

RAIDS FOR SLAVES

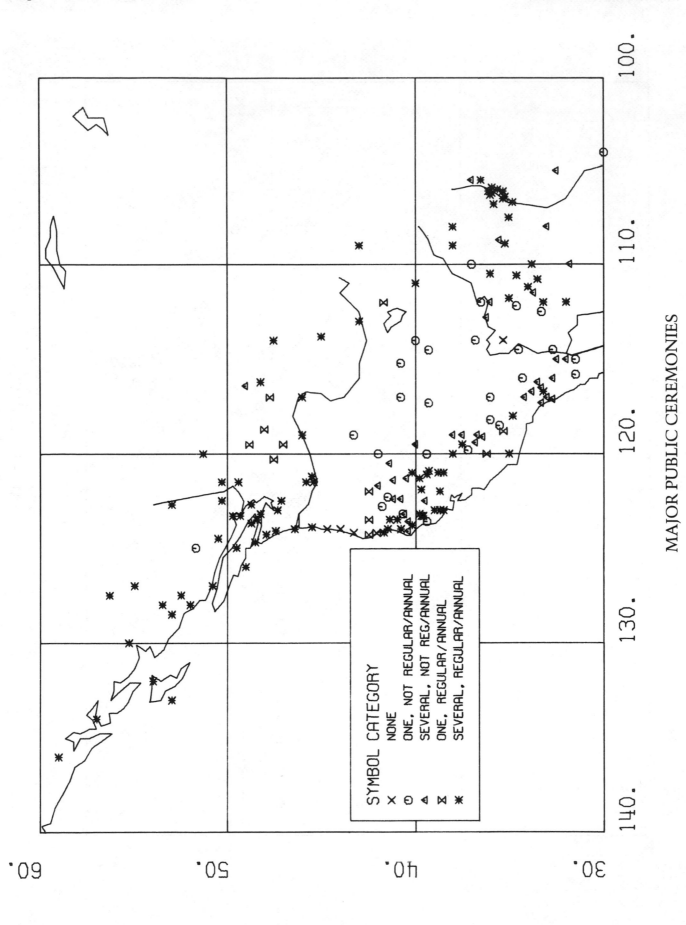

MAJOR PUBLIC CEREMONIES

SYMBOL CATEGORY
X   NONE
⊖   ONE, NOT REGULAR/ANNUAL
◁   SEVERAL, NOT REG/ANNUAL
⋈   ONE, REGULAR/ANNUAL
✳   SEVERAL, REGULAR/ANNUAL

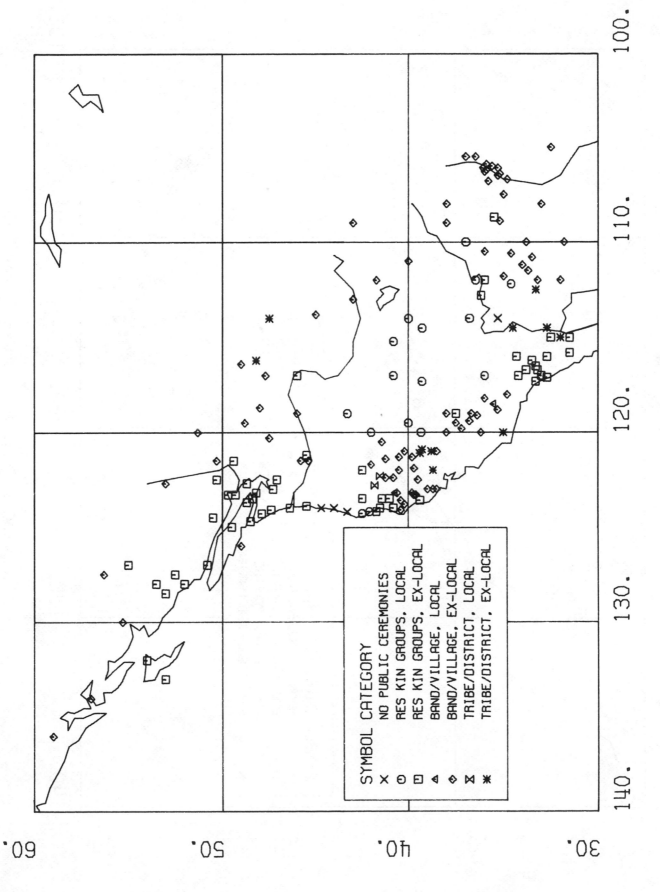

ATTENDANCE AT LARGEST PUBLIC CEREMONY

SYMBOL CATEGORY

NO PUBLIC CEREMONIES   X
RES KIN GROUPS, LOCAL   ⊖
RES KIN GROUPS, EX-LOCAL   ⊡
BAND/VILLAGE, LOCAL   △
BAND/VILLAGE, EX-LOCAL   ◇
TRIBE/DISTRICT, LOCAL   ⋈
TRIBE/DISTRICT, EX-LOCAL   ✳

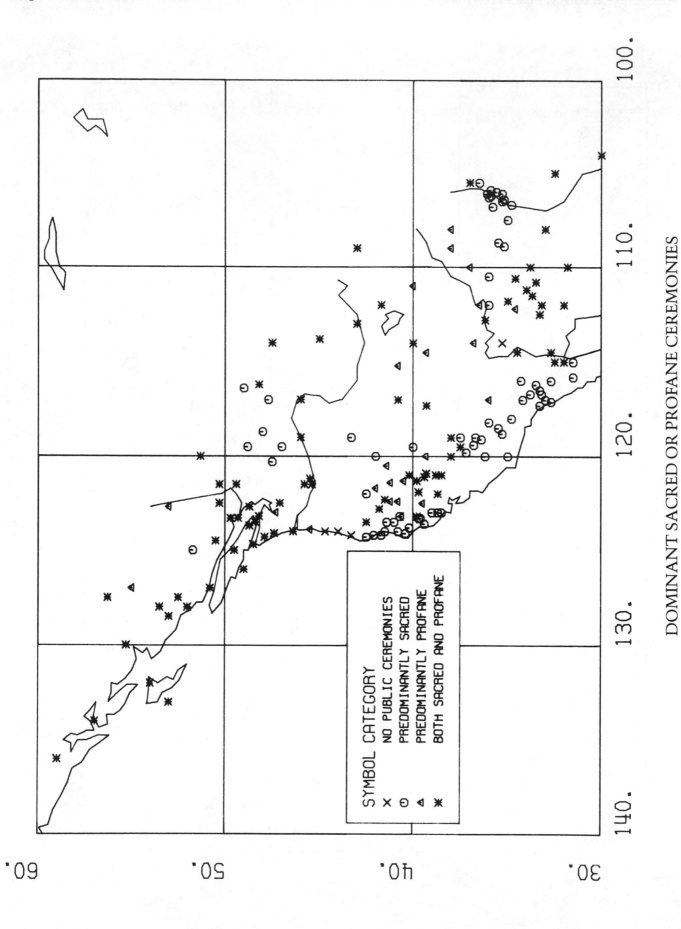

DOMINANT SACRED OR PROFANE CEREMONIES

SYMBOL CATEGORY
X   NO PUBLIC CEREMONIES
⊖   PREDOMINANTLY SACRED
◁   PREDOMINANTLY PROFANE
✳   BOTH SACRED AND PROFANE

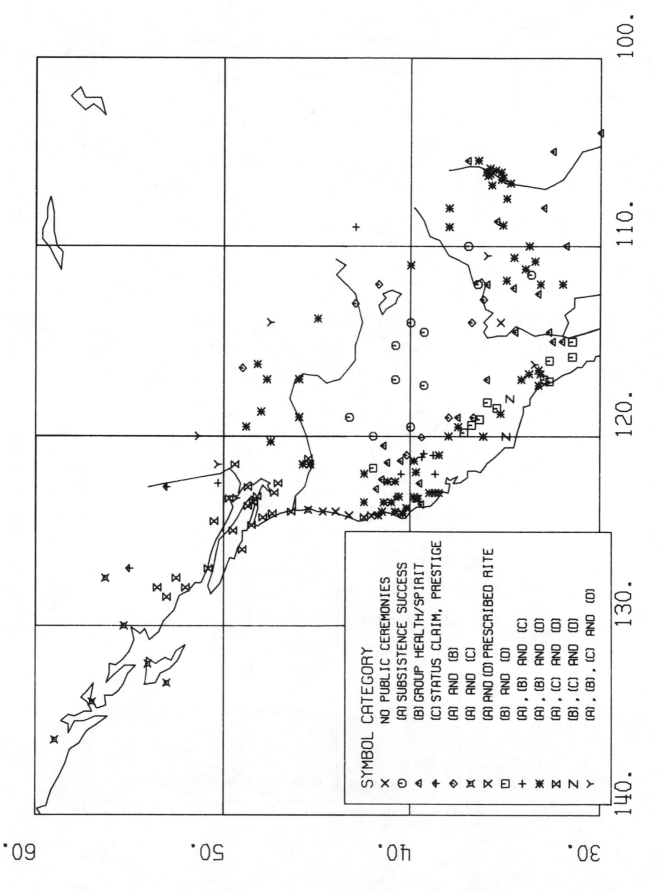

REASONS FOR PERFORMING PUBLIC CEREMONIES

SYMBOL CATEGORY

X	NO PUBLIC CEREMONIES
⊖	(A) SUBSISTENCE SUCCESS
◁	(B) GROUP HEALTH/SPIRIT
✦	(C) STATUS CLAIM, PRESTIGE
◇	(A) AND (B)
⋈	(A) AND (C)
⋉	(A) AND (D) PRESCRIBED RITE
⊟	(B) AND (D)
+	(A), (B) AND (C)
✳	(A), (B) AND (D)
⋈	(A), (C) AND (D)
N	(B), (C) AND (D)
Y	(A), (B), (C) AND (D)

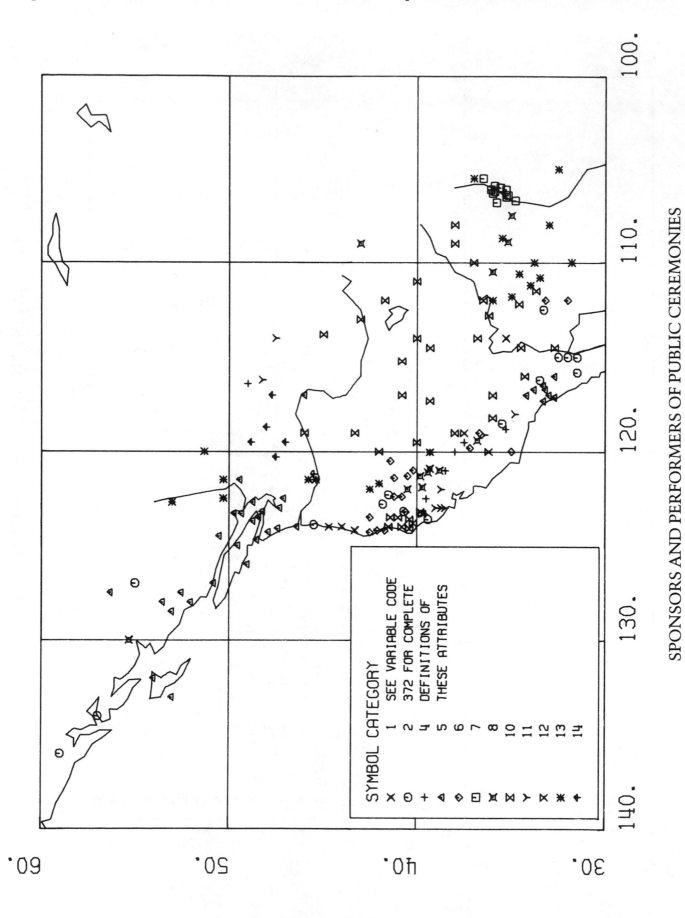

SPONSORS AND PERFORMERS OF PUBLIC CEREMONIES

SYMBOL CATEGORY

	1	SEE VARIABLE CODE
X	2	372 FOR COMPLETE
⊖	4	DEFINITIONS OF
+	5	THESE ATTRIBUTES
◁	6	
◇	7	
▣	8	
⋈	10	
⋈	11	
Y	12	
⋊	13	
✳	14	
✦		

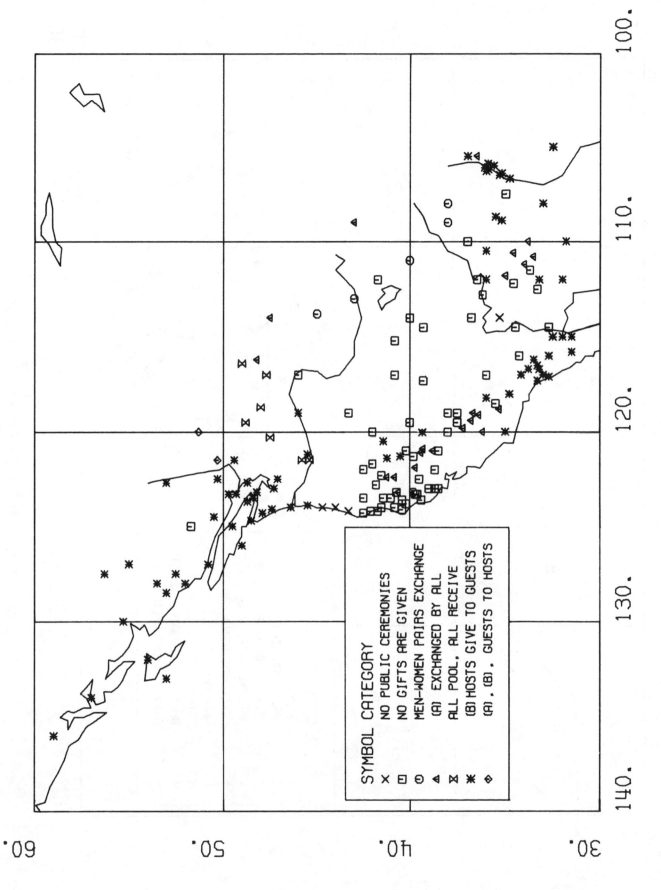

SYMBOL CATEGORY

X	NO PUBLIC CEREMONIES
⊟	NO GIFTS ARE GIVEN
⊖	MEN-WOMEN PAIRS EXCHANGE
◁	(A) EXCHANGED BY ALL
⋈	ALL POOL, ALL RECEIVE
✳	(B) HOSTS GIVE TO GUESTS
◇	(A), (B), GUESTS TO HOSTS

GIFT-GIVING AT PUBLIC CEREMONIES

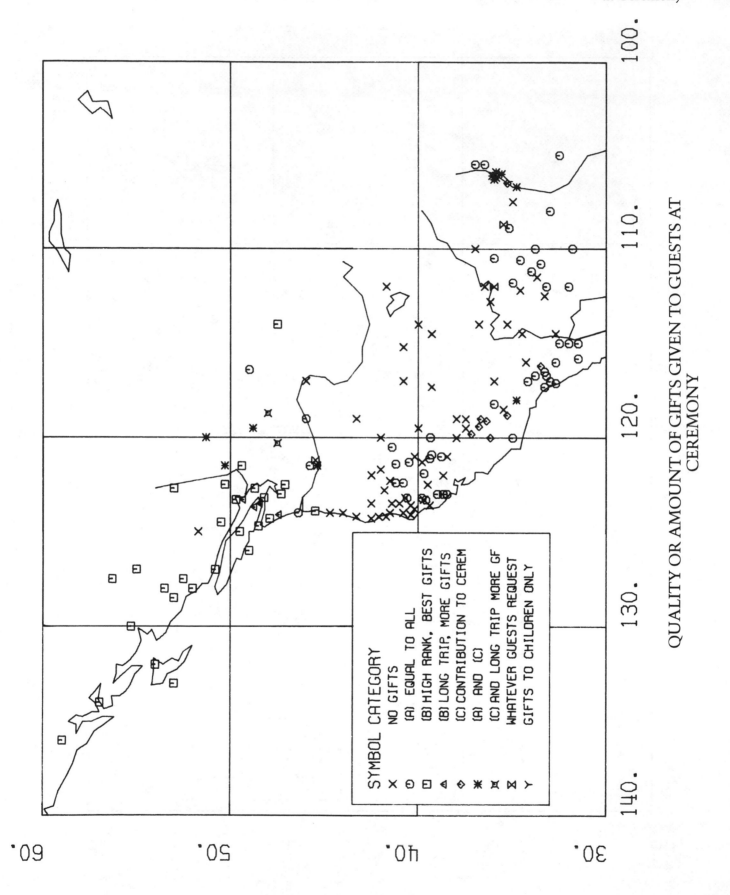

QUALITY OR AMOUNT OF GIFTS GIVEN TO GUESTS AT
CEREMONY

SYMBOL CATEGORY
X   NO GIFTS
⊖   (A) EQUAL TO ALL
⊟   (B) HIGH RANK, BEST GIFTS
▲   (B) LONG TRIP, MORE GIFTS
◇   (C) CONTRIBUTION TO CEREM
✳   (A) AND (C)
⋈   (C) AND LONG TRIP MORE GF
⊠   WHATEVER GUESTS REQUEST
Y   GIFTS TO CHILDREN ONLY

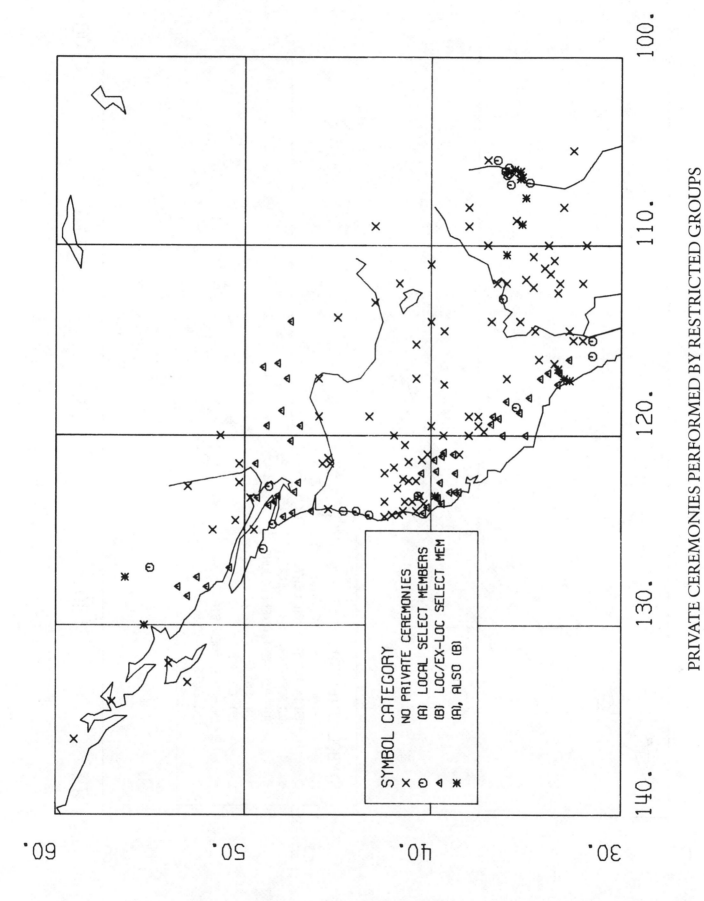

SYMBOL CATEGORY
X	⊖	◁	✳
NO PRIVATE CEREMONIES			
(A) LOCAL SELECT MEMBERS			
(B) LOC/EX-LOC SELECT MEM			
(A), ALSO (B)			

PRIVATE CEREMONIES PERFORMED BY RESTRICTED GROUPS

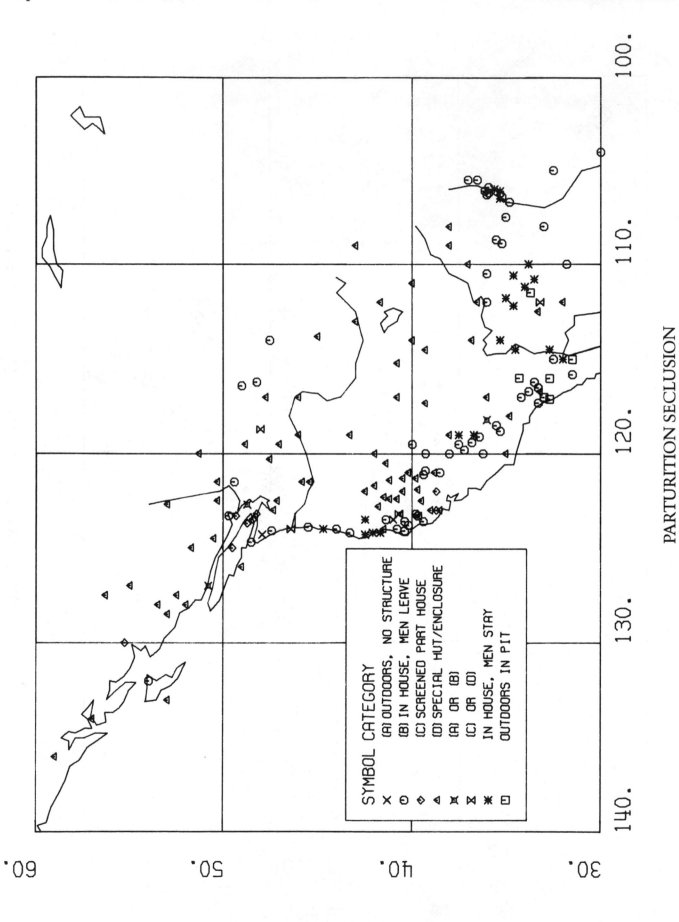

PARTURITION SECLUSION

SYMBOL CATEGORY
(A) OUTDOORS, NO STRUCTURE
(B) IN HOUSE, MEN LEAVE
(C) SCREENED PART HOUSE
(D) SPECIAL HUT/ENCLOSURE
(A) OR (B)
(C) OR (D)
IN HOUSE, MEN STAY
OUTDOORS IN PIT

X ⊖ ◇ ◁ ⋈ ⋈ ✻ ▢

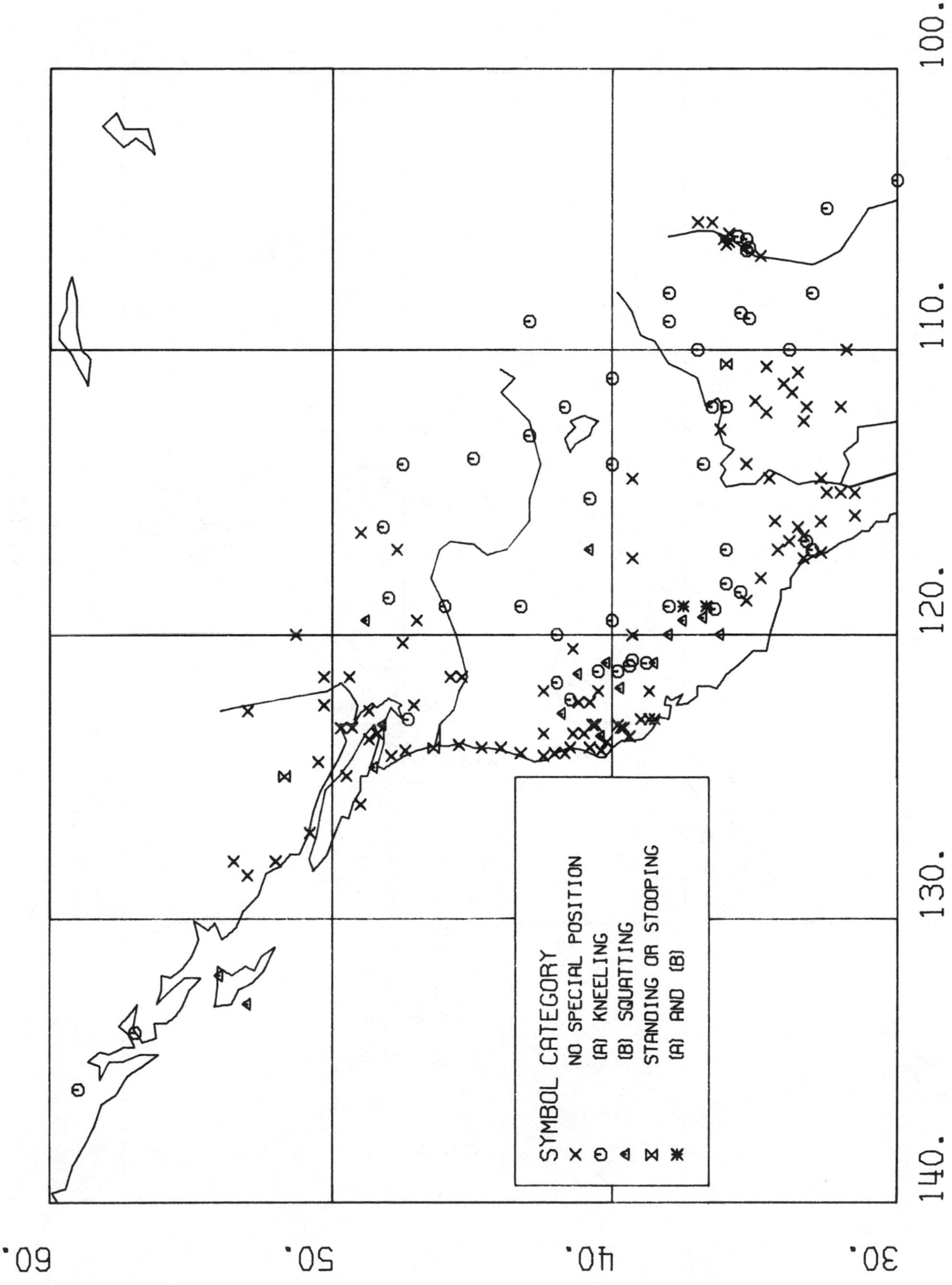

PARTURITION POSITION, A

SYMBOL CATEGORY

✕	NO SPECIAL POSITION
⊖	(A) KNEELING
◁	(B) SQUATTING
⋈	STANDING OR STOOPING
✳	(A) AND (B)

SYMBOL CATEGORY
× NO SPECIAL POSITION
⊖ (A) SITTING
◁ (B) LYING OR RECLINING
✱ (A) AND (B)
100.
110.
120.
130.
140.
60.
50.
40.
30.

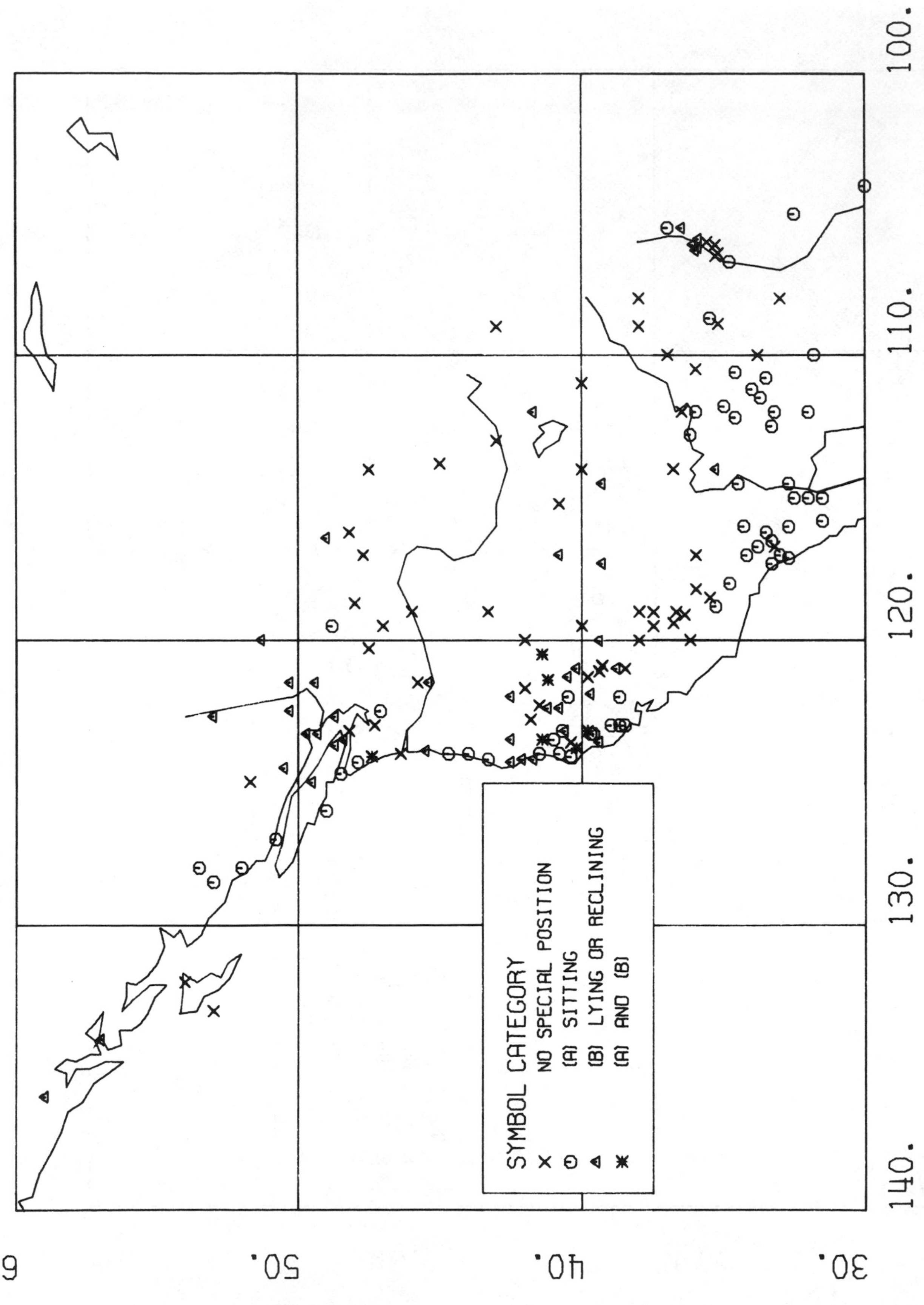

PARTURITION POSITION, B

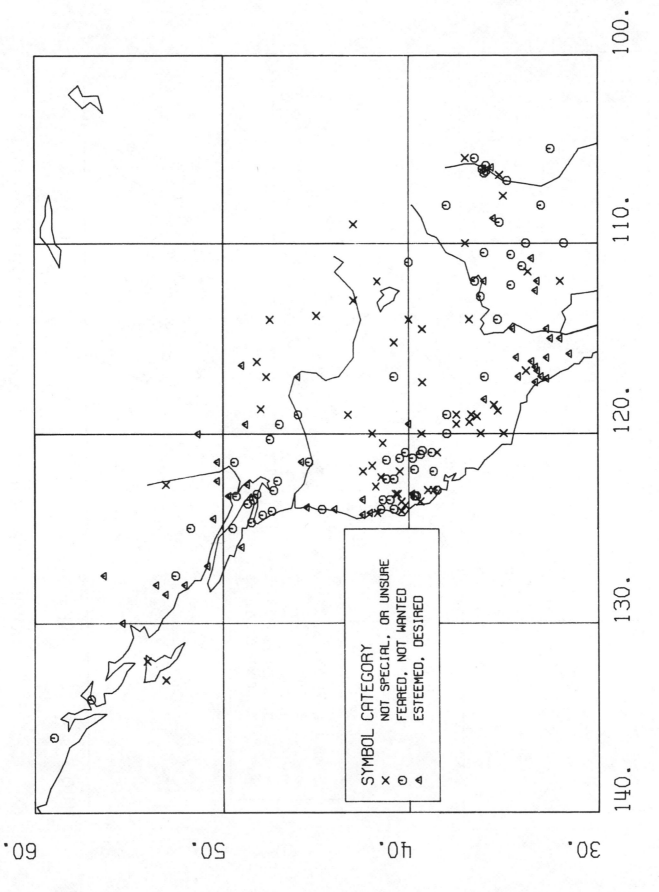

ATTITUDES TOWARD TWIN BIRTHS

SYMBOL CATEGORY
X   NOT SPECIAL, OR UNSURE
Θ   FEARED, NOT WANTED
◁   ESTEEMED, DESIRED

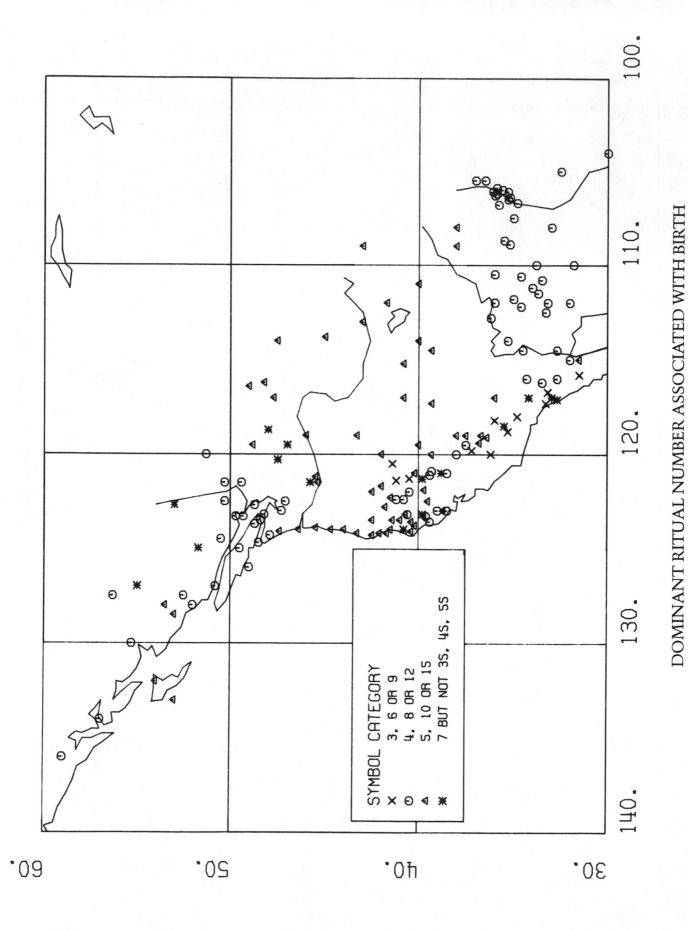

DOMINANT RITUAL NUMBER ASSOCIATED WITH BIRTH

SYMBOL CATEGORY
X   3, 6 OR 9
Θ   4, 8 OR 12
◁   5, 10 OR 15
✳   7 BUT NOT 3S, 4S, 5S

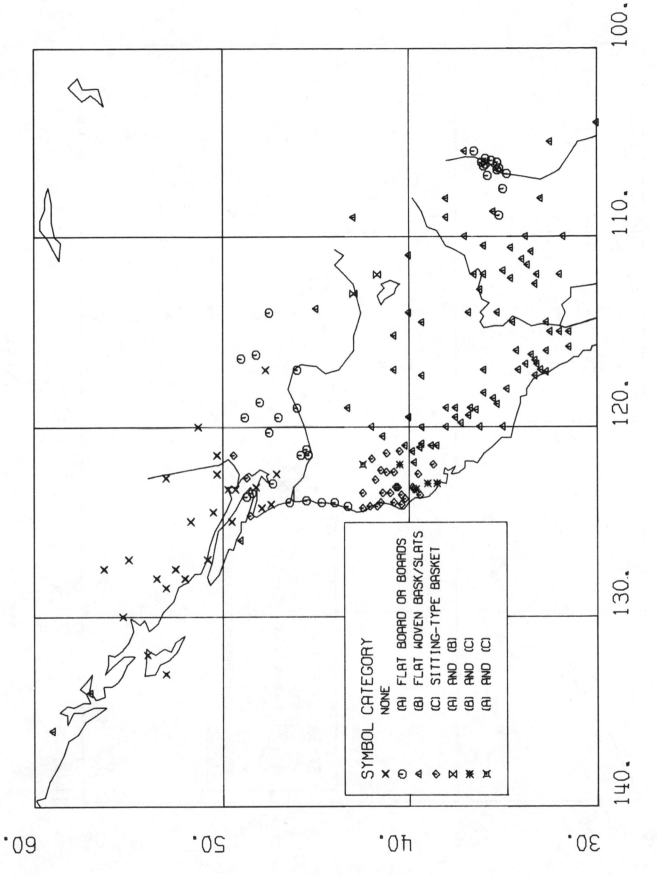

CRADLES, TYPE A

SYMBOL CATEGORY

NONE
× (A) FLAT BOARD OR BOARDS
Ⓘ (B) FLAT WOVEN BASK/SLATS
◁ (C) SITTING-TYPE BASKET
◇ (A) AND (B)
⋈ (B) AND (C)
✳ (A) AND (C)
⋈ (A) AND (C)

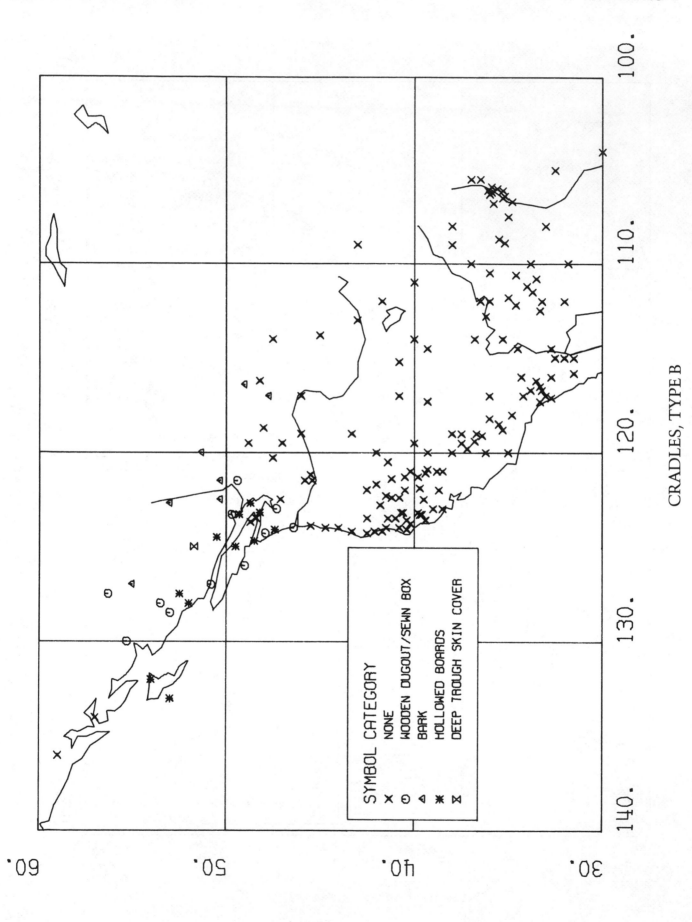

CRADLES, TYPE B

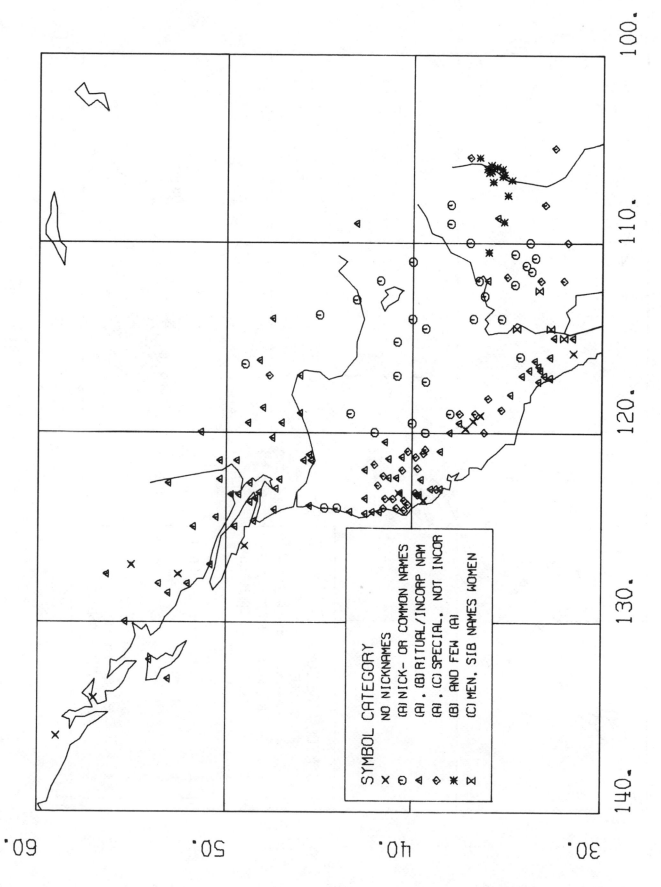

KINDS OF NAMES BESTOWED ON INDIVIDUALS

SYMBOL CATEGORY
X   NO NICKNAMES
⊖   (A) NICK- OR COMMON NAMES
◁   (A) . (B) RITUAL/INCORP NAM
◇   (A) . (C) SPECIAL. NOT INCOR
✳   (B) AND FEW (A)
⋈   (C) MEN. SIB NAMES WOMEN

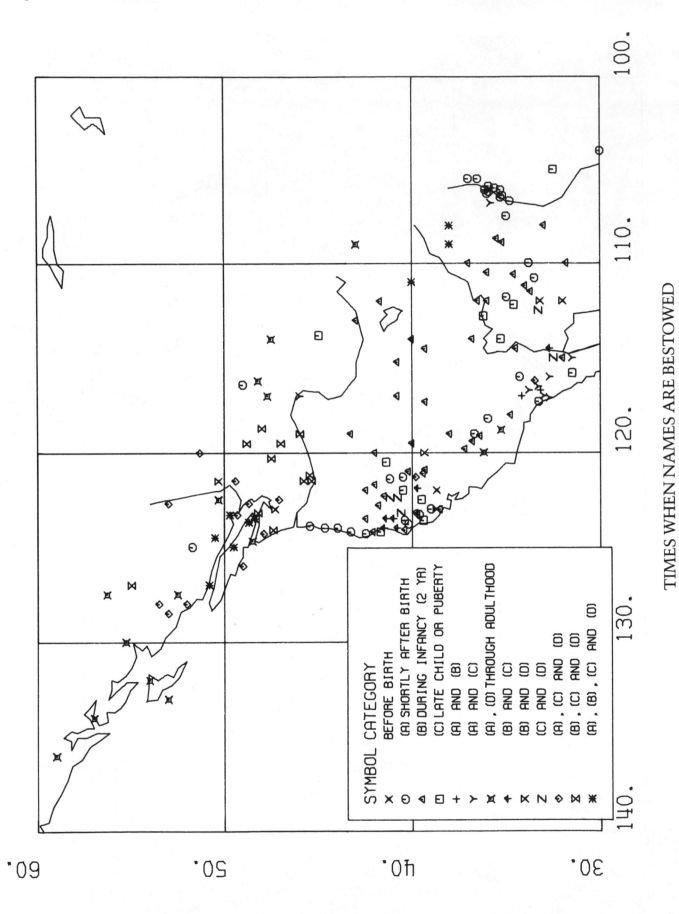

SYMBOL CATEGORY

BEFORE BIRTH

(A) SHORTLY AFTER BIRTH

(B) DURING INFANCY (2 YR)

(C) LATE CHILD OR PUBERTY

(A) AND (B)

(A) AND (C)

(A) , (D) THROUGH ADULTHOOD

(B) AND (C)

(B) AND (D)

(C) AND (D)

(A) , (C) AND (D)

(B) , (C) AND (D)

(A) , (B) , (C) AND (D)

TIMES WHEN NAMES ARE BESTOWED

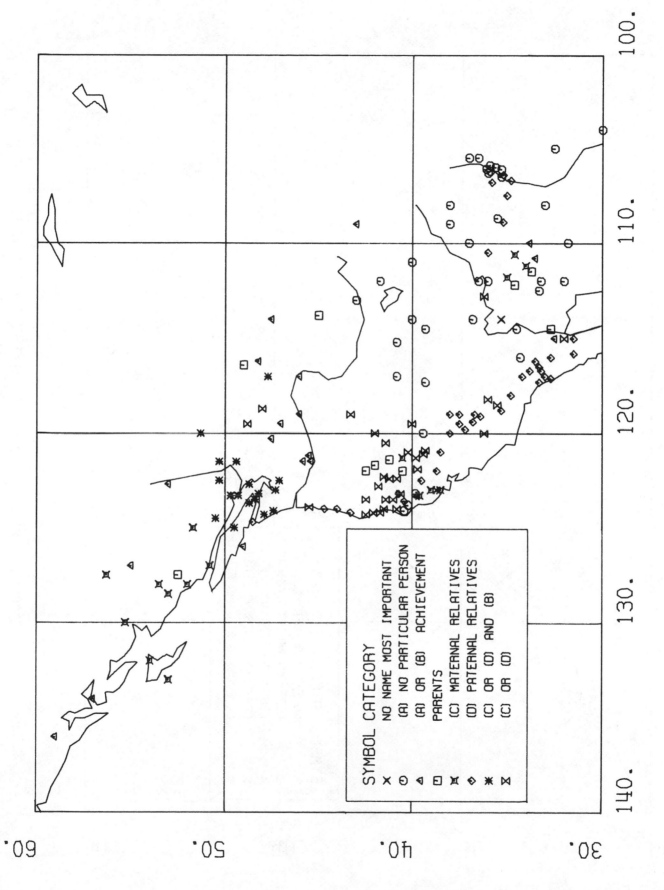

DONOR OF PERSON'S MOST IMPORTANT NAME

SYMBOL CATEGORY
- X   NO NAME MOST IMPORTANT
- ⊖   (A) NO PARTICULAR PERSON
- ◁   (A) OR (B) ACHIEVEMENT
- ▣   PARENTS
- ⋈   (C) MATERNAL RELATIVES
- ◇   (D) PATERNAL RELATIVES
- ✳   (C) OR (D) AND (B)
- ⋈   (C) OR (D)

Kind of Public Ceremony Held at Time of
Most Important Naming

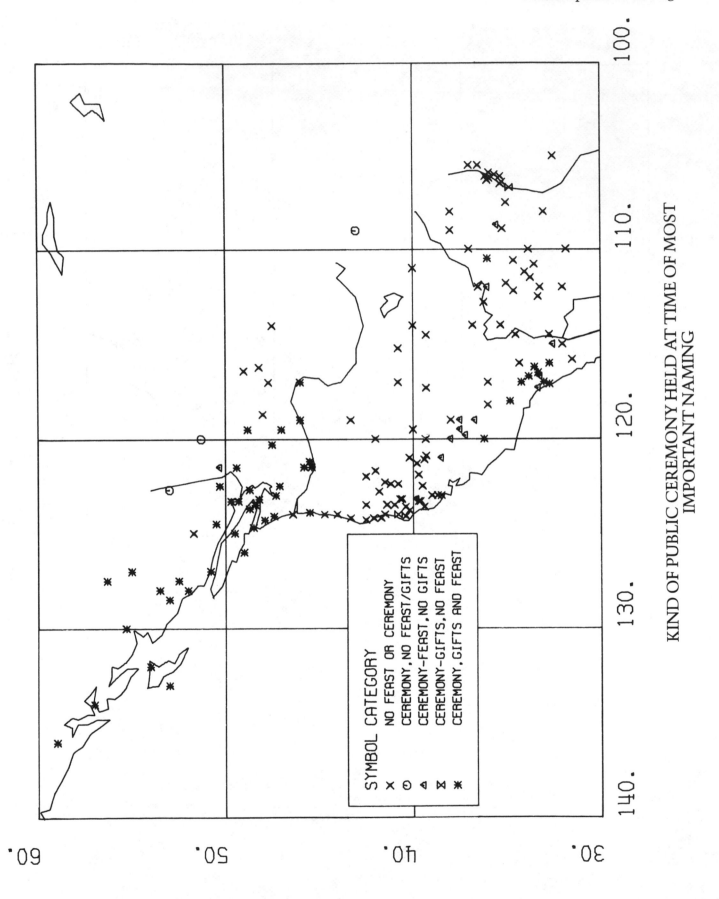

KIND OF PUBLIC CEREMONY HELD AT TIME OF MOST
IMPORTANT NAMING

SYMBOL CATEGORY
X   NO FEAST OR CEREMONY
⊖   CEREMONY,NO FEAST/GIFTS
◁   CEREMONY-FEAST,NO GIFTS
⋈   CEREMONY-GIFTS,NO FEAST
✳   CEREMONY,GIFTS AND FEAST

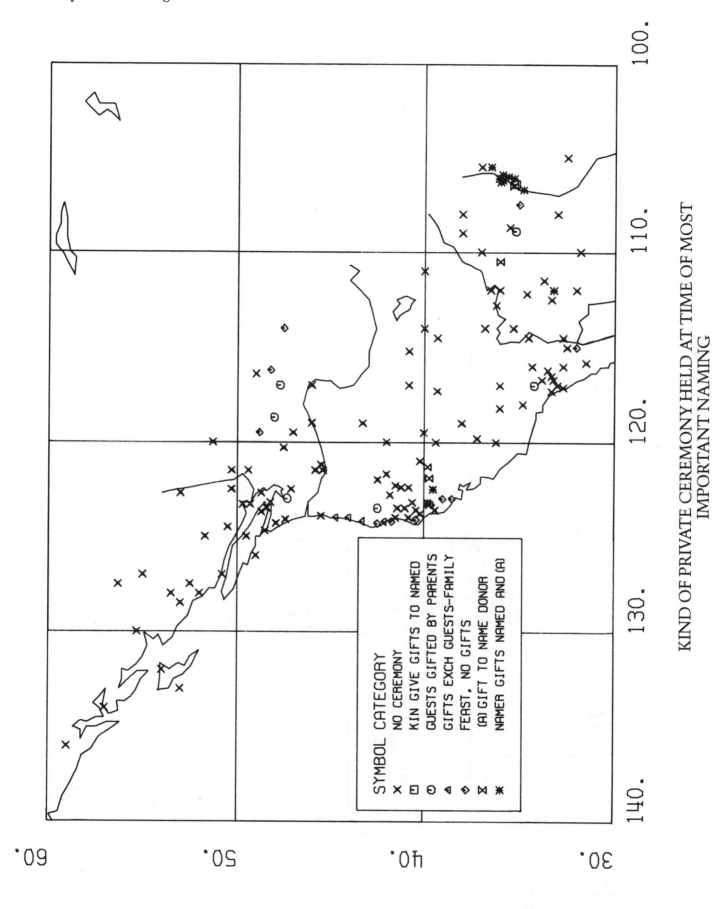

KIND OF PRIVATE CEREMONY HELD AT TIME OF MOST
IMPORTANT NAMING

SYMBOL CATEGORY
X   NO CEREMONY
⊟   KIN GIVE GIFTS TO NAMED
⊖   GUESTS GIFTED BY PARENTS
◁   GIFTS EXCH GUESTS-FAMILY
◇   FEAST, NO GIFTS
⋈   (A) GIFT TO NAME DONOR
✳   NAMER GIFTS NAMED AND (A)

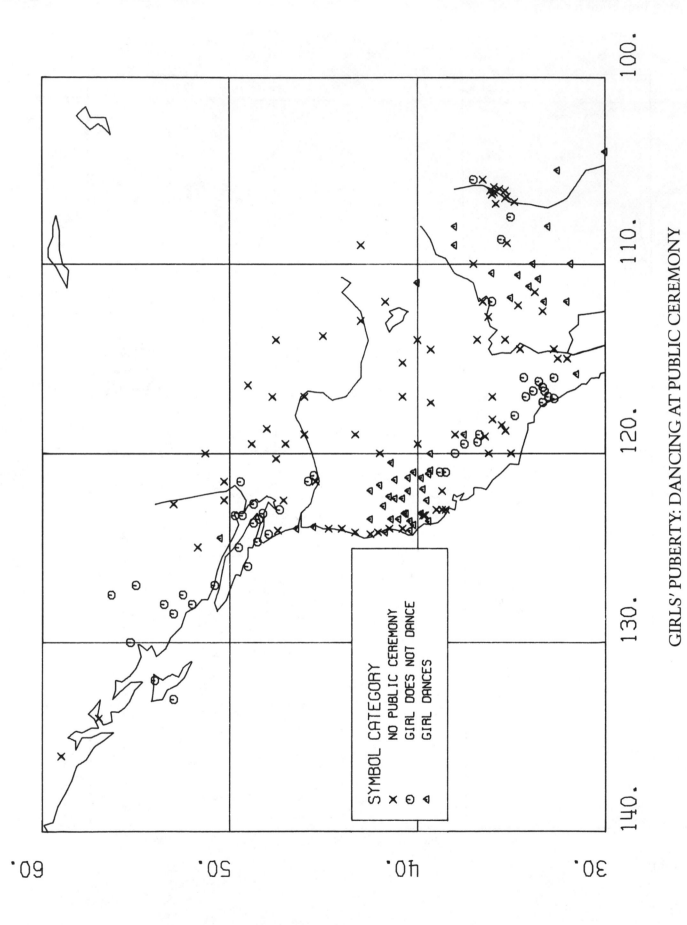

GIRLS' PUBERTY: DANCING AT PUBLIC CEREMONY

SYMBOL CATEGORY
× NO PUBLIC CEREMONY
⊖ GIRL DOES NOT DANCE
◁ GIRL DANCES

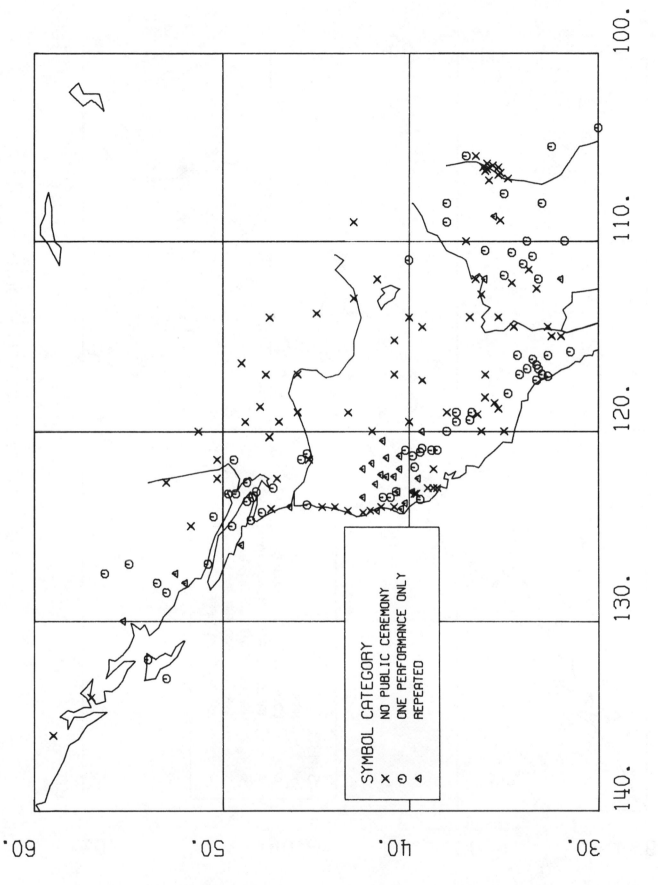

GIRLS' PUBERTY: REPETITION OF PUBLIC CEREMONY

SYMBOL CATEGORY
X   NO PUBLIC CEREMONY
⊖   ONE PERFORMANCE ONLY
◁   REPEATED

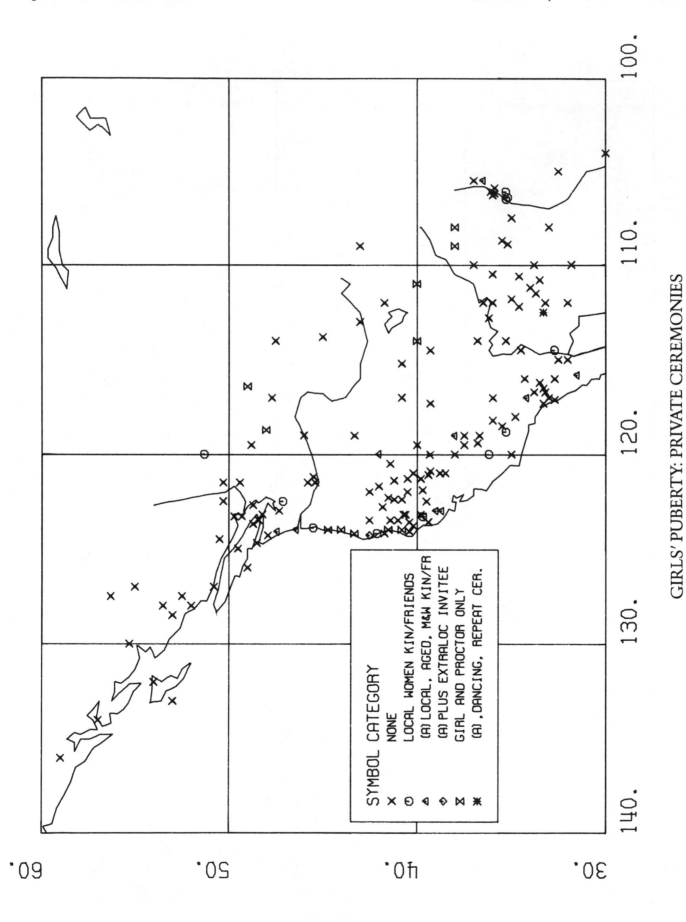

GIRLS' PUBERTY: PRIVATE CEREMONIES

SYMBOL CATEGORY
NONE
LOCAL WOMEN KIN/FRIENDS
(A)LOCAL, AGED, M&W KIN/FR
(A)PLUS EXTRALOC INVITEE
GIRL AND PROCTOR ONLY
(A),DANCING, REPEAT CER.

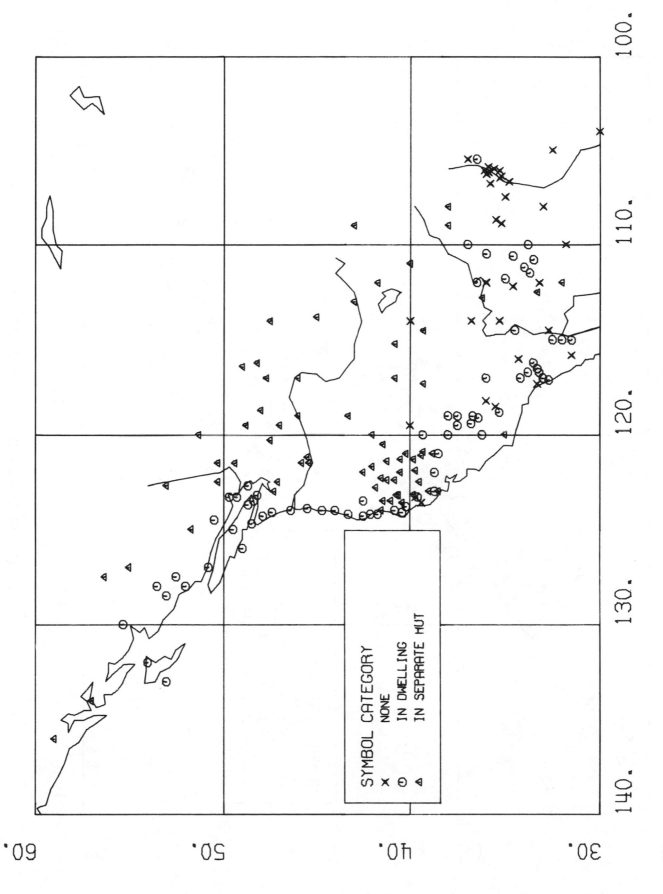

GIRLS' PUBERTY: PLACE OF SECLUSION, A

SYMBOL CATEGORY
X   NONE
⊖   IN DWELLING
◁   IN SEPARATE HUT

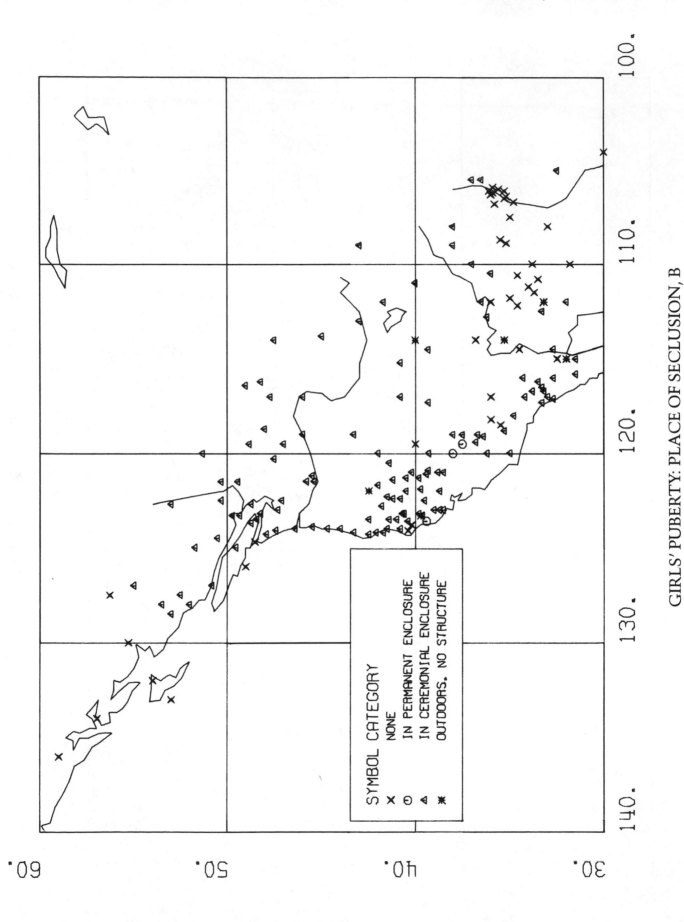

GIRLS' PUBERTY: PLACE OF SECLUSION, B

SYMBOL CATEGORY

X   NONE
⊖   IN PERMANENT ENCLOSURE
◁   IN CEREMONIAL ENCLOSURE
✳   OUTDOORS, NO STRUCTURE

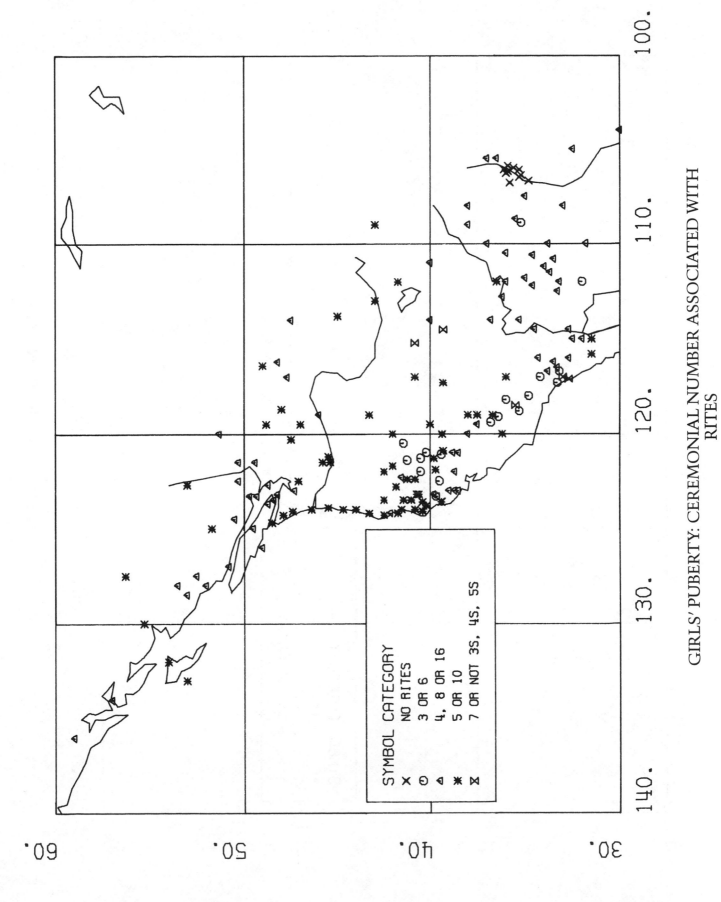

GIRLS' PUBERTY: CEREMONIAL NUMBER ASSOCIATED WITH RITES

SYMBOL CATEGORY
X   NO RITES
Θ   3 OR 6
◁   4, 8 OR 16
✳   5 OR 10
⋈   7 OR NOT 3S, 4S, 5S

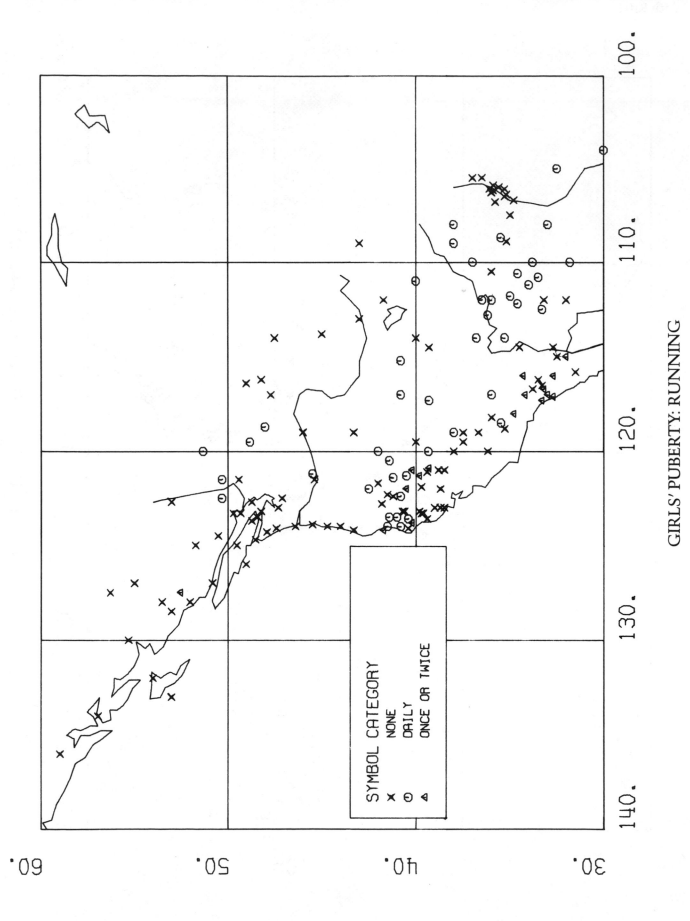

SYMBOL CATEGORY

NONE   ✗
DAILY   ⊖
ONCE OR TWICE ◁

GIRLS' PUBERTY: RUNNING

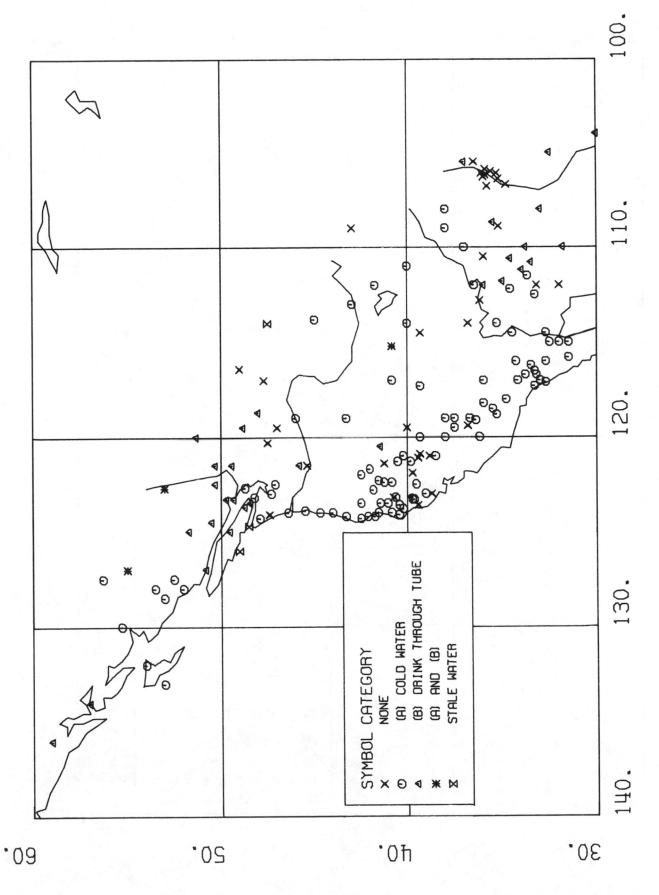

GIRLS' PUBERTY: DRINK TABOOS

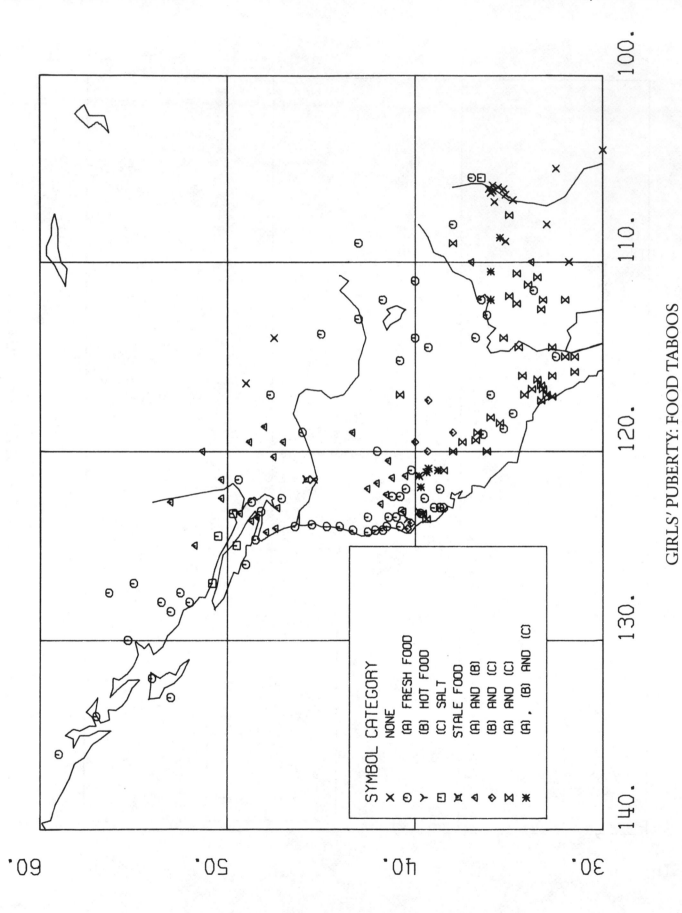

GIRLS' PUBERTY: FOOD TABOOS

SYMBOL CATEGORY
NONE
(A) FRESH FOOD
(B) HOT FOOD
(C) SALT
STALE FOOD
(A) AND (B)
(B) AND (C)
(A) AND (C)
(A), (B) AND (C)

X   ⊖   Y   ⊟   ⋈   ◁   ◇   ⋈   ✳

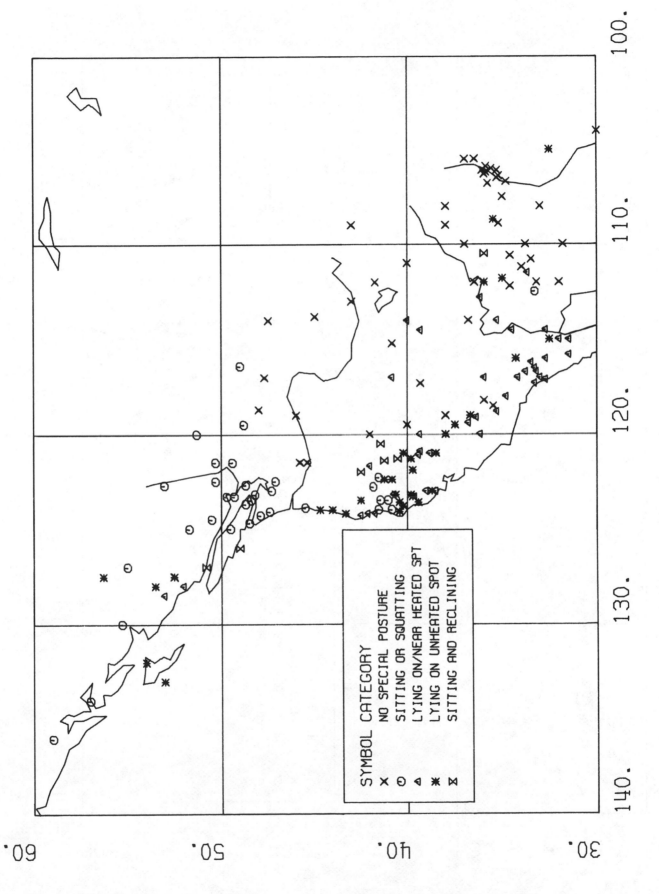

GIRLS' PUBERTY: POSTURE IN SECLUSION

SYMBOL CATEGORY
✕ NO SPECIAL POSTURE
⊖ SITTING OR SQUATTING
◁ LYING ON/NEAR HEATED SPT
✳ LYING ON UNHEATED SPOT
⋈ SITTING AND RECLINING

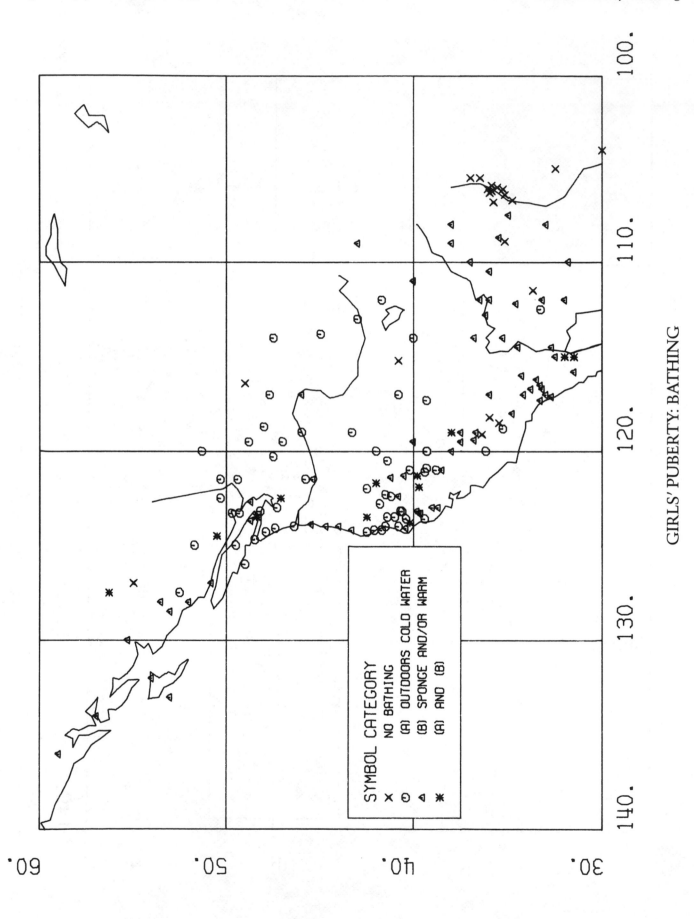

GIRLS' PUBERTY: BATHING

SYMBOL CATEGORY

	NO BATHING
×	(A) OUTDOORS COLD WATER
⊖	(B) SPONGE AND/OR WARM
◁	(A) AND (B)
✳	

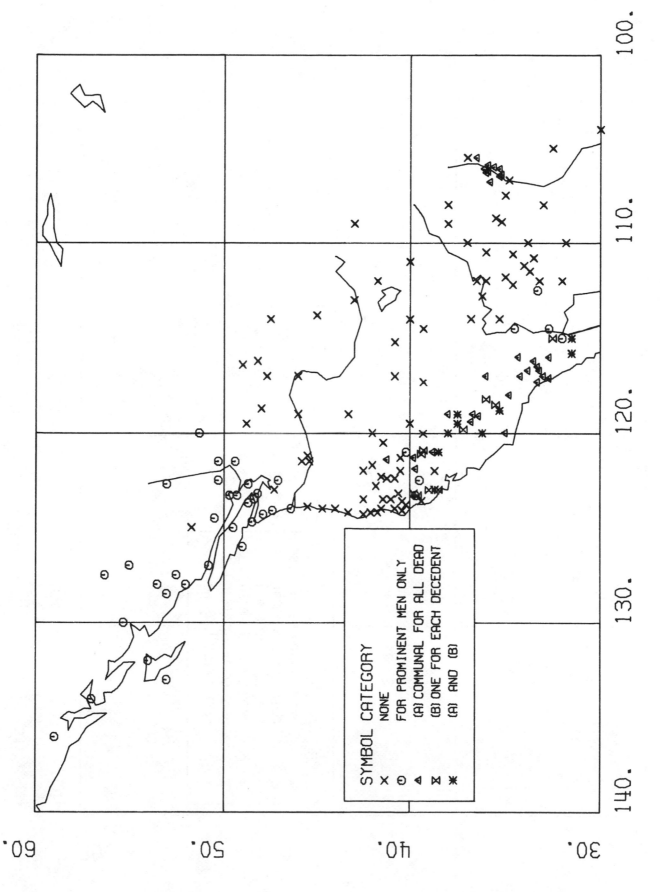

PERIODIC MOURNING CEREMONY AFTER FUNERAL

SYMBOL CATEGORY

X   NONE

⊖   FOR PROMINENT MEN ONLY

◁   (A) COMMUNAL FOR ALL DEAD

⧓   (B) ONE FOR EACH DECEDENT

✳   (A) AND (B)

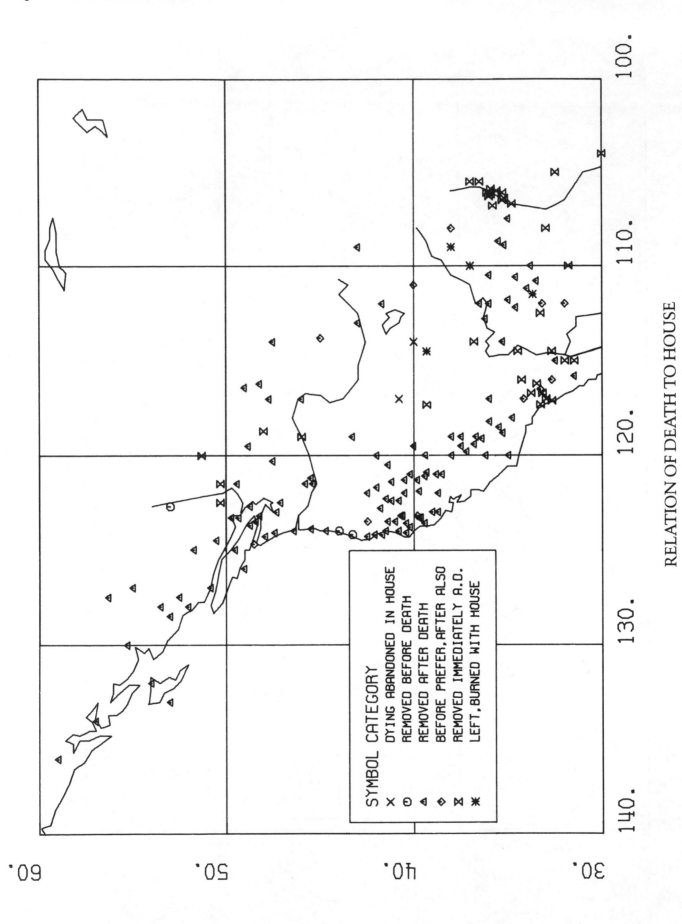

RELATION OF DEATH TO HOUSE

SYMBOL CATEGORY
X DYING ABANDONED IN HOUSE
Θ REMOVED BEFORE DEATH
◁ REMOVED AFTER DEATH
◇ BEFORE PREFER,AFTER ALSO
⋈ REMOVED IMMEDIATELY A.D.
✳ LEFT,BURNED WITH HOUSE

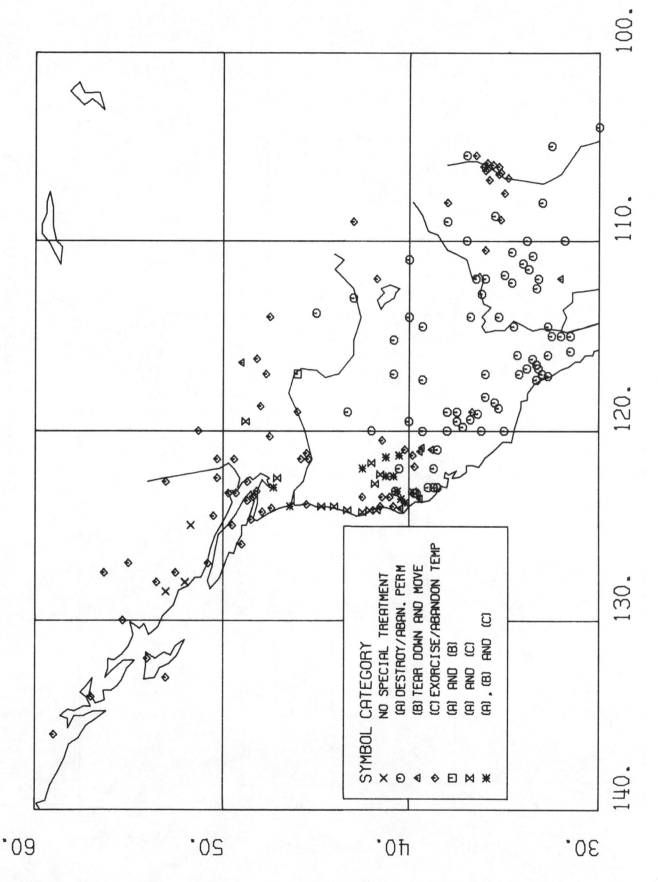

SYMBOL CATEGORY
- X　　NO SPECIAL TREATMENT
- ⊖　　(A) DESTROY/ABAN. PERM
- ◁　　(B) TEAR DOWN AND MOVE
- ◇　　(C) EXORCISE/ABANDON TEMP
- ⊟　　(A) AND (B)
- ⋈　　(A) AND (C)
- ✳　　(A) , (B) AND (C)

TREATMENT OF HOUSE FOLLOWING DEATH

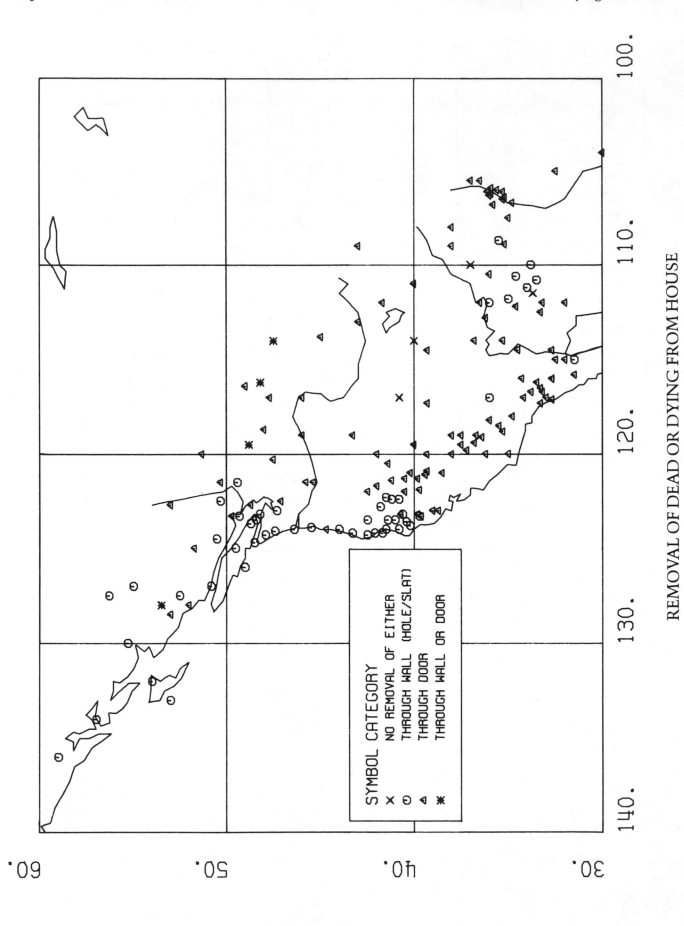

REMOVAL OF DEAD OR DYING FROM HOUSE

SYMBOL CATEGORY
X NO REMOVAL OF EITHER
⊖ THROUGH WALL (HOLE/SLAT)
◁ THROUGH DOOR
✳ THROUGH WALL OR DOOR

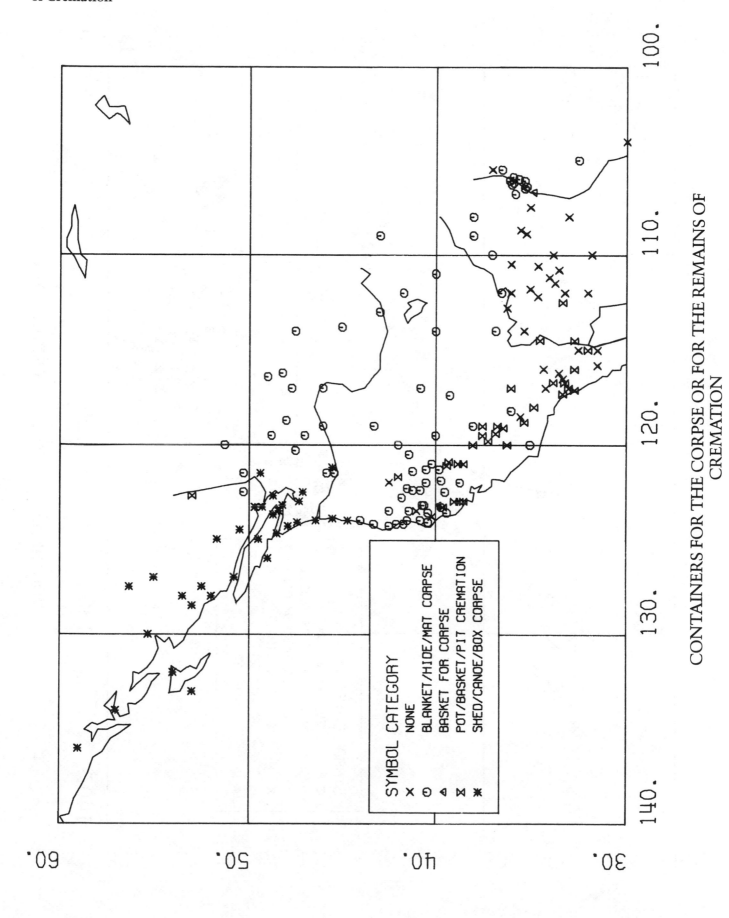

CONTAINERS FOR THE CORPSE OR FOR THE REMAINS OF CREMATION

SYMBOL CATEGORY
X NONE
⊖ BLANKET/HIDE/MAT CORPSE
◁ BASKET FOR CORPSE
⋈ POT/BASKET/PIT CREMATION
✱ SHED/CANOE/BOX CORPSE

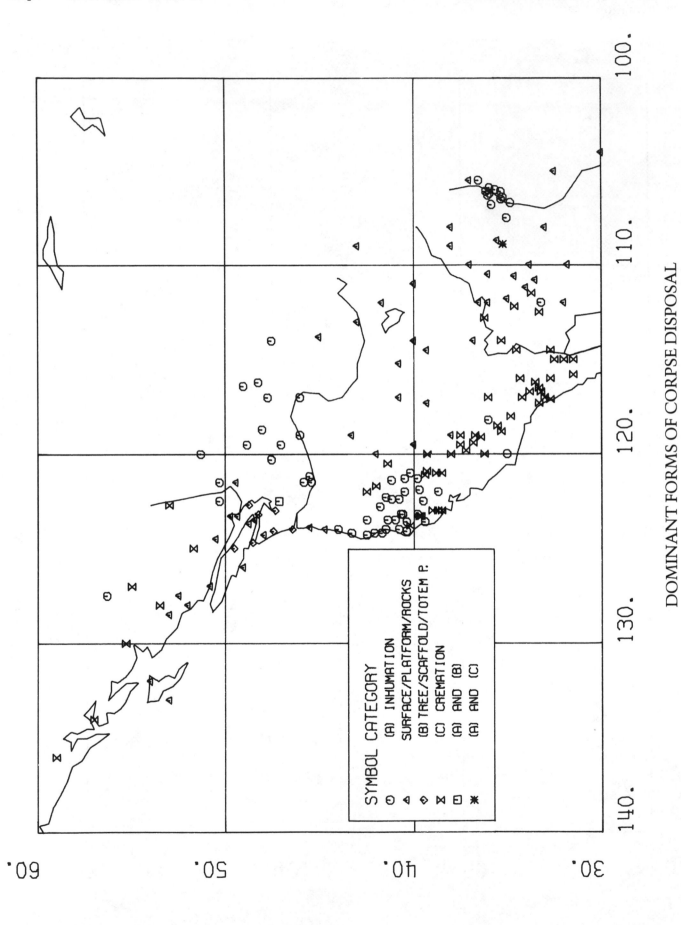

DOMINANT FORMS OF CORPSE DISPOSAL

SYMBOL CATEGORY
(A) INHUMATION
SURFACE/PLATFORM/ROCKS
(B) TREE/SCAFFOLD/TOTEM P.
(C) CREMATION
(A) AND (B)
(A) AND (C)

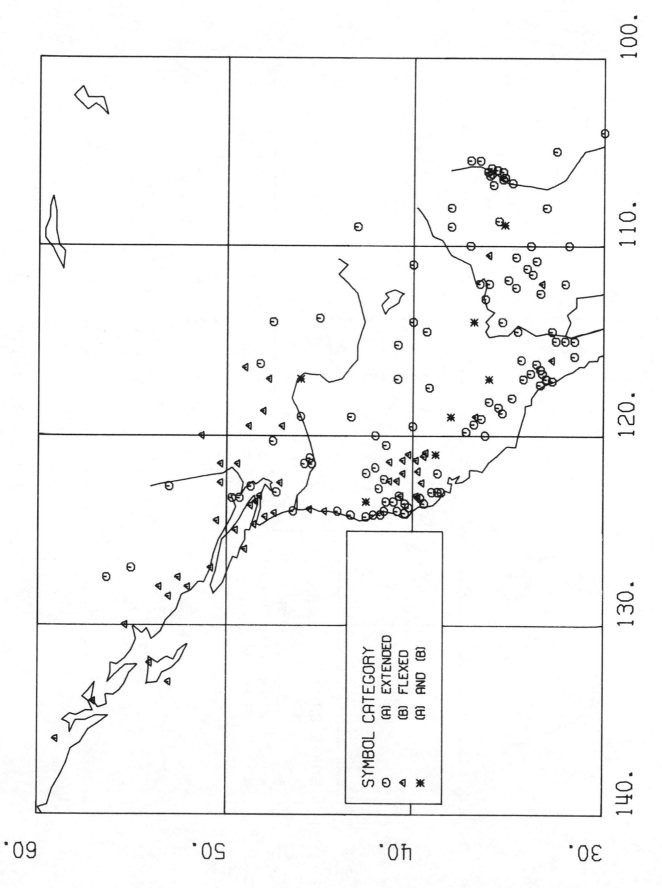

BURIAL POSITION OF CORPSE

SYMBOL CATEGORY
Θ (A) EXTENDED
◁ (B) FLEXED
✳ (A) AND (B)

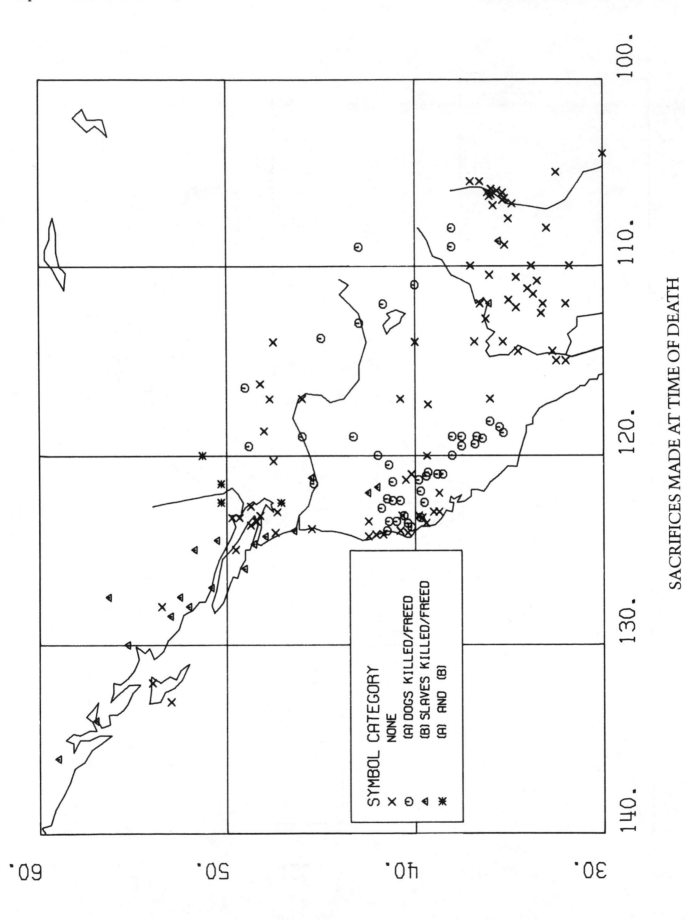

SYMBOL CATEGORY

X	NONE
⊖	(A) DOGS KILLED/FREED
◁	(B) SLAVES KILLED/FREED
✳	(A) AND (B)

SACRIFICES MADE AT TIME OF DEATH

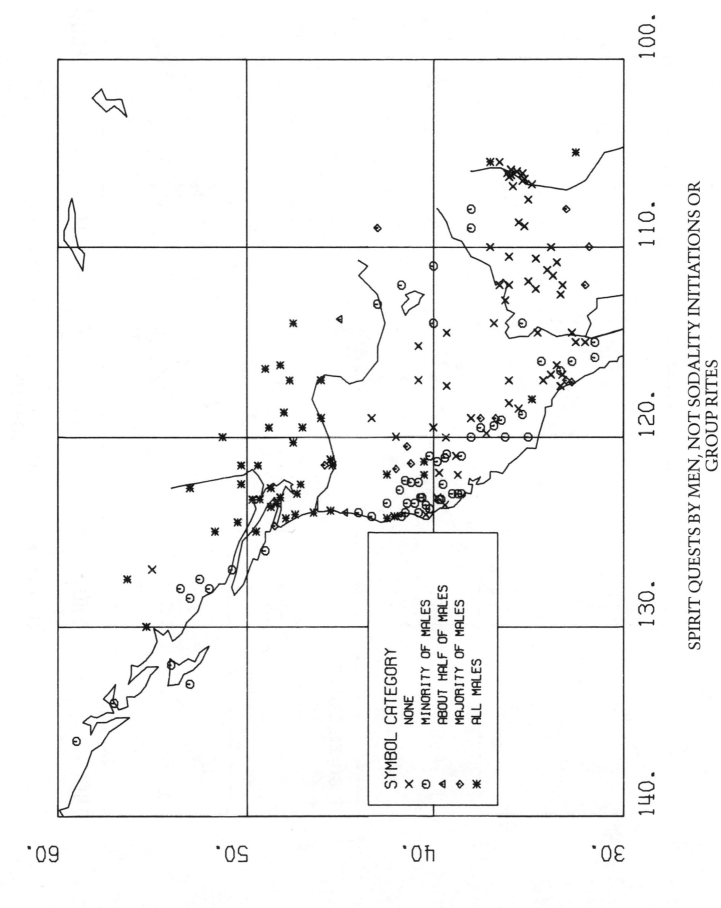

SPIRIT QUESTS BY MEN, NOT SODALITY INITIATIONS OR GROUP RITES

SYMBOL CATEGORY
X NONE
⊖ MINORITY OF MALES
△ ABOUT HALF OF MALES
◇ MAJORITY OF MALES
✳ ALL MALES

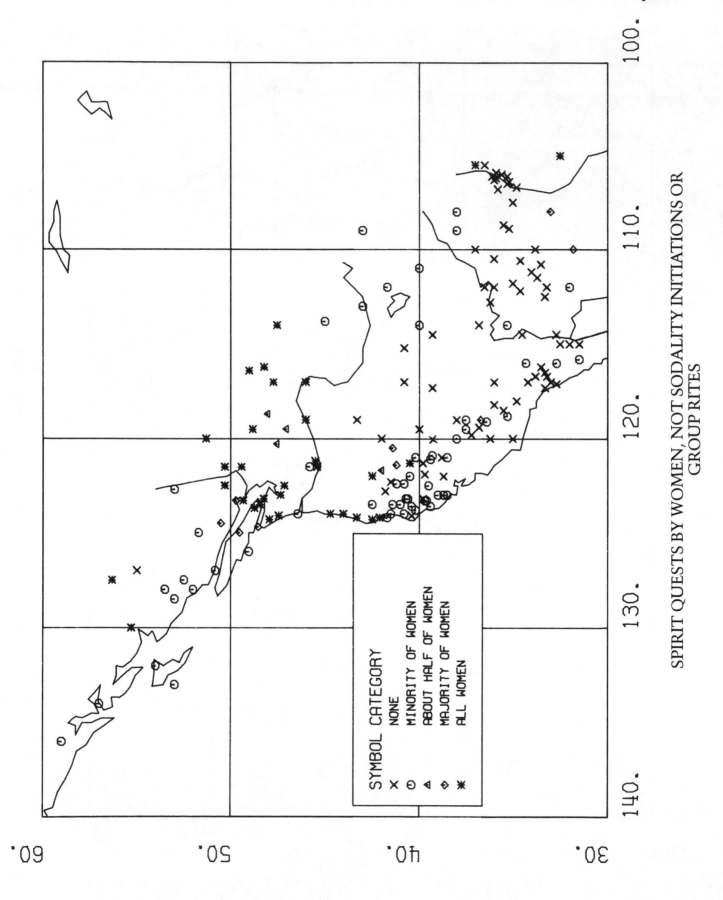

SPIRIT QUESTS BY WOMEN, NOT SODALITY INITIATIONS OR
GROUP RITES

SYMBOL CATEGORY

NONE   X
MINORITY OF WOMEN   ⊖
ABOUT HALF OF WOMEN   ◁
MAJORITY OF WOMEN   ◇
ALL WOMEN   ✳

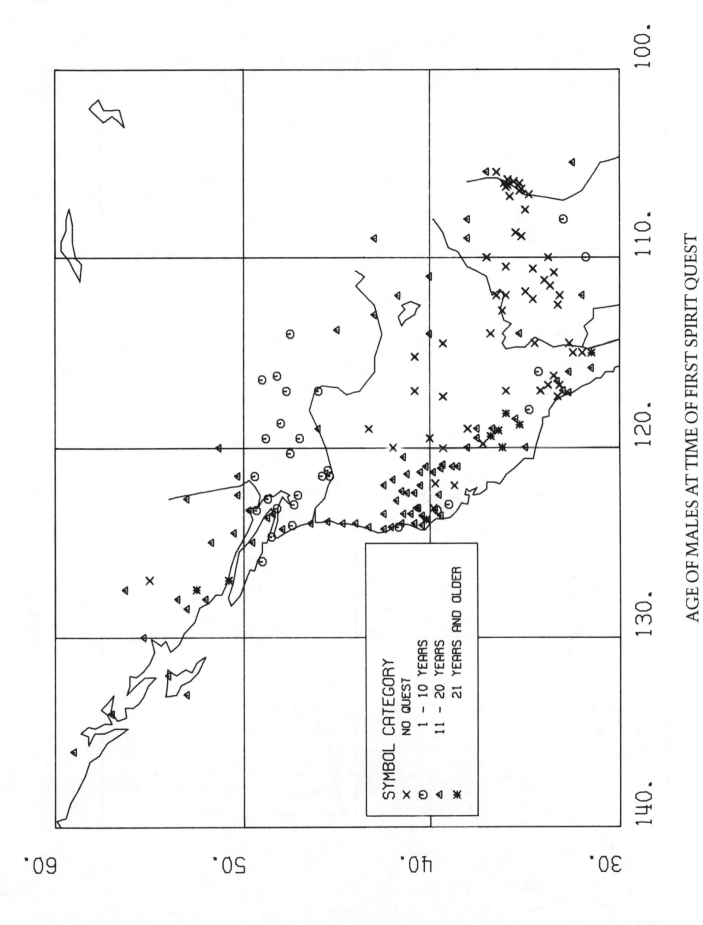

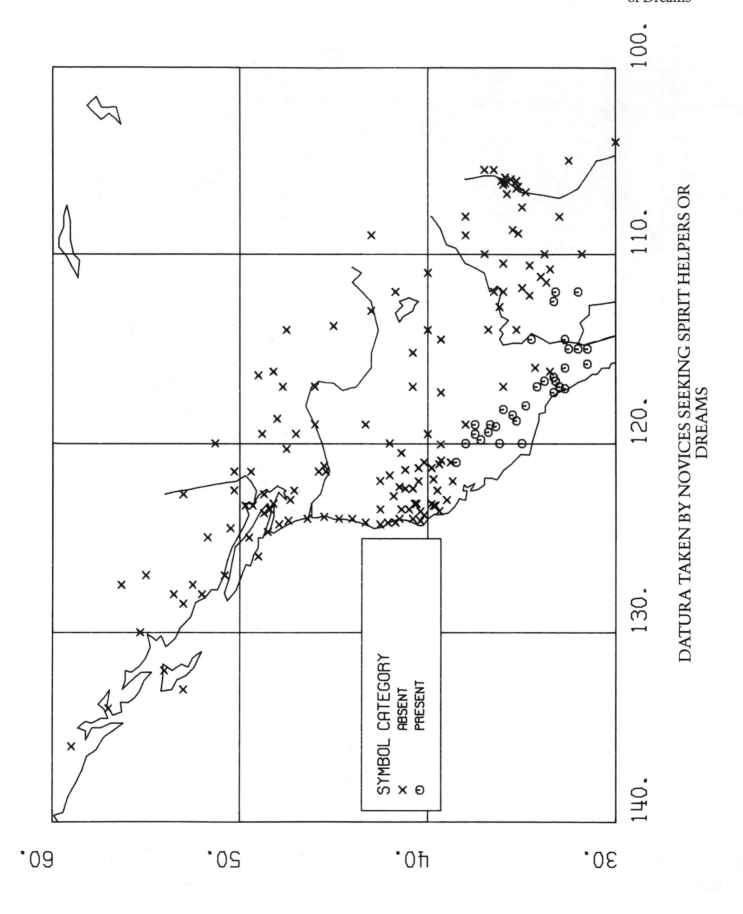

DATURA TAKEN BY NOVICES SEEKING SPIRIT HELPERS OR DREAMS

SYMBOL CATEGORY

× ABSENT
⊖ PRESENT

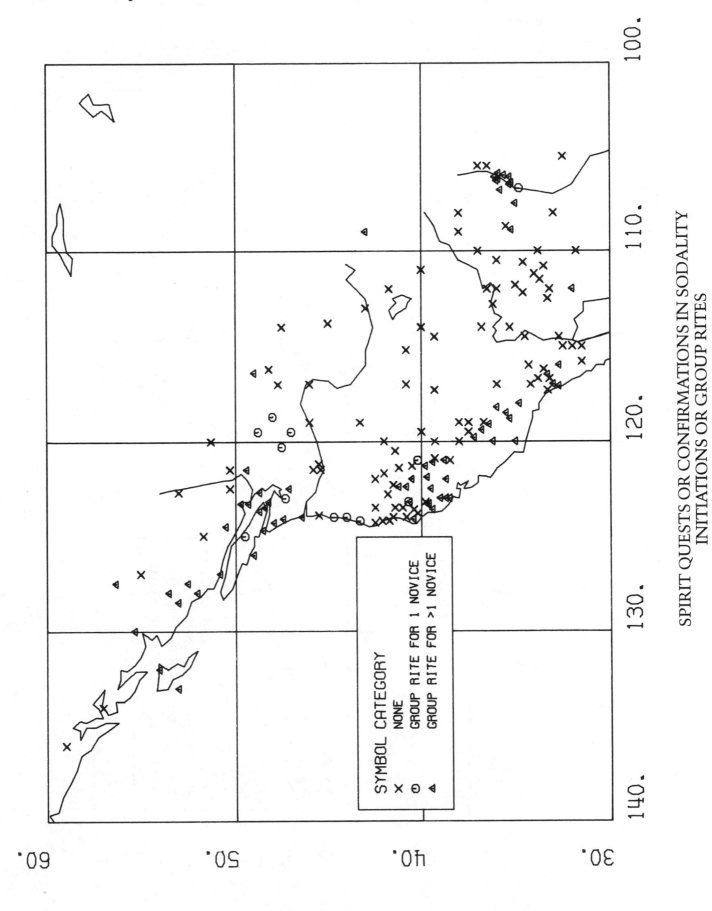

SPIRIT QUESTS OR CONFIRMATIONS IN SODALITY
INITIATIONS OR GROUP RITES

SYMBOL CATEGORY

X	NONE
⊖	GROUP RITE FOR 1 NOVICE
◁	GROUP RITE FOR >1 NOVICE

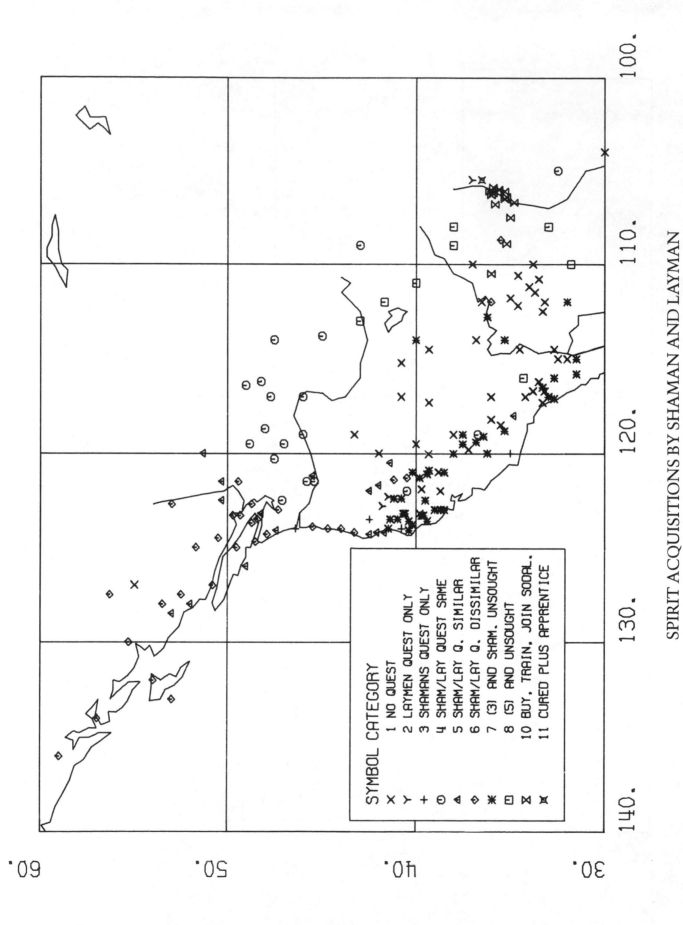

SPIRIT ACQUISITIONS BY SHAMAN AND LAYMAN

SYMBOL CATEGORY
1 NO QUEST
2 LAYMEN QUEST ONLY
3 SHAMANS QUEST ONLY
4 SHAM/LAY QUEST SAME
5 SHAM/LAY Q. SIMILAR
6 SHAM/LAY Q. DISSIMILAR
7 (3) AND SHAM. UNSOUGHT
8 (5) AND UNSOUGHT
10 BUY, TRAIN, JOIN SODAL.
11 CURED PLUS APPRENTICE

X Y + ⊖ ◁ ◇ ✳ ⊟ ⋈ ⋈

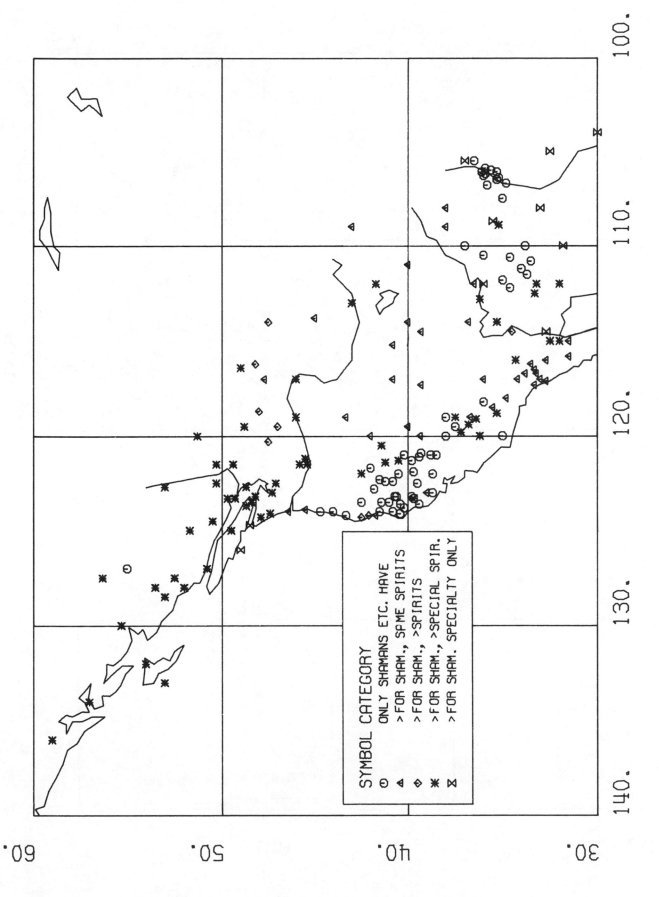

POWER POSSESSED BY SHAMAN AND LAYMAN

SYMBOL CATEGORY

ONLY SHAMANS ETC. HAVE
>FOR SHAM., SPME SPIRITS
>FOR SHAM., >SPIRITS
>FOR SHAM., >SPECIAL SPIR.
>FOR SHAM. SPECIALTY ONLY

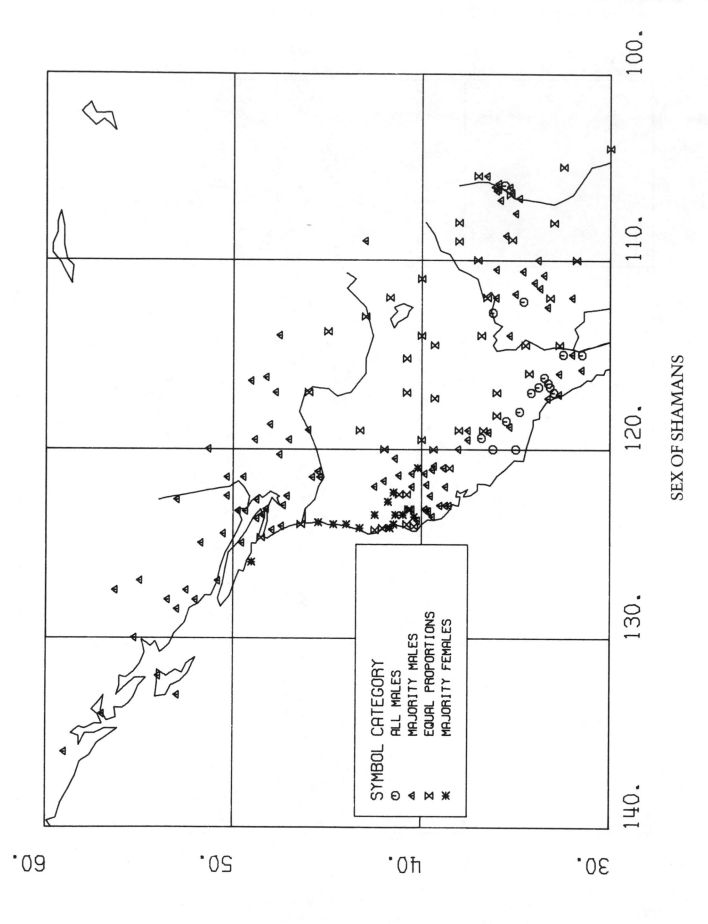

SEX OF SHAMANS

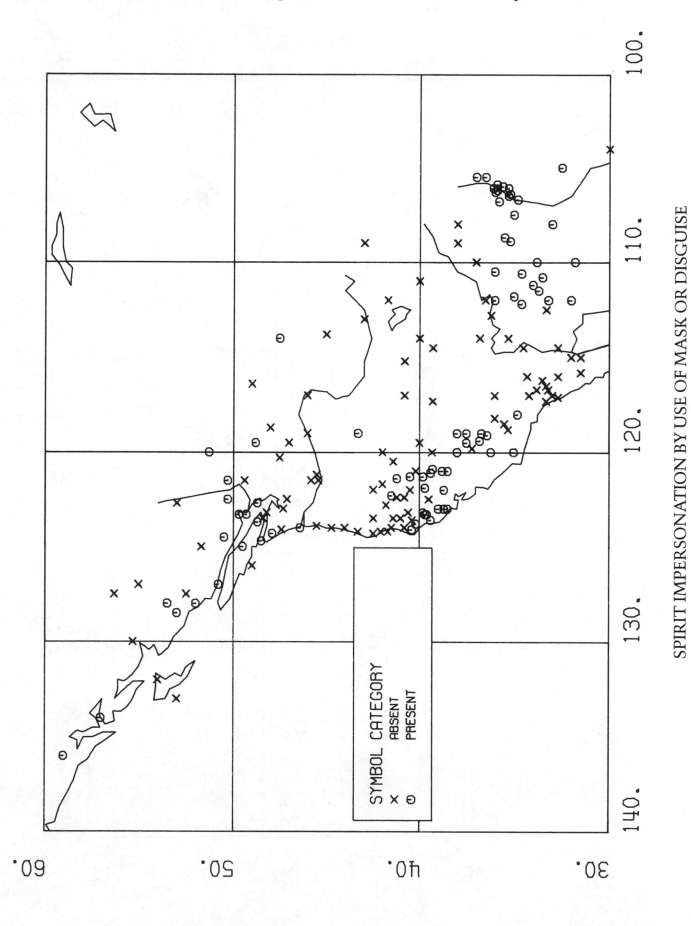

SPIRIT IMPERSONATION BY USE OF MASK OR DISGUISE

SYMBOL CATEGORY
X   ABSENT
Θ   PRESENT

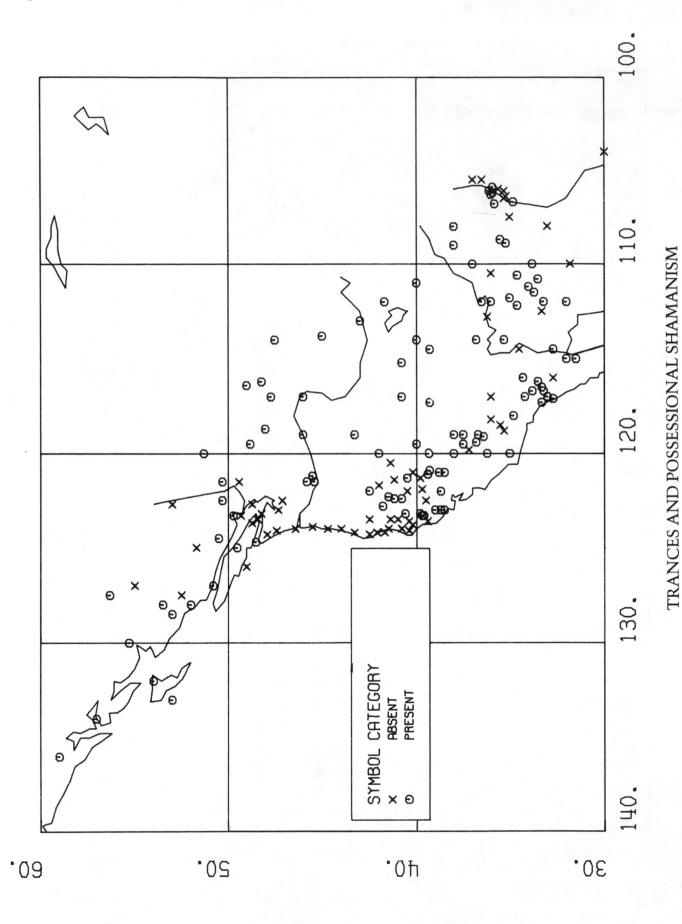

TRANCES AND POSSESSIONAL SHAMANISM

SYMBOL CATEGORY
ABSENT
PRESENT
×
⊖

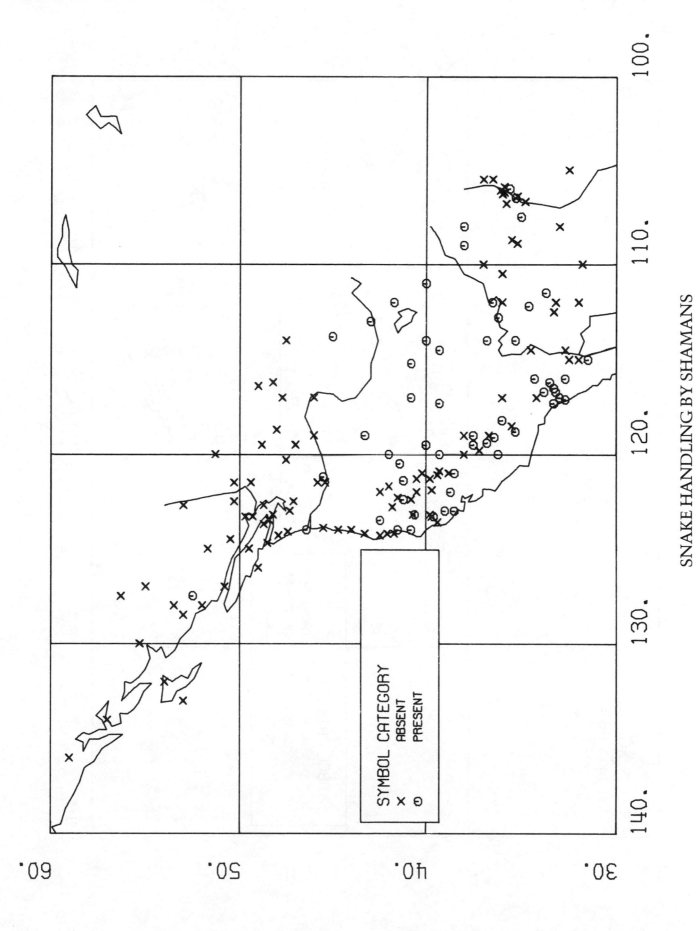

SNAKE HANDLING BY SHAMANS

SYMBOL CATEGORY

X   ABSENT

⊖   PRESENT

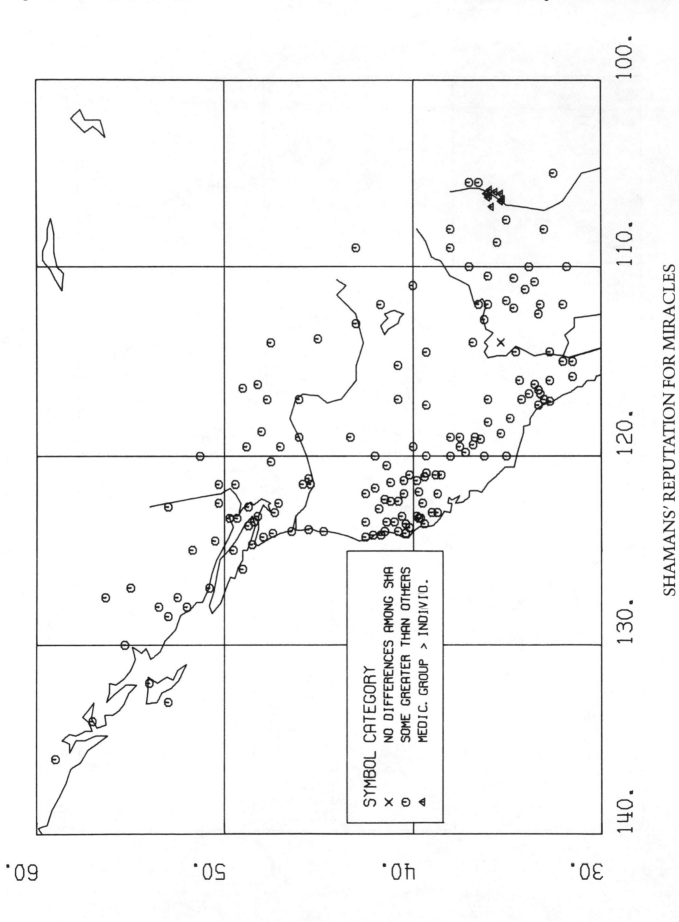

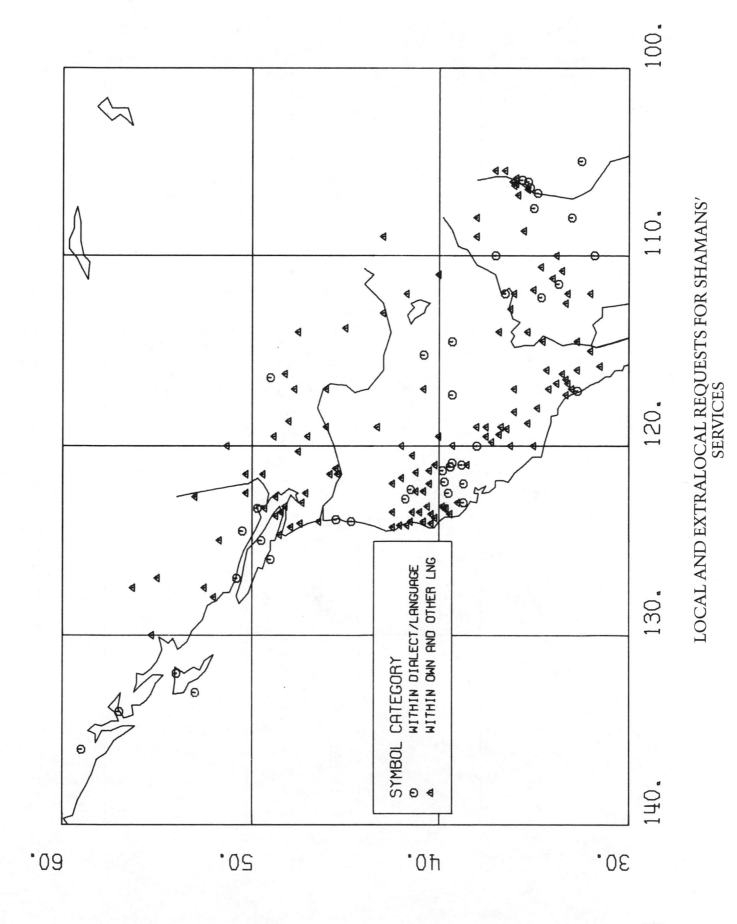

LOCAL AND EXTRALOCAL REQUESTS FOR SHAMANS' SERVICES

SYMBOL CATEGORY
⊖ WITHIN DIALECT/LANGUAGE
◁ WITHIN OWN AND OTHER LNG

Belief in Illness Caused by Intrusion of
Foreign Objects or Spirits

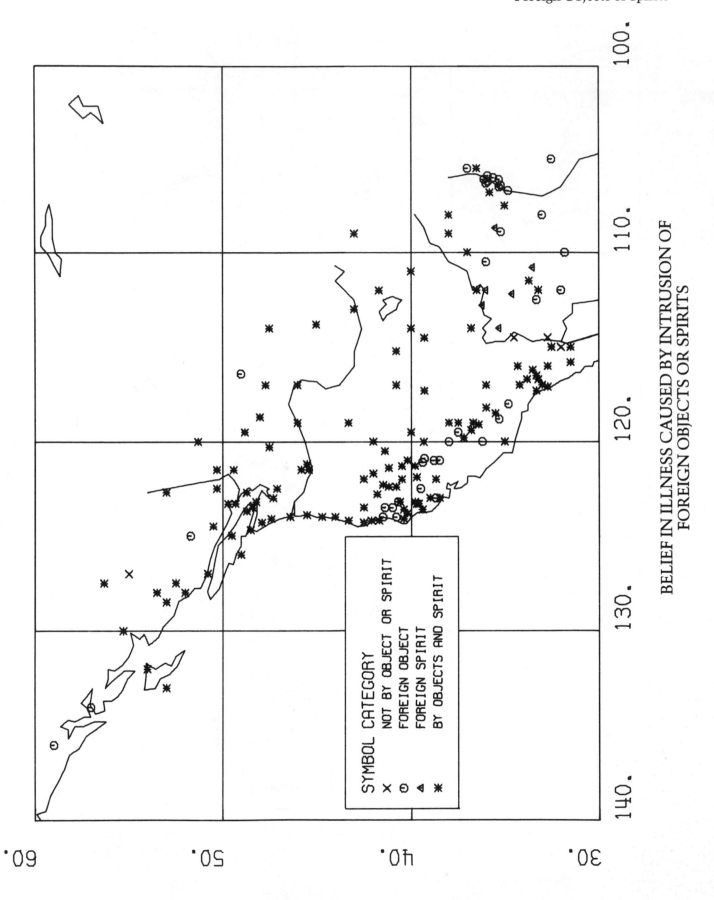

BELIEF IN ILLNESS CAUSED BY INTRUSION OF
FOREIGN OBJECTS OR SPIRITS

SYMBOL CATEGORY
X   NOT BY OBJECT OR SPIRIT
⊖   FOREIGN OBJECT
◄   FOREIGN SPIRIT
✳   BY OBJECTS AND SPIRIT

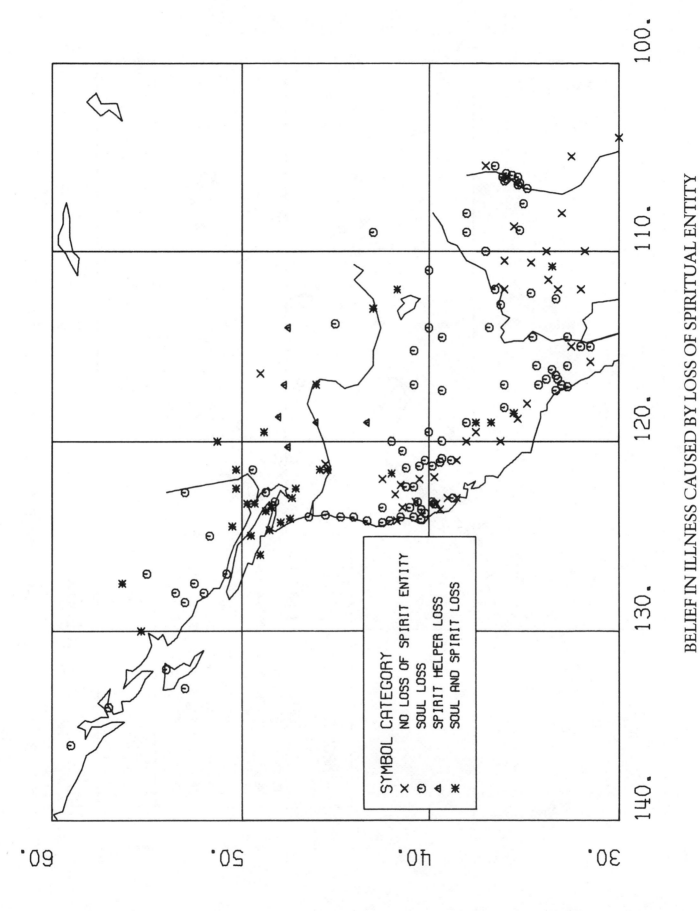

BELIEF IN ILLNESS CAUSED BY LOSS OF SPIRITUAL ENTITY

SYMBOL CATEGORY
X   NO LOSS OF SPIRIT ENTITY
⊖   SOUL LOSS
◁   SPIRIT HELPER LOSS
✳   SOUL AND SPIRIT LOSS

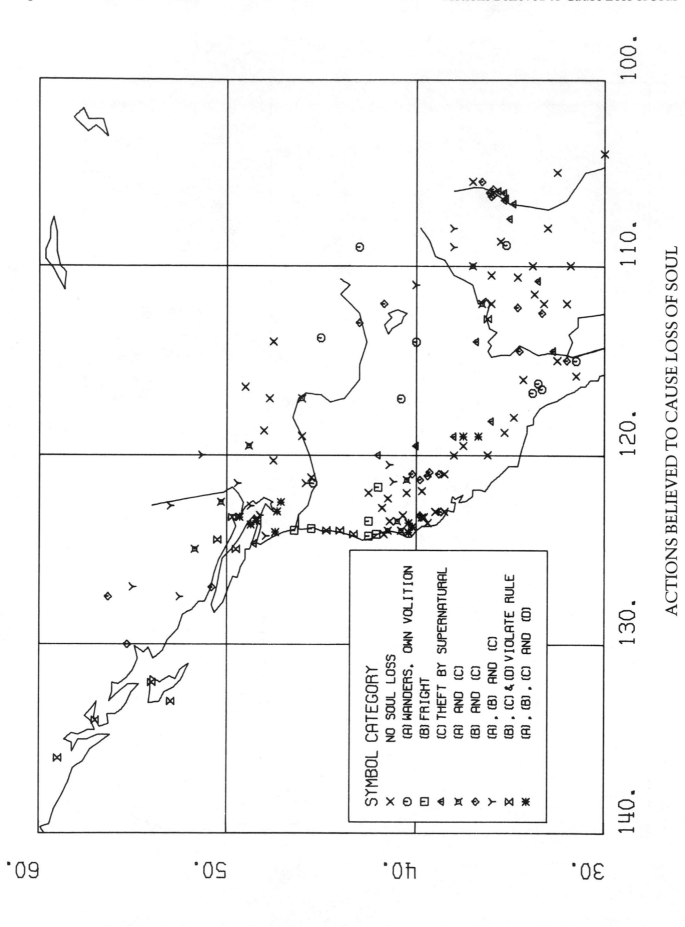

ACTIONS BELIEVED TO CAUSE LOSS OF SOUL

SYMBOL CATEGORY

NO SOUL LOSS
(A) WANDERS, OWN VOLITION
(B) FRIGHT
(C) THEFT BY SUPERNATURAL
(A) AND (C)
(B) AND (C)
(A), (B) AND (C)
(B), (C) & (D) VIOLATE RULE
(A), (B), (C) AND (D)

X   ⊖   ⊡   ◁   ⋈   ◇   Y   ⋉   ✳

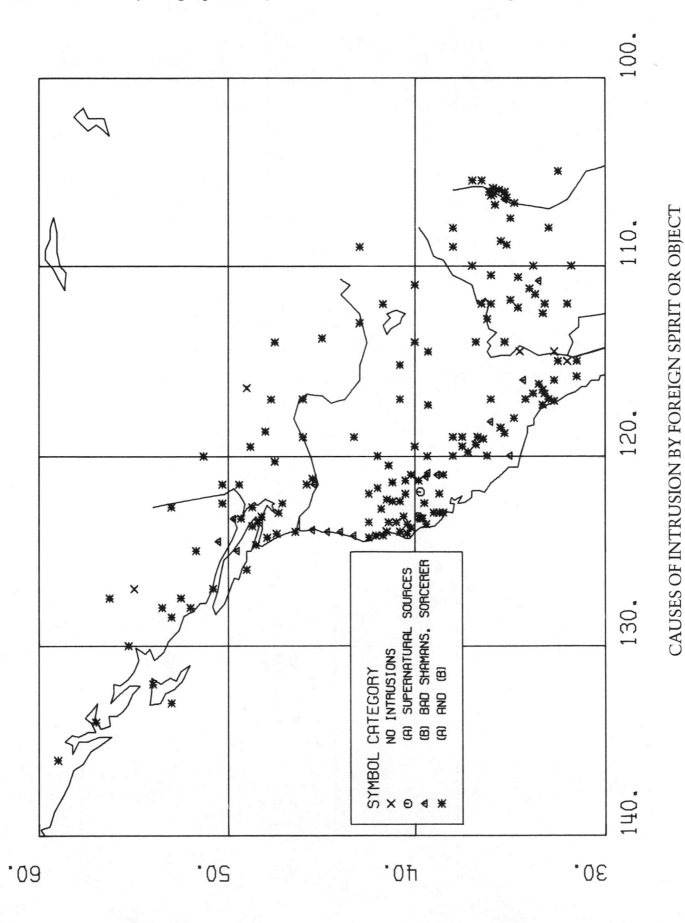

CAUSES OF INTRUSION BY FOREIGN SPIRIT OR OBJECT

SYMBOL CATEGORY
X   NO INTRUSIONS
Θ   (A) SUPERNATURAL SOURCES
◁   (B) BAD SHAMANS, SORCERER
＊   (A) AND (B)

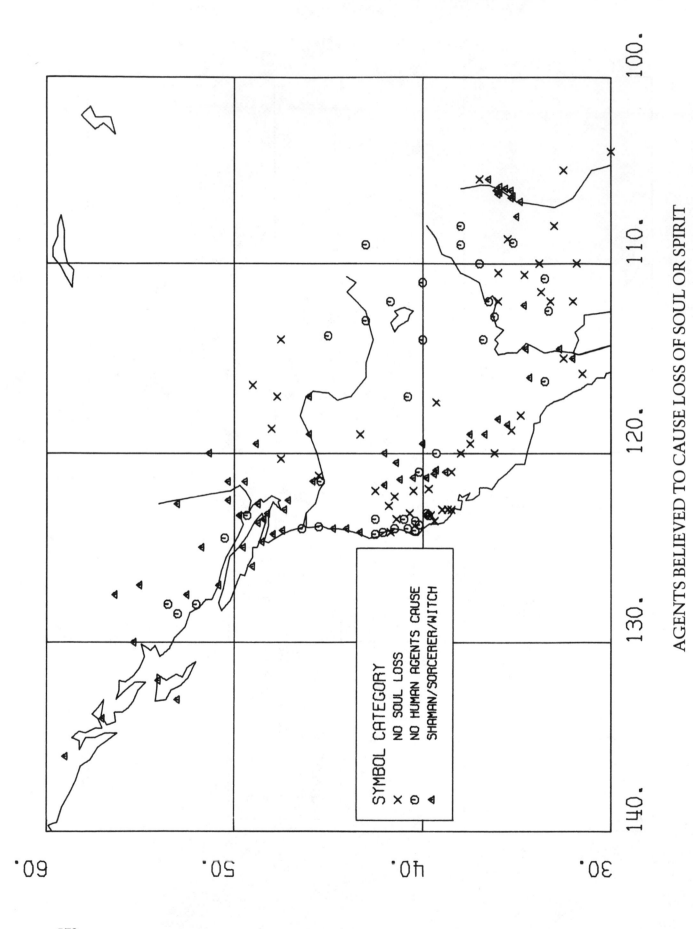

AGENTS BELIEVED TO CAUSE LOSS OF SOUL OR SPIRIT

SYMBOL CATEGORY
X   NO SOUL LOSS
⊖   NO HUMAN AGENTS CAUSE
◄   SHAMAN/SORCERER/WITCH

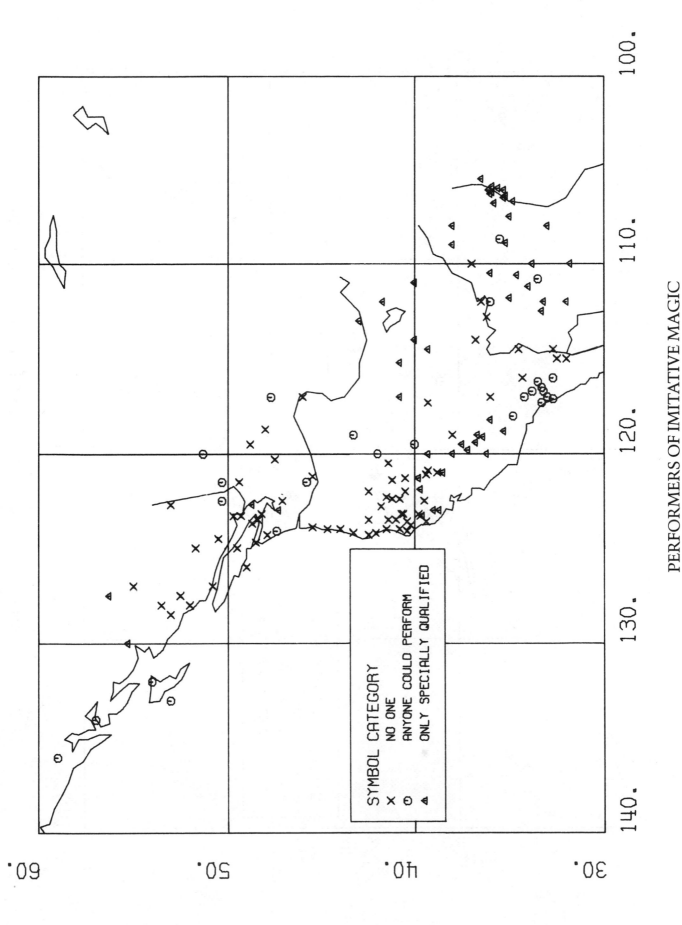

PERFORMERS OF IMITATIVE MAGIC

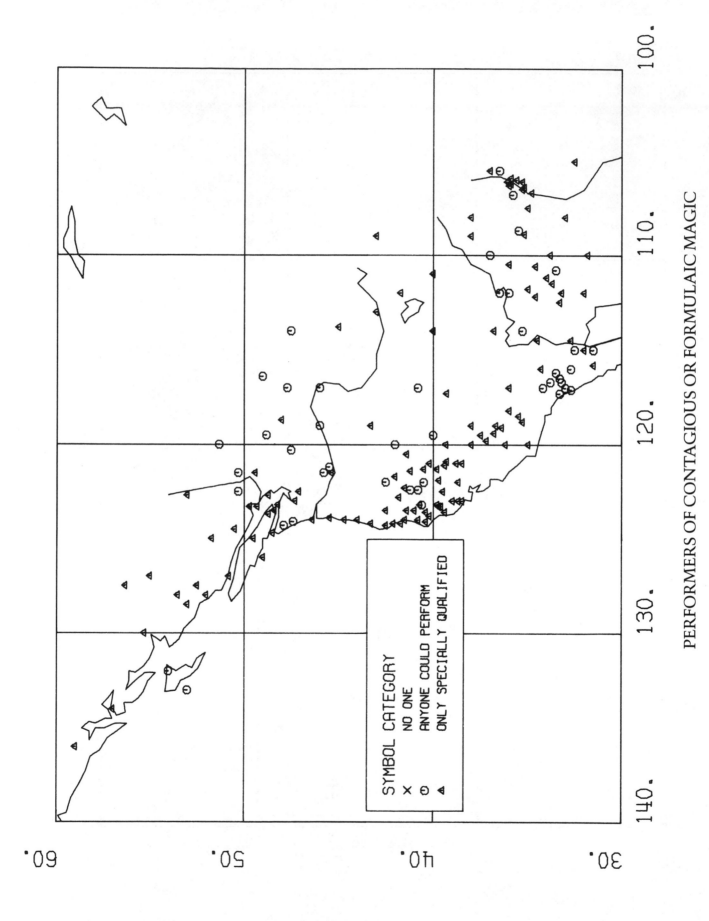

PERFORMERS OF CONTAGIOUS OR FORMULAIC MAGIC

SYMBOL CATEGORY
X   NO ONE
⊖   ANYONE COULD PERFORM
◁   ONLY SPECIALLY QUALIFIED

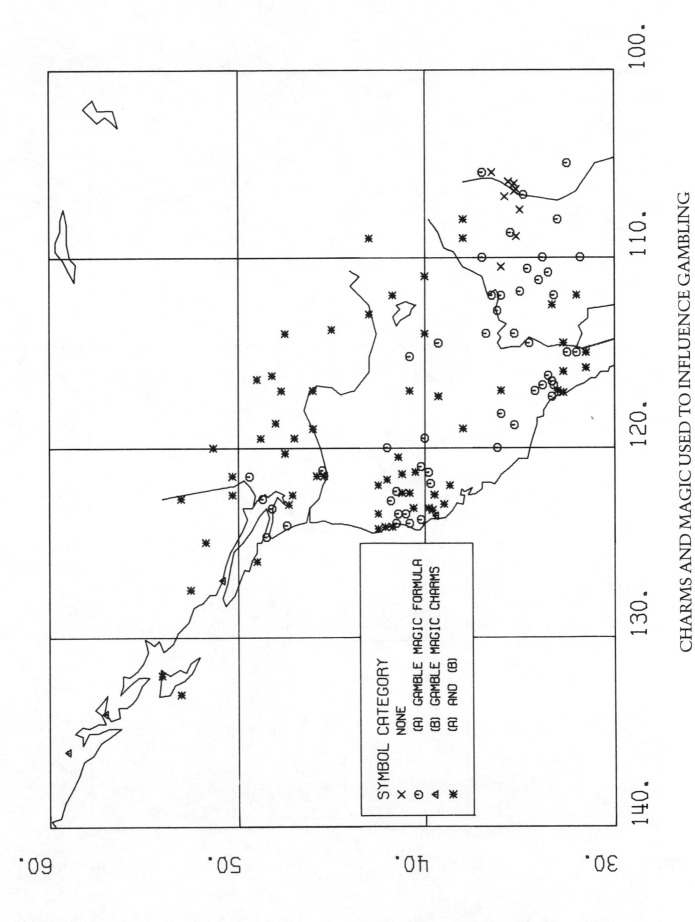

CHARMS AND MAGIC USED TO INFLUENCE GAMBLING

SYMBOL CATEGORY
NONE
X   (A) GAMBLE MAGIC FORMULA
Θ   (B) GAMBLE MAGIC CHARMS
▵   (A) AND (B)
✳

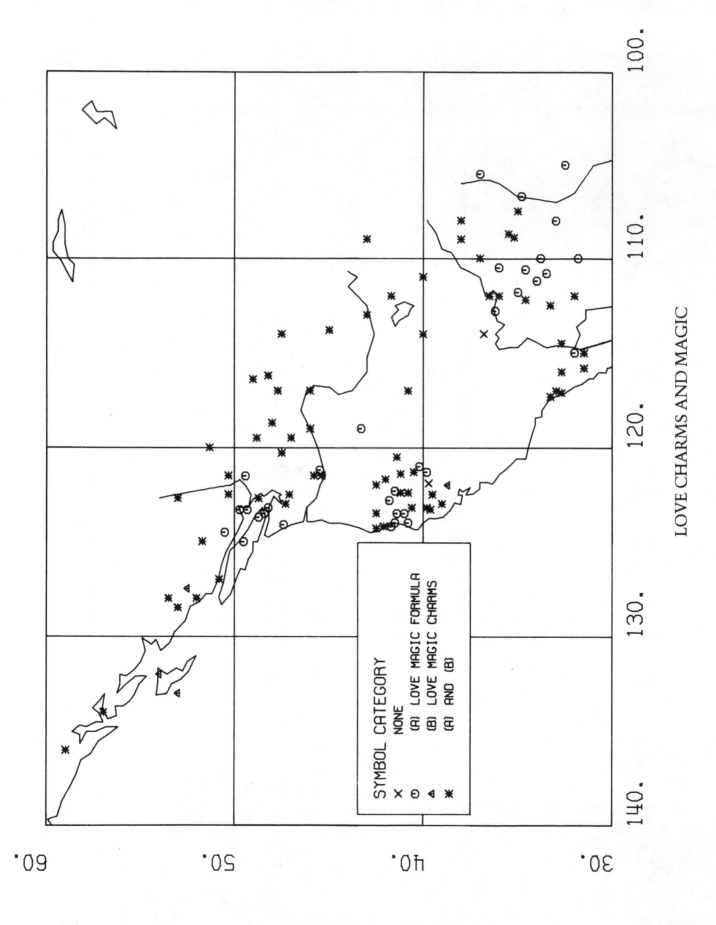

SYMBOL CATEGORY

X	NONE
⊖	(A) LOVE MAGIC FORMULA
◁	(B) LOVE MAGIC CHARMS
✳	(A) AND (B)

LOVE CHARMS AND MAGIC

Appendix E

Guide to the Variables and Definitions of Variables

DEFINITIONS OF THE VARIABLES

I. Natural Environment

I-A. Physiography and Climate

1. Tribal longitude in five-degree intervals

1. 100–105 degrees.
2. 105–110 degrees.
3. 110–115 degrees.
4. 115–120 degrees.
5. 120–125 degrees.
6. 125–130 degrees.
7. 130–135 degrees.
8. 135–140 degrees.
9. No information.

FROM: Driver et al. (1953); latitude and longitude lines added later, at every two-degree interval.

2. Tribal latitude in five-degree intervals

1. 30–35 degrees.
2. 35–40 degrees.
3. 40–45 degrees.
4. 45–50 degrees.
5. 50–55 degrees.
6. 55–60 degrees.
9. No information.

FROM: Driver et al. (1953); latitude and longitude lines added later, at every two-degree interval.

3. Tribal altitude in 1,000- and 2,000-foot intervals

1. 0–1,000 feet.
2. 1,000–2,000 feet.
3. 2,000–4,000 feet.
4. 4,000–6,000 feet.
5. 6,000–8,000 feet.
9. No information.

FROM: Shantz and Zon (1936); and Canadian Department of Mines and Technical Surveys (1957), Map 11.

4. Tribal area average annual precipitation (a 20-year average) p. 318

1. 0–10 inches.
2. 10–20 inches.
3. 20–40 inches.
4. 40–60 inches.
5. 60–100 inches.
6. Over 100 inches.
9. No information.

FROM: Shantz and Zon (1936), "Precipitation and Humidity," p. 6; and Canadian Department of Mines and Technical Surveys (1957), Map 25.

5. Tribal natural vegetation area p. 319

1. Western pines: yellow pine, sugar pine, lodgepole pine, douglas-fir.
2. Northwestern conifers: western larch, western white pine, Douglas-fir, redwood.
3. Sagebrush.
4. Creosote bush and mesquite.
5. Chaparral (broadleaf forest and scrub forest).
6. Pinon–juniper.
7. Bunchgrass.
8. Short grass.
9. No information.
10. Tundra.
11. 4 and 6 (creosote, mesquite, and juniper).
12. 6 and 8 (pinon–juniper and bunch grass).

FROM: Shantz and Zon (1936), "Natural Vegetation," pp. 4–5; and Canadian Department of Mines and Technical Surveys (1957), Map 38.

6. Tribal area average temperature in January p. 320

1. 0–10° F.
2. 10–20° F.
3. 20–30° F.
4. 30–40° F.
5. 40–50° F.
6. 50–60° F.
9. No information.

FROM: Canadian Department of Mines and Technical Surveys (1957), Map 21; and Shantz and Zon (1936), "Climate," p. 10.

7. Tribal area average temperature in July p. 321

1. 50–60° F.
2. 60–70° F.
3. 70–80° F.
4. 80–90° F.
5. 90–100° F.
9. No information.

FROM: Canadian Department of Mines and Technical Surveys (1957), Map 21; and Shantz and Zon (1936), "Climate," p. 16.

I-B. Wild Plants, Natural Flora

8. California white oak or valley oak, *Quercus lobata*

1. Absent.
2. Present.
3. Present and very frequent (a codominant species of the natural vegetation, after Kuchler, 1964).
4. Sufficiently frequent species to be sole representative of the genus shown on Kuchler's map of dominant natural vegetation.
9. No information.

9. Oregon white oak, *Quercus garryana*

1. Absent.
2. Present.
3. Very frequent.
4. Only representative of the genus shown on map of dominant vegetation.
9. No information.

10. Blue oak, *Quercus douglasii*

1. Absent.
2. Present.
3. Very frequent.
4. Only representative of the genus shown on map of dominant vegetation.
9. No information.

11. Maul oak or canyon live oak, *Quercus chrysolepis*

1. Absent.
2. Present.
3. Very frequent.
4. Only representative of the genus shown on map of dominant vegetation.
9. No information.

12. California live oak, *Quercus agrifolia*

1. Absent.
2. Present.
3. Very frequent.
4. Only representative of the genus shown on map of dominant vegetation.
9. No information.

13. Interior live oak, *Quercus wislizenii*

1. Absent.
2. Present.
3. Very frequent.
4. Only representative of the genus shown on map of dominant vegetation.
9. No information.

14. California black oak, *Quercus kelloggii*

1. Absent.
2. Present.
3. Very frequent.
4. Only representative of the genus shown on map of dominant vegetation.
9. No information.

15. Tan-oak, *Lithocarpus densiflora*

1. Absent.
2. Present.
9. No information.

16. Emory oak or scrub oak, *Quercus emoryi*

1. Absent.
2. Present.
3. Very frequent.

4. Only representative of the genus shown on map of dominant vegetation.
9. No information.

17. Gambel oak, *Quercus gambellii*

1. Absent.
2. Present.
3. Very frequent.
4. Only representative of the genus shown on map of dominant vegetation.
9. No information.

18. Evergreen oak, *Quercus undulata*

1. Absent.
2. Present.
3. Very frequent.
4. Only species represented on map of dominant vegetation.
9. No information.

19. Pinyon pine, *Pinus edulis*

1. Absent.
2. Present.
3. Very frequent.
4. Only species represented on map of dominant vegetation.
9. No information.

20. Single-leaf pinyon pine, *Pinus monophylla*

1. Absent.
2. Present.
3. Very frequent.
4. Only species represented on map of dominant vegetation.
9. No information.

21. Ponderosa or yellow pine, *Pinus ponderosa*

1. Absent.
2. Present.
9. No information.

22. Lodgepole pine, *Pinus contorta*

1. Absent.
2. Present.
9. No information.

23. Sugar pine, *Pinus lambertiana*

1. Absent.
2. Present.
9. No information.

24. Giant sahuaro cactus, *Carnegiea gigantea*

1. Absent.
2. Present.
9. No information.

25. Honey mesquite, *Prosopis juliflora* **(and other mesquite spp.)**

1. Absent.
2. Present.
3. Very frequent.
4. Only representative of genus shown on map of dominant vegetation.
9. No information.

26. Screwbean, *Prosopis pubescens*

1. Absent.
2. Present.
9. No information.

27. Mescal, *Agave parryi*

1. Absent.
2. Present.
9. No information.

28. Mescal, *Agave deserti*

1. Absent.
2. Present.
9. No information.

29. Mescal, *Agave utahensis*

1. Absent.
2. Present.
9. No information.

30. Mescal, *Agave palmeri*

1. Absent.
2. Present.
9. No information.

31. Mescal, *Agave conseii*

1. Absent.
2. Present.
9. No information.

32. Mescal, *Agave neomexicana*

1. Absent.
2. Present.
9. No information.

33. Soapweed, *Yucca glauca,* **or Datil,** *Y. baccata*

1. Absent.
2. Present.
9. No information.

34. Sotol, *Dasylerion wheeleri*

1. Absent.
2. Present.
9. No information.

35. Prickly-pear cactus, *Opuntia engelmannii* **(and other prickly-pear spp.)**

1. Absent.
2. Present.
3. Very frequent.
4. Only representative of genus on map of natural vegetation.
9. No information.

36. Cholla cactus, *Opuntia arborescens* **(and other cholla spp.)**

1. Absent.
2. Present.
3. Very frequent.
4. Only representative of genus on map of natural vegetation.
9. No information.

37. Sand-root, *Ammobroma sonorae*

1. Absent.
2. Present.
9. No information.

38. Pigweed, *Amaranthus retroflexus*

1. Absent.
2. Present.
9. No information.

39. Serviceberry, *Amelanchier alnifolia*

1. Absent.
2. Present.
9. No information.

40. Lambsquarter, *Chenopodium album*

1. Absent.
2. Present.
9. No information.

41. Saltbush, *Atriplex argentea*

1. Absent.
2. Present.
3. Very frequent.
4. Only genus represented on map of dominant vegetation.
9. No information.

42. Western hackberry, *Celtis douglasii*

1. Absent.
2. Present.
9. No information.

43. Guaco, *Cleome serrulata*

1. Absent.
2. Present.
9. No information.

44. Indian millet, *Eriocoma cuspidata*

   1. Absent.
   2. Present.
   9. No information.

45. Common purslane, *Portulaca oleracea*

   1. Absent.
   2. Present.
   9. No information.

46. Wild potato, *Solanum triflorum* **and other potato spp.**

   1. Absent.
   2. Present.
   9. No information.

47. Yamp, *Carum gairdneri*

   1. Absent.
   2. Present.
   9. No information.

48. Thistle, *Cirsium acaule,* **and other** *Cirsium* **spp.**

   1. Absent.
   2. Present.
   9. No information.

49. Wild rye, *Elymus condensatus* **or** *sibiricus*

   1. Absent.
   2. Present.
   9. No information.

50. Sunflower, *Helianthus annuus*

   1. Absent.
   2. Present.
   9. No information.

51. Sunflower, *Helianthus* **(all other spp.)**

   1. Absent.
   2. Present.
   9. No information.

52. Broomrape, genus *Orobanche*

   1. Absent.
   2. Present.
   9. No information.

53. Sand bunchgrass, Rice Grass, *Oryzopis* **spp.**

   1. Absent.
   2. Present.
   9. No information.

54. Tobacco-root or Bitterroot, *Valeriana edulis*

   1. Absent.
   2. Present.
   9. No information.

55. Camass, genus *Camassia*

   1. Absent.
   2. Present.
   9. No information.

56. Braken fern, *Pteridium aquilinum*

   1. Absent.
   2. Present.
   9. No information.

57. Western hazelnut or filbert, *Corylus californica*

   1. Absent.
   2. Present.
   9. No information.

58. Lupine, *Lupinus polyphyllus*

   1. Absent.
   2. Present.
   9. No information.

59. Salal, *Gaultheria shallon*

   1. Absent.
   2. Present.
   9. No information.

60. Tiger-lily, *Lilium* **spp.**

   1. Absent.
   2. Present.
   9. No information.

61. Wokas or Water-lily, *Nymphaea polysepala*

   1. Absent.
   2. Present.
   9. No information.

62. Life Zones in Tribal Territory

   1. Lower Austral.
   2. Upper Austral.
   3. Transition.
   4. Canadian.
   5. 1 and 2.
   6. 2 and 3.
   7. 3 and 4.
   8. 1 and 2 and 3.
   9. No information.
  10. 2 and 3 and 4.

I-C. Sea Mammals

63. Baird's beaked whale, *Berardius bairdii*

   1. Absent or very rare.
   2. Present.
   9. No information.

64. Pacific beaked whale, *Mesoplodon stejnegeri*

1. Absent or very rare.
2. Present.
9. No information.

65. Goose-beaked whale, *Ziphius cavirostris*

1. Absent or very rare.
2. Present.
9. No information.

66. Sperm whale, *Physeter catodon*

1. Absent or very rare.
2. Present.
9. No information.

67. Pygmy sperm whale, *Kogia breviceps*

1. Absent or very rare.
2. Present.
9. No information

68. California gray whale, *Eschrichtius gibbosus*

1. Absent or very rare.
2. Present.
9. No information.

69. Fin-backed whale, *Balaenoptera physalus*

1. Absent or very rare.
2. Present.
9. No information.

70. Sei whale, *Balaenoptera borealis*

1. Absent or very rare.
2. Present.
9. No information.

71. Blue whale or Sulphur-bottomed whale, *Sibbaldus musculus*

1. Absent or very rare.
2. Present.
9. No information.

72. Hump-backed whale, *Megaptera novaengliae*

1. Absent or very rare.
2. Present.
9. No information.

73. Pacific Right whale, *Eubalaena sieboldii*

1. Absent or very rare.
2. Present.
9. No information.

74. Gray's porpoise or spotted dolphin, *Stenella styx*

1. Absent or very rare.
2. Present.
9. No information.

75. Pacific dolphin, *Delphinius bairdii*

1. Absent or very rare.
2. Present.
9. No information.

76. Gill's bottle-nosed dolphin, *Tursiops gillii*

1. Absent or very rare.
2. Present.
9. No information.

77. Pacific bottle-nosed dolphin, *Tursiops nuuanu*

1. Absent or very rare.
2. Present.
9. No information.

78. Northern right-whale dolphin, *Lissodelphus borealis*

1. Absent or very rare.
2. Present.
9. No information.

79. Pacific white-sided dolphin, *Lagenorhynchus obliquidens*

1. Absent or very rare.
2. Present.
9. No information.

80. Pacific killer-whale, *Grampus rectipinna*

1. Absent or very rare.
2. Present.
9. No information.

81. False killer-whale, *Pseudorca crassidens*

1. Absent or very rare.
2. Present.
9. No information.

82. Pacific blackfish or pilot whale, *Globicephala scammonii*

1. Absent or very rare.
2. Present.
9. No information.

83. Pacific harbor porpoise, *Phocoena vomerina*

1. Absent or very rare.
2. Present.
9. No information.

84. Dall's porpoise, *Phocoenoides dalli*

1. Absent or very rare.
2. Present.
9. No information.

85. Sea-otter, *Enhydra lutris*

1. Absent or very rare.
2. Present.
9. No information.

86. Northern or Alaska fur-seal, *Callorhinus ursinus*

1. Absent or very rare.
2. Present.
9. No information.

87. Guadalupe fur-seal, *Arctophoca townsendii*

1. Absent or very rare.
2. Present.
9. No information.

88. Northern sea-lion, *Eumetopias jubata*

1. Absent or very rare.
2. Present.
9. No information.

89. California sea-lion, *Zalophus californianus*

1. Absent or very rare.
2. Present.
9. No information.

90. Harbor seal, *Phoca vitulina*

1. Absent or very rare.
2. Present.
9. No information.

91. Northern elephant-seal, *Mirounga angustirostris*

1. Absent or very rare.
2. Present.
9. No information.

92. Total number of types of the 29 sea mammals available in tribal area   **p. 332**

1. None.
2. 1–5.
3. 6–10.
4. 11–15.
5. 16–20.
6. 21–25.
7. 26–30.
9. No information.

I-D. Land Mammals

93. Cottontail rabbit, *Sylvilagus* **spp.**

1. Absent or very rare.
2. Present.
9. No information.

94. Jack rabbit, *Lepus* **spp.**

1. Absent or very rare.
2. Present.
9. No information.

95. Beaver, *Castor canadensis*

1. Absent or very rare.
2. Present.
9. No information.

96. Porcupine, *Erethizon dorsatum*

1. Absent or very rare.
2. Present.
9. No information.

97. Coyote, *Canis latrans*

1. Absent or very rare.
2. Present.
9. No information.

98. Wolf, *Canis lupus*

1. Absent or very rare.
2. Present.
9. No information.

99. Bear, *Ursus americanus,* **and other** *Ursus* **spp.**

1. Absent or very rare.
2. Present.
9. No information.

100. Mountain lions, *Felis concolor*

1. Absent.
2. Present.
9. No information.

101. Lynx, *Lynx canadensis*

1. Absent or very rare.
2. Present.
9. No information.

102. Bobcat, *Lynx rufus*

1. Absent or very rare.
2. Present.
9. No information.

103. Wapiti (Elk), *Cervus* **spp.**

1. Absent or very rare.
2. *C. canadensis* present.
3. *C. nannodes* present.
4. *C. merriami* present.
9. No information.

104. Black-tailed deer or mule deer, *Odocoileus hemionus*

1. Absent or very rare.
2. Present.
9. No information.

105. White-tailed deer, *Odocoileus virginiana*

1. Absent or very rare.
2. Present.
9. No information.

106. Moose, *Alces alces*

1. Absent or very rare.
2. Present.
9. No information.

107. Caribou, *Rangifer* **spp.**

1. Absent or very rare.
2. Present.
9. No information.

108. Pronghorn antelope, *Antilocapra americana*

1. Absent or very rare.
2. Present.
9. No information.

109. Bison, *Bison bison*

1. Absent or very rare.
2. Present.
9. No information.

110. Mountain goat, *Oreamnos americanus*

1. Absent or very rare.
2. Present.
9. No information.

111. Mountain sheep, *Ovis canadensis*

1. Absent or very rare.
2. Present.
9. No information.

112. Total number of 19 species of land mammals available in tribal area   **p. 327**

1. Absent or very rare.
2. 1–5.
3. 6–10.
4. 11–15.
5. 16–19.
9. No information.

I-E. Fish: Freshwater, Saltwater, and Anadromous

113. Western sea-lamprey, *Entosphenus tridentatus*

1. Absent.
2. Present.
9. No information.

114. White sturgeon, *Acipenser transmontanus*

1. Absent.
2. Present.
9. No information.

115. Cutthroat trout, *Salmo clarkii,* **and Rainbow trout,** *S. gairdnerii*

1. Absent.
2. Present.
9. No information.

116. Dolly Varden char, *Salvelinus malma*

1. Absent.
2. Present.
9. No information.

117. Rocky Mountain whitefish, *Coregonus* **spp., and lake whitefish,** *Prosopium* **spp.**

1. Absent.
2. Present.
9. No information.

118. Suckers, family Catostomidae, *Catostomus* **spp.,** *Chamistes* **spp.,** *Deltistes* **spp.,** *Pantosteus* **spp.,** *Xyrauchen texanus*

1. Absent.
2. Present.
9. No information.

119. Chinook or king salmon, *Oncorhynchus tshawytscha*

1. Absent or very rare.
2. Present.
9. No information.

120. Coho or silver salmon, *Oncorhynchus kisutch*

1. Absent or very rare.
2. Present.
9. No information.

121. Pink or humpback salmon, *Oncorhynchus gorbuscha*

1. Absent or very rare.
2. Present.
9. No information.

122. Sockeye or red salmon, *Oncorhynchus nerka*

1. Absent or very rare.
2. Present.
9. No information.

123. Chum or dog salmon, *Oncorhynchus keta*

1. Absent or very rare.
2. Present.
9. No information.

124. Steelhead trout, *Salmon gairdnerii irideus, S. g. newberryi*

1. Absent or very rare.
2. Present.
9. No information.

125. Number of salmon and steelhead anadromous species present in tribal area   **p. 329**

1. 0.
2. 1.
3. 2.
4. 3.
5. 4.
6. 5.
7. 6.
9. No information.

126. Herring, *Clupea pallasii*

1. Absent or very rare.

2. Present.
9. No information.

---

127. Sardine or California pilchard, *Sardinops sagax*

1. Absent or very rare.
2. Present.
9. No information.

---

128. Eulachon or candlefish, *Thaleichthys pacificus*

1. Absent or very rare.
2. Present.
9. No information.

---

129. Pacific halibut, *Hippoglossus stenolepis*

1. Absent or very rare.
2. Present.
9. No information.

---

130. Pacific cod, *Gadus macrocephalus*

1. Absent or very rare.
2. Present.
9. No information.

---

131. Surf smelt, *Hypomesus pretiosus*

1. Absent or very rare.
2. Present.
9. No information.

---

132. Quantity of fish available in tribal territory; average annual production in pounds per square mile of territory   p. 328

1. Fishless or very nearly so.
2. Less than 50.
3. 50–100.
4. 100–200.
5. 200–300.
6. 400–600.
7. 800–1000.
9. No information.

---

133. Relative amount of fish used as food by tribe

1. Tribe reported as never eating fish.
2. Fish contributed very little to diet.
3. Fish commonly eaten, but a supplement and not a staple.
4. Fish a staple but no more important than game or plants.
5. Fish the most important staple.
9. No information.

I-F. Game Birds

---

134. Swans, *Olor* spp.

1. Absent or very rare.
2. Present.
9. No information.

---

135. Canada goose, *Branta canadensis*

1. Absent or very rare.
2. Present.
9. No information.

---

136. Mallard duck, *Amas platyrhynchos*

1. Absent or very rare.
2. Present.
9. No information.

---

137. Turkey, *Meleagris gallopavo*

1. Absent or very rare.
2. Present.
9. No information.

II. Technology and Material Culture

II-A. Hunting

---

138. Harpoon for hunting sea mammals   p. 333

1. Harpoon probably absent.
2. Harpoon without float.
3. Harpoon with inflated float.
9. No information.

---

139. Devices used to direct or restrict land mammal movement   p. 335

1. Probably neither fences nor nets were used.
2. A stationary fence or enclosure was used.
3. A portable net.
4. Both.
9. No information.

---

140. Pitfalls for snaring land mammals   p. 336

1. Probably absent.
2. Present.
9. No information.

---

141. Deadfalls for snaring land mammals   p. 337

1. Probably absent.
2. Stone only.
3. Logs, or combination of logs and stones, but not stones alone.
4. Stones, or logs, or combination of logs and stones.
9. No information.

II-B. Fishing

---

142. Fish nets and seines   p. 338

1. Probably no nets.
2. Only small hand nets.
3. Gill nets and seines.
9. No information.

---

143. Fish weirs and traps   p. 339

1. Probably no weirs and traps.
2. Simple pens or obstructions, or traps without weirs.

3. Weirs equipped with traps.
9. No information.

144. Fish spears   p. 340

1. Leister probably absent.
2. Leister present.
9. No information.

145. Fish harpoons   p. 341

1. Probably no fish harpoons.
2. Single point.
3. Double point.
4. Both single and double point.
9. No information.

II-C. Gathering Wild Plants

146. Containers for gathering seeds   p. 342

1. Probably no seeds gathered or no report of seed-gathering containers.
2. Basketry.
3. Hide.
4. Both basketry and hide.
5. Both pottery and basketry.
9. No information.

147. Kinds of digging sticks   p. 346

1. Probably absent.
2. Crutch-handled.
3. Straight-handled.
4. Both crutch-handled and straight-handled sticks used.
9. No information.

148. Poles, tongs, and cutters   p. 347

1. Probably all absent.
2. Gathering poles.
3. Cactus tongs.
4. End-bladed mescal cutter.
5. Both gathering poles and cactus tongs.
6. Both gathering poles and end-bladed mescal cutters.
7. All three devices: poles, tongs, and cutters.
9. No information.

II-D. Horticulture

149. Maize cultivated at time of first contact with Europeans   p. 352

1. Probably not cultivated.
2. Cultivated.
9. No information.

150. Irrigation of cultivated plants   p. 353

1. Probably no irrigation.
2. Only natural flood irrigation.
3. Wing fences, dykes, dams to control runoff.
4. Irrigation ditches dug and maintained (item (B) in symbol category of Map Cu-23).

5. Both wing fences, etc., and ditches (items (B) and (C) in symbol category of Map Cu-23).
6. Both natural flood and ditches.
7. Both natural flood and wing fences.
9. No information.

151. Sticklike farming tools   p. 354

1. None of the below.
2. Pointed stick.
3. End-bladed stick.
4. Swordlike tool.
5. Both pointed stick and end-bladed stick.
6. Both pointed stick and swordlike tool.
7. All three: pointed, end-bladed, swordlike.
9. No information.

II-E. Food Preparation and Preservation

152. Method of boiling food   p. 345

1. Boiling done directly over fire, in pottery or steatite containers
2. Heated stones dropped into container.
3. Both direct fire and stone boiling.
9. No information.

153. Acorn preparation   p. 348

1. Acorns not eaten.
2. Eaten without leaching.
3. Ground before leaching.
4. Whole kernel immersed in cold water or buried in mud.
5. Boiled whole with lye to leach.
6. Both ground before leaching and whole kernel immersed in cold water or buried.
9. No information.

154. Stone food mortars   p. 350

1. Probably no stone food mortars.
2. Portable hollowed mortar.
3. Portable slab or block mortar.
4. Both hollowed and slab or block.
9. No information.

155. Wooden food mortars   p. 349

1. Probably no wooden food mortars.
2. In end of log.
3. In side of log.
4. Slab, block, or plank.
5. Both in end of log and side of log.
9. No information.

156. Milling stones   p. 344

1. Probably no milling stones used.
2. Milling stones had round or oval shape; not set within a bin.
3. Rectangloid slab, not in a bin.
4. Rectangloid trough.
5. Round or oval and rectangloid shapes used, not in bin.

6. Rectangloid slab in wooden bin.
7. Three types used: round or oval, rectangloid slab not in bin, and rectangloid trough.
9. No information.

157. Method of drying meat   p. 351

1. Meat dried only in sun or air, or smoking not reported.
2. Meat smoked or fire dried.
9. No information.

158. Seed-parching implements   p. 343

1. Probably no parching of seeds done.
2. Parched on flat stone.
3. In basketry container.
4. In pottery container.
5. In both basketry and pottery containers.
9. No information.

159. Salt (sodium chloride) added to food   p. 385

1. Probably absent.
2. Present.
9. No information.

II-F. Boats

160. Dominant boat types: those most frequent or preferred   p. 334

1. No boats or rafts of any kind.
2. Log or pole raft.
3. Balsa.
4. Round hide boat.
5. Bark canoe.
6. Dugout canoe.
7. Plank canoe.
8. Both log or pole raft and dugout canoe.
9. No information.

II-G. Housing

161. Dominant house type: the type preferred for winter dwelling   p. 356

1. Double lean-to.
2. Crude conical tipi, covered with brush, bark, and perhaps unsewn hides.
3. Mohave-type with four-pitch roof.
4. Plains type of conical tipi, with sewn hide cover in nineteenth century.
5. Rectangular plank house with vertical walls.
6. Domed house.
7. Semisubterranean, circular, earth-covered lodge.
8. Pueblo type: rectangular, vertical walls, nearly flat roof, multiple stories, and multiple rooms clustered together.
9. No information.

162. Conical and subconical dwellings   p. 357

1. No conical or subconical dwellings.
2. No specified number of poles, or number of poles not mentioned.

3. Three-pole foundation.
4. Four-pole foundation.
5. Both three-pole and four-pole foundation.
9. No information.

163. House-covering made of hide and thatch   p. 358

1. Neither hide nor thatch house covering.
2. House covering of hide.
3. House covering of thatch.
4. Both hide and thatch house covering.
9. No information.

164. House covering made of bark or mats   p. 359

1. Neither bark nor mat house covering.
2. Bark house covering.
3. Woven or sewn mat house covering.
4. Both bark and mat house covering.
9. No information.

165. House-covering or exterior made of stone or earth materials   p. 360

1. Neither stone, adobe, wattle, nor sod.
2. Covering of unprocessed earth or sod.
3. Walls of stone, adobe, or mud wattle.
9. No information.

166. House floor-level and entrance   p. 361

1. Neither semisubterranean floor nor tunnel entrance.
2. Semisubterranean floor.
3. Tunnel entrance.
4. Both semisubterranean floor and tunnel entrance.
9. No information.

II-H. Clothing

167. Headgear of woven plant materials   p. 362

1. No headgear of woven plant materials.
2. Rainhat with brim worn by both sexes.
3. Brimless or less-brimmed cap worn by both sexes.
4. Brimless or less-brimmed cap worn only by women.
9. No information.

168. Headgear made of hide or fur   p. 365

1. No headgear of hide or fur.
2. Brimless fur cap.
3. Fur cap with visor.
4. Buckskin cap.
5. Brimless fur cap and buckskin cap.
6. Brimless fur cap and fur cap with visor.
9. No information.

169. Robes or capes made of fur   p. 372

1. No robes or capes made of fur.
2. Made of single large hide with fur.
3. Of multiple small hides with fur, sewn together.
4. Both single large and multiple small hides with fur.
9. No information.

170. Robes or capes made of buckskin or of strips of small furs fastened together but not sewn together   p. 366

1. Absent.
2. Of twined, woven, netted strips of fur.
3. Of buckskin (dehaired).
4. Both twined and dehaired buckskin.
9. No information.

171. Robes or capes made of wool, hair, or feathers   p. 363

1. Absent.
2. Of woven wool or hair.
3. Of feather covering over woven or netted foundation.
4. Both woven wool or hair and feathers used as covering over woven or netted foundation.
9. No information.

172. Robes or capes made of plant materials   p. 364

1. Absence of these.
2. Were made of woven plant materials.
3. Made of unwoven plant materials.
4. Made of both woven plant materials and unwoven plant materials.
9. No information.

173. Shirts and dresses   p. 373

1. Neither Plains type nor pueblo type of shirts and dresses.
2. Pueblo type of women's dress of woven cotton.
3. Plains type of men's buckskin shirt with flaps to elbow.
4. Plains type of women's buckskin dress with flaps to elbow.
5. Plains type of apparel worn by both men and women.
6. Both Pueblo type of women's apparel and Plains type of men's apparel worn.
9. No information.

174. Breechclout   p. 367

1. No breechclout of hide or plant material.
2. Of hide.
3. Of plant material.
4. Both hide and plant material.
9. No information.

175. Skirt or kilt made of animal materials   p. 368

1. No skirt or kilt of animal material.
2. Of hide or fur.
3. Of woven wool or hair.
4. Both hide or fur and woven wool or hair.
9. No information.

176. Skirt or kilt made of plant materials   p. 369

1. No skirt or kilt of plant material.
2. Of spun and woven materials.
3. Of unspun and unwoven plant materials.
4. Both spun and woven, and unspun and unwoven materials.
9. No information.

177. Material used for apron   p. 370

1. No apron.
2. Made of hide or fur.
3. Made of plant materials.
4. Made of woven wool.
5. Both hide or fur and plant materials used.
6. Both hide or fur and woven wool used.
7. Hide or fur, plant materials, and woven wool all used.
9. No information.

178. Position of apron   p. 371

1. No apron.
2. Front apron.
3. Back apron.
4. Both front and back apron.
9. No information.

179. Moccasins   p. 374

1. Neither hard- nor soft-soled moccasins.
2. Hard- (separate-)soled.
3. Soft- (continuous-)soled.
4. Both hard- and soft-soled.
9. No information.

180. Sandals   p. 376

1. Neither hide nor plant material used in sandals.
2. Hide used as material for sandals.
3. Plant material used for sandals.
4. Both hide and plant material used for sandals.
9. No information.

181. Mittens and muffs   p. 375

1. Neither mittens nor muffs.
2. Hide or fur mittens.
3. Fur muff.
4. Both mittens and muffs.
9. No information.

II-I. Weaving

182. Basketry weaves   p. 377

1. Twining done exclusively, or definitely was more frequent.
2. Coiling done exclusively, or definitely was more frequent.
3. Both twining and coiling.
4. Both twining and coiling absent.
9. No information.

183. Weaving devices   p. 378

1. No weaving device.
2. One-bar or one-cord device, suspended warp.
3. Two-bar frame without heddles.
4. Two-bar frame with heddles.
5. Both one-bar and two-bar devices without heddles.
6. Both two-bar with and two-bar devices without heddles.
9. No information.

III. Subsistence Economy

III-A. Agriculture

184. Agricultural and Horticultural production   p. 379

1. No agriculture is practiced.
2. Incipient horticulture of food crops practiced only.
3. Incipient horticulture of nonfood crops only.
4. Both 2 and 3.
5. Agriculture confined to nonfood crops.
6. Agriculture is practiced, but does not produce the dominant foodstuffs in the average diet. (Less than half the total foodstuffs.)
7. Agriculture is practiced, and produces the dominant foodstuffs in the average diet. (More than half the total foodstuffs.)
9. No information.

185. Agricultural products and incipient horticulture done not for food   p. 380

1. Neither cotton nor tobacco grown.
2. Cotton grown.
3. Tobacco grown.
4. Cotton and tobacco grown.
9. No information

186. Agricultural products grown for food   p. 381

1. No edible agricultural products grown.
2. Maize only.
3. Maize and squash.
4. Maize, beans, squashes grown.
5. Maize, beans, squashes, and any of the following are grown: pigweed (*Amaranthus retroflexus*), or sunflower *Helianthus* spp., or panicgrass (*Panicum* spp.), or barnyard grass (*Echinochloa* spp.), or maguey (*Agave* spp.).
6. Maize, beans, squashes and all of the following species are grown: *Amaranthus*, *Helianthus*, and *Panicum*, and *Echinochloa*, and/or *Agave*.
9. No information.

187. Agricultural products grown for beverages

1. No beverage crops grown.
2. *Agave* spp. (maguey) or *Dasylerion wheeleri* (sotol).
3. Maguey, sotol, and cacti.
4. Mesquite or screwbean.
5. Mesquite or screwbean and maize.
6. Mesquite or screwbean and cacti.
7. Mesquite or screwbean, and cacti, and either maguey or sotol.
8. Mesquite or screwbean, and maize, and cacti, and either maguey or sotol.
9. No information.

188. External sources of agricultural products for food   p. 382

1. No extralocal trade for agricultural food stuffs.
2. Maize, beans, squash are predominant foods traded for (bartered, received as gifts, etc.) extralocally.
3. *Amaranthus* spp. and/or *Helianthus* spp. and/or *Agave* spp., and/or grasses are predominant foods traded for extralocally.

4. Maize, beans, squash, and one or more of items listed in 3 are traded for extralocally in about equal amounts.
9. No information.

189. External sources of agricultural products for beverages

1. No extralocal trade for agricultural beverage crops.
2. *Agave* spp., *Dasylerion* spp., or cacti are predominant beverage crops traded for (bartered, received as gifts, etc.) extralocally.
3. Mesquite or screwbean are predominant beverage crops traded for extralocally.
4. *Agave* spp., or *Dasylerion* spp., cacti, mesquite, or screwbean are traded for extralocally in about equal amounts.
9. No information.

190. Probable percentage of diet contributed by agricultural foodstuffs acquired locally   p. 383

1. 0 percent.
2. 1–10 percent.
3. 11–25 percent.
4. 26–50 percent.
5. 51–100 percent.
9. No information.

191. Probable percentage of diet contributed by agricultural foodstuffs acquired extralocally   p. 384

1. 0 percent.
2. 1–10 percent.
3. 11–25 percent.
4. 26–50 percent.
5. 51–100 percent.
9. No information.

192. External sources of agricultural products used as nonfood or for beverages

1. No extralocal trade for nonfood agricultural products.
2. Cultivated tobacco traded for (bartered, received as gifts, and so forth) extralocally.
3. Cotton traded for extralocally.
4. Tobacco and cotton traded for extralocally.
9. No information.

193. Animal husbandry—before contact with Europeans   p. 386

1. No pre-Contact domesticates.
2. Pre-Contact use of domesticated dogs (for eating, ceremonial eating, transportation, watchdogs, sources of wool, or for hunting).
3. Pre-Contact use of domesticated fowl or other small animals (for eating or ceremonialism).
4. Pre-Contact use of domesticated dogs and one or more other small animals.
9. No information.

III-B. Fishing, Sea-Mammal Hunting, and Shellfish Collecting

194. Local "fishing"—procurement of all types of aquatic animals (shellfish, aquatic mammals, and fish)   p. 387

1. "Fishing" is minimal or not practiced at all. If practiced it contributes less than five percent to the normal diet (less than 5 percent).
2. "Fishing" is practiced and contributes a tertiary food source in the average diet (approximately between a twentieth and a quarter of the normal diet, 5 percent to 25 percent).
3. "Fishing" is practiced and contributes a secondary food source in the average diet (approximately between a quarter and a half of the normal diet, 25 percent to 50 percent).
4. "Fishing" is practiced and contributes the dominant foodstuffs in the average diet (more than half of the normal diet, 50 percent to 100 percent).
9. No information.

195. **Predominant aquatic animals for which groups fish or hunt or collect**   **p. 388**

1. No fishing or other kinds of procurement of aquatic animals present.
2. Fishing consists predominantly in catching fish (salmon, halibut, and so forth).
3. "Fishing" consists predominantly in collecting shellfish and other small aquatic fauna.
4. "Fishing" consists predominantly in capturing large aquatic animals (seals, whales, and so forth).
5. "Fishing" consists in about equal catches of fish and collections of shellfish, neither amount predominating.
6. "Fishing" consists in about equal catches of fish and large aquatic mammals, neither amount predominating.
7. "Fishing" consists in about equal collections of shellfish and catches of large aquatic mammals, neither amount predominating.
8. "Fishing" consists in about equal collections and catches of shellfish, fish, and large aquatic mammals, the amounts of no single type predominating.
9. No information.

196. **Probable percentage of diet contributed by fish, shellfish, and large aquatic mammals procured locally**

1. 0 percent.   **p. 389**
2. 1–10 percent.
3. 11–25 percent.
4. 26–50 percent.
5. 51–100 percent.
9. No information.

197. **External sources of fish, shellfish, and large aquatic animals**   **p. 390**

1. No extralocal trade for fish, shellfish, or large aquatic animals.
2. Fish or fish byproducts traded for (by bartering, gift exchange, and so forth) extralocally.
3. Large aquatic animals traded for (by bartering, gift exchange, and so forth) extralocally.
4. Shellfish and small aquatic animals traded for extralocally.
5. Fish and large aquatic animals traded for extralocally.
6. Fish and shellfish traded for extralocally.
7. Large aquatic animals and shellfish traded for extralocally.

8. Fish, shellfish, and large aquatic animals traded for extralocally.
9. No information.

198. **Probable percentage of diet contributed by fish, shellfish, and large aquatic animals procured extralocally**   **p. 391**

1. 0 percent.
2. 1–10 percent.
3. 11–25 percent.
4. 26–50 percent.
5. 51–100 percent.
9. No information.

III-C. Hunting

199. **Local hunting—procurement of all types of game (fowl, large mammals, etc.)**   **p. 392**

1. Hunting is minimal or not practiced at all. If practiced it contributes less than five percent to the normal diet.
2. Hunting is practiced and contributes a tertiary food source in the average diet (approximately between a twentieth and a quarter of the normal diet).
3. Hunting is practiced and contributes a secondary food source in the average diet (approximately between a quarter and a half of the normal diet).
4. Hunting is practiced and contributes the dominant foodstuffs in the average diet (more than half of the normal diet).
9. No information.

200. **Predominant types of animals for which groups hunt**   **pp. 393, 394**

1. No hunting present.
2. Hunting is predominantly for fowl or other birds (such as sage chickens, ducks, geese, or swans).
3. Hunting is predominantly for small land-mammals which are not herd animals (such as rabbits, hares, rats, gophers, or beavers).
4. Hunting is predominantly for large-sized (e.g., moose, elk) and medium-sized land-mammals (e.g., deer, big-horn sheep, mountain goats, antelopes) that live in medium or small herds.
5. Hunting is predominantly for large land-mammals that live in large herds (such as bison or caribou).
6. Hunting is equally types 2 and 3 above, no single type dominant.
7. Hunting is equally types 2 and 4 above, no single type dominant.
8. Hunting is equally types 2 and 5 above, no single type dominant.
9. No information.
10. Hunting is equally types 3 and 4 above, no single type dominant.
11. Hunting is equally types 3 and 5 above, no single type dominant.
12. Hunting is equally types 4 and 5 above, no single type dominant.
13. Hunting is equally types 2, 3 and 4 above, no single type dominant.
14. Hunting is equally types 2, 4, and 5 above, no single type dominant.
15. Hunting is equally types 2, 3, and 5 above, no single type dominant.

16. Hunting is equally types 3, 4, and 5 above, no single type dominant.
17. Hunting is equally types 2, 3, 4, and 5 above, no single type dominant.

201. Probable percentage of diet contributed by procuring (hunting) large game, small animals, and fowl locally   p. 395

1. 0 percent.
2. 1–10 percent.
3. 11–25 percent.
4. 26–50 percent.
5. 51–100 percent.
9. No information.

202. External sources of game, small mammals, or fowl   p. 396

1. No extralocal trade for animals procured by hunting.
2. Fowl and other birds traded for extralocally.
3. Small mammals (beaver, rats, rabbits, or hares, etc.) traded for extralocally.
4. Medium-sized game (deer, mountain sheep, mountain goats, antelopes) traded for extralocally.
5. Large game (elk, caribou, bison, moose, or bear) traded for extralocally (trade includes barter, gift exchange, and so forth).
6. Both 2 and 3.
7. Both 2 and 4.
8. Both 2 and 5.
9. No information.
10. Both 3 and 4.
11. Both 3 and 5.
12. Both 4 and 5.
13. 2, 3, and 4.
14. 2, 3, and 5.
15. 2, 4, and 5.
16. 3, 4, and 5.
17. 2, 3, 4, and 5.

203. Probable percentage of diet contributed by large game, small mammals, and fowl procured extralocally   p. 397

1. 0 percent.
2. 1–10 percent.
3. 11–25 percent.
4. 26–50 percent.
5. 51–100 percent.
9. No information.

III-D. Gathering or Extracting

204. Local gathering—all food sources (nuts, seeds, berries, and roots)   p. 398

1. Gathering is not practiced, or it makes no appreciable contribution to the food supply.
2. Gathering is practiced, and it contributes a tertiary food source in the average diet (approximately between a twentieth and a quarter of the normal diet).
3. Gathering is practiced, and it contributes a secondary food source in the average diet (approximately between a quarter and a half of the normal diet).
4. Gathering is practiced, and it contributes the dominant foodstuffs to the average diet (more than half of the normal diet).
9. No information.

205. Predominant types of foods gathered.   p. 400

1. No foods of consequence in the diet are collected.
2. Gathering consists predominantly in the collecting of wild herbs, or roots, or tubers, or all of these.
3. Gathering consists predominantly in the collecting of wild seeds, or wild berries, or wild fruits (e.g., plums), or all of these.
4. Gathering consists predominantly in the collecting of wild nuts or leaves, or both.
5. Gathering consists of 2 and 3, neither being dominant.
6. Gathering consists of 2 and 4, neither being dominant.
7. Gathering consists of 3 and 4, neither being dominant.
8. Gathering consists of 2, 3, and 4, none being clearly dominant.
9. No information.

206. External sources of roots, nuts, seeds, berries, fruit, tubers, or leaves, etc.   p. 401

1. No extralocal trade (through barter, gift exchange, etc.) for roots, nuts, etc.
2. Wild herbs, roots, or tubers traded for extralocally.
3. Wild seeds, berries, or fruits traded for extralocally.
4. Wild nuts or leaves traded for extralocally.
5. Both 2 and 3.
6. Both 2 and 4.
7. Both 3 and 4.
8. 2, 3, and 4.
9. No information.

207. Probable percentage of diet contributed by roots, seeds, berries, nuts, leaves, tubers, etc., procured extralocally   p. 402

1. 0 percent.
2. 1–10 percent.
3. 11–25 percent.
4. 26–50 percent.
5. 51–100 percent.
9. No information.

208. Probable percentage of diet contributed by roots, seeds, berries, nuts, leaves, or tubers, etc., procured locally   p. 399

1. 0 percent.
2. 1–10 percent.
3. 11–25 percent.
4. 26–50 percent.
5. 51–100 percent.
9. No information.

III-E. Transportation

209. Dominant land-transportation of food or other goods   p. 403

1. No appreciable land-transport of any subsistence goods.
2. Land-transport of subsistence goods is done exclu-

sively by human carriers (using, perhaps, a tumpline, carrying stick, etc.).

3. Land-transport of subsistence goods is done exclusively by dogs (with either packs or travois, or with both).

4. Land-transport of subsistence goods is done by humans and dogs.

9. No information.

210. Dominant water-transportation of food or other goods   p. 404

1. Watercraft are not used for transport.

2. Small watercraft are used to carry light loads (about 200 lb) for short distances over placid water (20 feet to ½ mile).

3. Watercraft are used to carry medium loads (about 300–600 lb) for medium distances (from 20 feet to several miles, across lakes, rivers, or even for short distances at sea) over turbulent water.

4. Watercraft are used to carry large loads (about 600–3,000 lb) for long distances (up to hundreds of miles) over turbulent waters (especially on large rivers and on the Pacific Ocean).

5. Watercraft are used to carry large loads medium distances.

9. No information.

III-F. Local Resource Availability

211. General availability of local subsistence resources

1. The food resources utilized by the society are notably constant from year to year, season to season, and day to day, so that an adequate supply for daily needs is regularly available by the expenditure of a reasonable amount of effort.

2. The food resources are constant from year to year and from season to season, but there is substantial diurnal variation in the available supply, owing to chance factors such as the success or failure of hunters on particular days.

3. The food resources, though relatively constant from year to year, vary markedly from season to season depending upon such climatic and ecological factors as sharp contrasts between hot and cold or wet and dry seasons and great differences in the seasonal availability of plant or animal food, or both kinds of foods.

4. The food resources, whatever their diurnal and seasonal variation, are markedly variable from year to year, owing to extreme annual differences in rainfall or other recurrent but unpredictable climatic vicissitudes.

9. No information.

III-G. Food Storage

212. Major storage place for food: the place most preferred or frequently used   p. 355

1. No storage places.

2. In pits, caves, or rock shelters.

3. In dwelling or on high platform or house roof.

4. In special storage structure, such as masonry granary.

5. 3 and 4.

6. 2 and 3.

7. 2, 3 and 4.

8. 2 and 4.

9. No information.

213. Maximum length of time stored food is kept   p. 405

1. One month.

2. Two to six months.

3. Seven months to one year.

4. More than one year.

9. No information.

IV. Economic Organization

IV-A. Division of Labor

214. Weaving of nets, baskets, or mats   p. 426

1. No weaving of nets, baskets, or mats.

2. Weaving of nets, baskets, or mats is predominantly a female activity.

3. Weaving of nets, baskets, or mats is predominantly a male activity.

4. Weaving of nets, baskets, or mats is done by both sexes, neither clearly predominating.

9. No information.

215. Specialized weaving of nets, baskets, or mats   p. 427

1. No weaving of nets, baskets or mats.

2. No specialization in weaving of nets, baskets or mats other than sex.

3. Select people who possess either special skills or supernatural power, or both, do specialized weaving of nets, baskets or mats.

9. No information.

216. Production task-groups for weaving of nets, baskets, or mats

Task-groups are defined as units of coworkers who regularly—i.e., daily, seasonally, or annually—coalesce to accomplish some task(s) jointly. Each member need not provide the same resources, or skills, or labor to accomplish the task. Membership is rather stable over a period of a few years.

1. No local weaving of nets, baskets, or mats.

2. Weaving of nets, baskets or mats is practiced, but not by task-groups.

3. Weaving by task-groups whose members, male or female, are not necessarily related as kin or affines, nor are they necessarily relatives.

4. Task-groups are predominantly made up of male kin.

5. Task-groups predominantly male affines.

6. Task-groups predominantly female kin.

7. Task-groups predominantly female affines.

9. No information.

217. Weaving of cotton, wool, or hair into garments

1. No weaving of cotton, wool, or hair.

2. Predominantly a female activity.

3. Predominantly a male activity.
4. Weaving of cotton, wool, or hair into garments is done by both sexes, neither clearly predominating.
9. No information.

---

218. Specialized weaving of cotton, wool, or hair into garments

1. No weaving of cotton, wool, or hair into garments.
2. No specialization in weaving of cotton, wool, or hair, other than perhaps sex (see V-217 for sexual division of labor).
3. Select people who possess either special skills or supernatural power, or both, do specialized weaving of cotton, wool, or hair garments.
9. No information.

---

219. Production task-groups for weaving cotton, wool, or hair

See definition of task-groups at V-216.

1. No local weaving of cotton, wool, or hair.
2. Weaving of cotton, wool, or hair is practiced, but not by task-groups.
3. Weaving by task-groups whose members, male or female, are not necessarily related as kin or affines, nor are they necessarily relatives.
4. Task-groups predominantly male kin.
5. Task-groups predominantly male affines.
6. Task-groups predominantly female kin.
7. Task-groups predominantly female affines.
8. Task-groups male and female usually affinally related.
9. No information.

---

220. Leather-hide-working: dressing skins locally   p. 428

1. No leather-working is practiced locally.
2. Leather-working is predominantly men's work.
3. Leather-working is predominantly women's work.
4. Leather-working is done by both sexes, neither clearly predominating.
9. No information.

---

221. Specialized hide-working

1. No hide-working.
2. No specialization other than perhaps on the basis of sex (see V-220 for sexual division of labor).
3. Select people who possess either special skills or supernatural power, or both, specialize in hide working.
9. No information.

---

222. Production task-groups in leather-hide-working

See definition of task-groups at V-216.

1. No hides worked locally.
2. Hides are worked, but not by task-groups.
3. Hides are worked by task-groups whose members, male or female, are not necessarily related, and if related, are neither predominantly affines nor kin.
4. Hides are worked by male task-groups whose members are predominantly kin-related.
5. Hides are worked by male task-groups whose members are predominantly affine-related.
6. Hides are worked by female task-groups whose members are predominantly kin-related.
7. Hides are worked by female task-groups whose members are predominantly affine-related.
8. Hides are worked by male and female task-groups, neither group predominating; members are affinally related, primarily.
9. No information.

---

223. Pottery manufacture   p. 429

1. No pottery is manufactured locally.
2. Pottery manufacture is predominantly male work.
3. Pottery manufacture is predominantly female work.
4. Pottery manufacture is done by both sexes, neither clearly predominating.
9. No information.

---

224. Specialized pottery manufacture   p. 430

1. No pottery manufactured.
2. No specialization other than sex (see sexual division of pottery labor, V-223).
3. Select people who possess special skills or supernatural powers, or both, specialize in pottery manufacture.
9. No information.

---

225. Production task-groups for pottery

See definition of task-groups at V-216.

1. No pottery made locally.
2. Pottery made, but not by task-groups.
3. Pottery made by task-groups whose members, male or female, are not necessarily kin, or affines, or relatives at all.
4. Pottery made by task-groups of predominantly male kin.
5. Pottery made by task-groups of predominantly male affines.
6. Pottery made by task-groups of predominantly female kin.
7. Pottery made by task-groups of predominantly female affines.
9. No information.

---

226. Boat building: all types of watercraft   p. 431

1. No watercraft built locally.
2. Watercraft primarily built by women.
3. Watercraft primarily built by men.
4. Watercraft built by men and women, neither clearly predominating.
9. No information.

---

227. Specialization of boat building for all types of watercraft   p. 432

1. No watercraft is built.
2. No specialization other than sex (see sexual division of boat-building labor, V-226).
3. Select people who possess special skills or supernatural powers, or both, specialize in boat building.
9. No information.

228. Production task-groups in boat building

See definition of task-groups at V-216.

1. No boats built locally.
2. Boats are built, but not by task-groups.
3. Boats are built by task-groups whose members, male or female, are not necessarily related, and if related, are neither predominantly affines nor kin.
4. Boats are built by male task-groups whose members are predominantly kin-related.
5. Boats are built by male task-groups whose members are predominantly affine-related.
6. Boats are built by female task-groups whose members are predominantly kin-related.
7. Boats are built by task-groups whose members are predominantly affine-related.
9. No information.

229. House construction: dominant type or types in which people reside for the longest period each year   p. 433

1. Houses primarily built by women.
2. Houses primarily built by men.
3. Houses built by men and women, neither clearly predominating.
9. No information.

230. Specialization in house construction   p. 434

1. No specialization, or no specialization other than sex (see V-229).
2. Select people who possess special skills or supernatural powers, or both, specialize in house construction.
9. No information.

231. Production task-groups in house construction p. 435

See definition of task-groups at V-216.

1. Houses are not built by task-groups.
2. Houses are built by task-groups whose members, male or female, are not necessarily related, and if related, are neither predominantly affines or kin.
3. Houses are built by male task-groups whose members are predominantly kin-related.
4. Houses are built by male task-groups whose members are predominantly affine-related.
5. Houses are built by female task-groups whose members are predominantly kin-related.
6. Houses are built by female task-groups whose members are predominantly affine-related.
7. Houses are built by task-groups composed of male and female members primarily kin-related.
8. Houses are built by male task-groups both kin- and affine-related.
9. No information.

232. Division of labor of gathering of all types of foodstuffs

1. Gathering is not practiced.
2. Gathering is principally done by females.
3. Gathering is principally done by males.

4. Gathering is done by females and males, neither clearly predominating.
9. No information.

233. Specialization in gathering

1. No gathering practiced or no specialization in tasks.
2. No specialization in gathering other than those based on sex (see V-232).
3. Select people who possess special skills or supernatural powers, or both, specialize in gathering, if only as leaders or directors of the tasks.
9. No information.

234. Role of children and the aged in gathering

1. Children or the aged (or both groups) do *not* help in gathering.
2. Children or the aged (or both groups) *do* help in gathering.
9. No information.

235. Production task-groups in gathering   p. 436

See definition of task groups at V-216.

1. No gathering.
2. Gathering is not done by task-groups.
3. Gathering is done by task-groups whose members, male or female, are not necessarily related, and if related, are neither predominantly affines nor kin.
4. Gathering is done by female task-groups whose members are predominantly kin-related.
5. Gathering is done by female task-groups whose members are predominantly affine-related.
6. Gathering is done by female task-groups whose members are neither predominantly kin nor affine-related.
7. Gathering is done by male and female task-groups both kin- and affine-related.
9. No information.

236. Division of labor of hunting of all land mammals, fowl, etc.

1. No hunting is practiced.
2. Hunting is principally done by males.
3. Hunting is principally done by females.
4. Hunting is done by males and females, neither clearly predominating.
9. No information.

237. Role of children and the aged in hunting

1. No hunting practiced.
2. Neither children nor the aged help in hunting.
3. The aged help in hunting, but children do not.
4. Children help in hunting, but the aged do not.
5. Both children and the aged help in hunting.
9. No information.

238. Specialization in hunting.

1. No hunting is practiced, or there is no specialization in tasks.

2. No hunting specialization other than that which is based on sex (see V-236).
3. Select people who possess special skills or supernatural powers, or both, specialize in hunting, if only as leaders or directors of the tasks.
9. No information.

239. Production task-groups in hunting   p. 437

See definition of task-groups at V-216.

1. No hunting.
2. Hunting is not done by task-groups.
3. Hunting is done by task-groups whose members, male or female, are not necessarily related, and if related, are neither predominantly affines nor kin.
4. Hunting is done by male task-groups whose members are predominantly kin-related.
5. Hunting is done by male task-groups whose members are predominantly affine-related.
6. 3 and 4.
7. 4 and 5.
9. No information.

240. Division of labor of fishing: all forms of animal extraction from water, including true fishing, capturing of sea-mammals, and shellfishing   p. 438

1. No extraction of animals from water is practiced.
2. Fishing is principally done by males.
3. Fishing is principally done by females.
4. Fishing is done by males and females, neither clearly predominating.
9. No information.

241. Role of children and the aged in fishing   p. 439

1. No extraction of animals from water is practiced.
2. Neither children nor the aged help in fishing.
3. The aged help in fishing, but children do not.
4. Children help in fishing, but the aged do not.
5. Both children and the aged help in fishing.
9. No information.

242. Production task-groups in fishing

See definition of task groups at V-216.

1. No fishing.
2. Fishing is not done by task-groups.
3. Fishing is done by task-groups whose members, male or female, are not necessarily related, and if related, are neither predominantly affines nor kin.
4. Fishing is done by male task-groups whose members are predominantly kin-related.
5. Fishing is done by male task-groups whose members are predominantly affine-related.
6. Fishing is done by female task-groups whose members are predominantly kin-related.
7. Fishing is done by female task-groups whose members are predominantly affine-related.
9. No information.

243. Specialization in fishing or in hunting for sea mammals   p. 440

1. No fishing is practiced, or there is no specialization in tasks.
2. No specialization of fishing or sea-mammal hunting other than that which is based on sex (see V-240).
3. Select people who possess special skills or supernatural powers, or both, specialize in fishing, if only as leaders and directors.
4. Select people who possess special skills or supernatural powers, or both, specialize in sea-mammal hunting, if only as leaders and directors.
5. Both 3 and 4.
9. No information.

244. Division of labor of animal husbandry

1. No animal husbandry practiced.
2. Animal husbandry is principally a male task.
3. Animal husbandry is principally a female task.
4. Animal husbandry is done by males and females, neither clearly predominating.
9. No information.

245. Role of children and the aged in agriculture

1. No agriculture is practiced.
2. Neither children nor the aged help in agriculture.
3. The aged help in agriculture, but the children do not.
4. The children help in agriculture, but the aged do not.
5. Both the children and the aged help in agriculture.
9. No information.

246. Specialization in agriculture   p. 442

1. No agriculture, or there is no specialization in tasks.
2. No agricultural specialization other than that which is based on sex (see V-248).
3. Select people who possess special skills or supernatural power, or both, specialize in agriculture, if only as leaders and directors.
9. No information.

247. Production task-groups in agriculture   p. 443

See definition of task groups at V-216.

1. No agriculture.
2. Agriculture is not done by task-groups.
3. Agriculture is done by task-groups whose members, male or female, are not necessarily related, and if related, are neither predominantly affines nor kin.
4. Agriculture is done by male task-groups whose members are predominantly kin-related.
5. Agriculture is done by male task-groups whose members are predominantly affine-related.
6. Agriculture is done by female task-groups whose members are predominantly kin-related.
7. Agriculture is done by female task-groups whose members are predominantly affine-related.
9. No information.

248. Division of Labor of agriculture   p. 441

1. No agriculture is practiced.
2. Agriculture is predominantly female work.
3. Agriculture is predominantly male work.

4. Agriculture is done by males and females, neither clearly predominating.
9. No information.

IV-B. Economic Distribution

Economic distribution includes all forms of distribution of expropriated goods and products within and among societies.

---

249. Reciprocity distribution of food and chattels within a society (intracommunity or local residence-group) p. 411

1. There is no reciprocity within the society.
2. Food and/or chattels are predominantly distributed on a *balanced* or equal basis, i.e., donors and recipients reverse roles on a fairly equal basis and contribute and receive food and/or chattels more or less equally.
3. Food and/or chattels are predominantly distributed on a *generalized* basis, i.e., some people possess or have access to much more food and/or many more chattels than other people. A pattern obtains where the possessors of plenty are generalized donors and those who possess less are generalized recipients. The recipients do not reciprocate to the donors in amount.
4. Food and/or chattels are predominantly distributed on a *negative* basis, i.e., some people possess or have access to much more food and/or many more chattels than other people. A pattern obtains where the possessors of plenty provide for the needy as the exigencies dictate; but the needy recipients, in turn, pay back a greater quantity of food and/or chattels to the original donor than they received. (The return payment may be deferred for a season or more.)
5. Both 2 and 3 obtain; neither clearly predominates.
6. Both 2 and 4 obtain; neither clearly predominates.
7. Both 3 and 4 obtain; neither clearly predominates.
8. 2, 3, and 4 obtain; none clearly predominates.
9. No information.

---

250. Redistribution of chattels and food within a society (intracommunity or local residence-group) p. 412

1. No redistribution of chattels and/or food.
2. Food and/or chattels are collected predominantly by individuals who are not necessarily lineage, deme, nor household heads, and these objects are then redistributed among the people in the local residence group—among kin and/or nonkin.
3. Food and/or chattels are collected predominantly by individuals who are lineage, deme, or household heads, and these objects are then redistributed among the people in the local residence group—among kin and/or nonkin.
4. Food and/or chattels are collected predominantly by individuals who represent the local residence group as a whole (such as chief, village headman, and the like) rather than simply a deme, lineage, or household, and these objects are then redistributed among the people in the local residence group—among kin and/or nonkin.
5. Both 2 and 3 are practiced; neither clearly predominates.
6. Both 2 and 4 are practiced; neither clearly predominates.

7. Both 3 and 4 are practiced; neither clearly predominates.
8. 2, 3, and 4 are practiced; none clearly predominates.
9. No information.

---

251. Sharing of access to local food resources as a form of distribution within the society (intracommunity or local residence-group) p. 415

1. Most local food resources are viewed as being either communal property or free and available to all.
2. Most local food resources such as animals on specific tidewater flats, roots on specific grounds, fields of corn, are viewed as being private properties of units within the local community, such as demes, lineages, or households, yet access to these resources is provided to other units within the local community.
3. Most local food resources, such as fish and shellfish on tidewater flats, roots on specific grounds, fields of corn and beans, are viewed as being private properties of units within the local community such as demes, lineages, or households, and access to these resources is *not* provided to other units within the local community.
4. Most local food resources are viewed as being private properties of individual persons within the local communities, yet access to these resources is provided to other people within the local community.
5. Most local food resources are viewed as being private properties of individual persons, and access to these resources is *not* provided to other people within the local community.
6. Both 2 and 4 are present; neither clearly predominates.
7. Both 2 and 5 are present; neither clearly predominates.
8. Both 3 and 4 are present; neither clearly predominates.
9. No information.
10. Both 3 and 5 are present; neither clearly predominates.
11. 1, 2 and 4 present; none clearly predominates.

---

252. Ceremonialism or etiquette in intracommunity reciprocity of food and/or chattels p. 417

1. No reciprocity.
2. Reciprocity, but no ceremonialism of any sort.
3. Ceremonialism is present when food and/or chattels are reciprocated; e.g., the recipient returns food and/or chattels to the original donor in a particular way at an appropriate time.
4. Both reciprocity without ceremonialism, and ceremonialism.
9. No information.

---

253. Ceremonialism or etiquette in intracommunity redistribution of food and/or chattels p. 418

1. No redistribution of food and/or chattels.
2. Redistribution in which there is no ceremonialism of any sort and in which recipients of food and/or chattels are treated about equally.
3. Redistribution in which there is ceremonialism and in

which recipients of food and/or chattels are treated about equally.

4. Redistribution in which there is some ceremonialism and in which recipients receive food and/or chattels differentially; e.g., nonkin receive more than kin or vice versa, the people of highest rank receive more than those of lowest rank, the people with the greatest prestige are the first to receive goods, and so forth.

5. Redistribution with ceremony in which the donor provides food for the ceremony, and all who attend receive about equal shares regardless of differences in status, rank, or kinship.

6. Both 2 and 3.

7. Both 2 and 5.

9. No information.

---

254. Ceremonialism or etiquette in intracommunity use of privately owned food resources and/or chattels p. 416

1. No or few privately owned food resources and/or chattels.

2. No intracommunity use of privately owned food resources and/or chattels permitted; therefore no ceremonialism.

3. No ceremonialism or etiquette is involved in exploiting food resources or using chattels recognized as belonging to others.

4. Some ceremonialism or etiquette is involved in gaining access to the food resources or the use of chattels recognized as belonging to others; e.g., invitations are extended, use is requested, affines are expected to use the resources and/or chattels, and so forth.

5. Both 3 and 4.

9. No information.

---

255. Reciprocity distribution of food and/or chattels between (or among) societies (intercommunity or extralocal residence-group reciprocity)   p. 419

1. There is no reciprocity between or among extralocal groups.

2. Food and/or chattels are predominantly distributed on a *balanced* or equal basis, i.e., donors and recipients reverse roles on a fairly equal basis and contribute and receive food and/or chattels more or less equally.

3. Food and/or chattels are predominantly distributed on a *generalized* basis, i.e., people in the local group possess or have access to much more food and/or many more chattels than people in another local group. A pattern obtains where these possessors of plenty are *generalized donors* and those who possess less are generalized recipients. The recipients do not reciprocate to the donors in amount.

4. Food and/or chattels are predominantly distributed on a *negative* basis, i.e., people in the local group possess or have access to much more food and/or many more chattels than people in other local groups. A pattern obtains where these possessors of plenty provide for the needy as the exigencies dictate; but the needy recipients, in turn, pay back as *negative donors* a greater quantity of food and/or chattels to the original donor than they received. (The return payment may be deferred for a season or more.)

5. Generalized reciprocity (see item 3) in which the local group is the *generalized recipient* rather than the donor.

6. Negative reciprocity (see item 4) in which the local group is the *negative recipient* of food and/or chattels from a group that possesses plenty (or from several groups), rather than being the possessors and donors of plenty themselves.

7. Both 2 and 3 obtain; neither clearly predominates.

8. Both 3 and 4 obtain; neither clearly predominates.

9. No information.

---

256. Redistribution of chattels and food between (or among) societies (intercommunity or extralocal residence-group redistribution)

1. No extralocal redistribution of chattels and/or food involves the local group as donor or as recipient.

2. Members of the local group receive food and/or chattels redistributed by members of other communities (extralocal groups), but the local group does not redistribute—i.e., does not serve as donor.

3. Food and/or chattels are collected predominantly by individual persons who are *not* necessarily lineage, deme, or household heads, and these objects are then redistributed among people from *other* communities (extralocal residence-groups).

4. Food and/or chattels are collected predominantly by individual persons who *are* lineage, deme, or household heads, and these objects are then redistributed among people from *other* communities (extralocal residence-groups).

5. Food and/or chattels are collected predominantly by individual persons who represent the local residence-group as a whole (such as chief, village headman, and the like) rather than simply a deme, lineage, or household, and these objects are then redistributed among people from other communities (extralocal residence-groups).

9. No information.

---

257. Sharing of access to local food resources as a form of distribution between (or among) societies (intercommunity or extralocal residence-group redistribution)   p. 421

1. No access to local food resources is given to people from different extralocal groups.

2. Most local food resources are viewed as being communal property, or as free and available to all, and access to these resources is extended to people from other communities (extralocal groups).

3. Most local food resources are viewed as being private properties of units within the local community, such as demes, lineages, or households, yet access to these resources is provided to people from other communities (extralocal groups).

4. Most local food resources are viewed as being private properties of individuals within the local community, yet access to these resources is provided to people from other communities (extralocal groups).

5. Both 2 and 3 are present; neither clearly predominates.

6. Both 3 and 4 are present; neither clearly predominates.

9. No information.

258. **Ceremonialism or etiquette in intercommunity reciprocity of food and/or chattels**   **p. 420**

1. No intercommunity reciprocity.
2. Reciprocity between individuals from different communities, but no ceremonialism of any sort.
3. Ceremonialism is present when food and/or chattels are reciprocated, e.g., the recipient from one community returns food and/or chattels to the original donor in another community in a particular way at an appropriate time.
4. Reciprocity between ceremonial or political leaders of localized community units, such as patrilineages and patriclans, patridemes, the matriunits, and less structured communities.
5. Both 2 and 4.
6. Both 2 and 3.
7. Both 3 and 4.
9. No information.

259. **Ceremonialism or etiquette in intercommunity redistribution of food and/or chattels**

1. No intercommunity redistribution of food and/or chattels.
2. Redistribution among people from more than one community accompanied with no ceremonialism of any sort; the recipients of food and/or chattels are treated about equally by the donor.
3. Redistribution among people from more than one community accompanied with some ceremonialism; recipients receive food and/or chattels differentially, e.g., affines receive more than kin or vice versa, the people of higher rank receive more than the people of lesser rank, the people with the greatest prestige are the first to recieve goods, or the people who have travelled the farthest to visit the hosts are the first to receive goods, or they receive the most goods, or both.
4. Redistribution among people from more than one community accompanied with ceremonialism; the recipients of food and/or chattels are treated about equally by donor.
5. Both 2 and 4.
9. No information.

260. **Ceremonialism or etiquette in intercommunity use of privately owned food resources and/or chattels** **p. 422**

1. No privately owned food resources and/or chattels.
2. No intercommunity use of privately owned or communally owned resources and/or chattels.
3. No ceremonialism nor etiquette is involved in allowing people from other communities (extralocal groups) to exploit food resources or use chattels recognized as belonging to the host-group (or members of the host-group).
4. Some ceremonialism or etiquette is involved in allowing people from other communities to exploit food resources or to use chattels recognized as belonging to the host-group (or members of the host-group), e.g., invitations are extended or requests are granted, affines are expected to use the hosts' resources and/or chattels, joint use or exploitation is accompanied by feasting, dancing, and so forth.

5. Both 3 and 4.
9. No information.

261. **Barter or trade within communities for food and/or chattels (intracommunity or local residence-group)**   **p. 413**

1. Barter or trade, replete with higgle-haggle over value, does not occur.
2. Barter or trade, but no mention of standardized values or higgle-haggle.
3. Barter or trade as reciprocal gift-giving between friends, but with bargaining between strangers.
4. Barter or trade replete with higgle-haggle over value for food and/or chattels occurs, but only between people who are not close kin.
5. Barter for food and/or chattels occurs among kin and nonkin, especially between craft specialists and their clients.
6. Both 4 and 5.
9. No information.

262. **Gift exchange within communities for food and/or chattels (intracommunity or local residence-group)**   **p. 414**

1. No gift exchange occurs, or if it occurs it is negligible.
2. Gift exchange regardless of kinship or rank.
3. Gift exchange of food and/or chattels occurs predominantly between kin and affines (exchange may be deferred).
4. Gift exchange of food and/or chattels occurs predominantly between people of similar rank.
5. Both 3 and 4 obtain, neither clearly predominating.
9. No information.

263. **Barter or trade between (or among) communities for food and/or chattels (intercommunity or extralocal residence-groups)**   **p. 423**

1. Barter or trade, replete with higgle-haggle over value, does not occur.
2. Barter or trade, but no mention of standardized values or higgle-haggle.
3. Barter or trade as reciprocal gift-giving between friends, but with bargaining between strangers.
4. Barter or trade occurs, but values are standardized and higgle-haggle does not occur.
5. Barter or trade, replete with higgle-haggle over value, does occur.
6. Both 4 and 5.
9. No information.

264. **Agents of barter or trade between communities (intercommunity or extralocal residence-groups)**   **p. 424**

1. No agents or barter or trade.
2. Intercommunity barter or trade is conducted by producers with anyone who wishes to trade.
3. Intercommunity barter or trade is conducted by specially designated traders.
4. Intercommunity barter or trade is conducted between trade partners (trade partners may use kinship terms).
5. Intercommunity barter or trade conducted by headmen, chiefs, or other permanent leaders.
6. Both 2 and 3, neither clearly predominating.

7. Both 2 and 4, neither clearly predominating.
8. Both 3 and 4, neither clearly predominating.
9. No information.
10. 2, 3, and 4, none clearly predominating.

11. No predominance of either individual or group ownership, but both.
12. Both 1 and 8.
13. Both 2 and 8.

---

265. Gift exchange between (or among) communities for food and/or chattels (intercommunity or extralocal residence-groups)   p. 425

1. No gift exchange occurs, or if it occurs it is negligible.
2. Gift exchange between individuals in different communities regardless of kinship or rank.
3. Gift exchange occurs predominantly between kin and affines (exchange may be deferred).
4. Gift exchange occurs predominantly between people of similar rank (exchange may be deferred).
5. Both 3 and 4 obtain, neither clearly predominates.
6. Gift exchange between ceremonial or political leaders of localized communities, such as patrilineages, patrisibs, patridemes, parallel matriunits, and multiple kin-group communities.
9. No information.

IV-C. Ownership of Property

---

266. Ownership of key gathering sites, i.e., root grounds, berry bushes, seed grounds, cacti, wild trees, etc.   p. 406

1. No gathering sites, or if there are gathering sites, they are not predominantly recognized as private property.
2. Gathering sites for key extractive resources predominantly recognized as property belonging to ambilocal households and/or larger ambilocal units.
3. Gathering sites for key extractive resources (e.g., acorn trees, or root grounds, or cactus plants) are predominantly recognized as properties belonging to patridemes or patrihouseholds.
4. Gathering sites for key extractive resources are predominantly recognized as properties belonging to matridemes or matrihouseholds.
5. Gathering sites for key extractive resources are predominantly recognized as properties belonging to patrilineages or patrisibs.
6. Gathering sites for key extractive resources are predominantly recognized as properties belonging to matrilineages, or matrisibs.
7. Gathering sites for key extractive resources are predominantly recognized as the property of women (owned individually or by task-groups) and not as property of matridemes, matrihouseholds, matrilineages, or matrisibs.
8. Gathering sites for key extractive resources are predominantly recognized as the property of men (owned individually or by task-groups) and not as property of patridemes, patrihouseholds, patrilineages, or patrisibs.
9. No information.
10. Some gathering sites for key extractive resources are owned by men (individually or by task-groups) and some by women (individually or by task-groups), neither clearly predominating. (The resources on male-owned sites may be different in kind from those on female-owned sites.)

---

267. Ownership of key hunting sites, i.e., deadfalls, deer runs, sites for catching eagles, fowl nesting areas, game tracts, etc.   p. 407

1. No hunting sites, or if there are hunting sites, such as large game tracts, they are not regarded as private property.
2. Hunting sites for key extractive resources are predominantly recognized as properties belonging to ambilocal households and/or demes.
3. Hunting sites for key extractive resources (e.g., deer, elk, mountain sheep, rabbit, moose, or duck, etc.) are predominantly recognized as properties belonging to patridemes or patrihouseholds.
4. Hunting sites for key extractive resources are predominantly recognized as properties belonging to matridemes or matrihouseholds.
5. Hunting sites for key extractive resources are predominantly recognized as properties belonging to patrilineages or patrisibs.
6. Hunting sites for key extractive resources are predominantly recognized as properties belonging to matridemes or matrisibs.
7. Hunting sites for key extractive resources are predominantly recognized as the property of men (owned individually or by task-groups) and not as property of patrihouseholds, patridemes, patrilineages, or patrisibs.
8. Some hunting sites are owned by men (individually or by task-groups) and some by patrihouseholds, patridemes, patrilineages, or patrisibs, none clearly predominating. (The resources on individually owned sites may be different in kind from the resources on sites owned by kinship-groups.)
9. No information.
10. No predominance of individual or group ownership, but both.

---

268. Ownership of key fishing and other aquatic animal extraction-sites (including all forms of animal extraction from water, tidewater flats, sections of river banks, or from weirs and impounds)   p. 408

1. No fishing sites, or if there are fishing sites, they are not predominantly recognized as private property.
2. Fishing sites for key extractive resources are predominantly recognized as belonging to ambilocal households and large ambilocal groups.
3. Fishing sites for key extractive resources (e.g., shellfish, seals, anadromous fishes) are predominantly recognized as properties belonging to patridemes or patrihouseholds.
4. Fishing sites for key extractive resources are predominantly recognized as properties belonging to matridemes or matrihouseholds.
5. Fishing sites for key extractive resources are predominantly recognized as properties belonging to patrilineages or patrisibs.
6. Fishing sites for key extractive resources are predom-

inantly recognized as properties belonging to men born into matrilineages or matrisibs.

7. Fishing sites for key extractive resources are predominantly recognized as properties belonging to women (owned individually or by task-groups) and not matrihouseholds, matridemes, matrisibs, or matrilineages.

8. Fishing sites for key extractive resources are predominantly recognized as properties belonging to men (owned individually or by task-groups) and not patrihouseholds, patridemes, patrilineages, or patrisibs.

9. No information.

10. Some fishing sites for key extractive resources are owned by men (individually or by task-groups) and some by women (individually or by task-groups), neither clearly predominating. (The resources on male-owned sites may be different in kind from those on female-owned sites.)

11. Some fishing sites are owned by individual men or women and others are owned by kinship units (households, demes, lineages, or clans), neither individual nor group ownership clearly predominating. (Individually-owned resources may differ in kind from resources owned by kinship units.

12. Both 1 and 7.

---

269. Ownership of farming sites, including cultivated trees, but not tobacco plots   p. 409

1. No farming sites.

2. Farming sites are communal and available to anyone who wishes to use them.

3. Farming sites are owned by nuclear or polygynous families.

4. Farming sites are predominantly recognized as belonging to patridemes or patrihouseholds.

5. Farming sites are predominantly recognized as belonging to matridemes or matrihouseholds.

6. Farming sites are predominantly recognized as belonging to patrilineages or patrisibs.

7. Farming sites are predominantly recognized as belonging to matrilineages or matrisibs.

8. Farming sites are predominantly recognized as belonging to men (owned individually or by task-groups) and not patrihouseholds, patridemes, patrilineages, or patrisibs.

9. No information.

10. Farming sites are predominantly recognized as belonging to women (owned individually or by task-groups) and not matrihouseholds, matridemes, matrilineages, or matrisibs.

11. Some farming sites are owned by individual men or women and some by kinship units (households, demes, lineages, or sibs), neither individual nor group ownership clearly predominating. (Individually owned resources may differ in kind from resources owned by kinship units.)

12. Both 8 and 10.

---

270. Ownership of house   p. 410

1. House owned (perhaps only temporarily) by the individual (male or female) who constructs and cares for it.

2. House owned jointly by man and wife.

3. House owned (perhaps only temporarily) by family household that occupies it.

4. House owned by patrihousehold or patrideme.

5. House owned by matrihousehold or matrideme.

6. House owned by patrilineage or patrisib.

7. House owned by matrilineage or matrisib.

9. No information.

---

271. Ownership of men's chattels (movable property such as canoes, blankets, bows, knives, slaves, etc.)

1. There is no male ownership or exclusive usufruct of chattels.

2. Males have usufruct rights over some chattels, but not clear ownership.

3. Males have ownership rights over some chattels, though they do not retain the right to dispose of chattels as they see fit.

4. Males have ownership rights over some chattels, retaining the right to dispose of the chattels as they see fit.

5. Both 3 and 4 obtain, neither clearly predominating.

9. No information.

---

272. Ownership of women's chattels (movable property such as coppers, blankets, clothes, tools, etc.)

1. There is no female ownership or exclusive usufruct of chattels.

2. Females have usufruct rights over some chattels, but not clear ownership.

3. Females have ownership rights over some chattels, though they do not retain the right to dispose of the chattels as they see fit.

4. Females have ownership rights over some chattels, retaining the right to dispose of the chattels as they see fit.

5. Both 3 and 4 obtain, neither clearly predominating.

9. No information.

---

273. Ownership of common property following divorce

1. There is little or no common property and it is not a consideration at divorce.

2. Women and men divide property at divorce, more or less equally.

3. Compensation in shell trade or other material wealth is paid by relatives of spouse considered to be at fault. Innocent spouse retains bulk of common property.

4. Men take most of the common property at divorce.

5. Women take most of the common property at divorce.

6. Men take all of the common property at divorce.

7. Women take all of the common property at divorce.

9. No information.

IV-D.   Inheritance of Property

---

274. Inheritance of gathering sites

1. No specific gathering sites and/or no inheritance.

2. Gathering sites are retained communally by all kinship groups in the community (local residence-group), not by individual persons, specific task-groups, or kinship units.

3. Gathering sites are inherited (even if only to be

supervised) by the oldest son or daughter of the recognized leader of the kinship unit (household, deme, lineage, sib) that owns the sites.

4. Gathering sites are inherited (even if only to be supervised) by the most competent son or daughter, not necessarily the oldest, of the recognized leader of the kinship unit (household, deme, lineage, sib) that owns the sites.

5. Gathering sites are inherited (even if only to be supervised) by the most competent kin (lineal or collateral, so not necessarily a son or daughter) of the recognized leader of the kinship unit that owns the sites.

6. Gathering sites are inherited by the sons or daughters of the person or the members of the task-group that owns the sites.

7. Gathering sites are disposed of, or bequeathed, in any manner chosen by the owner(s).

8. Gathering sites are inherited by daughters only, then sons if no daughters.

9. No information.

10. Gathering sites are inherited by the son-in-law of a male owner.

11. Both 2 and 6.

275. Inheritance of hunting sites

1. No specific hunting sites and no inheritance.

2. Hunting sites are retained by all the kinship groups in the community (local residence-group), not by individual persons, specific task-groups, or kinship units.

3. Hunting sites are inherited (even if only to be supervised) by the oldest son or daughter of the recognized leader of the kinship unit (household, deme, lineage, or sibs) that owns the sites.

4. Hunting sites are inherited (even if only to be supervised) by the most competent son or daughter, not necessarily the oldest, of the recognized leader of the kinship unit that owns the sites.

5. Hunting sites are inherited (even if only to be supervised) by the most competent kin (lineal or collateral, so not necessarily son or daughter) of the recognized leader of the kinship unit that owns the sites.

6. Hunting sites are inherited by the sons or daughters of the person or the members of the task-group that owns the sites.

7. Hunting sites are disposed of, or bequeathed, in any manner chosen by the owner(s).

8. Hunting sites are inherited by a man's sister's son.

9. No information.

10. Both 2 and 3.

11. Hunting sites are inherited by the son-in-law of a male owner.

276. Inheritance of fishing and other aquatic animal extraction sites

1. No specific fishing sites and no fishing-site inheritance.

2. Fishing sites are retained by all the kinship groups in the community (local residence-group), not by individuals, specific task-groups, or kinship units.

3. Fishing sites are inherited (even if only to be supervised) by the oldest son or daughter of the recog-

nized leader of the kinship unit (household, deme, lineage, or sib) that owns the sites.

4. Fishing sites are inherited (even if only to be supervised) by the most competent son or daughter, not necessarily the oldest, of the recognized leader of the kinship unit that owns the sites.

5. Fishing sites are inherited (even if only to be supervised) by the most competent kin (either lineal or collateral, so not necessarily son or daughter) of the recognized leader of the kinship unit that owns the sites.

6. Fishing sites are inherited by the sons or daughters of the person or the members of the task-group that owns the sites.

7. Fishing sites are disposed of, or bequeathed, in any manner chosen by the owner(s).

8. Fishing sites are inherited by a man's sister's son.

9. No information.

10. Combination of 2, 3, or 6.

11. Fishing sites are inherited by the son-in-law of a male owner.

277. Inheritance of farming sites

1. No farming practiced.

2. Farming sites are retained by the community (local residence-group), not by individual persons, specific task-groups, or kinship units.

3. Farming sites are inherited (even if only to be supervised) by the oldest son or daughter of the recognized leader of the kinship unit (household, deme, lineage, or sib) that owns the sites.

4. Farming sites are inherited (even if only to be supervised) by the most competent son or daughter of the recognized leader of the kinship unit that owns the sites.

5. Farming sites are inherited by the most competent kin (either lineal or collateral, so not necessarily son or daughter) of the recognized leader of the kinship unit that owns the sites.

6. Farming sites are inherited by the sons or daughters of the person or members of the task-group that owns the sites.

7. Farming sites are disposed of, or bequeathed, in any manner chosen by the owner(s).

8. Farming sites inherited by son-in-law of male owner.

9. No information

278. Inheritance of houses

1. No inheritance of house. (The house may be a temporary structure, it may be disposed of at the death of the owner, or it may be occupied by the first person who claims it.)

2. House inherited by (even if only as supervisor) the oldest son or daughter of the recognized leader of the kinship unit (household, deme, lineage, or clan) that owns the house.

3. House inherited by (even if only as supervisor) the most competent son or daughter (not necessarily the oldest) of the recognized leader of the kinship unit that owns the house.

4. House inherited by (even if only as supervisor) the most competent kin (either lineal or collateral, so not necessarily son or daughter) of the recognized leader of the kinship unit that owns the house.

5. House inherited by the son(s) or daughter(s) of the person who owns the house.
6. House is retained by the community. (It may be dismantled, reassigned, or both.)
7. House is inherited by whomever designated by owner as the heir.
8. House is inherited by a man's sister's son.
9. No information.
10. Both 1 and 2.
11. House inherited by surviving spouse.

279. Inheritance of men's chattels

1. No male chattels of consequence and no inheritance of men's chattel's.
2. Male chattels inherited more or less equally by all available sons, some perhaps being given to more distant collaterals, friends, or affines.
3. Male chattels are predominantly inherited by sons.
4. Male chattels are predominantly inherited by the oldest son.
5. Male chattels are disposed of at death, or are bequeathed or sold in any manner elected by the owner before death.
6. Male chattels are predominantly inherited by a man's sister's son.
7. Male chattels are predominantly inherited by child regardless of sex.
8. Both 3 and 5.
9. No information.
10. Both 4 and 5.
11. Male chattels disposed of at death, or given to non-relatives.
12. Male chattels inherited by brother.
13. Both 2 and 5.
14. Male chattels predominantly inherited by sisters, brothers, and other members of man's matrisib.

280. Inheritance of women's chattels

1. No female chattels of consequence and no inheritance of women's chattels.
2. Female chattels inherited more or less equally by all available daughters, some perhaps being given to more distant collaterals, friends, or affines.
3. Female chattels are predominantly inherited by daughters.
4. Female chattels are predominantly inherited by oldest daughter.
5. Female chattels are disposed of at death, or are bequeathed or sold in any manner elected by the owner before death.
6. Female chattels predominantly inherited by any child regardless of sex.
7. Both 2 and 5.
8. Both 3 and 5.
9. No information.
10. Female chattels disposed of at death, or given to non-relatives.

V. Settlement Pattern, Demography, and Community Organization

V-A. Settlement Pattern

The community is defined as "the maximal group of persons who normally reside together in face-to-face association" (G. P. Murdock, C. S. Ford, A. E. Hudson, R. Kenne-day, L. W. Simmons, and J. W. M. Whiting, 1945, *Outline of Cultural Materials*, Human Relations Area Files Press, p. 29). This definition of the community is used throughout this code unless otherwise specified in the individual codes (as, for example, at "Ceremonialism" variables).

281. Fixity of settlement   p. 444

1. Degree of settlement of the community is that of migratory or nomadic bands occupying temporary camps for brief periods successively throughout the year.
2. That of seminomadic communities occupying temporary camps for much of the year but aggregated in a fixed settlement at some season or seasons, e.g., recurrently occupied winter quarters.
3. Rotating settlements, i.e., two or more permanent or semipermanent settlements occupied successively at different seasons.
4. Semisedentary settlements occupied throughout the year by at least a nucleus of the community's population, but from which a substantial proportion of the population departs seasonally to occupy shifting camps, e.g., on extended hunting or fishing trips or during pastoral transhumance.
5. Impermanent settlements occupied throughout the year but periodically moved for ecological reasons, as under conditions of shifting cultivation.
6. Impermanent settlements occupied throughout the year but moved from time to time for nonecological reasons, e.g., because of untoward events like an epidemic or the death of a headman.
7. Permanent settlements occupied throughout the year and for long or indefinite periods. [In default of definite evidence of impermanence, raters were instructed to use 7 rather than 5 or 6.]
9. No information.

282. Compactness of settlement   p. 445

This variable assesses the degree to which the local pattern of settlement is dispersed or concentrated. For societies with seasonal differences in settlement pattern, raters were instructed to specify the pattern prevailing for the longest period of the year (and to indicate the alternate pattern in parentheses).

1. Settlements are compact, e.g., nucleated villages or concentrated camps.
2. Settlements are dispersed, e.g., neighborhoods of isolated family homesteads or bands whose members live in dispersed family camps.
3. Settlements are composed of spatially separate hamlets or subsettlements.
4. Settlements are partially dispersed, e.g., a central village or town core with outlying satellite hamlets or family homesteads.
5. Settlements are straggling, e.g., dwellings or homesteads strung out along a river bank, the seashore, or the like, in a rather continuous distribution. Such settlements merge into one another, but are considered distinct settlements by the occupants, nevertheless.
9. No information.

V-B. Demography

283. Size of community population (the size of the typical community in the focal area)   p. 446

1. Fewer than 50 persons.
2. From 50 to 99 persons.
3. From 100 to 199 persons.
4. From 200 to 399 persons.
5. From 400 to 799 persons.
6. From 800 to 1,599 persons.
7. From 1,600 to 3,199 persons.
8. Over 3,200 persons.
9. No information.

284. Density of community organization p. 447

This variable assesses the nature and degree of urbanization within the indigenous society of which the focal area is a part. Raters were instructed to ascertain which indigenous pre-European-contact settlement was largest, shared the broader culture of the focal community or area, and exercised significant effects on, or relationships with, the focal area.

284. Density of community organization

1. Within the culture being examined (focal area), the society is mostly rural; the largest communities have none of the characteristics of administrative, ceremonial, or mercantile centers.
2. The largest settlement is primarily a ceremonial or religious center for the focal area (which is perhaps a larger and more densely populated region).
3. The largest settlement is primarily an administrative or political center for the focal area (which is perhaps a larger and more densely populated region).
4. The largest settlement is a major mercantile or trade center for the region, whether or not it is also a ceremonial or administrative center.

285. Population density within territory controlled by community

This variable assesses the density of population within the territory exploited or controlled by a focal or typical community. [For purposes of conversion, a square mile is equivalent to 640 acres or 2.59 square kilometers; a kilometer is equal to .621 miles, and a mile is equal to 1.61 kilometers.]

1. Less than one person per five square miles.
2. From one person per square mile to one per five square miles.
3. From one to five persons per square mile.
4. From five to 25 persons per square mile.
5. From 25 to 100 persons per square mile.
6. From 100 to 500 persons per square mile.
7. Over 500 persons per square mile.
9. No information.

V-C. Community Organization

286. Community structure

1. There are no structures in the community that are larger or more impressive than the usual residential dwellings.
2. The most impressive structure (or type of structure) in the community is the residence of a category of influential persons, e.g., a mansion, palace, or large structure occupied by the local headman, a noble, or a wealthy landowner.
3. The most impressive structure (or type of structure) is an assembly hall, a men's house, or other essentially secular or public building.
4. The most impressive structure (or type of structure) is a temple, church, or other essentially religious or ceremonial edifice.
5. The most impressive structure (or type of structure) is a fort, citadel, massive defensive wall, or other military installation.
6. There are two or more types of impressive structures other than dwellings; no one type clearly preponderates.
9. No information.

287. Community segmentation

1. There are no local subdivisions of the typical or focal community other than family households.
2. The community is divided into local moieties, i.e., into *two* contrasting or opposing subdivisions, or into two subdivisions that lack the characteristics of moieties.
3. The community is divided into *three* or more local subdivisions (wards, barrios, residential districts, or other).
4. The community is organized so that, other than family households, at least two larger types of local subdivisions are present and these are hierarchical; e.g., precincts or districts exist within larger wards or parishes.
9. No information.

288. Intracommunity residence pattern

1. Residence in particular segments of the community is determined primarily by voluntary choice.
2. Residence in particular segments of the community is determined primarily by kinship ties, as in the case of localized clans or ramages.
3. Residence in particular local segments is determined primarily by ethnic considerations, e.g., race, tribal membership, or national origins.
4. Residence in particular local segments is determined primarily by political factors, e.g., ideological factions, adherence to particular chiefs.
5. Residence in particular local segments is determined primarily by religious affiliations, e.g., sect or cult-group membership.
6. Residence in particular local segments is determined primarily by status differentials, e.g., wealth, occupation, social class, or caste membership.
7. Residence in particular local segments is determined approximately equally by two or more types of consideration, among which kinship ties are relatively unimportant.
8. Residence in particular local segments is determined approximately equally by two or more types of consideration, among which kinship ties are important.
9. No information

289. Community integration

1. The focal or typical community is notably lacking in social integration, at least as compared with its constituent local segments or with some larger political unit of which it forms a part.
2. The focal community is distinguished from other

neighboring communities by ethnic factors, e.g., by belonging to a different tribe or speaking a different language.

3. The focal or typical community is primarily a kinship unit, its members (or at least those of the sex that does not shift residence in marriage) belonging preponderantly to a single kinship unit, e.g., a clan or localized lineage, sib, or deme.

4. The focal or typical community is integrated by multiple ties among a plurality of kinship groups, where the basic ties are kinship.

5. The focal or typical community is integrated primarily by common social status, its members belonging preponderantly to a single social class, caste, or occupational group and differing in this respect from at least some of its neighboring communities.

6. The focal or typical community is integrated primarily (not incidentally) by common political ties, e.g., through allegiance to a particular chief, or by political and economic interdependencies, e.g., through patron-client relationships.

7. The focal or typical community is integrated primarily by a common cult or religious affiliation not shared by neighboring communities, or by a civil–religious system of offices; in either case, the religious element transcends in importance all other types of local bonds.

8. The focal or typical community is primarily integrated, not by common kinship, social status, worship, or political allegiance, but by the choice, fact, or accident of common residence, shifts in residence from one community to another being relatively easy and frequent.

9. No information.

VI. Social and Kinship Organization

VI-A. Marriage

---

290. Form of marriage (dominant form is about 60 percent or more of all marriages)

1. Monogamy: marriage of one woman and one man.
2. Polygyny: marriage of two or more women to one man.
9. No information.

---

291. Estimated incidence of polygamy, or plural marriage (all forms of polygamy, polygyny, and polyandry) p. 454

1. No polygamy, or it is very rare.
2. 5–10 percent.
3. 11–25 percent.
4. 26–50 percent.
5. Over 50 percent.
9. No information

---

292. Dominant form of polygamy p. 453

1. No polygamy, or it is rare.
2. Sororal polygyny wherein wives are sisters, or stand in roughly equivalent relationship to one another (such as classificatory sisters).
3. Nonsororal polygyny wherein wives are not sisters nor do they stand in any equivalent relationship to each other.

4. General polygyny wherein wives may be sisters or unrelated.
5. Polyandry: marriage of several men to one woman.
9. No information.

---

293. Secondary marriage

By secondary marriage is meant any marriage where the selection of a new spouse is contingent on the relationship between the selectee and a prior spouse of the selector. Sororal polygyny and fraternal polyandry rated present if practiced at all.

1. No secondary marriages.
2. Sororal polygyny.
3. Sororate: marriage of a man to his deceased wife's sister or "sister."
4. Levirate: marriage of a woman to her deceased husband's brother or "brother."
5. Both 2 and 3.
6. Both 3 and 4.
7. 2, 3, and 4.
8. Fraternal polyandry.
9. No information.
10. 2, 3, 4, and 8.
11. 3, 4, and 8.

---

294. First-cousin marriage is approved (or dominant, or preferred, or prescribed) p. 448

1. No first-cousin marriage of any form is approved, etc.
2. Matrilateral cross-cousin marriage is approved, etc.
3. Patrilateral cross-cousin marriage is approved, etc.
4. Patrilateral parallel-cousin marriage is approved, etc.
5. Bilateral cross-cousin marriage is approved, etc.
6. Matrilateral cross-cousin marriage and matrilateral parallel-cousin marriage are both approved.
7. 4 and 5.
9. No information.

---

295. Second-cousin marriage is approved (or dominant, or preferred, or prescribed). p. 449

1. No second-cousin marriage of any form is approved.
2. Matrilateral cross-cousin marriage is approved, etc.
3. Patrilateral cross-cousin marriage is approved, etc.
4. Patrilateral parallel-cousin marriage is approved, etc.
5. Bilateral cross-cousin marriage is approved, etc.
6. Matrilateral cross-cousin marriage and matrilateral parallel-cousin marriage are both approved.
7. 4 and 5.
8. Any second-cousin marriage is approved.
9. No information.

---

296. Nonlateral marriage is approved (or dominant, or preferred, or prescribed) p. 450

1. Nonlateral marriage is not approved (or dominant, or preferred, or prescribed).
2. Nonlateral marriage is approved, etc. (No marriage of any first and/or second cousins.)
3. Nonlateral marriage, including cousins of third degree or beyond the third degree, is approved, etc. [Rated present only if explicit statement of such. Thus, the statement "blood relatives cannot marry," without

additional information on what degree of relationships constitutes "blood" relationship, is rated 2.]

9. No information.

---

297. Special marriages other than cousin marriages p. 452

1. None.
2. Brother–sister-exchange (or exchange of their terminological equivalents), includes "sister-exchange" and "two men exchange sisters."
3. Pseudo cross-cousin marriage (i.e., marriage to either mother's brother's or father's sister's stepchild).
4. Both 2 and 3.
9. No information.

---

298. Community marriage patterns: the prevalence of local exogamy, endogamy, or agamy   p. 451

Local community boundaries may be rather definite or rather diffuse, merging into a fairly continuous population. The local community is that one recognized by the ethnographers, the informants, or both.

1. Marriage patterns are those of agamous communities, where there is no marked tendency or rule toward either exogamy or endogamy.
2. Those of exogamous communities, where there is a marked tendency or rule for marriage partners to come from different communities.
3. Those of endogamous communities, where there is a marked tendency or rule for marriage partners to come from the same community.
9. No information.

**299. Exchange of gifts (goods and services) between relatives of the bride and groom at marriage: initial exchanges made prior to and through the nuptial rite
                p. 455**

1. There is no exchange of gifts or services at marriage, or the exchange is negligible.
2. Gift exchanges between the relatives of the bride and the groom are reciprocal and roughly equal in goods, services, or both.
3. Unequal gift exchanges which tend to approach bride-prices.
4. Unequal gift exchanges which tend to approach dowries.
9. No information.

**300. Exchange of gifts (goods and services) between relatives of the bride and groom after the nuptial rite
                p. 456**

1. No exchange or negligible exchange after the nuptial rite.
2. Gift exchanges continue for about one year, or until the first child is born.
3. Gift exchanges continue beyond approximately a year, *or* throughout the duration of the marriage.
9. No information.

---

301. Bride service, in which a man performs services for his bride's (or prospective bride's) family (usually as options to other forms of marriage obligations) p. 457

1. No bride service.
2. Bride service is performed before the marriage.

3. Bride service continues for up to one year after the marriage is recognized.
4. Bride service continues beyond one year.
9. No information.

VI-B.   Family and Household

---

302. Forms of the family which are predominant in the society (these family units do not necessarily co-reside)

1. No family type clearly predominates. Several forms are present.
2. Independent families, or nuclear families composed of a man, wife, and their unmarried offspring.
3. Polygynous families composed of a man, his wives, and their unmarried offspring.
4. Polyandrous families composed of a woman, her husbands, and their unmarried offspring.
5. Stem families, which normally include only two related families of procreation (disregarding polygamous unions), the two being of adjacent generations.
6. Lineal families, which normally include one family of procreation in the senior generation, but include at least two such families in the next generation.
7. Extended families, which normally include at least two related families of procreation in at least two adjacent generations.
9. No information.

---

303. Forms of the family which occur often, but which do not predominate

The family type in question is either the modal type, but less than 50 percent, or second in frequency to the dominant form. Not necessarily co-residential.

1. No modal or secondary family form. [Analysts used this attribute unless secondary form was explicitly stated or indicated.]
2. Independent.
3. Polygynous.
4. Polyandrous.
5. Stem.
6. Lineal.
7. Extended.
9. No information.

---

304. Dominant family household forms, or co-residential units (not necessarily under same roof) which tend to share some domestic functions, such as distribution of food, child rearing and training, preparation of meals, etc.   p. 461

1. Nuclear family household is independent.
2. Each polygynous family unit is independent with a separate house for each wife.
3. Polygynous family co-resides with all wives living in same house.
4. Polyandrous family co-resides with all husbands living in same house.
5. Stem family household co-resides.
6. Lineal family household co-resides.
7. Extended family co-resides.
9. No information.

305. Dominant form of postnuptial household residence
p. 458

The dominant form is the one that probably more than 50 percent of the households observe. Residence can be within, or adjacent to, the house of the mother, father, male kinsman, etc., in a unilocal situation. This typology is used to classify "household units." Residence terms will also be used to classify "community settlement patterns." It is important to keep household and community separate.

1. Ambilocal household, where husband and wife live with (or near) the kin of one or the other, choice being based on relative need, advantage, etc.
2. Neolocal household, where husband and wife set up independent residence without respect to placement of families of orientation.
3. Virilocal household, where husband and wife live with (or near) his kinsmen, but not necessarily his father.
4. Uxorilocal household, where husband and wife live with (or near) her kinsmen, but not necessarily her mother.
5. Patrilocal household, where husband and wife live with (or near) his father.
6. Matrilocal household, where husband and wife live with (or near) her mother.
7. Avunculocal household, where husband and wife live with his mother's brother.
9. No information.

306. Secondary form or modal form of postnuptial household residence where no form represents 50 percent of all practices, or where the secondary form occurs frequently, but does not dominate   **p. 459**

1. No secondary or modal, yet subordinate, form.
2. Ambilocal.
3. Neolocal.
4. Virilocal.
5. Uxorilocal.
6. Patrilocal.
7. Matrilocal.
8. Avunculocal.
9. No information.

307. Initial temporary form of postnuptial household residence   **p. 460**

Initial form of residency can last a week, a month, a year, until the first child is born, etc. The important point is that the initial form is regarded as temporary and that a permanent form follows.

1. No initial temporary form.
2. Matrilocal or uxorilocal.
3. Patrilocal or virilocal.
4. Avunculocal.
9. No information.

VI-C. Descent and Descent Groups

308. Forms of descent probably observed   **p. 462**

This is an ideological variable which stresses how individuals recognize and assign kin. This is not the same as descent groups, household residence forms, etc. Descent can be *stipulated* or *demonstrated*. Where descent is stipulated, membership in the line establishes a putative kinship bond between any two members. Where descent is demonstrated, or reckoned, claim to membership in the unit is validated by an acceptable demonstration of genealogical connection with another member of the line; the "demonstration" need not coincide with the actual genealogical tree.

1. Bilateral descent, or nonunilineal descent: a person is considered equally related to kin traced through males or through females; distance, that is, number of links, rather than sex of connecting link, is used to differentiate kin.
2. Patrilineal descent: a person emphasizes membership within a descent line traced through males.
3. Matrilineal descent: a person emphasizes membership within a descent line traced through females.
9. No information.

309. Forms of kinship units   **p. 463**

Kinship units can be described by reference to marriage, descent, and residence. They can also be described by reference to location, internal relationships, activities, ownership of property, and relationships between units. Variables follow which control for all of these properties. Descent units are demonstrated, and are unilineal or nonunilineal.

1. No descent units beyond the ego-oriented kindred of bilateral kinsmen. Kindreds differ for each member of the society except siblings.
2. A deme is a group of people *demonstrating* descent from a common ancestor regardless of sex of connecting ascendants, which is united by some additional criterion (such as collective ownership, common residence, and so on). *De facto*, some of the recognized descendants of a given ancestor are potential members and others are actual members of the unit.
3. A matrilineage is a lineage in which descent is *demonstrated* through the female line.
4. A patrilineage is a lineage in which descent is *demonstrated* through the male line.
9. No information.

310. Stipulated descent units, bilateral or unilineal **p. 473**

1. No stipulated descent units. Kinship units are either demonstrated or nonexistent, i.e., nothing beyond the ego-oriented kindred.
2. Septs are demes which are linked through presumed (stipulated) relatives.
3. Sibs are unilineal groups (matrilineal or patrilineal) that are linked through presumed (stipulated) descent.
9. No information.

311. Kinship units beyond sibs and septs   **p. 471**

1. No classification of kinship units, or none beyond demes and lineages, or none beyond sibs and septs.
2. Moieties: there are only two units, or several units (bilateral or unilineal) are grouped into two divisions.
3. Phratries: any grouping of kinship units other than moiety.
9. No information.

312. **Location of dominant postnuptial residence with regard to demonstrated kinship units—bilateral or unilineal**   p. 464
  1. No demonstrated kinship units.
  2. Residence is ambilocal (ambilocal demes of a special type are called *ramages*).
  3. Residence is patrilocal (or virilocal).
  4. Matrilocal (or uxorilocal).
  5. Avunculocal.
  9. No information.

313. **Localization of demonstrated kinship units**   p. 465
  1. No demonstrated kinship units (only kindreds).
  2. Members of kinship unit are dispersed in several communities.
  3. Members of kinship unit are localized in one community.
  9. No information.

314. **Localization of stipulated kinship units**   p. 474
  1. No stipulated kinship units.
  2. Members of kinship unit are dispersed in several communities.
  3. Members of kinship unit are localized in one community.
  9. No information.

315. **Relationships within the demonstrated kinship unit**   p. 466
  1. No demonstrated kinship units.
  2. Egalitarian relations: internal statuses are differentiated solely on the basis of generation, sex, and age.
  3. Ranked relations: internal statuses are differentiated on the basis of considerations other than generation or age (birth order, and so forth).
  9. No information.

316. **Relationships within the stipulated kinship unit**   p. 475
  1. No stipulated kinship units.
  2. Egalitarian relations.
  3. Ranked relations.
  9. No information.

317. **Activities of the demonstrated kinship unit**   p. 467
  Activities are organized and include one or more things, such as the performance of ceremonies, conduct of government, acceptance of joint liability, etc.
  1. No demonstrated kinship units.
  2. Unorganized demonstrated kinship units: no joint activity is carried out (such as ceremonies, and so forth).
  3. Organized demonstrated kinship units: the unit carries out joint activities.
  9. No information.

318. **Activities of the stipulated kinship unit**   p. 479
  1. No stipulated kinship units.
  2. Unorganized.
  3. Organized.
  9. No information.

319. **Activities of moieties and phratries**   p. 472
  These activities include performance of ceremonies, marriage regulation, and the like.
  1. No moiety or phratry.
  2. Unorganized.
  3. Organized, but only to regulate marriage.
  4. Organized to perform special rituals (including religious rituals, games, feasts, and so forth).
  5. Both 3 and 4.
  6. Organized to perform rituals and regulate political affairs.
  9. No information.

320. **Relationships between demonstrated kinship units**   p. 468
  1. No demonstrated kinship units.
  2. Nonhierarchical: demonstrated kinship units are not differentiated with respect to prestige, power, or privilege.
  3. Minimal hierarchy: units are differentiated on the basis of prestige alone.
  4. Moderate hierarchy: units form a set, one member of which has differential power or privilege.
  5. Hierarchical: a set of kinship units are differentiated with respect to power or privilege.
  9. No information.

321. **Relationships among stipulated kinship units**
  See definitions of hierarchy V-320.   p. 476
  1. No stipulated kinship units.
  2. Nonhierarchical.
  3. Minimal hierarchy.
  4. Moderate hierarchy.
  5. Hierarchy.
  9. No information.

322. **Ownership of corporeal property by demonstrated kinship units**   p. 469
  1. No demonstrated kinship units.
  2. No corporeal property, movable or not, such as hunting territory, fishing stations, houses, etc., is owned by demonstrated kinship units.
  3. Movable corporeal property, such as houses, boats, fish traps and weirs, etc.
  4. Unmovable corporeal property, such as fishing stations, farm land, berry patches, etc.
  5. Both 3 and 4.
  9. No information.

323. **Ownership of corporeal property by stipulated kinship units**   p. 477
  1. No stipulated kinship units.
  2. No corporeal property.
  3. Movable corporeal property.
  4. Unmovable corporeal property.
  5. Both 3 and 4.
  9. No information.

324. **Ownership of incorporeal property by demonstrated kinship units**   p. 470

Incorporeal property includes special privileges, heirlooms, special rituals, dances, ceremonial objects, etc.

1. No demonstrated kinship units.
2. No incorporeal property owned by demonstrated kinship units.
3. Incorporeal property includes privileges, heirlooms, rituals, songs, dances, crests, myths, names, and the like.
9. No information.

325. Ownership of incorporeal property by stipulated kinship units   p. 478

1. No stipulated kinship units.
2. No incorporeal property.
3. Incorporeal property.
9. No information.

VI-D. Kinship Terms

The following terminological classifications are drawn from G. P. Murdock's typologies: see Murdock (1970: 165–208).

326. Kinship term patterns for grandparents   p. 480

1. Bisexual Pattern, where two terms, distinguished by sex, can be glossed as "grandparent."
2. Merging Pattern, where a single undifferentiated term can be glossed as "grandparent."
3. Bifurcate Bisexual Pattern, where four terms, distinguished by both sex and the sex of the connecting relative, can be glossed as "paternal grandfather," "maternal grandfather," "paternal grandmother," and "maternal grandmother."
4. Matriskewed Pattern, where three terms distinguished by sex and, for females, distinguished also by the sex of the connecting relative, can be glossed as "grandfather," "paternal grandmother" (or, for female, "mother's husband's mother"), and "maternal grandmother." (NOTE: This is Murdock's "K.")
5. Bifurcate Pattern where, two terms distinguished by the sex of the connecting relative can be glossed as "paternal grandparent" and "maternal grandparent." (NOTE: This is Murdock's "M.")
6. A rare pattern distinguishing between grandparent of ego's sex, Gr Fa (grandfather, woman speaking), and Gr Mo (grandmother, man speaking). (NOTE: This is Murdock's "T.") In Map Cu-152, this is termed "Ego Same-Sex Distinction."
7. A rare pattern intermediate between Bifurcate and Bifurcate Bisexual patterns, which distinguishes between Fa Pa (father's parents), Mo Fa (mother's father), and Mo Mo (mother's mother). (NOTE: This is Murdock's "U.") In Map Cu-152, this is termed "Inter Bif/Bif Bisex M."
8. Opposite of 7: Three terms are Mo Pa (mother's parents), Fa Mo, and Fa Fa. In Map Cu-152, this is termed "Inter Bif/Bif Bisex F."
9. No information.
10. Three terms: (1) Gr Mo (man speaking) and Gr Fa (woman speaking), (2) Gr Fa (man speaking), and (3) Gr Mo (woman speaking).

327. Kinship term patterns for grandchildren pp. 481, 482

1. Merging Pattern, where a single undifferentiated term can be glossed as "grandchild." (Map Cu-153).
2. Bisexual Pattern, where two terms, distinguished by sex, can be glossed as "grandson" and "granddaughter." (Map Cu-153.)
3. Self-reciprocal Pattern, where grandparental terms, either with or without diminutive affixes, are applied to grandchildren—a grandchild being invariably called by the same term which he applies to the speaker (Map Cu-153).
4. Bifurcate-Bisexual Pattern, where four terms, distinguished by both the sex of the grandchild and the sex of the connecting relative, can be glossed as "son's son," "son's daughter," "daughter's son," and "daughter's daughter." (Map Cu-154.)
5. Bifurcate Pattern, where two terms, distinguished by the sex of the connecting relative, can be glossed as "son's child" and "daughter's child." (NOTE: This is Murdock's "M.") (Map Cu-153.)
6. Bifurcate Speaker's-Sex Pattern, where four terms, differentiated by the sex both of the speaker and of the connecting relative, can be glossed as "son's child" (man speaking), "son's child" (woman speaking), "daughter's child" (man speaking), and "daughter's child" (woman speaking). (NOTE: This is Murdock's "N.") (Map Cu-153.)
7. A rare pattern between Bifurcate and Bifurcate Bisexual patterns, where So Ch, Da So, and Da Da are distinguished. (Murdock's "R.") (In Map Cu-154 this is termed "Inter Bif/Bif Bisexual.")
8. A rare pattern between Bifurcate and Bifurcate Speaker's-Sex patterns, where distinction is made between So Ch, Da Ch (woman speaking), and Da Ch (man speaking). (NOTE: This is Murdock's "S.") (In Maps Cu-153 and Cu-154 this is termed "Inter Bif/Bif Spkr Sex A.")
9. No information.
10. Maximal Differentiation Pattern for woman speaker and man speaker. Each has set of terms for So So, So Da, Da So, Da Da. (Murdock's "Y.") (Map Cu-154.)
11. Terms are So Ch (man speaking), So Ch (woman speaking), and Da Ch (both sexes speaking). (In Maps Cu-153 and Cu-154 this termed "Inter Bif/Bif Spkr Sex B.")
12. "Grandchild" (man speaking), "son's child" (woman speaking), "daughter's child" (woman speaking). (In Map Cu-154 this is termed "Three Terms.")

328. Kinship term patterns for uncles   p. 483

1. Simple Bifurcate Merging Pattern, where a single term can be glossed as "mother's brother," paternal uncles being terminologically equated with father.
2. Simple Bifurcate Collateral Pattern, where two special terms, distinguished by the sex of the connecting relative, can be glossed as "paternal uncle" and "maternal uncle."
3. Skewed Bifurcate Collateral Pattern, where three special terms, distinguished by the sex (mother or father) of the connecting person and also by age relative to that person, can be glossed as, in the case of paternal uncles, "father's elder brother," "father's younger brother," and "mother's brother."

4. Lineal pattern, where a special single term can be glossed as "uncle," applying to both the father's and the mother's brothers and distinguishing them from the father.

5. Age-Differentiated Bifurcate Collateral Pattern, where four terms, distinguished by both relative age and the sex of the connecting person, can be glossed as "father's elder brother," "father's younger brother," "mother's elder brother," and "mother's younger brother." (NOTE: This is Murdock's "K.")

6. Speaker-Differentiated Bifurcate-Merging Pattern, where paternal uncles are terminologically equated with father, while maternal uncles are called by two special terms, differentiated by the sex of the speaker, which can be glossed as "mother's brother" (man speaking), and "mother's brother" (woman speaking). (NOTE: This is Murdock's "M.")

7. Speaker-Differentiated Bifurcate-Collateral Pattern, where four special terms, differentiated by the sex of the connecting person and sex of the speaker, can be glossed as "father's brother" (man speaking), "father's brother" (woman speaking), "mother's brother" (man speaking), and "mother's brother" (woman speaking). (NOTE: This is *not* Murdock's "N.")

9. No information.

---

329. Kinship term patterns for aunts   p. 484

1. Simple Bifurcate Collateral Pattern, where two special terms, distinguished by the sex of the connecting relative, can be glossed as "paternal aunt" and "maternal aunt."

2. Bifurcate Merging Pattern, where a single special term can be glossed as "father's sister," maternal aunts being terminologically equated with mother.

3. Lineal Pattern, where a single special term can be glossed as "aunt," applying to both the father's and the mother's sisters and distinguishing them from mother.

4. Generation Pattern, where special terms are lacking for both maternal and paternal aunts, who are terminologically equated with mother.

5. Skewed Bifurcate Collateral Pattern, where three special terms, distinguished by the sex (mother or father) of the connecting person and also by age relative to that person, can be glossed as, in the case of maternal aunts, "mother's elder sister," "mother's younger sister," and "father's sister."

6. Age-Differentiated Bifurcate Collateral Pattern, where four terms, distinguished by both relative age and the sex of the connecting person, can be glossed as "father's elder sister," "father's younger sister," "mother's elder sister," and "mother's younger sister." (NOTE: This is Murdock's "L.")

7. Speaker-Differentiated Bifurcate Collateral Pattern, where three special terms, differentiated by the sex of the connecting relative and for paternal aunts also by the sex of the speaker, can be glossed as "father's sister" (man speaking), "father's sister" (woman speaking), and "mother's sister." (NOTE: This is Murdock's "M.")

8. Speaker-Differentiated Bifurcate Merging Pattern (unique to Sia Pueblo).

9. No information.

10. A rare pattern similar to the Age-Differentiated Bifurcate Collateral Pattern (6) where Fa El Si, Mo El Si, and Fa Yo Si are distinguished, but Mo Yo Si is not. (NOTE: This is Murdock's "U.")

11. Speaker-Differentiated Bifurcate Collateral Pattern, where three special terms, differentiated by the sex of the connecting relative and, for maternal aunts, also by the sex of the speaker, can be glossed as "mother's sister" (man speaking), "mother's sister" (woman speaking), and "father's sister." (NOTE: This is converse of 7, and is *not* described by Murdock.)

---

330. Kinship term patterns for siblings   pp. 485, 486

1. Dravidian Pattern, where four terms, distinguished by both sex and relative age of the sibling, can be glossed as "elder brother," "younger brother," and "elder sister," and "younger sister." (Map Cu-157.)

2. Yoruban Pattern, where two terms, distinguished by relative age of sibling, can be glossed as "elder sibling," and "younger sibling." (NOTE: This is Murdock's "C.") (Map Cu-157).

3. Algonkian Pattern, where three terms, distinguished by relative age of sibling and, for elder siblings, also by sex, can be glossed as "elder brother," "elder sister," and "younger sibling." (NOTE: This is Murdock's "D.")

4. Kordofanian Pattern, where a single undifferentiated term can be glossed as "sibling." (NOTE: This is Murdock's "E.") (Map Cu-157.)

5. Southern Bantu Pattern, where three terms, distinguished by sex and, for siblings of the speaker's sex, also by age relative to the speaker, can be glossed as "elder sibling of the speaker's sex," "younger sibling of the speaker's sex," and "sibling of the opposite sex." (NOTE: This is Murdock's "F.") (Map Cu-158.)

6. East Polynesian Pattern, where four terms, distinguished by sex and, for siblings of the speaker's sex, also by age relative to the speaker, can be glossed as "elder sibling of the speaker's sex," "younger sibling of the speaker's sex," "brother" (woman speaking), and "sister" (man speaking). (NOTE: This is Murdock's "G.") (Map Cu-157.)

7. Quechuan Pattern, where four terms, distinguished by both sex of sibling and sex of speaker, can be glossed as "brother" (man speaking), "brother" (woman speaking), "sister" (man speaking), and "sister" (woman speaking). (NOTE: This is Murdock's "H.") (Map Cu-157.)

8. Siouan Pattern: any pattern with extensive differentiation by sex of sibling, sex of speaker, and age relative to the speaker, which results in a total of seven or eight distinct terms for siblings. (NOTE: This is Murdock's "L".) (Map Cu-158.)

9. No information.

10. Caddoan Pattern, where six terms, distinguished by sex of sibling, sex of speaker and, for siblings of the speaker's sex, also by age relative to the speaker, which can be glossed as "elder brother" (man speaking), "younger brother" (man speaking), "brother" (woman speaking), "sister" (man speaking), "elder sister" (woman speaking), and "younger sister" (woman speaking). (NOTE: This is Murdock's "M.") (Map Cu-158.)

11. Malagasy Pattern, where three terms, distinguished by sex of sibling and also by sex of speaker, can be

glossed as "siblings of the speaker's sex," "brother" (woman speaking), and "sister" (man speaking). (NOTE: This is Murdock's "N".) (Does not appear in Map Cu-157 or Map Cu-158).

12. Jivaran Pattern, where three terms, distinguished by sex of sibling and also by whichever sex is opposite that of speaker, can be glossed as "brother" (man speaking), "sister" (woman speaking), and "sibling of the opposite sex." (NOTE: This is Murdock's "O.") (Map Cu-158.)

13. Voltaic Pattern, where three terms, distinguished by sex of sibling and, for brothers, also by age relative to the speaker, can be glossed as "elder brother," "younger brother," and "sister." (NOTE: This is Murdock's "P.") (Map Cu-158.)

14. Yukian Pattern, where three terms, distinguished by relative age and, for younger siblings, also by sex, can be glossed as "elder sibling," "younger brother," and "younger sister." (NOTE: This is Murdock's "Q.") (Map Cu-157.)

15. A rare pattern distinguishing Br (man speaking), Br (woman speaking), El Si, and Yo Si. (NOTE: This is Murdock's "R.") (Does not appear in Map Cu-157 or Map Cu-158.)

16. A rare pattern distinguishing El Br (man speaking), El Br (woman speaking), Yo Br (man speaking), El Si, and Yo Si=Yo Br (woman speaking). (NOTE: This is Murdock's "V.") (Does not appear in Map Cu-157 or Map Cu-158.)

17. A rare pattern distinguishing El Br (man speaking), El Br (woman speaking), Yo Br, Yo Si (woman speaking), El Si (woman speaking), and Si (man speaking). (NOTE: This is Murdock's "W.") (Appears as "Age-Difference" in Map Cu-158.)

18. A rare pattern where three terms can be glossed "elder sister," "younger sister," and "brother." (Extrapolated from E. B. Gifford 1922, p. 18, and applied to Chimariko and Shasta tribes). (Appears as "Age-Sex Differences" in Map Cu-158.)

19. European Pattern, where two terms, distinguished by sex, can be glossed "brother" and "sister." (NOTE: This is Murdock's "B.")

20. Four terms: "older sibling," "younger sibling," "brother," and "sister." (Appears as "Four Terms" in Map Cu-158.)

21. Three terms: "brother" (man speaking), "sister" (woman speaking), and a third term meaning "brother" (woman speaking) or "sister" (man speaking). (Appears as "Three Terms" in Map Cu-158.)

22. "Older sibling," "younger sibling," "sister" (man speaking), "older sister" (man speaking). (Appears as "Age-Diff Three Terms" in Map Cu-158.)

---

331. Kinship term patterns for cross-cousins and parallel cousins   p. 487

1. Hawaiian Pattern: siblings, cross-, and parallel cousins are called by the same term. ×c = ||c = sib

2. Iroquois Pattern, where one or more special terms for first cross-cousins differ from those for siblings, parallel cousins, and avuncular and nepotic relatives. sib = ||c ≠ ×c

3. Eskimo Pattern, where one or more special terms for first cross-cousins differ from those for siblings, but do not distinguish cross from parallel cousins. ×c = ||c ≠ sib

4. Omaha Pattern, where the children of a mother's brother and of a father's sister (cross-cousins) are terminologically distinguished from siblings, parallel cousins, and each other but are not designated by special terms. Instead, a mother's brother's children are terminologically equated with relatives of an ascending generation, normally with the mother and her brother, and a father's sister's children are equated with relatives of a descending generation, normally with a man's sister's children and his own children.

5. Crow Pattern: the mirror image of the Omaha pattern, with a mother's brother's children terminologically equated with relatives of a descending generation, normally with a man's own children and a woman's brother's children, while a father's sister's children are equated with relatives of an ascending generation, normally with father and father's sister.

9. No information.

VII. Political Organization, Sodalities, Warfare

VII-A. Leadership and Succession

---

332. Type and complexity of political leadership in the focal local community   p. 489

1. The focal or typical community lacks centralized leadership, political authority being dispersed among its component households or other segments, which remain essentially autonomous.

2. The community has a single leader or headman but lacks other political offices other than, at most, an informal council of elders.

3. The community has a single leader or headman with one or more functional assistants and/or a formal council or assembly, but lacks an elaborate or hierarchical political organization.

4. The community has a single leader or headman plus an elaborate or hierarchical system of subordinate political statuses.

5. The community lacks a single political head but is governed collectively by a committee, a council, an age-grade organization, or the like.

6. The local political organization is theocratic, authority being vested not in secular officials but in a priesthood, a secret society, or other religious functionaries.

7. The community has a dual system of leadership, combining secular and religious offices of comparable influence and authority, e.g., headman and shaman or priest, council and secret society. [This code is not applicable unless the religious functionaries exercise important judicial or other *political* functions as well as strictly religious ones.]

8. The community has dual or plural headmen with distinct but coordinate authority and one or more functional assistants, etc., but lacks a complex system of subordinate political statuses. (Eastern Pomo, Northern Pomo, and some Yokuts.)

9. No information.

10. Two sets of village chiefs with elaborate hierarchy of political status, etc., divided jurisdiction by season. (Tewa.)

---

333. Mode of succession to political leadership within the focal or typical local community   p. 496

1. No political authorities and no succession to the job.
2. Succession to the office of headman, if such or an approximate equivalent exists, is through appointment (not merely acquiescence) by some higher political authority.
3. Succession is not appointive or hereditary but is achieved (by means of informal consensus or election) primarily through the acquisition of personal influence, leadership qualities, prestige, or wealth.
4. Succession is based primarily upon seniority or age, as under gerontocracy. (Does not appear on Map Cu-169.)
5. Succession tends to be hereditary by a son or other patri- kinsman of the preceding headman. (Appears as "Patri Inheritance" in Map Cu-169.)
6. Succession tends to be hereditary, by a sister's son or other matri- kinsman of the predecessor. (Appears as "Matri Inheritance" in Map Cu-169.)
7. Succession tends to be hereditary, not by a particular category of kinsman but by a member of a privileged group selected for his personal qualifications by some electoral or appointive procedure. (Appears as "Privileged Group Inherit" in Map Cu-169.)
8. Item 6 ideally, actually tempered by 3 (qualities of personal influence, leadership qualities, prestige, or wealth). (Appears as "(A) and (B)" in Map Cu-169.)
9. No information.
10. Item 7 tempered by 3 (qualities of personal influence, prestige, or wealth) or by recognition of leadership qualities as determined through either informal consensus or formal elections. (Eastern Pomo, Haida.) (Appears as "(A) and (C)" in Map Cu-169.)
11. Succession based on divination, dreams, or the like. (Lower Kutenai.) (Does not appear in Map Cu-169.)
12. Nonhereditary: informally acknowledged by dream power. (Mohave and Yuma.)
13. Informally acknowledged by dream power and general qualities of leadership, with tendency toward patrilineal heredity. (Maricopa.) (Appears as "(A), (B), and Dreaming" in Map Cu-169.)

VII-B. Local and Extralocal Government

334. Government and territory   p. 488

See also: "Criteria of Government," Category VII-C.

1. Local society (or focal community) has no territorial organization larger than the residential kin group. True political organization is lacking.
2. Local society is composed of several residential kin groups which are *formally united* into villages or bands. (This is termed "tribelet" in Kroeber's and Driver's usage.) There is no organization larger than the village or band, which can be a seasonal (e.g., winter village or summer band) co-residence group rather than a year-around co-residence group.
3. Local society is composed of several residential kin groups which are formally united into villages or bands, and this political unit is further combined with others to form a tribe (several bands or several villages, the latter often being referred to as "districts"). These larger units may or may not convene *in toto.*
9. No information.

VII-C. Criteria of Government

335. Political organization and common defense   p. 490

1. No organization beyond the residential kin group joins together in common defense during warfare *or* raids.
2. No organization beyond the local society—village or band, whether predominantly kin or nonkin—joins together in common defense during warfare and raids; yet extralocal groups do not customarily join together in common defense.
3. Local and extralocal organization (tribe or district of villages) commonly and customarily join together for common defense against warfare and raids.
9. No information.

336. Political organization and the distribution of food in times of scarcity   p. 491

1. No organization beyond the residential kin group joins together to distribute food in times of scarcity.
2. No organization beyond the local society—village or band—joins together to distribute food in times of scarcity. [The rating "2" is applied also to villages wherein village chief had storehouse and duty to feed needy, if *formal* village chief was present.]
3. Extralocal organizations, such as tribes or districts, commonly and customarily join together to distribute food in times of scarcity.
9. No information.

337. Political organization and the allocation of access to important means for producing sustenance   p. 492

This variable refers to intragroup area resources e.g., land for farming, water for irrigation, hunting, fishing, gathering rights etc., and whether or not these resources are allocated internally among families or kin groups by some political authority above kin group headmen. This does not include question of whether or not village boundaries are maintained and resources are "jealously guarded against poaching by outsiders."

1. No organization beyond the residential kin group joins together to allow access to the important subsistence resources.
2. No organization beyond the village or band which joins together to allow access to the important subsistence resources.
3. The extralocal tribe or district organization commonly and customarily joins together to allow access to the important subsistence resources.
9. No information.

338. Political organization and the allocation of civic duties such as labor or military conscription   p. 494

1. No political organization. [Always "1" if Variable 337 is rated "kin group," or "1".]
1. No political organization is invoked to allocate civic duties.
3. The village or band organization is invoked to allocate civic duties.

4. The tribe or district organization is invoked to allocate civic duties.
9. No information.

339. Political organization and the formation of alliances with other groups (extralocal communities)   p. 493

1. No alliances are formed with other groups.
2. Residential kin groups form alliances with other groups from time to time.
3. Village or band organization is invoked to form alliances with other groups.
4. Tribe or district organization is invoked to form alliances with other groups.
9. No information.

340. Political organization and the punishment of crimes   p. 495

1. No political organization or third-party arbitration between litigants.
2. No political organization, but mediation or arbitration between litigants by third party occurs.
3. Village or band organization is invoked to punish crimes.
4. Tribal or district organization is invoked to punish crimes.
9. No information.

VII-D. Sodalities

341. Nature of tribal sodalities   p. 497

A sodality is a subdivision of a society whose members are not primarily determined by kinship or by co-residence. Membership in these groups of "associates," "friends," "comrades," etc., is generally voluntary and not ascribed at birth, though older relations may exert pressures to persuade a person to join the sodality that they consider to be the proper one. The tribal sodality is the most encompassing type, and it entails some procedure of initiation and education either in tribal lore, religious secrets, or both.

1. No tribal sodality.
2. A tribal sodality that includes all mature males in the society. It excludes all others from membership.
3. A tribal sodality that includes all mature women in the society. It excludes all others from membership.
4. Both male and female tribal sodalities, one for each sex.
5. A single tribal sodality that is composed of all the mature males *and* females in the society.
6. A tribal sodality that is composed of all the mature males *and* females in the society, but there are several different chapters of the sodality in the local community (e.g., Western Pueblo Kachina cults).
7. A tribal sodality that is composed of all mature *males* in the society, but there are several different chapters of the sodality in the local community. (Kutenai, Zuni.)
9. No information.

342. Restricted sodalities   p. 498

The term "restricted sodality" applies to an organization with membership restricted to only a part of the mature males, or the mature females, or a mixture of both short of the totality. Restricted sodalities may also have initiation

ceremonies, as well as other rituals, with content and meaning unknown to the nonmembers in the remainder of the population.

1. No restricted sodalities.
2. Restricted sodality or sodalities for men only.
3. Restricted sodality or sodalities for women only.
4. Restricted sodality or sodalities for a select (sometimes self-selected) number of men and women.
5. 2 and 3.
6. 2 and 4.
7. 2, 3, and 4.
9. No information.

343. Sex-dominance of restricted sodalities   p. 501

1. No restricted sodalities.
2. No dominance in numbers of sodalities or functions of sodalities by male groups over female groups.
3. Male sodalities outnumber and were more important in function than female sodalities.
4. Female sodalities outnumber and were more important in function than male sodalities.
9. No information.

344. Functions of restricted sodalities   p. 499

1. No restricted sodalities.
2. Performed religious rituals (including rituals for fertility, weather control, etc.), dances, songs, etc.
3. Performed health and curing ceremonies.
4. Performed political services including, perhaps, defending the larger society or conducting raids for the larger society.
5. Both 2 and 3.
6. Both 2 and 4.
7. Both 3 and 4.
8. All 2, 3, and 4.
9. No information.
10. Performed economic services, e.g., hunting for larger society, in addition to 2, 3 and 4.

345. Restricted sodality: participants and spectators   p. 500

1. No restricted sodalities.
2. Sodality members performed all sodality functions in secret—not for the public.
3. Sodality members performed all sodality functions (except initiations) in public.
4. Some restricted sodality functions were performed in secret; some were partly public.
9. No information.

346. Objects of restricted sodality functions   p. 502

Do sodalities function only for members, or do they function for nonmembers?

1. No restricted sodalities.
2. Restricted sodalities perform for the benefit of members only (e.g., personal dances, spirit seekings, health improvement, and the like).
3. Restricted sodalities perform for the benefit of nonmembers in the society at large (e.g., to cure nonmembers, to insure good crops or rain, to entertain with fine dances, and so forth).
4. Restricted sodalities perform at times for the benefit of members and at times for the benefit of nonmembers.

5. The society has some restricted sodalities that are wholly for the benefit of members, and some that are for the benefit of members and nonmembers.
9. No information.

347. Clubs and age-classes

Clubs and age-classes are informal sodalities without any secrets. Age-classes are special types of sodalities that include any division of a population into organized age-groups of a more or less permanent nature.)

1. No clubs or age-classes.
2. Club(s) are present but are not divided into age-classes.
3. Club(s) are divided into age-classes.
9. No information.

348. Club and age-class membership

1. No clubs.
2. Members are men only.
3. Members are women only.
4. Members are men or women.
5. Some for men only, some for women only.
9. No information.

VII-E. Warfare

349. Duels between members of the same society

This refers to encounters between two individuals.

1. No duels between members of the same community.
2. Duels between members of the same community, but never or rarely between kin.
3. Duels between members of the same village, band, district, or tribe, both between kin and nonkin.
9. No information.

350. Feuds within the local community or extralocal organization   p. 508

Feuds refer to conflicts between two families, lineages, clans, sibs, demes, or other kinship groups. They are often protracted series of reprisals that are not settled, mainly because there is no mechanism to settle them.

1. No feuding.
2. Feuding is confined to kinship groups in the local community only.
3. Feuding is confined to kinship groups in either the local community or the extralocal organization (tribe or district) only.
4. Feuding occurs among kinship groups in the local community and extralocal organization, and between kinship groups which do not belong to the same local or extralocal organizations.
5. Feuding occurs among extralocal groups only.
9. No information.

Raiding

Raids are single, small military engagements of short duration. They are motivated by desire for booty, women, slaves, prestige, vengeance of a slain warrior, or to fulfill a vision or instructions received through dreams. A raiding

party has a leader and from as few as five to as many as 50 people.

351. Raids motivated by desire for economic booty such as hides, pottery, food, etc.   p. 511

1. No raids conducted.
2. Raids, but not for booty.
3. Raids conducted for booty.
9. No information.

352. Raids motivated by desire for women (wife-stealing)   p. 514

1. No raids conducted.
2. Raids, but not for women.
3. Raids conducted for women.
9. No information.

353. Raids motivated by desire for slaves (separate from wife-stealing)   p. 515

1. No raids conducted.
2. Raids, but not for slaves.
3. Raids conducted for slaves.
9. No information.

354. Raids motivated by desire for prestige   p. 512

1. No raids conducted.
2. Raids, but not for prestige.
3. Raids conducted for prestige.
9. No information.

355. Raids motivated by a desire to fulfill visions or dream instructions   p. 513

1. No raids conducted.
2. Raids, but not to fulfill visions or dream instructions.
3. Raids to fulfill visions or dream instructions.
9. No information.

356. Raids motivated by desire to avenge the death of a warrior   p. 509

1. No raids conducted.
2. Raids, but not to avenge a death.
3. Raids to avenge the death of a warrior.
9. No information.

357. Raids motivated by the desire to avenge poaching   p. 510

1. No raids conducted.
2. Raids, but not to avenge poaching.
3. Raids to avenge poaching.
9. No information.

358. Incidence of raiding   p. 503

1. Offensive raids are either rare or never occur (0–1 per year).
2. Offensive raids are moderate (2–4 per year).
3. Offensive raids are frequent (>4 per year).
9. No information.

359. Incidence of defense against raiding   p. 504

1. Never or rarely raided by another group.

2. Raided moderately (2–4 per year).
3. Raided frequently (>4 per year).
9. No information.

360. Presence of buffer zones

A buffer zone is defined as "no man's land" between subsistence areas owned by different groups. If members of either group enter the buffer zone to hunt, fish, farm, or gather, it is possible that they could suffer an attack from the opposing group, and both groups recognize the danger of entering the buffer zones, even if they did so frequently.

1. No buffer zones present or mentioned in the literature.
2. A buffer zone is recognized with another society (a different band or village if no tribal organization, a different tribe or district if tribal organization).
3. Buffer zones are recognized with more than one society (different bands or villages if no tribal or district organization, different tribes or districts if tribal organization).
9. No information.

361. Incidence of warfare

Warfare is defined as conflicts between two factions with true political organization, each of which possesses definite leadership, some kind of military tactics, and at least the hope of being able to weather a series of battles.

1. Warfare not present.
2. Warfare very rarely engaged in, but if so it was primarily restricted to one part of the year.
3. Warfare very rarely engaged in, but it occurred at any time during the year.
4. Warfare commonly engaged in, but when so it was restricted to one part of the year.
5. Warfare commonly engaged in during any time of the year.
9. No information.

362. Motives for engaging in warfare

Desire for territorial expansion, access to strategic resources, glory and prestige, among other motives are said to prompt men to go to war. Each society is rated for all of the motives that seem to have prompted its warfare.

1. No warfare.
2. Territorial expansion.
3. Maintenance of own territory.
4. Access to important resources.
5. Booty.
6. Slaves.
7. Glory and prestige.
8. Religious prescription.
9. No information.
10. Some combination of 2, 3, 4, and 5 only.
11. 5 and 6 only.
12. Some combination of 5, 6, 7, and 8 only.
13. Some combination of all items 2 through 8.

363. Permanent military organizations   p. 505

These are defined as restricted sodalities or armies, conscripted or freely joined, with definite leadership.

1. No permanent military organizations.
2. One permanent military organization.
3. More than one permanent military organization, but no ultimate leader.
4. More than one permanent military organization with an ultimate leader (or council or leaders) with authority over all.
9. No information.

364. Special fighting regalia   p. 506

These are defined as special weapons, armament, dress, or insignias.

1. No special fighting regalia.
2. Special weapons.
3. Special armament.
4. Special dress. (Does not appear in Map Cu-179.)
5. Special insignias. (Does not appear in Map Cu-179.)
6. Some combination of 2, 3, 4, and 5. (Appears as "(A) (B) Dress and Insignia" in Map Cu-179.)
9. No information.

365. Public ceremonies associated with warfare or raids
p. 507

These ceremonies can be performed before or after a conflict, but are performed in public and not merely for the participants.

1. No public ceremonies associated with warfare or raids.
2. Public ceremonies associated with preparation for conflicts only.
3. Public ceremonies associated with postconflict period only.
4. Public ceremonies performed both before and after conflict.
9. No information.

VIII. Ceremonialism, Including Life Cycle

VIII-A. Ceremonialism

Ceremonies are public or private (for the entire focal community or for a select membership within the community), sacred or profane or both (some sacred ceremonies are accompanied by profane acts and diversions), and major or minor (in size and meaning to the community that performs and attends). Moreover, some ceremonies are performed for an entire tribe or district, whereas still others are attended by people from beyond the membership of the (1) residential kin group if it is the largest sovereign unit, (2) village or band if it is the largest sovereign unit, and (3) tribe or district if it is the largest sovereign unit.

366. Major public ceremonies performed for people other than members of religious sodalities and the like
p. 516

A "major" ceremony draws all or most members of the sponsoring group together for its performance, and is considered major in importance by the participants.

1. No major public ceremonies are performed.
2. One major public ceremony is performed in the cultural repertoire, but not on a regular, annual basis.
3. More than one major public ceremony is performed, but not necessarily on an annual basis.

4. One major public ceremony is performed on a regular, at least annual, basis.
5. More than one major public ceremony is performed each year.
9. No information.

---

367. Attendance at largest public ceremony   p. 517

The "largest" public ceremony would be the one having the largest attendance, the most splendid event in the cultural repertoire, the one having the greatest number of ancillary activities, or a ceremony having some combination of these three attributes.

1. No public ceremony.
2. Where residential kin group is the largest sovereign group, ceremonies are performed for self and other kin groups from local area only.
3. Where residential kin group is the largest sovereign group, ceremonies are performed not only for self and other kin groups from local area, but for people from distant areas as well—perhaps people of different dialects, languages, etc.
4. Where band or village is the largest sovereign group, ceremonies are performed for that group only.
5. Where band or village is the largest sovereign group, ceremonies are performed for that group as well as for people from distant (other) groups.
6. Where tribe or district is largest sovereign group, ceremonies are performed for that group only.
7. Where tribe or district is largest sovereign group, ceremonies are performed for that group as well as for people from different (other) groups.
9. No information.

---

368. Dominant sacred or profane nature of major public ceremonies   p. 518

The variable assesses whether major public ceremonies are by nature more sacred (dealing with supernatural acts and beliefs for supernatural ends), more profane (dealing with more mundane, less supernatural acts and ideology), or whether they are accompanied by both types of acts and ideology and there is no clear evidence to show that one dominates the other.

1. No public ceremony.
2. Major public ceremony(s) predominantly sacred.
3. Major public ceremony(s) predominantly profane.
4. Major public ceremony(s) both sacred and profane.
9. No information.

---

369. Reasons for performing public ceremonies of all kinds (according to the sponsors)   p. 519

1. No public ceremonies.
2. Public ceremonies for success at farming, fishing, hunting, or gathering (this includes replenishment of subsistence resources).
3. Public ceremonies for the health and well-being of the community (this includes avenging a death).
4. Public ceremonies to substantiate a claim to a new status, or to gain prestige, or both.
5. Public ceremonies to fulfill ritual prescriptions.
6. 2 and 3 only.
7. 2 and 4 only.

8. 2 and 5 only.
9. No information.
10. 3 and 4 only.
11. 3 and 5 only.
12. 2, 3, and 4 only.
13. 2, 3, and 5 only.
14. 2, 4, and 5 only.
15. 3, 4, and 5 only.
16. 2, 3, 4, and 5.

---

370. Gift-giving at public ceremonies   p. 521

1. No public ceremonies.
2. No gifts are given at public ceremonies.
3. Male-female pairs exchange gifts at some ceremonials. Most ceremonials have no gift exchange.
4. Gifts are exchanged at public ceremonies.
5. Gifts are pooled at ceremonies by *everyone* who attends—locals or not—then distributed to all who attend or participate, including the local hosts.
6. Gifts are given by hosts (sponsors) to those in attendance. There is no immediate exchange.
7. Gifts are exchanged at some ceremonies, given from hosts to guests at some ceremonies, and given from guests to hosts at some ceremonies.
9. No information.

---

371. Quality or amount of gifts given at public ceremony if gifts are given by hosts to guests   p. 522

1. No gifts.
2. All guests receive, in theory, equal gifts.
3. Guests receive more or better gifts depending on their rank.
4. Guests receive more or better gifts depending on the distance they travel to attend the ceremony.
5. Guests receive gifts in an order related to the distance they have travelled: the farther they travel, the earlier they receive a gift during the distribution of gifts.
6. Both 3 and 4.
7. Both 3 and 5.
8. Guests (or reciprocants) receive gifts consonant with their contribution to the ceremony—material or spiritual.
9. No information.
10. Both 2 and 8.
11. Both 8 and 4.
12. Guests receive whatever they request.
13. Gifts to children only.

---

372. Sponsorship and performance of all public ceremonies   p. 520

1. No public ceremonies.
2. Public ceremonies sponsored and performed by kinship groups only.
3. Public ceremonies sponsored and performed by restricted sodalities only.
4. Public ceremonies sponsored and performed under the leadership of political (or theocratic) authorities—anyone in band, village, tribe, or district can be called into service in the conduct of the ceremony.
5. Society has several public ceremonies, some are 2, some 3, and some are both 2 *and* 3.

6. Society has several public ceremonies, some are 2 and some 4.
7. Society has several public ceremonies, some are 3 and some 4.
8. Society has several public ceremonies, some are 2, some 3, and some 4.
9. No information.
10. Public ceremonies not sponsored in the formal sense, though directed by a ritualist or shaman with the economic help of the community (nominal sponsorship of chief or headman).
11. Society has several ceremonies, some are 3, some 4, and some are both 3 *and* 4.
12. Public ceremonies sponsored and performed by moieties under the leadership of moiety chiefs.
13. Society has several ceremonies, some are sponsored and performed by kinship groups (2), and some are sponsored nominally by shamans (or spiritual leaders).
14. The formal sponsor is any individual, the actual director is a shaman, and the entire community contributes to ceremony; also, kinship groups (2) sponsor and perform such ceremonies as marrying and naming feasts.

373. Private ceremonies performed by restricted sodalities or the like   p. 523

These ceremonies are not open to the entire local community. (See the "Sodalities" variables, Category VII-D.)

1. No private ceremonies.
2. Private ceremonies restricted to local members of a select organization.
3. Private ceremonies restricted to members of select local organization and their counterparts in other communities.
4. Some private ceremonies restricted to local members (2), and some include counterparts in other communities (3).
9. No information.

VIII-B. Life Cycle: Birth

374. Parturition seclusion   p. 524

1. Outdoors, no structure of any kind.
2. In entire house, men leave.
3. In a screened off part of house.
4. In a special hut or enclosure.
5. Outdoors or in house vacated by men.
6. In hut or in screened off part of house.
7. In entire house, men do not leave.
8. Outdoors in pit.
9. No information.

375. Parturition position, A   p. 525

1. No special position.
2. Kneeling.
3. Squatting.
4. Standing or stooping.
5. Both kneeling and squatting.
9. No information.

376. Parturition position, B   p. 526

1. No special position.
2. Sitting.
3. Lying on back or reclining backwards.
4. Both sitting and lying on back or reclining backwards.
9. No information.

377. Twins   p. 527

1. No special attitude or ambivalent attitude toward twins reported.
2. Feared or not wanted or one killed.
3. Esteemed or desired.
9. No information.

378. Most frequent ritual number associated with birth

1. 3, 6, or 9.   p. 528
2. 4, 8, or 12.
3. 5, 10, or 15.
4. 7 or some number other than a multiple of 3, 4, or 5.
9. No information.

379. Cradles, A   p. 529

1. None.
2. Flat board(s).
3. Flat, but made of rods, slats, or basketry materials woven together.
4. Upright type of basketry cradle.
5. Both flat board(s) and flat woven types.
6. Upright type and flat type basketry cradles.
7. Flat board and sitting basket.
9. No information.

380. Cradles, B   p. 530

1. None.
2. Wood container, dugout, or sewn box.
3. Bark.
4. Hollowed boards—neither flat nor dugout.
5. Deep trough frame covered with buckskin.
9. No information.

VIII-C. Life Cycle: Naming

381. Names bestowed on individuals: nicknames or common names of address, plus special names bestowed on individuals   p. 531

1. No nicknames or common names of address.
2. Nicknames or common names of address only.
3. Nicknames or common names of address, plus special names with ritual significance or incorporeal property significance.
4. Nicknames plus special names that were *not* regarded as having incorporeal property significance.
5. Special names treated as being ritually significant or as having incorporeal property significance; very few nicknames.
6. Special sib names for women, plus 4 for men.
9. No information.

382. Time of bestowal of name(s) on a person   p. 532

If more than one name is acquired throughout lifetime, those periods in which they are most apt to be acquired are assessed by this variable.

1. Name is bestowed on infant before birth.
2. Name is bestowed shortly after birth (a few days).
3. Name is bestowed during infancy (up to about 2 years).
4. Name is bestowed sometime during late childhood or puberty.
5. Names are acquired throughout adult life, and include teknonymy.
6. 2 and 3.
7. 2 and 4.
8. 2 and 5.
9. No information.
10. 3 and 4.
11. 3 and 5.
12. 4 and 5.
13. 2, 4, and 5.
14. 3, 4, and 5.
15. 2, 3, 4, and 5.

383. By whom the most important name of a person is bestowed   p. 533

The "most important name" is that name which the tribe considers as most important. It can be a name of address, a name of reference, or a name that is recognized as possessing special properties and, in the owner's lifetime, in some societies it might never be used in reference or address.

1. No name considered most important.
2. Most important name is not necessarily bestowed by any relative.
3. Most important name is not necessarily bestowed by any particular kinsman or affine, but can be achieved by a person for himself (herself) through great deeds—economic (potlatch, for example), warfare, religious, spirit quest, and so on.
4. Most important name is bestowed by parents.
5. Most important name is bestowed by maternal relatives.
6. Most important name is bestowed by paternal relatives.
7. Most important name is bestowed by paternal *or* maternal relatives, but also must be achieved through great deeds—economic, warfare, religious, spirit quest, and so forth.
8. Most important name is from maternal or paternal relatives, achievement not critical.
9. No information.

384. Feast or public ceremony at most important naming event   p. 534

"Public ceremony" here means that people other than kinsmen or affines are invited to witness the most important naming ceremony. Feasting and gift-giving may be associated with this ceremony.

1. No feast or public ceremony.
2. Public ceremony, but no feast or giving of gifts.

3. Public ceremony accompanied by feast but no giving of gifts.
4. Public ceremony accompanied by giving of gifts but no feast.
5. Public ceremony accompanied by both giving of gifts and feasting.
9. No information.

385. Private ceremony accompanying the most important naming event   p. 535

A private ceremony for name bestowal is attended by kin and affines only.

1. No private ceremony.
2. Private ceremony in which kin offer gifts to person named only.
3. Private ceremony in which gifts are given to those in attendance by the parents or grandparents of the person named only.
4. Private ceremony in which gifts are exchanged between nuclear family of the named and those in attendance.
5. Private ceremony with feast, but no gifts.
6. Private ceremony where gift is given to the namer(s) only.
7. Private ceremony where namer gives gift to child, child's parents might defer reciprocation or return a gift immediately.
9. No information.

VIII-D. Life Cycle: Girls' Puberty Rites or Female Initiations Near Puberty

386. Place of seclusion, A   p. 539

1. None.
2. In dwelling.
3. In separate hut.
4. Both.
9. No information.

387. Place of seclusion, B   p. 540

1. None.
2. In permanent ceremonial structure.
3. In ceremonial enclosure.
4. Outdoors, no structure or enclosure.
9. No information.

388. Most frequent ritual number associated with girls' puberty rites   p. 541

1. No rites.
2. 3 or 6.
3. 4, 8, or 16.
4. 5 or 10.
5. 7 or a multiple of some number other than 3, 4, or 5.
9. No information.

389. Running   p. 542

1. No running.
2. Running daily.
3. Running once or twice.
9. No information.

390. Drink taboos   p. 543

1. None.
2. Cold water taboo.
3. Must drink through tube.
4. Cold water taboo, *and* must drink through tube.
5. Stale water taboo.
6. Stale water taboo, *and* must drink through tube.
9. No information.

391. Food taboos   p. 544

1. None.
2. Fresh food taboo.
3. Hot food taboo.
4. Salt taboo.
5. Stale food taboo.
6. Both hot food and fresh food taboo.
7. Both hot food taboo and salt taboo.
8. Fresh food (meat) and salt taboo.
9. No information.
10. Fresh food, hot food, and salt taboo.

392. Posture in seclusion   p. 545

1. No special posture.
2. Sitting or squatting.
3. Lying on or near heated spot.
4. Lying on unheated spot.
5. Sitting and reclining (sometimes day/night differences).
9. No information.

393. Bathing   p. 546

1. No bathing.
2. Outdoors in cold water.
3. Indoors with sponge bath and/or warm water.
4. Both outdoors in cold water and indoors with sponge bath and/or warm water.
9. No information.

394. Dancing at public ceremony   p. 536

1. No public ceremony.
2. Girl does not dance at public ceremony.
3. Girl dances at public ceremony.
9. No information.

395. Repetition of public ceremony   p. 537

1. No public ceremony.
2. Not repeated, given only once.
3. Repeated.
9. No information.

396. Private ceremony   p. 538

1. No private ceremony.
2. Private ceremony for pubescent girl and a few close female friends and/or relations, usually from within the community.
3. Private ceremony for pubescent girl and some near kin and/or friends, both sexes, usually aged, usually from within the community.
4. Same as 2, yet extralocal invitees.

5. Same as 3, yet extralocal invitees.
6. Private ceremony for girl and proctor only.
7. Private ceremony for kin and friends, as at 3; girl and others dance; ceremony is repeated.
9. No information.

VIII-E. Life Cycle: Death

397. Dominant containers for corpse or cremation remains
                                                   p. 551

1. None.
2. Only blanket, hide, or mat around corpse.
3. Basket.
4. Pot, or basket, or pit for remains of cremation.
5. Small shed houses, canoes, or boxes.
9. No information.

398. Dominant forms of corpse disposal   p. 552

1. Inhumation.
2. On surface, or on slightly raised platform or in rock crevice, rock shelter, or cave.
3. In tree or on high scaffold, or top of totem pole.
4. Cremation.
5. Tree or scaffold, followed by inhumation.
6. Inhumation and cremation.
9. No information.

399. Burial position of corpse   p. 553

1. Extended.
2. Flexed.
3. Either extended or flexed.
9. No information.

400. Removal of dying person or corpse from house p. 550

1. No removal of dying person or corpse from house.
2. Through wall of house.
3. Through door of house.
4. Through wall or door.
9. No information.

401. Relation of death to house   p. 548

1. Dying person abandoned in house.
2. Dying person removed from house before death.
3. Corpse removed from house after death.
4. Remove before death if possible, otherwise immediately after death.
5. Removed immediately upon death.
6. If person dies in house, house and corpse are burned.
9. No information.

402. Treatment of dominant house type after death p. 549

1. No special treatment.
2. Destroyed, burned, or abandoned permanently.
3. Torn down and moved.
4. Exorcised and/or abandoned only temporarily.
5. Either 2 or 3.
6. Either 2 or 4.
7. Either 3 or 4.
8. Items 2 and 3 and 4.
9. No information.

403. Sacrifice at death   p. 554

1. None.
2. Dogs and/or other (pre-European) domesticated animals killed (or freed or given away).
3. Slaves or captives killed (or freed, if this is prestigious).
4. Dogs killed or given away, *and* slaves killed or freed.
9. No information.

404. Periodic mourning ceremony, distinct from funeral, at later date   p. 547

1. None.
2. Only for chief or prominent man (includes memorial potlatch).
3. For all dead of entire community.
4. Each deceased person has one mourning ceremony distinct from funeral.
5. Both tribal mourning for all deceased, and one or more special mournings for each deceased person.
9. No information.

IX. Spirit Quest, Shamanism, Causes of Illness, and Magic

IX-A. Spirit Quest

405. Spirit quests by individual males: not associated with sodality initiations or group rites   p. 555

1. No quest by males.
2. Minority of males.
3. About half of males.
4. Majority of males.
5. All males.
9. No information.

406. Spirit quests by individual females: not associated with sodality initiations or group rites   p. 556

1. No quest by females.
2. Minority of females.
3. About half of females.
4. Majority of females.
5. All females.
9. No information.

407. Age of first spirit quest made by males (because better reported)   p. 557

1. No quest by males.
2. 1–10 years of age.
3. 11–20 years of age.
4. Over 20 years of age.
9. No information.

408. Datura (Jimsonweed) taken by novices seeking spirit helpers or dreams   p. 558

1. Absent.
2. Present.
9. No information.

409. Spirit quests or confirmations in sodality initiations or other group rites involving persons other than the novice   p. 559

1. No group rite.
2. A group rite for one novice.
3. A group rite for more than one novice.
9. No information.

410. Differences between shamans' and laymen's spirit quests   p. 560

1. No specific spirit quest for shaman or layman.
2. Spirit quests for laymen only.
3. No spirit or vision quest for layman, but quest by shaman.
4. Spirit quests for shaman and layman are identical.
5. Spirit quests for shaman and layman are rather similar, though duration of shaman's quest is somewhat longer and has some more specialized activities than that of the layman.
6. Spirit quests of shaman and layman are dissimilar. Specialized spirits are sought by shaman and inheritance or sponsorship is often necessary to acquire these spirits.
7. Power comes to the shaman sought or unsought; shaman must also train with another shaman; power does not come to layman unsought. Some laymen seek special hunting abilities or the like.
8. Most spirits come unsought, but shamans and laymen can seek spirits or dreams in the same fashion (especially by drinking a concoction made from Jimson weed).
9. No information.
10. Power comes through purchase and training with shaman (or medium societies); initiation to shaman or curing society is usually required as well. (Purchase is made with gifts or feasts. Moreover, sick often pledge themselves to society or cause if they are cured.)
11. Power comes through sickness and cure, plus apprenticeship to shaman who cures the person.

411. Differences between shamans' and laymen's spirit and power possession   p. 561

1. Only shamans, priests, ritualists, and the like receive power.
2. Shamans possess greater power than laymen, but not a greater number of different kinds of spirits than laymen.
3. Shaman possesses greater general power than layman, usually because he acquires a greater number of spirits, but not because the spirits have specific functions.
4. Shamans possesses greater power as well as more specific spirits than laymen over specific functions, such as spirits to cure specific maladies.
5. Shamans possess different powers than laymen, but not necessarily greater power in anything but their specialties. Shamans, for instance, cure the sick, but do not have the supernatural powers of some ritualists over other functions.
9. No information.

IX-B. Shamanism

412. Sex of shamans   p. 562

1. All males.
2. Majority males, minority females.
3. Proportion of sexes about equal.
4. Majority females, minority males.
5. All females.
9. No information.

413. Spirit impersonation with mask or disguise   p. 563

1. Absent.
2. Present.
9. No information.

414. Snake-handling by shamans   p. 565

1. Absent.
2. Present.
9. No information.

415. Possessional shamanism (including trances)   p. 564

1. Absent.
2. Present.
9. No information.

416. Shamans' reputations for miraculous powers for curing, controlling weather, etc.   p. 566

1. No differences among shamans.
2. Some shamans reported to have greater power than others.
3. Medicine societies reported to have greater power in concert than any particular shaman. (Whole medicine society called upon to work for cure if shaman fails.)
9. No information.

417. Local and extralocal requests for shamans' services   p. 567

1. Shaman's services called on in home community only.
2. Shamans' services (or some shamans' services) requested in communities other than their home communities, but within their own dialect or language area.
3. Shamans' services (or some shamans' services) requested in home community, in other communities within same language, and other language-speaking communities on occasion.
9. No information.

IX-C. Causes of Illness

418. Illness caused by foreign intrusion   p. 568

1. Caused by neither foreign object nor foreign spirit.
2. Foreign object.
3. Foreign spirit.
4. Both foreign object and foreign spirit.
9. No information.

419. Illness caused by loss of spiritual entity   p. 569

1. Not caused by loss of spiritual entity.
2. Soul-loss.
3. Loss of spirit helper.
4. Both soul-loss and loss of spirit helper.
9. No information.

420. Actions which cause soul-loss   p. 570

1. No soul-loss.
2. Loss by wandering of soul, usually on own volition.
3. Loss by fright.
4. Loss by theft, usually by a ghost or some other supernatural agent (not a sorcerer, or witch, or bad medicine man).
5. Loss by violation of an interdiction.
6. 2 and 3.
7. 2 and 4.
8. 2 and 5.
9. No information.
10. 3 and 4.
11. 4 and 5.
12. 2, 3, and 4.
13. 3, 4, and 5.
14. 2, 3, 4, and 5.

421. Causes of foreign spirit or object intrusion   p. 571

1. No foreign intrusions.
2. Intrusions caused by supernatural sources only, no human agents involved.
3. Intrusions caused by bad shamans, sorcerers, etc.
4. Intrusions caused both by supernatural agents and sorcerers, etc.
9. No information.

422. Agents who cause soul- or spirit-loss   p. 572

1. No soul-loss.
2. No human agents cause soul-loss.
3. Souls stolen by shamans, or sorcerers, or witches.
9. No information.

IX-D. Magic

423. White imitative magic used to bring good health, or kill animals, or insure good crops, or the like

1. No white imitative magic.
2. White imitative magic, such as shooting with arrows or poison darts, wooing through entreating, coaxing, or gesturing, or stabbing an animal effigy, or simulating crop growth, and so forth, is practiced.
9. No information.

424. Black imitative magic used to harm humans

1. No black imitative magic.
2. Black imitative magic used to harm humans.
9. No information.

425. Performers of imitative magic   p. 573

1. No one performed imitative magic.
2. Anyone could perform imitative magic.
3. Only specially qualified people such as shamans or

evil shamans (witches, sorcerers) could perform imitative magic.
9. No information.

426. **White contagious or formulaic magic for good purposes**

1. No white contagious or formulaic magic.
2. White contagious or formulaic magic used for good purposes.
9. No information.

427. **Black contagious or formulaic magic used to harm humans**

1. No black contagious or formulaic magic.
2. Black contagious or formulaic magic to harm humans.
9. No information.

428. **Performers of contagious or formulaic magic   p. 574**

1. No one performed contagious or formulaic magic.
2. Anyone could perform contagious or formulaic magic.
3. Only specifically qualified people such as shamans or evil shamans (sorcerers) could perform contagious or formulaic magic.
9. No information.

429. **Charms or magic to make persons reckless in gambling, or to make person successful in gambling**

p. 575
1. No gambling magic techniques or charms.
2. Gambling magic techniques but not charms.
3. Gambling charms but not magical techniques.
4. Both gambling magic techniques and charms.
9. No information.

430. **Charms or magical techniques to make persons receptive to love   p. 576**

1. No love magic techniques or charms.
2. Love magic techniques but not charms.
3. Love charms but not magic techniques.
4. Both love magic techniques and charms.
9. No information.

431. **Total number of 11 species of oaks available in tribal territory   p. 322**

1. 0.
2. 1–3.
3. 4–6.
4. 7–9.
5. 10–11.
9. No information,

432. **Total number of 5 species of pines available in tribal territory   p. 323**

1. 0.
2. 1
3. 2.
4. 3.
5. 4.
6. 5.
9. No information.

433. **Total number of 13 species of cactus, mescal, mesquite, and yucca available in tribal territory   p. 324**

1. 0.
2. 1–2.
3. 4–6.
4. 7–9.
5. 10–12.
6. 13.
9. No information.

434. **Total number of 12 species of grasses available in tribal territory   p. 325**

1. 0.
2. 1–2.
3. 3–4.
4. 5–6.
5. 7–8.
6. 9–10.
7. 11–12.
9. No information.

435. **Total number of 11 types of roots, lilies, nuts, and berries available in tribal territory   p. 326**

1. 0.
2. 1–2.
3. 3–4.
4. 5–6.
5. 7–8.
6. 9–10.
7. 11.
9. No information.

436. **Total number of herbs, roots, and tubers available**

1. 0.
2. 1–2.
3. 3–4.
4. 5–6.
5. 7–8.
6. 9–11.

437. **Total number of seeds, pods, beans, berries, and fruits available**

1. 0.
2. 1–4.
3. 5–8.
4. 9–13.
5. 14–18.
6. 19–23.
9. No information.

438. **Total number of nuts and leaves available**

1. 0.
2. 1–5.
3. 6–10.
4. 11–15.
5. 16–20.
6. 21–25.
9. No information.

439. Small land mammals available (rabbits, hares, gophers, beavers, rats)

1. 0.
2. 1.
3. 2.
4. 3.
5. 4.

440. Large land mammals available (nonherding or small-herd kinds, including moose, elk, deer, sheep, goats, antelopes, bear)

1. 0.
2. 1–2.
3. 3–4.
4. 5–6.
5. 7–8.

441. Large land mammals available (large herds including caribou and bison)

1. 0.
2. 1.
3. 2.

442. Total number of 8 species of saltwater fishes in tribal territory   p. 330

1. 0.
2. 1–2.
3. 3–4.
4. 5–6.
5. 7–8.
9. No information.

443. Total number of 4 species of freshwater fishes in tribal territory   p. 331

1. 0.
2. 1.
3. 2.
4. 3.
5. 4.
9. No information.

Appendix F

Tribal Names and Sample Numbers

TRIBAL NAMES	TRIBAL SAMPLE NUMBER	TRIBAL NAMES	TRIBAL SAMPLE NUMBER
Northern or Chilkat Tlingit	001	Tillamook Salish	028
Southern or *Xuts! Nuwu* Tlingit	002	Alsea	029
Northern or Massett Haida	003	Siuslaw	030
Southern or Skidegate Haida	004	Coos	031
Tsimshian	005	Tututni	032
Gitksan	006	Chetco	033
Haisla Kwakiutl	007	Galice Creek 1	034
Haihais or China Hat Kwakiutl	008	Tolowa	035
Bella Bella Kwakiutl	009	Yurok	036
Southern or Fort Rupert Kwakiutl	010	Karok	037
Bella Coola Salish	011	Hupa	038
Clayoquot Nootka	012	Wiyot	039
Makah Nootka	013	Sinkyone	040
Klahuse Salish	014	Mattole	041
Pentlatch Salish	015	Nongatl (Van Duzen)	042
Squamish Salish	016	Kato	043
Cowichan Salish	017	East Shasta	044
West Sanetch Salish	018	West Shasta	045
Upper Stalo or Upper Fraser Salish	019	Chimariko	046
Lower Fraser Salish	020	Trinity River Wintu	047
Lummi Salish	021	McCloud River Wintu	048
Klallam Salish	022	Sacramento River Wintu	049
Twana Hood Canal Salish	023	Nomlaki	050
Quinault Salish	024	East Achomawi	051
Puyallup-Nisqually Salish	025	West Achomawi	052
Quileute or Chemakuan	026	Atsugewi	053
Lower Chinook	027	Valley Maidu	054

TRIBAL NAMES	TRIBAL SAMPLE NUMBER	TRIBAL NAMES	TRIBAL SAMPLE NUMBER
Foothill Maidu	055	Shuswap	096
Mountain Maidu	056	Upper Lillooet	097
Foothill Nisenan	057	Upper Thompson	098
Mountain Nisenan	058	Southern or Sinkaietk Okanagon	099
Southern Nisenan	059	Sanpoil-Nespelem	100
Coast Yuki	060	Columbia	101
Yuki	061	Wenatchi	102
Yana	062	Coeur d'Alene	103
Northern Pomo	063	Kalispel	104
Eastern Pomo	064	Flathead	105
Southern Pomo	065	Kutenai	106
Wappo	066	Nez Percé	107
Patwin or Southern Wintu	067	Umatilla	108
Northern Miwok	068	Klikitat	109
Central Miwok	069	Wishram	110
Southern Miwok	070	Tenino	111
San Joaquin or Northern Western Mono	071	Klamath	112
Kings River or Southern-Western Western Mono	072	Modoc	113
Chukchansi or San Joaquin Yokuts	073	Wada-Dokado or Malheur Lake Northern Paiute	114
Kings River or Choinimni and Kocheyali Yokuts	074	Kiyui-Dokado or Surprise Valley Northern Paiute	115
Kaweah or Wukchamni Yokuts	075	Kuyui-Dokado or Truckee River and Pyramid Lake Northern Paiute	116
Lake or Tachi Yokuts	076		
Yauelmani or Southern Yokuts	077	Owens Valley Paiute or Eastern Mono Northern Paiute	117
Tubatulabal	078		
Kawaiisu	079	Panamint Shoshone	118
Salinan	080	Washo	119
Gabrieliño	081	Reese River Shoshone	120
Luiseño	082	Spring Valley Shoshone	121
Cupeño	083	Ruby Valley Shoshone	122
Serraño or Saboba	084	Battle Mountain Shoshone	123
Desert Cahuilla	085	Gosiute Shoshone	124
Pass Cahuilla	086	Bohogue or Fort Hall Shoshone	125
Mountain Cahuilla	087	Agaiduku or Lemhi Shoshone	126
Mountain Diegueño	088	Hukundika Shoshone	127
Western Diegueño	089	Wind River Shoshone	128
Desert Diegueño	090	Uintah or Tompanowots Ute	129
Kaliwa	091	Uncompaghre or Taviwatsiu and Mowataviwatsiu Ute	130
Akwa'ala	092		
Alkatcho or Skeena Drainage and Bulkley River Carrier	093	Wimonuch or Wimonuntsi, Wemenuis and Navajo Springs Ute	131
Lower or Fraser Drainage Carrier	094	Shivwits Southern Paiute	132
		Kaibab Southern Paiute	133
Chilcotin	095	San Juan Southern Paiute	134

TRIBAL NAMES	TRIBAL SAMPLE NUMBER	TRIBAL NAMES	TRIBAL SAMPLE NUMBER
Chemehuevi Southern Paiute	135	Mescalero Apache	154
Havasupai	136	Lipan Apache	155
Walapai	137	Jicarilla Apache	156
Northeast or Verde Valley Yavapai	138	Western Navajo	157
Southeast Yavapai	139	Eastern Navajo	158
Mohave	140	Hopi	159
Yuma	141	Zuni	160
Kamia	142	Acoma Western Keres	161
Cocopa	143	Sia Eastern Keres	162
Maricopa	144	Santa Ana Eastern Keres	163
Pima	145	Santa Domingo Eastern Keres	164
Papago	146	Cochiti Eastern Keres	165
North Tonto Western Apache	147	San Juan Tewa	166
South Tonto Western Apache	148	San Ildefonso Tewa	167
San Carlos Western Apache	149	Santa Clara Tewa	168
Cibecue Western Apache	150	Nambe Tewa	169
White Mountain Western Apache	151	Taos Tiwa	170
Warm Springs Chiricahua Apache	152	Isleta Tiwa	171
Huachuca Chiricahua Apache	153	Jemez Towa	172

General Bibliography

KEY TO ABBREVIATIONS

Journals and series frequently cited in the bibliography are abbreviated as shown below, following the format established in George P. Murdock's, *Ethnographic Bibliography of North America*, 1960, 3rd edition. Places in which these references are published are listed here rather than in the bibliography.

A   Anthropos. Mödling and Vienna, Austria.

AA   American Anthropologist. Washington, D.C., New York, N.Y., Lancaster, Penn., and Menasha, Wisc.

AAn   American Antiquity. Menasha, Wisc., and Salt Lake City, Utah.

ABC   Anthropology in British Columbia. Victoria, B.C.

ABCM   Anthropology in British Columbia: Memoirs. Victoria, B.C.

AE   American Ethnologist. Washington, D.C.

AI   American Indigena. Mexico City, Mexico.

AL   Anthropological Linguistics. Bloomington, Ind.

APAM   Anthropological Papers of the American Museum of Natural History. New York, N.Y.

APUA   Anthropological Papers of the University of Arizona. Tucson, Ariz.

APUU   Anthropological Papers of the University of Utah. Salt Lake City, Utah.

AR   Anthropological Records. Berkeley, Calif.

ARBAE   Annual Reports of the Bureau of American Ethnology. Washington, D.C.

ARSI   Annual Reports of the Board of Regents of the Smithsonian Institution. Washington, D.C.

BAMNH   Bulletin of the American Museum of Natural History. New York, N.Y.

BBAE   Bulletins of the Bureau of American Ethnology. Washington, D.C.

BPMCM   Bulletins of the Public Museum of the City of Milwaukee. Milwaukee, Wisc.

CA   Current Anthropology. Chicago, Ill.

CUAS   Catholic University of America Anthropological Series. Washington, D.C.

CUCA   Columbia University Contributions to Anthropology. New York, N.Y.

DJA   Davidson Journal of Anthropology. Seattle, Wash.

E   Ethnohistory. Bloomington, Ind.

EP   El Palacio. Santa Fe, N. Mex.

Ey   Ethnology. Pittsburgh, Penn.

GR   Geographical Review. New York, N.Y.

GSA   General Series in Anthropology. Menasha, Wisc.

IA   Ibero-Americana. Berkeley, Calif.

ICSL   International Conference on Salishan Languages. Seattle, Wash.; Victoria, B.C.; Vancouver, B.C.

IJAL   International Journal of American Linguistics. New York, N.Y., and Baltimore, Md.

IUPAL   Indiana University Publications in

Anthropology and Linguistics. Bloomington, Ind.

IUP-LSM   Indiana University Publications Language Science Monographs. Bloomington, Ind.

JAFL   Journal of American Folk-Lore. Boston, Mass., and New York, N.Y.

JAI   Journal of the (Royal) Anthropological Institute of Great Britain and Ireland. London, England.

Lg   Language. Baltimore, Md., and Menasha, Wisc.

M   Masterkey. Los Angeles, Calif.

MAAA   Memoirs of the American Anthropological Association. Menasha, Wisc.

MAES   Monographs of the American Ethnological Society. New York, N.Y.

MAFLS   Memoirs of the American Folk-Lore Society. Boston, Mass.

MAMNH   Memoirs of the American Museum of Natural History. New York, N.Y.

MIJL   Memoirs of the International Journal of American Linguistics. Bloomington, Ind.

MLA   Memoirs of the Laboratory of Anthropology. Santa Fe, N. Mex.

MNMNA   Museum Notes of the Museum of Northern Arizona. Flagstaff, Ariz.

MPR   Miscellanea Paul Rivet Octogenario Dicata. LXIV (2 vols., 1610 pp). 1958. Mexico City, Mexico.

MSAA   Memoirs of the Society for American Archaeology. Menasha, Wisc., and Salt Lake City, Utah.

NARN   Northwest Anthropological Research Notes. Moscow, Idaho.

NLAUN   Notebook of the Laboratory of Anthropology of the University of Nebraska. Lincoln, Neb.

NMA   New Mexico Anthropologist. Albuquerque, N. Mex.

P   Plateau. Flagstaff, Ariz.

PAA   Proceedings of the American Academy of Arts and Sciences. Boston, Mass.

PAES   Publications of the American Ethnological Society. New York, N.Y., Seattle, Wash.

PAPS   Proceedings of the American Philosophical Society. Philadelphia, Penn.

PHAPF   Publications of the Frederick Webb Hodge Anniversary Publication Fund, Southwest Museum. Los Angeles, Calif.

PMP   Peabody Museum Papers (Archeological and Ethnological Papers of the Peabody Museum, Harvard University). Cambridge, Mass.

PNQ   Pacific Northwest Quarterly. Seattle, Wash.

RUCAS   Reports of the University of California Archaeological Survey. Berkeley, Calif.

RUSMN   Reports of the United States National Museum. Washington, D.C.

SCA   Smithsonian Contributions to Anthropology. Washington, D.C.

SCK   Smithsonian (Institution) Contributions to Knowledge. Washington, D.C.

SJA   Southwestern Journal of Anthropology. Albuquerque, N. Mex.

SMC   Smithsonian (Institution) Miscellaneous Collections. Washington, D.C.

TAPS   Transactions of the American Philosophical Society. Philadelphia, Penn.

TCI   Transactions of the (Royal) Canadian Institute. Toronto, Ontario.

TNYAS   Transactions of the New York Academy of Sciences. New York, N.Y.

UCP   University of California Publications in American Archeology and Ethnology. Berkeley, Calif.

UCPG   University of California Publications in Geography. Berkeley, Calif.

UCPL   University of California Publications in Linguistics. Berkeley, Calif.

UNMB   University of New Mexico Bulletin, Anthropological Series. Albuquerque, N. Mex.

UNMBB   University of New Mexico Bulletin, Biological Series. Albuquerque, N. Mex.

UNMPA   University of New Mexico Publications in Anthropology. Albuquerque, N. Mex.

UOSA   University of Oregon Monographs. Studies in Anthropology. Eugene, Ore.

UTMMB   University of Texas Memorial Museum Bulletins. Austin, Tex.

UWPA   University of Washington Publications in Anthropology. Seattle, Wash.

VFPA   Viking Fund Publications in Anthropology. New York, N.Y.

YUPA   Yale University Publications in Anthropology. New Haven, Conn.

REFERENCES

Except for deletion of the names of cities in which journals and series are published and the addition of the full names of authors, the citations in this bibliography follow the style established by Murdock (1960).

Aberle, David F.
1961a Matrilineal Descent in Cross-Cultural Perspective.

In David Schneider and Kathleen Gough, eds., pp. 665–727.

1961b Navajo. *In* David Schneider and Kathleen Gough, eds., pp. 96–201.

Abrams, Leroy
1923–1960 *Illustrated Flora of the Pacific States.* 4 vols. Stanford University Press: Stanford, Calif.

Adams, John W.
1973 *The Gitksan Potlatch: Population Flux, Resource Ownership and Reciprocity.* Holt, Rinehart and Winston: Toronto.

Aginsky, Burt W.
1943 Central Sierra. *AR* **8**: 393–468.

Anastasio, Angelo
1972 The Southern Plateau: An Ecological Analysis of Intergroup Relations *NARN* **6**: 109–229.

Anderson, James
1925 *Trees and Shrubs: Food Medicinal, and Poisonous Plants of British Columbia.* Victoria Museum: Victoria, B.C.

Aoki, Haruo
1962 Nez Percé and Northern Sahaptin: A Binary Comparison. *IJAL* **28**: 172–182.
1966 Nez Percé and Proto-Sahaptin Kinship Terms. *IJAL* **32**: 357–368.
1975 The East Plateau Linguistic Diffusion Area. *IJAL* **41**: 183–199.

Aro, K. V., and M. P. Shepard
1967 Pacific Salmon in Canada. International North Pacific Fisheries Commission. *Bulletin 23:* 225–327. Victoria, B.C.

Bailey, Alfred M., and Robert J. Niedrach
1965 *Birds of Colorado.* Denver Museum of Natural History. 2 vols.: Denver, Colo.

Barbeau, Marius
1917 Parallels between the Northwest Coast and Iroquoian Clans and Phratries. *AA* **19**: 403–405.

Barnett, Homer G.
1937 Oregon Coast. *AR* **1**: 155–204.
1938 The Coast Salish of Canada. *AA* **40**: 118–141.
1939 Gulf of Georgia Salish. *AR* **1**: 221–295. Berkeley.
1955 The Coast Salish of British Columbia. *UOSA* **4**: 1–333.
1968 *The Nature and Function of the Potlatch.* [Originally published in 1938.] Department of Anthropology, University of Oregon: Eugene, Ore.

Barrett, Samuel A.
1910 The Material Culture of the Klamath Lake and Modoc Indians. *UCP* **5**: 239–60.
1917 The Washo Indians. *BPMCM* **2**: 1–52.
1952 Material Aspects of Pomo Culture. *BPMCM* **20**: 1–508.

Barrett, Samuel A., and Edward W. Gifford
1933 Miwok Material Culture. *BPMCM* **2**: 117–376.

Barrows, David P.
1900 *The Ethnobotany of the Coahuilla Indians of Southern California.* University of Chicago Press: Chicago.

[Reprinted in 1967 by Malki Museum Press: Banning, Calif.]

Basehart, Harry W.
1960 *Mescalero Apache Subsistence Patterns and Socio-Political Organization.* The University of New Mexico Mescalero-Chiricahua Land Claims Project (mimeograph). Albuquerque, N. Mex.
1967 The Resource Holding Corporation among the Mescalero Apache. *SJA* **23**: 277–291.
1970 Mescalero Apache Band Organization and Leadership. *SJA* **26**: 87–106.
1971 Mescalero Apache Band Organization and Leadership. *In* Basso and Opler, eds., pp. 35–49.

Basso, Keith H.
1969 Western Apache Witchcraft. *APUA* **15**: 1–75.
1970 *The Cibecue Apache.* Holt, Rinehart and Winston: New York.

Basso, Keith H., ed.
1971 *Western Apache Raiding and Warfare: From the Notes of Grenville Goodwin.* University of Arizona Press: Tucson, Ariz.

Basso, Keith H., and Morris E. Opler, eds.
1971 Apachean Culture History and Ethnology. *APUA* **21**: 1–168.

Baumhoff, Martin A.
1958 California Athabascan Groups. *AR* **16**: 157–237.
1963 Ecological Determinants of Aboriginal California Populations. *UCP* **49**: 155–236.

Baumhoff, Martin A., and David L. Olmsted
1963 Palaihniham: Radiocarbon Support for Glottochronology. *AA* **65**: 278–284.
1964 Notes on Palaihnihan Culture History: Glottochronology and Archaeology. *In* William Bright, ed., pp. 1–12.

Beaglehole, Ernest
1937 Notes on Hopi Economic Life. *YUPA* **15**: 1–88.

Beals, Ralph L.
1933 Ethnology of the Nisenan. *UCP* **31**: 335–410.

Bean, Lowell J.
1972 *Mukat's People: The Cahuilla Indians of Southern California.* University of California Press: Berkeley, Calif.

Bean, Lowell J., and Harry Lawton
1976 Some Explanations for the Rise of Cultural Complexity in Native California with Comments on Proto-Agriculture and Agriculture. *In* Lowell J. Bean and Thomas C. Blackburn, eds., pp. 19–48.

Bean, Lowell J., and Thomas C. Blackburn, eds.
1976 *Native Californians, A Theoretical Retrospective.* Ballena Press: Ramona, Calif.

Bee, Robert L.
1963 Changes in Yuman Social Organization. *Ey* **2**: 207–227.

Beeler, Madison S.
1961 Northern Costanoan. *IJAL* **27**: 191–197.
1970 Sibilant Harmony in Chumash. *IJAL* **36**: 14–17.

Behle, Wm. H.
1958   *The Bird of Life of Great Salt Lake*. University of Utah Press: Salt Lake City, Utah.

Bell, Willis H., and Edward F. Castetter
1937   The Utilization of Mesquite and Screwbean by the Aborigines in the American Southwest. *UNMBB* 5, No. 2.
1941   The Utilization of Yucca, Sotol, and Beargrass by the Aborigines in the American Southwest. *UNMBB* 5, No. 5

Benedict, Ruth
1924   A Brief Sketch of Serraño Culture. *AA* 26: 366–392.
1934   *Patterns of Culture*. Little, Brown: Boston.

Bergsland, Knut, and Hans Vogt
1962   On the Validity of Glottochronology. *CA* : 115–159.

Boas, Franz
1897   The Social Organization and Secret Societies of the Kwakiutl Indians. *RUSNM* 1895: 311–738.
1909   The Kwakiutl of Vancouver Island. *MAMNH* 8: 307–515.
1966   *Kwakiutl Ethnography*. Edited and abridged by Helen Codere. University of Chicago Press: Chicago.

Bowman, Isaiah
1911   *Forest Physiography*. (Life Zones from Plate I.) Wiley: New York.

Bright, Jane O., and William Bright
1965   Semantic Structures in Northwestern California and the Sapir-Whorf Hypothesis. *AA* 67(2): 249–258.

Bright, William, ed.
1964   Studies in California Linguistics. *UCPL* 34.

Bright, William, and Jane Hill
1967   Linguistic History of the Cupeño. *In* Dell Hymes and William Bittle, eds. pp. 351–371.

Broadbent, Silvia, and Catherine Callaghan
1960   Comparative Miwok: A Preliminary Study. IJAL 20: 301–316.

Brooks, Allan, and Harry S. Smith
1925   *A Distribution List of the Birds of British Columbia*. Cooper Ornithological Club: Berkeley, Calif.

Brown, Robert
1868   On the Vegetable Products Used by the Northwest American Indians as Food and Medicine. *Transactions of the Botanical Society of Edinburgh*, 9: 378–396. Edinburgh, Scotland.

Bryan, Kirk
1929   Floodwater Farming. *GR* 19: 444–456.

Bunzell, Ruth L.
1932   Introduction to Zuni Ceremonialism. *ARBAE* 47: 467–544.

Bye, Robert A., Jr.
1972   Ethnobotany of the Southern Paiute Indians in the 1870s: With a Note on the Early Ethnobotanical Contributions of Dr. Edward Palmer. *In* Don D. Fowler, ed., pp. 87–104.

Callaghan, Catherine A.
1962   Comparative Miwok-Mutsun with Notes on Rumsen. *IJAL* 28: 97–107.
1964   Phonemic Borrowing in Lake Miwok. *In* William Bright, ed., pp. 46–53.
1967   Miwok-Costanoan as a Subfamily of Penutian. *IJAL* 33: 224–227.

Canadian Department of Mines and Technical Surveys
1957   *Atlas of Canada*. Ottawa, Ontario.

Carneiro, Robert
1970   Scale Analysis, Evolutionary Sequences, and the Ratings of Cultures. *In* Raoul Naroll and Ronald Cohen, eds., pp. 834–871.

Castetter, Edward F.
1935   Uncultivated Native Plants Used as Sources of Food. *UNMBB* 4, No. 1.

Castetter, Edward F., and Willis H. Bell
1937   The Aboriginal Utilization of the Tall Cacti in the American Southwest. *UNMBB* 5, No. 1.
1942   *Pima and Papago Indian Agriculture*. Inter-American Studies, 1: 1–245. University of New Mexico Press: Albuquerque, N. Mex.
1951   *Yuman Indian Agriculture*. University of New Mexico Press: Albuquerque, N. Mex.

Castetter, Edward F., Willis H. Bell, and Alvin R. Grone
1938   The Early Utilization and the Distribution of Agave in the American Southwest. *UNMBB* 5, No. 4.

Castetter, Edward F., and Morris Opler
1936   The Ethnobiology of the Chiricahua and Mescalero Apache. *UNMBB* 4, No. 5.

Castetter, Edward F., and Ruth Underhill
1935   The Ethnobiology of the Papago Indians. *UNMBB* 4, No. 3.

Chamberlain, A. F.
1892   Report on the Kootenay Indians of South-Eastern British Columbia. *In* Report for The British Association for The Advancement of Science, pp. 549–624. London, England.

Clemens, W. A., and G. V. Wilby
1961   *Fishes of the Pacific Coast of Canada*. Fisheries Research Board of Canada: Victoria, B.C.

Clements, Forrest E.
1954   Use of Cluster Analysis with Anthropological Data. *AA* 56: 180–199.

Cline, Walter, *et al.*
1938   The Sinkaietk or Southern Okanagon of Washington. L. Spier, gen. ed., *GSA* 6: 1–262.

Codere, Helen
1950   Fighting With Property. *MAES* 18.

Colson, Elizabeth
1953   *The Makah Indians*. University of Minnesota Press: Minneapolis, Minn.
1974   *Autobiographies of Three Pomo Women*. Archaeological Research Facility, Department of Anthropology, University of California: Berkeley, Calif.

Cook, Sherburne F.
1956   The Aboriginal Population of the North Coast of California. *AR* **16**: 81–130.
1964   The Aboriginal Population of Upper California. *Actas y Memorias: XXXV International Congress of Americanists*; Mexico City, 1962, Vol. 2: 397–403.

Curtis, Edward S.
1926   The North American Indian 16: 65–248. Plimpton Press, Norwood, Mass. [Reprinted by Johnson Reprint, 1970.]

Cushing, Frank
1896   Outline of Zuni Creation Myths. *ARBAE* **13**: 321–447.

Davis, Irvine
1959   Linguistic Clues to Northern Rio Grande Prehistory. *EP* **66**: 73–84.

Davis, Ray J.
1952   *Flora of Idaho*. Brown: Dubuque, Iowa.

Davis, Wilbur A.
1966   Theoretical Problems in Western Prehistory. *In* Warren L. d'Azevedo, ed., pp. 147–166.

d'Azevedo, Warren, ed.
1966   *The Current Status of Anthropological Research in the Great Basin*. Desert Research Institute Technical Report Series S–H, No. 1: Reno, Nev.

de Josselin de Jong, P. E.
1967   The Participants' View of Their Culture. *In* Jongmans and Gutkind, eds., pp. 89–101.

den Hollander, A. N. J.
1967   Social Description: The Problem of Reliability and Validity. *In* Jongmans and Gutkind, eds., pp. 1–34.

Diamond, Stanley, ed.
1960   *Culture in History*. Columbia University Press: New York.

Diebold, A. Richard
1960   Determining the Centers of Dispersal of Language Groups. *IJAL* **26**: 1–10.

Dixon, Roland B.
1905   The Northern Maidu. *BAMNH* **17**: 119–346.
1907   The Shasta. *BAMNH* **17**: 381–498.
1910   The Chimariko Indians and Language. *UCP* **5**: 293–380.

Downs, James F.
1966   *The Two Worlds of the Washo*. Holt, Rinehart and Winston: New York.

Dozier, Edward P.
1954   The Hopi-Tewa of Arizona. *UCP* **44**: 259–376.
1966   Factionalism at Santa Clara Pueblo. *Ey* **15**: 172–185.
1970   *The Pueblo Indians of North America*. Holt, Rinehart and Winston: New York.

Driver, Harold E.
1936   Wappo Ethnography. *UCP* **36**: 179–220.
1937   Southern Sierra Nevada. *AR* **1**: 53–154.
1938   The Reliability of Culture Element Data. *AR* **1**: 205–209.

1939   Northwest California. *AR* **1**: 297–433.
1941   Girls' Puberty Rites in Western North America. *AR* **6**: 21–90.
1956   An Integration of Functional, Evolutionary, and Historical Theories by Means of Correlations. *IUPAL* **12**: 1–36.
1962   The Contribution of A. L. Kroeber to Culture Area Theory and Practice. *MIJL* **18**.
1966   Geographical-Historical vs. Psycho-Functional Explanations of Kin Avoidances. *CA* **7**: 131–182.

Driver, Harold E., and James L. Coffin
1975   Classification and Development of North American Indian Cultures: A Statistical Analysis of the Driver–Massey Sample. *TAPS* **65**(3): 1–120.

Driver, Harold E., William Cooper, Erich Kirchoff, William Massey, Dorothy Libby, and Robert Spier
1953   Indian Tribes of North America (map). *IUPAL* **9**.

Driver, Harold E., James A. Kennedy, Herschel C. Hudson, and Ora May Engle
1972   Statistical Classification of North American Indian Ethnic Units. *Ey* **11**: 311–39.

Driver, Harold E., and William C. Massey
1957   Comparative Studies of North American Indians. *TAPS* **47**(2): 165–456.

Driver, Harold E., and Karl F. Schuessler
1957   Factor Analysis of Ethnographic Data. *AA* **59**: 655–663.

Drucker, Philip
1936   A Karuk World-Renewal Ceremony at Panamiuk. *UCP* **35**: 23–28.
1937a   Southern California. *AR* **1**: 1–52.
1937b   The Tolowa and Their Southwest Oregon Kin. *UCP* **36**: 221–300.
1939   Contributions to Alsea Ethnography. *UCP* **35**: 81–102.
1940   Kwakiutl Dancing Societies. *AR* **2**: 201–30.
1941   Yuman-Piman. *AR* **6**: 91–230.
1950   Northwest Coast. *AR* **9**: 157–294.
1951   *The Northern and Central Nootkan Tribes*. *BBAE* **144**.
1965   *Cultures of the North Pacific Coast*. Chandler Press: San Francisco.

Drucker, Philip, and Robert F. Heizer
1967   *To Make My Name Good*. University of California Press: Berkeley, Calif.

Du Bois, Constance
1908   The Religion of the Luiseño Indians. *UCP* **8**: 70–174.

Du Bois, Cora
1932   Tolowa Notes. *AA* **34**: 248–262.
1935   Wintu Ethnography. *UCP* **36**: 1–148.
1936   The Wealth Concept as an Integrative Factor in Tolowa-Tututni Culture. *In* Julian Steward, ed., pp. 49–65.

Duff, Wilson
1951   Notes on Carrier Social Organization. *ABC* **2**: 28–34.
1952   The Upper Stalo Indians of the Fraser Valley. British Columbia. *ABCM* **1**: 1–136.

Dumarest, Noel
1919   Notes on Cochiti. *MAAA* **6**: 137–237.

Durkheim, Emile
1912   *The Elementary Forms of the Religious Life* (1965 edition). The Free Press: New York.

Dyen, Isidore
1962   The Lexicostatistically Determined Relationship of a Language Group. *IJAL* **28**: 153–161.
1963   Lexicostatistically Determined Borrowing and Taboo. *Lg* **39**: 60–66.
1973a   The Impact of Lexicostatistics on Comparative Linguistics. *In* Isidore Dyen, ed., pp. 75–84.

Dyen, Isidore, ed.
1973b   *Lexicostatistics in Genetic Linguistics.* Mouton and Co.: The Hague, Netherlands.

Dyen, Isidore, and David F. Aberle
1974   *Lexical Reconstruction: The Case of the Proto-Athapaskan Kinship System.* Cambridge University Press: New York.

Eggan, Fred
1950   *Social Organization of the Western Pueblos.* University of Chicago Press: Chicago.
1966   *The American Indian, Perspectives for the Study of Social Change.* Aldine Publishing Company: Chicago.

Eggan, Fred, ed.
1937   *Social Anthropology of North American Tribes.* University of Chicago Press: Chicago.

Ellis, Florence Hawley
1964   A Reconstruction of the Basic Jemez Pattern of Social Organization, with Comparisons to other Tanoan Social Structures. *UNMPA* **11**: 1–69.

Elmendorf, W. E.
1948   The Cultural Setting of the Twana Secret Society. *AA* **50**: 625–630.
1951   World Taboo and Lexical Change in Coast Salish. *IJAL* **17**: 205–208.
1960   The Structure of Twana Culture with Comparative Notes on the Structure of Yurok Culture. *Research Studies of Washington State University.* Vol. 28, No. 3 Pullman, Wash.
1961   System Change in Salish Kinship Terminologies. *SJA* **17**: 365–382.
1962a   Lexical Innovation and Persistence in Four Salish Dialects. *IJAL* **28**: 85–96.
1962b   Lexical Relation Models as a Possible Check on Lexicostatistic Inferences. *AA* **64**: 760–770.
1963   Yukian-Siouan Lexical Similarities. *IJAL* **29**: 300–309.
1964   Item and Set Comparisons in Yuchi, Siouan and Yukian. *IJAL* **30**: 328–340.
1965   Review of A. L. Kroeber's Yokuts Dialect Survey (1963). *AA* **67**: 1017–1018.
1968   Lexical and Cultural Change in Yukian. *AL* **10**(7): 1–41.
1969   Geographical Ordering, Subgrouping and Olympic Salish. *IJAL* **35**: 220–225.
1976   Personal Communication (letter) re: Northwest Coast and Plateau Languages and Cultures. November 20.

Elsasser, Albert B., and Robert F. Heizer
1966   Excavation of Two Northwestern California Coastal Sites. *RUCAS* **67**.

Essene, Frank
1942   Round Valley. *AR* **8**: 1–97.

Euler, Robert C.
1954   Notes on Land Tenure at Isleta Pueblo. *EP* **61**: 368–373.
1966   Southern Paiute Ethnohistory. *APUU* **78**: 1–139.

Ezell, Frank
1961   Hispanic Acculturation of Gila River Pima. *MAAA* **90**: 1–171.

Fairbanks, Gordon H.
1955   A Note on Glottochronology. *IJAL* **21**: 116–120.

Fathauer, George H.
1954   The Structure and Causation of Mohave Warfare. *SJA* **10**: 97–118.

Fenton, William N.
1957   Factionalism at Taos Pueblo, New Mexico. *BBAE* **154**: 297–344.

Fontana, Bernard, William J. Robinson, Charles W. Cormack, and Ernest E. Leavitt, Jr.
1962   *Papago Indian Pottery.* University of Washington Press: Seattle.

Ford, Clellan S.
1941   *Smoke From Their Fires.* Yale University Press: New Haven

Ford, Richard I.
1972   An Ecological Perspective on the Eastern Pueblos. *In* Alfonso Ortiz, ed., pp. 1–17.

Ford, Richard, Albert H. Schroeder, and Stewart L. Peckham
1972   Three Perspectives on Puebloan Prehistory. *In* Alfonso Ortiz, ed., pp. 19–40.

Forde, C. Daryll
1931   Ethnography of the Yuma Indians. *UCP* **28**: 83–278.

Foster, George M.
1944   A Summary of Yuki Culture. *AR* **5**: 155–244.

Fowler, Don D., ed.
1972   *Great Basin Cultural Ecology: A Symposium.* Desert Research Institute Publications in the Social Sciences, No. 8. University of Nevada: Reno, Nev.

Fowler, Don D., and Catherine S. Fowler, eds.
1971   Anthropology of the Numa: John Wesley Powell's Manuscripts on the Numic Peoples of Western North America, 1868–1880. *SCA* **14**.

Fox, Robin
1967   *The Keresan Bridge.* London School of Economics Monographs on Social Anthropology, No. 35. London.

Frachtenberg, Leo J.
1921   The Ceremonial Societies of the Quileute Indians. *AA* **23**: 320–352.

Frazier, Sir James
1922 *The Golden Bough* (abridged). Macmillan: New York.

Freed, Stanley A.
1963 A Reconstruction of Aboriginal Washo Social Organization. *APUU* 67: 8–24.

Freilich, Morris, ed.
1970 *Marginal Natives: Anthropologists at Work.* Harper and Row: New York.

French, David
1961 Wasco-Wishram. *In* E. Spicer, ed., pp. 337–429.

Garfield, Viola E.
1939 Tsimshian Clan and Society. *UWPA* 7: 167–349.
1947 Historical Aspects of Tlingit Clans in Angoo, Alaska. *AA* **49**: 438–452.

Garfield, Viola, and Paul S. Wingert.
1950 The Tsimshian Indians and Their Arts. *PAE* **18**: 96 pp.

Garth, Thomas R.
1944 Kinship Terminology, Marriage Practices and Behavior Toward Kin among the Atsugewi. *AA* **46**: 348–362.
1953 Atsugewi Ethnography. *AR* **14**: 123–212.

Gayton, Ann H.
1930 Yokuts-Mono Chiefs and Shamans. *UCP* **24**: 361–420.
1945 Yokuts and Western Mono Social Organization. *AA* **47**: 409–426.
1946 Culture-Environment Integration. *SJA* **2**: 252–268.
1948a Yokuts and Western Mono Ethnography. Tulare Lake, Southern Valley, and Central Foothill Yokuts. *AR* **10**: 1–143.
1948b Yokuts and Western Mono Ethnography. Northern Foothill Yokuts and Western Mono. *AR* **10**: 143–301.

Gifford, Edward W.
1916 Dichotomous Social Organization in South Central California. *UCP* **11**: 291–296.
1918 Clans and Moieties in Southern California. *UCP* **14**: 167–174.
1922 California Kinship Terminologies. *UCP* **18**: 1–285.
1923 Pomo Lands on Clear Lake. *UCP* **20**: 77–92.
1926a Clear Lake Pomo Society. *UCP* **18**: 287–390.
1926b Miwok Cults. *UCP* **18**: 391–408.
1926c Miwok Lineages and the Political Units in Aboriginal California. *AA* **28**: 389–401.
1927 Southern Maidu Religious Ceremonies. *AA* **29**: 214–257.
1931 The Kamia of Imperial Valley. *BBAE* 97: 1–88.
1932a The Northfork Mono. *UCP* **31**: 15–65.
1932b The Southeastern Yavapai. *UCP* **29**: 177–252.
1933 The Cocopa. *UCP* **31**: 257–334.
1936 Northeastern and Western Yavapai. *UCP* **34**: 247–354.
1936 California Balanophagy. *In* Julian Steward, ed., pp. 87–98.
1939 The Coast Yuki. *A* **34**: 292–375.
1940 Apache-Pueblo. *AR* **4**: 1–207.

1944 Miwok Lineages. *AA* **46**: 376–381.
1955 Central Miwok Ceremonies. *AR* **14**: 261–318.

Gifford, Edward W., and Stanislaw Klimek
1936 Yana. *UCP* **37**: 71–100.

Gifford, Edward W., and A. L. Kroeber
1937 Pomo. *UCP* **37**: 117–254.

Gifford, Edward W., and Robert H. Lowie
1928 Notes on the Akwa'ala Indians. *UCP* **23**: 339–352.

Goddard, Pliny E.
1902 Life and Culture of the Hupa. *UCP* **1**: 1–88.

Goldfrank, Esther S.
1927 The Social and Ceremonial Organization of Cochiti. *MAAA* **33**: 1–129.

Goldman, Irving
1937a The Kwakiutl Indians of Vancouver Island. *In* Margaret Mead, ed., pp. 180–209.
1937b The Zuni Indians of New Mexico. *In* Margaret Mead, ed., pp. 313–353.
1940 The Alkatcho Carrier of British Columbia. *In* Ralph Linton, ed., pp. 333–389.
1941 The Alkatcho Carrier: Historical Background of Crest Prerogatives. *AA* **43**: 396–418.

Goldschmidt, Walker
1951 Nomalki Ethnography. *UCP* **42**: 303–443.

Goldschmidt, Walter R., and Harold E. Driver
1940 The Hupa White Deerskin Dance. *UCP* **35**: 103–42.

Golla, V. K.
1964 Comparative Yokuts Phonology. *In* William Bright, ed.

Goodman, Leo A., and William H. Kruskal
1954 Measures of Association for Cross Classification. *Journal of the American Statistical Association* **49**: 732–764.

Goodwin, Grenville
1935 Social Divisions and Economic Life of the Western Apache. *AA* **37**: 55–64.
1937 The Characteristics and Function of Clan in a Southern Athapascan Culture. *AA* **39**: 394–407.
1942 *The Social Organization of the Western Apache.* University of Chicago Press: Chicago.
1971 *Western Apache Raiding and Warfare.* Keith H. Basso, ed. University of Arizona Press: Tucson, Ariz.

Goss, James A.
1965 Ute Linguistics and Anasazi Abandonment of the Four Corners Area. *MSAA* **31**: 73–81.
1966 Internal Diversity in Southern Numic. *In* Warren d'Azevedo, ed., pp. 265–272.
1968 Cultural-Historical Inference from Utaztekan Linguistic Evidence. *Occasional Papers of the Idaho State Museum* **22**: 1–42. Pocatello, Idaho.

Gould, Richard A.
1976 Ecology and Adaptive Responses Among the Tolowa Indians of Northwestern California. *In* Lowell J. Bean and Thomas C. Blackburn, eds., pp. 49–78.

Grant, Blanche C.
1925 *Taos Indians.* Taos.

Griffin, P. Bion, Mark P. Leone, and Keith H. Basso
1971   Western Apache Ecology: From Horticulture to Agriculture. *In* Keith H. Basso and Morris E. Opler, eds., pp. 69–76.

Grinnell, Joseph, and Alden H. Miller
1944   *The Distribution of the Birds of California.* Cooper Ornithological Club: Berkeley, Calif.

Gunnerson, James, and Dolores Gunnerson
1971   Apachean Culture: A Study in Unity and Diversity. *In* Keith H. Basso and Morris E. Opler, eds., pp. 7–27.

Gunther, Erna
1927   Klallam Ethnography. *UWPA* 1: 171–314.
1945   Ethnobotany of Western Washington. *UWPA* **10**: 1–62.
1972   *Indian Life on the Northwest Coast of North America, as Seen by the Early Explorers and Fur Traders during the Last Decades of the Eighteenth Century.* University of Chicago Press: Chicago.

Guttman, L.
1968   A General Nonmetric Technique for Finding the Smallest Coordinate Space for a Configuration of Points. *Psychometrika* **33**: 469–506.

Haas, Mary R.
1966   Wiyot-Yurok-Algonkin and Problems of Comparative Algokian. *IJAL* **32**: 101–107.
1969   Internal Reconstruction of Nootka-Nitinat Pronominal Suffixes. *IJAL* **35**: 108–124.
1970   Consonant Symbolism in Northwestern California: A Problem in Diffusion. *In* Earl H. Swanson, ed., pp. 86–96.

Haeberlin, H., and E. Gunther
1930   The Indians of Puget Sound. *UWPA* **4**.

Haile, Berard
1954   Property Concepts of the Navajo Indians. *CUAS* **17**: 1–64.

Haines, Francis
1955   *The Nez Percés.* University of Oklahoma Press: Norman, Okla.

Hale, Kenneth
1958   Internal Diversity in Uto-Aztecan: I. *IJAL* **24**: 101–107.
1959   Internal Diversity of Uto-Aztecan: II. *IJAL* **25**: 114–121.
1962   Jemez and Kiowa Correspondences in Reference to Kiowa-Tanoan. *IJAL* **28**: 1–5.
1967   Toward a Reconstruction of Kiowa-Tanoan Phonology. *IJAL* **33**: 112–120.

Hall, Eugene Raymond, and Keith R. Kelson.
1959   *Mammals of North America.* Ronald Press: New York.

Halpern, A. M.
1964   A Report on a Survey of the Pomo Languages. *In* William Bright, ed., pp. 88–93.

Halseath, Odd S.
1924   Report of Economic and Social Survey of the Keres Pueblo of Sia. *EP* **16**: 67–75.

Hamp, Eric P.
1970   Wiyot and Yurok Correspondences. *In* Earl H. Swanson, Jr., ed., pp. 107–112.

Harrington, H. D.
1954   *Manual of the Plants of Colorado.* Sage Books: Denver, Colo.

Harrington, John P.
1912   Tewa Relationship Terms. *AA* **14**: 472–498.
1916   The Ethnography of the Tewa Indians. *ARBAE* **29**: 29–618.
1942   Central California Coast. *AR* **7**: 1–46.

Harrington, M. R.
1955   Ancient Life among the Southern California Indians. *M* **29**: 79–88, 117–129, 153–167.

Harris, J. S.
1940   The White Knife Shoshoni of Nevada. *In* Ralph Linton, ed., pp. 39–118.

Harris, Marvin
1978   Cannibals and Kings. Macmillan: New York.

Hawley, Florence M.
1937   Pueblo Social Organization as a Lead to Pueblo History. *AA* **39**: 504–523.
1950   Keresan Patterns of Kinship and Social Organization. *AA* **52**: 499–512.

Heizer, Robert F.
1971   The Western Coast of North America. *In* Robert F. Heizer and M. A. Whipple, eds., pp. 131–143.

Heizer, Robert F., ed.
1966   *Aboriginal California. Three Studies in Culture History.* University of California Archeological Research Facility: Berkeley, Calif.

Heizer, Robert F., and M. A. Whipple, eds.
1971   *The California Indians. A Source book.* University of California Press: Berkeley, Calif.

Helm, June, ed.
1968   Essays on the Problem of the Tribe. *PAES* Spring Meeting 1966, Seattle.

Hieb, Louis A.
1972   Meaning and Mismeaning: Toward an Understanding of the Ritual Clown. *In* Alfonso Ortiz, ed., pp. 163–196.

Hill, Jane H., and Kenneth C. Hill
1968   Stress in the Cupan (Uto-Aztecan) Languages. *IJAL* **34**: 232–241.

Hill, Willard W.
1936   Notes on Pima Land Law and Tenure. *AA* **38**: 586–589.
1938   The Agricultural and Hunting Methods of the Navajo Indians. *YUPA* **18**: 1–194.

Hill-Tout, Charles
1902   Ethnological Studies of the Mainland Halkomelem. *British Association of Advanced Science* **72**: 355–490. London.
1907   *British North America, 1: The Far West, The Home of the Salish and Dene.* Archibald Constable: London.

Hobson, Richard
1954   Navajo Acquisitive Values. *PMP* **42**(3): 1–45.

Hoebel, E. Adamson
 1935   The Sun Dance of the Hekandika Shoshone. *AA* **37**: 570–581.
 1939   Comanche and Hekandika Shoshone Relationship Systems. *AA* **41**: 440–457.

Hoijer, Harry
 1956a The Chronology of the Athapaskan Languages. *IJAL* **22**: 219–232.
 1956b Lexicostatistics: a Critique. *Lg* **32**: 49–60.
 1960   Athapaskan Language of the Pacific Coast. Stanley Diamond, ed., pp. 960–976.
 1962   Linguistic Subgrouping by Glottochronology and by the Comparative Method. *Lingua* **II**: 192–198.
 1963   The Athapaskan Languages. *UCPL* **29**: 1–29.
 1971   The Positions of the Apachean Languages in the Athapaskan Stock. *In* Keith Basso and Morris E. Opler, eds., pp. 3–6.

Holt, Catherine
 1946   Shasta Ethnography. *AR* **3**: 299–349.

Hooper, Lucille
 1920   The Cahuilla Indians. *UCP* **16**: 315–380.

Hulten, Eric
 1968   *Flora of Alaska and Neighboring Territories.* Stanford University Press: Stanford, Calif.

Hymes, Dell
 1957   A Note on Athapaskan Glottochronology. *IJAL* **23**: 291–296.
 1966   Some Points of Siuslaw Phonology. *IJAL* **32**: 328–342.

Hymes, Dell, and William Bittle, eds.
 1967   *Studies in Southwestern Ethnolinguistics.* Mouton and Co.: The Hague, Netherlands.

Inglis, Gordon B.
 1970   Northwest American Matriliny: The Problem of Origins. *Ey* **9**: 149–159.

Jacobs, Melville
 1937   Historic Perspective in Indian Languages of Oregon and Washington. *PNQ* **28**: 55–74.
 1939   Coos Narrative and Ethnologic Texts. *UWPA* **8**: 1–125.
 1954   The Areal Spread of Sound Features in the Language of Northwest California. *UCPL* **10**: 46–56.

Jacobsen, William H., Jr.
 1966   Washo Linguistic Studies. *In* Warren d'Azevedo, ed., pp. 113–136.
 1969   Origin of Nootka Pharyngeals. *IJAL* **35**: 125–153.

James, Harry C.
 1960   *The Cahuilla Indians.* Westernlore Press: Los Angeles.

Jenness, Diamond
 1943   The Carrier Indians of the Bulkley River: Their Social and Religious Life. *BBAE* **133**: 469–587.
 1955   The Faith of a Coast Salish Indian. *ABCM* **3**: 1–92.

Jennings, Jesse D.
 1974   *Prehistory of North America.* Second Edition. McGraw-Hill, Inc.: New York.

Jepson, Willis L.
 1925   *A Manual of Flowering Plants of California.* Independent Press Room and Williams: San Francisco.

Jewett, Stanley G., Walter P. Taylor, Wm. T. Shaw, and John W. Aldrich
 1953   *Birds of Washington State.* University of Washington Press: Seattle.

Johnston, Bernice Eastman
 1964   *California's Gabrieliño Indians.* Southwest Museum: Los Angeles.

Johnston, B. J.
 1955–1956   The Gabrieliño Indians of Southern California. *M* **29** and **30**.

Jones, Livingston F.
 1914   *A Study of the Thlingets of Alaska.* New York.

Jongmans, D. G., and P. C. W. Gutkind, eds.
 1967   *Anthropologists in the Field.* Van Gorcum and Co.: Assen, Netherlands.

Jorgensen, Joseph G.
 1964   *The Ethnohistory and Acculturation of the Northern Ute.* Ph.D. Dissertation. Indiana University. Bloomington.
 1966   Geographical Clusterings and Functional Explanations of In-Law Avoidances: An Analysis of Comparative Methods. *CA* **7**: 161–169.
 1969   Salish Language and Culture: A Statistical Analysis of Internal Relationship, History and Evolution. *IUP-LSM* **3**: 173 pp.
 1972   *The Sun Dance Religion.* University of Chicago Press: Chicago.
 1974   On Continuous Area and World-Wide Studies in Formal Comparative Ethnology. *In* Joseph G. Jorgensen, ed., pp. 195–204.
 n.d.   Comparative Traditional Economics and Ecological Adaptations. To appear In *Handbook of North American Indians,* William Sturtevant, General Editor; Alfonso Ortiz, Series Editor, The Southwest.

Jorgensen, Joseph G., ed.
 1974   *Comparative Studies by Harold E. Driver and Essays in His Honor.* Human Relations Area Files Press: New Haven, Conn.

Joseph, A., R. Spicer, and J. Chesky
 1949   *The Desert People.* University of Chicago Press: Chicago.

Kaut, Charles R.
 1957   The Western Apache Clan System. *UNMPA* **9**: 1–99.
 1966   Western Apache Clan and Phratry Organization. *AA* **58**: 140–147.
 1974   The Clan System as an Epiphenomenal Element of Western Apache Social Organization. *Ey* **13**: 45–70.

Kearney, Thomas H., and Robert H. Peebles
 1960   *Arizona Flora.* University of California Press: Berkeley, Calif.

Kelly, Isabel T.
 1932   Ethnography of the Surprise Valley Paiute. *UCP* **31**: 67–210.

1934 Southern Paiute Bands. *AA* **36**: 548–560.
1938 Band Organization of the Southern Paiute. *AA* **40**: 633–634.
1939 Southern Paiute Shamanism. *AR* **2**: 151–167.
1964 Southern Paiute Ethnography. *APUU* **69**: 194 pp.

Kelly, W. H.
1942 Cocopa Gentes. *AA* **44**: 675–691.

King, Chester
1976 Chumash Inter-Village Economic Exchange. *In* Lowell J. Bean and Thomas C. Blackburn, eds., pp. 289–319.

Kinkade, Dale, and Clarence D. Sloat
1969 Proto-Interior Salish Vowels. Paper presented at 4th *ICSL*, Victoria, B.C.

Klimek, Stanislaw
1935 The Structure of California Indian Culture. *UCP* **37**: 1–70.

Kluckholn, Clyde, and Dorothea Leighton
1946 *The Navajo.* Harvard University Press: Cambridge, Mass.

Kniffen, Fred B.
1928 Achomawi Geography. *UCP* **23**: 297–332.
1939 Pomo Geography. *UCP* **26**: 353–400.

Köbben, A. J. F.
1967a Participation and Quantification: Field Work among the Djuka (Bush Negroes of Surinam). *In* Jongmans and Gutkind, eds., pp. 35–55.
1967b Why Exceptions? The Logic of Cross-Cultural Analysis *CA* **8**: 3–34.

Koppert, Vincent A.
1930 Contributions to Clayoquot Ethnology. *CUAS* **1**: 1–124.

Krause, Aurel
1956 *The Tlingit Indians,* translated by Erna Gunther. University of Washington Press: Seattle.

Krauss, Michael
1973 Na-Dene. *In* Thomas A. Sebeok, ed. Mouton and Co.: The Hague, Netherlands.

Kroeber, Alfred L.
1908a Ethnography of the Cahuilla Indians. *UCP* **8**: 29–68.
1908b Notes on the Luiseños. *UCP* **8**: 174–187.
1917 Zuni Kin and Clan. *APAM* **18**: 39–204.
1920 Yuman Tribes of the Lower Colorado. *UCP* **16**: 475–491.
1925 *Handbook of the Indians of California. BBAE* **78**.
1929 The Valley Nisenan. *UCP* **24**: 253–290.
1932 The Patwin and Their Neighbors. *UCP* **29**: 253–364.
1935 Walapai Ethnography. *MAAA* **42**: 1–293.
1939 *Cultural and Natural Areas of Native North America. UCP* **38**: 1–242.
1945 A Yurok War Reminiscence. *SJA* **1**: 318–332.
1955 Linguistic Time Depths So Far and Their Meaning. *IJAL* **21**: 91–104.
1959a Possible Athapascan Influences on Yuki. *IJAL* **25**: 59.

1959b Reflections on Athapaskan Glottochronology. *UCP* **47**: 241–258.
1963 Yokuts Dialect Survey. *AR* **11**: 177–251.
1966 The Nature of Land-Holding Groups in Aboriginal California. *In* Robert F. Heizer, ed., pp. 81–120.

Kroeber, Alfred L., and Samuel A. Barrett
1960 Fishing among the Indians of Northwestern California. *AR* **21**: 1–210.

Kroeber, Alfred L., and Edward W. Gifford
1949 World Renewal: A Cult System of Native California. *AR* **13**: 1–155.

Kroeber, Alfred L., and George W. Grace
1960 The Sparkman Grammar of Luiseño. *UCPL* **16**.

Kuchler, A. W.
1964 Potential Natural Vegetation of the Coterminus United States. (Most detailed and largest map, 3×5 feet.) Special Publication No. 36. American Geographical Society: New York.

Kuipers, Aert H.
1967a On Divergence, Interaction and Merging of Salish Language Communities. Paper presented at 2nd *ICSL*, Seattle, Wash.
1967b *The Squamish Language.* Janua Linguarum Series Practica 73. Part 1. Mouton and Co.: The Hague, Netherlands.
1969a *The Squamish Language: Grammar, Texts Dictionary.* Janua Linguarum Series Practica 73. Part 2. Mouton and Co.: The Hague, Netherlands.
1969b Towards a Salish Etymological Dictionary. Paper presented at 4th *ICSL*, Victoria, B.C.

Kurath, Gertrude P.
1970 *Music and Dance of the Tewa Pueblos.* Museum of New Mexico Research Records, No. 8. Santa Fe, N. Mex.

Laguna, Frederica de
1960 The Story of a Tlingit Community. *BBAE* **172**.

Lamb, Sydney
1958 Linguistic Prehistory in the Great Basin. *IJAL* **24**: 95–100.
1964 The Classification of the Uto-Aztecan Languages. *In* William Bright, ed., pp. 106–125.

Lamphere, Louise
1969 Symbolic Elements in Navajo Ritual. *SJA* **25**: 279–305.

Landberg, Leif C. W.
The Chumash Indians of Southern California. Southwest Museum papers **19**. 158 pp. Los Angeles.

Langdon, Margaret
1970 A Grammar of Diegueño: The Mesa Grande Dialect. *UCPL* **66**.

Langdon, Margaret, ed.
1973 *Papers from the Conference on Hokan Languages.* Janua Linguarum. Mouton and Co.: The Hague, Netherlands.

Lange, Charles H.
1959 *Cochiti.* University of Texas Press: Austin, Tex.

Laski, Vera
1959   Seeking Life. *MAFLS*, No. 50.

Latta, F. F.
1949   *Handbook of Yokuts Indians*. Kern County Museum: Oildale, Calif.

Leach, Edmund, ed.
1967   *The Structural Study of Myth and Totemism*. Lairstock: London.

Leacock, Eleanor, and Nancy O. Lurie, eds.
1971   *North American Indians in Historical Perspective*. Random House: New York.

Lees, Robert B.
1953   The Basis of Glottochronology. *Lg* **29**: 113–127.

Leonhardy, Frank C., and David G. Rice
1970   A Proposed Culture Typology for the Lower Snake River Region, Southeastern Washington. *NARN* **4**: 1–29.

Lessa, William, and Evon Vogt, eds.
1972   *Reader in Comparative Religion*. Third Edition. Harper and Row: New York.

Levine, Robert
1976   Haida-Tlingit Relations. Paper presented at 2nd *ICSL*, Seattle, Wash.

Levi-Strauss, Claude
1967   The Story of Asdiwal. *In* Edmund Leach, ed., pp. 1–47.

Ligon, J. Stokley
1961   *New Mexico Birds and Where to Find Them*. University of New Mexico Press: Albuquerque, N. Mex.

Lingoes, J. C.
1965   An IBM-7090 Program for Guttman–Lingoes Smallest Space Analysis: I. *Behavioral Science* **10**: 183–184.
1968   The Multivariate Analysis of Qualitative Data. *Multivariate Behavior Research* **3**: 61–94.
1971   Some Boundary Conditions for a Monotone Analysis of Symmetric Matrices. *Psychometrika* **36**: 195–203.

Lingoes, J. C., and Roskam, E.
1971   A Mathematical and Empirical Study of Two Multidimensional Scaling Algorithms. *Michigan Mathematical Psychology Program, MMPP* **1**: 1–169. Ann Arbor, Mich.

Linsdale, Jean M.
1936   *The Birds of Nevada*. Cooper Ornithological Club: Berkeley, Calif.

Linton, Ralph, ed.
1940   *Acculturation in Seven American Indian Tribes*. Appleton-Century: New York.

Little, Elbert L., Jr.
1971   *Atlas of United States Trees*. Miscellaneous Publication No. 1146, United States Department of Agriculture: Washington, D.C.

Loeb, Edwin M.
1926   Pomo Folkways. *UCP* **19**: 149–405.

1932   The Western Kuksu Cult. *UCP* **33**: 1–138.
1933   The Eastern Kuksu Cult. *UCP* **33**: 139–232.

Longacre, William A., ed.
1970   *Reconstructing Historic Pueblo Societies*. A School of American Research Book. University of New Mexico Press: Albuquerque, N. Mex.

Lopatin, Ivan Alexis
1945   Social Life and Religion of the Indians in Kitimat, British Columbia. *University of Southern California Social Science Series* **26**: 1–118. Los Angeles.

Loud, Llewellyn
1918   Ethnography and Archeology of the Wiyot Territory. *UCP* **14**: 221–436.

Lowie, Robert H.
1908   The Northern Shoshone. *APAM* **2**: 169–306.
1924   Notes on Shoshonean Ethnography. *APAM* **20**: 185–314.
1939   Ethnographic Notes on the Washo. *UCP* **36**: 301–352.

McClellan, Catherine
n.d.   Personal communication (letter) to David F. Aberle re: Tlingit-Tagish relations. Letter in possession of Aberle.

McIllwraith, Thomas F.
1948   *The Bella Coola Indians*. 2 vols. University of Toronto Press: Toronto, Ontario.

McKern, Will Carleton
1922   Functional Families of the Patwin. *UCP* **13**: 235–258.

McNett, Charles W., Jr.
1968   A Suggested Method of Drawing Random Samples in Cross-Cultural Surveys. *AA* **70**: 50–55.

Manners, Robert A.
1959   Habitat, Technology, and Social Organization of the Southern Paiute. *AI* **19**: 179–197.

Mason, John A.
1912   The Ethnology of the Salinan Indians. *UCP* **10**: 97–240.

Marsh, Gordon
n.d.   Personal communication (letter) to David F. Aberle re: Tagish language. Letter in possession of F. Aberle.

Mason, Otis T.
1896   Influence of Environment upon Human Industries or Arts. *ARSI* **1895**: 639–665.

Mead, Margaret, ed.
1937   *Cooperation and Competition among Primitive Peoples*. New York.

Meigs, Peveril
1939   The Kiliwa Indians of Lower California. *IA* **15**: 1–114.

Miller, Wick R.
1963   Proto-Keresan. *IJAL* **29**: 310–330.
1965   Acoma Grammar and Texts. *UCPL* **40**: 259 pp.
1966   Anthropological Linguistics in the Great Basin. *In* d'Azevedo, ed., pp. 17–36.

1970   Western Shoshoni Dialects. *In* Earl H. Swanson, J. ed., pp. 17–36.

Miller, Wick, James L. Tanner, and Laurence P. Foley
1971   A Lexicostatistic study of Shoshone Dialects. *AL* **13**(4): 142–164. Bloomington.

Mitchell, Donald H.
1971   Archeology of the Gulf of Georgia Area: A Natural Region and Its Cultural Types. *Syesis* **4**: 228 pp. British Columbia Provincial Museum, Victoria B.C.

Morice, Adrien Gabriel
1893   Notes Archeological, Industrial, and Sociological on the Western Denes. *TCI* **4**: 1–222.

Moziño, Jose Mariano
1970   Noticas de Nutka: An Account of Nootka Sound in 1792. Translated and edited by I. H. Wilson. *PAES* **50**: 150 pp.

Murdock, George P.
1934a   Kinship and Social Behavior among the Haida. *AA* **36**: 355–385.
1934b   *Our Primitive Contemporaries.* Macmillan: New York.
1936   Rank and Potlatch Among the Haida. *YUPA* **13**: 1–20.
1938   Notes on the Tenino, Molala, and Paiute of Oregon. *AA* **40**: 395–402.
1949   *Social Structure.* Macmillan: New York, N.Y.
1955   North American Social Organization. *DJA* **1**: 85–95.
1958   Social Organization of the Tenino. *MPR* **1**: 299–315.
1960   *Ethnographic Bibliography of North America.* 3rd edition. Human Relations Area Files Press: New Haven, Conn.
1965   Tenino Shamanism. *Ey* **4**: 165–171.
1967   Ethnographic Atlas. *Ey* **6**: 108–236.
1970   Kin Term Patterns and Their Distribution. *Ey* **9**: 165–208.

Murdock, George P. *et al.*
1961   Outline of Cultural Materials. Human Relations Area Files Press: New Haven, Conn.

Murdock, George P., and Douglas R. White
1969   Standard Cross-Cultural Sample. *Ey* **8**: 329–369.

Naroll, Raoul
1962   *Data Quality Control—A New Research Technique.* The Free Press: Glencoe, Ill.
1964   On Ethnic Unit Classification. *CA* **5**: 283–312.
1970   Data Quality Control in Cross Cultural Surveys. *In* Naroll and Cohen, eds., pp. 927–945.

Naroll, Raoul, and Ronald Cohen, eds.
1970   *A Handbook of Method in Cultural Anthropology.* Natural History Press: New Haven.

Newman, Stanley
1964   Comparison of Zuni and California Penutian. *IJAL* **30**: 1–13.

Nomland, Gladys A.
1935   Sinkyone Notes. *UCP* **36**: 149–178.

Nomland, G. A., and A. L. Kroeber

1936   Wiyot Towns. *UCP* **35**: 39–48.

Norbeck, Edward
1961   *Religion in Primitive Society.* Harper and Row: New York.

Olmsted, David L.
1965   Phonemic Change and Subgrouping: Some Hokan Data. *Lg* **41**: 303–307.

Olson, Ronald L.
1933   Clan and Moiety in Native America. *UCP* **33**: 351–422.
1936a   The Quinault Indians. *UWPA* **6**: 1–190.
1936b   Some Trading Customs of the Chilkat Tlingit. *In* Julian H. Steward, ed., pp. 211–214.
1940   The Social Organization of the Haisla. *AR* **2**: 169–200.
1955   Notes on the Bella Bella Kwakiutl. *AR* **14**: 319–348.
1967   Social Structure and Social Life of the Tlingit in Alaska. *AR* **26**: 1–123.

Opler, Marvin K.
1940   The Southern Ute of Colorado. *In* Ralph Linton, ed., pp. 119–206.

Opler, Morris E.
1936a   The Kinship Systems of the Southern Athapascan-Speaking Tribes. *AA* **38**: 620–633.
1936b   A Summary of Jicarilla Apache Culture. *AA* **38**: 202–223.
1937   An Outline of Chiricahua Apache Social Organization. *In* Fred Eggan, ed., pp. 172–239.
1940   Myths and Legends of the Lipan Apache Indians. *MAFLS* **36**: 296 pp.
1941   *An Apache Lifeway.* University of Chicago Press: Chicago.
1943   The Character and Derivation of Jicarilla Holiness Rites. *UNMB* **4**(3), 1–98.
1945   The Lipan Apache Death Complex. *SJA* **1**: 122–142.
1946   Childhood and Youth in Jicarilla Apache Society. *PHAPF* **5**: 1–170.
1955   An Outline of Chiracahua Apache Social Organization. *In* Fred Eggan, ed., pp. 173–242.
1969   *Apache Odyssey: A Journey Between Two Worlds.* Holt, Rinehart and Winston: New York.
1971a   Jicarilla Apache Territory, Economy, and Society in 1850. *SJA* **27**: 309–329.
1971b   Pots, Apache, and the Dismal River Aspect. *In* Keith H. Basso and Morris E. Opler, eds., pp. 29–33.

Ortiz, Alfonso
1969   *The World of the Tewa Indians.* University of Chicago Press, Chicago.

Ortiz, Alfonso, ed.
1972   *New Perspectives on the Pueblos.* A School of American Research Book. University of New Mexico Press: Albuquerque, N. Mex.

Oswalt, Robert L.
1964   The Internal Relationships of the Pomo Family of Languages. *Actas y Memorias: XXXV International Congress of Americanists;* Mexico City, 1962. Vol. 2: 413–421.

1973   Comparative Verb Morphology in Pomo. *In* Margaret Langdon, ed.

Park, Willard Z.
1938   The Organization and Habitat of Paviotso Bands. *AA* **40**: 622–626.

Parsons, Elsie C.
1919   Mothers and Children at Zuni. *Man* **19**: 168–173.
1924   Tewa Kin, Clan, and Moiety. *AA* **26**: 333–339.
1925   *The Pueblo of Jemez.* Yale University Press: New Haven.
1929   The Social Organization of the Tewa of New Mexico. *MAAA* **36**: 1–309.
1930   Isleta. *ARBAE* **47**: 193–446.
1932   The Kinship Nomenclature of the Pueblo Indians. *AA* **34**: 377–390.
1936   Taos Pueblo. *GSA* **2**: 1–120.
1939   Pueblo Indian Religion. 2 vols. University of Chicago Press: Chicago.

Peck, Morton E.
1961   *A Manual of the Higher Plants of Oregon.* Second edition. Binfords and Mort: Portland, Ore.

Pelto, Pertti J.
1970   *Anthropological Research. The Structure of Inquiry.* Harper and Row: New York.

Pettit, George A.
1950   The Quileute of La Push. *AR* **14**: 1–120.

Phillips, Allan, Joe Marshall, and Gale Monson
1964   *The Birds of Arizona.* University of Arizona Press: Tucson, Ariz.

Piddocke, Stuart
1965   The Potlatch System of the Southern Kwakiutl: A New Perspective. *SJA* **21**: 244–264.

Pierce, Joe E.
1962   Possible Electronic Computation of Typological Indices for Linguistic Structures. *IJAL* **28**: 215–226.
1965   Hanis and Miluk: Dialects or Unrelated Languages. *IJAL* **31**: 323–325.
1966   Genetic Comparisons of Hanis, Miluk, Alsea, Siuslaw and Takelma. *IJAL* **32**: 379–387.

Pitkin, Harvey.
1962   A Bibliography of the Wintun Family of Languages. *IJAL* **28**: 43–54.

Price, John A.
1962   *Washo Economy.* Nevada State Museum Anthropological Papers, No. 6. Reno, Nev.

Radin, Paul
1924   Wappo Texts. *UCP* **19**: 1–147.

Ray, Verne F.
1932   The Sanpoil and Nespelem. *UWPA* **5**: 1–237.
1938   Lower Chinook Ethnographic Notes. *UWPA* **7**: 29–165.
1939   *Cultural Relations of the Plateau of North America.* Southwest Museum: Los Angeles.
1942   Plateau. *AR* **8**: 99–257.
1963   *Primitive Pragmatists: The Modoc Indians of Northern California.* University of Washington Press: Seattle.

Reichard, Gladys
1928   Social Life of the Navajo Indians. *CUCA* **7**: 1–239.

Reiter, Paul
1938   *The Jemez Pueblo of Unshagi.* School of American Research Monographs **5**: 1–92; **6**: 97–211. Santa Fe, N. Mex.

Rigsby, Bruce
1965   *Linguistic Relations in the Southern Plateau.* Unpublished Ph.D. Dissertation in Anthropology, University of Oregon: Eugene, Ore.
1966   On Cayuse-Molala Relatability. *IJAL* **32**: 369–378.
1969   *Some Linguistic Insights into Recent Tsimshian Prehistory.* Manuscript in possession of William E. Elmendorf.
1970   A Note on Gitksan Speech Play. *IJAL* **36**: 211–215.

Robbins, Wilfred W., *et al*
1916   Ethnobotany of the Tewa Indians. *BBAE* **55**: 118 pp.

Roberts, John M.
1951   Three Navajo Households. *PMP* **40**: 101 pp.
1956   Zuni Daily Life. *NLAUN* **3**: 1–143.

Rockwell, Wilson
1956   *The Utes.* Sage Books: Denver.

Rohner, Ronald
1965   *The People of Guilford.* Queen's Printer: Ottawa, Ontario.

Rohner, Ronald P., and Leonard Katz
1970   Testing for Validity and Reliability in Cross-Cultural Research. *AA* **72**: 1068–1072.

Rohner, Ronald P., and Evelyn C. Rohner
1970   *The Kwakiutl.* Holt, Rinehart and Winston: New York.

Roskam, E., and Lingoes, J. C.
1970   Minissa-I: A Fortran IV (G) Program for the Smallest Space Analysis of Square Symmetric Matrices. *Behavioral Science* **15**: 204–205.

Rosman, Abraham, and Paula Rubel
1971   *Feasting with Mine Enemy.* Columbia University Press: New York.

Rostlund, Erhard
1952   Freshwater Fish and Fishing in Native North America. *UCPG* **9**: 1–314.

Russell, Frank
1908   The Pima Indians. *ARBAE* **26**: 3–390.

St. John, Harold
1963   *Flora of Southeastern Washington and Adjacent Idaho.* Edwards Brothers: Escondido, California.

Sanger, David
1967   Prehistory of the Pacific Northwest Plateau as seen from the Interior of British Columbia. *AAn* **32**: 186–197.

Sapir, Edward
1907   Preliminary Report on the Language and Mythology of the Upper Chinook. *AA* **9**: 533–544.
1920   Nass River Terms of Relationship. *AA* **22**: 261–271.

1930 Texts of the Kaibab Paiutes and Uintah Utes. *PAA* **45**: 297–535.

Sapir, Edward, and Leslie Spier
1943 Notes on the Culture of the Yana. *AR* 3: 239–297.

Saxton, Dean
1963 Papago Phonemes. *IJAL* **29**: 29–35.

Schneider, David M., and Kathleen Gough, eds.
1961 *Matrilineal Kinship*. University of California Press: Berkeley, Calif.

Schneider, David M., and John M. Roberts
1956 Zuni Kin Terms. *NLAUN* 3: 29 pp.

Schroeder, Albert H.
1965 A Brief History of the Southern Utes. *Southwestern Lore* **30**: 53–78.

Sebeok, Thomas A., ed.
1973 *Current Trends in Linguistics: X*. Mouton and Co.: The Hague, Netherlands.

Service, Elman R.
1947 Recent Observations on Havasupai Land Tenure. *SJA* 3: 360–366.
1962 *Primitive Social Organization: An Evolutionary Perspective*. Harper and Row: New York.

Shafer, Robert
1952 Notes on Penutian. *IJAL* **18**: 211–216.

Shantz, Homer L., and Raphael Zon
1936 *Atlas of American Agriculture, Land Relief*. U.S. Department of Agriculture: Washington, D.C.

Sherzer, Joel
1973 Areal Linguistics in North America. *In* T. A. Sebeok, ed., pp. 749–795.

Shimkin, Demitri B.
1947a Childhood and Development among the Wind River Shoshone. *AR* 5: 289–326.
1947b Wind River Shoshone Ethnogeography. *AR* **5**: 245–288.

Shipek, Florence C.
1968 *The Autobiography of Delfina Cuero*. Dawson's Book Shop: Los Angeles.

Shipley, William
1961 Maidu and Nisenan: A Binary Comparison. *IJAL* **27**: 46–51.
1966 The Relation of Klamath to California Penutian. *Lg* **42**: 489–498.
1969 Proto-Takelman. *IJAL* **35**: 226–230.
1970 Proto-Kalapuyan. *In* Earl H. Swanson, ed., pp. 97–106.

Silverstein, Michael
1974 Dialectical Developments in Chinookan Tense. Aspect Systems: An Areal-Historical Analysis. *MIJL* **29**.

Sjoberg, Andree F.
1953 Lipan Apache Culture in Historical Perspective. *SJA* **9**: 76–98.

Smith, Anne M.
1974 *Ethnography of the Northern Ute*. Museum of New Mexico Papers in Anthropology, 17. 288 pp. Santa Fe, N. Mex.

Smith, Janet Hugie
1972 Native Pharmacopoeia of the Eastern Great Basin: A Report on Work in Progress. *In* Don D. Fowler, ed., pp. 73–86.

Smith, Marian W.
1940 The Puyallup-Nisqually. *CUCA* **32**: 336 pp.

Sonnichsen, C. L.
1958 *The Mescalero Apaches*. University of Oklahoma Press: Norman, Okla.

Sparkman, Philip S.
1908 The Culture of the Luiseño Indians. *UCP* **8**: 187–234.

Spicer, Edward
1962 *Cycles of Conquest*. University of Arizona Press: Tucson, Ariz.

Spicer, Edward, ed.
1961 *Perspectives in American Indian Culture Change*. University of Chicago Press: Chicago.

Spier, Leslie
1923 Southern Diegueño Customs. *UCP* **20**: 297–358.
1928 Havasupai Ethnography. *APAM* **29**: 83–392.
1930 Klamath Ethnography. *UCP* **30**: 1–338.
1933 *Yuman Tribes of the Gila River*. University of Chicago Press: Chicago.
1936 Cultural Relations of the Gila River and Lower Colorado Tribes. *YUPA* 3: 22 pp.

Spier, Leslie, and Edward Sapir
1930 Wishram Ethnography. *UWPA* 3: 151–300.

Spinden, Herbert J.
1908 The Nez Percé Indians. *MAAA* **2**: 165–274.

Stern, Bernard J.
1934 The Lummi Indians of Northwest Washington. *CUCA* **17**: 1–127.

Stern, Theodore
1966 *The Klamath Tribe*. University of Washington Press: Seattle.

Stevenson, Matilda C.
1894 The Sia. *ARBAE* **11**: 9–157.
1904 The Zuni Indians. *ARBAE* **23**: 13–608.

Steward, Julian H.
1933 Ethnography of the Owens Valley Paiute. *UCP* **33**: 233–350.
1937 Ecological Aspects of Southwestern Society. *A* **32**: 87–104.
1938 Basin-Plateau Aboriginal Sociopolitical Groups. *BBAE* **120**: 1–346.
1941 Nevada Shoshone *AR* 4: 209–259.
1943 Northern and Gosiute Shoshoni. *AR* 8: 203–392.
1970 Foundations of Basin-Plateau Shoshonean Society. *In* Earl H. Swanson, Jr. ed., pp. 113–151.
1936 Steward, Julian H., ed.
Essays in Anthropology Presented to A. L. Kroeber. University of California Press: Berkeley, Calif.

Stewart, Kenneth M.
1947 Mohave Warfare. *SJA* 3: 257–278.

Stewart, Omer C.
1941   Northern Paiute. *UCP* **4**: 361–446.
1942   Ute-Southern Paiute. *AR* **6**: 231–355.
1943   Notes on Pomo Ethnography. *UCP* **40**: 29–62.

Strong, William D.
1929   Aboriginal Society in Southern California. *UCP* **26**: 274–328.

Suttles, Wayne
1955   Katzie Ethnographic Notes. *ABCM* **2**: 31 pp.
1958   Private Knowledge, Morality, and Social Classes Among the Coast Salish. *AA* **60**: 497–507.
1960a   Affinal Ties, Subsistence, and Prestige Among the Coast Salish. *AA* **62**: 296–305.
1960b   Variation in Habitat and Culture in the Northwest Coast. *Akten des 34 Internationalean Amerikannishen-Kongresses, Wein,* 1960: 522–537.
1965   Multiple Phonological Correspondence in Two Adjacent Salish Languages and Their Implications. Paper presented at 18th Northwest Anthropological Conference, Bellingham, Washington.

Swadesh, Morris
1950   Salish Internal Relationships. *IJAL* **16**: 157–167.
1951   Diffusional Cumulation and Archaic Residue. *SJA* **7**: 14–21.
1952   Lexicostatistic Dating of Prehistoric Ethnic Contacts. *PAPS* **94**: 452–463.
1953a   Jicaque as a Hokan Language. *IJAL* **19**: 216–222.
1953b   Mosan I: Problems of Remote Comparison. *IJAL* **19**: 26–44.
1953c   Mosan II: Comparative Vocabulary. *IJAL* **20**: 123–133.
1953d   Salish-Wakashan Lexical Comparisons Noted by Boas. *IJAL* **19**: 290–291.
1954a   Review of "The Language of the Papago Indians" by J. Alden Mason. *Word* **10** (1).
1954b   Time Depths of American Linguistic Groupings. *AA* **56**: 361–364.
1955   Chemakum Lexicon Compared with Quileute. *IJAL* **21**: 60–72.
1956   Problems of Long Range Comparison in Penutian. *Lg* **32**: 17–41.
1962   Afinidades de Las Lenguas Amerindias. *Internationalen Amerikanisten-Kongresses, Wein,* 729–738.
1965   Kalapuya and Takelman. *IJAL* **31**: 237–240.
1967   Linguistic Classification in the Southwest. *In* Dell Hymes and William Bittle, eds., pp. 281–309.

Swan, James G.
1857   The Northwest Coast. Harper Bros: New York.
1870   The Indians of Cape Flattery. *SCK* **16**: 1–108.

Swanson, Earl H. Jr., ed.
1970   *Languages and Cultures in Western North America. Essays in Honor of Sven Liljeblad.* Idaho State University Press: Pocatello, Idaho.

Swanson, Guy R.
1960   *Birth of the Gods.* University of Michigan Press: Ann Arbor, Mich.

Swanton, John R.
1908   Social Condition, Beliefs, and Linguistic Relationship of the Tlingit Indians. *ARBAE* **26**: 391–486.
1909   Contributions to the Ethnology of the Haida. *MAMNH* **8**: 1–300.

Tax, Sol
1937   Some Problems of Social Organization. *In* Fred Eggan, ed., pp. 3–15.

Taylor, Walter W.
1961   Archaeology and Language in Western North America. *AAn* **27**: 71–81.

Teeter, Karl V.
1964   The Wiyot Language. *UCPL* **37**.
1965   The Algonquian Verb: Notes toward a Reconsideration. *IJAL* **31**: 221–225.

Teit, James A.
1900   The Thompson Indians. *MAMNH* **2**: 163–192.
1906   The Lillooet Indians. *MAMNH* **4**: 193–300.
1907   Notes on the Chilcotin Indians. *MAMNH* **4**: 759–789.
1909   The Shuswap. *MAMNH* **4**: 447–758.
1928   The Middle Columbia Salish. *UWPA* **2**: 83–128.
1930   The Salishan Tribes of the Western Plateaus. *ARBAE* **45**: 37–396.

Thomas, David H.
1972   Western Shoshone Ecology: Settlement Patterns and Beyond. *In* Don D. Fowler, ed., pp. 135–154.

Thomas, L. L., J. Z. Kronenfeld, and D. B. Kronenfeld
1976   Asdiwal Crumbles: A Critique of Levi-Straussian Myth Analysis. *AE* **3**: 147–173.

Thompson, Laurence C.
1965   More on Comparative Salish. Paper presented at 4th Conference on American Indian Languages, Denver.
1973   The Northwest. *In* Thomas A. Sebeok, ed.

Thompson, Laurence C., and M. Terry Thompson
1972   *Language Universals, Nasals, and the Northwest Coast. In* M. Estellie Smith, ed. *Studies in Linguistics in Honor of George L. Trager. Janua Linguarum* **52**: 441–456.

Tidestrom, Ivar
1925   *Flora of Utah and Nevada.* Contributions from the United States National Herbarium, Vol. 25: Washington, D.C.

Titiev, Mischa
1944   Old Oraibi. *PMP* **22**: 1–277.
1956   Shamans, Witches and Chiefs Among the Hopi. *Tomorrow* **4**(3): 51–56. New York.

Trager, George L.
1967   The Tanoan Settlement of the Rio Grande Area: A Possible Chronology. *In* Dell Hymes and William Bittle, eds., pp. 335–350.
1969   Taos and Picuris—How Long Separated? *IJAL* **35**: 180–182.

Turney-High, Harry H.
1937   The Flathead Indians of Montana. *MAAA* **48**: 1–161.
1941   Ethnography of the Kutanai. *MAAA* **56**: 1–202.

Tylor, Edward B.
1889   On a Method of Investigating the Development of Institutions: Applied to Laws of Marriage and Descent. *JAI* **18**: 245–272.

Ultan, Russel
1964   Proto-Maiduan Phonology. *IJAL* **30**: 355–370.

Underhill, Ruth M.
1939   Social Organization of the Papago Indians. *CUCA* **30**: 1–280.
1946   *Papago Indian Religion.* Columbia University Press: New York.
1956   *The Navajos.* University of Oklahoma Press: Norman, Okla.

U.S. Department of Commerce, National Marine Fisheries Service
n.d.   Maps of Columbia Drainage Fish. Columbia Fisheries Program Office: Portland, Oregon.

Van Gennep, Arnold
1960   *The Rites of Passage.* University of Chicago Press: Chicago.

Vayda, Andrew P.
1961   A Re-examination of Northwest Coast Economic Systems. *TNYAS* **23**: 618–624.
1966   Pomo Trade Feasts. *Humanities: Cahiers de l'Institut de Science Economique Appliques,* pp. 1–6. Paris, France.

Velten, Harry
1943   The Nez Percé Verb. *PNQ* **34**: 271–292.

Vivian, R. Gwinn
1970   An Inquiry into Prehistoric Social Organization in Chaco Canyon, New Mexico. *In* William A. Longacre, ed., pp. 59–83.

Voegelin, C. F., and F. M. Voegelin
1973   Southwest and Great Basin Languages. *In* Thomas A. Sebeok, ed.

Voegelin, C. F., F. M. Voegelin, and Kenneth L. Hale
1962   Typological and Comparative Grammar of Uto-Aztecan: I (Phonology). *IUPAL* **17**.

Voegelin, C. F., F. M. Voegelin, and Noel W. Schutz, Jr.
1967   The Language Situation in Arizona as Part of the Southwest Culture Area. *In* Dell Hymes and William Bittle, eds., pp. 403–451.

Voegelin, Erminie W.
1938   Tubatulabal Ethnography. *AR* **2**: 1–84.
1942   Northeast California. *AR* **7**: 47–251.

Voegelin, Erminie W., and Julian H. Steward
1954   *The Northern Paiute Indians.* Indian Claims Commission: Washington, D.C.

Von Bertalanffy, Ludwig
1968   *General Systems Theory.* Revised Edition. Brazillier: New York, N.Y.

Walker, Deward E., Jr.
1967   Nez Percé Sorcery. *Ey* **6**: 66–96.
1968   *Conflict and Schism in Nez Percé Acculturation: A Study of Religion and Politics.* Washington State University Press: Pullman, Wash.

Wallace, W. J.
1949   Hupa Warfare. *M* **23**: 71–77, 101–106.

Wallace, W. J., and E. S. Taylor
1950   Hupa Sorcery. *SJA* **6**: 188–196.

Wares, Alan C.
1968   *A Comparative Study of Yuman Consonantism.* Mouton and Co.: The Hague, Netherlands.

Waterman, Thomas T.
1910   The Religious Practices of the Diegueño Indians. *UCP* **8**: 271–358.
1918   The Yana Indians. *UCP* **13**: 35–70.
1925   Village Sites in Tolowa and Neighboring Areas. *AA* **27**: 528–543.

Waterman, T. T., and A. L. Kroeber
1934   Yurok Marriages. *UCP* **35**: 1–14.

Webb, Nancy M.
1972   A Statement of Some Phonological Correspondences among the Pomo Languages. *MIJL* **26**: 55 pp.

Wenger, Patrick M.
1968   Phonotactical Indices: A Test Case in Macro-Penutian Classification. Unpublished Master's Thesis in Anthropology: University of Oregon, Eugene.
1973   Numerical Taxonomy and Linguistic Classification: West Coast Languages as a Test Case. Unpublished Ph.D. Dissertation: University of California, Davis.

White, Douglas R.
1975   Process, Statistics and Anthropological Theory: An Appreciation of Harold E. Driver. *Reviews in Anthropology* **2**: 295–314. Storrs, Conn.

White, Leslie A.
1930   The Acoma Indians. *ARBAE* **47**: 17–192.
1935   The Pueblo of Santa Domingo. *MAAA* **43**: 1–210.
1942   The Pueblo of Santa Ana. *MAAA* **60**: 1–360.
1943   New Material From Acoma. *BBAE* **136**: 301–360.
1949   *The Science of Culture.* Farrar, Strauss, Giroux: New York.
1962   The Pueblo of Sia, New Mexico. *BBAE* **184**: 1–327.
1963   The Ethnography and Ethnology of Franz Boas. *UTMMB* **6**.

Whiting, Alfred F.
1939   Ethnobotany of the Hopi. Bulletin 15. Museum of Northern Arizona. Flagstaff, Ariz.

Whiting, Beatrice B.
1950   Paiute Sorcery. *VFPA* **15**: 1–110.

Whitman, William
1947   The Pueblo Indians of San Ildefonso: A Changing Culture. *CUCA* **34**: 1–164.

Whorf, Benjamin L., and George L. Trager
1937   The Relationship of Uto-Aztecan and Tanoan. *AA* **39**: 609–624.

Wike, Joyce
1958   Social Stratification among the Nootka. *E* **5**: 219–241.

Winter, Werner
  1957   Yuman Language I: First Impressions. *IJAL* **23**:
         18–23.
  1967   The Identity of the Paipai (Akwa'ala). *In* Dell
         Hymes and William Bittle, eds., pp. 372–378.
Wissler, Clark
  1926   The Relation of Nature to Man in Aboriginal
         America. McMurtrie: New York. 249 pp.
Wittfogel, Karl A., and Esther S. Goldfrank
  1943   Some Aspects of Pueblo Mythology and Society.
         JAFL **56**: 17–30.

Wooton, E. D., and Paul C. Standley
  1915   *Flora of New Mexico*. Contributions from the United
         States National Herbarium. Vol. 19: Washington,
         D.C.
Zigmond, Maurice L.
  1938   Kawaiisu Territory. *AA* **40**: 634–638.

Bibliographic References Arranged by Tribe

References pertaining to the tribes in the left-hand column have been merged in the bibliographic listings for the tribes specified in the right-hand column.

Central Miwok	= Miwok
Chemehuevi	= Southern Paiute
Chukchansi Yokuts	= Yokuts
Cibecue	= Western Apache
Eastern Navajo	= Navajo
East Pomo	= Pomo
Foothill Maidu	= Maidu
Foothill Nisenan	= Nisenan
Kaibab	= Southern Paiute
Kaweah Yokuts	= Yokuts
Kings River Mono	= Mono, Western
Kings River Yokuts	= Yokuts
Lake Yokuts	= Yokuts
Mountain Maidu	= Maidu
Mountain Nisenan	= Nisenan
Northern Miwok	= Miwok
Northern Pomo	= Pomo
Northern Chilkat Tlingit	= Tlingit
North Tonto	= Western Apache
Pentlatch	= Klahuse
San Carlos	= Western Apache
San Joaquin Mono	= Mono, Western
San Juan Southern Paiute	= Southern Paiute
Shivwits	= Southern Paiute
Southern Diegueño	= Diegueño
Southern Miwok	= Miwok
Southern Nisenan	= Nisenan
Southern Pomo	= Pomo
Southern or *Xuts! Nuwu* Tlingit	= Tlingit
South Tonto	= Western Apache
Squamish	= Klahuse
Valley Maidu	= Maidu
Western Diegueño	= Diegueño
Western Navajo	= Navajo
White Mountain	= Western Apache
Yauelmani Yokuts	= Yokuts

REFERENCES CITED BY TRIBE

Achomawi
  Kniffen 1928; Kroeber 1925; Voegelin 1942.

Acoma
  Curtis 1926; Eggan 1950; White 1930, 1943.

Agaiduku (Lemhi) Shoshone
  Lowie 1908; Steward 1938, 1943.

Akwa'ala
  Drucker 1937a; Gifford and Lowie 1928.

Alsea
  Barnett 1937; Drucker 1939.

Atsugewi
  Garth 1944, 1953; Voegelin 1942.

Battle Mountain (White Knife) Shoshone
  Harris 1940; Steward 1938, 1941.

Bella Bella Kwakiutl
  Drucker 1940, 1950; Lopatin 1945; Olson 1955.

Bella Coola
  Drucker 1940, 1950; McIlwraith 1948; Rosman and Rubel 1971.

Bohogue (Fort Hall) Shoshone
  Steward 1938, 1943.

Cahuilla
  Drucker 1937a; Hooper 1920; James 1960; Kroeber 1908a, 1925; Strong 1929.

Carrier
  Aro and Shepard 1967; Duff 1951; Goldman 1940, 1941; Hill-Tout 1907; Jenness 1943; Morice 1893; Ray 1942.

Chetco
  Barnett 1937; Drucker 1937b.

Chilcotin
  Aro and Shepard 1967; Morice 1893; Ray 1942; Teit 1907.

Chimariko
  Dixon 1910; Driver 1939.

Chiricahua Apache
  Gifford 1940; Opler 1937, 1941, 1955.

Clayoquot Nootka
  Drucker 1940, 1950, 1951; Koppert 1930; Moziño 1970; Wike 1958.

Coast Yuki
  Baumhoff 1963; Driver 1939; Gifford 1939; Loeb 1932.

Cochiti
  Dumarest 1919; Fox 1967; Goldfrank 1927; Hawley 1950; Lange 1959.

Cocopa
  Drucker 1941; Gifford 1933; Kelly 1942.

Coeur d'Alene
  Ray 1942; Teit 1930.

Columbia
  Ray 1942; Teit 1928.

Coos
  Barnett 1937; Jacobs 1939.

Cowichan
  Barnett 1938, 1939, 1955; Hill-Tout 1902; Suttles 1960.

Cupeño
  Drucker 1937a; Gifford 1918; Strong 1929.

Diegueño
  Drucker 1937a, 1941; DuBois 1908; Gifford 1918; Shipek 1968; Spier 1923; Waterman 1910.

Flathead
  Ray 1942; Teit 1930; Turney-High 1937.

Fort Rupert Kwakiutl
  Boas 1897, 1909, 1966; Codere 1950; Drucker 1940, 1950; Drucker and Heizer 1967; Ford 1941; Goldman 1937a; Rohner 1965; Rohner and Rohner 1970; Rosman and Rubel 1971.

Gabrieliño
  Harrington 1942; Johnston 1964; Johnston 1955–1956; Kroeber 1925.

Galice Creek
  Barnett 1937; Drucker 1937b.

Gitksan
  Drucker 1950; Garfield 1939; Garfield and Wingert 1950; Sapir 1920.

Gosiute
  Steward 1938, 1943; Stewart 1942.

Haida
  Drucker 1940, 1950, 1965; Krause 1956; Murdock 1934a, 1934b, 1936; Rosman and Rubel 1971; Swanton 1909.

Haihais Kwakiutl
  Drucker 1940, 1950.

Haisla Kwakiutl
  Barnett 1968; Boas 1909; Codere 1950; Drucker 1940, 1950; Drucker and Heizer 1967; Lopatin 1945; Olson 1940; Rohner and Rohner 1970; Rosman and Rubel 1971.

Havasupai
  Service 1947; Spier 1928.

Hopi
  Beaglehole 1937; Dozier 1970; Eggan 1950; Titiev 1944, 1956.

Hukundika (Promontory) Shoshone
  Hoebel 1935, 1939; Steward 1938, 1943.

Hupa
  Baumhoff 1958, 1963; Driver 1939; Goddard 1903; Goldschmidt and Driver 1940; Kroeber and Gifford 1949; Wallace 1949; Wallace and Taylor 1950.

Isleta
  Euler 1954; Parsons 1930.

Jemez
  Ellis 1964; Parsons 1925; Reiter 1938.

Jicarilla Apache
  Gifford 1940; Opler 1936b, 1943, 1946, 1971.

Kalispel
  Ray 1942; Teit 1930.

Kaliwa
  Meigs 1939.

Kamia
  Drucker 1941; Gifford 1931; Kroeber 1920.

Karok
  Baumhoff 1963; Driver 1939; Drucker 1936; Kroeber 1925; Kroeber and Gifford 1949.

Kato
  Driver 1939; Essene 1942; Kroeber 1925; Loeb 1932.

Kawaiisu
  Driver 1937; Kroeber 1925; Zigmond 1938.

Kidu-Dokado Northern Paiute
  Kelly 1932; Stewart 1941.

Klahuse, Pentlatch, Squamish Georgia Salish
  Barnett 1939, 1955; Suttles 1958.

Klallam
  Gunther 1927.

Klamath
  Barrett 1910; Kroeber 1925; Spier 1930; Stern 1966; Voegelin 1942.

Klikitat
    Ray 1939, 1942.

Kutenai
    Chamberlain 1892; Ray 1942; Turney-High 1941.

Kuyui-Dokado Northern Paiute
    Lowie 1924; Park 1938; Stewart 1941.

Lillooet, Upper
    Aro and Shepard 1967; Ray 1942; Teit 1906.

Lipan Apache
    Gifford 1940; Opler 1940, 1945; Opler 1936a; Sjoberg 1953.

Lower Chinook
    Ray 1938; Swan 1857.

Lower Fraser (Musqueam)
    Barnett 1938, 1955; Hill-Tout 1902; Jenness 1955; Suttles 1955, 1960.

Luiseño
    Drucker 1937a; DuBois 1908; Gifford 1919; Harrington 1955; Kroeber 1908b, 1925; Sparkman 1908; Strong 1929.

Lummi
    Stern 1934; Suttles 1960.

Maidu
    Dixon 1905; Loeb 1933; Voegelin 1942.

Makah
    Colson 1953; Drucker 1940; Swan 1870; Wike 1958.

Maricopa
    Drucker 1941; Spier 1933.

Mattole
    Baumhoff 1958, 1963; Driver 1939; Kroeber and Barrett 1960.

Mescalero Apache
    Basehart 1960, 1967, 1970, 1971; Gifford 1940; Opler, M. E. 1969; Sonnichsen 1958.

Miwok
    Aginsky 1943; Barrett and Gifford 1933; Baumhoff 1963; Gifford 1926b, 1926c, 1944, 1955; Kroeber 1925.

Modoc
    Barrett 1910; Kroeber 1925; Ray 1963; Voegelin 1942.

Mohave
    Castetter and Bell 1951; Drucker 1941; Fathauer 1954; Kroeber 1925; Spier 1936; Stewart 1947.

Mono, Western
    Aginsky 1943; Baumhoff 1963; Driver 1937; Gayton 1930, 1945, 1948b; Gifford 1932a.

Nambe
    Dozier 1954, 1970; Harrington 1916, Ortiz 1969; Parsons 1924, 1929.

Navajo
    Aberle 1961b; Haile 1954; Hill 1938; Hobson 1954; Kluckholn and Leighton 1946; Reichard 1928; Roberts 1951; Underhill 1956.

Nez Percé
    Haines 1955; Spinden 1908; Walker 1967, 1968.

Nisenan
    Beals 1933; Dixon 1905; Gifford 1927; Kroeber 1929; Loeb 1933; Voegelin 1942.

Nomlaki
    Goldschmidt 1951.

Nongatl
    Baumhoff 1958; Driver 1939; Kroeber 1925; Kroeber and Barrett 1960.

Owens Valley Paiute
    Driver 1937; Steward 1933, 1941.

Panamint (California Shoshone)
    Driver 1937; Steward 1938, 1941.

Papago
    Castetter and Bell 1942; Drucker 1941; Joseph, Spicer, and Chesky 1949; Underhill 1939, 1946.

Patwin
    Gifford and Kroeber 1937; Kroeber 1932; Loeb 1932; McKern 1922.

Pima
    Castetter and Bell 1942; Drucker 1941; Ezell 1961; Hill 1936; Russell 1908; Spier 1936.

Pomo
    Barrett 1952; Baumhoff 1963; Gifford 1923, 1926a; Gifford and Kroeber 1937; Kniffen 1939; Kroeber 1925, 1932; Loeb 1926, 1932; Stewart 1943.

Puyallup-Nisqually
    Haeberlin and Gunther 1930; Smith 1940.

Quileute
    Drucker 1940; Frachtenberg 1921; Pettit 1950.

Quinault
    Olson 1936a.

Reese River Shoshone
    Steward 1938, 1941.

Ruby Valley Shoshone
    Steward 1938, 1941.

Salinan
    Harrington 1942; Mason 1912.

San Ildefonso
    Dozier 1970; Ortiz 1969; Parsons 1929; Whitman 1947.

San Juan Tewa
    Dozier 1954; Kurath 1970; Laski 1959; Ortiz 1969; Parsons 1929.

Sanpoil-Nespelem
    Ray 1932, 1942; Teit 1930.

Santa Ana
    White 1942.

Santa Clara Tewa
    Dozier 1966, 1970; Ortiz 1969; Parsons 1929.

Santa Domingo
    White 1935.

Serraño
    Benedict 1924; Drucker 1937a; Gifford 1918; Kroeber 1925; Strong 1929.

Shasta
    Dixon 1907; Holt 1946; Voegelin 1942.

Shuswap
    Aro and Shepard 1967; Ray 1942; Teit 1909.

Sia
Halseath 1924; Stevenson 1894; White 1962.

Sinkyone
Baumhoff 1958; Driver 1939; Kroeber and Barrett 1960; Nomland 1935.

Siuslaw
Barnett 1937.

Southern Okanagon
Cline 1938; Ray 1942; Teit 1930.

Southern Paiute
Drucker 1937a, 1941; Euler 1966; Kelly 1934, 1938, 1939, 1964; Kroeber 1925; Lowie 1924; Opler 1940; Sapir 1930; Stewart 1942.

Spring Valley Shoshone
Steward 1938, 1941.

Taos
Fenton 1957; Grant 1925; Parsons 1936.

Tenino
Murdock 1958, 1965; Ray 1942.

Thompson, Upper
Aro and Shepard 1967; Ray 1942; Teit 1900.

Tillamook
Barnett 1937.

Tlingit
Barnett 1968; de Laguna 1960; Drucker 1950; Drucker and Hiezer 1967; Garfield 1947; Jones 1914; Krause 1956; Olson 1936b, 1967; Rosman and Eubel 1971; Swanton 1908.

Tolowa
Barnett 1937; Baumhoff 1963; Drucker 1937b, Du Bois 1932, 1936; Waterman 1925.

Tsimshian
Barnett 1968; Drucker 1940, 1950, 1965; Garfield 1939; Garfield and Wingert 1950; Rosman and Rubel 1971.

Tubatulabal
Driver 1937; Voegelin 1938.

Tututni
Barnett 1937; Drucker 1936; Du Bois 1936.

Twana
Elmendorf 1948, 1960.

Uintah Ute (Tompanowots)
Jorgensen 1964; Lowie 1924; Sapir 1930; Smith 1974; Stewart 1942.

Umatilla
Ray 1939, 1942.

Uncompaghre Utes (Taviwatsiu, Mowatavivatsiu)
Jorgensen 1964; Rockwell 1956; Smith 1974; Stewart 1942.

Upper Stalo
Duff 1952; Hill-Tout 1902.

Wada-Dokado Northern Paiute
Stewart 1941; Voegelin and Steward 1954; Whiting 1950.

Walapai
Drucker 1941; Kroeber 1935.

Wappo
Baumhoff 1963; Driver 1936; Loeb 1933; Radin 1924.

Washo
Barrett 1917; Downs 1966; Freed 1963; Lowie 1939; Price 1962.

Wenatchi
Ray 1942; Teit 1928.

Western Apache
Basso 1969, 1970; Basso and Opler 1971; Gifford 1940; Goodwin 1935, 1937, 1942, 1971; Kaut 1957, 1966; Opler 1971b.

West Sanetch
Barnett 1939, 1955.

Wimonuch Utes (Ute Mountain Ute, Wimonutsi, Navajo Springs)
Gifford 1940; Lowie 1924; Opler, M. K. 1940; Stewart 1942.

Wind River Shoshone
Lowie 1924; Shimkin 1947a, 1947b.

Wintu
Du Bois 1935; Voegelin 1942.

Wishram
French 1961; Spier and Sapir 1930.

Wiyot
Baumhoff 1963; Cook 1956; Driver 1939; Kroeber 1925; Kroeber and Gifford 1949; Loud 1918; Nomland and Kroeber 1936.

Yana
Gifford and Klimek 1936; Sapir and Spier 1943; Waterman 1918.

Yavapai
Drucker 1941; Gifford 1932, 1936.

Yokuts
Aginski 1943; Baumhoff 1963; Driver 1937; Gayton 1930, 1945, 1946, 1948; Latta 1949.

Yuki
Baumhoff 1963; Essene 1942; Foster 1944; Loeb 1932a.

Yuma
Bee 1963; Castetter and Bell 1951; Forde 1931; Kroeber 1925.

Yurok
Baumhoff 1963; Driver 1939; Elmendorf 1960; Kroeber 1925, 1945; Kroeber and Gifford 1949; Waterman and Kroeber 1934.

Zuni
Bunzell 1932; Cushing 1896; Eggan 1950; Goldman 1937; Kroeber 1917; Parsons 1919; Roberts 1956; Schneider and Roberts 1956; Stevenson 1904.

Index of Languages and Linguistics

Index of Species

Index of Authors

Names of authors specifically cited in the text appear here. All authors whose research publications have been consulted in rating data for the societies and topics analyzed in this book appear in the General Bibliography and the Bibliographic References Arranged by Tribe.

Subject Index

This subject index includes references to cultural and environmental topics and references to relations among environment, language, and culture. For language and linguistic topics, species classifications, and authors mentioned in the text, see Index of Languages and Linguistics, Index of Species, and Index of Authors.